ONTARIO SUPERIOR COURT PRACTICE

2021

ANNOTATED SMALL CLAIMS COURT RULES AND RELATED MATERIALS

Todd L. Archibald
Justice of the Superior Court of Justice

P. Tamara Sugunasiri
Master of the Superior Court of Justice

Andrew James
Research Editor

M. Gosia Balowska
Index Contributor

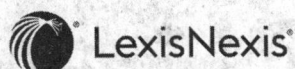

Ontario Superior Court Practice, Annotated Small Claims Court Rules and Related Materials, 2021 Edition

Library and Archives of Canada Cataloguing in Publication

Archibald, Todd

Ontario Superior Court Practice, 2013 Edition

Annual.

2021 ed.-

ISBN 978-0-433-50613-3 (bound)
ISBN 978-0-433-50662-1 (pbk.)

1. Civil Procedures—Ontario   2. Court rules—Ontario   3. Courts—Ontario
4. Ontario. Superior Court of Justice—Rules and practice   4. Forms (Law)—Ontario
I. Title

KEO1061.A329O5   347.713'05'02636   C00-9000964-7

Published by LexisNexis Canada, a member of the LexisNexis Group
LexisNexis Canada Inc.
111 Gordon Baker Road, Suite 900
Toronto, Ontario
M2H 3R1

Customer Service
Telephone: (905) 479-2665 • Fax: (905) 479-2826
Toll-Free Phone: 1-800-668-6481 • Toll-Free Fax: 1-800-461-3275
Email: customerservice@lexisnexis.ca
Web Site: www.lexisnexis.ca

Printed and bound in Canada.

ABOUT THE AUTHORS

The Honourable Mr. Justice Todd L. Archibald has been a Superior Court Justice since 1999. He is currently an Adjunct Professor at Osgoode Hall Law School and the Co-Director of Osgoode's Civil LL.M. program. He is also the co-author of *Regulatory and Corporate Liability: From Due Diligence to Risk Management* (published by Canada Law Book, updated annually) and *Discovery in Canadian Common Law: Practice, Techniques and Strategies* (published by LexisNexis Canada, 2017). He is Editor of the national *Annual Review of Civil Litigation* (Thomson Reuters) and a former Litigation Partner with Borden & Elliot. Justice Archibald graduated in law from the University of Toronto in 1977 and was called to the Bar of Ontario in 1979. He obtained a Master of Laws from Osgoode Hall Law School in 1985. He has been a member of the Ontario Civil Rules Committee since 2013. He received the Ontario Attorney General's 2015 David Mundell medal for legal scholarship.

Master P. Tamara Sugunasiri was appointed a Master of the Superior Court of Justice on March 1, 2017. Prior to that, she was a senior litigator at the Department of Justice, practising in the areas of tort, administrative law and commercial litigation. Master Sugunasiri graduated from Windsor Law in 1998, having completed a Master's degree in Philosophy in 1995 with a focus on access to justice. She was called to the Ontario Bar in 2000. Master Sugunasiri has taught paralegal courses in civil litigation and legal writing and research for Humber College, and she continues to be faculty for various courses and CPD programs, including Osgoode Hall's part-time Civil LL.M. course.

ENHANCED FORMS

Did you know? Our e-books contain links to fillable electronic forms. Follow the instructions on the sticker on the inside cover of the main volume to download your e-book. Once you have downloaded your e-book, navigate to the Forms section. From there, you will have access to forms which can be filled out and saved to your computer for future reference.

LEGISLATIVE CURRENCY

Note: The legislation reproduced in this consolidation is current to the Ontario Gazette, Vol. 153, Issue 28 (July 10, 2020).

Changes to legislation not in force are reproduced as shaded text.

TABLE OF CONTENTS

TABLE OF CONTENTS

TABLE OF CASES

COURTS OF JUSTICE ACT

RULES OF THE SMALL CLAIMS COURT

(O. Reg. 258/98)

Amendments: O. Reg. 461/01; O. Reg. 330/02; O. Reg. 440/03; O. Reg. 78/06; O. Reg. 574/07, s. 1; O. Reg. 56/08; O. Reg. 393/09, ss. 1-24; O. Reg. 440/10, ss. 1-7; O. Reg. 56/12; O. Reg. 400/12; O. Reg. 230/13, ss. 1-17; O. Reg. 44/14, ss. 1-14; O. Reg. 171/14, s. 1; O. Reg. 194/15, s. 3; O. Reg. 38/16, ss. 1-8; O. Reg. 488/16, s. 1; O. Reg. 202/17, s. 1; O. Reg. 345/19.

CONTENTS

OVERVIEW

The Small Claims Court accommodates 50% of the civil litigation in Ontario. It is designed to be an expeditious and informal forum for the resolution of disputes. An overriding principle is that the disputes it has jurisdiction to deal with are to be dealt with quickly, cheaply and with less reliance on formal rules.[1]

With the threshold increasing from $10,000 to $25,000 on January 1, 2010,[2] the Small Claims Court now plays a much larger role in the adjudication of civil disputes in the province. The statutory basis of the court lies in ss. 22-33.1 of the *Courts of Justice Act*, R.S.O. 1990, c. C.43 ("CJA"). Procedure in the court is governed by the Small Claims Court Rules ("SCCR").

The basic process in Small Claims Court has three steps: pleadings, settlement conference and trial.[3]

Authority The Small Claims Court shall hear and determine in a summary way all questions of law and fact and may make such order as is considered just and agreeable to good conscience.[4] This does not abrogate basic principles of procedural fairness, jurisdiction or statutory interpretation.[5] Such power should not result in the procedural unfairness which is visited upon a party when it is deprived of a meaningful opportunity to prepare an argument and address the court on an issue.[6]

Generally, the Small Claims Court shall hear and determine all questions of law relating to the court, including proceedings with respect to the issue of authority to order cross-examination on an affidavit in support of a motion. It would be commenced by a Notice of Motion in that court.[7] The Small Claims Court is a branch of the Superior Court of Justice by virtue of CJA s. 22(1). Therefore, other statutes which direct that proceedings be brought in the Superior Court of Justice are deemed to confer jurisdiction on the Small Claims Court for claims within its monetary jurisdiction.[8] While there is no provision in the CJA that Deputy Judges are also Judges of the General Division, there is no doubt that they are Judges of a Branch of the General Division.[9]

The Small Claims Court has jurisdiction to award legal or equitable relief where the relief requested is a monetary payment under the limit of $25,000 or the return of personal property valued within that limit. This includes jurisdiction to grant relief based on a claim of unjust enrichment. Sections 23, 96(1) and 96(3) of the CJA are to be read as a coherent package. Section 23 of the CJA is broad enough to allow the Small Claims Court to deal with claims in common law and equity. Under s. 96(1), the courts, including the Small Claims Court, are authorized to concurrently administer all rules of equity and the common law. The phrase "where otherwise provided" in s. 96(3) must mean that the Small Claims Court is able to grant equitable relief within the limits of its jurisdiction set out in s. 23; namely, to order the payment of money or the return of personal property.[10]

The Small Claims Court has an inherent jurisdiction to control its own process. The scheduling of trials falls within that inherent jurisdiction. Inherent jurisdiction also covers the discretion to order trial together. The court has the authority to consolidate trials consistent with the principle expressed in CJA s. 138 that "As far as possible, multiplicity of proceedings shall be avoided."[11] A deputy judge has the jurisdiction to alter the time deadlines otherwise provided under the *Small Claims Court Rules* and even to dismiss an action.[12]

Specific types of proceedings An action against the federal Crown can be maintained in the Small Claims Court. As a branch of what is now the Superior Court of Justice, the court is conferred such jurisdiction by virtue of the combined effect of s. 21 of the *Crown Liability and Proceedings Act*, R.S.C. 1985, c. C-50 and the definition of "superior court" in s. 35(1) of the federal *Interpretation Act*, R.S.C. 1985, c. I-21.[13] The Small Claims Court has jurisdiction to consider a trust claim under the *Construction Lien Act* provided that the amount involved is within its monetary jurisdiction. Any declaration under ss. 8 and 13 of the *Construction Lien Act*, R.S.O. 1990, c. C.30 is incidental to the substantive remedy of damages — *i.e.*, the court makes findings that a trust exists and that moneys are owed.[14]

While what is now s. 134 of the *Condominium Act, 1998*, S.O. 1998, c. 19 indicates that disputes regarding duties under the Act are to be determined by the Superior Court of Justice, there is no express statutory requirement that such disputes shall be heard by a Judge appointed under s. 96 of the *Constitution Act, 1867*. Where an application involves the interpretation of the condominium agreement as opposed to imposition of a duty on the condominium, it may be decided by a Judge of the Small Claims Court, provided the claim is within the court's monetary jurisdiction.[15]

The procedures of the Small Claims Court were never intended to deal with a complex action involving the duties owed by stock exchanges to investors.[16] Similarly, it was not appropriate to bring a complex medical malpractice action in Small Claims Court, although only $10,000 was claimed. D hospital had the right to make a full answer and defence as its reputation was at stake, and D's experts would need the evidence obtained on discovery in order to properly formulate their opinions.[17]

Proceedings in Ontario for debt owing in the amount of $25,000 or less, based on a foreign judgment from a non-reciprocating state, should be brought by action in the Small Claims Court.[18]

The Small Claims Court has jurisdiction to hear applications under s. 67 of the PPSA.[19] However, it has been noted that the Legislature chose the word "application" in s. 67(1) of the PPSA carefully. It has the same meaning as in s. 1 of the CJA. Such proceedings should therefore be commenced by application and not by way of action.[20] Similarly, an application under s. 23 of the *Repair and Storage Liens Act* may proceed as an application under the Small Claims Court Rules. The application language of RSLA ss. 23 and 25 should read as meaning Plaintiff's Claim.[21]

The Ontario small claims court is now authorized under the *Ontario Human Rights Code* to determine whether D has breached the Code if the plaintiff is litigating in the small claims court on a related non-Code matter.[22]

Family law cases, if such a case is channelled through the Family Law Rules, must be heard by a family court. The amount claimed does not drive that analysis because Family Law Rules deal with types of claims rather than amounts claimed. A claim to vary the Cohabitation Agreement, which is a "domestic contract" within the meaning of Part IV of the Family Law Act, must proceed in a family court.[23]

The Small Claims Court has no jurisdiction over a *Solicitors Act* assessment, and no power to consolidate proceedings before it with proceedings under the *Solicitors Act*, or direct that one be stayed pending determination of the other.[24]

Fees The absence of a statutory mechanism for the waiver or reduction of fees in limited circumstances was a breach of the rule of law and was unconstitutional. At common law, there is a constitutional right of access to the courts, and indigent persons should not be denied access to the Small Claims Court when their claims or defences are meritorious and their inability to pay the prescribed fees is proven on a balance of probabilities.[25]

Language The right conferred on francophone citizens in Ontario under s. 126 to a bilingual proceeding is a substantive right, and is applicable to proceedings in Small Claims Court despite the direction in CJA s. 25 that such cases are to be heard in a manner which will keep costs low and procedure simple.[26]

Rules As the Small Claims Court is a special subset of the Superior Court to accommodate small claims with simplicity and expediency, and with smaller risk of costs, the procedures throughout are significantly different than the Superior Court. The Rules of the court are simplified. The procedure is simplified; for example, it already being a summary court, there is no summary judgment procedure in the court, there is no discovery process, and there is simplification of admissibility of documentary evidence. The Small Claims Court Rules need to be read as a whole and also in the context of the common law — this forms part of a contextual analysis where the factors of conduct, reasons for delay, and prejudice are considered.[27]

Representation A party may be represented in a proceeding in the Small Claims Court by a person authorized under the *Law Society Act*, R.S.O. 1990, c. L.8 to represent the party, but the court may exclude from a hearing anyone, other than a person licensed under the *Law Society Act*, appearing on behalf of the party if it finds that such person is not competent properly to represent the party, or does not understand and comply at the hearing with the duties and responsibilities of an advocate.[28]

Self-representation Judges of the Small Claims Court, its administrators and members of the Bar are required to conduct themselves in a manner so as to ensure that self-represented persons are provided with fair access and equal treatment by the court. This dictate, however, does not require the court to ameliorate all of the adverse consequences that so often arise when the self-represented litigant takes upon himself or herself the task of preparing pleadings, and prosecuting his or her own case. The assistance of the court in such cases ought to be restricted to the provision of legal information, not legal advice. The decision of the self-represented to act as their own counsel should not affect the court's obligation to apply the same legal principles, rules of evidence and standards of procedure to both sides.[29]

Discovery Discovery is not an isolated procedural step separately identified in Small Claims Court process, those steps being pleadings, settlement conference and trial. Instead, the SCCR create a limited form of document discovery woven into the pleading and settlement conference steps. The alternate document disclosure process ensures relevant documents are equally available to both parties by giving the power to order disclosure to the settlement conference judge without the need of a separate motion. This is more convenient for the self-represented litigant who must attend the settlement conference as part of the mandatory process and may not be aware of the motion process.[30]

Small Claims court is generally not a court of surprises.[31] The general rule in Small Claims Court Actions is that full and fair disclosure should take place as early as possible in the proceeding. Rules 7.01(2), 9.02(1) and 10.01(4) require that copies of all documents on which a party intends to rely be attached to the claim or defence. Such disclosure, timed as such, puts the parties on notice of the case that they have to meet. To the extent that it discloses the strengths and weaknesses of their respective cases, such disclosure promotes early settlement. This objective assists both the litigants and the court. As well, and to this end, r. 13.03(2) dictates an additional disclosure requirement. At least 14 days before the date set for the settlement conference, each party or his legal representative, must serve the other parties with copies of any documents (including any expert reports) that were not attached to the claim or defence, and file them with the court. Service and filing of a list of proposed witnesses of each party is also required at this stage (r. 13.03(2)(*b*)).[32] Then 30 or more days prior to trial each party may serve and file the documents that they plan to rely upon at the trial as evidence (rr. 18.02(1) and 18.02(2)2).[33]

There is an inconsistency in the case law and practice as to whether there is any "discovery" power beyond the specific provision of r. 13.05(2)(vi). It has been said that the only exception to the absence of discovery rights in Small Claims Court is the power of a settlement conference judge to make an order for the production of documents between the parties: see r. 13.05(2)(a)(vi).[34] There is no jurisdiction in the Small Claims court for a pre-trial motion to compel the production of documents.[35]

Determination of issues at trial Essentially, the litigants present a set of facts to the deputy judge, and it is left to the deputy judge to determine the legal issues that emerge from those facts and bring his or her legal expertise to bear in resolving those issues.[36]

Even if pleadings should be read liberally, they are still important in Small Claims Court, so that D has notice of the case to be met. This is particularly true now that damages of up to $25,000 can be awarded in Small Claims Court.[37] The Small Claims Court can grant relief that was not pleaded, but should do so only if (i) there is no need for evidence beyond that led at trial in support of the relief pled; and (ii) it is not unfair to grant such relief.[38]

Trial management What trial management tools are most appropriate is a fact-sensitive exercise of discretion having regard to the totality of the circumstances including the presence of self-represented litigants, the sophistication of the parties, the issues framed by the pleadings, the degree of organization of the case, time estimates provided to the court, the existence of agreed facts or admissions, etc. Approaches may include the following:

(1) at the outset, secure clear statements from the parties as to what aspects of the pleadings are live issues for trial and the means by which burdens of proof will be discharged

(2) seek presentation of a witness and exhibit list and the relevance of same to issues in the case

(3) obtain estimates from the parties respecting the time for witness examinations and oral arguments

(4) identify admissibility of evidence issues and determine whether an offer of proof or *voir dire* is required or whether the issue is really a matter of weight

(5) set time limits for oral argument

(6) maintain control of questioning, and in particular cross-examination, to limit the evidence to what is admissible and relevant to real issues in the proceeding, while avoiding repetitive or cumulative evidence

(7) exercise judicial intervention in addition to clarify evidence and relevance, and to avoid confusion or mistreatment of witnesses.

Judicial intervention should be undertaken without commandeering the case, without evidencing prejudgment or disbelief/belief in a witness's testimony, a closed mind or engaging in conduct giving an appearance of favouring either party. It is the quality of the intervention rather than the quantity that matters. Wherever possible, judicial intervention respecting the questioning of a witness should be reserved until the witness's testimony is at an end.

Persistent interference by a trial judge might well cause any reasonable bystander to conclude that the accused did not have a fair trial. Always having regard to the perceptions a self-represented litigant may reasonably have, a trial judge generally has greater liberty during argument or closing submissions to challenge a party's position or to express preliminary thoughts on issues.

Robust trial management cannot eliminate elements of a fair trial for the sake of efficiency for example, the right to be heard includes the opportunity to make submissions. The right to be heard, the *audi alteram partem* rule, is a fundamental component of natural justice.

Effective cross-examination is recognized as the core of a fair trial and the right to cross-examine witnesses, while not absolute, should be without significant and unwarranted restraint. That said, prolix, repetitive, confusing, abusive, irrelevant, unstructured and misleading cross-examinations are subject to judicial control.

The trial judge cannot place any restriction on the length of time to be consumed by cross-examination. The rulings of the trial judge should be made when questions are put or about to be put and should be confined to the propriety of the question or questions in issue. However, a timetable is essential so that the judge can exercise control and so that there is a clear target to aim at for the completion of the evidence of each witness. Moreover, the judge can and should indicate when cross-examination is irrelevant, unnecessary or time wasting. The judge may limit the time for further cross-examination of a particular witness.

While some jurisdictions have recently favoured time limits for the cross-examination of vulnerable witnesses, capping the duration of examinations is inappropriate. A trial court may inquire into the anticipated length of an examination and even set reasonable and flexible targets.

A trial judge is entitled to the presumption of integrity, which includes the presumption of impartiality. That said, a fine balance is to be drawn by judges who are expected both to conduct the process effectively and avoid creating in the mind of a reasonable, fair minded and informed person any impression of a lack of impartiality. The test for pre-judgment is whether a reasonable observer would conclude that the trial judge was engaged in premature decision-making.

Essential to the application of active trial management is maintenance of respect and civility through judicious demeanour. The court must preserve its neutrality and act with restraint in conducting a proceeding. Frustration with litigants or their questions or positions should not result in editorializing, sarcasm, ill-considered or discourteous language from a trial judge. Of course, dismissive or mocking conduct by the court is unacceptable.[39]

Evidence The Small Claims Court may admit as evidence at a hearing and act upon any oral testimony and any document or other thing so long as the evidence is relevant to the subject matter of the proceeding, but the court may exclude anything unduly repetitious. However, privileged information or evidence prohibited by statute is not admissible.[40] The Small Claims Court has a broad discretion to receive and act on evidence which might be inadmissible in other courts. Such evidence is before the court and the court is entitled to accept it for the truth of its contents, subject to the court's general discretion as to weight.[41]

Admissions The Small Claims Court Rules make no provision for requests to admit. Rule 51 of the Civil Rules does not apply to proceedings in the Small Claims Court, by virtue of r. 1.02(1) of the SCCR.[42] Despite this, recourse has been made to r. 51 of the Civil Rules, under which a party seeking to amend its pleading by withdrawing an admission must satisfy a three-part test. First, the proposed amendment must raise a triable issue. Second, the admission made was inadvertent. Third, the withdrawal will not cause an injustice.[43]

Costs An award of costs in the Small Claims Court, other than disbursements, shall not exceed 15% of the amount claimed or the value of the property sought to be recovered unless the court considers it necessary in the interests of justice to penalize a party or a party's representative for unreasonable behaviour in the proceeding.[44]

Appeals An appeal lies to the Divisional Court from a final order of the Small Claims Court only in an action for the payment of money in excess of $2,500, excluding costs, or for the recovery of possession of personal property exceeding $2,500 in value.[45] Section 31 of the CJA is the only provision that governs appeals from the Small Claims Court, and provides that appeals from the Small Claims Court lie only to the Divisional Court. Leave is not required in order to appeal to the Divisional Court. Where an order made by a judge of the Small Claims Court is interlocutory, and not final, there is no appeal to the Divisional Court or the Superior Court of Justice. Section 19(1)(b) of the CJA does not contemplate a procedure for appealing an interlocutory order of the Small Claims Court to the Divisional Court with leave from a judge of the Superior Court of Justice.[46]

Standard of review It is not true that a different and lesser standard of review applies to Small Claims Court reasons. In assessing the adequacy of the reasons, context matters. Appellate courts recognize that oral reasons ordinarily cannot be as thorough and detailed as written reasons. In moving under pressure from case to case, it is expected that oral judgments will contain much less than the complete line of reasoning leading to the result.[47]

---

[1] *Lahrkamp v. Metropolitan Toronto Condominium Corp. No. 932*, [2012] O.J. No. 5986, 2012 ONSC 6326 (Ont. Div. Ct.).

[2] Small Claims Court Jurisdiction and Appeal Limit, O. Reg. 626/00, s. 1.

[3] *Petrykowski v. 553562 Ontario Ltd.*, [2010] O.J. No. 1048 (Ont. Sm. Cl. Ct.).

[4] *Courts of Justice Act*, R.S.O. 1990, c. C.43, s. 25.

[5] *Princess Cruises v. Nicolazzo*, [2009] O.J. No. 2294, 97 O.R. (3d) 630 (Ont. Div. Ct.). See also *Wittenberg v. Fred Geisweller/Locomotive Investments Inc.*, [1999] O.J. No. 2351, 44 O.R. (3d) 626 (Ont. Div. Ct.).

[6] *Armellini v. Crook*, [2013] O.J. No. 3249, 2013 ONSC 4735 (Ont. S.C.J.).

[7] *Mayo v. Veenstra*, [2003] O.J. No. 37, 63 O.R. (3d) 194 (Ont. S.C.J.).

[8] *Brighton Heating & Air Conditioning Ltd. v. Savoia*, [2006] O.J. No. 250, 79 O.R. (3d) 386 (Ont. S.C.J.).

[9] *Stockey v. Peel Condominium Corp. No. 174*, [1996] O.J. No. 3248, 30 O.R. (3d) 464 (Ont. Div. Ct.).

[10] *Grover v. Hodgins*, [2011] O.J. No. 310, 2011 ONCA 72 (Ont. C.A.), leave to appeal to S.C.C. refused [2011] S.C.C.A. No. 142 (S.C.C.)

[11] *Oberbichler v. State Farm Mutual Automobile Insurance Co.*, [2013] O.J. No. 3898 (Ont. S.C.J. (Sm. Cl. Ct.)).

[12] *Hervieux v. Huronia Optical*, [2016] O.J. No. 3270, 2016 ONCA 294 (Ont. C.A.).

[13] *Luo v. Canada (Attorney General)*, [1997] O.J. No. 1581, 33 O.R. (3d) 300 (Ont. Div. Ct.).

[14] *Brighton Heating & Air Conditioning Ltd. v. Savoia*, [2006] O.J. No. 250, 79 O.R. (3d) 386 (Ont. S.C.J.).

[15] *Stockey v. Peel Condominium Corp. No. 174*, [1996] O.J. No. 3248, 30 O.R. (3d) 464 (Ont. Div Ct.). Note: *Stockey* was decided under s. 49 of the 1990 *Condominium Act*.

[16] *Vigna v. Toronto Stock Exchange*, [1998] O.J. No. 4924, 28 C.P.C. (4th) 318 (Ont. Div. Ct.).

[17] *Farlow v. Hospital for Sick Children*, [2009] O.J. No. 4847, 100 O.R. (3d) 213 (Ont. S.C.J.).

[18] *Lahrkamp v. Metropolitan Toronto Condominium Corp. No. 932*, [2012] O.J. No. 5986, 2012 ONSC 6326 (Ont. Div. Ct.).

[19] *Chrysler Financial Services Canada Inc. v. Misner*, [2012] O.J. No. 3779 (Ont. S.C.J.).

[20] *Paccar Financial Services Ltd. v. 2026125 Ontario Ltd.*, [2014] O.J. No. 291, 2014 ONSC 456 (Ont. S.C.J.).

[21] *1218897 Ontario Ltd. (c.o.b. Castle Auto Collision & Mechanical Service) v. McEachern*, [2016] O.J. No. 1702 (Ont. S.C.J.).

[22] *Friman v. Toledo Estates Ltd.*, [2013] O.J. No. 1908, 2012 ONSC 4609 (Ont. S.C.J. (Sm. Cl. Ct.)).

[23] *Kurtz v. Hueckroth*, [2014] O.J. No. 3506.

[24] *Wallis v. Steven D. Gadbois Professional Corp.*, [2015] O.J. No. 545 (Ont. S.C.J. (Sm. Cl. Ct.)).

[25] *Polewsky v. Home Hardware Stores Ltd.*, [2003] O.J. No. 2908, 66 O.R. (3d) 600 (Ont. Div. Ct.).

[26] *Wittenberg v. Fred Geisweller/Locomotive Investments Inc.*, [1999] O.J. No. 2351, 44 O.R. (3d) 626 (Ont. Div. Ct.).

[27] *Sarkisian v. Chacon Properties Inc.*, [2013] O.J. No. 806 (Ont. S.C.J. (Sm. Cl. Ct.)).

[28] *Courts of Justice Act*, R.S.O. 1990, c. C.43, s. 26.

[29] *Crocker v. Ventawood Management Inc.*, [2013] O.J. No. 4588 (Ont. S.C.J. (Sm. Cl. Ct.)).

[30] *National Service Dog Training Centre Inc. v. Hall*, [2013] O.J. No. 3216 (Ont. S.C.J. (Sm. Cl. Ct.)).

[31] *Sterling Tile & Carpet v. Sierra Building Group Inc.*, [2015] O.J. No. 5136 (Ont. S.C.J.).

[32] *Crocker v. Ventawood Management Inc.*, [2013] O.J. No. 4588 (Ont. S.C.J. (Sm. Cl. Ct.)).

[33] *Sterling Tile & Carpet v. Sierra Building Group Inc.*, [2015] O.J. No. 5136 (Ont. S.C.J.).

[34] *Petrykowski v. 553562 Ontario Ltd.*, [2010] O.J. No. 1048 (Ont. S.C.J. (Sm. Cl. Ct.)). *Contra: Burke*

v. Lauzon Sound and Automation Inc., [2016] O.J. No. 2914 (Ont. Sm. Cl. Ct.).

35 *Cathers v. RBC Dominion Securities Inc.*, [2013] O.J. No. 5119 (Ont. S.C.J. (Sm. Cl. Ct.)).

36 *936464 Ontario Ltd. v. Mungo Bear Ltd.*, [2003] O.J. No. 3795, 74 O.R. (3d) 45 (Ont. S.C.J.)

37 *Salamon v. Toronto (City)*, [2011] O.J. No. 6251, 2011 ONSC 4192 (Ont. Div. Ct.).

38 *Brighton Heating & Air Conditioning Ltd. v. Savoia*, [2006] O.J. No. 250, 79 O.R. (3d) 386 (Ont. Div. Ct.).

39 *Chanachowicz v. Winona Wood Ltd.*, [2016] O.J. No. 37, 2016 ONSC 160 (Ont. S.C.J. (Sm. Cl. Ct.)).

40 *Courts of Justice Act*, R.S.O. 1990, c. C.43, s. 26.

41 *Lamka v. Waterloo (Regional Municipality) Police Services Board*, [2012] O.J. No. 5591 (Ont. S.C.J. (Sm. Cl. Ct.)).

42 *Metcalfe v. Khanna*, [2012] O.J. No. 34 (Ont. S.C.J. (Sm. Cl. Ct.)).

43 *Kinka Transport Inc. v. Rideway Transport Inc.*, [2012] O.J. No. 4081 (Ont. S.C.J. (Sm. Cl. Ct.)).

44 *Courts of Justice Act*, R.S.O. 1990, c. C.43, s. 29.

45 Small Claims Court Jurisdiction and Appeal Limit, O. Reg. 626/00, s. 2.

46 *Grainger v. Windsor-Essex Children's Aid Society*, [2009] O.J. No. 2872, 96 O.R. (3d) 711 (Ont. S.C.J.).

47 *Massoudinia v. Volfson*, [2013] O.J. No. 210, 2013 ONCA 29 (Ont. C.A.).

Rule 1 — General

1.01 CITATION — These rules may be cited as the Small Claims Court Rules.

1.02 DEFINITIONS — (1) In these rules,

"court" means the Small Claims Court;

"disability", where used in respect of a person or party, means that the person or party is,

(a)   a minor,

(b)   mentally incapable within the meaning of section 6 or 45 of the *Substitute Decisions Act, 1992* in respect of an issue in the proceeding, whether the person or party has a guardian or not, or

(c)   an absentee within the meaning of the *Absentees Act*;

"document" includes data and information in electronic form;

"electronic" includes created, recorded, transmitted or stored in digital form or in other intangible form by electronic, magnetic or optical means or by any other means that has capabilities for creation, recording, transmission or storage similar to those means, and "electronically" has a corresponding meaning;

"holiday" means,

(a)   any Saturday or Sunday,

(b)   New Year's Day,

(b.1)   Family Day,

(c)   Good Friday,

7

(d)   Easter Monday,

(e)   Victoria Day,

(f)   Canada Day,

(g)   Civic Holiday,

(h)   Labour Day,

(i)   Thanksgiving Day,

(j)   Remembrance Day,

(k)   Christmas Day,

(l)   Boxing Day, and

(m)   any special holiday proclaimed by the Governor General or the Lieutenant Governor,

and if New Year's Day, Canada Day or Remembrance Day falls on a Saturday or Sunday, the following Monday is a holiday, and if Christmas Day falls on a Saturday or Sunday, the following Monday and Tuesday are holidays, and if Christmas Day falls on a Friday, the following Monday is a holiday;

"information technology" [REVOKED: O. Reg. 78/06, s. 2(1), in force July 1, 2006.]

"order" includes a judgment.

"paralegal" means a person licensed under the *Law Society Act* to provide legal services in Ontario;

"proof of service" means, with respect to a document, proof of service of the document in accordance with rule 8.06;

"representative" means the lawyer, paralegal or other person representing a person in a proceeding under these rules;

"self-represented", when used in reference to a person, means that the person is not represented by a representative.

"territorial division" means,

(a)   a county, a district or a regional municipality, and

(b)   each of the following, as they existed on December 31, 2002:

    (i)   The combined area of County of Brant and City of Brantford.

    (ii)   Municipality of Chatham-Kent.

    (iii)   Haldimand County.

    (iv)   City of Hamilton.

    (v)   City of Kawartha Lakes.

    (vi)   Norfolk County.

(vii)   **City of Ottawa.**

(viii)   **County of Prince Edward.**

(ix)   **City of Toronto.**

(2) [REVOKED: O. Reg. 78/06, s. 2(3), in force July 1, 2006.]

[O. Reg. 461/01, s. 1(1); O. Reg. 330/02, s. 1; O. Reg. 440/03, s. 5; O. Reg. 78/06, s. 2; O. Reg. 574/07, s. 1; O. Reg. 393/09, s. 1; O. Reg. 230/13, s. 1; O. Reg. 44/14, s. 1.]

1.03 GENERAL PRINCIPLE — (1) These rules shall be liberally construed to secure the just, most expeditious and least expensive determination of every proceeding on its merits in accordance with section 25 of the *Courts of Justice Act*.

(2) MATTERS NOT COVERED IN RULES — If these rules do not cover a matter adequately, the court may give directions and make any order that is just, and the practice shall be decided by analogy to these rules, by reference to the *Courts of Justice Act* and the Act governing the action and, if the court considers it appropriate, by reference to the *Rules of Civil Procedure*.

[O. Reg. 78/06, s. 3.]

PRACTICE NOTES

§1.   Generally
§2.   Matters not covered in Rules

§1 Generally The Small Claims Court is often referred to as the "people's court". It is hospitable to litigants who are not represented by counsel. Its procedures are straightforward. Twenty-one rules govern an action from commencement to trial and enforcement. Costs related to Small Claims Court matters are significantly lower than is the case in the Superior Court. The court is geared to, and does, dispense justice quickly. The lack of formality, rules and procedures means that cases can make their way through the system more quickly than in Superior Court. The Small Claims Court is well suited to cases which can be dispensed with in a summary way, cases in which the evidence and legal issues are fairly straightforward. Proceedings in Small Claims Court are also less costly than proceedings in Superior Court. There are no examinations for discovery. There is a limit on costs awards.[1]

Rule 1.03(1) suggests that there should be a liberal interpretation of the rules leading to the just, most expeditious and least expensive, determination on its merits. Two things are notable — the first goal is "justice" and the final goal is determination on the merits as opposed to allowing procedural technicalities to resolve the matter. A justice priority and meritorious determination are consistent with the overriding authority set out in s. 25 of the *Courts of Justice Act* that determinations are to be just and agreeable to good conscience.[2]

The Small Claims Court is bound by the doctrine of *stare decisis* to follow cases binding on it. To do otherwise would lead to arbitrary and unpredictable results which would operate to promote litigation rather than give guidance and promote resolution.[3]

Litigants should not circumvent the *Small Claims Court Rules* and try to obtain relief prematurely in the Superior Court.[4]

[1] *Farlow v. Hospital for Sick Children*, [2009] O.J. No. 4847, 100 O.R. (3d) 213 (Ont. S.C.J. (Sm. Cl. Ct.)).

[2] *National Service Dog Training Centre Inc. v. Hall*, [2013] O.J. No. 3216 (Ont. S.C.J. (Sm. Cl. Ct.)).

[3] *Collins Barrow Leamington LLP v. Tiessen*, [2014] O.J. No. 5813 (Ont. S.C.J. (Sm. Cl. Ct.)).

[4] *Dauvin-Borja v. D.M. Robichaud Ltd.*, [2016] O.J. No. 3377, 2016 ONSC 4195 (Ont. S.C.J.).

§2 Matters not covered in Rules   The weight of authority is against the importation into Small Claims of those processes which are hostile to the objectives of the court. Production of documents is one of those processes. Rule 1.03(2) cannot be used to create an entirely new and substantial procedure — such as a summary judgment, which is not included in the Rules of the Small Claims Court.[1] The analogy rule provided by r. 1.03(2) can only be applied where those rules fail to cover a matter adequately.[2]

When a matter is not adequately covered by the rules, r. 1.03(2) empowers a deputy judge to give directions and make any order that is just. Notable in this rule is that the sole criterion is what is "just" and the range of available outcomes is wide being "any order". The trigger for application of r. 1.03(2) is inadequate coverage of a matter, suggesting that absence or partial coverage of a matter may be resolved under this rule.[3] The Small Claims Court has no jurisdiction to order cross-examination on affidavits,[4] nor has the jurisdiction to make a non-party production order.[5]

The Small Claims Court Rules cannot be said to fail to address the matter of discovery of non-party documents adequately, when they contain no attempt to address that matter at all. There is no discovery in the Small Claims Court — the Civil Rules Committee having made a decision to omit discovery from the streamlined, summary procedures of the Small Claims Court Rules. Therefore, the analogy rule does not apply.[6] However, the absence of any power to make non-party production orders prior to trial does not limit a party's right to summons such evidence for trial. The power to summons witnesses is provided in r. 18.03 of the Small Claims Court Rules, and r. 18.03(2) specifically provides that a summonsed witness may be required to produce documents at trial.[7]

Rule 15.01(6) suggests that a Small Claims Court judge has the jurisdiction to vary or clarify an order previously made. In any case, r. 1.04 makes it clear that the Small Claims Court can impose conditions on the orders which it makes. Even if this were not so, r. 1.03(2) can be invoked to include reference to r. 59.06 of the Civil Rules which deals with "amending, setting aside or varying" orders.[8]

Interim recovery of personal property   The Small Claims Court has no jurisdiction to make an order for the interim recovery of personal property, as such. In defended cases, it is only after a trial that the court can make an order for the recovery of possession of personal property, which is then enforceable by writ of delivery. The sole exception is where the P who claims recovery of possession of personal property can satisfy the court that judgment should be granted before trial under r. 12.02 of the Small Claims Court Rules. Such a judgment would be a final and not an interlocutory order.[9]

Even if the court can be found to have jurisdiction to make an order for the interim recovery of personal property, the "substantial grounds" test for interim recovery of personal property requires a high degree of assurance that P will be successful at trial. Claims supported by clear documentary evidence are more likely to meet the test; claims depending upon a finding of credibility are less likely to do so.[10]

Inspections   To make the authority to inspect a meaningful one, under r. 17.03 some expert assistance may be necessary in advance of the trial. This reality is not adequately covered by r. 17.03, and therefore a deputy judge has authority under r. 1.03(2) to make an order analogous to the type of order that could be made under r. 32.01 of the *Rules of Civil Procedure*.[11]

Representative orders   Rule 1.03 permits a court to rely on r. 12.07 of the Civil Rules to grant a representation order in Small Claims Court proceedings. There is no principled reason why the legislature would seek to prohibit a trade union from suing or being sued in the Small Claims Court. The legislature did not intend to omit representation orders under r. 12.07 of the Civil Rules. It is not apparent that the legislature decided that such motions take on significance for the parties where the result should only be determined by a judge of the Superior Court.[12]

[1] *Caprio v. Caprio*, [2009] O.J. No. 3695, 97 O.R. (3d) 312 (Ont. S.C.J. (Sm. Cl. Ct.)).

[2] *Lemont v. State Farm Mutual Automobile Insurance Co.*, [2011] O.J. No. 4601 (Ont. S.C.J. (Sm. Cl. Ct.)).

[3] *National Service Dog Training Centre Inc. v. Hall*, [2013] O.J. No. 3216 (Ont. S.C.J. (Sm. Cl. Ct.)).

[4] *Mayo v. Veenstra*, [2003] O.J. No. 37, 63 O.R. (3d) 194 (Ont. S.C.J. (Sm. Cl. Ct.)).

[5] *Damjanac v. Davis*, [2008] O.J. No. 5164 (Ont. S.C.J. (Sm. Cl. Ct.)).

[6] *Lemont v. State Farm Mutual Automobile Insurance Co.*, [2011] O.J. No. 4601 (Ont. S.C.J. (Sm. Cl. Ct.)).

[7] *Polymer Distribution Inc. v. Rasmussen*, [2011] O.J. No. 1281 (Ont. S.C.J. (Sm. Cl. Ct.)).

[8] *Lahrkamp v. Metropolitan Toronto Condominium Corp. No. 932*, [2012] O.J. No. 5986, 2012 ONSC 6326 (Ont. Div. Ct.).

[9] *Ever Fresh Direct Foods v. Schindler*, [2011] O.J. No. 3634 (Ont. S.C.J. (Sm. Cl. Ct.)).

[10] *Gunn v. Gunn*, [2013] O.J. No. 30 (Ont. S.C.J. (Sm. Cl. Ct.)).

[11] *Riddell v. Apple Canada Inc.*, [2017] O.J. No. 3605, 2017 ONCA 590 (Ont. C.A.), application for leave to appeal to S.C.C. filed December 10, 2017.

[12] *Kelava v. Spadacini*, [2019] O.J. No. 5578, 2019 ONSC 6314 (Ont. Div. Ct.). See also *Bruyea v. O'Regan*, [2019] O.J. No. 3847, 2019 ONCA 599 (Ont. C.A.).

1.04 ORDERS ON TERMS — When making an order under these rules, the court may impose such terms and give such directions as are just.

1.05 STANDARDS FOR DOCUMENTS — A document in a proceeding shall be printed, typewritten, written or reproduced legibly.

[O. Reg. 78/06, s. 4.]

1.05.1 (1) ELECTRONIC FILING, ISSUANCE OF DOCUMENTS — If these rules permit or require a document to be filed electronically, the software authorized by the Ministry of the Attorney General for the purpose shall be used for the filing.

  (2) If these rules permit or require a document to be issued electronically, the software authorized by the Ministry of the Attorney General for the purpose shall be used for the issuance.

  (3) A document issued using the authorized software is deemed to have been issued by the Small Claims Court.

  (4) REQUIREMENT FOR SIGNATURE — If a document is filed or issued electronically, a requirement in these rules that the document contain a person's signature is satisfied if the authorized software indicates on the document that the document has been electronically filed or issued, as the case may be.

  (5) DATE OF FILING, ISSUANCE — The date on which a document that is filed or issued electronically is considered to have been filed or issued, as the case may be, is the date indicated for the document by the authorized software.

  (6) FILING, ISSUANCE OUTSIDE OF BUSINESS HOURS — A document that is filed or issued electronically outside of regular business hours is deemed to have been filed or issued, as the case may be, on the next day that is not a holiday.

  (7) REQUIREMENT TO KEEP ORIGINAL — A person who electronically files an affidavit or other signed or certified document in accordance with these rules shall,

  (a)   keep the original document until the third anniversary of the electronic filing, until the clerk requests that the original document be filed or until these rules require that the original document be filed, whichever is earliest; and

(b)   file the original document on the clerk's request.

(8) **LIMIT ON APPLICATION OF RULE** — Despite subrules (1) and (2) and anything to the contrary in these rules, a rule permitting or requiring a document to be filed or issued electronically does not apply unless the Ministry of the Attorney General has authorized software to be used for the purpose for the court location at which the proceeding to which the document relates was or is to be commenced or to which it was transferred.

(9) **INCONSISTENCIES** — In the event of an inconsistency between a document filed electronically by a person using the authorized software and information provided by the person using the authorized software other than the electronically filed document,

(a)   the electronically filed document prevails; and

(b)   the clerk may request written clarification from the person respecting the inconsistency.

[O. Reg. 44/14, s. 2; O. Reg. 38/16, s. 1.]

1.06 FORMS — (1) The forms prescribed by these rules shall be used where applicable and with such variations as the circumstances require.

(2) **TABLE OF FORMS** — In these rules, when a form is referred to by number, the reference is to the form with that number that is described in the Table of Forms at the end of these rules and is available on the Internet through www.ontariocourtforms.on.ca.

(3) **ADDITIONAL PARTIES** — If a form does not have sufficient space to list all of the parties to the action on the first page, the remaining parties shall be listed in Form 1A, which shall be appended to the form immediately following the first page.

(4) **ADDITIONAL DEBTORS** — If any of the following forms do not have sufficient space to list all of the debtors in respect of which the form applies, the remaining debtors shall be listed in Form 1A.1, which shall be appended to the form:

1.   Certificate of judgment (Form 20A).

2.   Writ of seizure and sale of personal property (Form 20C).

3.   Writ of seizure and sale of land (Form 20D).

4.   Direction to enforce writ of seizure and sale of personal property (Form 20O).

(5) **AFFIDAVIT** — If these rules permit or require the use of an affidavit, Form 15B may be used for the purpose unless another form is specified.

[O. Reg. 330/02, s. 2; O. Reg. 440/03, s. 1; O. Reg. 78/06, s. 4; O. Reg. 393/09, s. 2.]

1.07 TELEPHONE AND VIDEO CONFERENCES – WHERE AVAILABLE — (1) If facilities for a telephone or video conference are available at the court, all or part of any of the following maybe heard or conducted by telephone or video conference as permitted by subrules (2) and (3):

1.   A settlement conference.

2.   A motion.

(1.1) If facilities for a video conference are available at the court, all or part of an examination of a debtor or other person under rule 20.10 may be conducted by video conference as permitted by subrules (2) and (3).

(2) REQUEST TO BE MADE — A settlement conference or motion may be heard or conducted by telephone or video conference or all or part of an examination under rule 20.10 may be conducted by video conference if a party files a request for the conference (Form 1B), indicating the reasons for the request, and the court grants the request.

(3) BALANCE OF CONVENIENCE — In deciding whether to direct a telephone or video conference, the judge shall consider,

(a)   the balance of convenience between the party that wants the telephone or video conference and any party that opposes it; and

(b)   any other relevant matter.

(4) ARRANGEMENTS FOR CONFERENCE — If an order directing a telephone or video conference is made, the court shall make the necessary arrangements for the conference and notify the parties of them.

(5) SETTING ASIDE OR VARYING ORDER — A judge presiding at a proceeding or step in a proceeding may set aside or vary an order directing a telephone or video conference.
[O. Reg. 78/06, s. 4; O. Reg. 393/09, s. 3.]

1.08 REPRESENTATION — For greater certainty, nothing in these rules permits or authorizes the court to permit a person to act as a representative if that person is not authorized to do so under the *Law Society Act*.
[O. Reg. 230/13, s. 2.]

Rule 2 — Non-Compliance with the Rules

2.01 EFFECT OF NON-COMPLIANCE — A failure to comply with these rules is an irregularity and does not render a proceeding or a step, document or order in a proceeding a nullity, and the court may grant all necessary amendments or other relief, on such terms as are just, to secure the just determination of the real matters in dispute.

2.02 COURT MAY DISPENSE WITH COMPLIANCE — If necessary in the interest of justice, the court may dispense with compliance with any rule at any time.

PRACTICE NOTES

§1 **General principles**   Rule 2.02 gives a judge a great deal of discretion in applying the rules so as to arrive at a fair and reasonable result. However, in order to decide whether the result is fair and reasonable the interests of the two parties must be weighed against each other.[1]

[1] *Vallières v. Samson*, [2009] O.J. No. 3230, 97 O.R. (3d) 761 (Ont. Div. Ct.).

Rule 3 — Time

3.01 COMPUTATION — If these rules or an order of the court prescribe a period of time for the taking of a step in a proceeding, the time shall be counted by excluding the first day and including the last day of the period; if the last day of the period of time falls on a holiday, the period ends on the next day that is not a holiday.

3.02 POWERS OF COURT — (1) The court may lengthen or shorten any time prescribed by these rules or an order, on such terms as are just.

(2) **CONSENT** — A time prescribed by these rules for serving or filing a document may be lengthened or shortened by filing the consent of the parties.

[O. Reg. 461/01, s. 3.]

Rule 4 — Parties Under Disability

4.01 PLAINTIFF'S LITIGATION GUARDIAN — (1) An action by a person under disability shall be commenced or continued by a litigation guardian, subject to subrule (2).

(2) **EXCEPTION** — A minor may sue for any sum not exceeding $500 as if he or she were of full age.

(3) **CONSENT** — A plaintiff's litigation guardian shall, at the time of filing a claim or as soon as possible afterwards, file with the clerk a consent (Form 4A) in which the litigation guardian,

(a)   states the nature of the disability;

(b)   in the case of a minor, states the minor's birth date;

(c)   sets out his or her relationship, if any, to the person under disability;

(d)   states that he or she has no interest in the proceeding contrary to that of the person under disability;

(e)   acknowledges that he or she is aware of his or her liability to pay personally any costs awarded against him or her or against the person under disability; and

(f)   states whether he or she is represented by a representative and, if so, gives that person's name and confirms that the person has written authority to act in the proceeding.

[O. Reg. 230/13, s. 3.]

4.02 DEFENDANT'S LITIGATION GUARDIAN — (1) An action against a person under disability shall be defended by a litigation guardian.

(2) A defendant's litigation guardian shall file with the defence a consent (Form 4A) in which the litigation guardian,

(a)   states the nature of the disability;

(b)   in the case of a minor, states the minor's birth date;

(c)   sets out his or her relationship, if any, to the person under disability;

(d)   states that he or she has no interest in the proceeding contrary to that of the person under disability; and

(e)   states whether he or she is represented by a representative and, if so, gives that person's name and confirms that the person has written authority to act in the proceeding.

(3) **If it appears to the court that a defendant is a person under disability and the defendant does not have a litigation guardian the court may, after notice to the proposed litigation guardian, appoint as litigation guardian for the defendant any person who has no interest in the action contrary to that of the defendant.**

[O. Reg. 78/06, s. 5; O. Reg. 230/13, s. 4.]

PRACTICE NOTES

§1 General principles A litigation guardian is required for D under r. 4.02. The litigation guardian may be any qualified person under r. 4.03(2)(*a*)(i), or, if no such person is available, the Children's Lawyer under r. 4.03(2)(*a*)(ii). The usual practice is that once a claim has been served, a motion is brought either by the proposed litigation guardian or by P to appoint the litigation guardian for the minor defendant. The rules relating to minors are designed to protect them pursuant to the court's traditional *parens patriae* jurisdiction. A further protection is the requirement under r. 11.01(2) for leave of the court before a person under disability may be noted in default. Rule 8.02(i) provides a special rule for service on a minor. The usual option for alternative service of a claim under r. 8.01(1) is not available for minors. The only available method for personal service on a minor is that provided under r. 8.02(i).[1]

[1]   *Co-Operators General Insurance Co. v. Jones*, [2018] O.J. No. 545 at paras. 14-18 (Ont. S.C.J. (Sm. Cl. Ct.)).

4.03 WHO MAY BE LITIGATION GUARDIAN — (1) Any person who is not under disability may be a plaintiff's or defendant's litigation guardian, subject to subrule (2).

(2) **If the plaintiff or defendant,**

(a)   **is a minor, in a proceeding to which subrule 4.01 (2) does not apply,**

    (i)   **the parent or person with lawful custody or another suitable person shall be the litigation guardian, or**

    (ii)   **if no such person is available and able to act, the Children's Lawyer shall be the litigation guardian;**

(b)   **is mentally incapable and has a guardian with authority to act as litigation guardian in the proceeding, the guardian shall be the litigation guardian;**

(c)   **is mentally incapable and does not have a guardian with authority to act as litigation guardian in the proceeding, but has an attorney under a power of attorney with that authority, the attorney shall be the litigation guardian;**

(d)   **is mentally incapable and has neither a guardian with authority to act as litigation guardian in the proceeding nor an attorney under a power of attorney with that power,**

    (i)   **a suitable person who has no interest contrary to that of the incapable person may be the litigation guardian, or**

> > (ii)   if no such person is available and able to act, the Public Guardian and Trustee shall be the litigation guardian;
>
> (e)   is an absentee,
>
> > (i)   the committee of his or her estate appointed under the Absentees Act shall be the litigation guardian,
> >
> > (ii)   if there is no such committee, a suitable person who has no interest contrary to that of the absentee may be the litigation guardian, or
> >
> > (iii)   if no such person is available and able to act, the Public Guardian and Trustee shall be the litigation guardian;
>
> (f)   is a person in respect of whom an order was made under subsection 72 (1) or (2) of the *Mental Health Act* as it read before April 3, 1995, the Public Guardian and Trustee shall be the litigation guardian.

4.04 DUTIES OF LITIGATION GUARDIAN — (1) A litigation guardian shall diligently attend to the interests of the person under disability and take all steps reasonably necessary for the protection of those interests, including the commencement and conduct of a defendant's claim.

(2) **PUBLIC GUARDIAN AND TRUSTEE, CHILDREN'S LAWYER** — The Public Guardian and Trustee or the Children's Lawyer may act as litigation guardian without filing the consent required by subrule 4.01 (3) or 4.02 (2).

4.05 POWER OF COURT — The court may remove or replace a litigation guardian at any time.

4.06 SETTING ASIDE JUDGMENT, ETC. — If an action has been brought against a person under disability and the action has not been defended by a litigation guardian, the court may set aside the noting of default or any judgment against the person under disability on such terms as are just, and may set aside any step that has been taken to enforce the judgment.

4.07 SETTLEMENT REQUIRES COURT'S APPROVAL — No settlement of a claim made by or against a person under disability is binding on the person without the approval of the court.

4.08 MONEY TO BE PAID INTO COURT — (1) Any money payable to a person under disability under an order or a settlement shall be paid into court, unless the court orders otherwise, and shall afterwards be paid out or otherwise disposed of as ordered by the court.

(2) If money is payable to a person under disability under an order or settlement, the court may order that the money shall be paid directly to the person, and payment made under the order discharges the obligation to the extent of the amount paid.

(3) **SUPPORTING AFFIDAVIT** — A motion for an order under this rule shall be supported by an affidavit in Form 4B rather than an affidavit in Form 15A.

(4) **COSTS** — In making an order under this rule, the court may order that costs pay-

able to the moving party be paid out of the money in court directly to the the moving party's representative.

[O. Reg. 230/13, s. 5.]

Rule 5 — Partnerships and Sole Proprietorships

5.01 PARTNERSHIPS — A proceeding by or against two or more persons as partners may be commenced using the firm name of the partnership.

PRACTICE NOTES

§1 Generally Where a partnership is sued using the firm name, r. 5.03 goes on to provide that a Notice to Alleged Partner (Form 5A) may be served with the claim. That procedure then permits enforcement of an eventual judgment against the property of individual partners (as opposed to the firm property), unless a partner defends the proceeding separately denying having been a partner at the material time (r. 5.03(2)), except if the person admits being a partner or is adjudged to have been a partner at that time (r. 5.05(2)). Where a party elects not to follow this procedure and instead two individual Ds as partners, it is an error to describe the two individuals as a single legal entity.[1]

[1] *All Canadian Mechanical and Electrical Inc. v. Henderson*, [2011] O.J. No. 1456 (Ont. S.C.J. (Sm. Cl. Ct.)).

5.02 DEFENCE — If a proceeding is commenced against a partnership using the firm name, the partnership's defence shall be delivered in the firm name and no person who admits being a partner at any material time may defend the proceeding separately, except with leave of the court.

5.03 NOTICE TO ALLEGED PARTNER — (1) In a proceeding against a partnership using the firm name, a plaintiff who seeks an order that would be enforceable personally against a person as a partner may serve the person with the claim, together with a notice to alleged partner (Form 5A).

(2) A person served as provided in subrule (1) is deemed to have been a partner at the material time, unless the person defends the proceeding separately denying having been a partner at the material time.

5.04 DISCLOSURE OF PARTNERS — (1) If a proceeding is commenced by or against a partnership using the firm name, any other party may serve a notice requiring the partnership to disclose immediately in writing the names and addresses of all partners constituting the partnership at a time specified in the notice; if a partner's present address is unknown, the partnership shall disclose the last known address.

(1.1)-(1.1.1) [REVOKED: O. Reg. 78/06, s. 6, in force July 1, 2006.]

(2) If a partnership fails to comply with a notice under subrule (1), its claim may be dismissed or the proceeding stayed or its defence may be struck out.

[O. Reg. 461/01, s. 4(1); O. Reg. 330/02, s. 3; O. Reg. 440/03, s. 5; O. Reg. 78/06, s. 6.]

5.05 ENFORCEMENT OF ORDER — (1) An order against a partnership using the firm name may be enforced against the partnership's property.

(2) An order against a partnership using the firm name may also be enforced, if the order or a subsequent order so provides, against any person who was served as provided in rule 5.03 and who,

(a)   under that rule, is deemed to have been a partner at the material time;

(b)   has admitted being a partner at that time; or

(c)   has been adjudged to have been a partner at that time.

(3) **AGAINST PERSON NOT SERVED AS ALLEGED PARTNER —** If, after an order has been made against a partnership using the firm name, the party obtaining it claims to be entitled to enforce it against any person alleged to be a partner other than a person who was served as provided in rule 5.03, the party may make a motion for leave to do so; the judge may grant leave if the person's liability as a partner is not disputed or, if disputed, after the liability has been determined in such manner as the judge directs.
[O. Reg. 78/06, s. 7.]

5.06 SOLE PROPRIETORSHIPS — (1) If a person carries on business in a business name other than his or her own name, a proceeding may be commenced by or against the person using the business name.

(2) Rules 5.01 to 5.05 apply, with necessary modifications, to a proceeding by or against a sole proprietor using a business name, as though the sole proprietor were a partner and the business name were the firm name of a partnership.

Rule 6 — Forum and Jurisdiction

6.01 PLACE OF COMMENCEMENT AND TRIAL — (1) An action shall be commenced,

(a)   in the territorial division,

    (i)   in which the cause of action arose, or

    (ii)   in which the defendant or, if there are several defendants, in which any one of them resides or carries on business; or

(b)   at the court's place of sitting that is nearest to the place where the defendant or, if there are several defendants, where any one of them resides or carries on business.

(2) An action shall be tried in the place where it is commenced, but if the court is satisfied that the balance of convenience substantially favours holding the trial at another place than those described in subrule (1), the court may order that the action be tried at that other place.

(3) If, when an action is called for trial or settlement conference, the judge finds that the place where the action was commenced is not the proper place of trial, the court may order that the action be tried in any other place where it could have been commenced under this rule.
[O. Reg. 78/06, s. 8(1).]

PRACTICE NOTES

§1 Generally The long-standing practice in Small Claims Court has been that P must, as a general rule, commence a proceeding in the county where D resides or carries on business. If there are several defendants, P may choose any county in which one of the defendants resides or carries on business. The exception is that the proceeding may be commenced where the cause of action arose, even if none of the defendants resides or carries on business there. The further exception is that P may commence at the court's place of sitting that is nearest to the defendant or one of several defendants. That would only apply if there was no Small Claims Court in a county in which a defendant or one of them resides or carries on business. That the contract in issue may have been formed in a different county based on application of the common law rules for determination of where contract formation occurred was irrelevant where the cause of action was not the formation of the contract but the alleged breach.[1]

The general rule, as reflected in r. 6, is that a claim must be commenced in the jurisdiction where D resides or carries on business. However, the claim may be commenced in the jurisdiction where the cause of action arose, even if D does not reside in that jurisdiction. As a general rule, a contract is formed where the acceptance is received. There is a distinction between where the contract is formed, and where the breach occurs. In a claim based on breach of contract, the cause of action emanates from the breach, not the situs of the formation of the contract.[2]

Rule 6.01 is a mandatory provision, and there is no provision therein that permits the parties to contract out of the mandatory effect of the Rule. In order to commence a claim in a jurisdiction where none of the defendants reside or carry on business, P must establish that the cause of action arose in that jurisdiction. When the cause of action is a non-payment, the action ought to be commenced in the jurisdiction where D resides or carries on business.[3]

The tort of misrepresentation occurs in the jurisdiction in which the information was received or acted or relied upon.[4] When the cause of action was D's outright refusal to pay, as opposed to a bounced cheque, the cause of action originated in the jurisdiction where D decided not to pay, that is, where D carries on business.[5]

Procedure Subrules 6.01(1) and (2) provide two different approaches to questions of venue in the Small Claims Court. Subrule (1) provides where a proceeding must be commenced. Subrule (2) presupposes that a proper venue for commencement has been selected, and provides that venue may nevertheless be changed on motion if the balance of convenience substantially favours some other venue. Subrule 6.01(3) clarifies this distinction by effectively providing that a trial judge or settlement conference judge who finds the place of commencement is incorrect, may transfer the case to the proper venue for trial. The court may change venue on motion under either of r. 6.01(1) or (2). In appropriate circumstances the court may order a change of venue as a term of making any other order. Where P had selected the wrong venue for commencement, the court should correct that error by sending the case back to where it ought to have been commenced. The policy behind r. 6.01 is that convenience to P is sacrificed in favour of convenience to D. P should not be permitted to ignore the rule and impose unwarranted travel cost on D with impunity.[6]

It would be open to the court to dismiss all proceedings which were commenced in the wrong venue, without prejudice to them being commenced afresh where the defendants reside. In that event, P would lose the costs incurred to date in all such cases, which might send a message, particularly to institutional plaintiffs, not to ignore the venue rule.[7]

Noting in default To commence in a wrong venue and transfer to the correct venue only after D has been served and noted in default does not cure the venue problem P has created. The noting of default in the wrong venue is an irregular noting in default and should not be permitted to support a default judgment. The appropriate remedy is to set aside the noting in default and give D the right to defend in the correct and local court office where the case ought to have proceeded to begin with. Such a remedy also tends to discourage all plaintiffs including institutional plaintiffs from commencing claims in the wrong venue.[8]

---

[1] *2055525 Ontario Ltd. v. Thirty Three Rosedale, Holdings Inc.*, [2013] O.J. No. 5350 (Ont. S.C.J. (Sm. Cl. Ct.)).

[2] *Abacus Chartered Professional Accountant Corp. v. Annzo Corp.*, [2015] O.J. No. 4915 (Ont. S.C.J. (Sm. Cl. Ct.)).

[3] *Indcom Leasing Inc. v. Economy Lube Mississauga #2 Inc.*, [2014] O.J. No. 4041 (Ont. S.C.J. (Sm. Cl. Ct.)).

[4] *Leonard v. GC Surplus*, [2014] O.J. No. 1906 (Ont. S.C.J.).

[5] *Loyalist Collection Services Inc. v. Aerosprays, Inc.*, [2014] O.J. No. 5685 (Ont. S.C.J. (Sm. Cl. Ct.)).

[6] *2055525 Ontario Ltd. v. Thirty Three Rosedale, Holdings Inc.*, [2013] O.J. No. 5350 (Ont. S.C.J. (Sm. Cl. Ct.)).

[7] *Cash 4 You Corp. v. Power*, [2014] O.J. No. 2131 (Ont. S.C.J. (Sm. Cl. Ct.)

[8] *TD Auto Finance (Canada) Inc. v. Vardy*, [2012] O.J. No. 2410 (Ont. S.C.J. (Sm. Cl. Ct.)).

6.02 A cause of action shall not be divided into two or more actions for the purpose of bringing it within the court's jurisdiction.

PRACTICE NOTES

§1 Cause of action   While there is no definition of "cause of action" under either the Rules of Civil Procedure or under the Small Claims Court Rules, *Black's Law Dictionary* offers two alternate definitions. The first is "a group of operative facts giving rise to one or more basis for suing"; the second is the "legal theory of a lawsuit".[1]

The cause of action where there has been a non payment of a debt is, in essence, one of breach of contract. P cannot therefore, bring several actions where there has been one breach of contract. If there are several contracts, it is equally clear, that multiple actions can be sustained. P could not bring multiple actions on multiple invoices where an overarching agreement or contract governed the relationship between the parties.[2]

[1] *KNP Headwear Inc. v. Levinson*, [2005] O.J. No. 5438 (Ont. Div. Ct.). See also *Pen Woodworking Ltd. v. Narenjkar*, [2015] O.J. No. 3487 (Ont. S.C.J.).

[2] *Staff Mountain Inc. v. Indis Inc. (c.o.b. Muir's Cartage)*, [2015] O.J. No. 7264 (Ont. S.C.J. (Sm. Cl. Ct.)).

6.03 [REVOKED: O. Reg. 78/06, s. 8(2), in force July 1, 2006.]

Rule 7 — Commencement of Proceedings

7.01 PLAINTIFF'S CLAIM — (1) An action shall be commenced by filing a plaintiff's claim (Form 7A) with the clerk, together with a copy of the claim for each defendant.

(2) CONTENTS OF CLAIM, ATTACHMENTS — The following requirements apply to the claim:

1.   **It shall contain the following information, in concise and non- technical language:**

   i.   **The full names of the parties to the proceeding and, if relevant, the capacity in which they sue or are sued.**

   ii.   **The nature of the claim, with reasonable certainty and detail, including the date, place and nature of the occurrences on which the claim is based.**

   iii. **The amount of the claim and the relief requested.**

   iv.   **The name, address, telephone number, fax number if any, and Law Society of Upper Canada registration number if any, of the representative representing the plaintiff or, if the plaintiff is self-represented, the plaintiff's address, telephone number and fax number if any.**

v.   **The address where the plaintiff believes the defendant may be served.**

2.   **If the plaintiff's claim is based in whole or in part on a document, a copy of the document shall be attached to each copy of the claim, unless it is unavailable, in which case the claim shall state the reason why the document is not attached.**

(3) [REVOKED: O. Reg. 78/06, s. 9(2), in force July 1, 2006.]

[O. Reg. 78/06, s. 9; O. Reg. 56/08, s. 1; O. Reg. 230/13, s. 6.]

PRACTICE NOTES

§1 Generally P is required to name individual defendants by their full legal names. Form 7A contains boxes for an individual defendant's surname, first name, second or middle name, and any "also known as" names. It is P's own error to use D's informal first name and to take out a default judgment using that name. It is not open to P to obtain an order to change D's name on the default judgment order without notice to D. Rule 60.07(10) of the Civil Rules only supports a motion, without notice, where the judgment creditor is using one or more names in a manner that might otherwise frustrate enforcement of a judgment debt. P is required to obtain an order with notice under SCCR 15.01(6).[1]

Representative orders Rule 1.03 of the SCCR permits a court to rely on r. 12.07 of the Civil Rules to grant a representation order in Small Claims Court proceedings. There is no principled reason why the legislature would seek to prohibit a trade union from suing or being sued in the Small Claims Court. The legislature did not intend to omit representation orders under r. 12.07 of the Civil Rules. It is not apparent that the legislature decided that such motions take on significance for the parties where the result should only be determined by a judge of the Superior Court.[2]

[1] *Mirt v. Gerber*, [2015] O.J. No. 2888 (Ont. S.C.J. (Sm. Cl. Ct.)).

[2] *Kelava v. Spadacini*, [2019] O.J. No. 5578, 2019 ONSC 6314 (Ont. Div. Ct.). See also *Bruyea v. O'Regan*, [2019] O.J. No. 3847, 2019 ONCA 599 (Ont. C.A.).

7.02 ELECTRONIC FILING OF CLAIM — (1) A plaintiff's claim may be filed with the clerk electronically in accordance with this rule, if the following conditions are satisfied:

1.   **[REVOKED: O. Reg. 38/16, s. 2 (1).]**

2.   **Any interest payable in relation to the claim is no greater than 35 per cent per year.**

3.   **The defendant is not a person under disability.**

4.   **The claim is one that may, under subrule 6.01 (1), be filed in a court location for which the software authorized by the Ministry of the Attorney General for the purpose may be used, as indicated by the Ministry.**

(2) The plaintiff's claim shall specify at which court location referred to in paragraph 4 of subrule (1) the action is being commenced, and that court location is deemed to be the place at which the action is commenced.

(3) An email address at which the plaintiff agrees to accept service or receipt of documents from the court must be specified when filing the plaintiff's claim.

(4) If a plaintiff's claim is filed electronically, the requirement in subrule 7.01 (1) to also file a copy of the claim for each defendant does not apply.

(5) REQUIREMENT TO FILE IN PAPER FORMAT — A plaintiff's claim that has been filed and issued electronically shall be filed with the clerk by the plaintiff in paper format, with proof of service, in the following circumstances and in accordance with the following rules:

1.   If a defence is filed disputing all or part of the claim, the documents shall be filed at least 14 days before the date of the settlement conference, for the purposes of subrule 13.03 (2).

2.   If the plaintiff files a request to clerk under subrule 9.03 (3) for a terms of payment hearing, the documents shall be filed together with the request.

3.   If a motion is filed in the proceeding, the documents shall be filed in accordance with the following:

   i.   In the case of a motion in writing for an assessment of damages filed in paper format under clause 11.03 (2) (a), the documents shall be filed together with the motion.

   ii.   In the case of a motion in writing for an assessment of damages filed electronically under clause 11.03 (2.1) (a), the documents shall be filed within 14 days after the day the motion is filed.

   iii.   In any other case, the documents shall be filed at least three days before the hearing date.

4.   If the plaintiff files a request to clerk under clause 11.03 (2) (b) or (2.1) (b) for an assessment hearing, the documents shall be filed at least three days before the hearing date.

5.   If a garnishment hearing is requested under subrule 20.08 (15), the documents shall be filed,

   i.   at the time the hearing is requested, if the plaintiff is making the request, or

   ii.   in any other case, at least three days before the hearing date.

6.   If the plaintiff requests an examination under subrule 20.10 (1), the documents shall be filed when making the request.

[O. Reg. 44/14, s. 3; O. Reg. 38/16, s. 2.]

7.03 ISSUING CLAIM — (1) On receiving the plaintiff's claim, the clerk shall immediately issue it by dating, signing and sealing it and assigning it a court file number.

(2) The original of the claim shall remain in the court file and the copies shall be given to the plaintiff for service on the defendant.

PRACTICE NOTES

§1 General principles In the Small Claims Court, a liberal, non-technical approach should be taken to pleadings. The small claims court may grant relief or allow a defence not asserted in the pleadings if supporting evidence is not needed beyond what was adduced at trial and it was not unfair, in all of the circumstances, to grant such relief or allow such a defence. This approach does not depend on whether the litigants are self-represented (or represented by non-lawyers). Otherwise, what happens where one party is self-represented and one has counsel? The informality of pleading is a function of the nature of the court and not of the quality of the representation.[1]

---

[1] *Brighton Heating & Air Conditioning Ltd. v. Savoia*, [2006] O.J. No. 250, 79 O.R. (3d) 386 (Ont. Div. Ct.).

7.04 ELECTRONIC ISSUANCE OF CLAIM — (1) A plaintiff's claim that is filed electronically under rule 7.02 shall be issued electronically.

(2) If a plaintiff's claim is issued electronically, subrule 7.03 (2) does not apply. Instead, the claim shall be retained electronically, and a copy shall be placed into the court file by the clerk only if a request is made by a person in accordance with section 137 of the *Courts of Justice Act* to see the claim.

[O. Reg. 44/14, s. 3.]

Rule 8 — Service
Service of Particular Documents

8.01 PLAINTIFF'S OR DEFENDANT'S CLAIM — (1) A plaintiff's claim or defendant's claim (Form 7A or 10A) shall be served personally as provided in rule 8.02 or by an alternative to personal service as provided in rule 8.03.

(2) **TIME FOR SERVICE OF CLAIM —** A claim shall be served within six months after the date it is issued, but the court may extend the time for service, before or after the six months has elapsed.

(3) [REVOKED: O. Reg. 44/14, s. 4(1), in force July 1, 2014.]

(3.1) [REVOKED: O. Reg. 78/06, s. 10, in force July 1, 2006.]

(4) **DEFAULT JUDGMENT —** A default judgment (Form 11B) shall be served by the clerk in accordance with the following:

1. The clerk shall serve the default judgment by mail or by fax on all parties named in the claim, subject to paragraph 2.

2. If a plaintiff's claim was issued electronically under rule 7.04, the clerk may instead serve the default judgment on the plaintiff by email to the email address provided by the plaintiff for the purpose.

(4.1) [REVOKED: O. Reg. 38/16, s. 3 (1).]

(4.1.1) [REVOKED: O. Reg. 78/06, s. 10, in force July 1, 2006.]

(5) **ASSESSMENT ORDER —** An order made on a motion in writing for an assessment of damages under subrule 11.03 (2) shall be served by the clerk in accordance with the following:

1. The clerk shall serve the order on the plaintiff by mail if the plaintiff provides a stamped, self-addressed envelope with the notice of motion and support affidavit, subject to paragraph 2.

2.   If the plaintiff's claim was issued electronically under rule 7.04, the clerk may instead serve the order on the plaintiff by email to the email address provided by the plaintiff for the purpose.

(6) **SETTLEMENT CONFERENCE ORDER** — An order made at a settlement conference shall be served by the clerk by mail or by fax, on all parties that did not attend the settlement conference.

(7) **SUMMONS TO WITNESS** — A summons to witness (Form 18A) shall be served personally by the party who requires the presence of the witness, or by the party's representative, at least 10 days before the trial date; at the time of service, attendance money calculated in accordance with the regulations made under the *Administration of Justice Act* shall be paid or tendered to the witness.

(8) **NOTICE OF GARNISHMENT** — A notice of garnishment (Form 20E) shall be served by the creditor,

(a)   together with a sworn affidavit for enforcement request (Form 20P), on the debtor, by mail, by courier, personally as provided in rule 8.02 or by an alternative to personal service as provided in rule 8.03; and

(b)   together with a garnishee's statement (Form 20F), on the garnishee, by mail, by courier, personally as provided in rule 8.02 or by an alternative to personal service as provided in rule 8.03.

(9) **NOTICE OF GARNISHMENT HEARING** — A notice of garnishment hearing (Form 20Q) shall be served by the person requesting the hearing on the creditor, debtor, garnishee and co-owner of the debt, if any, and any other interested persons by mail, by courier, personally as provided in rule 8.02 or by an alternative to personal services as provided in rule 8.03.

(10) **NOTICE OF EXAMINATION** — A notice of examination (Form 20H) shall be served by the creditor on the debtor or person to be examined personally as provided in rule 8.02 or by an alternative to personal service as provided in rule 8.03.

(11) **FINANCIAL STATEMENT** — If the person to be examined is the debtor and the debtor is an individual, the creditor shall serve the notice of examination on the debtor together with a blank financial information form (Form 20I).

(12) The notice of examination,

(a)   shall be served, together with the financial information form if applicable, at least 30 days before the date fixed for the examination; and

(b)   shall be filed, with proof of service, at least three days before the date fixed for the examination.

(13) **NOTICE OF CONTEMPT HEARING** — A notice of a contempt hearing shall be served by the creditor on the debtor or person to be examined personally as provided in rule 8.02.

(14) **DEFENCE AND OTHER DOCUMENTS** — The following documents may be

served by mail, by courier, by fax, personally as provided in rule 8.02 or by an alternative to personal service as provided in rule 8.03, unless the court orders otherwise:

1.   A defence.

2.   Any other document not referred to in subrules (1) to (13).

[O. Reg. 461/01, s. 7(1)-(3); O. Reg. 330/02, s. 4; O. Reg. 440/03, s. 5; O. Reg. 78/06, s. 10; O. Reg. 393/09, s. 4; O. Reg. 230/13, s. 7; O. Reg. 44/14, s. 4; O. Reg. 38/16, s. 3.]

PRACTICE NOTES

§1 Notice of contempt hearing   Rule 8 suggests that the evidence placed before the court on a contempt hearing triggered by the service should at least: (1) demonstrate service was effected on a debtor and was personal; and (2) address the issue of whether the person served is or is not of the age of majority and is not under a disability. Even without r. 8.01, a court should be extremely reluctant to make a finding of contempt in absence of personal service. However, r. 8 does not impose a requirement of personal service that is so absolute that actual notice is not sufficient to support a finding of contempt. However, at the very least, the court would have to be satisfied on the basis of credible and compelling evidence that D did have actual notice of the contempt hearing.[1]

[1] *Avco Financial Services v. Wall*, [2000] O.J. No. 194 (Ont. S.C.J. (Sm. Cl. Ct.)). See also *Gehres Windows and Doors Ltd. v. Diamond (c.o.b. Creative European Designs)*, [2012] O.J. No. 4167 (Ont. S.C.J. (Sm. Cl. Ct.)).

8.02 PERSONAL SERVICE —   If a document is to be served personally, service shall be made,

Individual

(a)   on an individual, other than a person under disability, by leaving a copy of the document with him or her;

Municipality

(b)   on a municipal corporation, by leaving a copy of the document with the chair, mayor, warden or reeve of the municipality, with the clerk or deputy clerk of the municipality or with a lawyer for the municipality;

Corporation

(c)   on any other corporation, by leaving a copy of the document with,

(i)   an officer, a director or another person authorized to act on behalf of the corporation, or

(ii)   a person at any place of business of the corporation who appears to be in control or management of the place of business;

Board or Commission

(d)   on a board or commission, by leaving a copy of the document with a member or officer of the board or commission;

Person Outside Ontario Carrying on Business in Ontario

(e)   on a person outside Ontario who carries on business in Ontario, by leaving a copy of the document with anyone carrying on business in Ontario for the person;

Crown in Right of Canada

(f)   on Her Majesty the Queen in right of Canada, in accordance with subsection 23 (2) of the *Crown Liability and Proceedings Act*(Canada);

Crown in Right of Ontario

(g)   on Her Majesty the Queen in right of Ontario, in accordance with section 10 of the *Proceedings Against the Crown Act*;

Absentee

(h)   on an absentee, by leaving a copy of the document with the absentee's committee, if one has been appointed or, if not, with the Public Guardian and Trustee;

Minor

(i)   on a minor, by leaving a copy of the document with the minor and, if the minor resides with a parent or other person having his or her care or lawful custody, by leaving another copy of the document with the parent or other person;

Mentally Incapable Person

(j)   on a mentally incapable person,

(i)   if there is a guardian or an attorney acting under a validated power of attorney for personal care with authority to act in the proceeding, by leaving a copy of the document with the guardian or attorney,

(ii)   if there is no guardian or attorney acting under a validated power of attorney for personal care with authority to act in the proceeding but there is an attorney under a power of attorney with authority to act in the proceeding, by leaving a copy of the document with the attorney and leaving an additional copy with the person,

(iii)   if there is neither a guardian nor an attorney with authority to act in the proceeding, by leaving a copy of the document bearing the person's name and address with the Public Guardian and Trustee and leaving an additional copy with the person;

Partnership

(k)   on a partnership, by leaving a copy of the document with,

(i)   any one or more of the partners, or

(ii)   a person at the principal place of business of the partnership who appears to be in control or management of the place of business; and

Sole Proprietorship

(l)   on a sole proprietorship, by leaving a copy of the document with,

(i)   the sole proprietor, or

(ii)   a person at the principal place of business of the sole proprietorship who

appears to be in control or management of the place of business.
[O. Reg. 56/12, ss. 1, 6(1); O. Reg. 230/13, s. 7.]

8.03 ALTERNATIVES TO PERSONAL SERVICE — (1) If a document is to be served by an alternative to personal service, service shall be made in accordance with subrule (2), (3) or (5); in the case of a plaintiff's claim or defendant's claim served on an individual, service may also be made in accordance with subrule (7).

(2) AT PLACE OF RESIDENCE — If an attempt is made to effect personal service at an individual's place of residence and for any reason personal service cannot be effected, the document may be served by,

(a)   leaving a copy in a sealed envelope addressed to the individual at the place of residence with anyone who appears to be an adult member of the same household; and

(b)   on the same day or the following day, mailing or sending by courier another copy of the document to the individual at the place of residence.

(3) CORPORATION — If the head office or principal place of business of a corporation or, in the case of an extra-provincial corporation, the attorney for service in Ontario cannot be found at the last address recorded with the Ministry of Government Services, service may be made on the corporation,

(a)   by mailing or sending by courier a copy of the document to the corporation or to the attorney for service in Ontario, as the case may be, at that address; and

(b)   by mailing or sending by courier a copy of the document to each director of the corporation as recorded with the Ministry of Government Services, at the director's address as recorded with that Ministry.

(4) WHEN EFFECTIVE — Service made under subrule (2) or (3) is effective on the fifth day after the document is mailed or verified by courier that it was delivered.

(5) ACCEPTANCE OF SERVICE BY LAWYER OR PARALEGAL — Service on a party who is represented by a lawyer may be made by leaving a copy of the document with the lawyer or an employee in the lawyer's office, but service under this subrule is effective only if the lawyer or employee endorses on the document or a copy of it an acceptance of service and the date of the acceptance.

(6) By accepting service the lawyer is deemed to represent to the court that he or she has the client's authority to accept service.

(7) SERVICE OF CLAIM — Service of a plaintiff's claim or defendant's claim on an individual against whom the claim is made may be made by sending a copy of the claim by registered mail or by courier to the individual's place of residence, if the signature of the individual or any person who appears to be a member of the same household, verifying receipt of the copy, is obtained.

(8) Service under subrule (7) is effective on the date on which receipt of the copy of the claim is verified by signature, as shown in a delivery confirmation provided by or obtained from Canada Post or the commercial courier, as the case may be.

(9) [REVOKED: O. Reg. 393/09, s. 5(4).]

[O. Reg. 78/06, s. 11; O. Reg. 393/09, s. 5; O. Reg. 440/10, s. 1; O. Reg. 230/13, s. 9.]

8.04 SUBSTITUTED SERVICE — If it is shown that it is impractical to effect prompt service of a claim personally or by an alternative to personal service, the court may allow substituted service.

PRACTICE NOTES

§1 General principles Substituted service or validation of service is the exception rather than the rule. The exception applies only where P has shown that reasonable efforts have been made to serve D personally and that it would be impractical to serve by face-to-face or hand-delivered means. Impractical is not a synonym for inconvenient. P may be allowed to substitute a method of service of a claim on D if P can establish that the alternative method used would result in the claim coming to the notice of D, including sending a private message to D's suspected Facebook account.[1]

"Service", in the context of r. 8.04, means providing copies of the documents to the other parties in a court case. It is obviously of critical importance to the fair administration of justice that a claim be received by D. In appropriate circumstances, the authority exists for a judge of the Small Claims Court to order substituted service by email under r. 8.04.[2] Substituted service requires P to establish, by evidence, that the proposed method of service is likely to bring the claim to D's attention.[3]

The Rules relating to substituted service are designed to permit a certain degree of discretion and flexibility. However, a judge is required to consider the rights of all parties, not simply the moving party, in deciding whether or not to grant the relief requested. P, in seeking such an order, must explain why he believes the address he proposed for service is a current and valid one. The entire legal system is based on the concept of "notice". Any address that counsel manages to get his hands on will not necessarily do for service. The onus is on P to show, on proper evidence, that the method they propose for substituted service will have "some likelihood" or a "reasonable possibility" of bringing the proceeding to D's attention. Service by Facebook message was permissible where:

i.   P had located a Facebook account in the same name as the person sought to be served.

ii.   The name was not a common name -- increasing the likelihood that the Facebook account holder and the person sought to be served were one and the same.

iii.   The Facebook profile included photographs which indicated that the account holder and the person to be served were one and the same.

iv.   Prior to filing the affidavit, a representative of P exchanged private messages with the Facebook account holder which indicated that this account belonged to the party sought to be served.

v.   The exchange of messages on the Facebook account a short time before the motion date indicated that the Facebook account was still active.

It was appropriate to order service via the *private* message feature on the Facebook account of the person to be served, to avoid unnecessary public exposure or embarrassment. In addition to evidence to support the finding that the Facebook account holder and the person to be served are one and the same, it is equally important to have evidence of some recent activity on the account. Service of notice to an abandoned Facebook account is no more likely to give actual notice of a claim to D than would mailing the claim to a physical address that is no longer occupied by D.[4]

Unlike the *Rules of the Small Claims Court*, the *Rules of Civil Procedure* only include service on a lawyer of record and do not include service on a paralegal as valid alternative service. On an application for leave to appeal to the Divisional Court from a costs order of the Small Claims Court, service on the other party's paralegal was insufficient.[5]

[1] *Eastview Properties Inc. v. Mohamed*, [2014] O.J. No. 4220 (Ont. S.C.J. (Sm. Cl. Ct.)).

[2] *Cash Flow Recoveries Inc. v. Stearns*, [2015] O.J. No. 5264 (Ont. S.C.J. (Sm. Cl. Ct.)).

[3] *Laframboise v. Woodward*, [2002] O.J. No. 1590, 59 O.R. (3d) 338 (Ont. S.C.J.). See also *Bobesich*

v. Nagulandran, [2017] O.J. No. 4702 (Ont. S.C.J. (Sm. Cl. Ct.)).

⁴ *Cash Flow Recoveries Inc. v. Crate*, [2017] O.J. No. 931 (Ont. S.C.J. (Sm. Cl. Ct.)), applying *Jewish Family and Child Services of Greater Toronto v. B. (K.)*, [2016] O.J. No. 2377, 2016 ONCJ 259 (Ont. C.J.).

⁴ *Tailored Foam Solutions (2013) Inc. v. Martindale Estate*, [2018] O.J. No. 1333, 2018 ONSC 1592 (Ont. Div. Ct.).

8.05 SERVICE OUTSIDE ONTARIO — If the defendant is outside Ontario, the court may award as costs of the action the costs reasonably incurred in effecting service of the claim on the defendant there.

[O. Reg. 78/06, s. 12.]

8.06 PROOF OF SERVICE — An affidavit of service (Form 8A) made by the person effecting the service constitutes proof of service of a document.

[O. Reg. 461/01, s. 8(1), (3); O. Reg. 330/02, s. 5; O. Reg. 440/03, s. 5; O. Reg. 78/06, s. 13.]

8.07 SERVICE BY MAIL — (1) If a document is to be served by mail under these rules, it shall be sent, by regular lettermail or registered mail, to the last address of the person or of the person's representative that is,

    (a)   on file with the court, if the document is to be served by the clerk;

    (b)   known to the sender, if the document is to be served by any other person.

    (2) WHEN EFFECTIVE — Service of a document by mail is deemed to be effective on the fifth day following the date of mailing.

    (3) EXCEPTION — This rule does not apply when a claim is served by registered mail under subrule 8.03 (7).

[O. Reg. 78/06, s. 14(E); O. Reg. 393/09, s. 6; O. Reg. 230/13, s. 10.]

8.07.1 SERVICE BY COURIER — (1) If a document is to be served by courier under these rules, it shall be sent by means of a commercial courier to the last address of the person or of the person's representative that is on file with the court or known to the sender.

    (2) WHEN EFFECTIVE — Service of a document sent by courier is deemed to be effective on the fifth day following the date on which the courier verifies to the sender that the document was delivered.

    (3) EXCEPTION — This rule does not apply when a claim is served by courier under subrule 8.03 (7).

[O. Reg. 78/06, s. 15; O. Reg. 393/09, s. 7; O. Reg. 230/13, s. 11.]

8.08 SERVICE BY FAX — (1) Service of a document by fax is deemed to be effective,

    (a)   on the day of transmission, if transmission takes place before 5 p.m. on a day that is not a holiday;

    (b)   on the next day that is not a holiday, in any other case.

    (2) A document containing 16 or more pages, including the cover page, may be served by fax only between 5 p.m. and 8 a.m. the following day, unless the party to be served consents in advance.

[O. Reg. 393/09, s. 8.]

8.09 NOTICE OF CHANGE OF ADDRESS — (1) A party whose address for service changes shall serve notice of the change on the court and other parties within seven days after the change takes place.

(2) Service of the notice may be proved by affidavit if the court orders that proof of service is required.

(3)-(5) [REVOKED: O. Reg. 78/06, s. 16, in force July 1, 2006.]

[O. Reg. 461/01, s. 9(1); O. Reg. 330/02, s. 6; O. Reg. 440/03, s. 5; O. Reg. 78/06, s. 16.]

8.10 FAILURE TO RECEIVE DOCUMENT — A person who has been served or who is deemed to have been served with a document in accordance with these rules is nevertheless entitled to show, on a motion to set aside the consequences of default, on a motion for an extension of time or in support of a request for an adjournment, that the document,

(a)   did not come to the person's notice; or

(b)   came to the person's notice only at some time later than when it was served or is deemed to have been served.

[O. Reg. 461/01, s. 9(1).]

Rule 9 — Defence

9.01 DEFENCE — A defendant who wishes to dispute a plaintiff's claim shall, within 20 days of being served with the claim,

(a)   serve on every other party a defence (Form 9A); and

(b)   file the defence, with proof of service, with the clerk.

[O. Reg. 461/01, s. 10(1), (2); O. Reg. 330/02, s. 7; O. Reg. 440/03, ss. 2, 5; O. Reg. 78/06, s. 17; O. Reg. 440/10, s. 2; O. Reg. 44/14, s. 5.]

9.02 CONTENTS OF DEFENCE, ATTACHMENTS — (1) The following requirements apply to the defence:

1.   It shall contain the following information:

   i.   The reasons why the defendant disputes the plaintiff's claim, expressed in concise non-technical language with a reasonable amount of detail.

   ii.   If the defendant is self-represented, the defendant's name, address and telephone number, and fax number if any.

   iii.   If the defendant is represented by a representative, that person's name, address and telephone number, and fax number if any, and Law Society of Upper Canada registration number if any.

2.   If the defence is based in whole or in part on a document, a copy of the document shall be attached to each copy of the defence, unless it is unavailable, in which case the defence shall state the reason why the document is not attached.

(2) [REVOKED: O. Reg. 78/06, s. 19, in force July 1, 2006.]

[O. Reg. 461/01, s. 11; O. Reg. 78/06, ss. 18, 19; O. Reg. 56/12, ss. 2, 6(1); O. Reg. 230/13, s. 12.]

9.03 ADMISSION OF LIABILITY AND PROPOSAL OF TERMS OF PAYMENT — (1) A defendant who admits liability for all or part of the plaintiff's claim but wishes to arrange terms of payment may in the defence admit liability and propose terms of payment.

(2) **WHERE NO DISPUTE —** If the plaintiff does not dispute the proposal within the 20-day period referred to in subrule (3),

(a)   the defendant shall make payment in accordance with the proposal as if it were a court order;

(b)   the plaintiff may serve a notice of default of payment (Form 20L) on the defendant if the defendant fails to make payment in accordance with the proposal; and

(c)   the clerk shall sign judgment for the unpaid balance of the undisputed amount on the filing of an affidavit of default of payment (Form 20M) by the plaintiff swearing,

(i)   that the defendant failed to make payment in accordance with the proposal,

(ii)   to the amount paid by the defendant and the unpaid balance, and

(iii) that 15 days have passed since the defendant was served with a notice of default of payment.

(3) **DISPUTE —** The plaintiff may dispute the proposal within 20 days after service of the defence by filing with the clerk and serving on the defendant a request to clerk (Form 9B) for a terms of payment hearing before a referee or other person appointed by the court.

(4) The clerk shall fix a time for the hearing, allowing for a reasonable notice period after the date the request is served, and serve a notice of hearing on the parties.

(4.1) **MANNER OF SERVICE —** The notice of hearing shall be served by mail or fax.

(4.2) **FINANCIAL INFORMATION FORM, DEFENDANT AN INDIVIDUAL —** The clerk shall serve a financial information form (Form 20I) on the defendant, together with the notice of hearing, if the defendant is an individual.

(4.3) Where a defendant receives a financial information form under subrule (4.2), he or she shall complete it and serve it on the creditor before the hearing, but shall not file it with the court.

(5) **ORDER —** On the hearing, the referee or other person may make an order as to terms of payment by the defendant.

(6) **FAILURE TO APPEAR, DEFAULT JUDGMENT —** If the defendant does not appear at the hearing, the clerk may sign default judgment against the defendant for the part of the claim that has been admitted and shall serve a default judgment (Form 11B) on the defendant in accordance with subrule 8.01(4).

(6.1) [REVOKED: O. Reg. 78/06, s. 20(5), in force July 1, 2006.]

(7) FAILURE TO MAKE PAYMENTS — Unless the referee or other person specifies otherwise in the order as to terms of payment, if the defendant fails to make payment in accordance with the order, the clerk shall sign judgment for the unpaid balance on the filing of an affidavit by the plaintiff swearing to the default and stating the amount paid and the unpaid balance.

[O. Reg. 461/01, s. 12(1), (3); O. Reg. 330/02, s. 8; O. Reg. 440/03, s. 5; O. Reg. 78/06, s. 20.]

PRACTICE NOTES

§1 General principles In the Small Claims Court, a liberal, non-technical approach should be taken to pleadings. The small claims court may grant relief or allow a defence not asserted in the pleadings if supporting evidence is not needed beyond what was adduced at trial and it was not unfair, in all of the circumstances, to grant such relief or allow such a defence. This approach does not depend on whether the litigants are self-represented (or represented by non-lawyers). Otherwise, what happens where one party is self-represented and one has counsel? The informality of pleading is a function of the nature of the court and not of the quality of the representation.[1]

[1] *Brighton Heating & Air Conditioning Ltd. v. Savoia*, [2006] O.J. No. 250, 79 O.R. (3d) 386 (Ont. Div. Ct.).

Rule 10 — Defendant's Claim

10.01 DEFENDANT'S CLAIM — (1) A defendant may make a claim,

(a)   against the plaintiff;

(b)   against any other person,

    (i)   arising out of the transaction or occurrence relied upon by the plaintiff, or

    (ii)   related to the plaintiff's claim; or

(c)   against the plaintiff and against another person in accordance with clause (b).

(2) The defendant's claim shall be in Form 10A and may be issued,

(a)   within 20 days after the day on which the defence is filed; or

(b)   after the time described in clause (a) but before trial or default judgment, with leave of the court.

(3) COPIES — The defendant shall provide a copy of the defendant's claim to the court.

(4) CONTENTS OF DEFENDANT'S CLAIM, ATTACHMENTS — The following requirements apply to the defendant's claim:

1.   It shall contain the following information:

    i.   The full names of the parties to the defendant's claim and, if relevant, the capacity in which they sue or are sued.

    ii.   The nature of the claim, expressed in concise non-technical language with a reasonable amount of detail, including the date, place and nature of the occurrences on which the claim is based.

iii.   The amount of the claim and the relief requested.

iv.   If the defendant is self-represented, the defendant's name, address and telephone number, and fax number if any.

v.   If the defendant is represented by a representative, that person's name, address and telephone number, and fax number if any, and Law Society of Upper Canada registration number if any.

vi.   The address where the defendant believes each person against whom the claim is made may be served.

vii.   The court file number assigned to the plaintiff's claim.

2.   If the defendant's claim is based in whole or in part on a document, a copy of the document shall be attached to each copy of the claim, unless it is unavailable, in which case the claim shall state the reason why the document is not attached.

(5) [REVOKED: O. Reg. 78/06, s. 21(4), in force July 1, 2006.]

(6) ISSUANCE — On receiving the defendant's claim, the clerk shall immediately issue it by dating, signing and sealing it, shall assign it the same court file number as the plaintiff's claim and shall place the original in the court file.

(7)-(8) [REVOKED: O. Reg. 78/06, s. 21(4), in force July 1, 2006.]

[O. Reg. 461/01, s. 13(1)-(4); O. Reg. 330/02, s. 9; O. Reg. 440/03, s. 3; O. Reg. 78/06, s. 21; O. Reg. 56/12, ss. 3, 6(1); O. Reg. 230/13, s. 13.]

10.02 SERVICE — A defendant's claim shall be served by the defendant on every person against whom it is made, in accordance with subrules 8.01 (1) and (2).

10.03 DEFENCE — A party who wishes to dispute the defendant's claim or a third party who wishes to dispute the plaintiff's claim shall, within 20 days after service of the defendant's claim,

(a)   serve on every other party a defence (Form 9A); and

(b)   file the defence, with proof of service, with the clerk.

[O. Reg. 461/01, s. 14(1), (2); O. Reg. 330/02, s. 10; O. Reg. 440/03, ss. 4, 5; O. Reg. 78/06, s. 22; O. Reg. 44/14, s. 6.]

10.04 DEFENDANT'S CLAIM TO BE TRIED WITH MAIN ACTION — (1) A defendant's claim shall be tried and disposed of at the trial of the action, unless the court orders otherwise.

(2) EXCEPTION — If it appears that a defendant's claim may unduly complicate or delay the trial of the action or cause undue prejudice to a party, the court may order separate trials or direct that the defendant's claim proceed as a separate action.

(3) RIGHTS OF THIRD PARTY — If the defendant alleges, in a defendant's claim, that a third party is liable to the defendant for all or part of the plaintiff's claim in the action, the third party may at the trial contest the defendant's liability to the plaintiff but only if the third party has filed a defence in accordance with subrule 10.03 (1).

[O. Reg. 78/06, s. 23.]

10.05 APPLICATION OF RULES TO DEFENDANT'S CLAIM — (1) These rules apply, with necessary modifications, to a defendant's claim as if it were a plaintiff's claim, and to a defence to a defendant's claim as if it were a defence to a plaintiff's claim.

(2) EXCEPTION — However, when a person against whom a defendant's claim is made is noted in default, judgment against that person may be obtained only in accordance with rule 11.04.

(3) EXCEPTION, ELECTRONIC FILING, ISSUANCE — Subrule (1) does not apply to rule 7.02 (electronic filing of claim) or rule 7.04 (electronic issuance of claim).

[O. Reg. 56/08, s. 2; O. Reg. 44/14, s. 7.]

PRACTICE NOTES

§1 General principles In the Small Claims Court, a liberal, non-technical approach should be taken to pleadings. The small claims court may grant relief or allow a defence not asserted in the pleadings if supporting evidence is not needed beyond what was adduced at trial and it was not unfair, in all of the circumstances, to grant such relief or allow such a defence. This approach does not depend on whether the litigants are self-represented (or represented by non-lawyers). Otherwise, what happens where one party is self-represented and one has counsel? The informality of pleading is a function of the nature of the court and not of the quality of the representation.[1]

[1] *Brighton Heating & Air Conditioning Ltd. v. Savoia*, [2006] O.J. No. 250, 79 O.R. (3d) 386 (Ont. Div. Ct.).

Rule 11 — Default Proceedings

11.01 NOTING DEFENDANT IN DEFAULT — (1) If a defendant to a plaintiff's claim or a defendant's claim fails to file a defence to all or part of the claim with the clerk within the prescribed time, the clerk may, when proof is filed that the claim was served within the territorial division, note the defendant in default.

(1.1) ELECTRONIC FILING — In the case of a plaintiff's claim that was issued electronically under rule 7.04, the plaintiff may file the proof referred to in subrule (1) electronically.

(2) LEAVE REQUIRED FOR PERSON UNDER DISABILITY — A person under disability may not be noted in default under subrule (1), except with leave of the court.

(3) SERVICE OUTSIDE TERRITORIAL DIVISION — If all the defendants have been served outside the court's territorial division, the clerk shall not note any defendant in default until it is proved by an affidavit for jurisdiction (Form 11A) submitted to the clerk, or by evidence presented before a judge, that the action was properly brought in that territorial division.

(4) ELECTRONIC FILING — In the case of a plaintiff's claim that was issued electronically under rule 7.04, the plaintiff may file the affidavit for jurisdiction electronically.

[O. Reg. 78/06, s. 24; O. Reg. 44/14, s. 8.]

PRACTICE NOTES

§1 Wrong venue To commence in a wrong venue and transfer to the correct venue only after D has been served and noted in default does not cure the venue problem P has created. The noting of default in the wrong venue is an irregular noting in default and should not be permitted to support a default judgment. The appropriate remedy is to set aside the noting in default and give D the right to defend in the correct and local court office where the case ought to have proceeded to begin with.[1]

---

[1] *TD Auto Finance (Canada) Inc. v. Vardy*, [2012] O.J. No. 2410 (Ont. S.C.J. (Sm. Cl. Ct.)).

11.02 DEFAULT JUDGMENT, PLAINTIFF'S CLAIM, DEBT OR LIQUIDATED DEMAND — (1) If a defendant has been noted in default, the clerk may sign default judgment (Form 11B) in respect of the claim or any part of the claim to which the default applies that is for a debt or liquidated demand in money, including interest if claimed.

(2) The fact that default judgment has been signed under subrule (1) does not affect the plaintiff's right to proceed on the remainder of the claim or against any other defendant for all or part of the claim.

(3) MANNER OF SERVICE OF DEFAULT JUDGMENT — A default judgment (Form 11B) shall be served in accordance with subrule 8.01 (4).

[O. Reg. 78/06, s. 24; O. Reg. 44/14, s. 9; O. Reg. 38/16, s. 4.]

11.03 DEFAULT JUDGMENT, PLAINTIFF'S CLAIM, UNLIQUIDATED DEMAND — **(1)** If all defendants have been noted in default, the plaintiff may obtain judgment against a defendant noted in default with respect to any part of the claim to which rule 11.02 does not apply.

(2) To obtain judgment, the plaintiff may,

(a)　　file a notice of motion and supporting affidavit (Form 15A) requesting a motion in writing for an assessment of damages, setting out the reasons why the motion should be granted and attaching any relevant documents; or

(b)　　file a request to clerk (Form 9B) requesting that an assessment hearing be arranged.

(2.1) ELECTRONIC FILING — If the plaintiff wishes to obtain judgment and the plaintiff's claim was issued electronically under rule 7.04,

(a)　　the plaintiff may file the documents referred to in clause (2) (a) electronically, subject to subrule (2.2); or

(b)　　if the plaintiff wishes to request an assessment hearing, the plaintiff may file a request with the clerk electronically, and the use of Form 9B is not required for the purpose.

(2.2) REQUIREMENT TO FILE IN PAPER FORMAT— Despite clause (2.1) (a), the documents referred to in clause (2) (a) shall be filed with the clerk by the plaintiff in paper format within 14 days after the day the documents are filed electronically.

(3) INADEQUATE SUPPORTING AFFIDAVIT — On a motion in writing for an assessment of damages under clause (2) (a), a judge who finds the plaintiff's affidavit inadequate or unsatisfactory may order that,

(a)   a further affidavit be provided; or

(b)   an assessment hearing be held.

(4) ASSESSMENT HEARING — If an assessment hearing is to be held under clause (2) (b) or (3) (b), the clerk shall fix a date for the hearing and send a notice of hearing to the plaintiff, and the assessment hearing shall proceed as a trial in accordance with rule 17.

(5) MATTERS TO BE PROVED — On a motion in writing for an assessment of damages or at an assessment hearing, the plaintiff is not required to prove liability against a defendant noted in default, but is required to prove the amount of the claim.

(6) SERVICE OF ORDER — An order made on a motion in writing for an assessment of damages shall be served by the clerk in accordance with subrule 8.01 (5).

(7) NO ASSESSMENT WHERE DEFENCE FILED — If one or more defendants have filed a defence, a plaintiff requiring an assessment of damages against a defendant noted in default shall proceed to a settlement conference under rule 13 and, if necessary, a trial in accordance with rule 17.
[O. Reg. 78/06, s. 24; O. Reg. 393/09, s. 9; O. Reg. 38/16, s. 5.]

PRACTICE NOTES

§1 General principles Rule 11 of the SCCR is worded differently from r. 19 of the *Rules of Civil Procedure*. The effect of r. 11.03(5) is that P is not always required to prove liability against D noted in default. However, where P's claim does not disclose any tenable or satisfactory basis for liability, where P's evidence falls short of establishing that the relief requested is warranted, and where, as sometimes occurs, P's materials actually disprove P's own case, the court is required to consider such difficulties in fashioning an order that is just and agreeable to good conscience. Shortcomings in the pleadings, whether a failure to disclose a reasonable cause of action or a pleading that is simply not directed at what in truth occurred, are not eliminated by the mere fact of D's failure to defend. The court should not be required to ignore the facts or the law, or both, and to grant judgments which are contrary to the facts, the law or both, merely because D has elected not to participate in the proceedings.[1] D's failure to defend cannot strengthen P's claim against D and does not compel the court to make a finding that is contrary to the evidence and therefore contrary to the truth of the matter. Rule 11.03(6) does not alter that position.[2]

Small Claims Court Judges have an overriding duty to the law and to the administration of justice to ensure that judgments granted by them reflect the principle that justice is indeed done and that manifestly unsustainable claims are not to be mechanically processed.[3]

Rule 11.03(3) of the SCCR confirms that when the Deputy Judge finds that the P's affidavit is inadequate or unsatisfactory, he or she may order that a further affidavit be provided or assessment hearing be held. It is not appropriate to dismiss P's claim without further notice to P. Rule 11.03(5) confirms that P was not required to prove liability against D who were noted in default.[4]

For r. 11.03(1) to apply, all the defendants must be noted in default. Where one of the defendants has filed a defence, the plain language of the rule suggests that default judgment against the other defendants is not available. However, it is possible that a Small Claims Court has jurisdiction to relieve against joinder and to effectively sever the claims as against the two defendants.[5] Rule 11.03 only applies to undefended actions. It does not apply where P seeks leave to discontinue the action at the start of trial.[6]

Assessment Where P sued on a contract without providing the contract language between the parties, it was open to the court to either grant in full or deny each claim as unproved based on the material filed, depending on the more appropriate assessment of the facts presented. It was preferable in the circumstances to invoke r. 11.03(3)(*b*) and send the matters on to an assessment hearing.[7]

Whether a claim could be identified as liquidated would depend on the answers to several questions:

(a)   Is it ascertainable by calculation or by referring to a fixed scale of charges?

(b)   Can the calculation be made by reference to the agreement between the parties itself, or at least implied by the agreement?

(c)   Was the price or method of calculation of the price agreed upon by the parties?

(d)   Has the defendant obliged himself/herself to pay a specific sum of money?

(e)   Was a reasonable estimated cost established by the parties?[8]

Rule 11.03 permits a judge to request further and better evidence when an assessment is in writing. Although one might argue that this should be available for oral hearings, the procedure is at the judge's discretion. Rule 11 must be read together with r. 19 of the *Rules of Civil Procedure*, which states that D who has been noted in default is deemed to admit the truth of all allegations of fact made in the claim. However, P is not entitled to judgment on a motion for judgment, or at trial, merely because the facts alleged in the statement of claim are deemed to be admitted. This is, of course, unless the facts entitle P to judgment. P must establish its entitlement to judgment as a matter of fact and law.[9]

[1] *Grand River Natural Stone Ltd. v. Armour Masonry*, [2011] O.J. No. 5707 (Ont. S.C.J. (Sm. Cl. Ct.)).

[2] *Northgate Properties Inc. v. United Spray Booths Ltd.*, [2012] O.J. No. 2407 (Ont. S.C.J. (Sm. Cl. Ct.)).

[3] *Jalo v. Scotia Bank Head Office*, [2014] O.J. No. 2507 (Ont. S.C.J. (Sm. Cl. Ct.)).

[4] *Action Auto Leasing & Gallery Inc. v. Crawford*, [2013] O.J. No. 4684, 2013 ONSC 6299 (Ont. S.C.J.).

[5] *Belair Insurance Co. v. Dias*, [2013] O.J. No. 715 (Ont. S.C.J. (Sm. Cl. Ct.)).

[6] *Ever Fresh Direct Foods Inc. v. Schindler*, [2012] O.J. No. 3673 (Ont. S.C.J. (Sm. Cl. Ct.)).

[7] *Canadian Tire Bank v. Ramkalawan*, [2013] O.J. No. 902 (Ont. S.C.J. (Sm. Cl. Ct.)).

[8] *Capital One Bank (Canada Branch) v. Toogood*, [2013] O.J. No. 4023, 2013 ONSC 5440 (Ont. Div. Ct.).

[9] *Stamm Investments Ltd. v. Hobbs*, [2016] O.J. No. 5226, 2016 ONSC 6223 (Ont. Div. Ct.)

11.04 DEFAULT JUDGMENT, DEFENDANT'S CLAIM — If a party against whom a defendant's claim is made has been noted in default, judgment may be obtained against the party only at trial or on motion.

[O. Reg. 78/06, s. 24.]

PRACTICE NOTES

§1 Generally   The fact of a representative's error with regards to the issue of a meritorious defence should be approached neutrally, since the client has the potential availability of a negligence claim against the representative.[1]

[1] *Barrios v. Sousa (c.o.b. Lets Talk House)*, [2014] O.J. No. 3306 (Ont. S.C.J. (Sm. Cl. Ct.)).

11.05 CONSEQUENCES OF NOTING IN DEFAULT — (1) A defendant who has been noted in default shall not file a defence or take any other step in the proceeding, except making a motion under rule 11.06, without leave of the court or the plaintiff's consent.

(2) Any step in the proceeding may be taken without the consent of a defendant who has been noted in default.

(3) A defendant who has been noted in default is not entitled to notice of any step in the

proceeding and need not be served with any other document, except the following:

1. Subrule 11.02 (3) (service of default judgment).

2. Rule 12.01 (amendment of claim or defence).

3. Subrule 15.01 (6) (motion after judgment).

4. Postjudgment proceedings against a debtor under rule 20.

[O. Reg. 78/06, s. 24.]

11.06 SETTING ASIDE NOTING OF DEFAULT BY COURT ON MOTION — The court may set aside the noting in default or default judgment against a party and any step that has been taken to enforce the judgment, on such terms as are just, if the party makes a motion to set aside and the court is satisfied that,

(a) **the party has a meritorious defence and a reasonable explanation for the default; and**

(b) **the motion is made as soon as is reasonably possible in all the circumstances.**

[O. Reg. 461/01, s. 15; O. Reg. 78/06, s. 24.]

PRACTICE NOTES

§1 Generally Motions by D to set aside a default judgment are routine in Small Claims Court and are usually unopposed. Whether opposed or not, there is usually little difficulty in determining that the action should proceed on the merits rather than keeping in place a judgment that often arose from doubtful service of the claim, or the inadvertence or genuine misunderstanding of a self-represented defendant. Where D is represented, however, the motion is not so simple.[1]

Test Rule 11.06 contains different wording than r. 19.08 of the Civil Rules and codifies the three-part test for setting aside. The Court of Appeal has set out five factors to consider as part of determining whether the interests of justice favours the granting of a set-aside order under RCP r. 19.08:

(a) whether the motion was brought promptly after D learned of the default judgment;

(b) whether there is a plausible excuse or explanation for D's default in complying with the Rules;

(c) whether the facts establish that D has an arguable defence on the merits;

(d) the potential prejudice to D should the motion be dismissed and the potential prejudice to P should the motion be allowed; and

(e) the effect of any order the court might make on the overall integrity of the administration of justice.

These factors are not intended to be treated as rigid rules, when considering the particular circumstances of each case.[2] D need not provide evidence in respect of each of the above elements. In order to set aside a default judgment, a court should consider whether the interests of justice favour an order setting aside the default judgment. To do this, a court should look at whether there is more potential prejudice to D or P in deciding whether to set aside the default judgment and how the potential order will affect the overall integrity of the administration of justice.[3] In other words, the Court of Appeal appears to be saying: "Let's look at all the factors and try to do the right thing, allowing the parties to have their day in court, with the least amount of damage being caused in the process."[4]

In the majority of cases, the most important factor on a typical motion will be the requirement to establish that the moving defendant has "a meritorious defence". If the record makes clear that D has no defence, there is little point in setting aside the default judgment as the net effect of doing so may simply be to increase D's liability by exposing him or her to the risk of a representation fee at trial. However, if there is a meritorious defence, the system favours a determination on the merits so both parties have a full opportunity to present their respective sides of the story.[5]

A "meritorious defence" means an arguable defence. It does not require the moving defendant to establish that the defence is likely to succeed at trial.

However, the level of discretion to set aside a default judgment that exists under RCP r. 19.08 where D has an arguable defence does not exist in Small Claims Court. While there is still an element of discretion as to whether a default will be set aside, the court must generally be satisfied that all three factors set out in r. 11.06 are met. In Small Claims Court, the motions judge cannot weigh the merits of the defence and potentially determine that they are so compelling that the other factors may be ignored.[6]

The tests governing the setting aside of default judgments are not to be applied rigidly. The tests are a guide and the governing principle is whether the interests of justice favour or do not favour setting aside the default judgment. The court must look at the potential prejudice not only to D but also to P and the impact of an order on the integrity of the administration of justice.[7]

There are two principles that must be kept in mind: first, the seemingly universal principle that, in most cases, it is preferable the parties be afforded the opportunity to have a full and complete hearing on the merits rather than a party be defeated on a procedural technicality. It pervades every attempt to set aside a default judgment and is particularly important in Small Claims Court where many people are self-represented. In the Small Claims Court, the large majority of such motions are successful and most involve a concern with the sufficiency of service of the Claim.

The second principle is that on a motion under r. 11.06 or r. 19.08 D has the onus of establishing all provisions of the rule are met. D must meet all three provisions in order to succeed in the Small Claims Court and in the full Superior Court of Justice.[8]

Writ of execution Rule 11.06 applies to a motion to set aside a default judgment, and also may apply to lift a writ of execution on terms. However, it does not give the court jurisdiction to order that part of the proceeds of D's property be held in trust pending determination of the litigation.[9]

Effect of delay A four-month delay from the time D became aware that P was seeking default judgment until service of the motion to set it aside was acceptable as an amount of time where D made efforts during that time to indicate his intention to defend the matter.[10]

Evidence On a summary judgment motion, the evidence is generally limited to the evidence contained in the affidavits and any exhibits annexed thereto, with few exceptions. However, CJA s. 27 permits the Small Claims Court at a hearing to admit as evidence and act upon any oral testimony or document whether or not that evidence is sworn or affirmed. Section 27 is a recognition that parties in the Small Claims Court are often self-represented and in need of some leeway. It is not an invitation to give voluminous evidence by a representative. Attempting to give voluminous evidence at the hearing by the representative has many disadvantages: it violates the rule that, in so far as it is possible, evidence must be limited to that contained in the filed affidavits and annexed exhibits; it ambushes the opposite party; it improperly and unnecessarily merges the differing roles of witness and advocate.[11]

A court is entitled to be skeptical of evidence that constitutes, or fails to constitute, a "reasonable explanation" for D failing to initially defend a proceeding, but it is legally unacceptable to make findings of credibility on a paper record if that can be avoided.[12]

Policy and procedure The wording difference between RCP 19.08 and r. 11.06 does not affect the underlying policy, which is to preclude appeals to the Divisional Court from the multitude of default judgments that are granted throughout the province in the Small Claims Court.[13]

Parties seeking to set aside a default judgment of the court should proceed under r. 11.06 rather than bring a motion to the Superior Court.[14] Rule 11.06 provides an expeditious remedy to set aside or vary default judgments without the need to institute an appeal to the Divisional Court. D in the Small Claims Court must exhaust the setting aside remedies of the Small Claims Court before an appeal lies to the Divisional Court. When a defence is struck for whatever reason and judgment thereafter obtained *ex parte*, the judgment is in the nature of a default judgment. Accordingly, r. 11.06 must then be pursued rather than an appeal to the Divisional Court.[15]

[1] *Adam MacArthur Electrical Contracting Ltd. v. Lamb Development Corp.*, [2017] O.J. No. 3143 at paras. 1-2 (Ont. S.C.J. (Sm. Cl. Ct.)).

[2] *Mountain View Farms Ltd. v. McQueen*, [2014] O.J. No. 1197, 2014 ONCA 194 at paras. 48-50 (Ont. C.A.).

[3] *Peterbilt of Ontario Inc. v. 1565627 Ontario Ltd.*, [2007] O.J. No. 1685, 2007 ONCA 333 at para. 2 (Ont. C.A.).

[4] *Khokhar v. Farhat*, [2017] O.J. No. 3853 at para. 7 (Ont. S.C.J. (Sm. Cl. Ct.)).

[5] *Hiley (c.o.b. Stagecoach House Woodsmiths) v. Hill*, [2018] O.J. No. 4623, 2018 ONSC 5315 (Ont. S.C.J.).

[6] *Adam MacArthur Electrical Contracting Ltd. v. Lamb Development Corp.*, [2017] O.J. No. 3143 at paras. 30 and 31 (Ont. S.C.J. (Sm. Cl. Ct.)). See also *Brideau v. Lennon*, [2017] O.J. No. 6701 (Ont. S.C.J. (Sm. Cl. Ct.)). But see *Thompson v. Hergott*, [2015] O.J. No. 2120 (Ont. S.C.J. (Sm. Cl. Ct.)), where the court downplayed any difference in application of the two rules, and *Khokhar v. Farhat*, [2017] O.J. No. 3853 (Ont. S.C.J. (Sm. Cl. Ct.)), where the court applied the *Mountain View Farms Ltd. v. McQueen* test (see [2014] O.J. No. 1197, 2014 ONCA 194 (Ont. C.A.)).]

[7] *2272546 Ontario Inc. v. Garnett (c.o.b. Hunstville Hotrod)*, [2013] O.J. No. 2159 (Ont. S.C.J. (Sm. Cl. Ct.)).

[8] *Thompson v. Hergott*, [2015] O.J. No. 2120 (Ont. S.C.J. (Sm. Cl. Ct.)).

[9] *Chhokar Law Office v. Nelson*, [2020] O.J. No. 1838, 2020 ONSC 2607 (Ont. S.C.J.).

[10] *Jane Doe 464533 v. D. (N.)*, [2016] O.J. No. 6876, 2016 ONSC 4920 at para. 16 (Ont. S.C.J.), leave to appeal refused [2017] O.J. No. 60, 2017 ONSC 127 (Ont. S.C.J.). See also *Adam MacArthur Electrical Contracting Ltd. v. Lamb Development Corp.*, [2017] O.J. No. 3143 (Ont. S.C.J. (Sm. Cl. Ct.)).

[11] *Thompson v. Hergott*, [2015] O.J. No. 2120 (Ont. S.C.J. (Sm. Cl. Ct.)).

[12] *Stratford (City) Treasurer, Ontario Works v. Ford*, [2014] O.J. No. 3730 (Ont. S.C.J. (Sm. Cl. Ct.)).

[13] *Thompson v. Hergott*, [2015] O.J. No. 2120 (Ont. S.C.J. (Sm. Cl. Ct.)).

[14] *Dauvin-Borja v. D.M. Robichaud Ltd.*, [2016] O.J. No. 3377, 2016 ONSC 4195 (Ont. S.C.J.).

[15] *2272546 Ontario Inc. v. Garnett (c.o.b. Hunstville Hotrod)*, [2013] O.J. No. 2159 at paras. 3 and 4 (Ont. S.C.J. (Sm. Cl. Ct.)).

Rule 11.1 — Dismissal by Clerk

11.1.01 DISMISSAL — (1) Unless the court orders otherwise, the clerk shall make an order dismissing an action for delay if, by the second anniversary of the commencement of the action,

(a)   **the action has not been disposed of by order; and**

(b)   **no step has been taken by the plaintiff under subrule 11.03 (2) or (2.1) to obtain judgment, nor has a trial date been requested.**

(2) EXCEPTIONS — Subrule (1) does not apply if,

(a)   **an offer to settle the action has been accepted and filed;**

(b)   **the defence contains an admission of liability for the plaintiff's claim in the action and a proposal of terms of payment under subrule 9.03 (1); or**

(c)   **at the time the clerk would otherwise be required under that subrule to dismiss the action, the plaintiff is under disability.**

(2.1) ELECTRONIC ISSUANCE — An order made under subrule (1) may be issued electronically.

(3) SERVICE OF ORDER — The clerk shall serve a copy of an order made under subrule (1) on the parties.

(4) [REVOKED: O. REG. 488/16, S. 1.]

[O. Reg. 78/06, s. 24; O. Reg. 56/08, s. 3; O. Reg. 393/09, s. 10; O. Reg. 56/12, s. 4; O. Reg. 194/15, ss. 1-3; O. Reg. 38/16, s. 6; O. Reg. 488/16, s. 1.]

Recent amendments: Rule 11.1 was amended by O. Reg. 194/15 and O. Reg. 38/16 to extend the permitted time period from 180 days to two years.

11.1.02 EFFECT OF DISMISSAL ON DEFENDANT'S CLAIM — If an action against a defendant who has made a defendant's claim is dismissed for delay under subrule 11.1.01 (1), the defendant's claim shall be deemed to be dismissed 60 days after the order under that subrule is served, unless the court orders otherwise during the 60-day period.

[O. Reg. 202/17, s. 1.]

PRACTICE NOTES

---

§1.   Generally
§2.   Counterclaims by D

---

§1 Generally Rule 11.1 signals the obvious interest of the administration of justice in containing expense and delay by containing the overall duration of civil proceedings in this court.[1] The rule-makers instituted r. 11 several years ago to assist the process in weeding out recalcitrant plaintiffs who fail to move forward in the litigation process. But it cannot have been intended to lay a trap for busy lawyers who are trying to keep costs down as they must in Small Claims Court and trying to move matters forward at an agreeable pace to the next step and to dates of mutual availability. Rule 13.07 of the Small Claims Court Rules suggests that the parties must set the matter down for trial with the clerk within 30 days of the settlement conference. A matter should not be administratively dismissed under r. 11.1.01(2) unless all settlement conferences have been finished and the parties have had an opportunity within those 30 days to set the matter for trial. Also, the parties should be afforded the 45-day notice of pending dismissal under r. 11.1.01(2) prior to the actual dismissal. In the absence of prejudice to D, delay caused by D failing to respond to P's reasonable request to set aside the administrative dismissal (with or without terms) should not prevent the court from setting aside the dismissal.[2]

A party seeking to set aside a dismissal order must address the following four issues:

i.   the litigation delay;

ii.   inadvertence in missing the deadline;

iii.   whether the motion to set aside was brought promptly; and

iv.   whether D will suffer prejudice.

A contextual approach should be taken such that the court should consider and weigh all relevant factors to determine the order that is just in the circumstances.[3]

[1] *Robb-Simand v. Re/Max Real Estate Centre Inc.*, [2012] O.J. No. 5232 (Ont. S.C.J. (Sm. Cl. Ct.)).

[2] *Sarkisian v. Chacon Properties Inc.*, [2013] O.J. No. 806 (Ont. S.C.J. (Sm. Cl. Ct.)).

[3] *Gilchrist v. Meraw*, [2016] O.J. No. 1195, 2016 ONSC 1645 (Ont. Div. Ct.).

§2 Counterclaims by D By analogy to the CJA, and particularly to CJA ss. 23(1) and 31, an "action" within the meaning of r. 11.1 does not incorporate D's counterclaim into a P's claim for purposes of the notice and dismissal order contemplated by that Rule. They are separate proceedings with separate rights of appeal. If the clerk issues a single notice under the P's claim, the clerk may proceed to dismiss only P's claim. If D's claim is eligible for such a notice and order, a separate notice and order are required setting out the different court file number and title of proceedings accordingly. It appears unfair to interpret r. 11.1 in a manner that would fail to give due notice to D who have issued counterclaims that their claims are in jeopardy of dismissal for delay. Giving proper notice to D who have made counterclaims would also tend to increase the chance that actions would be set down for trial prior to issuance of a r. 11.1 dismissal order, and to reduce the incidence of motions to set aside such orders.[1]

[1] *Evans v. Triserve Management Inc.*, [2013] O.J. No. 2651 (Ont. S.C.J. (Small Claims Ct.)).

Rule 11.2 — Request for Clerk's Order on Consent

11.2.01 CONSENT ORDER — (1) The clerk shall, on the filing of a request for clerk's order on consent (Form 11.2A), make an order granting the relief sought, including costs, if the following conditions are satisfied:

1.   **The relief sought is,**

i.   **amending a claim or defence less than 30 days before the originally scheduled trial date,**

ii.   **adding, deleting or substituting a party less than 30 days before the originally scheduled trial date,**

iii.   **setting aside the noting in default or default judgment against a party and any specified step to enforce the judgment that has not yet been completed,**

iv.   **restoring a matter that was dismissed under rule 11.1 to the list,**

v.   **noting that payment has been made in full satisfaction of a judgment or terms of settlement, or**

vi.   **dismissing an action.**

2.   **The request is signed by all parties (including any party to be added, deleted or substituted) and states,**

i.   **that each party has received a copy of the request, and**

ii.   **that no party that would be affected by the order is under disability.**

3., 4.   [REVOKED: O. Reg. 393/09, s. 11(3).]

(2) **SERVICE OF ORDER —** The clerk shall serve a copy of an order made under subrule (1) in accordance with subrule 8.01 (14) on a party that requests it and provides a stamped, self-addressed envelope.

(3) **SAME, REFUSAL TO MAKE ORDER —** Where the clerk refuses to make an order, the clerk shall serve a copy of the request for clerk's order on consent (Form 11.2A), with reasons for the refusal, on all the parties.

(4) **NOTICE OF SETTING ASIDE OF ENFORCEMENT STEP —** Where an order is made setting aside a specified step to enforce a judgment under subparagraph 1 iii of sub-

rule (1), a party shall file a copy of the order at each court location where the enforcement step has been requested.

[O. Reg. 78/06, s. 24; O. Reg. 393/09, s. 11.]

Rule 11.3 — Discontinuance

11.3.01 DISCONTINUANCE BY PLAINTIFF IN UNDEFENDED ACTION — (1) A plaintiff may discontinue his or her claim against a defendant who fails to file a defence to all or part of the claim with the clerk within the prescribed time by,

(a)   serving a notice of discontinued claim (Form 11.3A) on all defendants who were served with the claim; and

(b)   filing the notice with proof of service.

(2) A claim may not be discontinued by or against a person under disability, except with leave of the court.

(3) **ELECTRONIC FILING** — If the plaintiff's claim was issued electronically under rule 7.04, the plaintiff may file the notice of discontinued claim, with proof of service, electronically.

[O. Reg. 393/09, s. 12; O. Reg. 44/14, s. 10.]

11.3.02 EFFECT OF DISCONTINUANCE ON SUBSEQUENT ACTION — The discontinuance of a claim is not a defence to a subsequent action on the matter, unless an order granting leave to discontinue provides otherwise.

[O. Reg. 393/09, s. 12.]

Rule 12 — Amendment, Striking Out, Stay and Dismissal

12.01 RIGHT TO AMEND — (1) A plaintiff's or defendant's claim and a defence to a plaintiff's or defendant's claim may be amended by filing with the clerk a copy that is marked "Amended", in which any additions are underlined and any other changes are identified.

(1.1) **ELECTRONIC FILING** — In the case of a plaintiff's claim that was issued electronically under rule 7.04, the plaintiff may file the amended claim electronically if the claim being amended has not yet been served.

(1.2) **REQUIREMENT TO FILE IN PAPER FORMAT** — Subrule 7.02 (5) applies, with necessary modifications, to an amended plaintiff's claim that is filed electronically under subrule (1.1).

(2) **SERVICE** — The amended document shall be served by the party making the amendment on all parties, including any parties in default, in accordance with subrule 8.01 (14).

(3) **TIME** — Filing and service of the amended document shall take place at least 30 days before the originally scheduled trial date, unless,

(a)   the court, on motion, allows a shorter notice period; or

(b)   a clerk's order permitting the amendment is obtained under subrule 11.2.01 (1).

(4) SERVICE ON ADDED PARTY — A person added as a party shall be served with the claim as amended, except that if the person is added as a party at trial, the court may dispense with service of the claim.

(5) NO AMENDMENT REQUIRED IN RESPONSE — A party who is served with an amended document is not required to amend the party's defence or claim.

[O. Reg. 78/06, s. 25; O. Reg. 393/09, s. 13; O. Reg. 44/14, s. 11(1); O. Reg. 38/16, s. 7.]

PRACTICE NOTES

Rule 12.01 does not provide any guidance as to when or under what circumstances a motion under subr. (3)(*a*) can be granted. Rule 26.01 provides that such a motion can be brought at any stage of an action, and the court shall grant leave to amend a pleading on such terms as are just, unless prejudice would result that could not be compensated for by costs or an adjournment. Rule 26.01 is mandatory. An amendment is to be permitted even in the face of unfairness and prejudice unless the prejudice cannot be compensated for in costs.[1]

[1] *St. Clair Tavern (Sarnia) Ltd. v. Gresham*, [2015] O.J. No. 7078 (Ont. S.C.J. (Sm. Cl. Ct.)).

12.02 MOTION TO STRIKE OUT OR AMEND A DOCUMENT — (1) The court may, on motion, strike out or amend all or part of any document that,

(a)   discloses no reasonable cause of action or defence;

(b)   may delay or make it difficult to have a fair trial; or

(c)   is inflammatory, a waste of time, a nuisance or an abuse of the court's process.

(2) In connection with an order striking out or amending a document under subrule (1), the court may do one or more of the following:

1.   In the case of a claim, order that the action be stayed or dismissed.

2.   In the case of a defence, strike out the defence and grant judgment.

2.1   In the case of a motion, order that the motion be stayed or dismissed.

3.   Impose such terms as are just.

(3) GENERAL POWER TO STAY, DISMISS ACTION — The court may, on its own initiative, make the order referred to in paragraph 1 of subrule (2) staying or dismissing an action, if the action appears on its face to be inflammatory, a waste of time, a nuisance or an abuse of the court's process.

(4) Unless the court orders otherwise, an order under subrule (3) shall be made on the basis of written submissions in accordance with the following procedures:

1.   The court shall direct the clerk to send notice by mail to the plaintiff that the court is considering making the order.

2.   The plaintiff may, within 20 days after receiving the notice, file with the court a written submission, no more than four pages in length, responding to the notice.

3.   If the plaintiff does not file a written submission that complies with paragraph 2, the court may make the order without any further notice to the plaintiff or to any

other party.

4.   If the plaintiff files a written submission that complies with paragraph 2, the court may direct the clerk to send a copy of the submission by mail to any other party.

5.   A party who receives a copy of the plaintiff's submission may, within 10 days after receiving the copy, file with the court a written submission, no more than four pages in length, responding to the plaintiff's submission, and shall send a copy of the responding submission by mail to the plaintiff, and, on the request of any other party, to that party.

(5) The clerk shall send a copy of an order made under subrule (1) by mail to all the parties as soon as possible after the order is made.

(6) A document required under this rule to be sent by mail shall be mailed in the manner described in subrule 8.07 (1), and is deemed to have been received on the fifth day after it is mailed.

(7) **GENERAL POWER TO STAY, DISMISS MOTION** — The court may, on its own initiative, make the order referred to in paragraph 2.1 of subrule (2) staying or dismissing a motion, if the motion appears on its face to be inflammatory, a waste of time, a nuisance or an abuse of the court's process.

(8) Subrules (4) to (6) apply, with necessary modifications, to the stay or dismissal of a motion under subrule (7) and, for the purpose, a reference to the plaintiff shall be read as a reference to the moving party.

(9) **CLERK TO NOTIFY COURT** — If the clerk becomes aware that an action could be the subject of an order under subrule (3), or that a motion could be the subject of an order under subrule (7), the clerk shall notify the court.

[O. Reg. 78/06, s. 26; O. Reg. 44/14, s. 11(2), (3).]

PRACTICE NOTES

§1.   General principles
§2.   Appeals

§1 General principles Conceptually, r. 12.02 can be viewed as being somewhere between rr. 20 and 21 of the *Rules of Civil Procedure*. It is not a summary judgment motion involving extensive affidavits and a requirement such as contemplated in RCP r. 20, where the responding party must put his or her "best foot forward". It is more akin to a RCP r. 21 motion, although it is worded more broadly and does not have the same prohibition on the filing of affidavit evidence. It is a motion that is brought in the spirit of the summary nature of Small Claims Court proceedings and involves an analysis of whether a reasonable cause of action has been disclosed or whether the proceeding should be ended at an early stage because its continuation would be "inflammatory", a "waste of time" or a "nuisance." The references to actions that are inflammatory, a waste of time or a nuisance were intended to lower the very high threshold set by r. 21.01(3)(*d*)'s reference to actions that are frivolous, vexatious or an abuse of process. Rule 12.02 motions will often be brought and responded to by self-represented litigants who lack the extensive training of counsel. The test to be applied on such a motion ought to reflect this, and avoid the complex case law that has fleshed out the *Rules of Civil Procedure*. The failure to provide for summary judgment motions is not a gap in the *Rules of the Small Claims Court*, but rather is a deliberate omission. It is not up to the court to read in such a provision, particularly in light of the fact that r. 12.02 specifically addresses the ability to bring a motion in the nature of those contemplated by RCP rr. 20, 21 and 76. If a motion for summary judgment of the kind provided for in r. 20 is to be created, it is a matter for the Rules Committee and not the courts.[1]

Rule 12.02 serves a gatekeeper function, to permit claims or defences to be concluded by motion rather than proceeding to trial.[2]

In short, while the procedure for a motion for summary judgment is not available under the Small Claims Court Rules, a judge can make a decision with the same effect under r. 12.02. The failure to provide for summary judgment in Small Claims Court was not a gap to be filled through r. 1.03(2) but rather a deliberate omission.[3]

It is not correct to treat r. 12.02 as equivalent to r. 20 of the Civil Rules and thereby incorporate a summary judgment procedure into Small Claims Court, which would be neither necessary nor appropriate. However, neither is it correct to treat r. 12.02 as equivalent to r. 21: given the aversion to technical pleading requirements in this court, it would not be appropriate to require what could be highly technical arguments on the pleadings as the sole mechanism for an early dismissal of baseless claims.[4]

Timing A motion for dismissal of an action on the basis that the claim discloses no reasonable cause of action should be made on notice under r. 12.02 and not in the middle of trial. The motion also has to be brought in accordance with r. 15.01.[5]

Test The Small Claims Court has the jurisdiction to dismiss, stay and strike pleadings within the ambits of r. 12.02 of the Small Claims Court Rules. The question therefore is: Does the plaintiff's claim: (a) disclose no reasonable cause of action? (b) cause delays or make it difficult to have a fair trial? or (c) is it inflammatory, a waste of time, a nuisance or an abuse of the court's process? Before a court will strike or dismiss a pleading, it does so with great caution, sparingly and only where it is abundantly clear that there is no action.[6] The test to apply under (a) is whether the claim has no meaningful chance of success at trial.[7]

Complex law should not be a bar to a decision under r. 12. The law will be just as complicated at a trial, except that by then there would have been attendances on a settlement conference and then a trial with perhaps several hours of *viva voce* evidence, concluding with much of the same written and oral arguments given on the motion. A claim with an obvious limitation period that has run, should not have to go to trial.[8]

The following principles that must be brought to bear in proceedings under r. 12.02:

(1)   The allegations of fact in the statement of claim, unless patently ridiculous or incapable of proof, must be accepted as proven;

(2)   The moving party, in order to succeed, must show that it is plain, obvious and beyond doubt that the plaintiff could not succeed;

(3)   A claim will not be dismissed simply because it is novel; and

(4)   The claim must be read generously with allowance for inadequacies due to drafting deficiencies.[9]

Res judicata/Abuse of process A case may be dismissed under r. 12.02 where it is an abuse of process because it constitutes an attempt to re-litigate a matter that was decided previously.[10] The finality of a court's decision is intended to prevent a misuse of court procedure to avoid bringing the administration of justice into disrepute. The plea of *res judicata* generally applies not only to points upon which the court was actually required by the parties to form an opinion and pronounce a judgment upon, but also to every point that properly belonged to the subject matter of the litigation and which the parties, exercising reasonable diligence, might have brought forward at the time. The goal of the doctrine of abuse of process has as its goal the protection of the fairness and integrity of the administration of justice by preventing needless multiplicity of proceedings. This doctrine can be applied even where *res judicata* is not strictly available where allowing the litigation to proceed would violate principles such as judicial economy, consistency, finality and the integrity of the administration of justice.[11]

Comparison with Civil Rules Rule 12.02 combines the provisions of RCP rr. 21.01 and 25.11 with respect to failure to comply with the rules of pleading and lack of substantive validity. The language used in SCCR r. 12.02 is made more accessible to self-represented litigants: "frivolous" is replaced by "a waste of time"; "vexatious" is replaced by "a nuisance"; and "scandalous" is replaced by "inflammatory". In addition, "may prejudice or delay the fair trial of the action" in RCP r. 15.11 is replaced by "delay or make it difficult to have a fair trial" in SCCR r. 12.02. Both SCCR r. 12.02 and RCP r. 25.11 permit the court to strike out all or part of a pleading or other document on the grounds that they are frivolous (a waste of time), vexatious (a nuisance) or scandalous (inflammatory). Under SCCR r. 12.01, the court may amend the document rather than striking it out. Under RCP r. 25.11, the document may be struck out with or without leave to amend. By contrast, RCP r. 21.01 addresses the action as a whole and where it is found to be frivolous or vexatious, the entire action will be stayed or dismissed. With respect to substantive validity, both RCP r. 21.01(1)(b) and SCCR r. 12.02 permit the court to strike out a pleading on the ground that it discloses no reasonable cause of action or defence.[12]

Rules 20 and 21 of the Civil Rules govern such motions in the full Superior Court of Justice, and are much more detailed than SCCR r. 12.02. Rules 20 and 21 were markedly revised effective January 1, 2010, while r. 12.02 remains unchanged. Unlike the current Superior Court Rules, r. 12.02 neither requires nor specifically permits affidavits on a motion such as the one now before this court. Certainly, the rules of the Small Claims Court do not provide for cross-examination on affidavits.[13]

On January 23, 2014, the summary judgment procedure under r. 20 of the *Rules of Civil Procedure* was the subject of the Supreme Court of Canada's decision in *Hryniak v. Mauldin*.[14] In light of that decision, the question for Small Claims Court is whether the need for different nomenclature and analysis under r. 12.02 than under r. 20 has been completely undermined. All of the policy reasons which finds to support a liberal use of r. 20 would seem to apply in Small Claims Court. There is a good argument that the need to distance r. 12.02 from the jurisprudential baggage which had developed under rr. 20 and 21, at least as to r. 20, is gone. On the other hand it remains true that in Small Claims Court there are no cross-examinations on motion affidavits and no examinations of witnesses on a pending motion.[15]

Pleadings The whole purpose of r. 12.02 is to avoid going through a full trial when the pleadings do not support a valid claim, and where to proceed to trial on that pleading would be a waste of time.[16] The primary focus on a r. 12.02 motion is the pleadings, the issue being whether it is plain and obvious or beyond reasonable doubt that the pleadings disclose no reasonable cause of action. The law is clear that for this purpose the pleading is to be read generously, with accommodation for inadequacies resulting from drafting deficiencies. The court is not to take an overly technical approach to the pleading.[17]

Evidence/Supporting documents on the motion The prohibition on admitting evidence contained in r. 21.01(2) is absent from r. 12.02.[18] There is disagreement in the case law on this issue. In favour of a restrictive approach:

- It is doubtful that such evidence can be adduced given that there is no right to cross examine, and r. 12.02 does not authorize the court to make findings of fact. Allegations of fact in the claim must be accepted as proven unless patently ridiculous or incapable of proof. The moving party, in order to succeed, must show it is plain, obvious and beyond doubt that P could not succeed.[19]

In favour of a liberal approach:

- It is not true that the *Rules of the Small Claims Court* do not adequately accommodate or guide complex evidence-based motions, or that limitation period adjudications which are evidence-based are properly disposed of at trial.[20]

- A defence on a collections case can be struck as a "waste of time" where documentary evidence revealed that D had in fact authorized the debt transactions.[21]

Deficient pleadings/Self-represented parties Courts are required to be sensitive to the circumstances of a self-represented litigant. A court should not be too quick to dismiss an action on the basis of rigid formalities or on a strict application of the rules when dealing with parties that may be limited in means and/or may be lacking in the necessary skills, knowledge or experience. To do so would impede access to justice for many and would only serve to undermine the administration of justice. That being said, a jurist must consider the interests of all parties in applying the rules. It cannot merely stand by and watch a litigant be forced through the trial process when there is no merit to an action or there is no possibility for the action to succeed. There is no right to force a litigant through to the conclusion of a meritless claim. It is for this very reason that r. 12.02 exists.[22]

The higher standards of pleading in the Superior Court are simply unworkable in the Small Claims Court, where litigants are routinely unrepresented, and where legal concepts such as the many varieties of causes of action are completely foreign to the parties. Essentially, the litigants present a set of facts to the deputy judge, and it is left to the deputy judge to determine the legal issues that emerge from those facts and bring his or her legal expertise to bear in resolving those issues. On a motion to strike pleadings, a motions judge may, by questioning the responding party or otherwise, determine whether the facts upon which that party relies are capable of supporting a cause of action and then either amend the pleading or strike it out, as may be appropriate based upon the information received. Note that under SCCR r. 12.01, the court may amend the document rather than striking it out.[23]

The court can strike a statement of defence without either of the parties properly bringing the issue on motion under r. 15.01. Rule 15.03(1) permits a motion to be brought where "the nature or circumstances of the motion make notice unnecessary", such as when the Deputy Judge disposes of what is deemed to be the only reasonable defence disclosed in the statement.[24]

Leave to amend Where pleadings are to be struck on a r. 12.02 motion, leave to amend the pleading may be granted unless the pleading contains a radical defect incapable of being cured by amendment. For example, leave to amend will be refused and the action will be dismissed if it is statute-barred.[25]

Recovery of property before trial The Small Claims Court has no jurisdiction to make an order for the interim recovery of personal property, as such. The sole exception is where the P who claims recovery of possession of personal property can satisfy the court that judgment should be granted before trial under r. 12.02. Such a judgment would be a final and not an interlocutory order.[26]

Default in disclosure or undertakings The obligation of a litigant in Small Claims Court is to produce to the opposite party copies of all documents upon which they intend to rely at trial. This carries with it a clear discretion to be exercised by each litigant to determine what documents, if any, are necessary to prove their position to the trial judge. Parties who continually ignore court orders and refuse to answer undertakings should have their pleadings struck.[27] It would also be open to a deputy judge in the appropriate case to dismiss an action under r. 12.02 for a party's failure to comply with a court production order or any other order.[28]

A judge must follow r. 12.02(4). A judge can decide not to follow r. 12.02(4), but only if the judge "orders otherwise". An order made without a motion and notice to the parties was made without jurisdiction and in breach of principles of procedural fairness and natural justice.[29]

Authority of settlement conference judges Rule 13.05(2)(a)(iv) allows a settlement conference judge to make an order "striking out a claim . . . under subrule 12.02(1)". However, the power to dismiss an action comes from r. 12.02(2). Settlement conference judges had previously been given the authority to make an order dismissing an action by r. 13.05(2)(a)(v), which was revoked in 2014.[30] A settlement conference judge may make a ruling under r. 12.02. The wording of r. 12.02 is not an actual determination on the merits, but rather a motion that is brought in the spirit of the summary nature of Small Claims Court proceedings and involves an analysis of whether a reasonable cause of action has been disclosed or whether the proceeding should be ended at an early stage because its continuation would be "inflammatory", a "waste of time" or a "nuisance".[31]

[1] *Van de Vrande v. Butkowsky*, [2010] O.J. No. 1239, 2010 ONCA 230 (Ont. C.A.).

[2] *Carroca v. River Park (Village)*, [2014] O.J. No. 5462 (Ont. S.C.J. (Sm. Cl. Ct,)).

[3] *Hira v. Tulsiani Builders Inc.*, [2012] O.J. No. 1777 (Ont. S.C.J. (Sm. Cl. Ct.)).

[4] *Bonneville Electric Ltd. v. Shaw*, [2012] O.J. No. 4295 (Ont. S.C.J. (Sm. Cl. Ct.)). See also *O'Brien v. Ottawa Hospital (Civic Campus)*, [2011] O.J. No. 66, 2011 ONSC 231 (Ont. Div. Ct.).

[5] *Halton Regional Pound Facility v. Holland*, [2014] O.J. No. 3067, 2014 ONSC 3776 (Ont. Div. Ct.).

[6] *Vertolli v. YouTube, LLC*, [2012] O.J. No. 4275 (Ont. S.C.J. (Sm. Cl. Ct.)).

[7] *Bonneville Electric Ltd. v. Shaw*, [2012] O.J. No. 4295 (Ont. S.C.J. (Sm. Cl. Ct.)). See also *O'Brien*

v. Ottawa Hospital (Civic Campus), [2011] O.J. No. 66, 2011 ONSC 231 (Ont. Div. Ct.).

[8] *Camm v. Kirkpatrick*, [2013] O.J. No. 3830 (Ont. S.C.J. (Sm. Cl. Ct.)).

[9] *Schwartzentruber v. Wettlauffer Home Improvements and Contracting Inc.*, [2012] O.J. No. 128 (Ont. S.C.J. (Sm. Cl. Ct.)).

[10] *Fisher v. Ontario (Minister of Community and Social Services)*, [2014] O.J. No. 4975 (Ont. S.C.J. (Sm. Cl. Ct.)). See also *Vuong v. Toronto East General & Orthopaedic Hospital*, [2010] O.J. No. 5784, 328 D.L.R. (4th) 759 (Ont. Div. Ct.).

[11] *Ferguson v. Plate*, [2018] O.J. No. 3754 (Ont. S.C.J. (Sm. Cl. Ct.)).

[12] *Onwuachu v. Trans Union of Canada Inc.*, [2013] O.J. No. 923 (Ont. S.C.J. (Sm. Cl. Ct.)).

[13] *Tucker v. Vuteq Canada Inc.*, [2012] O.J. No. 3763 (Ont. S.C.J. (Sm. Cl. Ct.)).

[14] [2014] S.C.J. No. 7, 2014 SCC 7 (S.C.C.).

[15] *Tuka v. Butt*, [2014] O.J. No. 852 (Ont. S.C.J. (Sm. Cl. Ct.)).

[16] *Moses v. Mortgage Central*, [2019] O.J. No. 480 (Ont. S.C.J. (Sm. Cl. Ct.)).

[17] *Korb v. McCeachran*, [2014] O.J. No. 2527 (Ont. S.C.J.).

[18] *Van de Vrande v. Butkowsky*, [2010] O.J. No. 1239, 2010 ONCA 230 (Ont. C.A.).

[19] *Tucker v. Vuteq Canada Inc.*, [2012] O.J. No. 3763 (Ont. S.C.J. (Sm. Cl. Ct.)).

[20] *Moses v. Mortgage Central*, [2019] O.J. No. 480 (Ont. S.C.J. (Sm. Cl. Ct.)).

[21] *Canadian Tire Bank v. Barna*, [2019] O.J. No. 1193, 2019 ONSC 1533 (Ont. Div. Ct.).

[22] *Rill v. Adams*, [2017] O.J. No. 4644, 2017 ONSC 5297 at para. 32 (Ont. S.C.J.).

[23] *Onwuachu v. Trans Union of Canada Inc.*, [2013] O.J. No. 923 (Ont. S.C.J. (Sm. Cl. Ct.)). See also *936464 Ontario Ltd. (c.o.b. Plumbhouse Plumbing & Heating) v. Mungo Bear Ltd.*, [2003] O.J. No. 3795, 74 O.R. (3d) 45 (Ont. Div. Ct.).

[24] *Henry v. Greig*, [2015] O.J. No. 68, 2015 ONSC 168 (Ont. S.C.J.).

[25] *Moses v. Mortgage Central*, [2019] O.J. No. 480 (Ont. S.C.J. (Sm. Cl. Ct.)).

[26] *Ever Fresh Direct Foods v. Schindler*, [2011] O.J. No. 3634 (Ont. S.C.J. (Sm. Cl. Ct.)). See also *Venneri v. Streetpro Roadside Assistance Inc.*, [2012] O.J. No. 1264 (Ont. S.C.J. (Sm. Cl. Ct.)).

[27] *Hira v. Tulsiani Builders Inc.*, [2012] O.J. No. 1777 (Ont. S.C.J. (Sm. Cl. Ct.)).

[28] *Hervieux v. Huronia Optical*, [2016] O.J. No. 3270, 2016 ONCA 294 (Ont. C.A.).

[29] *Rizvi v. Urban Studio Inc. (c.o.b. Only Basements)*, [2018] O.J. No. 319, 2018 ONSC 484 at paras. 8 and 9 (Ont. Div. Ct.).

[30] *Elguindy v. St. Joseph's Health Care London*, [2017] O.J. No. 3615, 2017 ONSC 4247 at paras. 62-64 (Ont. Div. Ct.).

[31] *Elguindy v. St. Joseph's Health Care London*, [2017] O.J. No. 4661, 2017 ONSC 5360 at para. 58 (Ont. Div. Ct.), citing *Van de Vrande v. Butkowsky*, [2010] O.J. No. 1239, 2010 ONCA 230 at para. 19 (Ont. C.A.).

§2 Appeals   An order that purports to dismiss an action is a final order. The Divisional Court therefore has jurisdiction to hear an appeal of an order dismissing a claim under r. 12.02. Section 31 of the CJA provides that an appeal lies to the Divisional Court from a "final order of the Small Claims Court *in an action* for the payment of money in excess of $500, excluding costs". A dismissal of an action for a claim of over $500 is appealable on the same basis as an order granting judgment for P.[1]

Even if the Small Claims Court has a power similar to that of the Superior Court under r. 59.06 to set aside or vary a previous order of the court, that power should not be used to consider issues properly addressed by way of appeal, such as alleged errors of law.[2]

[1] *Kipiniak v. Dubiel*, [2011] O.J. No. 572, 2011 ONSC 825 (Ont. Div. Ct.).

[2] *Alexander v. Neville*, [2014] O.J. No. 1867 (Ont. S.C.J. (Sm. Cl. Ct.)).

12.03 STAY OR DISMISSAL IF NO LEAVE UNDER COURTS OF JUSTICE ACT — (1)
If the court determines that a person who is subject to an order under subsection 140 (1) of the Courts of Justice Act has instituted or continued an action without the order having been rescinded or leave granted for the action to be instituted or continued, the court shall make an order staying or dismissing the action.

(2) **REQUEST FOR ORDER** — Any party to the action may file with the clerk a written request for an order under subrule (1).

(3) **SERVICE OF ORDER** — An order under subrule (1) may be made without notice, but the clerk shall send a copy of the order by mail, in the manner described in subrule 8.07 (1), to every party to the action as soon as possible after the order is made.

[O. Reg. 44/14, s. 11(4).]

PRACTICE NOTES

§1 Generally Section 140 of the CJA does not authorize a Small Claims Court Judge to make an Order barring a litigant from instituting or continuing proceedings that are considered to be vexatious. That power has been reserved to the Superior Court Justices. However, once a litigant has been made the subject matter of an order under s. 140, the Small Claims Court Rules then may permit a Small Claims Court Judge to act if such a person is to be found to be continuing to initiate proceedings. Rule 12.03 of the Small Claims Court permits a judge of that court to stay or dismiss a claim where no leave has been obtained by a person against whom an order has been made under s. 140.[1]

[1] *Ferguson v. Plate*, [2018] O.J. No. 3754 (Ont. S.C.J. (Sm. Cl. Ct.)).

Rule 13 — Settlement Conferences

13.01 SETTLEMENT CONFERENCE REQUIRED IN DEFENDED ACTION — (1) A
settlement conference shall be held in every defended action.

(2) **DUTY OF CLERK** — The clerk shall fix a time, date and place for the settlement conference and serve a notice of settlement conference, together with a list of proposed witnesses (Form 13A), on the parties.

(3) **TIMING** — The settlement conference shall be held within 90 days after the first defence is filed.

(4) **EXCEPTION** — Subrules (1) to (3) do not apply if the defence contains an admission of liability for all of the plaintiff's claim and a proposal of terms of payment under subrule 9.03 (1).

[O. Reg. 78/06, s. 27.]

13.02 ATTENDANCE — (1) A party and the party's representative, if any, shall, unless
the court orders otherwise, participate in the settlement conference,

(a)   by personal attendance; or

(b)   by telephone or video conference in accordance with rule 1.07.

(2) AUTHORITY TO SETTLE — A party who requires another person's approval before agreeing to a settlement shall, before the settlement conference, arrange to have ready telephone access to the other person throughout the conference, whether it takes place during or after regular business hours.

(3) ADDITIONAL SETTLEMENT CONFERENCES — The court may order the parties to attend an additional settlement conference.

(4) The clerk shall fix a time and place for any additional settlement conference and serve a notice of settlement conference, together with a list of proposed witnesses (Form 13A) on the parties.

(5) FAILURE TO ATTEND — If a party who has received a notice of settlement conference fails to attend the conference, the court may,

(a)   impose appropriate sanctions, by way of costs or otherwise; and

(b)   order that an additional settlement conference be held, if necessary.

(6) If a defendant fails to attend a first settlement conference, receives notice of an additional settlement conference and fails to attend the additional settlement conference, the court may,

(a)   strike out the defence and dismiss the defendant's claim, if any, and allow the plaintiff to prove the plaintiff's claim; or

(b)   make such other order as is just.

(7) INADEQUATE PREPARATION, FAILURE TO FILE MATERIAL — The court may award costs against a person who attends a settlement conference if,

(a)   in the opinion of the court, the person is so inadequately prepared as to frustrate the purposes of the conference;

(b)   the person fails to file the material required by subrule 13.03 (2).

[O. Reg. 78/06, s. 27; O. Reg. 230/13, s. 14.]

PRACTICE NOTES

§1 Generally   There is no specific provision in the SCCR to set aside an order under r. 13.02(6). Rule 11.06 is not directly applicable. However, it is a principle of the Small Claims Court and of civil procedure generally that judgments or orders obtained by default or in the absence of the other party may be set aside by the same level of court, at least in appropriate circumstances. As much as possible, matters should be heard on their merits, with both sides presenting evidence and argument and able to challenge the submissions of the other side. The naturally concomitant power of the Small Claims Court in Ontario may be exercised to set aside an order at a settlement conference under r. 13.02(6), rendered as it is in the absence of the party against whom it is made. In doing so, the court may broadly apply the factors referred to in r. 11.06, namely: (i) is there a meritorious defence (or claim); (ii) is there a reasonable explanation for the default (or failure to attend); and (iii) was the proceeding to set aside the default taken as soon as practical in the circumstances.[1]

The Small Claims Court has jurisdiction to set aside an order made at the settlement conference in the absence of D, and hence a judgment in favour of P, without the necessity of an appeal to the Divisional Court. Policy and practicality demand this. Matters of process, such as orders obtained by default or in the absence of the other party, should be made in the first instance to the court having jurisdiction over that process.

Small Claims Court matters should not be brought to the Divisional Court except by way of a substantive appeal after a hearing on the merits to address errors of law or of mixed law and fact or of fact that may justify appellate intervention. Otherwise, there would be a multitude of appeals inundating the Divisional Court from the Small Claims Court.[2]

An order striking P's claim was a final order of the court. Such an order could have properly been the subject of an appeal to the Divisional Court but cannot be the subject of a motion to Small Claims Court to simply set aside the earlier order where there was no evidence to suggest anything irregular occurred in the scheduling of the conference in the normal course by the clerk, on notice to both parties pursuant to r. 13.01(2). Nor was there evidence to explain or excuse P's failure to attend that conference, and his failure to pay the costs as ordered by a deputy judge. Appropriate sanctions for P's failure to attend a settlement conference, by way of costs or otherwise includes the potential sanction of dismissal or striking of P's claim. It may be that r. 13.02(6) implies that in general, at least as to D's failure to attend a settlement conference, a striking or dismissal order may be appropriately deferred to a second conference. In other words a party who fails to attend may in some or many cases be given a "second chance". But that is only a generalization of how these situations are often but not always dealt with in practice. The settlement conference judge has jurisdiction to make a final order where a party fails to attend a first settlement conference, in appropriate cases.[3]

[1] *Maly v. Hanniman*, [2012] O.J. No. 5130 (Ont. S.C.J. (Sm. Cl. Ct.)).

[2] *Brighton Lee-Rich Enterprises v. Thompson*, [2013] O.J. No. 4970 (Ont. S.C.J. (Sm. Cl. Ct.)).

[3] *Mortazavi v. Monod*, 2020 CanLII 20492 (Ont. S.C.J.).

13.03 PURPOSES OF SETTLEMENT CONFERENCE — (1) The purposes of a settlement conference are,

(a)   to resolve or narrow the issues in the action;

(b)   to expedite the disposition of the action;

(c)   to encourage settlement of the action;

(d)   to assist the parties in effective preparation for trial; and

(e)   to provide full disclosure between the parties of the relevant facts and evidence.

(2) DISCLOSURE — At least 14 days before the date of the settlement conference, each party shall serve on every other party and file with the court,

(a)   a copy of any document to be relied on at the trial, including an expert report, not attached to the party's claim or defence; and

(b)   a list of proposed witnesses (Form 13A) and of other persons with knowledge of the matters in dispute in the action.

(3) At the settlement conference, the parties or their representatives shall openly and frankly discuss the issues involved in the action.

(4) FURTHER DISCLOSURE RESTRICTED — Except as otherwise provided or with the consent of the parties (Form 13B), the matters discussed at the settlement conference shall not be disclosed to others until after the action has been disposed of.

[O. Reg. 78/06, s. 27.]

PRACTICE NOTES

§1.   Confidentiality
§2.   Discovery

§1 Confidentiality   Disclosure of pre-trial conference discussions to the trial judge, even on consent, is prohibited. To compromise the sanctity of that process would discourage the full and frank discussion that is essential to its proper function and would therefore compromise its objective of encouraging settlement. The court should guard against any erosion of that sanctity. The action is not disposed of until the trial judge's function is completed. That includes the costs hearing. The rule requires formal consent to disclosure to others even after the action has been disposed of.[1]

[1] *Lucy v. Kitchener (City)*, [2013] O.J. No. 190, 6 M.P.L.R. (5th) 285 (Ont. Sm. Cl. Ct.)).

§2 Discovery   There is no jurisdiction in the Small Claims court for a pre-trial motion to compel the production of documents.[1]

[1] *Cathers v. RBC Dominion Securities Inc.*, [2013] O.J. No. 5119 (Ont. S.C.J. (Sm. Cl. Ct.)).

13.04 RECOMMENDATIONS TO PARTIES — The court may make recommendations to the parties on any matter relating to the conduct of the action, in order to fulfil the purposes of a settlement conference, including recommendations as to,

(a)   **the clarification and simplification of issues in the action;**

(b)   **the elimination of claims or defences that appear to be unsupported; and**

(c)   **the admission of facts or documents without further proof.**
[O. Reg. 78/06, s. 27.]

13.05 ORDERS AT SETTLEMENT CONFERENCE — (1) A judge conducting a settlement conference may make any order relating to the conduct of the action that the court could make.

(2) Without limiting the generality of subrule (1), the judge may,

(a)   **make an order,**

     (i)   **adding or deleting parties,**

     (ii)   **consolidating actions,**

     (iii)   **with written reasons, staying or dismissing the action,**

     (iv)   **amending or striking out a claim or defence under rule subrule 12.02(1),**

     (v)   **[REVOKED: O. Reg. 44/14, s. 12(3)]**

     (vi)   **directing production of documents,**

     (vii)   **changing the place of trial under rule 6.01,**

     (viii)   **directing an additional settlement conference under subrule 13.02 (3), and**

     (ix)   **ordering costs; and**

(b)   at an additional settlement conference, order judgment under subrule 13.02 (6).

(3) **RECOMMENDATIONS TO JUDGE** — If the settlement conference is conducted by a referee, a judge may, on the referee's recommendation, make any order that may be made under subrules (1) and (2).

(4) **CONSENT TO FINAL JUDGMENT** — A judge may order final judgment at a settlement conference where the matter in dispute is for an amount under the appealable limit and a party files a consent (Form 13B) signed by all parties before the settlement conference indicating that they wish to obtain final determination of the matter at the settlement conference if a mediated settlement is not reached.

(5) **SERVICE OF ORDER** — Within 10 days after the judge signs an order made at a settlement conference, the clerk shall serve the order on the parties that were not present at the settlement conference in accordance with subrule 8.01 (6).

[O. Reg. 78/06, s. 27; O. Reg. 44/14, s. 12.]

PRACTICE NOTES

§1 General principles Rule 13.05 does not appear to contemplate formal motions being brought at settlement conferences. The normal practice is for document requests at settlement conferences to be made either orally with prior notice to the other parties (usually by letter) or without prior notice, but without any formal motion. Production requests are not supposed to overtake the primary function of the settlement conference which is to discuss settlement. Rule 13.05(1) indicates that the powers of a settlement conference judge are those of the court, meaning that they cannot be more extensive than those of the court. The power of a settlement conference judge to order the production of documents is limited to production of documents between the parties. A Small Claims Court has no jurisdiction to make pre-trial orders for the production of documents by non-parties, whether on motion or at a settlement conference.[1]

With regard to r. 13.05(2)(a)(iii), the written reasons should be sufficient to serve a number of functional and inherently important purposes, including those of ensuring that parties are not left in doubt as to why a decision has been reached, and providing both the parties and an appellate court with a sufficient basis for exploring the merits of an appeal. This clause does not create an obligation to render sufficient reasons; it merely provides express confirmation of an obligation that already exists pursuant to fundamental principles of fairness and natural justice.[2]

In accordance with the provisions of r. 13.05(1) and (2)(a)(vi), it was open to a deputy judge during settlement conferences to require P to provide his expert evidence to the appellants in advance of the trial. Further, under r. 13.05(2), if the circumstances warranted it, the deputy judge, with written reasons, could have stayed or dismissed the action.[3]

Discovery power generally The proper interpretation of r. 13.05(2)(vi) is not that it *limits* production orders to settlement conferences, but rather that it affirms that a judge even at a settlement conference may make such a mandatory order, it being one of a type that the court *outside of a settlement conference* could make.[4]

Where production orders are made, it is consistent with the summary process of the Small Claims Court that the scope of production is generally limited to reliance as opposed to relevance. Reliance is a significantly narrower basis for disclosure than relevance. One of the ways that proceedings are conducted in a summary way in the Small Claims Court court is through the elimination of examinations for discovery. In addition there is no broad and mandatory requirement for document discovery as set out under r. 39 of the Civil Rules. Instead, the SCCR provide for three limited forms of document discovery. Those consist of: (i) the requirement to attach to the claim or defence copies of any documents on which the claim or defence is based; (ii) for the settlement conference, the requirement to attach to the List of Witnesses copies of any other documents to be relied on at trial and the related power of the settlement conference judge to order production of documents; and (iii) the requirement to serve copies of documents at least 30 days before trial where a party intends to introduce the documents through the hearsay exception in r. 18.02.[5]

Striking claims and dismissing actions Rule 13.05(2)(a)(iv) allows a settlement conference judge to make an order "striking out a claim . . . under subrule 12.02(1)". However, the power to dismiss an action comes from r. 12.02(2). Settlement conference judges had previously been given the authority to make an order dismissing an action by r. 13.05(2)(a)(v), which was revoked in 2014.[6]

Costs There is an obligation on litigants to prepare for and attend a settlement conference with a mind open to the position of the opposing litigant, and the views of the presiding judge. Failure to do so thwarts the legitimate purposes and objectives of the settlement conference and wastes the time and money of all involved. In such circumstances, an order for costs may well be warranted. On the other hand, parties to an action are entitled to maintain their positions during a settlement conference, and to have the matter proceed to trial. They are under no obligation to accept a settlement proposed by an opposing litigant, or the presiding judge, and are under no obligation to compromise. It would be an error to make a costs order solely because a party failed to better their initial settlement offer, but such an error would not amount to a breach of procedural fairness.[7]

[1] *Lemont v. State Farm Mutual Automobile Insurance Co.*, [2011] O.J. No. 4601 (Ont. S.C.J. (Sm. Cl. Ct.)).

[2] *Doerr v. Sterling Paralegal*, [2014] O.J. No. 1732, 2014 ONSC 2335 (Ont. Div. Ct.).

[3] *Hervieux v. Huronia Optical*, [2016] O.J. No. 3270, 2016 ONCA 294 (Ont. C.A.).

[4] *Burke v. Lauzon Sound and Automation Inc.*, [2016] O.J. No. 2914 (Ont. S.C.J. (Sm. Cl. Ct.)).

[5] *Cecchin v. Lander*, [2019] O.J. No. 5923 (Ont. S.C.J.).

[6] *Elguindy v. St. Joseph's Health Care London*, [2017] O.J. No. 3615, 2017 ONSC 4247 at paras. 62-64 (Ont. Div. Ct.).

[7] *Kovac v. Royal Botanical Gardens*, [2019] O.J. No. 3603, 2019 ONSC 4151 (Ont. Div. Ct.).

13.06 MEMORANDUM — (1) At the end of the settlement conference, the court shall prepare a memorandum summarizing,

    (a)   **recommendations made under rule 13.04;**

    (b)   **the issues remaining in dispute;**

    (c)   **the matters agreed on by the parties;**

    (d)   **any evidentiary matters that are considered relevant; and**

    (e)   **information relating to the scheduling of the remaining steps in the proceeding.**

(2) The memorandum shall be filed with the clerk, who shall give a copy to the trial judge.

[O. Reg. 78/06, s. 27.]

13.07 NOTICE OF TRIAL — At or after the settlement conference, the clerk shall provide the parties with a notice stating that one of the parties must request a trial date if the action is not disposed of within 30 days after the settlement conference, and pay the fee required for setting the action down for trial.

[O. Reg. 78/06, s. 27.]

PRACTICE NOTES

§1 Generally Rule 13.07 of the Small Claims Court Rules suggests that the parties must set the matter down for trial with the clerk within 30 days of the settlement conference.[1]

[1] *Sarkisian v. Chacon Properties Inc.*, [2013] O.J. No. 806 (Ont. S.C.J. (Sm. Cl. Ct.)).

13.08 JUDGE NOT TO PRESIDE AT TRIAL — A judge who conducts a settlement conference in an action shall not preside at the trial of the action.

[O. Reg. 78/06, s. 27.]

13.09 WITHDRAWAL OF CLAIM — After a settlement conference has been held, a claim against a party who is not in default shall not be withdrawn or discontinued by the party who brought the claim without,

(a)   the written consent of the party against whom the claim is brought; or

(b)   leave of the court.

[O. Reg. 78/06, s. 27.]

PRACTICE NOTES

§1 Generally Where P seeks leave to discontinue the action at the start of trial, r. 13.09 is the applicable provision. Leave of the court is a discretionary matter and that the Small Claims Court Rules provide no specific guidance on how that discretion should be exercised. The window to discontinue defended actions as of right is prior to completion of the settlement conference. Although the degree of progress of the action is not an exclusive factor for consideration, it will generally be more difficult for P to obtain leave to discontinue as an action progresses towards trial. The equities will accumulate in favour of D obtaining a termination of the action that will shield him from being vexed by the matter anew — whether by a judicial determination on the merits, a dismissal of the claim or a discontinuance on terms that no new action may be brought on the same cause.[1]

Before a settlement conference has been held, a claim in this court can be discontinued as of right. After a settlement conference has been held, consent or leave to discontinue is required under r. 13.09. The court has a discretion to grant or deny leave.[2]

[1] *Ever Fresh Direct Foods Inc. v. Schindler*, [2012] O.J. No. 3673 (Ont. S.C.J. (Sm. Cl. Ct.)).

[2] *Glycobiosciences Inc. v. Marcm Consulting Canada*, [2015] O.J. No. 4440 (On. S.C.J. (Sm. Cl. Ct.)).

13.10 COSTS — The costs of a settlement conference, exclusive of disbursements, shall not exceed $100 unless the court orders otherwise because there are special circumstances.

[O. Reg. 78/06, s. 27.]

Rule 14 — Offer to Settle

14.01 A party may serve on any other party an offer to settle a claim on the terms specified in the offer.

PRACTICE NOTES

§1 Generally Though e-mail is not a valid method of service under the Small Claims Court Rules, e-mail can be valid communication in writing indicating the acceptance of an offer to settle. If the party filed the Acceptance of Offer to Settle and communicated the acceptance through e-mail, but did not serve it on the opposing party, the failure to serve the proper form is immaterial to the question of when the offer was accepted.[1]

[1] *Ayr Hardwood Flooring Inc. v. Korczmarczyk*, [2015] O.J. No. 83 (Ont. S.C.J. (Sm. Cl. Ct.)).

14.01.1 WRITTEN DOCUMENTS — (1) An offer to settle, an acceptance of an offer to settle and a notice of withdrawal of an offer to settle shall be in writing.

(2) **USE OF FORMS** — An offer to settle may be in Form 14A, an acceptance of an offer to settle may be in Form 14B and a notice of withdrawal of an offer to settle may be in Form 14C.

(3) **TERMS OF SETTLEMENT** — The terms of an accepted offer to settle may be set out in terms of settlement (Form 14D).

[O. Reg. 78/06, s. 28.]

14.02 TIME FOR MAKING OFFER — (1) An offer to settle may be made at any time.

(2) **COSTS CONSEQUENCES** — The costs consequences referred to in rule 14.07 apply only if the offer to settle is served on the party to whom it is made at least seven days before the trial commences.

[O. Reg. 78/06, s. 29.]

14.03 WITHDRAWAL — (1) An offer to settle may be withdrawn at any time before it is accepted, by serving a notice of withdrawal of an offer to settle on the party to whom it was made.

(2) **DEEMED WITHDRAWAL** — If an offer to settle specifies a date after which it is no longer available for acceptance, and has not been accepted on or before that date, the offer shall be deemed to have been withdrawn on the day after that date.

(3) **EXPIRY WHEN COURT DISPOSES OF CLAIM** — An offer may not be accepted after the court disposes of the claim in respect of which the offer is made.

[O. Reg. 461/01, s. 16; O. Reg. 78/06, s. 29.]

14.04 NO DISCLOSURE TO TRIAL JUDGE — If an offer to settle is not accepted, no communication about it or any related negotiations shall be made to the trial judge until all questions of liability and the relief to be granted, other than costs, have been determined.

[O. Reg. 78/06, s. 29.]

14.05 ACCEPTANCE OF AN OFFER TO SETTLE — (1) An offer to settle may be accepted by serving an acceptance of an offer to settle on the party who made it, at any time before it is withdrawn or before the court disposes of the claim in respect of which it is made.

(2) **PAYMENT INTO COURT AS CONDITION** — An offer by a plaintiff to settle a claim in return for the payment of money by a defendant may include a term that the defendant pay the money into court; in that case, the defendant may accept the offer only by paying the money into court and notifying the plaintiff of the payment.

(3) If a defendant offers to pay money to a plaintiff in settlement of a claim, the plaintiff may accept the offer with the condition that the defendant pay the money into court; if the offer is so accepted and the defendant fails to pay the money into court, the plaintiff may proceed as provided in rule 14.06.

(4) **COSTS** — If an accepted offer to settle does not deal with costs, the plaintiff is en-

titled,

(a)   in the case of an offer made by the defendant, to the plaintiff's disbursements assessed to the date the plaintiff was served with the offer;

(b)   in the case of an offer made by the plaintiff, to the plaintiff's disbursements assessed to the date that the notice of acceptance was served.

[O. Reg. 78/06, s. 30.]

14.06 FAILURE TO COMPLY WITH ACCEPTED OFFER — If a party to an accepted offer to settle fails to comply with the terms of the offer, the other party may,

(a)   make a motion to the court for judgment in the terms of the accepted offer; or

(b)   continue the proceeding as if there had been no offer to settle.

PRACTICE NOTES

§1 Generally   Rule 14.06 provides that where a party to a settlement fails to comply with its terms, the other party may make a motion to enforce the settlement or may continue the proceeding as if there had been no settlement. In most situations involving an alleged breach of a settlement, it is relatively clear whether there has been a breach and it is relatively straightforward for the other party to make his or her election under that rule. However, where P disputes that D actually made the payment agreed to, the appropriate path is by way of a fresh proceeding in which that allegation can be tested through pleadings and a trial.[1]

Binding settlement   Rule 14.06 is a rough equivalent of r. 49.09 of the Civil Rules. For there to be a binding settlement agreement, the essential provisions must have been agreed upon and there must be a mutual intention to create a legally binding relationship. A statement of interest in settling and a near-promise to sign a document or documents probably not yet read do not provide the certainty required to constitute an acceptance.[2]

[1]   *Spylo v. Reyhani (c.o.b. Kitchen, Living and Beyond by Roya)*, [2013] O.J. No. 1690 (Ont. S.C.J. (Sm. Cl. Ct.)).

[2]   *Schwartzentruber v. Wettlauffer Home Improvements and Contracting Inc.*, [2012] O.J. No. 128 (Ont. S.C.J. (Sm. Cl. Ct.)).

14.07 COSTS CONSEQUENCES OF FAILURE TO ACCEPT — (1) When a plaintiff makes an offer to settle that is not accepted by the defendant, the court may award the plaintiff an amount not exceeding twice the costs of the action, if the following conditions are met:

1.   The plaintiff obtains a judgment as favourable as or more favourable than the terms of the offer.

2.   The offer was made at least seven days before the trial.

3.   The offer was not withdrawn and did not expire before the trial.

(2) When a defendant makes an offer to settle that is not accepted by the plaintiff, the court may award the defendant an amount not exceeding twice the costs awardable to a successful party, from the date the offer was served, if the following conditions are met:

1.   The plaintiff obtains a judgment as favourable as or less favourable than the terms of the offer.

2.   The offer was made at least seven days before the trial.

3.   The offer was not withdrawn and did not expire before the trial.

(3) If an amount is awarded under subrule (1) or (2) to a self-represented party, the court may also award the party an amount not exceeding $500 as compensation for inconvenience and expense.

[O. Reg. 78/06, s. 31.]

PRACTICE NOTES

§1 Generally The cost consequences of offers to settle should be reliably applied if they are to have the intended effect of encouraging settlements and discouraging unreasonable positions. However, the language of r. 14.07 of the Small Claims Court Rules is different than that of r. 49.10 of the Civil Rules, and the costs rules in Small Claims Court are of course significantly different in any event than the costs rules applicable in the Superior Court of Justice. Settlement conference discussions cannot be disclosed to the trial judge, even on consent. The litigants are responsible for their own assessments of the case and cannot simply rely on the assessment of a settlement conference judge, whose focus is on settlement and whose opinion would by definition be irrelevant to and not binding on the trial judge.[1]

An element of compromise is not an essential element of an offer to settle, but its absence can be a relevant factor to be taken into account. P's offer to settle waived interest and substantial legal costs incurred to the date of the offer had a sufficient element of compromise to conclude that P was entitled to enhanced costs under r. 14.07.[2]

Non-compliant offers The judge is entitled to consider anything properly relevant to a proper determination of costs, including taking into account an offer to settle, even if it may not be in strict compliance with r. 14.07(1)(3).[3]

Disclosure of such offers which do not comply with r. 14.07 is unobjectionable in itself. However, the court should not punish a party for failing to make, from the other party's perspective, a reasonable settlement offer. D is entitled to put P to the proof of its claim and there is no obligation to settle an action. D's offer to settle for nil does not qualify for cost consequences under r. 14.07(2).[4] However, see r. 19.06 regarding the potential costs consequences of accepting reasonable offers.

Double costs While r. 14.07 cannot conflict with CJA s. 29, s. 29 does not impose a rigid cap. Section 29 was not intended to cap the costs at 15% in the circumstances of an offer that gives rise to the cost consequences outlined in r. 14.07. Rule 14.07 is a specific instance of a party's "unreasonable behaviour in the proceeding" that may invite increased costs under s. 29. In this respect, r. 14.07 supplements s. 29, and does not conflict with it. It operates to encourage settlement of Small Claims Court proceedings. Section 29 is not limited to the amount claimed by the successful party. The amount claimed by the unsuccessful party may also be considered. There is no reason why the amount of D's claim should not be considered when determining costs under s. 29. Certainly, D would have insisted that costs be calculated on the amount of its claim had it been successful. Parties in Small Claims Court proceedings must understand that there are potential adverse costs consequences if they exaggerate or inflate their claims or advance unmeritorious counterclaims. This, too, promotes settlement. The Small Claims Court can award costs on the combined total of P's and D's claims even where that amount exceeds the $25,000 monetary limit of the Small Claims Court. Section 29 does not increase the monetary limit of the court, but sets out a method for calculating the maximum costs that the court can award in any particular case. Clearly, the cost associated with a case involving P's claim and D's claim will usually exceed the costs of a case with only one claim, and it is only logical that the deputy judge can take into account the value of both claims when determining the maximum costs that can be awarded.[5]

The Small Claims Court's discretion to award double costs under r. 14.07 can be applied in tandem with its jurisdiction to make a penalty costs award under s. 29, where the double costs would amount to more than 15% of the amount claimed.[6] Section 29 of the CJA was not intended to cap the costs at 15% in the circumstances of an offer that gives rise to the cost consequences outlined in r. 14.07. This seems to give meaning to the need to encourage the acceptance of reasonable settlement offers, while maintaining proportionality with the amounts in dispute and allowing the judge to consider what is fair and reasonable in all of the circumstances.[7] Rule 14.07 of the SCCR can therefore be applied to award double costs even if the doubled amount exceeds the 15% *prima facie* limit under CJA s. 29. In addition, under r. 19.01(1), P is entitled to recover its reasonable disbursements.[8] Of course, where no fees awarded, there was nothing to double under r. 14.07.[9] The double cost rule does not apply when P fails to recover anything and the action is dismissed.[10]

Unlike r. 49.10 of the Civil Rules, r. 14.07 does not provide for costs on an enhanced scale from the date of the offer. Rule 14.07 does not extend to Small Claims Court appeals.[11]

There is some controversy about the interplay of CJA s. 29 and r. 14.07. Some courts consider failure to accept a settlement offer which is then exceeded at trial to be an example of "unreasonable behaviour in the proceeding" permitting the costs to exceed 15% under s. 29. The effect of such reasoning is almost always the doubling of the costs otherwise determined. But the 15% is a ceiling, not a tariff, and does not obviate the determination of a reasonable representation fee in the circumstances of each case. The statutory provision and the rule must be dealt with in order, always keeping in mind that the statute limits the rule. First, the court must determine the costs exclusive of disbursements, which largely means determining a reasonable representation fee. If the conditions of r. 14.07(1) or (2) are met, the court must then determine by how much to increase that reasonable representation fee, within a range of 0% to 100%. The court must take into account what an unsuccessful party should reasonably expect to pay for his day in court considering the length and complexity of the case and the amount in issue. This amount is universally acknowledged, especially in the Small Claims Court, to be much less than the actual costs of the successful party in most cases. At the second stage, the reasonable expectations of the unsuccessful party take on far less significance because of its conduct in failing to accept a reasonable settlement offer. The expectations of an unsuccessful litigant who has refused a reasonable settlement offer should be higher than one who has not done that. Moreover, the application of the rule is intended to be somewhat punitive, in order to condition litigants to seriously consider settlement offers. Still, the increased fee must still be reasonable, even if that only means less than or equal to the successful party's actual costs. Then the court may turn to r. 19.06 and consider whether extra compensation should be ordered.

Those are the categories of costs which the court is authorized by the rules to award to represented litigants. Section 29 of the CJA does not authorize the awarding of another category or level of costs when its test is met. Rather, it authorizes awarding costs permitted by the Rules which exceed 15% of the amount claimed when its test is met. Otherwise, it sets an upper limit on the costs which are awardable under the Rules.

Therefore, if a reasonable representation fee, or an increased representation fee awarded under r. 14.07, or a representation fee, plain or increased, plus compensation under r. 19.06 exceeds 15% of the amount claimed, it must be reduced to 15% of the amount claimed unless the court considers it necessary to penalize a party for unreasonable behaviour in the proceeding. This is a separate determination from those involved in rr. 14.07 and 19.06. Section 29 represents the view of the legislature that costs in Small Claims Court, while properly following upon success, or failure to accept a reasonable settlement offer, must be kept within limits to preserve access to the court, and that costs exceeding 15% of the amount claimed would be punitive. Only when a penalty is warranted by the unreasonable behaviour of a party may the limit be exceeded.

In some cases, the simple failure to accept a reasonable settlement offer which is bettered after trial might be considered unreasonable behaviour warranting costs exceeding the limit. In other cases, it might not, but combined with other behaviour in the proceedings, the test might be met. In other cases, despite the absence of settlement offers, or where an offer is not less than the judgment (or more than the judgment in the case of defendants' offers), other unreasonable behaviour in the proceeding alone might meet the test in s. 29.[12]

[1] *Filippova v. Arvato Digital Services, Canada Inc.*, [2012] O.J. No. 3623 (Ont. S.C.J. (Sm. Cl. Ct.)).

[2] *Downtown Rental and Building Supplies Ltd. v. 2239004 Ontario Inc.*, [2015] O.J. No. 3486 (Ont. S.C.J. (Sm. Cl. Ct.)).

[3] *RPMS Property Management Inc. v. Twiddy*, [2015] O.J. No. 623 (Ont. S.C.J.).

[4] *Lucy v. Kitchener (City)*, [2013] O.J. No. 190, 6 M.P.L.R. (5th) 285 (Ont. S.C.J. (Sm. Cl. Ct.)).

[5] *10.1 Inc. v. 2248951 Ontario Inc.*, [2018] O.J. No. 168, 2018 ONSC 381 at paras. 50, 52, 53, 54 (Ont. Div. Ct.).

[6] *1604966 Ontario Ltd. v. Andsign International Management Inc.*, [2013] O.J. No. 2401 (Ont. S.C.J. (Sm. Cl. Ct.)).

[7] *Barrie Trim and Mouldings Inc. v. Dewsbury*, [2010] O.J. No. 1836, 2010 ONSC 2598 (Ont. Div. Ct.).

[8] *Barrie Trim and Mouldings Inc. v. Dewsbury*, [2010] O.J. No. 1836, 2010 ONSC 2598 (Ont. Div. Ct.). See also *Conestoga Roofing & Sheet Metal Ltd. v. Baranski*, [2012] O.J. No. 3371 (Ont. Div. Ct.); *McDonald's Restaurants of Canada Ltd. v. Harrison*, [2012] O.J. No. 5625 (Ont. S.C.J. (Sm. Cl. Ct.)); *Bedrock Stone Masonry v. Blake*, [2015] O.J. No. 3663 (Ont. S.C.J. (Sm. Cl. Ct.)); *E-Conomy Finance Group Ltd. v. FLS Transportation Services Inc.*, [2016] O.J. No. 2691 (Ont. S.C.J. (Sm. Cl. Ct.)).

[9] *Paquette Travers & Deutschmann v. Neil*, [2013] O.J. No. 719 (Ont. S.C.J. (Sm. Cl. Ct.)).

[10] *Prohaska v. Howe*, [2016] O.J. No. 13, 2016 ONSC 48 (Ont. S.C.J. (Sm. Cl. Ct.)). See also *Macdonald v. Genereux-Partridge*, [2016] O.J. No. 2816 (Ont. S.C.J. (Sm. Cl. Ct.)).

[11] *Caskanette v. Bong-Keun Choi Dentistry Professional Corp.*, [2016] O.J. No. 5291, 2016 ONSC 6448 (Ont. S.C.J.).

[12] *Coicici v. Ashton Pools, Ponds and Spas Inc.*, [2017] O.J. No. 4465 at paras. 6, 11-16 (Ont. S.C.J. (Sm. Cl. Ct.)) [footnotes omitted].

Rule 15 — Motions

15.01 NOTICE OF MOTION AND SUPPORTING AFFIDAVIT — (1) A motion shall be made by a notice of motion and supporting affidavit (Form 15A).

(2) The moving party shall obtain a hearing date from the clerk before serving the notice of motion and supporting affidavit under subrule (3).

(3) The notice of motion and supporting affidavit,

(a)   shall be served on every party who has filed a claim and any defendant who has not been noted in default, at least seven days before the hearing date; and

(b)   shall be filed, with proof of service, at least three days before the hearing date.

(4) **SUPPORTING AFFIDAVIT IN RESPONSE —** A party who prepares an affidavit (Form 15B) in response to the moving party's notice of motion and supporting affidavit shall serve it on every party who has filed a claim or defence and file it, with proof of service, at least two days before the hearing date.

(5) **SUPPLEMENTARY AFFIDAVIT —** The moving party may serve a supplementary affidavit on every party who has filed a claim or defence and file it, with proof of service, at least two days before the hearing date.

(6) **MOTION AFTER JUDGMENT SIGNED —** A motion that is made after judgment has been signed shall be served on all parties, including those who have been noted in default.

[O. Reg. 78/06, s. 32; O. Reg. 393/09, s. 14.]

PRACTICE NOTES

§1. Motion to vary a previous order
§2. Change names of parties
§3. Production by third party
§4. Discovery

§1 Motion to vary a previous order Rule 15.01(6) suggests that a Small Claims Court judge has the jurisdiction to vary or clarify an order previously made. In any case, r. 1.04 which makes clear that the Small Claims Court can impose conditions on the orders which it makes. Even if this were not so, r. 1.03(2) provides that where the Small Claims Court Rules do not adequately cover a matter, if the court considers it appropriate, it may consider it by reference the Rules of Civil Procedure. This would include reference to r. 59.06 of the Rules of Civil Procedure, which deals with "amending, setting aside or varying" orders.[1]

[1] *Lahrkamp v. Metropolitan Toronto Condominium Corp. No. 932*, [2012] O.J. No. 5986, 2012 ONSC 6326 (Ont. Div. Ct.).

§2 Change names of parties P is required to name individual defendants by their full legal names. Form 7A contains boxes for an individual defendant's surname, first name, second or middle name, and any "also known as" names. It is P's own error to use D's informal first name and to take out a default judgment using that name. It is not open to P to obtain an order to change D's name on the default judgment order without notice to D. Rule 60.07(10) of the Civil Rules only supports a motion, without notice, where the judgment creditor is using one or more names in a manner that might otherwise frustrate enforcement of a judgment debt. P is required to obtain an order with notice under SCCR 15.01(6).[1]

[1] *Mirt v. Gerber*, [2015] O.J. No. 2888 (Ont. S.C.J. (Sm. Cl. Ct.)).

§3 Production by third party There is no jurisdiction in the Small Claims Court to issue a third party order for production. In the absence of discovery in the Small Claims Court, there is no gap in the Rules which would permit incorporation of r. 30.10 of the *Rules of Civil Procedure*.[1]

[1] *Elguindy v. St. Joseph's Health Care*, [2016] O.J. No. 2742, 2016 ONSC 2847 (Ont. Div. Ct.)

§4 Discovery Prior Small Claims Court rules specifically prohibited documentary discovery, except with leave, whereas the current Rules specifically provide for documentary discovery in the context of a settlement conference (r. 13.05(2)(*a*)(vi)). There is a conflict in the case law regarding the existence of a power of a Small Claims Court to order discovery. It has been held that the proper interpretation of r. 13.05(2)(vi) is not that it *limits* production orders to settlement conferences, but rather that it affirms that a judge even at a settlement conference may make such a mandatory order, it being one of a type that the court *outside of a settlement conference* could make. If there were a real "contest" about documents, whether over relevance or privilege or burden or some other matter, it may be more appropriate on occasion that that be dealt with via motion with the requisite affidavit material and the like, rather than in the "without prejudice" mediation forum of a settlement conference. The court should therefore not be precluded from dealing with such issues via motion, whether at trial or on a motions list. Of course, the entire discovery regime of the Superior Court Rules cannot and should not be imported and applied in Small Claims Court.[1]

Where production orders are made, it is consistent with the summary process of the Small Claims Court that the scope of production is generally limited to reliance as opposed to relevance. Reliance is a significantly narrower basis for disclosure than relevance. One of the ways that proceedings are conducted in a summary way in the Small Claims Court is through the elimination of examinations for discovery. In addition there is no broad and mandatory requirement for document discovery as set out under r. 39 of the Civil Rules. Instead, the SCCR provide for three limited forms of document discovery. Those consist of: (i) the requirement to attach to the claim or defence copies of any documents on which the claim or defence is based; (ii) for the settlement conference, the requirement to attach to the List of Witnesses copies of any other documents to be relied on at trial and the related power of the settlement conference judge to order production of documents; and (iii) the requirement to serve copies of documents at least 30 days before trial where a party intends to introduce the documents through the hearsay exception in r. 18.02.[2]

[1] *Burke v. Lauzon Sound and Automation Inc.*, [2016] O.J. No. 2914 (Ont. S.C.J. (Sm. Cl. Ct.)). *Contra*: *Elguindy v. St. Joseph's Health Care*, [2016] O.J. No. 2742, 2016 ONSC 2847 (Ont. Div. Ct.) in *obiter*.

[2] *Cecchin v. Lander*, [2019] O.J. No. 5923 (Ont. S.C.J.).

§5 Supplementary affidavit Rule 15.01(5) deals with a moving party's right to deliver a "supplementary affidavit". A supplementary affidavit under r. 15.01(5) means a supplementary affidavit in reply to a responding affidavit delivered by a responding party under r. 15.01(4). A respondent is entitled to contemporaneous notice of both what orders the moving party seeks and what evidence is offered in support of the motion. The court is not required to accept unsworn material in support of a motion when the requirement for affidavit evidence is stipulated under r. 15. The court always has a discretion to reject evidence, including sworn evidence, on appropriate grounds. In practice in the Small Claims Court it would be most unusual for a moving party to be permitted to rely on a brief of unsworn documents to prove contested facts, in the complete absence of any supporting affidavit evidence.[1]

[1] *Mortazavi v. Monod*, 2020 CanLII 20492 (Ont. S.C.J.).

15.02 METHOD OF HEARING — (1) A motion may be heard,

(a)   in person;

(b)   by telephone or video conference in accordance with paragraph 2 of subrule 1.07 (1);

(c)   by a judge in writing under clause 11.03 (2) (a) or (2.1) (a);

(d)   by any other method that the judge determines is fair and reasonable.

(2) The attendance of the parties is not required if the motion is in writing under clause (1) (c).

[O. Reg. 78/06, s. 32; O. Reg. 38/16, s. 8.]

15.03 MOTION WITHOUT NOTICE — (1) Despite rule 15.01, a motion may be made without notice if the nature or circumstances of the motion make notice unnecessary or not reasonably possible.

(2) SERVICE OF ORDER — A party who obtains an order on motion without notice shall serve it on every affected party, together with a copy of the notice of motion and supporting affidavit used on the motion, within five days after the order is signed.

(3) MOTION TO SET ASIDE OR VARY MOTION MADE WITHOUT NOTICE — A party who is affected by an order obtained on motion without notice may make a motion to set aside or vary the order, within 30 days after being served with the order.

[O. Reg. 78/06, s. 32; O. Reg. 393/09, s. 15.]

15.04 NO FURTHER MOTIONS WITHOUT LEAVE — If the court is satisfied that a party has tried to delay the action, add to its costs or otherwise abuse the court's process by making numerous motions without merit, the court may, on motion, make an order prohibiting the party from making any further motions in the action without leave of the court.

[O. Reg. 78/06, s. 32.]

15.05 ADJOURNMENT OF MOTION — A motion shall not be adjourned at a party's request before the hearing date unless the written consent of all parties is filed when the request is made, unless the court orders otherwise.

[O. Reg. 78/06, s. 32.]

15.06 WITHDRAWAL OF MOTION — A motion shall not be withdrawn without,

   (a)   the written consent of all the parties; or

   (b)   leave of the court.

[O. Reg. 78/06, s. 32.]

15.07 COSTS — The costs of a motion, exclusive of disbursements, shall not exceed $100 unless the court orders otherwise because there are special circumstances.

[O. Reg. 78/06, s. 32.]

PRACTICE NOTES

§1 Generally   To award more than $100 exclusive of disbursements on a motion, a court must find that there are special circumstances warranting an award of elevated costs. The statutory reference in CJA to unreasonable behaviour in the proceedings echoes the basis upon which substantial indemnity costs are awarded under Superior Court proceedings and the Civil Rules. Misconduct and unreasonable behaviour is cited to provide the basis upon which the elevated and exceptional costs of substantial indemnity is awarded in lieu of the partial indemnity which are awarded in ordinary course.[1] Special circumstances may include a motion for summary judgment brought at the commencement of the trial which disposed of the claim in its entirety.[2]

Full indemnity costs   Full indemnification is likely to be ordered where the parties have entered into an agreement that provides for indemnification on this basis. In other cases, full indemnification is reserved for situations in which the court wishes to impose a penalty for reprehensible conduct on the part of the party against whom costs are awarded. Full indemnification should be provided only where there has been reprehensible, scandalous or outrageous conduct on the part of one of the parties. Re-litigating an issue by itself is not deserving of a full indemnity costs order.[3]

[1] *Karnas v. Orion Management*, [2015] O.J. No. 5104 (Ont. S.C.J. (Sm. Cl. Ct.)).

[2] *Tarko v. Metropolitan Toronto Condominium Corp. 626*, [2015] O.J. No. 693, 2015 ONSC 982 (Ont. S.C.J.).

[3] *Ferguson v. Plate*, [2018] O.J. No. 3754 (Ont. S.C.J. (Sm. Cl. Ct.)).

Rule 16 — Notice of Trial

16.01 CLERK FIXES DATE AND SERVES NOTICE — (1) The clerk shall fix a date for trial and serve a notice of trial on each party who has filed a claim or defence if,

   (a)   a settlement conference has been held; and

   (b)   a party has requested that the clerk fix a date for trial and has paid the required fee.

(2) MANNER OF SERVICE — **The notice of trial shall be served by mail or fax.**

[O. Reg. 461/01, s. 17(1); O. Reg. 330/02, s. 11; O. Reg. 440/03, s. 5; O. Reg. 78/06, s. 32.]

Rule 17 — Trial

17.01 FAILURE TO ATTEND — **(1) If an action is called for trial and all the parties fail to attend, the trial judge may strike the action off the trial list.**

(2) If an action is called for trial and a party fails to attend, the trial judge may,

(a)   **proceed with the trial in the party's absence;**

(b)   **if the plaintiff attends and the defendant fails to do so, strike out the defence and dismiss the defendant's claim, if any, and allow the plaintiff to prove the plaintiff's claim, subject to subrule (3);**

(c)   **if the defendant attends and the plaintiff fails to do so, dismiss the action and allow the defendant to prove the defendant's claim, if any; or**

(d)   **make such other order as is just.**

(2.1) In the case described in clause (2) (b) or (c), the person with the claim is not required to prove liability against the party who has failed to attend but is required to prove the amount of the claim.

(3) In the case described in clause (2) (b), if an issue as to the proper place of trial under subrule 6.01 (1) is raised in the defence, the trial judge shall consider it and make a finding.

(4) SETTING ASIDE OR VARIATION OF JUDGMENT — **The court may set aside or vary, on such terms as are just, a judgment obtained against a party who failed to attend at the trial.**

(5) CONDITIONS TO MAKING OF ORDER UNDER SUBRULE (4) — **The court may make an order under subrule (4) only if,**

(a)   **the party who failed to attend makes a motion for the order within 30 days after becoming aware of the judgment; or**

(b)   **the party who failed to attend makes a motion for an extension of the 30-day period mentioned in clause (a) and the court is satisfied that there are special circumstances that justify the extension.**

[O. Reg. 78/06, s. 33.]

PRACTICE NOTES

§1 Generally Rule 17.01(4) provides that the court has a discretion to set aside a judgment obtained against a party who failed to attend at trial. A failure to appear for trial is a default, regardless of whether the party who has failed to appear happens to be P or D. On a motion of this type, the analysis called for under r. 11.06 applies. Assuming the motion is brought promptly, the moving party must satisfactorily explain her default and establish a meritorious claim or in other words a claim which has a meaningful chance of success at trial. If a plaintiff fails to establish that hers is such a claim, there is no reason why the court would exercise its discretion under r. 17.01(4) to set aside the judgment dismissing the action.[1]

[1] *Bond v. Deeb*, [2013] O.J. No. 1524 (Ont. S.C.J. (Sm. Cl. Ct.)). See also *Sharma v. Giffen LLP*, [2012] O.J. No. 5800 (Ont. S.C.J. (Sm. Cl. Ct.)).

17.02 ADJOURNMENT — (1) The court may postpone or adjourn a trial on such terms as are just, including the payment by one party to another of an amount as compensation for inconvenience and expense.

(2) If the trial of an action has been adjourned two or more times, any further adjournment may be made only on motion with notice to all the parties who were served with the notice of trial, unless the court orders otherwise.

[O. Reg. 78/06, s. 34.]

PRACTICE NOTES

§1 Generally Rule 17.02(1) provides that a trial may be adjourned by the court. On a plain reading of that rule, two things should be obvious: (i) the power to adjourn is discretionary as indicated by the word "may"; and (ii) it is the court, meaning a judge of the court, who possesses that discretion. The clerk or other court staff are not "the court" for this purpose. There is nothing in the Small Claims Court Rules to suggest that parties have an automatic right to adjourn their trials. There is nothing in those rules or the forms to suggest that the court clerk has jurisdiction to adjourn trials, nor for that matter is there any provision for the parties to obtain a second settlement conference as of right. What the Rules do say is that if parties fail to show up for their own trial, the court may proceed in their absence (r. 17.01(2)(*a*)). Rule 11.1 signals the obvious interest of the administration of justice in containing expense and delay by containing the overall duration of civil proceedings in this court.[1]

The proper administration of justice requires that the court strive to avoid wasting valuable court time when adjournments are not truly necessary. It is the court that may grant or refuse an adjournment. The parties are not given the power to adjourn a trial, even on consent. The court has a discretion to grant or deny adjournments, regardless of consent. Parties who assume that an adjournment request will be granted, or who elect not to appear at trial based on such assumptions, take the risk that the adjournment may be denied. The intention of the Civil Rules Committee appears to be that third and subsequent adjournments should be categorically more difficult to obtain than first and second adjournments. The consent of the parties is not mentioned in r. 17.02(2). In effect, each adjournment request is and should be less likely to be granted when there has already been one or more previous adjournments. That is particularly so with trials in the Small Claims Court involving a full day or more of trial time, since last-minute adjournments result in the loss of valuable court time for other litigants. It is also particularly so in files where interlocutory battles seem to be causing undue expense and delay. The court has an interest in taking hold of problem files and resolving them promptly and finally rather than letting undue expense and delay continue unabated.[2]

In Small Claims Court as in other courts, there comes a point when justice unreasonably delayed is justice denied.[3] At each step along the way, and particularly given the limitations on costs orders, the value of the substantive dispute will tend to be eroded by unrecoverable costs losses which will increase if a matter suffers from delays and adjournments.[4] Court dates — especially trial dates — are precious. The Small Claims Court is a very busy court. That is particularly so after the increase in its monetary jurisdiction in January 2010. A contested adjournment of a trial is therefore reluctantly granted. Good, sufficient and compelling reasons must be provided.[5]

Unfortunately, lawyers and paralegals sometimes assume that a consent adjournment request in Small Claims Court will always be granted. Whether there are good reasons for the request or not, the assumption might prove to be correct or incorrect. Adjournments are after all a discretionary matter and one relevant factor is the proper administration of justice. It is not acceptable for a party to fail to appear for trial based on an assumption that an adjournment will be granted, even on consent. When a party fails to attend trial, that party runs the risk that the trial may proceed in that party's absence, under r. 17.01(2).[6]

Rule 17.02(2) signals that a third adjournment request will be scrutinized with greater care than prior adjournment requests. In addition, such a request must be supported by a motion and supporting affidavit evidence, or the court must be persuaded to dispense with that requirement.[7]

Consent requests There is nothing in the *Small Claims Court Rules* that requires consent adjournment requests to be granted in every case. Rule 17.02 refers to the court's discretion to grant or deny adjournment requests but makes no distinction between requests that are made on consent or otherwise.[8]

[1] *Robb-Simand v. Re/Max Real Estate Centre Inc.*, [2012] O.J. No. 5232 (Ont. S.C.J. (Sm. Cl. Ct.)).

[2] *Petrykowski v. 553562 Ontario Ltd. (c.o.b. Bell Cartage)*, [2010] O.J. No. 2574 (Ont. S.C.J. (Sm. Cl. Ct.)).

[3] *Toste v. Baker*, [2007] O.J. No. 835 (Ont. Div. Ct.).

[4] *1604966 Ontario Ltd. v. Andsign International Management Inc.*, [2013] O.J. No. 2401 (Ont. S.C.J. (Sm. Cl. Ct.)).

[5] *Holtzman v. Suite Collections Canada Inc.*, [2013] O.J. No. 3049, 2013 ONSC 4240 (Ont. Div. Ct.).

[6] *Taylor v. 2300474 Ontario Inc.*, [2015] O.J. No. 3440 (Ont. S.C.J. (Sm. Cl. Ct.)).

[7] *Snyder v. Physiomed Group Inc.*, [2014] O.J. No. 3947 (Ont. S.C.J. (Sm. Cl. Ct.)).

[8] *MarcM Consulting Canada v. GlycoBioSciences Inc.*, [2015] O.J. No. 5226 (Ont. S.C.J. (Sm. Cl. Ct.)).

17.03 INSPECTION — The trial judge may, in the presence of the parties or their representatives, inspect any real or personal property concerning which a question arises in the action.

PRACTICE NOTES

§1 Generally Rule 17.03 is a procedure for taking evidence at trial and is similar to r. 52.05 of the *Rules of Civil Procedure*. Pre-trial discovery by way of inspection of property is a separate issue. The fact that r. 32 of those rules does not apply in Small Claims Court is simply one aspect of the policy decision by the Civil Rules Committee that there is no discovery in Small Claims Court. There is no legislative gap to fill in the case of a request for production of personal property: the Small Claims Court does not have jurisdiction to grant such an order.[1]

The confines of a courtroom and the limited time available within the trial make r. 17.03 more suited to the inspection of an inanimate object that does not require expert assessment. Where an animal is the subject of the dispute between the parties, r. 17.03 is not adequate for the matter at hand and it is more appropriate for P to have a pre-trial inspection of the animal by analogy to r. 32 of the *Rules of Civil Procedure*.[2]

Ordering a pre-trial inspection of the property is not hostile to the objectives of the court, it is central to principles of natural justice. This is an issue of fundamental fairness which the court must be allowed to address in the context of controlling its own proceedings and to support the most just, agreeable and in good conscience determination. A question about the condition of the property cannot be determined on the merits if only one side is allowed to collect relevant evidence. A party will not perceive the justice system as fair if it is denied the basic opportunity afforded to the other party. The playing field must be level or the administration of justice will fall into disrepute.[3] There is nothing in the language of r. 17.03 that restricts its operation to an out of court examination or view. To make the authority to inspect a meaningful one, under r. 17.03 some expert assistance may be necessary. In the interests of an expeditious determination at trial, such expert assistance may need to be provided in advance of the trial. This reality is not adequately covered by r. 17.03, and therefore a Deputy Judge has authority under r. 1.03(2) to make an order analogous to the type of order that could be made under r. 32.01 of the *Rules of Civil Procedure*.[4]

[1] *Garg v. Raywal Limited Partnership (c.o.b. Raywal Cabinets)*, [2014] O.J. No. 3686

[2] *National Service Dog Training Centre Inc. v. Hall*, [2013] O.J. No. 3216 (Ont. S.C.J. (Sm. Cl. Ct.)).

[3] *National Service Dog Training Centre Inc. v. Hall*, [2013] O.J. No. 3216 at para. 31 (Ont. S.C.J. (Sm. Cl. Ct.)).

[4] *Riddell v. Apple Canada Inc.*, [2017] O.J. No. 3605, 2017 ONCA 590), application for leave to appeal to S.C.C. filed December 10, 2017.

17.04 MOTION FOR NEW TRIAL — (1) A party may make a motion for a new trial within 30 days after a final order is made.

(2) **TRANSCRIPT** — In addition to serving and filing the notice of motion and supporting affidavit (Form 15A) required under rule 15.01, the moving party shall serve and file proof that a request has been made for a transcript of,

(a)   the reasons for judgment; and

(b)   any other portion of the proceeding that is relevant.

(3) **SERVICE AND FILING OF TRANSCRIPT** — If available, a copy of the transcript shall, at least three days before the hearing date,

(a)   be served on all parties who were served with the original notice of trial; and

(b)   be filed, with proof of service.

(4) **POWERS OF COURT ON MOTION** — On the hearing of the motion, the court may,

(a)   if the party demonstrates that a condition referred to in subrule (5) is satisfied,

    (i)   grant a new trial, or

    (ii)   pronounce the judgment that ought to have been given at trial and order judgment accordingly; or

(b)   dismiss the motion.

(5) **CONDITIONS** — The conditions referred to in clause (4) (a) are:

1.   There was a purely arithmetical error in the determination of the amount of damages awarded.

2.   There is relevant evidence that was not available to the party at the time of the original trial and could not reasonably have been expected to be available at that time.

[O. Reg. 78/06, s. 35; O. Reg. 393/09, s. 16.]

PRACTICE NOTES

§1 Generally Rule 17.04(1) is restrictive and specific. It provides that a party may make a motion for a new trial within 30 days after a final order is made. The rule permits the motions judge to grant a new trial only if the moving party demonstrates that there was a purely mathematical error in the determination of the amount of damages awarded or that there is relevant evidence that was not available to the party at the time of the original trial and could not reasonably have been expected to be available at that time.[1]

Rule 17.04 was never intended as an appeal and does not give a litigant "a second bite of the apple". The strong general rule is that parties are entitled to one trial and only one trial of a particular dispute. A dissatisfied litigant may have a right of appeal to the Divisional Court, which may vary or reverse a judgment and may order a new trial, subject to the applicable principles of appellate review. But he or she cannot have a second trial merely because he does not like the result of the first one. There are only two exceptions under r. 17.04 which permit the trial court, as opposed to the Divisional Court, to set aside or vary a judgment and, if necessary, direct a new trial. A party asking for a new trial under r. 17.04 must establish a condition under subrule (5). If the party does so, the court then has a discretion to either vary the judgment, direct a new trial.[2]

Subsequent appeal The filing of the Small Claims Court motion to obtain a new trial and the ordering of transcripts shows an intention to challenge the decision within the appeal period and can be taken as an intention to appeal for purposes of granting an extension of the time for appealing.[3]

Motion to vary a previous order Rule 15.01(6) suggests that a Small Claims Court judge has the jurisdiction to vary or clarify an order previously made. In any case, r. 1.04 makes it clear that the Small Claims Court can impose conditions on the orders which it makes. Even if this were not so, r. 1.03(2) provides that where the Small Claims Court Rules do not adequately cover a matter, if the court considers it appropriate, it may consider it by reference the *Rules of Civil Procedure*. This would include reference to r. 59.06 of the *Rules of Civil Procedure* which deals with "amending, setting aside or varying" orders.[4]

Extension of time While r. 1.03(1) requires the court to construe r. 17 liberally in the way which secures the just, most expeditious and least expensive determination of the proceeding on its merits, it would be difficult to justify an extension of one year. Justice, fairness and the most expeditious and least expensive determination requires some finality to the proceedings. A party is entitled to close their file, not have to continue to litigate the case in which a decision has been released. That lawyers are busy cannot by itself be a sufficient reason to give a one year extension to bring a motion to set aside a trial order.[5]

[1] *Rourke v. Toronto (City)*, [2012] O.J. No. 1896, 2012 ONSC 2563 (Ont. Div. Ct.).

[2] *Petrykowski v. 553562 Ontario Ltd. (c.o.b. Bell Cartage)*, [2010] O.J. No. 2574 (Ont. S.C.J. (Sm. Cl. Ct.)).

[3] *Keshavarz v. Zarieh*, [2015] O.J. No. 5701, 2015 ONSC 6721 (Ont. Div. Ct.).

[4] *Lahrkamp v. Metropolitan Toronto Condominium Corp. No. 932*, [2012] O.J. No. 5986, 2012 ONSC 6326 (Ont. Div. Ct.).

[5] *Haeusler v. Canadian Mini-Warehouse Properties Co.*, [2016] O.J. No. 2427 (Ont. S.C.J.).

Rule 18 — Evidence at Trial

18.01 AFFIDAVIT — At the trial of an undefended action, the plaintiff's case may be proved by affidavit, unless the trial judge orders otherwise.

18.02 WRITTEN STATEMENTS, DOCUMENTS AND RECORDS — (1) A document or written statement or an audio or visual record that has been served, at least 30 days before the trial date, on all parties who were served with the notice of trial, shall be received in evidence, unless the trial judge orders otherwise.

(2) Subrule (1) applies to the following written statements and documents:

1.   The signed written statement of any witness, including the written report of an expert, to the extent that the statement relates to facts and opinions to which the witness would be permitted to testify in person.

2.   Any other document, including but not limited to a hospital record or medical report made in the course of care and treatment, a financial record, a receipt, a bill, documentary evidence of loss of income or property damage, and a repair esti-

mate.

(3) DETAILS ABOUT WITNESS OR AUTHOR — A party who serves on another party a written statement or document described in subrule (2) shall append to or include in the statement or document,

(a)   the name, telephone number and address for service of the witness or author; and

(b)   if the witness or author is to give expert evidence, a summary of his or her qualifications.

(4) A party who has been served with a written statement or document described in subrule (2) and wishes to cross-examine the witness or author may summon him or her as a witness under subrule 18.03 (1).

(5) WHERE WITNESS OR AUTHOR IS SUMMONED — A party who serves a summons to witness on a witness or author referred to in subrule (3) shall, at the time the summons is served, serve a copy of the summons on every other party.

(6) Service of a summons and the payment or tender of attendance money under this rule may be proved by affidavit (Form 8A).

(7) ADJOURNMENT — A party who is not served with a copy of the summons in accordance with subrule (5) may request an adjournment of the trial, with costs.

[O. Reg. 78/06, s. 36.]

PRACTICE NOTES

§1 Generally Rule 18.02 is only one method to admit documents in Small Claims Court. Documents which are unqualified for admission under this rule may still be admitted through a witness or under the general statutory discretion conferred by CJA s. 27. Rule 18.02 offers the simplicity and costs savings of admitting documents without calling an in-person witness. The rule provides that if the information required by r. 18.02(3) is provided, and if the document was served at least 30 days before trial, the document shall be admitted unless the trial judge orders otherwise under r. 18.02(1). This permits a party served with a document to serve a summons on its author if so advised, under r. 18.02(4), and cross-examine that witness at trial. The document then serves as examination-in-chief and the witness may be cross-examined and re-examined in the usual fashion. In fact, that option is rarely exercised, and that is unsurprising given the nature of proceedings in Small Claims Court.[1]

Statement of issues Although process in the Small Claims Court is informal, trial counsel should provide the court with a statement of the issues for the court to decide. This is a useful thing to do in any case where the statement of the issues is not obvious: it serves to focus the court's attention, ensures that the parties really do have a common view of the matters for adjudication, and is very helpful for the court in framing its reasons for judgment. Clarity over such things – particularly in a forum where pleadings are often barebones – is an aid to economy and efficiency.[2]

Hearsay evidence Rule 18.02 is a hearsay exception. It permits documents to be admitted at trial in Small Claims Court without an in-person witness to identify them. The court has a general discretion to admit hearsay under s. 27 of the CJA. However, r. 18.02 is only one method to admit documents in Small Claims Court. Documents which are unqualified for admission under r. 18.02 may still be admitted through a witness or under the general statutory discretion conferred by CJA s. 27. Rule 18.02 offers the simplicity and costs savings of admitting documents without calling an in-person witness. The Rule provides that if the information required by r. 18.02(3) is provided, and if the document was served at least 30 days before trial, the document shall be admitted unless the trial judge orders otherwise under r. 18.02(1). This permits a party served with a document to serve a summons on its author if so advised, under r. 18.02(4), and cross-examine that witness at trial. The document then serves as examination-in-chief and the witness may be cross-examined and re-examined in the usual fashion. In fact, that option is rarely exercised, and that is unsurprising given the nature of proceedings in Small Claims Court.[3]

The Small Claims Court has a broad discretion to receive and act on evidence which might be inadmissible in other courts. To the extent that hearsay evidence is contained in documents which are admitted into evidence, such evidence is before the court and the court is entitled to accept it for the truth of its contents, subject to the court's general discretion as to weight.[4] But while the Small Claims Court may decide cases on the basis of hearsay evidence to avoid additional cost and technical procedures, this does not mean that a trial judge must accept evidence upon which there has been no cross-examination or where the documentary evidence does not accord with the Small Claims Court Rules.[5]

Expert/opinion evidence Deputy Judges must have the authority to exercise a gatekeeping function to determine whether evidence should be admissible. A Small Claims Court judge is not required to hear the evidence before determining its admissibility. A Small Claims Court Judge does have discretion to determine how expert evidence will be placed before the court, and may consider, and even exclude, expert evidence before the expert testifies. Expert evidence is opinion evidence. Unless it meets certain requirements for admissibility, expert evidence is *prima facie* inadmissible. As a result, it is up to the party seeking to tender the evidence to demonstrate that the trier of fact should consider it. Given that expert evidence can often be lengthy, complex and technical, conducting the analysis of whether the evidence should be admitted is most efficiently done at the outset.

An expert will often provide the court with specialized information that is beyond the court's knowledge. Triers of fact must take care to ensure that they are not influenced by inadmissible opinions offered by third parties. As a result, the gatekeeping function should be exercised more vigilantly with expert evidence.[6]

A treating physician can provide expert opinion evidence for the truth of its contents without complying with the formal requirements of r. 53.03 of the *Rules of Civil Procedure*, in the following circumstances:

   i.   The opinion to be given is based on the witness's observation of or participation in the events at issue; and

   ii. The witness formed the opinion to be given as part of the ordinary exercise of his or her skill, knowledge, training and experience while observing or participating in such events.

It follows that under the *Small Claims Court Rules*, parties are not obliged to engage independent experts and provide formal expert reports in the same circumstances. To hold otherwise would undermine the fundamental objective of the Small Claims Court to provide easier and less expensive access to justice, especially to self-represented litigants who are the most frequent users of the Small Claims Court system.[7]

Opinion evidence Even the relaxed rules of the Small Claims Court do not permit a person with direct involvement in the matters in issue in the litigation to testify as an expert, because such a person clearly lacks the distance and impartiality necessary to provide an unbiased opinion to the court.[8]

Written reports There is no absolute obligation pursuant to the SCCR to file a written report prior to trial. The discretion to admit opinion evidence without a report having been filed in advance of trial lies with the trial judge. The provisions of r. 18.02 are permissive and not a prohibition. In the context of a Small Claims Court trial, it would be an error to apply r. 53.03 of the *Rules of Civil Procedure*. Given the nature of the proceedings in the Small Claims Court and the frequent presence of self-represented litigants, it is appropriate to have the trial judge retain jurisdiction for the admission of evidence as provided in CJA s. 27.[9]

Production during trial A trial is not an examination for discovery. Counsel is not entitled to ask on cross-examination for undertakings to produce documents during a trial as if it was an examination for discovery under the Rules, and then expect the trial to grind to a halt while the document is produced for counsel to review and consider what, if anything, to do with it. The suggestion that any and all relevant or potentially relevant evidence needs to be presented at trial flies in the face of common sense and proper trial management. Counsel have an obligation to exercise their professional judgment concerning what evidence is both relevant and necessary and thereby assist the court and their clients in conducting trials as expeditiously as possible while keeping cost and delay to a reasonable minimum. Proposing that everything remotely relevant must be made evidence at trial is an abdication of that responsibility and would senselessly prolong civil trials. Fishing around for evidence which may or may not be worth anything to anyone may be acceptable, to some limited extent, on examinations for discovery but is incompatible with the focused approach required at trial. And in Small Claims Court, there are no examinations for discovery. One of the most basic general rules of evidence is that the probative value of evidence must not be outweighed by the time required for its presentation. D's failure to disclose a technical problem with a USB memory stick – containing relevant video evidence served three months earlier – until day four of trial during cross-examination did not represent cooperation by D's counsel.[10]

[1] *Fakhoury v. Gurguis*, [2013] O.J. No. 1688 (Ont. S.C.J. (Sm. Cl. Ct.)).

[2] *Advantagewon Inc. v. Cover*, [2020] O.J. No. 35, 2020 ONSC 84 (Ont. Div. Ct.).

[3] *Fakhoury v. Gurguis*, [2013] O.J. No. 1688 (Ont. S.C.J. (Sm. Cl. Ct.)).

[4] *Lamka v. Waterloo (Regional Municipality) Police Services Board*, [2012] O.J. No. 5591 (Ont. S.C.J. (Sm. Cl. Ct.)).

[5] *Lourenco v. Elle Mortgage Corp.*, [2013] O.J. No. 1371, 2013 ONSC 1487 (Ont. S.C.J.).

[6] *Prohaska v. Howe*, [2016] O.J. No. 13, 2016 ONSC 48 (Ont. S.C.J.).

[7] *Hervieux v. Huronia Optical*, [2016] O.J. No. 3270, 2016 ONCA 294 (Ont. C.A.).

[8] *Solo Cable Solutions Inc. v. Canadian Shield Preservation Products Inc.*, [2013] O.J. No. 3332 (Ont. S.C.J. (Sm. Cl. Ct.)).

[9] *Untinen v. Dykstra (c.o.b. Dykstra Roofing & Renovations)*, [2016] O.J. No. 3933, 2016 ONSC 4721 (Ont. Div. Ct.).

[10] *Cecchin v. Lander*, [2019] O.J. No. 5923 (Ont. S.C.J.). See also *Riddell v. Apple Canada Inc.*, [2016] O.J. No. 4934, 2016 ONSC 4934 (Ont. Div. Ct.), affd without mentioning this point [2017] O.J. No. 3605, 139 O.R. (3d) 595 (Ont. C.A.), leave to appeal refused [2017] S.C.C.A. No. 470 (S.C.C.).

18.03 SUMMONS TO WITNESS — (1) A party who requires the attendance of a person in Ontario as a witness at a trial may serve the person with a summons to witness (Form 18A) requiring him or her to attend the trial at the time and place stated in the summons.

(2) The summons may also require the witness to produce at the trial the documents or other things in his or her possession, control or power relating to the matters in question in the action that are specified in the summons.

(3) A summons to witness (Form 18A) shall be served in accordance with subrule 8.01 (7).

(4) Service of a summons and the payment or tender of attendance money may be proved by affidavit (Form 8A).

(5) A summons to witness continues to have effect until the attendance of the witness is no longer required.

(5.1) INTERPRETER — If a party serves a summons on a witness who requires an interpreter, the party shall arrange for a qualified interpreter to attend at the trial unless the interpretation is from English to French or French to English and an interpreter is provided by the Ministry of the Attorney General.

(5.2) If a party does not comply with subrule (5.1), every other party is entitled to request an adjournment of the trial, with costs.

(6) FAILURE TO ATTEND OR REMAIN IN ATTENDANCE — If a witness whose

evidence is material to the conduct of an action fails to attend at the trial or to remain in attendance in accordance with the requirements of a summons to witness served on him or her, the trial judge may, by warrant (Form 18B) directed to all police officers in Ontario, cause the witness to be apprehended anywhere within Ontario and promptly brought before the court.

(6.1) **IDENTIFICATION FORM** — The party who served the summons on the witness may file with the clerk an identification form (Form 20K) to assist the police in apprehending the witness.

(7) On being apprehended, the witness may be detained in custody until his or her presence is no longer required or released on such terms as are just, and may be ordered to pay the costs arising out of the failure to attend or remain in attendance.

(8) **ABUSE OF POWER TO SUMMON WITNESS** — If satisfied that a party has abused the power to summon a witness under this rule, the court may order that the party pay directly to the witness an amount as compensation for inconvenience and expense.
[O. Reg. 78/06, s. 37.]

Rule 19 — Costs

19.01 DISBURSEMENTS — (1) A successful party is entitled to have the party's reasonable disbursements, including any costs of effecting service or preparing a plaintiff's or defendant's claim or a defence and expenses for travel, accommodation, photocopying and experts' reports, paid by the unsuccessful party, unless the court orders otherwise.

(1.1) For greater certainty, subrule (1) includes costs associated with the electronic filing or issuance of documents under these rules.

(2) The clerk shall assess the disbursements in accordance with the regulations made under the *Administration of Justice Act* and in accordance with subrules (3) and (4); the assessment is subject to review by the court.

(3) The amount of disbursements assessed for effecting service shall not exceed $60 for each person served unless the court is of the opinion that there are special circumstances that justify assessing a greater amount.

(4) The amount of disbursements assessed for preparing a plaintiff's or defendant's claim or a defence shall not exceed $100.
[O. Reg. 78/06, s. 38; O. Reg. 440/10, s. 3; O. Reg. 44/14, s. 13.]

PRACTICE NOTES

§1 Generally Rule 57 of the *Rules of Civil Procedure* can provide additional guidance as to the factors to consider in determining the appropriate amount of costs under r. 19.[1]

Reasonable disbursements for the cost of experts' reports do not require an expert to be explicitly "qualified" at trial. When the absence of objection to the evidence to be called by either counsel disposed of the need and requirement for an admissibility ruling at trial, the experts' costs should be reflected in disbursements.[2]

Tariff A of the *Rules of Civil Procedure* limits "overnight accommodation and meal allowance" for witnesses obliged to stay overnight to $75.00. Although there is no equivalent provision in the Small Claims Court Rules, in the absence of an itemized account and receipts, the same cap should apply.[3]

[1] *McIsaac v. Duval*, [2014] O.J. No. 177 (Ont. S.C.J. (Sm. Cl. Ct.)).

[2] *Mandarin Restaurant Franchise Corp. v. Figtree Construction Ltd.*, [2014] O.J. No. 5076 (Ont. S.C.J. (Sm. Cl. Ct.)).

[3] *2106449 Ontario Inc. (c.o.b. Pioneer 1 Steel Building) v. Fulford*, [2014] O.J. No. 1688 (Ont. S.C.J. (Sm. Cl. Ct.)).

19.02 LIMIT — Any power under this rule to award costs is subject to section 29 of the *Courts of Justice Act*, which limits the amount of costs that may be awarded.
[O. Reg. 78/06, s. 39.]

PRACTICE NOTES

§1 Generally Under r. 19.02, any power under r. 19 to award costs is subject to CJA, s. 29, which provides that Small Claims Court costs awards shall not exceed 15% of the amount claimed or the value of the property sought to be recovered, subject to a finding that a larger award is necessary in the interest of justice to penalize unreasonable behaviour.[1]

Potential litigants, with or without counsel, must be afforded the opportunity to pursue small claims knowing that costs are limited if successful, and without fear of risking high costs if they are less successful or not successful (and claim not hopeless or frivolous).[2]

Section 29 of the CJA provides that an award of costs in the Small Claims Court, other than disbursements, is not to exceed 15% of the amount claimed or the value of the property sought to be recovered unless the court considers it necessary in the interest of justice to penalize a party or a party's representative for unreasonable behaviour in the proceeding. For the purposes of establishing the amount against which the basic 15% ceiling for costs in the Small Claim Court set out in CJA s. 29 is applied, the amounts of both P's claim and D's claim are added together.[3]

An award of costs should not merely reflect the application of a mathematical formula, and should be fair and reasonable in the circumstances of the case, taking into account the amount of preparation required.[4] The court has discretion on the issue of costs subject to the limitations otherwise provided for. Section 29 of the CJA does not limit 1) by whom they are to be paid if so ordered, 2) to what extent the costs shall be paid, and 3) it does not specifically prohibit or limit to whom they might be ordered to be paid. In appropriate circumstances cost may be ordered against a solicitor, such as when he or she failed in his or her duty to the court to exercise reasonable competence and to be courteous and civil by not informing it that a trial would not be proceeding, and when the court has incurred costs as a result.[5]

Note that r. 19.06 of the SCCR authorizes the court to order a party to pay an amount as compensation to another party where it has unduly complicated or prolonged an action or has otherwise acted unreasonably.[6]

Appeals There are no limitations relating to the costs that can be awarded in the Divisional Court. Instead, costs are in the discretion of the court under s. 131(1) of the CJA. In exercising that discretion, the court must be guided by the principles set out in r. 57 of the Civil Rules. Successful self-represented litigants are entitled to be compensated for their opportunity cost in time spent preparing for the appeal. One hundred dollars per hour has been recognized as reasonable in many cases involving self-represented litigants.[7] Rule 19.02 provides guidance in the approach to take in determining costs in an appeal.[8]

Exercise of discretion The 15% referred to in CJA s. 29 is not a guideline for fixing costs. Rather it is a *prima facie* limit on costs which are fixed under rr. 19 and 14.07. Maximum awards are meant for maximum cases. The court is given a discretion to allow "a reasonable representation fee" under r. 19.04. The fixing of that fee may be driven by various factors including the length and complexity of trial, seniority of counsel, importance of the issues, and so on. Any award of costs is subject to the *prima facie* limit under s. 29.[9]

Condominiums The *Condominium Act* (Ont.) contains several provisions providing for full indemnity in favour of the condominium corporation, for example in actions against a unit owner to enforce a lien or in connection with the collection or attempted collection from a unit owner of an unpaid amount. It does not apply when the condominium corporation successfully defends an action in Small Claims Court, in which case the usual Small Claims Court Rules apply.[10]

[1] *Halpin v. Thibault*, [2020] O.J. No. 757, 2020 ONSC 1043 (Ont. Div. Ct.).

[2] *Bedrock Stone Masonry v. Blake*, [2015] O.J. No. 3663 (Ont. S.C.J. (Sm. Cl. Ct.)).

[3] *2Go Custom Kitchens Inc. v. Keon*, [2012] O.J. No. 616 (Ont. S.C.J. (Sm. Cl. Ct.)).

[4] *Parker v. Abbey*, [2014] O.J. No. 6189, 2014 ONSC 7451 (Ont. Div. Ct.).

[5] *HVAC Maximum Heating & Cooling Inc. v. 1693876 Ontario Inc.*, [2015] O.J. No. 387 (Ont. S.C.J. (Sm. Cl. Ct.)).

[6] *Fournier v. Cartier*, [2013] O.J. No. 3472 (Ont. S.C.J. (Sm. Cl. Ct.)).

[7] *Halpin v. Thibault*, [2020] O.J. No. 757, 2020 ONSC 1043 (Ont. Div. Ct.).

[8] *Fraser v. Coutu*, [2012] O.J. No. 3108, 2012 ONSC 3997 (Ont. S.C.J.).

[9] *De Fresne v. H.O.P.E. Systems Inc. (c.o.b. Stage Door Transportation)*, [2016] O.J. No. 5061 (Ont. S.C.J. (Sm. Cl. Ct.)).

[10] *Polkry's Mechanical Plumbing & Heating v. Jaszczysyzn*, [2016] O.J. No. 4573 (Ont. S.C.J. (Sm. Cl. Ct.)).

19.03 [REVOKED: O. Reg. 440/10, s. 4, in force January 1, 2011.]

19.04 REPRESENTATION FEE — If a successful party is represented by a lawyer, student-at-law or paralegal, the court may award the party a reasonable representation fee at trial or at an assessment hearing.

[O. Reg. 78/06, s. 39; O. Reg. 440/10, s. 5; O. Reg. 230/13, s. 15.]

PRACTICE NOTES

§1.   Generally
§2.   Appeals

§1 Generally   A representation fee under r. 19.04 is only available where a party is represented at a trial or assessment hearing by a lawyer, student-at-law or paralegal. Where one of the parties is a law firm and represented by a member of firm, the party is considered to be self-represented for this purpose and no representation fee is available. The rule can and should be no different for self-represented parties who happen to be lawyers than it is for other self-represented parties. An award under r. 19.05 or r. 19.06 may be available but such awards are not routinely made.[1]

A party who is a lawyer, but who is not suing for a matter related to his or her legal practice, is not entitled to a representation fee under r. 19.04, but may be entitled to an order for compensation for inconvenience and expense under r. 19.05.[2]

Quantum   The fact that the case was fact-driven and based on circumstantial evidence, that D was required to incur unnecessary time, effort and expense to defend himself, the restrictions imposed by the rules of court in this regard and the principle of proportionality were all factors that must be reflected in any costs award.[3]

***Pro bono* representation**   The court has authority to award costs to a law school operated community legal services program even though it did not charge a fee for its services.[4]

Failure to pay costs of a motion   The Small Claims Court Rules do not have an equivalent rule to r. 57.03(2) of the Civil Rules, which authorizes the court to "dismiss or stay the party's proceeding, strike out the party's defence or make such other order as is just" where the party fails to pay a costs order against it. Before r. 57.03 was put in place, it was generally the case that unless an order stated costs were payable

75

forthwith or within a certain time frame, that costs were payable at the conclusion of the litigation. It is open to a court to decide that the principles in r. 57.03(1)(a) to cost orders following motions in Small Claims court, and that the most reasonable interpretation an interlocutory costs order would be that costs were payable within 30 days.[5]

[1] *Paquette Travers & Deutschmann v. Neil*, [2013] O.J. No. 719 (Ont. S.C.J. (Sm. Cl. Ct.)). See also *Van Buskirk v. Karimianfar*, [2009] O.J. No. 1250 (Ont. S.C.J. (Sm. Cl. Ct.)).

[2] *Hill v. Queensbury Strategies Inc.*, [2014] O.J. No. 4411 (Ont. S.C.J.).

[3] *Pendrith v. Sefidi*, [2013] O.J. No. 2035 (Ont. S.C.J. (Sm. Cl. Ct.)).

[4] *1266704 Ontario Inc. (c.o.b. Larizza Enterprises) v. Morgan*, [2016] O.J. No. 4676 (Ont. S.C.J. (Sm. Cl. Ct.)).

[5] *Platinum Stairs Ltd. v. Laranjeira*, [2017] O.J. No. 5362, 2017 ONSC 6107 at paras. 19, 25 and 26 (Ont. Div. Ct.).

§2 Appeals Leave to appeal a costs order should be sparingly granted, and only if there has been an error in principle, or the costs award is clearly wrong. Moreover, the proposed appeal should raise an issue of some importance to the administration of justice that goes beyond the interests of the parties. These considerations are particularly important in the context of an appeal of a final order of the Small Claims Court, which can be brought only if the amount in dispute exceeds $2,500 excluding costs (see s. 31 of the *Courts of Justice Act* and O. Reg. 626/00, s. 2).[1]

[1] *Bougadis Chang LLP v. 1231238 Ontario Inc. (c.o.b. Billy's Souvlaki Place)*, [2012] O.J. No. 5433, 2012 ONSC 6409 (Ont. Div. Ct.).

19.05 COMPENSATION FOR INCONVENIENCE AND EXPENSE — The court may order an unsuccessful party to pay to a successful party who is self-represented an amount not exceeding $500 as compensation for inconvenience and expense.
[O. Reg. 78/06, s. 39; O. Reg. 440/10, s. 5.]

PRACTICE NOTES

§1 Generally Rule 19.05 of the Small Claims Court Rules has relevance when determining compensation in an appeal from a Small Claims Court judgment, though the judge of the Divisional Court is not bound by the $500 limitation.[1]

A self-represented litigant does not have an automatic right to recover costs. The matter remains fully within the discretion of the trial judge, and there are undoubtedly cases where the self-represented litigant's conduct of the proceedings is inappropriate. The trial judge maintains a discretion to make the appropriate costs award, including denial of costs. Self-represented litigants, be they legally trained or not, are not entitled to costs calculated on the same basis as those of the litigant who retains counsel. All litigants suffer a loss of time through their involvement in the legal process. The self-represented litigant should not recover costs for the time and effort that any litigant would have to devote to the case. Costs should only be awarded to those lay litigants who can demonstrate that they devoted time and effort to do the work ordinarily done by a lawyer retained to conduct the litigation, and that as a result, they incurred an opportunity cost by foregoing remunerative activity. A self-represented law litigant should receive only a "moderate" or "reasonable" allowance for the loss of time devoted to preparing and presenting the case. This excludes routine awards on a per diem basis to litigants who would ordinarily be in attendance at court in any event.[2]

[1] *Desjardins v. Van Iersel*, [2014] O.J. No. 5590, 2014 ONSC 6921 (Ont. Div. Ct.).

[2] *Pridham v. Noel*, [2015] O.J. No. 3589 (Ont. S.C.J. (Sm. Cl. Ct.)).

19.06 PENALTY — If the court is satisfied that a party has unduly complicated or pro-

longed an action or has otherwise acted unreasonably, the court may order the party to pay an amount as compensation to another party.

[O. Reg. 78/06, s. 39.]

PRACTICE NOTES

§1 Generally Penalty costs are appropriate when "unreasonable behaviour", such as allegations of fraud, dishonesty or other improper conduct seriously prejudicial to a party's character or reputation are made but not proved. Since the Small Claims Court lacks the terminology and a formula for determining punitive costs, the Rules of Civil Procedure definition of "substantial indemnity costs" as 1.5 of partial indemnity costs may be used.[1]

Rule 19.06, when it refers to "otherwise acting unreasonably", must be interpreted as referring to the conduct of a party within the proceeding. The rule is not intended to give the Small Claims Court a broad and unfettered discretion to make awards of compensation regarding the conduct of a party that is unrelated to the matter over which the Small Claims Court has jurisdiction. This interpretation is also consistent with the wording of s. 29 of the CJA to which all of the Small Claims Court rules are subject, that makes it clear that the conduct to be considered when assessing a penalty is conduct in the proceeding.[2]

The rejection by the unsuccessful party of reasonable written offers to settle constitutes unreasonable behaviour for the purposes of CJA s. 29 and r. 19.06.[3]

However, P's taking a repetitive approach to presenting evidence and failing to group similar evidence together did not attract a penalty where the trial was not extended significantly. This was not the nature of misconduct that s. 29 and r. 17.06 were intended to address.[4]

While the cost increase under r. 14.07 is capped at 100%, there is no such cap on compensation awarded under r. 19.06. The test for the awarding of compensation under r. 19.06 is very similar to the test under CJA s. 29, so it might be expected that a finding of unreasonable behaviour under r. 19.06 would always justify an affirmative finding under s. 29. However, the two tests are not identical. Rule 19.06 focuses on the need to compensate a party who has suffered excess costs as a result of the unreasonable behaviour of another party. Section 29 requires a further finding of a need to penalize the offending party. So compensation under r. 19.06, like increased costs under r. 14.07, are limited to 15% of the amount claimed unless the court finds that, beyond the criteria in those rules, there is both unreasonable conduct and a need to penalize the unreasonable party.[5]

Vexatious litigants The reasonable expectation of the unsuccessful party is one of the factors to be considered in determining an amount that is fair and reasonable. In awarding costs against a vexatious litigant who has driven the costs of the proceeding, the cost framework of the small claims court is an important consideration, and generally speaking it can be said that costs are "low" reflecting that it is the "People's Court" and access to justice is important. An unsuccessful litigant in Small Claims Court is not expecting to get hit with a massive legal bill if he or she loses at trial — a situation markedly different from litigation in the Superior Court. The 15% limitation on costs would be a factor in such expectation — even when dealing with a "penalty" provision that permits costs to be awarded in excess of 15% of the amount claimed. The fact the successful defendant spent in excess of $140,000 in legal fees is not of particular importance in assessing the penalty costs.[6]

[1] *Brander v. Backstage Bar and Grill Inc.*, [2014] O.J. No. 794 (Ont. S.C.J. (Sm. Cl. Ct.)).

[2] *Stewart v. Toronto Standard Condominium Corp. No. 1591*, [2014] O.J. No. 562, 2014 ONSC 795 (Ont. Div. Ct.). See also *Smith (Litigation guardian of) v. Croft*, [2015] O.J. No. 3264 (Ont. S.C.J. (Sm. Cl. Ct.)).

[3] *2Go Custom Kitchens Inc. v. Keon*, [2012] O.J. No. 616 (Ont. S.C.J. (Sm. Cl. Ct.)).

[4] *Fournier v. Cartier*, [2013] O.J. No. 3472 (Ont. S.C.J. (Sm. Cl. Ct.)).

[5] *Coicici v. Ashton Pools, Ponds and Spas Inc.*, [2017] O.J. No. 4465 at para. 17 (Ont. S.C.J. (Sm. Cl. Ct.)).

[6] *Lahrkamp v. Metropolitan Toronto Condominium Corp. No. 932*, [2017] O.J. No. 7038 (Ont. S.C.J.).

Rule 20 — Enforcement of Orders

20.01 DEFINITIONS — In rules 20.02 to 20.12,

"creditor" means a person who is entitled to enforce an order for the payment or recovery of money;

"debtor" means a person against whom an order for the payment or recovery of money may be enforced.

[O. Reg. 78/06, s. 40.]

20.02 POWER OF COURT — (1) The court may,

(a)   stay the enforcement of an order of the court, for such time and on such terms as are just; and

(b)   vary the times and proportions in which money payable under an order of the court shall be paid, if it is satisfied that the debtor's circumstances have changed.

(2) ENFORCEMENT LIMITED WHILE PERIODIC PAYMENT ORDER IN FORCE — While an order for periodic payment is in force, no step to enforce the judgment may be taken or continued against the debtor by a creditor named in the order, except issuing a writ of seizure and sale of land and filing it with the sheriff.

(3) SERVICE OF NOTICE OF DEFAULT OF PAYMENT — The creditor may serve the debtor with a notice of default of payment (Form 20L) in accordance with subrule 8.01 (14) and file a copy of it, together with an affidavit of default of payment (Form 20M), if the debtor fails to make payments under an order for periodic payment.

(4) TERMINATION ON DEFAULT — An order for periodic payment terminates on the day that is 15 days after the creditor serves the debtor with the notice of default of payment, unless a consent (Form 13B) in which the creditor waives the default is filed within the 15-day period.

[O. Reg. 78/06, s. 41.]

20.03 GENERAL — In addition to any other method of enforcement provided by law,

(a)   an order for the payment or recovery of money may be enforced by,

   (i)   a writ of seizure and sale of personal property (Form 20C) under rule 20.06,

   (ii)   a writ of seizure and sale of land (Form 20D) under rule 20.07, and

   (iii)   garnishment under rule 20.08; and

(b)   a further order as to payment may be made under subrule 20.10 (7).

PRACTICE NOTES

§1 Generally Rule 20 provides that judgments of the Small Claims Court may be enforced by the methods listed in that rule "in addition to any other method of enforcement provided by law". This reserves the authority of the Superior Court to enforce judgments of the Small Claims Court.[1]

[1] *Canaccede International Acquisitions Ltd. v. Abdullah*, [2015] O.J. No. 4635, 2015 ONSC 5553, 127 O.R. (3d) 779 (Ont. S.C.J. (Sm. Cl. Ct.)).

20.04 CERTIFICATE OF JUDGMENT — (1) If there is default under an order for the payment or recovery of money, the clerk shall, at the creditor's request, supported by an affidavit for enforcement request (Form 20P) stating the amount still owing, issue a certificate of judgment (Form 20A) to the clerk at the court location specified by the creditor.

(2) The certificate of judgment shall state,

(a)   the date of the order and the amount awarded;

(b)   the rate of postjudgment interest payable; and

(c)   the amount owing, including postjudgment interest.

[O. Reg. 393/09, s. 17.]

20.05 DELIVERY OF PERSONAL PROPERTY — (1) An order for the delivery of personal property may be enforced by a writ of delivery (Form 20B) issued by the clerk to a bailiff, on the request of the person in whose favour the order was made, supported by an affidavit of that person or someone acting on that person's authority stating that the property has not been delivered.

(2) **SEIZURE OF OTHER PERSONAL PROPERTY —** If the property referred to in a writ of delivery cannot be found or taken by the bailiff, the person in whose favour the order was made may make a motion to the court for an order directing the bailiff to seize any other personal property of the person against whom the order was made.

(3) Unless the court orders otherwise the bailiff shall keep personal property seized under subrule (2) until the court makes a further order for its disposition.

(4) **STORAGE COSTS —** The person in whose favour the order is made shall pay the bailiff's storage costs, in advance and from time to time; if the person fails to do so, the seizure shall be deemed to be abandoned.

[O. Reg. 78/06, s. 42; O. Reg. 230/13, s. 16.]

PRACTICE NOTES

§1 Generally The writ of delivery is a means to enforce an order for the delivery of personal property. In other words it only applies where an order for the delivery of personal property has been claimed and granted. Such orders are made under CJA s. 23(1)(*b*), in an "action for the recovery of possession of personal property . . .".[1]

[1] *Easyhome Ltd. v. Hookey*, [2016] O.J. No. 4769 (Ont. S.C.J. (Sm. Cl. Ct.)).

20.06 WRIT OF SEIZURE AND SALE OF PERSONAL PROPERTY — (1) If there is default under an order for the payment or recovery of money, the clerk shall, at the creditor's request, supported by an affidavit for enforcement request (Form 20P) stating the amount still owing, issue to a bailiff a writ of seizure and sale of personal property (Form 20C), and the bailiff shall enforce the writ for the amount owing, postjudgment interest and the bailiff's fees and expenses.

(1.1) If more than six years have passed since the order was made, a writ of seizure and sale of personal property may be issued only with leave of the court.

(1.2) If a writ of seizure and sale of personal property is not issued within one year after the date on which an order granting leave to issue it is made,

(a)   the order granting leave ceases to have effect; and

(b)   a writ of seizure and sale of personal property may be issued only with leave of the court on a subsequent motion.

(1.3) A writ of seizure and sale of personal property shall show the creditor's name, address and telephone number and the name, address and telephone number of the creditor's representative, if any.

(2) DURATION OF WRIT — A writ of seizure and sale of personal property remains in force for six years after the date of its issue and for a further six years after each renewal.

(3) RENEWAL OF WRIT — A writ of seizure and sale of personal property may be renewed before its expiration by filing a request to renew a writ of seizure and sale (Form 20N) with the bailiff.

(4) DIRECTION TO ENFORCE — The creditor may request enforcement of a writ of seizure and sale of personal property by filing a direction to enforce writ of seizure and sale of personal property (Form 20O) with the bailiff.

(5) INVENTORY OF PROPERTY SEIZED — Within a reasonable time after a request is made by the debtor or someone acting on the debtor's authority, the bailiff shall deliver an inventory of personal property seized under a writ of seizure and sale of personal property.

(6) SALE OF PERSONAL PROPERTY — Personal property seized under a writ of seizure and sale of personal property shall not be sold by the bailiff unless notice of the time and place of sale has been,

(a)   mailed, at least 10 days before the sale,

(i)   to the creditor at the address shown on the writ, or to the creditor's representative, and

(ii)   to the debtor at the debtor's last known address; and

(b)   advertised in a manner that is likely to bring it to the attention of the public.
[O. Reg. 78/06, s. 43; O. Reg. 393/09, s. 18; O. Reg. 230/13, s. 17.]

20.07 WRIT OF SEIZURE AND SALE OF LAND — (1) If an order for the payment or recovery of money is unsatisfied, the clerk shall at the creditor's request, supported by an affidavit for enforcement request (Form 20P) stating the amount still owing, issue to the sheriff specified by the creditor a writ of seizure and sale of land (Form 20D).

(1.1) If more than six years have passed since the order was made, a writ of seizure and sale of land may be issued only with leave of the court.

(1.2) If a writ of seizure and sale of land is not issued within one year after the date on which an order granting leave to issue it is made,

(a)   the order granting leave ceases to have effect; and

(b)   a writ of seizure and sale of land may be issued only with leave of the court on a subsequent motion.

(1.3) ELECTRONIC FILING, ISSUANCE — The following persons may electronically file a request under subrule (1) for a writ of seizure and sale of land, without the supporting affidavit for enforcement request:

1.   A lawyer or a paralegal.

2.   A person who has filed a requisition with the clerk to provide for the electronic filing and issuance of documents in relation to the enforcement of an order.

(1.4) If the request is filed electronically, the writ of seizure and sale of land shall be issued electronically.

(1.5) Subrule 1.05.1 (6) does not apply to an electronically filed request or an electronically issued writ.

(2) APPLICATION OF RULES OF CIVIL PROCEDURE TO ISSUED WRIT — Subject to subrules (3) and (4), the Rules of Civil Procedure apply for all purposes instead of these rules to an issued writ of seizure and sale of land, as if the writ were a writ of seizure and sale issued under rule 60.07 of those Rules.

(3) DURATION OF WRIT — A writ of seizure and sale of land remains in force for six years after the date of its issue and for a further six years after each renewal.

(4) ALTERNATIVE METHOD OF RENEWAL — Instead of being renewed under the Rules of Civil Procedure in accordance with subrule (2), a writ of seizure and sale of land may be renewed before its expiration by filing a request to renew a writ of seizure and sale (Form 20N) with the sheriff.
[O. Reg. 78/06, s. 44; O. Reg. 393/09, s. 19; O. Reg. 44/14, s. 14.]

PRACTICE NOTES

§1 Equitable execution A judicially supervised sale conducted by way of a reference as equitable relief to enforce judgments of the Small Claims Court is available only in the Superior Court of Justice.[1]

---

[1] *Canaccede International Acquisitions Ltd. v. Abdullah*, [2015] O.J. No. 4635, 2015 ONSC 5553, 127 O.R. (3d) 779 (Ont. S.C.J. (Sm. Cl. Ct.)).

20.08 GARNISHMENT — (1) A creditor may enforce an order for the payment or recovery of money by garnishment of debts payable to the debtor by other persons.

(2) JOINT DEBTS GARNISHABLE — If a debt is payable to the debtor and to one or more co-owners, one-half of the indebtedness or a greater or lesser amount specified in an order made under subrule (15) may be garnished.

(2.1) WHERE LEAVE REQUIRED — If more than six years have passed since the order was made, or if its enforcement is subject to a condition, a notice of garnishment may be issued only with leave of the court.

(2.2) If a notice of garnishment is not issued within one year after the date on which an order granting leave to issue it is made,

(a)   the order granting leave ceases to have effect; and

(b)   a notice of garnishment may be issued only with leave of the court on a subsequent motion.

(2.3) A notice of renewal of garnishment may be issued under subrule (5.3) without leave of the court before the original notice of garnishment or any subsequent notice of renewal of garnishment expires.

(3) OBTAINING NOTICE OF GARNISHMENT — A creditor who seeks to enforce an order by garnishment shall file with the clerk of a court in the territorial division in which the debtor resides or carries on business,

(a)   an affidavit for enforcement request (Form 20P) naming one debtor and one garnishee and stating,

(i)   the date of the order and the amount awarded,

(ii)   the territorial division in which the order was made,

(iii)   the rate of postjudgment interest payable,

(iv)   the total amount of any payments received since the order was granted,

(v)   the amount owing, including postjudgment interest,

(vi)   the name and address of the named garnishee to whom a notice of garnishment is to be directed,

(vii)   the creditor's belief that the named garnishee is or will become indebted to the debtor, and the grounds for the belief, and

(viii) any particulars of the debts that are known to the creditor; and

(b)   a certificate of judgment (Form 20A), if the order was made in another territorial division.

(4) On the filing of the documents required by subrule (3), the clerk shall issue a notice of garnishment (Form 20E) naming as garnishee the person named in the affidavit.

(5) A notice of garnishment issued under subrule (4) shall name only one debtor and only one garnishee.

(5.1) DURATION AND RENEWAL — A notice of garnishment remains in force for six years from the date of its issue and for a further six years from each renewal.

(5.2) A notice of garnishment may be renewed before its expiration by filing with the clerk of the court in which the notice of garnishment was issued a notice of renewal of garnishment (Form 20E.1), together with an affidavit for enforcement request (Form 20P).

(5.3) On the filing of the notice and affidavit required by subrule (5.2), the clerk shall issue the notice of renewal of garnishment (Form 20E.1) naming as garnishee the person named in the affidavit.

(5.4) The provisions of these rules that apply with respect to notices of garnishment also apply with respect to notices of renewal of garnishment.

(6) SERVICE OF NOTICE OF GARNISHMENT — The notice of garnishment (Form 20E) shall be served by the creditor in accordance with subrule 8.01 (8).

(6.1) The creditor shall serve the notice of garnishment on the debtor within five days of serving it on the garnishee.

(6.2) FINANCIAL INSTITUTION — If the garnishee is a financial institution, the notice of garnishment and all further notices required to be served under this rule shall be served at the branch at which the debt is payable.

(6.3) PROOF OF SERVICE — Service of the notice of garnishment may be proved by affidavit.

(7) GARNISHEE LIABLE FROM TIME OF SERVICE — The garnishee is liable to pay to the clerk any debt of the garnishee to the debtor, up to the amount shown in the notice of garnishment, within 10 days after service of the notice on the garnishee or 10 days after the debt becomes payable, whichever is later.

(8) For the purpose of subrule (7), a debt of the garnishee to the debtor includes,

    (a)   a debt payable at the time the notice of garnishment is served; and

    (b)   a debt payable (whether absolutely or on the fulfilment of a condition) after the notice is served and within six years after it is issued.

(9) PAYMENT BY GARNISHEE — A garnishee who admits owing a debt to the debtor shall pay it to the clerk in the manner prescribed by the notice of garnishment, and the amounts paid into court shall not exceed the portion of the debtor's wages that are subject to seizure or garnishment under section 7 of the *Wages Act*.

(10) EQUAL DISTRIBUTION AMONG CREDITORS — If the clerk has issued notices of garnishment in respect of a debtor at the request of more than one creditor and receives payment under any of the notices of garnishment, he or she shall distribute the payment equally among the creditors who have filed a request for garnishment and have not been paid in full.

(11) DISPUTING GARNISHMENT — A garnishee referred to in subrule (12) shall, within 10 days after service of the notice of garnishment, file with the court a statement (Form 20F) setting out the particulars.

(12) Subrule (11) applies to a garnishee who,

    (a)   wishes to dispute the garnishment for any reason; or

    (b)   pays to the clerk less than the amount set out in the notice of garnishment as owing by the garnishee to the debtor, because the debt is owed to the debtor and to one or more co-owners of the debt or for any other reason.

(13) **SERVICE ON CREDITOR AND DEBTOR —** The garnishee shall serve a copy of the garnishee's statement on the creditor and the debtor.

(14) **NOTICE TO CO-OWNER OF DEBT —** A creditor who is served with a garnishee's statement under subrule (13) shall forthwith send to any co-owners of the debt, in accordance with subrule 8.01 (14), a notice to co-owner of debt (Form 20G) and a copy of the garnishee's statement.

(15) **GARNISHMENT HEARING —** At the request of a creditor, debtor, garnishee, co-owner of the debt or any other interested person, the clerk shall fix a time and place for a garnishment hearing.

(15.1) **SERVICE OF NOTICE OF GARNISHMENT HEARING —** After having obtained a hearing date from the clerk, the party requesting the garnishment hearing shall serve the notice of garnishment hearing (Form 20Q) in accordance with subrule 8.01 (9).

(15.2) **POWERS OF COURT AT HEARING —** At the garnishment hearing, the court may,

(a)   if it is alleged that the garnishee's debt to the debtor has been assigned or encumbered, order the assignee or encumbrancer to appear and state the nature and particulars of the claim;

(b)   determine the rights and liabilities of the garnishee, any co-owner of the debt, the debtor and any assignee or encumbrancer;

(c)   vary or suspend periodic payments under a notice of garnishment; or

(d)   determine any other matter in relation to a notice of garnishment.

(16) **TIME TO REQUEST HEARING —** A person who has been served with a notice to co-owner of debt is not entitled to dispute the enforcement of the creditor's order for the payment or recovery of money or a payment made by the clerk unless the person requests a garnishment hearing within 30 days after the notice is sent.

(17) **ENFORCEMENT AGAINST GARNISHEE —** If the garnishee does not pay to the clerk the amount set out in the notice of garnishment and does not send a garnishee's statement, the creditor is entitled to an order against the garnishee for payment of the amount set out in the notice, unless the court orders otherwise.

(18) **PAYMENT TO PERSON OTHER THAN CLERK —** If, after service of a notice of garnishment, the garnishee pays a debt attached by the notice to a person other than the clerk, the garnishee remains liable to pay the debt in accordance with notice.

(19) **EFFECT OF PAYMENT TO CLERK —** Payment of a debt by a garnishee in accordance with a notice of garnishment is a valid discharge of the debt as between the garnishee and the debtor and any co-owner of the debt, to the extent of the payment.

(20) **DISTRIBUTION OF PAYMENTS —** When proof is filed that the notice of garnishment was served on the debtor, the clerk shall distribute a payment received under a notice of garnishment to a creditor in accordance with subrule (20.1), unless,

(a)   a hearing has been requested under subrule (15);

(b)   a notice of motion and supporting affidavit (Form 15A) has been filed under rule 8.10, 11.06 or 17.04; or

(c)   a request for clerk's order on consent (Form 11.2A) has been filed seeking the relief described in subparagraph 1 iii of subrule 11.2.01 (1).

(20.1) The clerk shall distribute the payment,

(a)   in the case of the first payment under the notice of garnishment, 30 days after the date it is received; and

(b)   in the case of every subsequent payment under the notice of garnishment, as they are received.

(20.2) NOTICE ONCE ORDER SATISFIED — Once the amount owing under an order that is enforced by garnishment is paid, the creditor shall immediately serve a notice of termination of garnishment (Form 20R) on the garnishee and on the clerk.

(21) PAYMENT IF DEBT JOINTLY OWNED — If a payment of a debt owed to the debtor and one or more co-owners has been made to the clerk, no request for a garnishment hearing is made and the time for doing so under subrule (16) has expired, the creditor may file with the clerk, within 30 days after that expiry,

(a)   proof of service of the notice to co-owner; and

(b)   an affidavit stating that the creditor believes that no co-owner of the debt is a person under disability, and the grounds for the belief.

(22) The affidavit required by subrule (21) may contain statements of the deponent's information and belief, if the source of the information and the fact of the belief are specified in the affidavit.

(23) If the creditor does not file the material referred to in subrule (21) the clerk shall return the money to the garnishee.

[O. Reg. 461/01, s. 18; O. Reg. 78/06, s. 45(1) to (4), (5)(E) and (6) to (9); O. Reg. 393/09, s. 20.]

PRACTICE NOTES

§1 Generally Garnishment is only available where a debt is or will be legally owed by the garnishee to the judgment-debtor. That a non-party may hold income property in trust for the judgment debtor is not a garnishable debt. P would have to obtain a judgment in the Superior Court of Justice establishing the judgment-debtor's interest in such real properties before enforcement against such an interest would be available. This Small Claims Court has no jurisdiction to make a judgment declaring ownership of real property. Dressing up such a remedy as a garnishment order would be substantively and procedurally impossible.[1]

Law firm as garnishee Where the garnishee is the law firm of the judgment debtor, and the firm's retainer has not been terminated and continued at least with respect to trust funds to conclude a pending settlement between the judgment debtor with a third party, there is no potential balance to be paid to the judgment-debtor. The trust funds therefore are not a debt owed by the law firm garnishee to the judgment-debtor and were accordingly not subject to garnishment. There is no principled reason why retainer funds for a civil matter should be treated differently than those for a criminal matter.[2]

[1] *Sangwan v. Marsh*, [2019] O.J. No. 5117 (Ont. S.C.J.).

[2] *Superior Hardwood Flooring v. Iron Horse Construction Corp.*, [2019] O.J. No. 5119 (Ont. S.C.J.).

Social Assistance Payments exempted Section 23 of the *Ontario Works Act, 1997*, S.O. 1997, c. 25, Sched. A provides that basic financial assistance is not subject to garnishment even if the amount has been paid into the person's account at a financial institution.

20.09 CONSOLIDATION ORDER — (1) A debtor against whom there are two or more unsatisfied orders for the payment of money may make a motion to the court for a consolidation order.

(2) The debtor's notice of motion and supporting affidavit (Form 15A) shall set out, in the affidavit portion,

(a)   the names and addresses of the creditors who have obtained an order for the payment of money against the debtor;

(b)   the amount owed to each creditor;

(c)   the amount of the debtor's income from all sources, identifying them; and

(d)   the debtor's current financial obligations and any other relevant facts.

(3) NOTICE OF MOTION — For the purposes of clause 15.01 (3) (a), the notice of motion and supporting affidavit shall be served on each of the creditors mentioned in it at least seven days before the hearing date.

(4) CONTENTS OF CONSOLIDATION ORDER — At the hearing of the motion, the court may make a consolidation order setting out,

(a)   a list of unsatisfied orders for the payment of money against the debtor, indicating in each case the date, court and amount and the amount unpaid;

(b)   the amounts to be paid into court by the debtor under the consolidation order; and

(c)   the times of the payments.

(5) The total of the amounts to be paid into court by the debtor under a consolidation order shall not exceed the portion of the debtor's wages that are subject to seizure or garnishment under section 7 of the *Wages Act*.

(6) CREDITOR MAY MAKE SUBMISSIONS — At the hearing of the motion, a creditor may make submissions as to the amount and times of payment.

(7) FURTHER ORDERS OBTAINED AFTER CONSOLIDATION ORDER — If an order for the payment of money is obtained against the debtor after the date of the consolidation order for a debt incurred before the date of the consolidation order, the creditor may file with the clerk a certified copy of the new order; the creditor shall be added to the consolidation order and shall share in the distribution under it from that time.

(8) A consolidation order terminates immediately if an order for the payment of money is obtained against the debtor for a debt incurred after the date of the consolidation order.

(9) ENFORCEMENT LIMITED WHILE CONSOLIDATION ORDER IN FORCE — While the consolidation order is in force, no step to enforce the judgment may be taken or continued against the debtor by a creditor named in the order, except issuing a writ of seizure and sale of land and filing it with the sheriff.

(10) TERMINATION ON DEFAULT — A consolidation order terminates immediately if the debtor is in default under it for 21 days.

(11) EFFECT OF TERMINATION — If a consolidation order terminates under sub-rule (8) or (10), the clerk shall notify the creditors named in the consolidation order, and no further consolidation order shall be made in respect of the debtor for one year after the date of termination.

(11.1) MANNER OF SENDING NOTICE — The notice that the consolidation order is terminated shall be served by mail or fax.

(11.2)-(11.3) [REVOKED: O. Reg. 78/06, s. 46 (2), in force July 1, 2006.]

(12) EQUAL DISTRIBUTION AMONG CREDITORS — All payments into a consolidation account belong to the creditors named in the consolidation order, who shall share equally in the distribution of the money.

(13) The clerk shall distribute the money paid into the consolidation account at least once every six months.
[O. Reg. 461/01, s. 19(1), (2); O. Reg. 330/02, s. 12; O. Reg. 440/03, s. 5; O. Reg. 78/06, s. 46; O. Reg. 393/09, s. 21.]

PRACTICE NOTES

§1 Generally Where there are multiple judgment-creditors, the usual rule would be for equal distribution between them, consistent with the procedure under a consolidation order.[1]

[1] *Superior Hardwood Flooring v. Iron Horse Construction Corp.*, [2019] O.J. No. 5119 (Ont. S.C.J.).

20.10 EXAMINATION OF DEBTOR OR OTHER PERSON — (1) If there is default under an order for the payment or recovery of money, the clerk of a court in the territorial division in which the debtor or other person to be examined resides or carries on business shall, at the creditor's request, issue a notice of examination (Form 20H) directed to the debtor or other person.

(2) The creditor's request shall be accompanied by,

(a)   an affidavit for enforcement request (Form 20P) setting out,

    (i)   the date of the order and the amount awarded,

    (ii)   the territorial division in which the order was made,

    (iii)   the rate of postjudgment interest payable,

    (iv)   the total amount of any payments received since the order was granted, and

    (v)   the amount owing, including postjudgment interest; and

(b)   a certificate of judgment (Form 20A), if the order was made in another territorial jurisdiction.

(3) SERVICE OF NOTICE OF EXAMINATION — The notice of examination shall be served in accordance with subrules 8.01 (10), (11) and (12).

(4) The debtor, any other persons to be examined and any witnesses whose evidence the court considers necessary may be examined in relation to,

(a)   the reason for nonpayment;

(b)   the debtor's income and property;

(c)   the debts owed to and by the debtor;

(d)   the disposal the debtor has made of any property either before or after the order was made;

(e)   the debtor's present, past and future means to satisfy the order;

(f)   whether the debtor intends to obey the order or has any reason for not doing so; and

(g)   any other matter pertinent to the enforcement of the order.

(4.1) DUTIES OF PERSON TO BE EXAMINED — A person who is served with a notice of examination shall,

(a)   inform himself or herself about the matters mentioned in subrule (4) and be prepared to answer questions about them; and

(b)   in the case of an examination of a debtor who is an individual, complete a financial information form (Form 20I) and,

(i)   serve it on the creditor requesting the examination, but not file it with the court, and

(ii)   provide a copy of it to the judge presiding at the examination hearing.

(4.2) A debtor required under clause (4.1) (b) to complete a financial information form (Form 20I) shall bring such documents to the examination hearing as are necessary to support the information that he or she provides in the financial information form.

(5) WHO MAY BE EXAMINED — An officer or director of a corporate debtor, or, in the case of a debtor that is a partnership or sole proprietorship, the sole proprietor or any partner, may be examined on the debtor's behalf in relation to the matters set out in subrule (4).

(5.1) ATTENDANCE — A person required to attend an examination may attend,

(a)   in person; or

(b)   by video conference in accordance with rule 1.07.

(6) EXAMINATIONS PRIVATE, UNDER OATH AND RECORDED — The exami-

nation shall be,

  (a)   **held in the absence of the public, unless the court orders otherwise;**

  (b)   **conducted under oath; and**

  (c)   **recorded.**

  (7) **ORDER AS TO PAYMENT** — **After the examination or if the debtor's consent is filed, the court may make an order as to payment.**

  (8) **ENFORCEMENT LIMITED WHILE ORDER AS TO PAYMENT IN FORCE** — **While an order as to payment is in force, no step to enforce the judgment may be taken or continued against the debtor by a creditor named in the order, except issuing a writ of seizure and sale of land and filing it with the sheriff.**

  (9)-(15) [REVOKED: O. Reg. 78/06, s. 47(5), in force July 1, 2006.]

[O. Reg. 461/01, s. 20(1), (2); O. Reg. 330/02, s. 13; O. Reg. 440/03, s. 11; O. Reg. 78/06, s. 47; O. Reg. 393/09, s. 22; O. Reg. 440/10, s. 6.]

PRACTICE NOTES

§1 Generally This rule provides that a creditor may examine a debtor if there is a default in payment under an order. The rule goes on to list the subjects upon which the debtor can be examined including the debtor's income and the debtor's present, past and future means to satisfy the order. There is nothing in the Small Claims Court Rules that carves out of their application the situation where a debtor is receiving social assistance or welfare of some kind. It may be that if that is the debtor's situation, the creditor may not have any enforcement remedies available but that is a different question. The purpose underlying the examination is to find out just that type of information. There is also, of course, always the possibility that the examination may unearth information regarding the debtor's assets of which the government agency that granted the social assistance or welfare was unaware.[1]

Examination of non-parties Unlike r. 60.18(6) of the Civil Rules, r. 20.10 of the *Small Claims Court Rules* does not require leave of the court to examine a non-party in aid of execution. Examinations of a judgment-debtor's spouse, or an alleged transferee of a judgment-debtor's property, are not unheard of.[2]

The privacy and other individual rights of non-parties not to be unjustifiably intruded upon by a compulsory court examination process without cause are no less worthy of protection by the court than the right of creditors to pursue payment of their judgments. Protecting non-party rights requires that clear and express authorization to examine a non-party must be found in the Rules, for any examination to be confined to relevant matters and for such non-party to be afforded an opportunity to be heard regarding the request examination before any examination proceeds. The most important factor in interpreting r. 20.10 (1) is to consider how limited the wording in that rule is and how it contrasts with the clear wording of the only two sub-rules which do authorize non-party examinations: rr. 20.10(5) and 20.10(4). With respect to the wording of r. 20.10(1), the only "shall" in the subrule is the one directed to the clerk of the court. There is no directive to the court or to any judge presiding on judgment debtor examinations. There is no directive to the parties to the action or to any third party reading the rule. By its terms, r. 20.10(1) is limited to the clerical mechanics or administrative process of issuing the notice and booking an attendance. On its face and at its highest, the subrule might be read as allowing a Notice of Examination to be issued to a non-party but that is not the same thing as authorizing an examination of that non-party. At its highest, the effect of issuing a notice to a non-party who is not caught by r. 20.10(5) and whose examination has not been authorized by r. 20.10(4) is to put the issue of what, if any, examination should proceed before the court on the same date as the date booked for the proposed examination. It would be reasonable for a creditor to await a motion under r. 20.10(4) being heard and ruled on before requesting the court clerk to issue a Notice of Examination for any non-party not caught by r. 20.10(5). The express authorization in subr. (5) creates a class of non-party "other persons to be examined" to which the administrative process of issuing a Notice of Examination in r. 20.10(1) can be reasonably seen to apply. The right to examine non-party "witnesses" set out in r. 20.10(4) is express and clear and unequivocal but is expressly and clearly and unequivocally conditional on the court first making a finding that the examination is "necessary". The reference to "any other persons to be examined" in r. 20.10(4) is also reasonably regarded as a reference to those non-parties caught by r. 20.10(5) who are examinable as of right on the judgment debtor's behalf. An interpretation of r. 20.10(4), (5) and (1) which limits non-party examinations to those authorized under r. 20.10(5) or found to be necessary under r. 20.10(4) is in harmony with the approach to non-party examinations under r. 60.18(6) of the Civil Rules. There is no "gap" to be filled by analogy to the Civil Rules, and r. 20.10(4) expressly requires necessity to be shown before an examination of a non-party not caught by r. 20.10(5) is permitted. However, r. 60.18 provides relevant context for any interpretation of the Small Claims Court's rules. The case law on the interpretation of r. 60.18(6), while the test differs in wording from SCCR r. 20.10(4), is also instructive about how the courts should balance the rights and interests of the parties in deciding to allow a non-party examination to proceed.[3]

Unlike rule 60.18(6) of the Civil Rules, rule 20.10 of the Small Claims Court Rules does not require leave of the court to examine a non-party in aid of execution. Examinations of a judgment-debtor's spouse, or an alleged transferee of a judgment-debtor's property, are not unheard of.[4]

Forms Form 20I is only applicable where the person to be examined is a judgment-debtor: see r. 20.10(4.1)(*b*).[5]

[1] *Zeppieri & Associates v. Jabbari*, [2014] O.J. No. 592, 2014 ONSC 818 (Ont. Div. Ct.).

[2] *Sangwan v. Marsh*, [2019] O.J. No. 5117 (Ont. S.C.J.).

[3] *Premier Brands Ltd. v. Monk's Group of Pubs Inc. (c.o.b. The Monk's Hearth)*, [2015] O.J. No. 4565 (Ont. S.C.J. (Sm. Cl. Ct.)).

[4] *Sangwan v. Marsh*, 2019 CanLII 93996 (Ont. S.C.S.M.).

[5] *All Canadian Mechanical and Electrical Inc. v. Henderson*, [2011] O.J. No. 1456 (Ont. S.C.J. (Sm. Cl. Ct.)).

20.11 CONTEMPT HEARING — (1) If a person on whom a notice of examination has been served under rule 20.10 attends the examination but refuses to answer questions or to produce records or documents, the court may order the person to attend before it for a contempt hearing.

(2) SAME — If a person on whom a notice of examination has been served under rule 20.10 fails to attend the examination, the court may order the person to attend before it for a contempt hearing under subsection 30 (1) of the *Courts of Justice Act*.

(3) NOTICE OF CONTEMPT HEARING — If the court makes an order for a contempt hearing

(a)   the clerk shall provide the creditor with a notice of contempt hearing setting out the time, date and place of the hearing; and

(b)   the creditor shall serve the notice of contempt hearing on the debtor or other person in accordance with subrule 8.01 (13) and file the affidavit of service at least seven days before the hearing.

(4) SETTING ASIDE ORDER FOR CONTEMPT HEARING — A person who has been ordered to attend a contempt hearing under subsection 30(1) of the *Courts of Justice Act* may make a motion to set aside the order, before or after receiving the notice of con-

tempt hearing but before the date of the hearing and, on the motion, the court may set aside the order and order that the person attend another examination under rule 20.10.

(5) **FINDING OF CONTEMPT OF COURT** — At a contempt hearing held under subrule (1), the court may find the person to be in contempt of court if the person fails to show cause why the person should not be held in contempt for refusing to answer questions or produce records or documents.

(6) **SAME** — The finding of contempt at a hearing held under subsection 30 (1) of the *Courts of Justice Act* is subject to subsection 30 (2) of that Act.

(7) **OTHER POWERS OF COURT AT CONTEMPT HEARING** — At a contempt hearing, the court may order that the person,

(a)   attend an examination under rule 20.10;

(b)   be jailed for a period of not more than five days;

(c)   attend an additional contempt hearing under subrule (1) or subsection 30 (1) of the *Courts of Justice Act*, as the case may be; or

(d)   comply with any other order that the judge considers necessary or just.

(8) **WARRANT OF COMMITTAL** — If a committal is ordered under clause (7) (b),

(a)   the creditor may complete and file with the clerk an identification form (Form 20K) to assist the police in apprehending the person named in the warrant of committal; and

(b)   the clerk shall issue a warrant of committal (Form 20J), accompanied by the identification form, if any, directed to all police officers in Ontario to apprehend the person named in the warrant anywhere in Ontario and promptly bring the person to the nearest correctional institution.

(9) **DISCHARGE** — A person in custody under a warrant issued under this rule shall be discharged from custody on the order of the court or when the time prescribed in the warrant expires, whichever is earlier.

(10) **DURATION AND RENEWAL** — A warrant issued under this rule remains in force for 12 months after the date of issue and may be renewed by order of the court on a motion made by the creditor for 12 months at each renewal, unless the court orders otherwise.

(11) [REVOKED: O. Reg. 440/10, s. 7, in force January 1, 2011.]

[O. Reg. 78/06, s. 48; O. Reg. 440/10, s. 7.]

20.12 SATISFACTION OF ORDER — If payment is made in full satisfaction of an order,

(a)   where all parties consent, a party may file a request for clerk's order or consent (Form 11.2A) indicating that payment has been made in full satisfaction of the order or terms of settlement; or

(b)   the debtor may make a motion for an order confirming that payment has been made in full satisfaction of the order or terms of settlement.

[O. Reg. 78/06, s. 48; O. Reg. 393/09, s. 23.]

Rule 21 — Referee

21.01 (1) A person assigned the powers and duties of a referee under subsection 73(2) of the *Courts of Justice Act* may, if directed by the regional senior justice or his or her designate,

(a)   hear disputes of proposals of terms of payment under rule 9.03;

(b)   conduct settlement conferences under rule 13;

(c)   hear motions for consolidation orders under rule 20.09; and

(d)   assess receipted disbursements for fees paid to the court, an authorized court transcriptionist or a sheriff under the regulations made under the *Administration of Justice Act*.

(2) Except under subrule 9.03 (5) (order as to terms of payment), a referee shall not make a final decision in any matter referred to him or her but shall report his or her findings and recommendations to the court.

[O. Reg. 78/06, s. 49; O. Reg. 393/09, s. 24; O. Reg. 171/14, s. 1.]

Rule 22 — Payment Into and Out of Court

22.01 DEFINITIONS — In this Rule,

  "Accountant" means the Accountant of the Superior Court of Justice;

  "clerk" means the clerk in the location where the proceeding was commenced.

22.02 NON-APPLICATION OF RULE — This Rule does not apply to money paid or to be paid into court,

(a)   under an order or proposal for payment made under rule 9.03;

(b)   under an offer to settle a claim in return for the payment of money; or

(c)   for the enforcement of an order for the payment or recovery of money under Rule 20, including enforcement by garnishment.

22.03 PAYMENT INTO COURT — (1) Subject to subrule (7), a party who is required to pay money into court shall do so in accordance with subrules (2) to (6).

(2) FILING WITH CLERK OR ACCOUNTANT — The party shall file the following documents with the clerk or the Accountant:

1.   If the payment into court is under a statutory provision or rule, a written request for payment into court that refers to that provision or rule.

2.   If the payment into court is under an order, a written request for payment into court and a copy of the order that bears the court's seal.

(3) DIRECTION — On receiving the documents required to be filed under subrule (2), the clerk or Accountant shall give the party a direction to receive the money, addressed to a bank listed in Schedule I or II to the *Bank Act*(Canada) and specifying the account in the

Accountant's name into which the money is to be paid.

(4) CLERK TO FORWARD DOCUMENTS — If the documents are filed with the clerk, the clerk shall forward the documents to the Accountant.

(5) PAYMENT — On receiving the direction referred to in subrule (3), the party shall pay the money into the specified bank account in accordance with the direction.

(6) BANK'S DUTIES — On receiving the money, the bank shall give a receipt to the party paying the money and immediately send a copy of the receipt to the Accountant.

(7) PAYMENT TO ACCOUNTANT BY MAIL — A party may pay money into court by mailing to the Accountant the applicable documents referred to in subrule (2), together with the money that is payable; the written request for payment into court referred to in that subrule shall include the party's name and mailing address.

(8) ACCOUNTANT TO PROVIDE RECEIPT — On receiving money under subrule (7), the Accountant shall send a receipt to the party paying the money.

(9) PROOF OF PAYMENT — A party who pays money into court shall, immediately after receiving a receipt from the bank under subrule (6) or from the Accountant under subrule (8), as the case may be, send to every other party a copy of the receipt and file a copy of the receipt with the court.

22.04 PAYMENT OUT OF COURT — (1) Money may only be paid out of court under an order.

(2) DOCUMENTS TO BE FILED — A person who seeks payment of money out of court shall file with the Accountant,

(a)   a written request for payment out and supporting affidavit, in the form provided by the Ministry; and

(b)   a copy of the order for payment out that bears the court's seal.

(3) PAYMENT OUT, CHILDREN'S LAWYER OR PUBLIC GUARDIAN AND TRUSTEE — If the person seeking payment out is the Children's Lawyer or the Public Guardian and Trustee,

(a)   the written request need not be in the form provided by the Ministry and a supporting affidavit is not required; and

(b)   a single written request that deals with more than one proceeding may be filed.

(4) PAYMENT OUT, MINOR ATTAINING AGE OF MAJORITY — Despite subrule (2), money in court to which a party is entitled under an order once the party attains the age of majority may be paid out to the party on filing with the Accountant, in the forms provided by the Accountant,

(a)   a written request for payment out; and

(b)   an affidavit proving the identity of the party and that the party has attained the age of majority.

(5) ACCOUNTANT'S DUTIES — If the requirements of subrule (2) or (4), as the case may be, are met, the Accountant shall pay the money to the person named in the order for payment out, and the payment shall include any accrued interest, unless a court orders otherwise.

22.05 TRANSITION — This Rule applies to the payment into and out of court of money paid into court on and after the day on which Ontario Regulation 400/12 comes into force.

[O. Reg. 400/12, s. 2.]

COURTS OF JUSTICE ACT

FAMILY LAW RULES

(O. Reg. 114/99)

Amendments: O. Reg. 544/99; O. Reg. 202/01; O. Reg. 337/02; O. Reg. 56/03; O. Reg. 91/03; O. Reg. 92/03; O. Reg. 89/04; O. Reg. 76/06; O. Reg. 519/06; O. Reg. 120/07; O. Reg. 439/07; O. Reg. 561/07; O. Reg. 151/08; O. Reg. 386/09, s. 1; O. Reg. 6/10, ss. 1-9; O. Reg. 51/10, s. 1; O. Reg. 52/10, s. 1; O. Reg. 383/11; O. Reg. 186/12; O. Reg. 388/12; O. Reg. 389/12; O. Reg. 322/13; O. Reg. 142/14; O. Reg. 69/15; O. Reg. 140/15, ss. 1-2, 4-5; O. Reg. 235/16, ss. 1-7; O. Reg. 226/17; O. Reg. 298/18; O. Reg. 385/18; O. Reg. 418/18; O. Reg. 535/18; O. Reg. 93/19; O. Reg. 250/19; CTR 12 FE 20(F) - 2.

CONTENTS

Rule 1 — General

1. CITATION — (1) These rules may be cited as the Family Law Rules.

(2) CASES AND COURTS TO WHICH RULES APPLY — These rules apply to all family law cases in the Family Court of the Superior Court of Justice, in the Superior Court of Justice and in the Ontario Court of Justice,

(a)   under,

    (i)   the *Change of Name Act*,

    (ii)   Parts V, VII and VIII of the *Child, Youth and Family Services Act, 2017*,

    (iii)   the *Children's Law Reform Act*, except sections 59 and 60,

    (iii.1)   the *Civil Marriage Act* (Canada),

    (iv)   the *Divorce Act* (Canada),

    (iv.1)   the *Family Homes on Reserves and Matrimonial Interests or Rights Act* (Canada),

    (v)   the *Family Law Act*, except Part V,

    (vi)   the *Family Responsibility and Support Arrears Enforcement Act, 1996*,

    (vii)   section 6 of the *Marriage Act*, and

    (viii)   the *Interjurisdictional Support Orders Act, 2002*;

(b)   for the interpretation, enforcement or variation of a marriage contract, cohabitation agreement, separation agreement, paternity agreement, family arbitration agreement or family arbitration award;

(c)   for a constructive or resulting trust or a monetary award as compensation for unjust enrichment between persons who have cohabited;

(d)   for annulment of a marriage or a declaration of validity or invalidity of a marriage;

(e)   for appeals of family arbitration awards under the *Arbitration Act, 1991*; and

(f)   for proceedings under First Nation laws made under,

    (i)   the *Family Homes on Reserves and Matrimonial Interests or Rights Act* (Canada), or

    (ii)   the *First Nations Land Management Act* (Canada), with respect to the effect of relationship breakdown on matrimonial real property.

(2.1) [REVOKED: O. Reg. 89/04, s. 1(2).]

(3) CASE MANAGEMENT IN FAMILY COURT OF SUPERIOR COURT OF JUSTICE — Despite subrule (2), rule 39 (case management in the Family Court of the Superior Court of Justice) applies only to cases in the Family Court of the Superior Court of

Justice, which has jurisdiction in the following municipalities:

1. **Regional Municipality of Durham.**

2. **County of Elgin.**

3. **County of Frontenac.**

4. **Regional Municipality of Haldimand-Norfolk.**

5. **County of Haliburton.**

6. **City of Hamilton.**

7. **County of Hastings.**

8. **City of Kawartha Lakes.**

9. **County of Lanark.**

10. **United Counties of Leeds and Grenville.**

11. **County of Lennox and Addington.**

12. **County of Middlesex.**

13. **Territorial District of Muskoka.**

14. **Regional Municipality of Niagara.**

15. **County of Northumberland.**

16. **City of Ottawa.**

17. **County of Peterborough.**

18. **United Counties of Prescott and Russell.**

19. **County of Prince Edward.**

20. **County of Renfrew.**

21. **County of Simcoe.**

22. **United Counties of Stormont, Dundas and Glengarry.**

23. **Regional Municipality of Waterloo.**

24. **Regional Municipality of York.**

(4) CASE MANAGEMENT IN ONTARIO COURT OF JUSTICE — Despite subrule (2), rule 40 (case management in the Ontario Court of Justice) applies only to cases in the Ontario Court of Justice.

(4.1) CASE MANAGEMENT IN THE SUPERIOR COURT OF JUSTICE — Despite subrule (2), rule 41 (case management in the Superior Court of Justice, other than the Family Court of the Superior Court of Justice) applies only to cases in the Superior Court of Justice that are not in the Family Court of the Superior Court of Justice.

(5) FAMILY LAW CASE COMBINED WITH OTHER MATTER — If a case in the court combines a family law case to which these rules apply with another matter to which these rules would not otherwise apply, the parties may agree or the court on motion may order that these rules apply to the combined case or part of it.

(6) CONDITIONS AND DIRECTIONS — When making an order, the court may impose conditions and give directions as appropriate.

(7) MATTERS NOT COVERED IN RULES — If these rules do not cover a matter adequately, the court may give directions, and the practice shall be decided by analogy to these rules, by reference to the Courts of Justice Act and the Act governing the case and, if the court considers it appropriate, by reference to the *Rules of Civil Procedure*.

(7.1) CERTAIN ORDERS THAT MAY BE MADE AT ANY TIME — For greater certainty, a court may make an order under subrule (7.2), (8), (8.1) or (8.2) at any time during a case, and the power to make such an order,

(a)   is in addition to any other power to make an order that these rules may specify in the circumstances; and

(b)   exists unless these rules expressly provide otherwise.

(7.2) PROCEDURAL ORDERS — For the purposes of promoting the primary objective of these rules as required under subrules 2 (4) and, particularly, (5), the court may make orders giving such directions or imposing such conditions respecting procedural matters as are just, including an order,

(a)   that a party give to another party an affidavit listing documents that are relevant to the issues in a case and that are in the party's control or available to the party on request, or that a party make any other disclosure, within a specified time;

(b)   limiting the number of affidavits that a party may file, or limiting the length of affidavits that a party may file (excluding any exhibits);

(c)   that any motions be brought within a specified time;

(d)   that a statement setting out what material facts are not in dispute be filed within a specified time (in which case the facts are deemed to be established unless a judge orders otherwise);

(e)   that questioning be conducted in accordance with a plan established by the court, be subject to a time limit or be limited with respect to scope;

(f)   limiting the number of witnesses;

(g)   that all or part of an affidavit or any other evidence filed at any stage in a case, and any cross-examinations on it, may be used at a hearing;

(h)   that a party serve and file, within a specified time, a written summary of the anticipated evidence of a witness;

(i)   that a witness give all or part of his or her evidence by affidavit or another method not requiring the witness to attend in person;

(j)   that oral evidence be presented, or that any oral evidence be subject to a time limit;

(k)   that any expert witnesses for the parties meet to discuss the issues, and prepare a joint statement setting out the issues on which they agree and the issues that are in dispute;

(l)   that a party serve and file a summary of argument;

(m)   that a party provide to the court a draft order (Form 25, 25A, 25B, 25C or 25D) setting out the relief that he or she is seeking;

(n)   identifying the issues to be decided at a particular hearing;

(o)   that the parties appear before the court by a specified date;

(p)   that a case be scheduled for trial or that a trial management conference be conducted; and

(q)   that a trial be limited to a specified number of days and apportioning those days between the parties.

(7.3) **EFFECT OF ORDER AT TRIAL** — An order made under clause (7.2) (i) does not apply to the giving of evidence on cross-examination unless the order states so expressly.

(7.4) An order made under subrule (7.2) respecting how a trial is to proceed applies unless the trial judge orders otherwise.

(8) **FAILURE TO OBEY ORDER** — If a person fails to obey an order in a case or a related case, the court may deal with the failure by making any order that it considers necessary for a just determination of the matter, including,

(a)   an order for costs;

(b)   an order dismissing a claim;

(c)   an order striking out any application, answer, notice of motion, motion to change, response to motion to change, financial statement, affidavit, or any other document filed by a party;

(d)   an order that all or part of a document that was required to be provided but was not, may not be used in the case;

(e)   if the failure to obey was by a party, an order that the party is not entitled to any further order from the court unless the court orders otherwise;

(f)   an order postponing the trial or any other step in the case; and

(g)   on motion, a contempt order.

(8.1) **FAILURE TO FOLLOW RULES** — If a person fails to follow these rules, the court may deal with the failure by making any order described in subrule (8), other than a contempt order under clause (8) (g).

(8.2) DOCUMENT THAT MAY DELAY OR IS INFLAMMATORY, ETC. — The court may strike out all or part of any document that may delay or make it difficult to have a fair trial or that is inflammatory, a waste of time, a nuisance or an abuse of the court process.

(8.3) [REVOKED: O. Reg. 69/15, s. 1(2).]

(8.4) CONSEQUENCES OF STRIKING OUT CERTAIN DOCUMENTS — If an order is made striking out a party's application, answer, motion to change or response to motion to change in a case, the following consequences apply unless a court orders otherwise:

1.   The party is not entitled to any further notice of steps in the case, except as provided by subrule 25 (13) (service of order).

2.   The party is not entitled to participate in the case in any way.

3.   The court may deal with the case in the party's absence.

4.   A date may be set for an uncontested trial of the case.

(9) REFERENCE TO FORMS — In these rules, when a form is referred to by number, the reference is to the form with that number that is described in the Table of Forms at the end of these rules and is available on the Internet through www.ontariocourtforms.on.ca.

(9.1) USE OF FORMS — The forms authorized by these rules and set out in the Table of Forms shall be used where applicable and may be adjusted as needed to fit the situation.

(9.2) REQUIREMENTS FOR COMPLETING FORMS — A party who is required by these rules to provide a form shall, subject to subrule (9.1),

(a)   follow the instructions set out in the form;

(b)   fully complete all portions of the form; and

(c)   attach to the form any documents that the form requires.

(10) FORMAT OF WRITTEN DOCUMENTS — Every written document in a case,

(a)   shall be legibly typed or printed; and

(b)   in the case of a document in paper format,

  (i)   shall be on white paper, or on white or nearly white paper with recycled paper content, and

  (ii)   may appear on one or both sides of the page.

(c)   [REVOKED: O. Reg. 142/14, s. 1.]

(11) PRACTICE DIRECTIONS — In subrules (12), (12.1) and (12.2),

"practice direction" means a direction, notice, memorandum or guide for the purpose of governing, subject to these rules, the conduct of cases in any area.

(12) REQUIREMENTS FOR PRACTICE DIRECTION — A practice direction shall be approved in advance by the Chief Justice or Chief Judge of the court, filed with the secretary of the Family Rules Committee and posted on the Ontario Courts website.

(12.1) EFFECTIVE DATE OF PRACTICE DIRECTION — A practice direction does not come into effect before it is filed and posted as described in subrule (12).

(12.2) OLD PRACTICE DIRECTIONS — Practice directions that were issued before these rules take effect no longer apply.

(13) GENERAL TRANSITION RULES, CYFSA — The following rules apply in relation to cases commenced but not concluded under the *Child, Youth and Family Services Act* before its repeal:

1.   If regulations made under paragraph 11 of subsection 339(1) of the Child, Youth and Family Services Act, 2017 provide for the continued application of any portion of the repealed Act to such cases, these rules, as they read immediately before the Act's repeal, continue to apply with respect to the continued application of that part of the repealed Act.

2.   If regulations made under paragraph 11 of subsection 339(1) of the *Child, Youth and Family Services Act, 2017* provide that a reference in that Act to a matter shall be read as including a matter in the *Child and Family Services Act*, a reference in these rules to that matter in the *Child, Youth and Family Services Act, 2017* shall be read as including that matter in the *Child and Family Services Act*.

(14) [REVOKED: O. Reg. 76/06, s. 1(2).]

[O. Reg. 441/99, s. 1; O. Reg. 202/01, s. 1; O. Reg. 56/03, s. 1; O. Reg. 89/04, s. 1; O. Reg. 76/06, s. 1; O. Reg. 561/07, s. 1; O. Reg. 388/12, s. 1; O. Reg. 322/13, s. 1; O. Reg. 142/14, s. 1; O. Reg. 69/15, s. 1; O. Reg. 226/17, s. 1; O. Reg. 298/18, s. 1; O. Reg. 385/18, s. 1; O. Reg. 93/19, s. 1.]

Rule 1.1 — Electronic Filing and Issuance of Documents

1.1 AUTHORIZED SOFTWARE — (1) If these rules permit or require a document to be filed or issued electronically, the software authorized by the Ministry of the Attorney General for the purpose shall be used for the filing or issuance.

(2) **AGREEMENT** — A rule that provides that a document may be filed electronically does not apply unless the party filing the document agrees to the terms of use of the authorized software and provides an email address at which he or she agrees to accept documents from the court electronically.

(3) **DEEMED ISSUANCE** — A document issued electronically using the authorized software is deemed to have been issued by the court.

(4) **DATE OF ELECTRONIC FILING, ISSUANCE** — The date on which a document that is filed or issued electronically is considered to have been filed or issued, as the case may be, is the date indicated for the document by the authorized software.

(5) **SAME, OUTSIDE OF BUSINESS HOURS** — If a document is filed or issued electronically outside of regular business hours, the authorized software shall indicate that the document was filed or issued, as the case may be, on the next day on which court offices are open.

(6) INCONSISTENCIES — In the event of an inconsistency between information provided in a document filed electronically by a person using the authorized software and information provided by the person using the authorized software that is not in the electronically filed document,

(a)   the information in the electronically filed document prevails, except with respect to the municipality specified by the person for the purposes of rule 5 where the information that is not in the electronically filed document prevails; and

(b)   the clerk may request from the person clarification, in the manner specified by the clerk, respecting the inconsistency, and the person shall promptly provide it.

(7) REQUIREMENT TO KEEP ORIGINAL — A person who, in accordance with these rules, electronically files a document that was originally signed, certified or commissioned in paper format shall,

(a)   retain the original document until the day on which the case is finally disposed of or, if no notice of appeal is served in the case, the time for serving the notice has expired, subject to any requirement in these rules to give the document to the clerk before that day; and

(b)   promptly make the original document available for inspection and copying on the request of the court or of any party to the case.

[O. Reg. 298/18, s. 2.]

Rule 2 — Interpretation

2. DEFINITIONS — (1) In these rules,

"address" means a person's street or municipal address, mailing address, telephone number, fax number and email address;

"appellant" means a person who starts an appeal;

"applicant" means a person who starts an application;

"application" means, as the context requires, the document that starts a case or the procedure by which new cases are brought to the court for a final order or provisional order;

"arbitration agreement" means an agreement by which two or more persons agree to submit to arbitration a dispute that has arisen or may arise between them;

"authorized software" means the software referred to in rule 1.1 (electronic filing and issuance of documents);

"bond" includes a recognizance, and expressions that refer to the posting of a bond include the act of entering into a recognizance;

"case" means an application or any other method allowed in law for bringing a matter to the court for a final order or provisional order, and includes all motions, enforcements and appeals;

"change", when used to refer to an order or agreement, means to vary, suspend or discharge, or a variation, suspension or discharge (depending on whether the word is used as a verb or as a noun);

"child" means a child as defined in the Act governing the case or, if not defined in that

Act, a person under the age of 18 years, and in a case under the *Divorce Act* (Canada) includes a "child of the marriage" within the meaning of that Act;

"child protection case" means a case under Part V of the *Child, Youth and Family Services Act, 2017*;

"child support guidelines" means Ontario Regulation 391/97 (Child Support Guidelines) made under the *Family Law Act*, or the Federal Child Support Guidelines, as the case may be;

"clerk" means a person who has the authority of a clerk or a registrar of the court;

"contempt motion" means a motion for a contempt order;

"contempt order" means an order finding a person in contempt of court;

"continuing record" means the record made under Rule 9 containing, in accordance with these rules, written documents in a case that are filed with the court;

"corporation" [*French version only*]

"court" means the court in which a case is being heard;

"default hearing" means a hearing under section 41 of the *Family Responsibility and Support Arrears Enforcement Act, 1996* in which a payor is required to come to court to explain why payment has not been made as required by a support order;

"Director of the Family Responsibility Office" means the Director of the Family Responsibility Office under the *Family Responsibility and Support Arrears Enforcement Act, 1996*, and "Director" has the same meaning, unless the context requires otherwise;

"document" means information, sound or images recorded by any method;

"enforcement" means the use of one or more remedies mentioned in rule 26 (enforcement of orders) to enforce an order;

"family arbitration" means an arbitration that,

(a)   deals with matters that could be dealt with in a marriage contract, separation agreement, cohabitation agreement or paternity agreement under Part IV of the *Family Law Act*, and

(b)   is conducted exclusively in accordance with the law of Ontario or of another Canadian jurisdiction;

"family arbitration agreement" and "family arbitration award" have meanings that correspond to the meaning of "family arbitration";

"file" means to file with proof of service,

(a)   in the court office in the municipality where the case or enforcement is started or to which the case or enforcement is transferred, or

(b)   electronically in accordance with these rules;

"final order" means an order, other than a temporary order, that decides a claim in an application, including,

(a)   an order made on motion that changes a final order,

(b)   a judgment, and

(c)   an order that decides a party's rights, in an issue between the parties or between a party and a non-party;

"government agency" means the Crown, a Crown agency, a municipal government or agency, a children's aid society or any other public body;

"income source" has the same meaning as in the *Family Responsibility and Support Arrears Enforcement Act, 1996*;

"lawyer" means a person authorized under the *Law Society Act* to practise law in Ontario;

"legal aid rate" means the rate payable by the Ontario Legal Aid Plan on an account submitted by a lawyer for copying in the lawyer's office;

"mail", when used as a noun, means ordinary or regular mail, and when used as a verb means to send by ordinary or regular mail;

"municipality" means a county, district, district municipality, regional municipality, the City of Toronto or a municipal corporation formed from the amalgamation of all the municipalities of a county, district, district municipality or regional municipality, and includes,

(a)   an Indian reserve within the territorial area of a municipality, and

(b)   the part of The Regional Municipality of Niagara that was the County of Lincoln as it existed on December 31, 1969;

"on motion" means on motion of a party or a person having an interest in the case;

"payment order" means a temporary or final order, but not a provisional order, requiring a person to pay money to another person, including,

(a)   an order to pay an amount under Part I or II of the *Family Law Act* or the corresponding provisions of a predecessor Act,

(b)   a support order,

(c)   a support deduction order,

(d)   an order under section 108 or subsection 213 (2) of the *Child Youth, and Family Services Act, 2017,* or under the corresponding provision of a predecessor Act,

(e)   a payment order made under rules 26 to 32 (enforcement measures) or under section 41 of the *Family Responsibility and Support Arrears Enforcement Act, 1996,*

(f)   a fine for contempt of court,

(g)   an order of forfeiture of a bond or recognizance,

(h)   an order requiring a party to pay the fees and expenses of,

(i)   an assessor, mediator or other expert named by the court, or

(ii)   a person conducting a blood test to help determine a child's parentage, and

(i)   the costs and disbursements in a case;

"payor" means a person required to pay money under an order or agreement, and includes the estate trustee of a payor who died;

"periodic payment" means an amount payable at regular intervals and includes an amount payable in instalments;

"property claim" means a claim,

(a)   under Part I of the *Family Law Act*,

(b)   for a constructive or resulting trust, or

(c)   for a monetary award as compensation for unjust enrichment;

"provisional order" means an order that is not effective until confirmed by a court;

"recipient" means a person entitled to receive money or costs under a payment order or agreement, including,

(a)   a guardian or person with custody of a child who is entitled to money for the child's benefit under an order,

(b)   in the case of a support order made under the *Family Law Act*, an agency referred to in subsection 33 (3) of that Act,

(c)   in the case of a support order made under the *Divorce Act* (Canada), an agency referred to in subsection 20.1 (1) of that Act,

(d)   a children's aid society entitled to money under an order made under section 108 or subsection 213 (2) of the *Child, Youth and Family Services Act, 2017*, or the corresponding provision in a predecessor Act,

(e)   an assessor, mediator or other expert entitled to fees and expenses from the party named in the order, and

(f)   the estate trustee of a person who was entitled to money under an order at the time of his or her death;

"Registrar General" means the Registrar General under the *Vital Statistics Act*;

"respondent" means a person against whom a claim is made in an application, answer or appeal;

"special party" means a party, other than a child party, who is or appears to be mentally incapable for the purposes of the *Substitute Decisions Act, 1992* in respect of an issue in the case and who, as a result, requires legal representation;

"support deduction order" means a support deduction order as defined in section 1 of the *Family Responsibility and Support Arrears Enforcement Act, 1996*;

"support order" means an order described in subsection 34 (1) of the *Family Law Act* or a support order as defined in subsection 2 (1) of the *Divorce Act* (Canada) or in section 1 of the *Family Responsibility and Support Arrears Enforcement Act, 1996*;

"temporary order" means an order that says it is effective only for a limited time, and includes an interim order;

"trial" includes a hearing;

"uncontested trial" means a trial at which only the party making the claim provides evidence and submissions.

(1.1) TEMPORARY ORDERS — For the purposes of the definition of "temporary order" in subrule (1), temporary orders include orders made under subsection 94 (2) (custody during adjournment) of the *Child, Youth and Family Services Act, 2017* but do not include an order made under paragraph 2 of subsection 101 (1) (interim society care and custody) of that Act.

(2) PRIMARY OBJECTIVE — The primary objective of these rules is to enable the court to deal with cases justly.

(3) DEALING WITH CASES JUSTLY — Dealing with a case justly includes,

(a)   ensuring that the procedure is fair to all parties;

(b)   saving expense and time;

(c)   dealing with the case in ways that are appropriate to its importance and complexity; and

(d)   giving appropriate court resources to the case while taking account of the need to give resources to other cases.

(4) DUTY TO PROMOTE PRIMARY OBJECTIVE — The court is required to apply these rules to promote the primary objective, and parties and their lawyers are required to help the court to promote the primary objective.

(5) DUTY TO MANAGE CASES — The court shall promote the primary objective by active management of cases, which includes,

(a)   at an early stage, identifying the issues, and separating and disposing of those that do not need full investigation and trial;

(b)   encouraging and facilitating use of alternatives to the court process;

(c)   helping the parties to settle all or part of the case;

(d)   setting timetables or otherwise controlling the progress of the case;

(e)   considering whether the likely benefits of taking a step justify the cost;

(f)   dealing with as many aspects of the case as possible on the same occasion; and

(g)   if appropriate, dealing with the case without parties and their lawyers needing to come to court, on the basis of written documents or by holding a telephone or video conference.

[O. Reg. 544/99, s. 2; O. Reg. 76/06, s. 2; O. Reg. 439/07, s. 2; O. Reg. 388/12, s. 2; O. Reg. 142/14, s. 2; O. Reg. 69/15, s. 2; O. Reg. 140/15, s. 4; O. Reg. 298/18, s. 3; O. Reg. 250/19, s. 1.]

Rule 3 — Time

3. COUNTING DAYS — (1) In these rules or an order, the number of days between two events is counted as follows:

1.   The first day is the day after the first event.

2.   The last day is the day of the second event.

(2) COUNTING DAYS — SHORT PERIODS — If a rule or order provides a period of less than seven days for something to be done, Saturdays, Sundays and other days when all court offices are closed do not count as part of the period.

(3) DAY WHEN COURT OFFICES CLOSED — If the last day of a period of time under these rules or an order falls on a day when court offices are closed, the period ends on the next day they are open.

(4) COUNTING DAYS — EXAMPLES — The following are examples of how time is counted under these rules:

1.   Notice of a motion must be served not later than six days before the motion date (see subrule 14 (11)). Saturday and Sunday are not counted, because the notice period is less than seven days (see subrule (2)). Service on the day set out in the left column below is in time for the motion to be heard on the day set out in the right column below.

Service on	Motion may be heard on the following
Monday	The second following Tuesday
Tuesday	The second following Wednesday
Wednesday	The second following Thursday
Thursday	The second following Friday
Friday	The second following Monday
Saturday	The second following Tuesday
Sunday	The second following Tuesday

2.   A respondent who is served with an application in Canada has 30 days to serve an answer (see subrule 10 (1)). A respondent who is served with an application on October 1 is in time if the answer is served on or before October 31. A respondent served on November 1 is in time if the answer is served on or before December 1.

3.   If the last day for doing something under these rules or an order is New Year's Day, January 1, which is a day when court offices are closed, the time expires on January 2. If January 2 is a Saturday, Sunday or other day when court offices are closed, the time expires on January 3. If January 3 is a day when court offices are closed, the time expires on January 4.

(5) ORDER TO LENGTHEN OR SHORTEN TIME — The court may make an order to lengthen or shorten any time set out in these rules or an order, except that it may lengthen a time set out in subrule 33 (1) (timetable for child protection cases) only if the best interests of the child require it.

(6) WRITTEN CONSENT TO CHANGE TIME — The parties may, by consent in writing, change any time set out in these rules, except that they may not change a time set out in,

(a)   clause 14 (11) (e) (confirmation of motion);

(b)   clause 17 (14) (c) (confirmation of conference);

(c)   subrule 33 (1) (timetable for child protection cases);

(d)   rule 39 (case management in Family Court of Superior Court of Justice);

(e)   rule 40 (case management in Ontario Court of Justice); or

(f)   rule 41 (case management in the Superior Court of Justice (other than the Family Court of the Superior Court of Justice)).

(7) LATE DOCUMENTS REFUSED BY COURT OFFICE — The staff at a court office shall refuse to accept a document that a person asks to file after,

(a)   the time specified in these rules; or

(b)   the later time specified in a consent under subrule (6), a statute that applies to the case, or a court order.

[O. Reg. 544/99, s. 3; O. Reg. 202/01, s. 2; O. Reg. 76/06, s. 3; O. Reg. 298/18, s. 4 (2), (3).]

Rule 4 — Representation

4. DEFINITION — (0.1) In this rule,

"limited scope retainer" means the provision of legal services by a lawyer for part, but not all, of a party's case by agreement between the lawyer and the party.

(1) REPRESENTATION FOR A PARTY — A party may,

(a)   act in person;

(b)   be represented by a lawyer; or

(c)   be represented by a person who is not a lawyer, but only if the court gives permission in advance.

(1.1) INTERPRETATION, ACTING IN PERSON — Where a party acts in person, anything these rules require or permit a lawyer or other representative to do shall be done by the party.

(1.2) LIMITED SCOPE RETAINER — Clause (1) (b) permits a party to be represented by a lawyer acting under a limited scope retainer.

(1.3) INTERPRETATION, LIMITED SCOPE RETAINER — A party who is represented by a lawyer acting under a limited scope retainer is considered for the purposes of these rules to be acting in person, unless the lawyer is acting as the party's lawyer of record.

(2) **PRIVATE REPRESENTATION OF SPECIAL PARTY OR CHILD PARTY** — The court may authorize a person to represent a special party or a child party if the person is,

(a)   appropriate for the task; and

(b)   willing to act as representative.

(3) **PUBLIC LAW OFFICER TO REPRESENT SPECIAL PARTY OR CHILD PARTY** — If there is no appropriate person willing to act as a representative for a special party or a child party, the court may, on the consent of the official, authorize the representation of the special party or child party by,

(a)   the Public Guardian and Trustee, in the case of a special party; or

(b)   the Children's Lawyer, in the case of a child party.

(3.1) **COURT TO CONSIDER REPRESENTION OF CHILD PARTY** — The court shall consider what, if any, representation is required for a child party and shall make an order under this rule accordingly.

(4) **SERVICE OF AUTHORIZATION TO REPRESENT** — An order under subrule (2) or (3) shall be served immediately, by the person who asked for the order or by any other person named by the court,

(a)   on the representative; and

(b)   on every party in the case.

(5) **REPRESENTATION OF PARTY WHO DIES** — If a party dies after the start of a case, the court may make the estate trustee a party instead, on motion without notice.

(6) **AUTHORIZING REPRESENTATIVE FOR PARTY WHO DIES** — If the party has no estate trustee, the court may authorize an appropriate person to act as representative, with that person's consent, given in advance.

(7) **LAWYER FOR CHILD** — In a case that involves a child who is not a party, the court may authorize a lawyer to represent the child, and then the child has the rights of a party, unless the court orders otherwise.

(8) **CHILD'S RIGHTS SUBJECT TO STATUTE** — Subrule (7) is subject to section 78 (legal representation of child, protection hearing) and subsection 161 (6) (legal representation of child, secure treatment hearing) of the *Child, Youth and Family Services Act, 2017*.

(9) **CHOICE OF LAWYER** — A party who is acting in person may choose a lawyer by serving on every other party and filing a notice of change in representation (Form 4) containing the lawyer's consent to act.

(9.1) **NON-APPLICATION** — Subrule (9) does not apply if the party chooses a lawyer acting under a limited scope retainer and that lawyer is not the lawyer of record for the party.

(10) **CHANGE IN REPRESENTATION** — Except as subrule (10.1) provides, a party

represented by a lawyer may, by serving on every other party and filing a notice of change in representation (Form 4),

    (a)   change lawyers; or

    (b)   act in person.

    (10.1) EXCEPTION, CHILD PROTECTION CASE SCHEDULED FOR TRIAL — In a child protection case that has been scheduled for trial or placed on a trial list, a party may act under clause (10) (b) only with the court's permission, obtained in advance by motion made with notice.

    (11) NOTICE OF CHANGE IN REPRESENTATION — A notice of change in representation shall,

    (a)   contain the party's address for service, if the party wants to appear without a lawyer; or

    (b)   show the name and address of the new lawyer, if the party wants to change lawyers.

    (12) LAWYER'S REMOVAL FROM THE CASE — A lawyer may make a motion for an order to be removed from the case, with notice to the client and to,

    (a)   the Children's Lawyer, if the client is a child;

    (b)   the Public Guardian and Trustee, if the client is or appears to be mentally incapable in respect of an issue in the case.

    (13) NOTICE OF MOTION TO REMOVE LAWYER — Notice of a motion to remove a lawyer shall also be served on the other parties to the case, but the evidence in support of the motion shall not be served on them, shall not be put into the continuing record and shall not be kept in the court file after the motion is heard.

    (14) AFFIDAVIT IN SUPPORT OF MOTION TO REMOVE LAWYER — The affidavit in support of the motion shall indicate what stage the case is at, the next event in the case and any scheduled dates.

    (15) CONTENTS AND SERVICE OF ORDER REMOVING LAWYER — The order removing the lawyer from the case shall,

    (a)   set out the client's last known address for service; and

    (b)   be served on all other parties, served on the client by mail, fax or email at the client's last known address and filed immediately.

[O. Reg. 91/03, s. 1; O. Reg. 322/13, s. 2; O. Reg. 140/15, s. 4; O. Reg. 298/18, s. 5; O. Reg. 250/19, s. 2.]

Rule 5 — Where a Case Starts and Is to Be Heard

5. WHERE CASE STARTS — (1) Subject to sections 21.8 and 21.11 of the *Courts of Justice Act* (territorial jurisdiction — Family Court), a case shall be started,

    (a)   in the municipality where a party resides;

(b)   if the case deals with custody of or access to a child, in the municipality where the child ordinarily resides, except for cases described in,

    (i)   section 22 (jurisdiction of an Ontario court) of the *Children's Law Reform Act*, and

    (ii)   subsection 91 (2) (place for child protection hearing) and subsection 203 (1) (place for adoption proceeding) of the *Child, Youth and Family Services Act, 2017*; or

(c)   in a municipality chosen by all parties, but only with the court's permission given in advance in that municipality.

(2) **STARTING CASE — DANGER TO CHILD OR PARTY —** Subject to sections 21.8 and 21.11 of the *Courts of Justice Act*, if there is immediate danger that a child may be removed from Ontario or immediate danger to a child's or party's health or safety, a party may start a case in any municipality and a motion may be heard in that municipality, but the case shall be transferred to a municipality referred to in subrule (1) immediately after the motion is heard, unless the court orders otherwise.

(3) **CLERK TO REFUSE DOCUMENTS IF CASE IN WRONG PLACE —** The clerk shall refuse to accept an application for filing unless,

(a)   the case is started in the municipality where a party resides;

(b)   the case deals with custody of or access to a child and is started in the municipality where the child ordinarily resides;

(c)   the case is started in a municipality chosen by all parties and the order permitting the case to be started there is filed with the application; or

(d)   the lawyer or party asking to file the application says in writing that the case is one that is permitted by clause (1) (b) or subrule (2) to be started in that municipality.

(4) **PLACE FOR STEPS OTHER THAN ENFORCEMENT —** All steps in the case, other than enforcement, shall take place in the municipality where the case is started or transferred.

(5) **PLACE FOR ENFORCEMENT — PAYMENT ORDERS —** All steps in enforcement of a payment order, including a motion to suspend a support deduction order, shall take place,

(a)   in the municipality where the recipient resides;

(b)   if the recipient does not reside in Ontario, in the municipality where the order is filed with the court for enforcement;

(c)   if the person enforcing the order so chooses, in the municipality where the payor resides; or

(d)   in a motion under section 26 (income source dispute) of the *Family Responsibility and Support Arrears Enforcement Act, 1996*, in the municipality where the income source resides.

(6) **PLACE FOR ENFORCEMENT — OTHER ORDERS —** All steps in the enforcement of an order other than a payment order shall take place,

(a)   if the order involves custody of or access to a child,

    (i)   in the municipality where the child ordinarily resides, or

    (ii)   if the child does not ordinarily reside in Ontario, in the municipality to which the child has the closest connection;

(b)   if the order involves property, in the municipality where the person enforcing the order resides or the municipality where the property is located; or

(c)   in a municipality chosen by all parties, but only with the court's permission given in advance in that municipality.

(6.1) **FILING WRIT WITH SHERIFF —** Despite subrules (5) and (6), a writ of seizure and sale (Form 28) may be filed with a sheriff in a different municipality.

(7) **ALTERNATIVE PLACE FOR ENFORCEMENT — ORDER ENFORCED BY CONTEMPT MOTION —** An order, other than a payment order, that is being enforced by a contempt motion may also be enforced in the municipality in which the order was made.

(7.1) **PLACE FOR ENFORCEMENT — ELECTRONIC WRIT —** A writ of seizure and sale that is issued electronically under rule 28 (seizure and sale),

(a)   shall specify the municipality in which the enforcement is taking place under subrule (5), (6) or (7), as the case may be; and

(b)   is deemed to have been issued in that municipality.

(8) **TRANSFER TO ANOTHER MUNICIPALITY —** If it is substantially more convenient to deal with a case or any step in the case in another municipality, the court may, on motion, order that the case or step be transferred there.

(9) **CHANGE OF PLACE FOR CHILD PROTECTION CASE —** Notice of a motion under subsection 91 (3) of the *Child, Youth and Family Services Act, 2017* to transfer a case to a place within the jurisdiction of another children's aid society shall be served on the parties and the other children's aid society, with the evidence in support of the motion.

[O. Reg. 322/13, s. 3; O. Reg. 142/14, s. 3; O. Reg. 298/18, s. 6.]

Rule 6 — Service of Documents

6. METHODS OF SERVICE — (1) Service of a document under these rules may be carried out by regular service or by special service in accordance with this rule, unless an Act, rule or order provides otherwise.

(1.1) **AGE RESTRICTION —** No person shall serve a document under these rules unless he or she is at least 18 years of age.

(2) **REGULAR SERVICE —** Regular service of a document on a person is carried out

by,

(a)   mailing a copy to the person's lawyer or, if none, to the person;

(b)   sending a copy by same- or next-day courier to the person's lawyer or, if none, to the person;

(c)   depositing a copy at a document exchange to which the person's lawyer or, if none, the person belongs;

(c.1)   if the person consents or the court orders, using an electronic document exchange;

(d)   faxing a copy to the person's lawyer or, if none, to the person; or

(e)   if the person consents or the court orders, emailing a copy to the person's lawyer or, if none, to the person.

(3) **SPECIAL SERVICE** — Special service of a document on a person is carried out by,

(a)   leaving a copy,

    (i)   with the person to be served,

    (ii)   if the person is or appears to be mentally incapable in respect of an issue in the case, with the person and with the guardian of the person's property or, if none, with the Public Guardian and Trustee,

    (iii)   if the person is a child, with the child and with the child's lawyer, if any,

    (iv)   if the person is a corporation, with an officer, director or agent of the corporation, or with a person at any place of business of the corporation who appears to be managing the place, or

    (v)   if the person is a children's aid society, with an officer, director or employee of the society;

(b)   leaving a copy with the person's lawyer of record in the case, or with a lawyer who accepts service in writing on a copy of the document;

(c)   mailing a copy to the person, together with an acknowledgment of service in the form of a prepaid return postcard (Form 6), all in an envelope that is addressed to the person and has the sender's return address (but service under this clause is not valid unless the return postcard, signed by the person, is filed in the continuing record); or

(d)   leaving a copy at the person's place of residence, in an envelope addressed to the person, with anyone who appears to be an adult person resident at the same address and, on the same day or on the next, mailing another copy to the person at that address.

(4) **SPECIAL SERVICE – DOCUMENTS THAT COULD LEAD TO IMPRISONMENT** — Special service of the following documents shall be carried out only by a method set out in (3) (a), unless the court orders otherwise:

FAMILY LAW RULES

1. A notice of contempt motion.

2. A summons to witness.

3. A notice of motion or notice of default hearing in which the person to be served faces a possibility of imprisonment.

(4.1) SPECIAL SERVICE – RESTRICTION ON WHO MAY SERVE — Subject to subrule (4.2), special service of the following documents shall be carried out by a person other than the party required to serve the document:

1. An application (Form 8, 8A, 8B, 8B.1, 8B.2, 8C, 8D, 8D.1, 34L or 34N).

2. A motion to change (Form 15) and change information form (Form 15A) or affidavit permitted under subrule 15 (22), with required attachments.

3. A document listed in subrule (4).

(4.2) EXCEPTIONS — Subrule (4.1) does not apply if,

(a) the party required to serve the document or the person being served is a person referred to in clause 8 (6) (c) (officials, agencies, *etc.*); or

(b) the court orders otherwise.

(5) REGULAR SERVICE AT ADDRESS ON LATEST DOCUMENT — Regular service may be carried out at the address for service shown on the latest document filed by the person to be served.

(6) NOTICE OF ADDRESS CHANGE — A party whose address for service changes shall immediately serve notice of the change on the other parties and file it.

(7) SERVICE BY MAIL, WHEN EFFECTIVE — Service of a document by mail is effective on the fifth day after it was mailed.

(8) SERVICE BY COURIER, WHEN EFFECTIVE — Service of a document by courier is effective on,

(a) the day after the day the courier picks it up, in the case of same-day courier service; or

(b) two days after the day the courier picks it up, in the case of next-day courier service.

(9) SERVICE BY DOCUMENT EXCHANGE, WHEN EFFECTIVE — Service of a document by deposit at a document exchange is effective only if the copy deposited and an additional copy of the document are date-stamped by the document exchange in the presence of the person depositing the copy, and then service is effective on the day after the date on the stamp.

(10) SERVICE BY ELECTRONIC DOCUMENT EXCHANGE, WHEN EFFECTIVE — Service of a document through an electronic document exchange is effective only if the electronic document exchange provides a record of service showing the date and time of service, as well as the information listed in subrule (11.4), and then service is effective on,

(a)   the date shown on the record of service; or

(b)   if the record of service shows that the document was served after 4 p.m., the following day.

(11) SERVICE BY FAX OR EMAIL, WHEN EFFECTIVE — Service of a document by fax or email is effective on,

(a)   the date shown on the first page of the fax or in the email message, as the case may be; or

(b)   if the first page of the fax or the email message shows that the document was served after 4 p.m., the following day.

(11.1) SPECIAL SERVICE BY LEAVING COPY, WHEN EFFECTIVE — Special service of a document under clause (3) (a) or (b) is effective on the day the copy of the document was left in accordance with those clauses or, if the document was left after 4 p.m., the following day.

(11.2) SPECIAL SERVICE BY LEAVING COPY AND MAILING, WHEN EFFECTIVE — Special service of a document under clause (3) (d) is effective on the fifth day after it was mailed.

(11.3) EXCEPTION, IF EFFECTIVE DATE IS A HOLIDAY — Despite subrules (7) to (11.2), if the effective date of service under one of those subrules would be a day on which court offices are closed, service is instead effective on the next day on which they are open.

(11.4) INFORMATION TO BE INCLUDED IN RECORD OF SERVICE — A record of service for service of a document through an electronic document exchange shall, in addition to the date and time of service, include,

(a)   the total number of pages served;

(b)   the name and email address of the person who served the document;

(c)   the name of the person or lawyer who was served; and

(d)   the title or a description of the nature of the document.

(12) INFORMATION TO BE INCLUDED WITH DOCUMENT SERVED BY FAX — A document that is served by fax shall show, on its first page,

(a)   the sender's name, telephone number and fax number;

(b)   the name of the person or lawyer to be served;

(c)   the date and time of the fax;

(d)   the total number of pages faxed; and

(e)   the name and telephone number of a person to contact in case of transmission difficulties.

(13) MAXIMUM LENGTH OF DOCUMENT THAT MAY BE FAXED — Service of a document or documents relating to a single step in a case may be carried out by fax only

if the total number of pages (including any cover page or back sheet) is not more than 20, unless the parties consent in advance or the court orders otherwise.

(14) DOCUMENTS THAT MAY NOT BE FAXED — A trial record, appeal record, factum or book of authorities may not be served by fax at any time unless the person to be served consents in advance.

(14.1) INFORMATION TO BE INCLUDED WITH DOCUMENT SERVED BY EMAIL — Unless the court orders otherwise, the email message to which a document served by email is attached shall include,

(a)   the name of the person or lawyer to be served;

(b)   the title or a description of the nature of the document;

(c)   the date and time of the email; and

(d)   the name and telephone number of a person to contact in case of transmission difficulties.

(15) SUBSTITUTED SERVICE — The court may order that a document be served by substituted service, using a method chosen by the court, if the party making the motion,

(a)   provides detailed evidence showing,

    (i)   what steps have been taken to locate the person to be served, and

    (ii)   if the person has been located, what steps have been taken to serve the document on that person; and

(b)   shows that the method of service could reasonably be expected to bring the document to the person's attention.

(15.1) SAME, NOTICE — An order under subrule (15) may be obtained on motion without notice, except where the person to be served is a government agency.

(16) SERVICE NOT REQUIRED — The court may, on motion without notice, order that service is not required if,

(a)   reasonable efforts to locate the person to be served have not been or would not be successful; and

(b)   there is no method of substituted service that could reasonably be expected to bring the document to the person's attention.

(17) SERVICE BY ADVERTISEMENT — If the court orders service by advertisement, Form 6A shall be used.

(18) APPROVING IRREGULAR SERVICE — When a document has been served by a method not allowed by these rules or by an order, the court may make an order approving the service if the document,

(a)   came to the attention of the person to be served; or

(b)   would have come to the person's attention if the person had not been evading service.

(19) PROOF OF SERVICE — Service of a document may be proved by,

(a)   an acceptance or admission of service, written by the person to be served or the person's lawyer;

(b)   an affidavit of service (Form 6B);

(c)   the return postcard mentioned in clause (3) (c);

(d)   the date stamp on a copy of the document served by deposit at a document exchange; or

(e)   a record of service provided by an electronic document exchange that meets the requirements of this rule.

(20) DOCUMENT THAT WAS NOT SEEN ON EFFECTIVE DATE — The court may, on motion, lengthen a time, set aside the consequences of failing to take a step by a specified time, order an adjournment, or make any other order that is just, if, despite service of a document having been effected on a person in accordance with this rule, the person shows that the document,

(a)   did not come to his or her notice; or

(b)   came to his or her notice only after the effective date of service.

[O. Reg. 6/10, s. 1; O. Reg. 322/13, s. 4; O. Reg. 140/15, s. 1; O. Reg. 235/16, s. 1.]

Rule 7 — Parties

7. WHO ARE PARTIES – CASE — (1) A person who makes a claim in a case or against whom a claim is made in a case is a party to the case.

(2) WHO ARE PARTIES – MOTION — For purposes of a motion only, a person who is affected by a motion is also a party, but this does not apply to a child affected by a motion relating to custody, access, child protection, adoption or child support.

(3) PERSONS WHO MUST BE NAMED AS PARTIES — A person starting a case shall name,

(a)   as an applicant, every person who makes a claim;

(b)   as a respondent,

    (i)   every person against whom a claim is made, and

    (ii)   every other person who should be a party to enable the court to decide all the issues in the case.

(4) PARTIES IN CASES INVOLVING CHILDREN — In any of the following cases, every parent or other person who has care and control of the child involved, except a foster parent under the *Child, Youth and Family Services Act, 2017*, shall be named as a party, unless the court orders otherwise:

1.   A case about custody of or access to a child.

2.   A child protection case.

3.   A secure treatment case (Part VII of the *Child, Youth and Family Services Act, 2017*).

(4.1) MOTION TO CHANGE ORDER, S. 102 OF THE CYFSA — In a motion to change an order made under section 102 of the *Child, Youth and Family Services Act, 2017*, the children's aid society that was a party to the case in which the order was made is not a party to the motion to change the order, unless the court orders otherwise.

(5) PARTY ADDED BY COURT ORDER — The court may order that any person who should be a party shall be added as a party, and may give directions for service on that person.

(5.1) RESTRICTION ON ADDING CHILD AS A PARTY — A child who is the subject of a custody, access, child protection, adoption or child support case but is not a party to the case may not be added as a party unless the court orders otherwise.

(5.2) ADDITIONAL PARTIES IN CERTAIN CHILD SUPPORT CASES — In a case involving a child party in which a claim is made for support of the child, the court shall order that any persons who may be obligated to provide support for the child and who are not already parties to the case be added as parties in relation to the claim, and may give directions for service on such persons.

(6) PERMANENT CASE NAME AND COURT FILE NUMBER — The court file number given to a case and the description of the parties as applicants and respondents in the case shall remain the same on a motion to change an order, a status review application, an application (general) for *Child, Youth and Family Services Act, 2017* cases other than child protection and status review, an application for an openness order, an enforcement or an appeal, no matter who starts it, with the following exceptions:

1.   In an enforcement of a payment order, the parties may be described instead as payors, recipients and garnishees.

2.   In an appeal, the parties shall also be described as appellants and respondents.

3.   When a case is transferred to another municipality, it may be given a new court file number.

4.   An application under section 207 of the *Child, Youth and Family Services Act, 2017* to change or terminate an openness order shall be given a new court file number.

5.   In a motion to change an order made under section 102 of the *Child, Youth and Family Services Act, 2017*,

    i.   the person making the motion shall be named as the applicant and every other party to the motion shall be named as the respondents, and

    ii.   the motion shall be given a new court file number.

6.   [REVOKED: O. Reg. 298/18, s. 7(7).]

[O. Reg. 519/06, s. 1; O. Reg. 383/11, s. 1; O. Reg. 186/12, s. 1; O. Reg. 298/18, s. 7; O. Reg. 535/18, s. 1(F); O. Reg. 250/19, s. 3.]

Rule 8 — Starting a Case

8. FILING AN APPLICATION — (1) To start a case, a person shall file an application (Form 8, 8A, 8B, 8B.1, 8B.2, 8C, 8D, 8D.1, 34L or 34N).

(1.1) ENFORCEMENT OF FAMILY ARBITRATION AWARD — Despite subrule (1), a person who is entitled to the enforcement of a family arbitration award and who wants to ask the court to enforce the award under section 59.8 of the *Family Law Act* may do so by filing a request to enforce a family arbitration award (Form 32.1) under rule 32.1.

(1.2) WHEN REQUIRED TO PROCEED BY MOTION — Despite subrules (1) and (1.1), if there is already a family law case to which these rules apply between the parties to the family arbitration agreement in the Superior Court of Justice or the Family Court of the Superior Court of Justice, the party entitled to enforcement shall make a motion in that case rather than an application under this rule or a request under rule 32.1, and subrule 14 (24) applies in respect of the motion.

(2) CHANGE TO FINAL ORDER OR AGREEMENT — Subject to subrule 25 (19) (changing order — fraud, mistake, lack of notice), a party who wants to ask the court to change a final order or an agreement for support filed under section 35 of the *Family Law Act* may do so only by a motion under rule 15 (if permitted to do so by that rule).

(2.1) EXCEPTION — Despite subrule (2), if a party who wants to ask the court to change a final order or agreement to which rule 15 applies also wants to make one or more related claims to which rule 15 does not apply, the party may file an application under subrule (1) to deal with the request for a change together with the related claim or claims and, in that case, subrules 15 (11) to (13) apply with necessary changes to the request.

(3) CLAIMS IN APPLICATION — An application may contain,

(a)   a claim against more than one person; and

(b)   more than one claim against the same person.

(3.1) CLAIM FOR CUSTODY OR ACCESS — An application containing a claim for custody of or access to a child shall be accompanied by the applicable documents referred to in Rule 35.1.

(3.2) CLAIM RELATING TO FAMILY ARBITRATION — An application containing a claim under the *Arbitration Act, 1991* or the *Family Law Act* relating to a family arbitration, family arbitration agreement or family arbitration award shall be accompanied by,

(a)   copies of the certificates of independent legal advice required by the *Family Law Act* for the parties;

(b)   a copy of the family arbitration agreement; and

(c)   if an award has been made, the original award or a certified copy.

(4) COURT DATE SET WHEN APPLICATION FILED — When an application is filed, the clerk shall,

(a)   set a court date, except as provided by subrule 39 (7) (case management, standard track) and subrule 41 (4) (case management, clerk's role); and

(b)   seal the application with the court seal.

(5) SERVICE OF APPLICATION — The application shall be served immediately on every other party, and special service shall be used unless the party is listed in subrule (6).

(6) SERVICE ON OFFICIALS, AGENCIES, ETC. — The application may be served, subject to subrule (8.1),

(a)   on a foster parent, at the foster parent's residence;

(b)   on a representative of a band or First Nations, Inuit or Métis community, by serving the chief or other person who appears to be in charge of its management;

(c)   on any of the following persons, at their place of business:

1.   A Director appointed under section 53 of the *Child, Youth and Family Services Act, 2017*.

2.   A local director appointed under section 38 of the *Child and Family Services Act, 2017*.

3.   An administrator in charge of a secure treatment program under Part VII of the *Child, Youth and Family Services Act, 2017*.

4.   A children's aid society.

5.   The Minister of Community and Social Services.

6.   An agency referred to in subsection 33 (3) of the *Family Law Act* or subsection 20.1 (1) of the *Divorce Act* (Canada).

7.   The Director of the Family Responsibility Office.

8.   The Children's Lawyer.

9.   The Public Guardian and Trustee.

10.   The Registrar General.

(7) SERVING PROTECTION APPLICATION ON CHILD — In a child protection case in which the child is entitled to notice, the application shall be served on the child by special service.

(8) SERVING SECURE TREATMENT APPLICATION ON CHILD — An application for secure treatment (Part VII of the *Child, Youth and Family Services Act, 2017*) shall be served on the child by special service.

(8.1) SERVING OPENNESS APPLICATIONS — An application for an openness order or an application to change or terminate an openness order (Part VIII of the *Child,*

Youth and Family Services Act, 2017) shall be served by special service on,

(a) the child, if he or she is 12 years of age or older;

(b) the child's lawyer, if any; and

(c) the Children's Lawyer.

(9) SERVING APPLICATION ON CHILD'S LAWYER — If an order has been made for legal representation of a child under section 78 or subsection 161 (6) of the *Child, Youth and Family Services Act, 2017* or under subrule 4 (7), the applicant, or another party directed by the court, shall serve all documents in the continuing record and any status review application on the child's lawyer.

(10) SERVING PROTECTION APPLICATION BEFORE START OF CASE — If a child is brought to a place of safety (section 81, 82, 84 or 85 of the *Child, Youth and Family Services Act, 2017*), an application may be served without being sealed by the clerk, if it is filed on or before the court date.

(11) APPLICATION NOT SERVED ON OR BEFORE COURT DATE — If an application is not served on a respondent on or before the court date, at the applicant's request the clerk shall set a new court date for that respondent and the applicant shall make the necessary change to the application and serve it immediately on that respondent.

[O. Reg. 89/04, s. 2; O. Reg. 519/06, ss. 1, 2; O. Reg. 151/08, s. 1; O. Reg. 6/10, s. 2; O. Reg. 388/12, s. 3; O. Reg. 142/14, s. 4; O. Reg. 140/15, s. 5; O. Reg. 298/18, s. 8; O. Reg. 535/18, s. 2(F).]

Rule 8.1 — Mandatory Information Program

8.1 APPLICATION OF RULE — (1) This rule applies to cases started after August 31, 2011 that deal with any of the following:

1. A claim for custody of or access to a child under the *Divorce Act* (Canada) or Part III of the *Children's Law Reform Act.*

2. A claim respecting net family property under Part I of the *Family Law Act.*

3. A claim respecting a matrimonial home under Part II of the *Family Law Act.*

4. A claim for support under the *Divorce Act* (Canada) or Part III of the *Family Law Act.*

5. A restraining order under the *Family Law Act* or the *Children's Law Reform Act.*

6. A motion to change a final order or agreement under rule 15, except motions that deal only with changing child or spousal support.

(2) EXCEPTION — Subrules (4) to (7) do not apply to,

(a) a person or agency referred to in subsection 33 (3) of the *Family Law Act*;

(b) the Director of the Family Responsibility Office.

(c) parties in cases that are proceeding on consent;

(d) parties in cases in which the only claims made are for a divorce, costs or the in-

121

corporation of the terms of an agreement or prior court order;

(d.1)   parties to an application in which the only claims made in the application and any answer relate to a family arbitration, family arbitration agreement or family arbitration award, unless the court orders otherwise; or

(e)   parties who have already attended a mandatory information program.

(3) CONTENT OF PROGRAM — The program referred to in this rule shall provide parties to cases referred to in subrule (1) with information about separation and the legal process, and may include information on topics such as,

(a)   the options available for resolving differences, including alternatives to going to court;

(b)   the impact the separation of parents has on children; and

(c)   resources available to deal with problems arising from separation.

(4) ATTENDANCE COMPULSORY — Each party to a case shall attend the program no later than 45 days after the case is started.

(5) APPOINTMENTS TO ATTEND — The applicant shall arrange his or her own appointment to attend the program, obtain an appointment for the respondent from the person who conducts the program, and serve notice of the respondent's appointment with the application.

(6) CERTIFICATE — The person who conducts the program shall provide for each party who attends a certificate of attendance, which shall be filed as soon as possible, and in any event not later than 2 p.m. on the second day before the day of the case conference, if one is scheduled.

(7) NO OTHER STEPS — A party shall not take any step in the case before his or her certificate of attendance is filed, except that a respondent may serve and file an answer and a party may make an appointment for a case conference.

(8) EXCEPTION — The court may, on motion, order that any or all of subrules (4) to (7) do not apply to the party because of urgency or hardship or for some other reason in the interest of justice.

(9) [REVOKED: O. Reg. 561/07, s. 2.]

[O. Reg. 89/04, s. 3; O. Reg. 561/07, s. 2; O. Reg. 383/11, s. 2; O. Reg. 388/12, s. 4.]

Rule 9 — Continuing Record

9. CONTINUING RECORD CREATED — (1) A person starting a case shall,

(a)   prepare a single continuing record of the case, to be the court's permanent record of the case; and

(b)   serve it on all other parties and file it, along with the affidavits of service or other documents proving that the continuing record was served.

(2) [REVOKED: O. Reg. 519/06, s. 3(1).]

(3) **SUPPORT ENFORCEMENT CONTINUING RECORD** — If a support order is filed with the Director of the Family Responsibility Office, the person bringing the case before the court shall prepare the continuing record, and the continuing record shall be called the support enforcement continuing record.

(4) **CHILD PROTECTION CONTINUING RECORD** — In an application for a child protection order or an application for a status review of a child protection order, the continuing record shall be called the child protection continuing record.

(5) [REVOKED: O. Reg. 76/06, s. 4(3).]

(6) **FORMAL REQUIREMENTS OF CONTINUING RECORD** — In preparing and maintaining a continuing record and support enforcement continuing record under this rule, the parties shall meet the requirements set out in the document entitled "Formal Requirements of the Continuing Record under the Family Law Rules", dated October 21, 2013, published by the Family Rules Committee and available on the Internet through www.ontariocourtforms.on.ca.

(6.1) **FORMAL REQUIREMENTS OF CHILD PROTECTION CONTINUING RECORD** — In preparing and maintaining a child protection continuing record under this rule, the parties shall meet the requirements set out in the document entitled "Formal Requirements of the Child Protection Continuing Record under the Family Law Rules", dated November 1, 2005, published by the Family Rules Committee and available on the Internet through www.ontariocourtforms.on.ca.

(7) **SEPARATION OF SINGLE RECORD** — Instead of the single continuing record mentioned in subrule (1), the continuing record may be separated into separate records for the applicant and the respondent, in accordance with the following:

1.   In a case other than a child protection case, the court may order separate records on its own initiative or at the request of either party on motion or at a case conference, settlement conference or trial management conference.

2.   [REVOKED: O. Reg. 519/06, s. 3(3).]

3.   If the court orders separate records and there is more than one applicant and respondent, the court may order separate records for each applicant and respondent.

4.   If the record consists of separate records, the separate records are called the applicant's record and the respondent's record.

(8) **COMBINING SEPARATED RECORDS** — If the continuing record has been separated, the court may order the records to be combined into a single record on its own initiative or at the request of either party at a case conference, settlement conference or trial management conference.

(9) **COMBINING SEPARATED RECORDS ON CONSENT** — If the continuing record has been separated, the parties may, if they agree, combine the separate records into a single continuing record, in which case the parties shall arrange together for the combining of the records.

(10) BY WHOM RECORD IS SEPARATED OR COMBINED — If the court orders that the continuing record,

(a)   be separated or combined on its own initiative, the court shall give directions as to which party shall separate or combine the record, as the case requires;

(b)   be separated or combined at the request of a party at a case conference, settlement conference or trial management conference, the party that makes the request shall separate or combine the record, as the case requires, unless the court orders otherwise.

(11) MAINTAINING CONTINUING RECORD — The parties are responsible, under the clerk's supervision, for adding to a continuing record that has not been separated all documents filed in the case and, in the case of separated records, each party is responsible, under the clerk's supervision, for adding the documents the party files to the party's own record.

(12) DUTIES OF PARTY SERVING DOCUMENTS — A party serving documents shall,

(a)   if the continuing record has not been separated,

    (i)   serve and file any documents that are not already in the continuing record, and

    (ii)   serve with the documents an updated cumulative table of contents listing the documents being filed; and

(b)   if the continuing record has been separated,

    (i)   serve and file any documents that are not already in the party's separate record, and

    (ii)   serve with the documents an updated cumulative table of contents listing the documents being filed in the party's separate record.

(13) NO SERVICE OR FILING OF DOCUMENTS ALREADY IN RECORD — A party shall not serve or file any document that is already in the record, despite any requirement in these rules that the document be served and filed.

(14) [REVOKED: O. Reg. 519/06, s. 3(4).]

(15) DOCUMENTS REFERRED TO BY TAB IN RECORD — A party who is relying on a document in the record shall refer to it by its tab in the record, except in a support enforcement continuing record.

(16) DOCUMENTS NOT TO BE REMOVED FROM RECORD — No document shall be removed from the continuing record except by order.

(17) WRITTEN REASONS FOR ORDER — If the court gives written reasons for making an order,

(a)   they may be endorsed by hand on an endorsement sheet, or the endorsement may be a short note on the endorsement sheet saying that written reasons are being given separately;

(b)   the clerk shall add a copy of the reasons to the endorsements section of the record; and

(c)   the clerk shall send a copy to the parties by mail, fax or email.

(18) [REVOKED: O. Reg. 519/06, s. 3(5).]

(19) APPEAL — If a final order is appealed, only the notice of appeal and any order of the appeal court (and no other appeal document) shall be added to the record.

(20) TRANSFER OF RECORD IF CASE TRANSFERRED — If the court transfers a case to another municipality the clerk shall, on request, transfer the record to the clerk at the court office in the other municipality, and the record shall be used there as if the case had started in the other municipality.

(21) CONFIRMATION OF SUPPORT ORDER — When a provisional support order or a provisional change to a support order is sent to a court in Ontario for confirmation,

(a)   if the provisional order or change was made in Ontario, the clerk shall send the continuing record to the court office where the confirmation is to take place and the respondent shall update it as this rule requires; and

(b)   if the provisional order or change was not made in Ontario, the clerk shall prepare the continuing record and the respondent shall update it as this rule requires.

(22) CASES STARTED BEFORE JANUARY 1, 2007 — Despite this rule, if a case was started before January 1, 2007, the version of this rule that applied to the case on December 31, 2006 as its application may have been modified by the court continues, subject to subrule (23), to apply to the case unless the court orders otherwise.

(23) EXCEPTION, CASES STARTED BEFORE JANUARY 1, 2007 — If a motion to change a final order is made on or after January 1, 2007 in respect of a case started before that date, this rule shall apply to the motion and to all documents filed afterwards.

(24) [REVOKED: O. Reg. 519/06, s. 3(6).]

[O. Reg. 89/04, s. 4; O. Reg. 76/06, s. 4; O. Reg. 519/06, s. 3; O. Reg. 322/13, s. 5; O. Reg. 140/15, s. 4.]

Rule 10 — Answering a Case

10. SERVING AND FILING ANSWER — (1) A person against whom an application is made shall serve an answer (Form 10, 33B, 33B.1 or 33B.2) on every other party and file it within 30 days after being served with the application.

(2) TIME FOR ANSWER — APPLICATION SERVED OUTSIDE CANADA OR U.S.A. — If an application is served outside Canada or the United States of America, the time for serving and filing an answer is 60 days.

(2.1) EXCEPTION — PLACEMENT FOR ADOPTION — In an application to dispense with a parent's consent before adoption placement, (Form 8D.1), the time for serving

125

the answer is,

  (a)   **20 days, if the application is served in Canada or the United States of America;**

  (b)   **40 days, if the application is served outside Canada or the United States of America.**

  (3) **ANSWER MAY INCLUDE CLAIM** — A respondent may include in the answer,

  (a)   a claim against the applicant;

  (b)   a claim against any other person, who then also becomes a respondent in the case.

  (4) **ANSWER BY ADDED RESPONDENT** — Subrules (1) to (3) apply to a respondent added under subrule (3), except that the time for serving and filing an answer is 14 days after service on the added respondent, or 30 days if the added respondent is served outside Canada or the United States of America.

  (4.1) **CLAIM FOR CUSTODY OR ACCESS** — An answer that includes a claim for custody of or access to a child shall be accompanied by the applicable documents referred to in Rule 35.1.

  (5) **NO ANSWER** — The consequences set out in paragraphs 1 to 4 of subrule 1 (8.4) apply, with necessary changes, if a respondent does not serve and file an answer.

  (6) **REPLY** — A party may, within 10 days after being served with an answer, serve and file a reply (Form 10A) in response to a claim made in the answer.

[O. Reg. 337/02, s. 2; O. Reg. 91/03, s. 2; O. Reg. 519/06, s. 4; O. Reg. 6/10, s. 3; O. Reg. 322/13, s. 6; O. Reg. 142/14, s. 5; O. Reg. 535/18, s. 3(F).]

Rule 11 — Amending an Application, Answer or Reply

11. AMENDING APPLICATION WITHOUT COURT'S PERMISSION — (1) An applicant may amend the application without the court's permission as follows:

  1.   If no answer has been filed, by serving and filing an amended application in the manner set out in rule 8 (starting a case).

  2.   If an answer has been filed, by serving and filing an amended application in the manner set out in rule 8 and also filing the consent of all parties to the amendment.

  (2) **AMENDING ANSWER WITHOUT COURT'S PERMISSION** — A respondent may amend the answer without the court's permission as follows:

  1.   If the application has been amended, by serving and filing an amended answer within 14 days after being served with the amended application.

  2.   If the application has not been amended, by serving and filing an amended answer and also filing the consent of all parties to the amendment.

  (2.1) **CHILD PROTECTION, AMENDMENTS WITHOUT COURT'S PERMISSION** — In a child protection case, if a significant change relating to the child happens after the original document is filed,

126

(a)   the applicant may serve and file an amended application, an amended plan of care or both; and

(b)   the respondent may serve and file an amended answer and plan of care.

(3) AMENDING APPLICATION OR ANSWER WITH COURT'S PERMISSION — On motion, the court shall give permission to a party to amend an application, answer or reply, unless the amendment would disadvantage another party in a way for which costs or an adjournment could not compensate.

(3.1) CLAIM FOR CUSTODY OR ACCESS — If an application or answer is amended to include a claim for custody of or access to a child that was not in the original application or answer, the amended application or amended answer shall be accompanied by the applicable documents referred to in rule 35.1.

(4) HOW AMENDMENT IS SHOWN — An amendment shall be clearly shown by underlining all changes, and the rule or order permitting the amendment and the date of the amendment shall be noted in the margin of each amended page.

[O. Reg. 91/03, s. 3; O. Reg. 6/10, s. 4.]

Rule 12 — Withdrawing, Combining or Splitting Cases

12. WITHDRAWING APPLICATION, ANSWER OR REPLY — **(1)** A party who does not want to continue with all or part of a case may withdraw all or part of the application, answer or reply by serving a notice of withdrawal (Form 12) on every other party and filing it.

(2) WITHDRAWAL — SPECIAL PARTY OR CHILD PARTY — The application, answer or reply of a special party or a child party may be withdrawn (whether in whole or in part) only with the court's permission, and the notice of motion for permission shall be served on every other party and on,

(a)   the Public Guardian and Trustee, in the case of a special party; or

(b)   the Children's Lawyer, in the case of a child party.

(3) COSTS PAYABLE ON WITHDRAWAL — A party who withdraws all or part of an application, answer or reply shall pay the costs of every other party in relation to the withdrawn application, answer, reply or part, up to the date of the withdrawal, unless the court orders or the parties agree otherwise.

(4) COSTS ON WITHDRAWAL BY GOVERNMENT AGENCY — Despite subrule (3), if the party is a government agency, costs are in the court's discretion.

(5) COMBINING AND SPLITTING CASES — If it would be more convenient to hear two or more cases, claims or issues together or to split a case into two or more separate cases, claims or issues, the court may, on motion, order accordingly.

(6) SPLITTING DIVORCE FROM OTHER ISSUES — The court may, on motion, make an order splitting a divorce from the other issues in a case if,

(a)   neither spouse will be disadvantaged by the order; and

   (b)   reasonable arrangements have been made for the support of any children of the marriage.

[O. Reg. 250/19, s. 4.]

Rule 13 — Financial Disclosure

13. FINANCIAL STATEMENT WITH APPLICATION, ANSWER OR MOTION — (1) If an application, answer or motion contains a claim for support, a property claim, or a claim for exclusive possession of the matrimonial home and its contents,

   (a)   the party making the claim shall serve and file a financial statement (Form 13 or 13.1) with the document that contains the claim; and

   (b)   the party against whom the claim is made shall serve and file a financial statement within the time for serving and filing an answer, reply or affidavit or other document responding to the motion, whether the party is serving an answer, reply or affidavit or other document responding to the motion or not.

  (1.1) FORM 13 FOR SUPPORT CLAIM WITHOUT PROPERTY CLAIM — If the application, answer or motion contains a claim for support but does not contain a property claim or a claim for exclusive possession of the matrimonial home and its contents, the financial statement used by the parties under these rules shall be in Form 13.

  (1.2) FORM 13.1 FOR PROPERTY CLAIM WITH OR WITHOUT SUPPORT CLAIM — If the application, answer or motion contains a property claim or a claim for exclusive possession of the matrimonial home and its contents, the financial statement used by the parties under these rules shall be in Form 13.1, whether a claim for support is also included or not.

  (1.3) EXCEPTION, CERTAIN SUPPORT CLAIMS — If the only claim for support contained in the application, answer or motion is a claim for child support in the amount specified in the table of the applicable child support guidelines, the party making the claim is not required to file a financial statement, unless the application, answer or motion also contains a property claim or a claim for exclusive possession of the matrimonial home and its contents.

  (1.4) EXCEPTION, FAMILY ARBITRATION CLAIM — If the only claim contained in the application, answer or motion is a claim under the *Arbitration Act, 1991* or the *Family Law Act* relating to a family arbitration, family arbitration agreement or family arbitration award, the party making the claim is not required to file a financial statement, unless the court orders otherwise.

  (2) CLAIM FOR PAYMENT ORDER UNDER CYFSA — If an application, answer or notice of motion contains a claim for a payment order under section 108 of the *Child, Youth and Family Services Act, 2017*, clause (1) (a) does not apply to the children's aid society but clause (1) (b) applies to the party against whom the claim is made.

  (3) FINANCIAL STATEMENTS IN CUSTODY AND ACCESS CASES — If an application, answer or motion contains a claim for custody of or access to a child and this rule does not otherwise require the parties to serve and file financial statements, the court may order each party to serve and file a financial statement in Form 13 within the time decided

by the court.

(3.1) ADDITIONAL REQUIRED FINANCIAL DISCLOSURE, SUPPORT CLAIM — A party who is required under subrules (1) to (3) to serve and file a financial statement in relation to a claim for support shall, before the deadline set out in subrule (3.2), serve with the financial statement the following information, unless the court orders otherwise:

1. The income and financial information referred to in subsection 21 (1) of the child support guidelines.

2. If the party became unemployed within the last three years,

    i.   a complete copy of the party's Record of Employment, or other evidence of termination, and

    ii. a statement of any benefits or income that the party is still entitled to receive from his or her former employer despite or as a result of the termination.

3. In the case of a claim for the support of a child, proof of the amount of any special or extraordinary expenses, within the meaning of section 7 of the child support guidelines.

(3.2) TIMING OF REQUIREMENT — The party shall serve the information referred to in subrule (3.1),

(a) with the financial statement, if the application, answer or motion contains a claim for support but does not contain a property claim; or

(b) with the documents required to be served under subrule (3.3) or (3.4), as the case may be, if the application, answer or motion contains a property claim.

(3.3) ADDITIONAL REQUIRED FINANCIAL DISCLOSURE, CLAIM UNDER PART I OF THE *FAMILY LAW ACT* — A party who is required under subrules (1) to (3) to serve and file a financial statement in relation to a claim under Part I of the *Family Law Act* shall, no later than 30 days after the day by which the financial statement is required to be served, serve on the other party the following information, unless the court orders otherwise:

1. The statement issued closest to the valuation date for each bank account or other account in a financial institution, pension, registered retirement or other savings plan, and any other savings or investments in which the party had an interest on that date.

2. A copy of an application or request made by the party to obtain a valuation of his or her own pension benefits, deferred pension or pension, as the case may be, if any, as of the valuation date.

3. A copy of the Municipal Property Assessment Corporation's assessment of any real property in Ontario in which the party had a right or interest on the valuation date, for the year in which that date occurred.

4. If the party owned a life insurance policy on the valuation date, the statement is-

sued closest to that date showing the face amount and cash surrender value, if any, of the policy, and the named beneficiary.

5. If the party had an interest in a sole proprietorship or was self-employed on the valuation date, for each of the three years preceding that date,

   i. the financial statements of the party's business or professional practice, other than a partnership, and

   ii. a copy of every personal income tax return filed by the party, including any materials that were filed with the return.

6. If the party was a partner in a partnership on the valuation date, a copy of the partnership agreement and, for each of the three years preceding the valuation date,

   i. a copy of every personal income tax return filed by the party, including any materials that were filed with the return, and

   ii. the financial statements of the partnership.

7. If the party had an interest in a corporation on the valuation date, documentation showing the number and types of shares of the corporation and any other interests in the corporation that were owned by the party on that date.

8. If the corporation in which a party had an interest was privately held, for each of the three years preceding the valuation date,

   i. the financial statements for the corporation and its subsidiaries, and

   ii. if the interest was a majority interest, a copy of every income tax return filed by the corporation.

9. If the party was a beneficiary under a trust on the valuation date, a copy of the trust settlement agreement and the trust's financial statements for each of the three years preceding that date.

10. Documentation showing the value, on the valuation date, of any property not referred to in paragraphs 1 to 9 in which the party had an interest on that date.

11. Documentation that supports a claim, if any, for an exclusion under subsection 4 (2) of the *Family Law Act*.

12. The statements or invoices issued closest to the valuation date in relation to any mortgage, line of credit, credit card balance or other debt owed by the party on that date.

13. Any available documentation showing the value, on the date of marriage, of property that the party owned or in which he or she had an interest on that date, and the amount of any debts owed by the party on that date.

(3.4) **ADDITIONAL REQUIRED FINANCIAL DISCLOSURE, OTHER PROPERTY CLAIMS** — A party who is required under subrules (1) to (3) to serve and file a financial statement in relation to a property claim other than a claim under Part I of the *Family Law*

Act shall, no later than 30 days after the day by which the financial statement is required to be served, serve on the other party any information necessary to support the claim, unless the court orders otherwise.

(4) FINANCIAL STATEMENT WITH MOTION TO CHANGE TEMPORARY SUPPORT ORDER — Subject to subrule (1.3), the following rules respecting financial statements apply if a motion contains a request for a change in a temporary support order:

1. The party making the motion shall serve and file a financial statement (Form 13 or 13.1) with the notice of motion.

2. The party responding to the motion shall serve and file a financial statement as soon as possible after being served with the notice of motion, but in any event no later than two days before the motion date. Any affidavit in response to the motion shall be served and filed at the same time as the financial statement.

(4.1) EXCEPTION — BY CONSENT — Parties to a consent motion to change a temporary support order do not need to serve and file financial statements if they file a consent agreeing not to serve and file them.

(4.2) FINANCIAL STATEMENT WITH MOTION TO CHANGE FINAL SUPPORT ORDER OR SUPPORT AGREEMENT — Subject to subrule (1.3), the following rules respecting financial statements apply if a motion is made under rule 15 requesting a change to a final support order or a support agreement:

1. The party making the motion shall serve and file a financial statement (Form 13 or 13.1) with the motion to change (Form 15).

2. The party responding to the motion shall serve and file a financial statement within the time for serving and filing the response to motion to change (Form 15B) or returning the consent motion to change (Form 15C) to the party making the motion, as set out in subrule 15 (10). Any response to motion to change (Form 15B) shall be served and filed at the same time as the financial statement.

3. Parties who bring the motion by filing a consent motion to change (Form 15C) shall each file a financial statement with the form, unless they indicate in the form that they agree not to do so.

4. Parties who bring the motion by filing a consent motion to change child support (Form 15D) do not need to serve or file financial statements.

(4.3) FINANCIAL STATEMENT REQUIRED BY RESPONSE — Subrules (4) and (4.1), or subrule (4.2), as the case may be, apply with necessary changes if a party makes a motion to change an order or agreement for which the party is not required by this rule to file a financial statement, and the party responding to the motion requests a change to a support order or support agreement.

(5) NO FINANCIAL STATEMENT FROM ASSIGNEE — The assignee of a support order is not required to serve and file a financial statement under subrule (4) or (4.2).

(5.0.1) ADDITIONAL REQUIRED FINANCIAL DISCLOSURE, MOTION TO CHANGE SUPPORT — A party who is required under subrules (4) to (4.3) to serve and file a financial statement shall serve with the financial statement the following information, unless the court orders otherwise:

1.   The documents referred to in subrule (3.1).

2.   A current statement of arrears from the Family Responsibility Office.

3.   One of the following for each year for which the party is seeking to change or cancel arrears, as proof of the party's income:

      i.   The party's income tax return and,

            A.   the party's notice of assessment and, if any, notice of reassessment, or

            B.   if a notice of assessment and a notice of reassessment are unavailable for the year, a copy of the Income and Deductions printout provided by the Canada Revenue Agency for the party.

      ii.   If the party is not required to and has chosen not to file an income tax return because of the *Indian Act* (Canada), some other proof of income.

(5.0.2) **REQUIREMENT TO CERTIFY FINANCIAL DISCLOSURE** — A party who is required to serve documents under subrule (3.1), (3.3), (3.4) or (5.0.1) shall confirm service by,

(a)   serving a certificate of financial disclosure (Form 13A) together with the documents; and

(b)   filing the certificate no later than,

      (i)   seven days before a case conference, in the case of the applicant or the party making the motion, as the case may be, and

      (ii)   four days before the case conference, in the case of the other party.

(5.1) **FINANCIAL STATEMENT WITH MOTION TO REFRAIN** — A payor who makes a motion to require the Director of the Family Responsibility Office to refrain from suspending the payor's driver's licence shall, in accordance with subsection 35 (7) of the *Family Responsibility and Support Arrears Enforcement Act, 1996*, serve and file with the notice of motion,

(a)   a financial statement (Form 13 or 13.1) or a financial statement incorporated as Form 4 in Ontario Regulation 167/97 (General) made under that Act; and

(b)   the proof of income specified in section 15 of the regulation referred to in clause (a).

(6) [REVOKED: O. Reg. 69/15, s. 3(6).]

(7) **REQUIREMENTS FOR FILING** — The clerk shall not accept the financial statement of a party making or responding to a claim for support unless the following are attached to the form:

1.   Proof of the party's current income.

2.   One of the following, as proof of the party's income for the three previous years:

    i.   For each of the three previous taxation years,

        A.   the party's notice of assessment and, if any, notice of reassessment, or

        B.   if a notice of assessment and a notice of reassessment are unavailable for a taxation year, a copy of the Income and Deductions printout provided by the Canada Revenue Agency for the party for the taxation year.

    ii.   If the party swears or affirms a statement in the form that he or she is not required to and has chosen not to file an income tax return because of the *Indian Act (Canada)*, some other proof of income for the three previous years.

(7.0.1) EXCEPTION — Subrule (7) does not apply to a financial statement filed under subrule (5.1).

(7.1) DOCUMENTS THAT ARE NOT REQUIRED TO BE FILED — The following documents are not required to be filed in the continuing record unless the court orders otherwise:

1.   Income tax returns, except in the case of a filing under subrule (5.1).

2.   Any other document referred to in subrule (3.1), (3.3), (3.4) or (5.0.1), unless these rules provide otherwise.

(8) NO FINANCIAL DISCLOSURE BY CONSENT — SPOUSAL SUPPORT IN DIVORCE — Parties to a claim for spousal support under the *Divorce Act* (Canada) do not need to serve and file financial statements or provide additional financial disclosure under this rule if they file a consent,

(a)   agreeing to not serve and file financial statements or provide additional financial disclosure under this rule; or

(b)   agreeing to a specified amount of support, or to no support.

(9)   [REVOKED: O. Reg. 151/08, s. 2(8).]

(10) DOCUMENTS NOT TO BE FILED WITHOUT FINANCIAL STATEMENT — The clerk shall not accept a document for filing without a financial statement if these rules require the document to be filed with a financial statement.

(11) INSUFFICIENT FINANCIAL INFORMATION — If a party believes that the financial disclosure provided by another party under this rule, whether in a financial statement or otherwise, does not provide enough information for a full understanding of the other party's financial circumstances,

(a)   the party shall ask the other party to give the necessary additional information; and

(b) if the other party does not give it within seven days, the court may, on motion, order the other party to give the information or to serve and file a new financial statement.

(11.1) SAME — For greater certainty, a motion form (Form 14B) may be used if making a motion for an order under subrule (3.1), (3.3), (3.4) or (5.0.1) or an order under clause (11) (b).

(12) UPDATING FINANCIAL STATEMENT — Before any case conference, motion, settlement conference or trial, each party shall update the information in any financial statement that is more than 30 days old by serving and filing,

(a) a new financial statement; or

(b) an affidavit saying that the information in the last statement has not changed and is still true.

(12.1) MINOR CHANGES — If there have been minor changes but no major changes to the information in a party's past statement, the party may serve and file, instead of a new financial statement, an affidavit with details of the changes.

(12.2) TIME FOR UPDATING — The material described in subrules (12) and (12.1) shall be served and filed as follows:

1. For a case conference or settlement conference requested by a party, the requesting party shall serve and file at least seven days before the conference date and the other party shall serve and file at least four days before that date.

2. For a case conference or settlement conference that is not requested by a party, the applicant shall serve and file at least seven days before the conference date and the respondent shall serve and file at least four days before that date.

3. For a motion, the party making the motion shall serve and file at least seven days before the motion date and the other party shall serve and file at least four days before that date.

4. For a trial, the applicant shall serve and file at least seven days before the trial date and the respondent shall serve and file at least four days before that date.

(13) QUESTIONING ON FINANCIAL STATEMENT — A party may be questioned under rule 20 on a financial statement provided under this rule, but only after a request for information has been made under clause (11) (a).

(13.1) UPDATING CERTIFICATE OF FINANCIAL DISCLOSURE — Before any settlement conference or trial management conference, a party who has served a corrected, updated or new version of a document referred to in subrule (3.1), (3.3), (3.4) or (5.0.1) in accordance with subrule (15), or additional documents in accordance with subrule (16), shall serve and file an updated certificate of financial disclosure (Form 13A), no later than,

(a) seven days before the conference, in the case of the party requesting the conference or, if the conference is not requested by a party, the applicant or the party making the motion, as the case may be; and

(b)   four days before the conference, in the case of the other party.

(14) NET FAMILY PROPERTY STATEMENT — Each party to a property claim under Part I of the *Family Law Act* shall serve and file a net family property statement (Form 13B) or, if the party has already served a net family property statement, an affidavit saying that the information in that statement has not changed and is still true,

(a)   not less than 30 days before a settlement conference; and

(b)   not more than 30 days and not less than seven days before a trial.

(14.1) EXCEPTION, FAMILY ARBITRATION CLAIM — Subrule (14) does not apply if the property claim arises within a claim under the *Arbitration Act, 1991* or the *Family Law Act* relating to a family arbitration, family arbitration agreement or family arbitration award.

(14.2) COMPARISON OF NET FAMILY PROPERTIES, JOINT — Parties who have served and filed net family property statements in accordance with subrule (14) shall file a joint comparison of net family property statements (Form 13C) no later than seven days before a settlement conference, subject to subrule (14.3).

(14.3) COMPARISON OF NET FAMILY PROPERTIES, SEPARATE — If the parties fail to agree on a joint comparison of net family properties, each party shall serve and file his or her own comparison of net family property statements (Form 13C) no later than,

(a)   seven days before a settlement conference, in the case of the party requesting the conference or, if the settlement conference is not requested by a party, the applicant or the party making the motion, as the case may be; and

(b)   four days before the settlement conference, in the case of the other party.

(15) DUTY TO CORRECT, UPDATE DOCUMENTS — As soon as a party discovers that a document that he or she has served under this rule is incorrect, incomplete or out of date, the party shall serve on the other party and, if applicable, file, a corrected, updated or new document, as the circumstances require.

(16) DUTY TO ADDRESS OMISSIONS IN FINANCIAL DISCLOSURE — As soon as a party discovers that he or she failed to serve a document required to be served under subrule (3.1), (3.3), (3.4) or (5.0.1), the party shall serve the document on the other party.

(17) ORDER, IF DOCUMENT NOT PROVIDED — If a party has not served or filed a document in accordance with the requirements of this rule or an Act or regulation, the court may on motion order the party to serve or file the document and, if the court makes that order, it shall also order the party to pay costs.

(18) OTHER OBLIGATIONS CONTINUE TO APPLY — The duty to provide information under this rule does not affect any other duty set out in any other Act or regulation for the party to provide information to the other party in relation to a claim to which this rule applies.

[O. Reg. 202/01, s. 3; O. Reg. 92/03, s. 1; O. Reg. 76/06, s. 5; O. Reg. 151/08, s. 2; O. Reg. 52/10, s. 1; O. Reg. 388/12, s. 5; O. Reg. 142/14, s. 6; O. Reg. 69/15, s. 3; O. Reg. 298/18, s. 9.]

Rule 14 — Motions for Temporary Orders

14. WHEN TO MAKE MOTION — (1) A person who wants any of the following may make a motion:

1. A temporary order for a claim made in an application.

2. Directions on how to carry on the case.

3. A change in a temporary order.

(2) WHO MAY MAKE MOTION — A motion may be made by a party to the case or by a person with an interest in the case.

(3) PARTIES TO MOTION — A person who is affected by a motion is also a party, for purposes of the motion only, but this does not apply to a child affected by a motion relating to custody, access, child protection, adoption or child support.

(4) NO MOTION BEFORE CASE CONFERENCE ON SUBSTANTIVE ISSUES COMPLETED — No notice of motion or supporting evidence may be served and no motion may be heard before a conference dealing with the substantive issues in the case has been completed.

(4.1) [REVOKED: O. Reg. 89/04, s. 6(3).]

(4.2) URGENCY, HARDSHIP ETC. — Subrule (4) does not apply if the court is of the opinion that there is a situation of urgency or hardship or that a case conference is not required for some other reason in the interest of justice.

(5) [REVOKED: O. Reg. 89/04, s. 6(5).]

(6) OTHER MOTIONS — Subrule (4) does not apply to a motion,

(a) to change a temporary order under subrule 25 (19) (fraud, mistake, lack of notice);

(b) for a contempt order under rule 31 or an order striking out a document under subrule (22);

(c) for summary judgment under rule 16;

(d) to require the Director of the Family Responsibility Office to refrain from suspending a licence;

(e) to limit or stay a support order, the enforcement of arrears under a support order, or an alternative payment order under the *Family Responsibility and Support Arrears Enforcement Act, 1996*; (e.1) in a child protection case;

(e.2) made without notice, made on consent, that is unopposed or that is limited to procedural, uncomplicated or unopposed matters (Form 14B);

(e.3) made in an appeal;

(f) for an oral hearing under subrule 32.1 (10), 37 (8) or 37.1 (8); or

(g)   to set aside the registration of an interjurisdictional support order made outside Canada.

(7) MOTION INVOLVING COMPLICATED MATTERS — The judge who hears a motion involving complicated matters may,

(a)   order that the motion or any part of it be heard as a trial; and

(b)   give any directions that are necessary.

(8) MOTION BY TELEPHONE OR VIDEO CONFERENCE — A party who wants a motion to be heard by telephone or video conference shall,

(a)   obtain an appointment from the clerk for the hearing of the motion;

(b)   make the necessary arrangements;

(c)   serve a notice of the appointment and arrangements on all other parties, and file it; and

(d)   participate in the motion as the notice specifies.

(9) DOCUMENTS FOR A MOTION — A motion, whether made with or without notice,

(a)   requires a notice of motion (Form 14) and an affidavit (Form 14A); and

(b)   may be supported by additional evidence.

(10) PROCEDURAL, UNCOMPLICATED OR UNOPPOSED MATTERS — MOTION FORM — If a motion is limited to procedural, uncomplicated or unopposed matters, the party making the motion may use a motion form (Form 14B) instead of a notice of motion and affidavit.

(10.1) [REVOKED: O. Reg. 298/18, s. 10(1).]

(10.2) [REVOKED: O. Reg. 298/18, s. 10(1).]

(11) MOTION WITH NOTICE — A party making a motion with notice shall,

(a)   serve the documents mentioned in subrule (9) or (10) on all other parties, not later than four days before the motion date;

(b)   file the documents as soon as possible after service, but not later than two days before the motion date;

(c)   file a confirmation (Form 14C) not later than 2 p.m. two days before the motion date;

(d)   before giving the clerk confirmation of the motion in Form 14C under clause (e), give a copy of the confirmation of motion to every other party using mail, fax, email or any other method, except in a child protection case: and

(e)   not later than 2 p.m. three days before the motion date, give the clerk the confirmation of motion (Form 14C) by,

    (i)   delivering it to the court office, or

    (ii)   if available in the court office, sending it by fax or by email.

(11.1) EFFECT OF FAILURE TO CONFIRM — Unless the court orders otherwise, a motion shall not be heard if confirmation of the motion is not given to the clerk in accordance with clause (11) (e).

(11.2) PARTY TO UPDATE CONFIRMATION — If a party who has given a confirmation of motion determines at any time before the motion is heard that the confirmation is no longer correct, the party shall, if possible, immediately,

    (a)   give a copy of the corrected confirmation of motion in Form 14C to every other party using a method listed in clause (11) (d) and subsequently give the clerk the corrected confirmation of motion by a method listed in clause (11) (e); or

    (b)   in a child protection case, give the clerk a corrected confirmation of motion in Form 14C by a method listed in clause (11) (e).

(11.3) RESPONSE TO NOTICE TO MOTION — A response by a person to a motion made using a notice of motion (Form 14) shall be served and filed not later than four days before the motion date.

(11.4) RESPONSE TO MOTION FORM — A response by a person to a motion made using a motion form (Form 14B) shall be served and filed not later than four days after the motion form is served on the person.

(11.5) REPLY TO RESPONSE PERMITTED, NOTICE OF MOTION — A party who uses a notice of motion (Form 14) and who is served with a response to it may serve and file a reply not later than 2 p.m. three days before the motion date.

(11.6) REPLY TO RESPONSE NOT PERMITTED, MOTION FORM — A party who uses a motion form (Form 14B) and who is served with a response to it may not serve or file a reply.

(12) MOTION WITHOUT NOTICE — A motion may be made without notice if,

    (a)   the nature or circumstances of the motion make notice unnecessary or not reasonably possible;

    (b)   there is an immediate danger of a child's removal from Ontario, and the delay involved in serving a notice of motion would probably have serious consequences;

    (c)   there is an immediate danger to the health or safety of a child or of the party making the motion, and the delay involved in serving a notice of motion would probably have serious consequences; or

    (d)   service of a notice of motion would probably have serious consequences.

(13) FILING FOR MOTION WITHOUT NOTICE — The documents for use on a motion without notice shall be filed on or before the motion date, unless the court orders otherwise.

(14) ORDER MADE ON MOTION WITHOUT NOTICE — An order made on motion without notice (Form 14D) shall require the matter to come back to the court and, if possible, to the same judge, within 14 days or on a date chosen by the court.

(15) SERVICE OF ORDER MADE WITHOUT NOTICE — An order made on motion without notice shall be served immediately on all parties affected, together with all documents used on the motion, unless the court orders otherwise.

(16) WITHDRAWING A MOTION — A party making a motion may withdraw it in the same way as an application or answer is withdrawn under rule 12.

(17) EVIDENCE ON A MOTION — Evidence on a motion may be given by any one or more of the following methods:

1.   An affidavit or other admissible evidence in writing.

2.   A transcript of the questions and answers on a questioning under rule 20.

3.   With the court's permission, oral evidence.

(18) AFFIDAVIT BASED ON PERSONAL KNOWLEDGE — An affidavit for use on a motion shall, as much as possible, contain only information within the personal knowledge of the person signing the affidavit.

(19) AFFIDAVIT BASED ON OTHER INFORMATION — The affidavit may also contain information that the person learned from someone else, but only if,

(a)   the source of the information is identified by name and the affidavit states that the person signing it believes the information is true; and

(b)   in addition, if the motion is a contempt motion under rule 31, the information is not likely to be disputed.

(20) RESTRICTIONS ON EVIDENCE — The following restrictions apply to evidence for use on a motion, unless the court orders otherwise:

1.   The party making the motion shall serve all the evidence in support of the motion with the notice of motion.

2.   The party responding to the motion shall then serve all the evidence in response.

3.   The party making the motion may then serve evidence replying to any new matters raised by the evidence served by the party responding to the motion.

4.   No other evidence may be used.

(21) NO MOTIONS WITHOUT COURT'S PERMISSION — If a party tries to delay the case or add to its costs or in any other way to abuse the court's process by making numerous motions without merit, the court may order the party not to make any other motions in the case without the court's permission.

(22)-(23) [REVOKED: O. Reg. 322/13, s. 8(2).]

(24) MOTION RELATING TO FAMILY ARBITRATION — A party who wishes to make a claim under the *Arbitration Act, 1991* or the *Family Law Act* relating to a family arbitration, family arbitration agreement or family arbitration award that must or may be commenced by way of a motion may do so under this rule, even if the order being sought is a final order and, for the purpose, this rule applies with the following and any other necessary changes:

1. In addition to the documents referred to in subrule (9) or (10), the motion also requires,

    i.   copies of the certificates of independent legal advice required by the *Family Law Act* for the parties,

    ii. a copy of the family arbitration agreement, and

    iii. if an award has been made, the original award or a certified copy.

2. The documents referred to in subparagraphs 1 i, ii and iii shall be served and filed in accordance with subrule (11).

3. In the case of a motion to enforce a family arbitration award under section 59.8 of the *Family Law Act*, subrules (12) to (15) do not apply.

[O. Reg. 544/99, s. 6; O. Reg. 202/01, s. 4; O. Reg. 56/03, s. 2; O. Reg. 91/03, s. 4; O. Reg. 89/04, s. 6; O. Reg. 151/08, s. 3; O. Reg. 383/11, s. 3; O. Reg. 388/12, s. 6; O. Reg. 322/13, s. 8; O. Reg. 142/14, s. 7; O. Reg. 298/18, s. 10.]

Rule 15 — Motions to Change a Final Order or Agreement

15. (1) DEFINITION — In this rule,

"assignee" means an agency or person to whom a support order or agreement that is the subject of a motion under this rule is assigned under the *Family Law Act* or the *Divorce Act* (Canada).

(2) APPLICATION — Subject to subrule (3), this rule only applies to a motion to change,

(a) a final order; or

(b) an agreement for support filed under section 35 of the *Family Law Act*.

(2.1) SAME, NOTICE OF RECALCULATION — Subrule (2) applies regardless of whether a child support obligation set out in the order or agreement has been recalculated under section 39.1 of the *Family Law Act*.

(3) EXCEPTION — This rule does not apply to a motion or application to change an order made under the *Child, Youth and Family Services Act, 2017*, other than a final order made under section 39.1 of that Act.

(4) PLACE OF MOTION — Rule 5 (where a case starts) applies to a motion to change a final order or agreement as if the motion were a new case.

(5) MOTION TO CHANGE — Subject to subrules (17) and (18), a party who wants to ask the court to change a final order or agreement shall serve and file,

(a) a motion to change (Form 15); and

(b)   a change information form (Form 15A), with all required attachments.

(5.1) CLAIM FOR CUSTODY OR ACCESS — If the motion includes a claim for custody of or access to a child, the documents referred to in subrule (5) shall be accompanied by the applicable documents referred to in Rule 35.1.

(6) SERVICE TO INCLUDE BLANK FORMS — The party making the motion shall serve on the other party a blank response to motion to change (Form 15B) and a blank consent motion to change (Form 15C) together with the documents referred to in subrule (5).

(7) SPECIAL SERVICE — The documents referred to in subrules (5), (5.1) and (6) shall be served by special service (subrule 6 (3)), and not by regular service.

(8) EXCEPTION — Despite subrule (7), service on the persons mentioned in subrule 8 (6) (officials, agencies, etc.) may be made by regular service.

(8.1) SERVICE ON FAMILY RESPONSIBILITY OFFICE REQUIRED — The documents referred to in subrule (5) shall be served on the Director of the Family Responsibility Office if the motion to change includes a request to change a child support obligation that,

(a)   is set out in an order made under the *Divorce Act* (Canada); and

(b)   was recalculated under section 39.1 of the *Family Law Act* within the 35-day period before the motion is filed.

(9) RESPONSE OR CONSENT TO MOTION — The following rules apply to a party who is served with a motion to change a final order or agreement:

1.   If the party does not agree to the change or if the party wants to ask the court to make an additional or a different change to the final order or agreement, the party shall serve and file a response to motion to change (Form 15B), with all required attachments, within the time set out in clause (10) (a) or (b), as the case may be.

2.   If the party agrees to the change or if the parties agree to a different change, the party shall complete the applicable portions of the consent motion to change (Form 15C) and shall, within the time set out in clause (10) (a) or (b), as the case may be,

    i.   return a signed copy of the consent motion to change to the party making the motion, and

    ii.   provide a copy of the signed consent motion to change to the assignee, if any.

(10) SAME — The documents referred to in paragraphs 1 and 2 of subrule (9) shall be served and filed or returned and provided,

(a)   no later than 30 days after the party responding to the motion receives the motion to change and the supporting documents, if that party resides in Canada or the United States of America; or

(b)   no later than 60 days after the party responding to the motion receives the motion to change and the supporting documents, in any other case.

(11) SERVICE ON ASSIGNEE REQUIRED — In a motion to change a final order or agreement that has been assigned to an assignee, a party shall, in serving documents under subrule (5) or paragraph 1 of subrule (9), serve the documents on the assignee as if the assignee were also a party.

(12) ASSIGNEE MAY BECOME PARTY — On serving and filing a notice claiming a financial interest in the motion, an assignee becomes a respondent to the extent of the financial interest.

(13) SANCTIONS IF ASSIGNEE NOT SERVED — If an assignee is not served as required by subrule (11), the following rules apply:

1. The court may at any time, on motion by the assignee with notice to the other parties, set aside the changed order to the extent that it affects the assignee's financial interest.

2. The party who asked for the change has the burden of proving that the changed order should not be set aside.

3. If the changed order is set aside, the assignee is entitled to full recovery of its costs of the motion to set aside, unless the court orders otherwise.

(14) NO RESPONSE OR CONSENT — The consequences set out in paragraphs 1 to 4 of subrule 1 (8.4) apply, with necessary changes, if a party does not serve and file a response to motion to change (Form 15B) or return a consent motion to change (Form 15C) to the party making the motion as required under subrule (9).

(15) SAME, REQUEST FOR ORDER — If a party does not serve and file a response to motion to change (Form 15B) or return a consent motion to change (Form 15C) to the party making the motion as required under subrule (9), or if the party's response is struck out by an order, the party making the motion to change may file a motion form (Form 14B) asking that the court make the order requested in the materials filed by the party, unless an assignee has filed a notice of financial interest in the motion and opposes the change.

(16) CONSENT TO MOTION — If a party returns to the party making the motion a consent motion to change (Form 15C) in accordance with subparagraph 2 i of subrule (9), the party making the motion shall complete and file the consent motion to change and, unless any assignee refuses to consent to the change being requested, the party making the motion shall file with the consent motion to change,

(a) a motion form (Form 14B) asking that the court make the order described in the consent motion to change;

(b) five copies of a draft order;

(c) a stamped envelope addressed to each party and to the assignee, if any; and

(d) if the order that is agreed on relates in whole or in part to a support obligation,

(i) a support deduction order information form prescribed under the *Family Responsibility and Support Arrears Enforcement Act, 1996*, and

(ii)   a draft support deduction order.

(17) **MOTION TO CHANGE ON CONSENT** — Subject to subrule (18), if the parties to a final order or agreement want to ask the court to change the final order or agreement and the parties and any assignee agree to the change, the parties shall file,

(a)   a change information form (Form 15A), with all required attachments;

(b)   a consent motion to change (Form 15C);

(c)   a motion form (Form 14B) asking that the court make the order described in the consent motion to change;

(d)   five copies of a draft order;

(e)   a stamped envelope addressed to each party and to the assignee, if any; and

(f)   if the order that is agreed on relates in whole or in part to a support obligation,

(i)   a support deduction order information form prescribed under the *Family Responsibility and Support Arrears Enforcement Act, 1996*, and

(ii)   a draft support deduction order.

(18) **MOTION TO CHANGE ON CONSENT – CHILD SUPPORT ONLY** — If the parties to a final order or agreement want to ask the court to change the final order or agreement in relation only to a child support obligation, and the parties and any assignee agree to the change, the parties shall file,

(a)   a consent motion to change child support (Form 15D), with all required attachments;

(b)   five copies of a draft order;

(c)   a stamped envelope addressed to each party and to the assignee, if any;

(d)   a support deduction order information form prescribed under the *Family Responsibility and Support Arrears Enforcement Act, 1996*; and

(e)   a draft support deduction order.

(19) **CONSENT AFTER RESPONSE FILED** — If, at any time after a party has served and filed a response under paragraph 1 of subrule (9) and before the motion to change is heard, the parties and any assignee agree to an order that changes the final order or agreement that is the subject of the motion, the parties may proceed on consent by filing,

(a)   a consent motion to change (Form 15C);

(b)   a motion form (Form 14B) asking that the court make the order described in the consent motion to change;

(c)   five copies of a draft order;

(d)   a stamped envelope addressed to each party and to the assignee, if any; and

(e)   if the order that is agreed on relates in whole or in part to a support obligation,

> (i)   a support deduction order information form prescribed under the *Family Responsibility and Support Arrears Enforcement Act, 1996*, and
>
> (ii) a draft support deduction order.

(20) ORDER, AGREEMENT TO BE ATTACHED — A copy of any existing order or agreement that deals with custody, access or support shall be attached to every change information form (Form 15A) or consent motion to change child support (Form 15D).

(21) CHANGE NOT IN ACCORDANCE WITH CHILD SUPPORT GUIDELINES — Unless a motion to change a child support order or agreement is proceeding on the consent of the parties and any assignee, if a party asks that an order be made under this rule that is not in accordance with the tables in the applicable child support guidelines, the support recipient and the support payor shall each serve and file the evidence required by the following sections of the applicable child support guidelines, or the evidence that is otherwise necessary to satisfy the court that it should make the order asked for:

1.   Section 4 (income over $150,000).

2.   Section 5 (spouse in place of a parent).

3.   Section 7 (special expenses).

4.   Section 8 (split custody).

5.   Section 9 (shared custody).

6.   Section 10 (undue hardship).

7.   Section 21 (income and financial information) subject to subrule (21.1).

(21.1) FINANCIAL DISCLOSURE — Subrule (21) does not require that any documents already served on the other party under subrule 13 (5.0.1) be served again, but any such documents are required to be filed.

(22) AFFIDAVIT MAY BE FILED — A party or parties who want to ask the court to change a final order or agreement may, instead of using a change information form (Form 15A), use an affidavit containing evidence necessary to satisfy the court that it should make the order asked for and, in that case, these rules apply to the affidavit as if it were a change information form.

(23) SAME — A party who responds to a motion to change a final order or agreement by serving and filing a response to motion to change (Form 15B) may use an affidavit to provide evidence supporting his or her position instead of relying on the relevant portions of the form to provide the evidence or in addition to those portions of the form and, in that case, the affidavit is deemed to be part of the form.

(24) REQUIREMENTS FOR AFFIDAVIT — Subrules 14 (18) and (19) apply with necessary changes, to an affidavit provided in accordance with subrule (22) or (23).

(25) POWERS OF COURT — MOTION ON CONSENT OR UNOPPOSED — If a motion to change a final order or agreement proceeds on the consent of the parties and any assignee or is unopposed, the clerk shall present the filed materials to a judge and the judge may,

    (a)   **make the order asked for;**

    (b)   **require one or both parties to file further material; or**

    (c)   **require one or both parties to come to court.**

(26) **POWERS OF COURT – DIRECTIONS** — If the court is of the opinion that a motion, whether proceeding on consent or not, cannot be properly dealt with because of the material filed, because of the matters in dispute or for any other reason, the court may give directions, including directions for a trial.

(27) **APPLICATION OF SUBRULE 14(21)** — Subrule 14(21) applies with necessary changes.

(28) **MOTION UNDER RULE 14** — A motion under rule 14 may be made on a motion to change a final order or agreement.

(29) **ACCESS TO LISTED DOCUMENTS** — Subrule 19 (2) (access to listed documents) applies with necessary changes to a document mentioned in a form or affidavit used under this rule.

[O. Reg. 89/04, s. 7; O. Reg. 519/06, s. 5; O. Reg. 151/08, s. 4; O. Reg. 6/10, s. 6; O. Reg. 322/13, s. 9; O. Reg. 142/14, s. 8; O. Reg. 69/15, s. 4; O. Reg. 235/16, s. 2; O. Reg. 298/18, s. 11; O. Reg. 535/18, s. 4.]

Rule 16 — Summary Judgment

16. WHEN AVAILABLE — (1) After the respondent has served an answer or after the time for serving an answer has expired, a party may make a motion for summary judgment for a final order without a trial on all or part of any claim made or any defence presented in the case.

(2) **AVAILABLE IN ANY CASE EXCEPT DIVORCE** — A motion for summary judgment under subrule (1) may be made in any case (including a child protection case) that does not include a divorce claim.

(3) **DIVORCE CLAIM** — In a case that includes a divorce claim, the procedure provided in rule 36 (divorce) for an uncontested divorce may be used, or the divorce claim may be split from the rest of the case under subrule 12 (6).

(4) **EVIDENCE REQUIRED** — The party making the motion shall serve an affidavit or other evidence that sets out specific facts showing that there is no genuine issue requiring a trial.

(4.1) **EVIDENCE OF RESPONDING PARTY** — In response to the affidavit or other evidence served by the party making the motion, the party responding to the motion may not rest on mere allegations or denials but shall set out, in an affidavit or other evidence, specific facts showing that there is a genuine issue for trial.

(5) **EVIDENCE NOT FROM PERSONAL KNOWLEDGE** — If a party's evidence is not from a person who has personal knowledge of the facts in dispute, the court may draw conclusions unfavourable to the party.

(6) **NO GENUINE ISSUE FOR TRIAL —** If there is no genuine issue requiring a trial of a claim or defence, the court shall make a final order accordingly.

(6.1) **POWERS —** In determining whether there is a genuine issue requiring a trial, the court shall consider the evidence submitted by the parties, and the court may exercise any of the following powers for the purpose, unless it is in the interest of justice for such powers to be exercised only at a trial:

1.   Weighing the evidence.

2.   Evaluating the credibility of a deponent.

3.   Drawing any reasonable inference from the evidence.

(6.2) **ORAL EVIDENCE (MINI-TRIAL) —** The court may, for the purposes of exercising any of the powers set out in subrule (6.1), order that oral evidence be presented by one or more parties, with or without time limits on its presentation.

(7) **ONLY ISSUE AMOUNT OF ENTITLEMENT —** If the only genuine issue is the amount to which a party is entitled, the court shall order a trial to decide the amount.

(8) **ONLY ISSUE QUESTION OF LAW —** If the only genuine issue is a question of law, the court shall decide the issue and make a final order accordingly.

(9) **ORDER GIVING DIRECTIONS —** If the court does not make a final order, or makes an order for a trial of an issue, the court may, in addition to exercising a power listed in subrule 1 (7.2),

(a)   specify what facts are not in dispute, state the issues and give directions about how and when the case will go to trial (in which case the order governs how the trial proceeds, unless the trial judge orders otherwise);

(b)   give directions; and

(c)   impose conditions (for example, require a party to pay money into court as security, or limit a party's pretrial disclosure).

(10) [REVOKED: O. Reg. 69/15, s. 5(4).]

(11) [REVOKED: O. Reg. 69/15, s. 5(4).]

(12) **MOTION FOR SUMMARY DECISION ON LEGAL ISSUE —** The court may, on motion,

(a)   decide a question of law before trial, if the decision may dispose of all or part of the case, substantially shorten the trial or save substantial costs;

(b)   strike out an application, answer or reply because it sets out no reasonable claim or defence in law; or

(c)   dismiss or suspend a case because,

(i)   the court has no jurisdiction over it,

(ii)   a party has no legal capacity to carry on the case,

(iii)   there is another case going on between the same parties about the same matter, or

(iv)   the case is a waste of time, a nuisance or an abuse of the court process.

(13) EVIDENCE ON MOTION FOR SUMMARY DECISION OF LEGAL ISSUE — On a motion under subrule (12), evidence is admissible only if the parties consent or the court gives permission.

[O. Reg. 91/03, s. 5; O. Reg. 69/15, s. 5.]

Rule 17 — Conferences

17. CONFERENCES IN DEFENDED CASES — (1) Subject to subrule (1.1), in each case in which an answer is filed, a judge shall conduct at least one conference.

(1.1) EXCEPTION, CASE CONFERENCE OPTIONAL IN CHILD PROTECTION CASE — In a child protection case, a case conference may be conducted if,

(a)   a party requests it; or

(b)   the court considers it appropriate.

(2) UNDEFENDED CASES — If no answer is filed,

(a)   the clerk shall, on request, schedule a case conference or set a date for an uncontested trial or, in an uncontested divorce case, prepare the documents for a judge; and

(b)   a settlement conference or trial management conference shall be conducted only if the court orders it.

(3) MOTIONS TO CHANGE FINAL ORDER OR AGREEMENT — Subrule (1) applies, with necessary changes, to a motion to change a final order or agreement under rule 15, unless the motion is proceeding on the consent of the parties and any assignee or is unopposed.

(4) PURPOSES OF CASE CONFERENCE — The purposes of a case conference include,

(a)   exploring the chances of settling the case;

(b)   identifying the issues that are in dispute and those that are not in dispute;

(c)   exploring ways to resolve the issues that are in dispute;

(d)   ensuring disclosure of the relevant evidence;

(d.1)   identifying any issues relating to any expert evidence or reports on which the parties intend to rely at trial;

(e)   noting admissions that may simplify the case;

(f)   setting the date for the next step in the case;

(g)   setting a specific timetable for the steps to be taken in the case before it comes to

147

trial;

(h)   organizing a settlement conference, or holding one if appropriate; and

(i)   giving directions with respect to any intended motion, including the preparation of a specific timetable for the exchange of material for the motion and ordering the filing of summaries of argument, if appropriate.

(4.1) CASE CONFERENCE NOTICE — A party who asks for a case conference shall serve and file a case conference notice (Form 17).

(5) PURPOSES OF SETTLEMENT CONFERENCE — The purposes of a settlement conference include,

(a)   exploring the chances of settling the case;

(b)   settling or narrowing the issues in dispute;

(c)   ensuring disclosure of the relevant evidence;

(c.1)   settling or narrowing any issues relating to any expert evidence or reports on which the parties intend to rely at trial;

(d)   noting admissions that may simplify the case;

(e)   if possible, obtaining a view of how the court might decide the case;

(f)   considering any other matter that may help in a quick and just conclusion of the case;

(g)   if the case is not settled, identifying the witnesses and other evidence to be presented at trial, estimating the time needed for trial and scheduling the case for trial; and

(h)   organizing a trial management conference, or holding one if appropriate.

(6) PURPOSES OF TRIAL MANAGEMENT CONFERENCE — The purposes of a trial management conference include,

(a)   exploring the chances of settling the case;

(b)   arranging to receive evidence by a written report, an agreed statement of facts, an affidavit or another method, if appropriate;

(c)   deciding how the trial will proceed;

(c.1)   exploring the use of expert evidence or reports at trial, including the timing requirements for service and filing of experts' reports;

(d)   ensuring that the parties know what witnesses will testify and what other evidence will be presented at trial;

(e)   estimating the time needed for trial; and

(f)   setting the trial date, if this has not already been done.

(7) COMBINED CONFERENCE — At any time on the direction of a judge, part or all of a case conference, settlement conference and trial management conference may be combined.

(8) ORDERS AT CONFERENCE — At a case conference, settlement conference or trial management conference the judge may, if it is appropriate to do so,

(a)   make an order for document disclosure (rule 19), questioning (rule 20) or filing of summaries of argument on a motion, set the times for events in the case or give directions for the next step or steps in the case;

(a.0.1) make an order about expert opinion evidence, including,

    (i)   the engagement of an expert by or for one or more parties,

    (ii)   the use of expert opinion evidence in a case, or

    (iii) the provision, service or filing of experts' reports or written opinions;

(a.1) make an order requiring the parties to file a trial management endorsement or trial scheduling endorsement in a form determined by the court;

(b)   make an order requiring one or more parties to attend,

    (i)   a mandatory information program,

    (ii)   a case conference or settlement conference conducted by a person named under subrule (9),

    (iii) an intake meeting with a court-affiliated mediation service, or

    (iv)   a program offered through any other available community service or resource;

(b.1) if notice has been served, make a final order or any temporary order, including any of the following temporary orders to facilitate the preservation of the rights of the parties until a further agreement or order is made:

    (i)   an order relating to the designation of beneficiaries under a policy of life insurance, registered retirement savings plan, trust, pension, annuity or a similar financial instrument,

    (ii)   an order preserving assets generally or particularly,

    (iii) an order prohibiting the concealment or destruction of documents or property,

    (iv)   an order requiring an accounting of funds under the control of one of the parties,

    (v)   an order preserving the health and medical insurance coverage for one of the parties and the children of the relationship, and

    (vi)   an order continuing the payment of periodic amounts required to preserve an asset or a benefit to one of the parties and the children;

  (c)   make an unopposed order or an order on consent; and

  (d)   on consent, refer any issue for alternative dispute resolution.

(9) CONFERENCES WITH A NON-JUDGE — A case conference or settlement conference may be conducted by a person referred to in subrule (9.1) who has been named for the purpose by the appropriate regional senior judge, unless a party requests a conference with a judge.

(9.1) SAME — For the purposes of subrule (9), the following persons may conduct a conference:

  1.   A person who is licensed under the *Law Society Act* to practice law in Ontario as a barrister and solicitor and whose licence is not suspended, if he or she has at least 10 years experience in the practice of family law.

  2.   A person who was licensed under the *Law Society Act* to practice law in Ontario as a barrister and solicitor but who has since retired, if, at the time of retirement,

        i.   his or her license was not suspended, and

        ii.   he or she had at least 10 years experience in the practice of family law.

  3.   A master or retired master of the Superior Court of Justice.

  4.   A retired judge of the Superior Court of Justice.

(10) SETTLEMENT CONFERENCE WITH JUDGE BEFORE CASE SET FOR TRIAL — A case shall not be scheduled for trial unless,

  (a)   a settlement conference has been conducted; or

  (b)   a judge has ordered that the case be scheduled for trial.

(11) ADDITIONAL REQUIREMENTS, TRIAL IN SUPERIOR COURT OF JUSTICE, FAMILY COURT OF THE SUPERIOR COURT OF JUSTICE — In addition to the requirements of subrule (10), unless the court orders otherwise in advance, a case in the Superior Court of Justice of the Family Court of the Superior Court of Justice shall not be scheduled for trial until the trial scheduling endorsement form referred to in clause (8) (a.1) has been completed be the parties and endorsed by the Court.

(11.1) SAME, EXCEPTIONAL CIRCUMSTANCES — An order under subrule (11) may only be made in exceptional circumstances.

(11.2) SAME, EXCEPTIONS — Subrule (11) does not apply with respect to any of the following cases, unless an order under clause (8) (a.1) requires the filing the trial scheduling endorsement form in the case:

  1.   A child protection case.

  2.   A case to be scheduled for an uncontested trial.

  3.   A case referred to in subrule (12).

(12) WHEN CONFERENCES OPTIONAL — A case conference, settlement conference or trial management conference is not required, but may be held at a party's request or on a judge's direction in the following circumstances:

1.   In an enforcement.

2.   In a request to enforce a family arbitration award under rule 32.1.

(13) **PARTIES TO SERVE DOCUMENTS FOR CONFERENCE** — Each party shall, within the times required under subrule (13.1), serve and file the following documents for the purposes of a conference:

1.   For a case conference, a case conference brief (Form 17A or 17B).

2.   For a settlement conference, a settlement conference brief (Form 17C or 17D).

3.   For a trial management conference held in the Ontario Court of Justice, a trial management conference brief (Form 17E).

4.   For a trial management conference held in the Superior Court of Justice or the Family Court of the Superior Court of Justice, the following documents, subject to paragraph 5:

   i.   The trial scheduling endorsement form referred to in clause (8) (a.1), completed by the parties and endorsed by the court, if it has not already been filed.

   ii.   An offer to settle all outstanding claims in the case.

   iii.   An outline of the party's opening statement.

5.   For a trial management conference held in the Superior Court of Justice or the Family Court of the Superior Court of Justice in relation to a case to which subrule (11) does not apply by virtue of subrule (11.2), a trial management conference brief (Form 17E).

(13.0.1) **CASE CONFERENCE BRIEF IN CHILD PROTECTION CASE** — In a child protection case, a case conference brief shall be served and filed only if a case conference is being held under subrule (1.1).

(13.1) **TIME FOR SERVICE OF BRIEFS** — The party requesting the conference (or, if the conference is not requested by a party, the applicant or party making the motion) shall serve and file the documents required to be filed for the conference under subrule (13) not later than six days before the date scheduled for the conference and the other party shall do so not later than four days before that date.

(14) **PARTIES TO CONFIRM ATTENDANCE** — Each party shall,

(a)   confer or attempt to confer orally or in writing with every other party about the issues that are in dispute, subject to a party being prohibited from such communication by court order;

(b)   before giving the clerk confirmation of the conference in Form 17F under clause (c), give a copy of the confirmation of conference to every other party using mail, fax, email or any other method, except in a child protection case; and

(c)   not later than 2 p.m. three days before the conference date, give the clerk the confirmation of conference (Form 17F) by,

  (i)   delivering it to the court office, or

  (ii)   if available in the court office, sending it by fax or by email.

(14.1) EFFECT OF FAILURE TO CONFIRM — Unless the court orders otherwise, a conference shall not be held if confirmation of the conference is not given to the clerk in accordance with clause (14) (c).

(14.1.1) PARTIES TO UPDATE CONFIRMATION — If a party who has given a confirmation of conference determines at any time before the conference is held that the confirmation is no longer correct, the party shall, if possible, immediately,

(a)   give a copy of the corrected confirmation of conference in Form 17F to every other party using a method listed in clause (14) (b) and subsequently give the clerk the corrected confirmation of conference by a method listed in clause (14) (c); or

(b)   in a child protection case, give the clerk a corrected confirmation of conference in Form 17F by a method listed in clause (14) (c).

(14.2) REQUIREMENT TO BRING DOCUMENTS TO SETTLEMENT CONFERENCE — The following documents shall be brought to a settlement conference:

1.   Any document that supports a party's position in respect of a dispute regarding the value of property or regarding the amount of a debt, in the case of a property claim under Part I of the *Family Law Act*.

2.   Any document required to be served under rule 13 (financial disclosure), if there is a dispute as to whether it was served.

(15) PARTIES AND LAWYERS TO COME TO CONFERENCE — The following shall come to each conference:

1.   The parties, unless the court orders otherwise.

2.   For each represented party, the lawyer with full knowledge of and authority in the case.

(16) PARTICIPATION BY TELEPHONE OR VIDEO CONFERENCE — With permission obtained in advance from the judge who is to conduct a conference, a party or lawyer may participate in the conference by telephone or video conference.

(17) SETTING UP TELEPHONE OR VIDEO CONFERENCE — A party or lawyer who has permission to participate by telephone or video conference shall,

(a)   make the necessary arrangements;

(b)   serve a notice of the arrangements on all other parties and file it; and

(c)   participate in the conference as the notice specifies.

(18) COSTS — Costs shall not be awarded at a conference unless a party to the conference was not prepared, did not serve the required documents, did not make any required disclosure, otherwise contributed to the conference being unproductive or otherwise did not follow these rules, in which case the judge shall, despite subrule 24 (10),

(a)   order the party to pay the costs of the conference immediately;

(b)   decide the amount of the costs; and

(c)   give any directions that are needed.

(18.1) COSTS MAY BE AWARDED LATER — Subrule (18) does not prevent the court from awarding costs in relation to the conference at a later stage in the case, if costs are not awarded at the conference.

(19) CONFERENCE AGREEMENT — No agreement reached at a conference is effective until it is signed by the parties, witnessed and, in a case involving a special party or a child party, approved by the court.

(20) AGREEMENT FILED IN CONTINUING RECORD — The agreement shall be filed as part of the continuing record, unless the court orders otherwise.

(21) CONTINUING RECORD, TRIAL MANAGEMENT CONFERENCE BRIEFS — Trial management conference briefs form part of the continuing record.

(22) CONTINUING RECORD, CASE CONFERENCE BRIEFS — Case conference briefs do not form part of the continuing record unless the court orders otherwise and shall be returned at the end of the conference to the parties who filed them or be destroyed by court staff immediately after the conference.

(22.1) DELETIONS FROM CASE CONFERENCE BRIEF INCLUDED IN RECORD — If the court orders that a case conference brief form part of the continuing record, that portion of the brief that deals with settlement of the case shall be deleted.

(22.2) CONTINUING RECORD, SETTLEMENT CONFERENCE BRIEFS — Settlement conference briefs do not form part of the continuing record and shall be returned at the end of the conference to the parties who filed them or be destroyed by the court staff immediately after the conference.

(23) CONFIDENTIALITY OF SETTLEMENT CONFERENCE — No brief or evidence prepared for a settlement conference and no statement made at a settlement conference shall be disclosed to any other judge, except in,

(a)   an agreement reached at a settlement conference; or

(b)   an order.

(24) SETTLEMENT CONFERENCE JUDGE CANNOT HEAR ISSUE — A judge who conducts a settlement conference about an issue shall not hear the issue, except as subrule (25) provides.

(25) EXCEPTION, CHILD PROTECTION CASE — In a child protection case, if a finding that the child is in need of protection is made without a trial and a trial is needed

153

to determine which order should be made under section 101 of the *Child, Youth and Family Services Act, 2017*, any judge who has not conducted a settlement conference on that issue may conduct the trial.

[O. Reg. 544/99, s. 8; O. Reg. 202/01, s. 5; O. Reg. 91/03, s. 6(4); O. Reg. 89/04, s. 8; O. Reg. 151/08, s. 5; O. Reg. 6/10, s. 7; O. Reg. 383/11, s. 4; O. Reg. 388/12, s. 7; O. Reg. 322/13, s. 10; O. Reg. 142/14, s. 9; O. Reg. 69/15, s. 6; O. Reg. 235/16, s. 3; O. Reg. 298/18, s. 12; O. Reg. 535/18, s. 5; O. Reg. 250/19, s. 5.]

Rule 18 — Offers to Settle

18. DEFINITION — (1) In this rule,

"offer" means an offer to settle one or more claims in a case, motion, appeal or enforcement, and includes a counter-offer.

(2) APPLICATION — This rule applies to an offer made at any time, even before the case is started.

(3) MAKING AN OFFER — A party may serve an offer on any other party.

(4) OFFER TO BE SIGNED BY PARTY AND LAWYER — An offer shall be signed personally by the party making it and also by the party's lawyer, if any.

(5) WITHDRAWING AN OFFER — A party who made an offer may withdraw it by serving a notice of withdrawal, at any time before the offer is accepted.

(6) TIME-LIMITED OFFER — An offer that is not accepted within the time set out in the offer is considered to have been withdrawn.

(7) OFFER EXPIRES WHEN COURT BEGINS TO GIVE DECISION — An offer may not be accepted after the court begins to give a decision that disposes of a claim dealt with in the offer.

(8) CONFIDENTIALITY OF OFFER — The terms of an offer,

(a)   shall not be mentioned in any document filed in the continuing record; and

(b)   shall not be mentioned to the judge hearing the claim dealt with in the offer, until the judge has dealt with all the issues in dispute except costs.

(9) ACCEPTING AN OFFER — The only valid way of accepting an offer is by serving an acceptance on the party who made the offer, at any time before,

(a)   the offer is withdrawn; or

(b)   the court begins to give a decision that disposes of a claim dealt with in the offer.

(10) OFFER REMAINS OPEN DESPITE REJECTION OR COUNTER-OFFER — A party may accept an offer in accordance with subrule (9) even if the party has previously rejected the offer or made a counter-offer.

(11) COSTS NOT DEALT WITH IN OFFER — If an accepted offer does not deal with costs, either party is entitled to ask the court for costs.

(12) OFFERS INVOLVING SPECIAL PARTY OR CHILD PARTY — An offer may be made, withdrawn or accepted by a special party or a child party, but neither a party's acceptance of a special party's or child party's offer nor the special party's or child party's acceptance of another party's offer are binding on the special party or child party until the court approves.

(13) FAILURE TO CARRY OUT TERMS OF ACCEPTED OFFER — If a party to an accepted offer does not carry out the terms of the offer, the other party may,

(a)   make a motion to turn the parts of the offer within the court's jurisdiction into an order; or

(b)   continue the case as if the offer had never been accepted.

(14) COSTS CONSEQUENCES OF FAILURE TO ACCEPT OFFER — A party who makes an offer is, unless the court orders otherwise, entitled to costs to the date the offer was served and full recovery of costs from that date, if the following conditions are met:

1.   If the offer relates to a motion, it is made at least one day before the motion date.

2.   If the offer relates to a trial or the hearing of a step other than a motion, it is made at least seven days before the trial or hearing date.

3.   The offer does not expire and is not withdrawn before the hearing starts.

4.   The offer is not accepted.

5.   The party who made the offer obtains an order that is as favourable as or more favourable than the offer.

(15) COSTS CONSEQUENCES — BURDEN OF PROOF — The burden of proving that the order is as favourable as or more favourable than the offer to settle is on the party who claims the benefit of subrule (14).

(16) COSTS — DISCRETION OF COURT — When the court exercises its discretion over costs, it may take into account any written offer to settle, the date it was made and its terms, even if subrule (14) does not apply.

[O. Reg. 250/19, s. 6.]

Rule 19 — Document Disclosure

19. AFFIDAVIT LISTING DOCUMENTS — **(1)** Subject to subrule (1.1), every party shall, within 10 days after another party's request, give the other party an affidavit listing every document that is,

(a)   relevant to any issue in the case; and

(b)   in the party's control, or available to the party on request.

(1.1) EXCEPTIONS — Subrule (1) does not apply

(a)   to the Office of the Children's Lawyer or to children's aid societies; and

(b)   in respect of documents required to be served under rule 13 (financial disclosure).

(2) ACCESS TO LISTED DOCUMENTS — The other party is entitled, on request,

(a)   to examine any document listed in the affidavit, unless it is protected by a legal privilege; and

(b)   to receive, at the party's own expense at the legal aid rate, a copy of any document that the party is entitled to examine under clause (a).

(3) ACCESS TO DOCUMENTS MENTIONED IN COURT PAPERS — Subrule (2) also applies, with necessary changes, to a document mentioned in a party's application, answer, reply, notice of motion or affidavit.

(4) DOCUMENTS PROTECTED BY LEGAL PRIVILEGE — If a party claims that a document is protected by a legal privilege, the court may, on motion, examine it and decide the issue.

(5) USE OF PRIVILEGED DOCUMENTS — A party who claims that a document is protected by a legal privilege may use it at trial only,

(a)   if the other party has been allowed to examine the document and been supplied with a copy, free of charge, at least 30 days before the settlement conference; or

(b)   on the conditions the trial judge considers appropriate, including an adjournment if necessary.

(6) DOCUMENTS OF SUBSIDIARY OR AFFILIATED CORPORATION — The court may, on motion despite clause 1(7.2)(a), order a party to give another party an affidavit listing the documents that are,

(a)   relevant to any issue in the case; and

(b)   in the control of, or available on request to a corporation that is controlled, directly or indirectly, by the party or by another corporation that the party controls directly or indirectly.

(6.1) DOCUMENTS OF OFFICE OF THE CHILDREN'S LAWYER OR CHILDREN'S AID SOCIETY — The court may, on motion despite clause 1 (7.2)(a), order the Office of the Children's Lawyer or a children's aid society to give another party an affidavit listing the documents that are,

(a)   relevant to any issue in the case; and

(b)   in the control of, or available on request to, the Office of the Children's Lawyer or the Children's Aid Society.

(7) ACCESS TO LISTED DOCUMENTS — Subrule (2) also applies, with necessary changes, to any document listed in an affidavit ordered under subrule (6) or (6.1).

(8) DOCUMENTS OMITTED FROM AFFIDAVIT OR FOUND LATER — A party who, after serving an affidavit required under subrule (1), (6) or (6.1), finds a document that should have been listed in it, or finds that the list is not correct or not complete, shall immediately serve on the other party a new affidavit listing the correct information.

(9) ACCESS TO ADDITIONAL DOCUMENTS — The other party is entitled, on request,

156

(a)   to examine any document listed in an affidavit served under subrule (8), unless it is protected by a legal privilege; and

(b)   to receive, free of charge, a copy of any document that the party is entitled to examine under clause (a).

(10) **FAILURE TO FOLLOW RULE 19 OR OBEY ORDER** — If a party does not follow this rule or obey an order made under this rule, the court may, in addition to any power to make an order under subrule 1 (8) or (8.1):

(a)   order the party to give another party an affidavit, let the other party examine a document or supply the other party with a copy free of charge;

(b)   order that a document favourable to the party's case may not be used except with the court's permission; or

(c)   order that the party is not entitled to obtain disclosure under these rules until the party follows the rule or obeys the order.

(11) **DOCUMENT IN NON-PARTY'S CONTROL** — If a document is in a non-party's control, or is available only to the non-party, and is not protected by a legal privilege, and it would be unfair to a party to go on with the case without the document, the court may, on motion with notice served on every party and served on the non-party by special service,

(a)   order the non-party to let the party examine the document and to supply the party with a copy at the legal aid rate; and

(b)   order that a copy be prepared and used for all purposes of the case instead of the original.

[O. Reg. 383/11, s. 5; O. Reg. 322/13, s. 11; O. Reg. 69/15, s. 7.]

Rule 20 — Questioning a Witness and Disclosure

20. QUESTIONING – PROCEDURE — (1) Questioning under this rule shall take place orally under oath or affirmation.

(2) **CROSS-EXAMINATION** — The right to question a person includes the right to cross-examine.

(3) **CHILD PROTECTION CASE – AVAILABLE AS OF RIGHT** — In a child protection case, a party is entitled to obtain information from another party about any issue in the case,

(a)   by questioning the other party, in which case the party shall serve the other party with a summons to witness (Form 23) by special service in accordance with subrule 6 (4); or

(b)   by affidavit or by another method, in which case the party shall serve the other party with a request for information (Form 20).

(4) **OTHER CASES – CONSENT OR ORDER** — In a case other than a child protection case, a party is entitled to obtain information from another party about any issue

in the case,

(a)   with the other party's consent; or

(b)   by an order under subrule (5).

(5) ORDER FOR QUESTIONING OR DISCLOSURE — The court may, on motion, order that a person (whether a party or not) be questioned by a party or disclose information by affidavit or by another method about any issue in the case, if the following conditions are met:

1.   It would be unfair to the party who wants the questioning or disclosure to carry on with the case without it.

2.   The information is not easily available by any other method.

3.   The questioning or disclosure will not cause unacceptable delay or undue expense.

(6) QUESTIONING SPECIAL PARTY OR CHILD PARTY — If a person to be questioned is a special party or a child party, the court may, on motion, order that someone else be questioned in addition to or in place of the person.

(7) QUESTIONING ABOUT AFFIDAVIT OR NET FAMILY PROPERTY STATEMENT — The court may make an order under subrule (5) that a person be questioned or disclose details about information in an affidavit or net family property statement.

(8) QUESTIONING OR DISCLOSURE – PRECONDITIONS — A party who wants to question a person or obtain information by affidavit or by another method may do so only if the party,

(a)   has served and filed any answer, financial statement or net family property statement that these rules require; and

(b)   promises in writing not to serve or file any further material for the next step in the case, except in reply to the answers or information obtained.

(9) NOTICE AND SUMMONS TO NON-PARTY — The court may make an order under this rule affecting a non-party only if the non-party has been served with the notice of motion, a summons to witness (Form 23) and the witness fee required by subrule 23 (4), all by special service (subrules 6 (3) and (4)).

(10) PENALTY FOR FAILURE TO OBEY SUMMONS — Subrule 23 (7) (failure to obey summons to witness) applies, with necessary changes, if a person summoned under subrule (9) fails to obey the summons.

(11) PLACE OF QUESTIONING — The questioning shall take place in the municipality in which the person to be questioned lives, unless that person and the party who wants to do the questioning agree to hold it in another municipality.

(12) OTHER ARRANGEMENTS FOR QUESTIONING — If the person to be questioned and the party who wants to do the questioning do not agree on one or more of the following matters, the court shall, on motion, make an order to decide the matter:

1. The date and time for the questioning.

2. The person responsible for recording the questioning.

3. The method for recording the questioning.

4. Payment of the expenses of the person to be questioned, if a non-party.

(13) **NOTICE TO PARTIES** — The parties shall, not later than three days before the questioning, be served with notice of the name of the person to be questioned and the address, date and time of the questioning.

(14) **QUESTIONING PERSON OUTSIDE ONTARIO** — If a person to be questioned lives outside Ontario and will not come to Ontario for questioning, the court may decide,

(a) the date, time and place for the questioning;

(b) how much notice the person should be given;

(c) the person before whom the questioning will be held;

(d) the amount of the witness fee to be paid to the person to be questioned;

(e) the method for recording the questioning;

(f) where necessary, that the clerk shall issue,

    (i) an authorization to a commissioner (Form 20A) who is to supervise the questioning outside Ontario, and

    (ii) a letter of request (Form 20B) to the appropriate court or authorities outside Ontario, asking for their assistance in getting the person to be questioned to come before the commissioner; and

(g) any other related matter.

(15) **COMMISSIONER'S DUTIES** — A commissioner authorized under subrule (14) shall,

(a) supervise the questioning according to the terms of the court's authorization, these rules and Ontario's law of evidence, unless the law of the place where the questioning is to be held requires some other manner of questioning;

(b) make and keep a copy of the record of the questioning and, if possible, of the exhibits, if any;

(c) deliver the original record, any exhibits and the authorization to the clerk who issued it; and

(d) notify the party who asked for the questioning that the record has been delivered to the clerk.

(16) **ORDER TO BRING DOCUMENTS OR THINGS** — An order for questioning and a summons to witness may also require the person to bring any document or thing that is,

(a)   relevant to any issue in the case; and

(b)   in the person's control or available to the person on request.

(17) **OTHER RULES APPLY** — Subrules 19 (2), (4) and (5) (right to examine document and obtain copy, documents protected by legal privilege, use of privileged documents) apply, with necessary changes, to the documents mentioned in the order.

(18) **SCOPE OF QUESTIONS** — Unless the court orders otherwise a person to be questioned may be asked about,

(a)   the names of persons who might reasonably be expected to know about the claims in the case and, with the court's permission, their addresses;

(b)   the names of the witnesses whom a party intends to call at trial and, with the court's permission, their addresses;

(c)   the names, addresses, findings, conclusions and opinions of expert witnesses whom a party intends to call or on whose reports the party intends to rely at trial;

(d)   if it is relevant to the case, the existence and details of any insurance policy under which the insurance company may be required to pay all or part of an order for the payment of money in the case or to pay back to a party money that the party has paid under an order; and

(e)   any other matter in dispute in the case.

(19) **REFUSAL TO ANSWER QUESTION** — If a person being questioned refuses to answer a question,

(a)   the court may, on motion,

    (i)   decide whether the question is proper,

    (ii)   give directions for the person's return to the questioning, and

    (iii)   make a contempt order against the person; and

(b)   if the person is a party or is questioned on behalf or in place of a party, the party shall not use the information that was refused as evidence in the case, unless the court gives permission under subrule (20).

(20) **COURT'S PERMISSION** — The court shall give permission unless the use of the information would cause harm to another party or an unacceptable delay in the trial, and may impose any appropriate conditions on the permission, including an adjournment if necessary.

(21) **DUTY TO CORRECT OR UPDATE ANSWERS** — A person who has been questioned or who has provided information in writing by affidavit or by another method and who finds that an answer or information given was incorrect or incomplete, or is no longer correct or complete, shall immediately provide the correct and complete information in writing to all parties.

(22) **LAWYER ANSWERING** — If there is no objection, questions may be answered

by the lawyer for a person being questioned, and the answer shall be taken as the person's own answer unless the person corrects or changes it before the questioning ends.

(23) METHOD FOR RECORDING QUESTIONING — All the questions and answers at a questioning shall be recorded electronically or manually.

(24) OBLIGATION TO KEEP INFORMATION CONFIDENTIAL — When a party obtains evidence under this rule, rule 13 (financial disclosure) or rule 19 (document disclosure), the party and the party's lawyer may use the evidence and any information obtained from it only for the purposes of the case in which the evidence was obtained, subject to the exceptions in subrule (25).

(25) USE OF INFORMATION PERMITTED — Evidence and any information obtained from it may be used for other purposes,

(a)   if the person who gave the evidence consents;

(b)   if the evidence is filed with the court, given at a hearing or referred to at a hearing;

(c)   to impeach the testimony of a witness in another case; or

(d)   in a later case between the same parties or their successors, if the case in which the evidence was obtained was withdrawn or dismissed.

(26) COURT MAY LIFT OBLIGATION OF CONFIDENTIALITY — The court may, on motion, give a party permission to disclose evidence or information obtained from it if the interests of justice outweigh any harm that would result to the party who provided the evidence.

[O. Reg. 322/13, s. 12; O. Reg. 69/15, s. 8; O. Reg. 250/19, s. 7.]

Rule 20.1 — Duty of Experts

20.1 APPLICATION — (1) This rule applies to,

(a)   a person who is a litigation expert within the meaning of rule 20.2; and

(b)   an expert who is appointed by the court under rule 20.3.

(2) DUTY OF EXPERT — It is the duty of every expert to whom this rule applies to,

(a)   provide opinion evidence that is fair, objective and non-partisan;

(b)   provide opinion evidence that is related only to matters that are within the expert's area of expertise; and

(c)   provide such additional assistance as the court may reasonably require to determine a matter in issue.

(3) DUTY PREVAILS — In the case of a litigation expert, the duty in subrule (2) prevails over any obligation owed by the expert to a party.

[O. Reg. 250/19, s. 8.]

Rule 20.2 — Expert Opinion Evidence

20.2 DEFINITIONS — (1) In this rule,

"joint litigation expert" means a litigation expert engaged to provide expert opinion evidence for two or more parties;

"litigation expert" means a person engaged for the purposes of litigation to provide expert opinion evidence;

"participant expert" means a person who is not engaged to provide expert opinion evidence for the purposes of litigation, but who provides expert opinion evidence based on the exercise of his or her skills, knowledge, training or experience while observing or participating in the events at issue.

(2) EXPERT WITNESS REPORTS — A party who wishes to call a litigation expert as a witness at trial shall, at least six days before the settlement conference, serve on all other parties and file a report signed by the expert and containing, at a minimum, the following:

1.   The expert's name, address and area of expertise.

2.   The expert's qualifications, including his or her employment and educational experiences in his or her area of expertise.

3.   The nature of the opinion being sought and each issue in the case to which the opinion relates.

4.   The instructions provided to the expert in relation to the case.

5.   The expert's opinion on each issue and, where there is a range of opinions given, a summary of the range and the reasons for the expert's own opinion within that range.

6.   The expert's reasons for his or her opinion, including,

     i.   a description of the factual assumptions on which the opinion is based,

     ii.   a description of any research or test conducted by or for the expert, or of any independent observations made by the expert, that led him or her to form the opinion, and, for each test,

         A.   an explanation of the scientific principles underlying the test and of the meaning of the test results, and

         B.   a description of any substantial influence a person's gender, socio-economic status, culture or race had or may have had on the test results or on the expert's assessment of the test results, and

     iii.   a description and explanation of every document or other source of information directly relied on by the expert in forming the opinion.

7.   An acknowledgement of expert's duty (Form 20.2) signed by the expert.

(3) SAME, MORE THAN ONE PARTY — If two or more parties wish to call a joint litigation expert as a witness at trial, subrule (2) applies with necessary modifications.

(4) **SUPPLEMENTARY REPORT** — Any supplementary report by a litigation expert must be signed by the expert, and shall be served on all other parties and filed,

(a)   at least 30 days before the start of the trial; or

(b)   in a child protection case, at least 14 days before the start of the trial.

(5) **DOCUMENTS TO ACCOMPANY REPORT** — The following documents shall accompany a report when it is served on a party under subrule (2), (3) or (4), unless the documents have already been served on the party:

1.   A copy of any written statement of facts on which the litigation expert's opinion is based.

2.   A copy of any document relied on by the litigation expert in forming his or her opinion.

(6) **RESTRICTION ON TESTIMONY** — Unless a judge orders otherwise, a litigation expert may not testify about an issue at trial unless the substance of the testimony is set out in a report that meets the requirements of this rule.

(7) **CROSS-EXAMINATION** — A joint litigation expert may be cross-examined at trial by any party.

(8) **WHEN JOINT LITIGATION EXPERT REQUIRED** — Litigation expert opinion evidence concerning the following matters may only be presented by a joint litigation expert:

1.   A claim for custody of or access to a child under the *Divorce Act* (Canada) or the *Children's Law Reform Act*, unless the court orders otherwise.

2.   Any other matter specified by the court.

(9) **MOTION FOR DIRECTIONS** — If parties who wish or are required to engage a joint litigation expert do not agree on a matter relating to the engagement, any one of them may make a motion for directions.

(10) **ORDER RE JOINT LITIGATION EXPERT** — The court may, on motion under subrule (9) or otherwise, make an order engaging a joint litigation expert for two or more parties.

(11) **SAME** — In making an order under subrule (10), the court shall ensure that the matters listed in subrule 20.3 (2) are either set out in the order or are otherwise addressed by the order.

(12) **COOPERATION** — Parties who engage a joint litigation expert, or for whom a joint litigation expert is engaged, shall cooperate fully with the expert and make full and timely disclosure of all relevant information and documents to the expert, and the court may draw any inference it considers reasonable from a party's failure to do so.

(13) **RESTRICTION ON EXPERTS ON SAME ISSUE** — If a joint litigation expert provides opinion evidence on an issue for a party, no other litigation expert may present opinion evidence on that issue for that party, unless the court orders otherwise.

(14) PARTICIPANT EXPERT — A party who wishes to call a participant expert as a witness at trial shall,

(a)   at least six days before the settlement conference,

    (i)   serve notice of the fact on all other parties, and

    (ii)   if the party wishes to submit any written opinion prepared by the expert as evidence in the trial, serve the written opinion on all other parties and file it; and

(b)   serve on any other party, at that party's request, a copy of any documents supporting the opinion evidence the participant expert plans to provide.

(15) APPLICATION TO MOTIONS FOR TEMPORARY ORDERS OR FOR SUMMARY JUDGMENT — Unless the court orders otherwise, this rule applies, with the following modifications, to the use of expert opinion evidence on a motion for a temporary order under rule 14 or a motion for summary judgment under rule 16:

1.   Expert witness reports and any supplementary reports shall be served and filed as evidence on the motion in accordance with the requirements of subrules 14 (11), (11.3), (13) and (20), as applicable.

2.   Any other necessary modifications.

    [O. Reg. 250/19, s. 8.]

Rule 20.3 — Court-Appointed Experts

20.3 APPOINTMENT OF EXPERT BY COURT — (1) The court may, on motion or on its own initiative, appoint one or more independent experts to inquire into and report on any question of fact or opinion relevant to an issue in a case.

(2) REQUIREMENTS OF ORDER — An order under subrule (1) shall,

(a)   name the expert being appointed, who shall be a person agreed on by the parties if possible;

(b)   specify the instructions to the expert; and

(c)   require the parties to pay the expert's fees and expenses and specify the proportions or amounts of the fees and expenses that each party is required to pay.

(3) SERIOUS FINANCIAL HARDSHIP — Despite clause (2) (c), the court may relieve a party from a requirement to pay any of the expert's fees or expenses if the court is satisfied that requiring the payment would cause serious financial hardship to the party.

(4) SECURITY — If a motion is made under subrule (1) that is opposed, the court may, as a condition of the appointment, require the party making the motion to give such security for the expert's fees and expenses as is just.

(5) ADDITIONAL ORDERS — In making an order under subrule (1), the court may make any further order it considers necessary to enable the expert to carry out the specified instructions, including,

(a)   an order for the inspection of property; or

(b)   an order under section 105 of the *Courts of Justice Act* (physical or mental examination of a person), if the requirements of that section are met.

(6) **REPORT** — The expert shall prepare a report of the results of his or her inquiry containing, at a minimum, the information listed in paragraphs 1 to 6 of subrule 20.2 (2) and an acknowledgement of expert's duty (Form 20.2) signed by the expert, and shall file the report with the clerk and provide a copy of it to each of the parties.

(7) **ADMISSIBILITY OF REPORT** — The expert's report is admissible in evidence in the case.

(8) **CROSS-EXAMINATION** — An expert appointed under this rule may be cross-examined at trial by any party.

(9) **NON-APPLICATION** — This rule does not apply to requests by the court that the Children's Lawyer act under subsection 112 (1) of the *Courts of Justice Act* or to appointments of persons by the court under,

(a)   subsection 30 (1) of the *Children's Law Reform Act* (assessment of needs of child); or

(b)   subsection 98 (4) or (5) of the *Child, Youth and Family Services Act, 2017* (assessment orders).

(10) **EXCEPTION** — Despite clause (9) (a), the report required under subsection 30 (1) of the *Children's Law Reform Act* shall contain, at a minimum, the information listed in paragraphs 1 to 6 of subrule 20.2 (2), unless the court orders otherwise.

[O. Reg. 250/19, s. 8.]

Rule 21 — Report of Children's Lawyer

21. REPORT OF CHILDREN'S LAWYER — When the Children's Lawyer investigates and reports on custody of or access to a child under section 112 of the *Courts of Justice Act*,

(a)   the Children's Lawyer shall first serve notice on the parties and file it;

(b)   the parties shall, from the time they are served with the notice, serve the Children's Lawyer with every document in the case that involves the child's custody, access, support, health or education, as if the Children's Lawyer were a party in the case;

(c)   the Children's Lawyer has the same rights as a party to document disclosure (rule 19) and questioning witnesses (rule 20) about any matter involving the child's custody, access, support, health or education;

(d)   within 90 days after serving the notice under clause (a), the Children's Lawyer shall serve a report on the parties and file it;

(e)   within 30 days after being served with the report, a party may serve and file a statement disputing anything in it; and

(f)   the trial shall not be held and the court shall not make a final order in the case until the 30 days referred to in clause (e) expire or the parties file a statement giving up their right to that time.

Rule 22 — Admission of Facts

22. MEANING OF ADMISSION THAT DOCUMENT GENUINE — (1) An admission that a document is genuine is an admission,

    (a)   if the document is said to be an original, that it was written, signed or sealed as it appears to have been;

    (b)   if it is said to be a copy, that it is a complete and accurate copy; and

    (c)   if it is said to be a copy of a document that is ordinarily sent from one person to another (for example, a letter, fax or electronic message), that it was sent as it appears to have been sent and was received by the person to whom it is addressed.

(2) REQUEST TO ADMIT — At any time, by serving a request to admit (Form 22) on another party, a party may ask the other party to admit, for purposes of the case only, that a fact is true or that a document is genuine.

(3) COPY OF DOCUMENT TO BE ATTACHED — A copy of any document mentioned in the request to admit shall be attached to it, unless the other party already has a copy or it is impractical to attach a copy.

(4) RESPONSE REQUIRED WITHIN 20 DAYS — The party on whom the request to admit is served is considered to have admitted, for purposes of the case only, that the fact is true or that the document is genuine, unless the party serves a response (Form 22A) within 20 days,

    (a)   denying that a particular fact mentioned in the request is true or that a particular document mentioned in the request is genuine; or

    (b)   refusing to admit that a particular fact mentioned in the request is true or that a particular document mentioned in the request is genuine, and giving the reasons for each refusal.

(5) WITHDRAWING ADMISSION — An admission that a fact is true or that a document is genuine (whether contained in a document served in the case or resulting from sub-rule (4)), may be withdrawn only with the other party's consent or with the court's permission.

Rule 23 — Evidence and Trial

23. TRIAL RECORD — (1) At least 30 days before the start of the trial, the applicant shall serve and file a trial record containing a table of contents and the following documents:

    1.   The application, answer and reply, if any.

    2.   Any agreed statement of facts.

    3.   If relevant to an issue at trial, financial statements and net family property statements by all parties, completed not more than 30 days before the record is served.

3.1   If the trial involves a claim for custody of or access to a child, the applicable documents referred to in Rule 35.1.

4.   Any assessment report ordered by the court or obtained by consent of the parties.

5.   Any temporary order relating to a matter still in dispute.

6.   Any order relating to the trial.

7.   The relevant parts of any transcript on which the party intends to rely at trial.

8.   Any evidence that is the subject of an order made under clause 1(7.2) (g).

9.   Any trial scheduling endorsement form completed by the parties and endorsed by the court.

(2) **RESPONDENT MAY ADD TO TRIAL RECORD** — Not later than seven days before the start of the trial, a respondent may serve, file and add to the trial record any document referred to in subrule (1) that is not already in the trial record.

(3) **SUMMONS TO WITNESS** — A party who wants a witness to give evidence in court or to be questioned and to bring documents or other things shall serve on the witness a summons to witness (Form 23) by special service in accordance with subrule 6 (4), together with the witness fee set out in subrule (4).

(4) **WITNESS FEE** — A person summoned as a witness shall be paid, for each day that the person is needed in court or to be questioned,

(a) $50 for coming to court or to be questioned;

(b)   travel money in the amount of,

   (i) $5, if the person lives in the city or town where the person gives evidence,

   (ii)   30 cents per kilometre each way, if the person lives elsewhere but within 300 kilometres of the court or place of questioning,

   (iii)   the cheapest available air fare plus $10 a day for airport parking and 30 cents per kilometre each way from the person's home to the airport and from the airport to the court or place of questioning, if the person lives 300 or more kilometres from the court or place of questioning; and

(c) $100 per night for meals and overnight stay, if the person does not live in the city or town where the trial is held and needs to stay overnight.

(4.1) **MEANING OF "CITY OR TOWN"** — For the purposes of subrule (4), a municipality shall be considered a city or town if it was a city or town on December 31, 2002.

(5) **CONTINUING EFFECT OF SUMMONS** — A summons to witness remains in effect until it is no longer necessary to have the witness present.

(6) **SUMMONS FOR ORIGINAL DOCUMENT** — If a document can be proved by a certified copy, a party who wants a witness to bring the original shall not serve a summons on the witness for that purpose without the court's permission.

(7) FAILURE TO OBEY SUMMONS — The court may issue a warrant for arrest (Form 32B) to bring a witness before the court if,

(a)   the witness has been served as subrule (3) requires, but has not obeyed the summons; and

(b)   it is necessary to have the witness present in court or at a questioning.

(8) INTERPROVINCIAL SUMMONS TO WITNESS — A summons to a witness outside Ontario under the *Interprovincial Summonses Act* shall be in Form 23A.

(9) SETTING ASIDE SUMMONS TO WITNESS — The court may, on motion, order that a summons to witness be set aside.

(10) ATTENDANCE OF A PRISONER — If it is necessary to have a prisoner come to court or to be questioned, the court may order (Form 23B) the prisoner's custodian to deliver the prisoner on payment of the fee set out in the regulations under the *Administration of Justice Act*.

(11) CALLING OPPOSING PARTY AS WITNESS — A party may call the opposing party as a witness and may cross-examine the opposing party.

(11.1) ATTENDANCE OF OPPOSING PARTY — A party who wishes to call an opposing party as a witness may have the opposing party attend,

(a)   by serving a summons under subrule (3) on the opposing party; or

(b)   by serving on the opposing party's lawyer, at least 10 days before the start of the trial, a notice of intention to call the opposing party as a witness.

(12) OPPOSING PARTY DISOBEYING SUMMONS — When an opposing party has been served with a summons under subrule (3), the court may make a final order in favour of the party calling the witness, adjourn the case or make any other appropriate order, including a contempt order, if the opposing party,

(a)   does not come to or remain in court as required by the summons; or

(b)   refuses to be sworn or to affirm, to answer any proper question or to bring any document or thing named in the summons.

(13) READING OPPOSING PARTY'S ANSWERS INTO EVIDENCE — An answer or information given under rule 20 (questioning) by an opposing party may be read into evidence at trial if it is otherwise proper evidence, even if the opposing party has already testified at trial.

(14) READING OTHER PERSON'S ANSWERS INTO EVIDENCE — Subrule (13) also applies, with necessary changes, to an answer or information given by a person questioned on behalf of or in place of an opposing party, unless the trial judge orders otherwise.

(15) USING ANSWERS — SPECIAL CIRCUMSTANCES — Subrule (13) is subject to the following:

1.   If the answer or information is being read into evidence to show that a witness's testimony at trial is not to be believed, answers or information given by the wit-

ness earlier must be put to the witness as sections 20 and 21 of the *Evidence Act* require.

2. At the request of an opposing party, the trial judge may direct the party reading the answer or information into evidence to read in, as well, any other answer or information that qualifies or explains what the party has read into evidence.

3. The answer or information of a special party or a child party may be read into evidence only with the trial judge's permission.

(16) **REBUTTING ANSWERS** — A party who has read answers or information into evidence at trial may introduce other evidence to rebut the answers or information.

(17) **USING ANSWERS OF WITNESS NOT AVAILABLE FOR TRIAL** — The trial judge may give a party permission to read into evidence all or part of the answers or information given under rule 20 (questioning) by a person who is unable or unwilling to testify at the trial, but before doing so the judge shall consider,

(a) the importance of the evidence;

(b) the general principle that trial evidence should be given orally in court;

(c) the extent to which the person was cross-examined; and

(d) any other relevant factor.

(18) **TAKING EVIDENCE BEFORE TRIAL** — The court may order that a witness whose evidence is necessary at trial may give evidence before trial at a place and before a person named in the order, and then may accept the transcript as evidence.

(19) **TAKING EVIDENCE BEFORE TRIAL OUTSIDE ONTARIO** — If a witness whose evidence is necessary at trial lives outside Ontario, subrules 20 (14) and (15) (questioning person outside Ontario, commissioner's duties) apply, with necessary changes.

(20) **EVIDENCE BY AFFIDAVIT, OTHER METHOD** — A party may request that the court make an order under clause 1 (7.2) (i) permitting the evidence of a witness to be heard by affidavit or another method not requiring the witness to attend in person.

(20.1) [REVOKED: O. Reg. 69/15, s. 9(2).]

(21) **CONDITIONS FOR USE OF AFFIDAVIT OR ELECTRONIC RECORDING** — Evidence at trial by affidavit or another method not requiring a witness to attend in person may be used only if,

(a) the use is in accordance with an order under clause 1 (7.2) (i);

(b) the evidence is served at least 30 days before the start of the trial; and

(c) the evidence would have been admissible if given by the witness in court.

(22) **AFFIDAVIT EVIDENCE AT UNCONTESTED TRIAL** — At an uncontested trial, evidence by affidavit in Form 14A or Form 23C, and, if applicable, Form 35.1 may be used without an order under clause 1 (7.2) (i), unless the court directs that oral evidence must be given.

(23)-(27) [REVOKED: O. Reg. 250/19, s. 9(2).]

[O. Reg. 544/99, s. 9; O. Reg. 202/01, s. 6; O. Reg. 92/03, s. 2; O. Reg. 6/10, s. 8; O. Reg. 322/13, s. 13; O. Reg. 69/15, s. 9; O. Reg. 535/18, s. 6; O. Reg. 250/19, s. 9.]

Rule 24 — Costs

24. SUCCESSFUL PARTY PRESUMED ENTITLED TO COSTS — (1) There is a presumption that a successful party is entitled to the costs of a motion, enforcement, case or appeal.

(2) NO PRESUMPTION IN CHILD PROTECTION CASE OR IF PARTY IS GOVERNMENT AGENCY — The presumption does not apply in a child protection case or to a party that is a government agency.

(3) COURT'S DISCRETION – COSTS FOR OR AGAINST GOVERNMENT AGENCY — The court has discretion to award costs to or against a party that is a government agency, whether it is successful or unsuccessful.

(4) SUCCESSFUL PARTY WHO HAS BEHAVED UNREASONABLY — Despite subrule (1), a successful party who has behaved unreasonably during a case may be deprived of all or part of the party's own costs or ordered to pay all or part of the unsuccessful party's costs.

(5) DECISION ON REASONABLENESS — In deciding whether a party has behaved reasonably or unreasonably, the court shall examine,

(a)   the party's behaviour in relation to the issues from the time they arose, including whether the party made an offer to settle;

(b)   the reasonableness of any offer the party made; and

(c)   any offer the party withdrew or failed to accept.

(6) DIVIDED SUCCESS — If success in a step in a case is divided, the court may apportion costs as appropriate.

(7) ABSENT OR UNPREPARED PARTY — If a party does not appear at a step in the case, or appears but is not properly prepared to deal with the issues at that step or otherwise contributes to that step being unproductive, the court shall award costs against the party unless the court orders otherwise in the interests of justice.

(8) BAD FAITH — If a party has acted in bad faith, the court shall decide costs on a full recovery basis and shall order the party to pay them immediately.

(9) COSTS CAUSED BY FAULT OF LAWYER OR AGENT — If a party's lawyer or agent has run up costs without reasonable cause or has wasted costs, the court may, on motion or on its own initiative, after giving the lawyer or agent an opportunity to be heard,

(a)   order that the lawyer or agent shall not charge the client fees or disbursements for work specified in the order, and order the lawyer or agent to repay money that the client has already paid toward costs;

(b)   order the lawyer or agent to repay the client any costs that the client has been or-

dered to pay another party;

(c)   order the lawyer or agent personally to pay the costs of any party; and

(d)   order that a copy of an order under this subrule be given to the client.

(10) DECIDING COSTS — Promptly after dealing with a step in the case, the court shall,

(a)   determine who, if anyone, is entitled to costs in relation to that step and set the amount of any costs; or

(b)   expressly reserve the decision on costs for determination at a later stage in the case.

(10.1) [REVOKED: O. Reg. 298/18, s. 14.]

(11) SAME — The failure of the court to act under subrule (10) in relation to a step in a case does not prevent the court from awarding costs in relation to the step at a later stage in the case.

(12) SETTING COSTS AMOUNTS — In setting the amount of costs, the court shall consider,

(a)   the reasonableness and proportionality of each of the following factors as it relates to the importance and complexity of the issues:

(i)   each party's behaviour,

(ii)   the time spent by each party,

(iii)   any written offers to settle, including offers that do not meet the requirements of rule 18,

(iv)   any legal fees, including the number of lawyers and their rates,

(v)   any expert witness fees, including the number of experts and their rates,

(vi)   any other expenses properly paid or payable; and

(b)   any other relevant matter.

(12.1) SUPPORTING MATERIALS — Any claim for costs respecting fees or expenses shall be supported by documentation satisfactory to the court.

(13) ORDER FOR SECURITY FOR COSTS — A judge may, on motion, make an order for security for costs that is just, based on one or more of the following factors:

1.   A party ordinarily resides outside Ontario.

2.   A party has an order against the other party for costs that remains unpaid, in the same case or another case.

3.   A party is a corporation and there is good reason to believe it does not have enough assets in Ontario to pay costs.

4.   There is good reason to believe that the case is a waste of time or a nuisance and that the party does not have enough assets in Ontario to pay costs.

5.   A statute entitles the party to security for costs.

(14) AMOUNT AND FORM OF SECURITY — The judge shall determine the amount of the security, its form and the method of giving it.

(15) EFFECT OF ORDER FOR SECURITY — Until the security has been given, a party against whom there is an order for security for costs may not take any step in the case, except to appeal from the order, unless a judge orders otherwise.

(16) FAILURE TO GIVE SECURITY — If the party does not give the security as ordered and, as a result, a judge makes an order dismissing the party's case or striking out the party's answer or any other document filed by the party, then subrule (15) no longer applies.

(17) SECURITY MAY BE CHANGED — The amount of the security, its form and the method of giving it may be changed by order at any time.

(18) PAYMENT OF EXPENSES — The court may make an order that a party pay an amount of money to another party to cover part or all of the expenses of carrying on the case, including a lawyer's fees.

[O. Reg. 544/99, s. 10; O. Reg. 322/13, s. 14; O. Reg. 235/16, s. 4; O. Reg. 298/18, s. 14; O. Reg. 418/18, s. 1.]

Rule 25 — Orders

25. CONSENT ORDER — (1) If the parties agree, the court may make an order under these rules or an Act without having the parties or their lawyers come to court.

(2) SUCCESSFUL PARTY PREPARES DRAFT ORDER — The party in whose favour an order is made shall prepare a draft of the order (Form 25, 25A, 25B, 25C or 25D), unless the court orders otherwise.

(3) OTHER PARTY MAY PREPARE DRAFT ORDER — If the party in whose favour an order is made does not have a lawyer or does not prepare a draft order within 10 days after the order is made, any other party may prepare the draft order, unless the court orders otherwise.

(4) APPROVAL OF DRAFT ORDER — A party who prepares an order shall serve a draft, for approval of its form and content, on every other party who was in court or was represented when the order was made (including a child who has a lawyer).

(5) SETTLING CONTENTS OF DISPUTED ORDER — Unless the court orders otherwise, a party who disagrees with the form or content of a draft order shall serve, on every party who was served under subrule (4) and on the party who served the draft order,

(a)   a notice disputing approval (Form 25E);

(b)   a copy of the order, redrafted as proposed; and

(c)   notice of a time and date at which the clerk will settle the order by telephone conference.

(6) **TIME AND DATE** — The time and date shall be set by the clerk and shall be within five days after service of the notice disputing approval.

(7) **DISPUTED ORDER** — **SETTLEMENT BY JUDGE** — If unable to settle the order at the telephone conference, the clerk shall, as soon as possible, refer the order to the judge who made it, to be settled at a further telephone conference, unless the judge orders the parties to come to court for settlement of the order.

(8) **NO APPROVAL REQUIRED IF NO RESPONSE FROM OTHER PARTY** — If no approval or notice disputing approval (Form 25E) is served within 10 days after the draft order is served for approval, it may be signed without approval.

(9) **NO APPROVAL REQUIRED FOR CERTAIN ORDERS** — If an order dismisses a motion, case or appeal, without costs, or is prepared by the clerk under subrule (11), it may be signed without approval.

(10) **NO APPROVAL REQUIRED IN EMERGENCIES** — If the delay involved in getting an order approved would have serious consequences, the judge who made it may sign it without approval.

(11) **WHEN CLERK PREPARES ORDER** — The clerk shall prepare the order for signature,

(a)   within 10 days after it is made, if no party has a lawyer;

(b)   as soon as it is made,

    (i)   if it is a support deduction order or alternative payment order under the *Family Responsibility and Support Arrears Enforcement Act, 1996* or an order under the *Interjurisdictional Support Orders Act, 2002,*

    (i.1)   if it is a restraining order under section 35 of the *Children's Law Reform Act* or section 46 of the *Family Law Act,*

    (i.2)   if it is an order terminating a restraining order referred to in subclause (i.1), or

    (ii)   if the judge directs the clerk to do so.

(11.1) **RESTRAINING ORDERS** — A restraining order referred to in subclause 11 (b) (i.1) shall be in Form 25F or 25G.

(11.2) An order terminating a restraining order referred to in subclause 11(b) (i.1) shall be in Form 25H.

(12) **WHO SIGNS ORDER** — An order may be signed by the judge who made it or by the clerk.

(13) **SERVICE OF ORDER** — Unless the court orders otherwise, the person who prepared an order shall serve it,

(a)   on every other party, including a party to whom paragraph 1 of subrule 1 (8.4) (no notice to party) applies;

(b)   if a child involved in the case has a lawyer, on the lawyer; and

(c)   on any other person named by the court.

(14) SUPPORT DEDUCTION ORDER NOT SERVED — A support deduction order under the *Family Responsibility and Support Arrears Enforcement Act, 1996* does not have to be served.

(15) SERVICE OF EXTENDED SOCIETY CARE ORDER — An order for extended society care under Part V of the *Child, Youth and Family Services Act, 2017* shall be served on the following persons, in addition to the ones mentioned in subrule (13):

1.   The child, if that Act requires notice to the child.

2.   Any foster parent or other person who is entitled to notice under subsection 79 (3) of that Act.

3.   A Director appointed under that Act.

(16) SERVICE OF SECURE TREATMENT ORDER — An order for secure treatment under Part VII of the *Child, Youth and Family Services Act, 2017* shall be served on the administrator of the secure treatment program, in addition to the persons mentioned in subrule (13).

(17) SERVICE OF ADOPTION ORDER — An adoption order shall be served on the following persons, in addition to the ones mentioned in subrule (13):

1.   The adopted child, if the child gave consent under subsection 180 (6) of the *Child, Youth and Family Services Act, 2017.*

2.   The persons mentioned in subsection 222 (3) of that Act.

(18) EFFECTIVE DATE — An order is effective from the date on which it is made, unless it states otherwise.

(19) CHANGING ORDER – FRAUD, MISTAKE, LACK OF NOTICE — The court may, on motion, change an order that,

(a)   was obtained by fraud;

(b)   contains a mistake;

(c)   needs to be changed to deal with a matter that was before the court but that it did not decide;

(d)   was made without notice; or

(e)   was made with notice, if an affected party was not present when the order was made because the notice was inadequate or the party was unable, for a reason satisfactory to the court, to be present.

(20) SAME — Rule 14 applies with necessary changes to a motion to change a final order under subrule (19) and, for the purpose, clause 14 (6) (a) shall be read as if the ref-

erence to a temporary order were a reference to a final order.

[O. Reg. 56/03, s. 3; O. Reg. 76/06, s. 6; O. Reg. 151/08, s. 6; O. Reg. 386/09, s. 1; O. Reg. 322/13, s. 15; O. Reg. 142/14, s. 10; O. Reg. 140/15, s. 2; O. Reg. 298/18, s. 15; O. Reg. 535/18, s. 7(F).]

Rule 25.1 — Payment into and out of Court

25.1 DEFINITION — (1) In this rule,

"Accountant" means the Accountant of the Superior Court of Justice.

(2) NON-APPLICATION OF RULE — This rule does not apply to,

(a) money paid or to be paid into court for the enforcement of an order for the payment or recovery of money, including enforcement by garnishment; or

(b) money for the support of a child or spouse that is paid or to be paid into court by the payor on behalf of a recipient.

(3) PAYMENT INTO COURT, FILING IN PERSON WITH CLERK OR ACCOUNTANT — Subject to subrule (9), a party who is required to pay money into court shall do so in accordance with subrules (4) to (8).

(4) DOCUMENTS TO BE FILED — The party shall file with the clerk or Accountant a written request for payment into court and a copy of the order under which the money is payable.

(5) DIRECTION — On receiving the documents filed under subrule (4), the clerk or Accountant shall give the party a direction to receive the money, addressed to a bank listed in Schedule I or II to the *Bank Act* (Canada) and specifying the account in the Accountant's name into which the money is to be paid.

(6) CLERK TO FORWARD DOCUMENTS — If the documents are filed with the clerk, the clerk shall forward the documents to the Accountant.

(7) PAYMENT — On receiving from the clerk or Accountant the direction referred to in subrule (5), the party shall pay the money into the specified bank account in accordance with the direction.

(8) BANK'S DUTIES — On receiving the money, the bank shall give a receipt to the party paying the money and immediately send a copy of the receipt to the Accountant.

(9) PAYMENT INTO COURT, PAYMENT BY MAIL TO ACCOUNTANT — A party may pay money into court by mailing to the Accountant the documents referred to in subrule (4), together with the money that is payable.

(10) ACCOUNTANT TO PROVIDE RECEIPT — On receiving money under subrule (9), the Accountant shall give a receipt to the party paying the money.

(11) PAYMENT OUT OF COURT, AUTHORITY — Money may only be paid out of court under an order or on consent of all parties.

(12) PAYMENT OUT UNDER AN ORDER — A person who seeks payment of money out of court under an order shall file with the Accountant,

(a)   a written request for payment out naming the person to whom the money is to be paid under the order;

(b)   the original order for payment out or a copy certified by an official of the court, unless one or the other has already been filed with the Accountant; and

(c)   an affidavit stating that the order for payment out is not under appeal and that the time for appealing the order has expired, or that any appeal of the order has been disposed of.

(13)   **CHILDREN'S LAWYER, PUBLIC GUARDIAN AND TRUSTEE** — If the person seeking payment out under an order is the Children's Lawyer or the Public Guardian and Trustee, the documents referred to in clauses (12) (a) and (c) are not required to be filed.

(14)   **PAYMENT OUT ON CONSENT** — A person who seeks payment of money out of court on consent shall file with the Accountant,

(a)   a written request for payment out naming the person to whom the money is to be paid, and an affidavit stating that neither the person making the request nor the person to whom the money is to be paid is a special party, a child party or a child under the age of 18 years who is not a party, with copies of the following attached as exhibits:

(i)   photo identification of the requesting person,

(ii)   proof of that person's date of birth,

(iii)   proof of that person's current address; and

(b)   the affidavit of each party or each of the other parties, as the case may be, stating that the party consents to the payment out as set out in the request and that neither the party nor the person to whom the money is to be paid is a special party, a child party or a child under the age of 18 years who is not a party, with copies of the documents referred to in subclauses (a) (i), (ii) and (iii), as they relate to the party providing the affidavit, attached as exhibits.

(15)   **ACCOUNTANT'S DUTIES** — If the requirements of subrule (12) or (14), as the case may be, are met, the Accountant shall pay the money to the person named in the order or request for payment out, and the payment shall include any accrued interest, unless a court orders otherwise.

(16)   **ORDER FOR PAYMENT OUT, SPECIAL PARTY OR CHILD** — The court may, on motion, order payment out of court of money for or on behalf of a special party or child.

(17)   **WHERE NOTICE IS NOT REQUIRED** — A motion under subrule (16) by the Children's Lawyer or the Public Guardian and Trustee may be made without notice, unless the court orders otherwise.

(18)   **COSTS** — In making an order under subrule (16), the court may order that costs payable to the person who made the motion be paid directly to that person's representative out of the money in court.

(19) **APPLICATION** — This rule applies to the payment into and out of court of money paid into court on and after the day on which Ontario Regulation 389/12 comes into force.

[O. Reg. 389/12, s. 1; O. Reg. 250/19, s. 10]

Rule 26 — Enforcement of Orders

26. WHERE TO ENFORCE AN ORDER — (1) The place for enforcement of an order is governed by 5 (5), (6), (7) and (7.1) (place for starting enforcement).

(2) **HOW TO ENFORCE AN ORDER** — An order that has not been obeyed may, in addition to any other method of enforcement provided by law, be enforced as provided by subrules (3) and (4).

(3) **PAYMENT ORDERS** — A payment order may be enforced by,

(a)   a request for a financial statement (subrule 27 (1));

(b)   a request for disclosure from an income source (subrule 27 (7));

(c)   a financial examination (subrule 27 (11));

(d)   seizure and sale (rule 28);

(e)   garnishment (rule 29);

(f)   a default hearing (rule 30), if the order is a support order;

(g)   the appointment of a receiver under section 101 of the *Courts of Justice Act*; and

(h)   registration under section 42 of the *Family Responsibility and Support Arrears Enforcement Act, 1996.*

(4) **OTHER ORDERS** — An order other than a payment order may be enforced by,

(a)   a writ of temporary seizure of property (subrule 28 (10));

(b)   a contempt order (rule 31); and

(c)   the appointment of a receiver under section 101 of the *Courts of Justice Act.*

(5) **STATEMENT OF MONEY OWED** — A statement of money owed shall be in Form 26, with a copy of the order that is in default attached.

(6) **SPECIAL FORMS FOR STATEMENT OF MONEY OWED** — Despite subrule (5),

(a)   if the *Family Responsibility and Support Arrears Enforcement Act, 1996* applies, a statement of arrears in the form used by the Director may be used instead of Form 26;

(b)   if the *Interjurisdictional Support Orders Act, 2002* applies, a document receivable under section 49 of that Act may be used instead of Form 26.

(7) **RECIPIENT'S OR DIRECTOR'S ENTITLEMENT TO COSTS** — Unless the court orders otherwise, the recipient or the Director is entitled to the costs,

(a)   of carrying out a financial examination; and

(b)   of issuing, serving, filing and enforcing a writ of seizure and sale, a writ of temporary seizure and a notice of garnishment and of changing them by statutory declaration.

(8) ENFORCEMENT OF ADMINISTRATIVE COSTS — For the purpose of subrule (7), the recipient or the Director may collect under a writ of seizure and sale, a notice of garnishment or a statutory declaration changing either of them,

(a)   the amounts set out in the regulations under the *Administration of Justice Act* and awarded under rule 24 (costs) for filing and renewing with the sheriff a writ of seizure and sale or a writ of temporary seizure;

(b)   payments made to a sheriff, clerk, official examiner, authorized court transcriptionist or other public officer in accordance with the regulations under the *Administration of Justice Act* and awarded under rule 24 (costs), on filing with the sheriff or clerk a copy of a receipt for each payment or an affidavit setting out the payments made; and

(c)   the actual expense for carrying out a financial examination, or any other costs to which the recipient or the Director is entitled under subrule (7), on filing with the sheriff or clerk an affidavit (Form 26A) setting out the items of expense in detail.

(9) AFFIDAVIT FOR FILING DOMESTIC CONTRACT — An affidavit for filing a domestic contract under subsection 35 (1) of the *Family Law Act* shall be in Form 26B.

(10) DIRECTOR'S STATUS — If the Director enforces an order under the *Family Responsibility and Support Arrears Enforcement Act, 1996*, anything in these rules relating to enforcement by the person in whose favour the order was made applies to the Director.

(11) FILING AND REFILING WITH THE DIRECTOR — A person who files or refiles a support order in the Director's office shall immediately send notice of the filing, by mail, fax or email, to the clerk at any court office where the recipient is enforcing the order.

(12) TRANSFERRING ENFORCEMENT FROM RECIPIENT TO DIRECTOR — A recipient who files a support order in the Director's office shall, on the Director's request, assign to the Director any enforcement that the recipient has started, and then the Director may continue with the enforcement as if the Director had started it.

(13) TRANSFERRING ENFORCEMENT FROM DIRECTOR TO RECIPIENT — If the parties withdraw a support order from the Director's office, the Director shall, on the recipient's request, given to the Director at the same time as the notice of withdrawal, assign to the recipient any enforcement that the Director has started, and then the recipient may continue with the enforcement as if the recipient had started it.

(14) NOTICE OF TRANSFER OF ENFORCEMENT — A person who continues an enforcement under subrule (12) or (13) shall immediately send a notice of transfer of enforcement (Form 26C), by mail, fax or email to,

(a)   all parties to the enforcement;

(b)   the clerk at every court office where the enforcement is being carried on; and

(c)   every sheriff who is involved with the enforcement at the time of transfer.

(15) PLACE OF REGISTRATION OF SUPPORT ORDER UNDER THE DIVORCE ACT (CANADA) — If a person wants to enforce an order for support made outside Ontario under the *Divorce Act* (Canada), the order shall be registered in a court, as defined in subsection 20 (1) of that Act, as follows:

1.   If the recipient resides in Ontario, in the municipality where the recipient resides.

2.   If the recipient does not reside in Ontario, in the municipality where the payor resides.

3.   If neither the recipient nor the payor resides in Ontario, in the municipality where any property owned by the payor is located or, if the payor doesn't have any property, in any municipality.

(16) PLACE OF REGISTRATION OF CUSTODY OR ACCESS ORDER UNDER THE DIVORCE ACT (CANADA) — If a person wants to enforce an order involving custody of or access to a child that is made outside Ontario under the *Divorce Act* (Canada), the order shall be registered in a court, as defined in subsection 20 (1) of that Act, in accordance with clause 5 (6) (a) of these rules.

(17) REGISTRATION REQUIREMENTS — The person requesting the registration shall send to the court a certified copy of the order and a written request that the order be registered under paragraph 20 (3) (a) of the *Divorce Act* (Canada).

[O. Reg. 544/99, s. 11; O. Reg. 56/03, s. 4; O. Reg. 89/04, s. 9; O. Reg. 142/14, s. 11; O. Reg. 140/15, s. 4; O. Reg. 235/16, s. 5.]

Rule 27 — Requiring Financial Information

27. REQUEST FOR FINANCIAL STATEMENT — (1) If a payment order is in default, a recipient may serve a request for a financial statement (Form 27) on the payor.

(2) EFFECT OF REQUEST FOR FINANCIAL STATEMENT — Within 15 days after being served with the request, the payor shall send a completed financial statement (Form 13) to the recipient by mail, fax or email.

(3) FREQUENCY OF REQUESTS FOR FINANCIAL STATEMENTS — A recipient may request a financial statement only once in a six-month period, unless the court gives the recipient permission to do so more often.

(4) APPLICATION OF RULE 13 — If a party is required under this rule to give a financial statement, the following subrules apply with necessary changes:

13   (6) (full disclosure)

13   (7) or (7.1) (income tax documents)

13   (11) (insufficient financial information)

13   (12) (updating financial statement)

13   (15) (correcting and updating)

13   (16) (order to file statement).

(5) ORDER FOR FINANCIAL STATEMENT — The court may, on motion, order a payor to serve and file a financial statement.

(6) FAILURE TO OBEY ORDER — If the payor does not serve and file a financial statement within 10 days after being served with the order, the court may, on motion with special service (subrule 6 (3)), order that the payor be imprisoned continuously or intermittently for not more than 40 days.

(7) REQUEST FOR STATEMENT OF INCOME FROM INCOME SOURCE — If a payment order is in default, the recipient may serve a request for a statement of income (Form 27A) on an income source of the payor, requiring the income source to prepare and send to the recipient, by mail, fax or email, a statement of income (Form 27B).

(8) FREQUENCY OF REQUESTS FOR STATEMENT OF INCOME — A recipient may request a statement of income from an income source only once in a six-month period, unless the court gives the recipient permission to do so more often.

(9) ORDER FOR STATEMENT OF INCOME — The court may, on the recipient's motion, order an income source to serve and file a statement of income.

(10) INCOME SOURCE'S FAILURE TO OBEY ORDER — If the income source does not serve and file a statement of income within 10 days after being served with the order, the court may, on the recipient's motion, order the income source to post a bond (Form 32).

(11) APPOINTMENT FOR FINANCIAL EXAMINATION — If a payment order is in default, the recipient may serve on the payor, by special service (subrule 6 (3)), an appointment for a financial examination (Form 27C), requiring the payor to,

(a)   come to a financial examination;

(b)   bring to the examination any document or thing named in the appointment that is in the payor's control or available to the payor on request, relevant to the enforcement of the order, and not protected by a legal privilege; and

(c)   serve a financial statement (Form 13) on the recipient, not later than seven days before the date of the examination.

(12) FINANCIAL EXAMINATION OF PERSON OTHER THAN PAYOR — If a payment order is in default and a person other than the payor may know about the matters listed in subrule (17), the recipient may require that person to come to a financial examination by serving a summons to witness (Form 23) and the witness fee (subrule 23 (4)) on the person by special service (subrules 6 (3) and (4)).

(13) PLACE WHERE FINANCIAL EXAMINATION HELD — A financial examination shall be held,

(a)   in a place where the parties and the person to be examined agree;

(b)   where the person to be examined lives in Ontario, in the municipality where the person lives; or

(c)   in a place chosen by the court.

(14) **OTHER RULES APPLY** — Subrules 19 (4), (5) and (8) (documents protected by legal privilege, use of privileged documents, documents omitted from affidavit) and 23 (7) (failure to obey summons) apply to a financial examination, with necessary changes.

(15) **NOTICE OF TIME AND PLACE OF EXAMINATION** — A payor who is served with an appointment or a person who is served with a summons for a financial examination shall have at least 10 days' notice of the time and place of the examination.

(16) **BEFORE WHOM EXAMINATION IS HELD, METHOD OF RECORDING** — A financial examination shall be held under oath or affirmation, before a person chosen by agreement of the payor and recipient or in accordance with subrule 20 (12) (other arrangements for questioning), and shall be recorded by a method chosen in the same way.

(17) **SCOPE OF EXAMINATION** — On a financial examination, the payor or other person may be questioned about,

(a)   the reason for the payor's default;

(b)   the payor's income and property;

(c)   the debts owed to and by the payor;

(d)   the disposal of any property by the payor either before or after the making of the order that is in default;

(e)   the payor's past, present and future ability to pay under the order;

(f)   whether the payor intends to obey the order, and any reason for not doing so; and

(g)   any other matter relevant to the enforcement of the order.

(18) **RESISTANCE TO EXAMINATION** — Subrule (19) applies if a payor who is served with an appointment or a person who is served with a summons for a financial examination,

(a)   does not come to the examination as required by the appointment or summons;

(b)   does not serve on the recipient a financial statement as required by the appointment;

(c)   comes to the examination, but does not bring a document or thing named in the appointment or summons; or

(d)   comes to the examination, but refuses to take an oath or affirm or to answer a question.

(19) **ORDER FOR ANOTHER EXAMINATION** — The court may, on motion, make an order and give directions for another financial examination of the payor or other person and may in addition require the payor or person to post a bond (Form 32).

(20) **IMPRISONMENT** — If a payor or other person, without sufficient excuse, fails to

obey an order or direction made under subrule (19), the court may, on motion with special service (subrule 6 (3)), order that the payor or person be imprisoned continuously or intermittently for not more than 40 days.

(21) IMPRISONMENT POWER IS ADDITIONAL — The court may exercise its power under subrule (20) in addition to or instead of its power of forfeiture under rule 32 (bonds, recognizances and warrants).

(22) FREQUENCY OF EXAMINATIONS — A recipient may conduct only one financial examination of a payor and one financial examination of any other person in a six-month period, or more often with the court's permission.

[O. Reg. 544/99, s. 12; O. Reg. 89/04, s. 10; O. Reg. 322/13, s. 16; O. Reg. 69/15, s. 10; O. Reg. 140/15, s. 4.]

Rule 28 — Seizure and Sale

28. ISSUE OF WRIT OF SEIZURE AND SALE — (1) The clerk shall issue a writ of seizure and sale (Form 28) if a recipient files,

(a)   a request for a writ of seizure and sale (Form 28A); and

(b)   a statement of money owed (subrules 26 (5) and (6)).

(1.1) ELECTRONIC FILING OF WRIT — Subject to subrule (11), a writ of seizure and sale issued under subrule (1) may be filed with a sheriff electronically.

(1.2) ELECTRONIC FILING OF REQUEST, ISSUANCE OF WRIT — Subject to subrule (11), a recipient may file a request for a writ of seizure and sale electronically, in which case,

(a)   clause (1) (b) does not apply to the request;

(b)   the writ shall be issued electronically; and

(c)   the issued writ shall automatically be filed electronically with the sheriff specified in the writ.

(1.3) [REVOKED: O. Reg. 298/18, s. 16.]

(1.4) ERROR IN WRIT ISSUED ELECTRONICALLY — If a person who obtained an electronically issued writ of seizure and sale discovers that the writ contains an error, the person may, no later than 5 p.m. eastern standard or daylight saving time, as the case may be, on the second day after the day on which the writ is considered under subrule (13) to have been filed with a sheriff, correct the error by using the software that was used for the issuance of the writ.

(2) STATUTORY DECLARATION UNDER THE *FAMILY RESPONSIBILITY AND SUPPORT ARREARS ENFORCEMENT ACT, 1996* — The statutory declaration to sheriff mentioned in section 44 of the *Family Responsibility and Support Arrears Enforcement Act, 1996* shall be in Form 28B.

(3) STATUTORY DECLARATION IF ORDER CHANGED — If a court changes a payment order that is being enforced by a writ of seizure and sale, a statutory declaration

to sheriff (Form 28B) may be filed with the sheriff and once filed, it has the same effect as a declaration mentioned in subrule (2).

(3.1) ELECTRONIC FILING — A statutory declaration referred to in subrule (2) or (3) may be filed electronically.

(4) DURATION OF WRIT — A writ of seizure and sale continues in effect until,

   (a)   the writ is withdrawn under subrule (6.5) or (7); or

   (b)   the court orders otherwise under subrule (8).

(5) WRIT ISSUED UNDER FORMER RULES — A writ directing the sheriff to seize and sell a payor's property that was issued by the court under the rules that applied before these rules take effect has the same legal effect as a writ of seizure and sale issued under these rules, and does not expire except as subrule (4) provides.

(6) NOTIFYING SHERIFF OF PAYMENT RECEIVED — If a writ of seizure and sale has been filed with a sheriff,

   (a)   the recipient shall, on the sheriff's request, provide a statutory declaration setting out details of all payments received by or on behalf of the recipient; and

   (b)   the sheriff shall update the writ accordingly.

(6.1) MAY BE FILED ELECTRONICALLY — Subject to subrule (11), the statutory declaration referred to in clause (6) (a) may be filed with the sheriff electronically.

(6.2) CHANGE OF ADDRESS — If the address of the recipient or his or her lawyer changes after a writ has been filed with a sheriff, the recipient shall give written notice of the new address to the sheriff, and the sheriff shall update the writ accordingly.

(6.3) MAY BE FILED ELECTRONICALLY — Subject to subrule (11), notice of the new address may be filed with the sheriff electronically.

(6.4) CONFIRMATION OF ELECTRONICALLY FILED WRIT — In order to confirm whether a writ of seizure and sale filed with a sheriff electronically has been properly issued and filed, the sheriff may require the recipient to provide to the sheriff, in the manner and within the time the sheriff specifies, a statement of money owed (subrule 26 (5) or (6)).

(6.5) WITHDRAWAL BY SHERIFF — The sheriff may withdraw an electronically filed writ of seizure and sale if,

   (a)   the sheriff determines that the writ was improperly issued or filed; or

   (b)   the recipient fails to comply with subrule (6.4).

(6.6) SAME — A writ may be withdrawn under subrule (6.5) at any time during its enforcement.

(6.7) CORRECTIONS BY SHERIFF — If the sheriff makes a determination that a writ of seizure and sale filed with the sheriff electronically was properly issued or filed but contains an error or otherwise differs from the order to which the writ relates, the sheriff may correct the writ to make it consistent with the order.

(6.8) NOTICE — The sheriff shall give notice of a withdrawal under subrule (6.5) or a correction under subrule (6.7) to the recipient.

(7) WITHDRAWING WRIT — The person who obtained a writ to enforce an order shall immediately withdraw it from every sheriff's office where it has been filed if,

   (a)   the person no longer wants to enforce the order by a writ;

   (b)   in the case of a payment order, the payor's obligation to make periodic payments under the order has ended and all other amounts owing under it have been paid; or

   (c)   in the case of any other order, the person against whom the writ was issued has obeyed the order.

(7.1) SAME — A writ may be withdrawn under subrule (7) by,

   (a)   giving written notice to the sheriff that the writ should be withdrawn; or

   (b)   subject to subrule (11), filing notice of a withdrawal of writ electronically.

(8) ORDER CHANGING, WITHDRAWING OR SUSPENDING WRIT — The court may, on motion, make an order changing the terms of a writ, withdrawing it or temporarily suspending it, even if the writ was issued by another court in Ontario.

(9) SERVICE OF ORDER — The person making the motion, or another person named by the court, shall serve a copy of the order on,

   (a)   every sheriff in whose office the writ has been filed; and

   (b)   if the writ was issued by the court in another place, or by another court, on the clerk of the court in the other place or the clerk of the other court.

(9.1) ELECTRONIC FILING OF CHANGES — If the court makes an order under subrule (8) making any of the following changes to a writ that has been filed with a sheriff, the person required to serve a copy of the order under subrule (9) may, subject to subrule (11), file the changes to the writ with the sheriff electronically instead of serving a copy of the order on the sheriff under clause (9) (a):

   1.   The name of a party.

   2.   The recipient's lawyer or other representative.

   3.   The amount owing under the writ.

(10) WRIT OF TEMPORARY SEIZURE OF PROPERTY — The court may, on motion with special service (subrule 6 (3)), give permission to issue a writ of temporary seizure (Form 28C) directing the sheriff to take possession of and hold all or part of the land and other property of a person against whom an order has been made and to hold any income from the property until the writ is withdrawn or the court orders otherwise.

(11) LIMIT ON WHO MAY FILE ELECTRONICALLY — The electronic filing and issuance of documents under this rule is only available for,

(a)   lawyers;

(b)   the Director of the Family Responsibility Office; and

(c)   Ministers or bodies acting under the authority of an Act of Canada or Ontario.

(12) [REVOKED: O. Reg. 298/18, s. 16.]

(13) [REVOKED: O. Reg. 298/18, s. 16.]

(14) ELECTRONIC FILING AND SIGNATURES, SWEARING — The following requirements are deemed to have been met if a document is filed or issued under this rule electronically using the authorized software:

1.   A requirement that the document be signed.

2.   A requirement that the document be sworn or affirmed.

[O. Reg. 544/99, s. 13; O. Reg. 89/04, s. 11; O. Reg. 142/14, s. 12; O. Reg. 298/18, s. 16.]

Rule 29 — Garnishment

29. ISSUE OF NOTICE OR NOTICES OF GARNISHMENT — **(1)** The clerk shall issue as many notices of garnishment (Form 29A or 29B) as a recipient requests if the recipient files,

(a)   a request for garnishment (Form 29) or an extra-provincial garnishment process referred to in section 50 of the *Family Responsibility and Support Arrears Enforcement Act, 1996*; and

(b)   a statement of money owed (subrules 26 (5) and (6)).

(2) ONE RECIPIENT AND ONE GARNISHEE PER NOTICE — Each notice of garnishment shall name only one recipient and one garnishee.

(3) SERVICE ON PAYOR AND GARNISHEE — The notice of garnishment shall be served on the payor and on the garnishee but the payor shall, in addition, be served with the documents filed under subrule (1).

(4) EFFECT OF NOTICE OF GARNISHMENT — A notice of garnishment attaches,

(a)   every debt that is payable by the garnishee to the payor at the time the notice is served; and

(b)   every debt that is payable by the garnishee to the payor,

(i)   after the notice is served, or

(ii)   on the fulfilment of a condition after the notice is served.

(5) DURATION — The notice of garnishment continues in effect from the time of service on the garnishee until it is withdrawn or stopped under this rule or until the court orders otherwise under this rule.

(6) FINANCIAL INSTITUTION — If the garnishee is a financial institution, the notice of garnishment and all further notices required to be served under this rule shall be served

185

at the branch of the institution where the debt to the payor is payable, unless subrule (6.1) applies.

(6.1) FEDERALLY REGULATED FINANCIAL INSTITUTION — GARNISHMENT RE SUPPORT — If the garnishee is a financial institution to which the *Bank Act* (Canada), the *Cooperative Credit Associations Act* (Canada) or the *Trust and Loan Companies Act* (Canada) applies and the garnishment enforces a support order, the notice of garnishment and all further notices required to be served under this rule,

(a)   shall be served at the designated office of the institution established for this purpose; and

(b)   shall be accompanied by a statement to garnishee financial institution re support (Form 29J).

(6.2) NEW ACCOUNTS — Subrules (4) and (5) do not apply to money in an account opened after a notice of garnishment is served as described in subrule (6) or (6.1).

(7) JOINT DEBTS GARNISHABLE — Subrules (4) and (5) also apply to debts owed to the payor and another person jointly.

(8) PROCEDURE WHEN JOINT DEBT GARNISHED — If a garnishee has been served with a notice of garnishment and the garnishee owes a debt to which subrules (4) and (5) apply to the payor and another person jointly,

(a)   the garnishee shall pay, in accordance with subrule (11), half of the debt, or the larger or smaller amount that the court orders;

(b)   the garnishee shall immediately send the other person a notice to co-owner of debt (Form 29C) by mail, fax or email, to the person's address in the garnishee's records; and

(c)   the garnishee shall immediately serve the notice to co-owner of debt on the recipient or the Director, depending on who is enforcing the order, and on the sheriff or clerk if the sheriff or clerk is to receive the money under subrule (11) or (12).

(9) JOINT DEBT – MONEY TO BE HELD — Despite subrule (12), if served with notice under clause (8) (c), the sheriff, clerk or Director shall hold the money received for 30 days, and may pay it out when the 30 days expire, unless the other person serves and files a dispute within the 30 days.

(10) PAYMENT OF ARREARS DOES NOT END GARNISHMENT — A notice of garnishment continues to attach future periodic payments even though the total amount owed when it was served is fully paid up.

(11) PERSONS TO WHOM GARNISHEE MAKES PAYMENTS — A garnishee who has been served with a notice of garnishment shall make the required payments to,

(a)   the Director, if the notice of garnishment relates to an order being enforced by the Director;

(b)   the clerk, if the notice of garnishment does not relate to an order being enforced by the Director.

(12) CLERK OR DIRECTOR TO PAY OUT MONEY — On receiving money under a notice of garnishment, the Director or clerk shall, even if a dispute has been filed, but subject to subrules (9) and (13), immediately pay,

(a)   to the recipient, any part of the money that comes within the priority created by subsection 2 (3) of the *Creditors' Relief Act, 2010*; and

(b)   to the sheriff, any part of the money that exceeds that priority.

(13) ORDER THAT SUBRULE (12) DOES NOT APPLY — The court may, at a garnishment hearing or on a motion to change the garnishment under this rule, order that subrule (12) does not apply.

(14) CHANGE IN GARNISHMENT, INDEXED SUPPORT — If a notice of garnishment enforces a support order that indexes periodic payments for inflation, the recipient may serve on the garnishee and on the payor a statutory declaration of indexed support (Form 29D) setting out the new amount to be paid under the order, and file the declaration with the court.

(15) EFFECT OF STATUTORY DECLARATION OF INDEXED SUPPORT — A statutory declaration of indexed support requires the garnishee to pay the new amount set out in the declaration from the time it is served on the garnishee.

(16) GARNISHMENT DISPUTE — Within 10 days after being served with a notice of garnishment or a statutory declaration of indexed support, a payor, garnishee or co-owner of a debt may serve on the other parties and file a dispute (Form 29E, 29F or 29G).

(17) NOTICE OF GARNISHMENT HEARING — The clerk shall, on request, issue a notice of garnishment hearing (Form 29H),

(a)   within 10 days after a dispute is served and filed; or

(b)   if the recipient says that the garnishee has not paid any money or has not paid enough money.

(18) SERVICE OF NOTICE — The clerk shall serve and file the notice not later than 10 days before the hearing.

(19) GARNISHMENT HEARING — At a garnishment hearing, the court may make one or more of the following temporary or final orders:

1.   An order dismissing the dispute.

2.   An order that changes how much is being garnished on account of a periodic payment order. The court may make an order under this paragraph even if it does not have the authority to change the payment order itself.

2.1   An order that changes how much is being garnished on account of a periodic payment order and that, at the same time, changes the payment order itself. The court may make an order under this paragraph only if,

   i.   the payment order is one that the court has the authority to change, and

   ii.   the parties to the payment order agree to the change, or one of those parties has served and filed notice of a motion to have the change made.

3.   An order changing how much is being garnished on account of a non-periodic payment order.

4.   An order suspending the garnishment or any term of it, while the hearing is adjourned or until the court orders otherwise.

5.   An order setting aside the notice of garnishment or any statutory declaration of indexed support.

6.   An order that garnished money held or received by the clerk, Director or sheriff be held in court.

7.   An order that garnished money that has been paid out in error to the recipient be paid into and held in court, returned to the garnishee or sent to the payor or to the co-owner of the debt.

8.   An order that garnished money held in court be returned to the garnishee or be sent to the payor, the co-owner of the debt, the sheriff, the clerk or the Director.

9.   An order deciding how much remains owing under a payment order that is being enforced by garnishment against the payor or garnishee.

10.   If the garnishee has not paid what was required by the notice of garnishment or statutory declaration of indexed support, an order that the garnishee pay all or part of what was required.

11.   An order deciding who is entitled to the costs of the garnishment hearing and setting the amount of the costs.

(20) **CHANGING GARNISHMENT AT OTHER TIMES** — The court may also use the powers listed in subrule (19), on motion or on its own initiative, even if the notice of garnishment was issued by another court,

(a)   on a motion under section 7 of the *Wages Act*;

(b)   if the court replaces a temporary payment order with a final payment order;

(c)   if the court indexes or changes a payment order; or

(d)   if the court allows an appeal.

(21) **CHANGING GARNISHMENT WHEN ABILITY TO PAY CHANGES** — If there has been a material change in the payor's circumstances affecting the payor's ability to pay, the court may, on motion, use the powers listed in subrule (19).

(22) **GARNISHEE'S PAYMENT PAYS DEBT** — Payment of a debt by a garnishee under a notice of garnishment or statutory declaration of indexed support pays off the debt between the garnishee and the payor to the extent of the payment.

(23) **NOTICE BY GARNISHEE – PAYOR NOT WORKING OR RECEIVING MONEY** — Within 10 days after a payor stops working for or is no longer receiving any money from a garnishee, the garnishee shall send a notice as subrule (27) requires,

(a)   saying that the payor is no longer working for or is no longer receiving any money from the garnishee;

(b)   giving the date on which the payor stopped working for or receiving money from the garnishee and the date of the last payment to the payor from the garnishee; and

(c)   giving the name and address of any other income source of the payor, if known.

(24) NOTICE BY GARNISHEE – PAYOR WORKING OR RECEIVING MONEY AGAIN — Within 10 days after the payor returns to work for or starts to receive money again from the garnishee, the garnishee shall send another notice as subrule (27) requires, saying that the payor has returned to work for or started to receive money again from the garnishee.

(25) NOTICE BY PAYOR – WORKING OR RECEIVING MONEY AGAIN — Within 10 days after returning to work for or starting to receive money again from the garnishee, the payor shall send a notice as subrule (27) requires, saying that the payor has returned to work for or started to receive money again from the garnishee.

(26) NOTICE BY PAYOR – NEW INCOME SOURCE — Within 10 days after starting to work for or receive money from a new income source, the payor shall send a notice as subrule (27) requires, saying that the payor has started to work for or to receive money from the new income source.

(27) NOTICE SENT TO CLERK AND RECIPIENT OR DIRECTOR — A notice referred to in subrule (23), (24), (25) or (26) shall be sent to the clerk, and to the recipient or the Director (depending on who is enforcing the order), by mail, fax or email.

(28) NOTICE BY CLERK — When the clerk receives a notice under subrule (26), the clerk shall immediately notify the recipient or the Director (depending on who is enforcing the order) by mail, fax or email.

(29) NEW NOTICE OF GARNISHMENT — If no written objection is received within 10 days of the clerk notifying the recipient or the Director that a notice under subrule (26) was received, the clerk shall,

(a)   issue a new notice of garnishment directed to the new garnishee, requiring the same deductions as were required to be made, under the previous notice of garnishment or statutory declaration of indexed support, on the day that the notice under subrule (26) was received; and

(b)   send a copy of the new notice of garnishment to the payor and the new garnishee, by mail, fax or email.

(30) EFFECT OF NEW NOTICE OF GARNISHMENT — Issuing a new notice of garnishment under clause (29) (a) does not cancel any previous notice of garnishment or statutory declaration of indexed support.

(31) NOTICE TO STOP GARNISHMENT — The recipient shall immediately send a notice to stop garnishment (Form 29I), by mail, fax or email, to the garnishee and payor and file it with the clerk if,

(a)   the recipient no longer wants to enforce the order by garnishment; or

(b)   the requirement to make periodic payments under the order has ended and all other amounts owing under the order have been paid.

(32) OLD ORDERS — This rule applies, with necessary changes, to,

(a)   an attachment order made under section 30 of the *Family Law Reform Act* (chapter 152 of the Revised Statutes of Ontario, 1980); and

(b)   a garnishment order issued by the court under the rules that were in effect before January 1, 1985.

[O. Reg. 544/99, s. 14; O. Reg. 56/03, s. 5; O. Reg. 76/06, s. 7; O. Reg. 322/13, s. 17; O. Reg. 140/15, s. 4.]

Rule 30 — Default Hearing

30. ISSUING NOTICE OF DEFAULT HEARING — **(1)** The clerk shall issue a notice of default hearing (Form 30),

(a)   if the support order is being enforced by the recipient, when the recipient files a request for a default hearing (Form 30A) and a statement of money owed (subrule 26 (5));

(b)   if it is being enforced by the Director, when the Director files a statement of money owed.

(2) SERVING NOTICE OF DEFAULT HEARING — The notice of default hearing shall be served on the payor by special service in accordance with subrule 6 (4) and filed.

(3) PAYOR'S DISPUTE — Within 10 days after being served with the notice, the payor shall serve on the recipient and file,

(a)   a financial statement (Form 13); and

(b)   a default dispute (Form 30B).

(4) UPDATING STATEMENT OF MONEY OWED — The recipient shall serve and file a new statement of money owed (subrule 26 (5)) not more than seven days before the default hearing.

(5) WHEN DIRECTOR TO UPDATE STATEMENT — Despite subrule 26 (10), subrule (4) applies to the Director only if,

(a)   the amount the Director is asking the court to enforce is greater than the amount shown in the notice of default hearing; or

(b)   the court directs it.

(6) STATEMENT OF MONEY OWED PRESUMED CORRECT — The payor is presumed to admit that the recipient's statement of money owed is correct, unless the payor has filed a default dispute stating that the statement of money owed is not correct and giving detailed reasons.

(7) ARREARS ENFORCEABLE TO DATE OF HEARING — At the default hearing, the court may decide and enforce the amount owing as of the date of the hearing.

(8) CONDITIONAL IMPRISONMENT — The court may make an order under clause **41 (10) (h)** or **(i)** of the *Family Responsibility and Support Arrears Enforcement Act, 1996,* suspending the payor's imprisonment on appropriate conditions.

(9) ISSUING WARRANT OF COMMITTAL — If the recipient, on a motion with special service in accordance with subrule 6 (4) on the payor, states by affidavit (or by oral evidence, with the court's permission) that the payor has not obeyed a condition that was imposed under subrule (8), the court may issue a warrant of committal against the payor, subject to subsection 41 (15) (power to change order) of the *Family Responsibility and Support Arrears Enforcement Act, 1996.*

[O. Reg. 76/06, s. 8; O. Reg. 322/13, s. 18.]

Rule 31 — Contempt of Court

31. WHEN CONTEMPT MOTION AVAILABLE — (1) An order, other than a payment order, may be enforced by a contempt motion made in the case in which the order was made, even if another penalty is available.

(2) NOTICE OF CONTEMPT MOTION — The notice of contempt motion (Form 31) shall be served together with a supporting affidavit, by special service in accordance with subrule 6 (4), unless the court orders otherwise.

(3) AFFIDAVIT FOR CONTEMPT MOTION — The supporting affidavit may contain statements of information that the person signing the affidavit learned from someone else, but only if the requirements of subrule 14 (19) are satisfied.

(4) WARRANT TO BRING TO COURT — To bring before the court a person against whom a contempt motion is made, the court may issue a warrant for the person's arrest if,

(a)   the person's attendance is necessary in the interest of justice; and

(b)   the person is not likely to attend voluntarily.

(5) CONTEMPT ORDERS — If the court finds a person in contempt of the court, it may order that the person,

(a)   be imprisoned for any period and on any conditions that are just;

(b)   pay a fine in any amount that is appropriate;

(c)   pay an amount to a party as a penalty;

(d)   do anything else that the court decides is appropriate;

(e)   not do what the court forbids;

(f)   pay costs in an amount decided by the court; and

(g)   obey any other order.

191

(6) WRIT OF TEMPORARY SEIZURE — The court may also give permission to issue a writ of temporary seizure (Form 28C) against the person's property.

(7) LIMITED IMPRISONMENT OR FINE — In a contempt order under one of the following provisions, the period of imprisonment and the amount of a fine may not be greater than the relevant Act allows:

1.   Section 38 of the *Children's Law Reform Act*.

2.   Section 49 of the *Family Law Act*.

3.   Section 53 of the *Family Responsibility and Support Arrears Enforcement Act, 1996*.

(8) CONDITIONAL IMPRISONMENT OR FINE — A contempt order for imprisonment or for the payment of a fine may be suspended on appropriate conditions.

(9) ISSUING WARRANT OF COMMITTAL — If a party, on a motion with special service (subrule 6 (3)) on the person in contempt, states by an affidavit in Form 32C (or by oral evidence, with the court's permission) that the person has not obeyed a condition imposed under subrule (8), the court may issue a warrant of committal against the person.

(10) PAYMENT OF FINE — A contempt order for the payment of a fine shall require the person in contempt to pay the fine,

(a)   in a single payment, immediately or before a date that the court chooses; or

(b)   in instalments, over a period of time that the court considers appropriate.

(11) CORPORATION IN CONTEMPT — If a corporation is found in contempt, the court may also make an order under subrule (5), (6) or (7) against any officer or director of the corporation.

(12) CHANGE IN CONTEMPT ORDER — The court may, on motion, change an order under this rule, give directions and make any other order that is just.

[O. Reg. 322/13, s. 19.]

Rule 32 — Bonds, Recognizances and Warrants

32. WARRANT TO BRING A PERSON TO COURT — (1) If a person does not come to court after being served with notice of a case, enforcement or motion that may result in an order requiring the person to post a bond,

(a)   the court may issue a warrant for the person's arrest, to bring the person before the court, and adjourn the case to await the person's arrival; or

(b)   the court may,

   (i)   hear and decide the case in the person's absence and, if appropriate, make an order requiring the person to post a bond, and

   (ii)   if the person has been served with the order and does not post the bond by the date set out in the order, issue a warrant for the person's arrest, on motion without notice, to bring the person before the court.

(2) **FORM OF BOND AND OTHER REQUIREMENTS** — A bond shall be in Form 32, does not need a seal, and shall,

    (a)   have at least one surety, unless the court orders otherwise;

    (b)   list the conditions that the court considers appropriate;

    (c)   set out an amount of money to be forfeited if the conditions are not obeyed;

    (d)   shall require the person posting the bond to deposit the money with the clerk immediately, unless the court orders otherwise; and

    (e)   name the person to whom any forfeited money is to be paid out.

(3) **PERSON BEFORE WHOM RECOGNIZANCE TO BE ENTERED INTO** — A recognizance shall be entered into before a judge, a justice of the peace or the clerk.

(4) **CHANGE OF CONDITIONS IN A BOND** — The court may, on motion, change any condition in a bond if there has been a material change in a party's circumstances since the date of the order for posting the bond or the date of an order under this subrule, whichever is more recent.

(5) **CHANGE IN BOND UNDER CHILDREN'S LAW REFORM ACT** — In the case of a bond under the *Children's Law Reform Act*, subrule (4) also applies to a material change in circumstances that affects or is likely to affect the best interests of the child.

(6) **REMOVAL OR REPLACEMENT OF SURETY** — The court may, on motion, order that a surety be removed or be replaced by another person as surety, in which case as soon as the order is made, the surety who is removed or replaced is free from any obligation under the bond.

(7) **MOTION TO ENFORCE BOND** — A person requesting the court's permission to enforce a bond under subsection 143 (1) (enforcement of recognizance or bond) of the *Courts of Justice Act* shall serve a notice of forfeiture motion (Form 32A), with a copy of the bond attached, on the person said to have broken the bond and on each surety.

(8) **FORFEITURE IF NO DEPOSIT MADE** — If an order of forfeiture of a bond is made and no deposit was required, or a deposit was required but was not made, the order shall require the payor or surety to pay the required amount to the person to whom the bond is payable,

    (a)   in a single payment, immediately or before a date that the court chooses; or

    (b)   in instalments, over a period of time that the court considers appropriate.

(9) **CHANGE IN PAYMENT SCHEDULE** — If time is allowed for payment under subrule (8), the court may, on a later motion by the payor or a surety, allow further time for payment.

(10) **ORDER FOR FORFEITURE OF DEPOSIT** — If an order of forfeiture of a bond is made and a deposit was required and was made, the order shall direct the clerk to pay the required amount immediately to the person to whom the bond is made payable.

(11) **CANCELLING BOND** — The court may, on motion, make an order under sub-

rule (4), or an order cancelling the bond and directing a refund of all or part of the deposit, if,

(a)   a payor or surety made a deposit under the bond;

(b)   the conditions of the bond have not been broken; and

(c)   the conditions have expired or, although they have not expired or do not have an expiry date, the payor or surety has good reasons for getting the conditions of the bond changed.

(12) FORM OF WARRANT FOR ARREST — A warrant for arrest issued against any of the following shall be in Form 32B:

1.   A payor who does not file a financial statement ordered under subsection 40 (4) of the *Family Responsibility and Support Arrears Enforcement Act, 1996* or under these rules.

2.   A payor who does not come to a default hearing under section 41 of the *Family Responsibility and Support Arrears Enforcement Act, 1996.*

3.   An absconding respondent under subsection 43 (1) or 59 (2) of the *Family Law Act.*

4.   An absconding payor under subsection 49 (1) of the *Family Responsibility and Support Arrears Enforcement Act, 1996.*

5.   A witness who does not come to court or remain in attendance as required by a summons to witness.

6.   A person who does not come to court in a case that may result in an order requiring the person to post a bond under these rules.

7.   A person who does not obey an order requiring the person to post a bond under these rules.

8.   A person against whom a contempt motion is made.

9.   Any other person liable to arrest under an order.

10.   Any other person liable to arrest for committing an offence.

(13) BAIL ON ARREST — Section 150 (interim release by justice of the peace) of the *Provincial Offences Act* applies, with necessary changes, to an arrest made under a warrant mentioned in paragraph 1, 2, 3 or 4 of subrule (12).

(14) AFFIDAVIT FOR WARRANT OF COMMITTAL — An affidavit in support of a motion for a warrant of committal shall be in Form 32C.

(15) FORM OF WARRANT OF COMMITTAL — A warrant of committal issued to enforce an order of imprisonment shall be in Form 32D.

Rule 32.1 — Enforcement of Family Arbitration Awards

32.1 REQUESTING ENFORCEMENT — (1) A party who is entitled to the enforcement of a family arbitration award and who wants to ask the court to enforce the award under section 59.8 of the *Family Law Act* may file a request to enforce a family arbitration award (Form 32.1), together with,

    (a)   copies of the certificates of independent legal advice required by the *Family Law Act* for the parties to the family arbitration agreement;

    (b)   a copy of the family arbitration agreement; and

    (c)   the original award or a certified copy.

(2) WHEN REQUIRED TO PROCEED BY MOTION — Despite subrule (1), if there is already a family law case to which these rules apply between the parties to the family arbitration agreement in the Superior Court of Justice or the Family Court of the Superior Court of Justice, the party entitled to enforcement shall make a motion in that case rather than a request under this rule, and subrule 14 (24) applies in respect of the motion.

(3) APPLICATION OF OTHER RULES — The rules that apply to an application apply to a request to enforce a family arbitration award that is proceeding under this rule, unless these rules provide otherwise.

(4) HEARING DATE — When a request to enforce a family arbitration award is filed, the clerk shall set a hearing date.

(5) SERVICE — The request shall be served immediately on every other party.

(6) REQUEST NOT SERVED ON OR BEFORE HEARING DATE — If a request to enforce a family arbitration award is not served on a respondent on or before the hearing date, the clerk shall, at the applicant's request, set a new hearing date for that respondent, and the applicant shall make the necessary change to the request and serve it immediately on that respondent.

(7) OPPOSING A REQUEST — Despite subrule 10 (1) (serving and filing answer), a respondent who wants to oppose a request to enforce a family arbitration award shall serve a dispute of request for enforcement (Form 32.1A) on every other party and file it,

    (a)   no later than 30 days after being served with the request; or

    (b)   if the request is served outside Canada or the United States of America, no later than 60 days after being served with the request.

(8) WRITTEN HEARING — Unless the court orders otherwise under subrule (10), the request shall be dealt with on the basis of written documents without the parties or their lawyers needing to come to court.

(9) REQUEST FOR ORAL HEARING — A respondent may request an oral hearing by filing a motion form (Form 14B) within seven days after being served with the request to enforce a family arbitration award.

(10) ORDER FOR ORAL HEARING — The court may order an oral hearing, on motion or on its own initiative, if it is satisfied that an oral hearing is necessary to deal with the case justly.

[O. Reg. 388/12, s. 8; O. Reg. 69/15, s. 11.]

Rule 33 — Child Protection

33. TIMETABLE — (1) Every child protection case, including a status review application, is governed by the following timetable:

Step in the case	Maximum time for completion, from the start of the case
First hearing, if child has been brought to a place of safety	5 days
Service and filing of answers and plans of care	30 days
Temporary care and custody hearing	35 days
Settlement conference	80 days
Hearing	120 days

(2) **CASE MANAGEMENT JUDGE** — Wherever possible, at the start of the case a judge shall be assigned to manage it and monitor its progress.

(3) **COURT MAY LENGTHEN TIMES ONLY IN BEST INTERESTS OF CHILD** — The court may lengthen a time shown in the timetable only if the best interests of the child require it.

(4) **PARTIES MAY NOT LENGTHEN TIMES** — The parties may not lengthen a time shown in the timetable by consent under subrule 3 (6).

(5) **PLAN OF CARE OR SUPERVISION TO BE SERVED** — A party who wants the court to consider a plan of care or supervision shall serve it on the other parties and file it not later than seven days before a conference, even if that is sooner than the timetable would require.

(6) **TEMPORARY CARE AND CUSTODY HEARING – AFFIDAVIT EVIDENCE** — The evidence at a temporary care and custody hearing shall be given by affidavit, unless the court orders otherwise.

(6.1) **STATUS REVIEW** — A status review application under clause 113 (2) (a) or (b) of the *Child, Youth and Family Services Act, 2017* shall be served at least 30 days before the date the order for society supervision or interim society care expires.

(7) **FORMS FOR CHILD PROTECTION CASES** — In a child protection case,

(a)   an information for a warrant to bring a child to a place of safety shall be in Form 33;

(b)   a warrant to bring a child to a place of safety shall be in Form 33A;

(c)   an applicant's plan of care for a child shall be,

    (i)   if the applicant is a children's aid society, in Form 33B, and

    (ii)   if the applicant is not a children's aid society, in Form 33B.1;

(c.1)   a respondent's answer and plan of care for a child shall be,

    (i)   if the respondent is not a children's aid society, in Form 33B.1,

    (ii)   if the respondent is a children's aid society, in Form 10 and Form 33B;

(d)   an agreed statement of facts in a child protection case shall be in Form 33C; and

(e)   an agreed statement of facts in a status review application shall be in Form 33D.

(8) FORMS FOR SECURE TREATMENT CASES — In an application under Part VII (secure treatment) of the *Child, Youth and Family Services Act, 2017*, a consent signed by the child shall be in Form 33E and a consent signed by any other person shall be in Form 33F.

(9) EXAMINATION OF EXPERT EVIDENCE ON MOTIONS (VOIR DIRE) — The court shall consider whether a preliminary examination of expert opinion evidence intended to be given on a motion in a child protection case is required in order to determine its admissibility.

[O. Reg. 91/03, s. 7; O. Reg. 76/06, s. 9; O. Reg. 298/18, s. 17; O. Reg. 250/19, s. 11.]

Rule 34 — Adoption

34. CYFSA DEFINITIONS APPLY — (1) The definitions in the *Child, Youth and Family Services Act, 2017* apply to this rule and, in particular,

"Director" means a Director within the meaning of the Act.

(2) MEANING OF "ACT" — In this rule,

"Act" means the *Child, Youth and Family Services Act, 2017;*

"old Act" means the *Child and Family Services Act,* as it read immediately before its repeal.

(2.1) USE OF INITIALS IN DOCUMENTS — An applicant or respondent may be referred to by only the first letter of his or her surname in any document in the case, except that,

(a)   the applicant's full names shall appear in the adoption order; and

(b)   the child's full names shall appear in the adoption order, unless the court orders that the child's first name and the first letter of his or her surname be used.

(3) CERTIFIED COPY OF ORDER FROM OUTSIDE ONTARIO — When this rule requires a copy of an order to be filed and the order in question was made outside Ontario, it shall be a copy that is certified by an official of the court or other authority that made it.

(4) MATERIAL TO BE FILED WITH ADOPTION APPLICATIONS — The following shall be filed with every application for an adoption:

1.   A certified copy of the statement of live birth of the child, or an equivalent that satisfies the court.

2.   If required, the child's consent to adoption (Form 34) or a notice of motion and supporting affidavit for an order under subsection 180 (9) of the Act dispensing with the child's consent.

3.   If the child is not in extended care, an affidavit of parentage (Form 34A) or any other evidence about parentage that the court requires from the child's parent or a person named by the court.

4.   If the applicant has a spouse who has not joined in the application, a consent to the child's adoption by the spouse (Form 34B).

5.   If required by the Act or by an order, a Director's or local director's statement on adoption (Form 34C) under subsection 202 (1) or (7) of the Act.

6.   An affidavit signed by the applicant (Form 34D) that includes details about the applicant's education, employment, health, background and ability to support and care for the child, a history of the relationship between the applicant and the child and any other evidence relating to the best interests of the child, and states whether the child is a First Nations, Inuk or Métis person.

(5) **REPORT OF CHILD'S ADJUSTMENT** — A report under subsection 202 (6) or (7) of the Act of the child's adjustment in the applicant's home shall also be filed with the application if the child is under 16 years of age, or is 16 years of age or older but has not withdrawn from parental control and has not married.

(6) **ADDITIONAL MATERIAL – CHILD IN EXTENDED SOCIETY CARE** — If the child is in extended society care, the following shall also be filed with the application:

1.   A Director's consent to adoption (Form 34E).

1.1   If an access order was made under Part V of the Act,

      0.i.   a copy of each access order,

      i.   copies of every notice given under subsection 195 (2) or 197 (2) of the Act or, if applicable, section 145.1.1 of the old Act,

      ii.   for each notice,

          A.   proof of service of the notice including, if applicable, a copy of an order permitting service by a method chosen by the court, or

          B.   a copy of an order that notice is not required, and

      iii. [REVOKED: O. Reg. 298/18, s. 18(12).]

      iv. an affidavit (Form 34G.1) signed by an employee of a children's aid society stating that,

    A. no application for an openness order has been filed, or

    B. if any applications for openness orders have been filed, the status of those applications, including details of any openness orders that have been made.

2. A copy of any order under Part V of the Act ending access to the child.

3. A copy of the order of extended society care.

4. Proof of service of the orders referred to in paragraphs 2 and 3, or a copy of any order dispensing with service.

5. An affidavit (Form 34G.1), signed by a person delegated by the local director of the children's aid society that has placed the child for adoption, stating,

    i. that the person has made reasonable inquiries as to whether there is any outstanding access order respecting the child and that, to the best of the person's knowledge, there is no such order, and

    ii. that there is no appeal in progress from an order referred to in paragraph 2 or 3, or that the appeal period has expired without an appeal being filed, or that an appeal was filed but has been withdrawn or finally dismissed.

6. If the child is a First Nations, Inuk or Métis person, proof that the written notice of intention to begin planning for the adoption of the child required under section 186 of the Act or, if applicable, section 141.2 of the old Act, was given.

(7) ADDITIONAL MATERIAL – CHILD NOT IN EXTENDED SOCIETY CARE — If the child is not in extended society care and is placed for adoption by a licensee or children's aid society, the following shall also be filed with the application:

1. A copy of any custody or access order that is in force and is known to the person placing the child, or to an applicant.

2. [REVOKED: O. Reg. 337/02, s. 3(4).]

3. A consent to adoption (Form 34F) under section 180 of the Act from every parent, other than the applicant, of whom the person placing the child or an applicant is aware. An order under section 181 of the Act dispensing with a parent's consent may be filed instead of the consent.

4. An affidavit (Form 34G) signed by the licensee or by an authorized employee of the children's aid society (depending on who is placing the child).

5. If the child is placed by a licensee, a copy of the licensee's licence to make the placement at the time of placing the child for adoption.

6. If the child is a First Nations, Inuk, or Métis person and is placed by a licensee, proof that any written notice of intention to place the child for adoption required by the regulations made under the Act or, if applicable, the old Act, was given.

7. If the child is a First Nations, Inuk, or Métis person and is placed by a children's aid society, proof that the written notice of intention to begin planning for the

adoption of the child required under section 186 of the Act or, if applicable, section 141.2 of the old Act, was given.

(8) **ADDITIONAL MATERIAL – RELATIVE OR STEP-PARENT** — If the applicant is the child's relative or the spouse of the child's parent and the child was a resident of Canada before being placed for adoption, an affidavit from each applicant (Form 34H) shall also be filed with the application.

(9) **APPLICATION BY STEP-PARENT OR RELATIVE** — An application by a relative of the child or the spouse of the child's parent,

(a)   shall not be commenced until the 21-day period referred to in subsection 180 (8) of the Act has expired; and

(b)   shall be accompanied by the applicant's affidavit confirming that he or she did not receive a withdrawal of consent during the 21-day period.

(10) **STEP-PARENT ADOPTION, PARENT'S CONSENT** — An application by the spouse of the child's parent shall be accompanied by the parent's consent (Form 34I).

(11) **INDEPENDENT LEGAL ADVICE, CHILD'S CONSENT** — The consent of a child to be adopted (Form 34) shall be witnessed by a representative of the Children's Lawyer, who shall complete the affidavit of execution and independent legal advice contained in the form.

(11.1) **INDEPENDENT LEGAL ADVICE, CONSENT OF PARENT UNDER 18** — The consent of a person under the age of 18 years who is a parent of the child to be adopted (Form 34F) shall be witnessed by a representative of the Children's Lawyer, who shall complete an affidavit of execution and independent legal advice (Form 34J).

(12) **INDEPENDENT LEGAL ADVICE, ADULT PARENT'S CONSENT** — The consent of an adult parent of the child to be adopted shall be witnessed by an independent lawyer, who shall complete the affidavit of execution and independent legal advice.

(13) **COPY OF CONSENT FOR PERSON SIGNING** — A person who signs a consent to an adoption shall be given a copy of the consent and of the affidavit of execution and independent legal advice.

(13.1) **WITHDRAWAL OF CONSENT BY PARENT** — A parent who has given consent to an adoption under subsection 180 (2) of the Act may withdraw the consent under subsection 180 (8) of the Act in accordance with the following:

1.   If the child is placed for adoption by a children's aid society, the parent who wishes to withdraw the consent shall ensure that the children's aid society receives the written withdrawal within 21 days after the consent was given.

2.   If the child is placed for adoption by a licensee, the parent who wishes to withdraw the consent shall ensure that the licensee receives the written withdrawal within 21 days after the consent was given.

3.   If a relative of the child or a spouse of a parent proposes to apply to adopt the child, the parent who wishes to withdraw the consent shall ensure that the rela-

tive or spouse receives the written withdrawal within 21 days after the consent was given.

(13.2) WITHDRAWAL OF CONSENT BY CHILD AGED SEVEN OR OLDER — A child who has given consent to an adoption under subsection 180 (6) of the Act may withdraw the consent under subsection 180 (8) of the Act in accordance with the following:

1. The withdrawal shall be signed within 21 days after the consent was given, and witnessed by the person who witnessed the consent under subrule (11) or by another representative of the Children's Lawyer.

2. The person who witnesses the withdrawal shall give the original withdrawal document to the child and promptly serve a copy on the children's aid society, licensee, relative or spouse, as the case may be.

(14) MOTION TO WITHDRAW CONSENT — Despite subrule 5 (4) (place for steps other than enforcement), a motion to withdraw a consent to an adoption under subsection 182 (1) of the Act shall be made in,

(a)   the municipality where the person who gave the consent lives; or

(b)   in any other place that the court decides.

(15) CLERK TO CHECK ADOPTION APPLICATION — Before the application is presented to a judge, the clerk shall,

(a)   review the application and other documents filed to see whether they are in order; and

(b)   prepare a certificate (Form 34K).

(16) DISPENSING WITH CONSENT BEFORE PLACEMENT — In an application to dispense with a parent's consent before placement for adoption,

(a)   the applicant may be the licensee, a parent, the children's aid society or the person who wants to adopt;

(b)   the respondent is the person who has not given consent;

(c)   if an order that service is not required is sought, the request shall be made in the application and not by motion;

(d)   if the application is being served, the applicant shall serve and file with it an affidavit (Form 14A) setting out the facts of the case;

(e)   if the application is not being served, the applicant shall file with it an affidavit (Form 14A) setting out the facts of the case, and the clerk shall send the case to a judge for a decision on the basis of affidavit evidence.

(17) FORMS FOR OPENNESS APPLICATIONS — In a case about an openness order under Part VIII of the Act,

(a)   an application for an openness order shall be in Form 34L;

(b)   a consent to an openness order under section 194 of the Act shall be in Form 34M;

(b.1)   a consent to an openness order under section 196 or 197 of the Act shall be in Form 34M.1;

(c)   an application to change or terminate an openness order shall be in Form 34N;

(d)   an answer to an application for an openness order or an answer to an application to change or terminate an openness order shall be in Form 33B.2;

(e)   the notice of intention to place a child for adoption to be served under subsection 195 (2) of the Act shall be in Form 8D.2;

(f)   the notice of intention to place a First Nations, Inuk or Métis child for adoption to be served under subsection 197 (2) of the Act on the child and on a representative chosen by each of the child's bands and First Nations, Inuit or Métis communities, shall be in Form 8D.3.

(g)   [REVOKED: O. Reg. 298/18, s. 18(27).]

(18) SERVICE OF NOTICE OF INTENTION TO PLACE A CHILD FOR ADOPTION — In an application for an order under subsection 195 (5) or clause 197 (4) (b) of the Act to allow another method of service of the notice of intention to place a child for adoption (Form 8D.2 or 8D.3), or for an order under subsection 195 (6) of the Act or clause 197 (4) (b) of the Act that notice is not required,

(a)   the applicant is the children's aid society;

(b)   the respondent is the person who is entitled to receive notice under subsection 195 (2) or 197 (2) of the Act;

(c)   the application shall be made using Form 8B.2 — Application (general) (*Child, Youth and Family Services Act, 2017* cases other than child protection and status review);

(d)   the application shall be filed in the same court file as the child protection case in which the child was ordered into extended society care;

(e)   the applicant shall file an affidavit (Form 14A) setting out the facts in support of the order being requested and the clerk shall send the case to a judge for a decision on the basis of the affidavit evidence.

(19) TIMELINES FOR OPENNESS APPLICATIONS — Every application for an openness order is governed by the following timetable:

Step in the case	Maximum time for completion, from the date the application is filed
Service and filing of answers	30 days
First hearing or settlement conference	50 days
Hearing	90 days

[O. Reg. 337/02, s. 3; O. Reg. 519/06, s. 6; O. Reg. 383/11, s. 7; O. Reg. 140/15, s. 5; O. Reg. 298/18, s. 18; O. Reg. 535/18, s. 8.]

Rule 35 — Change of Name

35. TIME FOR APPLICATION — **(1)** An application under subsection 7 (3) (application to court for change of name) of the *Change of Name Act* shall be made within 30 days after the applicant is notified that the Registrar General has refused to make the requested change of name.

(2) SERVICE ON THE REGISTRAR GENERAL — The applicant shall serve the application and any supporting material on the Registrar General by delivering or mailing a copy of the documents to the Deputy Registrar General.

(3) REGISTRAR GENERAL'S REASONS FOR REFUSAL — Within 15 days after being served under subrule (2), the Registrar General may file reasons for refusing to make the requested change of name.

Rule 35.1 — Custody and Access

35.1 (1) [REVOKED: O. Reg. 226/17, s. 2.]

(2) AFFIDAVIT IN SUPPORT OF CUSTODY OR ACCESS CLAIM — If an application, answer or motion to change a final order contains a claim for custody of or access to a child, the party making the claim shall serve and file an affidavit in support of claim for custody or access (Form 35.1), together with any other documents required by this rule, with the document that contains the claim.

(3) POLICE RECORDS CHECK — Every person who makes a claim for custody of a child and who is not a parent of the child shall attach to the affidavit in support of claim for custody or access,

   (a)   a police records check obtained not more than 60 days before the person starts the claim; or

   (b)   if the person requested the police records check for the purposes of the claim but has not received it by the time he or she starts the claim, proof of the request.

(4) SAME — If clause (3) (b) applies, the person shall serve and file the police records check no later than 10 days after receiving it.

(5) REQUEST FOR REPORT FROM CHILDREN'S AID SOCIETY — Every person required to submit a request under subsection 21.2 (2) of the *Children's Law Reform Act* for a report from a children's aid society shall provide to the court a copy of the request together with the affidavit in support of claim for custody or access.

(6) DOCUMENTS SHALL BE REFUSED — If these rules require a document to be accompanied by the applicable documents referred to in this rule, the clerk shall not accept the document for filing without,

   (a)   an affidavit in support of claim for custody or access; and

   (b)   the documents referred to in subrules (3) and (5), if applicable.

(7) CORRECTIONS AND UPDATES — As soon as a person discovers that information in his or her affidavit in support of claim for custody or access is incorrect or incomplete, or that there has been a change in the information provided in the affidavit, he or she shall immediately serve and file,

    (a)   a new affidavit in support of claim for custody or access (Form 35.1) containing the correct or updated information; or

    (b)   if the correction or change is minor, an affidavit in Form 14A describing the correction or change and indicating any effect it has on the person's plan for the care and upbringing of the child.

(8) ASSOCIATED CASES — If the clerk provides to a person making a claim for custody of a child information in writing under subsection 21.3 (1) of the *Children's Law Reform Act* respecting any current or previous family proceedings involving the child or any person who is a party to the claim and who is not a parent of the child, the person shall serve a copy of the written information on every other party.

(9) SAME — If the written information provided by the clerk contains information indicating that the person making the claim was or is involved in family proceedings in which he or she was or is not involved, the person making the claim may serve with the copy of the written information an affidavit identifying those proceedings.
[O. Reg. 6/10, s. 9; O. Reg. 226/17, s. 2; O. Reg. 535/18, s. 9(F).]

Rule 36 — Divorce

36. APPLICATION FOR DIVORCE — **(1)** Either spouse may start a divorce case by,

    (a)   filing an application naming the other spouse as a respondent; or

    (b)   filing a joint application with no respondent.

(2) JOINT APPLICATION — In a joint application, the divorce and any other order sought shall be made only with the consent of both spouses.

(3) ALLEGATION OF ADULTERY — In an application for divorce claiming that the other spouse committed adultery with another person, that person does not need to be named, but if named, shall be served with the application and has all the rights of a respondent in the case.

(4) MARRIAGE CERTIFICATE AND CENTRAL DIVORCE REGISTRY CERTIFICATE — The court shall not grant a divorce until the following have been filed:

    1.   A marriage certificate or marriage registration certificate, unless the application states that it is impractical to obtain a certificate and explains why.

    2.   A report on earlier divorce cases started by either spouse, issued under the *Central Registry of Divorce Proceedings Regulations* (Canada).

(5) DIVORCE BASED ON AFFIDAVIT EVIDENCE — An affidavit in Form 36 containing the following information shall be filed in accordance with subrule (5.1):

    1.   Confirmation that all the information in the application is correct, except as

stated in the affidavit.

2. If no marriage certificate or marriage registration certificate has been filed, sufficient information to prove the marriage.

3. Proof of any previous divorce or the death of a party's previous spouse, unless the marriage took place in Canada.

4. The information about arrangements for support of any children of the marriage required by paragraph 11 (1) (b) of the *Divorce Act* (Canada), and the income and financial information required by section 21 of the child support guidelines attached as exhibits.

5. Any other information necessary for the court to grant the divorce.

(5.1) **WHEN REQUIREMENT APPLIES** — The affidavit referred to in subrule (5) shall be filed,

(a) by the applicant, if the respondent files no answer or files an answer and later withdraws it; or

(b) in the case of a joint application, by the applicants.

(6) **DRAFT DIVORCE ORDER** — The applicant shall file with the affidavit,

(a) three copies of a draft divorce order (Form 25A);

(b) a stamped envelope addressed to each party; and

(c) if the divorce order is to contain a support order,

   (i) an extra copy of the draft divorce order for the clerk to file with the Director of the Family Responsibility Office, and

   (ii) two copies of a draft support deduction order.

(6.0.1) **ELECTRONIC FILING OF APPLICATION** — Subject to subrule (6.2), an application under clause (1) (a) may be filed electronically and, if they are filed together with the application, the following documents may also be filed electronically:

1. A marriage certificate or marriage registration certificate, unless it was issued outside Canada and not in electronic format.

2. Subject to paragraph 1 of subrule (6.3), any other document the party intends to file with the application, provided that it may be filed using the authorized software.

(6.1) **ELECTRONIC FILING OF JOINT APPLICATION** — Subject to subrules (6.2) and (6.2.1), a joint application under clause (1) (b) may be filed electronically, provided that the following documents are filed electronically together with the application:

1. The affidavits of the parties (Form 36).

2. A marriage certificate or marriage registration certificate, unless the application states that it is impractical to obtain a certificate and explains why.

3.   A draft divorce order (Form 25A).

4.   If the divorce order is to contain a support order,

     i.   a draft support deduction order,

     ii.   the support deduction order information form prescribed under the *Family Responsibility and Support Arrears Enforcement Act, 1996,* and

     iii.   the financial statements (Form 13 or 13.1) required by rule 13, if any.

4.1   If the divorce order is to contain an order respecting a property claim or a claim for exclusive possession of the matrimonial home and its contents, the financial statements (Form 13.1) required by rule 13, if any.

5.   If the divorce order is to contain an order for custody or access to a child, every affidavit in support of claim for custody or access (Form 35.1) required by rule 35.1.

6.   Any supporting documents required under these rules to be filed with a document referred to in paragraphs 1 to 5.

7.   Any other document the parties intend to file with the application, provided that it may be filed using the authorized software.

(6.2)   **WHERE ELECTRONIC FILING NOT AVAILABLE** — An application may not be filed electronically under subrule (6.0.1) or (6.1) if the authorized software does not permit electronic filing under the subrule for the municipality in which the application would otherwise be filed in paper format under rule 5.

(6.2.1)   A joint application may not be filed electronically under subrule (6.1) if,

(a)   the marriage certificate or marriage registration certificate was issued outside Canada and not in electronic format; or

(b)   the application contains, in addition to the claim for a divorce, a claim for relief other than a joint claim for,

     (i)   support,

     (ii)   an order respecting property or for exclusive possession of the matrimonial home and its contents, or

     (iii)   custody or access to a child.

(6.3)   **ELECTRONIC FILING AND RULE 36 REQUIREMENTS** — The following rules apply if an application for divorce is filed electronically:

1.   Despite electronic filing under subrule (6.0.1), the documents and materials required to be filed in accordance with subrules (5) and (6) may not be filed electronically and must be filed in paper format.

2.   If a joint application is filed electronically in accordance subrule (6.1), the requirements of subrule (6) are deemed to have been met.

(6.4) CONTINUING RECORD — Rule 9 (continuing record) does not apply to an application that is filed electronically in accordance with subrule (6.0.1) or (6.1) unless a party is required by subrule (6.6) to give documents to the clerk in paper format, in which case, unless the court orders otherwise, rule 9 applies as if the party were the person who started the case.

(6.5) ELECTRONIC ISSUANCE OF APPLICATION — An application that is filed electronically in accordance with subrule (6.0.1) or (6.1) may be issued electronically.

(6.6) REQUIREMENT TO GIVE DOCUMENTS IN PAPER FORMAT — If, after an application is filed electronically under subrule (6.0.1) or (6.1), a party intends or is required to file any other document in respect of the application, the party shall file the document in paper format and, unless the court orders otherwise, shall give to the clerk, in paper format, every document in the application that had previously been filed electronically.

(7) CLERK TO PRESENT PAPERS TO JUDGE — Once the requirements of subrules (4) to (6) have been met, the clerk shall prepare a certificate (Form 36A) and present the documents to a judge, who may,

(a)   grant the divorce as set out in the draft order;

(b)   have the clerk return the documents to the applicant to make any needed corrections; or

(c)   grant the divorce but make changes to the draft order, or refuse to grant the divorce, after giving the applicant a chance to file an additional affidavit or come to court to explain why the order should be made without change.

(8) DIVORCE CERTIFICATE — When a divorce takes effect, the clerk shall, on either party's request,

(a)   check the continuing record or, if there is no continuing record, the court file, to verify that,

    (i)   no appeal has been taken from the divorce order, or any appeal from it has been disposed of, and

    (ii)   no order has been made extending the time for an appeal, or any extended time has expired without an appeal; and

(b)   if satisfied of those matters, issue a divorce certificate (Form 36B) and mail it to the parties, unless the court orders otherwise.

(9) [REVOKED: O. Reg. 89/04, s. 12.]

[O. Reg. 89/04, s. 12; O. Reg. 298/18, s. 19; O. Reg. 535/18, s. 10.]

Rule 37 — *Interjurisdictional Support Orders Act, 2002*

37. APPLICATION — **(1)** This rule applies to cases under the Act.

(2) DEFINITIONS — In this rule,

"Act" means the *Interjurisdictional Support Orders Act, 2002*;

"appropriate authority" has the same meaning as in the Act;

"designated authority" has the same meaning as in the Act;

"general regulation" means Ontario Regulation 55/03;

"send", when used in reference to a person, means to,

(a)   mail to the person's lawyer or, if none, to the person,

(b)   send by courier to the person's lawyer or, if none, to the person,

(c)   deposit at a document exchange to which the person's lawyer belongs, or

(d)   fax to the person's lawyer or, if none, to the person.

(3) NOTICE OF HEARING — When the court receives a support application or a support variation application the clerk shall, under section 10 or 33 of the Act,

(a)   serve on the respondent, by special service,

    (i)   the notice of hearing mentioned in clause 10 (b) or 33 (b) of the Act (Form 37),

    (ii)   a copy of the documents sent by the designated authority, and

    (iii)   blank response forms; and

(b)   send to the designated authority a copy of the notice of hearing and an information sheet (Form 37A).

(4) INFORMATION AND DOCUMENTS TO BE PROVIDED BY RESPONDENT — The respondent shall file, within 30 days after service of the notice of hearing,

(a)   an answer in Form N under the general regulation,

    (i)   identifying any issues the respondent intends to raise with respect to the support application, and

    (ii)   containing the financial information referred to in subsection 21 (1) of Ontario Regulation 391/97 (Child Support Guidelines), if the support application includes a claim for child support;

(b)   an affidavit (Form 14A) setting out the evidence on which the respondent relies; and

(c)   a financial statement in Form K under the general regulation.

(5) RESPONDENT'S FINANCIAL STATEMENT — The respondent is required to file a financial statement whether he or she intends to dispute the claim or not.

(6) APPLICANT'S FINANCIAL STATEMENT — The fact that the applicant has provided financial information in a form different than that required by these rules does not affect the case.

(7) WRITTEN HEARING — Unless the court orders otherwise under subrule (9), the application shall be dealt with on the basis of written documents without the parties or

their lawyers needing to come to court.

(8) **REQUEST FOR ORAL HEARING** — The respondent may request an oral hearing by filing a motion form (Form 14B) within 30 days after being served with the notice of hearing.

(9) **ORDER FOR ORAL HEARING** — The court may order an oral hearing, on the respondent's motion or on its own initiative, if it is satisfied that an oral hearing is necessary to deal with the case justly.

(10) **DIRECTION TO REQUEST FURTHER INFORMATION OR DOCUMENTS** — A direction to request further information or documents under clause 11 (2) (a) or 34 (2) (a) of the Act shall be in Form 37B, and a statement of the court's reasons for requesting further evidence shall be attached to the direction.

(11) **DIRECTION TO BE SENT TO RESPONDENT** — When a direction is sent to the designated authority under clause 11 (2) (a) of the Act, the clerk shall also send a copy to the respondent.

(12) **ADJOURNMENT** — When the court adjourns the hearing under clause 11 (2) (b) or 34 (2) (b) of the Act, it shall specify the date on which the hearing is to continue.

(13) **COPIES OF FURTHER INFORMATION OR DOCUMENTS** — When the court receives the further information or documents, the clerk shall promptly prepare a notice of continuation of hearing (Form 37C) and send it, with copies of the information or documents, to the respondent and to the designated authority.

(14) **RESPONDENT'S AFFIDAVIT** — If the respondent wishes to respond to the further information or documents, he or she shall file an affidavit (Form 14A) containing the response with the court, within 30 days after receiving the notice of continuation of hearing.

(15) **PREPARATION OF ORDER** — The clerk shall prepare the order for signature as soon as it is made, in accordance with subrule 25 (11).

(16) **SENDING COPIES OF ORDER TO RESPONDENT AND DESIGNATED AUTHORITY** — The court shall send,

(a)   a copy of the order to the respondent, addressed to the respondent's last known address if sent by mail; and

(b)   a certified copy of the order to the designated authority.

(17) **SENDING COPY OF ORDER TO APPROPRIATE AUTHORITY** — The designated authority shall send the certified copy of the order to the appropriate authority.

(18) **NOTICE OF REGISTRATION, ORDER MADE OUTSIDE CANADA** — For the purpose of subsection 20 (1) of the Act, the clerk of the Ontario court shall give notice of the registration of an order made outside Canada by providing a notice in Form 37D, as described in subrule (19), to any party to the order who is believed to ordinarily reside in Ontario.

(19) **SENDING OR SPECIAL SERVICE** — If the party to whom notice is to be pro-

vided applied for the order in Ontario, the clerk shall send the notice to the party, but in any other case, the clerk shall serve the notice on the party by special service.

(20) **MOTION TO SET ASIDE REGISTRATION** — For the purpose of subsection 20 (3) of the Act, a party shall give notice of a motion to set aside the registration of an order made outside Canada by,

(a) filing in the Ontario court a notice of motion (Form 14) setting out the grounds for the motion;

(b) sending the notice of motion and supporting documents to the claimant at the address shown in the order; and

(c) serving the notice of motion and supporting documents on the designated authority at least 10 days before the motion hearing date.

(21) **DESIGNATED AUTHORITY NEED NOT APPEAR ON MOTION** — The designated authority is not required to appear on the motion to set aside registration.

(22) **NOTICE OF DECISION OR ORDER** — When the court makes a decision or order under section 20 of the Act, the clerk shall send copies of the order, with the court's reasons, if any,

(a) to each party, addressed to the party's last known address if sent by mail; and

(b) to the designated authority.

(23) **PARTY IN RECIPROCATING JURISDICTION** — If a party ordinarily resides in a reciprocating jurisdiction and the order was originally sent to Ontario for registration by the appropriate authority there, the clerk may send it to that appropriate authority rather than sending it to the party as set out in clause (22) (a).

(24) **PROVISIONAL ORDERS** — When the court makes a provisional order under section 7 or 30 of the Act, the clerk shall send the following to the designated authority, to be sent to the reciprocating jurisdiction:

1. One copy of,

  i. the application (Form A under the general regulation),

  ii. the applicant's financial statement (Form K under the general regulation), and

  iii. a statement giving any information about the respondent's identification, whereabouts, income, assets and liabilities.

2. Three certified copies of,

  i. the applicant's evidence and, if reasonably possible, the exhibits, and

  ii. the provisional order.

(25) **FURTHER EVIDENCE** — When the court that made a provisional order receives a request for further evidence from the confirming court under subsection 7 (4) or

30 (4) of the Act, the clerk shall send to the applicant a notice for taking further evidence (Form 37E) and a copy of the documents sent by the confirming court.

[O. Reg. 56/03, s. 6; O. Reg. 69/15, s. 12; O. Reg. 140/15, s. 5.]

Rule 37.1 — Provisional Orders and Confirmation of Provisional Orders — *Divorce Act, Family Law Act*

37.1 APPLICATION — (1) This rule applies to orders made under sections 18 and 19 of the *Divorce Act* (Canada) and under section 44 of the *Family Law Act*.

(2) DEFINITIONS — In this rule,

"confirming court" means,

(a) in the case of an order under section 19 of the *Divorce Act* (Canada), the court in Ontario or another province or territory of Canada that has jurisdiction to confirm a provisional variation of the order, or

(b) for the purpose of section 44 of the *Family Law Act*,

(i) the Ontario Court of Justice sitting in the municipality where the respondent resides, or

(ii) the Family Court of the Superior Court of Justice, if the respondent resides in an area where that court has jurisdiction;

"originating court" means,

(a) in the case of an order under section 18 of the *Divorce Act* (Canada), the court in Ontario or another province or territory of Canada that has jurisdiction under section 5 of that Act to deal with an application for a provisional variation of the order, or

(b) for the purpose of section 44 of the *Family Law Act*,

(i) the Ontario Court of Justice sitting in the municipality where the provisional order is made, or

(ii) the Family Court of the Superior Court of Justice when it makes the provisional order;

"send", when used in reference to a person, means to,

(a) mail to the person's lawyer or, if none, to the person,

(b) send by courier to the person's lawyer or, if none, to the person,

(c) deposit at a document exchange to which the person's lawyer belongs, or

(d) fax to the person's lawyer or, if none, to the person.

(3) DOCUMENTS TO BE SENT TO CONFIRMING COURT — When the court makes a provisional order under section 18 of the *Divorce Act* (Canada) or section 44 of the *Family Law Act*, the clerk shall send the following to the confirming court (if it is in Ontario) or to the Attorney General to be sent to the confirming court (if it is outside Ontario):

1.   One copy of,

     i.   the application (Form 8),

     ii.   the applicant's financial statement (Form 13),

     iii.   a statement giving any information about the respondent's identification, whereabouts, income, assets and liabilities, and

     iv.   if the confirming court is in another municipality in Ontario, proof that the application was served on the respondent.

2.   Three certified copies of,

     i.   the applicant's evidence and, if reasonably possible, the exhibits, and

     ii.   the provisional order.

(4) NO FINANCIAL STATEMENT FROM FOREIGN APPLICANT — When a confirming court in Ontario receives a provisional order made outside Ontario, the applicant does not have to file a financial statement.

(5) NOTICE OF CONFIRMATION HEARING — A clerk of a confirming court in Ontario who receives a provisional order shall,

    (a)   serve on the respondent, by special service (subrule 6 (3)),

     (i)   a notice of hearing (Form 37),

     (ii)   a copy of the documents sent by the originating court, and

     (iii)   blank response forms; and

    (b)   send a notice of hearing and an information sheet (Form 37A) to,

     (i)   the applicant,

     (ii)   the clerk of the originating court, and

     (iii)   the Attorney General, if the provisional order was made outside Ontario.

(6) RESPONDENT'S FINANCIAL STATEMENT — A respondent at a confirmation hearing under section 19 of the *Divorce Act* (Canada) shall serve and file a financial statement (Form 13) within 30 days after service of the notice of confirmation hearing.

(7) WRITTEN HEARING — Unless the court orders otherwise under subrule (9), the application shall be dealt with on the basis of written documents without the parties or their lawyers needing to come to court.

(8) REQUEST FOR ORAL HEARING — The respondent may request an oral hearing by filing a motion form (Form 14B) within 30 days after being served with the notice of hearing.

(9) ORDER FOR ORAL HEARING — The court may order an oral hearing, on the applicant's motion or on its own initiative, if it is satisfied that an oral hearing is necessary to deal with the case justly.

(10) COURT RECEIVES REQUEST FOR FURTHER EVIDENCE — When an originating court in Ontario receives a request for further evidence from the confirming court, the clerk shall send to the applicant a notice for taking further evidence (Form 37E) and a copy of the documents sent by the confirming court.

(11) COURT SENDS REQUEST FOR FURTHER EVIDENCE — When a confirming court in Ontario requests further evidence from the originating court,

(a)   the confirming court shall adjourn the confirmation hearing to a new date; and

(b)   the clerk shall send to the originating court two certified copies of the evidence taken in the confirming court.

(12) CONTINUING THE CONFIRMATION HEARING — When a confirming court in Ontario receives further evidence from the originating court, the clerk shall promptly prepare a notice of continuation of hearing (Form 37C) and send it, with copies of the evidence, to the respondent and, if the provisional order was made outside Ontario, to the Attorney General.

(13) RESPONDENT'S AFFIDAVIT — If the respondent wishes to respond to the further evidence, he or she shall file an affidavit containing the response with the court, within 30 days after receiving the notice of continuation of hearing.

[O. Reg. 56/03, s. 6; O. Reg. 69/15, s. 13.]

Rule 38 — Appeals

38. RULES THAT APPLY IN APPEALS TO DIVISIONAL COURT AND COURT OF APPEAL — (1) Rules 61, 62 and 63 of the *Rules of Civil Procedure* apply with necessary changes, including those modifications set out in subrules (2) and (3),

(a)   if an appeal lies to the Divisional Court or the Court of Appeal;

(b)   if leave to appeal to the Divisional Court or the Court of Appeal is required, in a family law case as described in subrule 1 (2).

(2) MODIFICATIONS IN CHILD PROTECTION APPEALS — If the appeal is brought in a case under the *Child, Youth and Family Services Act, 2017*, the following time periods apply instead of the time periods mentioned in the referenced provisions of the *Rules of Civil Procedure*:

1.   The time period referred to in clause 61.09 (1) (a) shall be 14 days after filing the notice of appeal if there is no transcript.

2.   The time period referred to in clause 61.09 (1) (b) shall be 30 days after receiving notice that the evidence has been transcribed.

3.   The time period referred to in clause 61.12 (2) shall be 30 days after service of the appeal book and compendium, exhibit book, transcript of evidence, if any, and appellant's factum.

4.   The time period referred to in clause 61.13 (2) (a) shall be 30 days after the registrar receives notice that the evidence has been transcribed.

5.   The time period referred to in clause 61.13 (2) (b) shall be six months after filing the notice of appeal.

6.   The time period referred to in subrule 62.02 (5) for serving the notice of motion for leave to appeal shall be 30 days.

(3) **APPEAL OF TEMPORARY ORDER IN CHILD AND FAMILY SERVICES ACT CASE** — In an appeal of a temporary order made in a case under the *Child, Youth and Family Services Act, 2017,* and brought to the Divisional Court under clause 19 (1) (b) of the *Courts of Justice Act*, the motion for leave to appeal shall be combined with the notice of appeal and heard together with the appeal.

(4) **APPEALS TO THE SUPERIOR COURT OF JUSTICE** — Subrules (5) to (45) apply to an appeal from an order of the Ontario Court of Justice to the Superior Court of Justice under,

(a)   section 48 of the *Family Law Act*;

(b)   section 73 of the *Children's Law Reform Act*;

(c)   sections 121 and 215 of the *Child, Youth and Family Services Act, 2017*;

(d)   section 40 of the *Interjurisdictional Support Orders Act, 2002*;

(e)   section 40 of the *Courts of Justice Act*; and

(f)   any other statute to which these rules apply, unless the statute provides for another procedure.

(5) **HOW TO START APPEAL** — To start an appeal from a final order of the Ontario Court of Justice to the Superior Court of Justice under any of the provisions listed in subrule (4), a party shall,

(a)   within 30 days after the date of the order or decision being appealed from, serve a notice of appeal (Form 38) on,

(i)   every other party affected by the appeal or entitled to appeal,

(ii)   the clerk of the court in the place where the order was made, and

(iii)   if the appeal is under section 121 of the *Child, Youth and Family Services Act, 2017*, every other person entitled to notice under subsection 79 (3) of that Act who appeared at the hearing; and

(b)   within 10 days after serving the notice of appeal, file it.

(6) **STARTING APPEAL OF TEMPORARY ORDER** — Subrule (5) applies to the starting of an appeal from a temporary order of the Ontario Court of Justice to the Superior Court of Justice except that the notice of appeal shall be served within seven days after the date of the temporary order.

(7) **SAME, CYFSA CASE** — To start an appeal from a temporary order of the Ontario Court of Justice to the Superior Court of Justice in a case under the *Child, Youth and Family Services Act, 2017*, subrule (5) applies and the notice of appeal shall be served within 30

days after the date of the temporary order.

(8) NAME OF CASE UNCHANGED — The name of a case in an appeal shall be the same as the name of the case in the order appealed from and shall identify the parties as appellant and respondent.

(9) APPEAL BY RESPONDENT — If the respondent in an appeal also wants to appeal the same order, this rule applies, with necessary changes, to the respondent's appeal, and the two appeals shall be heard together.

(10) GROUNDS STATED IN NOTICE OF APPEAL — The notice of appeal shall state the order that the appellant wants the appeal court to make and the legal grounds for the appeal.

(11) OTHER GROUNDS — At the hearing of the appeal, no grounds other than the ones stated in the notice of appeal may be argued unless the court gives permission.

(12) TRANSCRIPT OF EVIDENCE — If the appeal requires a transcript of evidence, the appellant shall, within 30 days after filing the notice of appeal, file proof that the transcript has been ordered.

(13) CONSULTATION WITH RESPONDENT — The appellant shall determine if the appeal requires a transcript of evidence in consultation with the respondent.

(14) AGREEMENT ON EVIDENCE TO BE TRANSCRIBED — If the appellant and respondent agree about what evidence needs to be transcribed, the appellant shall order the agreed evidence transcribed.

(15) NO AGREEMENT — If the appellant and respondent cannot agree, the appellant shall order a transcript of all of the oral evidence from the hearing of the decision under appeal unless the court orders otherwise.

(16) ONCE TRANSCRIPT COMPLETED — When the authorized court transcriptionist has completed the transcript, he or she shall promptly notify the appellant, the respondent and the court office in the court where the appeal will be heard.

(17) CONTENTS OF APPELLANT'S APPEAL RECORD — The appellant's appeal record shall contain a copy of the following documents, in the following order:

1. A table of contents describing each document, including each exhibit, by its nature and date and, for an exhibit, by exhibit number or letter.

2. The notice of appeal.

3. The order being appealed, as signed, and any reasons given by the court appealed from, as well as a further printed copy of the reasons if they are handwritten.

4. A transcript of the oral evidence.

5. Any other material that was before the court appealed from and that is necessary for the appeal.

(18) CONTENTS OF APPELLANT'S FACTUM — The appellant's factum shall be not more than 30 pages long, shall be signed by the appellant's lawyer or, if none, by the

appellant and shall consist of the following parts, containing paragraphs numbered consecutively from the beginning to the end of the factum:

1.   Part 1: Identification. A statement identifying the appellant and respondent and the court appealed from, and stating the result in that court.

2.   Part 2: Overview. A brief overview of the case and the issues on the appeal.

3.   Part 3: Facts. A brief summary of the facts relevant to the appeal, with reference to the evidence by page and line as necessary.

4.   Part 4: Issues. A brief statement of each issue, followed by a brief argument referring to the law relating to that issue.

5.   Part 5: Order. A precise statement of the order the appeal court is asked to make, including any order for costs.

6.   Part 6: Time estimate. An estimate of how much time will be needed for the appellant's oral argument, not including reply to the respondent's argument.

7.   Part 7: List of authorities. A list of all statutes, regulations, rules, cases and other authorities referred to in the factum.

8.   Part 8: Legislation. A copy of all relevant provisions of statutes, regulations and rules.

(19) RESPONDENT'S FACTUM AND APPEAL RECORD — The respondent shall, within the timeline set out in subrule (21) or (22), serve on every other party to the appeal and file,

(a)   a respondent's factum (subrule (20)); and

(b)   if applicable, a respondent's appeal record containing a copy of any material that was before the court appealed from which are necessary for the appeal but are not included in the appellant's appeal record.

(20) CONTENTS OF RESPONDENT'S FACTUM — The respondent's factum shall be not more than 30 pages long, shall be signed by the respondent's lawyer or, if none, by the respondent and shall consist of the following parts, containing paragraphs numbered consecutively from the beginning to the end of the factum:

1.   Part 1: Overview. A brief overview of the case and the issues on the appeal.

2.   Part 2: Facts. A brief statement of the facts in the appellant's factum that the respondent accepts as correct and the facts that the respondent says are incorrect, and a brief summary of any additional facts relied on by the respondent, with reference to the evidence by page and line as necessary.

3.   Part 3: Issues. A statement of the respondent's position on each issue raised by the appellant, followed by a brief argument referring to the law relating to that issue.

4.   Part 4: Additional issues. A brief statement of each additional issue raised by the respondent, followed by a brief argument referring to the law relating to that is-

sue.

5.   Part 5: Order. A precise statement of the order the appeal court is asked to make, including any order for costs.

6.   Part 6: Time estimate. An estimate of how much time will be needed for the respondent's oral argument.

7.   Part 7: List of authorities. A list of all statutes, regulations, rules, cases and other authorities referred to in the factum.

8.   Part 8: Legislation. A copy of all relevant provisions of statutes, regulations and rules not included in the appellant's factum.

(21) TIMELINES FOR SERVING AND FILING OF RECORDS AND FACTUMS OTHER THAN IN CYFSA CASES — Except for appeals in cases under the *Child, Youth and Family Services Act, 2017*, the following timelines for serving appeal records and factums apply:

1.   If a transcript is required, the appellant's appeal record and factum shall be served on the respondent and any other person entitled to be heard in the appeal and filed within 60 days from the date of receiving notice that evidence has been transcribed.

2.   If no transcript is required, the appellant's appeal record and factum shall be served on the respondent and any other person entitled to be heard in the appeal and filed within 30 days of filing of the notice of appeal.

3.   The respondent's appeal record and factum shall be served on the appellant and any other person entitled to be heard on the appeal and filed within 60 days from the serving of the appellant's appeal record and factum.

(22) TIMELINES FOR SERVING AND FILING OF RECORDS AND FACTUMS IN CYFSA CASES — For appeals of cases under the *Child, Youth and Family Services Act, 2017*, the following timelines for serving appeal records and factums apply:

1.   If a transcript is required, the appellant's appeal record and factum shall be served on the respondent and any other person entitled to be heard in the appeal and filed within 30 days from the date of receiving notice that evidence has been transcribed.

2.   If no transcript is required, the appellant's appeal record and factum shall be served on the respondent and any other person entitled to be heard in the appeal and filed within 14 days of filing of the notice of appeal.

3.   The respondent's appeal record and factum shall be served on the appellant and any other person entitled to be heard on the appeal and filed within 30 days from the serving of the appellant's appeal record and factum.

(23) SCHEDULING OF HEARING — When the appellant's appeal record and factum have been filed and the respondent's factum and appeal record, if any, have been filed, or the time for their filing has expired, the clerk shall schedule the appeal for hearing.

(24) PROMPT HEARING OF CYFSA APPEALS — An appeal under the *Child, Youth and Family Services Act, 2017* shall be heard within 60 days after the appellant's factum and appeal record are filed.

(25) MOTIONS IN APPEALS — If a person needs to bring a motion in an appeal, rule 14 applies with necessary changes to the motion.

(26) SECURITY FOR COSTS OF APPEAL — On a motion by the respondent for security for costs, the court may make an order for security for costs that is just, if it is satisfied that,

(a)   there is good reason to believe that the appeal is a waste of time, a nuisance, or an abuse of the court process and that the appellant has insufficient assets in Ontario to pay the costs of the appeal;

(b)   an order for security for costs could be made against the appellant under subrule 24 (13); or

(c)   for other good reason, security for costs should be ordered.

(27) DISMISSAL FOR FAILURE TO OBEY ORDER — If an appellant does not obey an order under subrule (26), the court may on motion dismiss the appeal.

(28) MOTION FOR SUMMARY JUDGMENT IN APPEAL — After the notice of appeal is filed, the respondent or any other person who is entitled to be heard on the appeal may make a motion for summary judgment or for summary decision on a legal issue without a hearing of the appeal, and rule 16 applies to the motion with necessary changes.

(29) MOTION TO RECEIVE FURTHER EVIDENCE — Any person entitled to be heard in the appeal may bring a motion to admit further evidence under clause 134 (4) (b) of the *Courts of Justice Act*.

(30) MOTION FOR DISMISSAL FOR DELAY — If the appellant has not,

(a)   filed proof that a transcript of evidence was ordered under subrule (12);

(b)   served and filed the appeal record and factum within the timelines set out in subrule (21) or (22) or such longer time as may have been ordered by the court,

the respondent may file a motion form (Form 14B) to have the appeal dismissed for delay.

(31) WITHDRAWAL OF APPEAL — The appellant may withdraw an appeal by serving a notice of withdrawal (Form 12) on every other party and filing it.

(32) DEEMED WITHDRAWAL — If a person serves a notice of appeal and does not file it within 10 days as required by clause (5) (b), the appeal shall be deemed to be withdrawn unless the court orders otherwise.

(33) AUTOMATIC STAYS PENDING APPEAL, SUPPORT ORDERS — The service of a notice of appeal from a temporary or final order does not stay a support order or an order that enforces a support order.

(34) OTHER PAYMENT ORDERS — The service of a notice of appeal from a temporary or final order stays, until the disposition of the appeal, any other payment order made under the temporary or final order.

(35) **STAY BY ORDER OF COURT** — A temporary or final order may be stayed on any conditions that the court considers appropriate,

(a)   by an order of the court that made the order;

(b)   by an order of the Superior Court of Justice.

(36) **EXPIRY OF STAY GRANTED BY COURT THAT MADE ORDER** — A stay granted under clause (35) (a) expires if no notice of appeal is served and the time for service has expired.

(37) **POWERS OF SUPERIOR COURT OF JUSTICE** — A stay granted under subrule (35) may be set aside or changed by the Superior Court of Justice.

(38) **EFFECT OF STAY GENERALLY** — If an order is stayed, no steps may be taken under the order or for its enforcement, except,

(a)   by order of the Superior Court of Justice; or

(b)   as provided in subrules (39) and (40).

(39) **SETTLING OF ORDER** — A stay does not prevent the settling or signing of the order.

(40) **WRIT OF EXECUTION** — A stay does not prevent the issue of a writ of seizure and sale or the filing of the writ in a sheriff's office or land registry office, but no instruction or direction to enforce the writ shall be given to a sheriff while the stay remains in effect.

(41) **CERTIFICATE OF STAY** — If an order is stayed, the clerk of the court that granted the stay shall, if requested by a party to the appeal, issue a certificate of stay in Form 63A under the *Rules of Civil Procedure* with necessary changes.

(42) **STAY OF SUPPORT ORDER** — A party who obtains a stay of a support order shall obtain a certificate of stay under subrule (41) and file it immediately in the office of the Director of the Family Responsibility Office if the stay relates to a support order being enforced by the Director.

(43) **CERTIFICATE FILED WITH SHERIFF'S OFFICE** — If a certificate of stay is filed with the sheriff's office, the sheriff shall not begin or continue enforcement of the order until satisfied that the stay is no longer in effect.

(44) **REQUEST FOR CERTIFICATE** — A request for a certificate of stay under subrule (41) shall state whether the stay is under subrule (34) or by order under subrule (35) and, if under subrule (35), shall set out the particulars of the order.

(45) **SETTING ASIDE WRIT OF EXECUTION** — The court may set aside the issue or filing of a writ of seizure and sale if the party making the motion or the appellant gives security satisfactory to the court.

(46) **APPEALS, FAMILY ARBITRATION AWARDS** — Subrules (5), (8) to (21), (23) and (25) to (32) apply, with necessary changes, including the modifications set out in subrules (47) to (55), to the appeal of a family arbitration award under section 45 of the *Ar-*

bitration Act, 1991 and, for the purpose,

(a)   a reference to the Ontario Court of Justice or to the court being appealed from shall be read as a reference to the arbitrator who made the family arbitration award; and

(b)   a reference to the order or decision being appealed from shall be read as a reference to the family arbitration award.

(47) **SAME, SERVICE** — In addition to the persons listed under clause (5) (a), the appellant shall serve the notice of appeal on the arbitrator.

(48) **SAME, CONTENTS OF APPELLANT'S APPEAL RECORD** — The material referred to in paragraph 5 of subrule (17) shall include,

(a)   copies of the certificates of independent legal advice required by the *Family Law Act* for the parties;

(b)   a copy of the family arbitration agreement; and

(c)   the original family arbitration award or a certified copy.

(49) **SAME, IF LEAVE REQUIRED** — If the appeal of a family arbitration award requires the leave of the court, rule 14 applies, with necessary changes, including the modifications set out in subrules (50) to (55), to the motion for leave to appeal, other than subrules 14 (4), (4.2), (6), (7), (10) to (15) and (17).

(50) **SAME** — The notice of motion (Form 14) shall,

(a)   be served on every other party affected by the appeal or entitled to appeal and on the arbitrator no later than 15 days after the making of the family arbitration award; and

(b)   be filed no later than five days after service.

(51) **SAME** — The affidavit (Form 14A) and any additional evidence mentioned in clause 14 (9) (b) shall be served and filed no later than 30 days after the filing of the notice of motion for leave to appeal, together with,

(a)   a copy of the notice of motion;

(b)   the documents listed in subrule (48); and

(c)   a factum consisting of a concise argument stating the facts and law relied on by the party making the motion.

(52) **SAME** — The notice of motion and factum shall set out the specific questions that it is proposed the court should answer on appeal if leave to appeal is granted.

(53) **SAME** — Any response to the motion for leave to appeal by a party shall be served and filed no later than 15 days after the materials referred to in subrule (51) were served on the party.

(54) **SAME** — The clerk shall fix a date for the hearing of the motion, which shall not,

except with the consent of the party responding to the motion, be earlier than 15 days after the filing of the materials referred to in subrule (51).

(55) **SAME** — If leave to appeal is granted,

(a)   the notice of appeal shall be served no later than seven days after the granting of leave; and

(b)   the 30-day deadline set out in clause (5) (a) does not apply, but the filing deadline set out in clause (5) (b) continues to apply.

[O. Reg. 89/04, s. 13; O. Reg. 76/06, s. 10; O. Reg. 388/12, s. 10; O. Reg. 142/14, s. 13; O. Reg. 69/15, s. 14; O. Reg. 140/15, s. 5; O. Reg. 298/18, s. 20.]

Rule 39 — Case Management in Family Court of Superior Court of Justice

39. CASE MANAGEMENT IN CERTAIN AREAS ONLY — (1) This rule applies only to cases in the Family Court of the Superior Court of Justice, which has jurisdiction in the municipalities listed in subrule 1 (3).

(2) **EXCLUDED CASES** — This rule does not apply to,

(a)   enforcements;

(b)   cases under rule 32.1, 37 or 37.1; or

(c)   cases under the *Child, Youth and Family Services Act, 2017.*

(3) **PARTIES MAY NOT LENGTHEN TIMES** — A time set out in this rule may be lengthened only by order of the case management judge and not by the parties' consent under subrule 3 (6).

(4) **FAST TRACK** — Applications to which this rule applies, except the ones mentioned in subrule (7), and motions to change a final order or agreement are fast track cases (subrules (5) and (6)).

(5) **FAST TRACK – FIRST COURT DATE** — In a fast track case the clerk shall, on or before the first court date,

(a)   confirm that all necessary documents have been served and filed;

(b)   refer the parties to sources of information about the court process, alternatives to court (including mediation), the effects of separation and divorce on children and community resources that may help the parties and their children;

(c)   if an answer has been filed in response to an application, or if a response to motion to change (Form 15B) or a notice of financial interest has been filed in a motion to change a final order or agreement under rule 15, confirm that the case is ready for a hearing, case conference or settlement conference and schedule it accordingly;

(d)   if no answer has been filed in response to an application, send the case to a judge for a decision on the basis of affidavit evidence or, on request of the applicant, schedule a case conference; and

221

(e)   if no response to motion to change (Form 15B), consent motion to change (Form 15C) or notice of financial interest is filed in response to a motion to change a final order or agreement under rule 15, send the case to a judge for a decision on the basis of the evidence filed in the motion.

(6) **FAST TRACK – CASE MANAGEMENT JUDGE ASSIGNED AT START** — In a fast track case, a case management judge shall be assigned by the first time the case comes before a judge.

(7) **STANDARD TRACK** — Applications in which the applicant makes any of the following claims are standard track cases (subrule (8)):

1.   A claim for divorce.

2.   A property claim.

3.   A claim under the *Arbitration Act, 1991* or the *Family Law Act* relating to a family arbitration, family arbitration agreement or family arbitration award.

(8) **FEATURES OF STANDARD TRACK** — In a standard track case,

(a)   the clerk shall not set a court date when the application is filed;

(b)   a case management judge shall be assigned when a case conference or a motion is scheduled, whichever comes first; and

(c)   the clerk shall schedule a case conference on any party's request.

(9) **FUNCTIONS OF CASE MANAGEMENT JUDGE** — The case management judge assigned to a case,

(a)   shall generally supervise its progress;

(b)   shall conduct the case conference and the settlement conference;

(c)   may schedule a case conference or settlement conference at any time, on the judge's own initiative; and

(d)   shall hear motions in the case, when available to hear motions.

(e)   [REVOKED: O. Reg. 76/06, s. 11(2).]

(10) **SUBSTITUTE CASE MANAGEMENT JUDGE** — If the case management judge is, for any reason, unavailable to continue as the case management judge, another case management judge may be assigned for part or all of the case.

(11) **NOTICE OF APPROACHING DISMISSAL AFTER 365 DAYS** — The clerk shall serve a notice of approaching dismissal (Form 39) for a case on the parties by mail, fax or email if the case has not been settled, withdrawn or scheduled or adjourned for trial before the 365th day after the date the case was started, and that time has not been lengthened by an order under subrule (3).

(11.1) **EXCEPTION** — Despite subrule (11), if a case conference or settlement conference is arranged before the 365th day after the date the case was started for a date on or later than the 365th day, the clerk shall not serve a notice of approaching dismissal except as set out in subrule (11.2).

(11.2) NOTICE SENT IF CONFERENCE DOES NOT TAKE PLACE — If a case conference or settlement conference is arranged for a date on or later than the 365th day after the date the case was started, but the hearing does not take place on that date and is not adjourned by a judge, the clerk shall serve the notice of approaching dismissal on the parties by mail, fax or email.

(12) DISMISSAL OF CASE — A case for which a notice of approaching dismissal has been served shall be dismissed without further notice, unless one of the parties, within 60 days after the notice is served,

(a)   obtains an order under subrule (3) to lengthen that time;

(b)   files an agreement signed by all parties and their lawyers, if any, for a final order disposing of all issues in the case, and a notice of motion for an order carrying out the agreement;

(c)   serves on all parties and files a notice of withdrawal (Form 12) that discontinues all outstanding claims in the case;

(d)   schedules or adjourns the case for trial; or

(e)   arranges a case conference or settlement conference for the first available date.

(12.1) SAME — If a case conference or settlement conference is arranged for a date as described in clause (12) (e), but the hearing does not take place on that date and is not adjourned by a judge, the case shall be dismissed without further notice.

(12.2) DISMISSAL AFTER NOTICE — The clerk shall dismiss a case under subrule (12) or (12.1) by preparing and signing an order dismissing the case, with no costs payable by any party.

(13) SERVICE OF DISMISSAL ORDER BY CLERK — The clerk shall serve the order on each party by mail, fax or email.

(14) SERVICE OF DISMISSAL ORDER BY LAWYER ON CLIENT — A lawyer who is served with a dismissal order on behalf of a client shall serve it on the client by mail, fax or email and file proof of service of the order.

(14.1) JUDGE MAY SET CLERK'S ORDER ASIDE — The case management judge or another judge may, on motion, set aside an order of the clerk under subrule (12).

(15) [REVOKED: O. Reg. 322/13, s. 20.]

[O. Reg. 89/04, s. 14; O. Reg. 76/06, s. 11; O. Reg. 439/07, s. 3; O. Reg. 151/08, s. 7; O. Reg. 388/12, s. 11; O. Reg. 322/13, s. 20; O. Reg. 140/15, s. 4; O. Reg. 298/18, s. 21.]

Rule 40 — Case Management in Ontario Court of Justice

40. CASE MANAGEMENT IN CERTAIN AREAS ONLY — (1) This rule applies only to cases in the Ontario Court of Justice.

(2) EXCLUDED CASES — This rule does not apply to,

(a)   enforcements;

(b)   cases under rule 37 or 37.1; or

(c)   cases under the *Child, Youth and Family Services Act, 2017*.

(3) PARTIES MAY NOT LENGTHEN TIMES — A time set out in this rule may be lengthened only by order and not by the parties' consent under subrule 3 (6).

(4) FIRST COURT DATE — The clerk shall, on or before the first court date,

(a)   confirm that all necessary documents have been served and filed;

(b)   refer the parties to sources of information about the court process, alternatives to court (including mediation), the effects of separation and divorce on children and community resources that may help the parties and their children;

(c)   if an answer has been filed in response to an application, or if a response to motion to change (Form 15B) or a notice of financial interest has been filed in a motion to change a final order or agreement under rule 15, confirm that the case is ready for a hearing, case conference or settlement conference and schedule it accordingly;

(d)   if no answer has been filed in response to an application, send the case to a judge for a decision on the basis of affidavit evidence or, on request of the applicant, schedule a case conference; and

(e)   if no response to motion to change (Form 15B), consent motion to change (Form 15C) or notice of financial interest is filed in response to a motion to change a final order or agreement under rule 15, send the case to a judge for a decision on the basis of the evidence filed in the motion.

(5) NOTICE OF APPROACHING DISMISSAL AFTER 365 DAYS — The clerk shall serve a notice of approaching dismissal (Form 39) for a case on the parties by mail, fax or email if the case has not been settled, withdrawn or scheduled or adjourned for trial before the 365th day after the date the case was started, and that time has not been lengthened by an order under subrule (3).

(5.1) EXCEPTION — Despite subrule (5), if a case conference or settlement conference is arranged before the 365th day after the date the case was started for a date on or later than the 365th day, the clerk shall not serve a notice of approaching dismissal except as set out in subrule (5.2).

(5.2) NOTICE SENT IF CONFERENCE DOES NOT TAKE PLACE — If a case conference or settlement conference is arranged for a date on or later than the 365th day after the date the case was started, but the hearing does not take place on that date and is not adjourned by a judge, the clerk shall serve the notice of approaching dismissal on the parties by mail, fax or email.

(6) DISMISSAL OF CASE — A case for which a notice of approaching dismissal has been served shall be dismissed without further notice, unless one of the parties, within 60 days after the notice is served,

(a)   obtains an order under subrule (3) to lengthen that time;

(b)   files an agreement signed by all parties and their lawyers, if any, for a final order disposing of all issues in the case, and a notice of motion for an order carrying out the agreement;

(c)   serves on all parties and files a notice of withdrawal (Form 12) that discontinues all outstanding claims in the case;

(d)   schedules or adjourns the case for trial; or

(e)   arranges a case conference or settlement conference for the first available date.

(6.1) **SAME** — If a case conference or settlement conference is arranged for a date as described in clause (6) (e), but the hearing does not take place on that date and is not adjourned by a judge, the case shall be dismissed without further notice.

(6.2) **DISMISSAL AFTER NOTICE** — The clerk shall dismiss a case under subrule (6) or (6.1) by preparing and signing an order dismissing the case, with no costs payable by any party.

(7) **SERVICE OF DISMISSAL ORDER BY CLERK** — The clerk shall serve the order on each party by mail, fax or email.

(8) **SERVICE OF DISMISSAL ORDER BY LAWYER ON CLIENT** — A lawyer who is served with a dismissal order on behalf of a client shall serve it on the client by mail, fax or email and file proof of service of the order.

(9) **JUDGE MAY SET CLERK'S ORDER ASIDE** — A judge may, on motion, set aside an order of the clerk under subrule (6).

(10) [REVOKED: O. Reg. 322/13, s. 21.]

[O. Reg. 202/01, s. 8; O. Reg. 89/04, s. 15; O. Reg. 439/07, s. 4; O. Reg. 151/08, s. 8; O. Reg. 388/12, s. 11; O. Reg. 322/13, s. 21; O. Reg. 140/15, s. 4; O. Reg. 298/18, s. 22.]

Rule 41 — Case Management in the Superior Court of Justice (other than the Family Court of the Superior Court of Justice)

41. CASE MANAGEMENT — (1) This rule applies only to cases in the Superior Court of Justice, other than cases in the Family Court of the Superior Court of Justice, started on or after July 1, 2004.

(2) **EXCLUDED CASES** — This rule does not apply to,

(a)   enforcements; or

(b)   cases under rule 32.1, 37 or 37.1.

(3) **PARTIES MAY NOT LENGTHEN TIMES** — A time set out in this rule may be lengthened only by order of the court and not by the parties' consent under subrule 3 (6).

(4) **CLERK'S ROLE** — The clerk shall not set a court date when the application is filed, and the case shall come before the court when a case conference or a motion is scheduled, whichever comes first, and the clerk shall schedule a case conference on any party's

request.

(5) NOTICE OF APPROACHING DISMISSAL AFTER 365 DAYS — The clerk shall serve a notice of approaching dismissal (Form 39) for a case on the parties by mail, fax or email if the case has not been settled, withdrawn or scheduled or adjourned for trial before the 365th day after the date the case was started, and that time has not been lengthened by an order under subrule (3).

(5.1) EXCEPTION — Despite subrule (5), if a case conference or settlement conference is arranged before the 365th day after the date the case was started for a date on or later than the 365th day, the clerk shall not serve a notice of approaching dismissal except as set out in subrule (5.2).

(5.2) NOTICE SENT IF CONFERENCE DOES NOT TAKE PLACE — If a case conference or settlement conference is arranged for a date on or later than the 365th day after the date the case was started, but the hearing does not take place on that date and is not adjourned by a judge, the clerk shall serve the notice of approaching dismissal on the parties by mail, fax or email.

(6) DISMISSAL OF CASE — A case for which a notice of approaching dismissal has been served shall be dismissed without further notice, unless one of the parties, within 60 days after the notice is served,

(a)   obtains an order under subrule (3) to lengthen that time;

(b)   files an agreement signed by all parties and their lawyers, if any, for a final order disposing of all issues in the case, and a notice of motion for an order carrying out the agreement;

(c)   serves on all parties and files a notice of withdrawal (Form 12) that discontinues all outstanding claims in the case;

(d)   schedules or adjourns the case for trial; or

(e)   arranges a case conference or settlement conference for the first available date.

(6.1) SAME — If a case conference or settlement conference is arranged for a date as described in clause (6) (e), but the hearing does not take place on that date and is not adjourned by a judge, the case shall be dismissed without further notice.

(6.2) DISMISSAL AFTER NOTICE — The clerk shall dismiss a case under subrule (6) or (6.1) by preparing and signing an order dismissing the case, with no costs payable by any party.

(7) SERVICE OF DISMISSAL ORDER — The clerk shall serve the order on each party by mail, fax or email.

(8) SERVICE OF DISMISSAL ORDER BY LAWYER ON CLIENT — A lawyer who is served with a dismissal order on behalf of a client shall serve it on the client by mail, fax or email and file proof of service of the order.

(9) JUDGE MAY SET CLERK'S ORDER ASIDE — A judge may, on motion, set aside an order of the clerk under subrule (6).

(10) [REVOKED: O. Reg. 322/13, s. 22.]

[O. Reg. 89/04, s. 16; O. Reg. 76/06, s. 13; O. Reg. 439/07, s. 5; O. Reg. 388/12, s. 12; O. Reg. 322/13, s. 22; O. Reg. 140/15, s. 4.]

Rule 42 — Appointment of Family Case Manager in the Family Court of the Superior Court of Justice in Ottawa

42. SCOPE — (1) This rule applies to cases in the Family Court of the Superior Court of Justice in the City of Ottawa if the cases relate to matters under the following Acts:

1.   [REVOKED: O. Reg. 235/16, s. 7.]

2.   The *Children's Law Reform Act*.

3.   The *Divorce Act* (Canada).

4.   The *Family Law Act*.

5.   The *Family Responsibility and Support Arrears Enforcement Act, 1996*.

(1.1) SAME — This rule applies in respect of a case regardless of whether it is a fast track case (rule 39) or a standard track case.

(2) PURPOSE — The purpose of this rule is to promote the active management, in accordance with subrule 2 (5), of cases to which this rule applies by conferring specified family law jurisdiction on a Family Case Manager.

(3) DEFINITION — In this rule,

"Family Case Manager" means a person appointed under section 86.1 of the *Courts of Justice Act* by the Lieutenant Governor in Council as a case management master who is assigned to manage cases for the purposes of this rule.

(4) FAMILY CASE MANAGER, POWERS AND DUTIES — In a case to which this rule applies,

(a)   the Family Case Manager may only exercise the powers and carry out the duties and functions that are specified in this rule; and

(b)   the exercise of those powers and the performance of those duties and functions are subject to the restrictions specified in subrule (5).

(5) NO JURISDICTION — The Family Case Manager has no jurisdiction in respect of,

(a)   a power, duty or function that is conferred exclusively on a judge of a superior court by law or expressly on a judge by an Act;

(b)   a case involving a special party or a child party;

(c)   the determination of a right or interest of a party in real property; or

(d)   the making of an order or hearing of a motion for an order,

    (i)   to change, set aside, stay or confirm an order of a judge,

(ii)   to find a person in contempt of court,

(iii)   to restrain the liberty of a person, including an order for imprisonment, a warrant for arrest or a warrant of committal,

(iv)   to dismiss all or part of a party's case for a failure by the party to follow these rules or obey an order in the case or a related case, if the *Family Responsibility and Support Arrears Enforcement Act, 1996* applies to the party's case,

(v)   to split a divorce from other issues in a case under subrule 12 (6), or

(vi)   [REVOKED: O. Reg. 235/16, s. 7.]

(vii) to grant summary judgment.

(6) [REVOKED: O. Reg. 235/16, s. 7.]

(7) MOTIONS UNDER RULE 14 — The Family Case Manager may hear motions under rule 14 relating to matters over which he or she has jurisdiction and, for the purpose, may exercise any power under that rule, other than a power under subrule 14 (21).

(8) ORDERS ON MOTION UNDER RULE 14 — If a motion under rule 14 is made in a case under an Act to which this rule applies, the Family Case Manager may make only the following orders:

0.1   Subject to subclause (5) (d) (iv), an order under subrule 1 (8), other than a contempt order under clause 1 (8) (g), and an order under subrule 1 (8.1).

0.2   An order under subrule 1 (8.2).

0.3   An order under subrule 1 (8.4), if the Family Case Manager made the order striking out the document.

1.   An order under rules 3, 4, 5, 6, 7, 9, 10, 11, 12, 13, 18, 19 and 20.

2.   An order for costs under rule 24 relating to a step in the case that the Family Case Manager dealt with.

3.   An order under rule 25 relating to an order made by the Family Case Manager.

3.1   An order under subrule 39 (3) or (14.1).

4.   An order to change a temporary order made by the Family Case Manager.

5.   An order under section 17.2 (Blood, DNA tests) of the *Children's Law Reform Act*.

6.   A temporary order for or relating to custody of or access to a child under section 21, 23, 25, 28, 29, 30, 32, 34, 39 or 40 of the *Children's Law Reform Act*.

7.   A temporary order for custody of or access to a child under section 16 of the *Divorce Act* (Canada).

8.   An order appointing a mediator under section 31 of the *Children's Law Reform Act* or section 3 (Mediation) of the *Family Law Act*.

9. A temporary order for or relating to support under section 33, clause 34 (1) (a), (e), (f), (g) or (h), subsection 34 (5) or section 37, 42 or 47 of the *Family Law Act*.

10. A temporary order for support under section 15.1 (Child support order) or 15.2 (Spousal support order) of the *Divorce Act* (Canada).

11. A temporary order under section 40 of the *Family Law Act*.

12. A temporary order dealing with property other than real property.

13. A support deduction order under section 10 (Support deduction orders to be made) of the *Family Responsibility and Support Arrears Enforcement Act, 1996*.

14. An order limiting or suspending a support deduction order.

15. An order under section 8 (Director to cease enforcement, termination of support obligation) of the *Family Responsibility and Support Arrears Enforcement Act, 1996* that terminates a support obligation or orders repayment from a person who received support.

15.1 An order under subsection 89 (3.1) or 112 (2) of the *Courts of Justice Act* requesting the Children's Lawyer to act.

16. An order that is necessary and incidental to the power to make a temporary order that is within the jurisdiction of the Family Case Manager.

(9) [REVOKED: O. Reg. 235/16, s. 7.]

(10) [REVOKED: O. Reg. 235/16, s. 7.]

(11) [REVOKED: O. Reg. 151/08, s. 9.]

(12) CONFERENCES — The Family Case Manager may conduct a case conference, settlement conference or trial management conference instead of a judge under rule 17.

(13) [REVOKED: O. Reg. 235/16, s. 7.]

(14) APPLICATION OF RULE 17 — At a case conference, settlement conference or trial management conference conducted by the Family Case Manager, rule 17 applies subject to the following changes:

1. In a case to which this rule applies, the Family Case Manager may make any order described in rule 17 and, with respect to the temporary and final orders referred to in clause 17 (8) (b),

   i. the only temporary or final orders that the Family Case Manager may make are those described in subrule (8) of this rule, and

   ii. the Family Case Manager shall not make a final order unless the parties consent to the order.

2. [REVOKED: O. Reg. 235/16, s. 7.]

3. A party to the conference may not request that the conference be conducted by a judge under subrule 17 (9).

4.   [REVOKED: O. Reg. 535/18, s. 11.]

(15) ENFORCEMENT POWERS — The Family Case Manager may exercise,

(a)   any power that a court may exercise under rule 27 (requiring financial information) other than a power to order a person imprisoned under subrule 27 (6), (20) or (21); and

(b)   the powers relating to garnishment orders set out in subrules 29 (5) and (19).

(16) SENSING CASE TO JUDGE — Despite anything to the contrary in this rule, the Family Case Manager may at any time order that a matter assigned to him or her be adjourned and sent to a judge.

(17) APPEAL FROM TEMPORARY ORDER — Subrules 38 (5) to (45) apply with necessary changes to an appeal from a temporary order of the Family Case Manager.

(18) APPEAL FROM FINAL ORDER — Subrules 38 (1), (2) and (3) apply with necessary changes to an appeal from a final order of the Family Case Manager.

(19) REVOCATION — This rule is revoked on July 1, 2021.

[O. Reg. 120/07, s. 1; O. Reg. 151/08, s. 9; O. Reg. 51/10, s. 1; O. Reg. 186/12, s. 2; O. Reg. 322/13, s. 23; O. Reg. 142/14, s. 14; O. Reg. 235/16, s. 7; O. Reg. 226/17, s. 3; O. Reg. 535/18, s. 11; O. Reg. 250/19, s. 12.]

43. Omitted (provides for coming into force of provisions of this Regulation).

SMALL CLAIMS COURT FORMS

TABLE OF CONTENTS

FORMS

Form Number	Form Title	Version Date	Effective Date	Page
20E.1	Notice of Renewal of Garnishment	May 1, 2019	Oct. 23, 2019	302
20F	Garnishee's Statement	May 1, 2019	Oct. 23, 2019	306
20G	Notice to Co-owner of Debt	May 1, 2019	Oct. 23, 2019	308
20H	Notice of Examination	Jan. 23, 2014	Jul. 18, 2014	310
20I	Financial Information Form	Jan. 23, 2014	Jul. 18, 2014	312
20J	Warrant of Committal	Jan. 23, 2014	Jul. 18, 2014	314
20K	Identification Form	Jan. 23, 2014	Jul. 18, 2014	316
20L	Notice of Default of Payment	Jan. 23, 2014	Jul. 18, 2014	318
20M	Affidavit of Default of Payment	Jan. 23, 2014	Jul. 18, 2014	320
20N	Request to Renew Writ of Seizure and Sale	Jan. 23, 2014	Jul. 18, 2014	322
20O	Direction to Enforce Writ of Seizure and Sale of Personal Property	Jan. 23, 2014	Jul. 18, 2014	323
20P	Affidavit for Enforcement Request	Jan. 23, 2014	Jul. 18, 2014	325
20Q	Notice of Garnishment Hearing	May 1, 2019	Oct. 23, 2019	328
20R	Notice of Termination of Garnishment	May 1, 2019	Oct. 23, 2019	331

Form 1A
Additional Parties

ONTARIO
Superior Court of Justice

PAGE 1A

Additional Parties
Form 1A Ont. Reg. No.: 258/98

Claim No.

☐ **Plaintiff No.**   ☐ **Defendant No.**

Last name, or name of company		
First name	Second name	Also known as
Address (street number, apt., unit)		
City/Town	Province	Phone no.
Postal code		Fax no.
Representative		LSUC #
Address (street number, apt., unit)		
City/Town	Province	Phone no.
Postal code		Fax no.

☐ **Plaintiff No.**   ☐ **Defendant No.**

Last name, or name of company		
First name	Second name	Also known as
Address (street number, apt., unit)		
City/Town	Province	Phone no.
Postal code		Fax no.
Representative		LSUC #
Address (street number, apt., unit)		
City/Town	Province	Phone no.
Postal code		Fax no.

☐ **Plaintiff No.**   ☐ **Defendant No.**

Last name, or name of company		
First name	Second name	Also known as
Address (street number, apt., unit)		
City/Town	Province	Phone no.
Postal code		Fax no.
Representative		LSUC #
Address (street number, apt., unit)		
City/Town	Province	Phone no.
Postal code		Fax no.

SCR 1.05-1A (January 23, 2014) CSD

Form 1A.1
Additional Debtors

ONTARIO
Superior Court of Justice

Additional Debtors
Form 1A.1 Ont. Reg. No.: 258/98

Claim No.

If a debtor has "also known as names", list each also known as name in a separate set of boxes below.

Last name of debtor, or name of company		
First name	Second name	Third name

Last name of debtor, or name of company		
First name	Second name	Third name

Last name of debtor, or name of company		
First name	Second name	Third name

Last name of debtor, or name of company		
First name	Second name	Third name

Last name of debtor, or name of company		
First name	Second name	Third name

Last name of debtor, or name of company		
First name	Second name	Third name

Last name of debtor, or name of company		
First name	Second name	Third name

SCR 1A.1 (January 23, 2014) CSD

Form 1B
Request for Telephone or Video Conference

ONTARIO
Superior Court of Justice

Request for Telephone or Video Conference
Form 1B Ont. Reg. No.: 258/98

Small Claims Court _____   Claim No. _____

Address _____

Phone number _____

BETWEEN

_____
Plaintiff(s)

and

_____
Defendant(s)

TO THE CLERK OF THE _____ **SMALL CLAIMS COURT:**
(Name of Small Claims Court location)

My name is _____ **and I request the court schedule the:**
(Name of requesting party)

(Check appropriate box(es)).   ☐ settlement conference

☐ motion

☐ examination of a debtor or other person *(examination of a debtor or other person cannot be conducted by telephone conference)*

in this case to be heard by   ☐ telephone conference

☐ video conference

where facilities are available and the court permits it.

My current telephone number is _____
(Telephone number with area code)

Where a judge directs a telephone or video conference, the clerk will make the necessary arrangements and notify the parties of them [R. 1.07(5)].

The reasons for my request are as follows:

_____ , 20 _____   _____
(Signature of party or representative)

NOTE: If you are requesting that a motion be heard by telephone or video conference, file this request together with your Notice of Motion and Supporting Affidavit (Form 15A) OR together with a copy of the Notice of Motion and Supporting Affidavit served on you by the opposing party.

Les formules des tribunaux sont affichées en anglais et en français sur le site www.ontariocourtforms.on.ca. Visitez ce site pour des renseignements sur des formats accessibles.

SCR 1.07-1B (January 23, 2014) CSD

FORM 1B   **PAGE 2**

_____
Claim No.

┌───┐
│ **DISPOSITION:** *(The judge will complete this section.)* │
│ Order to go as follows: │
│   │
│   │
│   │
│   │
│   │
│   │
│   │
│   │
│   │
│   │
│   │
│   │
│   │
│   │
└───┘

_____, 20 _____   _____
                                   (Signature of judge)

SCR 1.07-1B (January 23, 2014) CSD

238

Form 4A
Consent to Act as Litigation Guardian

ONTARIO
Superior Court of Justice

Consent to Act as Litigation Guardian
Form 4A Ont. Reg. No.: 258/98

Small Claims Court

Claim No.

Address

Phone number

BETWEEN

_____
Plaintiff(s)

and

_____
Defendant(s)

My name is	Name
And I live at	Street and number
	City, province, postal code
	Phone number and fax number

1. I consent to act as litigation guardian in this action for the

☐ plaintiff, named _____
(Name of plaintiff)

(Check one box only.)

and I acknowledge that I may be personally responsible for any costs awarded against me or against this person.

☐ defendant, named _____
(Name of defendant)

2. The above-named person is under the following disability:

☐ a minor whose birth date is _____
(State date of birth of minor)

(Check appropriate box(es).)

☐ mentally incapable within the meaning of Section 6 or Section 45 of the *Substitute Decisions Act, 1992* in respect of an issue in a proceeding.

☐ an absentee within the meaning of the *Absentees Act*.

3. My relationship to the person under disability is:
(State your relationship to the person under disability.)

Les formules des tribunaux sont affichées en anglais et en français sur le site www.ontariocourtforms.on.ca. Visitez ce site pour des renseignements sur des formats accessibles.

SCR 4.01-4.02-4A (January 23, 2014) CSD

239

FORM 4A   **PAGE 2**

_____
Claim No.

4. I have no interest in this action contrary to that of the person under disability.

5. I am

(Check one
box only.)

☐ represented and have given written authority to

_____
(Name of representative with authority to act in this
proceeding)

of _____
(Address for service)

_____
(Phone number and fax number)

to act in this proceeding.

☐ not represented by a representative.

_____, 20 _____

_____
(Signature of litigation guardian consenting)

_____
(Signature of witness)

_____
(Name of witness)

NOTE: Within seven (7) calendar days of changing your address for service, notify the court and all other parties in writing.

SCR 4.01-4.02-4A (January 23, 2014) CSD

Form 4B
Affidavit (Motion for Payment Out of Court)

ONTARIO
Superior Court of Justice

Affidavit (Motion for Payment Out of Court)
Form 4B Ont. Reg. No.: 258/98

Small Claims Court

Claim No.

Address

Phone number

BETWEEN

_____
Plaintiff(s)/Creditor(s)

and

_____
Defendant(s)/Debtor(s)

My name is _____
(Full name)

I live in _____
(Municipality & province)

I make this affidavit to support my motion for payment out of court of money belonging to

_____
(Name of person under disability)

of _____ ,
(Address)

who is _____
(State the nature of the disability)

and who was born on _____
(Date)

I am _____
(State your connection with the person under disability)

The Accountant has informed me that $ _____ , including interest accrued to

_____ , is in court.
(Date)

There has been previously paid out the sum of $ _____ on _____
(Date)

I propose that the sum of $ _____ should be paid out of court to _____
(Name of person)

for the following purpose: *(Set out what the person you named will do with the money.)*

Les formules des tribunaux sont affichées en anglais et en français sur le site
www.ontariocourtforms.on.ca. Visitez ce site pour des renseignements sur des
formats accessibles.

Continued on next page

FORM 4B   **PAGE 2**

Claim No.

I believe that this money should be paid out of court for the following reasons:
Set out your reasons in numbered paragraphs.

If more space is required, attach and initial extra pages.

Sworn/Affirmed before me at _____
                                              (Municipality)

in _____
                          (Province, state or country)

on _____ , 20 ____   _____
                                          Commissioner for taking affidavits
                                          (Type or print name below if signature is illegible.)

_____
Signature
(This form is to be signed in front of a
lawyer, justice of the peace, notary public
or commissioner for taking affidavits.)

WARNING: IT IS AN OFFENCE UNDER THE *CRIMINAL CODE* TO KNOWINGLY SWEAR OR AFFIRM A FALSE AFFIDAVIT.

SCR 4.08-4B (January 23, 2014) CSD

Form 5A
Notice to Alleged Partner

ONTARIO
Superior Court of Justice

Notice to Alleged Partner
Form 5A Ont. Reg. No.: 258/98

_____   _____
Small Claims Court   Claim No.

_____
Address

_____
Phone number

BETWEEN

_____
                                                          Plaintiff(s)

and

_____
                                                          Defendant(s)

TO:

Name of alleged partner
Street and number
City, province, postal code

YOU ARE ALLEGED TO HAVE BEEN A PARTNER on _____ , 20 ____

(or during the period) _____ , 20 ____ to _____ , 20 ____

in the partnership/business of _____ ,
                                              (Firm name)

a party named in this proceeding.

IF YOU WISH TO DENY THAT YOU WERE A PARTNER at any material time, you must defend this proceeding separately from the partnership, denying that you were a partner at the material time. If you fail to do so, you will be deemed to have been a partner on the date (or during the period) set out above.

CAUTION:	**AN ORDER AGAINST THE PARTNERSHIP MAY BE ENFORCED AGAINST YOU PERSONALLY** if you are deemed to have been a partner, if you admit that you were, or if the court finds that you were at the material time.

_____ , 20 ____   _____
                                  (Signature of plaintiff or representative)

Les formules des tribunaux sont affichées en anglais et en français sur le site www.ontariocourtforms.on.ca. Visitez ce site pour des renseignements sur des formats accessibles.

SCR 5.03-5A (January 23, 2014) CSD

Form 7A
Plaintiff's Claim

ONTARIO
Superior Court of Justice

Plaintiff's Claim
Form 7A Ont. Reg. No.: 258/98

Small Claims Court

Claim No.

Seal

Address

Phone number

Plaintiff No. 1 ☐ Additional plaintiff(s) listed on attached Form 1A. ☐ Under 18 years of age.

Last name, or name of company		
First name	Second name	Also known as
Address (street number, apt., unit)		
City/Town	Province	Phone no.
Postal code		Fax no.
Representative		LSUC #
Address (street number, apt., unit)		
City/Town	Province	Phone no.
Postal code		Fax no.

Defendant No. 1 ☐ Additional defendant(s) listed on attached Form 1A. ☐ Under 18 years of age.

Last name, or name of company		
First name	Second name	Also known as
Address (street number, apt., unit)		
City/Town	Province	Phone no.
Postal code		Fax no.
Representative		LSUC #
Address (street number, apt., unit)		
City/Town	Province	Phone no.
Postal code		Fax no.

Les formules des tribunaux sont affichées en anglais et en français sur le site www.ontariocourtforms.on.ca. Visitez ce site pour des renseignements sur des formats accessibles.

SCR 7.01-7A (November 1, 2016) CSD

Continued on next page

FORM 7A   **PAGE 2**

REASONS FOR CLAIM AND DETAILS

Explain what happened, including where and when. Then explain how much money you are claiming or what goods you want returned.

If you are relying on any documents, you **MUST** attach copies to the claim. If evidence is lost or unavailable, you **MUST** explain why it is not attached.

What happened?
Where?
When?

Continued on next page

FORM 7A   **PAGE 3**

Claim No.

How much? $ ....
                         (Principal amount claimed)

☐   ADDITIONAL PAGES ARE ATTACHED BECAUSE MORE ROOM WAS NEEDED.

The plaintiff also claims pre-judgment interest from _____ **under:**
                                                              (Date)

(Check only   ☐   **the *Courts of Justice Act***
one box)   ☐   **an agreement at the rate of** _____ **% per year**

and post-judgment interest, and court costs.

Prepared on: _____, 20 ____   _____
                                                 (Signature of plaintiff or representative)

Issued on: _____, 20 ____   _____
                                                 (Signature of clerk)

CAUTION TO DEFENDANT:	**IF YOU DO NOT FILE A DEFENCE** (Form 9A) and an Affidavit of Service (Form 8A) with the court within twenty (20) calendar days after you have been served with this Plaintiff's Claim, judgment may be obtained without notice and enforced against you. Forms and self-help materials are available at the Small Claims Court and on the following website: www.ontariocourtforms.on.ca.
CAUTION TO PARTIES:	Unless the court orders or the rules provide otherwise, **THIS ACTION WILL BE AUTOMATICALLY DISMISSED** if it has not been disposed of by order or otherwise two (2) years after it was commenced and a trial date or assessment under subrule 11.03(2) has not been requested.

For information on accessibility of court services for
people with disability-related needs, contact:
Telephone: 416-326-2220 / 1-800-518-7901   TTY: 416-326-4012 / 1-877-425-0575

SCR 7.01-7A (November 1, 2016) CSD

Instructions for Making a Claim

You can now file your claim online. Please visit: www.ontario.ca/smallclaims.

Step 1: COMPLETE the **Plaintiff's Claim** form. Be sure to get the defendant's name right. Explain what happened in detail. Include dates and places. State how much money you want or what goods you want returned. Attach copies of any documents that help your case. Examples are contracts, repair bills and photographs of damaged goods. If you want interest on money you are claiming, ask for it on the claim form. You and the defendant may have a contract that sets an annual interest rate. If so, use that rate. If not, claim the *Courts of Justice Act* interest rate posted on the Ministry of the Attorney General web-site at www.attorneygeneral.jus.gov.on.ca.

If there is more than one plaintiff or defendant, complete an **Additional Parties** form (Form 1A) and put it right behind page one of your plaintiff's claim form. You can get the additional parties form from the court office or at the following website: www.ontariocourtforms.on.ca.

Step 2: **FILE** the plaintiff's claim and related documents by taking it or mailing it to the Small Claims Court office. You must also file a copy for every defendant. There is a fee. Cheques or money orders are payable to the Minister of Finance. The fees are listed at the court office and online at: www.attorneygeneral.jus.gov.on.ca. The clerk will return stamped copies of the plaintiff's claim to you.

Step 3: **SERVE.** You must deliver a copy of the filed claim and your documents to each defendant. This is called "serving" the defendants. There are rules about how this must be done. See the Small Claims Court **"Guide to Serving Documents"** at the court office or online at www.attorneygeneral.jus.gov.on.ca.

Is it worth it? It is important to consider whether the person or company you are claiming from is likely to be able to pay. If they:

- are unemployed;
- are bankrupt;
- have no money of their own;
- have no personal property and have nothing else of value belonging to them (such as a car) which is not subject to a lease agreement;
- have ceased to carry on business; or
- have other debts to pay,

the court may not be able to help you get your money. However, you may be able to get your money if you are prepared to accept small instalments over a period of time. See the Small Claims Court **"After Judgment – Guide to Getting Results"** at the court office or online at www.attorneygeneral.jus.gov.on.ca.

DO NOT FILE THIS PAGE.

SCR 7.01-7A (November 1, 2016) CSD

Instructions for Completing the Affidavit of Service

In a court case, everyone involved must receive the key documents they need. "Serving" documents means giving copies to all the other parties. Generally speaking, this must be done at each step in the case. For example, the plaintiff must serve a copy of the plaintiff's claim form on the defendant. By serving documents, you tell the other parties about the step you are taking. They can then respond if they want to.

Step 1: SERVE the documents. You can serve the documents yourself. You can have a friend or co-worker do it for you. You can also hire someone, called a process server, to do it. If you have a representative, you can let them look after it. Different documents must be served in different ways. For example, the plaintiff's claim cannot be served on an individual by regular lettermail or fax. Check the Small Claims Court **"Guide to Serving Documents"** at court offices or online at www.attorneygeneral.jus.gov.on.ca to find out more about service rules. In general, a document can be served any day of the week.

Step 2: COMPLETE the **Affidavit of Service**. The person who serves the papers must keep careful notes. He or she will have to let the court know who was served and when and how this was done. These facts must be put on the **Affidavit of Service**. The person who fills out the form must swear or affirm that the facts are true.

DO NOT FILE THIS PAGE.

SCR 8.06-8A (November 1, 2015) CSD

Form 8A
Affidavit of Service

ONTARIO
Superior Court of Justice

Affidavit of Service
Form 8A Ont. Reg. No.: 258/98

Small Claims Court _____   Claim No. _____

Address _____

Phone number _____

BETWEEN

_____ Plaintiff(s)

and

_____ Defendant(s)

My name is _____
(Full name)

I live in _____
(Municipality & province)

and I swear/affirm that the following is true:

1. **I served** _____, **on** _____, 20 ____,
(Full name of person/corporation served)   (Date)

   at _____
   (Address (street and number, unit, municipality, province))

   which is
   ☐ the address of the person's home
   ☐ the address of the corporation's place of business
   ☐ the address of the person's or corporation's representative on record with the court
   ☐ the address on the document most recently filed in court by the party
   ☐ the address of the corporation's attorney for service in Ontario
   ☐ other address: _____
   (Specify.)

   with _____
   (Name(s) of document(s) served)

2. **I served the document(s) referred to in paragraph one by the following method:**
   (Tell how service took place by checking appropriate box(es).)

   Personal service
   ☐ leaving a copy with the person.
   ☐ leaving a copy with the _____ of the corporation.
   (Office or position)
   ☐ leaving a copy with:
   (Specify person's name and office/position.)
   at the place of business of the corporation who appeared to be in control or management of the place of business.

Les formules des tribunaux sont affichées en anglais et en français sur le site www.ontariocourtforms.on.ca. Visitez ce site pour des renseignements sur des formats accessibles.

SCR 8.06-8A (November 1, 2015) CSD

Continued on next page

FORM 8A   **PAGE 2**

Claim No.

Service at place of residence	☐ leaving a copy in a sealed envelope addressed to the person at the person's place of residence with a person who appeared to be an adult member of the same household, and sending another copy of the same document(s) to the person's place of residence on the same day or the following day by:

  ☐ regular lettermail.

  ☐ registered mail.

  ☐ courier.

Service by registered mail   ☐ registered mail.

(If a copy of a plaintiff's claim or defendant's claim was served by registered mail, attach a copy of the Canada Post delivery confirmation, showing the signature verifying delivery, to this affidavit.)

Service by courier   ☐ courier.

(If a copy of a plaintiff's claim or defendant's claim was served by courier, attach a copy of the courier's delivery confirmation, showing the signature verifying delivery, to this affidavit.)

Service on lawyer or paralegal   ☐ leaving a copy with a lawyer or paralegal or an employee in the lawyer's or paralegal's office, who accepted service on the person's behalf.

(Attach a copy of the document endorsed with an acceptance of service.)

Service by regular lettermail   ☐ regular lettermail.

Service by fax   ☐ fax sent at _____ at the following fax number: _____

                         (Time)   (Fax number)

Service to last known address of corporation or attorney for service, and to the directors   ☐ mail/courier to corporation or attorney for service at last known address recorded with the Ministry of Government Services, and

mail/courier to each director, as recorded with the Ministry of Government Services, as set out below:

Name of director	Director's address as recorded with the Ministry of Government Services (street & number, unit, municipality, province)

(Attach separate sheet for additional names if necessary.)

Substituted service   ☐ substituted service as ordered by the court on _____ , 20 _____ ,

                                                     (Date)

as follows: (Give details.)

Sworn/Affirmed before me at _____

                               (Municipality)

in _____

                           (Province, state, or country)

on _____ , 20 _____

                      Commissioner for taking affidavits
                      (Type or print name below if signature is illegible.)

_____
Signature
(This form is to be signed in front of a lawyer, justice of the peace, notary public or commissioner for taking affidavits.)

SCR 8.06-8A (November 1, 2015) CSD

Instructions for Filing a Defence to a Claim

Step 1: COMPLETE a **Defence** form. Make sure your name and address are right so you will receive documents about the case. State what you disagree with and why, and if there is anything you agree with. Attach copies of any documents that help your case. If you want to pay all or part of the amount owing, state how much you will pay and when you will pay.

If there is more than one plaintiff or defendant, complete an **Additional Parties** form (Form 1A) and put it right behind page one of your defence form. You can get the additional parties form and other forms at the court office or online at www.ontariocourtforms.on.ca.

Step 2: SERVE your completed Defence form and any attachments on every other party in the case and complete an Affidavit of Service (Form 8A). For more information, see the **"Guide to Serving Documents"** available at the court office and online at www.attorneygeneral.jus.gov.on.ca.

Step 3: FILE your Defence (Form 9A) and Affidavit of Service (Form 8A). Take the completed forms and related documents to the court office where the plaintiff filed the claim. You must do this within 20 days after you received the claim. If you miss the 20 day deadline, you can still file the defence as long as the plaintiff has not yet asked the court to have you noted in default, or with leave of the court if you have been noted in default. Pay the court filing fee. Cheques and money orders are payable to the Minister of Finance. The fees are listed at the court office and online at www.attorneygeneral.jus.gov.on.ca.

If you have been noted in default, you must take additional steps if you wish to file a defence. See the Small Claims Court **"Guide to Replying to a Claim"** referenced below for more information.

If your Defence contains a proposal of terms of payment and you fail to make payment in accordance with your proposal, judgment for the unpaid balance may be ordered against you.

What if the plaintiff owes me money or someone else is responsible for the loss?

If you wish to file a **Defendant's Claim** form (Form 10A) against the plaintiff or other person, you must file it no later than 20 days after you file your defence. If you miss this deadline, you can ask the court on motion for permission to file it later. There is a filing fee.

For more information about replying to a claim or making a defendant's claim, see the Small Claims Court **"Guide to Replying to a Claim"** available at the court office and online at www.attorneygeneral.jus.gov.on.ca. Also see the **Defendant's Claim** form online at www.ontariocourtforms.on.ca.

DO NOT FILE THIS PAGE.

Form 9A
Defence

ONTARIO
Superior Court of Justice

Defence
Form 9A Ont. Reg. No.: 258/98

Small Claims Court

Claim No.

Address

Phone number

Plaintiff No. 1 ☐ Additional plaintiff(s) listed on attached Form 1A. ☐ Under 18 years of age.

Last name, or name of company		
First name	Second name	Also known as
Address (street number, apt., unit)		
City/Town	Province	Phone no.
Postal code		Fax no.
Representative		LSUC #
Address (street number, apt., unit)		
City/Town	Province	Phone no.
Postal code		Fax no.

Defendant No. 1 ☐ Additional defendant(s) listed on attached Form 1A. ☐ Under 18 years of age.

Last name, or name of company		
First name	Second name	Also known as
Address (street number, apt., unit)		
City/Town	Province	Phone no.
Postal code		Fax no.
Representative		LSUC #
Address (street number, apt., unit)		
City/Town	Province	Phone no.
Postal code		Fax no.

Les formules des tribunaux sont affichées en anglais et en français sur le site www.ontariocourtforms.on.ca. Visitez ce site pour des renseignements sur des formats accessibles.

SCR 9.01-10.03-9A (January 23, 2014) CSD

FORM 9A   **PAGE 2**

Claim No.

THIS DEFENCE IS BEING FILED ON BEHALF OF: (Name(s) of defendant(s))

and I/we: (Check as many as apply)

☐   Dispute the claim made against me/us.

☐   Admit the full claim and propose the following terms of payment:

$ _____ per _____ commencing _____ , 20 ____ .
   (Amount)   (Week/month)

☐   Admit part of the claim in the amount of $ _____ and propose the following terms of payment:
                                                (Amount)

$ _____ per _____ commencing _____ , 20 ____ .
   (Amount)   (Week/month)

REASONS FOR DISPUTING THE CLAIM AND DETAILS:

Explain what happened, including where and when. Explain why you do not agree with the claim made against you.

If you are relying on any documents, you **MUST** attach copies to the Defence. If evidence is lost or unavailable, you **MUST** explain why it is not attached.

What happened?
Where?
When?

Continued on next page

FORM 9A   **PAGE 3**

_____
Claim No.

Why I/we disagree
with all or part of
the claim:

☐ **ADDITIONAL PAGES ARE ATTACHED BECAUSE MORE ROOM WAS NEEDED.**

Prepared on: _____ , 20 _____   _____
(Signature of defendant or representative)

NOTE:	Within seven (7) calendar days of changing your address for service, notify the court and all other parties in writing.

CAUTION TO PLAINTIFF(S):	If this Defence contains a proposal of terms of payment, you are deemed to have accepted the terms **unless** you file with the clerk and serve on the defendant(s) a Request to Clerk (Form 9B) for a terms of payment hearing **WITHIN TWENTY (20) CALENDAR DAYS** of service of this Defence [R. 9.03(3)].

Form 9B
Request to Clerk

ONTARIO
Superior Court of Justice

Request to Clerk
Form 9B Ont. Reg. No.: 258/98

Small Claims Court

Claim No.

Address

Phone number

BETWEEN

Plaintiff(s)

and

Defendant(s)

TO THE CLERK OF THE _____ **SMALL CLAIMS COURT:**
(Name of Small Claims Court location)

My name is _____ **and I request that the clerk of the court:**
(Name of party/representative)

(Check appropriate box(es).)

☐ note defendant(s) _____
(Name of defendant(s))
in default for failing to file a Defence (Form 9A) within the prescribed time period [R. 11.01(1)].

☐ schedule an assessment hearing (all defendants have been noted in default) [R. 11.03(2)(b)].

☐ schedule a terms of payment hearing because I dispute the defendant's proposed terms of payment contained in the Defence (Form 9A) [R. 9.03(3)].

☐ schedule a trial [R. 16.01(1)(b)].

☐ accept payment in the amount of $ _____ into court
(Amount)

    ☐ according to an order of the court, dated _____ , 20 ____ .

    ☐ for a person under disability according to an order or settlement dated
    _____ , 20 ____ [R. 4.08(1)].

    ☐ pursuant to the attached written offer to settle, dated _____ , 20 ____ [R. 14.05(2)].

    ☐ according to the following legislation:

_____
(Name of statute or regulation and section)

Les formules des tribunaux sont affichées en anglais et en français sur le site www.ontariocourtforms.on.ca. Visitez ce site pour des renseignements sur des formats accessibles.

SCR 4-9-11-14-16-9B (January 23, 2014) CSD

FORM 9B   **PAGE 2**

_____
Claim No.

☐ Other: (Specify.)

_____ , 20 ____   _____
(Signature of party or representative)

CAUTION: To obtain an assessment of damages, all defendants must be noted in default. If one or more defendants has filed a defence, the matter must proceed to a settlement conference. To bring a motion in writing for an assessment of damages, file a Notice of Motion and Supporting Affidavit (Form 15A). You can get forms at court offices or online at www.ontariocourtforms.on.ca.

SCR 4-9-11-14-16-9B (January 23, 2014) CSD

Instructions for Making a Defendant's Claim

As a defendant, you can also make a claim of your own against the plaintiff or someone else. This is called a **defendant's claim**. For example, the plaintiff may owe you money. Or you may believe someone else caused the plaintiff's loss and that person should have to pay. To make your claim against the plaintiff or another party take the following steps:

Step 1: COMPLETE the **Defendant's Claim** form. Fill in the claim number from the Plaintiff's Claim form in the top right hand corner. You are the "plaintiff by defendant's claim." Explain what happened in detail. Include dates and places. State how much money you want or what goods you want returned. Attach copies of any documents that help your case. Examples are contracts, repair bills and photographs of damaged goods. If you want interest on money you are claiming, ask for it on the claim form. You and the defendant may have a contract that sets an annual interest rate. If so, use that rate. If not, claim the *Courts of Justice Act* interest rate posted on the Ministry of the Attorney General website at www.attorneygeneral.jus.gov.on.ca.

If there is more than one plaintiff or defendant, complete an **Additional Parties** form (Form 1A) and put it right behind page one of your defendant's claim form. You can get the additional parties form from the court office or at the following website: www.ontariocourtforms.on.ca.

Step 2: FILE the defendant's claim form and related documents with the court office where the plaintiff's claim was filed. You must file your claim no later than 20 days after you file your defence, unless you have leave of the court. There is a filing fee. The clerk will return a stamped copy of the defendant's claim form and documents to you.

Step 3: SERVE the defendant's claim. You must deliver a copy of the filed defendant's claim and your documents to each of the persons you are claiming against. This is "serving" your claim. There are rules about how this must be done. See the Small Claims Court **"Guide to Serving Documents"** at the court office or online at www.attorneygeneral.jus.gov.on.ca. Each party will have 20 days to file a defence to your claim after receiving it.

DO NOT FILE THIS PAGE.

SCR 10.01-10A (January 23, 2014) CSD

257

Form 10A
Defendant's Claim

ONTARIO
Superior Court of Justice

Defendant's Claim
Form 10A Ont. Reg. No.: 258/98

Small Claims Court

Claim No.

Seal

Address

Phone number

Plaintiff by Defendant's Claim No. 1 ☐ Additional plaintiff(s) listed on attached Form 1A. ☐ Under 18 years of age.

Last name, or name of company		
First name	Second name	Also known as
Address (street number, apt., unit)		
City/Town	Province	Phone no.
Postal code		Fax no.
Representative		LSUC #
Address (street number, apt., unit)		
City/Town	Province	Phone no.
Postal code		Fax no.

Defendant by Defendant's Claim No. 1 ☐ Additional defendant(s) listed on attached Form 1A. ☐ Under 18 years of age.

Last name, or name of company		
First name	Second name	Also known as
Address (street number, apt., unit)		
City/Town	Province	Phone no.
Postal code		Fax no.
Representative		LSUC #
Address (street number, apt., unit)		
City/Town	Province	Phone no.
Postal code		Fax no.

Les formules des tribunaux sont affichées en anglais et en français sur le site www.ontariocourtforms.on.ca. Visitez ce site pour des renseignements sur des formats accessibles.

SCR 10.01-10A (January 23, 2014) CSD

FORM 10A
 PAGE 2

_____
Claim No.

REASONS FOR CLAIM AND DETAILS

Explain what happened, including where and when. Then explain how much money you are claiming or what goods you want returned.

If you are relying on any documents, you **MUST** attach copies to the claim. If evidence is lost or unavailable, you **MUST** explain why it is not attached.

What happened?
Where?
When?

Continued on next sheet

FORM 10A   **PAGE 3**

_____
Claim No.

How much? $ ....
                        (Principal amount claimed)

☐   **ADDITIONAL PAGES ARE ATTACHED BECAUSE MORE ROOM WAS NEEDED.**

The plaintiff by defendant's claim also claims pre-judgment interest from _____ **under:**
                                                                              (Date)

(Check only   ☐ **the** *Courts of Justice Act*
one box)
                 ☐ **an agreement at the rate of** _____ **% per year**

and post-judgment interest, and court costs.

Prepared on: _____, 20 _____   _____
                                                    (Signature of plaintiff or representative)

Issued on: _____, 20 _____   _____
                                                    (Signature of clerk)

CAUTION TO DEFENDANT BY DEFENDANT'S CLAIM:	**IF YOU DO NOT FILE A DEFENCE** (Form 9A) and an Affidavit of Service (Form 8A) with the court within twenty (20) calendar days after you have been served with this Defendant's Claim, judgment may be obtained by Defendant's Claim without notice and enforced against you. Forms and self-help materials are available at the Small Claims Court and on the following website: www.ontariocourtforms.on.ca.

For information on accessibility of court services for
people with disability-related needs, contact:
Telephone: 416-326-2220 / 1-800-518-7901   TTY: 416-326-4012 / 1-877-425-0575

SCR 10.01-10A (January 23, 2014) CSD

Form 11A
Affidavit for Jurisdiction

ONTARIO
Superior Court of Justice

Affidavit for Jurisdiction
Form 11A Ont. Reg. No.: 258/98

Small Claims Court _____

Claim No. _____

Address _____

Phone number _____

BETWEEN

_____
Plaintiff(s)

and

_____
Defendant(s)

My name is _____
(Full name)

I live in _____
(Municipality & province)

and I swear/affirm that the following is true:

1. In this action, I am the

   ☐ plaintiff

   ☐ representative of the plaintiff(s) _____
   (Name of plaintiff(s))

2. I make this affidavit in support of the plaintiff's request to note the defendant(s) in default, where all the defendants have been or will be served outside the court's territorial division [R. 11.01 (3)].

3. The plaintiff is entitled to proceed with this action in this territorial division because this is:

   ☐ where the event (cause of action) took place.

   ☐ where the defendant lives or carries on business.

   ☐ the court nearest to the place where the defendant lives or carries on business [R. 6.01].

Sworn/Affirmed before me at _____
(Municipality)

in _____
(Province, state or country)

on _____ , 20 ____

Commissioner for taking affidavits
(Type or print name below if signature is
illegible.)

Signature
(This form is to be signed in front of a
lawyer, justice of the peace, notary public
or commissioner for taking affidavits.)

WARNING: IT IS AN OFFENCE UNDER THE *CRIMINAL CODE* TO KNOWINGLY SWEAR OR AFFIRM A FALSE AFFIDAVIT.

Les formules des tribunaux sont affichées en anglais et en français sur le site www.ontariocourtforms.on.ca. Visitez ce site pour des renseignements sur des formats accessibles.

SCR 11.01-11A (January 23, 2014) CSD

Form 11B
Default Judgment

ONTARIO
Superior Court of Justice

Default Judgment
Form 11B Ont. Reg. No.: 258/98

Seal

Small Claims Court

Claim No.

Address

Phone number

Plaintiff No. 1   ☐ Additional plaintiff(s) listed on attached Form 1A.

Last name, or name of company		
First name	Second name	Also known as
Address (street number, apt., unit)		
City/Town	Province	Phone no.
Postal code		Fax no.
Representative		LSUC #
Address (street number, apt., unit)		
City/Town	Province	Phone no.
Postal code		Fax no.

Defendant No. 1   ☐ Additional defendant(s) listed on attached Form 1A.

Last name, or name of company		
First name	Second name	Also known as
Address (street number, apt., unit)		
City/Town	Province	Phone no.
Postal code		Fax no.
Representative		LSUC #
Address (street number, apt., unit)		
City/Town	Province	Phone no.
Postal code		Fax no.

Les formules des tribunaux sont affichées en anglais et en français sur le site www.ontariocourtforms.on.ca. Visitez ce site pour des renseignements sur des formats accessibles.

SCR 11.02-11B (January 23, 2014) CSD

Continued on next page

FORM 11B   **PAGE 2**

Claim No. _____

NOTICE TO THE DEFENDANT(S):
(Check one box only.)

☐ You have been noted in default according to Rule 11.01.

☐ You have defaulted in your payment according to Rule 9.03(2)(b), pursuant to

_____ dated _____, 20 ___ ,
               (Name of document)

and 15 days have passed since you were served with a Notice of Default of Payment (Form 20L).

DEFAULT JUDGMENT IS GIVEN against the following defendant(s):

Last name, or name of company		
First name	Second name	Also known as

Last name, or name of company		
First name	Second name	Also known as

Last name, or name of company		
First name	Second name	Also known as

☐ Additional defendant(s) listed on attached page (*list in same format*).

THE DEFENDANT(S) MUST PAY to the plaintiff(s) the following sums:

(A) **DEBT** (principal amount claimed minus any payments received since the plaintiff's
    claim was issued) $ _____

(B) **PRE-JUDGMENT INTEREST** calculated

    on the sum of $ _____ at the rate of _____ %

    per annum from _____, 20 ___ , to _____, 20 ___ ,

    being _____ days. $ _____

(C) **COSTS** to date (including the cost of issuing this judgment) $ _____

                                               TOTAL $ _____

This judgment bears post-judgment interest at _____ % per annum commencing this date.

_____, 20 ___   _____
                                              (Signature of clerk)

CAUTION TO DEFENDANT:	**YOU MUST PAY THE AMOUNT OF THIS JUDGMENT DIRECTLY TO THE PLAINTIFF(S) IMMEDIATELY.** Failure to do so may result in additional post-judgment interest and enforcement costs.

SCR 11.02-11B (January 23, 2014) CSD

Instructions for Getting Default Judgment

Step 1: NOTE the defendant in default. If you filed a claim and the defendant has not **served a defence and filed it with proof of service within 20 days after you served the claim**, ask the court clerk to find or "note" the defendant in default. You can do this by bringing or mailing a completed **Request to Clerk** form (Form 9B) to the court office.

If there is more than one plaintiff or defendant, complete an **Additional Parties** form (Form 1A) and put it right behind page one of your default judgment form. You can get the additional parties form from the court office or online at www.ontariocourtforms.on.ca.

Step 2: You can ask the court to order the defendant to pay money in one of two ways:

. if your claim is for a specified sum of money, ask the court clerk to sign a default judgment; or

. if your claim is for damages, ask a judge to make a judgment and assess your damages.

Court fees must be paid to take these steps.

How to ask a court clerk to sign default judgment

The court clerk can sign a default judgment in cases where the amount in dispute is stated under an agreement. The agreement does not have to be in writing. Examples include:

. unpaid accounts for goods or services sold and delivered

. unpaid loans

. back rent

To ask a clerk to sign a default judgment, you must fill out and file a **Default Judgment** form.

How to ask a judge to make a judgment and assess damages

A judge can make a judgment and assess damages in cases where the amount in dispute is not spelled out under an agreement. Examples include cases where your property has been damaged or you have been physically injured.

You can ask a judge to make a judgment and assess damages in one of two ways:

1. Make a written request, called a "motion in writing". To do this, you file a **Notice of Motion and Supporting Affidavit** form (Form 15A). In the affidavit you state the reasons why the motion should be granted. Attach all relevant documents. You do not have to go to court to speak to the judge. The judge will read all the documents and then decide the case.

2. Ask for an **assessment hearing** before a judge. To do this, fill out a **Request to Clerk** form (Form 9B) and file it with the court. A hearing is like a trial, except that the defendant is not in court. You and your witnesses are the only people who will be present before the judge. You must prove the amount that the defendant should pay. You can call witnesses and present evidence such as photos of damaged goods and receipts for repairs. The judge will then make a decision about the case.

See the following Small Claims Court guides at the court office or online at www.attorneygeneral.jus.gov.on.ca:

. for default judgments, see the **"Guide to Making a Claim"**

. for a motion in writing, see the **"Guide to Motions and Clerk's Orders"**

. for assessment hearings, see the **"Guide to Getting Ready for Court"**

DO NOT FILE THIS PAGE.

SCR 11.02-11B (January 23, 2014) CSD

Form 11.2A
Request for Clerk's Order on Consent

ONTARIO
Superior Court of Justice

Request for Clerk's Order on Consent
Form 11.2A Ont. Reg. No.: 258/98

Small Claims Court _____

Claim No. _____

Address _____

Phone number _____

Plaintiff No. 1 ☐ Additional plaintiff(s) listed on attached Form 1A.

Last name, or name of company		
First name	Second name	Also known as
Address (street number, apt., unit)		
City/Town	Province	Phone no.
Postal code		Fax no.
Representative		LSUC #
Address (street number, apt., unit)		
City/Town	Province	Phone no.
Postal code		Fax no.

Defendant No. 1 ☐ Additional defendant(s) listed on attached Form 1A.

Last name, or name of company		
First name	Second name	Also known as
Address (street number, apt., unit)		
City/Town	Province	Phone no.
Postal code		Fax no.
Representative		LSUC #
Address (street number, apt., unit)		
City/Town	Province	Phone no.
Postal code		Fax no.

NOTE: This request must be signed by all parties and anyone being added, deleted or substituted.

Les formules des tribunaux sont affichées en anglais et en français sur le site www.ontariocourtforms.on.ca. Visitez ce site pour des renseignements sur des formats accessibles.

SCR 11.2.01-11.2A (January 23, 2014) CSD

FORM 11.2A   **PAGE 2**

_____
Claim No.

TO THE PARTIES:

THIS REQUEST IS FILED BY: _____
(Name of party)

I state that:

☐ Each party has received a copy of this form.

☐ No party that would be affected by the order is under disability.

☐ This form has been signed and consented to by all parties, including any parties to be added, deleted or substituted.

I request that the clerk make the following order(s) on the consent of all parties:
(Check appropriate boxes.)

☐ set aside the noting in default of _____
(Name of defendant(s))

☐ set aside Default Judgment against _____
(Name of defendant(s))

☐ restore to the list the following matter that was dismissed under Rule 11.1: (Specify.)

_____

☐ cancel the examination hearing regarding _____
(Name of person to be examined)

☐ with respect to the following step(s) taken to enforce the default judgment that are not yet completed:

☐ withdraw the Writ of Seizure and Sale of Land issued against: (Name of debtor(s))

_____

and directed to the sheriff of the _____ :
(Name of county/region in which the sheriff (enforcement office) is located)

_____
(Provide instructions about what is to be done with any proceeds held or property seized by the sheriff.)

☐ withdraw the Writ of Seizure and Sale of Personal Property issued against: (Name of debtor(s))

_____

and directed to the bailiff of the _____ :
(Small Claims Court location)

_____
(Provide instructions about what is to be done with any proceeds held by the clerk of the court or property that has been seized by the bailiff.)

SCR 11.2.01-11.2A (January 23, 2014) CSD

Continued on next page

FORM 11.2A   **PAGE 3**

_____
Claim No.

☐ terminate the Notice of Garnishment or Notice of Renewal of Garnishment issued against:

_____
(Name of debtor(s))

and directed to _____ :

(Name of garnishee)

_____
(Provide instructions about what is to be done with any money held by the clerk of the court.)

☐ note that payment has been made in full satisfaction of an order or terms of settlement

☐ dismiss the: ☐ Plaintiff's Claim   ☐ Defendant's Claim

☐ costs in the amount of $ _____ , to be paid to _____

(Amount)   (Name of party(ies))

_____ by _____
(Name of party(ies))

The originally scheduled trial date is less than 30 days away and I request that the clerk make the following order(s) on the consent of all parties and any person to be added or substituted :
(Check appropriate boxes.)

☐ amend a Plaintiff's Claim issued on _____ , 20 ____ .
    (Attach two (2) copies of the amended Plaintiff's Claim.)

☐ amend a Defence filed on _____ , 20 ____ .
    (Attach two (2) copies of the amended Defence.)

☐ amend a Defendant's Claim issued on _____ , 20 ____ .
    (Attach two (2) copies of the amended Defendant's Claim.)

☐ add _____
                              (Name of party)

to the   ☐ Plaintiff's Claim   ☐ Defendant's Claim

as a   ☐ defendant   ☐ Plaintiff

☐ delete _____
                              (Name of party)

from the   ☐ Plaintiff's Claim   ☐ Defendant's Claim

☐ substitute _____
                              (Name of party)

with _____
                              (Name of party)

in the   ☐ Plaintiff's Claim   ☐ Defendant's Claim

Continued on next page

FORM 11.2A PAGE 4

Claim No. _____

_____ , 20 ____

(Signature of party consenting)

(Name of party consenting)

(Signature of witness)

(Name of witness)

_____ , 20 ____

(Signature of party consenting)

(Name of party consenting)

(Signature of witness)

(Name of witness)

_____ , 20 ____

(Signature of party consenting)

(Name of party consenting)

(Signature of witness)

(Name of witness)

_____ , 20 ____

(Signature of party consenting)

(Name of party consenting)

(Signature of witness)

(Name of witness)

DISPOSITION: *The clerk of the court will complete this section.*

☐ order to go as asked

☐ order refused because:

_____ , 20 ____   _____

(Signature of clerk)

SCR 11.2.01-11.2A (January 23, 2014) CSD

Form 11.3A
Notice of Discontinued Claim

ONTARIO
Superior Court of Justice

Notice of Discontinued Claim
Form 11.3A Ont. Reg. No.: 258/98

Small Claims Court

Claim No.

Address

Phone number

BETWEEN

_____
Plaintiff(s)

and

_____
Defendant(s)

TAKE NOTICE that the plaintiff discontinues the claim against the following defendant(s) who did not file a defence:

Last name, or name of company		
First name	Second name	Also known as

Last name, or name of company		
First name	Second name	Also known as

Last name, or name of company		
First name	Second name	Also known as

☐ Additional defendant(s) listed in attached page *(list in same format)*.

_____ , 20 _____   _____
                                 (Signature of plaintiff or representative)

                                 _____
                                 (Name, address and phone number of party or representative)

NOTE: **THIS NOTICE** must be served on all defendants who were served with the claim, and filed with the court with proof of service. A claim may not be discontinued by or against a person under disability, except with leave of the court.

Les formules des tribunaux sont affichées en anglais et en français sur le site www.ontariocourtforms.on.ca. Visitez ce site pour des renseignements sur des formats accessibles.

SCR 11.3-11.3A (January 23, 2014) CSD

Form 13A
List of Proposed Witnesses

ONTARIO
Superior Court of Justice

List of Proposed Witnesses
Form 13A Ont. Reg. No.: 258/98

Small Claims Court

Claim No.

Address

Phone number

BETWEEN

Plaintiff(s)

and

Defendant(s)

My name is _____
(Name of party/representative)

The following is my list of proposed witnesses in this case:

Name of witness	Address, phone and fax numbers
1.	
2.	
3.	

Les formules des tribunaux sont affichées en anglais et en français sur le site www.ontariocourtforms.on.ca. Visitez ce site pour des renseignements sur des formats accessibles.

SCR 13.01-13A (January 23, 2014) CSD

270

FORM 13A   **PAGE 2**

Claim No. _____

4. _____   _____
_____
_____
_____
_____

5. _____   _____
_____
_____
_____

The following is my list of other persons with knowledge of the matter in dispute in this case:

Name of person	**Address, phone and fax numbers**
1. _____	_____
	_____
	_____
	_____
2. _____	_____
	_____
	_____
	_____

(Attach a separate sheet in the above format for additional witnesses or other persons.)

_____ , 20____   _____
                                        (Signature of party or representative)

_____   _____
                              (Name, address and phone number of party or representative)

NOTE: **EACH PARTY MUST SERVE THIS LIST** on all other parties and file it with the court at least fourteen (14) days before the settlement conference [R. 13.03(2)(b)].

SCR 13.01-13A (January 23, 2014) CSD

Form 13B
Consent

ONTARIO
Superior Court of Justice

Consent
Form 13B Ont. Reg. No.: 258/98

Small Claims Court   Claim No.

Address

Phone number

BETWEEN

_____ Plaintiff(s)

and

_____ Defendant(s)

I/We, _____ ,
(Name of party(ies))

consent to the following:

The parties do not need to sign this consent on the same day, but each must sign in the presence of his or her witness who signs a moment later. (For additional parties' signatures, attach a separate sheet in the format below.)

_____ , 20 ___	_____ , 20 ___
(Signature of party consenting)	(Signature of party consenting)
(Name of party consenting)	(Name of party consenting)
(Signature of witness)	(Signature of witness)
(Name of witness)	(Name of witness)

Les formules des tribunaux sont affichées en anglais et en français sur le site www.ontariocourtforms.on.ca. Visitez ce site pour des renseignements sur des formats accessibles.

SCR 3-8-11-14-20-13B (January 23, 2014) CSD

Form 14A
Offer to Settle

ONTARIO
Superior Court of Justice

Offer to Settle
Form 14A Ont. Reg. No.: 258/98

Small Claims Court _____

Claim No. _____

Address _____

Phone number _____

BETWEEN

_____
Plaintiff(s)

and

_____
Defendant(s)

My name is _____
(Full name)

1. In this action, I am the

☐ Plaintiff

☐ Defendant

☐ representative of _____
(Name of party(ies))

2. I offer to settle this action against _____
(Name of party(ies))

on the following terms: *(Set out terms in numbered paragraphs, or on an attached sheet.)*

Les formules des tribunaux sont affichées en anglais et en français sur le site www.ontariocourtforms.on.ca. Visitez ce site pour des renseignements sur des formats accessibles.

SCR 14.01.1-14A (January 23, 2014) CSD

FORM 14A   **PAGE 2**

_____

Claim No.

3. This offer to settle is available for acceptance until _____ , 20 _____ .

This offer to settle may be accepted by serving an acceptance of offer to settle (Form 14B may be used) on the party who made it, at any time before it is withdrawn or before the court disposes of the claim to which the offer applies [R. 14.05(1)]. You can get forms at court offices or online at www.ontariocourtforms.on.ca.

_____ , 20 _____   _____

                                            (Signature of party or representative making offer)

                                            _____

                                            (Name, address and phone number of party or representative)

NOTE:	**IF YOU ACCEPT AN OFFER TO SETTLE, THEN FAIL TO COMPLY WITH ITS TERMS,** judgment in the terms of the accepted offer may be obtained against you on motion to the court, or the action may continue as if there has been no offer to settle [R. 14.06].

NOTE:	**IF THIS OFFER TO SETTLE IS NOT ACCEPTED, IT SHALL NOT BE FILED WITH THE COURT OR DISCLOSED** to the trial judge until all questions of liability and relief (other than costs) have been determined [R. 14.04].

SCR 14.01.1-14A (January 23, 2014) CSD

Form 14B
Acceptance of Offer to Settle

ONTARIO
Superior Court of Justice

Acceptance of Offer to Settle
Form 14B Ont. Reg. No.: 258/98

Small Claims Court | Claim No.

Address

Phone number

BETWEEN

_____
Plaintiff(s)

and

_____
Defendant(s)

My name is _____
(Full name)

1. In this action, I am the
   ☐ plaintiff
   ☐ defendant
   ☐ representative of _____
   (Name of party(ies))

2. I accept the offer to settle from _____
   (Name of party(ies))

   dated _____ , 20 _____ .

3. This offer to settle has not expired and has not been withdrawn.

_____ , 20 _____   _____
                                          (Signature of party or representative accepting offer)

                                          _____
                                          (Name, address and phone number of party or representative)

CAUTION:	IF YOU ACCEPT AN OFFER TO SETTLE, THEN FAIL TO COMPLY WITH ITS TERMS, judgment in the terms of the accepted offer may be obtained against you on motion to the Court, or this action may continue as if there has been no offer to settle [R. 14.06].

Les formules des tribunaux sont affichées en anglais et en français sur le site www.ontariocourtforms.on.ca. Visitez ce site pour des renseignements sur des formats accessibles.

SCR 14.01.1-14B (January 23, 2014) CSD

Form 14C
Notice of Withdrawal of Offer to Settle

ONTARIO
Superior Court of Justice

Notice of Withdrawal of Offer to Settle
Form 14C Ont. Reg. No.: 258/98

Small Claims Court _____   Claim No. _____

Address _____

Phone number _____

BETWEEN

_____   Plaintiff(s)

and

_____   Defendant(s)

My name is _____
(Full name)

1. In this action, I am the

    ☐ plaintiff

    ☐ defendant

    ☐ representative of _____
    (Name of party(ies))

2. I withdraw the offer to settle provided to _____
    (Name of party(ies))

    dated _____, 20 _____, which has not been accepted.

_____, 20 _____   _____
(Signature of party or representative withdrawing offer)

_____
(Name, address and phone number of party or representative)

Les formules des tribunaux sont affichées en anglais et en français sur le site www.ontariocourtforms.on.ca. Visitez ce site pour des renseignements sur des formats accessibles.

SCR 14.01.1-14C (January 23, 2014) CSD

Form 14D
Terms of Settlement

ONTARIO
Superior Court of Justice

Terms of Settlement
Form 14D Ont. Reg. No.: 258/98

_____
Small Claims Court

Claim No. _____

_____
Address

_____
Phone number

BETWEEN

_____
Plaintiff(s)

and

_____
Defendant(s)

We have agreed to settle this action on the following terms:

1. _____ shall pay to
(Name of party(ies))

_____ the sum of
(Name of party(ies))

$ _____ as follows as full and final settlement of the claim, inclusive of interest and costs:
(Provide terms of payment such as start date, frequency, amount and duration.)

Put a line through any blank space and initial.

Les formules des tribunaux sont affichées en anglais et en français sur le site
www.ontariocourtforms.on.ca. Visitez ce site pour des renseignements sur des
formats accessibles.

FORM 14D   **PAGE 2**

_____
Claim No.

2.   This claim (and Defendant's Claim, if any) is withdrawn.

3.   If a party to these terms of settlement fails to comply, judgment in the terms of settlement may be obtained against that party on motion to the court or this action may continue as if there has been no settlement.

4.   Provided that the terms of settlement are complied with, the parties above fully and finally release one another from all claims related to the facts and issues raised in this action.

The parties do not need to sign terms of settlement on the same day, but each must sign in the presence of his or her witness who signs a moment later. (For additional parties' signatures, attach a separate sheet in the below format.)

_____ , 20 _____   _____ , 20 _____

_____   _____
(Signature of party)   (Signature of party)

_____   _____
(Name of party)   (Name of party)

_____   _____
(Signature of witness)   (Signature of witness)

_____   _____
(Name of witness)   (Name of witness)

_____ , 20 _____   _____ , 20 _____

_____   _____
(Signature of party)   (Signature of party)

_____   _____
(Name of party)   (Name of party)

_____   _____
(Signature of witness)   (Signature of witness)

_____   _____
(Name of witness)   (Name of witness)

SCR 14D (January 23, 2014) CSD

Instructions for Making a Motion in Small Claims Court

A motion is a request to a judge to make an order about a case. For example, a defendant could ask the court for more time to send in a defence or a defendant's claim. Or either party could ask for more time to serve documents.

Motions can help the parties in a case. They can also make the case take longer and cost more money. If the judge grants your motion, you can ask the judge to make the other party pay some of your costs. These costs can include court filing fees, lawyer or agent fees, and expenses for witnesses, photocopying, faxing and delivery of documents.

Step 1: EXPLAIN what you are asking the judge to do and why. This is done by filling out a **Notice of Motion and Supporting Affidavit** form. Contact the clerk of the court to choose a time and date when the court could hear the motion. The clerk of the court will provide a hearing date and time. Put the date and time on the form.

Step 2: SERVE. The form must then be served on the other parties at least 7 days before the hearing date. There are rules about how this must be done. See the Small Claims Court **"Guide to Serving Documents"** at the court office or online at www.attorneygeneral.jus.gov.on.ca. Copies of documents attached to the form must also be served.

Step 3: FILE the **Notice of Motion and Supporting Affidavit** form at the court at least 3 days before the hearing date. There is a filing fee. Also file an **Affidavit of Service** (Form 8A) proving that the other parties were served.

Motion in Writing for an Assessment of Damages

If all defendants have been noted in default after failing to file a defence, you can bring a motion in writing for an assessment of damages. You do not have to attend the motion. The judge will make a decision based on the documents that you filed. If the judge thinks the documents you filed are inadequate, the court may order you to provide a further affidavit or to attend an assessment hearing. You can also request an assessment hearing.

For more information, see the **"Guide to Motions and Clerk's Orders"** at the court office or online at www.attorneygeneral.jus.gov.on.ca.

DO NOT FILE THIS PAGE

RSCC-15A-E (2015/11)

Form 15A
Notice of Motion and Supporting Affidavit

ONTARIO
Superior Court of Justice

Notice of Motion and Supporting Affidavit
Form 15A Ont. Reg. No.: 258/98

Small Claims Court	Claim No.
Address	
Phone Number	

Plaintiff No. 1 ☐ Additional plaintiff(s) listed on attached Form 1A.

Last name, or name of company		
First Name	Second Name	Also Known as
Address (street number, apt., unit)		
City/Town	Province	Phone no.
Postal Code		Fax no.
Representative		LSUC #
Address (street number, apt., unit)		
City/Town	Province	Phone no.
Postal Code		Fax no.

Defendant No. 1 ☐ Additional defendant(s) listed on attached Form 1A.

Last name, or name of company		
First Name	Second Name	Also Known as
Address (street number, apt., unit)		
City/Town	Province	Phone no.
Postal Code		Fax no.
Representative		LSUC no.
Address (street number, apt., unit)		
City/Town	Province	Phone no.
Postal Code		Fax no.

Les formules des tribunaux sont affichées en anglais et en français sur le site www.ontariocourtforms.on.ca. Visitez ce site pour des renseignements sur des formats accessibles.

RSCC-15A-E (2015/11)

FORM 15A   **PAGE 2**   _____
                                                             Claim No.

Complete Part A or Part B below, then complete the affidavit in support of motion on page 3.

A. THIS COURT WILL HEAR A MOTION on _____ , 20 _____ , at _____ ,
                                                                                  (Time)

or as soon as possible after that time, at _____
                                          (Address of court location and courtroom number)

_____

This motion will be made in person by _____ ,
                                          (Name of party)

   for the following order:

    ☐ the court's permission to extend time to (Specify)

    _____

    _____

    ☐ set aside default judgment and noting in default.

    ☐ set aside noting in default.

    ☐ permission to file a Defence.

    ☐ permission to file a Defendant's Claim.

    ☐ set aside order dismissing claim as abandoned.

    ☐ terminate garnishment and/or withdraw writ(s).

    ☐ Other:

    _____

    _____

    _____

    _____

☐ **ADDITIONAL PAGES ARE ATTACHED BECAUSE MORE ROOM WAS NEEDED.**

☐ **DOCUMENTS ARE ATTACHED.**

NOTE: **IF YOU FAIL TO ATTEND AN IN-PERSON MOTION,** an order may be made against you, with costs, in your absence. If you want to attend the motion by telephone or video conference, complete and file a Request for Telephone or Video Conference (Form 1B). If the court permits it, the clerk will make the necessary arrangements and notify the parties [R. 1.07(5)].

B. This motion in writing for an assessment of damages is made by

_____ ,
                   (Name of plaintiff)

who asks the court for an order assessing damages against

_____
                 (Name of defendant(s))

who have/has been noted in default.

RSCC-15A-E (2015/11)
                                     Continued on next page

FORM 15A
PAGE 3
_____
Claim No.

AFFIDAVIT IN SUPPORT OF MOTION

My name is _____
(Full Name)

I live in _____
(Municipality and Province)

I swear/affirm that the following is true:

Set out the facts in numbered paragraphs. If you learned a fact from someone else, you must give that person's name and state that you believe that fact to be true.

_____
_____
_____
_____
_____
_____
_____
_____
_____
_____
_____
_____
_____
_____
_____
_____
_____
_____
_____
_____
_____
_____
_____
_____
_____
_____
_____

RSCC-15A-E (2015/11)

Continued on next page

FORM 15A   PAGE 4   _____
                                                                Claim No.

AFFIDAVIT IN SUPPORT OF MOTION, continued

_____
_____
_____
_____
_____
_____
_____
_____
_____
_____
_____
_____
_____
_____
_____
_____
_____
_____
_____
_____
_____

If more space is required, attach and initial extra pages.

Sworn/Affirmed before me at _____
                                    (Municipality)

in _____
              (Province, state or country)   _____
                                                                                        Signature

on _____ , 20 _____   (This form is to be signed in front of a lawyer, justice of
                              Commissioner for taking affidavits   the peace, notary public or commissioner for taking
                              (Type or print name below if signature is   affidavits.)
                                          illegible.)

WARNING:	IT IS AN OFFENCE UNDER THE *CRIMINAL CODE* TO KNOWINGLY SWEAR OR AFFIRM A FALSE AFFIDAVIT.

For information on accessibility of court services for
people with disability-related needs, contact:
Telephone: 416-326-2220 / 1-800-518-7901 TTY: 416-326-4012 / 1-877-425-0575

| Save Form | Print Form | | Clear Form |

RSCC-15A-E (2015/11)

Form 15B
Affidavit

ONTARIO
Superior Court of Justice

Affidavit
Form 15B Ont. Reg. No.: 258/98

_____
Small Claims Court

Claim No.

_____
Address

_____
Phone number

BETWEEN

_____
Plaintiff(s)/Creditor(s)

and

_____
Defendant(s)/Debtor(s)

My name is _____
(Full name)

I live in _____
(Municipality & province)

I make this affidavit in relation to: _____
(Specify why the affidavit is being filed with the court.)

and I swear/affirm that the following is true:
Set out the facts in numbered paragraphs. If you learned a fact from someone else, you must give that person's name and state that you believe that fact to be true.

Les formules des tribunaux sont affichées en anglais et en français sur le site www.ontariocourtforms.on.ca. Visitez ce site pour des renseignements sur des formats accessibles.

SCR 15.01-15B (January 23, 2014) CSD

FORM 15B

PAGE 2

Claim No. _____

If more space is required, attach and initial extra pages.

Sworn/Affirmed before me at _____
(Municipality)

in _____
(Province, state or country)

on _____ , 20 ____   _____
Commissioner for taking affidavits
(Type or print name below if signature is illegible.)

_____
Signature
(This form is to be signed in front of a
lawyer, justice of the peace, notary public
or commissioner for taking affidavits.)

**WARNING: IT IS AN OFFENCE UNDER THE *CRIMINAL CODE* TO KNOWINGLY SWEAR OR
AFFIRM A FALSE AFFIDAVIT.**

SCR 15.01-15B (January 23, 2014) CSD

Form 18A
Summons to Witness

ONTARIO
Superior Court of Justice

Summons to Witness
Form 18A Ont. Reg. No.: 258/98

Seal

Small Claims Court

Claim No.

Address

Phone number

BETWEEN

_____
Plaintiff(s)

and

_____
Defendant(s)

TO: _____
(Name of witness)

YOU ARE REQUIRED TO ATTEND AND TO GIVE EVIDENCE IN COURT at the trial of this action on

_____, 20 _____ **at** _____, **at**
(Time)

_____
(Address of court location)

and to remain until your attendance is no longer required. You may be required to return to court from time to time.

YOU ARE ALSO REQUIRED TO BRING WITH YOU AND PRODUCE AT THE TRIAL the following documents or other things in your possession, control or power: (Identify and describe particular documents and other things required)

Les formules des tribunaux sont affichées en anglais et en français sur le site www.ontariocourtforms.on.ca. Visitez ce site pour des renseignements sur des formats accessibles.

SCR 18.03-18A (January 23, 2014) CSD

FORM 18A

PAGE 2

_____
Claim No.

and all other documents or other things in your possession, control or power relating to the action.

_____   has requested the clerk to issue this summons.
(Name of party)

_____ , 20 _____   _____
(Signature of clerk)

| NOTE: | **THIS SUMMONS MUST BE SERVED** personally, at least 10 days before the trial date, on the person to be summoned together with attendance money calculated in accordance with the Small Claims Court Schedule of Fees, which is a regulation under the _Administration of Justice Act_. To obtain a copy of the regulation, attend the nearest Small Claims Court or access the following website: www.e-laws.gov.on.ca. |

| CAUTION: | **IF YOU FAIL TO ATTEND OR REMAIN IN ATTENDANCE AS REQUIRED BY THIS SUMMONS, A WARRANT MAY BE ISSUED FOR YOUR ARREST.** |

For information on accessibility of court services for people with disability-related needs, contact:
Telephone: 416-326-2220 / 1-800-518-7901   TTY: 416-326-4012 / 1-877-425-0575

SCR 18.03-18A (January 23, 2014) CSD

Form 18B
Warrant for Arrest of Defaulting Witness

ONTARIO
Superior Court of Justice

Warrant for Arrest of Defaulting Witness
Form 18B Ont. Reg. No.: 258/98

Small Claims Court   Claim No.

Seal

Address

Phone number

BETWEEN

_____
Plaintiff(s)

and

_____
Defendant(s)

TO ALL POLICE OFFICERS IN ONTARIO AND TO THE OFFICERS OF ALL CORRECTIONAL INSTITUTIONS IN ONTARIO:

The witness _____
(Name)

of _____
(Address)

was served with a Summons to Witness (Form 18A) to give evidence at the trial of this action, and the prescribed attendance money was paid or tendered.

The witness failed to attend or to remain in attendance at the trial, and I am satisfied that the evidence of this witness is material to this proceeding.

YOU ARE ORDERED TO ARREST AND BRING this person before the court to give evidence in this action, and if the court is not then sitting or if the person cannot be brought before the court immediately, to deliver the person to a provincial correctional institution or other secure facility, to be admitted and detained there until the person can be brought before the court.

I FURTHER ORDER YOU TO HOLD this person in custody and to detain him/her only so long as necessary to bring this person before a court as ordered above.

_____, 20_____   _____
(Signature of judge)

Les formules des tribunaux sont affichées en anglais et en français sur le site www.ontariocourtforms.on.ca. Visitez ce site pour des renseignements sur des formats accessibles.

SCR 18.03-20.11-18B (January 23, 2014) CSD

Form 20A
Certificate of Judgment

ONTARIO
Superior Court of Justice

Certificate of Judgment
Form 20A Ont. Reg. No.: 258/98

Seal

Small Claims Court _____

Claim No. _____

Address _____

Phone number _____

BETWEEN

_____

Creditor(s)

and

_____

Debtor(s)

A judgment was made in this action on _____ **, 20** _____ **, in the**

_____
(Name of court where judgment was made)

against

Last name of debtor, or name of company		
First name	Second name	Third name
Address		

Last name of debtor, or name of company		
First name	Second name	Third name
Address		

Last name of debtor, or name of company		
First name	Second name	Third name
Address		

☐ Additional debtor(s) and also known as names are listed on attached Form 1A.1.

Les formules des tribunaux sont affichées en anglais et en français sur le site www.ontariocourtforms.on.ca. Visitez ce site pour des renseignements sur des formats accessibles.

SCR 20.04-20A (January 23, 2014) CSD

289

FORM 20A   **PAGE 2**

_____
                                                                    Claim No.

Judgment was made for the following sums:

(A) **AMOUNT OF JUDGMENT** (debt and pre-judgment interest) $ _____

(B) **COSTS** to date of judgment $ _____

Post-judgment interest continues to accrue at _____ % per annum.
                                              (Interest rate)

_____ , 20 _____   _____
                                                              (Signature of clerk)

TO THE CLERK OF THE _____ **SMALL CLAIMS COURT:**
                        (Name of court to where the judgment is to be filed)

The person requesting this certificate is _____
                                          (Name of party requesting certificate)

_____
                              (Address of party requesting certificate)

SCR 20.04-20A (January 23, 2014) CSD

Form 20B
Writ of Delivery

ONTARIO	**Writ of Delivery**
Superior Court of Justice	Form 20B Ont. Reg. No.: 258/98

Seal

Small Claims Court _____

Claim No. _____

Address _____

Phone number _____

BETWEEN

_____
Plaintiff(s)

and

_____
Defendant(s)

TO THE BAILIFF OF _____ **SMALL CLAIMS COURT:**
(Name of Small Claims Court location)

Under an order of this court made on _____ , 20 _____

YOU ARE DIRECTED to seize from _____
(Name of person against whom the order was made)

and to deliver without delay to

Name of person in whose favour the order was made
Street and number
City, province, postal code
Phone number and fax number, if any

possession of the following personal property:
(According to the court order, set out a description of the property to be delivered. Identify any marks or serial numbers. If the order refers to items set out in the issued claim, attach a copy of the issued claim.)

Les formules des tribunaux sont affichées en anglais et en français sur le site www.ontariocourtforms.on.ca. Visitez ce site pour des renseignements sur des formats accessibles.

SCR 20.05-20B (January 23, 2014) CSD

291

FORM 20B   **PAGE 2**

_____
Claim No.

The above personal property is located at: _____

(Address)

If the address provided does not clearly identify where the items are located, please attach a detailed map that shows the nearest intersection.

(To be completed by the clerk of the court.)	☐	**THE COURT HAS EXPRESSLY ORDERED** that you are authorized to use reasonable force to enter a private dwelling to execute this writ of delivery, if necessary [_Execution Act_, s. 20(2)]. A copy of the court's order on the endorsement record is attached.

_____, 20 _____   _____

(Signature of clerk)

SCR 20.05-20B (January 23, 2014) CSD

Form 20C
Writ of Seizure and Sale of Personal Property

FORMS

ONTARIO

Superior Court of Justice

Writ of Seizure and Sale of Personal Property
Form 20C Ont. Reg. No.: 258/98

Seal

Small Claims Court   Claim No.

Address

Phone number

Creditor No. 1   ☐ Additional party(ies) listed on attached Form 1A.

Last name, or name of company		
First name	Second name	Also known as
Address (street number, apt., unit)		
City/Town	Province	Phone no.
Postal code		Fax no.
Representative		LSUC #
Address (street number, apt., unit)		
City/Town	Province	Phone no.
Postal code		Fax no.

Debtor No. 1   ☐ Additional party(ies) listed on attached Form 1A.

Last name, or name of company		
First name	Second name	Also known as
Address (street number, apt., unit)		
City/Town	Province	Phone no.
Postal code		Fax no.
Representative		LSUC #
Address (street number, apt., unit)		
City/Town	Province	Phone no.
Postal code		Fax no.

Les formules des tribunaux sont affichées en anglais et en français sur le site www.ontariocourtforms.on.ca. Visitez ce site pour des renseignements sur des formats accessibles.

SCR 20.06-20C (January 23, 2014) CSD

FORM 20C

PAGE 2

Claim No. _____

TO THE BAILIFF OF THE _____ **SMALL CLAIMS COURT:**

(Small Claims Court location)

Under an order of this court made on _____ , 20 _____ , in favour of

_____

(Name of creditor(s))

YOU ARE DIRECTED to seize and sell the personal property of

Last name, or name of company		
First name	Second name	Third name

☐ Additional debtor(s) and also known as names listed on attached Form 1A.1.

situated within your jurisdiction and to realize from the seizure and sale the following sums:

(A) **AMOUNT OF JUDGMENT** (debt and pre-judgment interest) $ _____

(B) **COSTS** to date of judgment $ _____

(C) **TOTAL AMOUNT OF PAYMENTS RECEIVED FROM DEBTOR** after
judgment (if any) $ _____

Post-judgment interest continues to accrue

at the rate of _____ % per annum from _____ , 20 _____ .

(D) **SUBSEQUENT COSTS** incurred after judgment (including the cost of issuing this writ) $ _____

(E) Your fees and expenses in enforcing this writ.

YOU ARE DIRECTED to calculate the amount owing at the time of enforcement and to pay the proceeds over to the clerk of this court for the creditor.

_____ , 20 _____ _____

(Signature of clerk)

Reasonable disbursements necessarily incurred to enforce this writ	$ ....
(Bailiff (enforcement office) fees and expenses)	(filled in and initialled by $ the enforcement office)

NOTE: **THIS WRIT REMAINS IN FORCE FOR SIX YEARS** after the date of its issue and for a further six years after each renewal. The writ may be renewed before it expires by filing a Request to Renew a Writ of Seizure and Sale (Form 20N) with the bailiff (enforcement office).

SCR 20.06-20C (January 23, 2014) CSD

Form 20D
Writ of Seizure and Sale of Land

ONTARIO
Superior Court of Justice

Writ of Seizure and Sale of Land
Form 20D Ont. Reg. No.: 258/98

Seal

Small Claims Court

Claim No.

Address

Phone number

Creditor No. 1   ☐ Additional party(ies) listed on attached Form 1A.

Last name, or name of company		
First name	Second name	Also known as
Address (street number, apt., unit)		
City/Town	Province	Phone no.
Postal code		Fax no.
Representative		LSUC #
Address (street number, apt., unit)		
City/Town	Province	Phone no.
Postal code		Fax no.

Debtor No. 1   ☐ Additional party(ies) listed on attached Form 1A.

Last name, or name of company		
First name	Second name	Also known as
Address (street number, apt., unit)		
City/Town	Province	Phone no.
Postal code		Fax no.
Representative		LSUC #
Address (street number, apt., unit)		
City/Town	Province	Phone no.
Postal code		Fax no.

NOTE: **THIS WRIT REMAINS IN FORCE FOR SIX YEARS** after the date of its issue and for a further six years after each renewal. The writ may be renewed before it expires by filing a Request to Renew a Writ of Seizure and Sale (Form 20N) with the sheriff (enforcement office.)

Les formules des tribunaux sont affichées en anglais et en français sur le site www.ontariocourtforms.on.ca. Visitez ce site pour des renseignements sur des formats accessibles.

SCR 20.07-20D (January 23, 2014) CSD

FORM 20D   **PAGE 2**

_____
Claim No.

TO THE SHERIFF OF _____ :
(Name of county/region in which the enforcement office is located)

Under an order of this court made on _____ , 20 _____ , in favour of

_____
(Name of creditor(s))

YOU ARE DIRECTED to seize and sell the real property of

Last name, or name of company		
First name	Second name	Third name

☐ Additional debtor(s) and also known as names listed on attached Form 1A.1.

situated within your jurisdiction and to realize from the seizure and sale the following sums:

(A) **AMOUNT OF JUDGMENT** (debt and pre-judgment interest) $ _____

(B) **COSTS** to date of judgment $ _____

(C) **TOTAL AMOUNT OF PAYMENTS RECEIVED FROM DEBTOR** after
    judgment (if any) $ _____

    Post-judgment interest continues to accrue

    at the rate of _____ % per annum from _____ , 20 _____ .

(D) **SUBSEQUENT COSTS** incurred after judgment (including the cost of issuing this writ) $ _____

(E) Your fees and expenses in enforcing this writ.

YOU ARE DIRECTED to calculate the amount owing at the time of enforcement and pay out the proceeds according to law and to report on the execution of this writ if required by a party who filed this writ.

_____ , 20 _____   _____
                                         (Signature of clerk)

SCR 20.07-20D (January 23, 2014) CSD

296

Instructions for Enforcing a Judgment using Garnishment

If you are the plaintiff and you win the case, the court may order the defendant to pay you money. If the defendant is ordered to pay you money, the defendant (called the "debtor" after judgment, and you are called the "creditor") may pay right away, or you may give the debtor more time to pay. If the debtor does not pay, there are steps you can take to get the money. This is called **enforcing** the judgment. There are fees for these steps.

If someone else owes the debtor money, you can ask the court to order that person to send the money to the court office. The court will then pay you. This is called garnishment. For example, if you know where the debtor has a bank account or where the debtor works, you can ask the court to have the debtor's bank or employer pay money to the court.

Step 1: COMPLETE and FILE a <u>Notice of Garnishment</u> form and an <u>Affidavit for Enforcement Request</u> (Form 20P) with the court office. The clerk will stamp the notice. There is a fee.

Step 2: SERVE. You then serve a copy of the stamped notice of garnishment and a blank <u>Garnishee's Statement</u> form (Form 20F) on the person or business that has the money (the "garnishee") owed to the debtor. You also serve a copy of the stamped notice and the affidavit on the debtor. There are rules about how this must be done. See the Small Claims Court **"Guide to Serving Documents"** at the court office or online at <u>www.attorneygeneral.jus.gov.on.ca</u>. You can get copies of forms at the court office or online at <u>www.ontariocourtforms.on.ca</u>.

Step 3: TERMINATE. Once the judgment has been paid in full, the rules of the court require you to serve a **Notice of Termination of Garnishment** (Form 20R) on the garnishee and the court clerk. There are rules about how this must be done. See the Small Claims Court **"Guide to Serving Documents"** at the court office or online at <u>www.attorneygeneral.jus.gov.on.ca</u>. There is no fee.

For more information about enforcing a judgment, see the Small Claims Court **"After Judgment – Guide to Getting Results"** at the court office or online at <u>www.attorneygeneral.jus.gov.on.ca</u>.

DO NOT FILE THIS PAGE.

SCR 20.08-20E (January 23, 2014) CSD

Form 20E
Notice of Garnishment

Instructions for Enforcing a Judgment using Garnishment

If you are the plaintiff and you win the case, the court may order the defendant to pay you money. If the defendant is ordered to pay you money, the defendant (called the "debtor" after judgment, and you are called the "creditor") may pay right away, or you may give the debtor more time to pay. If the debtor does not pay, there are steps you can take to get the money. This is called **enforcing** the judgment. There are fees for these steps.

If someone else owes the debtor money, you can ask the court to order that person to send the money to the court office. The court will then pay you. This is called garnishment. For example, if you know where the debtor has a bank account or where the debtor works, you can ask the court to have the debtor's bank or employer pay money to the court.

Step 1: COMPLETE and FILE a **Notice of Garnishment** form and an **Affidavit for Enforcement Request** (Form 20P) with the court office. The clerk will stamp the notice. There is a fee.

Step 2: SERVE. You then serve a copy of the stamped notice of garnishment and a blank **Garnishee's Statement** form (Form 20F) on the person or business that has the money (the "garnishee") owed to the debtor. You also serve a copy of the stamped notice and the affidavit on the debtor. There are rules about how this must be done. See the Small Claims Court **"Guide to Serving Documents"** at the court office or online at **www.ontario.ca/attorneygeneral**. You can get copies of forms at the court office or online at www.ontariocourtforms.on.ca.

Step 3: TERMINATE. Once the judgment has been paid in full, the rules of the court require you to serve a **Notice of Termination of Garnishment** (Form 20R) on the garnishee and the court clerk. There are rules about how this must be done. See the Small Claims Court **"Guide to Serving Documents"** at the court office or online at www.ontario.ca/attorneygeneral. There is no fee.

For more information about enforcing a judgment, see the Small Claims Court **"After Judgment – Guide to Getting Results"** at the court office or online at www.ontario.ca/attorneygeneral.

DO NOT FILE THIS PAGE

RSCC-20E-E (2019/05)

298

ONTARIO
Superior Court of Justice

Notice of Garnishment
Form 20E Ont. Reg. No.: 258/98

Seal

Small Claims Court

Address

Phone Number

Claim No.

Garnishment No. (Assigned by clerk)

Creditor

☐ Additional creditors listed on attached Form 1A.

Last name, or name of company		
First Name	Second Name	Also Known as
Address (street number, apt., unit)		
City/Town	Province	Phone Number
Postal Code		Fax Number
Representative		Law Society of Ontario Number
Address (street number, apt., unit)		
City/Town	Province	Phone Number
Postal Code		Fax Number

Debtor

Last name, or name of company		
First Name	Second Name	Also Known as
Address (street number, apt., unit)		
City/Town	Province	Phone Number
Postal Code		Fax Number

Garnishee

Last name, or name of company		
First Name	Second Name	Also Known as
Address (street number, apt., unit)		
City/Town	Province	Phone Number
Postal Code		Fax Number

NOTE: **THE CREDITOR SHALL SERVE THIS NOTICE** on the debtor with an Affidavit for Enforcement Request (Form 20P) and serve on the garnishee this notice with a blank Garnishee's Statement (Form 20F).

Les formules des tribunaux sont affichées en anglais et en français sur le site www.ontariocourtforms.on.ca. Visitez ce site pour des renseignements sur des formats accessibles.
RSCC-20E-E (2019/05)

FORM 20E   PAGE 2

_____
Claim No.

_____
Garnishment No.

TO THE GARNISHEE:

The creditor has obtained a court order against the debtor. The creditor claims that you owe or will owe the debtor a debt in the form of wages, salary, pension payments, rent, annuity or other debt that you pay out in a lump-sum, periodically or by instalments. (A debt to the debtor includes both a debt payable to the debtor alone and a joint debt payable to the debtor and one or more co-owners.)

YOU ARE REQUIRED TO PAY to the clerk of the _____ Small Claims Court
                                                          (Garnishment issuing court)

(a) all debts now payable by you to the debtor, **within 10 days** after this notice is served on you; **and**

(b) all debts that become payable by you to the debtor after this notice is served on you and **within 6 years** after this notice is issued, **within 10 days** after they become payable.

The total amount of all your payments to the clerk is not to exceed $ _____
                                                                              (Amount unsatisfied)

THIS NOTICE IS LEGALLY BINDING ON YOU until it expires or is changed, renewed, terminated or satisfied. If you do not pay the total amount or such lesser amount as you are liable to pay, you must serve a Garnishee's Statement (Form 20F) on the creditor and debtor, and file it with the clerk within 10 days after this notice is served on you.

EACH PAYMENT, payable to the Minister of Finance, MUST BE SENT with a copy of the attached garnishee's payment notice to the clerk at the above court address.

If your debt is jointly owed to the debtor and to one or more co-owners, you must pay the debtor's appropriate share of the amount now payable, or which becomes payable, or such a percentage as the court may order.

The amounts paid into court shall not exceed the portion of the debtor's wages that are subject to seizure or garnishment under Section 7 of the _Wages Act_ (information available at: ontario.ca/attorneygeneral and ontario.ca/laws). The portion of wages that can be garnished may be increased or decreased only by order of the court. If such a court order is attached to this notice or is served on you, you must follow the direction in that court order.

_____ , 20 _____   _____
                                                              (Signature of clerk)

CAUTION TO GARNISHEE:	**IF YOU FAIL TO PAY** to the clerk the amount set out in this notice and do not file a Garnishee's Statement (Form 20F) disputing garnishment, **JUDGMENT MAY BE OBTAINED AGAINST YOU BY THE CREDITOR** for payment of the amount set out above, plus costs. If you make a payment to anyone other than the clerk of the court, you may be liable to pay again [R. 20.08(17) and (18)].

NOTE:	Any party or interested person may complete and serve a Notice of Garnishment Hearing (Form 20Q) to determine any matter related to this notice. To obtain forms and self-help materials, attend the nearest Small Claims Court or access the following website: www.ontariocourtforms.on.ca.

                                    Continued on next page

FORM 20E   **PAGE 3**

_____
Claim No.

_____
Garnishment No.

The top portion of the garnishee's payment notice, below, is to be completed by the creditor before the Notice of Garnishment is issued. Where it is anticipated that more than one payment will be made by the garnishee, the creditor should supply extra copies of the garnishee's payment notice. Additional copies of the garnishee's payment notice are available at court offices or online at www.ontariocourtforms.on.ca (see Form 20E or 20E.1).

GARNISHEE'S PAYMENT NOTICE

Make payment by cheque or money order payable to the Minister of Finance and send it, along with this payment notice to the clerk of the court at the following address:

Court address: _____

Claim No.: _____

Garnishment No.: _____

Creditor: _____

Debtor: _____

Garnishee: _____

TO BE COMPLETED BY GARNISHEE FOR EACH PAYMENT

Date of payment: _____ , 20 _____

Amount enclosed: $ _____

[Save Form]   [Print Form]   [Clear Form]

RSCC-20E-E (2019/05)

Form 20E.1
Notice of Renewal of Garnishment

Instructions for Renewing a Notice of Garnishment

Your garnishment will expire 6 years after it is issued. If the amount owed to you has not been paid in full, you may wish to have the garnishment renewed to ensure that the garnishee will continue to make payments. This must be done before the garnishment expires.

Step 1: COMPLETE and FILE a Notice of Renewal of Garnishment form and an **Affidavit for Enforcement Request** (Form 20P) with the court office. The clerk will stamp the notice.

Step 2: SERVE. You then serve a copy of the stamped notice of renewal of garnishment and a blank **Garnishee's Statement** form (Form 20F) on the person or business that has the money (the "garnishee") owed to the debtor. You also serve a copy of the stamped notice and the affidavit on the debtor. There are rules about how this must be done. See the Small Claims Court **"Guide to Serving Documents"** at the court office or online at www.ontario.ca/attorneygeneral. You can get copies of forms at the court office or online at www.ontariocourtforms.on.ca.

Step 3: TERMINATE. Once the judgment has been paid in full, the rules of the court require you to serve a **Notice of Termination of Garnishment** (Form 20R) on the garnishee and the court clerk. There are rules about how this must be done. See the Small Claims Court **"Guide to Serving Documents"** at the court office or online at www.ontario.ca/attorneygeneral. There is no fee.

For more information about enforcing a judgment, see the Small Claims Court **"After Judgment – Guide to Getting Results"** at the court office or online at www.ontario.ca/attorneygeneral.

DO NOT FILE THIS PAGE

RSCC-20E-1-E (2019/05)

ONTARIO
Superior Court of Justice

Notice of Renewal of Garnishment
Form 20E.1 Ont. Reg. No.: 258/98

Seal

Small Claims Court

Claim No.

Garnishment No. (Assigned by clerk)

Address

Phone Number

Creditor

☐ Additional creditors listed on attached Form 1A.

Last name, or name of company		
First Name	Second Name	Also Known as
Address (street number, apt., unit)		
City/Town	Province	Phone Number
Postal Code		Fax Number
Representative		Law Society of Ontario no.
Address (street number, apt., unit)		
City/Town	Province	Phone Number
Postal Code		Fax Number

Debtor

Last name, or name of company		
First Name	Second Name	Also Known as
Address (street number, apt., unit)		
City/Town	Province	Phone Number
Postal Code		Fax Number

Garnishee

Last name, or name of company		
First Name	Second Name	Also Known as
Address (street number, apt., unit)		
City/Town	Province	Phone Number
Postal Code		Fax Number

Les formules des tribunaux sont affichées en anglais et en français sur le site www.ontariocourtforms.on.ca. Visitez ce site pour des renseignements sur des formats accessibles.

RSCC-20E-1-E (2019/05)

FORM 20E.1   **PAGE 2**

_____
Claim No.

_____
Garnishment No.

TO THE GARNISHEE:

The creditor has renewed the garnishment issued or last renewed on _____ , 20 _____ .

              (Date)

The creditor has obtained a court order against the debtor. The creditor claims that you owe or will owe the debtor a debt in the form of wages, salary, pension payments, rent, annuity or other debt that you pay out in a lump-sum, periodically or by instalments. (A debt to the debtor includes both a debt payable to the debtor alone and a joint debt payable to the debtor and one or more co-owners.)

YOU ARE REQUIRED TO PAY to the clerk of the _____ Small Claims Court

              (Garnishment issuing court)

 (a) all debts now payable by you to the debtor, **within 10 days** after this notice is served on you; **and**

 (b) all debts that become payable by you to the debtor after this notice is served on you and **within 6 years** after this notice is issued, **within 10 days** after they become payable.

The total amount of all your payments to the clerk is not to exceed $ _____

         (Amount unsatisfied)

THIS NOTICE IS LEGALLY BINDING ON YOU until it expires or is changed, renewed, terminated or satisfied. If you do not pay the total amount or such lesser amount as you are liable to pay, you must serve a Garnishee's Statement (Form 20F) on the creditor and debtor, and file it with the clerk within 10 days after this notice is served on you.

EACH PAYMENT, payable to the Minister of Finance, MUST BE SENT with a copy of the attached garnishee's payment notice to the clerk at the above court address.

If your debt is jointly owed to the debtor and to one or more co-owners, you must pay the debtor's appropriate share of the amount now payable, or which becomes payable, or such percentage as the court may order.

The amounts paid into court shall not exceed the portion of the debtor's wages that are subject to seizure or garnishment under Section 7 of the _Wages Act_ (information available at: www.ontario.ca/attorneygeneral and www.ontario.ca/laws). The portion of wages that can be garnished may be increased or decreased only by order of the court. If such a court order is attached to this notice or is served on you, you must follow the direction in that court order.

_____ , 20 _____   _____

                                       (Signature of clerk)

CAUTION TO GARNISHEE: **IF YOU FAIL TO PAY** to the clerk the amount set out in this notice and do not file a Garnishee's Statement (Form 20F) disputing garnishment, **JUDGMENT MAY BE OBTAINED AGAINST YOU BY THE CREDITOR** for payment of the amount set out above, plus costs. If you make a payment to anyone other than the clerk of the court, you may be liable to pay again [R. 20.08(17) and (18)].

NOTE: Any party or interested person may complete and serve a Notice of Garnishment Hearing (Form 20Q) to determine any matter related to this notice. To obtain forms and self-help materials, attend the nearest Small Claims Court or access the following website: www.ontariocourtforms.on.ca.

FORM 20E.1 PAGE 3

Claim No. _____

Garnishment No. _____

The top portion of the garnishee's payment notice, below, is to be completed by the creditor before the Notice of Renewal of Garnishment (Form 20E.1) is issued. Where it is anticipated that more than one payment will be made by the garnishee, the creditor should supply extra copies of the garnishee's payment notice. Additional copies of the garnishee's payment notice are available at court offices or online at www.ontariocourtforms.on.ca (see Form 20E or 20E.1).

GARNISHEE'S PAYMENT NOTICE

Make payment by cheque or money order payable to the Minister of Finance and send it, along with this payment notice to the clerk of the court at the following address:

Court address: _____

Claim No.: _____

Garnishment No.: _____

Creditor: _____

Debtor: _____

Garnishee: _____

TO BE COMPLETED BY GARNISHEE FOR EACH PAYMENT

Date of payment: _____ , 20 _____

Amount enclosed: $ _____

| Save Form | Print Form | | Clear Form |

RSCC-20E-1-E (2019/05)

Form 20F
Garnishee's Statement

ONTARIO
Superior Court of Justice

Garnishee's Statement
Form 20F Ont. Reg. No.: 258/98

Small Claims Court _____

Claim No. _____

_____

Garnishment No. (Assigned by clerk) _____

Address _____

Phone Number _____

BETWEEN

_____

Creditor(s)

and

_____

Debtor(s)

Name of Garnishee _____
(Full legal name of garnishee)

A Notice of Garnishment was issued on _____ , 20 _____ , naming me/us as garnishee in relation to the debtor

_____
(Name of debtor)

☐ **I/WE DO NOT OWE** and do not expect to owe to the debtor the amount set out in the Notice of Garnishment for the following reason(s):

_____

_____

_____

_____

_____

_____

☐ **I/WE OWE OR WILL OWE** the debtor (or the debtor and one or more co-owners), wages or periodic payments based on the terms explained below:

(State the amount(s) and how often the debtor is paid. If the debtor is paid wages, state the gross amount of the debtor's wages before any deductions required by law and the net amount after those deductions, and attach a copy of a pay slip. If you owe or will owe the debtor a lump sum, state when and how much will be paid.)

_____

_____

_____

_____

_____

_____

Les formules des tribunaux sont affichées en anglais et en français sur le site www.ontariocourtforms.on.ca. Visitez ce site pour des renseignements sur des formats accessibles.

RSCC-20F-E (2019/05)

Continued on next page

FORM 20F **PAGE 2**

_____
Claim No.

_____
Garnishment No.

☐ **I/We are making payment of less than** the amount stated because the debt is owed to the debtor and to one or more co-owners, or for another reason explained below:

_____
(Identify the amount(s) and percentage owed to the debtor and each co-owner)

Co-owner(s) of the debt: _____
(Full legal name(s))

_____
(Address (street & number, unit, municipality, province))

☐ **I/We are not making a payment at this time or are making a payment of less than the amount stated** because I/we have been served with other notice(s) of garnishment against the debtor. (Provide details below.)

Name of creditor	Name of issuing court	Location of court or Sheriff's Office where payment is currently being made	Date Notice of Garnishment received
_____	_____	_____	_____
_____	_____	_____	_____
_____	_____	_____	_____

☐ **I/We will dispute the garnishment** by completing and serving a Notice of Garnishment Hearing (Form 20Q) on the creditor, debtor and co-owner(s) of the debt (if any) and any other interested person, and filing it with the clerk of the court.

_____ , 20 _____   _____
(Signature of garnishee or representative)

_____
(Address, phone and fax number of garnishee or representative)

_____

NOTE TO GARNISHEE:	The garnishee must serve a copy of the Garnishee's Statement on the creditor and the debtor and file it with the court. You can get an electronic version of this form online at www.ontariocourtforms.on.ca.

NOTE TO CREDITOR:	A creditor who is served with a Garnishee's Statement must send it to the co-owners of the debt, if any, together with a Notice to Co-owner of Debt (Form 20G). You can get forms at court offices or online at www.ontariocourtforms.on.ca.

[Save Form]   [Print Form]   [Clear Form]

RSCC-20F-E (2019/05)

Form 20G
Notice to Co-owner of Debt

ONTARIO
Superior Court of Justice

Notice to Co-owner of Debt
Form 20G Ont. Reg. No.: 258/98

Small Claims Court	Claim No.
	Garnishment No.
Address	
Phone Number	

Creditor ☐ Additional creditors listed on attached Form 1A.

Last name, or name of company		
First Name	Second Name	Also Known as
Address (street number, apt., unit)		
City/Town	Province	Phone Number
Postal Code		Fax Number
Representative		Law Society of Ontario No.
Address (street number, apt., unit)		
City/Town	Province	Phone Number
Postal Code		Fax Number

Debtor

Last name, or name of company		
First Name	Second Name	Also Known as
Address (street number, apt., unit)		
City/Town	Province	Phone Number
Postal Code		Fax Number

Garnishee

Last name, or name of company		
First Name	Second Name	Also Known as
Address (street number, apt., unit)		
City/Town	Province	Phone Number
Postal Code		Fax Number

NOTE: **THIS NOTICE SHALL BE SERVED BY THE CREDITOR** on each co-owner of debt together with a copy of the Garnishee's Statement (Form 20F) received from the garnishee.

Les formules des tribunaux sont affichées en anglais et en français sur le site www.ontariocourtforms.on.ca. Visitez ce site pour des renseignements sur des formats accessibles.

RSCC-20G-E (2019/05)

FORM 20G   **PAGE 2**

_____
Claim No.

_____
Garnishment No.

TO:

Name of co-owner(s) of debt
Street and number
City, province, postal code

(Attach a separate sheet, in the same format, for additional co-owners of debt.)

The creditor has obtained a court order against the debtor. The creditor has served a Notice of Garnishment

(Form 20E), dated _____ , 20 _____ , on _____ ,

(Name of garnishee)

claiming that the garnishee owes or will owe the debtor a debt in the form of wages, salary, pension payments, rent, annuity, or other debt that the garnishee pays out in a lump-sum, periodically or by instalments. (A debt to the debtor includes both a debt payable to the debtor alone and a joint debt payable to the debtor and one or more co-owners.)

The garnishee has set out in the attached Garnishee's Statement (Form 20F) that you are a co-owner of debt. Under the Notice of Garnishment, the garnishee has paid or will pay to the clerk of the Small Claims Court the appropriate share of the amount payable or such a percentage as the court may order.

IF YOU HAVE A CLAIM to the money being paid to the clerk of the Small Claims Court by the garnishee, you have 30 days from service of this notice to request a garnishment hearing by completing and serving a Notice of Garnishment Hearing (Form 20Q) on the creditor, debtor and garnishee, and filing it with the clerk. If you fail to do so, you are not entitled to dispute the enforcement of the creditor's order for the payment or recovery of money and the funds may be paid out to the creditor unless the court orders otherwise.

To obtain forms and self-help materials, attend the nearest Small Claims Court or access the following website: www.ontariocourtforms.on.ca.

_____ , 20 _____   _____
(Signature of creditor or representative)

NOTE:	Within seven (7) calendar days of changing your address for service, notify the court and all other parties in writing.

[Save Form]   [Print Form]   [Clear Form]

RSCC-20G-E (2019/05)

309

Form 20H
Notice of Examination

ONTARIO

Superior Court of Justice

Notice of Examination
Form 20H Ont. Reg. No.: 258/98

(Seal)

Small Claims Court

Claim No.

Address

Phone number

BETWEEN

_____
Creditor(s)

and

_____
Debtor(s)

TO: _____
(Name of person to be examined)

of _____
(Address of person to be examined)

The creditor _____ of _____
(Name of creditor)   (Address of creditor)

has obtained a judgment against _____ on _____ ,
(Name of debtor)

20 _____ , in the _____ Small Claims Court.
(Name of court where judgment was made)

According to the supporting affidavit filed by the creditor, the total due on the judgment is

$ _____ . *(This amount must match the total amount identified in the supporting affidavit.)*
(Total)

This total due takes into account all money received, accrued post-judgment interest and costs to

this date: _____ , 20 _____ . *(This date must match the date of the supporting affidavit.)*

YOU ARE REQUIRED TO ATTEND AN EXAMINATION HEARING to explain how the debtor will pay this judgment and if there are any reasons for not doing so.

Les formules des tribunaux sont affichées en anglais et en français sur le site www.ontariocourtforms.on.ca. Visitez ce site pour des renseignements sur des formats accessibles.

Continued on next page

FORMS

FORM 20H   **PAGE 2**   _____
                                                                          Claim No.

THIS COURT WILL HOLD AN EXAMINATION HEARING

on _____ , 20 _____ , at _____ or as soon as possible after that time, at
                                          (Time)

_____
                         (Address of court location)

_____
                          (Courtroom number)

_____ , 20 _____   _____
                                                (Signature of clerk)

CAUTION TO PERSON BEING EXAMINED:	If you fail to attend the examination hearing or attend and refuse to answer questions or produce documents, you may be ordered to attend a contempt hearing. At the contempt hearing, you may be found in contempt of court and the court may order you to be jailed.

NOTE TO DEBTOR:	A debtor who is an individual must serve on the creditor a completed Financial Information Form (Form 20I) prior to the hearing. This form must **not** be filed with the court. The debtor must provide a completed copy of this form to the judge at the examination hearing. The debtor must also bring to the hearing documents that support the information given in this form.

For information on accessibility of court services for
people with disability-related needs, contact:
Telephone: 416-326-2220 / 1-800-518-7901   TTY: 416-326-4012 / 1-877-425-0575

SCR 20.10-20H (January 23, 2014) CSD

Form 20I
Financial Information Form

FINANCIAL INFORMATION FORM
Form 20I Ont. Reg. No.: 258/98

This form is to be completed by the debtor and served on the creditor.

This form is not to be filed at the court office. The debtor must provide a completed copy of this form to the judge at the examination hearing. The debtor must also bring to the hearing documents that support the information given in this form.

MONTHLY INCOME		MONTHLY EXPENSES	
Employer(s) _____		Rent/Mortgage	$_____
Employer(s) _____		Maintenance/Support Payments	$_____
Net salary	$_____	Property taxes	$_____
Commissions	$_____	Utilities (heat, water & light)	$_____
Tips and gratuities	$_____	Phone	$_____
Employment insurance	$_____	Cable	$_____
Pension income	$_____	House/Tenant insurance	$_____
Investment income	$_____	Life insurance	$_____
Rental income	$_____	Food	$_____
Business income	$_____	Childcare/Babysitting	$_____
Child tax benefit	$_____	Motor vehicle (lease or loan) (licence, insurance, fuel & maintenance)	$_____
Maintenance (if any)	$_____		
Monthly income of other adult household members	$_____	Transportation (public)	$_____
Other	$_____		
Income assistance	$_____		
INCOME TOTAL	$_____	**EXPENSES TOTAL**	$_____

Les formules des tribunaux sont affichées en anglais et en français sur le site www.ontariocourtforms.on.ca. Visitez ce site pour des renseignements sur des formats accessibles.

Continued on next page

FORMS

MONTHLY DEBTS	VALUE OF ASSETS	
Credit card(s) payments *(please specify)*:	Real estate equity	$ _____
_____ $ _____	Market value $ _____	
_____ $ _____	Mortgage balance $ _____	
_____ $ _____	Automobile equity	$ _____
Bank or finance company loan payments *(please specify)*:	Make and year _____	
	Loan balance $ _____	
_____ $ _____	Bank or other account balance(s) *(include RRSPs)*	$ _____
_____ $ _____	Stocks & bonds	$ _____
Department store(s) payments *(please specify)*:	Life insurance (cash value)	$ _____
_____ $ _____	Money owing to you	$
_____ $ _____	Name of debtor _____	
DEBTS TOTAL $ _____	Personal property	$ _____
	Cash	$ _____
	Other	$ _____
	TOTAL VALUE OF ASSETS $ _____	

_____
(Name)

_____
(Signature)

SCR 9.03-20.10-20I (January 23, 2014) CSD

Form 20J
Warrant of Committal

ONTARIO
Superior Court of Justice

Warrant of Committal
Form 20J Ont. Reg. No.: 258/98

Seal

Small Claims Court

Claim No.

Address

Phone number

BETWEEN

_____

Plaintiff(s)

and

_____

Defendant(s)

TO ALL POLICE OFFICERS IN ONTARIO AND TO THE OFFICERS OF ALL CORRECTIONAL INSTITUTIONS IN ONTARIO:

THIS WARRANT IS FOR THE COMMITTAL OF

Last name		
First name	Second name	Also known as
Address (street number, apt., unit)		
City/Town	Province	Phone no.
Postal code		Fax no.

A Notice of Contempt Hearing was issued from this court which required

_____
(Name of person required to attend contempt hearing)

to attend the sittings of this court at _____ on _____ , 20 _____ .
(Time)   (Date)

Les formules des tribunaux sont affichées en anglais et en français sur le site www.ontariocourtforms.on.ca. Visitez ce site pour des renseignements sur des formats accessibles.

SCR 20.11-20J (January 23, 2014) CSD

FORM 20J   **PAGE 2**

_____

Claim No.

At the contempt hearing, it was duly proven that the Notice of Contempt Hearing was properly served, and this court found this person to be in contempt of court because he/she:

(Check appropriate box.)

☐ wilfully failed to attend an examination hearing as required by a Notice of Examination (Form 20H), which was properly served.

☐ attended the examination hearing, refused to answer questions or produce documents or records, and failed to show cause why he/she should not be held in contempt for refusing to answer questions or produce documents or records.

At the contempt hearing, a judge of this court ordered this person to be committed.

YOU ARE ORDERED to take the person named above to the nearest correctional institution and admit and

detain him or her there for _____ days.

This warrant expires twelve (12) months from the date of issue, unless renewed by court order. If renewed, the warrant expires twelve (12) months from the date of the renewal.

_____ , 20 _____   _____

(Signature of clerk)

SCR 20.11-20J (January 23, 2014) CSD

Form 20K
Identification Form

ONTARIO
Superior Court of Justice

Identification Form
Form 20K Ont. Reg. No.: 258/98

_____
Small Claims Court

Claim No.

_____
Address

_____
Phone number

BETWEEN

_____
Plaintiff(s)/Creditor(s)

and

_____
Defendant(s)/Debtor(s)

TO HELP PROCESS A CIVIL WARRANT FOR COMMITTAL, the following information, or **as much information as is reasonably available should be provided**. This is necessary for the police to identify the person to be arrested. Without this information it will be difficult to enforce the warrant.

1. Name _____
   (Last name of individual)   (First name)   (Second name)

2. Also known as names (if any) _____

3. Last known address and telephone number

4. (a) Date of birth *(d, m, y)* _____

5. Physical description

   (a) Gender _____ (b) Height _____ (c) Weight _____ (d) Build _____

   (e) Colour of eyes _____ (f) Hair colour _____ (g) Complexion _____

   (h) Clean-shaven _____ (i) Wears glasses _____

   (j) Clothing habits and tastes _____

   (k) Distinguishing marks, scars, tattoos, etc. _____

   (l) Other _____
                                        (Specify)

Les formules des tribunaux sont affichées en anglais et en français sur le site www.ontariocourtforms.on.ca. Visitez ce site pour des renseignements sur des formats accessibles.

SCR 20.11-20K (January 23, 2014) CSD

FORM 20K   **PAGE 2**

_____
Claim No.

6. Usual occupation _____

7. Last known place of employment _____

8. Vehicle description

(a) Make, model and year _____ (b) Colour _____

(c) Licence plate number _____ Province or state _____

(d) Driver's licence number _____ Province or state _____

(e) Distinguishing features on the vehicle (dents, car stereo, etc.)

_____

9. Other information _____

10. Photograph of the person provided in the box below, if available.

The information supplied above is true to the best of my knowledge and belief.

_____
(Signature of party)

_____
(Name of party)

_____ , 20 _____

Form 20L
Notice of Default of Payment

ONTARIO
Superior Court of Justice

Notice of Default of Payment
Form 20L Ont. Reg. No.: 258/98

Small Claims Court

Claim No.

Address

Phone number

BETWEEN

_____
Plaintiff(s)/Creditor(s)

and

_____
Defendant(s)/Debtor(s)

TO: _____
(Name of defendant(s)/debtor(s))

TAKE NOTICE that you defaulted in your payment(s) to

_____
(Name of plaintiff(s)/creditor(s))

(Check appropriate box.)

☐ under an order for periodic payment, dated _____ , 20 _____ .

According to Rule 20.02(4) of the *Rules of the Small Claims Court*, the order for periodic payment terminates on the day that is 15 days after the creditor serves the debtor with this notice, unless before that date, a Consent (Form 13B) is filed in which the creditor waives the default.

☐ under a proposal of terms of payment in the Defence (Form 9A) dated _____ , 20 _____ .

According to Rule 9.03(2)(c) the clerk may sign judgment for the unpaid balance of the undisputed amount on the day that is 15 days after the plaintiff serves the defendant with this notice.

Les formules des tribunaux sont affichées en anglais et en français sur le site www.ontariocourtforms.on.ca. Visitez ce site pour des renseignements sur des formats accessibles.

SCR 20.02-20L (January 23, 2014) CSD

318

FORM 20L   **PAGE 2**
                                                                    _____
                                                                    Claim No.

You can get forms and self-help materials at the Small Claims Court or online at: www.ontariocourtforms.on.ca.

NOTE TO DEFENDANT/DEBTOR:

If you

- failed to make payments but intend to do so; or

- made payments but the payments were not received by the creditor;

contact the plaintiff/creditor to make payment arrangements or correct the reason for non-receipt of payments. You may obtain the plaintiff/creditor's written consent (Form 13B may be used) to waive the default and file it with the court within 15 days of being served with this notice. Failure to do so may result in the following:

- in the case of default under a proposal of terms of payment in the Defence (Form 9A), the plaintiff may obtain default judgment for the unpaid balance of the undisputed amount; or

- in the case of default under an order for periodic payment, the order will terminate and the creditor may take other steps to enforce the order.

_____, 20 _____   _____
                                                (Signature of plaintiff/creditor or representative)

                                                _____
                                                (Name, address and phone number of plaintiff/creditor or representative)

SCR 20.02-20L (January 23, 2014) CSD

Form 20M
Affidavit of Default of Payment

ONTARIO
Superior Court of Justice

Affidavit of Default of Payment
Form 20M Ont. Reg. No.: 258/98

Small Claims Court   Claim No.

Address

Phone number

BETWEEN

_____
Plaintiff(s)/Creditor(s)

and

_____
Defendant(s)/Debtor(s)

My name is _____
(Full name)

I live in _____
(Municipality & province)

and I swear/affirm that the following is true:

1. In this action, I am the

(Check one box only.)
☐ plaintiff/creditor.
☐ representative of the plaintiff(s)/creditor(s) _____
(Name of plaintiff(s)/creditor(s))

2. To date, I have received from the defendant(s)/debtor(s) $ _____ , the last payment being made
(Amount)

on or about _____ , 20 _____ .

3. I make this affidavit in support of a request that:

☐ the clerk of the court issue a Default Judgment (Form 11B) [R. 9.03(2)(c)]. The defendant(s)

_____
(Name(s) of defendant(s))

(Check appropriate box and complete paragraph.)
failed to make payment in accordance with the proposed terms of payment in the Defence
(Form 9A) dated _____ , 20 _____ and fifteen (15) days have passed since the
defendant was served with a Notice of Default of Payment (Form 20L) at the following address(es):

_____
(Address(es) of defendant(s))

☐ the clerk of the court issue a Default Judgment (Form 11B) [R. 9.03(7)]. The defendant(s)

_____
(Name of defendant(s))

failed to make payment in accordance with the terms of payment order
dated _____ , 20 _____ .

Les formules des tribunaux sont affichées en anglais et en français sur le site
www.ontariocourtforms.on.ca. Visitez ce site pour des renseignements sur des
formats accessibles.

SCR 9.03-20M (January 23, 2014) CSD

FORM 20M   **PAGE 2**   _____
                                                                Claim No.

☐ I may enforce the judgment [R. 20.02(3)]. The debtor(s)

_____
(Name(s) of debtor(s))

(Check appropriate box and complete paragraph.)

failed to make payment in accordance with the order for periodic payment dated

_____ , 20 _____ , and fifteen (15) days have passed since the debtor(s) has/have

been served with a Notice of Default of Payment (Form 20L) at the following address(es):

_____
(Address(es) of debtor(s))

A Consent (Form 13B) in which the creditor waives the default has not been filed.

4. The unpaid balance is calculated as follows:

(A) **DEBT** $ _____

(B) **PRE-JUDGMENT INTEREST** calculated

on the sum of $ _____   at the rate of _____ %

per annum from _____ , 20 ____ to _____ , 20 ____ ,

being _____ days. $ _____

> **NOTE:** Calculation of interest is always on the amount owing from time to time as payments are received. This is true for both pre-judgment and post-judgment interest. Attach a separate sheet setting out how you calculated the total amount of any pre/post-judgment interest.

SUBTOTAL (amount of judgment) $ ....

(C) **COSTS** to date of judgment $ _____

(D) **TOTAL AMOUNT OF PAYMENTS RECEIVED FROM DEBTOR**
     after judgment (if any)   (minus) $ _____

(E) **POST-JUDGMENT INTEREST** to date calculated

on the sum of $ _____   at the rate of _____ %

per annum from _____ , 20 ____ to _____ , 20 ____ ,

being _____ days. $ _____

(F) **SUBSEQUENT COSTS** incurred after judgment (including the cost of serving
     the Notice of Default of Payment (Form 20L)) $ _____

TOTAL DUE $ ....

Sworn/Affirmed before me at _____

_____
(Municipality)

in _____

_____
(Province, state, or country)

on _____ , 20 ____

_____
Commissioner for taking affidavits
(Type or print name below if signature is illegible.)

_____
Signature
(This form is to be signed in front of a lawyer, justice of the peace, notary public or commissioner for taking affidavits.)

> **WARNING:**   IT IS AN OFFENCE UNDER THE *CRIMINAL CODE* TO KNOWINGLY SWEAR OR AFFIRM A FALSE AFFIDAVIT.

SCR 9.03-20M (January 23, 2014) CSD

Form 20N
Request to Renew Writ of Seizure and Sale

ONTARIO
Superior Court of Justice

Request to Renew Writ of Seizure and Sale
Form 20N Ont. Reg. No.: 258/98

Small Claims Court _____ Claim No. _____

Address _____

Phone number _____

BETWEEN

_____
Creditor(s)

and

_____
Debtor(s)

TO THE SHERIFF/BAILIFF OF _____ :
(Name of county/region and city/town in which the enforcement office is located)

YOU ARE REQUESTED TO RENEW the ☐ Writ of Seizure and Sale of Personal Property (Form 20C)

☐ Writ of Seizure and Sale of Land (Form 20D)

issued on _____ , 20 ____ , in this proceeding and filed in your office for a period of six

years from the date of renewal.

_____ , 20 ____   _____
(Signature of creditor or representative)

_____
(Name, address and phone number of creditor or representative)

NOTE: **A WRIT OF SEIZURE AND SALE OF LAND OR OF PERSONAL PROPERTY** remains in force
for six years after the date of its issue and for a further six years after each renewal.

Les formules des tribunaux sont affichées en anglais et en français sur le site
www.ontariocourtforms.on.ca. Visitez ce site pour des renseignements sur des
formats accessibles.

SCR 20.06-20.07-20N (January 23, 2014) CSD

Form 20O
Direction to Enforce Writ of Seizure and Sale of Personal Property

ONTARIO
Superior Court of Justice   **Direction to Enforce Writ of Seizure and Sale of Personal Property**

Form 20O Ont. Reg. No.: 258/98

Small Claims Court _____   Claim No. _____

Address _____

Phone number _____

BETWEEN

_____   Creditor(s)

and

_____   Debtor(s)

My name is _____

(Full name)

1. In this action, I am the

   (Check one box only.)   ☐ creditor.

   ☐ representative of the creditor(s).

   A Writ of Seizure and Sale of Personal Property (Form 20C) directed to the bailiff of the

   _____ Small Claims Court was issued on:

   (Small Claims Court location)

   _____, 20 _____, in favour of _____

   (Name of creditor)

2. I am filing this direction to enforce the Writ of Seizure and Sale of Personal Property, and direct the bailiff to seize and sell (if required) the personal property belonging to the following debtor(s):

Last name, or name of company		
First name	Second name	Third given name (individual only) (if applicable)

   ☐ Additional debtor(s) and also known as names are listed on attached Form 1A.1.

   Set out a description of the property to be seized. Identify any marks or serial numbers.

Les formules des tribunaux sont affichées en anglais et en français sur le site www.ontariocourtforms.on.ca. Visitez ce site pour des renseignements sur des formats accessibles.

SCR 20.06-20O (January 23, 2014) CSD

FORM 20O   **PAGE 2**

Claim No. _____

3. The above personal property is located at: _____

_____
(Address)

If the address provided does not clearly identify where the property is located, please attach a detailed map showing the nearest intersection.

4. From the date that the Writ of Seizure and Sale of Personal Property was issued, the following payments have been received from the debtor and/or subsequent costs incurred by the creditor:

(A) **PAYMENTS RECEIVED FROM DEBTOR**

             Date of Payment   Payment Amount

_____ $ _____

_____ $ _____

_____ $ _____

                          $ _____

☐ List of additional payments attached

(B) **SUBSEQUENT COSTS** incurred since issuance of Writ of Seizure and Sale of Personal Property

           Reason cost was incurred   Cost Amount

_____ $ _____

_____ $ _____

_____ $ _____

_____ $ _____

☐ List of additional costs attached

The bailiff will calculate the amount owing based on the information provided within the Writ of Seizure and Sale of Personal Property and the details provided above. This amount will include any reasonable disbursements necessarily incurred to enforce this writ.

_____, 20 _____   _____
                                                  (Signature of creditor or representative)

                                          _____
                             (Name, address and phone number of creditor or representative)

SCR 20.06-20O (January 23, 2014) CSD

Form 20P
Affidavit for Enforcement Request

ONTARIO
Superior Court of Justice

Affidavit for Enforcement Request
Form 20P Ont. Reg. No.: 258/98

_____
Small Claims Court

Claim No. _____

_____
Address

_____
Phone number

BETWEEN

_____
Plaintiff(s)/Creditor(s)

and / et

_____
Defendant(s)/Debtor(s)

My name is _____
(Full name)

I live in _____
(Municipality & province)

and I swear/affirm that the following is true:

1. **In this action, I am the**

   (Check one box only.)
   ☐ plaintiff/creditor.
   ☐ representative of the plaintiff(s)/creditor(s).

   I make this affidavit in support of a request that the clerk of the court issue the following enforcement process(es):

   ☐ Certificate of Judgment (Form 20A) to the clerk of the _____
   (Name of court where the judgment is to be filed)

   Small Claims Court.

   ☐ Writ of Seizure and Sale of Personal Property (Form 20C) directed to the bailiff of

   _____ Small Claims Court.
   (Name of court location)

   ☐ Writ of Seizure and Sale of Land (Form 20D) directed to the sheriff of _____
   (Name of county/region in which the enforcement office is located)

Les formules des tribunaux sont affichées en anglais et en français sur le site www.ontariocourtforms.on.ca. Visitez ce site pour des renseignements sur des formats accessibles.

FORM 20P   **PAGE 2**

Claim No. _____

☐ Notice of Garnishment (Form 20E)/Notice of Renewal of Garnishment (Form 20E.1).

I believe that the garnishee _____

(Name of garnishee)

at _____

(Address of garnishee)

is indebted to the debtor or will become indebted to the debtor for the following reasons:

The Notice will be served on the debtor _____

(Name of debtor)

at _____

(Address of debtor for service)

within five days of serving it on the garnishee.

☐ Notice of Examination (Form 20H).

☐ Writ of Delivery (Form 20B).

☐ Other *(Set out the nature of your request):*

Complete this section if you are requesting a Writ of Delivery.

2. An order for the delivery of the following personal property:
   (According to the court order, set out a description of the property to be delivered. Identify any marks or serial numbers.)

was made in this action against: _____

(Name of person against whom the order was made)

on _____ , 20 ____ , in the _____

(Name of court location where order was made)

Small Claims Court. Since the above listed personal property has not been delivered, I make this affidavit in support of a request that the clerk of the court issue a Writ of Delivery (Form 20B) to the bailiff of the

_____ Small Claims Court.

(Name of court location)

Continued on next page

FORM 20P   **PAGE 3**

....
Claim No.

Complete this section if you are requesting a Certificate of Judgment, Writ of Seizure and Sale of Personal Property, Writ of Seizure and Sale of Land, Notice of Garnishment, Notice of Renewal of Garnishment or Notice of Examination.

3. A judgment was made in this action against _____
                                              (Name of debtor(s))

on _____ , 20 ____ in the _____
                                     (Name of court where judgment was made)

Small Claims Court for the following sums:

(A) **DEBT** $ _____

(B) **PRE-JUDGMENT INTEREST** calculated

   on the sum of $ _____ at the rate of _____ %

   per annum from _____ , 20 ____ to _____ , 20 ____ ,

   being _____ days. $ _____

                     SUBTOTAL (Amount of Judgment) $ ....

(C) **COSTS** to date of judgment $ _____

(D) **TOTAL AMOUNT OF PAYMENTS RECEIVED FROM DEBTOR**
    after judgment (if any)   (minus) $ _____

(E) **POST-JUDGMENT INTEREST** to date calculated

   on the sum of $ _____ at the rate of _____ %

   per annum from _____ , 20 ____ to _____ , 20 ____ ,

   being _____ days. $ _____

> **NOTE:** Calculation of interest is always on the amount owing from time to time as payments are received. This is true for both pre-judgment and post-judgment interest. Attach a separate sheet setting out how you calculated the total amount of any pre/post-judgment interest.

(F) **SUBSEQUENT COSTS** incurred after judgment (including the cost of issuing
    the requested enforcement(s)) $ _____

                                      TOTAL DUE $ ....

Sworn/Affirmed before me at _____
                                     (Municipality)

in _____
              (Province, state or country)

on _____ , 20 ____ _____
                               Commissioner for taking affidavits
                               (Type or print name below if signature is illegible.)

_____
Signature
(This form is to be signed in front of a
lawyer, justice of the peace, notary public
or commissioner for taking affidavits.)

WARNING: IT IS AN OFFENCE UNDER THE *CRIMINAL CODE* TO KNOWINGLY SWEAR OR
                AFFIRM A FALSE AFFIDAVIT.

SCR 20.04-10-20P (January 23, 2014) CSD

Form 20Q
Notice of Garnishment Hearing

ONTARIO
Superior Court of Justice

Notice of Garnishment Hearing
Form 20Q Ont. Reg. No.: 258/98

Small Claims Court	Claim No.
	Garnishment No.
Address	
Phone Number	

Creditor ☐ Additional creditor(s) listed on the attached Form 1A.

Last name, or name of company		
First Name	Second Name	Also Known as
Address (street number, apt., unit)		
City/Town	Province	Phone no.
Postal Code		Fax no.
Representative		Law Society of Ontario no.
Address (street number, apt., unit)		
City/Town	Province	Phone no.
Postal Code		Fax no.

Debtor

Last name, or name of company		
First Name	Second Name	Also Known as
Address (street number, apt., unit)		
City/Town	Province	Phone no.
Postal Code		Fax no.
Representative		Law Society of Ontario no.
Address (street number, apt., unit)		
City/Town	Province	Phone no.
Postal Code		Fax no.

NOTE:	The Notice of Garnishment Hearing must be served by the person requesting the hearing on the creditor, debtor, garnishee, co-owner of debt, if any, and any other interested person [R. 8.01(9)].

Les formules des tribunaux sont affichées en anglais et en français sur le site www.ontariocourtforms.on.ca. Visitez ce site pour des renseignements sur des formats accessibles.

RSCC-20Q-E (2019/05)

FORM 20Q   **PAGE 2**

Claim No. _____

Garnishment No. _____

Garnishee

Last name, or name of company		
First Name	Second Name	Also Known as
Address (street number, apt., unit)		
City/Town	Province	Phone no.
Postal Code		Fax no.
Representative		Law Society of Ontario no.
Address (street number, apt., unit)		
City/Town	Province	Phone no.
Postal Code		Fax no.

Co-Owner of Debt (if any)   ☐ Additional co-owner(s) listed on the attached Form 1A.

Last name, or name of company		
First Name	Second Name	Also Known as
Address (street number, apt., unit)		
City/Town	Province	Phone no.
Postal Code		Fax no.
Representative		Law Society of Ontario no.
Address (street number, apt., unit)		
City/Town	Province	Phone no.
Postal Code		Fax no.

Other Interested Person (if any)   ☐ Additional interested person(s) listed on the attached Form 1A.

Last name, or name of company		
First Name	Second Name	Also Known as
Address (street number, apt., unit)		
City/Town	Province	Phone no.
Postal Code		Fax no.
Representative		Law Society of Ontario no.
Address (street number, apt., unit)		
City/Town	Province	Phone no.
Postal Code		Fax no.

RSCC-20Q-E (2019/05)   Continued on next page

FORM 20Q   **PAGE 3**

Claim No. _____

Garnishment No. _____

TO THE PARTIES:
(The person requesting this garnishment hearing or the person's representative must contact the clerk of the court to choose a time and date when the court could hold this garnishment hearing.)

THIS COURT WILL HOLD A GARNISHMENT HEARING on _____ , 20 _____ , **at**

_____ , **or as soon as possible after that time, at** (Address of court location and courtroom number)
(Time)

_____

_____

_____

because (Check the appropriate box.)

☐ the creditor   ☐ the debtor   ☐ the garnishee   ☐ the co-owner of debt

☐ other interested person: _____
(Specify)

states the following: *(In numbered paragraphs, provide details of your dispute and the order(s) requested.)*

_____

_____

_____

_____

_____

_____

_____

_____

_____

_____

_____

_____

_____

_____

☐ Additional pages are attached because more space was needed.

_____ , 20 _____   _____
(Signature of party or representative)

NOTE: If you fail to attend this garnishment hearing, an order may be made in your absence and enforced against you.

For information on accessibility of court services for people with disability-related needs, contact:
Telephone: 416-326-2220 / 1-800-518-7901   TTY: 416-326-4012 / 1-877-425-0575

Save Form   Print Form   Clear Form
RSCC-20Q-E (2019/05)

330

Form 20R
Notice of Termination of Garnishment

ONTARIO
Superior Court of Justice

Notice of Termination of Garnishment
Form 20R Ont. Reg. No.: 258/98

Small Claims Court _____   Claim No. _____

_____   Garnishment No. _____

Address

Phone Number _____

BETWEEN

_____
Creditor(s)

and

_____
Debtor(s)

TO _____
(Name of garnishee)

AND TO the clerk of the _____ **Small Claims Court:**
(Name of court location)

The Notice of Garnishment/Notice of Renewal of Garnishment dated _____ , 20 _____

served on you with respect to the debt of

Last name of debtor, or name of company		
First Name	Second Name	Also Known as
Address		

is terminated and you are not to make any further payments under it.

_____ , 20 _____   _____
(Signature of creditor or representative)

_____
(Name, address and phone number of creditor or representative)

_____

_____

NOTE:	The creditor must serve this notice on the garnishee and on the court clerk.

Les formules des tribunaux sont affichées en anglais et en français sur le site
www.ontariocourtforms.on.ca. Visitez ce site pour des renseignements sur des formats
accessibles.

Save Form	Print Form		Clear Form

RSCC-20R-E (2019/05)

RULES OF CIVIL PROCEDURE FORMS

TABLE OF CONTENTS

16A	Acknowledgment of Receipt Card	Nov. 1, 2005	Jul. 1, 2006	378
16B	Affidavit of Service	May 1, 2016	Aug. 1, 2016	379
16C	Certificate of Service by Sheriff	Nov. 1, 2005	Jul. 1, 2006	381
17A	Request for Service Abroad of Judicial or Extrajudicial Documents	Nov. 1, 2005	Jul. 1, 2006	382
17B	Summary of the Document to be Served	Nov. 1, 2005	Jul. 1, 2006	384
17C	Notice and Summary of Document	Nov. 1, 2005	Jul. 1, 2006	385
18A	Statement of Defence	Jul. 1, 2007	Jul. 1, 2008	387
18B	Notice of Intent to Defend	Jul. 1, 2007	Jul. 1, 2008	388
19A	Default Judgment (Debt or Liquidated Demand)	Nov. 1, 2005	Jul. 1, 2006	389
19B	Default Judgment (Recovery of Possession of Land)	Nov. 1, 2005	Jul. 1, 2006	390
19C	Default Judgment (Recovery of Possession of Personal Property)	Nov. 1, 2005	Jul. 1, 2006	391
19D	Requisition for Default Judgment	Jul. 1, 2007	Jul. 1, 2008	392
22A	Special Case	Jul. 1, 2007	Jul. 1, 2008	395
23A	Notice of Discontinuance	Jul. 1, 2007	Jul. 1, 2008	396
23B	Notice of Election to Proceed with Counter-claim	Jul. 1, 2007	Jul. 1, 2008	397
23C	Notice of Withdrawal of Defence	Jul. 1, 2007	Jul. 1, 2008	398
24.1A	Notice of Name of Mediator and Date of Session	Apr. 11, 2012	Jul. 1, 2012	399
24.1B	Notice by Assigned Mediator	Nov. 1, 2005	Jul. 1, 2006	400
24.1C	Statement of Issues	Nov. 1, 2005	Jul. 1, 2006	401
24.1D	Certificate of Non-Compliance	Nov. 1, 2005	Jul. 1, 2006	402
25A	Reply	Jul. 1, 2007	Jul. 1, 2008	403
27A	Counterclaim (Against Parties to Main Action Only)	Jul. 1, 2007	Jul. 1, 2008	404

27B	Counterclaim (Against Plaintiff and Person not Already Party to Main Action)	Jul. 1, 2007	Jul. 1, 2008	405
27C	Defence to Counterclaim	Jul. 1, 2007	Jul. 1, 2008	407
27D	Reply to Defence to Counterclaim	Jul. 1, 2007	Jul. 1, 2008	408
28A	Crossclaim	Jul. 1, 2007	Jul. 1, 2008	409
28B	Defence to Crossclaim	Jul. 1, 2007	Jul. 1, 2008	410
28C	Reply to Defence to Crossclaim	Jul. 1, 2007	Jul. 1, 2008	411
29A	Third Party Claim	Jul. 1, 2007	Jul. 1, 2008	412
29B	Third Party Defence	Jul. 1, 2007	Jul. 1, 2008	414
29C	Reply to Third Party Defence	Jul. 1, 2007	Jul. 1, 2008	415
30A	Affidavit of Documents (Individual)	Nov. 1, 2008	Jan. 1, 2010	416
30B	Affidavit of Documents (Corporation or Partnership)	Nov. 1, 2008	Jan. 1, 2010	418
30C	Request to Inspect Documents	Jul. 1, 2007	Jul. 1, 2008	420
34A	Notice of Examination	Jul. 1, 2007	Jul. 1, 2008	421
34B	Summons to Witness (Examination out of Court)	Jul. 1, 2007	Jul. 1, 2008	422
34C	Commission	Nov. 1, 2005	Jul. 1, 2006	424
34D	Letter of Request	Nov. 1, 2005	Jul. 1, 2006	427
34E	Order for Commission and Letter of Request	Nov. 1, 2005	Jul. 1, 2006	428
35A	Questions on Written Examination for Discovery	Jul. 1, 2007	Jul. 1, 2008	429
35B	Answers on Written Examination for Discovery	Nov. 1, 2005	Jul. 1, 2006	430
37A	Notice of Motion	Jul. 1, 2007	Jul. 1, 2008	431
37B	Confirmation of Motion	Sep. 1, 2018	Jan. 1, 2019	432
37C	Refusals and Undertakings Chart	Nov. 1, 2005	Jul. 1, 2006	433
38A	Notice of Appearance	Jul. 1, 2007	Jul. 1, 2008	434
38B	Confirmation of Application	Jul. 1, 2007	Jul. 1, 2008	435
42A	Certificate of Pending Litigation	Nov. 1, 2005	Jul. 1, 2006	436

FORMS

43A	Interpleader Order - General	Nov. 1, 2005	Jul. 1, 2006	437
44A	Bond - Interim Recovery of Personal Property	Nov. 1, 2005	Jul. 1, 2006	439
47A	Jury Notice	Jul. 1, 2007	Jul. 1, 2008	440
48C	Status Notice	Jul. 1, 2007	Jul. 1, 2008	441
48C.1	Status Notice: Action Not on a Trial List	Jul. 30, 2009	Jan. 1, 2010	442
48C.2	Status Notice: Action Struck from Trial List	Nov. 1, 2008	Jan. 1, 2010	444
48D	Order Dismissing Action for Delay	Nov. 1, 2016	Dec. 23, 2016	445
48E	Notice That Action Will Be Dismissed	Jul. 30, 2009	Jan. 1, 2010	446
48F	Order Dismissing Action as Abandoned	Jul. 30, 2009	Jan. 1, 2010	447
49A	Offer to Settle	Jul. 1, 2007	Jul. 1, 2008	448
49B	Notice of Withdrawal of Offer	Jul. 1, 2007	Jul. 1, 2008	449
49C	Acceptance of Offer	Jul. 1, 2007	Jul. 1, 2008	450
49D	Offer to Contribute	Jul. 1, 2007	Jul. 1, 2008	451
51A	Request to Admit	Jul. 1, 2007	Jul. 1, 2008	452
51B	Response to Request to Admit	Jul. 1, 2007	Jul. 1, 2008	453
53	Acknowledgment of Expert's Duty	July 22, 2014	Mar. 31, 2015	454
53A	Summons to Witness (at Hearing)	Jul. 1, 2007	Jul. 1, 2008	455
53B	Warrant for Arrest (Defaulting Witness)	Nov. 1, 2005	Jul. 1, 2006	456
53C	Summons to a Witness Outside Ontario	Jul. 1, 2007	Jul. 1, 2008	457
53D	Order for Attendance of Witness in Custody	Nov. 1, 2005	Jul. 1, 2006	458
55A	Notice of Hearing for Directions	Jul. 1, 2007	Jul. 1, 2008	459
55B	Notice to Party Added on Reference	Jul. 1, 2007	Jul. 1, 2008	460
55C	Report on Reference (Administration of Estate)	Nov. 1, 2005	Jul. 1, 2006	461
55D	Notice of Contested Claim	Jul. 1, 2007	Jul. 1, 2008	463
55E	Notice to Creditor	Apr. 11, 2012	Jul. 1, 2012	464
55F	Conditions of Sale	Jul. 1, 2007	Jul. 1, 2008	465
55G	Interim Report on Sale	Nov. 1, 2005	Jul. 1, 2006	466

56A	Order for Security for Costs	Nov. 1, 2005	Jul. 1, 2006	467
57A	Bill of Costs	Nov. 1, 2005	Jul. 1, 2006	468
57B	Costs Outline	Jul. 1, 2007	Jul. 1, 2008	469
58A	Notice of Appointment for Assessment of Costs	Jul. 1, 2007	Jul. 1, 2008	471
58B	Notice to Deliver a Bill of Costs for Assessment	Jul. 1, 2007	Jul. 1, 2008	472
58C	Certificate of Assessment of Costs	Nov. 1, 2005	Jul. 1, 2006	473
59A	Order	Jul. 1, 2007	Jul. 1, 2008	474
59B	Judgment	Jul. 1, 2007	Jul. 1, 2008	475
59C	Order on Appeal	Jul. 1, 2007	Jul. 1, 2008	477
59D	Notice of Appointment to Settle Order	Nov. 1, 2016	Mar. 27, 2017	478
60A	Writ of Seizure and Sale	Jul. 1, 2007	Jul. 1, 2008	479
60B	Writ of Sequestration	Nov. 1, 2005	Jul. 1, 2006	482
60C	Writ of Possession	Nov. 1, 2005	Jul. 1, 2006	483
60D	Writ of Delivery	Nov. 1, 2005	Jul. 1, 2006	484
60E	Request to Renew	Jul. 1, 2007	Jul. 1, 2008	485
60F	Direction to Enforce Writ of Seizure and Sale	Nov. 1, 2005	Jul. 1, 2006	486
60G	Requisition for Garnishment	Nov. 1, 2005	Jul. 1, 2006	488
60G.1	Requisition for Renewal of Garnishment	Nov. 1, 2005	Jul. 1, 2006	489
60H	Notice of Garnishment	May 1, 2019	Oct. 23, 2019	490
60H.1	Notice of Renewal of Garnishment	May 1, 2019	Oct. 23, 2019	492
60I	Garnishee's Statement	Nov. 1, 2005	Jul. 1, 2006	494
60I.1	Notice to Co-owner of the Debt	Apr. 11, 2012	Jul. 1, 2012	495
60J	Notice of Termination of Garnishment	Jul. 1, 2007	Jul. 1, 2008	496
60K	Warrant for Arrest (Contempt)	Nov. 1, 2005	Jul. 1, 2006	497
60L	Warrant of Committal	Nov. 1, 2005	Jul. 1, 2006	498
60M	Notice of Claim	Jul. 1, 2007	Jul. 1, 2008	499
60N	Sheriff's Report	Jul. 1, 2007	Jul. 1, 2008	500
60O	Request to Withdraw a Writ	Nov. 1, 2005	Jul. 1, 2006	501
61A	Notice of Appeal to an Appellate Court	Sept. 1, 2018	Dec. 21, 2018	502
61A.1	Notice of Appeal to the Divisional Court	Sept. 1, 2018	Dec. 21, 2018	503

61B	General Heading in Proceedings in Appellate Courts	Nov. 1, 2005	Jul. 1, 2006	504
61C	Appellant's Certificate Respecting Evidence	Nov. 1, 2005	Jul. 1, 2006	505
61D	Respondent's Certificate Respecting Evidence	Nov. 1, 2005	Jul. 1, 2006	506
61E	Notice of Cross-Appeal	Jul. 1, 2007	Jul. 1, 2008	507
61F	Supplementary Notice of Appeal (or Cross-Appeal)	Jul. 1, 2007	Jul. 1, 2008	508
61G	Notice of Listing for Hearing (Appeal)	Nov. 1, 2005	Jul. 1, 2006	509
61H	Certificate of Complete-ness of Appeal Book and Compendium	Jul. 1, 2007	Jul. 1, 2008	510
61I	Order Dismissing Appeal or Cross-Appeal for Delay	Nov. 1, 2016	Mar. 27, 2017	511
61I.1	Order Dismissing Appeal to Divisional Court for Delay	Sep. 1, 2018	Dec. 21, 2018	512
61J	Order Dismissing Motion for Leave to Appeal for Delay	Jul. 30, 2009	Jan. 1, 2010	513
61J.1	Order Dismissing Motion for Delay	Jul. 30, 2009	Jan. 1, 2010	514
61K	Notice of Abandonment of Appeal or Cross-Appeal	Jul. 1, 2007	Jul. 1, 2008	515
61L	Notice of Election to Proceed with Cross-Appeal	Jul. 1, 2007	Jul. 1, 2008	516
62A	Notice of Appeal to a Judge	Jul. 1, 2007	Jul. 1, 2008	517
63A	Certificate of Stay	Nov. 1, 2005	Jul. 1, 2006	518
63B	Certificate of Stay	Nov. 1, 2005	Jul. 1, 2006	519
64A	Request to Redeem	Jul. 1, 2007	Jul. 1, 2008	520
64B	Default Judgment for Foreclosure with a Reference	Nov. 1, 2005	Jul. 1, 2006	521
64C	Default Judgment for Immediate Foreclosure	Nov. 1, 2005	Jul. 1, 2006	523
64D	Default Judgment for Foreclosure without a Reference	Jul. 1, 2007	Jul. 1, 2008	524
64E	Final Order of Foreclosure	Jul. 1, 2007	Jul. 1, 2008	526

64F	Request for Sale	Jul. 1, 2007	Jul. 1, 2008	529
64G	Default Judgment for Sale with a Redemption Period (Action Converted from Foreclosure to Sale)	Nov. 1, 2005	Jul. 1, 2006	530
64H	Default Judgment for Immediate Sale (Action Converted from Foreclosure to Sale)	Nov. 1, 2005	Jul. 1, 2006	532
64I	Default Judgment for Sale Conditional on Proof of Claim (Action Converted from Foreclosure to Sale)	Nov. 1, 2005	Jul. 1, 2006	534
64J	Default Judgment for Immediate Sale	Nov. 1, 2005	Jul. 1, 2006	536
64K	Default Judgment for Sale with a Redemption Period	Nov. 1, 2005	Jul. 1, 2006	538
64L	Final Order for Sale	Jul. 1, 2007	Jul. 1, 2008	540
64M	Default Judgment for Redemption	Nov. 1, 2005	Jul. 1, 2006	541
64N	Notice of Reference to Subsequent Encumbrancer Added on Reference	Nov. 1, 2005	Jul. 1, 2006	542
64O	Notice of Reference to Subsequent Encumbrancer Named as Original Party	Nov. 1, 2005	Jul. 1, 2006	544
64P	Notice of Reference to Original Defendants	Nov. 1, 2005	Jul. 1, 2006	546
64Q	Notice to Added Defendant Having Interest in Equity	Nov. 1, 2005	Jul. 1, 2006	548
65A	Judgment for Administration of Estate	Nov. 1, 2005	Jul. 1, 2006	550
66A	Judgment for Partition or Sale	Nov. 1, 2005	Jul. 1, 2006	551
68A	Notice of Application to Divisional Court for Judicial Review	Sep. 1, 2018	Dec. 21, 2018	552
68B	Notice of Listing for Hearing (Judicial Review)	Nov. 1, 2005	Jul. 1, 2006	554
68C	Order Dismissing Application for Judicial Review	Jul. 30, 2009	Jan. 1, 2010	555

68D	Order Dismissing Application for Judicial Review for Delay	Sep. 1, 2018	Dec. 21, 2018	556
72A	Notice of Payment into Court	Jul. 1, 2007	Jul. 1, 2008	557
72B	Affidavit (Motion for Payment Out of Court)	Jul. 1, 2007	Jul. 1, 2008	558
72C	Stop Order	Jul. 1, 2007	Jul. 1, 2008	559
73A	Notice of Application for Registration of United Kingdom Judgment	Apr. 11, 2012	Jul. 1, 2012	560
74.1	Notice to Estate Registrar of Deposit of Will or Codicil	Nov. 1, 2005	Jul. 1, 2006	563
74.2	Notice to Estate Registrar of Withdrawal of Will or Codicil	Nov. 1, 2005	Jul. 1, 2006	565
74.3	Request for Notice of Commencement of Pro-ceeding	Nov. 1, 2005	Jul. 1, 2006	567
74.4	Application for Certifi-cate of Appointment of Estate Trustee with a Will (Individual Applicant)	Sep. 1, 2018	Dec. 21, 2018	568
74.4.1	Application for Certifi-cate of Appointment of Estate Trustee with a Will (Individual Applicant) Limited to the Assets Referred to in the Will	Sep. 1, 2018	Dec. 21, 2018	571
74.5	Application for Certifi-cate of Appointment of Estate Trustee with a Will (Corporate Applicant)	Sep. 1, 2018	Dec. 21, 2018	574
74.5.1	Application for Certifi-cate of Appointment of Estate Trustee with a Will (Corporate Applicant) Limited to the Assets Referred to in the Will	Sep. 1, 2018	Dec. 21, 2018	577
74.6	Affidavit of Service of Notice	Nov. 1, 2005	Jul. 1, 2006	580

74.7	Notice of an Application for a Certificate of Appointment of Estate Trustee with a Will	Feb. 1, 2015	Jan. 1, 2016	582
74.8	Affidavit of Execution of Will or Codicil	Nov. 1, 2005	Jul. 1, 2006	584
74.9	Affidavit Attesting to the Handwriting and Signature of a Holograph Will or Codicil	Nov. 1, 2005	Jul. 1, 2006	585
74.10	Affidavit of Condition of Will or Codicil	Oct. 27, 2017	Dec. 22, 2017	586
74.11	Renunciation of Right to a Certificate of Appointment of Estate Trustee (or Succeeding Estate Trustee) with a Will	Nov. 1, 2005	Jul. 1, 2006	587
74.12	Consent to Applicant's Appointment as Estate Trustee with a Will	Nov. 1, 2005	Jul. 1, 2006	588
74.12.1	Consent to Applicant's Appointment as Estate Trustee With a Will Limited to the Assets Referred to in the Will	Feb. 1, 2015	Jan. 1, 2016	589
74.13	Certificate of Appointment of Estate Trustee with a Will	Feb. 1, 2015	Jan. 1, 2016	590
74.13.1	Certificate of Appointment of Estate Trustee with a Will Limited to the Assets Referred to in the Will	Feb. 1, 2015	Jan. 1, 2016	591
74.13.2	Order for a Certificate of Appointment of (Succeeding) Estate Trustee with a Will Limited to the Assets Referred to in the Will	Apr. 11, 2012	Jul. 1, 2012	593
74.14	Application for Certificate of Appointment of Estate Trustee without a Will (Individual Applicant)	Sep. 1, 2018	Dec. 21, 2018	594
74.15	Application for Certificate of Appointment of Estate Trustee without a Will (Corporate Applicant)	Sep. 1, 2018	Dec. 21, 2018	597

74.16	Affidavit of Service of Notice	Nov. 1, 2005	Jul. 1, 2006	599
74.17	Notice of an Application for a Certificate of Appointment of Estate Trustee without a Will	Nov. 1, 2005	Jul. 1, 2006	600
74.18	Renunciation of Prior Right to a Certificate of Appointment of Estate Trustee without a Will	Nov. 1, 2005	Jul. 1, 2006	602
74.19	Consent to Applicant's Appointment as Estate Trustee without a Will	Nov. 1, 2005	Jul. 1, 2006	603
74.20	Certificate of Appointment of Estate Trustee without a Will	Nov. 1, 2005	Jul. 1, 2006	604
74.20.1	Application for Certificate of Appointment of a Foreign Estate Trustee's Nominee as Estate Trustee without a Will	Feb. 1, 2015	Jul. 9, 2015	605
74.20.2	Nomination of Applicant by Foreign Estate Trustee	Nov. 1, 2005	Jul. 1, 2006	608
74.20.3	Certificate of Appointment of Foreign Estate Trustee's Nominee as Estate Trustee without a Will	Nov. 1, 2005	Jul. 1, 2006	609
74.21	Application for Certificate of Appointment as Succeeding Estate Trustee with a Will	Nov. 1, 2005	Jul. 1, 2006	610
74.21.1	Application for Certificate of Appointment as Succeeding Estate Trustee with a Will Limited to the Assets Referred to in the Will	Apr. 11, 2012	Jul. 1, 2012	613
74.22	Consent to Applicant's Appointment as Succeeding Estate Trustee with a Will	Nov. 1, 2005	Jul. 1, 2006	616
74.22.1	Consent to Applicant's Appointment as Succeeding Estate Trustee with a Will Limited to the Assets Referred to in the Will	Apr. 11, 2012	Jul. 1, 2012	617

74.23	Certificate of Appointment of Succeeding Estate Trustee with a Will	Feb. 1, 2015	Jan. 1, 2016	618
74.23.1	Certificate of Appointment of Succeeding Estate Trustee with a Will Limited to the Assets Referred to in the Will	Feb. 1, 2015	Jan. 1, 2016	619
74.24	Application for Certificate of Appointment as Succeeding Estate Trustee without a Will	Nov. 1, 2005	Jul. 1, 2006	620
74.25	Consent to Applicant's Appointment as Succeeding Estate Trustee without a Will	Nov. 1, 2005	Jul. 1, 2006	623
74.26	Certificate of Appointment of Succeeding Estate Trustee without a Will	Nov. 1, 2005	Jul. 1, 2006	624
74.27	Application for Confirmation by Resealing of Appointment or Certificate of Ancillary Appointment of Estate Trustee	Feb. 1, 2015	Jul. 9, 2015	625
74.28	Confirmation by Resealing of Appointment of Estate Trustee	Feb. 1, 2015	Jan. 1, 2016	627
74.29	Certificate of Ancillary Appointment of Estate Trustee with a Will	Nov. 1, 2005	Jul. 1, 2006	628
74.30	Application for Certificate of Appointment of Estate Trustee During Litigation	Sept. 1, 2018	Dec. 21, 2018	629
74.31	Certificate of Appointment of Estate Trustee During Litigation	Nov. 1, 2005	Jul. 1, 2006	631
74.32	Bond - Insurance or Guarantee Company	Nov. 1, 2005	Jul. 1, 2006	632
74.33	Bond - Personal Sureties	Nov. 1, 2005	Jul. 1, 2006	634
74.34	Registrar's Notice to Estate Trustee Named in a Deposited Will of Application for Certificate of Appointment of Estate Trustee with a Will	Nov. 1, 2005	Jul. 1, 2006	637

345

74.35	Registrar's Notice to Estate Trustee Named in a Deposited Will of Application for Certificate of Appointment of Estate Trustee without a Will	Nov. 1, 2005	Jul. 1, 2006	638
74.36	Order to Accept or Refuse Appointment as Estate Trustee with a Will	Nov. 1, 2005	Jul. 1, 2006	639
74.37	Order to Accept or Refuse Appointment as Estate Trustee without a Will	Nov. 1, 2005	Jul. 1, 2006	640
74.38	Order to Consent or Object to a Proposed Appointment of an Estate Trustee with or without a Will	Jul. 1, 2007	Jul. 1, 2008	641
74.39	Order to File a Statement of Assets of the Estate	Nov. 1, 2005	Jul. 1, 2006	642
74.40	Order to Beneficiary Witness	Nov. 1, 2005	Jul. 1, 2006	643
74.41	Order to Former Spouse	Nov. 1, 2005	Jul. 1, 2006	644
74.42	Order to Pass Accounts	Nov. 1, 2005	Jul. 1, 2006	645
74.43	Affidavit Verifying Estate Accounts	Nov. 1, 2005	Jul. 1, 2006	646
74.44	Notice of Application to Pass Accounts	Jan. 1, 2016	May 26, 2016	647
74.45	Notice of Objection to Accounts	Jul. 1, 2007	Jul. 1, 2008	649
74.45.1	Request for Further Notice in Passing of Accounts	May 1, 2017	Jul. 1, 2017	650
74.46	Notice of No Objection to Accounts	Jul. 1, 2007	Jul. 1, 2008	651
74.46.1	Notice of Non-Participation in Passing of Accounts	Jul. 1, 2007	Jul. 1, 2008	652
74.47	Affidavit in Support of Unopposed Judgment on Passing of Accounts	Nov. 1, 2005	Jul. 1, 2006	653
74.48	Notice of Withdrawal of Objection	Jul. 1, 2007	Jul. 1, 2008	655
74.49	Request for Costs (Person other than Children's Lawyer or Public Guardian and Trustee)	Jul. 1, 2007	Jul. 1, 2008	656

74.49.1	Request for Costs (Children's Lawyer or Public Guardian and Trustee)	Jul. 1, 2007	Jul. 1, 2008	657
74.49.2	Request for Increased Costs (Estate Trustee)	Apr. 11, 2012	Jul. 1, 2012	658
74.49.3	Request for Increased Costs (Person other than Estate Trustee)	Apr. 11, 2012	Jul. 1, 2012	659
74.49.4	Reply to Notice of Objection to Accounts	Feb. 1, 2015	Jan. 1, 2016	661
74.50	Judgment on Unopposed Passing of Accounts	Apr. 11, 2012	Jul. 1, 2012	662
74.51	Judgment on Contested Passing of Accounts	Apr. 11, 2012	Jul. 1, 2012	664
75.1	Notice of Objection	Jul. 1, 2007	Jul. 1, 2008	666
75.2	Notice that Objection has been Filed	Jul. 1, 2007	Jul. 1, 2008	667
75.3	Notice to Objector	Jul. 1, 2007	Jul. 1, 2008	668
75.4	Notice of Appearance	Jul. 1, 2007	Jul. 1, 2008	669
75.5	Notice of Application for Directions	Jul. 1, 2007	Jul. 1, 2008	670
75.6	Notice of Motion for Directions	Jul. 1, 2007	Jul. 1, 2008	672
75.7	Statement of Claim Pursuant to Order Giving Directions	Nov. 1, 2005	Jul. 1, 2006	673
75.8	Order Giving Directions Where Pleadings Directed	Jul. 1, 2007	Jul. 1, 2008	674
75.9	Order Giving Directions Where Trial of Issues Directed	Jul. 1, 2007	Jul. 1, 2008	676
75.10	Statement of Submission of Rights to the Court	Jul. 1, 2007	Jul. 1, 2008	678
75.11	Notice of Settlement	Jul. 1, 2007	Jul. 1, 2008	679
75.12	Rejection of Settlement	Jul. 1, 2007	Jul. 1, 2008	680
75.13	Notice of Contestation	Jul. 1, 2007	Jul. 1, 2008	681
75.14	Claim Against Estate	Nov. 1, 2005	Jul. 1, 2006	682
75.1A	Request for Assignment of Mediator	Nov. 1, 2005	Jul. 1, 2006	684
75.1B	Notice by Mediator	Nov. 1, 2005	Jul. 1, 2006	685
75.1C	Statement of Issues	Nov. 1, 2005	Jul. 1, 2006	686
75.1D	Certificate of Non-Compliance	Nov. 1, 2005	Jul. 1, 2006	687
76A	Notice Whether Action Under Rule 76	Nov. 1, 2008	Jan. 1, 2010	688

76B	Simplified Procedure Motion Form	Nov. 1, 2005	Jul. 1, 2006	689
76C	Notice of Readiness for Pre-Trial Conference	Nov. 1, 2005	Jul. 1, 2006	692
76D	Trial Management Checklist	May 1, 2019	Jan. 1, 2020	693

FORM 2.1A

Courts of Justice Act

NOTICE THAT PROCEEDING (OR MOTION) MAY BE STAYED OR DISMISSED

(General heading)

NOTICE THAT PROCEEDING (OR MOTION) MAY BE STAYED OR DISMISSED

TO THE PLAINTIFF OR APPLICANT (OR MOVING PARTY)

The court is considering making an order staying or dismissing this proceeding (*or* motion) under Rule 2.1.01 (*or* Rule 2.1.02) because it appears on its face to be frivolous or vexatious or otherwise an abuse of the process of the court.

THIS PROCEEDING (*or* MOTION) WILL BE STAYED OR DISMISSED unless, within 15 days of receiving this notice, you file with the court a written submission, no more than 10 pages in length, responding to this notice. If you do not file a written submission that complies with this notice and Rule 2.1.01(*or* Rule 2.1.02), the court may order this proceeding (*or* motion) stayed or dismissed without further notice.

A copy of your submission may be given to any other party if the court directs it.

Date _____   Signed by _____

Local registrar
(Address of court office)

TO   *(Name and address of lawyer or plaintiff/applicant/moving party)*

RCP-E 2.1A (January 23, 2014)

349

FORM 4A

Courts of Justice Act

GENERAL HEADING OF DOCUMENTS — ACTIONS

(Court file no.)

ONTARIO

SUPERIOR COURT OF JUSTICE

BETWEEN:

(name)

Plaintiff

and

(name)

Defendant

(Title of document)

(Text of document)

(For the title of the proceeding in the case of a,

(a) *counterclaim against a person who is not already a party to the main action, follow Form 27B;*

(b) *third or subsequent party claim in an action, follow Form 29A in all documents in the main action and the third or subsequent party action;*

(c) *garnishment, follow Form 60H; or*

(d) *mortgage action in which defendants are added on a reference, follow Form 64N.*

(For the general heading in a proceeding in an appellate court, follow Form 61B.)

RCP-E 4A (November 1, 2005)

FORM 4B

Courts of Justice Act

GENERAL HEADING OF DOCUMENTS — APPLICATIONS

(Court file no.)

ONTARIO SUPERIOR COURT OF JUSTICE

B E T W E E N:

(name)

Applicant

and

(name)

Respondent

APPLICATION UNDER *(statutory provision or rule under which the application is made)*

(Title of document)

(Text of document)

(In a proceeding in an appellate court, follow Form 61B.)

RCP-E 4B (April 11, 2012)

FORM 4C

Courts of Justice Act

BACKSHEET

(Short title of proceeding)   *(Court file no.)*

(Name of Court)

PROCEEDING COMMENCED AT *(place)*

(Title of document)

(if affidavit, indicate name of deponent and date sworn)

(Name, address, telephone number, fax number (if any) and e-mail address (if any) of lawyer or party)

(Law society membership number of lawyer)

(Fax number, if known, and e-mail address, if known, of person on whom document is to be served)

RCP-E 4C (May 1, 2016)

FORM 4D

Courts of Justice Act

AFFIDAVIT

(General heading)

AFFIDAVIT OF *(name)*

I, *(full name of deponent)*, of the *(*City, Town, *etc.)* of.., in the *(*County, Regional Municipality, *etc.)* of..; *(where the deponent is a party or the lawyer, officer, director, member or employee of a party, set out the deponent's capacity)*, MAKE OATH AND SAY *(or* AFFIRM*)*:

1. *(Set out the statements of fact in consecutively numbered paragraphs, with each paragraph being confined as far as possible to a particular statement of fact.)*

Sworn *(or* Affirmed*)* before me at the *(*City, Town, *etc.)* of .... in the *(*County, Regional Municipality, *etc.)* of .... , on *date).*	
.... **Commissioner for Taking Affidavits** *(or as may be)*	.... *(Signature of deponent)*

RCP-E4D (July 1, 2007)

FORM 4E

Courts of Justice Act

REQUISITION

(General heading)

REQUISITION

TO THE LOCAL REGISTRAR at *(place)*

I REQUIRE *(Set out a concise statement of what is sought and include all particulars necessary for the registrar to act. Where what is sought is authorized by an order, refer to the order in the requisition and attach a copy of the entered order. Where an affidavit or other document must be filed with the requisition, refer to it in the requisition and attach it.)*

(Date)   *(Name, address and telephone number of lawyer or other person filing requisition)*

(The following are examples of different kinds of requisition.)

(Simple requisition)

I REQUIRE a certified copy of the *(identify document by nature and date).*

(Order attached)

I REQUIRE, in accordance with the order dated *(date),* a copy of which is attached, a commission authorizing the taking of evidence before the commissioner named in the order and a letter of request.

I REQUIRE, in accordance with the order dated *(date),* a copy of which is attached, a certificate of pending litigation in respect of the land described in the statement of claim.

(Affidavit attached)

I REQUIRE an order to continue this action with *(name)* as plaintiff and *(name)* as defendants. An affidavit stating that the defendant *(name)* has reached the age of majority is attached.

RCP-E 4E (July 1, 2007)

FORM 4F

Courts of Justice Act

NOTICE OF CONSTITUTIONAL QUESTION

(General heading)

NOTICE OF CONSTITUTIONAL QUESTION

The *(identify party)* intends to question the constitutional validity *(or applicability)* of *(identify the particular legislative provisions or the particular rule of common law) (or* to claim a remedy under subsection 24 (1) of the *Canadian Charter of Rights and Freedoms* in relation to an act or omission of the Government of Canada *(or* Ontario*))*.

The question is to be argued on *(day), (date), at (time), at (address of court house)*.

The following are the material facts giving rise to the constitutional question: *(Set out concisely the material facts that relate to the constitutional question. Where appropriate, attach pleadings or reasons for decision.)*

The following is the legal basis for the constitutional question: *(Set out concisely the legal basis for each question, identifying the nature of the constitutional principles to be argued.)*

(Date)   *(Name, address and telephone number of lawyer or party)*

TO   The Attorney General of Ontario *(as required by section 109 of the Courts of Justice Act)*
Constitutional Law Branch
4th floor
720 Bay Street
Toronto, Ontario M5G 2K1
fax: (416) 326-4015

The Attorney General of Canada *(as required by section 109 of the Courts of Justice Act)*
120 Adelaide Street West
Suite 400
Toronto, Ontario M5H 1T1
fax: (416) 952-0298

(or Justice Building
234 Wellington Street
Ottawa, Ontario K1A 0H8
fax: (613) 954-1920*)*

*(Names and addresses of lawyers
for all other parties and of all
other parties acting in person)*

*(This notice must be served as soon as the circumstances requiring it become known and, in any
event, at least 15 days before the question is to be argued, unless the court orders otherwise.)*

RCP-E 4F (April 27, 2020)

FORM 7A

Courts of Justice Act

REQUEST FOR APPOINTMENT OF LITIGATION GUARDIAN

(General heading)

REQUEST FOR APPOINTMENT OF LITIGATION GUARDIAN

THE PLAINTIFF *(or as may be)* BELIEVES THAT YOU ARE UNDER A LEGAL DISABILITY. As a party under disability, you must have a litigation guardian appointed by the court to act on your behalf in defending this proceeding.

YOU ARE REQUIRED to have some proper person make a motion to this court forthwith to be appointed as your litigation guardian.

IF YOU FAIL TO DO SO WITHIN TEN DAYS after service of this request, the plaintiff *(or as may be)* may move without further notice to have the court appoint a litigation guardian to act on your behalf.

(Date)   *(Name, address and telephone number of lawyer or party)*

TO: *(Name and address of party under disability)*

RCP-E 7A (July 1, 2007)

FORM 7B

Courts of Justice Act

ORDER TO CONTINUE (MINOR REACHING AGE OF MAJORITY)

(General heading)

(Court seal)

ORDER TO CONTINUE

On the requisition of *(identify party)* and on reading the affidavit of *(name)*, filed, which states that the minor *(name of party)* reached the age of majority on *(date)*,

IT IS ORDERED that this proceeding continue by *(or* against*) (name of party)* without a litigation guardian and that the title of the proceeding be amended accordingly in all documents issued, served or filed after the date of this order.

Date _____   Signed by   _____

                                                                   Local registrar

Address of   _____
court office

                                                         _____

RCP-E 7B (November 1, 2005)

FORM 8A

Courts of Justice Act

NOTICE TO ALLEGED PARTNER

(General heading)

NOTICE TO ALLEGED PARTNER

YOU ARE ALLEGED TO HAVE BEEN A PARTNER on *(date) (or* during *(period))* in the partnership of *(firm name)* named as a party to this proceeding.

IF YOU WISH TO DENY THAT YOU WERE A PARTNER at any material time, you must defend this proceeding separately from the partnership, denying that you were a partner at the material time. If you fail to do so, you will be deemed to have been a partner on the date *(or* during the period) set out above.

AN ORDER AGAINST THE PARTNERSHIP MAY BE ENFORCED AGAINST YOU PERSONALLY if you are deemed to have been a partner, if you admit that you were a partner or if the court finds that you were a partner at the material time.

(Date)   *(Name, address and telephone number of plaintiff's lawyer or plaintiff)*

TO: *(Name and address of alleged partner)*

RCP-E 8A (July 1, 2007)

FORM 11A

Courts of Justice Act

ORDER TO CONTINUE (TRANSFER OR TRANSMISSION OF INTEREST)

(General heading)

(Court seal)

ORDER TO CONTINUE

On the requisition of *(identify party or person)* and on reading the affidavit of *(name)*, filed, which indicates that on *(date)*, *(recite the details of the transfer or transmission of interest or liability)*,

IT IS ORDERED that this proceeding continue and that the title of the proceeding in all documents issued, served or filed after the date of this order be as follows: *(Set out new title of proceeding, deleting name of party whose interest is transferred or transmitted and showing name of new party.)*

Date _____   Signed by   _____

                                                        Local registrar

                              Address of   _____
                              court office

                                            _____

A party who wishes to set aside or vary this order must make a motion to do so forthwith after the order comes to the party's attention.

Where a transmission of interest occurs by reason of bankruptcy, leave of the bankruptcy court may be required under section 69.4 of the *Bankruptcy and Insolvency Act* (Canada) before the proceeding may continue.

RCP-E 11A (November 1, 2005)

FORM 14A

Courts of Justice Act

STATEMENT OF CLAIM (GENERAL)

(General heading)

(Court seal)

STATEMENT OF CLAIM

TO THE DEFENDANT

A LEGAL PROCEEDING HAS BEEN COMMENCED AGAINST YOU by the plaintiff. The claim made against you is set out in the following pages.

IF YOU WISH TO DEFEND THIS PROCEEDING, you or an Ontario lawyer acting for you must prepare a statement of defence in Form 18A prescribed by the Rules of Civil Procedure, serve it on the plaintiff's lawyer or, where the plaintiff does not have a lawyer, serve it on the plaintiff, and file it, with proof of service in this court office, WITHIN TWENTY DAYS after this statement of claim is served on you, if you are served in Ontario.

If you are served in another province or territory of Canada or in the United States of America, the period for serving and filing your statement of defence is forty days. If you are served outside Canada and the United States of America, the period is sixty days.

Instead of serving and filing a statement of defence, you may serve and file a notice of intent to defend in Form 18B prescribed by the Rules of Civil Procedure. This will entitle you to ten more days within which to serve and file your statement of defence.

IF YOU FAIL TO DEFEND THIS PROCEEDING, JUDGMENT MAY BE GIVEN AGAINST YOU IN YOUR ABSENCE AND WITHOUT FURTHER NOTICE TO YOU. IF YOU WISH TO DEFEND THIS PROCEEDING BUT ARE UNABLE TO PAY LEGAL FEES, LEGAL AID MAY BE AVAILABLE TO YOU BY CONTACTING A LOCAL LEGAL AID OFFICE.

(Where the claim made is for money only, include the following:)

IF YOU PAY THE PLAINTIFF'S CLAIM, and $ . . . . for costs, within the time for serving and filing your statement of defence you may move to have this proceeding dismissed by the court. If you believe the amount claimed for costs is excessive, you may pay the plaintiff's claim and $400 for costs and have the costs assessed by the court.

TAKE NOTICE: THIS ACTION WILL AUTOMATICALLY BE DISMISSED if it has not been set down for trial or terminated by any means within five years after the action was commenced unless otherwise ordered by the court.

Date _____   Issued by   _____

                                                 Local registrar

                                   Address of   _____
                                   court office

                                                 _____

TO   *(Name and address of each defendant)*

(In an action under the simplified procedure provided in Rule 76, add:)

THIS ACTION IS BROUGHT AGAINST YOU UNDER THE SIMPLIFIED PROCEDURE PROVIDED IN RULE 76 OF THE RULES OF CIVIL PROCEDURE.

CLAIM

1. The plaintiff claims: *(State here the precise relief claimed.)*

(Then set out in separate, consecutively numbered paragraphs each allegation of material fact relied on to substantiate the claim.)

(Where the statement of claim is to be served outside Ontario without a court order, set out the facts and the specific provisions of Rule 17 relied on in support of such service.)

(Date of issue)   *(Name, address and telephone number of law-
                                 yer or plaintiff)*

RCP-E 14A (June 9, 2014)

FORM 14B

Courts of Justice Act

STATEMENT OF CLAIM (MORTGAGE ACTION — FORECLOSURE)

(General heading)

(Court seal)

STATEMENT OF CLAIM (MORTGAGE ACTION — FORECLOSURE)

TO THE DEFENDANT

A LEGAL PROCEEDING HAS BEEN COMMENCED AGAINST YOU by the plaintiff. The claim made against you is set out in the following pages.

IF YOU WISH TO DEFEND THIS PROCEEDING, you or an Ontario lawyer acting for you must prepare a statement of defence in Form 18A prescribed by the Rules of Civil Procedure, serve it on the plaintiff's lawyer or, where the plaintiff does not have a lawyer, serve it on the plaintiff, and file it, with proof of service, in this court office, WITHIN 20 DAYS after this statement of claim is served on you, if you are served in Ontario.

If you are served in another province or territory of Canada or in the United States of America, the period for serving and filing your statement of defence is 40 days. If you are served outside Canada and the United States of America, the period is 60 days.

Instead of serving and filing a statement of defence, you may serve and file a notice of intent to defend in Form 18B prescribed by the Rules of Civil Procedure. This will entitle you to 10 more days within which to serve and file your statement of defence.

(Where payment of the mortgage debt is claimed, add:)

IF YOU PAY THE PLAINTIFF'S CLAIM, and $ . . . . for costs, within the time for serving and filing your statement of defence, you may move to have this proceeding dismissed by the court. If you believe the amount claimed for costs is excessive, you may pay the plaintiff's claim and $400 for costs and have the costs assessed by the court.

REQUEST TO REDEEM

Whether or not you serve and file a statement of defence, you may request the right to redeem the mortgaged property by serving a request to redeem (Form 64A) on the plaintiff and filing it in this court office within the time for serving and filing your statement of defence or at any time before being noted in default. If you do so, you will be entitled to seven days notice of the taking of the account of the amount due to the plaintiff, and to 60 days from the taking of the account within which to redeem the mortgaged property.

If you hold a lien, charge or encumbrance on the mortgaged property subsequent to the mortgage in question, you may file a request to redeem, which must contain particulars of your claim verified by an affidavit, and you will be entitled to redeem only if your claim is not disputed or, if disputed, is proved on a reference.

REQUEST FOR SALE

If you do not serve and file a statement of defence, you may request a sale of the mortgaged property by serving a request for sale (Form 64F) on the plaintiff and filing it in this court office within the time for serving and filing your statement of defence, or at any time before being noted in default. If you do so, the plaintiff will be entitled to obtain a judgment for a sale with a reference and you will be entitled to notice of the reference.

If you hold a lien, charge or encumbrance on the mortgaged property subsequent to the mortgage in question and you do not serve and file a request to redeem, you may file a request for sale which must contain particulars of your claim verified by an affidavit, and must be accompanied by a receipt showing that $250 has been paid into court as security for the costs of the plaintiff(s) and of any other party having carriage of the sale.

DEFAULT JUDGMENT

IF YOU FAIL TO SERVE AND FILE A STATEMENT OF DEFENCE, JUDGMENT MAY BE GIVEN AGAINST YOU WITHOUT FURTHER NOTICE. IF YOU WISH TO DEFEND THIS PROCEEDING BUT ARE UNABLE TO PAY LEGAL FEES, LEGAL AID MAY BE AVAILABLE TO YOU BY CONTACTING A LOCAL LEGAL AID OFFICE.

TAKE NOTICE: THIS ACTION WILL AUTOMATICALLY BE DISMISSED if it has not been set down for trial or terminated by any means within five years after the action was commenced unless otherwise ordered by the court.

Date _____ Issued by _____

Local registrar

Address of
court office _____

_____

TO: *(Name and address of each defendant)*

REQUEST TO REDEEM . . . . (sale action) . . . .

Whether or not you serve and file a statement of defence, you may request the right to redeem the mortgaged property by serving a request to redeem (Form 64A) on the plaintiff and filing it in this court office within the time for serving and filing your statement of defence, or at any time before being noted in default. If you do so, you will be entitled to seven days notice of the taking of the account of the amount due to the plaintiff, and to 60 days from the taking of the account within which to redeem the mortgaged property.

DEFAULT JUDGMENT

IF YOU FAIL TO SERVE AND FILE A STATEMENT OF DEFENCE, JUDGMENT MAY BE GIVEN AGAINST YOU WITHOUT FURTHER NOTICE. IF YOU WISH TO DEFEND THIS PROCEEDING BUT ARE UNABLE TO PAY LEGAL FEES, LEGAL AID MAY BE AVAILABLE TO YOU BY CONTACTING A LOCAL LEGAL AID OFFICE.

TAKE NOTICE: THIS ACTION WILL AUTOMATICALLY BE DISMISSED if it has not been set down for trial or terminated by any means within five years after the action was commenced unless otherwise ordered by the court.

Date _____   Issued by _____

Local registrar

Address of
court office _____

_____

TO: *(Name and address of each defendant)*

(Subsequent encumbrancers are not to be named as defendants in this statement of claim in a sale action.)

(In an action under the simplified procedure provided in Rule 76, add:)

THIS ACTION IS BROUGHT AGAINST YOU UNDER THE SIMPLIFIED PROCEDURE PROVIDED IN RULE 76 OF THE RULES OF CIVIL PROCEDURE.

CLAIM

1. The plaintiff claims:

(foreclosure)

   (a)   that the equity of redemption in the property secured by the mortgage mentioned below be foreclosed;

(or)

(sale)

   (a)   that the property secured by the mortgage mentioned below be sold and proceeds of sale applied towards the amount due under the mortgage, and payment to the plaintiff by the defendant *(name of defendant against whom payment of any deficiency is claimed)* personally of any deficiency if the sale proceeds are not sufficient to pay the amount found due to the plaintiff;

(possession)

   (b)   possession of the mortgaged property;

(payment of mortgage debt)

   (c)   payment by the defendant *(name of defendant against whom payment of mortgage debt is claimed)* of the sum of $. . . . . *(from paragraph 6 below)* now due under the mortgage together with interest at the rate of *(mortgage rate)* per cent per year until judgment;

(interest)

   (d)   post-judgment interest in accordance with the *Courts of Justice Act (or where the mortgage provides for interest after judgment at the mortgage rate, substitute:* post-judgment interest at the rate of *(mortgage rate)* per cent per year in accordance with the mortgage); and

(costs)

   (e)   the costs of this action *(on a substantial indemnity basis if the mortgage so provides, or if it provides for costs on a solicitor and client basis).*

365

2. The plaintiff's claim is on a mortgage dated *(date)*, made between *(name of mortgagor)* and *(name of mortgagee)*, and registered *(give particulars of registration and of any assignment of the mortgage)*, under which the defendant *(or as may be)* mortgaged the property described below for a term of . . . . . . years securing the sum of $ . . . . and interest on that sum at the rate of . . . . . . per cent per year. The mortgage provides for the payment of principal and interest as follows: *(Set out terms of payment. Add a reference to provisions in the mortgage for solicitor and client costs and post-judgment interest if applicable.)*

3. The mortgage provides that on default of payment of any sum required to be paid under the mortgage, the principal becomes due and payable and the plaintiff is entitled to possession of the mortgaged property and to foreclosure of the equity of redemption in the mortgaged property *(or sale of the mortgaged property or as may be)*.

4. *(Where a claim for payment is made under section 20 of the* Mortgages Act *against a person other than the original mortgagor, add:)* The defendant *(name)* became liable under section 20 of the *Mortgages Act* to pay the amount of the mortgage debt to the plaintiff by reason of *(set out particulars of the transfer of the mortgaged property from the original mortgagor to this defendant)*.

5. Default in payment of principal and interest *(or as may be)* occurred on *(date)*, and still continues.

6. There is now due under the terms of the mortgage:

(a)	for principal	$ _____
(b)	for taxes paid	$ _____
(c)	for premiums of insurance paid	$ _____
(d)	for maintenance costs paid	$ _____
(e)	for heating costs paid	$ _____
(f)	for utility costs paid	$ _____
	(add any other costs in similar fashion)	
(g)	for interest *(set out particulars)*	$ _____

Total now due: $ _____

The defendant *(name)* is liable to pay these sums and subsequent interest at the rate of _____ per cent per year.

7. The following is a description of the mortgaged property: *(Set out a description sufficient for registration. For Land Titles land, include the parcel number.)*

(In a foreclosure action where one or more subsequent encumbrancers are named as defendants, add:)

8. The defendant *(name)* has been made a party to this action as a subsequent encumbrancer.

(Where the statement of claim is to be served outside Ontario without a court order, set out the facts and the specific provisions of Rule 17 relied on in support of the service.)

(Date)   *(Name, address and telephone number of plaintiff's lawyer or plaintiff)*

RCP-E 14B (June 9, 2014)

FORM 14C

Courts of Justice Act

NOTICE OF ACTION

(General heading)

(Court seal)

NOTICE OF ACTION

TO THE DEFENDANT

A LEGAL PROCEEDING HAS BEEN COMMENCED AGAINST YOU by the plaintiff. The claim made against you is set out in the statement of claim served with this notice of action.

IF YOU WISH TO DEFEND THIS PROCEEDING, you or an Ontario lawyer acting for you must prepare a statement of defence in Form 18A prescribed by the Rules of Civil Procedure, serve it on the plaintiff's lawyer or, where the plaintiff does not have a lawyer, serve it on the plaintiff, and file it, with proof of service, in this court office, WITHIN TWENTY DAYS after this notice of action is served on you, if you are served in Ontario.

If you are served in another province or territory of Canada or in the United States of America, the period for serving and filing your statement of defence is forty days. If you are served outside Canada and the United States of America, the period is sixty days.

Instead of serving and filing a statement of defence, you may serve and file a notice of intent to defend in Form 18B prescribed by the Rules of Civil Procedure. This will entitle you to ten more days within which to serve and file your statement of defence.

IF YOU FAIL TO DEFEND THIS PROCEEDING, JUDGMENT MAY BE GIVEN AGAINST YOU IN YOUR ABSENCE AND WITHOUT FURTHER NOTICE TO YOU. IF YOU WISH TO DEFEND THIS PROCEEDING BUT ARE UNABLE TO PAY LEGAL FEES, LEGAL AID MAY BE AVAILABLE TO YOU BY CONTACTING A LOCAL LEGAL AID OFFICE.

(Where the claim made is for money only, include the following:)

IF YOU PAY THE PLAINTIFF'S CLAIM, and $ . . . . for costs, within the time for serving and filing your statement of defence, you may move to have this proceeding dismissed by the court. If you believe the amount claimed for costs is excessive, you may pay the plaintiff's claim and $400 for costs and have the costs assessed by the court.

TAKE NOTICE: THIS ACTION WILL AUTOMATICALLY BE DISMISSED if it has not been set down for trial or terminated by any means within five years after the action was commenced unless otherwise ordered by the court.

Date _____   Issued by   _____

                                                    Local registrar

                                     Address of   _____
                                     court office

                                                    _____

TO: *(Name and address of each defendant)*

(In an action under the simplified procedure provided in Rule 76, add:)

THIS ACTION IS BROUGHT AGAINST YOU UNDER THE SIMPLIFIED PROCEDURE PROVIDED IN RULE 76 OF THE RULES OF CIVIL PROCEDURE.

CLAIM

The plaintiff's claim is for *(set out a short statement of the nature of the plaintiff's claim).*

(Date)   *(Name, address and telephone number of law-
                                   yer or plaintiff)*

                                                    RCP-E 14C (June 9, 2014)

FORM 14D

Courts of Justice Act

STATEMENT OF CLAIM (ACTION COMMENCED BY NOTICE OF ACTION)

(General heading)

STATEMENT OF CLAIM

Notice of action issued on *(date)*

(In an action under the simplified procedure provided in Rule 76, add:)

THIS ACTION IS BROUGHT AGAINST YOU UNDER THE SIMPLIFIED PROCEDURE PROVIDED IN RULE 76 OF THE RULES OF CIVIL PROCEDURE.

1. The plaintiff claims: *(State here the precise relief claimed).*

(Then set out in separate, consecutively numbered paragraphs each allegation of material fact relied on to substantiate the claim.)

(Where the statement of claim is to be served outside Ontario without a court order, set out the facts and the specific provisions of Rule 17 relied on in support of such service.)

(Date)   *(Name, address and telephone number of law-*
                                   yer or plaintiff)

RCP-E 14D (July 1, 2007)

369

FORM 14E

Courts of Justice Act

NOTICE OF APPLICATION

(General heading)

(Court seal)

NOTICE OF APPLICATION

TO THE RESPONDENT

A LEGAL PROCEEDING HAS BEEN COMMENCED by the applicant. The claim made by the applicant appears on the following page.

THIS APPLICATION will come on for a hearing on *(day)*, *(date)*, at *(time)*, at *(address of court house)*.

IF YOU WISH TO OPPOSE THIS APPLICATION, to receive notice of any step in the application or to be served with any documents in the application, you or an Ontario lawyer acting for you must forthwith prepare a notice of appearance in Form 38A prescribed by the Rules of Civil Procedure, serve it on the applicant's lawyer or, where the applicant does not have a lawyer, serve it on the applicant, and file it, with proof of service, in this court office, and you or your lawyer must appear at the hearing.

IF YOU WISH TO PRESENT AFFIDAVIT OR OTHER DOCUMENTARY EVIDENCE TO THE COURT OR TO EXAMINE OR CROSS-EXAMINE WITNESSES ON THE APPLICA-TION, you or your lawyer must, in addition to serving your notice of appearance, serve a copy of the evidence on the applicant's lawyer or, where the applicant does not have a lawyer, serve it on the applicant, and file it, with proof of service, in the court office where the application is to be heard as soon as possible, but at least two days before the hearing.

IF YOU FAIL TO APPEAR AT THE HEARING, JUDGMENT MAY BE GIVEN IN YOUR ABSENCE AND WITHOUT FURTHER NOTICE TO YOU. IF YOU WISH TO OPPOSE THIS APPLICATION BUT ARE UNABLE TO PAY LEGAL FEES, LEGAL AID MAY BE AVAILABLE TO YOU BY CONTACTING A LOCAL LEGAL AID OFFICE.

Date _____   Issued by   _____

                                                                      Local registrar

                                        Address of   _____
                                        court office

                                                       _____

TO   *(Name and address of each respondent)*

APPLICATION

1. The applicant makes application for: *(State here the precise relief claimed.)*

2. The grounds for the application are: *(Specify the grounds to be argued, including a reference to any statutory provision or rule to be relied on.)*

3. The following documentary evidence will be used at the hearing of the application: *(List the affidavits or other documentary evidence to be relied on.)*

(Where the notice of application is to be served outside Ontario without a court order, state the facts and the specific provisions of Rule 17 relied on in support of such service.)

(Date of issue)   *(Name, address and telephone number of lawyer or applicant)*

RCP-E 14E (March 31, 2010)

FORM 14E.1

Courts of Justice Act

NOTICE OF APPLICATION UNDER SUBSECTION 140(3) OF THE *COURTS OF JUSTICE ACT*

(General heading)

(Court seal)

NOTICE OF APPLICATION UNDER SUBSECTION 140(3) OF THE *COURTS OF JUSTICE ACT*

TO THE ATTORNEY GENERAL OF ONTARIO AND THE RESPONDENT(S)

AN APPLICATION UNDER SUBSECTION 140(3) OF THE *COURTS OF JUSTICE ACT* HAS BEEN COMMENCED by the applicant. The claim made by the applicant appears on the following page.

THIS APPLICATION shall be heard in writing without the attendance of the parties, unless the court orders otherwise. An order under subsection 140(4) of the *Courts of Justice Act* granting leave to institute or continue a proceeding, or rescinding an order made under subsection 140(1) of that Act, shall not be made without an opportunity being provided to the Attorney General of Ontario and the respondents to serve and file a respondent's application record and factum.

Date _____ Issued by _____

                                                   Local registrar

                              Address of   _____
                              court office

                                              _____

TO   Crown Law Office (Civil Law)
            Ministry of the Attorney General
            720 Bay Street, 8th Floor
            Toronto, Ontario M7A 2S9
            *(Names and addresses of
            lawyers for all other parties and of all
            other parties acting in person)*

APPLICATION UNDER SUBSECTION 140(3) OF THE *COURTS OF JUSTICE ACT*

1. The applicant makes application for: *(State here the precise relief claimed.)*

2. The grounds for the application are: *(Specify the grounds to be argued, including a reference to any statutory provision or rule to be relied on.)*

(Where the notice of application is to be served outside Ontario without a court order, state the facts and the specific provisions of Rule 17 relied on in support of such service.)

(Date of issue)   *(Name, address and telephone number of law-*
                                     yer or applicant)

RCP-E 14E.1 (January 23, 2014)

FORM 14F

Courts of Justice Act

INFORMATION FOR COURT USE

ONTARIO

SUPERIOR COURT OF JUSTICE

(General heading)

INFORMATION FOR COURT USE

1. This proceeding is an: [ ] action   [ ] application

2. Has it been commenced under the *Class Proceedings Act, 1992*?   [ ] yes   [ ] no

3. If the proceeding is an action, does Rule 76 (Simplified Procedure) apply?   [ ] yes   [ ] no
Note: *Subject to the exceptions found in subrule 76.01(1), it is MANDATORY to proceed under Rule 76 for all cases in which the money amount claimed or the value of real or personal property claimed is $200,000 or less.*

4. The claim in this proceeding (action or application) is in respect of:

*(Select the **one** item that **best** describes the nature of the main claim in the proceeding.)*

Bankruptcy or insolvency law	[ ]	Motor vehicle accident	[ ]
Collection of liquidated debt	[ ]	Municipal law	[ ]
Constitutional law	[ ]	Partnership law	[ ]
Construction law (other than construction lien)	[ ]	Personal property security	[ ]
Construction lien	[ ]	Product liability	[ ]
Contract law	[ ]	Professional malpractice (other than medical)	[ ]
Corporate law	[ ]	Real property (including leases; excluding mortgage or charge)	[ ]
Defamation	[ ]	Tort: economic injury (other than from medical or professional malpractice)	[ ]
Employment or labour law	[ ]		
Intellectual property law	[ ]	Tort: human trafficking (*Prevention of and Remedies for Human Trafficking Act, 2017*)	[ ]
Judicial review	[ ]	Tort: personal injury (other than from motor vehicle accident)	[ ]
Medical malpractice	[ ]	Trusts, fiduciary duty	[ ]
Mortgage or charge	[ ]	Wills, estates	[ ]

CERTIFICATION

I certify that the above information is correct, to the best of my knowledge.

Date: _____

_____
Signature of lawyer
(if no lawyer, party must sign)

Print Form

RCP-14F-E (2019/05)

374

FORM 15A

Courts of Justice Act

NOTICE OF CHANGE OF LAWYER

(General heading)

NOTICE OF CHANGE OF LAWYER

The plaintiff *(or as may be)*, formerly represented by *(name of former lawyer)*, has appointed *(name of new lawyer)* as lawyer of record.

(Date)   *(Name, address and telephone number of new lawyer)*

TO   *(Name and address of former lawyer)*
AND TO   *(Names and addresses of lawyers for all other parties, or names and addresses of all other parties)*

RCP-E 15A (July 1, 2007)

FORM 15B

Courts of Justice Act

NOTICE OF APPOINTMENT OF LAWYER

(General heading)

NOTICE OF APPOINTMENT OF LAWYER

The plaintiff *(or as may be)* has appointed *(name)* as lawyer of record.

(Date)   *(Name, address and telephone number of lawyer of record)*

TO   *(Names and addresses of lawyers for all other parties, or names and addresses of all other parties)*

RCP-E 15B (July 1, 2007)

FORM 15C

Courts of Justice Act

NOTICE OF INTENTION TO ACT IN PERSON

(General heading)

NOTICE OF INTENTION TO ACT IN PERSON

The plaintiff *(or as may be)*, formerly represented by *(name)* as lawyer of record, intends to act in person.

(complete if filed by the lawyer of record) The plaintiff *(or as may be)* consents to the filing of this form by the lawyer of record on his/her behalf.

Date _____   Signed by _____

(print name of plaintiff (or as may be))

(complete if filed by the lawyer of record) I *(name of lawyer of record)* confirm that I have explained the purpose of this form to *(name of the plaintiff or as may be)* and have confirmed his/her intention to act in person in place of me. The plaintiff *(or as may be)* signed this form at the time he/she consented to act in person.

Date _____   Signed by _____

(print name of lawyer of record and Law Society registration number)

(Date)   *(Name, address for service and telephone number of party intending to act in person)*

TO   *(Name and address of former lawyer of record)*

AND TO   *(Names and addresses of lawyers for all other parties, or names and addresses of all other parties)*

RCP-E 15C (July 1, 2007)

FORM 16A

Courts of Justice Act

ACKNOWLEDGMENT OF RECEIPT CARD

(General heading)

TO *(full name)*

You are served by mail with the documents enclosed with this card in accordance with the Rules of Civil Procedure.

You are requested to sign the acknowledgment below and mail this card immediately after you receive it. If you fail to do so, the documents may be served on you in another manner and you may have to pay the costs of service.

ACKNOWLEDGMENT OF RECEIPT

I ACKNOWLEDGE that I have received a copy of the following documents: *(To be completed in advance by the sender of the documents. Include sufficient particulars to identify each document.)*

_____

Signature of person served

(The reverse side of this card must bear the name and address of the sender and the required postage.)

RCP-E 16A (November 1, 2005)

FORM 16B

Courts of Justice Act

AFFIDAVIT OF SERVICE

(If a separate document insert general heading)

AFFIDAVIT OF SERVICE

I, *(full name)*, of the . . . . *(City, Town, etc.)* of . . . . , in the *(County, Regional Municipality, etc.)* of . . . ., MAKE OATH AND SAY *(or AFFIRM)*:

(Personal service)

1. On *(date)*, at *(time)*, I served *(identify person served)* with the *(identify documents served)* by leaving a copy with him *(or her)* at *(address where service was made)*. *(Where the rules provide for personal service on a corporation, etc. by leaving a copy of the document with another person, substitute:* by leaving a copy with *(identify person by name and title)* at *(address where service was made).)*

2. I was able to identify the person by means of *(state the means by which the person's identity was ascertained.)*

(Service by leaving a copy with an adult person in the same household as an alternative to personal service)

1. I served *(identify person served)* with the *(identify documents served)* by leaving a copy on *(date)*, at *(time)*, with a person *(insert name if known)* who appeared to be an adult member of the same household in which *(identify person served)* is residing, at *(address where service was made)*, and by sending a copy by regular lettermail *(or* registered mail*)* on *(date)* to *(identify person served)* at the same address.

2. I ascertained that the person was an adult member of the household by means of *(state how it was ascertained that the person was an adult member of the household).*

3. Before serving the documents in this way, I made an unsuccessful attempt to serve *(identify person)* personally at the same address on *(date)*. *(If more than one attempt has been made, add:* and again on *(date).)*

(Service by mail as an alternative to personal service)

1. On *(date)*, I sent to the *(identify person served)* by regular lettermail *(or* registered mail*)* a copy of the *(identify documents served)*.

2. On *(date)*, I received the attached acknowledgment of receipt card *(or* post office receipt*)* bearing a signature that purports to be the signature of *(identify person)*.

(Service by mail on a lawyer)

1. I served *(identify party served)* with the *(identify documents served)* by sending a copy by regular lettermail *(or* registered mail*)* on *(date)* to *(name of lawyer)*, the lawyer for the *(identify party)*, at *(full mailing address)*.

(Service on a lawyer by fax)

1. I served *(identify party served)* with the *(identify documents served)* by sending a copy by fax to *(fax number)* on *(date)* to *(name of lawyer)*, the lawyer for the *(identify party)*.

(Service on a lawyer by courier)

1. I served *(identify party served)* with the *(identify documents served)* by sending a copy by *(name of courier)*, a courier, to *(name of lawyer)*, the lawyer for the *(identify party)*, at *(full address of place for delivery)*.

2. The copy was given to the courier on *(date)*.

(Service by mail on a party acting in person or a non-party)

1. I served *(identify party or person served)* with the *(identify documents served)* by sending a copy by regular lettermail *(or registered mail)* on *(date)* to *(full mailing address)*, the last address for service provided by *(identify party or person)* *(or, where no such address has been provided:* the last known address of *(identify party or person).)*

(Service on a lawyer by e-mail)

1. *(On consent of the parties or by court order)*, I served *(identify party served)* with the *(identify documents served)* by sending a copy by e-mail to *(e-mail address)* on *(date)* to *(name of lawyer)*, the lawyer for the *(identify party)*.

(Service by e-mail on a party acting in person or a non-party)

1. *(On consent of the parties or by court order)*, I served *(identify party or person served)* with the *(identify documents served)* by sending a copy by e-mail to *(e-mail address)* on *(date)*.

SWORN *(etc.)*

RCP-E 16B (May 1, 2016)

FORM 16C

Courts of Justice Act

CERTIFICATE OF SERVICE BY SHERIFF

(If a separate document insert general heading)

CERTIFICATE OF SERVICE BY SHERIFF

(Personal service)

I, *(full name)*, Sheriff *(or* Sheriff's Officer*)* of the *(*County, District, *etc.)* of . . . .
, *(time)*, I served *(identify person served)* with *(identify documents served)* by leaving a copy
with him *(or* her*)* at *(address where service was made)*. *(Where the rules provide for personal
service on a corporation, etc., by leaving a copy of the document with another person, substitute:* by leaving a copy with *(identify person by name and title)* at *(address where service was
made).)*

I was able to identify the person by means of *(state the means by which the person's identity was
ascertained.)*

*(Service by leaving a copy with an adult person in the same household as an alternative to per-
sonal service)*

I, *(full name)*, Sheriff *(or* Sheriff's Officer*)* of the *(*County, District, *etc.)* of . . . .
, certify that I served *(identify person served)* with this document by leaving a copy in a sealed
envelope addressed to him *(or* her*)* on *(date)*, at *(time)*, with a person *(insert name if known)* who
appeared to be an adult member of the same household in which *(identify person served)* is residing at *(address where service was made)*, and by sending a copy by regular lettermail *(or* registered mail*)* on *(date)* to *(identify person served)* at the same address.

I ascertained that the person was an adult member of the household by means of *(state how it
was ascertained that the person was an adult member of the household)*.

Before serving the document in this way, I made an unsuccessful attempt to serve *(identify
person)* personally at the same address on *(date)*. *(If more than one attempt has been made, add:*
and again on *(date).)*

Date _____   _____

(Signature of sheriff or sheriff's officer)

RCP-E 16C (November 1, 2005)

FORM 17A

Courts of Justice Act

REQUEST FOR SERVICE ABROAD OF JUDICIAL OR EXTRAJUDICIAL DOCUMENTS

Convention on the service abroad of judicial and
extrajudicial documents in civil or commercial matters,
signed at The Hague, November 15, 1965.

Identity and address of the applicant   Address of receiving Authority
_____   _____

The undersigned applicant has the honour to transmit - in duplicate - the documents listed below and, in conformity with article 5 of the above-mentioned Convention, requests prompt service of one copy thereof on the addressee, *i.e.*

(identity and address) . . . .

. . . .

(a) in accordance with the provisions of sub-paragraph (a) of the first paragraph of article 5 of the Convention*;

(b) in accordance with the following particular method (sub-paragraph (b) of the first paragraph of article 5)*: . . . .

. . . .

(c) by delivery to the addressee, if the addressee accepts it voluntarily (second paragraph of article 5)*.

The authority is requested to return or to have returned to the applicant a copy of the documents - and of the annexes* - with a certificate as provided on the reverse side.

(List of Documents) _____

_____

_____

_____   Done at, _____,
                                            the _____

_____

_____   Signature or stamp.

*Delete if inappropriate

CERTIFICATE

The undersigned authority has the honour to certify, in conformity with article 6 of the Convention,

(1) that the document has been served*

- the (date) . . . .

- at (place, street, number) . . . .

- in one of the following methods authorized by article 5 -

   (a)   in accordance with the provisions of sub-paragraph (a) of the first paragraph of article 5 of the Convention*;

   (b)   in accordance with the following particular method*:

   . . . .

   . . . . ;

   (c)   by delivery to the addressee, who accepted it voluntarily.

The documents referred to in the request have been delivered to:

- (identity and description of person) . . . .

. . . .

- relationship to the addressee (family, business or other) . . . .

. . . .

(2) that the document has not been served, by reason of the following facts*:

. . . .

. . . .

In conformity with the second paragraph of article 12 of the Convention, the applicant is requested to pay or reimburse the expenses detailed in the attached statement*.

Annexes

Documents returned: _____

_____

_____ Done at _____ ,
                                    the _____

In appropriate cases, documents establish- Signature or stamp.
ing the service:

_____

*Delete if inappropriate

RCP-E 17A (November 1, 2005)

FORM 17B

Courts of Justice Act

SUMMARY OF THE DOCUMENT TO BE SERVED

Convention on the service abroad of judicial and extrajudicial documents in civil or commercial matters, signed at The Hague, November 15, 1965.

(article 5, fourth paragraph)

Name and address of the requesting authority: . . . .

Particulars of the parties*: . . . .

. . . .

JUDICIAL DOCUMENT**

Nature and purpose of the document: . . . .

. . . .

Nature and purpose of the proceedings and, where appropriate, the amount in dispute: . . .

. . . .

Date and place for entering appearance**: . . . .

. . . .

Court which has given judgment**: . . . .

. . . .

Date of judgment**: . . . .

. . . .

Time limits stated in the document**: . . . .

. . . .

EXTRAJUDICIAL DOCUMENT**

Nature and purpose of the document: . . . .

. . . .

Time limits stated in the document**: . . . .

. . . .

* If appropriate, identity and address of the person interested in the transmission of the document.

. . . .

** Delete if inappropriate.

RCP-E 17B (November 1, 2005)

FORM 17C

Courts of Justice Act

NOTICE AND SUMMARY OF DOCUMENT

identity and address of the addressee

. . . .

. . . .

IMPORTANT

THE ENCLOSED DOCUMENT IS OF A LEGAL NATURE AND MAY AFFECT YOUR RIGHTS AND OBLIGATIONS. THE SUMMARY OF THE DOCUMENT TO BE SERVED WILL GIVE YOU SOME INFORMATION ABOUT ITS NATURE AND PURPOSE. YOU SHOULD HOWEVER READ THE DOCUMENT ITSELF CAREFULLY. IT MAY BE NECESSARY TO SEEK LEGAL ADVICE.

IF YOUR FINANCIAL RESOURCES ARE INSUFFICIENT YOU SHOULD SEEK INFORMATION ON THE POSSIBILITY OF OBTAINING LEGAL AID OR ADVICE EITHER IN THE COUNTRY WHERE YOU LIVE OR IN THE COUNTRY WHERE THE DOCUMENT WAS ISSUED.

ENQUIRIES ABOUT THE AVAILABILITY OF LEGAL AID OR ADVICE IN THE COUNTRY WHERE THE DOCUMENT WAS ISSUED MAY BE DIRECTED TO:

. . . .

(It is recommended that the standard terms in the notice be written in English and French and where appropriate also in the official language, or in one of the official languages of the State in which the document originated. The blanks could be completed either in the language of the State to which the document is to be sent, or in English or French.)

SUMMARY OF THE DOCUMENT TO BE SERVED: . . . .

Name and address of the requesting authority: . . . .

. . . .

*Particulars of the parties: . . . .

. . . .

**JUDICIAL DOCUMENT: . . . .

Nature and purpose of the document: . . . .

. . . .

Nature and purpose of the proceedings and where appropriate, the amount in dispute: . . . .

**Date and place for entering appearance: . . . .

. . . .

**Court which has given judgment: . . . .

. . . .

**Date of judgment: . . . .

**Time limits stated in the document: . . . .

. . . .

**EXTRAJUDICIAL DOCUMENT: . . . .

Nature and purpose of the document: . . . .

. . . .

**Time limits stated in the document: . . . .

. . . .

* If appropriate, identity and address of the person interested in the transmission of the document

** Delete if inappropriate

RCP-E 17C (November 1, 2005)

FORM 18A

Courts of Justice Act

STATEMENT OF DEFENCE

(General heading)

STATEMENT OF DEFENCE

1. The defendant admits the allegations contained in paragraphs . . . . of the statement of claim.

2. The defendant denies the allegations contained in paragraphs . . . . of the statement of claim.

3. The defendant has no knowledge in respect of the allegations contained in paragraphs . . . . of the statement of claim.

4. *(Set out in separate, consecutively numbered paragraphs each allegation of material fact relied on by way of defence.)*

(Date)   *(Name, address and telephone number of defendant's lawyer or defendant)*

TO *(Name and address of plaintiff's lawyer or plaintiff)*

RCP-E 18A (July 1, 2007)

FORM 18B

Courts of Justice Act

NOTICE OF INTENT TO DEFEND

(General heading)

NOTICE OF INTENT TO DEFEND

The defendant (*or* defendant added by counterclaim or third party) intends to defend this action.

(Date)　　　　　　*(Name, address and telephone number of lawyer or party*
　　　　　　　　　serving notice)

TO *(Name and address of lawyer or party on whom notice is served)*

RCP-E 18B (July 1, 2007)

FORM 19A

Courts of Justice Act

DEFAULT JUDGMENT (DEBT OR LIQUIDATED DEMAND)

(General heading)

(Court seal)

JUDGMENT

On reading the statement of claim in this action and the proof of service of the statement of claim on the defendant, filed, and the defendant having been noted in default,

1. IT IS ORDERED AND ADJUDGED that the defendant pay to the plaintiff the sum of $ . . . . and the sum of $ . . . . for the costs of this action. *(Where costs are to be assessed, substitute* the costs of this action as assessed by the court.*)*

This judgment bears interest at the rate of . . . . . . per cent per year from its date.

Date _____   Signed by   _____

                                                    Local registrar

                          Address of   _____
                          court office

                                                  _____

RCP-E 19A (November 1, 2005)

FORM 19B

Courts of Justice Act

DEFAULT JUDGMENT (RECOVERY OF POSSESSION OF LAND)

(General heading)

(Court seal)

JUDGMENT

On reading the statement of claim in this action and the proof of service of the statement of claim on the defendant, filed, and the defendant having been noted in default,

1. IT IS ORDERED AND ADJUDGED that the defendant deliver to the plaintiff possession of the following land: *(Where the description of the land is very lengthy, substitute the land described in the attached schedule.)*

2. IT IS ORDERED AND ADJUDGED that the defendant pay to the plaintiff the sum of $ . . . . for the costs of this action. *(Where costs are to be assessed, substitute the costs of this action as assessed by the court.)*

The costs fixed by and payable under this judgment bear interest at the rate of . . . . . . per cent per year from its date.

Date _____   Signed by   _____

                                            Local registrar

                    Address of   _____
                    court office

                                            _____

RCP-E 19B (November 1, 2005)

FORM 19C

Courts of Justice Act

DEFAULT JUDGMENT (RECOVERY OF POSSESSION OF PERSONAL PROPERTY)

(General heading)

(Court seal)

JUDGMENT

On reading the statement of claim in this action and the proof of service of the statement of claim on the defendant, filed, and the defendant having been noted in default,

1. IT IS ORDERED AND ADJUDGED that the defendant deliver to the plaintiff possession of the following personal property: *(or* the personal property described in the attached schedule.*)*

2. IT IS ORDERED AND ADJUDGED that the defendant pay to the plaintiff the sum of $ . . . . for the costs of this action. *(Where costs are to be assessed, substitute* the costs of this action as assessed by the court.*)*

The costs fixed by and payable under this judgment bear interest at the rate of . . . . . . per cent per year from its date.

Date _____ Signed by _____

Local registrar

Address of _____
court office

_____

RCP-E 19C (November 1, 2005)

FORM 19D

Courts of Justice Act

REQUISITION FOR DEFAULT JUDGMENT

(General heading)

REQUISITION FOR DEFAULT JUDGMENT

TO THE LOCAL REGISTRAR AT *(place)*

(Where the defendant has not been noted in default, begin with: I REQUIRE you to note the defendant *(name)* in default in this action on the ground that *(state nature of default).)*

I REQUIRE default judgment to be signed against the defendant *(name)*.

Default judgement may properly be signed in this action because the claim is for:

[   ] a debt or liquidated demand in money

[   ] recovery of possession of land

[   ] recovery of possession of personal property

[   ] foreclosure, sale or redemption of a mortgage

(Debt or liquidated demand)

[   ] There has been no payment on account of the claim since the statement of claim was issued. *(Complete Parts B and C.)*

OR

[   ] The following payments have been made on account of the claim since the statement of claim was issued. *(Complete Parts A and C.)*

PART A — PAYMENT(S) RECEIVED BY PLAINTIFF

(Complete this part only where part payment of the claim has been received. Where no payment has been received on account of the claim, omit this part and complete Part B.)

1. Principal

Principal sum claimed in statement of claim (without interest) $ . . . .

Date of Payment	Amount of Payment	Payment Amount Principal	Applied to Interest	Principal Sum Owing
TOTAL	$ _____	$ _____	$ _____	$ _____

2. Prejudgment interest

(Under section 128 of the Courts of Justice Act, *judgment may be obtained for prejudgment interest from the date the cause of action arose, if claimed in the statement of claim.)*

Date on which statement of claim was issued . . . .

Date from which prejudgment interest is claimed . . . .

The plaintiff is entitled to prejudgment interest on the claim, calculated as follows:

(Calculate simple interest only unless an agreement relied on in the statement of claim speci-

fies otherwise. Calculate interest on the principal sum owing from the date of the last payment. To calculate the interest amount, count the number of days since the last payment, multiply that number by the annual rate of interest, multiply the result by the principal sum owing and divide by 365.)

Principal Sum Owing	Start Date	End Date (Date of Payment)	Number of Days	Rate	Interest Amount

(The last End Date should be the date judgment is signed.)

TOTAL B $ _____

Principal Sum Owing (Total A above) $ _____

Total Interest Amount (Total B above) $ _____

SIGN JUDGMENT FOR $ _____

PART B — NO PAYMENT RECEIVED BY PLAINTIFF

(Complete this part only where no payment has been received on account of the claim.)

1. Principal

   Principal sum claimed in statement of claim (without interest) A $ . . . .

2. Prejudgment interest

   (Under section 128 of the Courts of Justice Act, *judgment may be obtained for prejudgment interest from the date the cause of action arose, if claimed in the statement of claim.)*

   Date on which statement of claim was issued . . . .

   Date from which prejudgment interest is claimed . . . .

   The plaintiff is entitled to prejudgment interest on the claim, calculated as follows:

   (Calculate simple interest only unless an agreement relied on in the statement of claim specifies otherwise. To calculate the interest amount, count the number of days and multiply that number by the annual rate of interest, multiply the result by the principal sum owing and divide by 365.)

Principal Sum Owing	Start Date	End Date (Date of Payment)	Number of Days	Rate	Interest Amount

TOTAL B $ _____

Principal Sum Owing (Total A above) $ _____

Total Interest Amount (Total B above) $ _____

SIGN JUDGMENT FOR $ _____

PART C — POSTJUDGMENT INTEREST AND COSTS

1. Postjudgment interest

The plaintiff is entitled to postjudgment interest at the rate of . . . . per cent per year,

[ ] under the *Courts of Justice Act*, as claimed in the statement of claim.

OR

[ ] in accordance with the claim made in the statement of claim.

2. Costs

The plaintiff wishes costs to be,

[ ] fixed by the local registrar.

OR

[ ] assessed by an assessment officer.

Date _____   _____

(Signature of plaintiff's lawyer or plaintiff)

(Name, address and telephone number of plaintiff's lawyer or plaintiff)

RCP-E 19D (July 1, 2007)

FORM 22A

Courts of Justice Act

SPECIAL CASE

(General heading)

SPECIAL CASE

THE FOLLOWING CASE is stated for the opinion of the court:

1. *(Set out, in consecutively numbered paragraphs, the material facts of the case, as agreed on by the parties, that are necessary to enable the court to determine the questions stated. Refer to and include a copy of any relevant documents.)*

THE QUESTIONS for the opinion of the court are:

1. *(Set out the questions in consecutively numbered paragraphs.)*

THE RELIEF SOUGHT on the determination of the questions stated is:

1. *(Set out the relief sought, as agreed on by the parties, in respect of each possible answer to each of the questions stated, in a form that could readily be incorporated into an order.)*

(Date)   *(Signature of all lawyers or parties in the proceeding)*
(Names, addresses and telephone numbers of all lawyers or parties in the proceeding)

RCP-E 22A (July 1, 2007)

FORM 23A

Courts of Justice Act

NOTICE OF DISCONTINUANCE

(General heading)

NOTICE OF DISCONTINUANCE

The plaintiff wholly discontinues this action. *(Where applicable, add* against the defendant *(name).)*

(Or The plaintiff discontinues that part of this action relating to . . . . *Where applicable, add* against the defendant *(name).)*

(Date)   *(Name, address and telephone number of*
                                plaintiff's lawyer or plaintiff)

TO *(Name and address of defendant's lawyer or defendant)*

NOTE: If there is a counterclaim, the defendant should consider rule 23.02, under which the counterclaim may be deemed to be discontinued.

NOTE: If there is a crossclaim or third party claim, the defendant should consider rule 23.03, under which the crossclaim or third party claim may be deemed to be dismissed.

RCP-E 23A (July 1, 2007)

FORM 23B

Courts of Justice Act

NOTICE OF ELECTION TO PROCEED WITH COUNTERCLAIM

(General heading)

NOTICE OF ELECTION

The defendant elects to proceed with the counterclaim in this action.

(Date)   *(Name, address and telephone number of defendant's lawyer or defendant)*

TO *(Name and address of plaintiff's lawyer or plaintiff)*

RCP-E 23B (July 1, 2007)

FORM 23C

Courts of Justice Act

NOTICE OF WITHDRAWAL OF DEFENCE

(General heading)

NOTICE OF WITHDRAWAL

The defendant withdraws the statement of defence in this action.

(Or The defendant withdraws paragraphs . . . . of the statement of defence in this action.)

(Date)   *(Name, address and telephone number of defendant's lawyer or defendant)*

TO *(Name and address of plaintiff's lawyer or plaintiff)*

RCP-E 23C (July 1, 2007)

FORM 24.1A

Courts of Justice Act

(General heading)

NOTICE OF NAME OF MEDIATOR AND DATE OF SESSION

TO: MEDIATION CO-ORDINATOR

1. I certify that I have consulted with the parties and that the parties have chosen the following mediator for the mediation session required by Rule 24.1: *(name)*

2. The mediator is named in the list of mediators for *(name county).*

(or)

2. The mediator is not named in a list of mediators, but has been chosen by the parties under clause 24.1.08 (2) (c).

3. The mediation session will take place on *(date).*

(Date)   *(Name, address, telephone number and fax number of plaintiff's lawyer or of plaintiff)*

RCP-E 24.1A (April 11, 2012)

399

FORM 24.1B

Courts of Justice Act

(General heading)

NOTICE BY ASSIGNED MEDIATOR

TO:

AND TO:

The notice of name of mediator and date of session (Form 24.1A) required by rule 24.1.09 of the Rules of Civil Procedure has not been filed in this action. Accordingly, the mediation co-ordinator has assigned me to conduct the mediation session under Rule 24.1. I am a mediator named in the list of mediators for *(name county)*.

The mediation session will take place on *(date)*, from *(time)* to *(time)*, at *(place)*.

Unless the court orders otherwise, you are required to attend this mediation session. If you have a lawyer representing you in this action, he or she is also required to attend.

You are required to file a statement of issues (Form 24.1C) by *(date)* (seven days before the mediation session). A blank copy of the form is attached.

When you attend the mediation session, you should bring with you any documents that you consider of central importance in the action. You should plan to remain throughout the scheduled time. If you need another person's approval before agreeing to a settlement, you should make arrangements before the mediation session to ensure that you have ready telephone access to that person throughout the session, even outside regular business hours.

YOU MAY BE PENALIZED UNDER RULE 24.1.13 IF YOU FAIL TO FILE A STATEMENT OF ISSUES OR FAIL TO ATTEND THE MEDIATION SESSION.

(Date)   *(Name, address, telephone number and fax*
                                            number of mediator)

cc. Mediation co-ordinator

RCP-E 24.1B (November 1, 2005)

FORM 24.1C

Courts of Justice Act

(General heading)

STATEMENT OF ISSUES

(To be provided to mediator and parties at least seven days before the mediation session)

<u>1. Factual and legal issues in dispute</u>

The plaintiff *(or* defendant*)* states that the following factual and legal issues are in dispute and remain to be resolved.

(Issues should be stated briefly and numbered consecutively.)

<u>2. Party's position and interests (what the party hopes to achieve)</u>

(Brief summary.)

<u>3. Attached documents</u>

Attached to this form are the following documents that the plaintiff *(or* defendant*)* considers of central importance in the action: *(list)*

  (Date)   *(party's signature)*

                                      (Name, address, telephone number and fax number of lawyer of party filing statement of issues, or of party)

NOTE: When the plaintiff provides a copy of this form to the mediator, a copy of the pleadings shall also be included.

NOTE: Rule 24.1.14 provides as follows:

> All communications at a mediation session and the mediator's notes and records shall be deemed to be without prejudice settlement discussions.

RCP-E 24.1C (November 1, 2005)

FORM 24.1D

Courts of Justice Act

(General heading)

CERTIFICATE OF NON-COMPLIANCE

TO: MEDIATION CO-ORDINATOR

I, *(name)*, mediator, certify that this certificate of non-compliance is filed because:

( )   *(Identify party(ies))* failed to provide a copy of a statement of issues to the mediator and the other parties *(or* to the mediator *or* to *party(ies))*.

( )   *(Identify plaintiff)* failed to provide a copy of the pleadings to the mediator.

( )   *(Identify party(ies))* failed to attend within the first 30 minutes of a scheduled mediation session.

(Date)   *(Name, address, telephone number and fax number, if any, of mediator)*

RCP-E 24.1D (November 1, 2005)

FORM 25A

Courts of Justice Act

REPLY

(General heading)

REPLY

1. The plaintiff admits the allegations contained in paragraphs . . . . of the statement of defence.

2. The plaintiff denies the allegations contained in paragraphs . . . . of the statement of defence.

3. The plaintiff has no knowledge in respect of the allegations contained in paragraphs . . . . of the statement of defence.

4. *(Set out in separate, consecutively numbered paragraphs each allegation of material fact relied on by way of reply to the statement of defence.)*

  (Date)   *(Name, address and telephone number of plaintiff's lawyer or plaintiff)*

TO *(Name and address of defendant's lawyer or defendant)*

RCP-E 25A (July 1, 2007)

FORM 27A

Courts of Justice Act

COUNTERCLAIM (AGAINST PARTIES TO MAIN ACTION ONLY)

(Where the counterclaim includes as a defendant to the counterclaim a person who is not already a party to the main action, use Form 27B.)

(Include the counterclaim in the same document as the statement of defence, and entitle the document STATEMENT OF DEFENCE AND COUNTERCLAIM. *The counterclaim is to follow the last paragraph of the statement of defence. Number the paragraphs in sequence commencing with the number following the number of the last paragraph of the statement of defence.)*

COUNTERCLAIM

The defendant *(name if more than one defendant)* claims: *(State here the precise relief claimed.)*

(Then set out in separate, consecutively numbered paragraphs each allegation of material fact relied on to substantiate the counterclaim.)

(Where the defendant to the counterclaim is sued in a capacity other than that in which the defendant is a party to the main action, set out the capacity.)

 (Date)   *(Name, address and telephone number of plaintiff's lawyer or plaintiff)*

TO *(Name and address of lawyer for defendant to the counterclaim or of defendant to the counterclaim)*

RCP-E 27A (July 1, 2007)

FORM 27B

Courts of Justice Act

COUNTERCLAIM (AGAINST PLAINTIFF AND PERSON NOT ALREADY PARTY TO MAIN ACTION)

(Where all defendants to the counterclaim are already parties to the main action, use Form 27A.)

(General heading)

(Add a second title of proceeding, as follows:)

AND BETWEEN:

(name)

(Court seal)

Plaintiff by
counterclaim

and

(name)

Defendants to
the counterclaim

STATEMENT OF DEFENCE AND COUNTERCLAIM

TO THE DEFENDANTS TO THE COUNTERCLAIM

A LEGAL PROCEEDING has been commenced against you by way of a counterclaim in an action in this court. The claim made against you is set out in the following pages.

IF YOU WISH TO DEFEND THIS COUNTERCLAIM, you or an Ontario lawyer acting for you must prepare a defence to counterclaim in Form 27C prescribed by the Rules of Civil Procedure, serve it on the plaintiff by counterclaim's lawyer or, where the plaintiff by counterclaim does not have a lawyer, serve it on the plaintiff by counterclaim, and file it, with proof of service, in this court, WITHIN TWENTY DAYS after this statement of defence and counterclaim is served on you.

If you are not already a party to the main action and you are served in another province or territory of Canada or in the United States of America, the period for serving and filing your defence is forty days. If you are served outside Canada and the United States of America, the period is sixty days.

If you are not already a party to the main action, instead of serving and filing a defence to counterclaim, you may serve and file a notice of intent to defend in Form 18B prescribed by the Rules of Civil Procedure. This will entitle you to ten more days within which to serve and file your defence to counterclaim.

IF YOU FAIL TO DEFEND THIS COUNTERCLAIM, JUDGMENT MAY BE GIVEN AGAINST YOU IN YOUR ABSENCE AND WITHOUT FURTHER NOTICE TO YOU. IF YOU WISH TO DEFEND THIS PROCEEDING BUT ARE UNABLE TO PAY LEGAL FEES,

LEGAL AID MAY BE AVAILABLE TO YOU BY CONTACTING A LOCAL LEGAL AID OFFICE.

(Where the counterclaim is for money only, include the following:)

IF YOU PAY THE AMOUNT OF THE COUNTERCLAIM AGAINST YOU, and $ . . . . for costs, within the time for serving and filing your defence to counterclaim, you may move to have the counterclaim against you dismissed by the court. If you believe the amount claimed for costs is excessive, you may pay the amount of the counterclaim and $400 for costs and have the costs assessed by the court.

Date _____   Issued by   _____

                                         Local registrar

                            Address of   _____
                            court office

                                                _____

TO   *(Name and address of defendant to the counterclaim who is not already a party to the main action)*
      (Name and address of lawyer for other defendant to the counterclaim or of other defendant to the counterclaim)

(The counterclaim is to follow the last paragraph of the statement of defence. Number the paragraphs in sequence commencing with the number following the number of the last paragraph of the statement of defence.)

COUNTERCLAIM

The defendant *(name if more than one defendant)* claims: *(State here the precise relief claimed.)*

(Then set out in separate, consecutively numbered paragraphs each allegation of material fact relied on to substantiate the counterclaim.)

(Where a defendant to the counterclaim who is not already a party to the main action is to be served outside Ontario without a court order, set out the facts and the specific provisions of Rule 17 relied on in support of such service.)

 (Date of issue)   *(Name, address and telephone number of plaintiff by counterclaim's lawyer or plaintiff by counterclaim)*

                                                          RCP-E 27B (July 1, 2007)

FORM 27C

Courts of Justice Act

DEFENCE TO COUNTERCLAIM

(General heading, including second title of proceeding, if required)

(A plaintiff who delivers a reply in the main action must include the defense to counterclaim in the same document as the reply, and the document is to be entitled REPLY AND DEFENCE TO COUNTERCLAIM. *The defense to counterclaim is to follow immediately after the last paragraph of the reply and the paragraphs are to be numbered in sequence commencing with the number following the number of the last paragraph of the reply.)*

DEFENCE TO COUNTERCLAIM

1. The defendant to the counterclaim admits the allegations contained in paragraphs . . . . of the counterclaim.

2. The defendant to the counterclaim denies the allegations contained in paragraphs . . . . the counterclaim.

3. The defendant to the counterclaim has no knowledge in respect of the allegations contained in paragraphs . . . . of the counterclaim.

4. *(Set out in separate, consecutively numbered paragraphs each allegation of material fact relied on by way of defence to the counterclaim.)*

(Date)   *(Name, address and telephone number of lawyer for defendant counterclaim or plaintiff by counterclaim)*

TO *(Name and address of plaintiff by counterclaim's lawyer or of plaintiff by counterclaim)*

RCP-E 27C (July 1, 2007)

FORM 27D

Courts of Justice Act

REPLY TO DEFENCE TO COUNTERCLAIM

(General heading, including second title of proceeding, if required)

REPLY TO DEFENCE TO COUNTERCLAIM

1. The plaintiff by counterclaim admits the allegations contained in paragraphs . . . . of the defence to counterclaim.

2. The plaintiff by counterclaim denies the allegations contained in paragraphs . . . . of the defence to counterclaim.

3. The plaintiff by counterclaim has no knowledge in respect of the allegations contained paragraphs . . . . of the defence to counterclaim.

4. *(Set out in separate, consecutively numbered paragraphs each allegation of material fact relied on by way of reply to the defence to counterclaim.)*

(Date of issue)   *(Name, address and telephone number of plaintiff by counterclaim's lawyer or plaintiff by counterclaim)*

TO *(Name and address of lawyer for the defendant to the counterclaim or defendant to the counterclaim)*

RCP-E 27D (July 1, 2007)

FORM 28A

Courts of Justice Act

CROSSCLAIM

(Include the crossclaim in the same document as the statement of defence, and entitle the document STATEMENT OF DEFENCE AND CROSSCLAIM. The crossclaim is to follow the last paragraph of the statement of defence. Number the paragraphs in sequence commencing with the number following the number of the last paragraph of the statement of defence.)

CROSSCLAIM

The defendant *(name)* claims against the defendant *(name): (State here the precise relief claimed.)*

(Then set out in separate, consecutively numbered paragraphs each allegation of material fact relied on to substantiate the crossclaim.)

(Where a defendant to the crossclaim is sued in a capacity other than that in which the defendant is a party to the main action, set out the capacity. Where the statement of defence and crossclaim is to be served outside Ontario without a court order, include the facts and the specific provisions of Rule 17 relied on in support of such service.)

(Date)   *(Name, address and telephone number of cross-claiming defendant lawyer or crossclaiming defendant)*

TO *(Name and address of defendant to crossclaim's lawyer or defendant to crossclaim)*

RCP-E 28A (July 1, 2007)

FORM 28B

Courts of Justice Act

DEFENCE TO CROSSCLAIM

(General heading)

DEFENCE TO CROSSCLAIM

1. The defendant *(name)* admits the allegations contained in paragraphs
. . . . of the cross claim.

2. The defendant *(name)* denies the allegations contained in paragraphs
. . . . of the cross claim.

3. The defendant *(name)* has no knowledge in respect of the allegations contained in paragraphs . . . . of the cross claim.

4. *(Set out in separate, consecutively numbered paragraphs each allegation of material fact relied on by way of defence to the cross claim.)*

(Date)   *(Name, address and telephone number of defendant of cross claim's lawyer or defendant to cross claims)*

TO *(Name and address of cross claiming defendant's lawyer or cross claiming defendant)*

RCP-E 28B (July 1, 2007)

FORM 28C

Courts of Justice Act

REPLY TO DEFENCE TO CROSSCLAIM

(General heading)

REPLY TO DEFENCE TO CROSSCLAIM

1. The defendant *(name)* admits the allegations contained in paragraphs . . . . of the defence to crossclaim.

2. The defendant *(name)* denies the allegations contained in paragraphs . . . . of the defence to crossclaim.

3. The defendant *(name)* has no knowledge in respect of the allegations contained in paragraphs . . . . of the defence to crossclaim.

4. *(Set out in separate, consecutively numbered paragraphs each allegation of material fact relied on by way of reply to the defence to crossclaim.)*

(Date)   *(Name, address and telephone number of cross-claiming defendant's lawyer or crossclaiming defendant)*

TO *(Name and address of defendant to crossclaim's lawyer or defendant to crossclaim)*

RCP-E 28C (July 1, 2007)

411

FORM 29A

Courts of Justice Act

THIRD PARTY CLAIM

(Court file no.)

ONTARIO

SUPERIOR COURT OF JUSTICE

BETWEEN:

(name)

Plaintiff

and

(Court seal)

(name)

Defendant

and

(name)

Third Party

THIRD PARTY CLAIM

TO THE THIRD PARTY

A LEGAL PROCEEDING HAS BEEN COMMENCED AGAINST YOU by way of a third party claim in an action in this court.

The action was commenced by the plaintiff against the defendant for the relief claimed in the statement of claim served with this third party claim. The defendant has defended the action on the grounds set out in the statement of defence served with this third party claim. The defendant's claim against you is set out in the following pages.

IF YOU WISH TO DEFEND THIS THIRD PARTY CLAIM, you or an Ontario lawyer acting for you must prepare a third party defence in Form 29B prescribed by the Rules of Civil Procedure, serve it on the lawyers for the other parties or, where a party does not have a lawyer, serve it on the party, and file it, with proof of service, WITHIN TWENTY DAYS after this third party claim is served on you, if you are served in Ontario.

If you are served in another province or territory of Canada or in the United States of America, the period for serving and filing your third party defence is forty days. If you are served outside Canada and the United States of America, the period is sixty days.

Instead of serving and filing a third party defence, you may serve and file a notice of intent to defend in Form 18B prescribed by the Rules of Civil Procedure. This will entitle you to ten more days within which to serve and file your third party defence.

YOU MAY ALSO DEFEND the action by the plaintiff against the defendant by serving and filing a statement of defence within the time for serving and filing your third party defence.

IF YOU FAIL TO DEFEND THIS THIRD PARTY CLAIM, JUDGMENT MAY BE GIVEN AGAINST YOU IN YOUR ABSENCE AND WITHOUT FURTHER NOTICE TO YOU. IF YOU WISH TO DEFEND THIS PROCEEDING BUT ARE UNABLE TO PAY LEGAL FEES, LEGAL AID MAY BE AVAILABLE TO YOU BY CONTACTING A LOCAL LEGAL AID OFFICE.

(Where the third party claim is for money only, include the following:)

IF YOU PAY THE AMOUNT OF THE THIRD PARTY CLAIM AGAINST YOU, and $
. . . . for costs, within the time for serving and filing your third party defence, you may move to have the third party claim dismissed by the court. If you believe the amount claimed for costs is excessive, you may pay the amount of the third party claim and $400 for costs and have the costs assessed by the court.

Date _____   Issued by _____
                                                                        Local registrar

                                          Address of _____
                                          court office

                                                      _____

TO *(Name and address of third party)*

CLAIM

1. The defendant claims against the third party: *(State here the precise relief claimed.)*

(Then set out in separate, consecutively numbered paragraphs each allegation of material fact relied on to substantiate the third party claim.)

(Where the third party claim is to be served outside Ontario without a court order, set out the facts and the specific provisions of Rule 17 relied on in support of such service.)

(Date of issue)   *(Name, address and telephone number of defendant's lawyer or defendant)*

RCP-E 29A (July 1, 2007)

413

FORM 29B

Courts of Justice Act

THIRD PARTY DEFENCE

(General heading, with title of proceeding in accordance with Form 29A)

THIRD PARTY DEFENCE

1. The third party admits the allegations contained in paragraphs . . . . of the third party claim.

2. The third party denies the allegations contained in paragraphs . . . . of the third party claim.

3. The third party has no knowledge in respect of the allegations contained in paragraphs . . . . third party claim.

4. *(Set out in separate, consecutively numbered* paragraphs *each allegation of material fact relied on by way of defence to the third party claim.)*

(Date)   *(Name, address and telephone number of third party's lawyer or third party)*

TO *(Name and address of defendant's lawyer or defendant)*

RCP-E 29B (July 1, 2007)

FORM 29C

Courts of Justice Act

REPLY TO THIRD PARTY DEFENCE

(General heading, with title of proceeding in accordance with Form 29A)

REPLY TO THIRD PARTY DEFENCE

1. The defendant admits the allegations contained in paragraphs . . . . of the third party defence.

2. The defendant denies the allegations contained in paragraphs . . . . of the third party defence.

3. The defendant has no knowledge in respect of the allegations contained in paragraphs . . . . of the third party defence.

4. *(Set out in separate, consecutively numbered paragraphs each allegation of material fact relied on by way of reply to the third party defence.)*

(Date)   *(Name, address and telephone number of defen-*
                            dant's lawyer or defendant)

TO *(Name and address of third party's lawyer or third party)*

RCP-E 29C (July 1, 2007)

415

FORM 30A

Courts of Justice Act

AFFIDAVIT OF DOCUMENTS (INDIVIDUAL)

(General heading)

AFFIDAVIT OF DOCUMENTS

I, *(full name of deponent)*, of the (City, Town, *etc.)* of . . . . , in the (County, Regional Municipality, *etc.)* of . . . . the plaintiff *(or as may be)* in this action, MAKE OATH AND SAY *(or* AFFIRM*):*

1. I have conducted a diligent search of my records and have made appropriate enquiries of others to inform myself in order to make this affidavit. This affidavit discloses, to the full extent of my knowledge, information and belief, all documents relevant to any matter in issue in this action that are or have been in my possession, control or power.

2. I have listed in Schedule A those documents that are in my possession, control or power and that I do not object to producing for inspection.

3. I have listed in Schedule B those documents that are or were in my possession, control or power and that I object to producing because I claim they are privileged, and I have stated in Schedule B the grounds for each such claim.

4. I have listed in Schedule C those documents that were formerly in my possession, control or power but are no longer in my possession, control or power, and I have stated in Schedule C when and how I lost possession or control of or power over them and their present location.

5. I have never had in my possession, control or power any document relevant to any matter in issue in this action other than those listed in Schedules A, B and C.

6. I have listed in Schedule D the names and addresses of persons who might reasonably be expected to have knowledge of transactions or occurrences in issue. *(Strike out this paragraph if the action is not being brought under the simplified procedure.)*

SWORN *(etc.)*

. . . .

(Signature of deponent)

LAWYER'S CERTIFICATE

I CERTIFY that I have explained to the deponent,

(a) the necessity of making full disclosure of all documents relevant to any matter in issue in the action;

(b) what kinds of documents are likely to be relevant to the allegations made in the pleadings; and

(c) if the action is brought under the simplified procedure, the necessity of providing the list required under rule 76.03.

(Date) _____   _____

(Signature of lawyer)

416

Schedule A

Documents in my possession, control or power that I do not object to producing for inspection.

(Number each document consecutively. Set out the nature and date of the document and other particulars sufficient to identify it.)

Schedule B

Documents that are or were in my possession, control or power that I object to producing on the grounds of privilege.

(Number each document consecutively. Set out the nature and date of the document and other particulars sufficient to identify it.State the grounds for claiming privilege for each document.)

Schedule C

Documents that were formerly in my possession, control or power but are no longer in my possession, control or power.

(Number each document consecutively. Set out the nature and date of the document and other particulars sufficient to identify it. State when and how possession or control of or power over each document was lost, and give the present location of each document.)

Schedule D

(To be filled in only if the action is being brought under the simplified procedure.)

Names and addresses of persons who might reasonably be expected to have knowledge of transactions or occurrences in issue.

RCP-E 30A (November 1, 2008)

417

FORM 30B

Courts of Justice Act

AFFIDAVIT OF DOCUMENTS (CORPORATION OR PARTNERSHIP)

(General heading)

AFFIDAVIT OF DOCUMENTS

I, *(full name of deponent)*, of the *(City, Town, etc.)* of . . . . , in the *(County, Regional Municipality, etc.)* of . . . . , MAKE OATH AND SAY (or AFFIRM):

1. I am the *(state the position held by the deponent in the corporation or partnership)* of the plaintiff *(or as may be)*, which is a corporation *(or* partnership).

2. I have conducted a diligent search of the corporation's *(or* partnership's) records and made appropriate enquiries of others to inform myself in order to make this affidavit. This affidavit discloses, to the full extent of my knowledge, information and belief, all documents relevant to any matter in issue in this action that are or have been in the possession, control or power of the corporation *(or* partnership).

3. I have listed in Schedule A those documents that are in the possession, control or power of the corporation *(or* partnership) and that it does not object to producing for inspection.

4. I have listed in Schedule B those documents that are or were in the possession, control or power of the corporation *(or* partnership) and that it objects to producing because it claims they are privileged, and I have stated in Schedule B the grounds for each such claim.

5. I have listed in Schedule C those documents that were formerly in the possession, control or power of the corporation *(or* partnership) but are no longer in its possession, control or power and I have stated in Schedule C when and how it lost possession or control of or power over them and their present location.

6. The corporation *(or* partnership) has never had in its possession, control or power any documents relevant to any matter in issue in this action other than those listed in Schedules A, B and C.

7. I have listed in Schedule D the names and addresses of persons who might reasonably be expected to have knowledge of transactions or occurrences in issue. *(Strike out this paragraph if the action is not being brought under the simplified procedure.)*

SWORN *(etc.)*

. . . .

(Signature of deponent)

LAWYER'S CERTIFICATE

I CERTIFY that I have explained to the deponent,

(a)   the necessity of making full disclosure of all documents relevant to any matter in issue in the action;

(b)   what kinds of documents are likely to be relevant to the allegations made in the pleadings; and

(c)   if the action is brought under the simplified procedure, the necessity of providing the list required under rule 76.03.

(Date) _____   _____

(Signature of lawyer)

Schedule A

Documents in the corporation's *(or* partnership's*)* possession, control or power that it does not object to producing for inspection.

(Number each document consecutively. Set out the nature and date of the document and other particulars sufficient to identify it.)

Schedule B

Documents that are or were in the corporation's *(or* partnership's*)* possession, control or power that it objects to producing on the grounds of privilege.

(Number each document consecutively. Set out the nature and date of the document and other particulars sufficient to identify it. State the grounds for claiming privilege for each document.)

Schedule C

Documents that were formerly in the corporation's *(or* partnership's*)* possession, control or power but are no longer in its possession, control or power.

(Number each document consecutively. Set out the nature and date of the document and other particulars sufficient to identify it. State when and how possession or control of or power over each document was lost, and give the present location of each document.)

Schedule D

(To be filled in only if the action is being brought under the simplified procedure.)

Names and addresses of persons who might reasonably be expected to have knowledge of transactions or occurrences in issue.

RCP-E 30B (November 1, 2008)

FORM 30C

Courts of Justice Act

REQUEST TO INSPECT DOCUMENTS

(General heading)

REQUEST TO INSPECT DOCUMENTS

You are requested to produce for inspection all the documents listed in Schedule A of your affidavit of documents *(or* the following documents referred to in your *(identify pleading or affidavit):)*

(Date)   *(Name, address and telephone number of requesting lawyer or party)*

TO *(Name and address of lawyer or party requested to produce)*

RCP-E 30C (July 1, 2007)

FORM 34A

Courts of Justice Act

NOTICE OF EXAMINATION

(To be used only for a party to the proceeding, a person to be examined for discovery or in aid of execution on behalf or in place of a party or a person to be cross-examined on an affidavit. For the examination of any other person, use a summons to witness (Form 34B).)

(General heading)

NOTICE OF EXAMINATION

TO *(Name of person to be examined)*

YOU ARE REQUIRED TO ATTEND, on *(day)*, *(date)*, at *(time)*, at the office of *(name, address and telephone number of examiner)*, for *(choose one of the following):*

[ ]   Cross-examination on your affidavit dated *(date)*

[ ]   Examination for discovery

[ ]   Examination for discovery on behalf of or in place of *(identify party)*

[ ]   Examination in aid of execution

[ ]   Examination in aid of execution on behalf of or in place of *(identify party)*

(Examination for discovery of a party or a person examined on behalf or in place of a party)

YOU ARE REQUIRED TO BRING WITH YOU and produce at the examination the documents mentioned in subrule 30.04 (4) of the Rules of Civil Procedure, and the following documents and things: *(Set out the nature and date of each document and give particulars sufficient to identify each document and thing.)*

(Other examinations)

YOU ARE REQUIRED TO BRING WITH YOU and produce at the examination the following documents and things: *(Set out the nature and date of each document and give particulars sufficient to identify each document and thing.)*

(Date)   *(Name, address and telephone number of examining lawyer or party)*

TO *(Name and address of lawyer or of person to be examined)*

RCP-E 34A (July 1, 2007)

421

FORM 34B

Courts of Justice Act

SUMMONS TO WITNESS (EXAMINATION OUT OF COURT)

(General heading)

(Court seal)

SUMMONS TO WITNESS

TO *(Name and address of person to be examined)*

YOU ARE REQUIRED TO ATTEND, on *(day)*, *(date)*, at *(time)*, at the office of *(name, address and telephone number of examiner)*, for *(choose one of the following):*

[ ]   Cross-examination on your affidavit dated *(date)*

[ ]   Examination for discovery with leave of the court

[ ]   Examination out of court as witness before hearing

[ ]   Examination in aid of execution

[ ]   Taking evidence before trial

YOU ARE REQUIRED TO BRING WITH YOU and produce at the examination the following documents and things: *(Set out the nature and date of each document and give particulars sufficient to identify each document and thing.)*

ATTENDANCE MONEY for . . . . . . day(s) of attendance is served with this summons, calculated in accordance with Tariff A of the Rules of Civil Procedure, as follows:

Attendance allowance of $ _____ daily $ _____

Travel allowance $ _____

Overnight accommodation and meal $ _____
allowance

TOTAL   _____

  $ _____

If further attendance is required, you will be entitled to additional attendance money.

IF YOU FAIL TO ATTEND OR REMAIN UNTIL THE END OF THIS EXAMINATION, YOU MAY BE COMPELLED TO ATTEND AT YOUR OWN EXPENSE AND YOU MAY BE FOUND IN CONTEMPT OF COURT.

Date _____   Issued by _____

                                               Local registrar

                                  Address of   _____
                                  court office

                                                 _____

This summons was issued at the request of, and inquires my be directed to:

(Name, address and telephone number of examining lawyer or party)

RCP-E 34B (July 1, 2007)

FORM 34C

Courts of Justice Act

COMMISSION

(General heading)

(Court seal)

COMMISSION

TO *(Name and address of commissioner)*

YOU HAVE BEEN APPOINTED A COMMISSIONER for the purpose of taking evidence in this proceeding now pending in this court by order of the court made on *(date)*, a copy of which is attached.

YOU ARE GIVEN FULL AUTHORITY to do all things necessary for taking the evidence mentioned in the order authorizing this commission. *(Where the commission is issued under Rule 36, add:* You are also authorized, on consent of the parties, to take the evidence of any other witnesses who may be found in *(name of province, state or country).)*

You are to send to this court a transcript of the evidence taken, together with this commission, forthwith after the transcript is completed.

In carrying out this commission, you are to follow the terms of the attached order and the instructions contained in this commission.

THIS COMMISSION is signed and sealed by order of the court.

Date _____   Issued by   _____
                                               Local registrar

                                 Address of   _____
                                 court office

                                               _____

The registrar is to attach to this commission a copy of Rules 34 and 36 and section 45 of the Evidence Act.

INSTRUCTIONS TO COMMISSIONER

1. This commission is to be conducted in accordance with Rules 34 and 36 of the Ontario Rules of Civil Procedure, a copy of which is attached, to the extent that it is possible to do so. The law of Ontario applies to the taking of the evidence.

2. Before acting on this commission, you must take the oath *(or* affirmation) set out below. You may do so before any person authorized by section 45 of the *Evidence Act* of Ontario, a copy of which is attached, to take affidavits or administer oaths or affirmations outside Ontario.

I, _____ , swear *(or* affirm) that I will, according to the best of my skill and knowledge, truly and faithfully and without partiality to any of the parties to this proceeding, take the evidence of every witness examined under this commission, and cause the evidence to be transcribed and forwarded to the court. *(In an oath, conclude:* So help me God.)

424

Sworn *(or* Affirmed*)* before
me at the
(City, Town, etc.) of _____
_____, in
the *(Province, State, etc.)* of

_____,

_____,

on *(date)*.

_____
(Signature of
commissioner)

_____
(Signature and office of per-
son before whom oath or af-
firmation is taken)

3. The examining party is required to give the person to be examined at least . . . . . . days notice of the examination and, where the order so provides, to pay attendance money to the person to be examined.

4. You must arrange to have the evidence before you recorded and transcribed. You are to administer the following oath *(or* affirmation*)* to the person who records and transcribes the evidence:

> You swear *(or* affirm*)* that you will truly and faithfully record and transcribe all questions put to all witnesses and their answers in accordance with the directions of the commissioner. *(In an oath, conclude:* So help you God.*)*

On consent of the parties, or where the order for this commission provides for it, the examination may be recorded by videotape or other similar means.

5. You are to administer the following oath *(or* affirmation*)* to each witness whose evidence is to be taken:

> You swear *(or* affirm*)* that the evidence to be given by you touching the matters in question between the parties to this proceeding shall be the truth, the whole truth, and nothing but the truth. *(In an oath, conclude:* So help you God.*)*

6. Where a witness does not understand the language or is deaf or mute, the evidence of the witness must be given through an interpreter. You are to administer the following oath *(or* affirmation*)* to the interpreter:

You swear *(or* affirm*)* that you understand the _____ language
and the language in which the examination is to be conducted and that you will
truly interpret the oath *(or* affirmation*)* to
the witness, all questions put to the witness and the answers of the witness, to
the best of your skill and understanding.
(In an oath, conclude: So help you God.)

7. You are to attach to this commission the transcript of the evidence and the exhibits, and any videotape or other recording of the examination. You are to complete the certificate set out be-low, and mail this commission, the transcript, the exhibits and any videotape or other recording of the examination to the office of the court where the commission was issued. You are to keep a copy of the transcript and, where practicable, a copy of the exhibits until the court disposes of this proceeding. Forthwith after you mail this commission and the accompanying material to the court office, you are to notify the parties who appeared at the examination that you have done so.

CERTIFICATE OF COMMISSIONER
I, _____, certify that:
1. I administered the proper oath *(or* affirmation*)* to her person who recorded and transcribed the evidence, to the wit-ness the transcript of whose evidence is attached and to any interpreter through whom the evidence was given.
2. The evidence of the witness was properly taken.
3. The evidence of the witness was ac-curately transcribed.
Date _____ _____

*(Signature of
commissioner)*

RCP-E 34C (November 1, 2005)

FORM 34D

Courts of Justice Act

LETTER OF REQUEST

(General heading)

(Court seal)

LETTER OF REQUEST

TO THE JUDICIAL AUTHORITIES OF *(name of province, state or country)*

A PROCEEDING IS PENDING IN THIS COURT at the *(City, Town, etc.)* of . . . . , in the Province of Ontario, Canada, between *(name)*, plaintiff *(or as may be)*, and *(name)*, defendant *(or as may be)*.

IT HAS BEEN SHOWN TO THIS COURT that it appears necessary for the purpose of justice that a witness residing within your jurisdiction be examined there.

THIS COURT HAS ISSUED A COMMISSION to *(name of commissioner)* of *(address of commissioner)*, providing for the examination of the witness *(name of witness)*, of *(address of witness)*.

YOU ARE REQUESTED, in furtherance of justice, to cause *(name of witness) (where the commission was issued under Rule 36, add* and, on consent of the parties, any other witnesses who may be found in your jurisdiction*)* to appear before the commissioner by the means ordinarily used in your jurisdiction, if necessary to secure attendance, and to answer questions under oath or affirmation *(where desired, add:)* and to bring to and produce at the examination the following documents and things: *(Set out the nature and date of each document and give particulars sufficient to identify each document and thing)*.

YOU ARE ALSO REQUESTED to permit the commissioner to conduct the examination of the witness in accordance with the law of evidence and Rules of Civil Procedure of Ontario and the commission issued by this court.

AND WHEN YOU REQUEST IT, the courts of Ontario are ready and willing to do the same for you in a similar case.

THIS LETTER OF REQUEST is signed and sealed by order of the court made on *(date)*.

Date _____   Issued by   _____

Local registrar

Address of   _____
court office

_____

RCP-E 34D (November 1, 2005)

FORM 34E

Courts of Justice Act

ORDER FOR COMMISSION AND LETTER OF REQUEST

(Court file no.)

(Court)

(Name of judge or officer)   *(Day and date order made)*

(Court seal)

(Title of proceeding)

ORDER

(Recitals in accordance with Form 59A)

1. THIS COURT ORDERS *(give particulars of any directions given by the court under rule 34.07).*

2. THIS COURT ORDERS that the registrar prepare and issue a commission naming *(name)*, of *(address)*, as commissioner to take the evidence of the witness *(name of witness)* in *(name of province, state or country) (where the order is made under Rule 36, add* and, on consent of the parties, any other witness who may be found there) for use at trial *(or* on examination for discovery, *etc.)*

3. THIS COURT ORDERS that the registrar prepare and issue a letter of request addressed to the judicial authorities of *(name of province, state or country)*, requesting the issuing of such process as is necessary to compel the witness *(or* witnesses) to attend and be examined before the commissioner.

(Signature of judge, officer or registrar)

RCP-E 34E (November 1, 2005)

FORM 35A

Courts of Justice Act

QUESTIONS ON WRITTEN EXAMINATION FOR DISCOVERY

(General heading)

QUESTIONS ON WRITTEN EXAMINATION FOR DISCOVERY

THE *(identify examining party)* has chosen to examine the *(identify person to be examined)* for discovery *(where the person is not a party, state whether the person is examined on behalf or in place of or in addition to a party or under a court order)* by written questions and requires that the following questions be answered by affidavit in Form 35B prescribed by the Rules of Civil Procedure, served within fifteen days after service of these questions.

(Where a further list of questions is served under rule 35.04 substitute:)

The *(identify examining party)* requires that the *(identify person to be examined)* answer the following further questions by affidavit in Form 35B prescribed by the Rules of Civil Procedure, served within fifteen days after service of these questions.

1. *(Number each question. Where the questions are a further list under rule 35.04, number the questions in sequence following the last question of the previous list.)*

(Date)   *(Name, address and telephone number of examining party's lawyer or examining party)*

TO *(Name and address of lawyer for person to be examined or of person to be examined)*

RCP-E 35A (July 1, 2007)

429

FORM 35B

Courts of Justice Act

ANSWERS ON WRITTEN EXAMINATION FOR DISCOVERY

(General heading)

ANSWERS ON WRITTEN EXAMINATION FOR DISCOVERY

I, *(full name of deponent)*, of the *(City, Town, etc.)* of . . . . , in the *(County, Regional Municipality, etc.)* of . . . . , the *(identify the capacity in which the deponent makes the affidavit)*, MAKE OATH AND SAY *(or* AFFIRM*)* that the following answers to the questions dated *(date)* submitted by the *(identify examining party)* are true, to the best of my knowledge, information and belief:

1. *(Number each answer to correspond with the question. Where the deponent objects to answering a question, state*: I object to answering this question on the ground that it is irrelevant to the matters in issue *or* that the information sought is privileged because *(specify) or as may be.)*

SWORN *(etc.)*

RCP-E 35B (November 1, 2005)

FORM 37A

Courts of Justice Act

NOTICE OF MOTION

(General heading)

NOTICE OF MOTION

The *(identify moving party)* will make a motion to the court *(or* judge) on *(day), (date),* at *(time),* or soon after that time as the motion can be heard, at *(address of court house).*

PROPOSED METHOD OF HEARING: The motion is to be heard *(choose appropriate option)*

☐ in writing under subrule 37.12.1 (1) because it is *(insert one of on* consent, unopposed *or* made without notice);

☐ in writing as an opposed motion under subrule 37.12.1 (4);

☐ orally.

THE MOTION IS FOR *(state here the precise relief sought).*

THE GROUNDS FOR THE MOTION ARE *(specify the grounds to be argued, including a reference to any statutory provision or rule to be relied on).*

THE FOLLOWING DOCUMENTARY EVIDENCE will be used at the hearing of the motion: *(list the affidavits or other documentary evidence to be relied on).*

(Date)   *(Name, address and telephone number of moving party's lawyer or moving party)*

TO   *(Name and address of responding party's lawyer or responding party)*

RCP-E37A (July 1, 2007)

431

FORM 37B

Courts of Justice Act

CONFIRMATION OF MOTION

(General heading)

CONFIRMATION OF MOTION

Part A:

I, ... *(name)*, lawyer for the moving party, confirm that the moving party has conferred or attempted to confer with the other party and confirm that the motion to be heard on . . . . *(date)* will proceed on the following basis:

[ ] for an adjournment on consent to . . . . *(date)*

[ ] for a contested adjournment to . . . . *(date)*, for the following reason: *(specify who is requesting the adjournment and why, and who is opposing it and why)*

[ ] for a consent order

[ ]for a hearing of all the issues

[ ] for a hearing of the following issues only *(specify)*

The presiding judge will be referred to the following materials: *(please be specific)*

I estimate that the time required for the motion, including costs submissions, will be. . . . . . minutes for the moving party*(ies)* and . . . . . . minutes for the responding party*(ies)* for a total of . . . . . . minutes.

(Date)

TO *(Name and address of responding party's lawyer or responding party)*

Part B:

I, ... *(name)*, [lawyer for] the responding party, confirm that the moving party served a notice of motion but failed to send a copy of the Confirmation of Motion (Form 37B) in accordance with Rule 37.10.1 (1)(b). I will appear on the motion date to seek costs. I estimate the time required for costs submissions will be . . . . . . minutes. I confirm that I have sent a copy of this form to the other party by fax or email in accordance with subrule 37.10.1(2.1)(b).

RCP-E 37B (January 1, 2019)

FORM 37C

Courts of Justice Act

REFUSALS AND UNDERTAKINGS CHART

(General heading)

REFUSALS AND UNDERTAKINGS CHART

REFUSALS					
Refusals to answer questions on the examination of.................. , dated.......................					
Issue & relationship to pleadings or affidavit *(Group the questions by issues.)*	**Question No.**	**Page No.**	**Specific question**	**Answer or precise basis for refusal**	**Disposition by the Court**
1.					
2.					
3.					

UNDERTAKINGS					
Outstanding undertakings given on the examination of.............. , dated.......................					
Issue & relationship to pleadings or affidavit *(Group the undertakings by issues.)*	**Question No.**	**Page No.**	**Specific undertaking**	**Date answered or precise reason for not doing so**	**Disposition by the Court**
1.					
2.					
3.					

(Date)   *(Name, address and telephone and fax numbers of the party filing the refusals and undertakings chart)*

RCP-E 37C (November 1, 2005)

FORM 38A

Courts of Justice Act

NOTICE OF APPEARANCE

(General heading)

NOTICE OF APPEARANCE

The respondent intends to respond to this application.

(Date)   *(Name, address and telephone number of re-*
                                              spondent's lawyer or respondent)

TO *(Name and address of applicant's lawyer or applicant)*

RCP-E 38A (July 1, 2007)

FORM 38B

Courts of Justice Act

CONFIRMATION OF APPLICATION

(General heading)

CONFIRMATION OF APPLICATION

I, ... *(name),* lawyer for the applicant confirm that the application to be heard on . . . . *(date)* will proceed on the following basis:

[ ] for an adjournment on consent to . . . . (date)

[ ] for a contested adjournment to . . . . *(date),* for the following reason: *(specify who is requesting the adjournment and why, and who is opposing it and why)*

[ ] for a consent order

[ ] for hearing of all the issues

[ ] for hearing of the following issues only *(specify)*

I estimate that the time required for the application will be: . . . . . . minutes for the applicant*(s)* and . . . . . . minutes for the respondent*(s)* for a total of . . . . . . minutes.

(Date)

TO *(Name and address of respondent's lawyer or respondent)*

RCP-E 38B (July 1, 2007)

FORM 42A

Courts of Justice Act

CERTIFICATE OF PENDING LITIGATION

(General heading)

(Court seal)

CERTIFICATE OF PENDING LITIGATION

I CERTIFY that in this proceeding an interest in the following land is in question:

(Set out a description of the land sufficient for registration. Where the land is registered under the Land Titles Act, *include the parcel number. Attach a schedule if necessary.)*

This certificate is issued under an order of the court made on *(date)*.

Date _____   Issued by   _____

                                                   Local registrar

                             Address of   _____
                             court office
                                            _____

RCP-E 42A (November 1, 2005)

FORM 43A

Courts of Justice Act

INTERPLEADER ORDER — GENERAL

(Court file no.)

(Court)

(Name of judge or officer)   *(Day and date order made)*

(Court seal)

(Title of Proceeding)

INTERPLEADER ORDER

(Where an interpleader application results in a judgment, amend the form accordingly.)

   (Recitals in accordance with Form 59A or 59B)

Payment of money into court

1. THIS COURT ORDERS that the *(identify party)* pay into court the sum of $ . . . . , less costs fixed at $ . . . . , to await the outcome of a proceeding in this court between *(identify parties)* *(or to await the outcome of this proceeding)*.

2. THIS COURT DECLARES that on compliance with paragraph 1 of this order, the liability of *(identify party)* in respect of the above sum is extinguished.

3. THIS COURT ORDERS *(include any other order made by the court under rule 43.04)*.

Sale of property and payment of proceeds into court

1. THIS COURT ORDERS that *(identify property)* be sold by *(method of sale)* and that the proceeds, less expenses of sale and the costs of *(identify party)* fixed at $ . . . . , be paid into court to await the outcome of a proceeding in this court between *(identify parties)* *(or to await the outcome of this proceeding)*.

2. THIS COURT DECLARES that on compliance with paragraph 1 of this order, the liability of *(identify party)* in respect of the above sum is extinguished.

3. THIS COURT ORDERS *(include any other order made by the court under rule 43.04)*.

Deposit of property with an officer of the court

1. THIS COURT ORDERS that *(identify property)* be deposited with the Sheriff of the *(county or district)* *(or as may be)* to await the outcome of a proceeding in this court between *(identify parties)* *(or to await the outcome of this proceeding)*.

2. THIS COURT DECLARES that on compliance with paragraph 1 of this order, the liability of *(identify party)* in respect of the above property is extinguished.

3. THIS COURT ORDERS *(include any other order made by the court under rule 43.04)*.

Trial of an issue

(This paragraph will normally form part of an order for payment into court or deposit of property with an officer of the court.)

4. THIS COURT ORDERS that there be a trial of the issue of *(give particulars of issue to be tried),* in which *(identify party)* shall be plaintiff and *(identify party)* shall be defendant.

5. THIS COURT ORDERS *(include any directions given by the court respecting pleadings, discovery and other matters).*

(Signature of judge, officer or local registrar)

RCP-E 43A (November 1, 2005)

FORM 44A

Courts of Justice Act

BOND — INTERIM RECOVERY OF PERSONAL PROPERTY

(General heading)

BOND

WE, *(identify party)* and *(name of surety)*, jointly and severally bind ourselves and our successors to the Sheriff of the *(county or district)* in the sum of $ . . . . if *(identify party)* fails to return *(identify property)* to *(identify opposite party)* without delay when ordered to do so, and to pay any damages and costs that *(identify opposite party)* has sustained by reason of the interim order for recovery of possession of the property.

Date _____

Witness _____   _____ *(seal)*

Signature of party

Witness _____   _____ *(seal)*

Signature of surety

RCP-E 44A (November 1, 2005)

FORM 47A

Courts of Justice Act

JURY NOTICE

(General heading)

JURY NOTICE

THE *(identify party)* REQUIRES that this action be tried *(or* that the issues of fact *or* that the damages in this action be assessed)* by a jury.

(Date)   *(Name, address and telephone number of law-*
                                          yer or party delivering notice)

TO *(Name and address of lawyer or party receiving notice)*

RCP-E 47A (July 1, 2007)

FORM 48C

Courts of Justice Act

STATUS NOTICE

(General heading)

STATUS NOTICE

TO THE PARTIES AND THEIR LAWYERS

MORE THAN TWO YEARS HAVE PASSED since a statement of defence in this action was filed. According to the records in the court office, this action has not been placed on the trial list or terminated.

THIS ACTION WILL BE DISMISSED FOR DELAY unless within ninety days after the service of this notice: (a) it is set down for trial; (b) it is terminated; or (c) a judge presiding at a status hearing orders otherwise.

A party may request the registrar to arrange a status hearing.

IF A STATUS HEARING is held, the plaintiff must show cause why the action should not be dismissed for delay, and the presiding judge may set time periods for the completion of the remaining steps necessary to have the action placed on a trial list and may order that it be placed on a trial list within a specified time, or may adjourn the status hearing to a specified date, or may dismiss the action for delay.

Date _____   Signed by _____

                                                          Local registrar

                              Address of   _____
                              court office

                                            _____

TO *(Names and addresses of all lawyers and parties acting in person)*

RCP-E 48C (July 1, 2007)

FORM 48C.1

Courts of Justice Act

STATUS NOTICE: ACTION NOT ON A TRIAL LIST

(General heading)

STATUS NOTICE: ACTION NOT ON A TRIAL LIST

TO THE PARTIES AND THEIR LAWYERS

1. According to the records in the court office:

    (a) more than 2 years have passed since a defence in this action was filed;

    (b) this action has not been placed on a trial list; and

    (c) this action has not been terminated by any means.

2. AS A RESULT, THIS ACTION SHALL BE DISMISSED FOR DELAY, with costs, unless within 90 days of service of this Notice,

    (a) the action is set down for trial;

    (b) the action is terminated by any means;

    (c) documents have been filed in accordance with subrule 48.14(10); or

    (d) a judge or case management master orders otherwise.

NOTE: A "defence" means a statement of defence, a notice of intent to defend, or a notice of motion in response to a proceeding, other than a motion challenging the court's jurisdiction.

NOTE: You may request that the registrar arrange a status hearing to show cause why the action should not be dismissed. Unless the presiding judge or case management master orders otherwise, a status hearing may be held in writing by filing, at least 7 days before the day of the hearing, a timetable signed by all the parties to the action that contains the information set out in subrule 48.14(11) and a draft order establishing the timetable.

NOTE: Unless the court orders otherwise, where the plaintiff is a party under a disability, an action may not be dismissed for delay under rule 48.14 unless the defendant gives notice to the Children's Lawyer or, if the Public Guardian and Trustee is litigation guardian of the plaintiff, to the Public Guardian and Trustee.

Date _____   Signed by   _____

                                                          Local registrar

                                         Address of   _____
                                         court office

                                                       _____

TO *(Names and addresses of all lawyers and parties acting in person)*

RCP-E 48C.1 (July 30, 2009)

FORM 48C.2

Courts of Justice Act

STATUS NOTICE: ACTION STRUCK FROM TRIAL LIST

(General heading)

STATUS NOTICE: ACTION STRUCK FROM TRIAL LIST

TO THE PARTIES AND THEIR LAWYERS

1. According to the records in the court office:

    (a)   this action was placed on a trial list and was subsequently struck off; and

    (b)   this action was not restored to the trial list within 180 days after being struck off.

2. AS A RESULT, THIS ACTION SHALL BE DISMISSED FOR DELAY, with costs, unless within 90 days of service of this Notice,

    (a)   the action is restored to a trial list;

    (b)   the action is terminated by any means;

    (c)   documents have been filed in accordance with subrule 48.14(10); or

    (d)   a judge or case management master orders otherwise.

NOTE: You may request that the registrar arrange a status hearing to show cause why the action should not be dismissed. Unless the presiding judge or case management master orders otherwise, a status hearing may be held in writing by filing, at least 7 days before the day of the hearing, a timetable signed by all the parties to the action that contains the information set out in subrule 48.14(11) and a draft order establishing the timetable.

NOTE: Unless the court orders otherwise, where the plaintiff is a party under a disability, an action may not be dismissed for delay under rule 48.14 unless the defendant gives notice to the Children's Lawyer or, if the Public Guardian and Trustee is litigation guardian of the plaintiff, to the Public Guardian and Trustee.

Date _____   Signed by   _____
                                                                      Local registrar

                                          Address of
                                          court office   _____

                                                                      _____

TO *(Names and addresses of all lawyers and parties acting in person)*

                                                            RCP-E 48C.2 (November 1, 2008)

FORM 48D

Courts of Justice Act

ORDER DISMISSING ACTION FOR DELAY

(General heading)

ORDER DISMISSING ACTION

The plaintiff has not *(give particulars of plaintiff's default under rule 48.14)* and has not cured the default.

IT IS ORDERED that this action be dismissed for delay.

Date _____ Signed by _____

Local registrar
(Address of court office)

NOTE: An order under rule 48.14 dismissing an action may be set aside under rule 37.14.

NOTE TO DEFENDANT(S) (AND OTHER PARTIES): When an order under rule 48.14 is made dismissing an action, rule 48.14(9) provides that any counterclaim, crossclaim or third party claim will be dismissed within 30 days thereafter in accordance with rules 24.03 and 24.04. Under rule 24.03, any counterclaim is deemed to be discontinued without costs unless the defendant delivers a notice of election to proceed with the counterclaim (Form 23B) within thirty days after the dismissal. Under rule 24.04(1) any crossclaim or third party claim made by a defendant is deemed to be dismissed, unless the court orders otherwise.

RCP-E 48D (November 1, 2016)

FORM 48E

Courts of Justice Act

NOTICE THAT ACTION WILL BE DISMISSED

(General heading)

NOTICE THAT ACTION WILL BE DISMISSED

TO THE PARTIES AND THEIR LAWYERS

According to the records in the court office:

(a)   180 days have passed since the originating process was issued,

(b)   no defence has been filed,

(c)   the action has not been disposed of by final order or judgment, and

(d)   the action has not been set down for trial.

Pursuant to subrule 48.15(1), THIS ACTION WILL BE DISMISSED AS ABANDONED unless, within 45 days of being served with this notice:

(a)   a defence is filed,

(b)   it is disposed of by final order or judgment, or

(c)   it is set down for trial.

NOTE: A "defence" means a statement of defence, a notice of intent to defend, or a notice of motion in response to a proceeding, other than a motion challenging the court's jurisdiction.

Date _____   Signed by _____

local registrar
(Address of court office)

TO *(Names and addresses of all lawyers and parties acting in person)*

RCP-E 48E (July 30, 2009)

FORM 48F

Courts of Justice Act

ORDER DISMISSING ACTION AS ABANDONED

(General heading)

ORDER DISMISSING ACTION AS ABANDONED

According to the records in the court office, more than 180 days have passed since the originating process was issued, no defence has been filed, the action has not been disposed of by final order or judgment, the action has not been set down for trial, and the registrar has given 45 days notice that the action will be dismissed as abandoned.

IT IS ORDERED that pursuant to subrule 48.15(1) this action be dismissed as abandoned.

Date _____ Signed by _____

Local registrar
(Address of court office)

NOTE: A "defence" means a statement of defence, a notice of intent to defend, or a notice of motion in response to a proceeding, other than a motion challenging the court's jurisdiction.

NOTE: An order under rule 48.15 dismissing an action may be set aside under rule 37.14.

TO *(Names and addresses of all lawyers and parties acting in person)*

RCP-E 48F (July 30, 2009)

FORM 49A

Courts of Justice Act

OFFER TO SETTLE

(General heading)

OFFER TO SETTLE

The *(identify party)* offers to settle this proceeding *(or* the following claims in this proceeding*)* on the following terms: *(Set out terms in consecutively numbered paragraphs.)*

(Date)   *(Name, address and telephone number of lawyer or party making offer)*

TO *(Name and address of lawyer or party to whom offer is made)*

RCP-E 49A (July 1, 2007)

FORM 49B

Courts of Justice Act

NOTICE OF WITHDRAWAL OF OFFER

(General heading)

NOTICE OF WITHDRAWAL OF OFFER

The *(identify party)* withdraws the offer to settle dated *(date)*.

(Date)   *(Name, address and telephone number of law-
                                       yer or party giving notice)*

TO *(Name and address of lawyer or party to whom notice is given)*

RCP-E 49B (July 1, 2007)

FORM 49C

Courts of Justice Act

ACCEPTANCE OF OFFER

(General heading)

ACCEPTANCE OF OFFER

The *(identify party)* accepts your offer to settle dated *(date)*.

(Date)   *(Name, address and telephone number of law-*
                                                 yer or party accepting offer)

TO *(Name and address of lawyer or party whose offer is accepted)*

RCP-E 49C (July 1, 2007)

FORM 49D

Courts of Justice Act

OFFER TO CONTRIBUTE

(General heading)

OFFER TO CONTRIBUTE

The defendant *(name of defendant making offer)* offers to contribute to a settlement of the plaintiff's claim on the following terms: *(Set out terms in consecutively numbered paragraphs.)*

(Date)   *(Name, address and telephone number of law-yer or defendant making offer)*

TO *(Name and address of lawyer or defendant to whom offer is made)*

RCP-E 49D (July 1, 2007)

FORM 51A

Courts of Justice Act

REQUEST TO ADMIT

(General heading)

REQUEST TO ADMIT

YOU ARE REQUESTED TO ADMIT, for the purposes of this proceeding only, the truth of the following facts: *(Set out facts in consecutively numbered paragraphs.)*

YOU ARE REQUESTED TO ADMIT, for the purposes of this proceeding only, the authenticity (see rule 51.01 of the Rules of Civil Procedure) of the following documents: *(Number each document and give particulars sufficient to identify each. Specify whether the document is an original or a copy and, where the document is a copy of a letter, telegram or telecommunication, state the nature of the document.)*

Attached to this request is a copy of each of the documents referred to above. *(Where it is not practicable to attach a copy or where the party already has a copy, state which documents are not attached and give the reason for not attaching them.)*

YOU MUST RESPOND TO THIS REQUEST by serving a response to request to admit in Form 51B prescribed by the Rules of Civil Procedure WITHIN TWENTY DAYS after this request is served on you. If you fail to do so, you will be deemed to admit, for the purposes of this proceeding only, the truth of the facts and the authenticity of the documents set out above.

(Date)   *(Name, address and telephone number of law-*
                                           yer or party serving request)

TO *(Name and address of lawyer or party on whom request is served)*

RCP-E 51A (July 1, 2007)

FORM 51B

Courts of Justice Act

RESPONSE TO REQUEST TO ADMIT

(General heading)

RESPONSE TO REQUEST TO ADMIT

In response to your request to admit dated *(date)*, the *(identify party responding to the request):*

1. Admits the truth of facts numbers . . . .

2. Admits the authenticity of documents numbers . . . .

3. Denies the truth of facts numbers . . . .

4. Denies the authenticity of documents numbers . . . .

5. Refuses to admit the truth of facts numbers . . . . for the following reasons: *(Set out reason for refusing to admit each fact.)*

6. Refuses to admit the authenticity of documents numbers . . . . for the following reasons: *(Set out reason for refusing to admit each document.)*

(Date)　　　　　　　　　　*(Name, address and telephone number of lawyer or party serving response)*

TO *(Name and address of lawyer or party on whom response is served)*

RCP-E 51B (July 1, 2007)

453

FORM 53

Courts of Justice Act

ACKNOWLEDGMENT OF EXPERT'S DUTY

(General heading)

ACKNOWLEDGMENT OF EXPERT'S DUTY

1. My name is . . . . *(name)*. I live at . . . . *(city)*, in the . . . . *(province/state)* of . . . . *(name of province/state)*.

2. I have been engaged by or on behalf of . . . . *(name of party/parties)* to provide evidence in relation to the above-noted court proceeding.

3. I acknowledge that it is my duty to provide evidence in relation to this proceeding as follows:

    (a)   to provide opinion evidence that is fair, objective and non-partisan;

    (b)   to provide opinion evidence that is related only to matters that are within my area of expertise; and

    (c)   to provide such additional assistance as the court may reasonably require, to determine a matter in issue.

4. I acknowledge that the duty referred to above prevails over any obligation which I may owe to any party by whom or on whose behalf I am engaged.

Date _____   _____

Signature

NOTE: This form must be attached to any report signed by the expert and provided for the purposes of subrule 53.03(1) or (2) of the *Rules of Civil Procedure*.

RCP-E 53 (July 22, 2014)

FORM 53A

Courts of Justice Act

SUMMONS TO WITNESS (AT HEARING)

(General heading)

(Court seal)

SUMMONS TO WITNESS

TO *(Name and address of witness)*

YOU ARE REQUIRED TO ATTEND TO GIVE EVIDENCE IN COURT at the hearing of this proceeding on *(day)*, *(date)*, at *(time)*, at *(address of court house)*, and to remain until your attendance is no longer required.

YOU ARE REQUIRED TO BRING WITH YOU and produce at the hearing the following documents and things: *(Set out the nature and date of each document and give particulars sufficient to identify each document and thing.)*

ATTENDANCE MONEY for . . . . . . day(s) of attendance is served with this summons, calculated in accordance with Tariff A of the Rules of Civil Procedure, as follows:

Attendance allowance of $ _____ daily $ _____

Travel allowance $ _____

Overnight accommodation and meal $ _____
allowance

TOTAL $ _____

If further attendance is required, you will be entitled to additional attendance money.

IF YOU FAIL TO ATTEND OR TO REMAIN IN ATTENDANCE AS REQUIRED BY THIS SUMMONS, A WARRANT MAY BE ISSUED FOR YOUR ARREST.

Date _____   Issued by   _____

                                                          Local registrar

                               Address of
                               court office   _____

                                              _____

This summons was issued at the request of, and inquiries may be directed to:

(Name, address and telephone number of lawyer or party serving summons)

RCP-E 53A (July 1, 2007)

FORM 53B

Courts of Justice Act

WARRANT FOR ARREST (DEFAULTING WITNESS)

(Court file no.)

(Court)

(Name of judge)

(Day and date)

(Court seal)

(Title of Proceeding)

WARRANT FOR ARREST

TO ALL POLICE OFFICERS in Ontario

AND TO the officers of all correctional institutions in Ontario

WHEREAS the witness *(name)*, of *(address)*, was served with a summons to witness to give evidence at the hearing of this proceeding, and the proper attendance money was paid or tendered,

AND WHEREAS the witness failed to obey the summons, and I am satisfied that the evidence of the witness is material to this proceeding,

YOU ARE ORDERED TO ARREST and bring the witness *(name of witness)* before the court to give evidence in this proceeding, and if the court is not then sitting or if the witness cannot be brought forthwith before the court, to deliver the witness to a provincial correctional institution or other secure facility, to be admitted and detained there until the witness can be brought before the court.

(Signature of judge)

RCP-E 53B (November 1, 2005)

FORM 53C

Courts of Justice Act

SUMMONS TO A WITNESS OUTSIDE ONTARIO

(General heading)

(Court seal)

SUMMONS TO A WITNESS OUTSIDE ONTARIO

TO *(Name and address of witness)*

YOU ARE REQUIRED TO ATTEND TO GIVE EVIDENCE (in court at the hearing of this proceeding, on an examination for discovery, on a cross-examination on your affidavit dated *(date), etc.)* on *(day), (date)*, at *(address of court house)*, and to remain until your attendance is no longer required.

YOU ARE REQUIRED TO BRING WITH YOU and produce at the hearing the following documents and things: *(Set out the nature and date of each document and give particulars sufficient to identify each document and thing.)*

ATTENDANCE MONEY for . . . . . . day(s) of attendance is served with this summons, calculated in accordance with the *Interprovincial Summonses Act* (Ontario), as follows:

Attendance allowance of $20 daily for each day of absence from your ordinary residence (not less than $60)	$ _____
Travel allowance	$ _____
Hotel accommodation allowance for not less than three days (not less than $60)	$ _____
Meal allowance for not less than three days (not less than $48)	$ _____
TOTAL	$ _____

If further attendance is required, you will be entitled to additional attendance money.

OBEDIENCE TO THIS SUMMONS may be compelled by the courts of your province under the *Interprovincial Summonses Act.*

Date _____   Issued by   _____
                                                 Local registrar

                              Address of
                              court office   _____

                                              _____

This summons was issued at the request of, and inquiries may be directed to:

(Name, address and telephone number of lawyer or party serving summons)

Attach or endorse the judge's certificate under section 5 of the Interprovincial Summonses Act

RCP-E 53C (July 1, 2007)

FORM 53D

Courts of Justice Act

ORDER FOR ATTENDANCE OF WITNESS IN CUSTODY

(Court file no.)

(Court)

(Name of judge or master)   *(Day and date order made)*

(Court seal)

(Title of Proceeding)

ORDER FOR ATTENDANCE OF WITNESS IN CUSTODY

TO THE OFFICERS OF *(name of correctional institution)*

AND TO ALL POLICE OFFICERS in Ontario

WHEREAS it appears that the evidence of the witness *(name)*, who is detained in custody, is material to this proceeding,

1. THIS COURT ORDERS that the witness *(name)* be brought before this court *(or as may be)* on *(day)*, *(date)*, at *(time)*, at *(address)*, to give evidence on behalf of the *(identify party)*, and that the witness be returned and readmitted immediately thereafter to the correctional institution or other facility from which the witness was brought.

(Signature of judge, officer or registrar)

RCP-E 53D (November 1, 2005)

FORM 55A

Courts of Justice Act

NOTICE OF HEARING FOR DIRECTIONS

(General heading)

NOTICE OF HEARING FOR DIRECTIONS

By order of the court, a copy of which is served with this notice, a reference was directed to *(person conducting reference)* for the purpose of *(set out purpose of reference)*.

The *(identify party)* has obtained an appointment with *(name of person conducting reference)* on *(day)*, *(date)*, at *(time)*, at *(address)* for a hearing to consider directions for the conduct of the reference in this proceeding.

IF YOU FAIL TO ATTEND, in person or by an Ontario lawyer acting for you, directions may be given and the reference may proceed in your absence and without further notice to you, and you will be bound by any order made in the proceeding.

(Date)   *(Name, address and telephone number of lawyer or party serving notice)*

TO *(Name and address of lawyer or party receiving notice)*

RCP-E 55A (July 1, 2007)

FORM 55B

Courts of Justice Act

NOTICE TO PARTY ADDED ON REFERENCE

(General heading)

NOTICE TO PARTY ADDED ON REFERENCE

TO *(Name of party added on reference)*

By order of the court, a copy of which is served with this notice, a reference was directed to *(person conducting reference)* for the purpose of *(set out purpose of reference)*.

YOU HAVE BEEN MADE A PARTY TO THIS PROCEEDING by order of *(name of person conducting reference)*, a copy of which is also served with this notice.

THE REFERENCE WILL PROCEED on *(day)*, *(date)*, at *(time)*, at *(address)*.

YOU MAKE A MOTION to a judge of this court WITHIN TEN DAYS *(or where the person is to be served outside Ontario, such further time as the referee directs)* after this notice is served on you to set aside or vary the order directing the reference or the order adding you as a party.

IF YOU FAIL TO DO SO OR IF YOU FAIL TO ATTEND ON THE REFERENCE, in person or by an Ontario lawyer acting for you, the reference may proceed in your absence and without further notice to you, and you will be bound by any order made in this proceeding.

(Date)   *(Name, address and telephone number of lawyer or party serving notice)*

TO *(Name and address of party added on reference)*

RCP-E 55B (July 1, 2007)

FORM 55C

Courts of Justice Act

REPORT ON REFERENCE (ADMINISTRATION OF ESTATE)

(General heading)

REPORT ON REFERENCE

In accordance with the order directing a reference dated *(date)*, I have disposed of the matters referred to me, and I report as follows:

1. The following parties were served with the order directing a reference and a notice of hearing for directions: *(Set out names). (Where applicable, add:* Service on the following parties was dispensed with: *(Set out names and the reason for dispensing with service).)* The following parties were added on the reference and were served with a notice to party added on reference: *(Set out names).*

2. The following parties did not attend on the reference: *(Set out names).*

3. The personal estate not specifically bequeathed by the testator received by the executors and for which they are chargeable amounts to $ . . . . , and they have paid or are entitled to be allowed the sum of $ . . . . , leaving a balance due from *(or* to*)* them of $ . . . . *(or, where applicable:* No personal estate has been received by the executors, nor are they chargeable with any.)*

4. The creditors' claims received in response to the advertisement for creditors and which I have allowed are set out in Schedule A and amount altogether to $ . . . . *(or, where applicable:* No creditor has sent in a claim in response to the advertisement for creditors, nor has any such claim been proved before me.)*

5. The funeral expenses of the testator amounting to $ . . . . have been paid by the executors and are allowed to them in the account of personal estate.

6. The legacies given by the testator are set out in Schedule B, and with the interest therein mentioned, remain due to the persons named *(or as the case may be).*

7. The personal estate of the testator outstanding or undisposed of is set out in Schedule C.

8. The real estate owned by the testator and the encumbrances affecting it are set out in Schedule D.

9. The rents and profits of the testator's real estate received by the executors and for which they are chargeable amount to $ . . . . and they have paid or are entitled to be allowed the sum of $ . . . . , leaving a balance due from *(or* to*)* them of $ . . . . *(or, where applicable:* No rents and profits have been received by the executors, nor are they chargeable with any).*

10. I have allowed the executors the sum of $ . . . . as compensation for their services in the management of the estate.

11. I have caused the real estate, other than *(identify property)*, which has specifically devised, to be sold and the purchasers have paid their purchase money into court.

12. In Schedule E, I have shown how the money in court is to be dealt with.

(Date)   *(Signature of referee)*

461

(All schedules should be as brief as possible. Only the general character of the things described should be shown. Land should be described without setting out a full legal description.)

(In Schedule C, the personal estate not specifically bequeathed should be set out separately from the other personal property outstanding or undisposed of. Where there is no specific bequest, the report should state that fact.)

RCP-E 55C (November 1, 2005)

FORM 55D

Courts of Justice Act

NOTICE OF CONTESTED CLAIM

(General heading)

NOTICE OF CONTESTED CLAIM

YOUR CLAIM IN THIS PROCEEDING IS BEING CONTESTED. You are required to prove your claim before the referee on *(day), (date), (time),* at *(address).*

IF YOU FAIL TO ATTEND AND PROVE YOUR CLAIM, YOUR CLAIM MAY BE DIS-ALLOWED.

(Date)   *(Name, address and telephone number of*
                                            party or lawyer serving notice)

TO *(Name and address of creditor)*

RCP-E 55D (July 1, 2007)

FORM 55E

Courts of Justice Act

NOTICE TO CREDITOR

(General heading)

NOTICE TO CREDITOR

YOU MAY OBTAIN PAYMENT of the amount allowed by the court in respect of your claim in this proceeding from the office of the Accountant of the Superior Court of Justice, 595 Bay Street, Suite 800, Toronto, ON M5G 2M6 *(or* the local registrar of this court at *(address))*.

(Date)   *(Name, address and telephone number of*
                                                          lawyer or party serving notice)

TO *(Name and address of creditor)*

RCP-E 55E (April 11, 2012)

FORM 55F

Courts of Justice Act

CONDITIONS OF SALE

1. No person shall advance the bidding in an amount less than $10 at any bidding under $500 nor in an amount less than $20 at any bidding over $500. No person shall be allowed to retract a bid.

2. The property shall be sold to the highest bidder. Where any dispute arises as to who is the last or highest bidder, the property shall be put up again.

3. All parties to the proceeding may bid, except the party having carriage of the sale and any trustee or agent for the party or other person in a fiduciary relationship to the party.

4. The purchaser shall, at the time of sale, pay to the party having carriage of the sale or to the party's lawyer a deposit of ten per cent of the purchase price and shall pay the balance of the purchase price on completion of the sale. On payment of the balance, the purchaser shall be entitled to receive a transfer and to take possession. The purchaser shall, at the time of sale, sign an agreement for the completion of the sale.

5. The purchaser shall have the transfer prepared at the purchaser's own expense and tender it to the party having carriage of the sale for execution.

6. Where the purchaser fails to comply with any of these conditions, the deposit and all other payments made shall be forfeited and the property may be resold. Any deficiency on the resale, together with all expenses incurred on the resale or caused by the default, shall be paid by the defaulting purchaser.

RCP-E 55F (July 1, 2007)

FORM 55G

Courts of Justice Act

INTERIM REPORT ON SALE

(General heading)

INTERIM REPORT ON SALE

1. In accordance with the order in this proceeding dated *(date)*, in the presence of *(or* after notice to*)* all parties concerned, I settled the form of an advertisement and the conditions of sale for the sale of the property referred to in the judgment.

2. The advertisement was published as directed, and the property was offered for sale by public auction by me *(or* by *(name)*, an auctioneer appointed by me for that purpose)* on *(date)*.

3. The sale was conducted in a fair, open and proper manner and *(name)* was declared the highest bidder for and became the purchaser of the property at the price of $ . . . . , payable as follows: *(Set out briefly the conditions of sale for payment of the purchase money.)*

(Date)   *(Signature of referee)*

RCP-E 55G (November 1, 2005)

FORM 56A

Courts of Justice Act

ORDER FOR SECURITY FOR COSTS

(Court file no.)

(Court)

(Name of judge or master)　　　　*(Day and date order made)*

(Court seal)

(Title of Proceeding)

ORDER FOR SECURITY FOR COSTS

(Recitals in accordance with Form 59A)

1. THIS COURT ORDERS that within . . . . . . days after this order is served on the plaintiff, *(or* applicant*)*, the plaintiff *(or* applicant*)* shall pay into court *(or* to *(name))* the sum of $ . . . . as security for the costs of this proceeding.

(Where a plaintiff or applicant is ordered to give security for costs in some other form, give a description of the security required and vary the form of the order accordingly.)

2. THIS COURT ORDERS that until the security required by this order has been given, the plaintiff *(or* applicant*)* may not take any step in this proceeding, except an appeal from this order *(or as otherwise ordered).*

(Signature of judge, master or registrar)

RCP-E 56A (November 1, 2005)

FORM 57A

Courts of Justice Act

BILL OF COSTS

(General heading)

BILL OF COSTS

AMOUNTS CLAIMED FOR FEES AND DISBURSEMENTS

(Following the items set out in Tariff A, itemize the claim for fees and disbursements. Indicate the names of the lawyers, students-at-law and law clerks who provided services in connection with each item.

In support of the claim for fees, attach copies of the dockets or other evidence.

In support of the claim for disbursements, attach copies of invoices or other evidence.)

STATEMENT OF EXPERIENCE

A claim for fees is being made with respect to the following lawyers:

Name of lawyer   Years of experience

TO: *(name and address of lawyer or party)*

RCP-E 57A (November 1, 2005)

FORM 57B

Courts of Justice Act

COSTS OUTLINE

ONTARIO

SUPERIOR COURT OF JUSTICE

COSTS OUTLINE

The *(identify party)* provides the following outline of the submissions to be made at the hearing in support of the costs the party will seek if successful:

Fees (as detailed below)	$
Estimated lawyer's fee for appearance	$
Disbursements (as detailed in the attached appendix)	$ _____
Total	$

The following points are made in support of the costs sought with reference to the factors set out in subrule 57.01(1):

• the amount claimed and the amount recovered in the proceeding

• the complexity of the proceeding

• the importance of the issues

• the conduct of any party that tended to shorten or lengthen unnecessarily the duration of the proceeding

• whether any step in the proceeding was improper, vexatious or unnecessary or taken through negligence, mistake or excessive caution

• a party's denial of or refusal to admit anything that should have been admitted

- the experience of the party's lawyer

[   ]

- the hours spent, the rates sought for costs and the rate actually charged by the party's lawyer

FEE ITEMS	PERSONS	HOURS	PARTIAL INDEMNITY RATE	ACTUAL RATE*
(e.g. pleadings, affidavits, cross-examinations, preparation, hearing, etc.)	*(identify the lawyers, students, and law clerks who provided services in connection with each item together with their year of call, if applicable)*	*(specify the hours claimed for each person identified in column 2)*	*(specify the rate being sought for each person identified in column 2)*	

* Specify the rate being charged to the client for each person identified in column 2. If there is a contingency fee arrangement, state the rate that would have been charged absent such arrangement.

- any other matter relevant to the question of costs

[   ]

LAWYER'S CERTIFICATE

I CERTIFY that the hours claimed have been spent, that the rates shown are correct and that each disbursement has been incurred as claimed.

Date...   ....
                                                                                    Signature of lawyer

RCP-E 57B (July 1, 2007)

FORM 58A

Courts of Justice Act

NOTICE OF APPOINTMENT FOR ASSESSMENT OF COSTS

(General heading)

NOTICE OF APPOINTMENT FOR ASSESSMENT OF COSTS

TO THE PARTIES

 I HAVE MADE AN APPOINTMENT to assess the costs of *(identify party)*, a copy of whose bill of costs is attached to this notice, on *(day)*, *(date)*, at *(time)*, at *(address)*.

Date _____   _____
                                                    Assessment officer

TO *(Name and address of lawyer or party on whom notice is served)*

RCP-E 58A (July 1, 2007)

FORM 58B

Courts of Justice Act

NOTICE TO DELIVER A BILL OF COSTS FOR ASSESSMENT

(General heading)

NOTICE TO DELIVER A BILL OF COSTS FOR ASSESSMENT

TO THE PARTIES

I HAVE MADE AN APPOINTMENT, at the request of *(identify party who obtained appointment)* to assess the costs of *(identify party entitled to costs and what costs are to be assessed)* on *(day)*, *(date)*, at *(time)*, at *(address)*.

TO *(identify party entitled to costs)*

YOU ARE REQUIRED to file your bill of costs with me and serve your bill of costs on every party interested in the assessment at least seven days before the above date.

Date _____   _____

Assessment officer

TO *(Name and address of lawyer or party on whom notice is served)*

RCP-E 58B (July 1, 2007)

FORM 58C

Courts of Justice Act

CERTIFICATE OF ASSESSMENT OF COSTS

(General heading)

CERTIFICATE OF ASSESSMENT OF COSTS

I CERTIFY that I have assessed the costs of *(identify party)* in this proceeding *(or as may be)* under the authority of *(give particulars of order or specify rule or statutory provision)*, and I ALLOW THE SUM OF $ . . . . . .

(Where postjudgment interest is payable, add:)

THE COSTS ALLOWED IN THIS ASSESSMENT BEAR INTEREST at the rate of . . . . . per cent per year commencing on *(date)*.

Date _____   _____
                                                                    Assessment officer

RCP-E 58C (November 1, 2005)

FORM 59A

Courts of Justice Act

ORDER

(Court file no.)

(Court)

(Name of judge or master)   *(Day and date order made)*

(Court seal)

(Title of Proceeding)

ORDER

THIS MOTION, made by *(identify moving party)* for *(state the relief sought in the notice of motion, except to the extent that it appears in the operative part of the order), (where applicable, add* made without notice,) was heard this day *(or* heard on *(date))*, at *(place), (recite any particulars necessary to understand the order).*

ON READING the *(give particulars of the material filed on the motion)* and on hearing the submissions of the lawyer(s) for *(identify parties), (where applicable, add (identify party)* appearing in person *or* no one appearing for *(identify party)*, although properly served as appears from *(indicate proof of service)),*

1. THIS COURT ORDERS that . . . .

2. THIS COURT ORDERS that . . . .

(In an order for the payment of money on which postjudgment interest is payable, add:)

THIS ORDER BEARS INTEREST at the rate of . . . . . . per cent per year commencing on *(date).*

(Signature of judge, officer or registrar)

RCP-E 59A (July 1, 2007)

FORM 59B

Courts of Justice Act

JUDGMENT

(Court file no.)

(Court)

(Name(s) of judge or officer)   *(Day and date judgment given)*

(Court seal)

(Title of Proceeding)

JUDGMENT

(Judgment after trial or hearing of application)

THIS ACTION *(or* APPLICATION) was heard this day *(or* heard on *(date))* without *(or* with) a jury at *(place)* in the presence of the lawyers for all parties *(where applicable, add (identify party)* appearing in person, *or* no one appearing for *(identify party)* although properly served as appears from *(indicate proof of service)),*

(Action) ON READING THE PLEADINGS AND HEARING THE EVIDENCE and the submissions of the lawyers for the parties,

(Application) ON READING THE NOTICE OF APPLICATION AND THE EVIDENCE FILED BY THE PARTIES, *(where applicable, add* on hearing the oral evidence presented by the parties,) and on hearing the submissions of the lawyers for the parties.

(Judgment on motion)

THIS MOTION, made by *(identify moving party),* for *(state the relief sought in the notice of motion, except to the extent that it appears in the operative part of the judgment), (where applicable, add* made without notice,) was heard this day *(or* heard on *(date)),* at *(place), (recite any particulars necessary to understand the judgment).*

ON READING THE *(give particulars of the material filed on the motion)* and on hearing the submissions of the lawyer(s) for *(identify parties), (where applicable, add (identify party)* appearing in person *or* no one appearing for *(identify party),* although properly served as appears from *(indicate proof of service)),*

1. THIS COURT ORDERS *(or* DECLARES, *if applicable) (where applicable, add:* AND ADJUDGES) that . . . .

2. THIS COURT ORDERS *(or as may be)* that . . . .

(In a judgment for the payment of money on which postjudgment interest is payable add:)

THIS JUDGMENT BEARS INTEREST at the rate of . . . . . . per cent per year commencing on *(date)*.

(Signature of judge, officer or registrar)

RCP-E 59B (July 1, 2007)

FORM 59C

Courts of Justice Act

ORDER ON APPEAL

(Court file no.)

(Court)

(Name(s) of judge(s))   *(Day and date order made)*

(Court seal)

(Title of Proceeding)

ORDER

THIS APPEAL by *(identify appellant)* for *(state the relief sought in the notice of appeal, except to the extent that it is stated in the operative part of the order)* was heard this day *(or* heard on *(date))*, at *(place)*, *(recite any particulars necessary to understand the order)*.

ON READING the *(give particulars of the material filed on the appeal)*, and on hearing the submissions of the lawyer(s) for *(identify parties)*, *(where applicable, add (identify party)* appearing in person *or* no one appearing for *(identify party)* although properly served as appears from *(indicate proof of service))*,

THIS COURT ORDERS *(or* CERTIFIES, *if applicable)* that . . . .

THIS ORDER BEARS INTEREST at the rate of . . . . . . per cent per year commencing on . . . . *(date)*

(Signature of judge or registrar)

RCP-E 59C (July 1, 2007)

477

FORM 59D

Courts of Justice Act

NOTICE OF APPOINTMENT TO SETTLE ORDER

(General heading)

NOTICE OF APPOINTMENT TO SETTLE ORDER

The *(identify party seeking appointment)* has scheduled an appointment to settle an order with the registrar on *(day)*, *(date)*, at *(time)*, or soon after that time as the motion can be heard, at *(address of court house)*.

PROPOSED METHOD OF HEARING: The appointment is to be heard *(choose appropriate option)*

☐ in writing;

☐ in writing as an opposed appointment;

☐ by teleconference;

☐ orally.

THE APPOINTMENT IS FOR *(state here the precise relief sought)*.

THE GROUNDS FOR THE APPOINTMENT ARE *(specify the grounds to be argued)*.

THE FOLLOWING DOCUMENTARY EVIDENCE will be used at the appointment: *(list the affidavits or other documentary evidence to be relied on)*.

(Date)

(Name, address and telephone number of lawyer of party seeking appointment or party seeking appointment)

TO *(Name and address of lawyer of other parties represented at hearing or other parties represented at hearing)*

RCP-E 59D (November 1, 2016)

FORM 60A

Courts of Justice Act

WRIT OF SEIZURE AND SALE

(Court file no.)

ONTARIO

SUPERIOR COURT OF JUSTICE

BETWEEN

AND

WRIT OF SEIZURE AND SALE

TO: the Sheriff of the *(name of county or district)*

Under an order of this court made on *(date)*, in favour of *(name of creditor)*, YOU ARE DIRECTED to seize and sell the real and personal property within your county or district of

Surname of individual or name of corporation/firm, etc.

First given name (individual only)	Second given name (individual only) (if applicable)	Third given name (individual only) (if applicable)

and to realize from the seizure and sale the following sums:

(a) $...............and interest at...............per cent per year commencing on *(date)*

   (Where the writ is for two or more periodic or instalment payments, substitute:)

   Amount of payment   Due Date

(b) $...............and interest at...............per cent per year on the payments in default commencing on the date of default;

(c) $...............for costs together with interest at...............per cent per year commencing on *(date);* and

(d)   your fees and expenses in enforcing this writ.

YOU ARE DIRECTED to pay out the proceeds according to law and to report on the execution of this writ if required by the party or lawyer who filed it.

Dated at..   Issued by ....

                                                     Registrar

on..

                                              Address of court office

                                           ....

                                           ....

                                           ....

FORM 60A Writ of Seizure and Sale, backsheet

(Short title of proceeding)   *(Court file no.)*

FEES

Fee	Item	Officer
	Paid for this writ	
$50	Lawyer's fee for issuing a writ	
	First renewal	
	Second renewal	
	Third renewal	

RENEWAL

Date	Officer

(Name of court)

PROCEEDING COMMENCED AT *(place)*

WRIT OF SEIZURE AND SALE

Creditor's name ....

Creditor's address ....

....

....

....

Lawyer's name ....

....

....

Lawyer's address and telephone no ....

....

....

RCP-E60A (July 1, 2007)

481

FORM 60B

Courts of Justice Act

WRIT OF SEQUESTRATION

(General heading)

(Court seal)

WRIT OF SEQUESTRATION

TO the Sheriff of the *(name of county or district)*

Under an order of this court made on *(date)* on motion of *(name of moving party)*, YOU ARE DIRECTED to take possession of and hold the following property within your county or district of *(name of person against whom order was made): (Set out a description of the property to be taken and held.)*

AND YOU ARE DIRECTED to collect and hold any income from the property until further order of this court.

Date _____   Issued by   _____
                                                    Local registrar

                                 Address of   _____
                                 court office

                                                _____

RCP-E 60B (November 1, 2005)

FORM 60C

Courts of Justice Act

WRIT OF POSSESSION

(General heading)

(Court seal)

WRIT OF POSSESSION

TO the Sheriff of the *(name of county or district)*

Under an order of this court made on *(date)* in favour of *(name of party who obtained order)*, YOU ARE DIRECTED to enter and take possession of the following land and premises in your county or district: *(Set out a description of the land and premises.)*

AND YOU ARE DIRECTED to give possession of the above land and premises without delay to *(name of party who obtained order)*.

Date _____   Issued by _____

                                                         Local registrar

                                 Address of _____
                                 court office

                                                         _____

Renewed by order made on *(date)*.

_____

Local register

RCP-E 60C (November 1, 2005)

FORM 60D

Courts of Justice Act

WRIT OF DELIVERY

(General heading)

(Court seal)

WRIT OF DELIVERY

TO the Sheriff of the *(name of county or district)*

Under an order of this court made on *(date)*, YOU ARE DIRECTED to seize from *(name of party)* and to deliver without delay to *(name of party who obtained order)* possession of the following personal property: *(Set out a description of the property to be delivered.)*

Date _____   Issued by   _____

Local registrar

Address of   _____
court office

_____

RCP-E 60D (November 1, 2005)

FORM 60E

Courts of Justice Act

REQUEST TO RENEW

(General heading)

REQUEST TO RENEW

TO the Sheriff of the *(name of county or district)*

YOU ARE REQUESTED TO RENEW the writ of seizure and sale issued on *(date)* in this proceeding and filed in your office for a period of six years from the date of renewal.

(Date)   *(Signature of party or lawyer)*
                                      (Name, address and telephone number of party or lawyer)

RCP-E 60E (July 1, 2007)

FORM 60F

Courts of Justice Act

DIRECTION TO ENFORCE WRIT OF SEIZURE AND SALE

(Sheriff's file no.)

(Court)

between :

(name)

Creditor(s)

and

(name)

Debtor(s)

DIRECTION TO ENFORCE WRIT

TO: the Sheriff of the *(name of county or district)*

Under an order of this court in favour of *(name of creditor)* made on *(date)*, *(name of debtor)* was ordered to pay the sum of $ . . . . *(where applicable, add each month or as may be)* with interest at the rate of . . . . . . per cent per year commencing on *(date)* and costs of $ . . . . *(as fixed or assessed)* with interest at the rate of . . . . . . per cent per year commencing on *(date)*. Since the order was made, the creditor has received the following payments:

Date of payment   Amount of payment

Under rule 60.19 of the *Rules of Civil Procedure*, the creditor is entitled to costs in the amount of,

(a) $50 for the preparation of documents in connection with issuing, renewing and filing with the sheriff the writ of execution or notice of garnishment;

(b) $ . . . . for disbursements paid to a sheriff, registrar, official examiner, court reporter or other public officer and to which the creditor is entitled under subrule 60.19 (1); *(Attach copy of all receipts.)*

(c) $ . . . . for an amount determined in accordance with Tariff A for conducting an examination in aid of execution; *(Attach affidavit confirming that examination was conducted, and a bill of costs.)*

(d) $ . . . . for any other costs to which the creditor is entitled under subrule 60.19 (1). *(Attach certificate of assessment.)*

YOU ARE DIRECTED to enforce the writ of seizure and sale issued on *(date)* and filed in your office for a sum sufficient to satisfy the total of the amounts set out above, together with subsequent interest, and your fees and expenses.

Date _____   _____

(Signature of party or lawyer)

*(Name, address and telephone number
of party or lawyer)*

RCP-E 60F (November 1, 2005)

FORM 60G

Courts of Justice Act

REQUISITION FOR GARNISHMENT

(General heading)

REQUISITION FOR GARNISHMENT

TO: the local registrar at *(place)*

I REQUIRE a notice of garnishment to be issued in this proceeding, in accordance with the attached draft Form 60H. The total amount to be shown in the notice of garnishment is $
. . . . , made up as follows:

1. $ . . . . for principal owing under the judgment or order, including prejudgment interest.

2. $ . . . . for the costs of the action.

3. $50 for the preparation of documents in connection with issuing, renewing and filing with the sheriff a writ of execution or notice of garnishment.

4. $ . . . . for disbursements paid to a sheriff, registrar, official examiner, court reporter or other public officer and to which the creditor is entitled under subrule 60.19 (1). *(Attach copies of all receipts.)*

5. $ . . . . for an amount determined in accordance with Tariff A for conducting an examination in aid of execution. *(Attach affidavit confirming that examination was conducted, and a bill of costs.)*

6. $ . . . . for any other costs to which the creditor is entitled under subrule 60.19 (1). *(Attach certificate of assessment.)*

7. $ . . . . for postjudgment interest to today's date. *(Calculate by counting the number of days that the principal sum has been owing, multiplying that number by the annual rate of interest, then multiplying by the principal sum owing and dividing by 365.)*

Date _____   _____

(Signature of creditor or creditor's lawyer)

(Name, address and telephone number of creditor or creditor's lawyer)

RCP-E 60G (November 1, 2005)

FORM 60G.1

Courts of Justice Act

REQUISITION FOR RENEWAL OF GARNISHMENT

ONTARIO

SUPERIOR COURT OF JUSTICE

(General heading)

REQUISITION FOR RENEWAL OF GARNISHMENT

TO: the local registrar at *(place)*

I REQUIRE a notice of renewal of garnishment to be issued in this proceeding, in accordance with the attached draft Form 60H.1. The total amount to be shown in the notice of renewal of garnishment is $ . . . . , made up as follows:

1. $ . . . . . . for principal owing under the judgment or order, including prejudgment interest.

2. $ . . . . . . for the costs of the action.

3. $50 for the preparation of documents in connection with issuing, renewing and filing with the sheriff a writ of execution or notice of garnishment.

4. $ . . . . . . for disbursements paid to a sheriff, registrar, official examiner, court reporter or other public officer and to which the creditor is entitled under subrule 60.19 (1). *(Attach copies of all receipts.)*

5. $ . . . . . . for an amount determined in accordance with Tariff A for conducting an examination in aid of execution. *(Attach affidavit confirming that examination was conducted, and a bill of costs.)*

6. $ . . . . . . for any other costs to which the creditor is entitled under subrule 60.19 (1). *(Attach certificate of assessment.)*

7. $ . . . . . . for postjudgment interest to today's date. *(Calculate by counting the number of days that the principal sum has been owing, multiplying that number by the annual rate of interest, then multiplying by the principal sum owing and dividing by 365.)*

Date _____   _____

(Signature of creditor or creditor's lawyer)

(Name, address and telephone number of creditor or creditor's lawyer)

RCP-E 60G.1 (November 1, 2005)

FORM 60H

Courts of Justice Act

NOTICE OF GARNISHMENT

(Court file no.)

(Garnishment no., assigned by registrar)

(Court)

BETWEEN

(name)

Creditor

(Court seal)

(and)

(name)

Debtor

(and)

(name)

Garnishee

NOTICE OF GARNISHMENT

TO *(name and address of garnishee)*

A LEGAL PROCEEDING in this court between the creditor and the debtor has resulted in an order that the debtor pay a sum of money to the creditor. The creditor claims that you owe a debt to the debtor. A debt to the debtor includes both a debt payable to the debtor and a debt payable to the debtor and one or more co-owners. The creditor has had this notice of garnishment directed to you as garnishee in order to seize any debt that you owe or will owe to the debtor. Where the debt is payable to the debtor and to one or more co-owners, you must pay one-half of the indebtedness or the greater or lesser amount specified in an order made under subrule 60.08 (16).

YOU ARE REQUIRED TO PAY to the Sheriff of the *(name of county or district)*,

(a) within 10 days after this notice is served on you, all debts now payable by you to the debtor; and

(b) within 10 days after they become payable, all debts that become payable by you to the debtor within 6 years after this notice is served on you,

subject to the exemptions provided by section 7 of the *Wages Act*. The total amount of all your payments to the sheriff is not to exceed $ .... less $10 for your costs of making each payment.

EACH PAYMENT MUST BE SENT with a copy of the attached garnishee's payment notice to the sheriff at the address shown below.

IF YOU DO NOT PAY THE TOTAL AMOUNT OF $ .... LESS $10 FOR YOUR COSTS OF MAKING EACH PAYMENT WITHIN 10 DAYS after this notice is served on you, because the debt is owed to the debtor and to one or more co-owners or for any other reason, you must within that time serve on the creditor and the debtor and file with the court a garnishee's statement in Form 60I attached to this notice.

IF YOU FAIL TO OBEY THIS NOTICE, THE COURT MAY MAKE AND ENFORCE AN ORDER AGAINST YOU for payment of the amount set out above and the costs of the creditor.

IF YOU MAKE PAYMENT TO ANYONE OTHER THAN THE SHERIFF, YOU MAY BE LIABLE TO PAY AGAIN.
TO THE CREDITOR, THE DEBTOR AND THE GARNISHEE.

RCP-60H-E (2019/05)

490

Any party may make a motion to the court to determine any matter in relation to this notice of garnishment.

Date .... Issued by ....
                                                                                        Local registrar

                                                                        Address of court office
                                                                        ....
                                                                        ....

Debtor's address
....
....

Sheriff's address
....
....

Creditor's address
....
....

telephone no. ....
....

(The top portion of the garnishee's payment notice is to be completed by the creditor before the notice of garnishment is issued. Where it is anticipated that more than one payment will be made by the garnishee, the creditor should provide extra copies of the payment notice.)

GARNISHEE'S PAYMENT NOTICE

Make payment by cheque or money order payable to the Sheriff of the *(the name of county or district)* and send it, along with a copy of this payment notice, to the *(address)*.

Court ....   File no ....

Office at ....   Garnishment no ....

Creditor ....

Debtor ....

Garnishee ....

TO BE COMPLETED BY GARNISHEE FOR EACH PAYMENT

Date of payment ....

Amount enclosed $ ....

Print Form

RCP-60H-E (2019/05)

491

FORM 60H.1

Courts of Justice Act

NOTICE OF RENEWAL OF GARNISHMENT

(Court file no.)

(Garnishment no., assigned by registrar)

(Court)

BETWEEN

(name)

Creditor

(Court seal)

(and)

(name)

Debtor

(and)

(name)

Garnishee

NOTICE OF RENEWAL OF GARNISHMENT

TO *(name and address of garnishee)*

   A LEGAL PROCEEDING in this court between the creditor and the debtor has resulted in an order that the debtor pay a sum of money to the creditor. The creditor claims that you owe a debt to the debtor. A debt to the debtor includes both a debt payable to the debtor and a debt payable to the debtor and one or more co-owners. The creditor has had this notice of renewal of garnishment directed to you as garnishee in order to seize any debt that you owe or will owe to the debtor. Where the debt is payable to the debtor and to one or more co-owners, you must pay one-half of the indebtedness or the greater or lesser amount specified in an order made under subrule 60.08 (16).

(Where appropriate, add: This notice of renewal of garnishment enforces an order for support.)

YOU ARE REQUIRED TO PAY to the Sheriff of the *(name of county or district)*,

(a) within 10 days after this notice is served on you, all debts now payable by you to the debtor; and

(b) within 10 days after they become payable, all debts that become payable by you to the debtor within 6 years after this notice is served on you,

subject to the exemptions provided by section 7 of the *Wages Act*. The total amount of all your payments to the sheriff is not to exceed $ .... less $10 for your costs of making each payment.

EACH PAYMENT MUST BE SENT with a copy of the attached garnishee's payment notice to the sheriff at the address shown below.

IF YOU DO NOT PAY THE TOTAL AMOUNT OF $ .... LESS $10 FOR YOUR COSTS OF MAKING EACH PAYMENT WITHIN 10 DAYS after this notice is served on you, because the debt is owed to the debtor and to one or more co-owners or for any other reason, you must within that time serve on the creditor and the debtor and file with the court a garnishee's statement in Form 60I attached to this notice.

IF YOU FAIL TO OBEY THIS NOTICE, THE COURT MAY MAKE AND ENFORCE AN ORDER AGAINST YOU for payment of the amount set out above and the costs of the creditor.

RCP-60H.1-E (2019/05)

RULES OF CIVIL PROCEDURE FORMS

IF YOU MAKE PAYMENT TO ANYONE OTHER THAN THE SHERIFF, YOU MAY BE LIABLE TO PAY AGAIN. TO THE CREDITOR, THE DEBTOR AND THE GARNISHEE.

Any party may make a motion to the court to determine any matter in relation to this notice of renewal of garnishment.

Date ....

Issued by ....
Local registrar

Address of court office

....

....

Debtor's address

....

....

Sheriff's address

....

....

Creditor's address

....

....

telephone no. ....

....

(The top portion of the garnishee's payment notice is to be completed by the creditor before the notice of renewal of garnishment is issued. Where it is anticipated that more than one payment will be made by the garnishee, the creditor should provide extra copies of the payment notice.)

GARNISHEE'S PAYMENT NOTICE

Make payment by cheque or money order payable to the Sheriff of the *(the name of county or district)* and send it, along with a copy of this payment notice, to the *(address)*.

Court ....

File no ....

Office at ....

Garnishment no ....

Creditor ....

Debtor ....

Garnishee ....

TO BE COMPLETED BY GARNISHEE FOR EACH PAYMENT

Date of payment ....

Amount enclosed $ ....

Print Form

RCP-60H.1-E (2019/05)

FORM 60I

Courts of Justice Act

GARNISHEE'S STATEMENT

(The general heading on this form is to be completed by the creditor and the form is to be attached to the notice of garnishment to be served on the garnishee before the notice of garnishment is issued.)

(General heading as in Form 60H)

GARNISHEE'S STATEMENT

1. I/We acknowledge that I/we owe or will owe the debtor or the debtor and one or more co-owners the sum of $ . . . . , payable on *(date)* because *(Give reasons why you owe the debtor or the debtor and one or more co-owners money. If you are making payment of less than the amount stated in line 2 of this paragraph because the debt is owed to the debtor and to one or more co-owners or for any other reason, give a full explanation of the reason. If you owe the debtor wages, state how often the debtor is paid. State the gross amount of the debtor's wages before any deductions and the net amount after all deductions and attach a copy of a pay slip.)*

1.1 *(If debt owed to debtor and one or more co-owners, check here and complete the following:)*

Co-owner(s) of the Debt (name, address). . . . .

2. *(If you do not owe the debtor money, explain why. Give any other information that will explain your financial relationship with the debtor.)*

3. *(If you have been served with any other notice of garnishment or a writ of execution against the debtor, give particulars.)*

Name of creditor   Location of Sheriff   Date of notice or writ   Date of service on you

4. *(If you have been served outside Ontario and you wish to object on the ground that service outside Ontario was improper, give particulars of your objection.)*

Date

Signature of or for gar-
nishee   _____

Name of garnishee   _____

Address   _____
                               _____
                               _____

Telephone number   _____

RCP-E 60I (November 1, 2005)

FORM 60I.1

Courts of Justice Act

NOTICE TO CO-OWNER OF THE DEBT

(General heading as in Form 60H)

TO   *(name and address of co-owner of the debt)*

A LEGAL PROCEEDING in this court between the creditor and the debtor has resulted in an order that the debtor pay a sum of money to the creditor. The creditor has given a notice of garnishment to *(name of garnishee)* claiming that the garnishee owes a debt to the debtor. A debt to the debtor includes both a debt payable to the debtor and a debt payable to the debtor and one or more other co-owners. The garnishee has indicated in the attached garnishee's statement that you are a co-owner. Under the notice of garnishment the garnishee has paid the greater of the debtor's ownership interest, as known to the garnishee, or one-half of the indebtedness to the sheriff.

IF YOU HAVE A CLAIM to the money being paid to the sheriff by the garnishee, you have 30 days from service of this notice to make a motion to the court for a garnishment hearing. If you fail to do so, you may not hereafter dispute the enforcement of the creditor's order for the payment or recovery of money under the Rules of Civil Procedure and the funds may be paid out in accordance with the *Creditors' Relief Act, 2010.*

Date _____

RCP-E 60I.1 (April 11, 2012)

FORM 60J

Courts of Justice Act

NOTICE OF TERMINATION OF GARNISHMENT

(General heading as in Form 60H)

NOTICE OF TERMINATION OF GARNISHMENT

TO *(name of garnishee)*

AND TO the Sheriff of the *(name of county or district)*

THE NOTICE OF GARNISHMENT DATED *(date)* SERVED ON YOU IS TERMINATED and you are not to make any further payments under it.

(Date)   *(Signature of creditor or lawyer)*
                            (Name, address and telephone number of creditor or lawyer)

RCP-E60J (July 1, 2007)

FORM 60K

Courts of Justice Act

WARRANT FOR ARREST (CONTEMPT)

(Court file no.)

(Court)

(Name of judge)   *(Day and date)*

(Court seal)

(Title of proceeding)

WARRANT FOR ARREST

TO ALL POLICE OFFICERS in Ontario

AND TO the officers of all correctional institutions in Ontario

WHEREAS it appears that *(name)*, of *(address)* may be in contempt of this court,

AND WHEREAS I am of the opinion that attendance of *(name)* at the hearing of the motion for a contempt order is necessary in the interest of justice and it appears that he *(or* she*)* is not likely to attend voluntarily,

YOU ARE ORDERED TO ARREST and bring *(name)* before the court for the hearing of the motion for a contempt order, and if the court is not then sitting or if he *(or* she*)* cannot be brought forthwith before the court, you are ordered to deliver him *(or* her*)* to a provincial correctional institution or other secure facility, to be admitted and detained there until he *(or* she*)* can be brought before the court.

(Signature of judge)

RCP-E 60K (November 1, 2005)

497

FORM 60L

Courts of Justice Act

WARRANT OF COMMITTAL

(Court file no.)

(Court)

(Name of judge)   *(Day and date)*

(Court seal)

(Title of proceeding)

WARRANT OF COMMITTAL

TO ALL POLICE OFFICERS in Ontario

AND TO THE OFFICERS OF *(name of correctional institution)*

WHEREAS I have found that *(name)* is in contempt of this court and have ordered imprisonment as punishment for the contempt,

YOU ARE ORDERED TO ARREST *(name)* and deliver him *(or* her*)* to a provincial correctional institution, to be detained there for *(or* until*) (give particulars of sentence).*

(Signature of judge)

RCP-E 60L (November 1, 2005)

FORM 60M

Courts of Justice Act

NOTICE OF CLAIM

(General heading)

TO THE CREDITORS OF *(name of debtor)*

I have received notice of a claim by *(name)*, of *(address)*, in respect of property or the proceeds of property taken or intended to be taken in execution against the debtor. Particulars of the claim are as follows: *(Give particulars.)*

You are required to give me notice in writing, within seven days after receiving this notice, stating whether you admit or dispute the claim.

(Date)   *(Name, address and telephone number of sheriff)*

TO   *(Name and address of each creditor or lawyer)*

RCP-E 60M (July 1, 2007)

FORM 60N

Courts of Justice Act

SHERIFF'S REPORT

(General heading)

SHERIFF'S REPORT

In response to your request of *(date)* concerning the execution of the writ of seizure and sale *(or* possession, delivery *or* sequestration) against *(name of party)* filed with me, I report that I have taken the following action, with the following results: *(Give particulars.)*

(Date)   *(Signature of sheriff)*

TO *(Name and address of creditor or lawyer)*

RCP-E 60N (July 1, 2007)

FORM 60O

Courts of Justice Act

REQUEST TO WITHDRAW A WRIT

ONTARIO

SUPERIOR COURT OF JUSTICE

(General heading)

REQUEST TO WITHDRAW A WRIT

TO: the Sheriff of the *(name of county or district)*

Under an order of this court in the favour of *(name of creditor)* made on *(date)*, *(name of debtor)* was ordered to pay the sum of $. . . . . . . *(where applicable, add* each month *or* as may be*)* with interest at the rate of . . . . . . per cent per year commencing on *(date)* and costs of $. . . . . . . *(as fixed or assessed)* with interest at the rate of . . . . . . per cent per year commencing on *(date)*.

(name of debtor) states as follows:

Order of Discharge

1. The order has been released by an order of discharge under the *Bankruptcy and Insolvency Act* (Canada). A certified copy of the order is attached.

2. The debtor has no debts under section 178 of that Act.

OR

Certificate of Full Performance

1. The order has been released by a certificate of full performance under the *Bankruptcy and Insolvency Act* (Canada). A copy of the certificate is attached.

2. The debtor has no debts under section 178 of that Act.

(name of debtor) requests that the writ of seizure and sale issued with respect to the order be withdrawn under rule 60.15 of the *Rules of Civil Procedure*.

Date _____   _____

(Signature of debtor)
*(Name, address and telephone number
of debtor or debtor's lawyer)*

RCP-E 60O (November 1, 2005)

FORM 61A

Courts of Justice Act

NOTICE OF APPEAL TO THE COURT OF APPEAL

(General heading in accordance with Form 61B)

NOTICE OF APPEAL

THE *(identify party)* APPEALS to the Court of Appeal from the judgment *(or* order*)* of *(name of judge, officer or tribunal)* dated *(date)* made at *(place)*.

THE APPELLANT ASKS that the judgment be set aside and a judgment be granted as follows *(or* that the judgment be varied as follows, *or as may be)*: *(Set out briefly the relief sought.)*

THE GROUNDS OF APPEAL are as follows: *(Set out briefly the grounds of appeal.)*

THE BASIS OF THE APPELLATE COURT'S JURISDICTION IS: *(State the basis for the appellate court's jurisdiction, including (i) any provision of a statute or regulation establishing jurisdiction, (ii) whether the order appealed from is final or interlocutory, (iii) whether leave to appeal is required an if so whether it has been granted, and (iv) any other facts relevant to establishing jurisdiction.)*

(Date)   *(Name, address and telephone and fax numbers of appellant's lawyer or of appellant)*

TO *(Name and address of respondent's lawyer or of respondent)*

RCP-E 61A (September 1, 2018)

FORM 61A.1

Courts of Justice Act

NOTICE OF APPEAL TO THE DIVISIONAL COURT

(General heading in accordance with Form 61B)

NOTICE OF APPEAL

THE *(identify party)* APPEALS to the Divisional Court from the judgment *(or* order*)* of *(name of judge, officer or tribunal)* dated *(date)* made at *(place)*.

THE APPELLANT ASKS that the judgment be set aside and a judgment be granted as follows *(or* that the judgment be varied as follows, *or as may be)*: *(Set out briefly the relief sought.)*

THE GROUNDS OF APPEAL are as follows: *(Set out briefly the grounds of appeal.)*

THE BASIS OF THE APPELLATE COURT'S JURISDICTION IS: *(State the basis for the appellate court's jurisdiction, including (i) any provision of a statute or regulation establishing jurisdiction, (ii) whether the order appealed from is final or interlocutory, (iii) whether leave to appeal is required an if so whether it has been granted, and (iv) any other facts relevant to establishing jurisdiction.)*

The appellant requests that this appeal be heard at *(place)*.

TAKE NOTICE: THIS APPEAL WILL AUTOMATICALLY BE DISMISSED if it has not been set down for hearing or terminated by any means within five years after the notice of appeal was filed with the court, unless otherwise ordered by the court.

(Date)   *(Name, address and telephone and fax numbers of appellant's lawyer or of appellant)*

TO *(Name and address of respondent's lawyer or of respondent)*

RCP-E 61A.1 (September 1, 2018)

FORM 61B

Courts of Justice Act

GENERAL HEADING IN PROCEEDINGS IN APPELLATE COURTS COURT OF APPEAL FOR ONTARIO *(or* DIVISIONAL COURT, SUPERIOR COURT OF JUSTICE*)*

(Appeal in an action)

BETWEEN:

(name)

Plaintiff
(Appellant) (or (Respondent))

and

(name)

Defendant (Respondent) (or (Appellant))

(Appeal in an application)

BETWEEN:

(name)

Applicant (Appellant) (or (Respondent in appeal))

and

(name)

Respondent (Respondent in appeal) (or (Appellant))

APPLICATION UNDER *(statutory provision or rule under which the application is made)*

(Where there are multiple parties in the proceeding at first instance and only some of them are parties to the appeal, include the names of all of the parties at first instance and underline the names of the parties to the appeal.)

RCP-E 61B (November 1, 2005)

FORM 61C

Courts of Justice Act

APPELLANT'S CERTIFICATE RESPECTING EVIDENCE

(General heading in accordance with Form 61B)

APPELLANT'S CERTIFICATE

The appellant certifies that the following evidence is required for the appeal, in the appellant's opinion:

1. Exhibits numbers . . . . . .

2. The affidavit evidence of *(names of deponents)*

3. The oral evidence of *(names of witnesses)*

(Date)   *(Name, address and telephone and fax numbers of appellant's lawyer or appellant)*

TO   *(Name and address of respondent's lawyer or respondent)*

RCP-E 61C (November 1, 2005)

FORM 61D

Courts of Justice Act

RESPONDENT'S CERTIFICATE RESPECTING EVIDENCE

(General heading in accordance with Form 61B)

RESPONDENT'S CERTIFICATE

The respondent confirms the appellant's certificate *(where necessary, add* except for the following:)

ADDITIONS

1. Exhibits numbers . . . . . . are required for the appeal.

2. The affidavit evidence of *(names of deponents)* is required for the appeal.

3. The oral evidence of *(names of witnesses)* is required for the appeal.

DELETIONS

4. Exhibits numbers . . . . . . are not required for the appeal.

5. The affidavit evidence of *(names of deponents)* is not required for the appeal.

6. The oral evidence of *(names of witnesses)* is not required for the appeal.

(Date)   *(Name, address and telephone and fax numbers of respondent's lawyer or respondent)*

TO *(Name and address of appellant's lawyer or appellant)*

RCP-E 61D (November 1, 2005)

FORM 61E

Courts of Justice Act

NOTICE OF CROSS-APPEAL

(General heading in accordance with Form 61B)

NOTICE OF CROSS-APPEAL

THE RESPONDENT CROSS-APPEALS in this appeal and asks that the judgment be set aside and judgment be granted as follows: *(or* that the judgment be varied as follows, *or as may be): (Set out briefly the relief sought.)*

THE GROUNDS FOR THIS CROSS-APPEAL are as follows: *(Set out briefly the grounds of cross-appeal.)*

(Date)   *(Name, address and telephone and fax numbers of respondent's lawyer or respondent)*

TO *(Name and address of appellant's lawyer or appellant)*

RCP-E 61E (July 1, 2007)

FORM 61F

Courts of Justice Act

SUPPLEMENTARY NOTICE OF APPEAL OR CROSS-APPEAL

(General heading in accordance with Form 61B)

SUPPLEMENTARY NOTICE OF APPEAL *(or* CROSS-APPEAL*)*

The appellant *(or* respondent*)* amends the notice of appeal *(or* cross-appeal*)* dated *(date)* in the following manner: *(Give particulars of the amendment.)*

(Date)   *(Name, address and telephone number of lawyer or party serving notice)*

TO *(Name and address of lawyer or party on whom notice is served)*

RCP-E 61F (July 1, 2007)

FORM 61G

Courts of Justice Act

NOTICE OF LISTING FOR HEARING (APPEAL)

(General heading in accordance with Form 61B)

NOTICE OF LISTING FOR HEARING

THIS APPEAL HAS BEEN PERFECTED and has been listed for hearing at *(place)*. You may ascertain from my office the approximate date of hearing.

Date _____ Signed by _____

> Registrar of the Court of Appeal *(or* Divisional Court *) (Address of court office)*

TO *(Name and address of every person listed in the certificate of perfection)*

RCP-E 61G (November 1, 2005)

509

FORM 61H

Courts of Justice Act

CERTIFICATE OF COMPLETENESS OF APPEAL BOOK AND COMPENDIUM

(General heading in accordance with Form 61B)

CERTIFICATE OF COMPLETENESS

I, *(name)*, lawyer for the appellant *(or* appellant*)*, certify that the appeal book and compendium in this appeal is complete and legible.

(Date)   *(Signature of appellant's lawyer or appellant)*

                             (Name, address and telephone number of appellant's lawyer or appellant)

RCP-E 61H (July 1, 2007)

FORM 61I

Courts of Justice Act

ORDER DISMISSING APPEAL OR CROSS-APPEAL FOR DELAY

(General heading in accordance with Form 61B)

ORDER DISMISSING APPEAL (*or* CROSS-APPEAL)

The appellant *(or* respondent*)* has not *(give particulars of appellant's or respondent's default under rule 61.13)* and has not cured the default, although any notice that may be required by rule 61.13 has been given.

IT IS ORDERED that this appeal *(or* cross-appeal*)* be dismissed for delay, with costs fixed at $750, despite rule 58.13.

Date _____ Signed by _____

Registrar of the Court of
Appeal (or Divisional
Court)

NOTE: If there is a cross-appeal, the appellant by cross-appeal should consider rule 61.15, under which the cross-appeal may be deemed to be abandoned.

RCP-E 61I (November 1, 2016)

FORM 61I.1

Courts of Justice Act

ORDER DISMISSING APPEAL TO DIVISIONAL COURT FOR DELAY

(General heading)

ORDER DISMISSING APPEAL

The appellant (or respondent) has not *(give particulars of appellant's or respondent's default under rule 61.13.0.1* and has not cured the default.

IT IS ORDERED that this appeal be dismissed for delay.

Date _____ Signed by _____

Local registrar
(Address of court office)

NOTE: An order under rule 61.13.0.1 dismissing an appeal may be set aside under rule 37.14.

NOTE: If there is a cross-appeal, the appellant by cross-appeal should consider rule 61.15, under which the cross-appeal may be deemed to be abandoned.

RCP-E 61I.1 (September 1, 2018)

FORM 61J

Courts of Justice Act

ORDER DISMISSING MOTION FOR LEAVE TO APPEAL FOR DELAY

(General Heading in accordance with Form 61B)

ORDER DISMISSING MOTION FOR LEAVE

The moving party on this motion for leave to appeal from the order (*or as may be*) of *(name of court or tribunal)* dated *(date)* has not served and filed the motion record, factum and *(if necessary)* transcripts in accordance with clause 61.13 (8) (a) (motion by responding party) (*or* clause 61.13 (8) (b) (Registrar's notice)) of the Rules of Civil Procedure.

IT IS ORDERED that this motion be dismissed for delay, with costs fixed at $750, despite rule 58.13.

Date _____   Signed by _____

Registrar of the Court of
Appeal (or Divisional
Court)

RCP-E 61J (July 30, 2009)

FORM 61J.1

Courts of Justice Act

ORDER DISMISSING MOTION FOR DELAY

(General heading in accordance with Form 61B)

ORDER DISMISSING MOTION FOR DELAY

The moving party on this motion has not served and filed the motion record, factum and other material in accordance with subrule 61.16 (4) of the Rules of Civil Procedure.

IT IS ORDERED that this motion be dismissed for delay, with costs fixed at $750, despite rule 58.13.

Date _____   Signed by _____

Registrar of the Court of Appeal (or Divisional Court)

RCP-E 61J.1 (July 30, 2009)

FORM 61K

Courts of Justice Act

NOTICE OF ABANDONMENT OF APPEAL OR CROSS-APPEAL

(General heading in accordance with Form 61B)

NOTICE OF ABANDONMENT

The appellant *(or* respondent*)* abandons this appeal *(or* cross-appeal*)*.

(Date)   *(Name, address and telephone number of lawyer or party serving notice)*

TO *(Name and address of lawyer or party on whom notice is served)*

NOTE: If there is a cross-appeal, the appellant by cross-appeal should consider rule 61.15, under which the cross-appeal may be deemed to be abandoned.

RCP-E 61K (July 1, 2007)

FORM 61L

Courts of Justice Act

NOTICE OF ELECTION TO PROCEED WITH CROSS-APPEAL

(General heading in accordance with Form 61B)

NOTICE OF ELECTION

The respondent elects to proceed with the cross-appeal.

(Date)   *(Name, address and telephone number of respondent's lawyer or respondent)*

TO *(Name and address of appellant's lawyer or appellant)*

RCP-E 61L (July 1, 2007)

FORM 62A

Courts of Justice Act

NOTICE OF APPEAL TO A JUDGE

(General heading)

NOTICE OF APPEAL

THE *(identify party)* APPEALS to a judge from the order *(or* certificate*)* of *(name of judge or officers)* dated *(date)*.

THE APPEAL WILL BE HEARD ON *(day)*, *(date)*, at *(time)* at *(address of court house)*.

THE *(identify party)* ASKS *(state the precise relief sought)*.

THE GROUNDS OF APPEAL are as follows: *(Set out briefly the grounds of appeal)*.

(Date)   *(Name, address and telephone number of law-*
                                              yer or party serving notice)

TO *(Name and address of lawyer or party on whom notice is served)*

RCP-E 62A (July 1, 2007)

FORM 63A

Courts of Justice Act

CERTIFICATE OF STAY

(General heading)

(Court seal)

CERTIFICATE OF STAY

The Registrar of the Court of Appeal *(or* Divisional Court*) (or* the local registrar of this court at *(place))* certifies that the order *(or* judgment*) of (name of judge or officer)* dated *(date)* have been stayed by the delivery of a notice of appeal from the order *(or* judgment*) (or* by order of *(name of judge)* dated *(date))*. *(Where an order is made under Rule 63 limiting the stay, give particulars.)*

Date _____   Issued by   _____

                                                 Registrar

                                 Address of   _____
                                 court office

                                              _____

RCP-E 63A (November 1, 2005)

FORM 63B

Courts of Justice Act

CERTIFICATE OF STAY

(General Heading)

(Court Seal)

CERTIFICATE OF STAY

The Registrar of the Divisional Court certifies that, under subsection 25 (1) of the *Statutory Powers Procedure Act*, the order of the Ontario Rental Housing Tribunal dated *(date)* has been stayed by an appeal to this court.

Date _____   Issued by _____

Registrar

RCP-E 63B (November 1, 2005)

FORM 64A

Courts of Justice Act

REQUEST TO REDEEM

(General Heading)

REQUEST TO REDEEM

The defendant *(name)* requests an opportunity to redeem the mortgaged property.

(Date)   *(Name, address and telephone number of defen-*
                                      dant's lawyer or defendant)

(Where the defendant is a subsequent encumbrancer, add:)

AFFIDAVIT VERIFYING CLAIM

I, *(full name of deponent)*, of the *(City, Town, etc.)* of . . . . , in the *(County, Re-gional Municipality, etc.)* of . . . . , *(where the deponent is a party or the lawyer, officer, director, member or employee of a party, set out the deponent's capacity)*, MAKE OATH AND SAY *(or AFFIRM)*:

1. There is now due to me under a mortgage on *(or an execution against or a construction lien registered against or as may be)* the mortgaged property,

(a) for principal	$ _____
(b) for interest *(set out particulars)*	$ _____
(c) *(set out particulars of any other amounts due)*	$ _____
Total now due	$ _____

Sworn *(etc.)*

RCP-E 64A (July 1, 2007)

520

FORM 64B

Courts of Justice Act

DEFAULT JUDGMENT FOR FORECLOSURE WITH A REFERENCE

(General heading)

(Court seal)

JUDGMENT

On reading the statement of claim in this action and the proof of service of the statement of claim on the defendant(s), filed, no request to redeem or request for sale having been served and filed *(or* the defendant(s) *(name(s))* having served and filed a request to redeem) and the defendant(s) having been noted in default, and the plaintiff wishing a reference *(or* the registrar having decided to sign judgment with a reference*)*,

1. IT IS ORDERED AND ADJUDGED that all necessary inquiries be made, accounts taken, costs fixed or assessed and steps taken for redemption or foreclosure of the equity of redemption in the mortgaged property described in the attached schedule, and that for these purposes this action be referred to the master *(or as may be)* at *(place)*. The mortgage is dated . . . . and made between *(name of mortgagor)* and *(name of mortgagee)*, and registered *(give particulars of registration and of any assignment of the mortgage)*.

(Where judgment is for possession, add:)

2. IT IS ORDERED AND ADJUDGED that the defendant *(name)* deliver to the plaintiff or as the plaintiff directs possession of the mortgaged property or of such part of it as is in the possession of the defendants.

(Where judgment is for payment of the mortgage debt and the registrar is to take the account, and the following two paragraphs:)

3. IT IS ORDERED AND ADJUDGED that the defendant *(name)* forthwith pay to the plaintiff the sum of $ . . . . . . , being the amount due to the plaintiff(s) today for principal, interest and costs; and on payment of the amount due to the plaintiff, the plaintiff convey the mortgaged property to the defendant or as the defendants directs, in accordance with section 2 of the *Mortgages Act*, and deliver up all documents relating to the mortgaged property.

THIS JUDGMENT BEARS INTEREST at the rate of *(rate claimed in the statement of claim)* per cent per year from its date.

(Where judgment is for payment of the mortgage debt and the plaintiff wishes the account to be taken on the reference or the registrar refers the taking of the account, substitute the following two paragraphs:)

3. IT IS ORDERED AND ADJUDGED that the defendant *(name)* pay to the plaintiff, forthwith after confirmation of the report on the reference, the amount found due for principal, interest and costs in accordance with the report, and on payment of the amount due to the plaintiff, the plaintiff convey the mortgaged property to the defendant or as the defendant directs, in accordance with section 2 of the *Mortgages Act*, and deliver up all documents relating to the mortgaged property.

THIS JUDGMENT BEARS INTEREST at the rate set out in the report on the reference from the date of confirmation of the report.

Date _____   Signed by   _____

                                                    Local registrar

                                      Address of   _____
                                      court office

                                                           _____

(The description of the mortgaged property in the attached schedule must be the same as in the statement of claim.)

RCP-E 64B (November 1, 2005)

FORM 64C

Courts of Justice Act

DEFAULT JUDGMENT FOR IMMEDIATE FORECLOSURE

(General heading)

(Court seal)

JUDGMENT

On reading the statement of claim in this action and the proof of service of the statement of claim on the defendant(s), filed, no request to redeem or request for sale having been served and filed, the defendant(s) having been noted in default, and the plaintiff not wishing a reference,

1. IT IS ORDERED AND ADJUDGED that the right, title and equity of redemption of the defendant(s) *(name(s))* to and in the mortgaged property described in the attached schedule are foreclosed. The mortgage is dated . . . . and made between *(name of mortgagor)* and *(name of mortgagee)*, and registered *(give particulars of registration and of any assignment of the mortgage)*.

(Where judgment is for possession, add:)

2. IT IS ORDERED AND ADJUDGED that the defendant *(name)* forthwith deliver to the plaintiff or as the plaintiff directs possession of the mortgaged property or of such part of it as is in the possession of the defendant.

(Where judgment is for payment of the mortgage debt, add the following two paragraphs:)

3. IT IS ORDERED AND ADJUDGED that the defendant *(name)* forthwith pay to the plaintiff the sum of $ . . . . , being the amount due to the plaintiff today for principal, interest and costs.

THIS JUDGMENT BEARS INTEREST at the rate of *(rate claimed in the statement of claim)* per cent per year from its date.

Date _____ Issued by _____

Local registrar

Address of _____
court office

_____

(The description of the mortgaged property in the attached schedule must be the same as in the statement of claim.)

RCP-E 64C (November 1, 2005)

FORM 64D

Courts of Justice Act

DEFAULT JUDGMENT FOR FORECLOSURE WITHOUT A REFERENCE

(General heading)

(Court seal)

JUDGMENT

On reading the statement of claim in this action and the proof of service of the statement of claim on the defendant(s), filed, no request for sale having been served and filed the defendant(s) *(name(s))* having served and filed a request to redeem and the defendant(s) having been noted in default, and the account having been taken in the presence of the lawyer(s) for the plaintiff(s) *(or* the plaintiff*)* and the lawyer(s) for the defendant(s) *(where applicable, add (identify party)* appearing in person *or* no one appearing for the defendant *(name)* although served with notice of the taking of the account as appears from the affidavit of *(name),* filed),

1. I FIND that the following sums are due to the plaintiff from the defendant *(name of owner of equity of redemption)* on *(redemption date),* the day I have fixed for payment under the mortgage in question in this action:

(a)	for principal	$_____
(b)	for taxes paid	$_____
(c)	for premiums of insurance paid	$_____
(d)	for maintenance costs paid	$_____
(e)	for heating costs paid	$_____
(f)	for utility costs paid *(add any other costs in similar fashion)*	$_____
(g)	for interest up to *(date of judgment)*	$_____
(h)	for costs of this action	$_____
(i)	for subsequent interest on the principal at the rate of ____per cent per year up to the day fixed for payment	$_____

making a total amount due on *(redemption date)* of $_____

2. IT IS ORDERED AND ADJUDGED that:

(a) on payment of the sum of $ . . . . *(total amount due from paragraph 1)* into the *(name of financial institution)* at *(address),* to the joint credit of the plaintiff and the Accountant of the Superior Court of Justice *(or* the local registrar*);* or

(b) on recovery by the plaintiff of the amount due under paragraph 6 of this judgment, together with post-judgment interest,

on or before *(redemption date),* the plaintiff shall convey the mortgaged property described in the attached schedule to the defendant *(name)* or as the defendant(s) direct(s), in accordance with section 2 of the *Mortgages Act,* and deliver up all documents relating to the mortgaged property. The mortgage is dated . . . . and made between *(name of mortgagor)* and *(name of mortgagee),* and registered *(give particulars of registration and of any assignment of the mortgage).*

(Delete clause (b) where the judgment does not order payment of the mortgage debt.)

524

(Where more than one party is entitled to redeem, add:)

3. IT IS ORDERED AND ADJUDGED that the defendant *(name of encumbrancer)* is entitled to the first right to redeem and the defendant *(name)* is entitled to the second right to redeem *(and so on)* and the defendant *(name of owner of equity of redemption)* is entitled to the last right to redeem.

(Foreclosure on default in payment)

4. IT IS ORDERED AND ADJUDGED that, on default in payment as required by paragraph 2, the right, title and equity of redemption of the defendant(s) to and in the mortgaged property described in the attached schedule are foreclosed.

(Where judgment is for possession, add:)

5. IT IS ORDERED AND ADJUDGED that the defendant *(name)* forthwith deliver to the plaintiff or as the plaintiff directs, possession of the mortgaged property, or of such part of it as is in the possession of the defendant.

(Where judgment is for payment of the mortgage debt, add the following two paragraphs:)

6. IT IS ORDERED AND ADJUDGED that the defendant *(name)* forthwith pay to the plaintiff(s) the sum of $ . . . . , being the amount due to the plaintiff today for principal, interest and costs.

   THIS JUDGMENT BEARS INTEREST at the rate of *(rate claimed in statement of claim)* per cent per year from its date.

Date _____   Issued by   _____

                                                 Local registrar

Address of   _____
court office

_____

(The description of the mortgaged property in the attached schedule must be the same as in the statement of claim.)

RCP-E 64D (July 1, 2007)

FORM 64E

Courts of Justice Act

FINAL ORDER OF FORECLOSURE

(Court file no.)

(Court)

(Name of judge or officer)   *(Day and date)*

(Court seal)

(Title of proceeding)

FINAL ORDER OF FORECLOSURE

THIS MOTION made by *(identify moving party)*, without notice, was heard this day.

(Order following judgment or report granting redemption period)

ON READING the judgment in this action dated *(date)*, *(where there is an order fixing a new day for payment, add:* the order for a new day for payment dated *(date))*, *(where a notice of change of account has been delivered, add:* the notice of change of account, with proof of service,) and the certificate of the *(title)* of the *(financial institution)* at *(place)*, with affidavit of execution, and the affidavit of the plaintiff, and on hearing the submissions of the lawyer for the plaintiff, and since the defendant(s) entitled to redeem has (have) not redeemed the mortgaged property,

1. IT IS ORDERED that the right, title and equity of redemption of the defendant(s) *(names of those who failed to serve and file a request to redeem, to attend and prove a claim on the taking of account or to redeem the mortgaged property)* to and in the mortgaged property described in the attached schedule are foreclosed. The mortgage is dated . . . . and made between *(name of mortgagor)* and *(name of mortgagee)*, and registered *(give particulars of registration and of any assignment of the mortgage)*.

(Order following report granting redemption period)

ON READING the judgment in this action dated *(date)*, and the report in this action dated *(date)* and confirmed on *(date)*, with proof of service, *(where there is an order fixing a new day for payment, add:* the order for a new day for payment dated *(date)*, with proof of service,) *(where a notice of change of account has been delivered, add:* the notice of change of account, with proof of service, and the certificate of the *(title)* of the *(financial institution)* at *(place)*, with affidavit of execution,) and the affidavit of the plaintiff, and on hearing the submissions of the lawyer for the plaintiff, and since the defendant(s) entitled to redeem has (have) not redeemed the mortgaged property,

1. IT IS ORDERED that the right, title and equity of redemption of the defendant(s) *(names of those who failed to serve and file a request to redeem, to attend and prove a claim on the reference or to redeem the mortgaged property)* to and in the mortgaged property described in the attached schedule are foreclosed. The mortgage is dated . . . . and made between *(name of mortgagor)* and *(name of mortgagee)*, and registered *(give particulars of registration and of any assignment of the mortgage)*.

(Order following report granting no redemption period)

ON READING the judgment in this action dated *(date)* and the report in this action dated *(date)* and confirmed on *(date)*, with proof of service, and the affidavit of the plaintiff, and on hearing the submissions of the lawyer for the plaintiff, and since no defendant is entitled to redeem,

1. IT IS ORDERED that the right, title and equity of redemption of the defendant(s) *(names)* to and in the mortgaged property described in the attached schedule are foreclosed. The mortgage is dated . . . . and made between *(name of mortgagor)* and *(name of mortgagee)*, and registered *(give particulars of registration and of any assignment of the mortgage)*.

(Order following redemption of plaintiff by encumbrancer)

ON READING the judgment in this action dated *(date)*, *(where there is a report, add:* the report on the reference in this action dated *(date)* and confirmed on *(date)*, with proof of service), the certificate of the *(title)* of the *(financial institution)* at *(place)*, with affidavit of execution, and the affidavit of the defendant *(name of defendant who has redeemed)*, on hearing the submissions of the lawyer for the defendant, and since the defendant has redeemed the plaintiff, and has obtained an assignment of the judgment and the mortgage and has registered the latter, and since the defendants *(names)* are in default,

1. IT IS ORDERED that the right, title and equity of redemption of the defendant(s) *(names of those failed to serve and file a request to redeem, to attend and prove a claim on the reference or to redeem the mortgaged property)* to and in the mortgaged property described in the attached schedule and foreclosed. The mortgage is dated . . . . and made between *(name of mortgagor)* and *(name of mortgagee)*, and registered *(give particulars of registration and of any assignment of the mortgage)*.

(Note: the preceding types of order in this form, which are for use in a foreclosure action, may be adapted for a redemption action by substituting "defendant" for "plaintiff" and "plaintiff" for "defendant", whenever those words appear.)

(Order following report in redemption action, where necessary to refer back to the master (or as may be) to complete redemption.)

ON READING the judgment in this action dated *(date)*, the report on the reference in this action dated *(date)* and confirmed on *(date)*, with proof of service, the certificate of the *(title)* of the *(financial institution)* at *(place)*, with affidavit of execution, and the affidavit of the defendant *(name)*, and on hearing the submissions of the lawyer for the defendant, and since the plaintiff has failed to redeem *(where there are subsequent encumbrancers and the defendant wishes to foreclose them, add:* and it is necessary to take accounts between the defendants*)*,

1. IT IS ORDERED that the right, title and equity of redemption of the plaintiff to and in the mortgaged property described in the attached schedule are foreclosed. The mortgage is dated . . . . and made between *(name of mortgagor)* and *(name of mortgagee)*, and registered *(give particulars of registration and of any assignment of the mortgage)*.

(Where subsequent encumbrancers are to be foreclosed)

2. IT IS ORDERED that all necessary inquiries be made, accounts taken, costs fixed or assessed and steps taken for redemption by or foreclosure against any subsequent encumbrancers, and that for these purposes this action be referred to the master *(or as may be)* at *(place)*.

(Where accounts are to be taken)

3. IT IS ORDERED that all necessary inquiries be made, accounts taken, costs fixed or assessed and steps taken for the adjustment of the respective rights and liabilities of the original defendants.

(Signature of judge, master or registrar)

(The description of the mortgaged property in the attached schedule must be the same as in the statement of claim.)

RCP-E 64E (July 1, 2007)

FORM 64F

Courts of Justice Act

REQUEST FOR SALE

(General heading)

REQUEST FOR SALE

The defendant *(name)* requests a sale of the mortgaged property.

(Where the defendant is a subsequent encumbrancer, add:)

Attached is a certificate of the Accountant of the Superior Court of Justice *(or* the local registrar of the court at *(place))* stating that the defendant has paid into court the sum of $250 as security for the costs of the plaintiff and of any other party having carriage of the sale.

(Date)   *(Name, address and telephone number of defendant's lawyer or defendant)*

(Where the defendant is a subsequent encumbrancer, add:)

AFFIDAVIT VERIFYING CLAIM

I, *(full name of deponent)*, of the (City, Town, *etc.)* of . . . . , in the (County Regional Municipality, *etc.)* of . . . . , *(where the deponent if a party or the lawyer, officer, director, member or employee of a party, set out the deponent's capacity)*, MAKE OATH AND SAY *(or* AFFIRM*)*:

1. There is now due to me under a mortgage on *(or* and execution against *or* a construction lien registered against *or as may be)* the mortgaged property,

(a)	for principal	$	_____
(b)	for interest *(set out particulars)*	$	_____
(c)	*(set out particulars of any other amounts due)*	$	_____
	Total now due	$	_____

SWORN *(etc.)*

RCP-E 64F (July 1, 2007)

529

FORM 64G

Courts of Justice Act

DEFAULT JUDGMENT FOR SALE WITH A REDEMPTION PERIOD (ACTION CONVERTED FROM FORECLOSURE TO SALE)

(General heading)

(Court seal)

JUDGMENT

On reading the statement of claim in this action and the proof of service of the statement of claim on the defendant(s), filed, the defendant *(name)* having served and filed a request for sale, the defendant(s) having been noted in default and the defendant(s) *(name(s))* having served and filed a request to redeem,

1. IT IS ORDERED AND ADJUDGED that all necessary inquiries be made, accounts taken, costs fixed or assessed and steps taken for redemption or sale of the mortgaged property described in the attached schedule, and that for these purposes this action be referred to the master *(or as may be)* at *(place)*.

(Where judgment is for possession, add:)

2. IT IS ORDERED AND ADJUDGED that the defendant *(name)* deliver to the plaintiff or as the plaintiff directs possession of the mortgaged property or of such part of it as is in the possession of the defendant.

(Where judgment is for payment of the mortgage debt and the registrar is to take the account, add the following two paragraphs:)

3. IT IS ORDERED AND ADJUDGED that the defendant *(name)* forthwith pay to the plaintiff the sum of $ . . . . , being the amount due to the plaintiff today for principal, interest and costs; and that, on payment of the amount due to the plaintiff before the sale takes place, the plaintiff convey the mortgaged property to the defendant or as the defendant directs, in accordance with section 2 of the *Mortgages Act*, and deliver up all documents relating to the mortgage property.

THIS JUDGMENT BEARS INTEREST at the rate of *(rate claimed in statement of claim)* per cent per year from its date.

(Where judgment is for payment of the mortgage debt and the plaintiff wishes the account to be taken on reference or the registrar refers the taking of the account, substitute the following two paragraphs:)

3. IT IS ORDERED AND ADJUDGED that the defendant *(name)* pay to the plaintiff, forthwith after the confirmation of the report on the reference, the amount found due for principal, interest and costs in accordance with the report; and that on payment of the amount due to the plaintiff before the sale takes place, the plaintiff convey the mortgaged property to the defendant or as the defendant directs, in accordance with section 2 of the *Mortgages Act,* and deliver up all documents relating to the mortgaged property.

THIS JUDGMENT BEARS INTEREST at the rate set out in the report on the reference from the date of confirmation of the report.

Date _____   Signed by   _____

Local registrar

Address of   _____
court office

                          _____

(The description of the mortgaged property in the attached schedule must be the same as in the statement of claim.)

RCP-E 64G (November 1, 2005)

FORM 64H

Courts of Justice Act

DEFAULT JUDGMENT FOR IMMEDIATE SALE (ACTION CONVERTED FROM FORECLOSURE TO SALE)

(General heading)

(Court seal)

JUDGMENT

On reading the statement of claim in this action and the proof of service of the statement of claim on the defendant(s), filed, the defendant *(name)* having served and filed a request for sale, the defendant(s) having been noted in default and no request to redeem having been served and filed *(or* a request to redeem having been served and filed by the defendant *(name of subsequent encumbrancer))*,

1. IT IS ORDERED AND ADJUDGED that all necessary inquiries be made, accounts taken, costs fixed or assessed and steps taken for the immediate sale of the mortgaged property described in the attached schedule without a redemption period, and that for these purposes this action be referred to the master *(or as may be)* at *(place)*.

2. IT IS ORDERED AND ADJUDGED that the purchasers pay the purchase money into court to the credit of this action and that the purchase money be applied in payment of what is found due to the plaintiff, together with subsequent interest and subsequent costs to be computed and fixed or assessed by the master *(or as may be)* and that the master *(or as may be)* also determine those parties or persons entitled to the balance of the money and the amounts to which they are entitled.

(Where judgment is for possession, add:)

3. IT IS ORDERED AND ADJUDGED that the defendant *(name)* forthwith deliver to the plaintiff or as the plaintiff directs possession of the mortgaged property, or of such part of it as is in the possession of the defendant.

(Where judgment is for payment of the mortgage debt and the registrar is to take the account, add the following two paragraphs:)

4. IT IS ORDERED AND ADJUDGED that the defendant *(name)* forthwith pay to the plaintiff the sum of $ . . . . , being the amount due to the plaintiff today for principal, interest and costs; and that on payment of the amount due to the plaintiff before the sale takes place, the plaintiff convey the mortgaged property to the defendant or as the defendant directs, in accordance with section 2 of the *Mortgages Act,* and deliver up all documents relating to the mortgaged property.

THIS JUDGMENT BEARS INTEREST at the rate of *(rate claimed in the statement of claim)* per cent per year from its date.

(Where judgment is for payment of the mortgage debt and the plaintiff wishes the account to be taken on the reference or the registrar refers the taking of account, substitute the following two paragraphs:)

4. IT IS ORDERED AND ADJUDGED that the defendant *(name)* pay to the plaintiff, forthwith after the confirmation of the report on the reference, the amount found due for principal, interest

and costs in accordance with the report, and on payment of the amount due to the plaintiff before the sale takes place, the plaintiff convey the mortgaged property to the defendant or as the defendant directs, in accordance with section 2 of the *Mortgages Act,* and deliver up all documents relating to the mortgaged property.

THIS JUDGMENT BEARS INTEREST at the rate set out in the report on the reference from the date of confirmation of the report.

Date _____ Signed by _____

Local registrar

Address of _____
court office

_____

(The description of the mortgaged property in the attached schedule must be the same as in the statement of claim.)

RCP-E 64H (November 1, 2005)

FORM 64I

Courts of Justice Act

DEFAULT JUDGMENT FOR SALE CONDITIONAL ON PROOF OF CLAIM (ACTION CONVERTED FROM FORECLOSURE TO SALE)

(General heading)

(Court seal)

JUDGMENT

On reading the statement of claim in this action and the proof of service of the statement of claim on the defendant(s), filed, no request to redeem having been served and filed *(or* the defendant *(name)* having served and filed a request to redeem), the defendant(s) having been noted in default, and the defendant *(name of subsequent encumbrancer)* having served and filed a request for sale and having paid into court the sum of $250 as security for costs,

1. IT IS ORDERED AND ADJUDGED that all necessary inquiries be made, accounts taken, costs fixed or assessed and steps taken for redemption or sale of the mortgaged property described in the attached schedule and that for these purposes this action be referred to the master *(or as may be)* at *(place).*

2. IT IS ORDERED AND ADJUDGED that, if the defendant *(name of subsequent encumbrancer)* fails to prove a claim on the reference for sale, the master *(or as may be)* shall proceed as on a reference for redemption or foreclosure.

(Where judgment is for possession, add:)

3. IT IS ORDERED AND ADJUDGED that the defendant *(name)* deliver to the plaintiff or as the plaintiff directs possession of the mortgaged property or of such part of it as is in the possession of the defendant.

(Where judgment is for payment of the mortgage debt and the registrar is to take the account, add the following two paragraphs:)

4. IT IS ORDERED AND ADJUDGED that the defendant *(name)* forthwith pay to the plaintiff the sum of $ . . . . , being the amount due to the plaintiff today for principal, interest and costs; and that on payment of the amount due to the plaintiff, the plaintiff convey the mortgaged property to the defendant or as the defendant directs, in accordance with section 2 of the *Mortgages Act*, and deliver up all documents relating to the mortgaged property.

THIS JUDGMENT BEARS INTEREST at the rate of *(rate claimed in statement of claim)* per cent per year from its date.

(Where judgment is for payment of the mortgage debt and the plaintiff wishes the account to be taken on the reference or the registrar refers the taking of the account, substitute the following two paragraphs:)

4. IT IS ORDERED AND ADJUDGED that the defendant *(name)* pay to the plaintiff, forthwith after the confirmation of the report on the reference, the amount found due for principal, interest and costs in accordance with the report, and on payment of the amount due to the plaintiff before the sale takes place, the plaintiff convey the mortgaged property to the defendant or as the defendant directs, in accordance with section 2 of the *Mortgages Act,* and deliver up all documents relating to the mortgaged property.

THIS JUDGMENT BEARS INTEREST at the rate set out in the report on the reference from the date of confirmation of the report.

Date _____   Signed by   _____

                                                            Local registrar

                                              Address of   _____
                                              court office

                                                             _____

(The description of the mortgaged property in the attached schedule must be the same as in the statement of claim.)

                                         RCP-E 64I (November 1, 2005)

FORM 64J

Courts of Justice Act

DEFAULT JUDGMENT FOR IMMEDIATE SALE

(General heading)

(Court seal)

JUDGMENT

On reading the statement of claim in this action and the proof of service of the statement of claim on the defendant(s), filed, no request to redeem having been served and filed and the defendant(s) having been noted in default,

1. IT IS ORDERED AND ADJUDGED that all necessary inquiries be made, accounts taken, costs fixed or assessed and steps taken for the immediate sale of the mortgaged property described in the attached schedule without a redemption period, and that for these purposes this action be referred to the master *(or as may be)* at *(place)*.

2. IT IS ORDERED AND ADJUDGED that the purchasers pay the purchase money into court to the credit of this action and that the purchase money be applied in payment of what is found due to the plaintiff, together with subsequent interest and subsequent costs to be computed and fixed or assessed by the master *(or as may be)* and that the master *(or as may be)* also determine those parties or persons entitled to the balance of the money and the amounts to which they are entitled.

(Where judgment is for possession, add:)

3. IT IS ORDERED AND ADJUDGED that the defendant *(name)* forthwith deliver to the plaintiff or as the plaintiff directs possession of the mortgaged property, or of such part of it as is in the possession of the defendant.

(Where judgment is for payment of the mortgage debt and the registrar is to take the account, add the following two paragraphs:)

4. IT IS ORDERED AND ADJUDGED that the defendant *(name)* forthwith pay to the plaintiff the sum of $ . . . . , being the amount due to the plaintiff today for principal, interest and costs; and that on payment of the amount due to the plaintiff before the sale takes place, the plaintiff convey the mortgaged property to the defendant or as the defendant directs, in accordance with section 2 of the *Mortgages Act,* and deliver up all documents relating to the mortgaged property.

THIS JUDGMENT BEARS INTEREST at the rate of *(rate claimed in statement of claim)* per cent per year from its date.

(Where judgment is for payment of the mortgage debt and the plaintiff wishes the account to be taken on the reference or the registrar refers the taking of the account, substitute the following two paragraphs:)

4. IT IS ORDERED AND ADJUDGED that the defendant *(name)* pay to the plaintiff, forthwith after the confirmation of the report on the reference, the amount found due for principal, interest and costs in accordance with the report, and on payment of the amount due to the plaintiff before the sale takes place, the plaintiff convey the mortgaged property to the defendant or as the defendant directs, in accordance with section 2 of the *Mortgages Act,* and deliver up all documents relating to the mortgaged property.

THIS JUDGMENT BEARS INTEREST at the rate set out in the report on the reference from the date of confirmation of the report.

Date _____ Signed by _____

                                                Local registrar

Address of   _____
court office

(The description of the mortgaged property in the attached schedule must be the same as in the statement of claim.)

RCP-E 64J (November 1, 2005)

FORM 64K

Courts of Justice Act

DEFAULT JUDGMENT FOR SALE WITH A REDEMPTION PERIOD

(General heading)

(Court seal)

JUDGMENT

On reading the statement of claim in this action and the proof of service of the statement of claim on the defendant(s), filed, the defendant(s) having been noted in default and the defendant *(name)* having served and filed a request to redeem,

1. IT IS ORDERED AND ADJUDGED that all necessary inquiries be made, accounts taken, costs fixed or assessed and steps taken for redemption or sale of the mortgaged property described in the attached schedule, and that for these purposes this action be referred to the master *(or as may be)* at *(place)*.

(Where judgment is for possession, add:)

2. IT IS ORDERED AND ADJUDGED that the defendant *(name)* deliver to the plaintiff or as the plaintiff directs possession of the mortgaged property or of such part of it as is in the possession of the defendant.

(Where judgment is for payment of the mortgage debt and the registrar is to take the account, add the following two paragraphs:)

3. IT IS ORDERED AND ADJUDGED that the defendant *(name)* forthwith pay to the plaintiff the sum of $ . . . . , being the amount due to the plaintiff today for principal, interest and costs; and on payment of the amount due to the plaintiff before the sale takes place, the plaintiff convey the mortgaged property to the defendant(s) or as the defendant directs, in accordance with section 2 of the *Mortgages Act*, and deliver up all documents relating to the mortgaged property.

THIS JUDGMENT BEARS INTEREST at the rate of *(rate claimed in statement of claim)* per cent per year from its date.

(Where judgment is for payment of the mortgage debt and the plaintiff wishes the account to be taken on the reference or the registrar refers the taking of the account, substitute the following two paragraphs:)

3. IT IS ORDERED AND ADJUDGED that the defendant *(name)* pay to the plaintiff(s), forthwith after confirmation of the report on the reference, the amount found due for principal, interest and costs in accordance with the report; and that on payment of the amount due to the plaintiff before the sale takes place, the plaintiff convey the mortgaged property to the defendant or as the defendant directs, in accordance with section 2 of the *Mortgages Act*, and deliver up all documents relating to the mortgaged property.

THIS JUDGMENT BEARS INTEREST at the rate set out in the report on the reference from the date of confirmation of the report.

Date _____ Signed by _____

Local registrar

Address of   _____
court office

                      _____

(The description of the mortgaged property in the attached schedule must be the same as in the statement of claim.)

RCP-E 64K (November 1, 2005)

FORM 64L

Courts of Justice Act

FINAL ORDER FOR SALE

(Court)

(Court file no.)

(Name of judge or officer)   *(Day and date)*

(Court seal)

(Title of proceeding)

FINAL ORDER FOR SALE

THIS MOTION made by the plaintiff, without notice, was heard this day.

ON READING the judgment in this action dated *(date)*, and the report in this action dated *(date)* and confirmed on *(date)*, with proof of service, the certificate of the *(title)* of the *(financial institution)* at *(place)*, with affidavit of execution, and the affidavit of the plaintiff, and on hearing the submissions of the lawyer for the plaintiff, and since the defendant(s) entitled to redeem has (have) not redeemed the mortgaged property,

1. IT IS ORDERED that the mortgaged property described in the attached schedule be sold forthwith as directed by the judgment in this action under the direction of the master *(or as may be)* at *(place)*.

(Where appropriate, add:)

2. IT IS ORDERED that the right, title and equity of redemption of the defendants *(names of subsequent encumbrancers who failed to attend and prove a claim on the reference)* to and in the mortgaged property described in the attached schedule are foreclosed.

(Signature of judge, master or registrar)

(The description of the mortgaged property in the attached schedule must be the same as in the statement of claim.)

RCP-E 64L (July 1, 2007)

FORM 64M

Courts of Justice Act

DEFAULT JUDGMENT FOR REDEMPTION

(General heading)

(Court seal)

JUDGMENT

On reading the statement of claim in this action and the proof of service of the statement of claim on the defendant(s), filed, and the defendant(s) having been noted in default,

1. IT IS ORDERED AND ADJUDGED that all necessary inquiries be made, accounts taken, costs fixed or assessed and steps taken for the redemption of the mortgaged property described in the attached schedule, and that for this purpose this action be referred to the master *(or as may be)* at *(place)*.

2. IT IS ORDERED AND ADJUDGED that, on the plaintiff paying to the defendant *(name of mortgagee)* the amount found due on the mortgage in question, or, if nothing is found due, then forthwith after the confirmation of the report on the reference, the defendant convey the mortgaged property to the plaintiff or as the plaintiff directs, in accordance with section 2 of the *Mortgages Act,* and deliver up all documents relating to the mortgaged property.

3. IT IS ORDERED AND ADJUDGED that if the plaintiff defaults in payment of the amount found due to the defendant *(name of mortgagee),* the defendant is entitled, on motion without notice, to a final order of foreclosure against the plaintiff or to an order dismissing the action with costs.

4. IT IS ORDERED AND ADJUDGED that if nothing is found due to the defendant *(name of mortgagee),* the defendant pay the plaintiff's costs of this action and, if any balance is found due from the defendant *(name of mortgagee)* to the plaintiff, that the defendant pay the balance to the plaintiff forthwith after confirmation of the report on the reference.

THIS JUDGMENT BEARS INTEREST at the rate set out in the report on the reference from the date of confirmation of the report.

Date _____   Signed by   _____

                                                              Local registrar

                                    Address of   _____
                                    court office

                                                  _____

(The description of the mortgaged property in the attached schedule must be the same as in the statement of claim.)

RCP-E 64M (November 1, 2005)

541

FORM 64N

Courts of Justice Act

NOTICE OF REFERENCE TO SUBSEQUENT ENCUMBRANCER ADDED ON REFERENCE

(Court file no.)

ONTARIO

SUPERIOR COURT OF JUSTICE

BETWEEN:

(name)

Plaintiff

and

(name(s))

Defendant(s)

and

(name(s))

Defendant(s) added on the reference

NOTICE OF REFERENCE

An action has been commenced by the plaintiff for the foreclosure *(or* sale*)* of the mortgaged property described in the attached schedule. I have been directed by the judgment in this action dated *(date)* *(where the judgment is for sale, insert:* to conduct a sale of the property and) to inquire whether any person other than the plaintiff has a lien, charge or encumbrance on the property subsequent to the plaintiff's claim. It appears that you may have a lien, charge or encumbrance on the property. I have therefore added you as a defendant in this action.

YOU ARE REQUIRED TO APPEAR before me and prove your claim, either in person or by an Ontario lawyer acting for you, on *(day), (date),* at *(time),* at *(address).* At that time, I shall determine the amount of the claim of the plaintiff, and of the encumbrancers who prove their claims before me. *(Where the judgment is for sale without a redemption period, add:* At the same time, I shall settle the conditions of sale and advertisement and make any other necessary preparations for the sale of the property.)

If you wish to set aside or vary my order adding you as a defendant or the judgment in this action, you must make a motion to the court within ten days after service on you of this notice *(or where the person is to be served outside Ontario, such further time as the referee directs).* If you fail to do so, you will be bound by the judgment and the subsequent steps in this action.

IF YOU FAIL TO ATTEND AND PROVE YOUR CLAIM at the time and place set out above, you will be treated as disclaiming all interest in the property and the action will proceed in your absence and without further notice to you. The property may be dealt with as if you had no claim, and your claim may be foreclosed.

(Date)   *(Signature of referee)*

TO *(Names and addresses of defendants added on reference who appear to be subsequent encumbrancers)*

(The description of the mortgaged property in the attached schedule must be the same as in the statement of claim.)

RCP-E 64N (November 1, 2005)

543

FORM 640

Courts of Justice Act

NOTICE OF REFERENCE TO SUBSEQUENT ENCUMBRANCER NAMED AS ORIGINAL PARTY

(Court file no.)

ONTARIO

SUPERIOR COURT OF JUSTICE

BETWEEN:

(name)

Plaintiff

and

(name)

Defendant(s)

and

(name(s))

Defendant(s) added

on the reference

NOTICE OF REFERENCE

The judgment in this action directs me *(where the judgment is for sale, insert:* to conduct a sale of the mortgaged property and*)* to inquire whether any person other than the plaintiff has a lien, charge or encumbrance on the mortgaged property in question in this action subsequent to the plaintiff's claim, and to take an account of the amount due to the plaintiff and any such person. It appears that you may have a lien, charge or encumbrance on the property.

YOU ARE REQUIRED TO APPEAR before me and prove your claim, either in person or by an Ontario lawyer acting for you, on *(day), (date),* at *(time),* at *(address).* At that time, I shall determine the amount of the claim of the plaintiff, and of the encumbrancers who prove their claims before me. (*Where the judgment is for sale without redemption period, add:* At the same time, I shall settle the conditions of sale and advertisement and make any other necessary preparations for the sale of the property.)

IF YOU FAIL TO ATTEND AND PROVE YOUR CLAIM at the time and place set out above, you will be treated as disclaiming any lien, charged or encumbrance on the property and the action will proceed in your absence and without further notice to you. The property may be dealt with as if you had no such claim and your claim may be foreclosed.

(Date)   *(Signature of referee)*

TO *(Names and addresses of defendants named in statement of claim who appear to be subsequent encumbrancers)*

RCP-E 64O (November 1, 2005)

FORM 64P

Courts of Justice Act

NOTICE OF REFERENCE TO ORIGINAL DEFENDANTS

(Court file no.)

ONTARIO

SUPERIOR COURT OF JUSTICE

BETWEEN:

(name)

Plaintiff

and

(name(s))

Defendant(s)

and

(name(s))

Defendant(s) added on the reference

NOTICE OF REFERENCE

The judgment in this action directs me *(where the judgment is for sale, insert:* to conduct a sale of the mortgaged property and*)* to inquire whether any person other than the plaintiff has a lien, charge or encumbrance on the mortgaged property in question in this action subsequent to the plaintiff's claim, and to take an account due to the plaintiff and any such person.

It appears that the persons named in the attached schedule may have a lien, charge or encumbrance on the property *(where the judgment directs the referee to add encumbrancers, add:* and I have therefore added as defendants those persons who were not already parties to this action).

YOU ARE REQUIRED TO APPEAR before me and prove your claim, either in person or by an Ontario lawyer acting for you, on *(day)*, *(date)*, at *(time)*, at *(address)*. At that time, I shall determine whether any of the parties have a lien, charge or encumbrance on the property and ascertain the amount of those claims and of the plaintiff's claim. *(Where the judgment is for sale without a redemption period, add:* At the same time, I shall settle the conditions of sale and advertisement and make any other necessary arrangements for the sale.)

(Where the judgment is for sale conditional on proof of a claim by a subsequent encumbrancer, add: The defendant *(name of subsequent encumbrancer)* has requested a sale of the property. If the defendant fails to attend and prove a claim before me, there will not be a sale of the property, and the claims of those who fail to appear before me may be foreclosed.)

IF YOU FAIL TO ATTEND at the time and place set out above, the action will proceed in your absence without further notice to you and your rights in the property may be foreclosed.

If you are a subsequent encumbrancer and fail to attend and prove your claim at the time and place set out above, you will be treated as disclaiming any lien, charge or encumbrance on the

546

property, the property may be dealt with as if you had no such claim and your claim may be foreclosed.

(Date)   *(Signature of referee)*

TO *(Names and addresses of defendants named in statement of claim)*

SCHEDULE OF ENCUMBRANCERS

Name of Encumbrancer	Nature of encumbrance	Instrument no.	Date of instrument	Date of registration

RCP-E 64P (November 1, 2005)

FORM 64Q

Courts of Justice Act

NOTICE TO ADDED DEFENDANT HAVING INTEREST IN EQUITY

(Court file no.)

ONTARIO

SUPERIOR COURT OF JUSTICE

BETWEEN:

(name)

Plaintiff

and

(name(s))

Defendant(s)

and

(name(s))

Defendant(s) added

on the reference

NOTICE TO ADDED DEFENDANT

An action has been commenced by the plaintiff for the foreclosure *(or* sale*)* of the mortgaged property described in the attached schedule. I have been directed by the judgment in this action dated *(date) (where the judgment is for sale, insert:* to conduct a sale of the property and*)* to inquire whether any person other than the plaintiff has a lien, charge or encumbrance on the property subsequent to the plaintiff's claim or whether any other person has an interest in the property. It appears that you may have an interest in the property. I have therefore added you as a defendant in this action. A copy of my order and the judgment in the action are attached to this notice.

If you wish to set aside or vary my order adding you as a defendant or the judgment in this action, you must make a motion to the court within ten days after service on you of this notice *(or where the defendant is to be served outside Ontario, such further time as the referee directs).* If you fail to do so, you will be bound by the judgment and the subsequent steps in this action.

IF YOU WISH AN OPPORTUNITY TO REDEEM the property, you are required to appear before me, either in person or by an Ontario lawyer acting for you, on *(day), (date),* at *(time),* at *(address).*

IF YOU FAIL TO ATTEND at the time and place set out above, you may be deemed to submit to an immediate foreclosure of your interest *(or* an immediate sale of the property*)* and the action may proceed in your absence and without further notice to you.

(Date)   *(Signature of referee)*

TO *(Names and addresses of defendants added on reference who appear to be interested in equity of redemption)*

(The description of the mortgaged property in the attached schedule must be the same as in the statement of claim.)

RCP-E 64Q (November 1, 2005)

FORM 65A

Courts of Justice Act

JUDGMENT FOR ADMINISTRATION OF ESTATE

(Court file no.)

(Court)

(Name of judge or officer)   *(Day and date judgment given)*

(Court seal)

(Title of proceeding)

JUDGMENT

(Recitals in accordance with Form 59B)

1. THIS COURT ORDERS AND ADJUDGES that all necessary inquiries be made, accounts taken, costs assessed and steps taken by the master *(or as may be)* at *(place)* for the administration and final winding up of the estate of *(name of deceased)* and for the adjustment of the rights of all parties interested in the property.

2. THIS COURT ORDERS AND ADJUDGES that any balance found due from the applicant or the respondent(s) to the estate be paid into court to the credit of this proceeding, subject to further order of the court.

3. THIS COURT ORDERS AND ADJUDGES that the property of the estate or such parts of it as the referee directs be sold as the referee directs and that the purchasers pay the purchase money into court to the credit of this proceeding, subject to the order of the court.

4. THIS COURT ORDERS AND ADJUDGES that the referee execute transfers for any party who is a minor.

(Signature of judge or registrar)

RCP-E 65A (November 1, 2005)

FORM 66A

Courts of Justice Act

JUDGMENT FOR PARTITION OR SALE

(Court file no.)

(Court)

(Name of judge or officer)   *(Day and date judgment given)*

(Court seal)

(Title of proceeding)

JUDGMENT

(Recitals in accordance with Form 59B)

1. THIS COURT ORDERS AND ADJUDGES that all necessary inquiries be made, accounts taken, costs assessed and steps taken by the master *(or as may be)* at *(place)* for the partition or sale, or for the partition of part and sale of the remainder, of the land described in the attached schedule in accordance with the interests of the parties entitled to share in it.

2. THIS COURT ORDERS AND ADJUDGES that the land, or such part of it as the referee thinks fit, be sold under the direction of the referee, free of the claims of encumbrancers, if any, who have consented to the sale, and subject to the claims of encumbrancers who have not consented to the sale, and that the purchaser pay the purchase money into court to the credit of this proceeding, subject to the order of the court.

3. THIS COURT ORDERS AND ADJUDGES that the referee execute a transfer for any party who is a minor.

4. THIS COURT ORDERS AND ADJUDGES that, if the land is partitioned or if part of the land is partitioned and the proceeds of the sale of the remainder are insufficient to pay the costs in full, the unpaid costs be paid by the parties according to their interests in the land *(where there are parties who are minors, add:* and that the portion of the costs payable by the parties who are minors be a lien on their respective shares, and that the plaintiff *(or* applicant) pay the costs of their litigation guardian and that those costs be added to the plaintiff's *(or* applicant's) costs.)

(Signature of judge, officer or registrar)

RCP-E 66A (November 1, 2005)

FORM 68A

Courts of Justice Act

NOTICE OF APPLICATION TO DIVISIONAL COURT FOR JUDICIAL REVIEW

(General heading)

(Court seal)

NOTICE OF APPLICATION TO DIVISIONAL COURT FOR JUDICIAL REVIEW

TO THE RESPONDENT

A LEGAL PROCEEDING HAS BEEN COMMENCED by the applicant. The claim made by the applicant appears on the following page.

THIS APPLICATION for judicial review will come on for a hearing before the Divisional Court on a date to be fixed by the registrar at the place of hearing requested by the applicant. The applicant requests that this application be heard at *(place where a Divisional Court sitting is scheduled).*

IF YOU WISH TO OPPOSE THIS APPLICATION, to receive notice of any step in the application or to be served with any documents in the application, you or an Ontario lawyer acting for you must forthwith prepare a notice of appearance in Form 38A prescribed by the Rules of Civil Procedure, serve it on the applicant's lawyer or, where the applicant does not have a lawyer, serve it on the applicant, and file it, with proof of service, in the office of the Divisional Court, and you or your lawyer must appear at the hearing.

IF YOU WISH TO PRESENT AFFIDAVIT OR OTHER DOCUMENTARY EVIDENCE TO THE COURT OR TO EXAMINE OR CROSS-EXAMINE WITNESSES ON THE APPLICATION, you or your lawyer must, in additional to serving your notice of appearance, serve a copy of the evidence on the applicant's lawyer or, where the applicant does not have a lawyer, serve it on the applicant, and file it, with proof of service, in the office of the Divisional Court within thirty days after service on you of the applicant's application record, or at least four days before the hearing, whichever is earlier.

IF YOU FAIL TO APPEAR AT THE HEARING, JUDGMENT MAY BE GIVEN TO IN YOUR ABSENCE AND WITHOUT FURTHER NOTICE TO YOU. IF YOU WISH TO DEFEND THIS PROCEEDING BUT ARE UNABLE TO PAY LEGAL FEES, LEGAL AID MAY BE AVAILABLE TO YOU BY CONTACTING A LOCAL LEGAL AID OFFICE.

TAKE NOTICE: THIS APPLICATION WILL AUTOMATICALLY BE DISMISSED if it has not been set down for hearing or terminated by any means within five years after the notice of application was filed with the court, unless otherwise ordered by the court.

Date

Issued by
Registrar

Address of court office

TO *(Name and address of each respondent)*

AND TO   Attorney General of Ontario *(as required by subsection 9(4) of the Judicial Review Procedure Act)*
Crown Law Office – Civil
720 Bay Street
8th Floor
Toronto, Ontario M7A 2S9

APPLICATION

1. The applicant makes application for: *(State here the precise relief claimed.)*

2. The grounds for the application are: *(Specify the grounds to be argued, including a reference to any statutory provision to be relied on.)*

   (Where the notice of application is to be served outside Ontario without a court order, state the facts and the specific provisions of Rule 17 relied on in support of such service.)

3. The following documentary evidence will be used at the hearing of the application: *(List the affidavits or other documentary evidence to be relied on.)*

(Date)   *(Name, address and telephone number of applicant's lawyer or applicant)*

RCP-E 68A (September 1, 2018)

553

FORM 68B

Courts of Justice Act

NOTICE OF LISTING FOR HEARING (JUDICIAL REVIEW)

(General heading)

NOTICE OF LISTING FOR HEARING

THIS APPLICATION FOR JUDICIAL REVIEW HAS BEEN PERFECTED and has been listed for hearing at *(place)*. You may ascertain from my office the approximate date of hearing.

Date _____ Signed by _____

Registrar of the
Divisional Court
(Address of court office)

TO *(Name and address of every person listed in the certificate of perfection)*

RCP-E 68B (November 1, 2005)

FORM 68C

Courts of Justice Act

ORDER DISMISSING APPLICATION FOR JUDICIAL REVIEW

(General heading)

(Court seal)

ORDER DISMISSING APPLICATION FOR JUDICIAL REVIEW

The applicant has not *(give particulars of applicant's default under rule 68.06)* and has not cured the default, although given notice under rule 68.06 to do so.

1. IT IS ORDERED that this application be dismissed for delay, with costs fixed at $750, despite rule 58.13.

Date _____ Signed by _____

Registrar of the
Divisional Court
(Address of court office)

RCP-E 68C (July 30, 2009)

FORM 68D

Courts of Justice Act

ORDER DISMISSING APPLICATION FOR JUDICIAL REVIEW FOR DELAY

(General heading)

ORDER DISMISSING APPLICATION

The applicant has not *(give particulars of applicant's default under rule 68.07)* and has not cured the default.

IT IS ORDERED that this application be dismissed for delay.

Date _____   Signed by _____

Local registrar
(Address of court office)

NOTE: An order under rule 68.07 dismissing an application may be set aside under rule 37.14.

RCP-E 68D (September 1, 2018)

FORM 72A

Courts of Justice Act

NOTICE OF PAYMENT INTO COURT

(General heading)

NOTICE OF PAYMENT INTO COURT

The *(identify party)* paid into court on *(date)* the sum of $ under the offer to settle *(or acceptance of offer)* dated *(date)*.

(Date)   *(Name, address and telephone number of lawyer or party giving notice)*

TO *(Name and address of lawyer or party receiving notice)*

RCP-E 72A (July 1, 2007)

FORM 72B

Courts of Justice Act

AFFIDAVIT (MOTION FOR PAYMENT OUT OF COURT)

(General heading)

AFFIDAVIT

I, *(full name of deponent)* of the *(*City, Town, *etc.)* of . . . . , in the *(*County, Regional Municipality, *etc.)* of . . . . , *(where the deponent is a party or the lawyer, officer, director, member or employee of a party, set out the deponent's capacity)*, MAKE OATH AND SAY *(or* AFFIRM*)*:

1. This affidavit is filed in support of a motion for payment out of court of money belonging to *(name of person under disability)*, of *(address)*, who is *(state the nature of the disability)* and who was born on *(date)*.

2. I am *(state the deponent's connection with the person under disability)*.

3. The Accountant *(or* local registrar at *(place))* has informed me that the sum of $ . . . . . . , including interest accrued to *(date)*, is in court. There has been previously paid out the sum of $ . . . . . . on *(date) (or as may be)*.

4. It is proposed that the sum of $ . . . . . . be paid out of court to *(name)* for the following purpose: *(Give particulars.)*

5. I believe that this expenditure is justified for the following reasons: *(Give particulars.)*

SWORN, *etc.*

RCP-E 72B (July 1, 2007)

FORM 72C

Courts of Justice Act

STOP ORDER

(Court file no.)

(Court)

(Name of judge or officer)   *(Day and date order made)*

(Court seal)

(Title of proceeding)

ORDER

(Recitals in accordance with Form 59A or 59B, followed by:) the *(identify applicant or moving party)* having undertaken through their lawyer to be bound by any order this court makes in respect of costs or damages caused by this order,

1. THIS COURT ORDERS that all money and securities held by the Accountant *(or* local registrar at *(place))* in this proceeding now or in the future, together with any interest, to which *(identify party)* is or becomes entitled shall not be dealt with except on notice to *(identify applicant or moving party)*.

(Signature of judge or officer)

RCP-E 72C (July 1, 2007)

FORM 73A

Courts of Justice Act

NOTICE OF APPLICATION FOR REGISTRATION OF UNITED KINGDOM JUDGMENT

(General heading)

(Court seal)

NOTICE OF APPLICATION

TO THE RESPONDENT

A LEGAL PROCEEDING HAS BEEN COMMENCED by the applicant for registration and enforcement in Ontario of a judgment granted against you by a court in the United Kingdom. The claim made by the applicant appears on the following pages.

THIS APPLICATION will come on for a hearing on (*day*), (*date*), at (*time*), at (*address of court house*).

IF YOU WISH TO OPPOSE THIS APPLICATION, to receive notice of any step in the application or to be served with any documents in the application, you or an Ontario lawyer acting for you must forthwith prepare a notice of appearance in Form 38A prescribed by the Rules of Civil Procedure, serve it on the applicant's lawyer or, where the applicant does not have a lawyer, serve it on the applicant, and file it, with proof of service, in this court office, and you or your lawyer must appear at the hearing.

IF YOU WISH TO PRESENT AFFIDAVIT OR OTHER DOCUMENTARY EVIDENCE TO THE COURT OR TO EXAMINE OR CROSS-EXAMINE WITNESSES ON THE APPLICATION, you or your lawyer must, in addition to serving your notice of appearance, serve a copy of the evidence on the applicant's lawyer or, where the applicant does not have a lawyer, serve it on the applicant, and file it, with proof of service, in the court office where the application is to be heard, as soon as possible, but at least four days before the hearing.

IF YOU FAIL TO APPEAR AT THE HEARING, THE UNITED KINGDOM JUDGMENT MAY BE REGISTERED AND ENFORCED AGAINST YOU WITHOUT FURTHER NOTICE.

Date...   Issued by...
                                                              Local registrar

                                                     Address of
                                                     court office ....

                                                     ....

TO   *(Name and address of each respondent)*

APPLICATION

The applicant applies under the *Reciprocal Enforcement of Judgments (U.K.) Act* for registration of the following judgment of a court in the United Kingdom:

(a) Name of court ....

(b) Plaintiff *(or* applicant*)* ....

....

(c) Defendant *(or* respondent*)* ....

....

(d) Date of judgment ....

(e) Amount awarded, in the currency of the judgment, in favour of each plaintiff *(or* applicant*)* and against each defendant *(or* respondent*)*

Judgment in favour of	Judgment against	Amount of judgment	Amount awarded for costs

(f) Post judgment interest

        Rate .... per year

        Commencing on *(date)* ....

        Payable on *(principal amount)* ....

(g) Amount unpaid, in the currency of the judgment, to each plaintiff *(or* applicant*)* and by each defendant *(or* respondent*)*

Payable to	Payable by	Amount unpaid on judgment, including interest	Amount unpaid on award of costs, including interest

561

2. The grounds for the application are:

(a) The judgment is one to which the Act and the Convention appearing as a schedule to the Act apply.

(b) The Act and the Convention do not preclude registration of the judgment.

( ) appeared

(c) The defendant *(or* respondent*)*

( ) did not appear

before the United Kingdom court that granted the judgement.

(If the defendant (or respondent) did not appear, explain in detail why registration is nevertheless permitted under the Reciprocal Enforcement of Judgments (U.K.) Act.)

(d) The applicant is entitled to register and enforce the judgment as,

( ) a plaintiff *(or* applicant*)* named in the judgment

( ) an assignee of the judgment

( ) other *(specify)* ....

....

3. The following documentary evidence is relied on in support of the application:

(a) the original or a certified copy of the judgment;

(b) the affidavit of..

(a) the original or a certified copy of proof of service of the originating process of the United Kingdom court.

4. The respondent in this application resides at:

....

(Date of issue)   *(Name, address and telephone number of lawyer or applicant)*

RCP-E 73A (April 11, 2012)

FORM 74.1

Courts of Justice Act

NOTICE TO ESTATE REGISTRAR OF DEPOSIT OF WILL OR CODICIL

ONTARIO

SUPERIOR COURT OF JUSTICE

NOTICE

TO THE ESTATE REGISTRAR FOR ONTARIO:

A will or codicil has been deposited in this office. Particulars of the document follow.

DETAILS ABOUT THE TESTATOR

Complete in full as applicable

First given name	Second given name	Third given name	Surname

And if the testator is known by any other name(s), state below the full name(s) used including surname.

First given name	Second given name	Third given name	Surname

Birth date of testator: _____ _____ _____
                              day   *month*   *year*

Date of will or codicil: _____ _____ _____
                              day   *month*   *year*

Estate trustees named in will or codicil:
    Name   Address

Date of deposit: _____ _____ _____
                        day   *month*   *year*

Office of deposit:

| day | month | year |

DATE:

| day | month | year |

_____
Registrar
Address of court office

RCP-E 74.1 (November 1, 2005)

FORM 74.2

Courts of Justice Act

NOTICE TO ESTATE REGISTRAR OF WITHDRAWAL OF WILL OR CODICIL

ONTARIO

SUPERIOR COURT OF JUSTICE

NOTICE

TO THE ESTATE REGISTRAR FOR ONTARIO:

A will or codicil has been withdrawn from this office. Particulars of the document follow.

DETAILS ABOUT THE TESTATOR

Complete in full as applicable

First given name	Second given name	Third given name	Surname

And if the testator is known by any other name(s), state below the full name(s) used including surname.

First given name	Second given name	Third given name	Surname

Birth date of testator: _____ _____ _____
                                day   *month*   *year*

Date of will or codicil: _____ _____ _____
                                day   *month*   *year*

Date of deposit: _____ _____ _____
                                day   *month*   *year*

Date of withdrawal: _____ _____ _____
                                day   *month*   *year*

Office of deposit: _____ _____ _____
                     day   month   year

DATE: _____ _____ _____
                     day   *month*   *year*

_____
Registrar
Address of court office

RCP-E 74.2 (November 1, 2005)

FORM 74.3

Courts of Justice Act

REQUEST FOR NOTICE OF COMMENCEMENT OF PROCEEDING

ONTARIO

SUPERIOR COURT OF JUSTICE

In the Estate of the deceased person described below:

DETAILS ABOUT THE DECEASED PERSON

Complete in full as applicable

First given name	Second given name	Third given name	Surname

And if the deceased was known by any other name(s), state below the full name(s) used including surname.

First given name	Second given name	Third given name	Surname

REQUEST FOR NOTICE OF COMMENCEMENT OF PROCEEDING

I have or appear to have a financial interest in the estate and desire to be informed of the commencement of any proceeding in the estate.

Notice of the commencement of any proceeding may be mailed to me at the address shown below.

DATE: _____   _____   _____
                   day   *month*   *year*

NAME OF INTERESTED PARTY: ADDRESS:

RCP-E 74.3 (November 1, 2005)

FORM 74.4

Courts of Justice Act

APPLICATION FOR CERTIFICATE OF APPOINTMENT OF ESTATE TRUSTEE
WITH A WILL (INDIVIDUAL APPLICANT)

ONTARIO

SUPERIOR COURT OF JUSTICE

**APPLICATION FOR CERTIFICATE OF
APPOINTMENT OF ESTATE TRUSTEE WITH A
WILL (INDIVIDUAL APPLICANT)**

(Form 74.4 Under the Rules)

at _____

This application is filed by (*insert name and address*)

DETAILS ABOUT THE DECEASED PERSON

Complete in full as applicable

First given name	Second given name	Third given name	Surname

And if the deceased was known by any other name(s), state below the full name(s) used including surname.

First given name	Second given name	Third given name	Surname

Date of birth of the deceased person, if known: (*day, month, year*)

Address of fixed place of abode (*street or postal address*) (*city or town*)	(*county or district*)

If the deceased person had no fixed place of abode in Ontario, did he or she have property in Ontario? ☐ No ☐ Yes	**Last occupation of deceased person**

Place of death (*city or town; county or district*)	**Date of death** (*day, month, year*)	**Date of last will** (marked as Exhibit "A") (*day, month, year*)

Was the deceased person 18 years of age or older at the date of the will (or 21 years of age or older if the will is dated earlier than September 1, 1971)? If not, explain why certificate is being sought. Give details in an attached schedule.	☐ No	☐ Yes

Date of codicil (marked as Exhibit "B") (*day, month, year*)	**Date of codicil** (marked as Exhibit "C") (*day, month, year*)

Marital Status ☐ Unmarried ☐ Married ☐ Widowed ☐ Divorced

Did the deceased person marry after the date of the will? If yes, explain why certificate is being sought. Give details in an attached schedule.	☐ No	☐ Yes
Was a marriage of the deceased person terminated by a judgment absolute of divorce, or declared a nullity, after the date of the will? If yes, give details in an attached schedule.	☐ No	☐ Yes
Is any person who signed the will or a codicil as witness or for the testator, or the spouse of such person, a beneficiary under the will? If yes, give details in an attached schedule.	☐ No	☐ Yes

RCP-E 74.4 (September 1, 2018)

VALUE OF ASSETS OF ESTATE

Note:

o   Under "Real estate, net of encumbrances", do not include any real estate in Ontario that is held jointly and passes by survivorship or any real estate outside Ontario.

o   Under "Personal Property", do not include money or property held jointly and passing by survivorship (such as a bank account), or money or property to which a person is entitled by virtue of a beneficiary designation under, for example, a life insurance contract, a registered pension plan, a registered retirement savings plans, a registered retirement income fund, a life income fund, a locked-in retirement account or a tax free savings account.

Personal Property	Real estate, net of encumbrances	Total
$	$	$

Is there any person entitled to an interest in the estate who is not an applicant?	☐ No ☐ Yes

If a person named in the will or a codicil as estate trustee is not an applicant, explain.

If a person not named in the will or a codicil as estate trustee is an applicant, explain why that person is entitled to apply.

If the spouse of the deceased is an applicant, has the spouse elected to receive the entitlement under section 5 of the *Family Law Act*? If yes, explain why the spouse is entitled to apply.	☐ No ☐ Yes

AFFIDAVIT(S) OF APPLICANT(S)
(Attach a separate sheet for additional affidavits, if necessary)

I, an applicant named in this application, make oath and say/affirm:

1. I am 18 years of age or older.
2. The exhibit(s) referred to in this application are the last will and each codicil (where applicable) of the deceased person and I do not know of any later will or codicil.
3. I will faithfully administer the deceased person's property according to law and render a complete and true account of my administration

when lawfully required.

4. If I am not named as estate trustee in the will or codicil, consents of persons who together have a majority interest in the value of the assets of the estate at the date of death are attached.
5. The information contained in this application and in any attached schedules is true, to the best of my knowledge and belief.

Name *(surname and forename(s))*	Occupation

Address *(street or postal address)*	*(city or town)*	*(province)*	*(postal code)*

Sworn/Affirmed before me at the ....

of ....

in the ....

of ....

this .... day of ...., 20.......

_____

Signature of applicant

_____

A Commissioner for taking Affidavits (*or as may be*)

RCP-E 74.4 (September 1, 2018)

Name *(surname and forename(s))*	Occupation	
Address *(street or postal address)* *(city or town)*	*(province)*	*(postal code)*

Sworn/Affirmed before me at the ....

of ....

in the ....

of ....   _____

this .... day of ...., 20.....   Signature of applicant

_____

A Commissioner for taking Affidavits *(or as may be)*

Notice to applicant: Information provided on this form related to the payment of estate administration tax may be forwarded to the Ministry of Finance pursuant to clause 39(1)(b) and 42(1)(c) of the *Freedom of Information and Protection of Privacy Act*. This includes the name of the deceased, name and address of estate trustee(s), value of the estate and any undertakings and tax payments made or refunded. This information will be used by the Ministry of Finance to determine the value of estates and the amount of estate administration tax payable. Questions about the collection of this information should be directed to the Senior Manager – Audit, Advisory and Compliance Branch, 33 King Street West, PO Box 625, Oshawa ON L1H 8H9, 1-866-668-8297.

RCP-E 74.4 (September 1, 2018)

FORM 74.4.1

Courts of Justice Act

APPLICATION FOR CERTIFICATE OF APPOINTMENT OF ESTATE TRUSTEE WITH A WILL (INDIVIDUAL APPLICANT) LIMITED TO THE ASSETS REFERRED TO IN THE WILL

ONTARIO

SUPERIOR COURT OF JUSTICE

APPLICATION FOR CERTIFICATE OF APPOINTMENT OF ESTATE TRUSTEE WITH A WILL (INDIVIDUAL APPLICANT) LIMITED TO THE ASSETS REFERRED TO IN THE WILL
(Form 74.4.1 Under the Rules)

at

This application is filed by *(insert name and address)*

DETAILS ABOUT THE DECEASED PERSON

Complete in full as applicable

First given name	Second given name	Third given name	Surname

And if the deceased was known by any other name(s), state below the full name(s) used including surname.

First given name	Second given name	Third given name	Surname

Date of birth of the deceased person, if known: *(day, month, year)*

Address of fixed place of abode *(street or postal address) (city or town)* | *(county or district)*

If the deceased person had no fixed place of abode in Ontario, did he or she have property in Ontario? ☐ No ☐ Yes	**Last occupation of deceased person**

Place of death *(city or town; county or district)*	**Date of death** *(day, month, year)*	**Date of last will** (marked as Exhibit "A") *(day, month, year)*

Was the deceased person 18 years of age or older at the date of the will (or 21 years of age or older if the will is dated earlier than September 1, 1971)?   ☐ No   ☐ Yes
If not, explain why certificate is being sought. Give details in an attached schedule.

Date of codicil (marked as Exhibit "B") *(day, month, year)*	**Date of codicil** (marked as Exhibit "C") *(day, month, year)*

| **Marital Status** ☐ Unmarried ☐ Married ☐ Widowed ☐ Divorced |

Did the deceased person marry after the date of the will?   ☐ No   ☐ Yes
If yes, explain why certificate is being sought. Give details in an attached schedule.

Was a marriage of the deceased person terminated by a judgment absolute of divorce, or declared a nullity, after the date of the will?   ☐ No   ☐ Yes
If yes, give details in an attached schedule.

Is any person who signed the will or a codicil as witness or for the testator, or the spouse of such person, a beneficiary under the will?   ☐ No   ☐ Yes
If yes, give details in an attached schedule.

RCP-E 74.4.1 (September 1, 2018)

VALUE OF ASSETS REFERRED TO IN ATTACHED WILL
(Marked as Exhibit "A" to this application)

Note:

   o   Under "Real estate, net of encumbrances", do not include any real estate in Ontario that is held jointly and passes by survivorship or any real estate outside Ontario.

   o   Under "Personal Property", do not include money or property held jointly and passing by survivorship (such as a bank account), or money or property to which a person is entitled by virtue of a beneficiary designation under, for example, a life insurance contract, a registered pension plan, a registered retirement savings plans, a registered retirement income fund, a life income fund, a locked-in retirement account or a tax free savings account.

Personal Property	Real estate, net of encumbrances	Total
$	$	$

Is there any person entitled to an interest in the estate who is not an applicant?   ☐ No   ☐ Yes

If a person named in the will or a codicil as estate trustee is not an applicant, explain.

If a person not named in the will or a codicil as estate trustee is an applicant, explain why that person is entitled to apply.

If the spouse of the deceased is an applicant, has the spouse elected to receive the entitlement under section 5 of the *Family Law Act*?   ☐ No   ☐ Yes
If yes, explain why the spouse is entitled to apply.

AFFIDAVIT(S) OF APPLICANT(S)
(Attach a separate sheet for additional affidavits, if necessary)

I, an applicant named in this application, make oath and say/affirm:

1. I am 18 years of age or older.
2. The exhibit(s) referred to in this application are the last will and each codicil (where applicable) of the deceased person relating to the assets referred to in the will and I do not know of any later will or codicil affecting those assets.
3. I will faithfully administer the deceased person's property according to law and render a complete and true account of my administration when lawfully required.
4. If I am not named as estate trustee in the will or codicil, consents of persons who together have a majority interest in the value of the assets of the estate at the date of death are attached.
5. The information contained in this application and in any attached schedules is true, to the best of my knowledge and belief.

Name *(surname and forename(s))*	Occupation

Address *(street or postal address)*	*(city or town)*	*(province)*	*(postal code)*

Sworn/Affirmed before me at the ....

of ....

in the ....

of ....

this .... day of .... , 20......

_____
Signature of applicant

_____
A Commissioner for taking Affidavits *(or as may be)*

RCP-E 74.4.1 (September 1, 2018)

Name *(surname and forename(s))*	Occupation		

Address *(street or postal address)*	*(city or town)*	*(province)*	*(postal code)*

Sworn/Affirmed before me at the ....

of ....

in the ....

of ....

this .... day of ...., 20.....

_____
Signature of applicant

_____
A Commissioner for taking Affidavits *(or as may be)*

Notice to applicant: Information provided on this form related to the payment of estate administration tax may be forwarded to the Ministry of Finance pursuant to clause 39(1)(b) and 42(1)(c) of the *Freedom of Information and Protection of Privacy Act*. This includes the name of the deceased, name and address of estate trustee(s), value of the estate and any undertakings and tax payments made or refunded. This information will be used by the Ministry of Finance to determine the value of estates and the amount of estate administration tax payable. Questions about the collection of this information should be directed to the Senior Manager – Audit, Advisory and Compliance Branch, 33 King Street West, PO Box 625, Oshawa ON L1H 8H9, 1-866-668-8297.

RCP-E 74.4.1 (September 1, 2018)

FORM 74.5

Courts of Justice Act

APPLICATION FOR CERTIFICATE OF APPOINTMENT OF ESTATE TRUSTEE
WITH A WILL (CORPORATE APPLICANT)

ONTARIO **SUPERIOR COURT OF JUSTICE**	**APPLICATION FOR CERTIFICATE OF APPOINTMENT OF ESTATE TRUSTEE WITH A WILL (CORPORATE APPLICANT)** *(Form 74.5 Under the Rules)*

At _____

This application is filed by *(insert name and address)*

DETAILS ABOUT THE DECEASED PERSON

Complete in full as applicable

First given name	Second given name	Third given name	Surname

And if the deceased was known by any other name(s), state below the full name(s) used including surname.

First given name	Second given name	Third given name	Surname

Date of birth of the deceased person, if known: *(day, month, year)*

Address of fixed place of abode *(street or postal address) (city or town)*	*(county or district)*

If the deceased person had no fixed place of abode in Ontario, did he or she have property in Ontario? ☐ No ☐ Yes	Last occupation of deceased person

Place of death *(city or town, county or district)*	Date of death *(day, month, year)*	Date of last will (marked as Exhibit "A") *(day, month, year)*

Was the deceased person 18 years of age or older at the date of the will (or 21 years of age or older if the will is dated earlier than September 1, 1971)? If not, explain why certificate is being sought. Give details in an attached schedule.	☐ No	☐ Yes

Date of codicil (marked as Exhibit "B") *(day, month, year)*	Date of codicil (marked as Exhibit "C") *(day, month, year)*

Marital Status	☐ Unmarried	☐ Married	☐ Widowed	☐ Divorced

Did the deceased person marry after the date of the will? If yes, explain why certificate is being sought. Give details in an attached schedule.	☐ No	☐ Yes
Was a marriage of the deceased person terminated by a judgment absolute of divorce, or declared a nullity, after the date of the will? If yes, give details in an attached schedule.	☐ No	☐ Yes
Is any person who signed the will or a codicil as witness or for the testator, or the spouse of such person, a beneficiary under the will? If yes, give details in an attached schedule.	☐ No	☐ Yes

RCP-E 74.5 (September 1, 2018)

VALUE OF ASSETS OF ESTATE

Note:

o   Under "Real estate, net of encumbrances", do not include any real estate in Ontario that is held jointly and passes by survivorship or any real estate outside Ontario.

o   Under "Personal Property", do not include money or property held jointly and passing by survivorship (such as a bank account), or money or property to which a person is entitled by virtue of a beneficiary designation under, for example, a life insurance contract, a registered pension plan, a registered retirement savings plans, a registered retirement income fund, a life income fund, a locked-in retirement account or a tax free savings account.

Personal property	Real estate, net of encumbrances	Total
$	$	$

Is there any person interested in the estate who is not an applicant?   ☐ No   ☐ Yes

If a person named in the will or a codicil as estate trustee is not an applicant, explain.

If a person not named in the will or a codicil a estate trustee is an applicant, explain why that person is entitled to apply.

If the spouse of the deceased is an applicant, has the spouse elected to receive the entitlement under
section 5 of the *Family Law Act*?   ☐ No   ☐ Yes
If yes, explain why the spouse is entitled to apply

AFFIDAVIT(S) OF APPLICANT(S)
(Attach a separate sheet for additional affidavits, if necessary)

I, a trust officer named in this application, make oath and say/affirm:

1. I am a trust officer of the corporate applicant.
2. I am 18 years of age or older.
3. The exhibit(s) referred to in this application are the last will and each codicil (where applicable) of the deceased person and I do not know of any later will or codicil.
4. The corporate applicant will faithfully administer the deceased person's property according to law and render a complete and true

account of its administration when lawfully required.

5. If the corporate applicant is not named as estate trustee in the will or codicil, consents of persons who together have a majority interest in the value of the assets of the estate at the date of death are attached.
6. The information contained in this application and in any attached schedules is true, to the best of my knowledge and belief.

Name of corporate applicant	Name of trust officer

Address of corporate applicant *(street or postal address)   (city or town)*   *(province)   (postal code)*

Sworn/Affirmed before me at the ....

of ....

in the ....

of ....

this .... day of ...., 20......

....
Signature of trust officer

....
A Commissioner for taking Affidavits *(or as may be)*

RCP-E 74.5 (September 1, 2018)

I, an applicant named in this application, make oath and say/affirm:

1. I am 18 years of age or older.
2. The exhibit(s) referred to in this application are the last will and each codicil (where applicable) of the deceased person and I do not know of any later will or codicil.
3. I will faithfully administer the deceased person's property according to law and render a complete and true account of my administration

when lawfully required.

4. If I am not named as estate trustee in the will or codicil, consents of persons who together have a majority interest in the value of the assets of the estate at the date of death are attached.
5. The information contained in this application and in any attached schedules is true, to the best of my knowledge and belief.

Name *(surname and forename(s))*	Occupation

Address *(street or postal address)*	*(city or town)*	*(province)*	*(postal code)*

Sworn/Affirmed before me at the ....

of ....

in the ....

of ....

this .... day of ...., 20...........

Signature of applicant

_____
A Commissioner for taking Affidavits *(or as may be)*

Notice to applicant: Information provided on this form related to the payment of estate administration tax may be forwarded to the Ministry of Finance pursuant to clause 39(1)(b) and 42(1)(c) of the *Freedom of Information and Protection of Privacy Act*. This includes the name of the deceased, name and address of estate trustee(s), value of the estate and any undertakings and tax payments made or refunded. This information will be used by the Ministry of Finance to determine the value of estates and the amount of estate administration tax payable. Questions about the collection of this information should be directed to the Senior Manager – Audit, Advisory and Compliance Branch, 33 King Street West, PO Box 625, Oshawa ON L1H 8H9, 1-866-668-8297.

RCP-E 74.5 (September 1, 2018)

FORM 74.5.1

Courts of Justice Act

APPLICATION FOR CERTIFICATE OF APPOINTMENT OF ESTATE TRUSTEE WITH A WILL (CORPORATE APPLICANT) LIMITED TO THE ASSETS REFERRED TO IN THE WILL

ONTARIO	**APPLICATION FOR CERTIFICATE OF APPOINTMENT OF ESTATE TRUSTEE WITH A WILL (CORPORATE APPLICANT) LIMITED TO THE ASSETS REFERRED TO IN THE WILL**
SUPERIOR COURT OF JUSTICE	*(Form 74.5.1 Under the Rules)*

at

This application is filed by *(insert name and address)*

DETAILS ABOUT THE DECEASED PERSON

Complete in full as applicable

First given name	Second given name	Third given name	Surname

And if the deceased was known by any other name(s), state below the full name(s) used including surname.

First given name	Second given name	Third given name	Surname

Date of birth of the deceased person, if known: *(day, month, year)*

Address of fixed place of abode *(street or postal address) (city or town)*	*(county or district)*

If the deceased person had no fixed place of abode in Ontario, did he or she have property in Ontario? ☐ No ☐ Yes	Last occupation of deceased person

Place of death *(city or town; county or district)*	Date of death *(day, month, year)*	Date of last will (marked as Exhibit "A") *(day, month, year)*

Was the deceased person 18 years of age or older at the date of the will (or 21 years of age or older if the will is dated earlier than September 1, 1971)?   ☐ No   ☐ Yes
If not, explain why certificate is being sought. Give details in an attached schedule.

Date of codicil (marked as Exhibit "B") *(day, month, year)*	Date of codicil (marked as Exhibit "C") *(day, month, year)*

Marital Status   ☐ Unmarried   ☐ Married   ☐ Widowed   ☐ Divorced

Did the deceased person marry after the date of the will?   ☐ No   ☐ Yes
If yes, explain why certificate is being sought. Give details in an attached schedule.

Was a marriage of the deceased person terminated by a judgment absolute of divorce, or declared a nullity, after the date of the will?   ☐ No   ☐ Yes
If yes, give details in an attached schedule.

Is any person who signed the will or a codicil as witness or for the testator, or the spouse of such person, a beneficiary under the will?   ☐ No   ☐ Yes
If yes, give details in an attached schedule.

RCP-E 74.5.1 (September 1, 2018)

VALUE OF ASSETS REFERRED TO IN ATTACHED WILL
(Marked as Exhibit "A" to this application)

Note:

o   Under "Real estate, net of encumbrances", do not include any real estate in Ontario that is held jointly and passes by survivorship or any real estate outside Ontario.

o   Under "Personal Property", do not include money or property held jointly and passing by survivorship (such as a bank account), or money or property to which a person is entitled by virtue of a beneficiary designation under, for example, a life insurance contract, a registered pension plan, a registered retirement savings plans, a registered retirement income fund, a life income fund, a locked-in retirement account or a tax free savings account.

Personal Property	Real estate, net of encumbrances	Total
$	$	$

Is there any person interested in the estate who is not an applicant?	☐ No	☐ Yes

If a person named in the will or a codicil as estate trustee is not an applicant, explain.

If a person not named in the will or a codicil as estate trustee is an applicant, explain why that person is entitled to apply.

If the spouse of the deceased is an applicant, has the spouse elected to receive the entitlement under section 5 of the *Family Law Act*?	☐ No	☐ Yes

If yes, explain why the spouse is entitled to apply.

AFFIDAVIT(S) OF APPLICANT(S)
(Attach a separate sheet for additional affidavits, if necessary)

I, a trust officer named in this application, make oath and say/affirm:

1.   I am a trust officer of the corporate applicant.
2.   I am 18 years of age or older.
3.   The exhibit(s) referred to in this application are the last will and each codicil (where applicable) of the deceased person relating to the assets referred to in the will and I do not know of any later will or codicil affecting those assets.
4.   The corporate applicant will faithfully administer the deceased person's property according to law and render a complete and true

account of its administration when lawfully required.
5.   If the corporate applicant is not named as estate trustee in the will or codicil, consents of persons who together have a majority interest in the value of the assets of the estate at the date of death are attached.
6.   The information contained in this application and in any attached schedules is true, to the best of my knowledge and belief.

Name of corporate applicant	Name of trust officer

Address of corporate applicant *(street or postal address)* *(city or town)*	*(province)*	*(postal code)*

Sworn/Affirmed before me at the ....

of ....

in the ....

of ....

this .... day of ...., 20.........

Signature of trust officer

A Commissioner for taking Affidavits *(or as may be)*

RCP-E 74.5.1 (September 1, 2018)

I, an applicant named in this application, make oath and say/affirm:

1. I am 18 years of age or older.
2. The exhibit(s) referred to in this application are the last will and each codicil (where applicable) of the deceased person relating to the assets referred to in the will and I do not know of any later will or codicil affecting those assets.
3. I will faithfully administer the deceased person's property according to law and render a complete and true account of my administration when lawfully required.

4. If I am not named as estate trustee in the will or codicil, consents of persons who together have a majority interest in the value of the assets of the estate at the date of death are attached.
5. The information contained in this application and in any attached schedules is true, to the best of my knowledge and belief.

Name *(surname and forename(s))*	Occupation

Address *(street or postal address)*	*(city or town)*	*(province)*	*(postal code)*

Sworn/Affirmed before me at the ....

of ....

in the ....

of ....

this .... day of ...., 20............

_____
Signature of applicant

_____
A Commissioner for taking Affidavits *(or as may be)*

Notice to applicant: Information provided on this form related to the payment of estate administration tax may be forwarded to the Ministry of Finance pursuant to clause 39(1)(b) and 42(1)(c) of the *Freedom of Information and Protection of Privacy Act.* This includes the name of the deceased, name and address of estate trustee(s), value of the estate and any undertakings and tax payments made or refunded. This information will be used by the Ministry of Finance to determine the value of estates and the amount of estate administration tax payable. Questions about the collection of this information should be directed to the Senior Manager – Audit, Advisory and Compliance Branch, 33 King Street West, PO Box 625, Oshawa ON L1H 8H9, 1-866-668-8297.

RCP-E 74.5.1 (September 1, 2018)

FORM 74.6

Courts of Justice Act

AFFIDAVIT OF SERVICE OF NOTICE

ONTARIO

SUPERIOR COURT OF JUSTICE

IN THE ESTATE OF   *(insert name)*   , deceased.

AFFIDAVIT OF SERVICE OF NOTICE

I,   *(insert name)* , of *(insert city or town and county or district of residence)* , make oath and say/affirm:

1.   I am an applicant for a certificate of appointment of estate trustee with a will in the estate.

2.   I have sent or caused to be sent a notice in Form 74.7, a copy of which is marked as Exhibit "A" to this affidavit, to all adult persons and charities named in the notice (except to an applicant who is entitled to share in the distribution of the estate), to the Public Guardian and Trustee if paragraph 6 of the notice applies, to a parent or guardian of the minor and to the Children's Lawyer if paragraph 4 applies, to the guardian or attorney if paragraph 5 applies, and to the Children's Lawyer if paragraph 7 applies, all by regular lettermail sent to the person's last known address.

3.   I have attached or caused to be attached to each notice the following:

    (A)   In the case of a notice sent to or in respect of a person entitled only to a specified item of property or stated amount of money, an extract of the part or parts of the will or codicil relating to the gift, or a copy of the will (and codicil(s), if any).

    (B)   In the case of a notice sent to or in respect of any other beneficiary, a copy of the will (and codicil(s), if any).

    (C)   In the case of a notice sent to the Children's Lawyer or the Public Guardian and Trustee, a copy of the will (and codicil(s), if any) and a statement of the estimated value of the interest of the person represented.

4.   The following persons and charities specifically named in the Will are not entitled to be served for the reasons shown:

Name of person (as it appears in will, if applicable)   **Reason not served**

If paragraph 4 does not apply insert "Not Applicable."

5.   The following persons named in the Will or being a member of a class of beneficiaries under the Will may be entitled to be served but have not been served for the reasons shown below:

580

Name of person (as it appears in will, if applicable)	**Reason not served**

If paragraph 5 does not apply insert "Not Applicable."

6.   To the best of my knowledge and belief, subject to paragraph 5 (if applicable), the persons named in the notice are all the persons who are entitled to share in the distribution of the estate.

Sworn/Affirmed before me at the ....)
)
of...)
)
in the...)
)
of...)
)   _____
this ....day of........................, 20...........)   Signature of applicant
)

_____
A Commissioner for taking Affidavits *(or as may be)*

RCP-E 74.6 (November 1, 2005)

FORM 74.7

Courts of Justice Act

NOTICE OF AN APPLICATION FOR A CERTIFICATE OF APPOINTMENT OF ESTATE TRUSTEE WITH A WILL

ONTARIO

SUPERIOR COURT OF JUSTICE

IN THE ESTATE OF _____ , deceased.

(insert name)

NOTICE OF AN APPLICATION FOR A CERTIFICATE OF APPOINTMENT OF ESTATE TRUSTEE WITH A WILL

1. The deceased died on _____ .

(insert date)

2. Attached to this notice are:

   (A) If the notice is sent to or in respect of a person entitled only to a specified item of property or stated amount of money, an extract of the part or parts of the will or codicil relating to the gift, or a copy of the will (and codicil(s), if any).

   (B) If the notice is sent to or in respect of any other beneficiary, a copy of the will (and codicil(s), if any).

   (C) If the notice is sent to the Children's Lawyer or the Public Guardian and Trustee, a copy of the will (and codicil(s), if any), and if it is not included in the notice, a statement of the estimated value of the interest of the person represented.

3. The applicant named in this notice is applying for a certificate of appointment of estate trustee with a will.

APPLICANT

Name	Address

4. The following persons who are less than 18 years of age are entitled, whether their interest is contingent or vested, to share in the distribution of the estate:

Name	Date of Birth *(day, month, year)*	Name and Address of Parent or Guardian	Estimated Value of Interest in Estate *

* Note: *The Estimated Value of Interest in Estate may be omitted in the form if it is included in a separate schedule attached to the notice sent to the Children's Lawyer.*

5. The following persons who are mentally incapable within the meaning of section 6 of the *Substitute Decisions Act, 1992* in respect of an issue in the proceeding, and who have guardians or attorneys acting under powers of attorney with authority to act in the proceeding, are entitled, whether their interest is contingent or vested, to share in the distribution of the estate:

Name and Address of Person	Name and Address of Guardian or Attorney *

* Specify whether guardian or attorney.

6. The following persons who are mentally incapable within the meaning of section 6 of the *Substitute Decisions Act, 1992* in respect of an issue in the proceeding, and who do not have guardians or attorneys acting under powers of attorney with authority to act in the proceeding, are entitled, whether their interest is contingent or vested, to share in the distribution of the estate:

Name and Address of Person	Estimated Value of Interest in Estate *

* Note: The Estimated Value of Interest in Estate may be omitted in the form if it is included in a separate schedule attached to the notice sent to the Public Guardian and Trustee.

7. Unborn or unascertained persons may be entitled to share in the distribution of the estate. *(Delete if not applicable)*

8. All other persons and charities entitled, whether their interest is contingent or vested, to share in the distribution of the estate are as follows:

Name	Address

9. This notice is being sent, by regular lettermail, to all adult persons and charities named above in this notice (except to an applicant who is entitled to share in the distribution of the estate), to the Public Guardian and Trustee if paragraph 6 applies, to a parent or guardian of the minor and to the Children's Lawyer if paragraph 4 applies, to the guardian or attorney if paragraph 5 applies, and to the Children's Lawyer if paragraph 7 applies.

10. The following persons named in the Will or being a member of a class of beneficiaries under the Will may be entitled to be served but have not been served for the reasons shown below:

Name of person (as it appears in will, if applicable)	Reason not served

If paragraph 10 does not apply insert "Not Applicable."

DATE

| Save Form | Print Form | | Clear Form |

FORM 74.8

Courts of Justice Act

AFFIDAVIT OF EXECUTION OF WILL OR CODICIL

ONTARIO

SUPERIOR COURT OF JUSTICE

In the matter of the execution of a will or codicil of *(insert name)*

AFFIDAVIT

I, *(insert name)*, of *(insert city or town and county or district, metropolitan or regional municipality of residence)*, make oath and say/affirm:

1. On *(date)*, I was present and saw the document marked as Exhibit "A" to this affidavit executed by *(insert name)*.

2. *(Insert name)* executed the document in the presence of myself and *(insert name of other witness and city or town, county or district, metropolitan or regional municipality of residence)*. We were both present at the same time, and signed the document in the testator's presence as attesting witnesses.

SWORN/AFFIRMED BEFORE)
me at the   of   )
in the   of   )
this   day of   , 20   .   ) ....
)
)
)
)

....
A Commissioner for Taking Affidavits *(or as may be)*

NOTE: If the testator was blind or signed by making his or her mark, add the following paragraph:

3. Before its execution, the document was read over to the testator, who (was blind) (signed by making his or her mark). The testator appeared to understand the contents.

WARNING: A beneficiary or the spouse of a beneficiary should not be a witness.

RCP-E 74.8 (November 1, 2005)

584

FORM 74.9

Courts of Justice Act

AFFIDAVIT ATTESTING TO THE HANDWRITING AND SIGNATURE OF A
HOLOGRAPH WILL OR CODICIL

ONTARIO

SUPERIOR COURT OF JUSTICE

IN THE ESTATE OF *(insert name)*, deceased.

AFFIDAVIT ATTESTING TO THE HANDWRITING
AND SIGNATURE OF A HOLOGRAPH WILL OR CODICIL

I, *(insert name)*, of *(insert city or town and county or district, metropolitan or regional municipality of residence)*, make oath and say/affirm:

1. I was well acquainted with the deceased and have frequently seen the deceased's signature and handwriting.

2. I believe the whole of the document dated *(insert date)*, now shown to me and marked as Exhibit "A" to this affidavit, including the signature, is in the handwriting of the deceased.

SWORN/AFFIRMED BEFORE	)
me at the of	)
in the of	)
this day of , 20 .	) ....
	)
	)
	)
	)

....
A Commissioner for Taking Affidavits *(or as may be)*

RCP-E 74.9 (November 1, 2005)

FORM 74.10

Courts of Justice Act

AFFIDAVIT OF CONDITION OF WILL OR CODICIL

ONTARIO

SUPERIOR COURT OF JUSTICE

IN THE ESTATE OF *(insert name)*, deceased.

AFFIDAVIT OF CONDITION OF WILL OR CODICIL

I, *(insert name)*, of *(insert city or town and county or district, metropolitan or regional municipality of residence)*, make oath and say/affirm:

1. On *(date)*, I was present and saw the document marked as Exhibit "A" to this affidavit executed by the deceased, in the presence of myself and *(insert name of other witness and city or town, county or district, metropolitan or regional municipality of residence)*. We were both present at the same time, and signed the document in the testator's presence as attesting witnesses.

2. The following alterations, erasures, obliterations or interlineations that have not been attested appear in the document:

3. The document is now in the same condition as when it was executed.

SWORN/AFFIRMED BEFORE	)
me at the of	)
in the of	)
this day of , 20	) ....
	)
	)
	)
	)

....
A Commissioner for Taking Affidavits *(or as may be)*

NOTE: If paragraph 3 is not correct, add the words "except that" and give details of the exceptions.

RCP-E 74.10 (October 24, 2017)

586

FORM 74.11

Courts of Justice Act

RENUNCIATION OF RIGHT TO A CERTIFICATE OF APPOINTMENT OF ESTATE TRUSTEE (OR SUCCEEDING ESTATE TRUSTEE) WITH A WILL

ONTARIO

SUPERIOR COURT OF JUSTICE

IN THE ESTATE OF *(insert name)*, deceased.

RENUNCIATION OF RIGHT TO A CERTIFICATE OF APPOINTMENT
OF ESTATE TRUSTEE (OR SUCCEEDING ESTATE TRUSTEE) WITH A WILL

The deceased died on *(date)*.

In that person's testamentary document dated *(date)*, I, *(insert name)*, was named an estate trustee.

I renounce my right to a certificate of appointment of estate trustee (or succeeding estate trustee) with a will.

DATE

```
                                          )
                                          )
                                          )
                                          )
                                          )
...............................................)  ...............................................
        Signature of witness              )      Signature of person renouncing
                                          )
                                          )
```

RCP-E 74.11 (November 1, 2005)

FORM 74.12

Courts of Justice Act

CONSENT TO APPLICANT'S APPOINTMENT AS ESTATE TRUSTEE WITH A WILL

ONTARIO

SUPERIOR COURT OF JUSTICE

IN THE ESTATE OF *(insert name)*, deceased.

CONSENT TO APPLICANT'S APPOINTMENT AS ESTATE TRUSTEE WITH A WILL

The deceased died on *(date)*.

No estate trustee named in a testamentary document of that person is applying for a certificate of appointment of estate trustee with a will.

I, *(insert name)*, am entitled to share in the distribution of the estate.

I consent to the application by *(insert name)* for a certificate of appointment of estate trustee with a will.

I consent to an order dispensing with the filing of a bond by the applicant *(delete if inapplicable)*.

DATE

```
                                    )
                                    )
                                    )
                                    )
                                    )
.........................................)  .............................................
      Signature of witness          )      Signature of person consenting
                                    )
                                    )
```

RCP-E 74.12 (November 1, 2005)

FORM 74.12.1

Courts of Justice Act

CONSENT TO APPLICANT'S APPOINTMENT AS ESTATE TRUSTEE WITH A WILL LIMITED TO THE ASSETS REFERRED TO IN THE WILL

ONTARIO

SUPERIOR COURT OF JUSTICE

IN THE ESTATE OF *(insert name)*, deceased.

CONSENT TO APPLICANT'S
APPOINTMENT AS ESTATE TRUSTEE WITH A WILL LIMITED TO THE ASSETS REFERRED TO IN THE WILL

The deceased died on *(date)*.

No estate trustee named in a testamentary document of that person is applying for a certificate of appointment of estate trustee with a will limited to the assets referred to in the will.

I, *(insert name)*, am entitled to share in the distribution of the estate.

I consent to the application by *(insert name)* for a certificate of appointment of estate trustee with a will limited to the assets referred to in the will.

I consent to an order dispensing with the filing of a bond by the applicant *(delete if inapplicable)*.

DATE

```
                              )
                              )
                              )
_____     )   _____
    Signature of witness      )         Signature of person consenting
                              )
                              )
```

Print Form

RCP-74-12-1-E (2015/02)

589

FORM 74.13

Courts of Justice Act

CERTIFICATE OF APPOINTMENT OF ESTATE TRUSTEE WITH A WILL

ONTARIO

SUPERIOR COURT OF JUSTICE

IN THE ESTATE OF .... , deceased,

late of

occupation

who died on

CERTIFICATE OF APPOINTMENT
OF ESTATE TRUSTEE WITH A WILL

Applicant	Address	Occupation

This CERTIFICATE OF APPOINTMENT OF ESTATE TRUSTEE WITH A WILL is hereby issued under the seal of the court to the applicant named above. Attached to this certificate is a copy of the deceased's last will dated .... (and codicil(s) dated ....).

DATE ....

Registrar

Address of court office

RCP-E 74.13 (February 1, 2015)

FORM 74.13.1

Courts of Justice Act

CERTIFICATE OF APPOINTMENT OF ESTATE TRUSTEE WITH A WILL LIMITED TO THE ASSETS REFERRED TO IN THE WILL

ONTARIO

SUPERIOR COURT OF JUSTICE

IN THE ESTATE OF   , deceased,

late of

occupation

who died on

CERTIFICATE OF APPOINTMENT OF ESTATE TRUSTEE WITH A WILL LIMITED TO THE ASSETS REFERRED TO IN THE WILL

Applicant	**Address**	**Occupation**

By the order of a judge of the Superior Court of Justice this grant of a certificate of appointment of estate trustee with a will is limited to the assets referred to in the will dated   (and codicils dated   ).

A copy of the will (and codicils) is attached. This will is the last will of the deceased dealing with those assets.

This CERTIFICATE OF APPOINTMENT OF ESTATE TRUSTEE WITH A WILL LIMITED TO THE ASSETS REFERRED TO IN THE WILL is hereby issued under the seal of the court to the applicant named above.

DATE _____   _____
                                                                                              Registrar

Address of court office

_____

_____

_____

RCP-74-13-1-E (2015/02)   Page 1 of 2

591

Court File No.

SUPERIOR COURT OF JUSTICE

at

IN THE ESTATE OF

, deceased

**CERTIFICATE OF APPOINTMENT
OF ESTATE TRUSTEE WITH A
WILLLIMITED TO THE ASSETS
REFERRED TO IN THE WILL**

Name, address, telephone number and fax number of
lawyer or applicant

Save Form   Print Form   Clear Form

RCP-74-13-1-E (2015/02)   Page 2 of 2

FORM 74.13.2

Courts of Justice Act

ORDER FOR CERTIFICATE OF APPOINTMENT OF (SUCCEEDING) ESTATE TRUSTEE WITH A WILL LIMITED TO THE ASSETS REFERRED TO IN THE WILL

(Court file no.)

(Court)

(Name of judge or officer)

(Day and date order made)

(Court seal)

In the Estate of *(insert name)*, deceased:

ORDER

UPON the Application for a Certificate of Appointment of *(Succeeding, delete if not applicable)* Estate Trustee with a Will Limited to the Assets Referred to in the Will in the Estate of . . . . , deceased,

1. IT IS ORDERED that a Certificate of Appointment of *(Succeeding, delete if not applicable)* Estate Trustee with a Will Limited to the Assets Referred to in the Will be issued for the Will of the deceased dated *(insert date)*.

RCP-E 74.13.2 (April 11, 2012)

FORM 74.14

Courts of Justice Act

APPLICATION FOR CERTIFICATE OF APPOINTMENT OF ESTATE TRUSTEE
WITHOUT A WILL (INDIVIDUAL APPLICANT)

ONTARIO **SUPERIOR COURT OF JUSTICE**	**APPLICATION FOR CERTIFICATE OF APPOINTMENT OF ESTATE TRUSTEE WITHOUT A WILL (INDIVIDUAL APPLICANT)** *(Form 74.14 Under the Rules)*

At _____

This application is filed by *(insert name and address)*

DETAILS ABOUT THE DECEASED PERSON

Complete in full as applicable

First given name	Second given name	Third given name	Surname

And if the deceased was known by any other name(s), state below the full name(s) used including surname.

First given name	Second given name	Third given name	Surname

Date of birth of the deceased person, if known: *(day, month, year)*

Address of fixed place of abode *(street or postal address) (city or town)*	*(county or district)*

If the deceased person had no fixed place of abode in Ontario, did he or she have property in Ontario? ☐ No ☐ Yes	Last occupation of deceased person

Place of death *(city or town; county or district)*	Date of death *(day, month, year)*

Marital Status	☐ Unmarried	☐ Married	☐ Widowed	☐ Divorced

Was the deceased person ever legally married?   ☐ Yes   ☐ No

If yes, attach a schedule and provide the following information:

- Name and current address of the deceased's spouse and of each former spouse.
- Whether any of the marriages was terminated and, if so, the method of termination of each marriage (that is, by divorce, by death or by declaration of nullity).
- Name and address of each child of each of the marriages.
- Name of each child who died before the deceased and the name and address of any issue of that deceased child.

Was the deceased person living with a person in a conjugal relationship outside marriage immediately before his or her death?   ☐ Yes   ☐ No

If yes, attach a schedule and provide the name and address of the person who was living with the deceased.

RCP-E 74.14 (September 1, 2018)

594

PERSONS ENTITLED TO SHARE IN THE ESTATE

(Attach a schedule if more space is needed. If a person entitled to share in the estate is not a spouse, child, parent, brother or sister of the deceased person, show how the relationship is traced.)

Name	Address	Relationship to deceased person	Age (if under 18)

VALUE OF ASSETS OF ESTATE

Note:

o   Under "Real estate, net of encumbrances", do not include any real estate in Ontario that is held jointly and passes by survivorship or any real estate outside Ontario.

o   Under "Personal Property", do not include money or property held jointly and passing by survivorship (such as a bank account), or money or property to which a person is entitled by virtue of a beneficiary designation under, for example, a life insurance contract, a registered pension plan, a registered retirement savings plans, a registered retirement income fund, a life income fund, a locked-in retirement account or a tax free savings account.

Personal property	Real estate, net of encumbrances	Total
$	$	$

Explain why the applicant is entitled to apply.

AFFIDAVIT(S) OF APPLICANT(S)
(Attach a separate sheet for additional affidavits, if necessary)

I, an applicant named in this application, make oath and say/affirm:

1.   I am 18 years of age or older and a resident of Ontario.
2.   I have made a careful search and inquiry for a will or other testamentary document of the deceased person, but none has been found. I believe that the person did not leave a will or other testamentary document.
3.   I will faithfully administer the deceased person's property according to law and render a complete and true account of my administration when lawfully required.
4.   Consents of persons who together have a majority interest in the value of the assets of the estate at the date of death are attached.
5.   The information contained in this application and in any attached schedules is true, to the best of my knowledge and belief.

Name (surname and forename(s))	Occupation

Address (street or postal address) (city or town)	(province) (postal code)

Sworn/Affirmed before me at the ....)

of ....)

in the ....)

of ....)

this .... day of ...., 20.........)

Signature of applicant

A Commissioner for taking Affidavits *(or as may be)*

RCP-E 74.14 (September 1, 2018)

Name *(surname and forename(s))*		Occupation		
Address *(street or postal address)*	*(city or town)*		*(province)*	*(postal code)*

Sworn/Affirmed before me at the ....)

of ....)

in the ....)

of ....)

this .... day of ...., 20.........)

_____
Signature of applicant

_____
A Commissioner for taking Affidavits *(or as may be)*

Notice to applicant: Information provided on this form related to the payment of estate administration tax may be forwarded to the Ministry of Finance pursuant to clause 39(1)(b) and 42(1)(c) of the *Freedom of Information and Protection of Privacy Act*. This includes the name of the deceased, name and address of estate trustee(s), value of the estate and any undertakings and tax payments made or refunded. This information will be used by the Ministry of Finance to determine the value of estates and the amount of estate administration tax payable. Questions about the collection of this information should be directed to the Senior Manager – Audit, Advisory and Compliance Branch, 33 King Street West, PO Box 625, Oshawa ON L1H 8H9, 1-866-668-8297.

RCP-E 74.14 (September 1, 2018)

FORM 74.15

Courts of Justice Act

APPLICATION FOR CERTIFICATE OF APPOINTMENT OF ESTATE TRUSTEE
WITHOUT A WILL (CORPORATE APPLICANT)

ONTARIO	**APPLICATION FOR CERTIFICATE OF APPOINTMENT OF ESTATE TRUSTEE WITHOUT A WILL (CORPORATE APPLICANT)**
SUPERIOR COURT OF JUSTICE	*(Form 74.15 Under the Rules)*

At

This application is filed by *(insert name and address)*

DETAILS ABOUT THE DECEASED PERSON

Complete in full as applicable

First given name	Second given name	Third given name	Surname

And if the deceased was known by any other name(s), state below the full name(s) used including surname.

First given name	Second given name	Third given name	Surname

Date of birth of the deceased person, if known: *(day, month, year)*

Address of fixed place of abode *(street or postal address) (city or town)*	*(county or district)*

If the deceased person had no fixed place of abode in Ontario, did he or she have property in Ontario? ☐ No ☐ Yes	Last occupation of deceased person

Place of death *(city or town, county or district)*	Date of death *(day, month, year)*

Marital Status	☐ Unmarried	☐ Married	☐ Widowed	☐ Divorced

Was the deceased person ever legally married?   ☐ Yes   ☐ No

If yes, attach a schedule and provide the following information:

- Name and current address of the deceased's spouse and of each former spouse.

- Whether any of the marriages was terminated and, if so, the method of termination of each marriage (that is, by divorce, by death or by declaration of nullity).

- Name and address of each child of each of the marriages.

- Name of each child who died before the deceased and the name and address of any issue of that deceased child.

Was the deceased person living with a person in a conjugal relationship outside marriage immediately before his or her death?   ☐ Yes   ☐ No

If yes, attach a schedule and provide the name and address of the person who was living with the deceased.

RCP-E 74.15 (September 1, 2018)

597

PERSONS ENTITLED TO SHARE IN THE ESTATE

(Attach a schedule if more space is needed. If a person entitled to share in the estate is not a spouse, child, parent, brother or sister of the deceased person, show how the relationship is traced.)

Name	Address	Relationship to deceased person	Age (if under 18)

VALUE OF ASSETS OF ESTATE

Note:

o   Under "Real estate, net of encumbrances", do not include any real estate in Ontario that is held jointly and passes by survivorship or any real estate outside Ontario.

o   Under "Personal Property", do not include money or property held jointly and passing by survivorship (such as a bank account), or money or property to which a person is entitled by virtue of a beneficiary designation under, for example, a life insurance contract, a registered pension plan, a registered retirement savings plans, a registered retirement income fund, a life income fund, a locked-in retirement account or a tax free savings account.

Personal property	Real estate, net of encumbrances	Total
$	$	$

Explain why the applicant is entitled to apply.

AFFIDAVIT(S) OF APPLICANT(S)
(Attach a separate sheet for additional affidavits, if necessary)

I, a trust officer named in this application, make oath and say/affirm:

1. I am a trust officer of the corporate applicant.
2. I am 18 years of age or older.
3. I have made a careful search and inquiry for a will or other testamentary document of the deceased person, but none has been found. I believe that the person did not leave a will or other testamentary document.
4. The corporate applicant will faithfully administer the deceased person's property according to law and render a complete and true account of my administration when lawfully required.
5. Consents of persons who together have a majority interest in the value of the assets of the estate at the date of death are attached.
6. The information contained in this application and in any attached schedules is true, to the best of my knowledge and belief.

Name of corporate applicant	Name of trust officer

Address of corporate applicant *(street or postal address)*   *(city or town)*   *(province)*   *(postal code)*

Sworn/Affirmed before me at the ....

of ....

in the ....

of ....

this .... day of ...., 20..........

_____
Signature of trust officer

_____
A Commissioner for taking Affidavits *(or as may be)*

Notice to applicant: Information provided on this form related to the payment of estate administration tax may be forwarded to the Ministry of Finance pursuant to clause 39(1)(b) and 42(1)(c) of the *Freedom of Information and Protection of Privacy Act.* This includes the name of the deceased, name and address of estate trustee(s), value of the estate and any undertakings and tax payments made or refunded. This information will be used by the Ministry of Finance to determine the value of estates and the amount of estate administration tax payable. Questions about the collection of this information should be directed to the Senior Manager – Audit, Advisory and Compliance Branch, 33 King Street West, PO Box 625, Oshawa ON L1H 8H9, 1-866-668-8297.

RCP-E 74.15 (September 1, 2018)

FORM 74.16

Courts of Justice Act

AFFIDAVIT OF SERVICE OF NOTICE

ONTARIO

SUPERIOR COURT OF JUSTICE

IN THE ESTATE OF   *(insert name)*   , deceased

AFFIDAVIT OF SERVICE OF NOTICE

I,   *(insert name)*   , of   *(insert city or town and county or district of residence)*, make oath and say/affirm:

1.   I am an applicant for a certificate of appointment of estate trustee without a will in the estate.

2.   I have sent or caused to be sent a notice in Form 74.17, a copy of which is marked as Exhibit "A" to this affidavit, to all adult persons named in the notice (except to an applicant who is entitled to share in the distribution of the estate), to a parent or guardian of the minor and to the Children's Lawyer if paragraph 3 of the notice applies, to the guardian or attorney if paragraph 4 applies and to the Public Guardian and Trustee if paragraph 5 applies, all by regular lettermail sent to the person's last known address.

3.   The following persons may be entitled to be served but have not been served for the reasons shown below:

Name of person (if applicable)   **Reason not served**

If paragraph 3 does not apply insert "Not Applicable."

4.   To the best of my knowledge and belief, subject to paragraph 3 (if applicable), the persons named in the notice are all the persons who are entitled to share in the distribution of the estate.

Sworn/Affirmed before me at the ....)

of..)

in the..)

of..)

this .... day of......................., 20..........)

_____
Signature of applicant

)

)

_____
A Commissioner for taking Affidavits *(or as may be)*

RCP-E 74.16 (November 1, 2005)

FORM 74.17

Courts of Justice Act

NOTICE OF AN APPLICATION FOR A

CERTIFICATE OF APPOINTMENT OF ESTATE TRUSTEE WITHOUT A WILL

ONTARIO

SUPERIOR COURT OF JUSTICE

IN THE ESTATE OF *(insert name)* , deceased.

NOTICE OF AN APPLICATION FOR A CERTIFICATE OF APPOINTMENT OF
ESTATE TRUSTEE WITHOUT A WILL

1. The deceased died on *(insert date)* , without a will.

2. The applicant named in this notice is applying for a certificate of appointment of estate trustee without a will.

APPLICANT

Name   **Address**

3. The following persons who are less than 18 years of age are entitled to share in the distribution of the estate:

Name	**Date of Birth** (day, month, year)	**Name and Address of Parent or Guardian**	**Estimated Value of Interest in Estate**

* Note: *The Estimated Value of Interest in Estate may be omitted in the form if it is included in a separate schedule attached to the notice sent to the Children's Lawyer.*

4. The following persons who are mentally incapable within the meaning of section 6 of the *Substitute Decisions Act, 1992* in respect of an issue in the proceeding, and who have guardians or attorneys acting under powers of attorney with authority to act in the proceeding, are entitled to share in the distribution of the estate:

Name and Address of Person   **Name and Address of Guardian or Attorney** *

* *Specify whether guardian or attorney.*

5. The following persons who are mentally incapable within the meaning of section 6 of the *Substitute Decisions Act, 1992* in respect of an issue in the proceeding, and who do not have guardians or attorneys acting under powers of attorney with authority to act in the proceeding, are entitled to share in the distribution of the estate:

Name and Address of Person   **Estimated Value of Interest in Estate**

600

* Note: *The Estimated Value of Interest in Estate may be omitted in the form if it is included in a separate schedule attached to the notice sent to the Public Guardian and Trustee.*

6. All other persons entitled to share in the distribution of the estate are as follows:

Name   **Address**

7. This notice is being sent, by regular lettermail, to all adult persons named above in this notice (except to an applicant who is entitled to share in the distribution of the estate), to a parent or guardian of the minor and to the Children's Lawyer if paragraph 3 applies, to the guardian or attorney if paragraph 4 applies, and to the Public Guardian and Trustee if paragraph 5 applies.

8. The following persons may be entitled to be served but have not been served for the reasons shown below:

Name of person   **Reason not served**

If paragraph 8 does not apply insert "Not Applicable."

DATE

RCP-E 74.17 (November 1, 2005)

FORM 74.18

Courts of Justice Act

RENUNCIATION OF PRIOR RIGHT TO A CERTIFICATE OF APPOINTMENT OF ESTATE TRUSTEE WITHOUT A WILL

ONTARIO

SUPERIOR COURT OF JUSTICE

IN THE ESTATE OF *(insert name)*, deceased.

RENUNCIATION OF PRIOR RIGHT TO A CERTIFICATE OF APPOINTMENT
OF ESTATE TRUSTEE WITHOUT A WILL

The deceased died on *(date)*, without a will.

I, *(insert name)*, am entitled to apply for a certificate of appointment of estate trustee without a will in priority to *(insert name)*.

I renounce my right to a certificate of appointment of estate trustee without a will in priority to *(insert name)*.

DATE

)

)

)

)

)

....) ....

Signature of witness   ) Signature of person renouncing

)

)

RCP-E 74.18 (November 1, 2005)

FORM 74.19

Courts of Justice Act

CONSENT TO APPLICANT'S APPOINTMENT AS ESTATE TRUSTEE WITHOUT A WILL

ONTARIO

SUPERIOR COURT OF JUSTICE

IN THE ESTATE OF *(insert name)*, deceased.

CONSENT TO APPLICANT'S APPOINTMENT AS ESTATE TRUSTEE WITHOUT A WILL

The deceased died on *(date)*, without a will.

I, *(insert name)*, am entitled to share in the distribution of the estate.

I consent to the application by *(insert name)* for a certificate of appointment of estate trustee without a will.

I consent to an order dispensing with the filing of a bond by the applicant *(delete if inapplicable)*.

DATE

```
                                              )
                                              )
                                              )
                                              )
                                              )
.................................................)   ..................................................
Signature of witness                          )   Signature of person renouncing
                                              )
                                              )
```

RCP-E 74.19 (November 1, 2005)

FORM 74.20

Courts of Justice Act

CERTIFICATE OF APPOINTMENT OF ESTATE TRUSTEE WITHOUT A WILL

Court file no.

ONTARIO

SUPERIOR COURT OF JUSTICE

IN THE ESTATE OF   , deceased,

late of

occupation

who died on

CERTIFICATE OF APPOINTMENT OF ESTATE TRUSTEE WITHOUT A WILL

Applicant   Address   Occupation

This CERTIFICATE OF APPOINTMENT OF ESTATE TRUSTEE WITHOUT A WILL is hereby issued under the seal of the court to the applicant named above.

DATE   _____
                                        Registrar
                                        Address of court office

RCP-E 74.20 (November 1, 2005)

FORM 74.20.1

Courts of Justice Act

APPLICATION FOR CERTIFICATE OF APPOINTMENT OF A FOREIGN ESTATE TRUSTEE'S NOMINEE AS ESTATE TRUSTEE WITHOUT A WILL

ONTARIO

SUPERIOR COURT OF JUSTICE

at _____

This application is filed by *(insert name)*

DETAILS ABOUT THE DECEASED PERSON

Complete in full as applicable

First given name	Second given name	Third given name	Surname

And if the deceased was known by any other name(s), state below the full name(s) used including surname.

First given name	Second given name	Third given name	Surname

Date of birth of the deceased person, if known: *(day, month, year)*

Address *(street or postal address) (city or town) (province or state) (country)*

Place of death *(city or town; country)*   **Date of death** *(day, month, year)*

Country of domicile

PARTICULARS OF FOREIGN CERTIFICATE

Country *(and province or state if applicable)* where issued	Issuing court	Date issued *(day, month, year)*

		Total
TOTAL VALUE OF ASSETS OF ESTATE	$	

VALUE OF ASSETS LOCATED IN ONTARIO

Personal property	Real estate, net of encumbrances	Total
$	$	$

AFFIDAVIT(S) OF APPLICANT(S)
(Attach a separate sheet for additional affidavits, if necessary)

I, an applicant named in this application, make oath and say/affirm:

1. I am the nominee of the foreign estate trustee appointed in the jurisdiction where the deceased was domiciled at the date of death.

2. A copy of the document appointing the foreign estate trustee, certified by the court that issued it, is marked as Exhibit "A" to this affidavit.

3. I am 18 years of age or older.

4. I will faithfully administer the deceased person's property according to law and render a complete and true account of my administration when lawfully required.

5. The information contained in this application and in any attached schedules is true, to the best of my knowledge and belief.

Name *(surname and forename(s))*	**Occupation**

Address *(street or postal address)*   *(city or town)*   *(province)*   *(postal code)*

Sworn/Affirmed before me at the _____

of _____

in the _____

of _____   _____

this _____ day of _____ , 20 _____   Signature of applicant

_____
A Commissioner for taking Affidavits *(or as may be)*

Name *(surname and forename(s))*

Occupation

Address *(street or postal address)*   *(city or town)*   *(province)*   *(postal code)*

Sworn/Affirmed before me at the _____

of _____

in the _____

of _____

this _____ day of _____, 20 _____

_____
Signature of applicant

_____
A Commissioner for taking Affidavits *(or as may be)*

Notice to applicant: Information provided on this form related to the payment of estate administration tax may be forwarded to the Ministry of Finance pursuant to clause 39(1)(b) and 42(1)(c) of the *Freedom of Information and Protection of Privacy Act*. This includes the name of the deceased, name and address of estate trustee(s), value of the estate and any undertakings and tax payments made or refunded. This information will be used by the Ministry of Finance to determine the value of estates and the amount of estate administration tax payable. Questions about the collection of this information should be directed to the Senior Manager – Audit, Advisory and Compliance Branch, 33 King Street West, PO Box 625, Oshawa ON L1H 8H9, 1-866-668-8297.

| Save Form | Print Form | | Clear Form |

FORM 74.20.2

Courts of Justice Act

NOMINATION OF APPLICANT BY FOREIGN ESTATE TRUSTEE

ONTARIO

SUPERIOR COURT OF JUSTICE

IN THE ESTATE OF *(insert name)*, deceased.

NOMINATION OF APPLICANT BY FOREIGN ESTATE TRUSTEE

1. The deceased died on *(insert date)*, without a will.

2. I, ... was appointed estate trustee by the . . . ., in the jurisdiction where the deceased was domiciled at the date of death, on the . . . . day of . . . . 20 . . . . . .

3. I nominate . . . . to apply in Ontario for a certificate of estate trustee without a will.

DATE:

_____   _____

Signature of witness   Signature of person nominating

RCP-E 74.20.2 (November 1, 2005)

FORM 74.20.3

Courts of Justice Act

CERTIFICATE OF APPOINTMENT OF FOREIGN ESTATE TRUSTEE'S NOMINEE AS ESTATE TRUSTEE WITHOUT A WILL

Court file no.

ONTARIO

SUPERIOR COURT OF JUSTICE

IN THE ESTATE OF   , deceased,

late of

occupation

who died on

CERTIFICATE OF APPOINTMENT OF FOREIGN ESTATE TRUSTEE'S NOMINEE AS ESTATE TRUSTEE WITHOUT A WILL

Applicant   Address   Occupation

   This CERTIFICATE OF APPOINTMENT OF FOREIGN ESTATE TRUSTEE'S NOMINEE AS ESTATE TRUSTEE WITHOUT A WILL is hereby issued under the seal of the court to the applicant named above.

DATE

_____
Registrar
Address of court office

RCP-E 74.20.3 (November 1, 2005)

FORM 74.21

Courts of Justice Act

APPLICATION FOR CERTIFICATE OF APPOINTMENT AS SUCCEEDING ESTATE TRUSTEE WITH A WILL

ONTARIO

SUPERIOR COURT OF JUSTICE

APPLICATION FOR CERTIFICATE OF APPOINTMENT AS SUCCEEDING ESTATE TRUSTEE WITH A WILL

(Form 74.21 Under the Rules)

at _____

This application is filed by *(insert name and address)*

DETAILS ABOUT THE DECEASED PERSON

Complete in full as applicable

First given name	Second given name	Third given name	Surname

And if the deceased was known by any other name(s), state below the full name(s) used including surname.

First given name	Second given name	Third given name	Surname

PARTICULARS OF FIRST CERTIFICATE

Name(s) of estate trustee(s)	Date issued *(day, month, year)*

VALUE OF UNDISTRIBUTED ASSETS OF ESTATE

Personal property	Real estate, net of encumbrances	Total
$	$	$

Explain why the applicant is entitled to apply.

610

AFFIDAVIT(S) OF APPLICANT(S)
(Attach a separate sheet for additional affidavits, if necessary.)

I, a trust officer named in this application, make oath and say/affirm:

1. I am a trust officer of the corporate applicant.
2. I am 18 years of age or older.
3. The corporate applicant will faithfully administer the deceased person's property according to law and render a complete and true account of its administration when lawfully required.
4. If the corporate applicant is not named as estate trustee in the will or codicil, consents of persons who together have a majority interest in the value of the undistributed assets of the estate at the date of this application are attached.
5. The information contained in this application and in any attached schedules is true, to the best of my knowledge and belief.

Name of corporate applicant	Name of trust officer

Address of corporate applicant *(city or town)*   *(province)*   *(postal code)*
(street or postal address)

Sworn/Affirmed before me at the..........................

of...

in the...

of...

this ....day of .... , 20...

_____
Signature of trust officer

_____
A Commissioner for taking Affidavits *(or as may be)*

I, an applicant named in this application, make oath and say/affirm:

1. I am 18 years of age or older.
2. I will faithfully administer the deceased person's property according to law and render a complete and true account of my administration when lawfully required.
3. If I am not named as estate trustee in the will or codicil, consents of persons who together have a majority interest in the value of the undistributed assets of the estate at the date of this application are attached.

4. The information contained in this application and in any attached schedules is true, to the best of my knowledge and belief.

Name *(surname and forename(s))*	**Occupation**

Address *(street or postal address)* *(city or town)*   *(province)*   *(postal code)*

Sworn/Affirmed before me at the.........................

of..

in the...

of..

this ....day of .... , 20..

_____
Signature of trust officer

_____
A Commissioner for taking Affidavits *(or as may be)*

RCP-E 74.21 (November 1, 2005)

FORM 74.21.1

Courts of Justice Act

APPLICATION FOR CERTIFICATE OF APPOINTMENT AS SUCCEEDING ESTATE
TRUSTEE WITH A WILL LIMITED TO THE ASSETS REFERRED TO IN THE WILL

ONTARIO

SUPERIOR COURT OF JUSTICE

at _____

**APPLICATION FOR CERTIFICATE OF
APPOINTMENT AS SUCCEEDING ESTATE
TRUSTEE WITH A WILL LIMITED TO THE
ASSETS REFERRED TO IN THE WILL**
(Form 74.21.1 Under the Rules)

This application is filed by *(insert name and address)*

DETAILS ABOUT THE DECEASED PERSON

Complete in full as applicable

First given name	Second given name	Third given name	Surname

*And if the deceased was known by any other name(s), state below the full name(s) used
including surname.*

First given name	Second given name	Third given name	Surname

Date of birth of the deceased person, if known: *(day, month, year)*

PARTICULARS OF FIRST CERTIFICATE

Name(s) of estate trustee(s)	Date issued *(day, month, year)*

VALUE OF UNDISTRIBUTED ASSETS OF ESTATE

Personal property	Real estate, net of encumbrances	Total
$	$	$

Explain why the applicant is entitled to apply.

613

AFFIDAVIT(S) OF APPLICANT(S)
(Attach a separate sheet for additional affidavits, if necessary.)

I, a trust officer named in this application, make oath and say/affirm:

1. I am a trust officer of the corporate applicant.
2. I am 18 years of age or older.
3. The corporate applicant will faithfully administer the deceased person's property according to law and render a complete and true account of its administration when lawfully required.
4. If the corporate applicant is not named as estate trustee in the will or codicil, consents of persons who together have a majority interest in the value of the undistributed assets of the estate at the date of this application are attached.
5. The information contained in this application and in any attached schedules is true, to the best of my knowledge and belief.

Name of corporate applicant	Name of trust officer

Address of corporate applicant *(city or town)*   *(province)*   *(postal code)*
(street or postal address)

Sworn/Affirmed before me at the ....

of...

in the...

of...

this .... day of......................., 20 ....

_____
Signature of trust officer

_____
A Commissioner for taking Affidavits *(or as may be)*

I, an applicant named in this application, make oath and say/affirm:

1. I am 18 years of age or older.
2. I will faithfully administer the deceased person's property according to law and render a complete and true account of my administration when lawfully required.
3. If I am not named as estate trustee in the will or codicil, consents of persons who together have a majority interest in the value of the undistributed assets of the estate at the date of this application are attached.

4. The information contained in this application and in any attached schedules is true, to the best of my knowledge and belief.

Name *(surname and forename(s))*	Occupation

Address *(street or postal (city or town)   (province)   (postal code) address)*

Sworn/Affirmed before me at the ....

of...

in the...

of..

this .... day of....................., 20 ....   _____
                                                                            Signature of applicant

_____
A Commissioner for taking Affidavits *(or as may be)*

RCP-E 74.21.1 (April 11, 2012)

FORM 74.22

Courts of Justice Act

CONSENT TO APPLICANT'S APPOINTMENT AS SUCCEEDING ESTATE TRUSTEE
WITH A WILL

ONTARIO

SUPERIOR COURT OF JUSTICE

IN THE ESTATE OF *(insert name)* , deceased.

CONSENT TO APPLICANT'S APPOINTMENT
AS SUCCEEDING ESTATE TRUSTEE WITH A WILL

The deceased died on *(date)*.

I, *(insert name)*, am entitled to share in the distribution of the remaining estate.

I consent to the application by *(insert name)* for a certificate of appointment of succeeding estate trustee with a will.

I consent to an order dispensing with the filing of a bond by the applicant *(delete if inapplicable)*.

DATE

)
)
)
)
....) ....
Signature of witness   ) Signature of person consenting
)
)
)

RCP-E 74.22 (November 1, 2005)

616

FORM 74.22.1

Courts of Justice Act

CONSENT TO APPLICANT'S APPOINTMENT AS SUCCEEDING ESTATE TRUSTEE
WITH A WILL LIMITED TO THE ASSETS REFERRED TO IN THE WILL

ONTARIO

SUPERIOR COURT OF JUSTICE

IN THE ESTATE OF *(insert name)*, deceased.

CONSENT TO APPLICANT'S APPOINTMENT
AS SUCCEEDING ESTATE TRUSTEE WITH A WILL LIMITED TO THE ASSETS
REFERRED TO IN THE WILL

The deceased died on *(date)*.

I, *(insert name)*, am entitled to share in the distribution of the remaining estate.

I consent to the application by *(insert name)* for a certificate of appointment of succeeding estate trustee with a will limited to the assets referred to in the will.

I consent to an order dispensing with the filing of a bond by the applicant *(delete if inapplicable)*.

DATE

```
                                                      )
                                                      )
                                                      )
                                                      )
                                                      )
..............................................................)  .........................................................
Signature of witness                                  )  Signature of person consenting
                                                      )
                                                      )
```

RCP-E 74.22.1 (April 11, 2012)

617

FORM 74.23

Courts of Justice Act

CERTIFICATE OF APPOINTMENT OF SUCCEEDING ESTATE TRUSTEE WITH A WILL

Court file no.

ONTARIO

SUPERIOR COURT OF JUSTICE

IN THE ESTATE OF   , deceased,

late of

occupation

who died on

CERTIFICATE OF APPOINTMENT OF SUCCEEDING ESTATE TRUSTEE WITH A WILL

Applicant: Address: Occupation:

This CERTIFICATE OF APPOINTMENT OF SUCCEEDING ESTATE TRUSTEE WITH A WILL is hereby issued under the seal of the court to the applicant named above. Attached to this certificate is a copy of the deceased's last will dated_____(and codicil(s) dated_____).

DATE

_____

Registrar

Address of court office

Print Form

RCP-74-23-E (2015/02)

618

FORM 74.23.1

Courts of Justice Act

CERTIFICATE OF APPOINTMENT OF SUCCEEDING ESTATE TRUSTEE WITH A WILL LIMITED TO THE ASSETS REFERRED TO IN THE WILL

ONTARIO

SUPERIOR COURT OF JUSTICE

IN THE ESTATE OF _____ deceased,

late of

occupation

who died on

CERTIFICATE OF APPOINTMENT OF SUCCEEDING ESTATE TRUSTEE WITH A WILL LIMITED TO THE ASSETS REFERRED TO IN THE WILL

Applicant: _____ Address: _____ Occupation: _____

By order of a judge of the Superior Court of Justice this grant of a certificate of appointment of estate trustee with a will is limited to the assets referred to in the will dated_____ (and codicils dated _____). A copy of the will (and codicils) is attached. This will is the last will of the deceased dealing with those assets.

This CERTIFICATE OF APPOINTMENT OF SUCCEEDING ESTATE TRUSTEE WITH A WILL LIMITED TO THE ASSETS REFERRED TO IN THE WILL is hereby issued under the seal of the court to the applicant named above.

DATE: _____   _____

                                        Registrar

                                        Address of court office

Print Form

RCP-74-23-1-E (2015/02)

619

FORM 74.24

Courts of Justice Act

APPLICATION FOR CERTIFICATE OF APPOINTMENT AS SUCCEEDING ESTATE TRUSTEE WITHOUT A WILL

ONTARIO **SUPERIOR COURT OF JUSTICE** at _____ This application is filed by *(insert name and address)*	**APPLICATION FOR CERTIFICATE OF APPOINTMENT AS SUCCEEDING ESTATE TRUSTEE WITHOUT A WILL** *(Form 74.24 Under the Rules)*

DETAILS ABOUT THE DECEASED PERSON

Complete in full as applicable

First given name	Second given name	Third given name	Surname

And if the deceased was known by any other name(s), state below the full name(s) used including surname.

First given name	Second given name	Third given name	Surname

PARTICULARS OF FIRST CERTIFICATE

Name(s) of estate trustee(s) or administrator(s)	Date issued *(day, month, year)*

PERSONS ENTITLED TO SHARE IN THE ESTATE
(at date of this application)

(Attach a schedule if more space is needed. If a person entitled to share in the estate is not a spouse, child, parent, brother or sister of the deceased person, show how the relationship is traced.)

Name	Address	Relationship to deceased person	Age (if under 18)

VALUE OF UNDISTRIBUTED ASSETS OF ESTATE

Personal property	Real estate, net of encumbrances	Total
$	$	$

Explain why the applicant is entitled to apply.

AFFIDAVIT(S) OF APPLICANT(S)
(Attach a separate sheet for additional affidavits, if necessary.)

I, a trust officer named in this application, make oath and say/affirm:

1. I am a trust officer of the corporate applicant.

2. I am 18 years of age or older.

3. The corporate applicant will faithfully administer the deceased person's property according to law and render a complete and true account of its administration when lawfully required.

4. Consents of persons who together have a majority interest in the value of the undistributed assets of the estate at the date of this application are attached.

5. The information contained in this application and in any attached schedules is true, to the best of my knowledge and belief.

Name of corporate applicant	Name of trust officer

Address of corporate applicant *(city or town)*   *(province)*   *(postal code)*
(street or postal address)

Sworn/Affirmed before me at the.............................

of...................................,..

in the..

of..

this.................. day of........................... , 20.........

_____
Signature of trust officer

_____
A Commissioner for taking Affidavits *(or as may be)*

I, an applicant named in this application, make oath and say/affirm:

1. I am 18 years of age or older and a resident of Ontario.
2. I will faithfully administer the deceased person's property according to law and render a complete and true account of my administration when lawfully required.
3. Consents of persons who together have a majority interest in the value of the undistributed assets of the estate at the date of this application are attached.
4. The information contained in this application and in any attached schedules is true, to the best of my knowledge and belief.

Name *(surname and forename(s))*	**Occupation**

Address *(street or postal(city or town) address)*	*(province)*	*(postal code)*

Sworn/Affirmed before me at the......................

of...

in the..

of..

this .... day of............................. , 20...

_____

A Commissioner for taking Affidavits *(or as may be)*

_____
Signature of trust officer

RCP-E 74.24 (November 1, 2005)

FORM 74.25

Courts of Justice Act

CONSENT TO APPLICANT'S APPOINTMENT AS SUCCEEDING ESTATE TRUSTEE
WITHOUT A WILL

ONTARIO

SUPERIOR COURT OF JUSTICE

IN THE ESTATE OF *(insert name)*, deceased.

CONSENT TO APPLICANT'S APPOINTMENT
AS SUCCEEDING ESTATE TRUSTEE WITHOUT A WILL

The deceased died on *(date)*, without a will.

I, *(insert name)*, am entitled to share in the distribution of the estate.

I consent to the application by *(insert name)* for a certificate of appointment of succeeding estate trustee without a will.

I consent to an order dispensing with the filing of a bond by the applicant *(delete if inapplicable)*.

DATE

```
                                      )
                                      )
                                      )
                                      )
                                      )
.......................................... ) ..................................................
Signature of witness                  ) Signature of person consenting
                                      )
```

RCP-E 74.25 (November 1, 2005)

FORM 74.26

Courts of Justice Act

CERTIFICATE OF APPOINTMENT OF SUCCEEDING ESTATE TRUSTEE WITHOUT A WILL

Court file no.

ONTARIO

SUPERIOR COURT OF JUSTICE

IN THE ESTATE OF   , deceased,

late of

occupation

who died on

CERTIFICATE OF APPOINTMENT OF SUCCEEDING ESTATE TRUSTEE WITHOUT A WILL

Applicant   Address   Occupation

   This CERTIFICATE OF APPOINTMENT OF SUCCEEDING ESTATE TRUSTEE WITH-OUT A WILL is hereby issued under the seal of the court to the applicant named above.

   DATE   _____

                                Registrar
                                Address of court office

RCP-E 74.26 (November 1, 2005)

FORM 74.27

Courts of Justice Act

APPLICATION FOR CONFIRMATION BY RESEALING OF APPOINTMENT OR CERTIFICATE OF ANCILLARY APPOINTMENT OF ESTATE TRUSTEE

ONTARIO

SUPERIOR COURT OF JUSTICE

at _____

This is an application for *(check one)*

☐ confirmation by resealing of the appointment of an estate trustee with (or without) a will.

☐ a certificate of ancillary appointment of an estate trustee with a will.

This application is filed by *(insert name and address)*

DETAILS ABOUT THE DECEASED PERSON

Complete in full as applicable

First given name	Second given name	Third given name	Surname

And if the deceased was known by any other name(s), state below the full name(s) used including surname.

First given name	Second given name	Third given name	Surname

Address *(street or postal address) (city or town) (province or state) (country)*

Place of death *(city or town; country)*	**Date of death** *(day, month, year)*

PARTICULARS OF PRIMARY CERTIFICATE OR GRANT

Country *(and province or state if applicable)* **where issued**	**Issuing court**	**Date issued** *(day, month, year)*

VALUE OF ASSETS LOCATED IN ONTARIO

Personal property	**Real estate, net of encumbrances**	**Total**
$	$	$

AFFIDAVIT(S) OF APPLICANT(S)

(Attach a separate sheet for additional affidavits, if necessary)

I, an applicant named in this application, make oath and say/affirm:

1. I am an estate trustee named in the primary certificate (*or* primary grant of letters probate or letters of administration), a copy of which, certified by the court that issued it, is Exhibit "A" to this affidavit.

2. I am 18 years of age or older.

3. I will faithfully administer the deceased person's property according to law and render a complete and true account of my administration when lawfully required.

render a complete and true account of my administration when lawfully required.

4. The primary certificate (*or* primary grant of letters probate or letters of administration) is still effective.

5. The information contained in this application and in any attached schedules is true, to the best of my knowledge and belief.

Name *(surname and forename(s))*	Occupation

Address *(street or postal address)*   *(city or town)*   *(province)*   *(postal code)*

Sworn/Affirmed before me at the _____

of _____

in the _____

of _____   _____

this _____ day of _____ , 20 _____   Signature of applicant

_____
A Commissioner for taking Affidavits *(or as may be)*

Notice to applicant: Information provided on this form related to the payment of estate administration tax may be forwarded to the Ministry of Finance pursuant to clause 39(1)(b) and 42(1)(c) of the *Freedom of Information and Protection of Privacy Act*. This includes the name of the deceased, name and address of estate trustee(s), value of the estate and any undertakings and tax payments made or refunded. This information will be used by the Ministry of Finance to determine the value of estates and the amount of estate administration tax payable. Questions about the collection of this information should be directed to the Senior Manager – Audit, Advisory and Compliance Branch, 33 King Street West, PO Box 625, Oshawa ON L1H 8H9, 1-866-668-8297.

Save Form	Print Form		Clear Form

RCP-74-27-E (2015/02)

Page 2 of 2

RULES OF CIVIL PROCEDURE FORMS

FORM 74.28

Courts of Justice Act

CONFIRMATION BY RESEALING OF APPOINTMENT OF ESTATE TRUSTEE

ONTARIO

SUPERIOR COURT OF JUSTICE

IN THE ESTATE OF *(insert name)*, deceased.

CONFIRMATION BY RESEALING OF APPOINTMENT OF ESTATE TRUSTEE

Sealed with the seal of the Superior Court of Justice by order of that court dated *(insert date)*, under subsection 52 (1) of the *Estates Act*.

DATE _____

Registrar
Address of court office

Print Form

RCP-74-28-E (2015/02)

627

FORM 74.29

Courts of Justice Act

CERTIFICATE OF ANCILLARY APPOINTMENT OF ESTATE TRUSTEE WITH A WILL

Court file no.

ONTARIO

SUPERIOR COURT OF JUSTICE

IN THE ESTATE OF   , deceased,

late of

occupation

who died on

CERTIFICATE OF ANCILLARY APPOINTMENT OF ESTATE TRUSTEE WITH A WILL

Applicant	Address	Occupation

Court of foreign grant

Date of foreign grant

This CERTIFICATE OF ANCILLARY APPOINTMENT OF ESTATE TRUSTEE WITH A WILL is hereby issued under the seal of the court to the applicant named above. A certified copy of the foreign grant, to which this certificate is ancillary, is attached.

DATE   _____

Registrar

Address of court office

RCP-E 74.29 (November 1, 2005)

FORM 74.30

Courts of Justice Act

APPLICATION FOR CERTIFICATE OF APPOINTMENT OF ESTATE TRUSTEE DURING LITIGATION

ONTARIO

SUPERIOR COURT OF JUSTICE

APPLICATION FOR CERTIFICATE OF APPOINTMENT OF ESTATE TRUSTEE DURING LITIGATION

(Form 74.30 Under the Rules)

At

This application is filed by *(insert name)*

DETAILS ABOUT THE DECEASED PERSON

Complete in full as applicable

First given name	Second given name	Third given name	Surname

And if the deceased was known by any other name(s), state below the full name(s) used including surname.

First given name	Second given name	Third given name	Surname

Date of birth of the deceased person, if known: *(day, month, year)*

Address of fixed place of abode *(street or postal address) (city or town)*   *(county or district)*

If the deceased person had no fixed place of abode in Ontario, did he or she have property in Ontario? ☐ No ☐ Yes	Last occupation of deceased person

Place of death *(city or town; county or district)*	Date of death *(day, month, year)*

VALUE OF ASSETS OF ESTATE

Note:

o   Under "Real estate, net of encumbrances", do not include any real estate in Ontario that is held jointly and passes by survivorship or any real estate outside Ontario.

o   Under "Personal Property", do not include money or property held jointly and passing by survivorship (such as a bank account), or money or property to which a person is entitled by virtue of a beneficiary designation under, for example, a life insurance contract, a registered pension plan, a registered retirement savings plans, a registered retirement income fund, a life income fund, a locked-in retirement account or a tax free savings account.

Personal property	Real estate, net of encumbrances	Total
$	$	$

This application is made pursuant to an order for the appointment of an estate trustee during litigation, made by

(name of judge)	*(day, month, year)*
	on

RCP-E 74.30 (September 1, 2018)

629

AFFIDAVIT(S) OF APPLICANT(S)
(Attach a separate sheet for additional affidavits, if necessary)

I, a trust officer named in this application, make oath and say/affirm:

1. I am a trust officer of the corporate applicant.
2. I am 18 years of age or older.
3. The corporate applicant will faithfully administer the deceased person's property according to law, make no distribution without

a court order, and render a complete and true account of its administration when lawfully required.
4. The information contained in this application and in any attached schedules is true, to the best of my knowledge and belief.

Name of corporate applicant	Name of trust officer

Address of corporate applicant *(street or postal address)*   *(city or town)*   *(province)*   *(postal code)*

Sworn/Affirmed before me at the ....

of ....

in the ....

of ....

this .... day of ...., 20......

Signature of trust officer

A Commissioner for taking Affidavits *(or as may be)*

I, an applicant named in this application, make oath and say/affirm:

1. I am 18 years of age or older.
2. I will faithfully administer the deceased person's property according to law, make no distribution without a court order and render a complete

and true account of my administration when lawfully required.
3. The information contained in this application and in any attached schedules is true, to the best of my knowledge and belief.

Name *(surname and forename(s))*	Occupation

Address *(street or postal address)*   *(city or town)*   *(province)*   *(postal code)*

Sworn/Affirmed before me at the ....

of ....

in the ....

of ....

this .... day of ...., 20......

Signature of applicant

A Commissioner for taking Affidavits *(or as may be)*

RCP-E 74.30 (September 1, 2018)

630

FORM 74.31

Courts of Justice Act

CERTIFICATE OF APPOINTMENT OF ESTATE TRUSTEE DURING LITIGATION

Court file no.

ONTARIO

SUPERIOR COURT OF JUSTICE

IN THE ESTATE OF   , deceased,

late of

occupation

who died on

CERTIFICATE OF APPOINTMENT OF ESTATE TRUSTEE DURING LITIGATION

Applicant   Address   Occupation

By order of the Superior Court of Justice, this CERTIFICATE OF APPOINTMENT OF ESTATE TRUSTEE DURING LITIGATION to determine the validity of a testamentary document of the deceased is hereby issued under the seal of the court to the applicant named above.

DATE

_____

Registrar
Address of court office

RCP-E 74.31 (November 1, 2005)

FORM 74.32

Courts of Justice Act

BOND — INSURANCE OR GUARANTEE COMPANY

ONTARIO

SUPERIOR COURT OF JUSTICE

BOND NO.   AMOUNT: $

IN THE ESTATE OF *(insert name)*, deceased.

The principal in this bond is *(insert name)*

The surety in this bond is *(insert name)*, an insurer licensed under the *Insurance Act* to write surety and fidelity insurance in Ontario.

The obligee in this bond is the Accountant of the Superior Court of Justice acting for the benefit of creditors and persons entitled to share in the estate of the deceased.

The principal and the surety bind themselves, their heirs, executors, successors and assigns jointly and severally to the Accountant of the Superior Court of Justice in the amount of . . . . Dollars ($ . . . .).

The principal as an estate trustee is required to prepare a complete and true inventory of all the property of the deceased, collect the assets of the estate, pay the debts of the estate, distribute the property of the deceased according to law, and render a complete and true accounting of these activities when lawfully required.

The primary obligation under this bond belongs to the principal. The principal is liable under this bond for any amount found by the court to be owing to any creditors of the estate and persons entitled to share in the estate to whom proper payment has not been made.

The surety, provided it has been given reasonable notice of any proceeding in which judgment may be given against the principal for failure to perform the obligations of this bond shall, on order of the court, and on default of the principal to pay any final judgment made against the principal in the proceeding, pay to the obligee the amount of any deficiency in the payment by the principal, but the surety shall not be liable to pay more than the amount of the bond.

The amount of this bond shall be reduced by and to the extent of any payment made under the bond pursuant to an order of the court.

The surety is entitled to an assignment of the rights of any person who receives payment or benefit from the proceeds of this bond, to the extent of such payment or benefit received.

DATE

SIGNED, SEALED AND DELIV-
ERED in the presence of:

_____
Principal

_____
Surety

RCP-E 74.32 (November 1, 2005)

FORM 74.33

Courts of Justice Act

BOND — PERSONAL SURETIES

ONTARIO

SUPERIOR COURT OF JUSTICE

BOND NO.   AMOUNT: $

IN THE ESTATE OF *(insert name)*, deceased.

The principal in this bond is *(insert name)*

The sureties in this bond are *(insert names)*

The obligee in this bond is the Accountant of the Superior Court of Justice acting for the benefit of creditors and persons entitled to share in the estate of the deceased.

The principal and the sureties bind themselves, their heirs, executors, successors and assigns jointly and severally to the Accountant of the Superior Court of Justice in the amount of .... Dollars ($ ....).

The principal as an estate trustee is required to prepare a complete and true inventory of all the property of the deceased, collect the assets of the estate, pay the debts of the estate, distribute the property of the deceased according to law, and render a complete and true accounting of these activities when lawfully required.

The primary obligation under this bond belongs to the principal. The principal is liable under this bond for any amount found by the court to be owing to any creditors of the estate and persons entitled to share in the estate to whom proper payment has not been made.

The sureties, provided they have been given reasonable notice of any proceeding in which judgment may be given against the principal for failure to perform the obligations of this bond shall, on order of the court, and on default of the principal to pay any final judgment made against the principal in the proceeding, pay to the obligee the amount of any deficiency in the payment by the principal, but the sureties shall not be liable to pay more than the amount of the bond.

The amount of this bond shall be reduced by and to the extent of any payment made under the bond pursuant to an order of the court.

634

The sureties are entitled to an assignment of the rights of any person who receives payment or benefit from the proceeds of this bond, to the extent of such payment or benefit received.

DATE

SIGNED, SEALED AND DELIVERED
in the presence of:

....
....
Principal

....
Surety

....
Surety

AFFIDAVIT OF SURETY

I, *(insert name)*, of *(insert city or town and county or district, metropolitan or regional municipality of residence)*, make oath and say/affirm:

I am a proposed surety on behalf of the intended estate trustees of the property of *(insert name)*, deceased, named in the attached bond.

I am eighteen years of age or over and own property worth $...................... over and above all encumbrances, and over and above what will pay my just debts and every sum for which I am now bail or for which I am liable as surety or endorser or otherwise.

SWORN/AFFIRMED BEFORE)
me at the   of   )
in the   of   )
)
this   day of   , 20 .   )
) ....
)
)
)

....
A Commissioner for Taking Affidavits *(or as may be)*

AFFIDAVIT OF SURETY

I, *(insert name)*, of *(insert city or town and county or district, metropolitan or regional municipality of residence)*, make oath and say/affirm:

I am a proposed surety on behalf of the intended estate trustees of the property of *(insert name)*, deceased, named in the attached bond.

I am eighteen years of age or over and own property worth $............................... over and above all encumbrances, and over and above what will pay my just debts and every sum for which I am now bail or for which I am liable as surety or endorser or otherwise.

SWORN/AFFIRMED BEFORE)
the at the   of   )
in the   of   )
this   day of   , 20 .)
)
) ....
)
)
)
)

....
A Commissioner for Taking Affidavits *(or as may be)*

RCP-E 74.33 (November 1, 2005)

FORM 74.34

Courts of Justice Act

REGISTRAR'S NOTICE TO ESTATE TRUSTEE NAMED IN A DEPOSITED WILL OF APPLICATION FOR CERTIFICATE OF APPOINTMENT OF ESTATE TRUSTEE WITH A WILL

ONTARIO

SUPERIOR COURT OF JUSTICE

NOTICE

Attached are a copy of an application for appointment of an estate trustee with a will in the estate of *(insert name)*, deceased, and a copy of a certificate of the Estate Registrar indicating that you were named as an estate trustee in a later will or codicil of the deceased that is on deposit in the Superior Court of Justice.

DATE _____   _____

Registrar
Address of court office

TO:

RCP-E 74.34 (November 1, 2005)

FORM 74.35

Courts of Justice Act

REGISTRAR'S NOTICE TO ESTATE TRUSTEE NAMED IN A DEPOSITED WILL OF APPLICATION FOR CERTIFICATE OF APPOINTMENT OF ESTATE TRUSTEE WITHOUT A WILL

ONTARIO

SUPERIOR COURT OF JUSTICE

NOTICE

Attached are a copy of an application for appointment of an estate trustee without a will in the estate of *(insert name)*, deceased, and a copy of a certificate of the Estate Registrar indicating that you were named as an estate trustee in a will or codicil of the deceased that is on deposit in the Superior Court of Justice.

DATE _____   _____

Registrar
Address of court office

TO:

RCP-E 74.35 (November 1, 2005)

FORM 74.36

Courts of Justice Act

ORDER TO ACCEPT OR REFUSE APPOINTMENT AS ESTATE TRUSTEE WITH A WILL

(Heading in accordance with Form 59A)

IN THE ESTATE OF *(insert name)*, deceased.

ORDER TO ACCEPT OR REFUSE APPOINTMENT

AS ESTATE TRUSTEE WITH A WILL

A motion for this order has been made by *(insert name of moving party)*. From an affidavit made by *(insert name of maker of affidavit)* that has been filed it appears that you are named as estate trustee in a will or codicil of the deceased dated *(insert date)*.

1. THIS COURT ORDERS THAT you file an application for a certificate of appointment of estate trustee with a will in the court office within . . . . days after this order is served on you.

2. THIS COURT ORDERS THAT if you do not do so within that time, you shall be deemed to have renounced your right to be appointed.

_____
Registrar
Address of court office

TO:

RCP-E 74.36 (November 1, 2005)

639

FORM 74.37

Courts of Justice Act

ORDER TO ACCEPT OR REFUSE APPOINTMENT AS ESTATE TRUSTEE WITHOUT A WILL

(Heading in accordance with Form 59A)

IN THE ESTATE OF *(insert name)*, deceased.

ORDER TO ACCEPT OR REFUSE APPOINTMENT

AS ESTATE TRUSTEE WITHOUT A WILL

A motion for this order has been made by *(insert name of moving party)*. From an affidavit made by *(insert name of maker of affidavit)* that has been filed it appears that you may have a prior right to be appointed estate trustee without a will in the deceased's estate.

1. THIS COURT ORDERS THAT you file an application for a certificate of appointment of estate trustee without a will in the court office within . . . . . . days after this order is served on you.

2. THIS COURT ORDERS THAT if you do not do so within that time, you shall be deemed to have renounced your right to be appointed.

_____

Registrar
Address of court office

TO:

RCP-E 74.37 (November 1, 2005)

640

FORM 74.38

Courts of Justice Act

ORDER TO CONSENT OR OBJECT TO A PROPOSED APPOINTMENT OF AN ESTATE TRUSTEE WITH OR WITHOUT A WILL

(Heading in accordance with Form 59A)

IN THE ESTATE OF *(insert name)*, deceased.

ORDER TO CONSENT OR OBJECT TO A PROPOSED APPOINTMENT

OF AN ESTATE TRUSTEE WITH OR WITHOUT A WILL

A motion for this order has been made by *(insert name of moving party)*. From an affidavit made by *(insert name of maker of affidavit)* that has been filed it appears that *(insert name)* is applying for a certificate of appointment as estate trustee with *(or* without*)* a will, that you are a person with a financial interest in the estate and that your consent to the appointment is being sought.

1. THIS COURT ORDERS THAT if you oppose that person's appointment as estate trustee, you must file a notice of objection to appointment of estate trustee, in the form attached as Schedule "A", in the court office within . . . . days after this order is served on you.

2. THIS COURT ORDERS THAT if you do not do so within that time, you shall be deemed to have consented to that person's appointment.

_____

Registrar
Address of court office

TO:

SCHEDULE "A"

ONTARIO

SUPERIOR COURT OF JUSTICE

IN THE ESTATE OF *(insert name)*, deceased.

NOTICE OF OBJECTION TO

APPOINTMENT OF ESTATE TRUSTEE

I, *(insert name)*, object to the appointment of *(insert name)* as estate trustee because *(indicate reason)*.

DATE

_____

(Name, address and telephone number of objecting person or lawyer for objecting person)

RCP-E 74.38 (July 1, 2007)

FORM 74.39

Courts of Justice Act

ORDER TO FILE A STATEMENT OF ASSETS OF THE ESTATE

(Heading in accordance with Form 59A)

IN THE ESTATE OF *(insert name)*, deceased.

ORDER TO A STATEMENT OF ASSETS OF THE ESTATE

A motion for this order has been made by *(insert name of moving party)*. From an affidavit made by *(insert name of maker of affidavit)* that has been filed it appears that you are an estate trustee of the estate and that you should provide further information about the assets of the estate.

THIS COURT ORDERS THAT you file a statement of the nature of each asset of the estate and its value at the date of death in the court office within . . . . days after this order is served on you.

_____
Registrar
Address of court office

TO:

RCP-E 74.39 (November 1, 2005)

FORM 74.40

Courts of Justice Act

ORDER TO BENEFICIARY WITNESS

(Heading in accordance with Form 59A)

IN THE ESTATE OF *(insert name)*, deceased.

ORDER TO BENEFICIARY WITNESS

A motion for this order has been made by *(insert name of moving party)*. From an affidavit made by *(insert name of maker of affidavit)*, it appears that *(insert name of moving party)* has made an application for a certificate of appointment of estate trustee with a will, that you are a beneficiary under the will or codicil dated *(insert date)* and that you or your spouse witnessed the will or codicil or signed for the testator.

1. THIS COURT ORDERS THAT if you wish the court to find that neither you nor your spouse exercised any improper or undue influence on the testator, you must make a motion, within . . . . . . days after this order is served on you, asking the court to make that finding.

2. THIS COURT ORDERS THAT if you do not make such a motion within that time, the applicant may proceed to obtain a certificate of appointment of estate trustee with a will, bearing a note stating that your benefits under the will are void under section 12 of the *Succession Law Reform Act*.

_____
Registrar
Address of court office

TO:

RCP-E 74.40 (November 1, 2005)

FORM 74.41

Courts of Justice Act

ORDER TO FORMER SPOUSE

(Heading in accordance with Form 59A)

IN THE ESTATE OF *(insert name)*, deceased.

ORDER TO FORMER SPOUSE

Subsection 17 (2) of the *Succession Law Reform Act* provides as follows:

"Except when a contrary intention appears by the will, where, after the testator makes a will, his or her marriage is terminated by a judgment absolute of divorce or is declared a nullity,

(a) a devise or bequest of a beneficial interest in property to his or her former spouse;

(b) an appointment of his or her former spouse as executor or trustee; and

(c) the conferring of a general or special power of appointment on his or her former spouse,

are revoked and the will shall be construed as if the former spouse had predeceased the testator."

A motion for this order has been made by *(insert name of moving party)*, who has also made an application for a certificate of appointment of estate trustee with a will. From the application it appears that the will is dated *(insert date) (and that the codicil(s) is (are) dated* . . . . *)*, that you are a former spouse of the testator and that your marriage was terminated by a judgment absolute of divorce or declared a nullity after the date of the will *(or codicil)*.

1. THIS COURT ORDERS THAT if you wish to take part in the determination of the question whether the provisions in the will that affect you are revoked under subsection 17 (2) of the *Succession Law Reform Act*, you must enter an appearance in the office of the registrar of the court within . . . . . . days after this order is served on you.

2. THIS COURT ORDERS THAT if you do not do so within that time, the question will be determined in your absence and you will be bound by the result.

_____

Registrar
Address of court office

TO:

RCP-E 74.41 (November 1, 2005)

FORM 74.42

Courts of Justice Act

ORDER TO PASS ACCOUNTS

(Heading in accordance with Form 59A)

IN THE ESTATE OF *(insert name)*, deceased.

ORDER TO PASS ACCOUNTS

A motion for this order has been made by *(insert name of moving party)*. From an affidavit made by *(insert name of maker of affidavit)* that has been filed it appears that you are an estate trustee of the estate and that you have made no accounting to the court of your dealings with the estate during the period from *(date)* to *(date)*.

THIS COURT ORDERS THAT you file accounts of the estate and an application to pass accounts, in accordance with rules 74.17 and 74.18 of the Rules of Civil Procedure, in the court office within . . . . . . days after this order is served on you.

_____
Registrar
Address of court office

TO:

RCP-E 74.42 (November 1, 2005)

FORM 74.43

Courts of Justice Act

AFFIDAVIT VERIFYING ESTATE ACCOUNTS

ONTARIO

SUPERIOR COURT OF JUSTICE

IN THE ESTATE OF *(insert name)*, deceased.

AFFIDAVIT VERIFYING ESTATE ACCOUNTS

I, *(insert name)*, of *(insert city or town and county or district, metropolitan or regional municipality of residence)*, make oath and say/affirm:

1. I am an estate trustee for this estate.

2. The accounts marked as Exhibit "A" to this affidavit are complete and correct.

3. The information contained in the notice of application to pass accounts with respect to this estate is true.

4. All persons having a financial interest in the estate are named as respondents in the notice of application to pass accounts.

5. For any party with a disability, a representative has been identified in the notice of application.

SWORN/AFFIRMED BEFORE)
me at the   of   )
in the   of   )
this   day of   , 20 .)
)   ....
)
)
)

....
A Commissioner for Taking Affidavits *(or as may be)*

RCP-E 74.43 (November 1, 2005)

FORM 74.44

Courts of Justice Act

NOTICE OF APPLICATION TO PASS ACCOUNTS

ONTARIO

SUPERIOR COURT OF JUSTICE

IN THE ESTATE OF *(insert name)*, deceased.

NOTICE OF APPLICATION TO PASS ACCOUNTS

This application to pass accounts will be heard on *(date)*, at *(time)*, at the court house at *(full address of court house)*, if any person with a financial interest in the estate objects to the accounts or to the compensation claimed and doesn't withdraw the objection, or if a request for increased costs is served and filed.

The deceased died on *(date)*.

A certificate of appointment of estate trustee was issued to *(insert name)* by this court on *(date)*.

The accounts are for the period from *(date)* to *(date)*.

The compensation claimed by the estate trustee, payable out of the estate, is *(insert amount)*.

The costs of the application claimed by the estate trustee under Tariff C are *(amount)*.

A person with a financial interest in the estate who retains a lawyer to review the accounts and makes no objection to them (or makes an objection and later withdraws it) but serves on the estate trustee and files with the court, with proof of service, a request for costs (Form 74.49 under the Rules of Civil Procedure) at least 10 days before the hearing date of the application, will be allowed one-half of the costs allowed to the estate trustee. However, where two or more persons are represented by the same lawyer, they are entitled to receive only one person's costs. If the Children's Lawyer or the Public Guardian and Trustee makes no objection to the accounts (or makes an objection and later withdraws it) but serves on the estate trustee and files with the court, with proof of service, a request for costs (Form 74.49.1) at least 10 days before the hearing date of the application, he or she will be allowed three-quarters of the costs allowed to the estate trustee.

Any person with a financial interest in the estate who wishes to object to the accounts shall do so by serving upon the estate trustee, or the lawyer for the estate trustee, a notice of objection to accounts (Form 74.45 under the Rules of Civil Procedure, a copy of which is attached to this notice of application), and by filing a copy of the notice in the court office at least 35 days before the hearing date specified in the notice of application [R.74.18 (7)].

Any person who wishes to withdraw a notice of objection to accounts shall, at least 15 days before the hearing date of the application, serve on the estate trustee, and file with proof of service, a notice of withdrawal of objection (Form 74.48) [R.74.18 (8.4)].

If the estate trustee or any person with a financial interest in the estate seeks costs of the application greater than the amount allowed in Tariff C, the estate trustee or other person shall serve on every other party a request for increased costs (Form 74.49.2 or 74.49.3 under the Rules of Civil Procedure) together with a Costs Outline in Form 57B, at least 15 days before the hearing date of the application [R.74.18 (11)].

Any person with a financial interest in the estate who wishes to object or consent to a request for increased costs shall do so by returning the completed form 74.49.2 or 74.49.3, as the case may be, to the person making the request so that he or she receives it at least 10 days before the hearing date of the application. The person making the request for increased costs shall, at least 5 days before the hearing date of the application, file with the court a supplementary record described in subrule 74.18 (11.3) containing (i) the documents served under subrule 74.18 (11), together with an affidavit of service of those documents, (ii) an affidavit containing a summary of the responses to the request for increased costs and a list of persons who failed to respond, and (iii) the factors that contributed to the increased costs [R.74.18 (11.3)].

Any person with a financial interest in the estate who does not wish to object to the accounts but wishes to receive notice of any further step in the application, including a request for costs or a request for increased costs, shall, at least 35 days before the hearing date specified in the notice of application, serve upon the estate trustee, and file with proof of service, a request for further notice in passing of accounts (Form 74.45.1), a copy of which is attached to this notice of application [R.74.18 (8)].

If one or more notices of objection to accounts are filed and not withdrawn, the estate trustee shall, at least **10 days** before the hearing date of the application, serve on the persons referred to in subrule 74.18 (11.6), and file with proof of service, (i) a consolidation of all the remaining notices of objection to accounts and (ii) a reply to notice of objection to accounts (Form 74.49.4) [R.74.18 (11.5)].

If the application to pass accounts proceeds to a hearing, the estate trustee shall, at least 5 days before the hearing date, file with the court a record containing the documents referred to in subrule 74.18 (11.7). If the applicant and every other person referred to under subrule 74.18 (11.6), agree to all of the terms of a draft order, the applicant shall indicate that it is a joint draft order.

If the applicant and other persons fail to agree to all of the terms of a draft order, the applicant shall indicate that it is the applicant's draft order. Any person referred to under clause 74.18 (11.6) (a) may file an alternative draft order at least 3 days before the hearing date of the application or, with leave of the court, at the hearing [R.74.18 (11.8) (11.9)].

At the hearing, the only issues upon which the court adjudicates are those raised in the notices of objection to accounts and requests for increased costs that have been filed, unless the court grants leave to a party to raise other issues [R.74.18 (12)].

If no notice of objection to accounts is served and filed, or all objections have been withdrawn, the estate trustee may, without a hearing, obtain a judgment passing the accounts and allowing the compensation and costs claimed [R.74.18 (8.5)].

On a request for increased costs, the court may, in consideration of the documents in the supplementary record, grant judgment without a hearing. If the court declines to grant a request for increased costs without a hearing, the hearing shall proceed on the date fixed [R.74.18 (11.4)].

Any person may contact the estate trustee or the estate trustee's lawyer to find out whether there will be a hearing. A copy of the accounts may be obtained from the estate trustee or the estate trustee's lawyer, or may be inspected in the court office during regular business hours.

DATE

_____

_____

Registrar

*(Name, address and telephone number of
estate trustee
or lawyer for the estate trustee)*

TO: *(Name and address of each person with a financial interest in the estate)*

(For a person under disability, also indicate name and address of personal representative)

(Attach blank copy of Form 74.45 (notice of objection to accounts).)

(Attach blank copy of Form 74.45.1 (request for further notice in passing of accounts).)

Print Form

FORM 74.45

Courts of Justice Act

NOTICE OF OBJECTION TO ACCOUNTS

ONTARIO

SUPERIOR COURT OF JUSTICE

IN THE ESTATE OF *(insert name)*, deceased.

NOTICE OF OBJECTION TO ACCOUNTS

1. I, *(insert name)*, object to the amount of compensation claimed by the estate trustee on the following grounds:

(If applicable, set out each objection in separate consecutively numbered paragraphs. Attach separate sheet if necessary.)

2. I, *(insert name)*, object to the accounts of the estate trustee on the following grounds:

(If applicable, set out each objection in separate consecutively numbered paragraphs. Attach separate sheet if necessary.)

DATE

> *(Name, address and telephone number of objecting person or lawyer for objecting person)*

TO: *(Name and address of estate trustee or lawyer for estate trustee)*

RCP-E 74.45 (July 1, 2007)

FORM 74.45.1

Courts of Justice Act

REQUEST FOR FURTHER NOTICE IN PASSING OF ACCOUNTS

ONTARIO

SUPERIOR COURT OF JUSTICE

IN THE ESTATE OF *(insert name)*, deceased.

REQUEST FOR FURTHER NOTICE IN PASSING OF ACCOUNTS

I *(insert name)* have been served with a notice of application to pass accounts. By serving this request for further notice, I acknowledge that:

I do not object to the accounts but wish to receive notice of any further step in the application, including a request for costs or a request for increased costs, and

I shall, at least 35 days before the hearing date specified in the notice of application, serve on the applicant, and file with proof of service, this request for further notice.

I further acknowledge that, unless the court orders otherwise, I am entitled to,

(a) receive notice of any further step in the application to pass accounts;

(b) receive any further document in the application;

(c) file material relating to a request for increased costs on the application at least 10 days before the hearing date of the application; and

(d) in the event of a hearing, be heard at the hearing, examine a witness and cross-examine on an affidavit, but with respect only to a request for increased costs.

DATE

(Name, address and telephone number of person requesting further notice or the lawyer for the person requesting further notice)

RCP-E 74.45.1 (May 1, 2017)

FORM 74.46

Courts of Justice Act

NOTICE OF NO OBJECTION TO ACCOUNTS

ONTARIO

SUPERIOR COURT OF JUSTICE

IN THE ESTATE OF *(insert name)*, deceased.

NOTICE OF NO OBJECTION TO ACCOUNTS

The (Public Guardian and Trustee) (Children's Lawyer) has no objection to the estate accounts and the claim for compensation by the estate trustee.

DATE

> *(Name, address and telephone number of Children's Lawyer or Public Guardian and Trustee, or lawyer for Children's Lawyer or Public Guardian and Trustee)*

TO: *(Name and address of estate trustee or lawyer for estate trustee)*

RCP-E 74.46 (July 1, 2007)

FORM 74.46.1

Courts of Justice Act

NOTICE OF NON-PARTICIPATION IN PASSING OF ACCOUNTS

ONTARIO

SUPERIOR COURT OF JUSTICE

IN THE ESTATE OF *(insert name)*, deceased.

NOTICE OF NON-PARTICIPATION IN PASSING OF ACCOUNTS

The (Public Guardian and Trustee) (Children's Lawyer) does not intend to participate in the passing of accounts.

DATE

> *(Name, address and telephone number of Children's Lawyer or Public Guardian and Trustee, or lawyer for Children's Lawyer or Public Guardian and Trustee)*

TO: *(Name and address of estate trustee or lawyer for the estate trustee)*

RCP-E 74.46.1 (July 1, 2007)

FORM 74.47

Courts of Justice Act

AFFIDAVIT IN SUPPORT OF UNOPPOSED JUDGMENT ON PASSING OF ACCOUNTS

ONTARIO

SUPERIOR COURT OF JUSTICE

IN THE ESTATE OF *(insert name)*, deceased.

AFFIDAVIT SUPPORT OF UNOPPOSED JUDGMENT
ON PASSING OF ACCOUNTS

I, *(insert name)*, of *(insert city or town and county or district, metropolitan or regional municipality of residence)*, make oath and say/affirm:

1. I am the applicant for an unopposed judgment on the passing of accounts in this estate with respect to estate accounts from *(date)* to *(date)*.

2. A copy of the estate accounts has been provided to each person who was served with the notice of application and who requested a copy of the accounts.

3. The time for filing notices of objection to the estate accounts has expired.

4. No notice of objection has been received from any person served with the notice of application.

OR

4. Any notice of objection that was received has been withdrawn by the filing of a notice of withdrawal of objection.

SWORN/AFFIRMED BEFORE   )
me at the   of   )
in the.   of   )
this   day of   , 20 .)
)   ....
)
)
)

....
A Commissioner for Taking Affidavits *(or as may be)*

NOTE: The two versions of paragraph 4 are in the alternative. Delete the one that does not apply.

RCP-E 74.47 (November 1, 2005)

FORM 74.48

Courts of Justice Act

NOTICE OF WITHDRAWAL OF OBJECTION

ONTARIO

SUPERIOR COURT OF JUSTICE

IN THE ESTATE OF *(insert name)*, deceased.

NOTICE OF WITHDRAWAL OF OBJECTION

I, *(insert name)*, filed a notice of objection to accounts and hereby withdraw that notice of objection.

DATE

> *(Name, address and telephone number of party or party's lawyer)*

TO: *(Name and address of estate trustee or lawyer for estate trustee)*

RCP-E 74.48 (July 1, 2007)

FORM 74.49

Courts of Justice Act

REQUEST FOR COSTS (PERSON OTHER THAN CHILDREN'S LAWYER OR PUBLIC GUARDIAN AND TRUSTEE)

ONTARIO

SUPERIOR COURT OF JUSTICE

IN THE ESTATE OF *(insert name)*, deceased.

REQUEST FOR COSTS (PERSON OTHER THAN CHILDREN'S LAWYER OR PUBLIC GUARDIAN AND TRUSTEE)

I, *(insert name)*, have retained *(insert name)* as my lawyer to review the estate accounts. I have no objection to the estate accounts and the claim for compensation by the estate trustee.

I request that I be awarded costs payable out of the estate in the amount of $ . . . ., representing one-half of the amount payable to the estate lawyer under Tariff C.

DATE

> *(Name, address and telephone number of party or party's lawyer)*

TO: *(Name and address of estate trustee or lawyer for estate trustee)*

RCP-E 74.49 (July 1, 2007)

656

FORM 74.49.1

Courts of Justice Act

REQUEST FOR COSTS (CHILDREN'S LAWYER OR PUBLIC GUARDIAN AND TRUSTEE)

ONTARIO

SUPERIOR COURT OF JUSTICE

IN THE ESTATE OF *(insert name)*, deceased.

REQUEST FOR COSTS (CHILDREN'S LAWYER OR PUBLIC GUARDIAN AND TRUSTEE)

The (Public Guardian and Trustee) (Children's Lawyer) has no objection to the estate accounts and the claim for compensation by the estate trustee.

The (Public Guardian and Trustee) (Children's Lawyer) requests that he or she be awarded costs payable out of the estate in the amount of $ . . . ., representing three-quarters of the amount payable to the estate lawyer under Tariff C.

DATE

> *(Name, address and telephone number of Children's Lawyer or Public Guardian and Trustee, or lawyer for Children's Lawyer or Public Guardian and Trustee)*

TO: *(Name and address of estate trustee or lawyer for the estate trustee)*

RCP-E 74.49.1 (July 1, 2007)

FORM 74.49.2

Courts of Justice Act

ONTARIO

SUPERIOR COURT OF JUSTICE

IN THE ESTATE OF *(insert name)*, deceased.

REQUEST FOR INCREASED COSTS (ESTATE TRUSTEE)

I request that I be awarded costs payable out of the estate in the amount of $ . . . . , in addition to the cost of attendance at a hearing, if required, which is greater than the amount of $ . . . . allowed under Tariff C. I understand that this request may require a hearing on the date specified in the notice of application, in the discretion of the presiding Judge.

DATE

> *(Name, address and telephone number of estate trustee or lawyer for estate trustee)*

TO: *(Name and address of each person with a financial interest in the estate)*

(For a person under disability, also indicate name and address of personal representative)

Response by person with a financial interest in the estate:

(A) I oppose this request for increased costs, for the following reasons:

-

-

OR

(B) I consent to this request for increased costs.

Date: _____

Signature of person
listed above

Any person with a financial interest in the estate who wishes to object or consent to a request for increased costs shall do so by returning the completed form 74.49.2 to the person making the request so that such person receives it at least 12 days before the date fixed for the hearing in the Notice of Application to Pass Accounts.

The person making the request for increased costs shall, at least 10 days before the date fixed for the hearing, file with the court a supplementary record described in subrule 74.18 (11.3) containing (i) the documents served under subrule 74.18 (11.1), together with an affidavit of service of those documents, (ii) an affidavit containing a summary of the responses to the request for increased costs and a list of persons who failed to respond, and (iii) the factors that contributed to the increased costs.

RCP-E 74.49.2 (April 11, 2012)

FORM 74.49.3

Courts of Justice Act

ONTARIO

SUPERIOR COURT OF JUSTICE

IN THE ESTATE OF *(insert name)*, deceased.

REQUEST FOR INCREASED COSTS (PERSON OTHER THAN ESTATE TRUSTEE)

1. I, *(insert name)*, have retained *(insert name)* as my lawyer to review the estate accounts. I have no objection to the estate accounts or to the claim for compensation by the estate trustee.

2. I request that I be awarded costs payable out of the estate in the amount of $ . . . . , in addition to the cost of attendance at a hearing, if required, which is greater than $ . . . . , being one-half the amount payable to the estate trustee under Tariff C. I understand that this request may require a hearing on the date specified in the notice of application, in the discretion of the presiding Judge.

DATE

(Name, address and telephone number of person or person's lawyer)

TO: *(Name and address of every other person with a financial interest in the estate)*

  (For a person under disability, also indicate name and address of personal representative)

  (Name and address of estate trustee or lawyer for estate trustee)

Response by Estate Trustee or person with a financial interest in the estate:

(A) I object to this request for increased costs, for the following reasons:

  -

  -

OR:

(B) I consent to this request for increased costs.

 Date: _____
                                                  Signature of person
                                                     listed above

Any person with a financial interest in the estate who wishes to object or consent to a request for increased costs shall do so by returning the completed form 74.49.3 to the person making the request so that such person receives it at least 12 days before the date fixed for the hearing in the Notice of Application to Pass Accounts.

The person making the request for increased costs shall, at least 10 days before the date fixed for the hearing, file with the court a supplementary record described in subrule 74.18 (11.3) containing (i) the documents served under subrule 74.18 (11.1), together with an affidavit of serviceof those documents, (ii) an affidavit containing a summary of the responses to the request for increased costs and a list of persons who failed to respond, and (iii) the factors that contributed to the increased costs.

RULES OF CIVIL PROCEDURE FORMS

FORM 74.49.4

Courts of Justice Act

REPLY TO NOTICE OF OBJECTION TO ACCOUNTS

ONTARIO

SUPERIOR COURT OF JUSTICE

IN THE ESTATE OF *(insert name)*, deceased.

REPLY TO NOTICE OF OBJECTION TO ACCOUNTS

1.   In the attached Notice of Objection to Accounts, *(insert name)* objected to the amount of compensation claimed by the estate trustee. The reply to the objection is as follows:

(If applicable, set out a reply to each objection in separate consecutively numbered paragraphs. Attach separate sheet if necessary.)

2.   In the attached Notice of Objection to Accounts, *(insert name)* objected to the accounts of the estate trustee. The reply to the objection is as follows:

(If applicable, set out a reply to each objection in separate consecutively numbered paragraphs. Attach separate sheet if necessary.)

DATE

(Name, address and telephone number of person or lawyer replying to the objection)

[Print Form]

FORM 74.50

Courts of Justice Act

JUDGMENT ON UNOPPOSED PASSING OF ACCOUNTS

(Heading in accordance with Form 59B)

IN THE ESTATE OF *(insert name)*, deceased.

JUDGMENT ON PASSING OF ACCOUNTS

THIS APPLICATION was read on *(date)*, at *(place)*.

ON READING THE NOTICE OF APPLICATION TO PASS ACCOUNTS, the affidavit of service and the affidavit in support of an unopposed judgment on passing of accounts, as filed, and as there are no objections to the accounts or the claim for compensation by the estate trustee,

1. THIS COURT DECLARES that the estate accounts, as filed by the applicant for the period from *(date)* to *(date)*, are hereby passed.

2. THIS COURT DECLARES that the capital receipts and capital disbursements of the applicant for the period are as follows:

CAPITAL ACCOUNT
Credit balance forward *(if applicable)* $ $

Receipts $ _____ $ _____ (total)

Debit balance forward *(if applicable)* $

Disbursements $ _____ $ _____ (total)

Credit (or debit) balance $ _____

3. THIS COURT DECLARES that the revenue receipts and revenue disbursements of the applicant for the period are as follows:

CAPITAL ACCOUNT
Credit balance forward *(if applicable)* $ $

Receipts $ _____ $ _____ (total)

Debit balance forward *(if applicable)* $

Disbursements $ _____ $ _____ (total)

Credit (or debit) balance $ _____

4. THIS COURT ORDERS that the estate trustee shall be paid as fair and reasonable compensation for services as estate trustee of the estate and for disbursements expended in administering the affairs of the estate during the period the total amount of $ . . . . . . (including H.S.T.), of which $ . . . . . . shall be paid out of the capital of the estate and $ . . . . . . shall be paid out of the revenue of the estate.

5. THIS COURT ORDERS that the costs of the passing of the accounts allowed in accordance with Tariff C, and payable out of the capital of the estate, are as follows:

To the estate trustee $ . . . . , and H.S.T. of $ . . . . for a total of $
. . . .

To *(insert names and amounts, showing each person awarded costs on a separate line)*

6. THIS COURT DECLARES that the accounts show that there remain in the estate trustee's hands the original assets as set out in Schedule "A", attached.

RCP-E 74.50 (April 11, 2012)

FORM 74.51

Courts of Justice Act

JUDGMENT ON CONTESTED PASSING OF ACCOUNTS

(Heading in accordance with Form 59B)

IN THE ESTATE OF *(insert name)*, deceased.

JUDGMENT ON PASSING OF ACCOUNTS

THIS APPLICATION was heard on *(date)*, at *(place)* in the presence of the lawyer(s) for *(insert name)* *(where applicable add* and *(insert name)* appearing in person) *(where applicable add* and no one appearing for *(insert name)*, although properly served as appears from the affidavit of service filed)*.

ON READING THE NOTICE OF APPLICATION TO PASS ACCOUNTS and on hearing the submissions made,

1. THIS COURT DECLARES that the estate accounts, as filed by the applicant for the period from *(date)* to *(date)*, are hereby passed.

2. THIS COURT DECLARES that the capital receipts and capital disbursements of the applicant for the period are as follows:

CAPITAL ACCOUNT

Credit balance forward *(if applicable)*	$	$
Receipts	$ _____	$ _____ (total)
Debit balance forward *(if applicable)*	$	
Disbursements	$ _____	$ _____ (total)
Credit (or debit) balance		$ _____

3. THIS COURT DECLARES that the revenue receipts and revenue disbursements of the applicant for the period are as follows:

CAPITAL ACCOUNT

Credit balance forward *(if applicable)*	$	$
Receipts	$ _____	$ _____ (total)
Debit balance forward *(if applicable)*	$	
Disbursements	$ _____	$ _____ (total)
Credit (or debit) balance		$ _____

4. THIS COURT ORDERS that the estate trustee shall be paid as fair and reasonable compensation for services as estate trustee of the estate and for disbursements expended in administering the affairs of the estate during the period the total amount of $ . . . . (including H.S.T.), of which $ . . . . shall be paid out of the capital of the estate and $ . . . . shall be paid out of the revenue of the estate.

5. THIS COURT ORDERS that the costs of the passing of the accounts allowed and payable out of the capital of the estate are as follows:

To the estate trustee $ . . . . , and H.S.T. of $ . . . . for a total of $ . . . .

To *(insert names and amounts, showing each person awarded costs on a separate line)*

6. THIS COURT DECLARES that the accounts show that there remain in the estate trustee's hands the original assets as set out in Schedule "A", attached.

RCP-E 74.51 (April 11, 2012)

FORM 75.1

Courts of Justice Act

NOTICE OF OBJECTION

ONTARIO

SUPERIOR COURT OF JUSTICE

In the Estate of the deceased person described below:

DETAILS ABOUT THE DECEASED PERSON

Complete in full as applicable

First given name	Second given name	Third given name	Surname

And if the deceased was known by any other name(s), state below the full name(s) used including surname.

First given name	Second given name	Third given name	Surname

IN THE MATTER OF an application for a certificate of appointment of estate trustee

NOTICE OF OBJECTION

I,   *(insert name)*   , object to the issuing of a certificate of appointment of estate trustee to   *(insert name of applicant)* without notice to me because   *(indicate reason, such as lack of testamentary capacity, undue influence or unfitness to act as estate trustee).*

The nature of my interest in the estate is: *(state relationship to the deceased and whether a named beneficiary under the will, or other basis for financial interest).*

DATE

(Name, address and telephone number of objector or lawyer for objector)

RCP-E 75.1 (July 1, 2007)

666

FORM 75.2

Courts of Justice Act

NOTICE THAT OBJECTION HAS BEEN FILED

ONTARIO

SUPERIOR COURT OF JUSTICE

IN THE ESTATE OF *(insert name)*, deceased.

IN THE MATTER OF an application for a certificate of appointment of estate trustee

NOTICE THAT OBJECTION HAS BEEN FILED

A notice of objection, a copy of which is attached, has been filed with the court.

No further action regarding issuing a certificate of a appointment to you will be taken until you have complied with subrule 75.03 (4) of the Rules of Civil Procedure.

DATE _____

Registrar
Address of court office

TO: *(Name, address and telephone number of applicant or lawyer for the applicant)*

RCP-E 75.2 (July 1, 2007)

FORM 75.3

Courts of Justice Act

NOTICE TO OBJECTOR

ONTARIO

SUPERIOR COURT OF JUSTICE

IN THE ESTATE OF *(insert name)*, deceased.

IN THE MATTER OF an application for a certificate of appointment of estate trustee

NOTICE TO OBJECTOR

AN APPLICATION for a certificate of appointment of estate trustee in the estate has been made by *(name of applicant)*.

IF YOU WISH TO OPPOSE this application, you or an Ontario lawyer acting for you must within 20 days of service on you of this notice to objector prepare a notice of appearance in Form 75.4 of the Rules of Civil Procedure, serve it on the applicant's lawyer, or where the applicant does not have a lawyer serve it on the applicant, and file it with proof of service in the court office at *(full court address where application for certificate of appointment was filed)*.

IF YOU FAIL to serve and file a notice of appearance, the application for certificate of appointment of estate trustee shall proceed as if your notice of objection had not been filed.

DATE

(Name, address and telephone number of applicant or lawyer for the applicant)

TO: *(Name and address of the objector or lawyer for the objector)*

RCP-E 75.3 (July 1, 2007)

668

FORM 75.4

Courts of Justice Act

NOTICE OF APPEARANCE

ONTARIO

SUPERIOR COURT OF JUSTICE

IN THE ESTATE OF *(insert name)*, deceased.

IN THE MATTER OF an application for a certificate of appointment of estate trustee

NOTICE OF APPEARANCE

I desire to oppose the issuing of a certificate of appointment of estate trustee for the reasons set out in the notice of objection filed.

DATE

(Name, address and telephone number of objector or lawyer for the objector)

TO: *(Name address and telephone number of applicant or lawyer for the applicant)*

RCP-E 75.4 (July 1, 2007)

FORM 75.5

Courts of Justice Act

NOTICE OF APPLICATION FOR DIRECTIONS

ONTARIO

SUPERIOR COURT OF JUSTICE

IN THE ESTATE OF *(insert name)*, deceased.

BETWEEN:

(Name)

Applicant

- and-

(Name)

Respondent

NOTICE OF APPLICATION FOR DIRECTIONS

TO THE RESPONDENT

A LEGAL PROCEEDING HAS BEEN COMMENCED by the applicant. The claim made by the applicant appears on the following page.

THIS APPLICATION will come on for a hearing before a judge on *(date)* at *(time)*, at the Court House at *(place)*.

IF YOU WISH TO OPPOSE THIS APPLICATION, you or an Ontario lawyer acting for you must forthwith prepare a notice of appearance in Form 38A prescribed by the Rules of Civil Procedure, serve it on the applicant's lawyer or, where the applicant does not have a lawyer, serve it on the applicant, and file it, with proof of service, in this court office, and you or your lawyer must appear at the hearing.

IF YOU WISH TO PRESENT AFFIDAVIT OR OTHER DOCUMENTARY EVIDENCE TO THE COURT OR TO EXAMINE OR CROSS-EXAMINE WITNESSES ON THE APPLICATION, you or your lawyer must, in addition to serving your notice of appearance, serve a copy of the evidence on the applicant's lawyer or, where the applicant does not have a lawyer, serve it on the applicant, and file it with proof of service, in the court office where the application is to be heard, as soon as possible, but not later than two days before the hearing.

IF YOU FAIL TO APPEAR AT THE HEARING, JUDGMENT MAY BE GIVEN IN YOUR ABSENCE AND WITHOUT FURTHER NOTICE TO YOU.

If you wish to oppose this application but are unable to pay legal fees, legal aid may be available to you by contacting a local Legal Aid office.

Date _____ Issued by _____

Local registrar

Address of court office

TO: *(Name and address of respondent, or lawyer for respondent)*

1.   The applicant makes application or directions from the court with respect to: *(state nature of proceeding).*

2.   The grounds for the application are rule 75.06 and *(include a reference to any statutory provision or Rule to be relied on).*

3.   The following documentary evidence will be used at the hearing of the application for directions: *(list the affidavits or other documentary evidence to be relied upon).*

RCP-E 75.5 (July 1, 2007)

FORM 75.6

Courts of Justice Act

NOTICE OF MOTION FOR DIRECTIONS

ONTARIO

SUPERIOR COURT OF JUSTICE

IN THE ESTATE OF *(insert name)*, deceased.

BETWEEN:

(Name)

Moving Party

- and -

(Name)

Respondent

NOTICE OF MOTION FOR DIRECTIONS

The moving party will make a motion to the court on *(date)*, at *(time)*, or so soon after that time as the motion can be heard at *(full address of Court House)*.

The motion is for directions with respect to:

(state nature of proceeding)

The grounds for the motion are rule 75.06 and *(specify the further grounds to be argued, including a reference to any statutory provision or Rule)*.

The following documentary evidence will be used at the hearing of the motion: *(list the affidavits or other documentary evidence to be relied on)*.

DATE

(Name, address and telephone number of applicant or lawyer for the applicant)

TO: *(Name and address of respondent or lawyer for the respondent)*

RCP-E 75.6 (July 1, 2007)

FORM 75.7

Courts of Justice Act

STATEMENT OF CLAIM PURSUANT TO ORDER GIVING DIRECTIONS

ONTARIO

SUPERIOR COURT OF JUSTICE

IN THE ESTATE OF *(insert name)*, deceased.

BETWEEN:

(Name)

Plaintiff

- and -

(Name)

Defendant

- and -

(Name)

Persons Submitting Rights to the Court

STATEMENT OF CLAIM PURSUANT TO ORDER GIVING DIRECTIONS

TO THE DEFENDANT

A LEGAL PROCEEDING HAS BEEN COMMENCED by the Plaintiff. The claim made is set out in the following pages.

IF YOU WISH TO DEFEND THIS PROCEEDING, you or an Ontario lawyer acting for you must prepare a statement of defence in Form 18A prescribed by the Rules of Civil Procedure, serve it on the plaintiff's lawyer, or, where the plaintiff does not have a lawyer, serve it on the plaintiff, and file it, with proof of service, in the court office, WITHIN 20 DAYS after this statement of claim is served upon you, if you are served in Ontario.

If you are served in another province or territory of Canada or in the United States of America, the period of serving and filing your statement of defence is 40 days. If you are served outside of Canada and the United States of America, the period is 60 days.

Instead of serving and filing a statement of defence, you may serve and file a Statement of Submission or Rights to the Court in Form 75.9 prescribed by the Rules of Civil Procedure.

IF YOU FAIL TO DEFEND THIS PROCEEDING, JUDGMENT MAY BE GIVEN AGAINST YOU IN YOUR ABSENCE AND WITHOUT FURTHER NOTICE TO YOU. IF YOU WISH TO DEFEND THIS PROCEEDING BUT ARE UNABLE TO PAY LEGAL FEES, LEGAL AID MAY BE AVAILABLE TO YOU BY CONTACTING A LOCAL LEGAL AID OFFICE.

1. The Plaintiff claims:

RCP-E 75.7 (November 1, 2005)

FORM 75.8

Courts of Justice Act

ORDER GIVING DIRECTIONS WHERE PLEADINGS DIRECTED

(Heading in accordance with Form 59A)

IN THE ESTATE OF *(insert name)*, deceased.

BETWEEN:

(Name)

Applicant
(Moving Party)

- and -

(Name)

Respondent
(Responding Party)

- and -

(Name)

Persons Submitting
Rights to the Court

ORDER GIVING DIRECTIONS

THIS APPLICATION *(or* MOTION*)* made by *(identify applicant or moving party)* for directions, was heard on *(date)*, at *(place),* in the presence of the lawyer(s) for *(insert name)*, and *(insert name)* appearing in person, and no one appearing for *(insert name)*, although properly served as appears from the affidavit of service, filed.

ON READING the notice of application *(or* notice of motion*)* and on hearing the submissions made,

1. THIS COURT ORDERS that *(insert name)* shall be plaintiff and *(insert name)* shall be defendant, and that *(insert names)* are submitting their rights to the court.

2. THIS COURT ORDERS that the plaintiff(s) shall serve upon the defendant(s) and file with the court a statement of claim in Form 75.7 within . . . . days after this order is entered, after which pleadings shall be served and filed under rule 75.07 of the Rules of Civil Procedure.

2.1 THIS COURT ORDERS that *(insert directions relating to mandatory mediation under Rule 75.1).*

3. THIS COURT ORDERS that the applicant and respondent shall serve and file affidavits of documents and attend and submit to examinations for discovery in accordance with the Rules of Civil Procedure.

4. THIS COURT ORDERS that on filing the appropriate documents with the court, *(insert name)* shall be appointed as estate trustee during litigation.

5. THIS COURT ORDERS that this order giving directions shall be served by an alternative to

personal service pursuant to rule 16.03 of the Rules of Civil Procedure, on the following persons: *(insert names)*

6. THIS COURT ORDERS that the issues be tried by a judge with *(or* without*)* a jury at *(place)* on a date to be fixed by the registrar.

7. THIS COURT ORDERS that the costs of this application *(or* motion*)* shall be *(insert amount)*

RCP-E 75.8 (July 1, 2007)

FORM 75.9

Courts of Justice Act

ORDER GIVING DIRECTIONS WHERE TRIAL OF ISSUES DIRECTED

(Headings in accordance with Form 59A)

IN THE ESTATE OF *(insert name)*, deceased.

BETWEEN:

(Name)

Applicant
(Moving Party)

- and -

(Name)

Respondent
(Responding Party)

- and -

(Name)

Persons Submitting Rights to the Court

ORDER GIVING DIRECTIONS

THIS APPLICATION *(or* MOTION*)* made by *(identify applicant or moving party)* for directions, was heard on *(date)*, at *(place)*, in the presence of the lawyer(s) for *(insert name)*, and *(insert name)* appearing in person, and no one appearing for *(insert name)*, although properly served as appears from the affidavit of service, filed.

ON READING the notice of application *(or* notice of motion*)* and on hearing the submissions made,

1. THIS COURT ORDERS that the parties to the proceeding and the issues to be tried be as follows:

    (a)   *(insert name)* affirms and *(insert name)* denies that *(state nature of allegation);*

    (b)   *(list each issue in a separate paragraph, specifying which parties affirm and which deny).*

2. THIS COURT ORDERS that *(insert names)* are submitting their rights to the court.

2.1 THIS COURT ORDERS that *(insert directions relating to mandatory mediation under Rule 75.1).*

3. THIS COURT ORDERS that the applicant and respondent shall serve and file affidavits of documents and attend and submit to examinations for discovery in accordance with the Rules of Civil Procedure.

4. THIS COURT ORDERS that on filing the appropriate documents with the court, *(insert name)* shall be appointed as estate trustee during litigation.

5. THIS COURT ORDERS that this order giving directions shall be served by an alternative to

676

personal service pursuant to rule 16.03 of the Rules of Civil Procedure, on the following persons: *(insert names)*

6. THIS COURT ORDERS that the issues be tried by a judge with *(or* without*)* a jury at *(place)* on a date to be fixed by the registrar.

7. THIS COURT ORDERS that the costs of this application *(or* motion*)* shall be *(insert amount)*

RCP-E 75.9 (July 1, 2007)

FORM 75.10

Courts of Justice Act

STATEMENT OF SUBMISSION OF RIGHTS TO THE COURT

ONTARIO

SUPERIOR COURT OF JUSTICE

IN THE ESTATE OF *(insert name)*, deceased.

BETWEEN:

(Name)

Applicant

- and-

(Name)

Respondent

STATEMENT OF SUBMISSION OF RIGHTS TO THE COURT

I, *(insert name),* submit my rights to the court and understand that pursuant to rule 75.07.1 of the Rules of Civil Procedure, the following consequences apply to me:

(a)   I shall not be entitled to receive any costs in the proceeding and shall not be liable to pay the costs of any party to the proceeding, except indirectly to the extent that costs are ordered by the court to be paid out of the estate;

(b)   I shall not receive notice of any step taken in the proceeding except the notice of trial and a copy of the judgment disposing of the matter;

(c)   If the proceeding is settled by agreement, a judgment on consent will not be given without notice to me.

DATE

(Name, address and telephone number of the person or lawyer acting for person)

TO: *(Name and address of plaintiff, or lawyer for plaintiff)*

RCP-E 75.10 (July 1, 2007)

678

FORM 75.11

Courts of Justice Act

NOTICE OF SETTLEMENT

ONTARIO

SUPERIOR COURT OF JUSTICE

IN THE ESTATE OF *(insert name)*, deceased.

BETWEEN:

(*Name*)

Applicant

- and -

(*Name*)

Respondent

- and -

(*Name*)

Persons Submitting
Rights to the Court

NOTICE OF SETTLEMENT

Pursuant to rule 75.07 of the Rules of Civil Procedure, attached as Schedule "A" is a copy of the settlement agreement that has been reached among the parties.

A judgment consistent with the settlement agreement will be sought. If you oppose that judgment, you or an Ontario lawyer acting for you must, within 10 days of service on you of this notice of settlement, serve a rejection of settlement in the form attached as Schedule "B" on the lawyer for the party serving this notice, or where the party serving this notice does not have a lawyer, serve it on the party serving this notice, and file it with proof of service in the court office at *(place)*.

If you fail to serve and file a rejection of settlement, the court will consider the request for judgment without further notice to you.

DATE

(Name, address and telephone number of party or lawyer for the party)

TO: *(Names and addresses of all persons who have submitted their rights to the court)*

RCP-E 75.11 (July 1, 2007)

FORM 75.12

Courts of Justice Act

REJECTION OF SETTLEMENT

ONTARIO

SUPERIOR COURT OF JUSTICE

IN THE ESTATE OF *(insert name)*, deceased.

BETWEEN:

(Name)

Applicant
(Plaintiff)

- and-

(Name)

Respondent
(Defendant)

- and-

(Name)

Persons Submitting
Rights to the Court

REJECTION OF SETTLEMENT

I, *(insert name)*, reject the settlement agreement attached to the notice of settlement dated *(insert date)*, for the following reasons: *(state reasons)*.

DATE

(Name, address and telephone number of person or lawyer for person)

TO: *(Name and address of party who served the notice of settlement or the lawyer for the party)*

RCP-E 75.12 (July 1, 2007)

FORM 75.13

Courts of Justice Act

NOTICE OF CONTESTATION

ONTARIO

SUPERIOR COURT OF JUSTICE

IN THE ESTATE OF *(insert name)*, deceased.

BETWEEN:

(Name)

Estate Trustee

- and -

(Name)

Claimant

NOTICE OF CONTESTATION

Pursuant to section 44 or 45 of the *Estates Act*, the estate trustee of the estate contests the claim made by you against the estate, on the following grounds:

(state grounds)

You may apply to this court at *(insert address of court office)* for an order allowing your claim and determining its amount. If you do not apply within 30 days after receiving this notice, or within 3 months after that date if the judge on application so allows, you shall be deemed to have abandoned your claim and your claim shall be forever barred.

DATE

(Name, address and telephone number of estate trustee or lawyer for estate trustee)

TO: *(Name and address of person submitting claim)*

RCP-E 75.13 (July 1, 2007)

FORM 75.14

Courts of Justice Act

CLAIM AGAINST ESTATE

ONTARIO

SUPERIOR COURT OF JUSTICE

IN THE ESTATE OF *(insert name)*, deceased.

BETWEEN:

(Name)

Claimant

- and -

(Name)

Estate Trustee

CLAIM AGAINST ESTATE

1. The claim against the estate is for $ .... for *(state grounds for claim)*.

* * *

AFFIDAVIT

I, *(name of claimant)*, of *(insert city or town and country or district, metropolitan or regional municipality of residence)*, MAKE OATH/AFFIRM AND SAY:

1. The grounds set out in this claim are true.

SWORN/AFFIRMED BEFORE me at the

	)
of , in the	)
, this day	)
of , 20 .	) ....
	)
	)
	)
	)

....

A Commissioner for taking Affidavits *(or as may be)*

RCP-E 75.14 (November 1, 2005)

FORM 75.1A

Courts of Justice Act

REQUEST FOR ASSIGNMENT OF MEDIATOR

ONTARIO

(Court file no.)

SUPERIOR COURT OF JUSTICE

IN THE ESTATE OF   deceased,

late of   ,

occupation   ,

who died on   .

REQUEST FOR ASSIGNMENT OF MEDIATOR

TO: Mediation co-ordinator for *(county)*

An order giving directions was made under rule 75.1.05 on *(date of order)*. A copy of the order is attached to this request.

The designated parties have not chosen a mediator under subrule 75.1.06 (1). The 30-day period mentioned in subrule 75.1.07 (1) has expired.

This is a request that you assign a mediator from the list for the county.

(Date)   *(Name, address, telephone number and fax number, if any, of lawyer of party filing request, or of party)*

RCP-E 75.1A (November 1, 2005)

FORM 75.1B

Courts of Justice Act

NOTICE BY MEDIATOR

ONTARIO

(Court file no.)

SUPERIOR COURT OF JUSTICE

IN THE ESTATE OF   deceased,

late of   ,

occupation   ,

who died on   .

NOTICE BY MEDIATOR

TO:

AND TO:

I am the mediator whom the mediation co-ordinator has appointed to conduct the mediation session under Rule 75.1. *(Delete this paragraph if mediator was chosen by designated parties under clause 75.1.06 (1) (a) or (c).)*

The mediation session will take place on *(date)*, from *(time)* to *(time)*, at *(place)*.

You are required to attend this mediation session. If you have a lawyer representing you in this proceeding, he or she is also required to attend.

You are required to file a statement of issues (Form 75.1C) by *(date)* (seven days before the mediation session). A blank copy of the form is attached.

When you attend the mediation session, you should bring with you any documents that you consider of central importance in the proceeding. You should plan to remain throughout the scheduled time. If you need another person's approval before agreeing to a settlement, you should make arrangements before the mediation session to ensure that you have ready telephone access to that person throughout the session, even outside regular business hours.

YOU MAY BE PENALIZED UNDER RULE 75.1.10 IF YOU FAIL TO FILE A STATE-MENT OF ISSUES OR FAIL TO ATTEND THE MEDIATION SESSION.

(Date)   *(Name, address, telephone number and fax number, if any, of mediator)*

RCP-E 75.1B (November 1, 2005)

FORM 75.1C

Courts of Justice Act

STATEMENT OF ISSUES

ONTARIO

(Court file no.)

SUPERIOR COURT OF JUSTICE

IN THE ESTATE OF   deceased,

late of   ,

occupation   ,

who died on   .

STATEMENT OF ISSUES

(To be provided to mediator and designated parties at least seven days before the mediation session)

1. Factual and legal issues in dispute

The undersigned designated party states that the following factual and legal issues are in dispute and remain to be resolved.

(Issues should be stated briefly and numbered consecutively.)

2. Party's position and interests (what the party hopes to achieve)

(Brief summary.)

3. Attached documents

Attached to this form are the following documents that the designated party considers of central importance in the proceeding: *(list)*

(Date)   *(party's signature)*

(Name, address, telephone number and fax number, if any, of
lawyer of party filing statement of issues, or of party)

NOTE: Rule 75.1.11 provides as follows:

All communications at a mediation session and the mediator's notes and records shall be deemed to be without prejudice settlement discussions.

RCP-E 75.1C (November 1, 2005)

FORM 75.1D

Courts of Justice Act

CERTIFICATE OF NON-COMPLIANCE

ONTARIO

(Court file no.)

SUPERIOR COURT OF JUSTICE

IN THE ESTATE OF   deceased,
late of   ,
occupation   ,
who died on   .

CERTIFICATE OF NON-COMPLIANCE

TO: *(court)*

I, *(name)*, mediator, certify that this certificate of non-compliance is filed because:

( ) *(Identify party(ies))* failed to provide a copy of a statement of issues to the mediator and the other parties *(or* to the mediator *or* to *party*(ies)).

( ) *(Identify party(ies))* failed to attend within the first 30 minutes of a scheduled mediation session.

(Date)   *(Name, address, telephone number and fax number, if any, of mediator)*

RCP-E 75.1D (November 1, 2005)

FORM 76A

Courts of Justice Act

NOTICE WHETHER ACTION UNDER RULE 76

(General heading)

NOTICE WHETHER ACTION UNDER RULE 76

The plaintiff states that this action and any related proceedings are:

(select one of the following:)

( ) continuing under Rule 76

( ) continuing as an ordinary procedure.

(Name, address and telephone and fax numbers of lawyer or plaintiff)

RCP-E 76A (November 1, 2008)

FORM 76B

Courts of Justice Act

SIMPLIFIED PROCEDURE MOTION FORM

Court File No.................

(General heading)

SIMPLIFIED PROCEDURE MOTION FORM

JURISDICTION   (   )   Judge
                        (   )   Master
                        (   )   Registrar

THIS FORM IS FILED BY *(Check appropriate boxes to identify the party filing this form as a moving/responding party on this motion AND to identify this party as plaintiff, defendant, etc. in the action)*

[   ]   moving party
[   ]   plaintiff

....

[   ]   responding party
[   ]   defendant

....

[   ]   Other — specify kind of party and name

....

MOTION MADE

[   ]   on consent of all parties   [   ]   on notice to all parties and unopposed
[   ]   without notice   [   ]   on notice to all parties and expected to be
                                                            opposed

Notice of this motion was served on (date):...

by means of:

....

METHOD OF HEARING REQUESTED

[   ]   by attendance
[   ]   in writing only, no attendance
[   ]   by fax
[   ]   by telephone conference under rule 1.08
[   ]   by video conference under rule 1.08

Date, time and place for conference call, telephone call or appearances

....
      (date)   (time)   (place)

ORDER SOUGHT BY THIS PARTY (Responding party is presumed to request dismissal of motion and costs)

[   ]   Extension of time — until (give specific date): ....
[   ]   serve claim
[   ]   file or deliver statement of defence
[   ]   Other relief — be specific

      ....
      ....

MATERIAL RELIED ON BY THIS PARTY

[   ]   this form
[   ]   pleadings
[   ]   affidavits — specify
[   ]   other — specify

      ....
      ....

GROUNDS IN SUPPORT OF/IN OPPOSITION TO MOTION (INCLUDING RULE AND STATUTORY PROVISIONS RELIED ON)

....
....

CERTIFICATION BY LAWYER

I certify that the above information is correct, to the best of my knowledge.
Signature of lawyer *(If no lawyer, party must sign)*

....
Date
....

THIS PARTY'S LAWYER *(If no lawyer, give party's name, address for service, telephone and fax number.)*

Name and firm:

Address:

Telephone: Fax:

THIS PARTY'S LAWYER *(If no lawyer, give party's name, address for service, telephone and fax number.)*

Name and firm:

Address:

Telephone: Fax:

OTHER LAWYER *(If no lawyer, give other party's name, address for service, telephone and fax number.)*

Name and firm:

Address:

Telephone: Fax:

OTHER LAWYER *(If no lawyer, give other party's name, address for service, telephone and fax number.)*

Name and firm:

Address:

Telephone: Fax:

DISPOSITION

[   ]   order to go as asked
[   ]   adjourned to
[   ]   order refused
[   ]   order to go as follows:

....
....

Hearing method ....   Hearing duration ....
                                                min.

Heard in: [   ] courtroom   [   ] office

[   ]   Successful party MUST prepare formal order for signature

[   ]   No copy of disposition to be sent to parties

[   ]   Other directions — specify

....
....

Date...............................   Name   Signature
                                           ....
                                           Judge/Master/Registrar

RCP-E 76B (November 1, 2005)

691

FORM 76C

Courts of Justice Act

NOTICE OF READINESS FOR PRE-TRIAL CONFERENCE

(General heading)

NOTICE OF READINESS FOR PRE-TRIAL CONFERENCE

The *(identify party)* is ready for a pre-trial conference and is setting this action down for trial. A pre-trial conference in the action will proceed as scheduled and the trial will proceed when the action is reached on the trial list, unless the court orders otherwise.

CERTIFICATE

I CERTIFY that there was a settlement discussion under rule 76.08.

Date   (Signature)

(Name, address and telephone and fax numbers of lawyer or party giving notice)

TO   *(Name and address of lawyer or party receiving notice)*

RCP-E 76C (November 1, 2005)

FORM 76D

Courts of Justice Act

TRIAL MANAGEMENT CHECKLIST

(General heading)

(Insert name of party filing this form)

TRIAL MANAGEMENT CHECKLIST

Trial Lawyer — Plaintiff (s):

Trial Lawyer — Defendant (s):

Filed by Plaintiff

Filed by Defendant

Filed by Subsequent Party

1.   Issues Outstanding

    (a)   liability:

    (b)   damages:

    (c)   other:

2.   Names of Plaintiff's Witnesses

3.   Names of Defendant's Witnesses

4.   Admissions

Are the parties prepared to admit any facts for the purposes of the trial?   ☐ yes   ☐ no

5.   Document Brief

Will there be a document brief?   ☐ yes   ☐ no

6.   Request to Admit

Will there be a request to admit?   ☐ yes   ☐ no

If so, have the parties agreed to a timetable?   ☐ yes   ☐ no

7.   Expert's Reports

Are any expert's reports anticipated?   ☐ yes   ☐ no

8.   Amendments to Pleadings

Are any amendments likely to be sought?   ☐ yes   ☐ no

9.   Factum of Law

Will the parties be submitting factums of law?   ☐ yes   ☐ no

Print Form

RCP-76D-E (2019/05)

FAMILY LAW FORMS

FORMS

TABLE OF CONTENTS

Commonly Used Forms at the Family Responsibility Office

Form	Description	Page
Freedom of Information Access or Correction Request	To help requesters get access to government records using the Freedom of Information and Protection of Privacy Act or to correct their personal information. For Freedom of Information requests, mail your request to: FIPPA Representative Family Responsibility Office Ministry of Community and Social Services P.O. Box 611 Steeles West Post Office Toronto, ON M3J 0K8 Please include a $5 cheque or money order payable to the Minister of Finance and mark the envelope as "private and confidential."	703
Affidavit for a Lost Cheque	The Family Responsibility Office will ask a support recipient to complete this form if they have not received a support cheque and believe that it has been lost.	705
Application to Discontinue Enforcement of Ongoing Support	This form is completed and submitted to the Family Responsibility Office by a support payor or an authorized third party who is claiming that support should end or has ended.	706
Cancellation of Third Party Authorization	This form stops all third party access to a client's case. Once the third party access is cancelled, only the payor or recipient will be able to receive information about their case.	708
Confirmation of Identity Letter Request	This is prepared by the Family Responsibility Office confirming that an individual is not one and the same as the support payor against whom the Family Responsibility Office has taken enforcement action. Most commonly, these letters are prepared in relation to writs of seizure and sale and real estate transactions.	709

Form	Description	Page
FRO Financial Statement (Form 4)	Support payors may be requested to complete this form to: • support a Voluntary Arrears Payment Schedule, or • because a payor is in default of his/her support obligations and the Family Responsibility Office has begun a default hearing. Documents to provide proof of income must be included with a financial statement, including: • pay stubs • income tax returns for the last three years, and • notices of assessment from the Canada Revenue Agency.	710
Notice of Re-Filing	Sometimes clients withdraw from the Family Responsibility Office and then decide to have their case reopened. Either party (the recipient or the payor) can complete this form and submit it to the Family Responsibility Office. If appropriate, the Family Responsibility Office will re-open the case and resume enforcement. If you withdrew your case on or after October 31, 2004, a $50 re-filing fee will be applied. You will also have to submit a registration package, if you have not submitted one already. If you want the Family Responsibility Office to enforce any arrears that may have accumulated since the case was closed, you will need to complete and submit a Statement of Arrears. If there has been a change in the status of a child (for example, the child is no longer eligible for support payments), you need to let the Family Responsibility Office know in writing.	717
Notice by Support Recipient of Unilateral Withdrawal	This form is used by support recipients who wish to withdraw from the Family Responsibility Office without the consent of the support payor. This form can only be used if the support payor is in arrears and the support recipient wishes to unilaterally withdraw from the Family Responsibility Office to pursue his or her own private enforcement actions.	718

Form	Description	Page
Notice of Withdrawal	This form is used when a payor and a recipient want to manage their support payments privately without the involvement of the Family Responsibility Office. Both the payor and the recipient must complete this form. When the Family Responsibility Office receives the form, the case will be closed and all enforcement action will stop.	719
Personal Pre-Authorized Debit (PAD) Application	This form authorizes the Family Responsibility Office to automatically deduct support payments from the support payor's bank account. This method of payment is only available to payors who do not have a regular source of income that makes support deductions on their behalf (for example, an employer).	720
Registration for Direct Deposit	This form allows the Family Responsibility Office to send support payments to the support recipient by direct deposit. The law now requires support recipients to register for direct deposit, so that they receive their money as quickly and securely as possible.	722
Registration Package	The Family Responsibility Office sends each recipient a Registration Package. All recipients must complete the package and send it back to the Family Responsibility Office so that it has the information it needs to start collecting support payments and enforcement if necessary.	723
Request for Director's Statement of Arrears	This is a statement of account. The first statement of account is free of charge. Subsequent requests cost $25.	729
Statement of Arrears	This form outlines the amount of support payments that a payor has missed and owes to a recipient. If a recipient wishes to claim arrears for a time before the Family Responsibility Office registered his or her support order, the recipient can complete a Statement of Arrears. This statement will include any unpaid support amounts that are due to the recipient.	730

Form	Description	Page
Third Party Authorization	This form authorizes a person other than the payor or recipient to act on the payor's or recipient's behalf. A Family Responsibility Office support payor or support recipient may designate this person to request and receive information from the Family Responsibility Office regarding their case.	738
Voluntary Arrears Payment Schedule Proposal	If the support payor has fallen behind in support payments, they may be able to negotiate a re-payment schedule. This is called a Voluntary Arrears Payment Schedule. This is an agreement where the support payor agrees to pay the support arrears to the Family Responsibility Office according to payment schedule negotiated between the support payor and the Family Responsibility Office. The payments made, based on this schedule, are in addition to the regular ongoing support payments.	739

Freedom of Information Access or Correction Request

 **Ontario** Ministry of Government and Consumer Services

Access or Correction Request
*Freedom of Information and
Protection of Privacy Act
Municipal Freedom of Information
and Protection of Privacy Act*

Personal information contained on this form is collected under the *Freedom of Information and Protection of Privacy Act* or *Municipal Freedom of Information and Protection of Privacy Act* and will be used to answer your request.

Questions about this collection should be directed to the Freedom of Information and Privacy Coordinator at the institution where you make the request.

Please see instructions on page 2 before filling out this form

Section A. Type of Request

☐ Access to general records (non-personal information)

☐ Access to own personal information

☐ Access to other's personal information by authorized party

☐ Correction of own personal information

Name of institution request made to

Section B. Requester's Information

Last Name		First Name	Middle Initial
Unit/Apartment Number	Street Number	Street Name	PO Box
City/Town		Province	Postal Code
Home phone no. (include area code)		Business/Mobile phone no. (include area code & extension) ext.	

Section C. Description of Records or Correction Requested

Time period of the records		Method of access	
From (yyyy/mm/dd)	To (yyyy/mm/dd)	☐ Receive copy ☐ Examine original (on site only)	

Section D. Payment and Signature

$5 application fee	Signature	Date (yyyy/mm/dd)
☐ Cheque ☐ Cash (in person only)		

Section E. Institution Use Only

Date Received (yyyy/mm/dd)	Request Number	Comments

Available on-line at www.ontario.ca. This form will be kept for 6 years from the date of completion. Once completed, this form has a sensitivity level of medium.

7540-1539E (2019/12)   © Queen's Printer for Ontario, 2019   Disponible en français   Page 1 of 2

Instructions for Completing Access or Correction Request

Informal Access to Records

Many records of public institutions are available to you without making a request under the *Freedom of Information and Protection of Privacy Act* or the *Municipal Freedom of Information and Protection of Privacy Act*. Contact the Freedom of Information and Privacy (FOIP) Coordinator at the institution that holds the records to determine whether you need to make a formal request.

Section A. Type of Request

Check the box that indicates what you are requesting. (Records that do not contain personal information are general records.)

The FOIP Coordinator is required to verify your identity before giving you access to your own personal information.

If you are requesting another person's personal information records, you must provide proof that you have the authority to act for them (e.g., power of attorney, guardian or trusteeship order).

Section B. Requester's Information

Please ensure you have entered your name, address and telephone numbers accurately.

Section C.   Description of Records or Correction Requested

Provide as much detail as possible about the requested general records, own personal information, other's personal information or correction of own personal information. Use a separate sheet of paper if you need more space and attach it to this form.

If you are requesting personal information records, provide the name that should appear on them.

Specify the time period for the records as precisely as possible, e.g., from 2008/07/21 to 2009/11/30.

If you are requesting a correction of your own personal information records, describe the correction you want and provide any supporting documents. If possible, provide copies of the information to be corrected and the information you wish to have it replaced with.

Check a box to indicate whether you want to examine original documents (which may only be done on site) or receive copies.

Section D. Payment and Signature

A $5 application fee is required. Please **do not** include any credit card information on this form. Cash payments must be made in person.

Make cheques payable to the appropriate payee of the institution that holds the records. The payee for Government of Ontario ministries is the Minister of Finance.

Sign and date the form and mail it or submit it in person to the institution that holds the records.

| Print Form | Clear Form |

7540-1539E (2019/12)

Affidavit for a Lost Cheque

 **Ontario**

Ministry of Community and Social Services

Family Responsibility Office
PO Box 200 Stn A
Oshawa ON L1H 0C5

Clear Form   Print Form

Affidavit for a Lost Cheque

I, _____
(Name in Full)

of _____
(Address, Street Name and Number, City/Town, Concession, Province and Postal Code)

in the County / District / Regional Municipality of _____ make oath and say as follows:

1. I certify that I _____ have not received, or have received and subsequently lost

    cheque number _____ dated _____ 20 _____ .

    For the sum of _____ $ _____
    (enter the sum in words)   (enter the sum in figures)

    alleged to have been drawn by the Family Responsibility Office on the ROYAL BANK OF CANADA, Toronto, Ontario

    In respect of Family Responsibility Office Case Number: _____

2. I further certify that I have not received payment of such amount by any other means.

3. In the event of a duplicate cheque being issued made payable to me, I agree not to cash, endorse, or transfer the original cheque should it ever come into my possession, but to return the same to the said Ministry of Community and Social Services.

4. I further agree that should the Minister of Finance suffer any loss whatsoever by reason of the issue of a duplicate cheque, I shall indemnify him against all costs, damages, interest and expenses which he may bear or incur as a result of any claims being made by me or my assignees, endorsees or transferees where such claim is made on the original cheque or the duplicate cheque, and I hereby authorize the Minister of Finance to withhold the amount of such loss for any future payment due me by him.

5. According to the best of my knowledge, information and belief, this cheque has not been cashed nor has same been deposited to any of my accounts.

_____   _____
Date of Signature   Claimant's Signature

_____   _____
Witness – Print Full Name (Witness must be 18 years or older)   Witness Signature

Instructions: Mail your completed form to: **Family Responsibility Office
PO Box 200 Stn A
Oshawa ON L1H 0C5**

***Please note:** Cheque number, cheque amount, date of cheque issuance, and case number can be obtained from the Family Responsibility Office to be included in the form prior to being witnessed. Please contact the Family Responsibility Office at 416 326-1817 or 1 800 267-4330 for further details.

FRO-13E (2009/08)   © Queen's Printer for Ontario, 2009

Application to Discontinue Enforcement of Ongoing Support

 **Ontario** ⬥

Ministry of Children,
Community and Social Services

Family Responsibility Office
PO Box 200 Stn A
Oshawa ON L1H 0C5

**Application to Discontinue
Enforcement of Ongoing Support**

Instructions

- This form is to be completed by the Support Payor or an Authorized Third Party. Complete this form **only** if you are claiming that ongoing support obligation should have ended.
- Before this form can be completed by an Authorized Third Party, the Family Responsibility Office (FRO) must have a completed "Third Party Authorization Form" on file before this form can be accepted by FRO.

Important: This form is a two-page document, please be sure to complete page two of this form.

FRO Case Number	I am the: ☐ person that pays support	☐ Authorized Third Party (provide contact information below)

Authorized Third Party Information (if applicable)

Last Name	First Name

Address

Unit Number	Street Number	Street Name	PO Box
City/Town		Province	Postal Code

Telephone Number Home	Business	ext.	Cell

Email Address

Support Payor Information

Last Name	First Name

Address

Unit Number	Street Number	Street Name	PO Box
City/Town		Province	Postal Code

Telephone Number Home	Business	ext.	Cell

Email Address

Support Recipient Information

Last Name	First Name

Address

Unit Number	Street Number	Street Name	PO Box
City/Town		Province	Postal Code

Telephone Number Home	Business	ext.	Cell

Email Address

FRO-031E (2019/05)   © Queen's Printer for Ontario, 2019   Disponible en français   Page 1 of 2

706

Application to Discontinue Enforcement of Ongoing Support

FRO Case Number

Support Order Information

Type of Support Order
☐ Spousal ☐ Child

Date of Order(s) (yyyy/mm/dd)

Reasons why the support payor is applying to discontinue support (but not limited to):

☐ A terminating event set out in the support order has occurred.

☐ The child is at or over the age of majority, is not enrolled in a full-time program of education, and is not intending to return to school.
Note: Age of majority in Ontario is 18 years of age as per the *Age of Majority and Accountability Act*.

☐ The child is at or over the age of majority and does not have an illness and/or a disability that prevents the child from leaving their custodial parent's care.

☐ The child is married/common-law status.

☐ The child is no longer living with the custodial parent / is not returning to live with them.

☐ The child is working full-time.

☐ Other (specify below)

Child Support Orders Only

If you are applying to discontinue child support, provide the following details for each child.

Name of Child (Last Name, First Name)	Date of Birth (yyyy/mm/dd)	Child Currently Lives with	Date Support Should Have ended (yyyy/mm/dd)
1.			
2.			
3.			
4.			
5.			
6.			
7.			

Spousal Support Orders Only

Name of Spouse		Date Support Should Have Ended (yyyy/mm/dd)
Last Name	First Name	

Signature

Note: By completing and signing this form, the support payor consents to FRO providing a photocopy of page 2 of this form to the support recipient.

Name of Support Payor or Authorized Third Party (Last Name, First Name) (Print)	Signature of Support Payor or Authorized Third Party	Date (yyyy/mm/dd)

Save Form   Print Form   Clear Form

FRO-031E (2019/05)

Page 2 of 2

707

Cancellation of Third Party Authorization

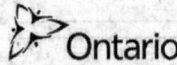 **Ontario**

Ministry of Community and
Social Services

Family Responsibility Office
PO Box 200 Stn A
Oshawa ON L1H 0C5

Cancellation of Third Party Authorization Form

Please complete this form to *CANCEL* Third Party Authorization on your case with the Family Responsibility Office (FRO).

A completed *Cancellation of Third Party Authorization Form* will STOP all third party access to your case file at FRO. Third Party Authorization can be set up again by completing a new *Third Party Authorization Form*.

| Name of FRO Client: | I am the: |
| | ☐ Person that pays support   ☐ Person that receives support |

| Street Address: | Apt#: | City: |

| Province: | Postal Code: | Work Phone or Cell # | Country: (if outside Canada) |

FRO Case Number:

My signature below indicates that I agree to the following:

1. I understand that by completing and signing this form I am asking the FRO to **CANCEL** the *Third Party Authorization Form* that I previously sent to FRO and **STOP** the Third Party from having access to my case.

2. I understand that once this *Cancellation of Third Party Authorization Form* is processed by FRO only I will receive or provide information to FRO concerning my case.

3. I understand that I will be required to complete a new *Third Party Authorization Form* and send it to FRO before a third party is provided ANY information concerning my case with FRO.

4. I understand that at FRO's discretion, they may contact me by telephone to verbally confirm this *Cancellation of Third Party Authorization Form* before canceling the Third Party's access to my case.

Please sign and date below to complete the *Cancellation of Third Party Authorization Form* for the FRO.

Please return the completed form to FRO by Mail or FAX

| FRO Client Signature: | Date: (DD/MM/YYYY) |
| **Return Completed Forms by Mail:**
Family Responsibility Office
PO Box 200 Stn A
Oshawa ON L1H 0C5 | **Return Completed Forms by Fax:**
(416)-240-2401 |

FRO – 015E (19/05/2004)   © Queen's Printer for Ontario, 2008

[Clear Form]   [Print Form]

708

Confirmation of Identity Letter Request

 **Ontario**

Ministry of Community
and Social Services

Family Responsibility Office
PO Box 200 Stn A
Oshawa ON L1H 0C5

**Confirmation of Identity
Letter Request**

(Pursuant to Ontario Regulation 160/00 made under the Family Responsibility and Support Arrears Enforcement Act, 1996)

- If you wish to receive a letter confirming that a person is not the same person who is named in a Writ of Seizure and Sale filed by the Director Family Responsibility Office with a Sheriff, please complete this form and return it to the Family Responsibility Office.

Family Responsibility Office, PO Box 622, Steeles West Post Office Toronto ON M3J 0K8

Fax (416) 240- 2468

Please do not send regular support payments to this address

Requestor's Name			
Address : Street and Number	City	Province	Postal Code
Telephone Number ( )		Facsimile Number ( )	
Signature:		Date:	

Third Party and Writ Information

Third Party's Name	Third Party's Date of Birth
Third Party's Social Insurance Number (SIN)	Third Party's Address

If a photocopy of the Writ is not included, please fill out the following section

Writ Number	Court of Issue
Writ Issue Date	Recipient's Name
Debtor's Name	FRO Case Number

Please return confirmation of identity letter by

☐ regular mail

☐ Fax to ( )_____

© Queen's Printer for Ontario, 2016

1

FRO Financial Statement (Form 4)

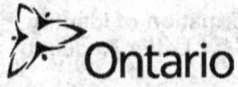 **Ontario**

FINANCIAL STATEMENT

Family Responsibility and Support Arrears Enforcement Act,
1996

Form 4

Case Number

You have 15 days to complete this form and return it to the Family Responsibility Office

I _____ , of _____

      Name of Payor   Address - Street and Number   Municipality

solemnly declare that all details of my financial situation are
_____ accurately set out below.

 Province   Postal Code

Part I - Employment Information
Occupation: What type of work do you do? _____
Are you self-employed?   ☐ Yes   ☐ No   If yes, financial statements for the past two years must be attached.
Are you now employed   ☐ Full-time   ☐ Part-time   ☐ Unemployed
Current employer: *(if more than one employer, provide details of other employers on a separate sheet)*
Name
Address: Street Name and Number   Municipality   Province   Postal Code
How long have you worked for this employer?

When are you paid? *(check one)*
         ☐ once a month   ☐ twice a month   ☐ once every two weeks
         ☐ weekly   ☐ other *(specify)* _____

If paid by commission, give details of the arrangement for payment that you have with your employer. Please tell us if you receive advances, how such advances are calculated, and if you are required to reimburse your employer should you fail to earn the commission or meet any production target.

FRO-010E (June 15, 2005)

If paid by commission, are the terms of the arrangement between you and your employer in writing? ☐ Yes ☐ No
If yes, attach a copy of the document. If no, when was the current arrangement reached? *(date)* _____
When will you next discuss changing the commission arrangements with your employer? *(date)* _____
Last employer: *(Complete only if not working now)*
Name
Address: Street Name and Number Municipality Province Postal Code
How long did you work for this employer? From_____ To _____
Reason employment ended *(specify)*

IMPORTANT: PLEASE FILL IN EITHER THE WEEKLY OR MONTHLY INCOME COLUMN, NOT BOTH.

If you receive or pay some money once a month, but are using the column for weekly income, divide the monthly amount by 4.33 to get the amount per week. If you receive or pay some money every week, but are using the column for monthly income, multiply the weekly amount by 4.33 to get the amount per month.

Part 2 – Income Information					
Income - A			Income Deductions - B		
Source of Income	Weekly $	Monthly $	Type of Deduction	Weekly $	Monthly $
Pay, Wages, Salary (before deductions)			Income Tax		
Bonuses			Canada Pension Plan		
Public Assistance			Employment Insurance		
Employment Insurance			Pension Plan Contributions		
Workers' Compensation Payments			Union or other dues		
Pensions			Group Insurance		
Rent, board you collect from others			Credit Union Loan		
Dividends			Credit Union Savings		
Interest			Other *(specify, i.e. charity)*		
Commissions			Total Deductions $ (B)	$	$
Support from others					
Family Allowance					
Other *(specify)*					

FRO-010E (June 15, 2005)

Total Income $ (A)	$	$	Take Home Income (A) – (B) = $

Part 3 - Expenses Information					
Expenses – C	**Weekly $**	**Monthly $**	**Expenses - D**	**Weekly $**	**Monthly $**
Groceries and Household Supplies			Public Transit, Taxis, etc.		
Meals outside home			Vehicle operation, gas and oil		
Clothing			Vehicle Insurance and Licence		
Laundry and Dry Cleaning			Maintenance		
Rent or Mortgage			Life Insurance		
Taxes			School Fees, Books, etc.		
Home Insurance			Music Lessons, Sports Fees, etc.		
Heating Fuel			Newspapers, Publications, Stationery		
Water			Entertainment, Recreation		
Hydro			Alcohol, Tobacco		
Telephone			Vacation		
Cable TV			Hairdresser, Barber		
Repairs and Maintenance			Toilet Articles (hairspray, soap, etc.)		
Other			Babysitting, Daycare		
Health and Medical Insurance			Children's Allowance, Gifts		
Drugs			Support Payments (actually being paid)		
Dental Care			Savings for future (exc. payroll ded.)		
Sub-total (C)	$	$	Other *(specify)*		
			Sub-total (D)	$	$

Total Expenses (Excluding Debt Payments) Add (C) + (D) = $ _____

Part 4 – Debt Information
If you own a car, are there still payments owing?   ☐ Yes   ☐ No
If yes, name of lender
Address

FRO-010E (June 15, 2005)

Date of Purchase

Initial amount financed? $ _____ Balance Owing $ _____ Monthly payments $ _____

Other Debts

If space not sufficient, use separate sheet

Type of Debt	Creditor (Name and Address)	Security	Full Amount Now Owing	Monthly Payments	Are Payments Currently Being Met
Bank or Trust Company Loans					☐ Yes ☐ No
					☐ Yes ☐ No
					☐ Yes ☐ No
					☐ Yes ☐ No
Finance Company Loan					☐ Yes ☐ No
					☐ Yes ☐ No
					☐ Yes ☐ No
					☐ Yes ☐ No
Credit Card Loans					☐ Yes ☐ No
					☐ Yes ☐ No
					☐ Yes ☐ No
					☐ Yes ☐ No
Other Debts					☐ Yes ☐ No
					☐ Yes ☐ No
					☐ Yes ☐ No
					☐ Yes ☐ No
					☐ Yes ☐ No
TOTALS					

FRO-010E (June 15, 2005)

Part 5 – Assets Information		
Type	Details – *(if space is not sufficient, use separate sheet)*	Value or Amount
	State Address of Property and Nature of Ownership	
Real Estate	1	•
	2	•
	3	•
	Year and Make	
Cars, Boats, Vehicles	1	•
	2	•
	3	•
	Address Where Located	
Household Goods and Furniture	1	•
	2	•
	3	•
	Description and Address Where Located	
Tools, Sports, Hobby Equipment	1	•
	2	•
	3	•
	Type – Issuer – Due Date – Number of Shares	
Bonds - Shares Term Deposits Investment Certificates	1	•
	2	•
	3	•
	Name and Address of Institution Account Number	
Bank Accounts	1	•
	2	•
	3	•
	Type and Issuer Account Number	
Savings Plans R.R.S.P. Pension Plans	1	•
	2	•
	3	•
	Type – Beneficiary – Face Amount	Cash Surrender Value ↓
Life Insurance	1	•
	2	•
	3	•
	Name and Address of Business	
Interest in Business *Attach separate financial statement for each business*	1	•
	2	•
	3	•

FRO-010E (June 15, 2005)

Name and Address of Debtors			
Money Owed to You	1		●
	2		●
	3		●
Description and Address of Location			
Other Assets	1		●
	2		●
	3		●
Total Estimated Value		$	●

Part 6 – Information

1.   The expenses shown on Part 3 of this form are for:

☐ Me alone

☐ Me and the following other persons: *(Give name(s) and relationship(s))*

_____

_____

2.   I understand that I am required to attach proof of my income to this form.

(a)   I attach to this statement proof of my current income, including my three most recent

☐ paycheque stubs   ☐ employment insurance benefits
☐ other *(specify)* _____

☐ workers' compensation payments   ☐ pension payments

Note: If you do not receive pay stubs or payment statements from an income source, attach a letter from the income source stating the amount of money received for the three consecutive payments made to you immediately before the date of the financial statement; **AND**

(b) ☐   I attach to this form a copy of my income tax returns that were filed with the Canada Revenue Agency for the past 3 taxation years, together with a copy of all material filed with the returns and a copy of any notices of assessment or re-assessment that I have received from the Agency for these years.

     ☐   I attach to this form a statement from the Canada Revenue Agency that I have not filed any income tax returns for the past 3 years.

     ☐   I am unable to attach my past 3 years' income tax returns and notices of assessment. I am attaching Canada Revenue Agency statements of my income and deductions for the past 3 years as proof of my income.

FRO-010E (June 15, 2005)

Sworn before me at the _____

_____ in the _____

of _____ on _____ 20 ___

_____
A Commissioner, etc.

}

_____
Signature
(This form is to be signed before a
lawyer, justice of the peace, notary
public or commissioner for taking
affidavits.)

AFTER REVIEWING THIS STATEMENT, THE DIRECTOR MAY REQUIRE OTHER EVIDENCE VERIFYING YOUR INCOME.

THE LAW REQUIRES THAT YOU MUST COMPLETE AND DELIVER THE COMPLETED FINANCIAL STATEMENT TO THE FAMILY RESPONSIBILITY OFFICE WITHIN 15 DAYS OF BEING SERVED WITH THE REQUEST TO COMPLETE IT.

IF, AFTER PROVIDING THE DIRECTOR WITH A COMPLETED FINANCIAL STATEMENT, YOU DISCOVER THAT SOME OF THE INFORMATION YOU PROVIDED WAS INCOMPLETE OR WRONG, THE LAW REQUIRES THAT YOU PROVIDE THE DIRECTOR WITH A CORRECT FINANCIAL STATEMENT WITHIN 10 DAYS OF THE DISCOVERY OF THE ERROR(S).

IF YOU FAIL TO COMPLY, YOU MAY BE ORDERED BY THE COURT TO COMPLY AND THE COURT MAY ORDER THAT **A WARRANT FOR YOUR ARREST** BE ISSUED.

IT IS AN OFFENCE TO KNOWINGLY FAIL TO COMPLY WITH THESE REQUIREMENTS. A PERSON CONVICTED OF AN OFFENCE IS LIABLE TO A FINE OF UP TO $10,000.

FRO-010E (June 15, 2005)

Notice of Re-Filing

 **Ontario**

Ministry of Community and
Social Services

Family Responsibility Office
PO Box 200 Stn A
Oshawa ON L1H 0C5

Notice of Re-Filing

Section A

Please complete this section to re-file your order with the Family Responsibility Office	FRO Case Number

Name:	I am the: ☐ Person that pays support ☐ Person that receives support

Street Address:	Apt#:	City:

Province:	Postal Code:	Country (if outside Canada)

Work Phone or Cell #	Home Phone #

FRO Client Signature:	Date: (DD/MM/YYYY)

Please select the option below that applies to you:

☐ I withdrew before October 31, 2004. (I do not need to complete Section B or pay a fee to re-file)

☐ I withdrew on or after October 31, 2004. (I need to complete section B and pay a fee of $50.00 to re-file)

If you cannot remember when you withdrew from the FRO, please call our office at 416-243-1909 or 1-888-815-2757

Section B

The fee for re-filing with the Family Responsibility Office is $50.00. Please select one payment method below:

☐ Cheque or Money Order (attached) Please make cheque or money order payable to the Minister of Finance

☐ Visa   ☐ MasterCard

Credit Card Number:

Expiry Date (MM/YY)	Name of Cardholder:

I, _____ authorize the Minister of Finance to charge my credit card for this
$50.00 re-filing fee.

Signature: _____   Date (DD/MM/YYYY) _____

Return Completed Forms by Mail: Family Responsibility Office PO Box 622 Steeles West Post Office Toronto ON M3J 0K8 www.ontario.ca/FRO	**Return Completed Forms by Fax:** (416)-240-2468

FRO – 016E (2017/01)

Notice by Support Recipient of Unilateral Withdrawal

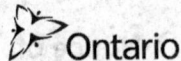 **Ontario**

Ministry of Community and
Social Services

Family Responsibility
Office
P.O. Box 200 Stn A
Oshawa, ON L1H 0C5

Notice by Support
Recipient of
Unilateral Withdrawal

USE THIS FORM ONLY IF:
- *YOU ARE A SUPPORT RECIPIENT WISHING TO UNILATERALY CLOSE YOUR CASE WITH FRO TO PURSUE YOUR OWN PRIVATE ENFORCEMENT MEASURES; AND*
- *YOUR CASE IS IN ARREARS BY AT LEAST ONE MONTH'S WORTH OF SUPPORT, PLUS $50.00.*

FRO Case Number

Recipient's Name

To: **Family Responsibility Office**

TAKE NOTICE that I

hereby withdraw the support provisions of the order / agreement /contract dated:

from the Family Responsibility Office, this includes the related Support Deduction Order if filed with the Director, Family Responsibility Office. I understand that I will be subject to a fee of $50.00 if I wish to re-file with the FRO at a later date.

It is recommended that you seek the advice of a lawyer regarding the transfer of certain enforcement from the Director of the Family Responsibility Office to yourself before you sign this form.

Date

Signature (Recipient)

Note:

If you have received social assistance from a municipality, district board, Indian Band or the Ministry of Community and Social Services since your support order was made, the *Family Responsibility and Support Arrears Enforcement Act, 1996* does not allow you to withdraw *except with the written consent of the Minister of Community and Social Services.*

The Minister of Community and Social Service hereby consents to the withdrawal of the order / agreement / contract.

Date

For the Minister of Community and Social Services

In order to partially offset the costs of re-opening a closed case, **a fee of $50.00 will be charged to both the Support Recipient and the Support Payor if you re-file with the FRO at a later date.** If you are considering withdrawing from the program or have questions about this fee, please call our office at 416-243-1909 or toll free 1-888-815-2757.

FRO-030E (2016/01)

© Queen's Printer for Ontario, 2016

Notice of Withdrawal

 **Ontario**

Ministry of Community and
Social Services

Family Responsibility Office
PO Box 200 Stn A
Oshawa ON L1H 0C5

Notice of Withdrawal

Case Number

| Recipient's Name | |
| Payor's Name | |

To: **Family Responsibility Office**

TAKE NOTICE that I

hereby withdraw the support provisions of the order / agreement /
contract dated:

from the Family Responsibility Office, this includes the related Support Deduction Order if filed with
the Director, Family Responsibility Office. We *understand that both the Support Payor and the
Support Recipient will be subject to a fee of $50.00 each if either wants to re-file with the FRO at a
later date.*

_____   _____
Date   Signature (Recipient)

_____   _____
Date   Signature (Payor)

Note: Both the Payor and the Recipient must sign this notice.

If you have received social assistance from a municipality, district board, Indian Band or the Ministry
of Community and Social Services since your support order was made, the *Family Responsibility and
Support Arrears Enforcement Act, 1996* does not allow you to withdraw except with the written
consent of the Minister of Community and Social Services.

The Minister of Community and Social Service hereby consents to the withdrawal of the order /
agreement / contract.

_____   _____
Date   For the Minister of Community and Social Services

In order to partially offset the costs of re-opening a closed case, **a fee of $50.00 will be charged to
both the Support Recipient and the Support Payor if you re-file with the FRO at a later date.** If
you are considering withdrawing from the program or have questions about this fee, please call our
office at 416 243-1909 or toll free 1 888 815-2757.

FRO-006E (2008/03)   © Queen's Printer for Ontario, 2008

[Print Form]   [Clear Form]

Personal Pre-Authorized Debit (PAD) Application

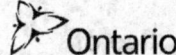 **Ontario**

Ministry of Community
and Social Services

Family Responsibility Office
PO Box 200 Stn A
Oshawa ON L1H 0C5
Tel. 1 800 267-4330 (Agent)
Tel. 416 326-1817 (GTA)
www.ontario.ca/FRO

Clear Form

**Personal Pre-Authorized
Debit (PAD) Application**
(Formerly Pre-authorized Payment or PAP)

For Family Responsibility Support Payments

IF YOUR EMPLOYER IS DEDUCTING SUPPORT PAYMENTS ON YOUR BEHALF, PLEASE IGNORE THIS FORM

Payor Last Name	Payor First Name	Payor Case Number
Branch Transit Number	Financial Institution Number	Bank Account Number

| Start Date: *(allow 15 days for processing)* (DD/MM/YYYY) | Amount of Withdrawal | |

Frequency you wish payments to be made. Choose one.

☐ **W** - Weekly   ☐ **M** - Monthly   ☐ **SM** - Semi-Monthly (1st + 15th)   ☐ **BW** - Bi-Weekly (every 2 weeks)

Home Telephone Number *(incl. Area Code)*	Business Telephone Number *(incl. Area Code)*	Fax Number *(incl. Area Code)*

DECLARATION:

1. Beginning on the above Start Date, I (the payor) authorize the Family Responsibility Office (the payee) to withdraw Pre-Authorized support payments from the designated bank account, of which I am the authorized signatory. If I am not the authorized signatory, the appropriate signature is also provided below.

2. I understand that I may cancel this agreement at any time by providing written notice to the Family Responsibility Office, at the address indicated above. This notification must be received ten (10) business days before the next scheduled debit. A sample cancellation form may be obtained from my financial institution or online at www.cdnpay.ca.

3. I agree to inform the Family Responsibility Office, in writing, at the address noted above, of any change in the above information (for example, Banking data / Withdrawal amount) before the next Pre-authorized Debit (PAD) is due.

4. I agree that if my support payments are affected by a cost of living adjustment (COLA), the Family Responsibility Office will automatically increase the amount of the withdrawal from my bank account. The amount of the increase will be equal to the amount of the cost of living adjustment that is in my support order or agreement. The Family Responsibility Office may also adjust the amount of withdrawal in the event of an order variation.

5. **I waive my right to receive pre-notification of the amount of the periodic PAD and agree that I do not require advance notice of the amount of PAD before a debit is processed.**

6. I agree to inform the Family Responsibility Office, in writing, to the above address, of any change in my employment status that results in an employer or income source remitting support on my behalf, which will make me ineligible for Pre-Authorized Debit method.

7. **I agree that, in the event of a non-negotiable payment (e.g. NSF), I will be liable to a charge of $35.**

8. I acknowledge that acceptance of this payment method is subject to the discretion of the Family Responsibility Office.

9. I agree that I may dispute a PAD only under the following conditions:
    (i) the PAD was not drawn in accordance with this PAD agreement
    (ii) the PAD agreement was revoked

10. **I have attached a copy of a cheque from the above designated bank account marked "VOID" for the purpose of this SIGNED Pre-Authorized Debit Application.**

Payor's Recourse/Reimbursement Statement
As a payor, you have certain recourse rights if any debit does not comply with this agreement. For example, you have the right to receive reimbursement for any debit that is not authorized or is not consistent with this PAD agreement. To obtain more information on your recourse rights, you may contact your financial institute or visit www.cdnpay.ca.

Signature of Payor	Date *(DD/MM/YYYY)*

Authorized Signature of Designated Bank Account Holder *(if not the payor)*

Print

Personal Pre-Authorized Debit Application
(Formerly Pre-authorized Payment or PAP)

For Family Responsibility Support Payments

Pre-Authorized Debit

The Family Responsibility Office is pleased to offer you a new and better way to pay your support payments: Pre-Authorized Debit or PAD.

It's Quick, It's Easy . . . and It's Convenient

With pre-Authorized Debit (PAD), you don't have to mail personal cheques to the Family Responsibility Office every week or month. Instead, your bank automatically withdraws the money from your bank account and sends it to us. No more keeping track of payment dates, writing post-dated cheques, or looking for a postage stamp.

To start using PAD

By completing the PAD Application Form with the required information, and signing the declaration, your Pre-Authorized Debit request can be processed.

Attach a cheque marked **VOID** to your completed, and **Signed** application form.

If you choose not to use the PAD method to pay your support payments, please use Telephone Banking or PC Banking. For more information on how to use these methods of payment, please contact your bank using the numbers listed below:

The Royal Bank of Canada	1 800 769-2511
The Bank of Montreal	1 800 363-9992
TD Canada Trust	1 866 567-8888
The Canadian Imperial Bank of Commerce	1 800 465-2422
The Bank of Nova Scotia	1 800 267-1234
Hong Kong Bank	1 800 889-4522
Credit Union Central of Ontario	Contact your Credit Union

FRO-001E (2009/12)

2 of 2

Registration for Direct Deposit

 **Ontario**

Ministry of Community
and Social Services

Family Responsibility Office
PO Box 200 Stn A
Oshawa ON L1H 0C5

Registration for Direct Deposit

FRO Case Number

When the Family Responsibility Office (FRO) receives a support payment that is owed to you, these funds will be sent by DIRECT DEPOSIT to your Canadian bank account. To ensure that you receive your money quickly, the following information must be provided. Incorrect information could result in your payment being sent to the wrong account.

Instructions

If you wish to have your support payments deposited into your **CHEQUING ACCOUNT, COMPLETE SECTION A** and **ATTACH A BLANK PERSONAL CHEQUE** with **"VOID"** written on it.

If, however, you wish to designate your **SAVINGS ACCOUNT**, complete **SECTION A**, take this form to your bank and ask them to complete **SECTION B** – Banking Data.

DO NOT FORGET TO SIGN THE BOTTOM OF THE FORM AUTHORIZING THE DIRECT DEPOSIT SERVICE.

Important notes about changing bank accounts

If your account number changes, or if you wish to have your support payments deposited to a different account, you must complete a new DIRECT DEPOSIT FORM and return it to FRO. After the changes have been processed, your support payments will be sent to your new account. **DO NOT CLOSE YOUR OLD ACCOUNT UNTIL YOU RECEIVE YOUR FIRST PAYMENT TO THE NEW ACCOUNT.**

PLEASE PRINT CLEARLY

Section A – Support Recipient Information

Last Name	First Name	Middle Initial

Address

Unit/Apt. Number	Street Number	Street Name	Lot, Concession or Township

City/Town	Province	Postal Code

Telephone number where you can be reached during the day (incl. area code)

NOTE: If attaching a VOID cheque, please tape the cheque over the Banking Information in Section B.

Section B – Banking Information (Must be completed by your bank if you are not attaching a VOID cheque)

Branch Number	Institution Number	Account Number

Name of Financial Institution

Branch

Branch Address

Place Bank Stamp

Bank Official's Signature and Position

Date (dd/mm/yyyy)

Until further notice, I authorize the direct deposit of my support payments to the account and financial institution designated in this form.

_____
Signature of Recipient

Date

0006-FRO-009E (2015/12)   © Queen's Printer for Ontario, 2015   Disponible en français   Clear Form   Print Form   Page 1 of 1

Registration Package

 **Ontario**

Ministry of Community
and Social Services

Family Responsibility Office
PO Box 200 Stn A
Oshawa ON L1H 0C5

Family Responsibility Office

Instructions for Recipients of Family Support

This filing package includes forms to be completed and returned to the Family Responsibility Office (FRO) as soon as possible. FRO must have this information for enforcement purposes.

1. **Recipient Information Form**

   You must provide the requested information that is available to you and indicate where we can contact you by mail and telephone.

   If your order or agreement is not already filed with FRO or if your order or agreement was previously withdrawn from FRO, you must complete this form and **attach a copy of your Order or Agreement.**

   NOTE: If you are filing a Domestic Contract, Separation Agreement, Cohabitation Agreement or Paternity Agreement with FRO, you must first file it with the Ontario Court of Justice or the Superior Court of Justice Family Court. When you file your Contract or Agreement with the court, you will be given an 'Affidavit for Filing Domestic Contract or Paternity Agreement with Court'. This Affidavit, stamped by the court, must be stapled to your Contract or Agreement. The Affidavit, your Contract or Agreement and the completed Registration forms must be submitted to FRO for enforcement purposes.

   YOU MUST SIGN THE RECIPIENT INFORMATION FORM AT THE BOTTOM WHERE SHOWN.

2. **Registration for Direct Deposit Form**

   Completion of this form authorizes FRO to deposit collected payments directly into your bank account. Funds will be received faster when payments are directly deposited into your bank account.

3. **Payor Information Form**

   Please answer all the questions as completely as possible and return the form to our office. If you cannot answer a question, write **"DO NOT KNOW"** as your answer, so that we know you saw the question but did not have the information at the time. If there is not enough space provided, please attach a separate sheet of paper including your name and FRO case number.

4. **Statement of Arrears Form**

   This form must be completed for FRO to begin collecting arrears owed to you prior to FRO enforcement. A copy of this form will be provided to the support payor (Payor) and this form becomes a court document if we take action to enforce support payments. It must therefore be accurate and signed in the presence of a **Commissioner for taking affidavits**, a **Justice of the Peace** or a **Notary Public.**

Check List

☐ **Recipient Information Form** *(Form must be signed)*

☐ **Registration for Direct Deposit** *(Section B must be completed OR void cheque attached)*

☐ **Payor Information Form** *(Provide as much information as possible)*

☐ **Statement of Arrears** *(Form must be signed and your signature witnessed and sworn)*

Ontario

Ministry of Community
and Social Services

Family Responsibility Office
PO Box 200 Stn A
Oshawa ON L1H 0C5

Recipient Information Form

FRO Case Number

Language Preferred ☐ English ☐ French

| Your Last Name (as written in the order) | Your First Name (as written in the order) | Your Middle Name(s) | ☐ Male ☐ Female |

Address

| Unit/Apt. Number | Street Number | Street Name | Lot, Concession or Township |

| City/Town | Province | Postal Code |

Date of Birth ___ / ___ / ___
Day Month Year

Home Telephone Number (incl. area code) | Cellular Telephone Number (incl. area code)

Employer

Social Insurance Number (SIN) | Work Telephone Number (incl. area code)

| Last Name of Payor (Person owing support) (as written in the order) | First Name of Payor (as written in the order) | Middle Name(s) of Payor |

My Support Provisions are contained in a (check one):

☐ Court Order ☐ Separation Agreement ☐ Domestic Contract
☐ Cohabitation Agreement ☐ Paternity Agreement

Date ___ / ___ / ___
Day Month Year

(Agreement/Contract must be filed with the Ontario Court of Justice or Superior Court of Justice Family Court)

Are you claiming spousal support for yourself? ☐ Yes ☐ No

Are you claiming support for the child(ren) named in the order/agreement? ☐ Yes ☐ No

If yes, list the name(s) of the child(ren) you are claiming support for *(use additional sheet if required)*

Last Name, First Name, Middle Name(s)	Date of Birth Day/Month/Year	Sex
		☐ Male ☐ Female
		☐ Male ☐ Female
		☐ Male ☐ Female
		☐ Male ☐ Female

Do you currently receive or have you applied for: ☐ Ontario Works ☐ Ontario Disability Support ☐ No

Do you have another case filed with FRO? If yes, please provide the name that the case is filed under and the case number.

| Name case is filed under | Case Number |

You must sign this form in order for FRO to enforce the support terms of your order/agreement/contract.

_____ Signature   _____ Date

008-FRO-005E (2015/12) © Queen's Printer for Ontario, 2015   Disponible en français   Page 2 of 10

724

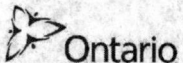

Ministry of Community and Social Services

Family Responsibility Office
PO Box 200 Stn A
Oshawa ON L1H 0C5

Registration for Direct Deposit

FRO Case Number

When the Family Responsibility Office (FRO) receives a support payment that is owed to you, these funds will be sent by **DIRECT DEPOSIT** to your Canadian bank account. To ensure that you receive your money quickly, the following information must be provided. Incorrect information could result in your payment being sent to the wrong account.

Instructions

If you wish to have your support payments deposited into your **CHEQUING ACCOUNT, COMPLETE SECTION A** and **ATTACH A BLANK PERSONAL CHEQUE** with **"VOID"** written on it.

If, however, you wish to designate your **SAVINGS ACCOUNT,** complete **SECTION A,** take this form to your bank and ask them to complete **SECTION B** – Banking Data.

DO NOT FORGET TO SIGN THE BOTTOM OF THE FORM AUTHORIZING THE DIRECT DEPOSIT SERVICE.

Important notes about changing bank accounts

If your account number changes, or if you wish to have your support payments deposited to a different account, you must complete a new DIRECT DEPOSIT FORM and return it to FRO. After the changes have been processed, your support payments will be sent to your new account. **DO NOT CLOSE YOUR OLD ACCOUNT UNTIL YOU RECEIVE YOUR FIRST PAYMENT TO THE NEW ACCOUNT.**

PLEASE PRINT CLEARLY

Section A – Support Recipient Information

Last Name	First Name	Middle Initial

Address

Unit/Apt. Number	Street Number	Street Name	Lot, Concession or Township

City/Town	Province	Postal Code

Telephone number where you can be reached during the day (incl. area code)

NOTE: If attaching a VOID cheque, please tape the cheque over the Banking Information in Section B.

Section B – Banking Information (Must be completed by your bank if you are not attaching a VOID cheque)

Branch Number	Institution Number	Account Number
Name of Financial Institution		
Branch		
Branch Address		
Bank Official's Signature and Position		Place Bank Stamp
Date (dd/mm/yyyy)		

Until further notice, I authorize the direct deposit of my support payments to the account and financial institution designated in this form.

_____   _____
Signature of Recipient   Date

008-FRO-005E (2015/12)   © Queen's Printer for Ontario, 2015   Disponible en français   Page 3 of 10

Ontario

Ministry of Community and Social Services

Family Responsibility Office
PO Box 200 Stn A
Oshawa ON L1H 0C5

Page 1 of 3

Payor Information Form
Information for Recipient to Complete

FRO Case Number

Payor's Last Name (as written in the order)	Payor's First Name (as written in the order)	Payor's Middle Name(s)	☐ Male ☐ Female

Payor's Address

Unit/Apt. Number	Street Number	Street Name		Lot, Concession or Township

City/Town	Province	Postal Code

Home Telephone Number (incl. area code)	Cellular Telephone Number (incl. area code)

Payor's Previous Address

Unit/Apt. Number	Street Number	Street Name		Lot, Concession or Township

City/Town	Province	Postal Code

Payor lived at this address from ___ / ___ / ___ to ___ / ___ / ___
Day / Month / Year   Day / Month / Year

Does the Payor use an alias or any other name(s)? If so, what name(s)?

Does the Payor have a Driver's Licence? ☐ Yes ☐ No ☐ Unknown

If the Payor has a Driver's Licence

Licence Number	Province

Payor's Social Insurance Number (This may be found on the Payor's tax return or your tax return)	Payor's Date of Birth ___ / ___ / ___ Day / Month / Year

Payor's mother's name before marriage

Payor's Marital Status
☐ Single ☐ Married ☐ Divorced ☐ Separated ☐ Cohabiting

Income Information

Indicate if the Payor is self-employed ☐ Yes ☐ No

If yes, give details of employment
_____ (e.g. Sole Owner, Partner, Family Business)

Payor's Current Employer/Income Source

Payor's Position	Date Started ___ / ___ / ___ Day / Month / Year

Employer's Address

Unit/Suite Number	Street Number and Street Name	City/Town

Province	Postal Code	Employer's Telephone Number (incl. area code)

Payor's Previous Employer/Income Source

Payor's Position	Date Started ___ / ___ / ___ Day / Month / Year

Employer's Address

Unit/Suite Number	Street Number and Street Name	City/Town

Province	Postal Code	Employer's Telephone Number (incl. area code)

Payor Information Form
Information for Recipient to Complete
Page 2 of 3

FRO Case Number

Property Information

Does the Payor own/lease/rent a car, truck, boat, snowmobile, farm equipment or recreational vehicle?

1. Vehicle Type | Model | Year | Colour

Licence Plate Number | Serial Number | ☐ Rent ☐ Own ☐ Lease

2. Vehicle Type | Model | Year | Colour

Licence Plate Number | Serial Number | ☐ Rent ☐ Own ☐ Lease

Does the Payor own (alone or jointly with another person/company) a house, cottage, farm, land, apartment building, office or investment property either in or outside of Canada?

1. Type of Property

Address
Apt. Number | Street Number | Street Name | Lot/Concession/Township

City/Town | Province | Postal Code

What is/are the name(s) of the person(s)/company who also own this property?

2. Type of Property

Address
Apt. Number | Street Number | Street Name | Lot/Concession/Township

City/Town | Province | Postal Code

What is/are the name(s) of the person(s)/company who also own this property?

Please attach additional information on a separate sheet of paper.

Other Information

Do you have the name and addresses of any of the Payor's relatives or friends who may help us locate the Payor if required?

1. Name | Relationship to Payor

Address: Street Number & Name/Apartment Number/City/Province/Postal Code | Telephone Number (incl. area code)

2. Name | Relationship to Payor

Address: Street Number & Name/Apartment Number/City/Province/Postal Code | Telephone Number (incl. area code)

Does the Payor belong to any professional or community groups, associations, clubs, unions that may help us to locate the Payor, if required? (Provide name of organization, address and telephone number if possible.)

Payor Information Form
Information for Recipient to Complete

Page 3 of 3

FRO Case Number

Does the Payor have other sources of income? *(e.g. Workplace Safety and Insurance Board Benefit, Employment Insurance Benefit, Disability Insurance, Pension Income.)* If yes, provide as much detail as possible, including claim numbers if known.

Please attach additional information *(e.g. business cards, business contacts)* on a separate sheet of paper.

Does the Payor frequently travel outside of Canada? If yes, for ☐ Business ☐ Pleasure

Passport Number

Does the Payor have any Federal Licences? *(e.g. Pilot Licence, Transport Licence)*

Type of Licence   Licence Number

Physical Description of the Payor (This information is required if we need to serve the Payor with Court Documents.)

If possible, include a current photograph of the Payor. Please attach the photograph to a separate sheet of paper and write the Payor's name, date the photograph was taken and your FRO case number.

Height	Weight	Build	Eye Colour	Eye Glasses ☐ Yes ☐ No
Hair Colour	Complexion (Skin Colour)	Distinguishing Marks or Features (e.g. Tattoos, Scars)		

Financial Information

Does the Payor have any Credit Cards?

Card Type	Card Type

Where does the Payor Bank?

1. Name of Financial Institution   Account Number

   Address

2. Name of Financial Institution   Account Number

   Address

List any other assets you are aware of *(e.g. Stocks, Bonds, Term Deposits, Life Insurance, Investment Certificates, RRSP).* If you require more space, please attach a separate sheet of paper.

Type of Asset	Location	Account/Policy/Serial Number

Request for Director's Statement of Arrears

 **Ontario**

Ministry of Community
and Social Services

Family Responsibility Office
PO Box 200 Stn A
Oshawa ON L1H 0C5

Statement of Arrears

Instructions

1. Complete the Statement of Arrears form, **in pen only**, if any support payments are owing to you at this time. The Family Responsibility Office (FRO) will begin the process of collecting these missed support payments (called "arrears") for you. A copy of this form will be provided to the support payor (Payor) and this form becomes a court document if we take action to enforce support payments. It must be signed in front of a Commissioner for taking affidavits, a Justice of the Peace or a Notary Public. A Commissioner is available at all court offices, community legal clinics and municipal or township offices. A Commissioner is also available at most law offices.

2. To complete the calculations on the Statement of Arrears form, write the date on which you were supposed to receive a support payment, starting with the first payment missed. The due dates for payment are found in your support order/agreement. If there is no due date, use the date of the order/agreement itself to calculate the dates payments are due. Then indicate if the payment was missed completely or if it was paid in part. List every support payment due after that, indicating if the payment was missed or paid in part. You must use a separate line for each payment. If you need more room, fill in a Schedule 'A' form and attach it to the Statement of Arrears. We will try to collect the total amount of arrears you claim is owed to you on this form.

3. If the arrears you are claiming include interest, please note that FRO will only take enforcement action on interest that has accrued as a result of the Payor's failure to comply with the support order. Where funds are being remitted to FRO through income source deductions, the Payor has no control over the schedule of payments by the income source. Therefore, FRO will not enforce any interest owing for delays in the receipt of support payments. To claim interest, please see **Instructions for Completing Interest Calculations**.

4. Some support orders and agreements say that support payments must be changed on a regular basis to reflect changes in the cost of living over the previous year. These provisions are called Cost of Living Adjustment (COLA) clauses. A COLA clause provides for the increase or decrease in the amount of support payments. In order to be enforced by FRO, support orders that contain a COLA clause must follow either the standard formula set out in Section 34(5) of the *Ontario Family Law Act* or Ontario Regulation 176/98.

   Please note that FRO cannot enforce COLA for child support orders made in accordance with the Child Support Guidelines. COLA does not apply to child support orders made under the federal *Divorce Act* on or after May 1, 1997 or to child support orders made under the *Ontario Family Law Act* on or after December 1, 1997.

5. If the arrears you are claiming are not for regular on-going support, but are for expenses, please note:

   - Depending on the terms of your Order or Agreement, these types of expenses may or may not be enforceable by FRO.

   - If the Order/Agreement doesn't include a clear requirement to pay or reimburse these expenses, they are likely not enforceable. If the expenses are enforceable, FRO requires a sworn Statement of Arrears, including the receipts.

Statement of Arrears

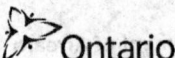 **Ontario**

Ministry of Community
and Social Services

Family Responsibility Office
PO Box 200 Stn A
Oshawa ON L1H 0C5

Instructions for Completing Interest Calculations

Please note that the Family Responsibility Office (FRO) will only take enforcement action on interest that has accrued as a result of the Payor's failure to comply with the support order. Where funds are being remitted to FRO through income source deductions, the Payor has no control over the schedule of payments by the income source. Therefore, FRO will not enforce any interest owing for delays in the receipt of support payments.

When determining the amount of interest owed to you, you should know the following:

i.   If your Ontario support order is dated after June 21, 1979, the interest rate must be stated in the order. For Ontario orders made before June 22, 1979, the rate of interest is five per cent (5%) and does not have to be stated in the order.

ii.   Prior to January 1, 1985, the Provincial Court (Family Division) could not award interest.

iii.   Under the *Courts of Justice Act*, interest accruing on a debt is simple interest and not compound interest.

iv.   Where the court provides that support be paid on a periodic basis (e.g. $500.00 per month), each payment in default will bear interest from the date that the payment was due. Therefore, the interest owing for each missed support payment must be calculated separately.

v.   Interest can be calculated by using the following formula:

$$\frac{\textbf{Principal} \; \times \; \textbf{Interest Rate} \; \times \; \textbf{Number of Days the Payment is in Arrears}}{\textbf{365 days}}$$

Where:
The principal is the outstanding individual support payment.
The Interest Rate, established by the *Courts of Justice Act* or its predecessor, is the rate that was in effect on the date that the court made the support order.

Example:
On January 27, 2011, the court made an order for support in the amount of $500.00 per month commencing February 1, 2011. The Payor has failed to make support payments for July 1, 2011 and September 1, 2011. The prescribed rate of interest for the first quarter of 2011 is three per cent (3%). As of October 1, 2011, the accrued interest is calculated as follows:

Interest on the July 1, 2011 payment is: $\dfrac{500 \;\times\; 3\% \;\times\; 92}{365} = \$3.78$

Interest on the September 1, 2011 payment is: $\dfrac{500 \;\times\; 3\% \;\times\; 30}{365} = \$1.23$

Total Interest = $\$3.78 + \$1.23 = \$5.01$

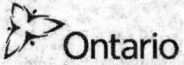

Ministry of Community and Social Services

Family Responsibility Office
PO Box 200 Stn A
Oshawa ON L1H 0C5

Statement of Arrears

FRO Case Number	

Support Recipient's Name

Last Name	First Name	Middle Initial

Support Payor's Name

Last Name	First Name	Middle Initial

1. I am the support recipient under the following
    Order

Date of Order	Court	Court File Number

Agreement filed with the Court

Date of Agreement	Court Agreement Filed With	Court File Number

2. The following amounts due under the order/agreement have not been paid. *(If you need more space, complete Schedule 'A')*
    Check if applicable. ☐ See Schedule 'A' attached

Date Payment Due Day/Month/Year	Amount Due	Date Paid Day/Month/Year	Amount Paid	Arrears

If you are entitled to interest on your support, *you must calculate the interest amount.* **Attach a copy of your calculations.**

If you are entitled to a COLA adjustment to your support, *you must include the adjustment in the amount due.* **Attach a copy of your calculations.**

Total Arrears $ _____ (a)

Total Interest to date (if any) $ _____ (b) **Applicable interest rate used** _____ %

My arrears as at: _____   TOTAL $ _____ (c)
            Date   (Add A and B)

You must sign this form in the presence of a lawyer, Justice of the Peace, Notary Public or Commissioner for taking affidavits.

Sworn before me at the _____ of _____

in the _____ of _____

this _____ day of _____, 20 _____

_____   _____
Signature of a commissioner, etc.   Signature of Support Recipient

731

Ministry of Community
and Social Services

Family Responsibility Office
PO Box 200 Stn A
Oshawa ON L1H 0C5

Schedule 'A'
To Statement of Arrears Form

FRO Case Number

Date Payment Due Day/Month/Year	Amount Due	Date Paid Day/Month/Year	Amount Paid	Arrears

Enter amount onto Statement of Arrears form.

Clear Form   Print Form

006-FRO-005E (2015/12)   © Queen's Printer for Ontario, 2015   Disponible en français

Ontario	Ministry of Community and Social Services
	Family Responsibility Office PO Box 200 Stn A Oshawa ON L1H 0C5

Request for Director's Statement of Arrears (Statement of Account)

(Pursuant to Ontario Regulation 160/00 made under the *Family Responsibility and Support Arrears Enforcement Act, 1996*)

- If you wish to receive a Director's Statement of Arrears (statement of account), please attach a cheque or money order for $25.00 to this form or fill out the credit card section.
- Make the cheque or money order payable to Family Responsibility Office.
- Mail payment and form to address below:

> **Family Responsibility Office**
> **PO Box 622**
> **Steeles West Post Office**
> **Toronto ON M3J 0K8**

Please do not send regular support payments to this address.

SECTION A

Please print your name

I am the
- ☐ Support Recipient
- ☐ Support Payor
- ☐ Solicitor for Support Recipient
- ☐ Solicitor for Support Payor
- ☐ Assignee

Case Number

Telephone Number
(   )

Address

Unit No.	Street No.	Street Name		PO Box

City/Town	Province	Postal Code

Support Payor's Name	Support Recipient's Name

Client Signature

SECTION B

$25.00 payment method
☐ Cheque/Money Order (attached)   *or*   ☐ Visa   ☐ MasterCard

Credit Card Number

Credit Card Expiry Date (MM/YY)   Name of Cardholder

Authorized Signature   Date (yyyy/mm/dd)

For urgent requests, **please fax this completed form to 416 240-2468.**

FRO-003E (2017/01)   © Queen's Printer for Ontario, 2017   Disponible en français

Ministry of Community
Statement of Arrears
and Social Services
Family Responsibility Office
PO Box 220
Downsview ON M3M 3A3

Instructions

1. Complete the Statement of Arrears form, **in pen only**, if any support payments are owing to you at this time. The Family Responsibility Office (FRO) will begin the process of collecting these missed support payments (called "arrears") for you. A copy of this form will be provided to the support payor (Payor) and this form becomes a court document if we take action to enforce support payments. It must be signed in front of a Commissioner for taking affidavits, a Justice of the Peace or a Notary Public. A Commissioner is available at all court offices, community legal clinics and municipal or township offices. A Commissioner is also available at most law offices.

2. To complete the calculations on the Statement of Arrears form, write the date on which you were supposed to receive a support payment, starting with the first payment missed. The due dates for payment are found in your support order/agreement. If there is no due date, use the date of the order/agreement itself to calculate the dates payments are due. Then indicate if the payment was missed completely or if it was paid in part. List every support payment due after that, indicating if the payment was missed or paid in part. You must use a separate line for each payment. If you need more room, fill in a Schedule 'A' form and attach it to the Statement of Arrears. We will try to collect the total amount of arrears you claim is owed to you on this form.

3. If the arrears you are claiming include interest, please note that FRO will only take enforcement action on interest that has accrued as a result of the Payor's failure to comply with the support order. Where funds are being remitted to FRO through income source deductions, the Payor has no control over the schedule of payments by the income source. Therefore, FRO will not enforce any interest owing for delays in the receipt of support payments. To claim interest, please see **Instructions for Completing Interest Calculations**.

4. Some support orders and agreements say that support payments must be changed on a regular basis to reflect changes in the cost of living over the previous year. These provisions are called Cost of Living Adjustment (COLA) clauses. A COLA clause provides for the increase or decrease in the amount of support payments. In order to be enforced by FRO, support orders that contain a COLA clause must follow either the standard formula set out in Section 34(5) of the *Ontario Family Law Act* or Ontario Regulation 176/98.

    Please note that FRO cannot enforce COLA for child support orders made in accordance with the Child Support Guidelines. COLA does not apply to child support orders made under the federal *Divorce Act* on or after May 1, 1997 or to child support orders made under the *Ontario Family Law Act* on or after December 1, 1997.

5. If the arrears you are claiming are not for regular on-going support, but are for expenses, please note:

    - Depending on the terms of your Order or Agreement, these types of expenses may or may not be enforceable by FRO.

    - If the Order/Agreement doesn't include a clear requirement to pay or reimburse these expenses, they are likely not enforceable. If the expenses are enforceable, FRO requires a sworn Statement of Arrears, including the receipts.

006 -FRO-007E (2012/09)

Ministry of Community and Social Services

Family Responsibility Office
PO Box 220
Downsview ON M3M 3A3

Statement of Arrears

Instructions for Completing Interest Calculations

Please note that the Family Responsibility Office (FRO) will only take enforcement action on interest that has accrued as a result of the Payor's failure to comply with the support order. Where funds are being remitted to FRO through income source deductions, the Payor has no control over the schedule of payments by the income source. Therefore, FRO will not enforce any interest owing for delays in the receipt of support payments.

When determining the amount of interest owed to you, you should know the following:

i.   If your Ontario support order is dated after June 21, 1979, the interest rate must be stated in the order. For Ontario orders made before June 22, 1979, the rate of interest is five per cent (5%) and does not have to be stated in the order.

ii.   Prior to January 1, 1985, the Provincial Court (Family Division) could not award interest.

iii.   Under the *Courts of Justice Act*, interest accruing on a debt is simple interest and not compound interest.

iv.   Where the court provides that support be paid on a periodic basis (e.g. $500.00 per month), each payment in default will bear interest from the date that the payment was due. Therefore, the interest owing for each missed support payment must be calculated separately.

v.   Interest can be calculated by using the following formula:

$$\frac{\text{Principal x Interest Rate x Number of Days the Payment is in Arrears}}{365 \text{ days}}$$

Where:

The principal is the outstanding individual support payment.

The Interest Rate, established by the *Courts of Justice Act* or its predecessor, is the rate that was in effect on the date that the court made the support order.

Example:

On January 27, 2011, the court made an order for support in the amount of $500.00 per month commencing February 1, 2011. The Payor has failed to make support payments for July 1, 2011 and September 1, 2011. The prescribed rate of interest for the first quarter of 2011 is three per cent (3%). As of October 1, 2011, the accrued interest is calculated as follows:

Interest on the July 1, 2011 payment is: $500 \times 3\% \times \frac{92}{365} = \$3.78$

Interest on the September 1, 2011 payment is: $500 \times 3\% \times \frac{30}{365} = \$1.23$

Total Interest = $\$3.78 + \$1.23 = \textbf{\$5.01}$

006 -FRO-007E (2012/09)

Ontario

Ministry of Community and Social Services

Family Responsibility Office
PO Box 220
Downsview ON M3M 3A3

Statement of Arrears

FRO Case Number

Support Recipient's Name

Last Name	First Name	Middle Initial

Support Payor's Name

Last Name	First Name	Middle Initial

1. I am the support recipient under the following:

Order

_____ _____ _____
Date of Order   Court   Court File Number

Agreement filed with the Court

_____ _____ _____
Date of Agreement   Court Agreement Filed With   Court File Number

2. The following amounts due under the order/agreement have not been paid. *(If you need more space, complete Schedule 'A')*

Check if applicable. ☐ See Schedule 'A' attached

Date Payment Due Day/Month/Year	Amount Due	Date Paid Day/Month/Year	Amount Paid	Arrears

If you are entitled to interest on your support, *you must calculate the interest amount.* **Attach a copy of your calculations.**

If you are entitled to a COLA adjustment to your support, *you must include the adjustment in the amount due.* **Attach a copy of your calculations.**

Total Arrears $ _____   (a)

Total Interest to date (if any) $ _____   (b) **Applicable interest rate used** _____ %

My arrears as at: _____ TOTAL $ _____ (c)
     Date   (Add A and B)

You must sign this form in the presence of a lawyer, Justice of the Peace, Notary Public or Commissioner for taking affidavits.

Sworn before me at the _____ of _____

in the _____ of _____

this _____ day of _____ , 20 _____

_____   _____
Signature of a commissioner, etc.   Signature of Support Recipient

006 -FRO-007E (2012/09)

736

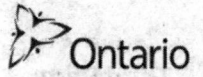

Ministry of Community and Social Services

Family Responsibility Office
PO Box 220
Downsview ON M3M 3A3

Schedule 'A'
To Statement of Arrears Form

FRO Case Number

Date Payment Due Day/Month/Year	Amount Due	Date Paid Day/Month/Year	Amount Paid	Arrears

Enter amount onto Statement of Arrears form.

006 -FRO-007E (2012/09)

Third Party Authorization

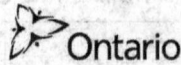

	Ministry of Community and Social Services	Family Responsibility Office PO Box 200 Stn A Oshawa ON L1H 0C5	**Third Party Authorization Form**

Please complete this form ONLY to designate a person other than yourself when it concerns: Providing information to the Family Responsibility Office (FRO) concerning your case and for receiving information from the FRO concerning your FRO case.

Name of FRO Client:	I am the: ☐ Person that pays support ☐ Person that receives support

Street Address:	Apt#:	City:

Province:	Postal Code:	Work Phone or Cell #	Country: (if outside Canada)

FRO Case Number:

My signature below indicates that I agree to the following:

1. I authorize the person named and listed below to act on my behalf regarding any inquiries relating to my case with the FRO.

2. This authorization allows the person named and listed below to provide any information to the FRO as it relates to my case.

3. This authorization allows the FRO and its agents to provide information to the person named and listed below as it relates to my case.

4. I understand that I must notify the FRO immediately, in writing, if I choose to no longer allow the person named and listed below to act as my Third Party. I realize I must complete the *Cancellation of Third Party Authorization Form* or provide FRO a signed letter to do so.

5. I understand there are legislative requirements I must comply with under the *Family Responsibility and Support Arrears Enforcement Act* which remain my responsibility as a support payor or support recipient (as the case may be).

I authorize the following person to act as my Third Party Person with FRO:	Authorized Third Party Person Date of Birth: (DD/MM/YYYY)

Authorized Third Party Street Address:	Apt#:	City:

Province:	Postal Code:	Country: (If outside of Canada)

Please sign and date below to complete the *Third Party Authorization Form* for the Family Responsibility Office

FRO Client Signature:	Date: (DD/MM/YYYY)

Return Completed Forms by Mail:	**Return Completed Forms by Fax:**
Family Responsibility Office PO Box 200 Stn A Oshawa ON L1H 0C5	(416)-240-2401

FRO – 014E (19/05/2004)   © Queen's Printer for Ontario, 2008

Clear Form	Print Form

Voluntary Arrears Payment Schedule Proposal

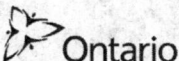

Ministry of Community and Social Services

Family Responsibility Office
PO Box 200, Station A
Oshawa ON L1H 0C5

**Voluntary Arrears Payment
Schedule (VAPS) Proposal**

FORMS

I would like to enter into a Voluntary Arrears Payment Schedule (VAPS) with the Family Responsibility Office (FRO)

FRO Case Number

Last name (as written in the support order)	First name (as written in the support order)	Middle Name(s)

My arrears balance is: $	As of this Date (yyyy/mm/dd)

Call FRO's automated line at 416-326-1818 or 1-800-267-7263 to get your current arrears balance.

Tip: You will need your seven-digit FRO Case Number and your six-digit PIN when you call.

I would like to propose the following payment plan to pay the arrears.

I propose to pay an extra: $ _____   In addition to my regular payment of: $ _____

☐ Daily	☐ Weekly	☐ Bi-Weekly	☐ Bi-Monthly	☐ Daily	☐ Weekly	☐ Bi-Weekly	☐ Bi-Monthly
☐ Monthly	☐ Quarterly	☐ Semi-Annually	☐ Annually	☐ Monthly	☐ Quarterly	☐ Semi-Annually	☐ Annually

If the current support obligation is to pay monthly, your proposal should be the same frequency.

Terms and Conditions

By signing this VAPS proposal, I understand and agree to the following:

- I will honour the payment terms of the VAPS. If I do not honour the VAPS, FRO may cancel it without notice to me and take the necessary steps to collect all arrears owing. I understand FRO may cancel or renegotiate the VAPS if:
  - FRO receives a new court order
  - the Support Recipient claims additional arrears not covered by the VAPS
  - my income increases significantly
- FRO has the authority to collect additional amounts towards the arrears, including my income tax refund, funds received from a Writ or Seizure and Sale or any other windfall (for example lottery winnings).
- If I have a Pre-Authorized Debit (PAD) payment method already in place, I agree it will be changed in accordance (to match) with this VAPS amount once accepted by FRO.

☐ I have attached my sworn financial statement and proof of income (see financial statement for requirements).

Suite/Unit/Apartment Number	Street Number	Street Name	
City		Province/State	Postal Code/Zip Code
Cellular Number (Including Area Code)	Home Number (Including Area Code)	Work Number (Including Area Code)	
Other Number (Including Area Code)		Email address	
Current Employer Name	Payroll Contact Name	Telephone number (Including Area Code)	
Signature of Support Payor		Date (yyyy/mm/dd)	

FRO-004E (2018/02)   © Queen's Printer for Ontario, 2018   Disponible en français   Print Form   Clear Form

Forms Regulated by the *Family Responsibility and Support Arrears Enforcement Act, 1996*

Form	Description	Page
Alternative Payment Order	An alternative payment order can be made, in limited circumstances, by a judge. The alternative payment order allows a support payor to pay by another method rather than by automatic income deductions under a support deduction order. If you are asking the court to make an alternative payment order, complete the appropriate sections of this form prior to your court date. If you or the support recipient has a lawyer, the lawyer will complete the rest of the form based on what the judge orders. If neither of you has a lawyer, provide the form to the court clerk and the court will complete the rest of the form based on what the judge orders.	743
Financial Statement	The financial statement must be completed by support payors in three situations: • when requested by the Family Responsibility Office in writing; • when asking the court for a refraining order (e.g., to prevent the Family Responsibility Office from suspending a driver's licence); and • when the Family Responsibility Office has served the support payor with a notice of default which requires the payor to appear in court to explain to a judge why support is not being paid. When this form is completed it should be provided to the Family Responsibility Office. If you are going to be in court, you must also file a copy of the completed financial statement with the court along with your other court documents.	746
Notice to Family Responsibility Office by Income Source	This notice is used by income sources (usually employers) to communicate with the Family Responsibility Office. This form can be used by an employer or other income source to let the Family Responsibility Office know that payments will be interrupted or stopped. This form can also be used to clarify that the income source or employer does not know the payor. If you are an employer or income source, complete the appropriate sections of this form and return it to the Family Responsibility Office.	754

Form	Description	Page
Refraining Order	This form must be used when a payor asks the court for a refraining order to prevent the Family Responsibility Office from suspending a driver's licence. If you are asking for a refraining order, complete the appropriate sections of this form prior to your court date, and provide it to the Family Responsibility Office lawyer. If you and the Family Responsibility Office lawyer can agree on what conditions should be set out in the refraining order, complete the form together and provide it to the court clerk for the judge's approval. If you and the Family Responsibility Office lawyer cannot agree, provide the form to the court clerk. The court will complete the rest of the information, based on what the judge orders. If you are asking for a refraining order, you should also complete a financial statement.	756
Support Deduction Order and Support Deduction Order Information Form	These two forms are used together each time a court makes a support order. The support deduction order allows the Family Responsibility Office to collect support by sending notice to a support payor's employer or other income source, requiring support to be deducted from the payor's income. If you are asking the court to make or change a support order, complete the appropriate sections of these forms prior to your court date, and provide them to the court clerk. The court will complete the rest of the information, based on what the judge orders.	760 762

Alternative Payment Order

ALTERNATIVE PAYMENT ORDER
ORDONNANCE DE PAIEMENT DE REMPLACEMENT

Family Responsibility and Support Arrears Enforcement Act, 1996
Loi de 1996 sur les obligations familiales et l'exécution des arriérés d'aliments

Form/Formule 3

Court File No. / *N° de dossier du tribunal*

_____
Name of Court / *Nom du tribunal*

_____
Location / *Lieu*

_____
Judge / *Juge*

_____
Date

Between / *Entre*

Applicant / Petitioner / Plaintiff
Requérant / Demandeur

and / *et*

Respondent / Defendant
Intimé / Défendeur

ALTERNATIVE PAYMENT ORDER / *ORDONNANCE DE PAIEMENT DE REMPLACEMENT*

COMPLETE 1 OR 2 / *REMPLIR LA PARTIE 1 OU 2*

1. THIS COURT ORDERS that the support deduction order dated *LE TRIBUNAL ORDONNE que l'ordonnance de retenue des aliments rendue le*

_____
(Date of Support Deduction Order)
(Date de l'ordonnance de retenue des aliments)

be suspended on the basis that it would be unconscionable, in all the circumstances, to require the payor,

soit suspendue du fait qu'il serait inadmissible, en tenant compte de toutes les circonstances, d'obliger le payeur

_____
(Name of Payor / *Nom du payeur*)

FRO-028 (June 15, 2005 /15 juin 2005)

to make support payments by
means of a support deduction
order.
*à verser des aliments au moyen
d'une ordonnance de retenue des
aliments.*

OR / *OU*

2.(a) <u>**To be completed only where the parties agree that they do not want support collected by means of a support deduction order**</u>
<u>Ne remplir que si les parties conviennent qu'elles ne veulent pas que les aliments soient perçus au moyen d'une ordonnance de retenue des aliments</u>

THIS COURT ORDERS THAT:
LE TRIBUNAL ORDONNE :

(i) the support deduction
order dated
*d'une part, que l'ordonnance
de retenue des aliments
rendue le*

be suspended on the
basis that the parties
agree that they
*soit suspendue du fait
que les parties
conviennent qu'elles*

_____
(Date of Support
Deduction Order)
*(Date de l'ordonnance
de retenue des aliments)*

do not want support payments collected by means of the support deduction order,
and
*ne veulent pas que les aliments soient perçus au moyen de l'ordonnance de retenue
des aliments,*

(ii) the payor
d'autre part, que le payeur

post with the Director of
the Family Responsibility
Office
*fournisse au directeur du
Bureau des obligations
familiales*

_____
(Name of Payor /
Nom du payeur)

security in an amount equal to the support payable for a four month period.
une sûreté d'un montant égal á la somme des aliments payables pour quatre mois.

2.(b) **THIS COURT ORDERS THAT** the security to be posted under subclause 2 (a) (ii) be paid to the Director of the Family Responsibility Office within 10 days following the date of this Order or by the next support payment due date, whichever occurs first.
LE TRIBUNAL ORDONNE QUE la sûreté exigée par l'alinéa 2 (a)(ii) soit fournie au directeur du Bureau des obligations familiales au plus tard 10 jours après la date de la présente ordonnance ou, s'il arrive en premier, au plus tard lejour où le prochain versement d'aliments est exigible.

FRO-028 (June 15, 2005 /15 juin 2005)

AND / *ET*

2.(c) **To be completed only where the court is ordering security to be posted above the prescribed amount**
Ne remplir que si le tribunal ordonne au payeur de fournir une sûreté en sus du montant prescrit

THIS COURT ORDERS THAT
LE TRIBUNAL ORDONNE QUE _____

(Name of Payor / *Nom du payeur*)

post additional security with the Director of the Family Responsibility Office in the amount of *fournisse au directeur du Bureau des obligations familiales une sûreté supplémentaire de* $ _____

to be paid to the Director of the Family Responsibility Office within 10 days following the date of this order or by the next support payment due date, whichever occurs first.
au plus tard 10 jours après la date de la présente ordonnance ou, s'il arrive en premier, au plus tard le jour où le prochain versement d'aliments est exigible.

3. The applicant (payor) shall make payments in accordance with the support order to the Director of the Family Responsibility Office.
Le requérant (payeur) fait les versements conformément à l'ordonnance alimentaire au directeur du Bureau des obligations familiales.

4. If the applicant (payor) fails to comply with the support order or this Alternative Payment Order, the Alternative Payment Order shall automatically terminate.
La présente ordonnance de paiement de remplacement prend fin automatiquement si le requérant (payeur) ne s'y conforme pas ou ne se conforme pas à l'ordonnance alimentaire.

_____

Signature of Judge, Registrar or Clerk of the Court / *Signature du juge ou du greffier du tribunal*

FRO-028 (June 15, 2005 /15 juin 2005)

Financial Statement

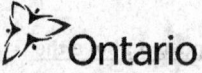 **Ontario**

FINANCIAL STATEMENT

Family Responsibility and Support Arrears Enforcement Act, 1996

Form 4

Case Number

You have 15 days to complete this form and return it to the Family Responsibility Office

I _____ , of _____

  Name of Payor   Address - Street and Number   Municipality

_____ solemnly declare that all details of my financial situation are
accurately set out below.

Province   Postal Code

Part I – Employment Information
Occupation: What type of work do you do? _____ Are you self-employed? ☐ Yes ☐ No If yes, financial statements for the past two years must be attached. Are you now employed ☐ Full-time ☐ Part-time ☐ Unemployed Current employer: *(if more than one employer, provide details of other employers on a separate sheet)*
Name
Address: Street Name and Number   Municipality   Province   Postal Code
How long have you worked for this employer?
When are you paid? *(check one)* ☐ once a month ☐ twice a month ☐ once every two weeks ☐ weekly ☐ other *(specify)* _____
If paid by commission, give details of the arrangement for payment that you have with your employer. Please tell us if you receive advances, how such advances are calculated, and if you are required to reimburse your employer should you fail to earn the commission or meet any production target.

FRO-010E (June 15, 2005)

If paid by commission, are the terms of the arrangement between you and your employer in writing?　☐ Yes　　☐ No	
If yes, attach a copy of the document. If no, when was the current arrangement reached? *(date)* _____	
When will you next discuss changing the commission arrangements with your employer? *(date)* _____	
Last employer: *(Complete only if not working now)*	
Name	
Address: Street Name and Number　　Municipality　Province　　Postal Code	
How long did you work for this employer? From_____　To_____	
Reason employment ended *(specify)*	

*IMPORTANT: PLEASE FILL IN EITHER THE WEEKLY OR MONTHLY INCOME COLUMN, **NOT BOTH.***

If you receive or pay some money once a month, but are using the column for weekly income, divide the monthly amount by 4.33 to get the amount per week. If you receive or pay some money every week, but are using the column for monthly income, multiply the weekly amount by 4.33 to get the amount per month.

Part 2 – Income Information					
Income - A			Income Deductions - B		
Source of Income	Weekly $	Monthly $	Type of Deduction	Weekly $	Monthly $
Pay, Wages, Salary (before deductions)			Income Tax		
Bonuses			Canada Pension Plan		
Public Assistance			Employment Insurance		
Employment Insurance			Pension Plan Contributions		
Workers' Compensation Payments			Union or other dues		
Pensions			Group Insurance		
Rent, board you collect from others			Credit Union Loan		
Dividends			Credit Union Savings		
Interest			Other *(specify, i.e. charity)*		
Commissions			Total Deductions $ (B)	$	$

FRO-010E (June 15, 2005)

Support from others				
Family Allowance				
Other *(specify)*				
Total Income $ (A)	$	$	**Take Home Income (A) – (B) = $** _____	

Part 3 – Expenses Information					
Expenses – C	**Weekly $**	**Monthly $**	**Expenses - D**	**Weekly $**	**Monthly $**
Groceries and Household Supplies			Public Transit, Taxis, etc.		
Meals outside home			Vehicle operation, gas and oil		
Clothing			Vehicle Insurance and Licence		
Laundry and Dry Cleaning			Maintenance		
Rent or Mortgage			Life Insurance		
Taxes			School Fees, Books, etc.		
Home Insurance			Music Lessons, Sports Fees, etc.		
Heating Fuel			Newspapers, Publications, Stationery		
Water			Entertainment, Recreation		
Hydro			Alcohol, Tobacco		
Telephone			Vacation		
Cable TV			Hairdresser, Barber		
Repairs and Maintenance			Toilet Articles (hairspray, soap, etc.)		
Other			Babysitting, Daycare		
Health and Medical Insurance			Children's Allowance, Gifts		
Drugs			Support Payments (actually being paid)		
Dental Care			Savings for future (exc. payroll ded.)		
Sub-total (C)	$	$	Other *(specify)*		
			Sub-total (D)	$	$
Total Expenses (Excluding Debt Payments) Add (C) + (D) = $ _____					

FRO-010E (June 15, 2005)

748

Part 4 – Debt Information

If you own a car, are there still payments owing? ☐ Yes ☐ No

If yes, name of lender

Address

Date of Purchase

Initial amount financed? $_____ Balance Owing $_____ Monthly payments $_____

Other Debts

If space not sufficient, use separate sheet

Type of Debt	Creditor (Name and Address)	Security	Full Amount Now Owing	Monthly Payments	Are Payments Currently Being Met
Bank or Trust Company Loans					☐ Yes ☐ No
					☐ Yes ☐ No
					☐ Yes ☐ No
					☐ Yes ☐ No
Finance Company Loan					☐ Yes ☐ No
					☐ Yes ☐ No
					☐ Yes ☐ No
					☐ Yes ☐ No
Credit Card Loans					☐ Yes ☐ No
					☐ Yes ☐ No
					☐ Yes ☐ No
					☐ Yes ☐ No

FRO-010E (June 15, 2005)

					☐ Yes ☐ No
					☐ Yes ☐ No
Other Debts					☐ Yes ☐ No
					☐ Yes ☐ No
					☐ Yes ☐ No
			TOTALS		

Part 5 – Assets Information		
Type	**Details – *(if space is not sufficient, use separate sheet)***	**Value or Amount**
	State Address of Property and Nature of Ownership	
Real Estate	1	•
	2	•
	3	•
	Year and Make	
Cars, Boats, Vehicles	1	•
	2	•
	3	•
	Address Where Located	
Household Goods and Furniture	1	•
	2	•
	3	•
	Description and Address Where Located	
Tools, Sports, Hobby Equipment	1	•
	2	•
	3	•
	Type – Issuer – Due Date – Number of Shares	
Bonds – Shares Term Deposits Investment Certificates	1	•
	2	•
	3	•
	Name and Address of Institution Account Number	
Bank Accounts	1	•
	2	•
	3	•

FRO-010E (June 15, 2005)

		Type and Issuer	Account Number	
Savings Plans R.R.S.P. Pension Plans	1			•
	2			•
	3			•
		Type – Beneficiary – Face Amount		Cash Surrender Value ↓
Life Insurance	1			•
	2			•
	3			•
		Name and Address of Business		
Interest in Business *Attach separate financial statement for each business*	1			•
	2			•
	3			•
		Name and Address of Debtors		
Money Owed to You	1			•
	2			•
	3			•
		Description and Address of Location		
Other Assets	1			•
	2			•
	3			•
		Total Estimated Value	$	•

FRO-010E (June 15, 2005)

751

Part 6 – Information

1. The expenses shown on Part 3 of this form are for:

☐ Me alone

☐ Me and the following other persons: *(Give name(s) and relationship(s))*

_____

_____

2. I understand that I am required to attach proof of my income to this form.
   (a) I attach to this statement proof of my current income, including my three most recent

   ☐ paycheque stubs   ☐ employment insurance benefits
   ☐ other *(specify)* _____

   ☐ workers' compensation payments   ☐ pension payments

   Note: If you do not receive pay stubs or payment statements from an income source, attach a letter from the income source stating the amount of money received for the three consecutive payments made to you immediately before the date of the financial statement; **AND**

   (b) ☐ I attach to this form a copy of my income tax returns that were filed with the Canada Revenue Agency for the past 3 taxation years, together with a copy of all material filed with the returns and a copy of any notices of assessment or re-assessment that I have received from the Agency for these years.

   ☐ I attach to this form a statement from the Canada Revenue Agency that I have not filed any income tax returns for the past 3 years.

   ☐ I am unable to attach my past 3 years' income tax returns and notices of assessment. I am attaching Canada Revenue Agency statements of my income and deductions for the past 3 years as proof of my income.

Sworn before me at the _____

_____in the _____

of _____ on _____ 20 ____

_____

A Commissioner, etc.

}

Signature
(This form is to be signed before a lawyer, justice of the peace, notary public or commissioner for taking affidavits.)

AFTER REVIEWING THIS STATEMENT, THE DIRECTOR MAY REQUIRE OTHER EVIDENCE VERIFYING YOUR INCOME.

THE LAW REQUIRES THAT YOU MUST COMPLETE AND DELIVER THE COMPLETED FINANCIAL STATEMENT TO THE FAMILY RESPONSIBILITY

FRO-010E (June 15, 2005)

OFFICE WITHIN 15 DAYS OF BEING SERVED WITH THE REQUEST TO COMPLETE IT.

IF, AFTER PROVIDING THE DIRECTOR WITH A COMPLETED FINANCIAL STATEMENT, YOU DISCOVER THAT SOME OF THE INFORMATION YOU PROVIDED WAS INCOMPLETE OR WRONG, THE LAW REQUIRES THAT YOU PROVIDE THE DIRECTOR WITH A CORRECT FINANCIAL STATEMENT WITHIN 10 DAYS OF THE DISCOVERY OF THE ERROR(S).

IF YOU FAIL TO COMPLY, YOU MAY BE ORDERED BY THE COURT TO COMPLY AND THE COURT MAY ORDER THAT **A WARRANT FOR YOUR ARREST** BE ISSUED.

IT IS AN OFFENCE TO KNOWINGLY FAIL TO COMPLY WITH THESE REQUIREMENTS. A PERSON CONVICTED OF AN OFFENCE IS LIABLE TO A FINE OF UP TO $10,000.

FRO-010E (June 15, 2005)

Notice to Family Responsibility Office by Income Source

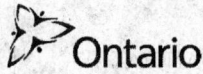

**NOTICE TO FAMILY RESPONSIBILITY OFFICE
BY INCOME SOURCE**

Family Responsibility and Support Arrears Enforcement Act, 1996
Form 5

Family Responsibility Office Case Number:_____

I,_____, have received a Support Deduction Notice dated_____, 20_____
(Name of income source)

regarding _____.
Name of Payor

DISPUTE BY INCOME SOURCE

I am not an income source of the payor named in the Support Deduction Notice for
the following reasons:

(check as many as apply)

- ☐   I do not owe any money or make any payments to the payor.
- ☐   The payor has never worked for me.
- ☐   Other *(specify)*

TERMINATION OR INTERRUPTION OF PAYMENTS

- ☐   The payor has worked for me, but stopped working for me on _____
  State reason why payor stopped working: Date

- ☐   Is termination permanent ☐ or a layoff   ☐ give date of recall, if
  known _____
- ☐   Other *(specify)*

RESUMPTION OF PAYMENTS

- ☐   Support deduction will resume as of_____
             State date of return to work

☐   I am not aware of any other employment held by the payor or any other
income source of the payor.

OR

☐   I am aware of other employment or income sources of the payor. If yes,
provide complete details:

_____

Name of Income Source: _____
           *Name of individual, corporation
or other organization*

FRO-018 (June 1, 2005)

Address (street & number)
Unit/Apt. No.

City   Province
                Postal Code

Name of Contact Person at Income Source:

Name

Position

Telephone Number

_____   _____
Date   Signature of Authorized Individual

If you receive a Support Deduction Notice in respect of a payor and you are not an income source for the payor, the law says that you must notify the Family Responsibility Office in writing of this fact. Anyone who fails to notify the Director can be found guilty of an offence and fined up to $10,000.

The law also says that, after receiving a Support Deduction Notice, an income source must make deductions and payments to the Family Responsibility Office. If the income source fails to make the deduction and payments without a proper reason, a court may order the income source to pay the amount that should have been deducted.

The law also says that you must write to the Family Responsibility Office if you were an income source but are no longer an income source for a payor or if you resume being an income source for a payor after deductions and payments are interrupted or terminated.

FRO-018 (June 1, 2005)

Refraining Order

REFRAINING ORDER
ORDONNANCE RESTRICTIVE
Family Responsibility and Support Arrears Enforcement Act, 1996
Loi de 1996 sur les obligations familiales et l'exécution des arriérés d'aliments
Form/Formule 6

Court File No. / *N°de dossier du tribunal*

Name of Court / *Nom du tribunal*

Location / *Lieu*

Judge / *Juge*

Date

Between / *Entre*

Applicant / Petitioner / Plaintiff
Requérant / Demandeur

and / *et*

Respondent / Defendant
Intimé / Défendeur

REFRAINING ORDER / *ORDONNANCE RESTRICTIVE*

1. **THIS COURT FINDS** that one of the following circumstances applies, as indicated:
    LE TRIBUNAL CONCLUT que l'une des circonstances suivantes s'applique, selon ce qui est indiqué :

    [ ] a motion by the applicant (payor) to change the support order has been made and not yet determined;*le requérant (payeur) a présenté une motion en modification de l'ordonnance alimentaire et il n'a pas encore été statué sur celle-ci;*

    [ ] the applicant (payor) has already started an appeal of the support order and the appeal has not yet been determined;
    le requérant (payeur) a interjeté appel de l'ordonnance alimentaire et il n'a pas encore été statué sur celui-ci;

    [ ] the applicant (payor) or his or her lawyer undertakes to obtain, within 20 days after the date of the refraining order, a court date for a motion to change the support order.
    le requérant (payeur) ou son avocat s'engage à obtenir, dans les 20 jours qui suivent la date de l'ordonnance restrictive, une date d'audience pour une motion en modification de l'ordonnance alimentaire.

2. **THIS COURT ORDERS THAT** the Director of the Family Responsibility Office refrain from directing the Registrar of Motor Vehicles to suspend the driver's licence of

FRO-020 (June 15, 2005 / 15 juin 2005)

LE TRIBUNAL ORDONNE QUE le directeur du Bureau des obligations familiales s'abstienne d'ordonner au registrateur des véhicules automobiles de suspendre le permis de conduire de

_____

(Name of Payor / *Nom du payeur*)

3. **THIS COURT ORDERS THAT** the applicant (payor) comply with the following term(s), as indicated:
LE TRIBUNAL ORDONNE QUE le requérant (payeur) se conforme aux conditions suivantes, selon ce qui est indiqué :

☐ Within 20 days after the date of this order, file with the court and the Director of the Family Responsibility Office the proof of income required by Ontario Regulation 167/97 (General), made under the *Family Responsibility and Support Arrears Enforcement Act, 1996.*

Dans les 20 jours qui suivent la date de la présente ordonnance, dépôt auprès du tribunal et du directeur du Bureau des obligations familiales les preuves relatives à son revenu qu'exige le Règlement de l'Ontario 167/97 (Dispositions générales), pris en application de la Loi de 1996 sur les obligations familiales et l'exécution des arriérés d'aliments.

☐ Pay ongoing support of
Versement des
obligations alimentaires   *(Time Period /*
courantes de $_____ per / *par* _____ *Période).*

☐ Pay on account of arrears
Versement, au titre des   *(Time Period /*
arriérés, de $_____ per / *par* _____ *Période).*

☐ Make lump sum
payment(s) of *Versement*
d'une/de somme(s)
forfaitaire(s) de $_____ by / *d'ici le* _____ *(Date).*

and / *et de* $_____ by / *d'ici le* _____ *(Date).*

4. **THIS ORDER TERMINATES** as follows:
LA PRÉSENTE ORDONNANCE PREND FIN comme suit :

i. it terminates automatically 20 days after the date it is made if the applicant (payor) or his or her lawyer undertook to obtain, within 20 days after the date this order is made, a court date for a motion to change the support order and failed to do so;

FRO-020 (June 15, 2005 / 15 juin 2005)

elle prend automatiquement fin 20 jours après avoir été rendue si le requérant (payeur) ou son avocat s'était engagé à obtenir, dans les 20 jours qui suivent la date de l'ordonnance, une date d'audience pour une motion en modification de l'ordonnance alimentaire et qu'il ne l'a pas obtenue;

ii.   if this order does not terminate under subparagraph i, it terminates on the earliest of the following:

si elle ne prend pas fin aux termes de la sous-disposition i, la présente ordonnance prend fin le premier en date des jours suivants :

(a) the day it is terminated under subsection 35 (9) of the Act,
le jour où elle est révoquée en vertu du paragraphe 35 (9) de la Loi,

(b) the day the motion to change the support order or the appeal of the support order is determined,
le jour où il est statué sur la motion en modification ou l'appel de l'ordonnance alimentaire,

(c) the day the support order is withdrawn from the Director's office,
le jour où l'ordonnance alimentaire est retirée du bureau du directeur,

(d) the day that is six months after the date of this order.
le jour qui tombe six mois après la date de la présente ordonnance

_____

Signature of Judge, Registrar or Clerk of the Court /
Signature du juge ou du greffier du tribunal

Notes: (see the Family Responsibility and Support Arrears Enforcement Act, 1996 for complete information)
Remarques : (consulter la Loi de 1996 sur les obligations familiales et l'exécution des arriérés d'aliments pour les renseignements complets)

1.   **The payment terms of this order do not change the payment terms of the support order. Arrears may continue to accrue under the support order and other enforcement actions may be taken by the Director unless the support order is changed.**

Les conditions de paiement de la présente ordonnance ne changent en rien celles de l'ordonnance alimentaire. L'arriéré peut continuer de s'accumuler aux termes de l'ordonnance alimentaire et le directeur peut prendre d'autres moyens d'exécution à moins que l'ordonnance alimentaire ne soit modifiée.

2.   **If you do not comply with the terms of this order, the Director of the Family Responsibility Office may issue a final notice to suspend your driver's licence.**

Si vous ne vous conformez pas aux conditions de la présente ordonnance, le directeur du Bureau des obligations familiales peut délivrer un dernier avis de suspension de votre permis de conduire.

FRO-020 (June 15, 2005 / 15 juin 2005)

3. This order may be extended, on motion to the court that made this order, for one further three or six month period, depending on the facts. A copy of the motion must be served on the Director. The motion to extend this order must be heard by the court before this order expires.

    La présente ordonnance peut être prorogée d'une période supplémentaire de trois mois ou de six mois, selon les circonstances, sur motion présentée devant le tribunal qui a rendu la présente ordonnance. Une copie de la motion doit être signifiée au directeur. La motion en prorogation doit être entendue par le tribunal avant que la présente ordonnance ne prenne fin.

FRO-020 (June 15, 2005 / 15 juin 2005)

Support Deduction Order and Support Deduction Order Information Form

SUPPORT DEDUCTION ORDER
ORDONNANCE DE RETENUE DES ALIMENTS
Family Responsibility and Support Arrears Enforcement Act, 1996
Loi de 1996 sur les obligations familiales et l'exécution des arriérés d'aliments
Form/Formule 1

Court File No. / *N°de dossier du tribunal*

_____
Name of Court / *Nom du tribunal*

_____
Location / *Lieu*

_____
Judge / *Juge*

_____
Date

Between / *Entre*

Applicant / Petitioner / Plaintiff
Requérant / Demandeur

and / *et*

Respondent / Defendant
Intimé / Défendeur

SUPPORT DEDUCTION ORDER / *ORDONNANCE DE RETENUE DES ALIMENTS*

Upon making an order this day which provides for the payment of support and on making the necessary inquiries required by section 11 of the *Family Responsibility and Support Arrears Enforcement Act, 1996:*

Après avoir rendu ce jour une ordonnance qui prévoit le versement d'aliments et après avoir fait les recherches nécessaires exigées par l'article 11 de la Loi de 1996 sur les obligations familiales et l'exécution des arriérés d'aliments :

1. **THIS COURT ORDERS THAT** *LE*
   TRIBUNAL ORDONNE QUE _____
   (Name of Payor / *Nom du payeur)*

   pay support as set out in the attached information form.
   verse des aliments comme le prévoit la formule de renseignements ci-jointe.

2. **THIS COURT ORDERS THAT** any income source that receives notice of this support deduction order make payments to the Director of the Family Responsibility Office in respect of the payor out of money owed to or paid by the income source to the payor.

FRO-019 (June 15, 2005 / 15 juin 2005)

LE TRIBUNAL ORDONNE *que toute source de revenu qui reçoit avis de la présente ordonnance fasse à l'égard du payeur des versements au directeur du Bureau des obligations familiales à même les sommes qu'elle doit au payeur ou qu'elle lui verse.*

_____
Signature of Judge, Registrar or Clerk of the Court /
Signature du juge ou du greffier du tribunal

FRO-019 (June 15, 2005 / 15 juin 2005)

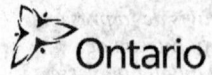 **Ontario**

SUPPORT DEDUCTION ORDER
INFORMATION FORM
Family Responsibility and Support Arrears Enforcement Act, 1996
Form 2

Name of Court _____

Court File No.

Location _____

NOTE: Please Print. Complete Parts A and B ONLY. Leave Parts C, D, E and F blank to be completed by court.

A. INFORMATION FOR THE FAMILY RESPONSIBILITY OFFICE

INFORMATION ON PARTIES   Family Responsibility Office Case Number *(if known)* _____

Payor

Payor Name	Birthdate (dd/mm/yyyy)	Sex ☐ M ☐ F
Street Number	Unit/Suite/Apt.	Street Name	
City/Town		Province	Postal Code
Social Insurance Number	Mother's Maiden Name	Language Preference
Home Telephone Number	Work/Business Telephone Number	Cell Phone Number

Recipient

Recipient Name	Birthdate (dd/mm/yyyy)	Sex ☐ M ☐ F
Street Number	Unit/Suite/Apt.	Street Name	
City/Town		Province	Postal Code
Social Insurance Number	Mother's Maiden Name	Language Preference
Home Telephone Number	Work/Business Telephone Number	Cell Phone Number

PAYOR'S EMPLOYMENT

Employer/Income Source Name

FRO-021E (June 15, 2005)

Payroll Office Address

Street Number	Unit/Suite/Apt.	Street Name		
City/Town			Province	Postal Code

☐ Self employed *(provide legal name of business and address)* _____
☐ Unemployed
☐ Receiving welfare, family benefits or other form of social assistance
☐ Receiving employment insurance benefits
☐ Other (i.e., workers' compensation, pension, etc.) _____
☐ Recipient does not know

SUPPORT ORDER INFORMATION

Is the support order a variation of a previous support order?   ☐ Yes   ☐ No
If "Yes", date of previous order ____

C, D, E and F to be COMPLETED BY COURTs

B. The attached support deduction order relates to a support order which says that: _____ is required to pay support Payor Name for the following persons:	**C. TYPE OF SUPPORT ORDER** ☐ Temporary ☐ Final

Name	Birthdate (dd/mm/yyyy)	Amount Payable	Frequency	Start Date (dd/mm/yyyy)	End Date (if any) (dd/mm/yyyy)
Spouse: a.		$			
Other Dependands b.		$			
c.		$			
d.		$			
e.		$			
f.		$			

D.   SPECIAL EXPENSES

FRO-021E (June 15, 2005)

Name of Child / Children	Birthdate (dd/mm/yyyy)	Amount	Frequency	Start Date (dd/mm/yyyy)	End Date (if any) (dd/mm/yyyy)
		$			
		$			
		$			
		$			
		$			

E. COST OF LIVING ADJUSTMENTS (DOES NOT APPLY TO CHILD SUPPORT)

Support is indexed in accordance with s. 34(5) of the *Family Law Act*   ☐ Yes ☐ No

If other indexing, explain method of calculation: _____

F. ARREARS – If the order is retroactive, if the order is a variation order or if the order provides for an arrears payment schedule,

are arrears owing as of the date of the order? ☐ No ☐ Yes. If "Yes", the amount of arrears = $ _____

and the arrears are to be paid as follows (if applicable) _____

PARTS A AND B COMPLETED BY: (please print)

Name	Title (If solicitor for a party, identify which party)	Telephone Number

FRO-021E (June 15, 2005)

Forms Required Under the *Interjurisdictional Support Orders Act, 2002*

Form Number	Form Title	Page
Form A	Support Application / Support Variation Application	766
Form B	Identification Information	770
Form C	Evidence of Parentage	772
Form D	Statements to Support a Declaration of Biological Parentage	773
Form E	Child Support Claim	776
Form F	Request for Support Order- If Respondent Does Not Provide Financial Information	777
Form G	Request for a Child Support Order – Different than Child Support Guidelines Table Amount	780
Form H	Special Expense Claim	783
Form I	Request to Pay Child Support – Different than Child Support Guidelines Table Amount	785
Form J	Support for Claimant / Applicant	788
Form K	Financial Statement	793
Form L	Child Status and Financial Statement	802
Form M	Evidence to Support Variation of a Support Order	806
Form N	Respondent's Answer to Application	809
Form O	Request for Enforcement	811

ISO FORMS

765

Form A

Support Application/Support Variation Application

A

Court File #: _____

Court Location: _____

REMO/RESO/ISO # _____

Office use only

This is a:

☐   **SUPPORT APPLICATION, or**

☐   **SUPPORT VARIATION APPLICATION.**

This application is made pursuant to the *Interjurisdictional Support Orders Act, 2002*
Statutes of Ontario 2002, Chapter 13.

Person applying for an order:

(Last Name)	(First Name)	(Middle Names)
(Street address and City/Town)		
(Province and Postal Code)		(daytime telephone)
(Mailing Address, if different than street address)		(fax number)
These are ☐ my own addresses, or ☐ c/o my lawyer, or ☐ c/o another person		

Person responding to this application (the respondent) is:

(Last Name)	(First Name)	(Middle Names)
(Street address and City/Town)		
(Province and Postal Code)		(daytime telephone)
(Mailing Address, if different than street address)		(fax number)
These are ☐ home addresses, or ☐ c/o a lawyer, or ☐ c/o another person		

*A government or government agency may wish to be informed of and/or participate in this
application (if its laws allow) because:* ☐ *I am receiving social assistance, or* ☐ *The
respondent is/may be receiving social assistance now, or has in the past*

I ask the Court to include in its order:

For SUPPORT

☐ A determination that the respondent

I ask the Court to include in its order:

For SUPPORT VARIATION

☐ A change or variation in the
amount of support in the current

Form A – March 31, 2003

is the parent of the child(ren) named in this application.

☐ Child support. If the respondent does not file sufficient financial information, or respond, a child support order for a total of $ _____ per month, starting as of _____

☐ That the respondent obtain and maintain medical and/or dental insurance coverage for the child(ren) and/or myself

☐ Support for myself of $ _____ per month, starting as of _____

☐ Other (specify):

order or agreement, from $ _____ per month, to $ _____

☐ A change in the amount of unpaid support arrears owing under the current support order(s) or agreement(s), and that the arrears be 'fixed' or set at $ _____ as of _____

☐ The termination of the obligation to (name) _____, as of _____

☐ Other (specify):

Legal Authority on which my application is based: (check one)

☐ A copy of the statute or legal authority is attached. I ask the Court to take notice of it when making its order.

☐ I rely on the law of the jurisdiction hearing this case.

Case History: Previous Court Orders or Agreements (check all that apply):

☐ There are no court orders or agreements involving the respondent, the child(ren) and me.

☐ There are court order(s) involving the respondent, the child(ren) and me. A copy of each court order is attached.

☐ There is a written agreement involving the respondent, the child(ren) and me. A copy of the agreement, and any changes to it, is attached.

☐ There is no Divorce action in progress.

☐ There is a Divorce action in progress. It does not include a claim for support.

☐ A Divorce order has been made; it does not deal with support. A copy is attached.

Family History (check all that apply):

☐ The respondent and I never lived together

☐ The respondent and I have a child or children together

☐ The respondent and I started living _____

☐ The respondent and I were married on _____

☐ The respondent and I entered into a formal, legally-recognized, relationship by registering our civil union or domestic partnership on _____

Form A – March 31, 2003

☐   The respondent and I separated on   _____

☐   The respondent and I were divorced by an order dated _____

The following documents are attached to and form part of the evidence in this application:

(check all that apply)

For Support and Support Variation applications		Office use only
☐ Identification Information (required)	Form B	
☐ Evidence of Parentage	Form C	
☐ Statements to Support a Declaration of Biological Parentage (disputed)	Form D	
☐ Child Support Claim	Form E	
☐ Request for a Support Order (if no financial information)	Form F	
☐ Request for a Child Support Order (different than child support guidelines)	Form G	
☐ Special Expense Claim	Form H	
☐ Request to Pay Child Support (different than child support guidelines)	Form I	
☐ Support for Claimant / Applicant	Form J	
☐ Financial Statement	Form K	
☐ Child Status and Financial Statement	Form L	
☐ Evidence to Support Variation of a Support Order	Form M	
Other Documents attached		
☐ Legal or Statutory Authority for application		
☐ All Support Orders or Written Agreements between the parties, or relating to any child for whom support is claimed		
☐ Documents required by the jurisdiction hearing this application		
☐ Other (list)		
☐		
☐		

Form A – March 31, 2003

☐		
☐		
☐		
☐		
☐		
☐		
☐		
☐		
☐		

I,_____ make oath or affirm and say that the information and facts contained in this application, including the attached forms, are true. I am making this application in good faith.

SWORN OR AFFIRMED BEFORE ME

At the _____ of_____

In the Province/Territory of _____   _____

On _____, 20___.   Claimant's/Applicant's signature
A Commissioner, etc.
Or a Notary Public

Form A – March 31, 2003

Form B

Identification Information

IDENTIFICATION INFORMATION

1. **INFORMATION ABOUT ME**

LAST NAME FIRST MIDDLE	SOCIAL INSURANCE #	SEX	DATE OF BIRTH
		☐ M ☐ F	D | M | Y

2. **CHILD(REN)** (if there are more than four children, attach additional page)

LAST NAME FIRST MIDDLE	Province/Territory /State of residence (last 6 mos)	Sex of child	DATE OF BIRTH DAY/ MONTH/ YEAR
1.		☐ M ☐ F	
2.		☐ M ☐ F	
3.		☐ M ☐ F	
4.		☐ M ☐ F	

3. **INFORMATION ABOUT THE RESPONDENT** (the other person)

LAST NAME FIRST MIDDLE	SOCIAL INSURANCE #	SEX	DATE OF BIRTH
		☐ M ☐ F	D | M | Y

ALIASES / OTHER NAMES USED	HEALTHCARE NUMBER	PERSON RESPONDENT LIVING WITH (spouse, common-law, or other partner)
OTHER IDENTIFICATION NUMBERS		RESPONDENT'S MOTHER'S MAIDEN (BIRTH) NAME
CURRENT, OR LAST KNOWN ADDRESS (STREET & NUMBER) CITY		THE RESPONDENT'S ADDRESS IS: ☐ CURRENT, or ☐ AS OF (date):
PROVINCE / TERRITORY / STATE COUNTRY POSTAL / ZIP CODE		AREA CODE & PHONE – HOME
☐ CURRENT OR ☐ LAST KNOWN EMPLOYER	USUAL OCCUPATION (INCLUDE UNION & LOCAL, TRADE OR PROFESSIONAL MEMBERSHIP)	
WORK ADDRESS (STREET & NUMBER) CITY		AREA CODE & PHONE – WORK
PROVINCE/TERRITORY/STATE COUNTRY POSTAL/ZIP CODE		AREA CODE & FAX – WORK

Form B – March 31, 2003

4. DESCRIPTION OF RESPONDENT

HEIGHT	WEIGHT	EYE COLOUR	HAIR COLOUR	COMPLEXION	WEARS GLASSES? ☐ Y ☐ No CONTACTS? ☐ Y ☐ N	PLACE OF BIRTH

VISIBLE DISTINGUISHING MARKS OR FEATURES (TATTOOS, BEAUTY MARKS, SCARS, ETC.)

FRIENDS AND/OR RELATIVES WHO KNOW WHERE TO CONTACT THE RESPONDENT

NAME	RELATION	ADDRESS	CITY	PROV/TERR/ STATE	POSTAL/ ZIP CODE	TELEPHONE
1.						
2.						
3.						

PHOTOGRAPH OF RESPONDENT IS ☐ NOT ATTACHED OR ☐ ATTACHED.

YEAR PHOTO TAKEN: _____

I have a Family Responsibility Office case number _____ . Other province/territory/state file number _____ .

This document is attached to, and forms part of the evidence in, my support application/support variation application/answer:

_____

Signature

Form B – March 31, 2003

Form C

Evidence of Parentage

EVIDENCE OF PARENTAGE

☐   I am entitled to claim support for the child named below.

☐   I ask the Court to declare that the respondent is a parent of the child:

Full name of child (Last, First, Middle)	Child's Date of Birth (day, month, year)

I claim that the respondent is a parent of the child because (*check all that apply*):

☐   The claimant and respondent were married to each other, or in a registered civil union, at the time of the child's birth

☐   The marriage of the claimant and respondent ended by a Court judgment or a divorce order within 300 days before the birth of the child

☐   The claimant and respondent married each other after the child was born, and the respondent said he is the father

☐   The respondent has said, in writing, that he is the father of the child (copy attached)

☐   The respondent is registered as the father of the child on the birth registration or Vital Statistics records (copy attached)

☐   The claimant and respondent lived together as a couple when the child was born, or the child was born within 300 days of the end of the relationship. The claimant and respondent had lived together for approximately
_____ (years, months)

☐   The claimant did not have sexual intercourse with any other man during the time 30 days before to 30 days after the date the child was conceived

☐   A genetic test was done to establish parentage. It shows the respondent is a parent of the child (copy attached)

☐   The respondent is not a biological parent of the child, but has acted as a parent to the child

☐   I believe the respondent will agree with a finding of parentage, or

☐   I believe the respondent may dispute parentage of the child. I attach Form D and / or additional documents to support my claim that the respondent is (or acted as) a parent of the child.

This document is attached to, and forms part of the evidence in, my support application/support variation application/answer:

_____
Signature

Form C – March 31, 2003

Form D

Statements to Support a Declaration of Biological Parentage

STATEMENTS TO SUPPORT A DECLARATION OF BIOLOGICAL PARENTAGE

☐ I am the mother of the child named below:

Child's Full Name (Last, First, Middle)	Date of Birth (day, month, year)	Place of Birth (City, Prov/Terr, Country)

1. I claim that the respondent is the father of the child, because:

I had sexual intercourse with the respondent: (City, Prov/Terr, Country)	(day, month, year OR from [date] to [date])	Full Term Pregnancy? ☐ Yes, or ☐ No (explain)

2. Other facts about my claim that the respondent is the father of the child *(check all that apply)*:

a	We lived together	☐ Yes ☐ No	Dates from to
b	I told social assistance officials that he is the father	☐ Yes ☐ No	
c	I told him that he was the father of the child	☐ Yes ☐ No	
d	He is named as the father on the birth registration	☐ Yes ☐ No	☐ certified copy attached
e	He admitted being the father of the child	☐ Yes ☐ No	
f	He signed an acknowledgement of paternity	☐ Yes ☐ No	☐ certified copy attached
g	He sent cards/letters/e-mails regarding the pregnancy and/or birth of the child	☐ Yes ☐ No	☐ copies attached
h	He was present when the child was born	☐ Yes ☐ No	
i	He visited the child at the hospital following birth	☐ Yes ☐ No	
j	He offered to pay for an abortion/medical expenses	☐ Yes ☐ No	
k	He paid for birth-related expenses	☐ Yes ☐ No	
l	He claimed the child on tax returns	☐ Yes ☐ No	☐ Don't know
m	He has provided food, clothes, gifts, or financial support for the child	☐ Yes ☐ No	If Yes, explain in #3
n	He lived with the child	☐ Yes ☐ No	If Yes, explain in #3

Form D – March 31, 2003

o	He visited the child	☐ Yes	☐ No	If Yes, explain in #3
p	The child looks like him ☐ Photo attached	☐ Yes	☐ No	If Yes, explain in #3
q	There are witnesses to my relationship with him. (If Yes, list names, addresses, and facts known by each person in #3)	☐ Yes	☐ No	If Yes, explain in #3

3. Other information in support of a declaration of parentage. Explanations for the 'yes' answers in question #2 are given below. ☐ Continued on attached sheets(s)

4. I agree to cooperate with a request for genetic testing of myself to confirm parentage. I agree to make the child, if in my custody, available for genetic testing.

5. I had sexual intercourse with a man other than the respondent during the time 30 days before to 30 days after the date the child was conceived
   ☐ No
   ☐ Yes (if yes, complete the following)

   a. The name(s) of the other man/men:

   b. The other man/men is/are blood relatives of the respondent (e.g. brother, cousin, uncle, etc.)
      ☐ No ☐ Yes (if yes, list relationship)

   c. I do not believe the other man / men could be the father because:

6. I was married to a man other than the respondent at the time of the child's birth
   ☐ No ☐ Yes (if yes, complete the following)

   a. Husband's name (first, middle, last) and last known address):

   b. I do not believe that the man I was married to is the father of the child because: (list reasons, and attach all supporting documents, including divorce order, blood test results, finding of non-paternity, if any)

Form D – March 31, 2003

_____
Signature

Form D – March 31, 2003

Form E

Child Support Claim

CHILD SUPPORT CLAIM

☐   I ask for child support for the following children:

Full name of child (Last, First, Middle)	Child's date of birth (day, month, year)

☐   I ask that the amount of child support be set using the child support guidelines or law of the jurisdiction where the respondent lives.

If the respondent lives in Canada:

    ☐   I ask for only the child support guidelines table amount for one or more children.

    ☐   I ask for child support in an amount different than the table amount. The form 'Request for a Child Support Order Different than Child Support Guidelines Table Amount' (Form G) is attached.

    ☐   I ask for additional child support, over the table or other amount. A 'Special Expense Claim' (Form H) is attached.
        I ask for additional child support of $ _____

☐   I ask for an order that the respondent obtain or maintain medical or dental insurance coverage for the child(ren).

This document is attached to, and forms part of the evidence in, my support application/support variation application/answer:

_____
Signature

Form E – March 31, 2003

Form F

Request for Support Order - If Respondent Does Not Provide Financial Information

REQUEST FOR SUPPORT ORDER
- IF RESPONDENT DOES NOT PROVIDE FINANCIAL INFORMATION -

☐   If the respondent does not provide sufficient, or any, financial information, I ask the Court to impute the respondent's income at $_____ per year. My evidence for this claim is in this form.

Based on the respondent's imputed income, I ask for an order for *(check all that apply)*:

☐ $ _____ per month for support for myself. My financial statement is attached.

☐   Child support of $_____ per month, or the amount payable under the child support guidelines table used by the Court.

☐   The respondent's share of special and/or extraordinary expenses. I have attached a Special Expense Claim form. A summary of my claim is:

Name of child	Type of special expense	Total $ paid for expense (after any subsidy deducted)	$ claimed for respondent's share of expense
		$_____ ☐ month or ☐ year	$_____ ☐ month or ☐ year
		$_____ ☐ month or ☐ year	$_____ ☐ month or ☐ year
		$_____ ☐ month or ☐ year	$_____ ☐ month or ☐ year
		$_____ ☐ month or ☐ year	$_____ ☐ month or ☐ year
		$_____ ☐ month or ☐ year	$_____ ☐ month or ☐ year

INFORMATION ABOUT THE RESPONDENT'S SOURCES OF INCOME:

1.   I believe the respondent has an annual income of about $_____

Form F – March 31, 2003

2.   The respondent's last known source of income is:

    ☐   Employment (include occupation, name and address of employer, other information)

    ☐   Self-employment (type of work, business address, any other information known)

    ☐   Employment Insurance (list dates on EI)

    ☐   Social Assistance (list dates known)

    ☐   Disability Insurance (list dates, reason, any other information known)

    ☐   Other (list dates, and details)

For boxes checked above, details of source(s) of income:

---

1.   The most recent information I have about the respondent's sources of income is attached. The information includes:

    ☐   Pay statements

    ☐   Income Tax Returns and/or Notices of Assessment

    ☐   Other (specify) _____

(Complete EITHER question 4 or 5, if applicable)

1.   I have no information or documents about the respondent's current income, but,

    ☐   In the past the respondent has worked: (list below)
        Type of work or occupation   *Dates of work*

    ☐   I have obtained statistical information from *(source)* _____ .
        It shows that a person employed as a *(work /*
        occupation respondent may have) _____
                    in your Court's jurisdiction may have an ___
                    _____ annual income of $_____

Form F – March 31, 2003

☐   I believe the respondent does/may own property or other assets that could produce some, or more, income. The property or asset is:

☐   Attached is a print-out from the website of Human Resources Development of an Occupational Profile – Labour Market Summary. I believe the print-out may assist the Court in imputing income to the respondent if sufficient financial information is not provided to the Court by the respondent.

☐   Attached are other documents that may assist the Court in imputing income to the respondent if sufficient financial information is not provided to the Court by the respondent. These documents include

I have no information about the respondent's sources of income, or past or present work or occupations, but,

☐   Attached is statistical information from *(source)* _____ . This information shows that the average annual income in your Court's jurisdiction is $ _____ .

☐   Attached is a print-out from the website of Statistics Canada. It shows the average family incomes in your Court's jurisdiction. I believe the attached print-out may assist the Court in imputing income to the respondent if sufficient financial information is not provided to the Court by the respondent.

☐   Attached are other documents that may assist the Court in imputing income to the respondent if sufficient financial information is not provided to the Court by the respondent. These documents include:

This document is attached to, and forms part of the evidence in, my support application/support variation application/answer:

_____
                                     Signature

Form F – March 31, 2003

Form G

Request for a Child Support Order – Different than Child Support Guidelines Table Amount

REQUEST FOR A CHILD SUPPORT ORDER
- DIFFERENT THAN CHILD SUPPORT GUIDELINES TABLE AMOUNT -

☐   I ask the Court for an order in an amount different than that in the child support guidelines table. My claim is based on the facts marked below. Documents to support each claim are attached.

1.   ☐   **CHILD OVER THE AGE OF MAJORITY:**

I ask for support for each child who is the age of majority or older. A Child Status and Financial Statement form is attached for each child. The amount requested for each child is:

NAME OF CHILD	DATE OF BIRTH (d/m/y)	AMOUNT FOR THIS CHILD

2.   ☐   **SPLIT CUSTODY**

There are 2 or more children, and at least one child lives with each of us. The custody arrangements are in the attached custody order, or are as follows:

I ask for child support of $ _____ per month for the support of the child(ren) living with me. My claim is based on the following calculations:

	Total income (known/ imputed in Form F)	Guideline Table for Prov/Terr of residence	Number of children	Amount Payable	Name(s) of Children
Respondent				$	
Claimant				$	
Subtract amount payable by claimant from amount payable by respondent to calculate amount claimed.				=$ 0.00	

Form G – March 31, 2003

3. ☐ **SHARED CUSTODY**

The child or children live with each of us at least 40% of the time during the year. Our custody arrangements are in the attached custody order, or are as follows:

I ask for child support of $ _____ per month for the following child(ren):

NAME OF CHILD	1.	2.	3.

4. ☐ **UNDUE HARDSHIP CLAIM:**

I ask the Court to determine that, if the child support guidelines table amount is ordered, I would have a lower household standard of living than the other parent. Part 5 of my Financial Statement (Form K) lists the income of the other people in my household.

I ask for support of $ _____ per month. I have attached documents to support each claim. The child support guidelines table amount would cause me or the child(ren) undue hardship because:

☐ I have large debts. The debts came from supporting our family before the other parent and I separated, or due to expenses for me to earn a living.

☐ My expenses for arranging the child(ren)'s visits to the other parent are high.

☐ I have a legal duty to support a child(ren) other than the child(ren) named in this application. The (or each) child is under the age of majority is not able to be self-supporting. Ages of child(ren) _____

☐ I have a legal duty to support another child and/or adult person. This duty is in a judgment, order, or written agreement. A copy is attached.

☐ I have a legal duty to support a person who is not able to be self-supporting.

Details of other reasons:

5. ☐ **I BELIEVE THE RESPONDENT'S INCOME IS OVER $150,000 PER YEAR:**

Form G – March 31, 2003

I ask for child support of $ _____ per month. I believe the respondent's income is over $150,000 per year. I have attached documents to support this belief.

This document is attached to, and forms part of the evidence in, my support application/support variation application/answer:

_____

_____

Signature

Form H

Special Expense Claim

SPECIAL EXPENSE CLAIM

☐   I ask the Court to make an order for additional child support. The additional amount is for the respondent's share of the following special expenses. I attach as evidence documents to show why these expenses are necessary.

My special expenses are for:

☐   1.   Childcare

☐   2.   Health-related expenses over $100.00 per year

☐   3.   Child's portion of medical and/or dental insurance premiums

☐   4.   Extraordinary expenses for education (grade school and high school)

☐   5.   Post-secondary education expenses (college or university)

☐   6.   Extraordinary expenses for extracurricular activities.

	Expense Type (1 to 6)	Brief description of expense	For (Name of Child)	Actual (or estimated) amount spent per Month or per Year (M/Y)	Net amount spent per YEAR (after any subsidy, benefit, tax deduction, or credit)
a					
b					
c					
d					
e					
f					
g					
h					
i					
j					
k					
l					
m					

Form H – March 31, 2003

n				
o				
p				
q				
r				
s				
t				
			Total of net amount spent (or estimated) per YEAR	$ 0.00

This document is attached to, and forms part of the evidence in, my support application/support variation application/answer:

_____

Signature

Form I

Request to Pay Child Support – Different than Child Support Guidelines Table Amount

I

REQUEST TO PAY CHILD SUPPORT
- DIFFERENT THAN CHILD SUPPORT GUIDELINES TABLE AMOUNT -

☐   I ask the Court for an order in an amount different than that in the child support guidelines table. My claim is based on the facts marked below. Documents to support each claim are attached.

1.   ☐   **UNDUE HARDSHIP CLAIM:**

I ask the Court to determine that, if the child support guidelines table amount is ordered, I would have a lower household standard of living than the other parent. Part 5 of my Financial Statement (Form K) lists the income of the other people in my household.

I ask to pay support of $ _____ per month. I have attached documents to support each claim. The child support guidelines table amount would cause me or the child(ren) undue hardship because:

     ☐   I have large debts. The debts came from supporting our family before the other parent and I separated, or due to expenses for me to earn a living.

     ☐   My expenses for arranging to visit the child(ren) are high.

     ☐   I have a legal duty to support a child(ren) other than the child(ren) named in this application. The (or each) child is under the age of majority or, if over the age of majority, is not able to be self-supporting. Ages of child(ren)._____.

     ☐   I have a legal duty to support another child and/or adult person. This duty is in a judgment, order, or written agreement. A copy is attached.

     ☐   I have a legal duty to support a person who is not able to be self-supporting.

     ☐   Details of other reasons:

2.   ☐   **CHILD OVER THE AGE OF MAJORITY:**

I ask to pay support of each child listed below who is the age of majority or older. The names of the child(ren) and date(s) of birth are:

Form I – March 31, 2003

NAME OF CHILD	DATE OF BIRTH (d/m/y)	AMOUNT FOR THIS CHILD

I ask the Court to take into account the attached document(s) and my reasons, which are:

☐ documents attached

3.   **SPLIT CUSTODY**

There are 2 or more children, and at least one child lives with each of us. The custody arrangements are in the attached custody order, or are as follows:

I ask to pay child support of $ _____ per month for the support of the child(ren) living with the respondent. My claim is based on the following calculations:

	Total income (known/ imputed in Form F)	Guideline Table for Prov/Terr of residence	Number of children	Amount Payable	Name(s) of Children
Respondent				$	
Claimant				$	
Subtract amount payable by claimant from amount payable by respondent to calculate amount claimed.				=$ 0.00	

Form I – March 31, 2003

786

4. ☐ **SHARED CUSTODY**

> The child or children live with each of us at least 40% of the time during the year. Our custody arrangements are in the attached custody order, or are as follows:

> I ask to pay child support of $ _____ per month for the following child(ren:

NAME OF CHILD	1.	2.	3.

This document is attached to, and forms part of the evidence in, my support application/support variation application/answer:

_____
Signature

Form I – March 31, 2003

Form J

Support for Claimant/Applicant

SUPPORT FOR CLAIMANT / APPLICANT

☐   I am the claimant / applicant and ask for support for myself. I ask the Court to order support of $ _____ per month. A Financial Statement (Form K) is included in my Application. My claim is based on the following facts:

FACTS ABOUT MY CLAIM:

1.	My date of birth is:	
2.	The children living with me are aged: *(if there is a child support order/agreement about any child, attach it)*	
3.	The respondent and I cohabited (lived together) in a marriage, marriage-like, common-law, civil union, or other domestic partnership: *(write details here)*	Start date: End date:
	The last place where we lived as a couple before separation is:	(city/country):
4.	During the time we were together, we separated for a total of *(years, months)* because:	Total time separated:
5.	The respondent and I lived together for a total of *(years, months)*:	
6.	My present status *(separated, divorced, married, common-law, single, other)*:	
MY EDUCATION:		
7.	The last grade I finished in school (before post-secondary school):	
8.	Year I completed this grade:	
9.	College / University level or year completed:	
10.	Year I completed this level:	
11.	Other training / certificate / diploma received:	
12.	Length of the training / certificate / diploma course (years, months)	
13.	Year I completed this course:	
MY WORK EXPERIENCE:		
14.	I did not work for pay while the respondent and I were together *(if this statement applies, put an X in box, and go to line 21)*	

Form J – March 31, 2003

15.	During the time the respondent and I were together, I worked for pay for a total of *(years, months)* *(attach work history list, with dates, employment, monthly pay)*	☐ work history list attached
16.	I worked for (%) of the time the respondent and I were together [example: if the entry on line 5 is 7 years + 2 months that equals (7x12)=84+2= 86 months. If the entry on line 15 is 3 years + 6 months that equals (3x12)+6=42 months. Then 42 /86 = 48.8%]	%
17.	The work I did was *(full time, or part time, or both)*	
18.	My normal employment was as: *(occupation)*	
19.	I also worked as *(other occupations)*	
20.	If part time, I worked an average of *(fraction)* of full time *[½, ¾, etc]*	
21.	I worked less than full time, or did not work for pay, because *(check any that apply)* ☐ I cared for the child(ren) when young *(dates)* ☐ I had a child at home with special needs *(dates)*	From: _____ To: _____ From: _____ To: _____
22.	☐ I needed to be home when the child(ren) returned from school ☐ We moved often *(how many times during relationship: _____)* ☐ I did not have the education/experience to get full time work ☐ There were no full time jobs available ☐ I did not want to work full time ☐ I was not able to work full time (due to medical condition) ☐ The respondent and I agreed that I would not work full time ☐ The respondent and I agreed that I would work only part time ☐ The respondent and I agreed that I would not work at all ☐ The respondent did not want me to work full time ☐ The respondent wanted me to work only part time ☐ The respondent did not want me to work at all ☐ Other reason(s):	

Form J – March 31, 2003

23.	Since the respondent and I separated, I have *(check any that apply)* ☐ Worked full time ☐ Worked part time ☐ Received social assistance ☐ Received income/benefits from employment insurance, disability, workers' compensation, investments (details) ☐ Received government grants or benefits (details) ☐ Other sources of income (details)	(dates and details)
24.	Since the respondent and I separated, I have not worked for pay at all because: *(reasons)*	
25.	Since the respondent and I separated, I have taken the following steps to improve my ability to support myself: *(courses, job training, education, re-location, etc.)*	

MEDICAL:

26.	I am not able to fully support myself because of a medical condition, disability, or special need which keeps me from working *(put short description in the box, and attach documents or doctor's letter giving details)*	☐ documents attached
27.	I am not able to fully support myself because a child or other person has a medical condition, disability, or special need which keeps me from working *(put name of person, relationship, and short description in the box, and attach documents or doctor's letter giving details)*	Name of person: Relationship to me: Condition / Special Need: ☐ documents attached

THE PRESENT, AND THE FUTURE:

28.	As of the date of this application, I am ☐ Not working ☐ Working full time *(occupation, monthly income)* ☐ Working part time *(occupation, monthly income)* ☐ Looking for work *(attach job search list)* ☐ Receiving social assistance *(monthly income)* ☐ Going to school *(type of course, how long, where)*	
29.	The respondent is paying support for me *($ monthly)*	
30.	The respondent agreed to pay support for me of *($ monthly, or other amount)* and has not paid the whole amount. There is now unpaid support of $ _____ owing	☐ agreement attached

Form J – March 31, 2003

31.	My other sources of income are (monthly) *(check any that apply and put amount in box at right)*	
	☐ rental of space / apartment in my home	
	☐ investment income *(savings, GICs, bonds, property)*	
	☐ support from a present spouse, or other former spouse *(attach order or agreement)*	
	☐ other *(details)*	
32.	Compared to the time the respondent and I were together, my standard of living is now	
	☐ much worse *(Details of the differences)*	
	☐ worse	
	☐ the same	
	☐ better	
	☐ much better	
33.	If the Court orders support for me, I plan to make myself self-supporting by:	
	☐ going to school to complete high school	
	☐ going to school to obtain a certificate / diploma / degree	
	☐ obtaining job / vocational training to get a job	
	I expect that when my plan is completed my standard of living will be *(pick one)*	
	☐ worse ☐ better ☐ the same, as when the respondent and I were together	
	☐ OR, I will not be able to become self-supporting because	
	Other	

Form J – March 31, 2003

34.	Details of my plan include: *(list name of course, where offered, length of time it takes, whether full of part time, costs, and results to be achieved. If the training/course has a brochure or curriculum, attach it.)*

[Mark each attached document with the line number to which the document relates]

☐   I have attached additional page(s) with more details about my claim, education, work experience, relationship with the respondent, medical information, present condition, and future plans, if applicable.

This document is attached to, and forms part of the evidence in, my support application/support variation application/answer:

_____

Signature

Form K

Financial Statement

FINANCIAL STATEMENT of _____
(name of person completing form)

I am the ☐ claimant/applicant or

☐ respondent in this application to make or vary a support order. My financial circumstances are:

1. My total annual income (before tax and other deductions) for this year will be approximately $_____

2. My source of income is: *(check any that apply, and write details in box below)*

    ☐   Employment *(occupation, name and address of employer, length of employment)*

    ☐   Self-employment *(occupation, name and address of business, length of employment)*

    ☐   Employment Insurance *(last date worked, and date benefits started)*

    ☐   Social Assistance *(date benefits started)*

    ☐   Disability insurance *(date benefits started, source of payment, reason for disability)*

    ☐   Other *(specify)*

Details of income sources checked above:

3. ☐ All or part of my income is not subject to income tax *(portion exempt, and reason)*

PART 1 - SOURCES OF INCOME

Line #		Amount
1.	Employment income (wages, salary, commissions, overtime, bonuses)	
2.	Other employment income (including tips and gratuities)	
3.	Old age security pension	
4.	Canada or Quebec Pension Plan benefits	

Form K – March 31, 2003

5.	Other pensions or superannuation				
6.	Employment insurance benefits				
7.	Taxable amount of dividends from taxable Canadian corporations				
8.	Interest and other investment income				
9.	Net partnership income	Gross		Net	
10.	Rental income				
11.	Taxable capital gains				
12.	Spousal support				
13.	Child support (taxable only)				
14.	Registered Retirement Savings Plan income				
15.	Business income	Gross		Net	
16.	Professional income	Gross		Net	
17.	Commission income	Gross		Net	
18.	Farming income	Gross		Net	
19.	Fishing income	Gross		Net	
20.	Workers Compensation benefits				
21.	Social Assistance payments				
22.	Net federal supplements				
23.	Other income (specify - see guide)				
24.	**(A) TOTAL ANNUAL INCOME**			$	0.00
25.	Total income in most recent personal income tax return (year:)	$			

ADJUSTMENTS TO INCOME

Line #	Additions	Amount
26.	Actual amount of dividends received from Canadian corporations	
27.	Actual capital gains realized in excess of actual capital losses	
28.	Salaries, benefits, or other payments paid to non-arm's-length persons, and deducted from self-employment income, unless necessary to earn self-employment income	
29.	Allowable capital cost allowance for real property	

Form K – March 31, 2003

30.	Employee stock options with a Canadian-controlled private corporation exercised (*Do not include if you dispose of the shares in the same year you exercise the option*)		
31.	Value of shares at the time the options are exercised		
32.	Less: Amount paid for the shares -		
33.	Amount paid to acquire the options to purchase the shares -		
34.		=	
35.	**(B) TOTAL ADDITIONS**	$	0.00
	Deductions		
36.	Union, professional dues, other employment expenses allowed under Child Support Guidelines		
37.	Child support received and included in total income above (line 13)		
38.	Spousal support received from the other parent and included in total income above (line 12)		
39.	Social assistance received by the parent for other members of the household		
40.	Taxable amount of dividends from taxable Canadian corporations		
41.	Taxable capital gains		
42.	Actual amount of business investment losses		
43.	Carrying charges and interest expenses		
44.	Self-employment income, net of reserves, including income for tax purposes in excess of the self-employment income for the 12 months ending on December 31 of the reporting year		
45.	Portion of partnership and sole proprietorship income that is required by the partnership to be re-invested		
46.	**(C) TOTAL DEDUCTIONS**	$	0.00

PART 2 - CHILD SUPPORT GUIDELINES TABLE AMOUNT CALCULATION

Annual Income for Child Support Guidelines Table Amount

47.	(A) Total Income (*from line 24*)		0.00		
48.	Plus (B) Total Additions (*from Line 35*) +		0.00		
49.	Minus (C) Total Deductions (*from line 46*) -		0.00		
50.	Annual Income for Child Support Guidelines Table Amount			$	0.00

Form K – March 31, 2003

	Annual Income for Special or Extraordinary Expenses Amount	
51.	Annual Income for Child Support Guidelines Table Amount *(from line 50)*	0.00
52.	Plus (if applicable) spousal support *received* from the other parent +	
53.	Minus (if applicable) spousal support *paid* to the other parent -	
54.	Annual Income for Special or Extraordinary Expenses Amount →	$ 0.00

PART 3 - EXPENSES

My monthly expenses are listed below. These expenses are for me, and the following members of my household:

(if you share an expense with another person, list only the amount that you pay. Convert all expenses to monthly amounts. List actual amounts - if impossible, give estimates, and mark as 'est')

		$ per Month			$ per Month
	Compulsory Deductions			**SUBTOTAL** *(from line 90)*	0.00
55.	Income Tax			**Adult Household Members**	
56.	Employment insurance		91.	Clothing	
57.	Canada Pension Plan		92.	Haircare	
58.	Employer pension		93.	Toiletries, cosmetics	
59.	Other *(specify)*		94.	Education fees, supplies	
	Household Expenses		95.	Entertainment & recreation	
60.	Groceries & household supplies		96.	Fitness	
61.	Meals outside the home		97.	Insurance	
62.	Furnishings and equipment		98.	Charitable donations	
63.	Telephone		99.	Gifts to others	
64.	Cable service		100.	Alcohol, tobacco	
65.	Laundry & dry cleaning			**Children**	
66.	Newspapers, periodicals		101.	Child care (regular expense)	
67.	Stationery, computer supplies		102.	Babysitting (occasional)	
68.	Vacation		103.	Clothing	
69.	Pet care		104.	Haircare	

Form K – March 31, 2003

	Housing (primary residence)					
			105.	Allowances		
70.	Rent or mortgage		106.	School fees & supplies		
71.	Taxes		107.	Entertainment & recreation		
72.	Home insurance		108.	Insurance		
73.	Heat		109.	Gifts (toys, books, etc.)		
74.	Electricity		110.	Activities, lessons, & supplies		
75.	Water		111.	Camp		
76.	House repairs & maintenance		112.	Gifts to other children		
77.	Yard maintenance			Savings for the future		
78.	Other (specify)		113.	RRSP		
	Health		114.	RESP		
79.	Medical Insurance		115.	Other		
80.	Drugs (after insurance coverage)		116.	Debt (other than mortgage)		
81.	Dental care (after insurance)		117.			
82.	Optical care (after insurance)		118.			
83.	Other (specify)		119.	Lease payments (specify)		
	Transportation		120.	Support payments to others (see note under *, below)		
84.	Public transit, taxis, etc.					
85.	Car operation		121.	Reserve for income taxes		
86.	Gas and oil		122.	Other (specify)		
87.	Insurance & licence		123.			
88.	Maintenance		124.			
89.	Parking		125.			
90.	SUBTOTAL	0.00	126.	TOTAL	0.00	

(* Note for line 120. Show support paid to persons **not** included in this application - example: support paid for a child of a past relationship between you and a parent who is not the claimant/applicant in this application. If paid, specify the

Name(s) of person(s) supported: _____. Are payments made

☐ Voluntarily, or ☐ due to a Court Order, or written agreement.

Do you deduct payments on your income tax return? ☐ Yes ☐ No.)

Form K – March 31, 2003

PART 4 – OTHER CHILD SUPPORT AND BENEFITS

Complete this part if ☐ you are claiming support for a child over the age of majority, and/or

☐ you are claiming an amount different than the child support guidelines table amount

A ☐ I receive child support for a child(ren) other than the child(ren) in this application:

Name(s) of child(ren)	Annual Amount Received	Taxable (Y/N

B ☐ I receive non-taxable benefits, allowances, or amounts. (*Example: use of a vehicle, childcare, or room and board. If the benefit is not an amount, include an estimate of the annual value of the benefit*)

Benefit received	Annual Amount or Estimate

PART 5 - HOUSEHOLD INCOME (not including children for whom support is claimed in this application)

Complete this part if

☐ you are living with another person **and**
☐ you are claiming support for yourself, **or**
☐ your child support application includes an undue hardship claim, **or**
☐ you believe the respondent may make an undue hardship claim.

A   I am living with: (*full name of person or persons - note: your living / marital relationship is not the issue; it is about sharing household responsibilities*)

B   A person named in 'A' has a child or children living in the home with us *(name and age of each child)*

C   For each person named in 'A', fill in the following information: (*add an extra page if more than 2 people*)

Name of Person #1   *Name of Person #2*

☐ Works at (name of employer, occupation)   ☐ Works at (name of employer, occupation)

Form K – March 31, 2003

☐ Earns $ _____ per _____	☐ Earns $ _____ per _____
☐ Pays for about_____% of household expenses	☐ Pays for about_____% of household expenses
☐ Does not work	☐ Does not work
☐ Has no earnings	☐ Has no earnings
☐ Contributes no money to the household expenses	☐ Contributes no money to the household expenses

PART 6 - ASSETS AND DEBTS

ASSETS

Real Estate	Description of Asset(s) - address, type of property	Your Equity	Market Value
Cars, boats, vehicles	Description of Asset(s) - year, make, model	Your Equity	Market Value
Pension Plan	Trustee/administrator of plan, date of valuation		Value
RRSPs	Financial institution, date of valuation		Value
Financial Assets	Bonds, shares, term deposits, investment certificates, mutual funds - list type, name of financial institution, when purchased		Value
Accounts	Bank or other accounts - type of account, name of financial institution		Value
Business	Name of business, address, nature and extent of ownership or interest		Value of Interest
Life Insurance	Company which issued policy		Cash Value

Form K – March 31, 2003

Debts to me	Description - name of person owing me money, reason for debt, repayment date		Value
Other	Description of other asset(s)		Value
		TOTAL VALUE OF ASSETS	$ 0.00

DEBTS

Mortgage	Institution / person holding mortgage	Date of last payment	Balance Owing
Credit Cards	Name/Company issuing card, and reason for borrowing	Date of last payment	Balance Owing
Bank/ Other	Financial Institution, and reason for borrowing	Date of last payment	Balance Owing
Other Debt	Description of any other debt(s) you owe	Date of last payment	Balance Owing
		TOTAL VALUE OF DEBTS	$ 0.00

Form K – March 31, 2003

PART 7 - DOCUMENTS ATTACHED TO THIS FINANCIAL STATEMENT

☐   My personal income tax return for each of the three most recent taxation years, and all documents attached to the returns.

☐   The income tax notice of assessment, or reassessment, I received for each of the three most recent tax years.

(Check each of the following statements that apply, and attach the listed documents)

☐   I am an employee. Attached is a statement showing my total earnings for this year, to date, including overtime. If this information is not shown on my pay stub, I attach a statement or letter from my employer with that information, including my rate of annual pay.

☐   I am receiving Employment Insurance benefits. My three most recent EIC benefits statements are attached.

☐   I am receiving Workers Compensation benefits. My three most recent WCB benefits statements are attached.

☐   I am receiving Social or Income Assistance. Attached is a statement showing the amount I receive.

☐   I am self-employed. For the three most recent taxation years, I attach:

         ☐   The financial statements of my business or professional practice, other than a partnership, and

         ☐   A statement showing a breakdown of salaries, wages, management fees, or other payments or benefits paid to, or on behalf of, persons or corporations with whom I do not deal at arm's length

☐   I am a partner in a partnership. I attach confirmation of my income and draw from, and capital in, the partnership for its three most recent taxation years.

☐   I control a corporation. I attach

         ☐   the financial statements of the corporation and its subsidiaries, and

         ☐   a statement showing a breakdown of all salaries, wages, management fees, or other payments or benefits paid to, or on behalf of, persons or corporations with which the corporation, and every related corporation, does not deal at arm's length

☐   I am the beneficiary under a trust. The trust settlement agreement and the trust's three most recent financial statements are attached.

Date this Financial Statement completed: _____.

This document is attached to, and forms part of the evidence in, my support application/support variation application/answer:

_____
                          Signature

Form K – March 31, 2003

Form L
Child Status and Financial Statement

CHILD STATUS AND FINANCIAL STATEMENT FOR _____

(name of child)

Child's date of birth *(dd/mm/yyyy)* _____

1. **Details of child's living arrangements:** *(include where child lives, whether child lives with other people)*

2. **Child's education status** *(check any that apply)*

☐   Is in high school, in grade _____

☐   Completed grade _____ in high school in
*(year)*_____, but did not graduate, and is not going to school now

☐   Has completed high school and is not going to school

☐   Has completed high school, and plans to attend post-secondary courses starting in: *(date)*_____

☐   Is taking full-time courses at community college or trade school

☐   Is taking part-time courses at community college or trade school

☐   Is taking full-time courses at university

☐   Is taking part-time courses at university

For each item checked in this section, give details (If the child is not in school, describe what the child is doing. If planning to attend, or attending post-secondary school, list name of school, location, level child is in, length of course or area of study until diploma/degree obtained)

Form L – March 31, 2003

802

Education details

---

3. **Child's financial and employment status** *(check any that apply)*. **The child:**

☐ Is not employed

☐ Is employed full-time

☐ Is employed part-time

☐ Has seasonal employment *(summer jobs)*

☐ Has filed an income tax return showing employment
income for *(years)* _____

☐ Has personal savings of approximately $ _____

☐ Receives gifts of money each year of approximately $ _____

☐ Is entitled to funds for education through an RESP or other savings plan
held by *(name of person(s) who holds the plan, type of plan, value if
known)*

☐ Is receiving, or is entitled to receive, government student loans

☐ Has personal income from investments, a trust, or other sources

☐ Other *(specify)*

*For any employment lines checked, give details (name of employer, child's
occupation, approximate wages/salary by hourly rate and monthly income, and how
long the child has worked for the employer. For other boxes checked, provide
details).*

ISO FORMS

> **Employment and income source details**

4.   **Child's education-related expenses:**

> *List expenses **directly** related to the child's education. For each, show who is paid, purpose of payment, amount paid per year, and who pays the amount. Put the **monthly** total (divide by 12) on line 106 of Form K.*

5.   **Reasons for child's continuing dependence:**
(The child is the age of majority or older. If the child is not working, and not going to school, provide details of any reasons that the child requires support from the parents. Attach an additional page if necessary, and supporting documents such as medical letters.)

☐ Supporting documents attached
☐ Additional page(s) attached

Form L – March 31, 2003

Form M

Evidence to Support Variation of a Support Order

EVIDENCE TO SUPPORT VARIATION OF A SUPPORT ORDER

I ask the Court to change (vary) the support order(s) or written agreement(s) between the respondent and me.

The order(s) or agreement(s) were made on the following dates, and are attached to my Support Variation Application (Form A). *(An application to change an order or agreement must be supported by documents to prove the change, and the current circumstances.)*

☐   person required to pay support (the payor), or

☐   person receiving support (the recipient).

☐ I ask the Court to **change** the amount of support to be paid for:	☐ I ask the Court to **end** support to be paid for:
☐ a child or children	☐ a child or children
☐ the recipient	☐ the recipient

1.   **Applicant's change in circumstances**

There has been a change in my circumstances since the date the order/agreement was made. *(Write details of the change, the date of the change, whether temporary or permanent. Attach an extra page if necessary.)*

Form M – March 31, 2003

2. Child's change in circumstances

There has been a change in the circumstances of a child(ren) named in the order/agreement. (*Write details of the change, the date of the change, whether temporary or permanent. Attach an extra page if necessary.*)

3. Respondent's change in circumstances

There has been a change in the respondent's circumstances since the date the order/agreement was made.
(*Write details of the change, the date of the change, whether temporary or permanent. Attach an extra page if necessary.*)

4. Applicant / Payor's application to reduce or cancel arrears

☐   As of today, the amount of unpaid support (arrears) is $_____.
A copy of a statement from the maintenance/support enforcement program is attached.

☐   If the Court orders a retroactive (back-dated) change in the amount of support, I ask that the support arrears be changed to show the change in the order.

☐   I have made the following efforts to pay the arrears:

☐   I will be able to pay any arrears the Court orders as follows:
(*Write the monthly amount available to pay arrears, or other sources of income/assets which could be used to pay arrears.*)

Form M – March 31, 2003

5.   **Applicant / Recipient's application to change support order**

☐   As of today, the amount of unpaid support (arrears) is
$_____. A copy of a statement from the maintenance/support
enforcement program is attached.

☐   If the Court orders a retroactive (back-dated) change in the amount of
support, I ask that the support arrears be changed to show the change in the
order.

Date this form
completed: _____

This document is attached to, and forms part of the evidence in, my support
application/support variation application/answer:

_____
           Signature

Form M – March 31, 2003

Form N

Respondent's Answer to Application

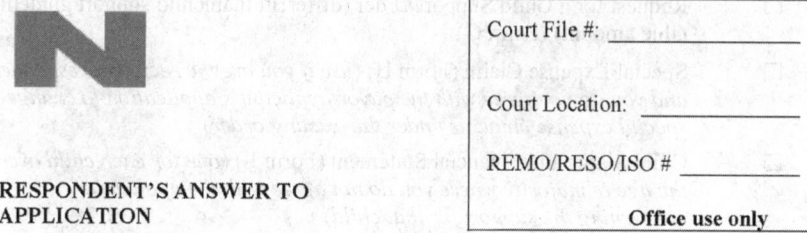

	Court File #: _____
RESPONDENT'S ANSWER TO APPLICATION	Court Location: _____
	REMO/RESO/ISO # _____
	Office use only

☐   I am the Respondent

☐   I am a person or agency or government with a legal right to participate in this application.

      My relationship is: _____.

I have been served with a Support Application, or Support Variation Application. My address for delivery of documents is

_____

(Last Name)   (First Name)   (Middle Names)

_____

(Street address and City/Town)

_____

(Province and Postal Code)   (daytime telephone)

_____

(Mailing Address, if different than street address)   (fax number)

_____

These are: ☐   my own addresses, or   ☐   c/o my lawyer, or   ☐   c/o another person

☐   I AGREE with the Application, and consent to an Order being made as requested.

      ☐   I agree to an order that I will pay support. My financial statement is attached to this Answer, or

      ☐   I am the support payor under the Order or Agreement the applicant wishes to change. My financial statement is attached to this Answer, or

      ☐   I am the support recipient under the Order or Agreement the applicant wishes to change. My financial information is not required to make a support variation Order.

☐   I DO NOT AGREE with the Application. My reasons for not agreeing are in the attached documents.

☐   I am filing this response with the court, including 3 copies of this Respondent's Answer to Application, and with copies of the following documents attached, where applicable:

      ☐   Financial Statement (Form K) *(required unless you are a support recipient who agrees to change an existing order)*

Form N – March 31, 2003

☐   Request to Pay Child Support (different than child support guidelines table amount) (Form I)

☐   Request for a Child Support Order (different than child support guidelines table amount) (Form G)

☐   Special Expense Claim (Form H) (*use if you are the recipient/respondent and you do not agree with the payor/applicant's application to change special expense amounts under the existing order*)

☐   Child Status and Financial Statement (Form L) (*one for each child over the age of majority where you do not agree with the application concerning the support for that child*)

☐   Other (specify):

☐   I have hired a lawyer. My lawyer's name, address, and telephone number are:

I, _____ make oath or affirm and say that the information and facts contained in this answer, including the attached forms and/or documents, are true. I am making this answer in good faith.

SWORN OR AFFIRMED BEFORE ME

At the _____ of _____

In the Province/Territory of _____   _____

On _____, 200___.   Respondent's signature

A Commissioner, etc

Form N – March 31, 2003

Form O

Request for Enforcement

REQUEST FOR ENFORCEMENT

USE THIS FORM IF:

- This is your first claim for support from this respondent
- You have a support order, and the respondent has moved to a new province, territory, or country
- You want the maintenance enforcement program to enforce a new, existing, or changed order.

ATTACH an extra copy of the Identification Information (Form B) to this Request. The information on the two forms will help the maintenance enforcement program to collect your monthly support and any unpaid arrears.

ARE YOU DEALING WITH A MAINTENANCE ENFORCEMENT PROGRAM ABOUT THIS ORDER OR AGREEMENT?

☐ NO   ☐ YES.

IF YES, PROGRAM HANDLING YOUR CASE _____

CASE/ACCOUNT NUMBER _____

ASSETS OF THE RESPONDENT / PAYOR

MOTOR VEHICLES (CARS, BOATS, RVs,)	YEAR	COLOUR	LICENCE PLATE NO / FROM WHAT PROV/TERR/STATE
1.			
2.			
3.			

REAL ESTATE (HOMES, COTTAGES, INVESTMENT PROPERTY) - STREET ADDRESS	CITY	PROV/TERR/STATE	LEGAL DESCRIPTION (IF KNOWN)
4.			
5.			

ASSETS / BANK / FINANCIAL INSTITUTION	ADDRESS	TYPE OF ACCOUNT	ACCOUNT NUMBER
6.			

Form O – March 31, 2003

7.			
8.			

CREDIT CARD ACCOUNTS - COMPANY NAME	ACCOUNT NUMBER
9.	
10.	
11.	
12	

IF THERE ARE MORE ASSETS, OR MORE DETAILS ABOUT ANY OF THESE ASSETS, PLEASE LIST BELOW, USING THE BOX NUMBER. (Example: if a piece of real estate listed in box 4 was paid for by the respondent, but is in the name of a current spouse.)

☐ ADDITIONAL PAGES, OR COPIES OF DOCUMENTS ARE ATTACHED

COURT: *DO NOT* SERVE THIS DOCUMENT ON RESPONDENT

Form O – March 31, 2003

Family Law Rules Forms

Form Number	Form Title	Version Date	Effective Date	Page
4	Notice of Change in Representation	Oct. 21, 2013	Jan. 1, 2014	821
6	Acknowledgement of Service	Sep. 1, 2005	May 1, 2006	822
6A	Advertisement	Mar. 19, 2015	Jun. 10, 2015	824
6B	Affidavit of Service	Apr. 12, 2016	Jul. 1, 2016	825
8	Application (General)	Apr. 12, 2016	Jul. 1, 2016	828
8A	Application (Divorce)	Apr. 12, 2016	Jul. 1, 2016	833
8B	Application (Child Protection and Status Review)	March 1, 2018	April 30, 2018	838
8B.1	Application (Status Review for Child in Extended Society Care and Child Formerly in Extended Society Care)	March 1, 2018	April 30, 2018	845
8B.2	Application (General) (*Child, Youth and Family Services Act, 2017* Cases other than Child Protection and Status Review)	March 1, 2018	April 30, 2018	850
8C	Application for Secure Treatment or Extension of Secure Treatment	March 1, 2018	April 30, 2018	854
8D	Application (Adoption)	March 1, 2018	April 30, 2018	856
8D.1	Application (Dispense with Parent's Consent to Adoption before Placement)	Nov. 1, 2018	Feb. 25, 2019	857
8D.2	Notice of Intention to Place Child(ren) for Adoption	March 1, 2018	April 30, 2018	859
8D.3	Notice of Intention to Place First Nations, Inuk or Métis Child for Adoption	March 1, 2018	April 30, 2018	862
10	Answer	March 1, 2018	April 30, 2018	863
10A	Reply	Sep. 1, 2005	May 1, 2006	867
12	Notice of Withdrawal	Sep. 1, 2005	May 1, 2006	869
13	Financial Statement (Support Claims)	Nov. 1, 2018	Feb. 25, 2019	871

FAMILY LAW RULES FORMS

Form Number	Form Title	Version Date	Effective Date	Page
13.1	Financial Statement (Property and Support Claims)	Nov. 1, 2018	Feb. 25, 2019	879
13A	Certificate of Financial Disclosure	Jan. 6, 2015	May 4, 2015	889
13B	Net Family Property Statement	May 15, 2009	Aug. 19, 2009	896
13C	Comparison of Net Family Property Statements	Jan. 6, 2015	May 4, 2015	900
14	Notice of Motion	March 1, 2018	July 1, 2018	905
14A	Affidavit (General)	Sep. 1, 2005	May 1, 2006	907
14B	Motion Form	Sep. 1, 2005	May 1, 2006	909
14C	Confirmation of Motion	March 1, 2018	July 1, 2018	911
14D	Order on Motion Without Notice	Sep. 1, 2005	May 1, 2006	913
15	Motion to Change	Apr. 12, 2016	Jul. 1, 2016	915
15A	Change Information Form	Nov. 1, 2018	Feb. 25, 2019	920
15B	Response to Motion to Change	Nov. 1, 2018	Feb. 25, 2019	929
15C	Consent Motion to Change	Apr. 12, 2016	Jul. 1, 2016	937
15D	Consent Motion to Change Child Support	Apr. 12, 2016	Jul. 1, 2016	941
17	Conference Notice	Nov. 1, 2018	Feb. 25, 2019	944
17A	Case Conference Brief – General	Nov. 1, 2018	Feb. 25, 2019	945
17B	Case Conference Brief for Protection Application or Status Review	March 1, 2018	April 30, 2018	949
17C	Settlement Conference Brief – General	Nov. 15, 2009	Mar. 1, 2010	955
17D	Settlement Conference Brief for Protection Application or Status Review	March 1, 2018	April 30, 2018	962
17E	Trial Management Conference Brief	Nov. 1, 2018	Jan. 1, 2019	967
17F	Confirmation of Conference	March 1, 2018	July 1, 2018	972
20	Request for Information	Sep. 1, 2005	May 1, 2006	975
20A	Authorization to Commissioner	Sep. 1, 2005	May 1, 2006	977
20B	Letter of Request	Sep. 1, 2005	May 1, 2006	984

Form Number	Form Title	Version Date	Effective Date	Page
20.2	Acknowledgement of Expert's Duty	Jun. 1, 2019	Sep. 1, 2019	987
22	Request to Admit	Sep. 1, 2005	May 1, 2006	988
22A	Response to Request to Admit	Sep. 1, 2005	May 1, 2006	990
23	Summons to Witness	Sep. 1, 2005	May 1, 2006	992
23A	Summons to Witness outside Ontario	Sep. 1, 2005	May 1, 2006	995
23B	Order for Prisoner's Attendance	Sep. 1, 2005	May 1, 2006	1000
23C	Affidavit for Uncontested Trial	Sep. 1, 2009	Oct. 15, 2009	1002
25	Order (General)	Sep. 1, 2005	May 1, 2006	1009
25A	Divorce Order	Sep. 1, 2005	May 1, 2006	1011
25B	Secure Treatment Order	March 1, 2018	April 30, 2018	1013
25C	Adoption Order	March 1, 2018	April 30, 2018	1015
25D	Order (Uncontested Trial)	Nov. 1, 2018	Feb. 25, 2019	1016
25E	Notice Disputing Approval of Order	Sep. 1, 2005	May 1, 2006	1020
25F	Restraining Order	Sep. 1, 2009	Oct. 15, 2009	1022
25G	Restraining Order on Motion without Notice	Sep. 1, 2009	Oct. 15, 2009	1024
25H	Order Terminating Restraining Order	Sep. 1, 2009	Oct. 15, 2009	1027
26	Statement of Money Owed	Apr. 12, 2016	Jul. 1, 2016	1029
26A	Affidavit of Enforcement Expenses	Apr. 12, 2016	Jul. 1, 2016	1035
26B	Affidavit for Filing Domestic Contract with Court	Apr. 12, 2016	Jul. 1, 2016	1037
26C	Notice of Transfer of Enforcement	Apr. 12, 2016	Jul. 1, 2016	1039
27	Request for Financial Statement	Apr. 12, 2016	Jul. 1, 2016	1041
27A	Request for Statement of Income	Apr. 12, 2016	Jul. 1, 2016	1042
27B	Statement of Income from Income Source	Sep. 1, 2005	May 1, 2006	1043
27C	Appointment for Financial Examination	Apr. 12, 2016	Jul. 1, 2016	1045
28	Writ of Seizure and Sale	Apr. 12, 2016	July 1, 2016	1047

Form Number	Form Title	Version Date	Effective Date	Page
28A	Request for Writ of Seizure and Sale	Sep. 1, 2005	May 1, 2006	1049
28B	Statutory Declaration to Sheriff	Jun. 15, 2007	Aug. 1, 2007	1051
28C	Writ of Temporary Seizure	Sep. 1, 2005	May 1, 2006	1053
29	Request for Garnishment	Apr. 12, 2016	Jul. 1, 2016	1055
29A	Notice of Garnishment (Lump-Sum Debt)	Apr. 12, 2016	Jul. 1, 2016	1057
29B	Notice of Garnishment (Periodic Debt)	Apr. 12, 2016	Jul. 1, 2016	1061
29C	Notice to Co-Owner of Debt	Sep. 1, 2005	May 1, 2006	1063
29D	Statutory Declaration of Indexed Support	Apr. 12, 2016	July 1, 2016	1065
29E	Dispute (Payor)	Sep. 1, 2005	May 1, 2006	1067
29F	Dispute (Garnishee)	Sep. 1, 2005	May 1, 2006	1070
29G	Dispute (Co-Owner of Debt)	Sep. 1, 2005	May 1, 2006	1073
29H	Notice of Garnishment Hearing	Sep. 1, 2005	May 1, 2006	1075
29I	Notice to Stop Garnishment	Sep. 1, 2005	May 1, 2006	1077
29J	Statement to Garnishee Financial Institution re Support	Apr. 12, 2016	Jul. 1, 2016	1079
30	Notice of Default Hearing	Apr. 12, 2016	Jul. 1, 2016	1081
30A	Request for Default Hearing	Sep. 1, 2005	May 1, 2006	1082
30B	Default Dispute	Sep. 1, 2005	May 1, 2006	1084
31	Notice of Contempt Motion	Sep. 1, 2005	May 1, 2006	1087
32	Bond (Recognizance)	Sep. 1, 2005	May 1, 2006	1089
32.1	Request to Enforce a Family Arbitration Award	Oct. 1, 2012	Jan. 1, 2013	1092
32.1A	Dispute of Request for Enforcement	Oct. 1, 2012	Jan. 1, 2013	1095
32A	Notice of Forfeiture Motion	Sep. 1, 2005	May 1, 2006	1096
32B	Warrant for Arrest	Apr. 12, 2016	Jul. 1, 2016	1098
32C	Affidavit for Warrant of Committal	Sep. 1, 2005	May 1, 2006	1100

Form Number	Form Title	Version Date	Effective Date	Page
32D	Warrant of Committal	Apr. 12, 2016	Jul. 1, 2016	1103
33	Information for Warrant to Bring a Child to a Place of Safety	March 1, 2018	April 30, 2018	1105
33A	Warrant to Bring a Child to a Place of Safety	March 1, 2018	April 30, 2018	1106
33B	Plan of Care for Child(ren) (Children's Aid Society)	March 1, 2018	April 30, 2018	1108
33B.1	Answer and Plan of Care (Parties other than Children's Aid Society)	March 1, 2018	April 30, 2018	1112
33B.2	Answer (*Child, Youth and Family Services Act, 2017* Cases other than Child Protection and Status Review)	March 1, 2018	April 30, 2018	1119
33C	Statement of Agreed Facts (Child Protection)	March 1, 2018	April 30, 2018	1124
33D	Statement of Agreed Facts (Status Review)	March 1, 2018	April 30, 2018	1127
33E	Child's Consent to Secure Treatment	Sep. 1, 2005	May 1, 2006	1130
33F	Consent to Secure Treatment (Person other than Child)	Nov. 1, 2018	Feb. 25, 2019	1133
34	Child's Consent to Adoption	Nov. 1, 2018	Feb. 25, 2019	1134
34A	Affidavit of Parentage, Sworn/Affirmed	March 1, 2018	April 30, 2018	1136
34B	Non-Parent's Consent to Adoption by Spouse	March 1, 2018	April 30, 2018	1139
34C	Director's or Local Director's Statement on Adoption	March 1, 2018	April 30, 2018	1141
34D	Affidavit of Adoption Applicant(s), Sworn/Affirmed	March 1, 2018	April 30, 2018	1143
34E	Director's Consent to Adoption	March 1, 2018	April 30, 2018	1146
34F	Parent's or Custodian's Consent to Adoption	Nov. 1, 2018	Feb. 25, 2019	1147
34G	Affidavit of Adoption Licensee or Society Employee, Sworn/Affirmed	March 1, 2018	April 30, 2018	1149

817

Form Number	Form Title	Version Date	Effective Date	Page
34G.1	Affidavit of Society Employee for Adoption of a Child in Extended Society Care, Sworn/Affirmed	March 1, 2018	April 30, 2018	1152
34H	Affidavit of Adopting Relative or Stepparent, Sworn/Affirmed	Nov. 1, 2018	Feb. 25, 2019	1155
34I	Parent's Consent to Adoption by Spouse	March 1, 2018	April 30, 2018	1158
34J	Affidavit of Execution and Independent Legal Advice (Children's Lawyer), Sworn/Affirmed	Nov. 1, 2018	Feb. 25, 2019	1160
34K	Certificate of Clerk (Adoption)	March 1, 2018	April 30, 2018	1161
34L	Application for Openness Order	March 1, 2018	April 30, 2018	1167
34M	Consent to Openness Order under s. 194 of the *Child, Youth and Family Services Act, 2017*	March 1, 2018	April 30, 2018	1170
34M.1	Consent to Openness Order under s. 196 or s. 197 of the *Child, Youth and Family Services Act, 2017*	March 1, 2018	April 30, 2018	1173
34N	Application to Change or Terminate Openness Order	March 1, 2018	April 30, 2018	1176
35.1	Affidavit in Support of Claim for Custody or Access, Dated	Nov. 1, 2018	Feb. 25, 2019	1181
36	Affidavit for Divorce	Sep. 1, 2005	May 1, 2006	1189
36A	Certificate of Clerk (Divorce)	Nov. 1, 2018	Feb. 25, 2019	1195
36B	Certificate of Divorce	Sep. 1, 2005	May 1, 2006	1197
37	Notice of Hearing	Sep. 1, 2005	May 1, 2006	1199
37A	Information Sheet	Sep. 1, 2005	May 1, 2006	1201
37B	Direction to Request Further Information	Sep. 1, 2005	May 1, 2006	1203
37C	Notice of Continuation of Hearing	Sep. 1, 2005	May 1, 2006	1205

Form Number	Form Title	Version Date	Effective Date	Page
37D	Notice of Registration of Order	Sep. 1, 2005	May 1, 2006	1207
37E	Notice for Taking Further Evidence	Sep. 1, 2005	May 1, 2006	1209
38	Notice of Appeal	Sep. 1, 2005	May 1, 2006	1211
39	Notice of Approaching Dismissal	Jun. 15, 2007	Sep. 1, 2007	1214

Form 4

Notice of Change in Representation

ONTARIO

Court File Number

_____
(Name of Court)

Form 4: Notice of Change in Representation

at _____
Court office address

Applicant(s)

Full legal name & address for service — street & number, municipality, postal code, telephone & fax numbers and e-mail address (if any).	Lawyer's name & address — street & number, municipality, postal code, telephone & fax numbers and e-mail address (if any).

Respondent(s)

Full legal name & address for service — street & number, municipality, postal code, telephone & fax numbers and e-mail address (if any).	Lawyer's name & address — street & number, municipality, postal code, telephone & fax numbers and e-mail address (if any).

Children's Lawyer

Name & address of Children's Lawyer's agent for service (street & number, municipality, postal code, telephone & fax numbers and e-mail address (if any)) and name of person represented.

TO ALL PARTIES AND THEIR LAWYERS

FROM *(name)* _____

(Name, address, telephone & fax numbers and e-mail address)

☐ I have chosen to be represented by a lawyer. See details in this box. →

☐ I have chosen a new lawyer. See details in this box. →

☐ I have decided to act in person. Documents can be served on me at the address set out in this box. →

☐ I have the court's permission to be represented by a person who is not a lawyer. See details in this box. →

☐ I have the court's permission to appear in person at a child protection trial. Documents can be served on me at the address set out in this box. →

_____   _____
Date of signature   *Signature*

Form 4:   **Notice of Change in Representation**   **(page 2)** | Court File Number

NOTES:

1.   *You must serve this notice on the lawyers for all of the other parties. If another party does not have a lawyer, you must serve it on the party. If you have been represented by a lawyer or other person who, because of this notice, is no longer going to represent you, you must also serve this notice on that lawyer or the other person who used to represent you.*

2.   *You can serve by any method set out in rule 6 of the Family Law Rules, including mail, courier and fax.*

3.   *When you have served this notice, you must file it with the clerk of the court together with proof of service (Form 6B). If you appeared without a lawyer and now you have chosen to be represented by a lawyer, you must attach that lawyer's consent to this notice.*

4.   *If a child protection case has been scheduled for trial, you must receive the court's permission to remove your lawyer and represent yourself.*

Form 6

Acknowledgement of Service

ONTARIO

Court File Number / Numéro de dossier du greffe

_____

(Name of Court/Nom du tribunal)

at
situé(e) au _____

Court office address/Adresse du reffe

Form 6: Acknowledgement of Service

Formule 6: Accusé de réception de la signification

You are asked to fill out and sign this card and to mail it immediately. If you do not return this card, the document(s) listed below may be personally served on you and you may be ordered to pay the costs of service.

Veuillez remplir et signer la présente carte et la mettre à la poste immédiatement. Si vous ne la retoumez pas, le ou les documents énumérés cidessous peuvent vous être signifiés à personne et il peut vous être ordonné de payer les frais de la signification.

My name is: *(full legal name)* / **Je m'appelle:** *(nom et prénom officiels* ....

I may be served at: *(address where court documents may be mailed to you)*

Les documents peuvent m'être signifiés au: *(adresse où les documents de procédure peuvent vous être envoyés)*

....

I acknowledge receiving a copy of the following document(s): / J'accuse réception d'une copie du ou des documents suivants:

□ Application dated / Demande datée du ....

□ Blank form of application / Exemplaire de la formule de demande

□ Financial statement dated / État financier daté du ....

□ Blank form of financial statement / Exemplaire de la formule d'état financier

□ Answer dated / Défense datée du ....

□ Blank form of answer / Exemplaire de la formule de defense ....

□ Affidavit of (name) / Affidavit de (nom) .... dated / daté du ....

□ Notice of motion dated / Avis de motion daté du

□ Statement of money owed dated / État des sommes dues daté du

....

□ *(Other. Give title and date of document.) / (Autre. Donnez le titre et la date du document.)*

□

□

□

_____   _____

Signature   *Date of signature / Date de la signature*

NOTICE: *The address that you give above will be used in future to serve documents by mail until you inform the other parties and the court office of a new address for service.*

REMARQUE: L'adresse que vous indiquez ci-dessus servira à l'avenir à vous signifier des documents par la poste jusqu'à ce que vous avisiez les autres parties et le greffe d'une nouvelle adresse aux fins de signification.

From/De ....

....

....

> **STAMP**
>
> **TIMBRE**

TO/À ....

....

....

Form 6A

Advertisement

FORM 6A

ADVERTISEMENT

ONTARIO

☐ **SUPERIOR COURT OF JUSTICE**
☐ **ONTARIO COURT OF JUSTICE**

NOTICE TO: *(full legal name)* _____

A CASE HAS BEEN STARTED AGAINST YOU IN COURT at *(address: street & number, municipality, postal code)*

The next court date is *(date)* _____ at _____ a.m.
or as soon as possible after that time.

The court may make an order in this case that may affect your rights. You can get more information about this case from the court office at *(Write or, if the court office is at a different address, give the street & number, municipality and postal code of the court office.)*

You may also get information about this case from *(name, address and telephone number of person publishing this advertisement)*

IF YOU DO NOT COME TO COURT, AN ORDER MAY BE MADE WITHOUT YOU AND BE ENFORCED AGAINST YOU.

| Save Form | Print Form | | Clear Form |

FLR-6A-E (2015/03)

Page 1 of 1

Form 6B

Affidavit of Service

ONTARIO

....	**Court File Number**
(Name of court)	
at	**Form 6B: Affidavit of Service**
Court office address	**sworn/affirmed**

Applicant(s)

Full legal name & address for service — street & number, municipality, postal code, telephone & fax numbers and e-mail address (if any).	Lawyer's name & address — street & number, municipality, postal code, telephone & fax numbers and e-mail address (if any).

Respondent(s)

Full legal name & address for service — street & number, municipality, postal code, telephone & fax numbers and e-mail address (if any).	Lawyer's name & address — street & number, municipality, postal code, telephone & fax numbers and e-mail address (if any).

My name is *(full legal name)* ....

I live in *(municipality & province)* ....

and I swear/affirm that the following is true:

1. On *(date)* .... , at *(time)* .... , I served *(name of person to be served)* .... with the following document(s) in this case:

Name of document	Author (if applicable)	Date when document signed, issued, sworn, etc.

List the documents served

NOTE: *You can leave out any part of this form that is not applicable.*

---

2. I served the documents mentioned in paragraph 1 by:

   ☐ special service. *(Go to paragraph 3 below if you used special service.)*

   ☐ mail. *(Go to paragraph 4 if you used mailed service.)*

   ☐ same day courier. *(Go to paragraph 5 if you used courier.)*

   Check one box only and go to indicated paragraph. ☐ next day courier. *(Go to paragraph 5 if you used courier.)*

   ☐ deposit at a document exchange. *(Go to paragraph 6 if you used a document exchange.)*

   ☐ an electronic document exchange. *(Go to paragraph 7 if you used an electronic document exchange.)*

   ☐ fax. *(Go to paragraph 8 if you used fax.)*

   ☐ email. *(Go to paragraph 9 if you used email.)*

   ☐ substituted service or advertisement. *(Go to paragraph 10 if you used substituted service or advertisement.)*

FLR 6B (April 12, 2016)

Page 1 of 3

Form 6B: sworn/affirmed	**Affidavit of Service**	(page 2)	Court File Number

3. I carried out special service of the document(s) on the person named in paragraph 1 at *(place or address)*

_____

by: ☐ leaving a copy with the person.

☐ leaving a copy with *(name)* _____

Check one box only. Strike out paragraphs 4 to 10 and go to paragraph 11.

    ☐ who is a lawyer who accepted service in writing on a copy of the document.

    ☐ who is the person's lawyer of record.

    ☐ who is the *(office or position)* _____

    of the corporation named in paragraph 1.

☐ mailing a copy to the person together with a prepaid return postcard in Form 6 in an envelope bearing the sender's return address. This postcard, in which receipt of the document(s) is acknowledged, was returned and is attached to this affidavit.

☐ leaving a copy in a sealed envelope addressed to the person at the person's place of residence with

(name) _____

who provided me with identification to show that he/she was an adult person residing at the same address and by mailing another copy of the same document(s) on the same or following day to the person named in paragraph 1 at that place of residence.

☐ other *(Specify. See rule 6 for details.)*

4. I mailed the document(s) to be served by addressing the covering envelope to the person named in paragraph 1 at:

(Set out address.) _____

which is the address ☐ of the person's place of business.

Check appropriate paragraph and strike out paragraphs 3, 5, 6, 7, 8, 9 and 10.

    ☐ of a lawyer who accepted service on the person's behalf.

    ☐ of the person's lawyer of record.

    ☐ of the person's home.

    ☐ on the document most recently filed in court by the person.

    ☐ other *(Specify.)* _____

5. The document(s) to be served was/were placed in an envelope that was picked up at _____ a.m./p.m. _____ on

(date) _____ by *(name of courier service)* _____

a private courier service, a copy of whose receipt is attached to this affidavit. The envelope was addressed to the person

named in paragraph 1 at: *(Set out address.)* _____

which is the address ☐ of the person's place of business.

    ☐ of a lawyer who accepted service on the person's behalf.

Check appropriate paragraph and strike out paragraphs 3, 4, 6, 7, 8, 9 and 10.

    ☐ of the person's lawyer of record.

    ☐ of the person's home.

    ☐ on the document most recently filed in court by the person.

    ☐ other *(Specify.)* _____

FLR 6B (April 12, 2016)   Page 2 of 3

Form 6B:	Affidavit of Service	(page 3)	Court File Number
sworn/affirmed			

6. The document(s) was/were deposited at a document exchange. The exchange's date stamp on the attached copy shows the date of deposit. *(Strike out paragraphs 3, 4, 5, 7, 8, 9, 10 and 13.)*

7. The documents were served through an electronic document exchange. The record of service from the exchange is attached to this affidavit. *(Strike out paragraphs 3, 4, 5, 6, 8, 9, 10 and 13.)*

8. The document(s) to be served was/were faxed. The fax confirmation is attached to this affidavit. *(Strike out paragraphs 3, 4, 5, 6, 7, 9, 10 and 13.)*

9. The documents were served by email. Attached to this Affidavit is a copy of the email that the document was attached to. *(Strike out paragraphs 3, 4, 5, 6, 7, 8, 10 and 13.)*

10. An order of this court made on *(date)* _____ allowed

    ☐ substituted service.

    ☐ service by advertisement. *(Attach advertisement.)*

    The order was carried out as follows: *(Give details. Then go to paragraph 13 if you had to travel to serve substitutionally or by advertisement.)*

11. My relationship to, or affiliation with, any party in this case is as follows:

12. I am at least 18 years of age.

13. To serve the document(s), I had to travel _____ kilometres. My fee for service of the document(s) is

    $ _____ including travel.

Sworn/Affirmed before me at _____

                                      municipality

in _____

                 province, state, or country

on _____   _____

          date   *Commissioner for taking affidavits*
                        *(Type or print name below if
                        signature is illegible.)*

_____
Signature
(This form is to be signed in front of a lawyer, justice of the peace, notary public or commissioner for taking affidavits.)

FAMILY LAW RULES FORMS

Form 8

Application (General)

ONTARIO

	Court File Number

(SEAL)

at _____
(Name of court)

_____
Court office address

**Form 8: Application
(General)**

Applicant(s)

Full legal name & address for service – street & number, municipality, postal code, telephone & fax numbers and e-mail address (if any).	Lawyer's name & address – street & number, municipality, postal code, telephone & fax numbers and e-mail address (if any).

Respondent(s)

Full legal name & address for service – street & number, municipality, postal code, telephone & fax numbers and e-mail address (if any).	Lawyer's name & address – street & number, municipality, postal code, telephone & fax numbers and e-mail address (if any).

TO THE RESPONDENT(S):

A COURT CASE HAS BEEN STARTED AGAINST YOU IN THIS COURT. THE DETAILS ARE SET OUT ON THE ATTACHED PAGES.

☐ **THE FIRST COURT DATE IS** *(date)* _____ **AT** _____ ☐ a.m. ☐ p.m.

or as soon as possible after that time, at: *(address)*

NOTE: *If this is a divorce case, no date will be set unless an Answer is filed. If you have also been served with a notice of motion, there may be an earlier court date and you or your lawyer should come to court for the motion.*

☐ **THIS CASE IS ON THE FAST TRACK OF THE CASE MANAGEMENT SYSTEM.** A case management judge will be assigned by the time this case first comes before a judge.

☐ **THIS CASE IS ON THE STANDARD TRACK OF THE CASE MANAGEMENT SYSTEM. No court date has been set for this case** but, if you have been served with a notice of motion, it has a court date and you or your lawyer should come to court for the motion. A case management judge will not be assigned until one of the parties asks the clerk of the court to schedule a case conference or until a motion is scheduled, whichever comes first.

IF, AFTER 365 DAYS, THE CASE HAS NOT BEEN SCHEDULED FOR TRIAL, the clerk of the court will send out a warning that the case will be dismissed within 60 days unless the parties file proof that the case has been settled or one of the parties asks for a case or a settlement conference.

IF YOU WANT TO OPPOSE ANY CLAIM IN THIS CASE, you or your lawyer must prepare an Answer (Form 10 – a blank copy should be attached), serve a copy on the applicant(s) and file a copy in the court office with an Affidavit of Service (Form 6B). **YOU HAVE ONLY 30 DAYS AFTER THIS APPLICATION IS SERVED ON YOU (60 DAYS IF THIS APPLICATION IS SERVED ON YOU OUTSIDE CANADA OR THE UNITED STATES) TO SERVE AND FILE AN ANSWER. IF YOU DO NOT, THE CASE WILL GO AHEAD WITHOUT YOU AND THE COURT MAY MAKE AN ORDER AND ENFORCE IT AGAINST YOU.**

FLR 8 (April 12, 2016)

Page 1 of 5

FAMILY LAW RULES FORMS

Form 8: Application (General) **(page 2)** Court File Number

Check the box of the paragraph that applies to your case

☐ This case includes a claim for support. It does not include a claim for property or exclusive possession of the matrimonial home and its contents. You **MUST** fill out a Financial Statement (Form 13 – a blank copy attached), serve a copy on the applicant(s) and file a copy in the court office with an Affidavit of Service even if you do not answer this case.

☐ This case includes a claim for property or exclusive possession of the matrimonial home and its contents. You **MUST** fill out a Financial Statement (Form 13.1 – a blank copy attached), serve a copy on the applicant(s) and file a copy in the court office with an Affidavit of Service even if you do not answer this case.

IF YOU WANT TO MAKE A CLAIM OF YOUR OWN, you or your lawyer must fill out the claim portion in the Answer, serve a copy on the applicant(s) and file a copy in the court office with an Affidavit of Service.

· If you want to make a claim for support but do not want to make a claim for property or exclusive possession of the matrimonial home and its contents, you **MUST** fill out a Financial Statement (Form 13), serve a copy on the applicant(s) and file a copy in the court office.

· However, if your only claim for support is for child support in the table amount specified under the Child Support Guidelines, you do not need to fill out, serve or file a Financial Statement.

· If you want to make a claim for property or exclusive possession of the matrimonial home and its contents, whether or not it includes a claim for support, you **MUST** fill out a Financial Statement (Form 13.1, not Form 13), serve a copy on the applicant(s), and file a copy in the court office.

YOU SHOULD GET LEGAL ADVICE ABOUT THIS CASE RIGHT AWAY. If you cannot afford a lawyer, you may be able to get help from your local Legal Aid Ontario office. *(See your telephone directory under LEGAL AID.)*

_____   _____
Date of issue   *Clerk of the court*

FAMILY LAW RULES FORMS

Form 8: Application (General)	(page 3)	Court file number

FAMILY HISTORY

APPLICANT: Age: _____   Birthdate: *(d, m, y)* _____

Resident in *(municipality & province)* _____

since *(date)* _____

Surname at birth: _____   Surname just before marriage: _____

Divorced before?   ☐ No   ☐ Yes *(Place and date of previous divorce)*

_____

RESPONDENT: Age: _____   Birthdate: *(d, m, y)* _____

Resident in *(municipality & province)* _____

since *(date)* _____

Surname at birth: _____   Surname just before marriage: _____

Divorced before?   ☐ No   ☐ Yes *(Place and date of previous divorce)*

_____

RELATIONSHIP DATES:

☐ Married on *(date)* _____   ☐ Started living together on *(date)* _____

☐ Separated on *(date)* _____   ☐ Never lived together   ☐ Still living together

THE CHILD(REN)

List all children involved in this case, even if no claim is made for these children.

Full legal name	Age	Birthdate *(d, m, y)*	Resident in *(municipality & province)*	Now Living With *(name of person and relationship to child)*

PREVIOUS CASES OR AGREEMENTS

Have the parties or the children been in a court case before?

☐ No   ☐ Yes

Have the parties made a written agreement dealing with any matter involved in this case?

☐ No   ☐ Yes *(Give date of agreement. Indicate which of its terms are in dispute.)*

FAMILY LAW RULES FORMS

Form 8:	Application (General)	(page 4)	Court file number

Has a Notice of Calculation and/or a Notice of Recalculation been issued by the online Child Support Service in this case?

☐ No   ☐ Yes *(Give date(s) of Notice(s) of Calculation or Recalculation.)*

If yes, are you asking the court to make an order for a child support that is different from the amount set out in the Notice?

☐ No   ☐ Yes *(Provide an explanation.)*

Have the parties arbitrated or agreed to arbitrate any matter involved in this case?

☐ No   ☐ Yes *(Give date of agreement and family arbitration award, if any.)*

CLAIM BY APPLICANT

I ASK THE COURT FOR THE FOLLOWING:
(Claims below include claims for temporary orders.)

Claims under the *Divorce Act* *(Check boxes in this column only if you are asking for a divorce and your case is in the Superior Court of Justice or Family Court of the Superior Court of Justice.)*	Claims under the *Family Law Act* or *Children's Law Reform Act*	Claims relating to property *(Check boxes in this column only if your case is in the Superior Court of Justice or Family Court of the Superior Court of Justice.)*
00 ☐ a divorce 01 ☐ support for me 02 ☐ support for child(ren) – table amount 03 ☐ support for child(ren) – other than table amount 04 ☐ custody of child(ren) 05 ☐ access to child(ren)	10 ☐ support for me 11 ☐ support for child(ren) – table amount 12 ☐ support for child(ren) – other than table amount 13 ☐ custody of child(ren) 14 ☐ access to child(ren) 15 ☐ restraining/non-harassment order 16 ☐ indexing spousal support 17 ☐ declaration of parentage 18 ☐ guardianship over child's property	20 ☐ equalization of net family properties 21 ☐ exclusive possession of matrimonial home 22 ☐ exclusive possession of contents of matrimonial home 23 ☐ freezing assets 24 ☐ sale of family property
Other claims 30 ☐ costs 31 ☐ annulment of marriage 32 ☐ prejudgment interest 33 ☐ claims relating to a family arbitration	50 ☐ Other *(Specify.)*	

Give details of the order that you want the court to make. *(Include any amounts of support (if known) and the names of the children for whom support, custody or access is claimed.)*

FLR 8 (April 12, 2016)   Page 4 of 5

831

Form 8:	Application (General)	(page 5)	Court File Number

IMPORTANT FACTS SUPPORTING MY CLAIM FOR DIVORCE

☐ **Separation:** The spouses have lived separate and apart since *(date)* .... and

    ☐ have not lived together again since that date in an unsuccessful attempt to reconcile.

    ☐ have lived together again during the following period(s) in an unsuccessful attempt to reconcile: *(Give dates.)*

☐ **Adultery:** The respondent has committed adultery. *(Give details. It is not necessary to name any other person involved but, if you do name the other person, then you must serve this application on the other person.)*

☐ **Cruelty:** The respondent has treated the applicant with physical or mental cruelty of such a kind as to make continued cohabitation intolerable. *(Give details.)*

IMPORTANT FACTS SUPPORTING MY OTHER CLAIM(S)
(Set out below the facts that form the legal basis for your other claim(s). Attach an additional page if you need more space.)

Put a line through any blank space left on this page. If additional space is needed, extra pages may be attached.

_____   _____
Date of signature   *Signature of applicant*

LAWYER'S CERTIFICATE
For divorce cases only

My name is:
and I am the applicant's lawyer in this divorce case. I certify that I have complied with the requirements of section 9 of the *Divorce Act*.

_____   _____
Date   *Signature of Lawyer*

For information on accessibility of court services for people with disability-related needs, contact:
Telephone: 416-326-2220 / 1-800-518-7901   TTY: 416-326-4012 / 1-877-425-0575

FLR 8 (April 12, 2016)   Page 5 of 5

Form 8A

Application (Divorce)

ONTARIO

SEAL at	**Court File Number**

_____
(Name of court)

_____
Court office address

Form 8A: Application (Divorce)

☐ **Simple (divorce only)**

☐ **Joint**

Applicant(s)

Full legal name & address for service – street & number, municipality, postal code, telephone & fax numbers and e-mail address (if any).	Lawyer's name & address – street & number, municipality, postal code, telephone & fax numbers and e-mail address (if any).

Respondent(s)

Full legal name & address for service – street & number, municipality, postal code, telephone & fax numbers and e-mail address (if any).	Lawyer's name & address – street & number, municipality, postal code, telephone & fax numbers and e-mail address (if any).

☐ **IN THIS CASE, THE APPLICANT IS CLAIMING DIVORCE ONLY.**

TO THE RESPONDENT(S): A COURT CASE FOR DIVORCE HAS BEEN STARTED AGAINST YOU IN THIS COURT. THE DETAILS ARE SET OUT ON THE ATTACHED PAGES.

THIS CASE IS ON THE STANDARD TRACK OF THE CASE MANAGEMENT SYSTEM. No court date has been set for this case but, if you have been served with a notice of motion, it has a court date and you or your lawyer should come to court for the motion. A case management judge will not be assigned until one of the parties asks the clerk of the court to schedule a case conference or until a motion is scheduled, whichever comes first.

IF, AFTER 365 DAYS, THE CASE HAS NOT BEEN SCHEDULED FOR TRIAL, the clerk of the court will send out a warning that the case will be dismissed within 60 days unless the parties file proof that the case has been settled or one of the parties asks for a case or a settlement conference.

IF YOU WANT TO OPPOSE ANY CLAIM IN THIS CASE, you or your lawyer must prepare an Answer (Form 10 – a blank copy should be attached), serve a copy on the applicant and file a copy in the court office with an Affidavit of Service (Form 6B). **YOU HAVE ONLY 30 DAYS AFTER THIS APPLICATION IS SERVED ON YOU (60 DAYS IF THIS APPLICATION IS SERVED ON YOU OUTSIDE CANADA OR THE UNITED STATES) TO SERVE AND FILE AN ANSWER. IF YOU DO NOT, THE CASE WILL GO AHEAD WITHOUT YOU AND THE COURT MAY MAKE AN ORDER AND ENFORCE IT AGAINST YOU.**

IF YOU WANT TO MAKE A CLAIM OF YOUR OWN, you or your lawyer must fill out the claim portion in the Answer, serve a copy on the applicant(s) and file a copy in the court office with an Affidavit of Service.

- If you want to make a claim for support but do not want to make a claim for property or exclusive possession of the matrimonial home and its contents, you **MUST** fill out a Financial Statement (Form 13), serve a copy on the applicant(s) and file a copy in the court office.
- However, if your only claim for support is for child support in the table amount specified under the Child Support Guidelines, you do not need to fill out, serve or file a Financial Statement.
- If you want to make a claim for property or exclusive possession of the matrimonial home and its contents, whether or not it includes a claim for support, you **MUST** fill out a Financial Statement (Form 13.1, not Form 13), serve a copy on the applicant(s), and file a copy in the court office.

YOU SHOULD GET LEGAL ADVICE ABOUT THIS CASE RIGHT AWAY. If you cannot afford a lawyer, you may be able to get help from your local Legal Aid Ontario office. *(See your telephone directory under LEGAL AID.)*

FAMILY LAW RULES FORMS

Form 8A: Application (Divorce)   **(page 2)**

Court File Number

☐ **THIS CASE IS A JOINT APPLICATION FOR DIVORCE. THE DETAILS ARE SET OUT ON THE ATTACHED PAGES.** The application and affidavits in support of the application will be presented to a judge when the materials have been checked for completeness.

If you are requesting anything other than a simple divorce, such as support or property or exclusive possession of the matrimonial home and its contents, then refer to page 1 for instructions regarding the Financial Statement you should file.

_____   _____
            Date of issue   *Clerk of the court*

Form 8A:	Application (Divorce)	(page 3)	Court file number

FAMILY HISTORY

APPLICANT: Age: _____ Birthdate: *(d, m, y)* _____

Resident in *(municipality & province)* _____

since *(date)* _____

Surname at birth: _____ Surname just before marriage: _____

Divorced before? ☐ No ☐ Yes *(Place and date of previous divorce)*

_____

RESPONDENT/JOINT APPLICANT: Age: _____ Birthdate: *(d, m, y)* _____

Resident in *(municipality & province)* _____

since *(date)* _____

Surname at birth: _____ Surname just before marriage: _____

Divorced before? ☐ No ☐ Yes *(Place and date of previous divorce)*

_____

RELATIONSHIP DATES:

☐ Married on *(date)* _____   ☐ Started living together on *(date)* _____

☐ Separated on *(date)* _____   ☐ Never lived together

THE CHILD(REN)
List all children involved in this case, even if no claim is made for these children.

Full legal name	Age	Birthdate *(d,m,y)*	Resident in *(municipality & province)*	Now Living With *(name of person and relationship to child)*

PREVIOUS CASES OR AGREEMENTS

Have the parties or the children been in a court case before?

☐ No   ☐ Yes

Have the parties made a written agreement dealing with any matter involved in this case?

☐ No   ☐ Yes *(Give date of agreement. Indicate which of its terms are in dispute. Attach an additional page if you need more space.)*

FAMILY LAW RULES FORMS

Form 8A:	Application (Divorce)	(page 4)	Court file number

Has a Notice of Calculation and/or a Notice of Recalculation been issued by the online Child Support Service in this case?

☐ No ☐ Yes *(Give date(s) of Notice(s) of Calculation or Recalculation.)*

If yes, are you asking the court to make an order for a child support that is different from the amount set out in the Notice?

☐ No ☐ Yes *(Provide an explanation.)*

CLAIMS

USE THIS FRAME ONLY IF THIS CASE IS A JOINT APPLICATION FOR DIVORCE

WE JOINTLY ASK THE COURT FOR THE FOLLOWING:

Claims under the *Divorce Act*

00 ☐ a divorce
01 ☐ spousal support
02 ☐ support for child(ren) – table amount
03 ☐ support for child(ren) – other than table amount
04 ☐ custody of child(ren)
05 ☐ access to child(ren)

Claims under the *Family Law Act* or *Children's Law Reform Act*

10 ☐ spousal support
11 ☐ support for child(ren) – table amount
12 ☐ support for child(ren) – other than table amount
13 ☐ custody of child(ren)
14 ☐ access to child(ren)
15 ☐ restraining/non-harassment order
16 ☐ indexing spousal support
17 ☐ declaration of parentage
18 ☐ guardianship over child's property

Claims relating to property

20 ☐ equalization of net family properties
21 ☐ exclusive possession of matrimonial home
22 ☐ exclusive possession of contents of matrimonial home
23 ☐ freezing assets
24 ☐ sale of family property

Other claims

30 ☐ costs
31 ☐ annulment of marriage
32 ☐ prejudgment interest
50 ☐ Other *(Specify)*

USE THIS FRAME ONLY IF THE APPLICANT'S ONLY CLAIM IN THIS CASE IS FOR DIVORCE.

I ASK THE COURT FOR:
(Check if applicable.)

00 ☐ a divorce   30 ☐ costs

IMPORTANT FACTS SUPPORTING THE CLAIM FOR DIVORCE

☐ **Separation:** The spouses have lived separate and apart since *(date)* .... and

☐ have not lived together again since that date in an unsuccessful attempt to reconcile.
☐ have lived together again during the following periods(s) in an unsuccessful attempt to reconcile: *(Give dates.)*

☐ **Adultery:** *(Name of spouse)* .... has committed adultery.
(Give details. It is not necessary to name any other person involved but if you do name the other person, then you must serve this application on the other person.)

Form 8A: **Application (Divorce)** **(page 5)** | Court File Number

☐ **Cruelty:** *(Name of spouse)* _____ has treated *(name of spouse)* _____ with physical or mental cruelty of such a kind as to make continued cohabitation intolerable. *(Give details.)*

USE THIS FRAME ONLY IF THIS CASE IS A JOINT APPLICATION FOR DIVORCE.

The details of the other order(s) that we jointly ask the court to make are as follows: *(Include any amounts of support and the names of the children for whom support, custody or access is to be ordered.)*

IMPORTANT FACTS SUPPORTING OUR CLAIM(S)
(Set out the facts that form the legal basis for your claim(s). Attach an additional page if you need more space.)

Put a line through any blank space left on this page.

Complete this section if your only claim is for a divorce. Your lawyer, if you are represented, must complete the Lawyer's Certificate below.

_____ _____
Date of signature   Signature of applicant

Complete this section if you are making a joint application for divorce. Your lawyer, if you are represented, must complete the Lawyer's Certificate below.

_____ _____
Date of signature   Signature of joint applicant

_____ _____
Date of signature   Signature of joint applicant

LAWYER'S CERTIFICATE

My name is: _____
and I am the lawyer for *(name)* _____ in this divorce case. I certify that I have complied with the requirements of section 9 of the *Divorce Act*.

_____ _____
Date   Signature of Lawyer

My name is: _____
and I am the lawyer for *(name)* _____ in this divorce case. I certify that I have complied with the requirements of section 9 of the *Divorce Act*.

_____ _____
Date   Signature of Lawyer

FLR 8A (April 12, 2016) Page 5 of 5

Form 8B

Application (Child Protection and Status Review)

ONTARIO

	Court File Number

SEAL at

(Name of court)

Court office address

Form 8B: Application
(Child Protection and
Status Review)

Applicant(s) *(In most cases, the applicant will be a children's aid society.)*

Full legal name & address for service — street & number, municipality, postal code, telephone & fax numbers and e-mail address (if any).	Lawyer's name & address — street & number, municipality, postal code, telephone & fax numbers and e-mail address (if any).

Respondent(s) *(In most cases, a respondent will be a "parent" within the meaning of section 74 of the Child, Youth and Family Services Act, 2017.)*

Full legal name & address for service — street & number, municipality, postal code, telephone & fax numbers and e-mail address (if any).	Lawyer's name & address — street & number, municipality, postal code, telephone & fax numbers and e-mail address (if any).

Children's Lawyer

Name & address of Children's Lawyer's agent for service (street & number, municipality, postal code, telephone & fax numbers and e-mail address (if any)) and name of person represented.

TO THE RESPONDENT(S):

A COURT CASE HAS BEEN STARTED AGAINST YOU IN THIS COURT. THE DETAILS ARE SET OUT ON THE ATTACHED PAGES.

THE FIRST COURT DATE IS *(date)* _____ **AT** _____ ☐ a.m. ☐ p.m.

or as soon as possible after that time, at: *(address)*

If you have also been served with a notice of motion, there may be an earlier court date and you or your lawyer should come to court for the motion.

IF YOU WANT TO OPPOSE ANY CLAIM IN THIS CASE, you or your lawyer must prepare an Answer and Plan of Care (Form 33B.1 – a blank copy should be attached), serve a copy on the children's aid society and all other parties and file a copy in the court office with an Affidavit of Service (Form 6B).

YOU HAVE ONLY 30 DAYS AFTER THIS APPLICATION IS SERVED ON YOU (60 DAYS IF THIS APPLICATION IS SERVED ON YOU OUTSIDE CANADA OR THE UNITED STATES) TO SERVE AND FILE AN ANSWER. IF YOU DO NOT, THE CASE WILL GO AHEAD WITHOUT YOU AND THE COURT MAY MAKE AN ORDER AND ENFORCE IT AGAINST YOU.

Check this box if this paragraph applies ☐ The children's aid society is also making a claim for child support. You **MUST** fill out a Financial Statement (Form 13 – a blank copy attached), serve a copy on the society and file a copy in the court office with an Affidavit of Service even if you do not answer this case.

FLR 8B (March 1, 2018)

Page 1 of 7

Form 8B: **Application (Child Protection**   (page 2)   Court File Number
               and Status Review)

WARNING: This case is subject to case management, which means that the case runs on a timetable. That timetable says that the following steps have to be finished by the following number of days from the start of this case:

Service and filing of answers and plans of care − *30 days*

Temporary care & custody hearing − *35 days*

Settlement conference − *80 days*

Hearing − *120 days*

You should consider getting legal advice about this case right away. If you cannot afford a lawyer, you may be able to get help from your local legal aid office. *(See your telephone directory under LEGAL AID).*

_____   _____
        Date of issue   *Clerk of the court*

Form 8B: **Application (Child Protection and Status Review)**   **(page 3)**   Court File Number

THE CHILD(REN): *(List all children involved in this case.)*

Child's Full Legal Name	Birthdate	Age	Sex	Full Legal Name(s) of Parent(s)	Is the Child First Nations, Inuk, or Métis?	Child's Bands and First Nations, Inuit, or Métis Communities

CLAIM BY APPLICANT

NOTE: *If this case is an application for a status review, strike out paragraph 1 and go immediately to paragraph 2.*

1. The applicant children's aid society asks the court to make a finding under Part V of the *Child, Youth and Family Services Act, 2017* that the child(ren) named in this application is/are in need of protection because:

   (Check the applicable box(es). In each checked paragraph, delete those portions of the text that are not relevant.)

   ☐ the child(ren) has/have suffered physical harm, inflicted by the person having charge of the child(ren) or caused by that person's

       ☐ failure to care for, provide for, supervise or protect the child(ren) adequately [subclause 74(2)*(a)(i)*].

       ☐ pattern of neglect in caring for, providing for, supervising or protecting the child(ren) [subclause 74(2)*(a)(ii)*].

   ☐ there is a risk that the child(ren) is/are likely to suffer physical harm inflicted by the person having charge of the child(ren) or caused by that person's

       ☐ failure to care for, provide for, supervise or protect the child(ren) adequately [subclause 74(2)*(b)(i)*].

       ☐ pattern of neglect in caring for, providing for, supervising or protecting the child(ren) [subclause 74(2)*(b)(ii)*].

   ☐ the child(ren) has/have been sexually abused or sexually exploited, by the person having charge of the child(ren) or by another person where the person having charge knows or should know of the possibility of sexual abuse or sexual exploitation and fails to protect the child(ren) [clause 74(2)*(c)*].

   ☐ there is a risk that the child(ren) is/are likely to be sexually abused or sexually exploited, by the person having charge of the child(ren) or by another person where the person having charge knows of should know of the possibility of sexual abuse or sexual exploitation and fails to protect the child(ren) [clause 74(2)*(d)*].

   ☐ the child(ren) require(s) treatment to cure, prevent or alleviate physical harm or suffering and the child(ren)'s parent or the person having charge of the child(ren) does not provide the treatment or access to the treatment, or, where the child(ren) is/are incapable of consenting to the treatment under the *Health Care Consent Act, 1996* and the parent is a substitute decision-maker for the child(ren), the parent refuses or is unavailable or unable to consent to the treatment on the child(ren)'s behalf [clause 74(2)*(e)*].

   ☐ the child(ren) has/have suffered emotional harm, demonstrated by serious anxiety, depression, withdrawal, self-destructive or aggressive behaviour, or delayed development and there are reasonable grounds to believe that the emotional harm suffered by the child(ren) results from the actions, failure to act or pattern of neglect on the part of the child(ren)'s parent or the person having charge of the child(ren) [clause 74(2)*(f)*].

   ☐ the child(ren) has/have suffered emotional harm, demonstrated by serious anxiety, depression, withdrawal, self-destructive or aggressive behaviour, or delayed development and the child(ren)'s parent or the person having charge of the child(ren) does not provide treatment or access to treatment, or, where the child(ren) is/are incapable of consenting to treatment under the *Health Care Consent Act, 1996*, refuses or is unavailable or unable to consent to the treatment to remedy or alleviate the harm [clause 74(2)*(g)*].

   ☐ there is a risk that the child(ren) is/are likely to suffer emotional harm, demonstrated by serious anxiety, depression, withdrawal, self-destructive or aggressive behaviour, or delayed development resulting from the actions, failure to act or pattern of neglect on the part of the child(ren)'s parent or the person having charge of the child(ren) [clause 74(2)*(h)*].

Form 8B: **Application (Child Protection and Status Review)** **(page 4)**

Court File Number [ ]

☐ there is a risk that the child(ren) is/are likely to suffer emotional harm, demonstrated by serious anxiety, depression, withdrawal, self-destructive or aggressive behaviour, or delayed development and that the child(ren)'s parent or the person having charge of the child(ren) does not provide treatment or access to treatment, or, where the child(ren) is/are incapable of consenting to treatment under the *Health Care Consent Act, 1996*, refuses or is unavailable or unable to consent to treatment to prevent the harm [clause 74(2)*(i)*].

☐ the child(ren) suffer(s) from a mental, emotional or developmental condition that, if not remedied, could seriously impair the child(ren)'s development and the child(ren)'s parent or the person having charge of the child(ren) does not provide treatment or access to treatment, or, where the child(ren) is/are incapable of consenting to treatment under the *Health Care Consent Act, 1996*, refuses or is unavailable or unable to consent to the treatment to remedy or alleviate the condition [clause 74(2)*(j)*].

☐ the child(ren)'s parent has died or is unavailable to exercise custodial rights over the child(ren) and has not made adequate provision for the child(ren)'s care and custody, or the child(ren) is/are in a residential placement and the parent refuses or is unable or unwilling to resume the child(ren)'s care and custody [clause 74(2)*(k)*].

☐ the child(ren) is/are younger than twelve and has/have killed or seriously injured another person or caused serious damage to another person's property, services or treatment are necessary to prevent a recurrence and the child(ren)'s parent or the person having charge of the child(ren) does not provide services or treatment or access to services or treatment, or, where the child(ren) is/are incapable of consenting to treatment under the *Health Care Consent Act, 1996*, refuses or is unavailable or unable to consent to treatment [clause 74(2)*(l)*].

☐ the child(ren) is/are less than twelve years old and has/have, on more than one occasion, injured another person or caused loss or damage to another person's property, with the encouragement of the person having charge of the child(ren) or because of that person's failure or inability to supervise the child(ren) adequately [clause 74(2)*(m)*].

☐ the child(ren)'s parent is unable to care for the child(ren) and the child(ren) is/are brought before the court with the parent's consent and, where the child(ren) is/are twelve years of age or older, with the child(ren)'s consent, for the matter to be dealt with under Part V of the *Child, Youth and Family Services Act, 2017* [clause 74(2)*(n)*].

☐ the child(ren) is/are sixteen or seventeen years of age and a prescribed circumstance or condition exists [clause 74(2)*(o)*].

2. *(name)* _____ asks for an order,

☐ that the child(ren) be placed with *(name of custodian)* _____

subject to the supervision of *(full legal name of supervising society)* _____

for a period of _____ months, on the terms and conditions set out in the Appendix on page 7 of this Application form.

☐ that the child(ren) be placed in the interim society care of *(full legal name of society)* _____

for a period of _____ months

☐ that the child(ren) be placed in the interim society care of *(full legal name of society)* _____

for a period of _____ months and then returned to *(name of custodian)* _____

subject to the supervision of *(full legal name of supervising society)* _____

for a period of _____ months, on the terms and conditions set out in the Appendix on page 7 of this Application form.

☐ that the child(ren) be placed in the extended society care of *(full legal name of caretaker society)* _____

Form 8B:	Application (Child Protection and Status Review)	(page 5)	Court File Number

☐ relating to access, the details of which are as follows:

☐ that *(name of person)*

be restrained under s. 137 of the *Child, Youth and Family Services Act, 2017* from having any contact with *(name of child(ren) and/or any other caregiver)*

☐ relating to payment of support while the child(ren) is/are in care or subject to an order of supervision, the details of which are as follows:

☐ for court costs.

☐ other *(Specify.)* _____

☐ that the child(ren) be placed in the custody of *(name of custodian – cannot be a foster parent of the child)*

(This order shall be deemed to be an order under s. 28 of the Children's Law Reform Act.)

☐ relating to access, the details of which are as follows:

(This order shall be deemed to be an order under s. 28 of the Children's Law Reform Act.)

☐ that *(name of person)* _____

be restrained under s. 102(3) of the *Child, Youth and Family Services Act, 2017* from having contact with *(name of child(ren) and/or any other caregiver)*

(This order shall be deemed to be an order under s. 35 of the Children's Law Reform Act.)

FLR 8B (March 1, 2018)

Page 5 of 7

842

Form 8B: **Application (Child Protection** **(page 6)** Court File Number
and Status Review)

3. To the applicant's best knowledge, the child(ren)

☐ has/have never before been in the care of a society under an out-of-court agreement under s. 75 of *Child, Youth and Family Services Act, 2017.*

☐ has/have been in the care of a society under an out-of-court agreement under s. 75 of *Child, Youth and Family Services Act, 2017.* The details are as follows: *(Set out the number of times each child was in society care, when the care began and how long it lasted.)*

4. To the applicant's best knowledge, the parties or the child(ren) ☐ have ☐ have not
been in a court case before relating to the supervision, interim or extended society care (guardianship) or custody of or access to the child(ren). *(Provide details of any existing custody order, including whether made by a superior court or under the Divorce Act.)*

5. The parties ☐ have ☐ have not
made a written agreement dealing with any matter involved in this case. *(If you checked the first box, give date of agreement and indicate which of its terms are in dispute. Attach an additional page if you need more space.)*

6. The following is a brief statement of the facts upon which the applicant is relying in this application.
(Set out the facts in numbered paragraphs. If you need more space, you may attach a page, but you must date and sign each additional page.)

Put a line through any blank space left on this page.

_____   _____
Date of signature   *Signature*

_____   _____
If applicant is a children's aid society,   *Print or type name.*
give office or position of person signing.

Form 8B: Application (Child Protection and Status Review)	(page 7)	Court File Number

APPENDIX

The terms and conditions proposed for the child(ren)'s supervision are as follows: *(Set out terms and conditions in numbered paragraphs. Omit this page if no supervision is sought.)*

Form 8B.1

Application (Status Review for Child in Extended Society Care and Child Formerly in Extended Society Care)

ONTARIO

SEAL at	_____ *(Name of court)* _____ *Court office address*

Court File Number

Form 8B.1: Application (Status Review for Child in Extended Society Care and Child Formerly in Extended Society Care)

Applicant(s) *(In most cases, the applicant will be a children's aid society.)*

Full legal name & address for service — street & number, municipality, postal code, telephone & fax numbers and e-mail address (if any).	Lawyer's name & address — street & number, municipality, postal code, telephone & fax numbers and e-mail address (if any).

Respondent(s) *(In most cases, a respondent will be a "parent" within the meaning of section 74 of the Child, Youth and Family Services Act, 2017.)*

Full legal name & address for service — street & number, municipality, postal code, telephone & fax numbers and e-mail address (if any).	Lawyer's name & address — street & number, municipality, postal code, telephone & fax numbers and e-mail address (if any).

Children's Lawyer

Name & address of Children's Lawyer's agent for service (street & number, municipality, postal code, telephone & fax numbers and e-mail address (if any)) and name of person represented.

TO THE RESPONDENT(S):

A COURT CASE HAS BEEN STARTED AGAINST YOU IN THIS COURT. THE DETAILS ARE SET OUT ON THE ATTACHED PAGES.

THE FIRST COURT DATE IS *(date)* _____ **AT** _____ ☐ a.m. ☐ p.m.

or as soon as possible after that time, at: *(address)*

If you have also been served with a notice of motion, there may be an earlier court date, and you or your lawyer should come to court for the motion.

IF YOU WANT TO OPPOSE ANY CLAIM IN THIS CASE, you or your lawyer must prepare an Answer and Plan of Care (Form 33B.1 – a blank copy should be attached), serve a copy on the children's aid society and all other parties and file a copy in the court office with an Affidavit of Service (Form 6B).

YOU HAVE ONLY 30 DAYS AFTER THIS APPLICATION IS SERVED ON YOU (60 DAYS IF THIS APPLICATION IS SERVED ON YOU OUTSIDE CANADA OR THE UNITED STATES) TO SERVE AND FILE AN ANSWER. IF YOU DO NOT, THE CASE WILL GO AHEAD WITHOUT YOU AND THE COURT MAY MAKE AN ORDER AND ENFORCE IT AGAINST YOU.

Check this box if this paragraph applies ☐ The children's aid society is also making a claim for child support. You **MUST** fill out a Financial Statement (Form 13 – a blank copy attached), serve a copy on the society and file a copy in the court office with an Affidavit of Service even if you do not answer this case.

FLR 8B.1 (March 1, 2018)

Page 1 of 5

Form 8B.1: **Application (Status Review for Child in**   **(page 2)**
Extended Society Care and Child
Formerly in Extended Society Care)

Court File Number

WARNING: This case is subject to case management, which means that the case runs on a timetable. That timetable says that the following steps have to be finished by the following number of days from the start of this case:

Service and filing of answers and plans of care – 30 days

Temporary care & custody hearing – 35 days

Settlement conference – 80 days

Hearing – 120 days

You should consider getting legal advice about this case right away. If you cannot afford a lawyer, you may be able to get help from your local legal aid office. *(See your telephone directory under LEGAL AID).*

_____
Date of issue

_____
Clerk of the court

FLR 8B.1 (March 1, 2018)

Page 2 of 5

846

Form 8B.1: Application (Status Review for Child in   **(page 3)**
        Extended Society Care and Child Formerly
        in Extended Society Care)

Court File Number

THE CHILD

Child's Full Legal Name	Birthdate	Age	Sex	Full Legal Name(s) of Parent(s)	Is the Child First Nations, Inuk, or Métis?	Child's Bands and First Nations, Inuit, or Métis Communities

CLAIM BY *(name and relationship to child, if applicable)* _____

1.   *(name)* _____ asks for an order,

    ☐   that the child be placed in the custody of *(name of custodian)* _____

        under s. 116(1)(b) of the *Child, Youth and Family Services Act, 2017.*

    ☐   that the child be placed with *(name of custodian)* _____

        subject to the supervision of *(full legal name of supervising society)*

        _____

        for a period of _____ months, on the terms and conditions set out in the Appendix on page 5

        of this Application form.

    ☐   that the child be placed in the extended society care of *(full legal name of caretaker society)*

        _____

    ☐   relating to access, the details of which are as follows:

    ☐   that *(name of person)* _____ be restrained under s. 137

        of the *Child, Youth and Family Services Act, 2017* from having any contact with *(name of child and/or any caregiver)*

        _____ *(Provide details of restraining order being sought.)*

    ☐   relating to payment of support while the child is in care or subject to an order of supervision, the details of which are as follows:

    ☐   terminating the order dated *(date of order)* _____ for *(type of order)*

    ☐   for court costs.

    ☐   other *(Specify.)*

FAMILY LAW RULES FORMS

Form 8B.1:	Application (Status Review for Child in Extended Society Care and Child Formerly in Extended Society Care)	(page 4)	Court File Number

2.   The details of the child's history in the care of a society are as follows:

(Set out number of times the child was in the care of a society, when the care began, how long it lasted and the date(s) of the order(s) for extended society care and access.)

3.   The following is a brief statement of the facts relied upon in this application.

(Set out the facts in numbered paragraphs. If you need more space, you may attach a page, but you must date and sign each additional page.)

Put a line through any blank space left on this page.

_____   _____
Date of signature   *Signature*

_____   _____
If applicant is a children's aid society,   *Print or type name.*
give office or position of person signing.

Form 8B.1: Application (Status Review for Child in   (page 5)
            Extended Society Care and Child
            Formerly in Extended Society Care)

Court File Number

APPENDIX

The terms and conditions proposed for the child's supervision are as follows: *(Set out terms and conditions in numbered paragraphs. Omit this page if no supervision is sought.)*

FLR 8B.1 (March 1, 2018)

Page 5 of 5

Form 8B.2

Application (General) (*Child, Youth and Family Services Act, 2017* Cases other than Child Protection and Status Review)

ONTARIO

		Court File Number
SEAL	at	

(Name of court)

Court office address

Form 8B.2: Application (General) (*Child, Youth and Family Services Act, 2017* Cases other than Child Protection and Status Review)

Applicant(s) *(In most cases, the applicant will be a children's aid society.)*

Full legal name & address for service — street & number, municipality, postal code, telephone & fax numbers and e-mail address (if any).	Lawyer's name & address — street & number, municipality, postal code, telephone & fax numbers and e-mail address (if any).

Respondent(s) *(In most cases, a respondent will be a "parent" within the meaning of section 74 of the Child, Youth and Family Services Act, 2017.)*

Full legal name & address for service — street & number, municipality, postal code, telephone & fax numbers and e-mail address (if any).	Lawyer's name & address — street & number, municipality, postal code, telephone & fax numbers and e-mail address (if any).

Children's Lawyer

Name & address of Children's Lawyer's agent for service (street & number, municipality, postal code, telephone & fax numbers and e-mail address (if any)) and name of person represented.

TO THE RESPONDENT(S):

A COURT CASE HAS BEEN STARTED AGAINST YOU IN THIS COURT. THE DETAILS ARE SET OUT ON THE ATTACHED PAGES.

THE FIRST COURT DATE IS *(date)* _____ **AT** _____ ☐ a.m. ☐ p.m.

or as soon as possible after that time, at: *(address)*

If you have also been served with a notice of motion, there may be an earlier court date and you or your lawyer should come to court for the motion.

IF YOU WANT TO OPPOSE ANY CLAIM IN THIS CASE, you or your lawyer must prepare an Answer (*Child, Youth and Family Services Act, 2017* Cases other than Child Protection and Status Review) (Form 33B.2 – a blank copy should be attached), serve a copy on the children's aid society and all other parties and file a copy in the court office with an Affidavit of Service (Form 6B).

YOU HAVE ONLY 30 DAYS AFTER THIS APPLICATION IS SERVED ON YOU (60 DAYS IF THIS APPLICATION IS SERVED ON YOU OUTSIDE CANADA OR THE UNITED STATES) TO SERVE AND FILE AN ANSWER. IF YOU DO NOT, THE CASE WILL GO AHEAD WITHOUT YOU AND THE COURT MAY MAKE AN ORDER AND ENFORCE IT AGAINST YOU.

Check this box if this paragraph applies ☐ The children's aid society is also making a claim for child support. You **MUST** fill out a Financial Statement (Form 13 – a blank copy attached), serve a copy on the society and file a copy in the court office with an Affidavit of Service even if you do not answer this case.

FLR 8B.2 (March 1, 2018)   Page 1 of 4

Form 8B.2:	Application (General) (*Child, Youth and* *Family Services Act, 2017* Cases other than Child Protection and Status Review)	(page 2)	Court File Number

WARNING: This case is subject to case management, which means that the case runs on a timetable. That timetable says that the following steps have to be finished by the following number of days from the start of this case:

Service and filing of answers and plans of care – 30 days

Settlement conference – 80 days

Hearing – 120 days

You should consider getting legal advice about this case right away. If you cannot afford a lawyer, you may be able to get help from your local legal aid office. *(See your telephone directory under LEGAL AID).*

_____   _____
Date of issue   Clerk of the court

FAMILY LAW RULES FORMS

Form 8B.2: Application (General) (*Child, Youth and Family Services Act, 2017* **Cases other than Child Protection and Status Review**)   (page 3)

Court File Number

THE CHILD(REN): *(List all children involved in this case.)*

Child's Full Legal Name	Birthdate	Age	Sex	Full Legal Name(s) of Parent(s)	Is the Child First Nations, Inuk, or Métis?	Child's Bands and First Nations, Inuit, or Métis Communities

CLAIM BY *(name and relationship to child, if applicable)* _____

1. *(name)* _____ asks for an order: *(Specify the order being sought and the grounds upon which the application is being brought)*

   ☐ relating to access, the details of which are as follows:

   ☐ that *(name of person)* _____ be restrained under s. 137 of the *Child, Youth and Family Services Act, 2017* from having any contact with *(name of child(ren) and/or any caregiver)*

                                             (Provide details of restraining order being sought.)

   ☐ relating to payment of support while the child(ren) is/are in care or subject to an order of supervision, the details of which are as follows:

   ☐ other *(Specify.)*

   ☐ for court costs of this application.

FLR 8B.2 (March 1, 2018)   Page 3 of 4

Form 8B.2: **Application (General)** (*Child, Youth and Family Services Act, 2017* Cases other than Child Protection and Status Review) **(page 4)**

Court File Number

2. The existing orders relating to the child(ren) are as follows:

3. The following is a brief statement of the facts relied upon in this application.
(Set out the facts in numbered paragraphs. If you need more space, you may attach a page, but you must date and sign each additional page.)

Put a line through any blank space left on this page.

_____
Date of signature

_____
Signature

_____
If applicant is a children's aid society, give office or position of person signing.

_____
Print or type name

FLR 8B.2 (March 1, 2018)

Page 4 of 4

Form 8C

Application for Secure Treatment or Extension of Secure Treatment

ONTARIO

	Court File Number

SEAL

at _____
(Name of court)

_____
Court office address

Form 8C: Application for
☐ **Secure Treatment**
☐ **Extension of Secure Treatment**

Applicant(s)

Full legal name & address for service — street & number, municipality, postal code, telephone & fax numbers and e-mail address *(if any)*.	Lawyer's name & address — street & number, municipality, postal code, telephone & fax numbers and e-mail address *(if any)*.

Respondent(s)

Full legal name & address for service — street & number, municipality, postal code, telephone & fax numbers and e-mail address *(if any)*.	Lawyer's name & address — street & number, municipality, postal code, telephone & fax numbers and e-mail address *(if any)*.

Child

Full legal name of child:	Lawyer's name & address — street & number, municipality, postal code, telephone & fax numbers and e-mail address *(if any)*.
Birth date (d, m, y):	
Sex:	

TO THE RESPONDENT(S) AND CHILD:

A COURT CASE HAS BEEN STARTED IN THIS COURT. THE DETAILS ARE SET OUT ON THE ATTACHED PAGES.

THE FIRST COURT DATE IS *(date)* _____ **AT** _____ ☐ a.m. ☐ p.m.

or as soon as possible after that time, at *(address)* _____

Check applicable box.

1. ☐ I/We am/are the child's parent(s). *(Attach the consent of the parent(s) in Form 33F. If the child is 16 or 17 years old, the child's consent – Form 33E – must also be attached. In an application to extend treatment, the consent of the program administrator in Form 33F must also be attached. If the "child" is 18 or more years old, the "child's" consent to extend treatment in Form 33F must also be attached.)*

   ☐ I am an authorized officer of the applicant children's aid society that has custody of the child under an order made under Part V of the *Child, Youth and Family Services Act, 2017*. *(Attach the officer's consent in Form 33F. If the child is 16 or 17 years old, the child's consent – Form 33E – must also be attached. In an application to extend treatment, the administrator's consent in Form 33F must also be attached.)*

   ☐ I am a person (other than an administrator of the secure treatment program) who is caring for the child. *(To be used only where the child is less than 16 years of age. A consent of the child's parent – Form 33F – must be attached. In an application to extend treatment, the administrator's consent in Form 33F must also be attached.)*

   ☐ I am the child in this case and I am 16 or 17 years old. *(The child's consent – Form 33E – must be attached. In an application to extend treatment, the administrator's consent in Form 33F must also be attached.)*

   ☐ I am the person who has been committed to the secure treatment program in this case and I am 18 or more years old. *(To be used only in an application to extend treatment. Attach the consent of the program administrator on Form 33F.)*

   ☐ I am a physician qualified under the law of Ontario to practise medicine. *(To be used in an application for secure treatment only where the child is 16 years of age or more. A physician can apply to extend treatment, but only if the "child" is 18 or more years of age and only if separate consents in Form 33F, both from the administrator of the program and from the "child" are attached.)*

FAMILY LAW RULES FORMS

Form 8C: **Application (secure treatment)**   **(page 2)** | Court File Number |

☐   I am the person in charge of the secure treatment program. *(To be used only in an application to extend secure treatment. Attach two consents in Form 33F – one from the administrator and the second from the child's parent or, if the child is in the care of a children's aid society, the society's consent. If the "child" is now 18 or more years old, the second consent in Form 33F must come from the "child".)*

2.   I/We ask for an order under Part VII of the *Child, Youth and Family Services Act, 2017*
   ☐   committing the child   ☐   extending the child's commitment
   to the secure treatment program at: *(Name and address of secure treatment program.)*

3.   I/We make this application because: *(NOTE: All three paragraphs – [a] and [b] and [c] – must be true in all cases.)*
   ☐   (a)   the child has a mental disorder;
   ☐   (b)   the secure treatment program would be effective to prevent the child from causing or attempting to cause serious bodily harm to himself/herself or to another person;
   ☐   (c)   no less restrictive method of providing treatment appropriate for the child's mental disorder is appropriate in the circumstances;

Use this frame only in an application for commitment to a secure treatment program.
In addition to paragraphs (a), (b) and (c) above, all three paragraphs below – (d) and (e) and (f) – must ALSO be true.

☐   d)   the child has, as a result of the mental disorder, within 45 days immediately before,

Check only one of these three boxes
   ☐   the date of this application for commitment to secure treatment,
   ☐   the child's detention or custody under the federal *Youth Criminal Justice Act* or Ontario's *Provincial Offences Act*,
   ☐   the child's admission as an involuntary patient to a psychiatric facility under the *Mental Health Act*,

   caused or attempted to cause serious bodily harm to himself/herself or to another person;

☐   e)   the child has:
   ☐   within the 12 months immediately before this application for secure treatment on an occasion different from the one mentioned in clause (b) above caused or attempted to cause or by words or conduct, made a substantial threat to cause serious bodily harm to himself/herself or to another person, OR
   ☐   caused or attempted to cause a person's death when causing or attempting to cause serious bodily harm to himself/herself or to another person; and

☐   f)   treatment appropriate for the child's mental disorder is available at the program named in paragraph 2 above.

Use this frame only in an application to extend the period of commitment to a secure treatment program.
In addition to paragraphs (a), (b) and (c) above, both paragraphs below – (d) and (e) – must ALSO be true.

☐   d)   the child is receiving,
   ☐   the treatment proposed when this court originally ordered commitment to the secure treatment program
   ☐   other appropriate treatment; and
☐   e)   there is an appropriate plan for the child's care on release from the secure treatment program.

---

4.   The following is a brief statement of the facts upon which this application is based. *(Set out the facts in numbered paragraphs with reference to the items in paragraph 3. If you need more space, you may attach a page, but you must date and sign each additional page.)*

Put a line through any blank space left on this page.

| Signature | Date of Signature |

| Signature | Date of Signature |

FLR 8C (March 1, 2018)   Page 2 of 2

Form 8D

Application (Adoption)

ONTARIO

SEAL	at _____ *(Name of court)* _____ Court office address	Court File Number _____

Form 8D: Application (Adoption)

Applicant(s) *(The first letter of the applicant's surname may be used)*

Full legal name & address for service — street & number, municipality, postal code, telephone & fax numbers and e-mail address (if any).	Lawyer's name & address — street & number, municipality, postal code, telephone & fax numbers and e-mail address (if any).

Respondent(s) *(If there is a respondent, the first letter of the respondent's surname may be used)*

Full legal name & address for service — street & number, municipality, postal code, telephone & fax numbers and e-mail address (if any).	Lawyer's name & address — street & number, municipality, postal code, telephone & fax numbers and e-mail address (if any).

The application is for a(n) *(check all boxes that apply):*

☐ adoption of a child in extended society care   ☐ licensed adoption   ☐ society adoption of a child who is not in extended society care   ☐ section 199(1)(b) adoption

☐ international adoption   ☐ relative adoption   ☐ stepparent adoption *(complete additional section below)*

THE APPLICANT(S) ASK FOR AN ORDER FOR THE ADOPTION OF: *(Give full legal name, date of birth, sex and birth registration number of person to be adopted. If this person is in extended society care or was placed for adoption by a licensee or children's aid society, you may use an initial for the surname.)*

_____   _____   _____   _____
Full legal name   Date of birth   Sex   Birth registration number

The applicant(s) also ask for an order that the person's name after adoption be: *(full legal name of person after adoption)*

_____

To be completed for a stepparent adoption:

If the adoption order is made, pursuant to s. 217(2)(b) of the *Child, Youth and Family Services Act, 2017*, the parents of the person will be:

YOU SHOULD CONSIDER GETTING LEGAL ADVICE ABOUT THIS RIGHT AWAY. If you cannot afford a lawyer, you may be able to get help from Legal Aid Ontario. Call **1-800-668-8258 toll-free** to get legal aid help in over 120 languages. For more information about the services available through Legal Aid Ontario, visit www.legalaid.on.ca.

Strike out the box below if it does not apply in this case.

NOTE TO THE RESPONDENTS: You are also being served with a notice of motion to dispense with your consent to the adoption. The details of the motion can be found on the notice of motion and the attached affidavit(s).

IF YOU WANT TO OPPOSE THIS ADOPTION, you or your lawyer must serve and file an *Answer* (Form 10). IF YOU **DO NOT DO SO, THE COURT MAY DISPENSE WITH YOUR CONSENT WITHOUT YOU AND YOU WILL GET NO FURTHER NOTICE.**

_____	_____
Date of signature	Signature of applicant

_____	_____
Date of signature	Signature of co-applicant

_____	_____
Date of issue by clerk of the court	Signature of clerk of the court

For information on accessibility of court services for people with disability-related needs, contact:
Telephone: 416-326-2220 / 1-800-518-7901   TTY: 416-326-4012 / 1-877-425-0575

FLR 8D (March 1, 2018)

Page 1 of 1

Form 8D.1

Application (Dispense with Parent's Consent to Adoption before Placement)

ONTARIO

SEAL

_____
(Name of court)

at _____
Court office address

Court File Number

Form 8D.1: Application (Dispense with Parent's Consent To Adoption Before Placement)

Applicant(s) *(The first letter of the applicant's surname may be used)*

Full legal name & address for service — street & number, municipality, postal code, telephone & fax numbers and e-mail address (if any).	Lawyer's name & address — street & number, municipality, postal code, telephone & fax numbers and e-mail address (if any).

Respondent(s) *(If there is a respondent, the first letter of the respondent's surname may be used)*

Full legal name & address for service — street & number, municipality, postal code, telephone & fax numbers and e-mail address (if any).	Lawyer's name & address — street & number, municipality, postal code, telephone & fax numbers and e-mail address (if any).

THE APPLICANT(S) ASK FOR AN ORDER DISPENSING WITH THE CONSENT OF THE RESPONDENT(S) TO THE ADOPTION OF THE CHILD: *(Give full legal name, date of birth, sex and birth registration number (if known) of person to be adopted. If this person is to be placed for adoption by a licensee or children's aid society, you may use an initial for the surname.)*

Full legal name	Date of birth	Sex	Birth registration number

☐ The applicant(s) also ask for an order that service of the application on the respondent(s) is not required.

NOTE TO THE RESPONDENT(S): A court case has been started against you in this court. The details are set out in the attached affidavit.

THE FIRST COURT DATE IS *(date)* _____ **at** _____ ☐ a.m. ☐ p.m.

or as soon as possible after that time, at: *(address)*

THIS CASE IS ON THE FAST TRACK OF THE CASE MANAGEMENT SYSTEM. A case management judge will be assigned by the time this case first comes before a judge.

IF YOU WANT TO OPPOSE THIS APPLICATION, you or your lawyer must prepare an *Answer* (Form 10 — a blank copy should be attached), serve a copy on the applicant(s) and file a copy in the court office with an *Affidavit of Service* (Form 6B). **YOU HAVE ONLY 20 DAYS AFTER THIS APPLICATION IS SERVED ON YOU (40 DAYS IF THIS APPLICATION IS SERVED ON YOU OUTSIDE CANADA OR THE UNITED STATES) TO SERVE AND FILE AN ANSWER. IF YOU DO NOT DO SO, THE COURT MAY DISPENSE WITH YOUR CONSENT WITHOUT YOU.**

FLR 8D.1 (November 1, 2018)

Page 1 of 2

Form 8D.1: **Application (Dispense with Parent's Consent** **(page 2)**
To Adoption Before Placement)

Court File Number

If you want to make a claim of your own, you or your lawyer must fill out the claim portion in the *Answer*, serve a copy on the applicant(s) and file a copy in the court office with an *Affidavit of Service*.

YOU SHOULD GET LEGAL ADVICE ABOUT THIS CASE RIGHT AWAY. If you cannot afford a lawyer, you may be able to get help from your local Legal Aid office. *(See your telephone directory under LEGAL AID).*

_____   _____
Date of signature   Signature of applicant

_____   _____
Date of signature   Signature of co-applicant

_____   _____
Date of issue by clerk of the court   Signature of clerk of the court

Form 8D.2

Notice of Intention to Place Child(ren) for Adoption

ONTARIO

	Court File Number

_____
(Name of court)

Form 8D.2: Notice of Intention to Place Child(ren) for Adoption

at _____
Court office address

TO: _____
(name of child being placed for adoption or person entitled to have access to the child)

This notice is to advise you that the *(name of children's aid society)* _____

is planning to: *(strike out the paragraph that does not apply. NOTE: in some cases, both paragraphs may apply.)*

☐ **place the following child(ren) for adoption:** *(full legal name(s) and date(s) of birth of child(ren)*

☐ **place you for adoption.**

This means that: *(Add more numbered lines as needed for each additional person.)*

1. Your access to _____ will end when _____ is placed for adoption.
   (name of the person to whom access is ending)   *(name or "you" as applicable)*

2. Your access to _____ will end when _____ is placed for adoption.
   (name of the person to whom access is ending)   *(name or "you" as applicable)*

3. Your access to _____ will end when _____ is placed for adoption.
   (name of the person to whom access is ending)   *(name or "you" as applicable)*

Strike out the box below if it does not apply in this case

You have been granted a right of access under the *Child, Youth and Family Services Act, 2017*. You have the right to apply for an openness order with respect to the following person(s): *(name(s) of person(s) to whom the person receiving this notice has a right of access and may apply for an openness order.)*

FLR 8D.2 (March 1, 2018)

FAMILY LAW RULES FORMS

Form 8D.2:	Notice of Intention to Place Child(ren) for Adoption	(page 2)	Court File Number

You must act within 30 days if you want to ask the court for an openness order.

If you want to have a right to contact any of the persons listed above through an openness order, you or your lawyer must, **within 30 days of receiving this notice**:

1. Prepare a Form 34L: Application for Openness Order. (A blank copy should be attached; if it is not, you can obtain a copy from the court office or at www.ontariocourtforms.on.ca.)

2. Serve a copy of the completed Form 34L on <u>all</u> of the following:

   a. The children's aid society to the attention of   at the following address:

   b. The Children's Lawyer at the Office of the Children's Lawyer, 393 University Avenue, 14th floor, Toronto, Ontario, M5G 1E6.

   c. The child's lawyer, if any.

   d. The person(s) with whom you are seeking openness, unless that person is a child under the age of 12.

3. File a copy of the completed Form 34L with a Form 6B: Affidavit of Service. You can obtain these forms from www.ontariocourtforms.on.ca or at the court office.

If you do not serve and file a Form 34L within 30 days of receiving this notice, you will not be able to apply to the court for any openness order.

Strike out the box below if it does not apply in this case

You are a person to whom access has been granted under *the Child, Youth and Family Services Act, 2017*. You do not have a right to apply for an openness order with respect to the following person(s):

Every person who has been granted a right of access under the *Child, Youth and Family Services Act, 2017* may seek an openness order within 30 days after notice is received.

Form 8D.2:   Notice of Intention to Place Child(ren) for Adoption   (page 3)

Court File Number

Information about the order(s) that will end

Court File Number	Court Office Address	Name(s) of Judge(s)	Date(s) of Order(s)

Details of Access Order(s) That Will End *(for example specify who has been granted a right of access and to which persons)*

You may get a lawyer to help you.

YOU SHOULD CONSIDER GETTING LEGAL ADVICE ABOUT THIS RIGHT AWAY. If you cannot afford a lawyer, you may be able to get help from Legal Aid Ontario. Call **1-800-668-8258 toll-free** to get legal aid help in over 120 languages. For more information about the services available through Legal Aid Ontario, visit www.legalaid.on.ca.

IF YOU ARE UNDER 18 YEARS OLD, the children's aid society must send a copy of this form to the Children's Lawyer at their place of business, which is the Office of the Children's Lawyer, 393 University Avenue, 14th floor, Toronto, Ontario, M5G 1E6. You can contact the Office of the Children's Lawyer at 416-314-8000 and ask to speak to a lawyer.

_____
Signature of children's aid society employee

_____
Date of signature

_____
(Name and position of children's aid society employee)

For information on accessibility of court services for people with disability-related needs, contact:
Telephone: 416-326-2220 / 1-800-518-7901   TTY: 416-326-4012 / 1-877-425-0575

Form 8D.3

Notice of Intention to Place First Nations, Inuk or Métis Child for Adoption

ONTARIO

	Court File Number

_____
(Name of court)

Form 8D.3: Notice of Intention to Place First Nations, Inuk or Métis Child for Adoption

at _____
Court office address

TO: _____
(name of child being placed for adoption or representative chosen by the child's band or First Nations, Inuit or Métis community)

This notice is to advise you that the *(name of children's aid society)* _____

is planning to:

☐ **place the child,** *(child's full legal name and date of birth)*

_____ , **for adoption.**

☐ **place you for adoption.**

You have a right to apply for an openness order within 30 days after receiving this notice.

If you want to have contact, you or your lawyer, **must within 30 days of receiving this notice:**

1. Prepare a Form 34L: Application for Openness Order. (A blank copy should be attached; if it is not, you can obtain a copy from the court office or at www.ontariocourtforms.on.ca.)

2. Serve a copy of the completed Form 34L on <u>all</u> the following:

   a. The children's aid society to the attention of _____

      at the following address: _____

   b. Any other person who could apply for an openness order under s. 197 of the *Child, Youth and Family Services Act, 2017* (Note: this could be the child, the child's lawyer, the Children's Lawyer, and/or the representative chosen by the child's band(s) or First Nations, Inuit or Métis communities.)

3. File a copy of the completed Form 34L with a Form 6B: Affidavit of Service (you can obtain a copy from the court office or at www.ontariocourtforms.on.ca) at the court office.

If you do not serve and file a Form 34L: Application for Openness Order within 30 days of receiving this notice, you will not be able to apply to the court for an openness order.

<u>**The children's aid society also has a right to apply for an openness order within 30 days after giving this notice.**</u>

YOU SHOULD CONSIDER GETTING LEGAL ADVICE ABOUT THIS NOTICE RIGHT AWAY.

IF YOU ARE UNDER 18 YEARS OLD the children's aid society must send a copy of this form to the Children's Lawyer at their place of business, which is the Office of the Children's Lawyer, 393 University Avenue, 14th floor, Toronto, Ontario, M5G 1E6. You can contact the Office of the Children's Lawyer at 416-314-8000 and ask to speak to a lawyer.

_____   _____
Signature of children's aid society employee   *Date of signature*

_____
(Name and position of children's aid society employee)

For information on accessibility of court services for people with disability-related needs, contact:
Telephone: 416-326-2220 / 1-800-518-7901   TTY: 416-326-4012 / 1-877-425-0575

FLR 8D.3 (March 1, 2018)

Page 1 of 1

Form 10

Answer

ONTARIO

	Court File Number
_____ *(Name of court)*	
at _____ *Court office address*	**Form 10: Answer**

Applicant(s)

Full legal name & address for service — street & number, municipality, postal code, telephone & fax numbers and e-mail address (if any).	Lawyer's name & address — street & number, municipality, postal code, telephone & fax numbers and e-mail address (if any).

Respondent(s)

Full legal name & address for service — street & number, municipality, postal code, telephone & fax numbers and e-mail address (if any).	Lawyer's name & address — street & number, municipality, postal code, telephone & fax numbers and e-mail address (if any).

Name & address of Children's Lawyer's agent for service (street & number, municipality, postal code, telephone & fax numbers and e-mail address (if any)) and name of person represented.

INSTRUCTIONS: Financial Statement

COMPLETE A FINANCIAL STATEMENT (Form 13) IF:

·   you are making or responding to a claim for spousal support; or

·   you are responding to a claim for child support; or

·   you are making a claim for child support in an amount different from the table amount specified under the Child Support Guidelines.

You must complete all parts of the form **UNLESS** you are **ONLY** responding to a claim for child support in the table amount specified under the Child Support Guidelines **AND** you agree with the claim. In that case, only complete Parts 1, 2 and 3.

COMPLETE A FINANCIAL STATEMENT (Form 13.1) IF:

·   you are making or responding to a claim for property or exclusive possession of the matrimonial home and its contents; or

·   you are making or responding to a claim for property or exclusive possession of the matrimonial home and its contents together with other claims for relief.

TO THE APPLICANT(S):

If you are making a claim against someone who is not an applicant, insert the person's name and address here.

AND TO: *(full legal name)* _____ **an added respondent,**

of *(address of added party)* _____

My name is *(full legal name)* _____

1.   I agree with the following claim(s) made by the applicant: *(Refer to the numbers alongside the boxes on page 4 of the application form.)*

Form 10:	Answer	(page 2)	Court File Number

2.   I do not agree with the following claim(s) made by the applicant: *(Again, refer to the numbers alongside the boxes on page 4 of the application form.)*

3.   ☐   I am asking that the applicant's claim (except for the parts with which I agree) be dismissed with costs.

4.   ☐   I am making a claim of my own.
(Attach a "Claim by Respondent" page and include it as page 3. Otherwise, do not attach it.)

5.   ☐   The FAMILY HISTORY, as set out in the application   ☐   is correct.
                                                                ☐   is not correct.
(If it is not correct, attach your own FAMILY HISTORY page and underline those parts that are different from the applicant's version.)

6.   The important facts that form the legal basis for my position in paragraph 2 are as follows:
(In numbered paragraphs, set out the facts for your position. Attach an additional sheet and number it if you need more space.)
   1.

Put a line through any blank space left on this page

_____   _____
Date of signature   Respondent's signature

864

Form 10:	Answer	(page 3)	Court File Number

CLAIM BY RESPONDENT

Fill out a separate claim page for each person against whom you are making your claim(s).

7.   THIS CLAIM IS MADE AGAINST

☐   THE APPLICANT

☐   AN ADDED PARTY, whose name is: *(full legal name)* _____

(If your claim is against an added party, make sure that this person's name appears on page 1 of this form.)

8.   I ASK THE COURT FOR THE FOLLOWING:
(Claims below include claims for temporary orders.)

Claims under the *Divorce Act* *(Check boxes in this column only if you are asking for a divorce and your case is in the Superior Court of Justice or Family Court of the Superior Court of Justice.)*		Claims relating to property *(Check boxes in this column only if your case is in the Superior Court of Justice or Family Court of the Superior Court of Justice.)*		Claims relating to child protection	
00	☐ a divorce	20	☐ equalization of net family properties	40	☐ access
01	☐ support for me			41	☐ lesser protection order
02	☐ support for child(ren) – table amount	21	☐ exclusive possession of matrimonial home	42	☐ return of child(ren) to my care
03	☐ support for child(ren)-other than table amount	22	☐ exclusive possession of contents of matrimonial home	43	☐ place child(ren) into care of *(name)* _____
04	☐ custody of child(ren)	23	☐ freezing assets	44	☐ interim society care and custody for _____ months
05	☐ access to child(ren)	24	☐ sale of family property	45	☐ society supervision of my child(ren) for _____ months

Claims under the *Family Law Act* or *Children's Law Reform Act*		Other claims			
10	☐ support for me	30	☐ costs		
11	☐ support for child(ren) – table amount	31	☐ annulment of marriage		
		32	☐ prejudgment interest		
12	☐ support for child(ren) – other than table amount	33	☐ claims relating to a family arbitration		
13	☐ custody of child(ren)				
14	☐ access to child(ren)				
15	☐ restraining/non-harassment order				
16	☐ indexing spousal support				
17	☐ declaration of parentage				
18	☐ guardianship over child's property				
50	☐ Other *(Specify.)*				

Give details of the order that you want the court to make. *(Include any amounts of support (if known) and the name(s) of the child(ren) for whom support, custody or access is claimed.)*

Form 10 : Answer	(page 4)	Court File Number

IMPORTANT FACTS SUPPORTING MY CLAIM(S)

(In numbered paragraphs, set out the facts that form the legal basis for your claim(s). Attach an additional page and number it if you need more space.)

Put a line through any blank space left on this page.

_____   _____
Date of signature   Respondent's signature

LAWYER'S CERTIFICATE

For divorce cases only

My name is _____

and I am the respondent's lawyer in this divorce case. I certify that I have complied with the requirements of section 9 of the *Divorce Act*.

_____   _____
Date   Signature of Lawyer

For information on accessibility of court services for people with disability-related needs, contact:
Telephone: 416-326-2220 / 1-800-518-7901   TTY: 416-326-4012 / 1-877-425-0575

Form 10A

Reply

ONTARIO

Court File Number

_____

(Name of court)

Form 10A: Reply by

☐ **applicant**

at _____

☐ **added respondent**

Court office address

Applicant(s) *(The first letter of the applicant's surname may be used)*

Full legal name & address for service — street & number, municipality, postal code, telephone & fax numbers and e-mail address (if any).	Lawyer's name & address — street & number, municipality, postal code, telephone & fax numbers and e-mail address (if any).

Respondent(s) *(If there is a respondent, the first letter of the respondent's surname may be used)*

Full legal name & address for service — street & number, municipality, postal code, telephone & fax numbers and e-mail address (if any).	Lawyer's name & address — street & number, municipality, postal code, telephone & fax numbers and e-mail address (if any).

Children's Lawyer

Name & address of Children's Lawyer's agent for service (street & number, municipality, postal code, telephone & fax numbers and e-mail address (if any)) and name of person represented.

INSTRUCTIONS: Financial Statement

COMPLETE A FINANCIAL STATEMENT (Form 13) IF:

- you are responding to a claim for spousal support; or
- you are responding to a claim for child support.

You must complete all parts of the form **UNLESS** you are **ONLY** responding to a claim for child support in the table amount specified under the Child Support Guidelines **AND** you agree with the claim. In that case, only complete Parts 1, 2 and 3.

COMPLETE A FINANCIAL STATEMENT (Form 13.1) IF:

- you are responding to a claim for property or exclusive possession of the matrimonial home and its contents; or
- you are responding to a claim for property or exclusive possession of the matrimonial home and its contents together with other claims for relief.

TO ALL PARTIES:

1. My name is *(full legal name)*..

2. I agree with the following claim(s) made by the respondent in his/her answer: *(Refer to the numbers alongside the boxes on page 3 of the answer form.)*

3. I do not agree with the following claim(s) made by the respondent: *(Again, refer to the numbers alongside the boxes on page 3 of the answer form.)*

4. ☐ I am asking that the respondent's claim (except for the parts with which I agree) be dismissed with costs.

5. The important facts supporting my position in paragraph 3 are as follows:

(In numbered paragraphs, set out the reasons for your position. Attach an additional sheet and number it if you need more space.)

Put a line through any space left on this page.

Date of signature	*Signature*

Form 12

Notice of Withdrawal

ONTARIO

_____
(Name of court)

at _____
Court office address

Court File Number

Form 12: Notice of Withdrawal

Applicant(s)

Full legal name & address for service — street & number, municipality, postal code, telephone & fax numbers and e-mail address (if any).	*Lawyer's name & address — street & number, municipality, postal code, telephone & fax numbers and e-mail address (if any).*

Respondent(s)

Full legal name & address for service — street & number, municipality, postal code, telephone & fax numbers and e-mail address (if any).	*Lawyer's name & address — street & number, municipality, postal code, telephone & fax numbers and e-mail address (if any).*

TO ALL PARTIES:

My name is *(full legal name)* ....

I withdraw this

- ☐ application dated *(date)* ....
- ☐ answer dated *(date)* ....
- ☐ notice of default hearing dated *(date)* ....
- ☐ notice of motion dated *(date)* ....
- ☐ *(Other; specify.)*

against *(names of parties against whom there is to be a withdrawal)*

....

....

- ☐ completely.
- ☐ regarding *(State limited nature of withdrawal.)*

_____   _____
Signature of party making withdrawal or of party's lawyer   *Date of signature*

NOTE TO OTHER PARTIES: If a case, an enforcement, a motion, etc., has been wholly or partly withdrawn against you by this notice, you are entitled to your costs from the party making the withdrawal unless the court orders otherwise or unless the parties agree otherwise.

Form 13

Financial Statement (Support Claims)

ONTARIO

_____
(Name of Court)

at _____
Court office address

Court File Number

Form 13: Financial
Statement (Support Claims)
sworn/affirmed

Applicant(s)

Full legal name & address for service — street & number, municipality, postal code, telephone & fax numbers and e-mail address (if any).	Lawyer's name & address — street & number, municipality, postal code, telephone & fax numbers and e-mail address (if any).

Respondent(s)

Full legal name & address for service — street & number, municipality, postal code, telephone & fax numbers and e-mail address (if any).	Lawyer's name & address — street & number, municipality, postal code, telephone & fax numbers and e-mail address (if any).

INSTRUCTIONS

You must complete this form if you are making or responding to a claim for child or spousal support or a claim to change support, unless your only claim for support is a claim for child support in the table amount under the *Child Support Guidelines*.

You may also be required to complete and attach additional schedules based on the claims that have been made in your case or your financial circumstances:

- If you have income that is not shown in Part I of the financial statement (for example, partnership income, dividends, rental income, capital gains or RRSP income), you must also complete **Schedule A**.
- If you have made or responded to a claim for child support that involves undue hardship or a claim for spousal support, you must also complete **Schedule B**.
- If you or the other party has sought a contribution towards special or extraordinary expenses for the child(ren), you must also complete **Schedule C**.

*NOTES: You must **fully and truthfully** complete this financial statement, including any applicable schedules. You must also provide the other party with documents relating to support and a Certificate of Financial Disclosure (Form 13A) as required by Rule 13 of the Family Law Rules.*

If you are making or responding to a claim for property, an equalization payment or the matrimonial home, you must complete Form 13.1: Financial Statement (Property and Support Claims) instead of this form.

1. **My name is** *(full legal name)* _____

   I live in *(municipality & province)* _____

   and I swear/affirm that the following is true:

PART 1: INCOME

2. **I am currently**

   ☐ employed by *(name and address of employer)*

   ☐ self-employed, carrying on business under the name of *(name and address of business)*

   ☐ unemployed since *(date when last employed)*

Page 1 of 8

Form 13: **Financial Statement (Support Claims)** **(page 2)**

Court file number

3. I attach proof of my year-to-date income from all sources, including my most recent *(attach all that are applicable)*:

☐ pay cheque stub ☐ social assistance stub ☐ pension stub ☐ workers' compensation stub

☐ employment insurance stub and last Record of Employment

☐ statement of income and expenses/ professional activities (for self-employed individuals)

☐ other (e.g. a letter from your employer confirming all income received to date this year)

4. Last year, my gross income from all sources was $ _____ *(do not subtract any taxes that have been deducted from this income).*

5. ☐ I am attaching all of the following required documents to this financial statement as proof of my income over the past three years, if they have not already been provided:

. a copy of my personal income tax returns for each of the past three taxation years, including any materials that were filed with the returns. *(Income tax returns must be served but should NOT be filed in the continuing record, unless they are filed with a motion to refrain a driver's license suspension.)*

. a copy of my notices of assessment and any notices of reassessment for each of the past three taxation years;

. where my notices of assessment and reassessment are unavailable for any of the past three taxation years or where I have not filed a return for any of the past three taxation years, an Income and Deductions printout from the Canada Revenue Agency for each of those years, whether or not I filed an income tax return.

Note: An Income and Deductions printout is available from Canada Revenue Agency. Please call customer service at 1-800-959-8281.

OR

☐ I am an Indian within the meaning of the *Indian Act* (Canada) and I have chosen not to file income tax returns for the past three years. I am attaching the following proof of income for the last three years *(list documents you have provided):*

(In this table you must show all of the income that you are currently receiving whether taxable or not.)

	Income Source	Amount Received/Month
1.	Employment income (before deductions)	$
2.	Commissions, tips and bonuses	$
3.	Self-employment income (Monthly amount before expenses: $)	$
4.	Employment Insurance benefits	$
5.	Workers' compensation benefits	$
6.	Social assistance income (including ODSP payments)	$
7.	Interest and investment income	$
8.	Pension income (including CPP and OAS)	$
9.	Spousal support received from a former spouse/partner	$
10.	Child Tax Benefits or Tax Rebates (e.g. GST)	$
11.	Other sources of income (e.g. RRSP withdrawals, capital gains) *(*attach Schedule A and divide annual amount by 12)*	$
12.	**Total monthly income from all sources:**	$
13.	**Total monthly income X 12 = Total annual income:**	$

Page 2 of 8

Form 13: Financial Statement (Support Claims) (page 3)

Court file number

14. Other Benefits

Provide details of any non-cash benefits that your employer provides to you or are paid for by your business such as medical insurance coverage, the use of a company car, or room and board.

Item	Details	Yearly Market Value
		$
		$
		$
		$

PART 2: EXPENSES

Expense	Monthly Amount	Expense	Monthly Amount
Automatic Deductions		**Transportation**	
CPP contributions	$	Public transit, taxis	$
EI premiums	$	Gas and oil	$
Income taxes	$	Car insurance and license	$
Employee pension contributions	$	Repairs and maintenance	$
Union dues	$	Parking	$
SUBTOTAL	$	Car Loan or Lease Payments	$
Housing		**SUBTOTAL**	$
Rent or mortgage	$	**Health**	
Property taxes	$	Health insurance premiums	$
Property insurance	$	Dental expenses	$
Condominium fees	$	Medicine and drugs	$
Repairs and maintenance	$	Eye care	$
SUBTOTAL	$	**SUBTOTAL**	$
Utilities		**Personal**	
Water	$	Clothing	$
Heat	$	Hair care and beauty	$
Electricity	$	Alcohol and tobacco	$

FAMILY LAW RULES FORMS

Page 3 of 8

873

Form 13:   **Financial Statement (Support Claims)**   **(page 4)**

Court file number

Utilities, continued		
Telephone	$	
Cell phone	$	
Cable	$	
Internet	$	
SUBTOTAL	$	
Household Expenses		
Groceries	$	
Household supplies	$	
Meals outside the home	$	
Pet care	$	
Laundry and Dry Cleaning	$	
SUBTOTAL	$	
Childcare Costs		
Daycare expense	$	
Babysitting costs	$	
SUBTOTAL	$	

Personal, continued		
Education (*specify*)	$	
Entertainment/recreation (including children)	$	
Gifts	$	
SUBTOTAL	$	
Other expenses		
Life Insurance premiums	$	
RRSP/RESP withdrawals	$	
Vacations	$	
School fees and supplies	$	
Clothing for children	$	
Children's activities	$	
Summer camp expenses	$	
Debt payments	$	
Support paid for other children	$	
Other expenses not shown above (*specify*)	$	
SUBTOTAL	$	

Total Amount of Monthly Expenses	$
Total Amount of Yearly Expenses	$

PART 3: ASSETS

Type		Details	Value or Amount
		State Address of Each Property and Nature of Ownership	
Real Estate	1		$
	2		$
	3		$
		Year and Make	
Cars, Boats, Vehicles	1		$
	2		$
	3		$

Page 4 of 8

874

Form 13: **Financial Statement (Support Claims)** **(page 5)**

Court file number

		Address Where Located	
Other Possessions of Value (e.g. computers, jewellery, collections)	1		$
	2		$
	3		$
		Type – Issuer – Due Date – Number of Shares	
Investments (e.g. bonds, shares, term deposits and mutual funds)	1		$
	2		$
	3		$
		Name and Address of Institution Account Number	
Bank Accounts	1		$
	2		$
	3		$
		Type and Issuer Account Number	
Savings Plans R.R.S.P.s Pension Plans R.E.S.P.s	1		$
	2		$
	3		$
		Type – Beneficiary – Face Amount Cash Surrender Value	
Life Insurance	1		$
	2		$
	3		$
		Name and Address of Business	
Interest in Business (*attach separate year-end statement for each business)	1		$
	2		$
	3		$
		Name and Address of Debtors	
Money Owed to You (for example, any court judgments in your favour, estate money and income tax refunds)	1		$
	2		$
	3		$
		Description	
Other Assets	1		$
	2		$
	3		$

Total Value of All Property	$

Page 5 of 8

FAMILY LAW RULES FORMS

Form 13:   **Financial Statement (Support Claims)**   **(page 6)** | Court file number |
| --- |

PART 4: DEBTS

Type of Debt	Creditor (name and address)	Full Amount Now Owing	Monthly Payments	Are Payments Being Made?
Mortgages, Lines of Credits or other Loans from a Bank, Trust or Finance Company		$	$	☐ Yes ☐ No
		$	$	☐ Yes ☐ No
		$	$	☐ Yes ☐ No
Outstanding Credit Card Balances		$	$	☐ Yes ☐ No
		$	$	☐ Yes ☐ No
		$	$	☐ Yes ☐ No
Unpaid Support Amounts		$	$	☐ Yes ☐ No
		$	$	☐ Yes ☐ No
		$	$	☐ Yes ☐ No
Other Debts		$	$	☐ Yes ☐ No
		$	$	☐ Yes ☐ No
		$	$	☐ Yes ☐ No

Total Amount of Debts Outstanding	$

PART 5: SUMMARY OF ASSETS AND LIABILITIES

Total Assets	$
Subtract Total Debts	$
Net Worth	$

NOTE: This financial statement must be updated no more than 30 days before any court event by either completing and filing:

- *a new financial statement with updated information, or*
- *an affidavit in Form 14A setting out the details of any minor changes or confirming that the information contained in this statement remains correct.*

Sworn/Affirmed before me at _____
                                                    municipality

in _____
                                province, state or country

on _____   _____
            date   *Commissioner for taking affidavits*
                                (Type or print name below if signature is illegible.)

_____
Signature
(This form is to be signed in front of a lawyer, justice of the peace, notary public or commissioner for taking affidavits.)

Schedule A
Additional Sources of Income

Line	Income Source	Annual Amount
1.	Net partnership income	$
2.	Net rental income (Gross annual rental income of $)	$
3.	Total amount of dividends received from taxable Canadian corporations	$
4.	Total capital gains ($) less capital losses ($)	$
5.	Registered retirement savings plan withdrawals	$
6.	Income from a Registered Retirement Income Fund or Annuity	$
7.	Any other income *(specify source)*	$

	Subtotal:	$

Schedule B
Other Income Earners in the Home

Complete this part only if you are making or responding to a claim for undue hardship or spousal support. Check and complete all sections that apply to your circumstances.

1. ☐ I live alone.

2. ☐ I am living with *(full legal name of person you are married to or cohabiting with)*

    _____

3. ☐ I/we live with the following other adult(s):

    _____

4. ☐ I/we have *(give number)* _____ child(ren) who live(s) in the home.

5. My spouse/partner ☐ works at *(place of work or business)* _____ .
    ☐ does not work outside the home.

6. My spouse/partner ☐ earns *(give amount)* $ _____ per _____ .
    ☐ does not earn any income.

7. ☐ My spouse/partner or other adult residing in the home contributes about $ _____ per
    _____ towards the household expenses.

Schedule C
Special or Extraordinary Expenses for the Child(ren)

Child's Name	Expense	Amount/yr.	Available Tax Credits or Deductions*
1.		$	$
2.		$	$
3.		$	$
4.		$	$
5.		$	$
6.		$	$
7.		$	$
8.		$	$
9.		$	$
10.		$	$

Total Net Annual Amount	$
Total Net Monthly Amount	$

* Some of these expenses can be claimed in a parent's income tax return in relation to a tax credit or deduction (for example childcare costs). These credits or deductions must be shown in the above chart.

☐ I earn $ _____ per year which should be used to determine my share of the above expenses.

NOTE:

Pursuant to the Child Support Guidelines, a court can order that the parents of a child share the costs of the following expenses for the child:

. Necessary childcare expenses;

. Medical insurance premiums and certain health-related expenses for the child that cost more than $100 annually;

. Extraordinary expenses for the child's education;

. Post-secondary school expenses; and,

. Extraordinary expenses for extracurricular activities.

Form 13.1

Financial Statement (Property and Support Claims)

ONTARIO

	Court File Number

_____
(Name of court)

at _____
Court office address

**Form 13.1: Financial
Statement (Property and
Support Claims)
sworn/affirmed**

Applicant(s)

Full legal name & address for service — street & number, municipality, postal code, telephone & fax numbers and e-mail address (if any).	Lawyer's name & address — street & number, municipality, postal code, telephone & fax numbers and e-mail address (if any).

Respondent(s)

Full legal name & address for service — street & number, municipality, postal code, telephone & fax numbers and e-mail address (if any).	Lawyer's name & address — street & number, municipality, postal code, telephone & fax numbers and e-mail address (if any).

INSTRUCTIONS

1. USE THIS FORM IF:
   - you are making or responding to a claim for property or exclusive possession of the matrimonial home and its contents; or
   - you are making or responding to a claim for property or exclusive possession of the matrimonial home and its contents together with other claims for relief.

2. USE FORM 13 INSTEAD OF THIS FORM IF:
   - you are making or responding to a claim for support but NOT making or responding to a claim for property or exclusive possession of the matrimonial home and its contents.

3. If you have income that is not shown in Part I of the financial statement (for example, partnership income, dividends, rental income, capital gains or RRSP income), you must also complete **Schedule A**.

4. If you or the other party has sought a contribution towards special or extraordinary expenses for the child(ren), you must also complete **Schedule B**.

NOTE: You must fully and truthfully complete this financial statement, including any applicable schedules. You must also provide the other party with documents relating to support and property and a Certificate of Financial Disclosure (Form 13A) as required by Rule 13 of the Family Law Rules.

---

1. **My name is** *(full legal name)* _____

   I live in *(municipality & province)* _____

   and I swear/affirm that the following is true:

PART 1: INCOME

2. I am currently

   ☐ employed by *(name and address of employer)*

   ☐ self-employed, carrying on business under the name of *(name and address of business)*

   ☐ unemployed since *(date when last employed)*

FAMILY LAW RULES FORMS

Form 13.1: Financial Statement (Property and Support Claims) **(page 2)**

Court file number

3. I attach proof of my year-to-date income from all sources, including my most recent *(attach all that are applicable)*:
   ☐ pay cheque stub   ☐ social assistance stub   ☐ pension stub   ☐ workers' compensation stub
   ☐ employment insurance stub and last Record of Employment
   ☐ statement of income and expenses/ professional activities (for self-employed individuals)
   ☐ other (e.g. a letter from your employer confirming all income received to date this year)

4. Last year, my gross income from all sources was $ _____ *(do not subtract any taxes that have been deducted from this income)*.

5. ☐ I am attaching all of the following required documents to this financial statement as proof of my income over the past three years, if they have not already been provided:
   . a copy of my personal income tax returns for each of the past three taxation years, including any materials that were filed with the returns. *(Income tax returns must be served but should NOT be filed in the continuing record, unless they are filed with a motion to refrain a driver's license suspension.)*
   . a copy of my notices of assessment and any notices of reassessment for each of the past three taxation years;
   . where my notices of assessment and reassessment are unavailable for any of the past three taxation years or where I have not filed a return for any of the past three taxation years, an Income and Deductions printout from the Canada Revenue Agency for each of those years, whether or not I filed an income tax return.
   Note: An Income and Deductions printout is available from Canada Revenue Agency. Please call customer service at 1-800-959-8281.

OR

☐ I am an Indian within the meaning of the *Indian Act* (Canada) and I have chosen not to file income tax returns for the past three years. I am attaching the following proof of income for the last three years *(list documents you have provided)*:

(In this table you must show all of the income that you are currently receiving whether taxable or not.)

	Income Source	Amount Received/Month
1.	Employment income (before deductions)	$
2.	Commissions, tips and bonuses	$
3.	Self-employment income (Monthly amount before expenses: $)	$
4.	Employment Insurance benefits	$
5.	Workers' compensation benefits	$
6.	Social assistance income (including ODSP payments)	$
7.	Interest and investment income	$
8.	Pension income (including CPP and OAS)	$
9.	Spousal support received from a former spouse/partner	$
10.	Child Tax Benefits or Tax Rebates (e.g. GST)	$
11.	Other sources of income (e.g. RRSP withdrawals, capital gains) (*attach Schedule A and divide annual amount by 12)	$
12.	**Total monthly income from all sources:**	$
13.	**Total monthly income X 12 = Total annual income:**	$

FLR 13.1 (November 1, 2018)

Page 2 of 10

880

Form 13.1: **Financial Statement (Property and** (page 3) | Court file number
Support Claims)

14. Other Benefits

Provide details of any non-cash benefits that your employer provides to you or are paid for by your business such as medical insurance coverage, the use of a company car, or room and board.

Item	Details	Yearly Market Value
		$
		$
		$
		$

PART 2: EXPENSES

Expense	Monthly Amount	Expense	Monthly Amount
Automatic Deductions		**Transportation**	
CPP contributions	$	Public transit, taxis	$
EI premiums	$	Gas and oil	$
Income taxes	$	Car insurance and license	$
Employee pension contributions	$	Repairs and maintenance	$
Union dues	$	Parking	$
SUBTOTAL	$	Car Loan or Lease Payments	$
Housing		**SUBTOTAL**	$
Rent or mortgage	$	**Health**	
Property taxes	$	Health insurance premiums	$
Property insurance	$	Dental expenses	$
Condominium fees	$	Medicine and drugs	$
Repairs and maintenance	$	Eye care	$
SUBTOTAL	$	**SUBTOTAL**	$
Utilities		**Personal**	
Water	$	Clothing	$
Heat	$	Hair care and beauty	$
Electricity	$	Alcohol and tobacco	$

ONTARIO SUPERIOR COURT PRACTICE RELATED MATERIALS

Form 13.1:	Financial Statement (Property and Support Claims)	(page 4)	Court file number

Utilities, continued		Personal, continued	
Telephone	$	Education (*specify*)	$
Cell phone	$	Entertainment/recreation (including children)	$
Cable	$	Gifts	$
Internet	$	**SUBTOTAL**	$
SUBTOTAL	$	**Other expenses**	
Household Expenses		Life Insurance premiums	$
Groceries	$	RRSP/RESP withdrawals	$
Household supplies	$	Vacations	$
Meals outside the home	$	School fees and supplies	$
Pet care	$	Clothing for children	$
Laundry and Dry Cleaning	$	Children's activities	$
SUBTOTAL	$	Summer camp expenses	$
Childcare Costs		Debt payments	$
Daycare expense	$	Support paid for other children	$
Babysitting costs	$	Other expenses not shown above (*specify*)	$
SUBTOTAL	$	**SUBTOTAL**	$

Total Amount of Monthly Expenses	$
Total Amount of Yearly Expenses	$

PART 3: OTHER INCOME EARNERS IN THE HOME

Complete this part only if you are making or responding to a claim for undue hardship or spousal support. Check and complete all sections that apply to your circumstances.

1. ☐ I live alone.
2. ☐ I am living with *(full legal name of person you are married to or cohabiting with)* _____
3. ☐ I/we live with the following other adult(s): _____
4. ☐ I/we have *(give number)* _____ child(ren) who live(s) in the home.
5. My spouse/partner ☐ works at *(place of work or business)* _____
   ☐ does not work outside the home.
6. My spouse/partner ☐ earns *(give amount)* $ _____ per _____
   ☐ does not earn any income.
7. My spouse/partner or other adult residing in the home contributes about $ _____ per _____
   towards the household expenses.

FLR 13.1 (November 1, 2018)

Page 4 of 10

882

Form 13.1:	Financial Statement (Property and Support Claims)	(page 5)	Court file number

PART 4: ASSETS IN AND OUT OF ONTARIO

If any sections of Parts 4 to 9 do not apply, do not leave blank, print "NONE" in the section.

The date of marriage is: *(give date)* _____

The valuation date is: *(give date)* _____

The date of commencement of cohabitation is (if different from date of marriage): *(give date)* _____

PART 4(a): LAND

*Include any interest in land **owned** on the dates in each of the columns below, including leasehold interests and mortgages. Show estimated market value of your interest, but do not deduct encumbrances or costs of disposition; these encumbrances and costs should be shown under Part 5, "Debts and Other Liabilities".*

Nature & Type of Ownership *(Give your percentage interest where relevant.)*	Address of Property	Estimated Market Value of YOUR Interest		
		on date of marriage	on valuation date	today
		$	$	$
15. TOTAL VALUE OF LAND		$		$

PART 4(b): GENERAL HOUSEHOLD ITEMS AND VEHICLES

Show estimated market value, not the cost of replacement for these items owned on the dates in each of the columns below. Do not deduct encumbrances or costs of disposition; these encumbrances and costs should be shown under Part 5, "Debts and Other Liabilities".

Item	Description	Indicate if NOT in your possession	Estimated Market Value of YOUR Interest		
			on date of marriage	on valuation date	today
Household goods & furniture			$	$	$
Cars, boats, vehicles			$	$	$
Jewellery, art, electronics, tools, sports & hobby equipment			$	$	$
Other special items			$	$	$
16. TOTAL VALUE OF GENERAL HOUSEHOLD ITEMS AND VEHICLES			$		$

FAMILY LAW RULES FORMS

Form 13.1:	Financial Statement (Property and Support Claims)	(page 6)	Court file number

PART 4(c): BANK ACCOUNTS, SAVINGS, SECURITIES AND PENSIONS

Show the items owned on the dates in each of the columns below by category, for example, cash, accounts in financial institutions, pensions, registered retirement or other savings plans, deposit receipts, any other savings, bonds, warrants, options, notes and other securities. Give your best estimate of the market value of the securities if the items were to be sold on the open market.

Category	INSTITUTION *(including location)/* DESCRIPTION *(including issuer and date)*	Account number	Amount/Estimated Market Value		
			on date of marriage	on valuation date	today
			$	$	$
17. TOTAL VALUE OF ACCOUNTS, SAVINGS, SECURITIES AND PENSIONS				$	$

PART 4(d): LIFE AND DISABILITY INSURANCE

List all policies in existence on the dates in each of the columns below.

Company, Type & Policy No.	Owner	Beneficiary	Face Amount	Cash Surrender Value		
				on date of marriage	on valuation date	today
				$	$	$
18. TOTAL CASH SURRENDER VALUE OF INSURANCE POLICIES					$	$

PART 4(e): BUSINESS INTERESTS

Show any interest in an unincorporated business owned on the dates in each of the columns below. An interest in an incorporated business may be shown here or under "BANK ACCOUNTS, SAVINGS, SECURITIES, AND PENSIONS" in Part 4(c). Give your best estimate of the market value of your interest.

Name of Firm or Company	Interest	Estimated Market Value of YOUR Interest		
		on date of marriage	on valuation date	today
		$	$	$
19. TOTAL VALUE OF BUSINESS INTERESTS			$	$

FLR 13.1 (November 1, 2018)

FAMILY LAW RULES FORMS

| Form 13.1: | Financial Statement (Property and Support Claims) | (page 7) | Court file number |

PART 4(f): MONEY OWED TO YOU

Give details of all money that other persons owe to you on the dates in each of the columns below, whether because of business or from personal dealings. Include any court judgments in your favour, any estate money and any income tax refunds owed to you.

Details	Amount Owed to You		
	on date of marriage	on valuation date	today
	$	$	$
20. TOTAL OF MONEY OWED TO YOU	$		$

PART 4(g): OTHER PROPERTY

Show other property or assets owned on the dates in each of the columns below. Include property of any kind not listed above. Give your best estimate of market value.

Category	Details	Estimated Market Value of YOUR interest		
		on date of marriage	on valuation date	today
		$	$	$
21. TOTAL VALUE OF OTHER PROPERTY		$		$
22. VALUE OF ALL PROPERTY OWNED ON THE VALUATION DATE *(Add items [15] to [21].)*		$		$

PART 5: DEBTS AND OTHER LIABILITIES

Show your debts and other liabilities on the dates in each of the columns below. List them by category such as mortgages, charges, liens, notes, credit cards, and accounts payable. Don't forget to include:
- *any money owed to the Canada Revenue Agency;*
- *contingent liabilities such as guarantees or warranties given by you (but indicate that they are contingent); and*
- *any unpaid legal or professional bills as a result of this case.*

Category	Details	Amount Owing		
		on date of marriage	on valuation date	today
		$	$	$
23. TOTAL OF DEBTS AND OTHER LIABILITIES		$		$

FAMILY LAW RULES FORMS

Form 13.1: Financial Statement (Property and Support Claims) (page 8)

Court file number

PART 6: PROPERTY, DEBTS AND OTHER LIABILITIES ON DATE OF MARRIAGE

Show by category the value of your property, debts and other liabilities, calculated as of the date of your marriage. (In this part, do not include the value of a matrimonial home or debts or other liabilities directly related to its purchase or significant improvement, if you and your spouse ordinarily occupied this property as your family residence at the time of separation.)

Category and details	Value on date of marriage	
	Assets	Liabilities
Land	$	$
General household items & vehicles	$	$
Bank accounts, savings, securities & pensions	$	$
Life & disability insurance	$	$
Business interests	$	$
Money owed to you	$	$
Other property *(Specify.)*	$	$
Debts and other liabilities *(Specify.)*	$	$
TOTALS	$	$
24. NET VALUE OF PROPERTY OWNED ON DATE OF MARRIAGE *(From the total of the "Assets" column, subtract the total of the "Liabilities" column.)*	$	
25. VALUE OF ALL DEDUCTIONS *(Add items [23] and [24].)*	$	

PART 7: EXCLUDED PROPERTY

Show by category the value of property owned on the valuation date that is excluded from the definition of "net family property" (such as gifts or inheritances received after marriage).

Category	Details	Value on valuation date
		$
26. TOTAL VALUE OF EXCLUDED PROPERTY		$

PART 8: DISPOSED-OF PROPERTY

Show by category the value of all property that you disposed of during the two years immediately preceding the making of this statement, or during the marriage, whichever period is shorter.

Category	Details	Value
		$
	27. TOTAL VALUE OF DISPOSED-OF PROPERTY	$

PART 9: CALCULATION OF NET FAMILY PROPERTY

	Deductions	BALANCE
Value of all property owned on valuation date *(from item [22] above)*		$
Subtract value of all deductions *(from item [25] above)*	$	$
Subtract total value of excluded property *(from item [26] above)*	$	$
28. NET FAMILY PROPERTY		$

NOTE: *This financial statement must be updated no more than 30 days before any court event by either completing and filing:*

- *a new financial statement with updated information, or*

- *an affidavit in Form 14A setting out the details of any minor changes or confirming that the information contained in this statement remains correct.*

Sworn/Affirmed before me at
                                             municipality

in _____

                   province, state or country

on _____ _____
        date   *Commissioner for taking affidavits*
                (Type or print name below if signature is illegible.)

_____
          Signature
(This form is to be signed in front of a lawyer, justice of the peace, notary public or commissioner for taking affidavits.)

Schedule A: Additional Sources of Income

Line	Income Source	Annual Amount
1.	Net partnership income	$
2.	Net rental income (Gross annual rental income of $)	$
3.	Total amount of dividends received from taxable Canadian corporations	$
4.	Total capital gains ($) less capital losses ($)	$
5.	Registered retirement savings plan withdrawals	$
6.	Income from a Registered Retirement Income Fund or Annuity	$
7.	Any other income (specify source)	$

Subtotal:	$

Schedule B: Special or Extraordinary Expenses for the Child(ren)

Child's Name	Expense	Amount/yr.	Available Tax Credits or Deductions*
1.		$	$
2.		$	$
3.		$	$
4.		$	$
5.		$	$
6.		$	$
7.		$	$
8.		$	$
9.		$	$
10.		$	$

Total Net Annual Amount	$
Total Net Monthly Amount	$

* Some of these expenses can be claimed in a parent's income tax return in relation to a tax credit or deduction (for example childcare costs). These credits or deductions must be shown in the above chart.

☐   I earn $ per year which should be used to determine my share of the above expenses.

NOTE: Pursuant to the Child Support Guidelines, a court can order that the parents of a child share the costs of the following expenses for the child:

- Necessary childcare expenses;
- Medical insurance premiums and certain health-related expenses for the child that cost more than $100 annually;
- Extraordinary expenses for the child's education;
- Post-secondary school expenses; and,
- Extraordinary expenses for extracurricular activities.

FLR 13.1 (November 1, 2018)   Page 10 of 10

Form 13A

Certificate of Financial Disclosure

ONTARIO

(Name of court)	**Court File Number**

at ....
Court office address

Form 13A: Certificate of Financial Disclosure

Applicant(s)

Full legal name & address for service — street & number, municipality, postal code, telephone & fax numbers and e-mail address (if any).	Lawyer's name & address — street & number, municipality, postal code, telephone & fax numbers and e-mail address (if any).

Respondent(s)

Full legal name & address for service — street & number, municipality, postal code, telephone & fax numbers and e-mail address (if any).	Lawyer's name & address — street & number, municipality, postal code, telephone & fax numbers and e-mail address (if any).

TO THE PARTIES

You must provide complete financial disclosure to the other parties in your case. A list of the documents you must provide to the other party is set out in Rule 13 of the Family Law Rules. You must list in this form all of the documents that you are providing to the other party in support of the information set out in your financial statement.

Once you have completed this form,

- if your case includes support with or without special expenses but does not include a claim under Part I of the Family Law Act (Family Property), you must:
  - attach all required documentation to the completed certificate.
  - serve this certificate (with attached documentation) on the other party with your completed Financial Statement.
- if your case includes a claim under Part I of the Family Law Act (Family Property) with or without a claim for support, you must:
  - attach all required documentation to the completed certificate.
  - serve this certificate (with attached documentation) on the other party within 30 days of the day that your Financial Statement was due to be served.

If you do not provide financial disclosure as required, a court may make an order against you.

You must file a copy of this certificate with the court. The documentation is not filed with the court. If you are the applicant or moving party in your case, you must file this certificate seven days before the case conference. If you are the respondent, you must serve it four days before the case conference.

If you have served any additional or updated financial disclosure before the settlement conference, you must prepare, serve and file an updated Certificate of Financial Disclosure.

Page 1 of 7

Form 13A: **Certificate of Financial Disclosure**   **(page 2)**

Court file number

Document Number	Document Description	Date of Document (yyyy/mm/dd)
Part A: Sources of Income		
Personal Income Tax Returns		
.		
.		
.		
.		
.		
Notices of Assessment and Reassessment		
.		
.		
.		
.		
.		
Employment Income		
.		
.		
.		
Self-Employment Income		
.		
.		
.		
.		
Partnership Income and Interests in a Partnership		
.		
.		
.		

Page 2 of 7

Form 13A: Certificate of Financial Disclosure   (page 3)

Court file number

Document Number	Document Description	Date of Document (yyyy/mm/dd)
Income from a Privately Held Corporation		
.		
.		
.		
.		
.		
Beneficial Income from, and Interest in, a Trust		
.		
.		
.		
.		
Income from Employment Insurance or Social Assistance		
.		
.		
.		
.		
Pensions and Annuities		
.		
.		
.		
.		
Income from Spousal Support		
.		
.		
.		
.		

Page 3 of 7

Form 13A: **Certificate of Financial Disclosure** (page 4)

Court file number

Document Number	Document Description	Date of Document (yyyy/mm/dd)
Tax Benefits or Rebates		
.		
.		
.		
.		
.		
Investment and Interest Income		
.		
.		
.		
.		
.		
Rental Income		
.		
.		
.		
.		
.		
Other Income		
.		
.		
.		
.		
.		
Part B: Special and Extraordinary Expenses		
.		
.		
.		
.		
.		

Form 13A: **Certificate of Financial Disclosure**   **(page 5)**   Court file number

Document Number	Document Description	Date of Document (yyyy/mm/dd)
Part C: Claim for Equalization of Net Family Property		
Assets and Liabilities at Valuation Date		
Real Estate		
.		
.		
.		
.		
.		
Savings and Investments		
.		
.		
.		
.		
.		
Pensions		
.		
.		
.		
.		
.		
Life Insurance Policies		
.		
.		
.		
.		
.		
Interest in a Sole Proprietorship		
.		
.		
.		
.		
.		

FAMILY LAW RULES FORMS

Form 13A: **Certificate of Financial Disclosure**   **(page 6)**   Court file number

Document Number	Document Description	Date of Document (yyyy/mm/dd)
Interest in a Partnership		
.		
.		
.		
.		
Interest in a Publically Held Corporation		
.		
.		
.		
.		
.		
Interest in a Privately Held Corporation		
.		
.		
.		
.		
Trust Interests		
.		
.		
.		
Property I own which does not belong in any of the other categories		
.		
.		
.		
.		
.		

Form 13A: **Certificate of Financial Disclosure**   **(page 7)**

Court file number

Document Number	Document Description	Date of Document (yyyy/mm/dd)
Liabilities		
.		
.		
.		
.		
.		
Assets and Liabilities at Marriage Date		
Assets		
.		
.		
.		
.		
Liabilities		
.		
.		
.		
.		
Excluded Property		
.		
.		
.		
.		

I am the Applicant/Respondent in this case. I certify that I have provided the opposing party with all of the documents that I have identified in this checklist.

Certified at _____ on _____

                 (City)   *(Date)*

_____

             (Signature of Party)

Page 7 of 7

Form 13B

Net Family Property Statement

ONTARIO

Court File Number

_____
(Name of court)

at _____

Court office address

Form 13B: Net Family Property Statement

Applicant(s)

Full legal name & address for service — street & number, municipality, postal code, telephone & fax numbers and e-mail address (if any).	Lawyer's name & address — street & number, municipality, postal code, telephone & fax numbers and e-mail address (if any).

Respondent(s)

Full legal name & address for service — street & number, municipality, postal code, telephone & fax numbers and e-mail address (if any).	Lawyer's name & address — street & number, municipality, postal code, telephone & fax numbers and e-mail address (if any).

My name is *(full legal name)* _____

The valuation date for the following material is *(date)* _____

(Complete the tables by filling in the columns for both parties, showing your assets, debts, etc., and those of your spouse.)

TABLE 1: Value of assets owned on valuation date *(List in the order of the categories in the financial statement.)*		
ITEM	**APPLICANT**	**RESPONDENT**
1.	$	$

	TOTAL 1	$	$

TABLE 2: Value of debts and liabilities on valuation date
(List in the order of the categories in the financial statement.)

ITEM	APPLICANT	RESPONDENT
1.	$	$
TOTAL 2	$	$

TABLE 3: Net value on date of marriage of property (other than a matrimonial home) after deducting debts or other liabilities on date of marriage (other than those relating directly to the purchase or significant improvement of a matrimonial home)
(List in the order of the categories in the financial statement.)

3(a)	PROPERTY ITEM	APPLICANT	RESPONDENT
		$	$
	TOTAL OF PROPERTY ITEMS	$	$
3(b)	DEBT ITEM		
	TOTAL OF DEBT ITEMS	$	$
	NET TOTAL 3 [3(a) *minus* 3(b)]	$	$

TABLE 4: Value or property excluded under subsection 4(2) of the *Family Law Act*
(List in the order of the categories in the financial statement.)

ITEM	APPLICANT	RESPONDENT
	$	$

TOTAL 4	$	$

TOTAL 2 *(from page 2)*	$	$
TOTAL 3 *(from page 2)*	$	$
TOTAL 4 *(from page 3)*	$	$
TOTAL 5 *([Total 2] + [Total 3] + [Total 4])*	$	$

TOTAL 1 *(from page 1)*	$	$
TOTAL 5 *(from above)*	$	$
TOTAL 6: NET FAMILY PROPERTY *([Total 1] minus [Total 5])*	$	$

_____   _____
Date of signature   *Signature*

Form 13C

Comparison of Net Family Property Statements

ONTARIO

Court File Number

_____
(Name of Court)

at _____
(Court office address)

Form 13C: Comparison of
Net Family Property Statements

This document must be completed once both parties have completed and exchanged Net Family Property Statements (Form 13B). This document can be completed jointly by the parties and filed with the court seven days before the settlement conference. If you and the other party are not able to agree on this document, then you each must prepare one, and serve it on the other party and file it with the court before the settlement conference. If you requested the settlement conference, you must serve and file the document seven days before the settlement conference, even if it is a joint statement. If no joint statement has been filed, the other party must serve and file the document four days before the settlement conference.

This form is being prepared by ☐ the Applicant

☐ the Respondent

☐ the Applicant and Respondent jointly

Applicant(s)

Full legal name & address for service — street & number, municipality, postal code, telephone & fax numbers and e-mail address (if any).	Lawyer's name & address — street & number, municipality, postal code, telephone & fax numbers and e-mail address (if any).

Respondent(s)

Full legal name & address for service — street & number, municipality, postal code, telephone & fax numbers and e-mail address (if any).	Lawyer's name & address — street & number, municipality, postal code, telephone & fax numbers and e-mail address (if any).

Valuation Date: _____   Statement Date: _____

1.   VALUE OF ASSETS OWNED ON VALUATION DATE

(a) LAND

NATURE & TYPE OF OWNERSHIP (State percentage interest where relevant)	NATURE & ADDRESS OF OWNERSHIP	COMMENTS	Document Number*	Applicant's Position		Respondent's Position	
				APPLICANT	RESPONDENT	APPLICANT	RESPONDENT
Matrimonial Home				$	$	$	$
				$	$	$	$
				$	$	$	$
(A) TOTALS: Value of Land				$	$	$	$

* Please use the number that you used for the document in your Certificate of Financial Disclosure (Form 13A)

Page 1 of 5

FAMILY LAW RULES FORMS

Comparison of Net Family Property Statements (Page 2)   Court file number

(b) GENERAL HOUSEHOLD ITEMS AND VEHICLES

ITEM	DESCRIPTION	COMMENTS	Document Number	Applicant's Position		Respondent's Position	
				APPLICANT	RESPONDENT	APPLICANT	RESPONDENT
Household goods & furniture				$	$	$	$
Cars, boats, vehicles				$	$	$	$
Jewellery, art, electronics, tools, sports & hobby, equipment				$	$	$	$
Other special items				$	$	$	$
				$	$	$	$
				$	$	$	$
(B) TOTALS: Value of General Household Items and Vehicles				$	$	$	$

(c) BANK ACCOUNTS AND SAVINGS, SECURITIES AND PENSIONS

CATEGORY (Savings, Checking, GIC, RRSP, Pensions, etc.)	INSTITUTION	ACCOUNT NUMBER	COMMENTS	Document Number	Applicant's Position		Respondent's Position	
					APPLICANT	RESPONDENT	APPLICANT	RESPONDENT
					$	$	$	$
					$	$	$	$
					$	$	$	$
(C) TOTALS: Value of Accounts and Savings					$	$	$	$

(d) LIFE AND DISABILITY INSURANCE

COMPANY TYPE & POLICY NO.	OWNER	BENEFICIARY	FACE AMOUNT ($)	COMMENTS	Document Number	Applicant's Position		Respondent's Position	
						APPLICANT	RESPONDENT	APPLICANT	RESPONDENT
			$			$	$	$	$
			$			$	$	$	$
			$			$	$	$	$
(D) TOTALS: Cash Surrender Value of Insurance Policies						$	$	$	$

(e) BUSINESS INTERESTS

NAME OF FIRM OR COMPANY	INTERESTS	COMMENTS	Document Number	Applicant's Position		Respondent's Position	
				APPLICANT	RESPONDENT	APPLICANT	RESPONDENT
				$	$	$	$

Page 2 of 5

901

Comparison of Net Family Property Statements (Page 3)   Court file number

				$	$	$	$
				$	$	$	$
(E) TOTALS: Value of Business Interests				$	$	$	$

(f) MONEY OWED TO YOU

DETAILS		COMMENTS	Document Number	Applicant's Position		Respondent's Position	
				APPLICANT	RESPONDENT	APPLICANT	RESPONDENT
				$	$	$	$
				$	$	$	$
				$	$	$	$
(F) TOTALS: Money Owed to You				$	$	$	$

(g) OTHER PROPERTY

CATEGORY	DETAILS	COMMENTS	Document Number	Applicant's Position		Respondent's Position	
				APPLICANT	RESPONDENT	APPLICANT	RESPONDENT
				$	$	$	$
				$	$	$	$
				$	$	$	$
(G) TOTALS: Value of Other Property				$	$	$	$

VALUE OF PROPERTY OWNED ON THE VALUATION DATE, (TOTAL 1) (Add: item A to item G inclusive)	$	$	$	$

2. **VALUE OF DEBTS AND OTHER LIABILITIES ON VALUATION DATE**

DEBTS AND OTHER LIABILITIES

CATEGORY	DETAILS	COMMENTS	Document Number	Applicant's Position		Respondent's Position	
				APPLICANT	RESPONDENT	APPLICANT	RESPONDENT
				$	$	$	$
				$	$	$	$
				$	$	$	$
TOTALS: Value of Debts and Other Liabilities, (TOTAL 2)				$	$	$	$

3.   NET VALUE OF PROPERTY (Other than a Matrimonial Home) AND DEBTS ON DATE OF MARRIAGE

PROPERTY, DEBTS AND OTHER LIABILITIES ON DATE OF MARRIAGE

CATEGORY AND DETAILS	COMMENTS	Document Number	Applicant's Position		Respondent's Position	
			APPLICANT	RESPONDENT	APPLICANT	RESPONDENT
Assets			$	$	$	$
			$	$	$	$
TOTAL OF PROPERTY ITEMS			$	$	$	$
Debts and other liabilities			$	$	$	$
			$	$	$	$
TOTAL OF DEBTS ITEMS			$	$	$	$
NET VALUE OF PROPERTY OWNED ON DATE OF MARRIAGE (NET TOTAL 3)			$	$	$	$

4.   VALUE OF PROPERTY EXCLUDED UNDER SUBS. 4(2) OF "FAMILY LAW ACT"

ITEM	COMMENTS	Document Number	Applicant's Position		Respondent's Position	
			APPLICANT	RESPONDENT	APPLICANT	RESPONDENT
			$	$	$	$
			$	$	$	$
			$	$	$	$
			$	$	$	$
			$	$	$	$
			$	$	$	$
TOTALS: Value of Excluded Property (TOTAL 4)			$	$	$	$

Comparison of Net Family Property Statements (Page 5)   Court file number _____

TOTAL 2: Debts and Other Liabilities	$	$	$	$
TOTAL 3: Value of Property Owned on the Date of Marriage	$	$	$	$
TOTAL 4: Value of Excluded Property	$	$	$	$
TOTAL 5: *(TOTAL 2 + TOTAL 3 + TOTAL 4)*	$	$	$	$

TOTAL 1: Value of Property Owned on Valuation Date	$	$	$	$
TOTAL 5: *(from above)*	$	$	$	$
TOTAL 6: NET FAMILY PROPERTY *(Subtract: TOTAL 1 minus TOTAL 5)*	$	$	$	$

	Applicant's Position		Respondent's Position	
	Applicant Pays To Respondent	Respondent Pays To Applicant	Applicant Pays To Respondent	Respondent Pays To Applicant
EQUALIZATION PAYMENTS	$	$	$	$

Form 14

Notice of Motion

ONTARIO

	Court File Number

(Name of court)

at _____

Court office address

Form 14: Notice of Motion

Applicant(s)

Full legal name & address for service — street & number, municipality, postal code, telephone & fax numbers and e-mail address *(if any)*.	Lawyer's name & address — street & number, municipality, postal code, telephone & fax numbers and e-mail address *(if any)*.

Respondent(s)

Full legal name & address for service — street & number, municipality, postal code, telephone & fax numbers and e-mail address *(if any)*.	Lawyer's name & address — street & number, municipality, postal code, telephone & fax numbers and e-mail address *(if any)*.

The person making this motion or the person's lawyer must contact the clerk of the court by telephone or otherwise to choose a time and date when the court could hear this motion.

TO THE PARTIES:

THE COURT WILL HEAR A MOTION on *(date)*

at _____ , **or as soon as possible after that time, at** *(place of hearing)*

This motion will be made by *(name of person making the motion)* _____
who will be asking the court for an order for the item(s) listed on page 2 of this notice.

☐ A copy of the affidavit(s) in support of this motion is/are served with this notice.

☐ A notice of a case conference is served with this notice to change an order.

If this material is missing, you should talk to the court office immediately.

The person making this motion is also relying on the following documents in the continuing record: *(List documents.)*

If you want to oppose this motion or to give your own views, you should talk to your own lawyer and prepare your own affidavit, serve it on all other parties and file it at the court office not later than 4 days before the date above. Only written and affidavit evidence will be allowed at a motion unless the court gives permission for oral testimony. You may bring your lawyer to the motion.

IF YOU DO NOT COME TO THE MOTION, THE COURT MAY MAKE AN ORDER WITHOUT YOU AND ENFORCE IT AGAINST YOU.

_____
Date of signature

_____
Signature of person making this motion or of person's lawyer

Typed or printed name of person or of person's lawyer, address for service, telephone & fax numbers and e-mail address (if any)

NOTE TO PERSON MAKING THIS MOTION: *You MUST file a confirmation (Form 14C) not later than 2:00 p.m. 3 days before the date set out above.*

If this is a motion to change past and future support payments under an order that has been assigned to a government agency, you must also serve this notice on that agency. If you do not, the agency can ask the court to set aside any order that you may get in this motion and can ask for costs against you.

FLR 14 (March 1, 2018)

Page 1 of 2

Form 14:   **Notice of Motion**   **(page 2)**   Court File Number

---

State the order or orders requested on this motion.

Form 14A

Affidavit (General)

ONTARIO

	Court File Number

_____

(Name of court)

Form 14A: Affidavit
(general) dated

at _____

Court office address

Applicant(s)

Full legal name & address for service — street & number, municipality, postal code, telephone & fax numbers and e-mail address (if any).	Lawyer's name & address — street & number, municipality, postal code, telephone & fax numbers and e-mail address (if any).

Respondent(s)

Full legal name & address for service — street & number, municipality, postal code, telephone & fax numbers and e-mail address (if any).	Lawyer's name & address — street & number, municipality, postal code, telephone & fax numbers and e-mail address (if any).

My name is *(full legal name)* ....

I live in *(municipality & province)*

....

and I swear/affirm that the following is true:

Set out the statements of fact in consecutively numbered paragraphs. Where possible, each numbered paragraph should consist of one complete sentence and be limited to a particular statement of fact. If you learned a fact from someone else, you must give that person's name and state that you believe that fact to be true.

1.

Put a line through any blank space left on this page.

Sworn/Affirmed before me at ....

municipality

In...

province, state, or country

on.................... _____

date

Commissioner for taking affidavits
(Type or print name below if signature is illegible.)

_____
Signature

(This form is to be signed in front of a lawyer, justice of the peace, notary public or commissioner for taking affidavits.)

Form 14B

Motion Form

ONTARIO

_____

(Name of court)

at _____

Court office address

Names of parties:

Applicant:.............................

Respondent:

....

Name of case

Hearing date: ....

management judge: ....

This form is filed by:

□ applicant □ respondent □ *(Other; specify.)* ....

This motion is made:

□ with the consent of all persons affected

□ with notice to all persons affected – opposition expected

□ with notice to all persons affected – unopposed

□ without notice

NOTE TO PERSON MAKING THIS MOTION: If this is a motion to change past and future support payments under an order that has been assigned to a government agency, you must also serve this motion form on that agency. If you do not, the agency can ask the court to set aside any order that you may get in this motion and can ask for court costs against you.

Order that you want the court to make: *(If you need more space, add an extra sheet but do not make any changes to this form.)*

Laws and rules on which you are relying: *(Give name of statute and section numbers; name of regulation and section numbers; and rule numbers.)*

I want the court to deal with this motion:

□ by relying only on written material.   □ in a hearing at which affected persons may attend personally.

□ by conference telephone call. *(An appointment for such a call must be arranged in advance; see rule 14 of the Family Law Rules.)*

At this motion, I am relying on the following material:

□ Tabs/pages .... of the continuing record

□ Pages .... of the transcript of the evidence of *(name of person)*

.................................., dated ....

(Relevant parts of the transcript must be highlighted.)

This party's lawyer *(Give lawyer's name, firm, telephone & fax number and e-mail address [if any]. If no lawyer, give party's name, and address for service, telephone & fax number and e-mail address [if any].)*	**Other party's lawyer** *(Give lawyer's name, firm, telephone & fax number and e-mail address [if any]. If no lawyer, give party's name, and address for service, telephone & fax number and e-mail address [if any].)*

Signature   *Date of signature*

Form 14C

Confirmation of Motion

ONTARIO

ONTARIO

	Court File Number

(Name of court)

at _____

Court office address

Form 14C: Confirmation of Motion

Applicant(s)

Full legal name & address for service — street & number, municipality, postal code, telephone & fax numbers and e-mail address (if any).	Lawyer's name & address — street & number, municipality, postal code, telephone & fax numbers and e-mail address (if any).

Respondent(s)

Full legal name & address for service — street & number, municipality, postal code, telephone & fax numbers and e-mail address (if any).	Lawyer's name & address — street & number, municipality, postal code, telephone & fax numbers and e-mail address (if any).

Name & address of Children's Lawyer's agent *(street & number, municipality, postal code, telephone & fax numbers and e-mail address (if any))* and name of person represented.

1. My name is *(full legal name)* _____

   and I am ☐ the lawyer for *(name)* _____

   ☐ the applicant in this case   ☐ the respondent in this case

   ☐ other *(specify)* _____

2. Have you conferred with the opposing counsel or party regarding the issues, motion material, and time estimates, as set out in paragraphs 3 to 10 below?

   ☐ Yes

   ☐ No, because *(provide reasons)*

NOTE: The *Family Law Rules* require the parties or their counsel to confer, or attempt to confer, orally or in writing with each other on the issues in dispute for a motion prior to filing Confirmations. The only exception is where a party is prohibited from such communication by court order. **Failure to comply with the *Family Law Rules* may result in a cost order.**

3. The scheduled date and time for this motion is *(date)* _____ at _____ a.m./p.m.

4. Has a case conference been held on the substantive issues in this case?

   ☐ Yes, a case conference was held before Justice _____

   ☐ No, a case conference has not been held on the substantive issues in this case.

Form 14C:	**Confirmation of Motion**	**(page 2)**	Court File Number

5. The case management judge for this case is Justice _____

6. This matter is

☐ going ahead on the issues listed in paragraph 7 below.

☐ going ahead for a consent order *(attach draft order)*.

☐ being adjourned on consent to *(date)* _____ for a *(event)* _____

because *(give reasons)*

☐ going ahead for a contested adjournment to *(date)* _____ asked for by *(name of person asking*

for adjournment) _____ because *(give reasons)*

7. What specific orders are you seeking on this motion? *(List the specific orders below)*
    a)
    b)
    c)
    d)
    e)
    f)

8. ☐ I confirm that I will bring a draft order to the motion.

9. The presiding judge will be referred to the following pages/tabs:

10. Time estimate: applicant: _____ minutes; respondent: _____ minutes; for a total of _____ minutes.

NOTE: The *Family Law Rules* require you to **deliver a copy** of this form to the opposing lawyer or party, unless this is a child protection matter. For clarification, regular or special service and an accompanying Affidavit of Service (Form 6B) under rule 6 of the *Family Law Rules* are not required. However, you must deliver this form by some method (including fax or e-mail) to the opposing lawyer or party prior to giving a copy to the court clerk.

_____   _____
      Date of signature   *Lawyer's or party's signature*

Form 14D
Order on Motion Without Notice

ONTARIO

SEAL	

_____
(Name of court)

Court File Number

Form 14D: Order on Motion without Notice

at _____
Court office address

Applicant(s)

Full legal name & address for service — street & number, municipality, postal code, telephone & fax numbers and e-mail address (if any).	Lawyer's name & address — street & number, municipality, postal code, telephone & fax numbers and e-mail address (if any).

Judge (print or type name)
_____

Respondent(s)

Full legal name & address for service — street & number, municipality, postal code, telephone & fax numbers and e-mail address (if any).	Lawyer's name & address — street & number, municipality, postal code, telephone & fax numbers and e-mail address (if any).

Date of order
_____

The court heard a motion made by *(name of person or persons who made the motion)*

....

without notice to *(name)* ....

The following persons were in court *(names of parties and lawyers in court at time of the motion)*

For this motion, the court read *(list the documents filed on the motion)*

The court also received and heard submissions on behalf of *(name or names)*

THIS COURT ORDERS THAT:

Put a line through any blank space left on this page.

_____   _____
      Date of signature   *Signature of judge or clerk of the court*

NOTICE TO *(name)* ....

This order has been made without notice to you. If you want the court to change this order, you must act as quickly as possible after the order comes to your attention, by serving an affidavit and a notice of motion on the other parties and by filing them together with proof of service at the court office.

Form 15

Motion to Change

ONTARIO

SEAL	Court File Number

_____
(Name of court)

at _____
Court office address

Form 15: Motion to Change

☐ **the order of Justice** _____ ,

dated _____

☐ **the agreement for support between the parties, dated** _____ ,

filed with the court on _____

Applicant(s)

Full legal name & address for service — street & number, municipality, postal code, telephone & fax numbers and e-mail address (if any).	Lawyer's name & address — street & number, municipality, postal code, telephone & fax numbers and e-mail address (if any).

Respondent(s)

Full legal name & address for service — street & number, municipality, postal code, telephone & fax numbers and e-mail address (if any).	Lawyer's name & address — street & number, municipality, postal code, telephone & fax numbers and e-mail address (if any).

Assignee (if applicable)

Full legal name & address for service — street & number, municipality, postal code, telephone & fax numbers and e-mail address (if any).	Lawyer's name & address — street & number, municipality, postal code, telephone & fax numbers and e-mail address (if any).

NOTE: *If you are seeking to change a support term in an agreement that has not already been filed with the court pursuant to s. 35 of the Family Law Act, you must file the agreement and Form 26B (Affidavit for Filing Domestic Contract with Court) before bringing this motion to change.*

You may use this form if you are seeking to change an order or agreement that has been recalculated by the online Child Support Service. You must serve a copy of this form on the Family Responsibility Office if the order you recalculated was made under the Divorce Act and the recalculation was completed within the last 35 days.

You may not use this form to change a Notice of Calculation made by the online Child Support Service.

If the order or agreement for support has been assigned to a person or agency, the assignee must be served with this form and the Change Information Form (Form 15A). The assignee's consent to change an order or agreement for support may be necessary. It is the responsibility of the person seeking the change to the order or agreement to determine if the order or agreement has been assigned. You can do this by submitting a Confirmation of Assignment form. The Confirmation of Assignment form is available through the Ministry of the Attorney General website or at the court office.

TO: *(name(s) of party(ies))* _____

(Name of party bringing motion) _____ has brought a motion to change

☐ the order of Justice _____ , dated _____

☐ recalculated by the online Child Support Service on _____ .

☐ the agreement between you and *(name of party bringing this motion)* _____ ,

dated _____ ☐ recalculated by the online Child Support Service on _____ .

Form 15:	Motion to Change Order or Agreement	(page 2)	Court File Number

☐ **THE FIRST COURT DATE IS** _____ , at _____ ☐ a.m. ☐ p.m.

or as soon as possible after that time, at *(address of court)*

☐ **NO COURT DATE HAS BEEN SET FOR THIS CASE.** A case management judge will not be assigned until one of the parties asks the clerk of the court to schedule a case conference and serves a Conference Notice (Form 17).

IF, AFTER 365 DAYS, THE CASE HAS NOT BEEN SCHEDULED FOR TRIAL, the clerk of the court will send out a warning that the case will be dismissed in 60 days unless the parties file proof that the case has been settled or one of the parties asks for a case or a settlement conference.

(To be completed by the party bringing this motion—check the box of any paragraph that applies to your case:)

☐ This case does not include any claim to change support, and a financial statement is therefore not attached.

☐ The case only includes a claim to change child support in accordance with the table amount specified under the Child Support Guidelines and a financial statement is therefore not attached.

☐ This case includes a claim to change support other than child support in the amount specified in the table of the applicable child support guidelines, and a financial statement is attached. You MUST fill out a Financial Statement (Form 13 or 13.1), serve a copy on the person(s) bringing the motion to change and file a copy in the court office with an Affidavit of Service (Form 6B) even if you do not respond to this case.

IF YOU CONSENT TO THE CHANGES BEING SOUGHT IN THIS MOTION, you or your lawyer must complete the Consent Motion to Change (Form 15C—a blank copy should be attached) and return a copy to the person(s) bringing the motion and any assignee, if applicable, within 30 days of being served (60 days if the motion to change is served on you outside Canada or the United States). The person(s) bringing the motion may then file the consent with the court and may obtain a court order based on the consent. If a first court date has been scheduled, you do not need to attend court on that date unless specifically directed by the court to do so.

IF YOU WANT TO OPPOSE ANY CHANGE BEING SOUGHT IN THIS MOTION OR WANT TO REQUEST A CHANGE OF YOUR OWN, you or your lawyer must complete the Response to Motion to Change (Form 15B—a blank copy should be attached), serve a copy on the person(s) bringing the motion and file a copy in the court office with an Affidavit of Service (Form 6B). **YOU HAVE ONLY 30 DAYS AFTER THIS MOTION TO CHANGE IS SERVED ON YOU (60 DAYS IF THE MOTION TO CHANGE IS SERVED ON YOU OUTSIDE CANADA OR THE UNITED STATES) TO SERVE AND FILE A RESPONSE TO A MOTION TO CHANGE. IF YOU DO NOT, THE CASE WILL GO AHEAD WITHOUT YOU AND THE COURT MAY MAKE AN ORDER AND ENFORCE IT AGAINST YOU.**

NOTE: If you want to make your own claim to change support, you MUST also fill out a Financial Statement (Form 13 or 13.1), serve a copy on the person(s) bringing the motion and file a copy in the court office with an Affidavit of Service (Form 6B) UNLESS your only claim for support is for child support in the table amount specified under the Child Support Guidelines.

YOU SHOULD GET LEGAL ADVICE ABOUT THIS CASE RIGHT AWAY. If you cannot afford a lawyer, you may be able to get help from your local Legal Aid Ontario Office. (See your telephone directory under LEGAL AID.)

Date of issue by the clerk of the court	*Clerk of the court*

Form 15:	Motion to Change Order or Agreement	(page 3)	Court File Number

CLAIM BY *(name(s) of person(s) bringing motion)* _____

I ASK THE COURT TO CHANGE THE EXISTING COURT ORDER OR SUPPORT AGREEMENT BY MAKING AN ORDER AS FOLLOWS: *(complete only those items that affect the terms of the order or agreement that you are seeking to change.)*

☐ 1. An order that *(name(s) of party(ies) or person(s))* _____

   have custody of the following child(ren): *(name(s) and birthdate(s) of child(ren))*

_____

☐ 2. An order that *(name(s) of party(ies) or person(s))* _____

   have access to the following child(ren): *(name(s) and birthdate(s) of child(ren))*

_____

   as follows: *(give details of access)*

_____

☐ 3. An order that *(name(s) of party(ies) and/or person(s))* _____

   and _____ have joint custody of the following child(ren):

   (name(s) and birthdate(s) of child(ren))

_____

☐ 4. An order for the following residential/access arrangements for the child(ren): *(name(s) and birthdate(s) of child(ren)*

_____

5. Order(s) dealing with child support as follows:

   ☐ Since the order/agreement for child support was made, a Notice of Recalculation was issued by the online Child Support Service dated _____ *(please attach)*.

   ☐ The order/agreement for child support, dated _____, be terminated for the following child(ren): *(insert name(s) and birthdate(s) of child(ren))*

_____

   effective *(date)* _____

   ☐ Based on the payor's annual income of $ _____, *(name of party)* _____

   pay *(name of party)* _____ $ _____ per month for the

   following child(ren): *(name(s) and birthdate(s) of child(ren))*

_____

   with payments to start on *(date)* _____

   ☐ This amount is the table amount listed in the Child Support Guidelines.

   ☐ This amount is more than the table amount listed in the Child Support Guidelines.

   ☐ This amount is less than the table amount listed in the Child Support Guidelines.

FAMILY LAW RULES FORMS

Form 15:   Motion to Change Order or Agreement   (page 4) | Court File Number

☐ Starting on *(date)* _____ , *(name of party)* _____

pay to *(name of party)* _____ $ _____

for the following special or extraordinary expenses:

Child's Name	Type of Expense	Total Amount of Expense	Payor's Share	Terms of Payment *(frequency of payment, date due, etc.)*
		$	$	
		$	$	
		$	$	
		$	$	
		$	$	

☐ Other: *(give details)*

6. ☐ Orders dealing with the outstanding child support owed as follows:

    ☐ The child support owed to *(name of recipient)* _____

    be fixed at $ _____ as of *(date)* _____

    ☐ *(Name of payor)* _____ pay to *(name of recipient)*

    _____ $ _____ per month, with

    payments to begin on *(date)* _____ until the full amount owing is paid.

    ☐ The child support owed to *(name of agency or other person)* _____

    be fixed at $ _____ as of *(date)* _____

    ☐ *(Name of payor)* _____ pay to *(name of agency or other person)*

    _____ $ _____ per month, with payments to

    begin on *(date)* _____ until the full amount owing is paid.

7. ☐ An order that the spousal support be changed as follows:

    ☐ The order/agreement for spousal support, dated _____ be terminated effective

    (date) _____ .

    ☐ *(Name of party)* _____ pay spousal support to

    (name of party) _____ in the amount of

    $ _____ per month, effective on *(date)* _____

    ☐ Other *(give details of the order you want the court to make)*

8. ☐ An order that the outstanding spousal support owed be paid as follows:

    ☐ The spousal support owed to *(name of recipient)* _____

    be fixed at $ _____ as of *(date)* _____ .

    ☐ *(Name of payor)* _____ pay to *(name of recipient)*

    _____ $ _____ per month, with

    payments to begin on *(date)* _____ until the full amount owing is paid.

Form 15:   **Motion to Change Order or Agreement**   **(page 5)**

Court File Number

☐ The spousal support owed to *(name of agency or other person)* _____

be fixed at $ _____ as of *(date)* _____ .

☐ *(Name of payor)* _____ pay to *(name of agency or other person)*

_____ $ _____ per month, with

payments to begin on *(date)* _____ until the full amount owing is paid.

9. ☐ I ask that the term(s) of the order of Justice *(name of judge)* _____ ,

dated _____ , for *(give details)* _____

be changed as follows: *(give details of the order you want the court to make)*

10. ☐ I ask the court for the following order:

The information and facts supporting my motion to change are set out in the Change Information Form (Form 15A) attached.

_____   _____
Date of signature   *Signature of person bringing the motion or person's lawyer*

FAMILY LAW RULES FORMS

Form 15A

Change Information Form

ONTARIO

	Court File Number

....
(Name of court)

Form 15A: Change
Information Form

at ....
Court office address

Applicant(s)

Full legal name & address for service — street & number, municipality, postal code, telephone & fax numbers and e-mail address (if any).	Lawyer's name & address — street & number, municipality, postal code, telephone & fax numbers and e-mail address (if any).

Respondent(s)

Full legal name & address for service — street & number, municipality, postal code, telephone & fax numbers and e-mail address (if any).	Lawyer's name & address — street & number, municipality, postal code, telephone & fax numbers and e-mail address (if any).

Assignee (if applicable)

Full legal name & address for service — street & number, municipality, postal code, telephone & fax numbers and e-mail address (if any).	Lawyer's name & address — street & number, municipality, postal code, telephone & fax numbers and e-mail address (if any).

PART 1 – GENERAL INFORMATION
(This part should be filled out to the best ability of the party asking for a change in an order or support agreement.)

My name is *(full legal name)* ....

I live in *(municipality & province)* ....

and I swear/affirm that the following is true:

1. I am the ☐ applicant ☐ Respondent

2. The applicant, *(applicant's full legal name)* ....

    was born on *(date of birth)* ....

    lives in *(municipality & province)* ....

    and, at the present time, is ☐ married ☐ living in a spousal relationship
    ☐ Separated ☐ other *(specify)* ....

    The applicant is the ☐ support recipient ☐ support payor

3. The respondent, *(respondent's full legal name)* ....

    was born on *(date of birth)* ....

    lives in *(municipality & province)* ....

    and, at the present time, is ☐ Married ☐ living in a spousal relationship
    ☐ Separated ☐ other *(specify)* ....

    The respondent is the ☐ support recipient ☐ support payor

Form 15A: **Change Information Form**   **(page 2)** | Court File Number |

4. This order/agreement   ☐ has never been assigned

☐ has been assigned to

☐ the Ontario Ministry of Community and Social Services

☐ Ontario Works in *(name of location)* _____

☐ the municipality of *(name)* _____

☐ other *(specify)* _____

The details of the assignment are: *(Give date of assignment, indicate whether it is still in effect, add any other relevant information known to you and attach a copy of the Confirmation of Assignment Form.)*

5. The applicant and the respondent:

☐ started living together on *(date)* _____

☐ were married on *(date)* _____

☐ never lived together

☐ separated on *(date)* _____

☐ were divorced on *(date)* _____

6. The following chart gives basic information about the child(ren) in this case:
(List all child(ren) involved in this case, even those for whom no support is being claimed.)

Child's full legal name	Age	Birthdate (d, m, y)	Lives in (municipality & province)	Now living with (name of person and relationship to child)	Support claimed for child? (YES or NO)

7. I attach a copy of the existing   ☐ court order   ☐ agreement that contains the term(s) to be changed.

921

Form 15A: **Change Information Form** **(page 3)** | Court File Number

8. The existing custody and access arrangements for the child(ren) are as follows:

Child's name	Custody/Access Arrangement

9. The details of the existing order/agreement with respect to support are as follows:

Date of order or agreement	Present child support payment	Other terms of child support	Present support payment (if any) for spouse
	$ ____ per ____		$ ____ per ____

10. The payment status of the existing order/agreement as of today is as follows:

☐ all payments have been made

☐ arrears are owing as follows:

Child support owed to recipient	Child support owed to other(s) (such as Ministry of Community and Social Services)	Spousal support owed to recipient	Spousal support owed to other(s) (such as Ministry of Community and Social Services)
$ ____	$ ____	$ ____	$ ____

CUSTODY/ACCESS
(Complete only if you are asking for a change in an order for custody or access.)

11. I ask that *(name(s) of party(ies) and/or person(s))* ____ have custody of the following child(ren) *(name(s) and birthdate(s) of child(ren))* ____

12. I ask that *(name of party)* ____ have access to the following child(ren) *(name(s) and birthdate(s) of child(ren))* ____

as follows: *(give details of access)*

OR

13. I ask that *(name(s) of party(ies) and/or person(s))* ____ and ____ have joint custody of the following child(ren) *(name(s) and birthdate(s) of child(ren))* ____

14. I ask for the following residential/access arrangements for the child(ren):

(name(s) and birthdate(s) of child(ren)) ____

Form 15A: **Change Information Form** **(page 4)** | Court File Number

15. The order I am asking the court to make is in the best interests of the child(ren) for the following reasons: *(give details)*

CHILD SUPPORT
(Complete this section only if you are asking for a change in child support.)

16. I am asking to change the child support in the order/agreement because:

☐ The order/agreement was made before the applicable Child Support Guidelines came into effect.

☐ The following change in circumstances has taken place: *(Give details of change in circumstances.)*

☐ The parties agree to the termination of the support order/agreement, dated _____ ,

for the following child(ren): *(name(s) and birthdate(s) of child(ren))*

_____ ,

as of *(date)* _____

☐ Other: *(give details)*

17. I ask that the child support be changed as follows:

☐ Since the order/agreement for child support was made, a Notice of Recalculation was issued by the online Child Support Service dated _____ *(please attach)*.

☐ The order/agreement for child support dated _____ be terminated for the following child(ren): *(insert name(s) and birthdate(s) of child(ren))* _____
effective *(date)* _____ .

☐ Based on the payor's income of $ _____ per year, *(name of party)* _____
pay child support to *(name of party)* _____
in the amount of $ _____ per month for the following child(ren) *(name(s) and birthdate(s) of child(ren))*

_____

with payments to start on *(date)* _____

☐ This amount is the table amount listed in the Child Support Guidelines.

☐ This amount is more than the table amount listed in the Child Support Guidelines.

☐ This amount is less than the table amount listed in the Child Support Guidelines. *(If this box is checked, you must complete paragraph 18.)*

☐ Starting on *(date)* _____ , *(name of party)* _____
pay to *(name of party)* _____ $ _____ for the following
special or extraordinary expenses:

Child's Name	Type of Expense	Total Amount of Expense	Payor's Share	Terms of Payment *(frequency of payment, date due, etc.)*
		$	$	
		$	$	
		$	$	
		$	$	
		$	$	
		$	$	

Form 15A:	Change Information Form	(page 5)	Court File Number

☐ Other: *(give details)*

18. ☐ I am asking that child support be changed to an amount that is less than the table amount listed in the Child Support Guidelines. The reason(s) for my request is/are that:

    ☐ The parties agree to a different amount.

        ☐ I have attached a separate sheet to this form that explains why this is an appropriate amount of child support.

        ☐ The recipient is getting social assistance payments from a public agency whose consent to this arrangement is needed. I am attaching the agency's consent to this form.

    ☐ As can be seen from paragraphs 6 and 8 above, the parties have shared custody of the child(ren) *(the payor has a child at least 40% of the time)*.

        ☐ I have attached a separate sheet to this form that compares the table amounts from the Child Support Guidelines for each of the parties, shows the increased cost of the shared custody arrangement, the financial circumstances of each party and of each child for whom support is claimed.

        ☐ The parties are agreeing to this arrangement and I have attached a separate sheet to this form that explains why this is an appropriate amount of child support.

    ☐ As can be seen from paragraphs 6 and 8 above, custody of the children is split between the parties. I have attached a separate sheet to this form that calculates the difference between the amount that each party would otherwise pay to the other under the Child Support Guidelines.

    ☐ A child is 18 or more years old and I attach to this form a separate sheet that calculates the amount of support for this child.

    ☐ A child contributes to his/her own support and I attach to this form a separate sheet showing the amount of the child's own income and/or assets.

    ☐ The payor's annual income is over $150,000 and I have attached to this form a separate sheet that calculates the amount of support that I want to be put in an order.

    ☐ Under the order/agreement, *(name(s) of child(ren))* _____

    is/are the subject of special provisions that I have detailed on a separate sheet that I have attached to this form.

    ☐ The payor stands in the place of a parent to *(name(s) of child(ren))* _____

    and I attach to this form a separate sheet that gives the details of another parent's duty to pay support for this/these child(ren), as well as the details of the calculation of the amount of support requested.

    ☐ The amount listed in the Child Support Guidelines would cause undue hardship to me or to the child(ren) for whom support is claimed. I attach to this form a separate sheet that compares the standards of living of the parties and calculates the amount of support that should be paid.

19. I ask that the outstanding child support owed be paid as follows:

    ☐ The child support owed to *(name of recipient)* _____

    be fixed at $ _____ as of *(date)* _____

    ☐ *(Name of payor)* _____ pay to *(name of recipient)* _____

    _____ $ _____ per month, with payments to begin on *(date)* _____

    until the full amount owing is paid.

    ☐ The child support owed to *(name of agency or other person)* _____

    be fixed at $ _____ as of *(date)* _____

Form 15A: **Change Information Form**   **(page 6)** | Court File Number

☐ *(Name of payor)* _____ pay to *(name of agency or other person)*
_____ $ _____ per month, with payments to begin on *(date)*
_____ until the full amount owing is paid.

SPOUSAL SUPPORT
(Complete only if you are asking for a change in spousal support.)

20. I am asking to change the spousal support in the order/agreement because:

     ☐ The following change in circumstances has taken place: *(give details of change in circumstances.)*

     ☐ Spousal support should no longer be paid as of *(date)* _____ for the following reasons:
        (give details)

     ☐ The parties consent to the termination of the spousal support order/agreement, dated _____ ,
        as of *(date)* _____ .

     ☐ Other *(give details)*:

21. I ask that the spousal support be changed as follows:

     ☐ The order/agreement for spousal support, dated _____ , be terminated
        effective *(date)* _____ .

     ☐ *(Name of party)* _____ pay spousal support to
        (name of party) _____ in the amount of $ _____ per month,
        effective on *(date)* _____ .

     ☐ Other *(give details of the order you want the court to make)*

22. I ask that the outstanding spousal support owed be paid as follows:

     ☐ The spousal support owed to *(name of recipient)*
        be fixed at $ _____ as of *(date)*

     ☐ *(Name of payor)* _____ pay to *(name of recipient)*
        $ _____ per month, with payments
        to begin on *(date)* _____ until the full amount owing is paid.

     ☐ The spousal support owed to *(name of agency or other person)*
        be fixed at $ _____ as of *(date)*

     ☐ *(Name of payor)* _____ pay to *(name of agency or other person)*
        $ _____ per month, with payments
        to begin on *(date)* _____ until the full amount owing is paid.

FAMILY LAW RULES FORMS

Form 15A:	Change Information Form	(page 7)	Court File Number

OTHER
(Complete if applicable.)

23. I ask that the term(s) of the order of Justice *(name of judge)* _____ ,

dated _____ , for *(give details)* _____

be changed as follows: *(give details of the order you want the court to make)*

24. I ask that the court make this order for the following reasons:

Sworn/Affirmed before me at _____	Signature
_____ *municipality*	*(This form is to be signed in front of a lawyer, justice of the peace, notary public or commissioner for taking affidavits.)*
in _____	
province, state or country	
on _____	
date _____	
Commissioner for taking affidavits	
(Type or print name below if signature is illegible.)	

Form 15A: Change Information Form   (page 8) | Court File Number |

PART 2 – INFORMATION FROM SUPPORT PAYOR

DO NOT COMPLETE THIS PART IF THE PARTIES ARE ONLY CONSENTING TO TERMINATE A SUPPORT OBLIGATION OR IF THE MOTION TO CHANGE DOES NOT INCLUDE A CLAIM TO CHANGE CHILD SUPPORT.

My name is *(full legal name)* _____

I live in *(municipality & province)* _____

and I swear/affirm that the following is true:

25.   I am the support payor in this case.

26.   I attach the following financial information about myself:

    (a) a copy of every personal income tax return that I filed with Canada Revenue Agency for the 3 most recent taxation years;

    (b) a copy of every notice of assessment or re-assessment from Canada Revenue Agency of those returns; and

    (c) ☐ *(applies only if you are an employee)* proof of this year's earnings from my employer as required by clause 21(1)(c) of the Child Support Guidelines.

       ☐ *(applies only if you are self-employed, or you are a partner in a partnership or you control a corporation or are a beneficiary under a trust)* the documents listed in clauses 21(1)(d), (e), (f) or (g) of the Child Support Guidelines.

27.   My total income

    ☐ will be $ _____ for this year;

    ☐ was $ _____ for last year; and

    ☐ was $ _____ for the year before that.

28.   On the basis of my annual income, the table amount from the Child Support Guidelines for *(number of child(ren))* _____ child(ren) is $ _____ per month.

29.   My financial statement   ☐ is attached.   ☐ is not attached.

Sworn/Affirmed before me at _____ *municipality* in _____ *province, state or country* on _____ *date* _____ *Commissioner for taking affidavits* *(Type or print name below* *if signature is illegible.)*	_____ *Signature* *(This form is to be signed in front of a lawyer,* *justice of the peace, notary public or* *commissioner for taking affidavits.)*

Form 15A: Change Information Form	(page 9)	Court File Number

PART 3 – INFORMATION FROM SUPPORT RECIPIENT

DO NOT COMPLETE THIS PART IF THE PARTIES ARE ONLY CONSENTING TO TERMINATE A SUPPORT OBLIGATION OR IF THE MOTION TO CHANGE DOES NOT INCLUDE A CLAIM TO CHANGE CHILD SUPPORT.

My name is *(full legal name)* _____

I live in *(municipality & province)* _____

and I swear/affirm that the following is true:

30. I am the support recipient in this case.

Fill in paragraphs 31 and 32 only if:

- *the change for which you are asking is for an amount that is different from the Child Support Guidelines;*
- *the change for which you are asking relates to a child*
  - *over the age of 18 years,*
  - *for whom the payor stands in the place of a parent, or*
  - *with respect to whom the payor has access or physical custody not less than 40% of the time over the course of the year;*
- *each party has custody of one or more children;*
- *the payor's annual income as determined under the guidelines is more than $150,000;*
- *either party claims that an order according to the guidelines would result in undue hardship; or*
- *there is a claim for special or extraordinary expenses.*

31. I attach the following financial information about myself:

  (a) a copy of every personal income tax return that I filed with Canada Revenue Agency for the 3 most recent taxation years;

  (b) a copy of every notice of assessment or re-assessment from Canada Revenue Agency of those returns; and

  (c) ☐ *(applies only if you are an employee)* proof of this year's earnings from my employer as required by clause 21(1)(c) of the Child Support Guidelines.

  ☐ *(applies only if you are self-employed, or you are a partner in a partnership or you control a corporation or are a beneficiary under a trust)* the documents listed in clauses 21(1)(d), (e), (f) or (g) of the Child Support Guidelines.

32. My total income

  ☐ will be $ _____ for this year;

  ☐ was $ _____ for last year; and

  ☐ was $ _____ for the year before that.

33. My financial statement   ☐ is attached.   ☐ is not attached.

Sworn/Affirmed before me at _____	
_____ *municipality*	Signature
in _____ *province, state or country*	*(This form is to be signed in front of a lawyer, justice of the peace, notary public or commissioner for taking affidavits.)*
on _____ *date* _____ *Commissioner for taking affidavits (Type or print name below if signature is illegible.)*	

Form 15B

Response to Motion to Change

ONTARIO

_____

(Name of court)

	Court File Number

at _____
Court office address

Form 15B: Response to Motion to Change

Applicant(s)

Full legal name & address for service — street & number, municipality, postal code, telephone & fax numbers and e-mail address (if any).	Lawyer's name & address — street & number, municipality, postal code, telephone & fax numbers and e-mail address (if any).

Respondent(s)

Full legal name & address for service — street & number, municipality, postal code, telephone & fax numbers and e-mail address (if any).	Lawyer's name & address — street & number, municipality, postal code, telephone & fax numbers and e-mail address (if any).

Assignee (if applicable)

Full legal name & address for service — street & number, municipality, postal code, telephone & fax numbers and e-mail address (if any).	Lawyer's name & address — street & number, municipality, postal code, telephone & fax numbers and e-mail address (if any).

PART 1 – GENERAL INFORMATION

My name is *(full legal name)* _____

I live in *(municipality and province)* _____

and I swear/affirm that the following is true:

1. I am the ☐ applicant ☐ Respondent

2. I am the ☐ support payor ☐ support recipient

3. This order/agreement ☐ has never been assigned

         ☐ has been assigned to

             ☐ the Ontario Ministry of Community and Social Services

             ☐ Ontario Works in *(name of location)* _____

             ☐ the municipality of *(name)* _____

             ☐ other *(specify)* _____

     The details of the assignment are: *(give date of assignment, indicate whether it is still in effect and add any other relevant information known to you.)*

4. ☐ Since the order/agreement for child support was made, a Notice of Recalculation was issued by the online Child Support Service dated _____ *(please attach).*

5. ☐ I agree with the information set out in paragraphs 1 through 10 of the Change Information Form (Form 15A), dated _____ .

     ☐ I agree with the information set out in paragraphs 1 through 10 of the Change Information Form (Form 15A), dated _____ EXCEPT as follows: *(give details of the information with which you do not agree and attach any documents that support your position.)*

Form 15B:	Response to Motion to Change	(page 2)	Court File Number

6. ☐ I agree with the claims made by *(name of person bringing motion to change)* _____

     in paragraphs _____ of the Motion to Change (Form 15), dated _____

     ☐ I disagree with the claims made by *(name of person bringing motion to change)* _____

     in paragraphs _____ of the Motion to Change (Form 15), dated _____

7. ☐ I am asking that the motion to change (except for the parts with which I agree) be dismissed with costs.

CLAIM BY RESPONDING PARTY
(Complete only if you are asking the court to change the existing order or support agreement.)

8. ☐ I am asking the court to make a change of my own, the details of which are set out below.

CUSTODY/ACCESS
(Complete only if you are asking for a change in a custody or access order.)

9. I ask that *(name of party)* _____

     have custody of the following child(ren): *(name(s) and birthdate(s) of child(ren))*

10. I ask that *(name of party)* _____

     have access to the following child(ren): *(name(s) and birthdate(s) of child(ren))*

     as follows: *(give details of access)*

OR

11. I ask that *(name(s) of party(ies) and/or person(s))* _____

     and _____

     have joint custody of the following child(ren): *(name(s) and birthdate(s) of child(ren))*

12. I ask for the following residential/access arrangements for the child(ren): *(include name(s) and birthdate(s) of child(ren))*

13. The order I am asking the court to make is in the best interests of the child(ren) for the following reasons: *(give details)*

CHILD SUPPORT
(Complete this section only if you are asking for a change in child support.)

14. I am asking to change the child support in the order/agreement because:

     ☐ the order/agreement was made before the applicable Child Support Guidelines came into effect.

     ☐ the following change in circumstances has taken place: *(give details of change in circumstances.)*

FLR 15B (November 1, 2018)

Form 15B: **Response to Motion to Change**   **(page 3)** | Court File Number

☐ the parties agree to the termination of the support order/agreement, dated .... ,
for the following child(ren): *(name(s) and birthdate(s) of child(ren))*

as of *(date)* ....

☐ Other: *(give details)*

15. I ask that the child support be changed as follows:

☐ The order/agreement for child support, dated .... be terminated for the
following child(ren): *(name(s) and birthdate(s) of child(ren))*

effective *(date)* ....

☐ Based on the payor's annual income of $ .... , *(name of party)* ....
pay child support to *(name of party)* .... in the amount of
$ .... per month for the following child(ren): *(name(s) and birthdate(s) of child(ren))*

with payments to start on *(date)* ....

☐ This amount is the table amount listed in the Child Support Guidelines.

☐ This amount is more than the table amount listed in the Child Support Guidelines.

☐ This amount is less than the table amount listed in the Child Support Guidelines. *(If this box is checked, you must complete paragraph 16.)*

☐ Starting on *(date)* .... , *(name of party)* ....
pay to *(name of party)* .... $ ....

for the following special or extraordinary expenses:

Child's Name	Type of Expense	Total Amount of Expense	Payor's Share	Terms of payment *(frequency of payment, date due, etc.)*
		$	$	
		$	$	
		$	$	
		$	$	
		$	$	

☐ Other: *(give details)*

16. I am asking that child support be changed to an amount that is less than the table amount listed in the Child Support Guidelines. The reason(s) for my request is/are that:

☐ The parties agree to a different amount.

☐ I have attached a separate sheet to this form that explains why this is an appropriate amount of child support.

☐ The recipient is getting social assistance payments from a public agency whose consent to this arrangement is needed. I am attaching the agency's consent to this form.

FLR 15B (November 1, 2018)   Page 3 of 8

Form 15B: **Response to Motion to Change**   **(page 4)**   Court File Number

☐ The parties have shared custody to the child(ren) *(the payor has a child at least 40% of the time)*.

    ☐ I have attached a separate sheet to this form that compares the table amounts from the Child Support Guidelines for each of the parties, shows the increased cost of the shared custody arrangement, the financial circumstances of each party and of each child for whom support is claimed.

    ☐ The parties are agreeing to this arrangement and I have attached a separate sheet to this form that explains why this is an appropriate amount of child support.

☐ Custody of the children is split between the parties. I have attached a separate sheet to this form that calculates the difference between the amount that each party would otherwise pay to the other under the Child Support Guidelines.

☐ A child is 18 or more years old and I attach to this form a separate sheet that calculates the amount of support for this child.

    ☐ A child contributes to his/her own support and I attach to this form a separate sheet showing the amount of the child's own income and/or assets.

☐ The payor's annual income is over $150,000 and I have attached to this form a separate sheet that calculates the amount of support that I want to be put in an order.

☐ Under the order/agreement, *(name(s) of child(ren))* _____

is/are the subject of special provisions that I have detailed on a separate sheet that I have attached to this form.

☐ The payor stands in the place of a parent to *(name(s) of child(ren)* _____

and I attach to this form a separate sheet that gives the details of another parent's duty to pay support for this/these child(ren), as well as the details of the calculation of the amount of support requested.

☐ The amount listed in the Child Support Guidelines would cause undue hardship to me or to the child(ren) for whom support is claimed. I attach to this form a separate sheet that compares the standards of living of the parties and calculates the amount of support that should be paid.

17. I ask that the outstanding child support owed be paid as follows:

    ☐ The child support owed to *(name of recipient)* _____

    be fixed at $ _____ as of *(date)* _____ and *(name of payor)*

_____ pay to *(name of recipient)*

_____ $ _____ per month,

with payments to begin on *(date)* _____ until the full amount owing is paid.

    ☐ The child support owed to *(name of agency or other person)* _____

    be fixed at $ _____ as of *(date)* _____ and *(name of payor)*

_____ pay to *(name of agency or other person)*

_____ $ _____ per month,

with payments to begin on *(date)* _____ until the full amount owing is paid.

SPOUSAL SUPPORT

(Complete only if you are asking for a change in spousal support.)

18. I am asking to change the spousal support in the order/agreement because:

    ☐ The following change in circumstances has taken place: *(give details of change in circumstances.)*

Form 15B: **Response to Motion to Change**   **(page 5)** | Court File Number |

☐ Spousal support should no longer be paid as of *(date)* _____ for the following reasons: *(give details)*

☐ The parties consent to the termination of the spousal support order/agreement, dated _____ ,
as of *(date)* _____ .

☐ Other *(specify)*

19. I ask that the spousal support be changed as follows:

☐ The order/agreement for spousal support, dated _____ , be terminated effective
(date) _____ .

☐ *(Name of party)* _____ pay spousal support to
(name of party) _____ in the amount of
$ _____ per month, effective on *(date)* _____ .

☐ Other: *(give details of the order you want the court to make)*

20. I ask that the outstanding spousal support owed be paid as follows:

☐ The spousal support owed to *(name of recipient)* _____
be fixed at $ _____ as of *(date)* _____ .

☐ *(Name of payor)* _____ pay to *(name of recipient)*
_____ $ _____ per month,
with payments to begin on *(date)* _____ until the full amount owing is paid.

☐ The spousal support owed to *(name of agency or other person)* _____
be fixed at $ _____ as of *(date)* _____ .

☐ *(Name of payor)* _____ pay to *(name of agency or other person)*
_____ $ _____ per month,
with payments to begin on *(date)* _____ until the full amount owing is paid.

OTHER
(Complete if applicable)

21. I ask that the term of the order of Justice *(name of judge)* _____ ,
dated _____ , for *(give details)* _____
be changed as follows: *(give details of the order you want the court to make)*

Form 15B: **Response to Motion to Change**   **(page 6)** | Court File Number

22. I ask that the court make the order set out in paragraph 21 for the following reasons:

23. I ask the court to make the following additional order:

24. I ask the court to make the order set out in paragraph 23 for the following reasons:

Sworn/Affirmed before me at ⎯⎯⎯⎯⎯⎯⎯⎯⎯⎯⎯⎯⎯⎯⎯⎯⎯⎯
municipality

in ⎯⎯⎯⎯⎯⎯⎯⎯⎯⎯⎯⎯⎯⎯⎯⎯⎯⎯⎯⎯⎯⎯⎯⎯⎯
province, state or country

on ⎯⎯⎯⎯⎯⎯⎯⎯⎯⎯ ⎯⎯⎯⎯⎯⎯⎯⎯⎯⎯⎯⎯⎯⎯⎯⎯
date   *Commissioner for taking affidavits*
(Type or print name below
if signature is illegible.)

⎯⎯⎯⎯⎯⎯⎯⎯⎯⎯⎯⎯⎯⎯⎯⎯⎯⎯⎯⎯⎯⎯⎯⎯
Signature
(This form is to be signed in front of a lawyer,
justice of the peace, notary public or
commissioner for taking affidavits.)

Form 15B: **Response to Motion to Change** (page 7) | Court File Number

PART 2 – INFORMATION FROM SUPPORT PAYOR

DO NOT COMPLETE THIS PART IF THE PARTIES ARE ONLY CONSENTING TO TERMINATE A SUPPORT OBLIGATION OR IF THE MOTION TO CHANGE DOES NOT INCLUDE A CLAIM TO CHANGE CHILD SUPPORT.

My name is *(full legal name)*

I live in *(municipality and province)*

and I swear/affirm that the following is true:

25. I am the support payor in this case.

26. I attach the following financial information about myself:

    (a) a copy of every personal income tax return that I filed with Canada Revenue Agency for the 3 most recent taxation years;

    (b) a copy of every notice of assessment or re-assessment from Canada Revenue Agency of those returns; and

    (c) ☐ *(applies only if you are an employee)* proof of this year's earnings from my employer as required by clause 21(1) (c) of the Child Support Guidelines.

    ☐ *(applies only if you are self-employed, or you are a partner in a partnership or you control a corporation or are a beneficiary under a trust)* the documents listed in clauses 21 (1)(d), (e), (f) or (g) of the Child Support Guidelines.

27. My total income

    ☐ will be $ _____ for this year;

    ☐ was $ _____ for last year; and

    ☐ was $ _____ for the year before that.

28. On the basis of my annual income, the table amount from the Child Support Guidelines for *(number of children)* _____ child(ren) is $ _____ per month.

29. My financial statement ☐ is attached. ☐ is not attached.

Sworn/Affirmed before me at _____
    municipality

in _____
    province, state or country

on _____
    date

    Commissioner for taking affidavits
    (Type or print name below if signature is illegible.)

_____
Signature
(This form is to be signed in front of a lawyer, justice of the peace, notary public or commissioner for taking affidavits.)

Form 15B: **Response to Motion to Change** (page 8)

Court File Number

PART 3 – INFORMATION FROM SUPPORT RECIPIENT

DO NOT COMPLETE THIS PART IF THE PARTIES ARE ONLY CONSENTING TO TERMINATE A SUPPORT OBLIGATION OR IF THE MOTION TO CHANGE DOES NOT INCLUDE A CLAIM TO CHANGE CHILD SUPPORT.

My name is *(full legal name)*

I live in *(municipality and province)*

and I swear/affirm that the following is true:

30. I am the support recipient in this case.

Fill in paragraphs 30 and 31 only if:

- *the change for which you are asking is for an amount that is different from the Child Support Guidelines;*
- *the change for which you are asking relates to a child*
  - *over the age of 18 years,*
  - *for whom the payor stands in the place of a parent, or*
  - *with respect to whom the payor has access or physical custody not less than 40% of the time over the course of the year;*
- *each party has custody of one or more children;*
- *the payor's annual income as determined under the guidelines is more than $150,000;*
- *either party claims that an order according to the guidelines would result in undue hardship; or*
- *there is a claim for special or extraordinary expenses.*

31. I attach the following financial information about myself:

    (a) a copy of every personal income tax return that I filed with Canada Revenue Agency for the 3 most recent taxation years;

    (b) a copy of every notice of assessment or re-assessment from Canada Revenue Agency of those returns; and

    (c) ☐ *(applies only if you are an employee)* proof of this year's earnings from my employer as required by clause 21(1) (c) of the Child Support Guidelines.

        ☐ *(applies only if you are self-employed, or you are a partner in a partnership or you control a corporation or are a beneficiary under a trust)* the documents listed in clauses 21 (1)(d), (e), (f) or (g) of the Child Support Guidelines.

32. My total income

    ☐ will be $ _____ for this year;

    ☐ was $ _____ for last year; and

    ☐ was $ _____ for the year before that.

33. My financial statement   ☐ is attached.   ☐ is not attached.

Sworn/Affirmed before me at _____

                municipality

in _____

        province, state or country

on _____

    date   *Commissioner for taking affidavits*
                (Type or print name below
                if signature is illegible.)

                Signature
        (This form is to be signed in front of a lawyer,
        justice of the peace, notary public or
        commissioner for taking affidavits.)

Form 15C

Consent Motion to Change

ONTARIO

(Name of court)	Court File Number

at _____

Court office address

Form 15C: Consent
Motion to Change

Applicant(s)

Full legal name & address for service — street & number, municipality, postal code, telephone & fax numbers and e-mail address (if any).	Lawyer's name & address — street & number, municipality, postal code, telephone & fax numbers and e-mail address (if any).

Respondent(s)

Full legal name & address for service — street & number, municipality, postal code, telephone & fax numbers and e-mail address (if any).	Lawyer's name & address — street & number, municipality, postal code, telephone & fax numbers and e-mail address (if any).

Assignee (if applicable)

Full legal name & address for service — street & number, municipality, postal code, telephone & fax numbers and e-mail address (if any).	Lawyer's name & address — street & number, municipality, postal code, telephone & fax numbers and e-mail address (if any).

YOU MAY USE THIS FORM IF YOU ARE SEEKING TO CHANGE AN ORDER OR AGREEMENT THAT HAS BEEN RECALCULATED BY THE ONLINE CHILD SUPPORT SERVICE. YOU MUST SERVE A COPY OF THIS FORM ON THE FAMILY RESPONSIBILITY OFFICE IF THE ORDER YOU RECALCULATED WAS MADE UNDER THE DIVORCE ACT AND THE RECALCULATION WAS COMPLETED WITHIN THE LAST 35 DAYS.

YOU MAY NOT USE THIS FORM TO CHANGE A NOTICE OF CALCULATION MADE BY THE ONLINE CHILD SUPPORT SERVICE.

EACH OF YOU SHOULD CONSIDER GETTING A LAWYER'S ADVICE BEFORE SIGNING THIS CONSENT.

IF YOU ARE SEEKING TO CHANGE A SUPPORT ORDER OR AGREEMENT THAT HAS BEEN ASSIGNED TO A PERSON OR AGENCY, YOU MUST SERVE ALL DOCUMENTS ON THE ASSIGNEE AND OBTAIN THE ASSIGNEE'S CONSENT TO ANY CHANGE THAT MAY AFFECT THE ASSIGNEE'S FINANCIAL INTEREST. FAILURE TO OBTAIN THE ASSIGNEE'S CONSENT MAY RESULT IN A COURT SETTING ASIDE AN ORDER AND ORDERING COSTS AGAINST THE PARTY WHO DID NOT PROVIDE NOTICE. IT IS THE RESPONSIBILITY OF THE PERSON SEEKING THE CHANGE TO DETERMINE IF THE ORDER HAS BEEN ASSIGNED. YOU CAN DO THIS BY SUBMITTING A CONFIRMATION OF ASSIGNMENT FORM. THE CONFIRMATION OF ASSIGNMENT FORM IS AVAILABLE THROUGH THE MINISTRY OF THE ATTORNEY GENERAL WEBSITE OR AT THE COURT OFFICE.

1. We know that each of us has the right to get advice from his or her own lawyer about this case and understand that signing this consent may result in a final court order that will be enforced.

2. ☐ We have filed/are filing Financial Statements (Form 13 or 13.1) with the court.

   ☐ We have agreed not to file any Financial Statements with the court.

3. ☐ We have attached the existing final order or support agreement and ask the court to make an order that changes that order or agreement as set out below.

   ☐ Since the order/agreement for child support was made, a Notice of Recalculation was issued by the

   online Child Support Service dated _____ *(please attach).*

   CUSTODY/ACCESS *(Complete only if the parties are asking for a change in a custody or access order.)*

4. ☐ We agree that *(name(s) of person(s) or party(ies))* _____

   shall have custody of the following child(ren):

Child's full legal name	Birthdate *(d, m, y)*	Age	Sex

Form 15C:	**Consent Motion to Change**	**(page 2)**	Court File Number

☐ We agree that *(name(s) of person(s) or party(ies))*

shall have access to: *(name(s) and birthdate(s) of child(ren))*

as follows: *(give details of access order)*

OR

5. ☐ We agree that *(names of parties or persons)*

and _____ shall have joint custody of the following child(ren):

Child's full legal name	Birthdate *(d, m, y)*	Age	Sex

☐ We agree that the residential/access arrangements for the child(ren) *(name(s) and birthdate(s) of child(ren))*

shall be as follows:

CHILD SUPPORT
(Complete only if the parties are asking for a change in child support.)

6. We agree to an order for child support that is:

☐ equal to or more than what is in the Child Support Guidelines.

☐ none (no child support).

☐ less than what is in the Child Support Guidelines for the following reasons:

7. The party receiving support ☐ is ☐ is not receiving social assistance.

8. We agree that child support shall be as follows:

☐ Based on the payor's annual income of $ _____ , *(name of party)* _____

shall pay to *(name of party)* _____ $ _____ per month

for the following child(ren) *(name(s) and birthdate(s) of child(ren))*

with payments to begin on *(date)* _____ .

☐ Starting on *(date)* _____ , *(name of party)* _____

shall pay *(name of party)* _____ $ _____ for the

following special or extraordinary expenses:

Form 15C: **Consent Motion to Change**   **(page 3)** | Court File Number |

Child's name	Type of expense	Total Amount of Expense	Payor's Share	Terms of Payment *(frequency of payment, date due, etc.)*
		$	$	
		$	$	
		$	$	
		$	$	
		$	$	

☐ *(Complete only if the parties are agreeing to special or extraordinary expenses.)* The recipient's total annual income is
$ _____ .

☐ The order or agreement for child support, with respect to the child(ren) *(name(s) and birthdate(s) of child(ren))*

_____ ,

dated _____ , shall be terminated as of *(date)* _____ .

Complete if applicable:

9. We also agree that the outstanding child support owed be paid off as follows:

☐ The child support owed to *(name of recipient)* _____ shall be

fixed at $ _____ as of *(date)* _____ and *(name of payor)* _____

shall pay *(name of recipient)* _____

$ _____ per month, with payments to begin on *(date)* _____ until the

full amount owing has been paid.

☐ The child support owed to *(name of agency or other person)* _____ shall be

fixed at $ _____ as of *(date)* _____ and *(name of payor)* _____

shall pay *(name of agency or other person)* _____

$ _____ per month, with payments to begin on *(date)* _____ until the

full amount owing has been paid.

SPOUSAL SUPPORT
(Complete only if the parties are seeking a change in spousal support.)

10. We agree that the spousal support payments should be as follows:

☐ *(Name of party)* _____ shall pay to

(name of party) _____ the amount of

$ _____ per month, with payments to begin on *(date)* _____

☐ The order or agreement for spousal support, dated _____ , shall be terminated as of

(date) _____ .

11. We agree that the outstanding spousal support owed be paid off as follows:

☐ The spousal support owed to *(name of recipient)* _____ shall be

fixed at $ _____ as of *(date)* _____ and *(name of payor)* _____

shall pay *(name of recipient)* _____

$ _____ per month, with payments to begin on *(date)* _____ until the

full amount owing has been paid.

FLR 15C (April 12, 2016)   Page 3 of 4

FAMILY LAW RULES FORMS

Form 15C:	**Consent Motion to Change**	**(page 4)**	Court File Number

☐ The spousal support owed to *(name of agency or other person)* _____

shall be fixed at $ _____ as of *(date)* _____ and *(name of payor)*

_____ shall pay *(name of recipient)* _____

$ _____ per month, with payments to begin on *(date)* _____ until the

full amount owing has been paid.

NOTE: If money is owed to an agency or other person (an assignee), a representative of that agency or the other person must consent to the change in the order.

OTHER
(Complete if applicable.)

12. We agree that paragraph(s) *(specify which paragraphs of the order are to be changed)* _____ of the order

of Justice *(name of judge)* _____ , dated _____ ,

shall be changed as follows: *(give details of the order you want the court to make)*

The parties do not need to sign this consent at the same time. Each party must sign in the presence of his or her witness who shall sign immediately after that party.

NOTE: The witness cannot be one of the parties. If the witness does not know the party, the witness should see identification that proves that the person signing the consent is the same person who is a party to the consent.

_____	_____
Applicant's signature	*Respondent's signature*
_____	_____
Date of applicant's signature	*Date of respondent's signature*
_____	_____
Signature of witness	*Signature of witness*
_____	_____
Type or print name of witness to applicant's signature	*Type or print name of witness to respondent's signature*
_____	_____
Address of witness	*Address of witness*
_____	_____
Telephone number of witness	*Telephone number of witness*

ASSIGNEE'S CONSENT

_____	_____
Signature of person authorized to sign on behalf of assignee	*Date of signature*

_____
Print name and title of person signing the consent

_____	_____
Witness's signature	*Name of witness (type or print legibly)*

FLR 15C (April 12, 2016)   Page 4 of 4

Form 15D

Consent Motion to Change Child Support

ONTARIO

	Court File Number
(Name of court)	

at _____

Court office address

Form 15D: Consent Motion to Change Child Support

Applicant(s)

Full legal name & address for service — street & number, municipality, postal code, telephone & fax numbers and e-mail address (if any).	Lawyer's name & address — street & number, municipality, postal code, telephone & fax numbers and e-mail address (if any).

Respondent(s)

Full legal name & address for service — street & number, municipality, postal code, telephone & fax numbers and e-mail address (if any).	Lawyer's name & address — street & number, municipality, postal code, telephone & fax numbers and e-mail address (if any).

Assignee (if applicable)

Full legal name & address for service — street & number, municipality, postal code, telephone & fax numbers and e-mail address (if any).	Lawyer's name & address — street & number, municipality, postal code, telephone & fax numbers and e-mail address (if any).

<u>Instructions to the Parties:</u>

IF YOU ARE SEEKING TO CHANGE A CHILD SUPPORT TERM IN AN AGREEMENT THAT HAS NOT ALREADY BEEN FILED WITH THE COURT PURSUANT TO SECTION 35 OF THE FAMILY LAW ACT, YOU MUST FILE THE AGREEMENT AND FORM 26B (Affidavit for Filing Domestic Contract with Court) BEFORE BRINGING THIS MOTION TO CHANGE.

YOU MAY USE THIS FORM IF YOU ARE SEEKING TO CHANGE AN ORDER OR AGREEMENT THAT HAS BEEN RECALCULATED BY THE ONLINE CHILD SUPPORT SERVICE. YOU MUST SERVE A COPY OF THIS FORM ON THE FAMILY RESPONSIBILITY OFFICE IF THE ORDER YOU RECALCULATED WAS MADE UNDER THE DIVORCE ACT AND THE RECALCULATION WAS COMPLETED WITHIN THE LAST 35 DAYS.

YOU MAY NOT USE THIS FORM TO CHANGE A NOTICE OF CALCULATION MADE BY THE ONLINE CHILD SUPPORT SERVICE.

EACH OF YOU SHOULD CONSIDER GETTING A LAWYER'S ADVICE BEFORE SIGNING THIS CONSENT.

IF YOU ARE SEEKING TO CHANGE A CHILD SUPPORT ORDER OR AGREEMENT THAT HAS BEEN ASSIGNED TO A PERSON OR AGENCY, YOU MUST OBTAIN THE ASSIGNEE'S CONSENT TO ANY CHANGE THAT MAY AFFECT THE ASSIGNEE'S FINANCIAL INTEREST. FAILURE TO OBTAIN THE ASSIGNEE'S CONSENT MAY RESULT IN A COURT SETTING ASIDE AN ORDER AND ORDERING COSTS AGAINST THE PARTY WHO DID NOT PROVIDE NOTICE. IT IS THE RESPONSIBILITY OF THE PERSON SEEKING THE CHANGE TO DETERMINE IF THE ORDER HAS BEEN ASSIGNED. YOU CAN DO THIS BY SUBMITTING A CONFIRMATION OF ASSIGNMENT FORM. THE CONFIRMATION OF ASSIGNMENT FORM IS AVAILABLE THROUGH THE MINISTRY OF THE ATTORNEY GENERAL WEBSITE OR AT THE COURT OFFICE.

TO THE COURT:

This motion to change child support is filed by the parties with the consent of the applicant and respondent and, if applicable, the assignee.

We ask the court to make the order requested in this motion by relying on this form only.

1. We know that each of us has the right to get advice from his or her own lawyer about this case and understand that signing this consent may result in a final court order that will be enforced.

2. We have attached the existing agreement or order for child support and ask the court to make an order that changes that order or agreement as set out below.

   ☐ Since the order/agreement for child support was made, a Notice of Recalculation was issued by the online Child Support Service dated _____ *(please attach)*.

Check the following box(es) that apply:

3. The total annual income of the person paying support is $ _____ .

   The payor ☐ is ☐ is not self-employed.

FLR 15D (April 12, 2016)

Page 1 of 3

Family Law Rules Forms

Form 15D: **Consent Motion to Change Child Support**   **(page 2)**   Court File Number

4. Proof of income for the payor was provided to the recipient by: *(check at least one)*
   - ☐ Most recent income tax return
   - ☐ Most recent notice of income tax assessment
   - ☐ Current pay stub
   - ☐ Business records
   - ☐ Other *(provide details)*

5. ☐ *(Name of party)* _____ shall pay to *(name of party)*
   $ _____ per month for the following
   child(ren) *(name(s) and birthdate(s) of child(ren))*

   with payments to begin on *(date)* _____ .

6. ☐ This amount is the table amount listed in the Child Support Guidelines.
   ☐ This amount is more than the table amount listed in the Child Support Guidelines.
   ☐ This amount is less than the table amount listed in the Child Support Guidelines for the following reasons: *(give details)*

7. ☐ Starting on *(date)* _____ , *(name of party)* _____
   shall pay *(name of party)* _____ $ _____
   for the following special or extraordinary expenses:

Child's name	Type of expense	Total Amount of Expense	Payor's Share	Terms of payment *(frequency of payment, date due, etc.)*
		$	$	
		$	$	
		$	$	
		$	$	
		$	$	

(Complete paragraphs 8 and 9 only if the parties are agreeing to special or extraordinary expenses.)

8. ☐ The recipient's total annual income is $ _____

9. Proof of income for the recipient was provided to the payor by: *(check at least one)*
   - ☐ Most recent income tax return
   - ☐ Most recent notice of income tax assessment
   - ☐ Current pay stub
   - ☐ Business records
   - ☐ Other *(provide details)*

10. ☐ The order or agreement for child support, with respect to the child(ren) *(name(s) and birthdate(s) of child(ren))*

    dated _____ , should be terminated as of *(date)* _____ .

FLR 15D (April 12, 2016)   Page 2 of 3

942

Form 15D: **Consent Motion to Change Child Support** (page 3)

Court File Number

Complete applicable paragraphs if there is outstanding child support owing

11. ☐ The child support owed to *(name of recipient)* .

shall be fixed at $ _____ as of *(date)* _____ .

12. ☐ *(Name of payor)* _____ shall pay *(name of recipient)*

_____ $ _____ per month, with payments

to begin on *(date)* _____ until the full amount owing is paid.

13. ☐ The child support owed to *(name of agency or other person)* _____

shall be fixed at $ _____ as of *(date)* _____ .

14. ☐ *(Name of payor)* _____ shall pay to *(name of agency or other person)*

_____ $ _____ per month, with payments to begin on *(date)*

_____ until the full amount owing is paid.

NOTE: If money is owed to an agency or other person (an assignee), a representative of that agency or the other person must consent to the change in the order.

The parties do not need to sign this consent at the same time. Each party must sign in the presence of his or her witness who shall sign immediately after that party.

NOTE: The witness cannot be one of the parties. If the witness does not know the party, the witness should see identification that proves that the person signing the consent is the same person who is a party to the consent.

_____	_____
Applicant's signature	*Respondent's signature*
_____	_____
Date of applicant's signature	*Date of respondent's signature*
_____	_____
Signature of witness	*Signature of witness*
_____	_____
Type or print name of witness to applicant's signature	*Type or print name of witness to respondent's signature*
_____	_____
Address of witness	*Address of witness*
_____	_____
Telephone number of witness	*Telephone number of witness*

ASSIGNEE'S CONSENT

_____	_____
Signature of person authorized to sign on behalf of assignee	*Date of signature*

_____
Print name and title of person signing the consent

_____	_____
Witness's signature	*Name of witness (type or print legibly)*

FLR 15D (April 12, 2016)

Page 3 of 3

Form 17

Conference Notice

ONTARIO

_____
(Name of court)

at _____
Court office address

Court File Number

**Form 17:
Conference
Notice**

Applicant(s)

Full legal name & address for service — street & number, municipality, postal code, telephone & fax numbers and e-mail address (if any).	Lawyer's name & address — street & number, municipality, postal code, telephone & fax numbers and e-mail address (if any).

Respondent(s)

Full legal name & address for service — street & number, municipality, postal code, telephone & fax numbers and e-mail address (if any).	Lawyer's name & address — street & number, municipality, postal code, telephone & fax numbers and e-mail address (if any).

Name & address of Children's Lawyer's agent (street & number, municipality, postal code, telephone & fax numbers and e-mail address (if any)) and name of person represented.

TO: *(name of party or parties or lawyer(s))*

A ☐ **CASE CONFERENCE** ☐ **SETTLEMENT CONFERENCE** ☐ **TRIAL MANAGEMENT CONFERENCE**

WILL BE HELD at *(place of conference)* _____

at _____ **on** *(date)* _____

The conference has been arranged at the request of

☐ the applicant ☐ the respondent
☐ the case management judge ☐ *(Other; specify.)* _____

to deal with the following issues:

_____

You must participate at the time and date by
☐ coming to court at the address set out above.
☐ video-conference or telephone at *(location of video terminal or telephone)* _____
as agreed under arrangements already made by *(name of person)* _____
for video/telephone conferencing.

IF YOU DO NOT PARTICIPATE AS SET OUT ABOVE, THE CASE MAY GO ON WITHOUT YOU OR THE COURT MAY DISMISS THE CASE.

_____ _____
Date of signature *Signature of clerk of the court*

NOTE: *The party requesting the conference (or, if the conference is not requested by a party, the applicant) must serve and file a case conference brief (Form 17A or 17B), settlement conference brief (Form 17C or 17D), trial management conference brief (Form 17E), or Trial Scheduling Endorsement Form, not later than six days before the date scheduled for the conference. The other party must serve and file their documents not later than four days before the conference date. Each party must also file a confirmation (Form 17F) not later than* **2 p.m. three days** *before the conference.*

FLR 17 (November 1, 2018) Page 1 of 1

Form 17A

Case Conference Brief – General

ONTARIO

	Court File Number
_____	
(Name of court)	**Form 17A:**
at _____	**Case Conference Brief –**
Court office address	**General**

Name of party filing this brief

Date of case conference

Applicant(s)

Full legal name & address for service — street & number, municipality, postal code, telephone & fax numbers and e-mail address (if any).	*Lawyer's name & address — street & number, municipality, postal code, telephone & fax numbers and e-mail address (if any).*

Respondent(s)

Full legal name & address for service — street & number, municipality, postal code, telephone & fax numbers and e-mail address (if any).	*Lawyer's name & address — street & number, municipality, postal code, telephone & fax numbers and e-mail address (if any).*

Name & address of Children's Lawyer's agent (street & number, municipality, postal code, telephone & fax numbers and e-mail address (if any)) and name of person represented.

PART 1: FAMILY FACTS

1. **APPLICANT:** Age: _____ Birthdate: *(d, m, y)* _____

2. **RESPONDENT:** Age: _____ Birthdate: *(d, m, y)* _____

3. **RELATIONSHIP DATES:**
   - ☐ Married on *(date)* _____
   - ☐ Separated on *(date)* _____
   - ☐ Started living together on *(date)* _____
   - ☐ Never lived together
   - ☐ Other *(Explain.)* _____

4. The basic information about the child(ren) is as follows:

Child's full legal name	Age	Birthdate *(d, m, y)*	Grade/Year and school	Now living with

FLR 17A (November 1, 2018)

Form 17A:	Case Conference Brief - General	(page 2)	Court File Number

PART 2: ISSUES

5. What are the issues in this case that **HAVE** been settled:

☐ child custody   ☐ spousal support   ☐ possession of home

☐ access   ☐ child support   ☐ equalization of net family property

☐ restraining order   ☐ ownership of property

☐ other *(Specify.)* _____

6. What are the issues in this case that have **NOT** yet been settled:

☐ child custody   ☐ spousal support   ☐ possession of home

☐ access   ☐ child support   ☐ equalization of net family property

☐ restraining order   ☐ ownership of property   *(Attach Net Family Property Statement, Form 13B)*

☐ other *(Specify.)* _____

7. If child or spousal support is an issue, give the income of the parties:

Applicant: $ _____ per year for the year 20 _____

Respondent: $ _____ per year for the year 20 _____

8. Have you explored any ways to settle the issues that are still in dispute in this case?

☐ No.   ☐ Yes. *(Give details.)*

9. Have any of the issues that have been settled been turned into a court order or a written agreement?

☐ No.

☐ Yes.   ☐ an order dated _____

          ☐ a written agreement that is attached.

10. Have the parents attended a family law or parenting education session?

☐ No. (Should they attend one? _____)

☐ Yes. *(Give details.)*

PART 3: ISSUES FOR THIS CASE CONFERENCE

11. What are the issues for this case conference? What are the important facts for this case conference?

Form 17A: **Case Conference Brief - General**   **(page 3)**

Court File Number

12.   What is your proposal to resolve these issues?

13.   Do you want the court to make a temporary or final order at the case conference about any of these issues?

        ☐ No.   ☐ Yes. *(Give details.)*

PART 4: FINANCIAL INFORMATION

NOTE: *If a claim for support has been made in this case, you must serve and file a new financial statement (Form 13 or 13.1), if it is different from the one filed in the continuing record or if the one in the continuing record is more than 30 days old. If there are minor changes but no major changes in your financial statement, you can serve and file an affidavit with details of the changes instead of a new financial statement. If you have not yet filed a financial statement in the continuing record, you must do it now. The page/tab number of the financial statement in the continuing record is* _____

14.   If a claim is being made for child support and a claim is made for special expenses under the child support guidelines, give details of those expenses or attach additional information.

15.   If a claim is made for child support and you claim that the Child Support Guidelines table amount should not be ordered, briefly outline the reasons here or attach an additional page.

Form 17A: **Case Conference Brief - General** **(page 4)**

Court File Number

PART 5: PROCEDURAL ISSUES

16. If custody or access issues are not yet settled:

    (a) Is a custody or access assessment needed?

    ☐ No.   ☐ Yes. *(Give names of possible assessors.)*

    (b) Does a child or a parent under 18 years of age need legal representation from the Office of the Children's Lawyer?

    ☐ No.   ☐ Yes. *(Give details and reasons.)*

17. Does any party need an order for the disclosure of documents, the questioning of witnesses, a property valuation or any other matter in this case?

    ☐ No.   ☐ Yes. *(Give details.)*

18. Are any other procedural orders needed?

    ☐ No.   ☐ Yes. *(Give details.)*

19. Have all the persons who should be parties in this case been added as parties?

    ☐ Yes.   ☐ No. *(Who needs to be added?)*

20. Are there issues that may require expert evidence or a report?

    ☐ No.   ☐ Yes. *(If yes, provide details such as: the type of expert evidence; whether the parties will be retaining a joint expert; who the expert will be; who will be paying the expert; how long it will take to obtain a report, etc.)*

21. Are there any other issues that should be reviewed at the case conference?

    ☐ No.   ☐ Yes. *(Give details.)*

_____   _____
Date of party's signature   *Signature of party*

_____   _____
Date of lawyer's signature   *Signature of party's lawyer*

Form 17B

Case Conference Brief for Protection Application or Status Review

ONTARIO

	Court File Number
(Name of court)	
at _____	**Form 17B: Case Conference Brief for**
Court office address	☐ **Protection Application**
	☐ **Status Review**

Name of party filing this brief	**Date of case conference**

Applicant(s)

Full legal name & address for service — street & number, municipality, postal code, telephone & fax numbers and e-mail address (if any).	Lawyer's name & address — street & number, municipality, postal code, telephone & fax numbers and e-mail address (if any).

Respondent(s)

Full legal name & address for service — street & number, municipality, postal code, telephone & fax numbers and e-mail address (if any).	Lawyer's name & address — street & number, municipality, postal code, telephone & fax numbers and e-mail address (if any).

Respondent(s)

Full legal name & address for service — street & number, municipality, postal code, telephone & fax numbers and e-mail address (if any).	Lawyer's name & address — street & number, municipality, postal code, telephone & fax numbers and e-mail address (if any).

Respondent(s)

Full legal name & address for service — street & number, municipality, postal code, telephone & fax numbers and e-mail address (if any).	Lawyer's name & address — street & number, municipality, postal code, telephone & fax numbers and e-mail address (if any).

Name & address of Children's Lawyer's agent (street & number, municipality, postal code, telephone & fax numbers and e-mail address (if any)) and name of person represented.

FAMILY LAW RULES FORMS

Form 17B:	Case Conference Brief for Protection Application or Status Review	(page 2)	Court File Number

– PART 1: BASIC INFORMATION ABOUT THE CHILD(REN) –

1. The basic information about the child(ren) is as follows:

Child's full legal name	Age	Birthdate (d, m, y)	Full legal name of every parent of child and relationship to child (See subsection 74(1) of the *Child, Youth and Family Services Act, 2017.*)	Date child was brought to a place of safety

2. Where is the child living at the time of this conference?

3. What is the total length of time that any child less than six years old has been in care? *(Attach more detail if necessary.)*
   Name of child _____ Total length of time _____

4. What is the total length of time any child six years old or more has been in care? *(Attach more details if necessary.)*
   Name of child _____ Total length of time _____

5. Is any child a First Nations, Inuk or Métis person?
   ☐ No. ☐ Yes.

5.a If the answer to question 6 is "Yes" and the child is a First Nations, Inuk or Métis person, give the name, address and telephone number of the representative chosen by each of the child's bands and First Nations, Inuit or Métis communities to which the child is a member or identifies with.

6. If the child was brought to a place of safety before the hearing, name the person from whose care and the place from which the child was removed.

7. Has everyone who is entitled to notice in this case been served?
   ☐ Yes. ☐ No. *(Do you want an order for substituted service on any person or an order that service is not required? Give details.)*

Form 17B:	Case Conference Brief for Protection Application or Status Review	(page 3)	Court File Number

– PART 2: OUTSTANDING ISSUES –

(Complete only Part 2A – Protection Application or Part 2B – Status Review, not both)

Part 2A – Protection Application

8. The parties have reached an agreement or the court has made an order on the following issues:

☐ findings of fact set out in Part 1 above
☐ temporary care and custody   ☐ access
☐ finding that child is in need of protection
☐ placing the child(ren) with *(name of person)* _____
     for _____ months under supervision.

☐ interim society care for _____ months.   ☐ extended society care with access

☐ *(Other. Specify.)*   ☐ extended society care without access

The details of this agreement or order are:

9. What are the issues in this case that have **NOT** yet been resolved?

☐ findings of fact set out in Part 1 above
☐ temporary care and custody   ☐ access
☐ finding that child is in need of protection
☐ placing the child(ren) with *(name of person)* _____
     for _____ months under supervision.

☐ interim society care for _____ months.   ☐ extended society care with access

☐ *(Other. Specify.)*   ☐ extended society care without access

Part 2B – Status Review

10. The parties have reached an agreement or the court has made an order on the following issues:

☐ temporary care and custody   ☐ access
☐ placing the child(ren) with *(name of person)* _____
     for _____ months under supervision.

☐ interim society care for _____ months.   ☐ extended society care with access

☐ *(Other. Specify.)*   ☐ extended society care without access

The details of this agreement or order are:

FLR 17B (March 1, 2018)   Page 3 of 5

Form 17B:	Case Conference Brief for Protection Application or Status Review	(page 3)	Court File Number

– PART 2: OUTSTANDING ISSUES –

(Complete only Part 2A – Protection Application or Part 2B – Status Review, not both)

Part 2A – Protection Application

8. The parties have reached an agreement or the court has made an order on the following issues:

☐ findings of fact set out in Part 1 above
☐ temporary care and custody   ☐ access
☐ finding that child is in need of protection
☐ placing the child(ren) with *(name of person)* _____

     for _____ months under supervision.

☐ interim society care for _____ months.   ☐ extended society care with access
☐ *(Other. Specify.)*   ☐ extended society care without access

The details of this agreement or order are:

9. What are the issues in this case that have **NOT** yet been resolved?

☐ findings of fact set out in Part 1 above
☐ temporary care and custody   ☐ access
☐ finding that child is in need of protection
☐ placing the child(ren) with *(name of person)* _____

     for _____ months under supervision.

☐ interim society care for _____ months.   ☐ extended society care with access
☐ *(Other. Specify.)*   ☐ extended society care without access

Part 2B – Status Review

10. The parties have reached an agreement or the court has made an order on the following issues:

☐ temporary care and custody   ☐ access
☐ placing the child(ren) with *(name of person)* _____

     for _____ months under supervision.

☐ interim society care for _____ months.   ☐ extended society care with access
☐ *(Other. Specify.)*   ☐ extended society care without access

The details of this agreement or order are:

Form 17B:	Case Conference Brief for Protection Application or Status Review	(page 4)	Court File Number

11. What are the issues in this case that have **NOT** yet been resolved?

☐ temporary care and custody   ☐ access

☐ placing the child(ren) with *(name of person)* _____

     for _____ months under supervision.

☐ interim society care for _____ months.   ☐ extended society care with access

☐ *(Other. Specify.)*   ☐ extended society care without access

– PART 3: ISSUES FOR THIS CASE CONFERENCE –

12. Have you explored any ways to settle the issues that are still in dispute in this case?

☐ No.   ☐ Yes. *(Give details.)*

13. What are the issues for this case conference? What are the important facts for this case conference?

14. What is your proposal to resolve these issues?

15. Are any of the issues in this case urgent?

☐ No.   ☐ Yes. *(Identify the issues and give details of why the issues are urgent.)*

– PART 4: PROCEDURAL ISSUES –

16. Does any party or the Children's Lawyer want an assessment?

☐ No.   ☐ Yes. *(Give names of possible assessors and the type of assessment recommended.)*

FAMILY LAW RULES FORMS

Form 17B:	Case Conference Brief for Protection Application or Status Review	(page 5)	Court File Number

17. Do the other parties agree with the proposal for an assessment?

☐ No. ☐ Yes. *(Give names of possible assessors, the type of assessment, who will be assessed, and how long it will take.)*

18. Have you served a plan of care on the other parties?

☐ No. ☐ Yes. *(A copy of the plan of care must be filed in the continuing record.)* The plan can be found at tab/page _____ of the continuing record.

19. Does a child or a parent under 18 years of age need legal representation from the Office of the Children's Lawyer?

☐ No. ☐ Yes. *(Give details and reasons.)*

20. Do you want an order for the disclosure of documents, the questioning of witnesses or any other matter in this case?

☐ No. ☐ Yes. *(Give details.)*

21. Are there issues that may require expert evidence or a report?

☐ No. ☐ Yes. *(If yes, provide details such as: the type of expert evidence; whether the parties will be retaining a joint expert; who the expert will be; who will be paying the expert; how long it will take to obtain a report, etc.)*

22. Are there any other issues that should be reviewed at the case conference?

☐ No. ☐ Yes. *(Give details.)*

_____
Date of party's signature

_____
Signature of party

_____
Date of lawyer's signature

_____
Signature of party's lawyer

Form 17C

Settlement Conference Brief – General

ONTARIO

Court File Number

_____

(Name of court)

at _____

Court office address

**Form 17C:
Settlement
Conference
Brief-General**

Name of party filing this brief	**Date of settlement conference**

Applicant(s)

Full legal name & address for service — street & number, municipality, postal code, telephone & fax numbers and e-mail address (if any).	*Lawyer's name & address — street & number, municipality, postal code, telephone & fax numbers and e-mail address (if any).*

Respondent(s)

Full legal name & address for service — street & number, municipality, postal code, telephone & fax numbers and e-mail address (if any).	*Lawyer's name & address — street & number, municipality, postal code, telephone & fax numbers and e-mail address (if any).*

Name & address of Children's Lawyer's agent (street & number, municipality, postal code, telephone & fax numbers and e-mail address (if any)) and name of person represented.

PART 1: FAMILY FACTS

1. **APPLICANT:**   Age: _____   Birthdate: *(d, m, y)* _____

2. **RESPONDENT:**   Age: _____   Birthdate: *(d, m, y)* _____

3. RELATIONSHIP DATES:

☐ Married on *(date)* _____

☐ Separated on *(date)* _____

☐ Started living together on *(date)* _____

☐ Never lived together

☐ Other *(Explain.)* _____

4. The basic information about the child(ren) is as follows:

Child's full legal name	Age	Birthdate *(d, m, y)*	Grade/Year and school	Now living with

PART 2: ISSUES

If you want to refer to anything else that is not in the continuing record and that does not need to be in the continuing record, you must attach it to this brief. In particular, attach any valuations or experts' reports that are not in the record.

If you want to refer to a report or document that has already been filed in the continuing record, just give the page number(s) or tab number of that document in the continuing record.

If you are updating a document that is already in the continuing record, you must file the updated document in the continuing record and then refer to it by the page number(s) or tab numbers of that update in the continuing record.

5. What are the issues in this case that **HAVE** been settled:

☐ child custody   ☐ spousal support   ☐ possession of home

☐ access   ☐ child support   ☐ equalization of net family property

☐ restraining order   ☐ ownership of property

☐ other *(Specify.)* _____

6. What are the issues in this case that have **NOT** yet been settled:

☐ child custody   ☐ spousal support   ☐ possession of home

☐ access   ☐ child support   ☐ equalization of net family
                                                   property

☐ restraining order   ☐ ownership of   *(Attach net family*
                          property   *property statement, Form*
                                                  13B)

☐ other *(Specify.)* _____

7. If child or spousal support is an issue, give the income of the parties:

Applicant: $ _____ per year for the year 20 _____

Respondent: $ _____ per year for the year 20 _____

8. What are the issues for this settlement conference? What are the important facts for this settlement conference?

_____

_____

_____

_____

9. Do you want the court to make a temporary or final order about any of these issues at the settlement conference?

☐ No   ☐ Yes. *(Give details.)* _____

_____

_____

_____

_____

10. Have any of these issues that have been settled been turned into a court order or a written agreement?

☐ No

☐ Yes   ☐ an order dated _____

         ☐ a written agreement that is attached.

11. Are any of the issues in this case urgent?

☐ No. ☐ Yes. *(Identify the issues and give details of why the issues are urgent.)*

_____

_____

_____

_____

_____

PART 3: PROCEDURAL MATTERS

12. If there is a custody or access assessment in this case, is it finished?

☐ Yes. *(If it is not already filed in the continuing record, file it now. Give the tab/page number(s) of the assessment:*

_____ *)*

☐ No. *(Explain why the assessment is not ready.)*

_____

_____

_____

_____

13. Are there issues that may require expert evidence or a report?

☐ No. ☐ Yes. *(If yes, provide details such as: the type of expert evidence; whether the parties will be retaining a joint expert; who the expert will be; who will be paying the expert; how long it will take to obtain a report, etc.)*

_____

_____

_____

14. Have all of the reports you intend to rely on been provided to all of the parties and the Children's Lawyer (if involved)?

☐ No. ☐ Yes.

If not, when will they be provided?

_____

_____

_____

15. If the Children's Lawyer is involved in this case, has the Children's Lawyer told the parties what its position is on the issues involving the children?

   ☐ Yes. *(What is the Children's Lawyer's position? Explain below.)*

   ☐ No. *(Explain below.)*

_____

_____

_____

_____

16. Have the parties finished the disclosing of documents and the questioning of witnesses?

   ☐ Yes.   ☐ No. *(State what has not been done.)*

_____

_____

_____

_____

_____

17. Are there any further procedural orders needed in this case?

   ☐ No.   ☐ Yes. *(Explain.)* _____

_____

_____

_____

_____

_____

_____

_____

18. I estimate that the trial time needed for my part of this trial is _____ days; the other side's part of this trial is _____ days.

PART 4: OFFER TO SETTLE

19. The following is my offer to settle the outstanding issues in this case:

☐ offer to settle all issues   ☐ offer to settle some of the issues

> **NOTE:** *If you have already made an offer and it is still open for acceptance, attach a copy to this brief. If you have not made an offer to settle, you must make one here. If you do not have enough information about all the issues, make a partial offer on those issues for which you do have enough information.*
>
> *The other side can accept your offer. And if the other side does accept it, the accepted offer becomes a binding contract and can be turned into a court order that can be enforced against you. The other side can make a counter-offer.*
>
> *In your offer for child support, give detailed calculations for any claim for special expenses or for undue hardship. If your offer deals with spousal support, it will be helpful to your case if you attach detailed calculations showing the effect of income tax on any proposed support order.*

_____

_____

_____

_____

_____

_____

_____

_____

_____

_____

_____

_____

_____

_____

_____

_____

_____

_____

_____

_____

_____

Put a line through any space left on this page. If additional space is needed, extra pages may be attached.

_____

_____	_____
Date of party's signature	*Signature of party*
_____	_____
Date of lawyer's signature	*Signature of party's lawyer*

Form 17D

Settlement Conference Brief for Protection Application or Status Review

ONTARIO

	Court File Number

_____
(Name of Court)

at _____
Court office address

**Form 17D: Settlement
Conference Brief for**
☐ **Protection Application**
☐ **Status Review**

Name of Party Filing this Brief

Date of settlement conference

Applicant(s)

Full legal name & address for service — street & number, municipality, postal code, telephone & fax numbers and e-mail address (if any).	Lawyer's name & address — street & number, municipality, postal code, telephone & fax numbers and e-mail address (if any).

Respondent(s)

Full legal name & address for service — street & number, municipality, postal code, telephone & fax numbers and e-mail address (if any).	Lawyer's name & address — street & number, municipality, postal code, telephone & fax numbers and e-mail address (if any).

Respondent(s)

Full legal name & address for service — street & number, municipality, postal code, telephone & fax numbers and e-mail address (if any).	Lawyer's name & address — street & number, municipality, postal code, telephone & fax numbers and e-mail address (if any).

Respondent(s)

Full legal name & address for service — street & number, municipality, postal code, telephone & fax numbers and e-mail address (if any).	Lawyer's name & address — street & number, municipality, postal code, telephone & fax numbers and e-mail address (if any).

Children's Lawyer

Name & address of Children's Lawyer's agent (street & number, municipality, postal code, telephone & fax numbers and e-mail address (if any)) and name of person represented.

FLR 17D (March 1, 2018)

Page 1 of 5

| Form 17D: | Settlement Conference Brief for | (page 2) | Court File Number |
| | Protection Application or Status Review | | |

PART 1: BASIC INFORMATION ABOUT THE CHILD(REN)

1. The basic information about the child(ren) is as follows:

Child's full legal name	Age	Birthdate (d, m, y)	Full legal name of every parent of child and relationship to child (See subsection 74(1) of the Child, Youth and Family Services Act, 2017.)	Date child was brought to a place of safety

2. Where is the child living at the time of this conference?

3. What is the total length of time that any child less than six years old has been in care? *(Attach more detail if necessary).*
   Name of child _____ Total length of time _____

4. What is the total length of time any child six years old or more has been in care? *(Attach more details if necessary.)*
   Name of child _____ Total length of time _____

5. Is any child a First Nations, Inuk or Métis person?
   ☐ No.   ☐ Yes.

5.a If the answer to question 5 if "Yes" and the child is a First Nations, Inuk or Métis person, give the name, address, and telephone number of the representative chosen by each of the child's bands and First Nations, Inuit or Métis communities to which the child is a member or identifies with.

6. If the child was brought to a place of safety before the hearing, name the person from whose care and the place from which the child was removed.

7. Has everyone who is entitled to notice in this case been served?
   ☐ Yes.   ☐ No. *(Do you want an order for substituted service on any person or an order that service is not required? Give details.)*

FAMILY LAW RULES FORMS

Form 17D:	Settlement Conference Brief for (page 3) Protection Application or Status Review	Court File Number

PART 2: OUTSTANDING ISSUES

NOTE: *If you want to refer to a report or document that has already been filed in the continuing record, just give the page number(s) or tab number of that document in the continuing record. If you are updating a document that is already in the continuing record, you must file the updated document in the continuing record and then refer to it by the page number(s) or tab numbers of that update in the continuing record. If you want to refer to anything else that is not in the continuing record and that does not need to be in the continuing record, you must attach it to this brief.*

(Complete only Part 2A – Protection Application or Part 2B – Status Review, not both)

Part 2A – Protection Application

8. The parties have reached an agreement or the court has made an order on the following issues:

☐ findings of fact set out in Part 1 above   ☐ payment order
☐ temporary care and custody   ☐ access
☐ finding that child is in need of protection
☐ placing the child(ren) with *(name of person)* _____
   for _____ months under supervision.
☐ Interim society care for _____ months.   ☐ extended society care with access
☐ *(Other. Specify.)*   ☐ extended society care without access

The details of this agreement or order are:

9. What are the issues in this case that have NOT yet been resolved and what needs to happen to resolve them?

10. Are any of the issues in this case urgent?

☐ No.   ☐ Yes. *(Identify the issues and give details of why the issues are urgent.)*

Part 2B – Status Review

11. The parties have reached an agreement or the court has made an order on the following issues:

☐ temporary care and custody   ☐ payment order
☐ placing the child(ren) with *(name of person)* _____
   for _____ months under supervision.
☐ interim society care for _____ months.   ☐ access
☐ *(Other. Specify.)*   ☐ extended society care with access
                                                     ☐ extended society care without access

The details of this agreement or order are:

12. What are the issues in this case that have NOT yet been resolved and what needs to happen to resolve them?

13. Are any of the issues in this case urgent?

☐ No.   ☐ Yes. *(Identify the issues and give details of why the issues are urgent.)*

FLR 17D (March 1, 2018)   Page 3 of 5

Form 17D:	Settlement Conference Brief for	(page 4)	Court File Number
	Protection Application or Status Review		

PART 3: PROCEDURAL ISSUES

14. If there is an assessment in this case, is it finished?

☐ Yes. *(If it is not already filed in the continuing record, file it now. Give the tab/page number(s) of the assessment:* _____ *)*

☐ No. *(Explain why the assessment is not ready.)*

15. Are there any other assessments necessary or not yet completed?

☐ No. ☐ Yes. *(Give details of the type of assessment, who will be assessed and any issues relating to the timing or completion of the assessment.)*

16. If the Children's Lawyer is involved in this case, has the Children's Lawyer told the parties what its position is on the issues involving the child(ren)?

☐ Yes. *(What is the Children's Lawyer's position? Explain below.)* ☐ No. *(Explain below.)*

17. Have you served and filed a plan of care?

☐ No. ☐ Yes. *(A copy of the plan of care must be filed in the continuing record.)* The plan can be found at tab/page _____ of the continuing record.

18. Have the parties finished the disclosing of documents and the questioning of witnesses?

☐ Yes. ☐ No. *(State what has not been done.)*

19. Are there issues that require expert evidence or a report?

☐ No. ☐ Yes. *(If yes, provide details such as: the type of expert evidence; whether the parties will be retaining a joint expert; who the expert will be; who will be paying the expert; how long it will take to obtain a report, etc.)*

20. Have all of the reports you intend to rely on been provided to all of the parties and the Children's Lawyer (if involved)?

☐ No. ☐ Yes.

If no, when will they be provided?

21. Are there any further procedural orders needed in this case?

☐ No. ☐ Yes. *(Explain.)*

22. Has an order been made for affidavit evidence at trial? *(Give details.)*

Form 17D: **Settlement Conference Brief for** **(page 5)**
Protection Application or Status Review

Court File Number

PART 4: OFFER TO SETTLE

23. The following is my offer to settle the outstanding issues in this case:

If you have already made an offer and it is still open for acceptance, attach a copy of this brief. The other side can accept your offer. And if the other side does accept it, the accepted offer becomes a binding contract and can be turned into a court order that can be enforced against you. The other side can make a counter-offer.

_____

Put a line through any space left on this page. If additional space is needed, extra pages may be attached.

_____   _____
Date of party's signature   Signature of party

_____   _____
Date of lawyer's signature   Signature of party's lawyer

Form 17E

Trial Management Conference Brief

ONTARIO

	Court File Number
_____ *(Name of court)*	
at _____ *Court office address*	**Form 17E: Trial Management Conference Brief**

Name of party filing this brief	**Date of trial management conference**

Applicant(s)

Full legal name & address for service — street & number, municipality, postal code, telephone & fax numbers and e-mail address (if any).	Lawyer's name & address — street & number, municipality, postal code, telephone & fax numbers and e-mail address (if any).

Respondent(s)

Full legal name & address for service — street & number, municipality, postal code, telephone & fax numbers and e-mail address (if any).	Lawyer's name & address — street & number, municipality, postal code, telephone & fax numbers and e-mail address (if any).

Name & address of Children's Lawyer's agent (street & number, municipality, postal code, telephone & fax numbers and e-mail address (if any)) and name of person represented.

Are any of the parties First Nations, Inuit, or Métis?

☐ No   ☐ Yes *(Who?)* _____

PART 1: THE ISSUES

1. What are the issues in this case that **HAVE** been settled or about which an order has been made:

Child protection cases

☐ access   ☐ finding in need of protection

☐ placing the child(ren) with *(name of person)* _____

for _____ months under supervision.

☐ interim society care for _____ months.   ☐ extended society care.

☐ other *(Specify.)* _____

All other cases

☐ child support   ☐ child custody

　☐ entitlement   　☐ joint vs sole custody

　☐ payor's income   　☐ primary residence

　☐ retroactive child support   ☐ child access

　☐ special or extraordinary expenses   ☐ spousal support

☐ restraining order   ☐ other *(Specify.)* _____

Attach a copy of any agreement that the judge should read to prepare for the trial management conference.

Form 17E: **Trial Management Conference Brief** (page 2)

Court File Number

2. Where is the child living at the time of this conference?

3. Are any of the issues in this case urgent?

☐ No. ☐ Yes. *(Identify the issues and give details of why the issues are urgent.)*

4. What are the issues in this case that have **NOT** yet been settled:

Child protection cases
☐ access ☐ finding in need of protection
☐ placing the child(ren) with *(name of person)*
for _____ months under supervision.
☐ interim society care for _____ months. ☐ extended society care.
☐ other *(Specify.)*

All other cases
☐ child support ☐ child custody
   ☐ entitlement   ☐ joint vs sole custody
   ☐ payor's income   ☐ primary residence
   ☐ retroactive child support   ☐ child access
   ☐ special or extraordinary expenses   ☐ spousal support
☐ restraining order ☐ other *(Specify.)*

PART 2: ISSUES FOR TRIAL

5. Attach an outline of your opening statement for the trial, including:
   (a) what you consider to be the undisputed facts;
   (b) the theory of your case on the disputed issues;
   (c) a brief summary of the evidence you plan to present at trial; and
   (d) the orders you are asking the trial judge to make.

6. (a) These are the witnesses whom I plan to have testify for me, the topics about which they will testify and my current estimate of the length of time for the testimony of each witness, including cross-examination:

Name of witness	Topic about which witness will testify	Current time estimate for witness

Form 17E: **Trial Management Conference Brief**   **(page 3)** | Court File Number |

(b) These are the expert witnesses whom I plan to have testify, their areas of expertise, and my current estimate of the length of time for the testimony of each witness, including cross-examination:

Name of expert	Expert report and CV filed? (Yes or No)	Area of expertise	Qualifications admitted? (Yes or No)	Current time estimate for witness

7. I estimate that the trial time needed for my part of this trial is .... days; the other side's part of this trial is .... days.

PART 3: PROCEDURAL MATTERS

8. Have the parties signed a statement of agreed facts?
    ☐ Yes. *(Attach a copy.)*   ☐ No. *(Explain why not.)*

9. Have the parties finished the disclosing of documents and the questioning of witnesses?
    ☐ Yes.   ☐ No. *(Indicate what has not been done.)*

10. Are there any expert reports that you intend to rely on at trial?
    ☐ No.   ☐ Yes. *(Give details about the reports such as who prepared them and the issues addressed.)*

11. Have all of the reports you intend to rely on been provided to all of the parties and the Children's Lawyer (if involved)?
    ☐ No.   ☐ Yes.
    If no, when will they be provided?

12. Attach a list of the relevant orders in this case.

13. Are there any orders or directions for trial that have not been carried out?
    ☐ No.   ☐ Yes. *(Explain.)*

Form 17E:	Trial Management Conference Brief	(page 4)	Court File Number

14. Have the parties produced a joint document brief?
☐ Yes. *(Attach a copy.)* ☐ No. *(Explain why not.)*

15. Has an order been made for affidavit evidence at trial?
☐ Yes. ☐ No. *(Explain.)*

16. Are there any preliminary or procedural matters that need to be dealt with before or at the start of the trial?
☐ No. ☐ Yes. *(Explain.)*

17. Have all parties been served?
☐ Yes. ☐ No. *(Explain.)*

Form 17E: **Trial Management Conference Brief** (page 5)

Court File Number

18. Have you served a request to admit?

☐ Yes. ☐ No. *(Explain.)*

_____   _____
Date of party's signature   Signature of party

_____   _____
Date of lawyer's signature   Signature of party's lawyer

Form 17F

Confirmation of Conference

ONTARIO

	Court File Number

....

(Name of court)

at ....

Court office address

Form 17F: Confirmation of Conference

Applicant(s)

Full legal name & address for service — street & number, municipality, postal code, telephone & fax numbers and e-mail address (if any).	Lawyer's name & address — street & number, municipality, postal code, telephone & fax numbers and e-mail address (if any).

Respondent(s)

Full legal name & address for service — street & number, municipality, postal code, telephone & fax numbers and e-mail address (if any).	Lawyer's name & address — street & number, municipality, postal code, telephone & fax numbers and e-mail address (if any).

Name & address of Children's Lawyer's agent (street & number, municipality, postal code, telephone & fax numbers and e-mail address (if any)) and name of person represented.

1. My name is *(full legal name)* ....

    and I am ☐ the lawyer for *(name)* ....

    ☐ the applicant in this case   ☐ the respondent in this case

    ☐ other *(specify)* ....

2. Have you conferred with the opposing counsel or party regarding the issues, conference material, and time estimates, as set out in paragraphs 3 to 9 below?

    ☐ Yes

    ☐ No, because *(provide reasons)*

NOTE: The *Family Law Rules* require the parties or their counsel to confer, or attempt to confer, orally or in writing with each other on the issues in dispute for a conference prior to filing Confirmations. The only exception is where a party is prohibited from such communication by court order. **Failure to comply with the *Family Law Rules* may result in a cost order.**

3. The scheduled date and time for this

    ☐ case conference   ☐ settlement conference   ☐ trial management conference

    is *(date)* .... at .... a.m./p.m.

4. The case management judge for this case is Justice

Form 17F: **Confirmation of Conference**   **(page 2)**

Court File Number

5. This matter is

☐ going ahead on the issues listed in paragraph 6 below.

☐ going ahead for a consent order regarding *(attach draft order)*.

☐ being adjourned on consent to *(date)* _____ for a *(event)* _____

because *(give reasons)*

☐ going ahead for a contested adjournment to *(date)* _____ asked for by *(name of person asking*

for adjournment) _____ because *(give reasons)*

6. What are the most important issues to be resolved at this step in the case? *(List the issues below)*
a)
b)
c)
d)
e)
f)

7. In addition to the case conference brief, the presiding judge will be referred to the following pages/tabs:

8. Time estimate: applicant: minutes; respondent: minutes; for a total of   minutes.

NOTE: The *Family Law Rules* require you to **deliver a copy** of this form to the opposing lawyer or party, unless this is a child protection matter. For clarification, regular or special service and an accompanying Affidavit of Service (Form 6B) under rule 6 of the *Family Law Rules* are not required. However, you must deliver this form by some method (including fax or e-mail) to the opposing lawyer or party prior to giving a copy to the court clerk.

_____   _____
Date of signature   Lawyer's or party's signature

FAMILY LAW RULES FORMS

Form 17A — Confirmation of Conference (page 2)

5. This matter is
☐ going ahead on the issues listed in paragraph 6 below;
☐ being fixed for a consent order hearing (short matters list)
☐ being adjourned on consent to ... for a reason
(because) (the reasons)

☐ being set up for a contested adjournment to (date) ... (asked for by) (name of person asking for the adjournment) (because) (give reasons)

6. What are the most important issues to be resolved at this step in the case? (list the issues below)
a)
b)
c)
d)
e)
f)

7. In addition to this case conference brief, the presiding judge will be referred to the following (specify):
a)
b)
c)

8. Time estimate: _____ minutes respondent; _____ minutes, for a total of _____ minutes.

NOTE: The Family Law Rules require you to deliver a copy of this form to the appropriate persons, unless this is a child protection matter. For contested or regular or special status and an appropriate form (Affidavit of service (Form 6B) under rule 6 of the Family Law Rules are not completed. However you must deliver this form by some method (including fax or e-mail) to the opposing lawyer or party prior to giving a copy to the court clerk.

(Date of signature) _____   (Lawyer's or party's signature) _____

Form 20

Form 20 Request for Information

ONTARIO

	Court File Number

_____
(Name of court)

Form 20: Request
for Information

at _____
Court office address

Applicant(s)

Full legal name & address for service — street & number, municipality, postal code, telephone & fax numbers and e-mail address (if any).	Lawyer's name & address — street & number, municipality, postal code, telephone & fax numbers and e-mail address (if any).

Respondent(s)

Full legal name & address for service — street & number, municipality, postal code, telephone & fax numbers and e-mail address (if any).	Lawyer's name & address — street & number, municipality, postal code, telephone & fax numbers and e-mail address (if any).

TO: *(name of party)* _____

This is a request for information in writing under subrule 20(3) of the *Family Law Rules*.

I request that the information be provided within _____ days by:

☐ an affidavit from *(name of person[s])* _____

☐ a letter from *(name of person[s])* _____

☐ *(Other; specify.)* _____

The information that I am requesting is as follows: *(Be as specific as possible. If you want more than one piece of information, number the requested pieces of information.)*

IF YOU DO NOT PROVIDE THE INFORMATION AS REQUESTED,

(1)   A SUMMONS MAY BE SERVED ON YOU, REQUIRING YOU TO BE QUESTIONED ABOUT IT; OR

(2)   A MOTION MAY BE MADE TO THE COURT FOR AN ORDER REQUIRING YOU TO PROVIDE THE INFORMATION AND YOU MAY BE ORDERED TO PAY THE COSTS OF THE MOTION.

_____   _____
              Signature   *Date of signature*

Form 20A
Authorization to Commissioner

ONTARIO

	Court File Number

SEAL

_____
(Name of court)

Form 20A:
Authorization to
Commissioner

at_____
Court office address

Applicant(s)

Full legal name & address for service — street & number, municipality, postal code, telephone & fax numbers and e-mail address (if any).	Lawyer's name & address — street & number, municipality, postal code, telephone & fax numbers and e-mail address (if any).

Respondent(s)

Full legal name & address for service — street & number, municipality, postal code, telephone & fax numbers and e-mail address (if any).	Lawyer's name & address — street & number, municipality, postal code, telephone & fax numbers and e-mail address (if any).

TO: *(full legal name and address of commissioner)*

_____

_____

_____

_____

THE COURT HAS NAMED YOU A COMMISSIONER to take evidence in this case. A copy of the order naming you is attached.

THE COURT GIVES YOU FULL POWER to take the necessary steps to take the evidence mentioned in the attached order.

If the parties consent, you also have the power to take the evidence of any other witnesses who may be found in *(name of province, territory, state or country)*

In carrying out your duties under this commission, you must follow,

    (a)   the terms of the attached order and

    (b)   the instructions set out below.

As soon as   ☐   an audio recording

               ☐   a video recording

               ☐   a transcript

of the evidence is finished, you must deliver it to the clerk of the court along with this commission.

_____   _____
             Signature   *Date of signature*

NOTE: *Attach the court's order naming the commissioner*

INSTRUCTIONS TO COMMISSIONER

1. You are to question the witness(es) according to subrules 20(14), (15), and 23(19) of the *Family Law Rules* to the extent that it is possible to do so. Subrules 20(14), (15), and 23(19) state as follows:

QUESTIONING PERSON OUTSIDE ONTARIO

20. – (14) If a person to be questioned lives outside Ontario and will not come to Ontario for questioning, the court may decide:

(a)	the date, the time and place for the questioning;
(b)	how much notice the person should be given;
(c)	the person before whom the questioning will be held;
(d)	the amount of the witness fee to be paid to the person to be questioned;
(e)	the method for recording the questioning;
(f)	where necessary, that the clerk shall issue,

    (i) an authorization to a commissioner (Form 20A) who is to supervise the questioning outside Ontario, and

    (ii) a letter of request (Form 20B) to the appropriate court or authorities outside Ontario, asking for their assistance in getting the person to be questioned to come before the commissioner; and

(g) any other related matter.

COMMISSIONER'S DUTIES

(15) A commissioner authorized under subrule (14) shall:

(a) supervise the questioning according to the terms of the court's authorization, these rules and Ontario's Law of evidence, unless the law of the place where the questioning is to be held requires some other manner of questioning;

(b) make and keep a copy of the record of the questioning and, where possible, of the exhibits, if any;

(c) deliver the original record, any exhibits and the authorization to the clerk who issued it; and

(d) notify the party who asked for the questioning that the record has been delivered to the clerk.

TAKING EVIDENCE BEFORE TRIAL OUTSIDE ONTARIO

23. – (19) If a witness whose evidence is necessary at trial lives outside Ontario, subrules 20(14) and (15) (questioning person outside Ontario, commissioner's duties) apply with necessary changes.

2. The law of Ontario applies to the taking of evidence, unless the law of the province, territory, state or country where you supervise the questioning requires you to follow some other manner of questioning.

3. Before you begin your duties under this commission, you yourself must take the following oath or affirmation:

I, *(commissioner's name)* _____

☐   swear

☐ affirm that I will,

(a) according to the best of my skill and knowledge, truly and faithfully and without bias to any of the parties to this case, take the evidence of every witness questioned under this commission, and

(b) cause the evidence to be ☐ recorded
☐ recorded and transcribed
and sent to the court.

(In an oath, add the words: "So help me God.")

Sworn/Affirmed before me at _____

municipality

in _____

province, state or country

on _____

date   *Commissioner for taking affidavits (Type or print name below if signature is illegible.)*

Signature

(This form is to be signed in front of a lawyer, justice of the peace, notary public or commissioner for taking affidavits.)

You may take this oath or affirmation before any person listed in section 45 of Ontario's *Evidence Act* who is authorized to take affidavits or to administer oaths or affirmations outside Ontario. Section 45 of the *Evidence Act* states:

45. Oaths, *etc.*, administered outside Ontario. – (1) An oath, affidavit, affirmation or statutory declaration administered, sworn, affirmed or made outside Ontario before:

(a) a judge;

(b) a magistrate;

(c) an officer of a court of justice;

(d) a commissioner for taking affidavits or other competent authority of the like nature;

(e) a notary public;

(f) the head of a city, town, village, township or other municipality;

(g) an officer of any of Her Majesty's diplomatic or consular services, including an ambassador, envoy, minister, chargé d'affaires, counsellor, secretary, attaché, consul-general, consul, vice-consul, pro-consul, consular agent, acting consul-general, acting consul, acting vice-consul, and acting consular agent;

(h) an officer of the Canadian diplomatic, consular or representative services, including, in addition to the diplomatic and consular officers mentioned in clause *(g)*, a high commissioner, permanent delegate, acting high commissioner, acting permanent delegate, counselor and secretary; or

(i) a Canadian Government trade commissioner or assistant trade commissioner,

980

exercising his or her functions or having jurisdiction or authority as such in the place in which it is administered, sworn, affirmed or made, is as valid and effectual to all intents and purposes as if it had been duly administered, sworn, affirmed or made in Ontario before a commissioner for taking affidavits in Ontario.

(2) *Idem.* – An oath, affidavit, affirmation or statutory declaration administered, sworn, affirmed or made outside Ontario before a notary public for Ontario or before a commissioner for taking affidavits in Ontario is as valid and effectual to all intents and purposes as if it had been duly administered, sworn, affirmed or made in Ontario before a commissioner for taking affidavits in Ontario.

(3) *Admissibility.* – A document that purports to be signed by a person mentioned in subsection (1) or (2) in testimony of an oath, affidavit, affirmation or statutory declaration having been administered, sworn, affirmed or made before him or her, and on which the person's office is shown below his or her signature, and

(a) in the case of a notary public, that purports to have impressed thereon or attached thereto his or her official seal;

(b) in the case of a person mentioned in clause (1) *(f)*, that purports to have impressed thereon or attached thereto the seal of the municipality;

(c) in the case of a person mentioned in clause (1) *(g)*, *(h)* or *(i)*, that purports to have impressed thereon or attached thereto his or her seal or the seal or stamp of his or her office or of the office to which he or she is attached.

is admissible in evidence without proof of his or her signature or of his or her office or official character or of the seal or stamp and without proof that he or she was exercising his or her functions or had jurisdiction or authority in the place in which the oath, affidavit, affirmation or statutory declaration was administered, sworn, affirmed or made.

4. The party who wants the witness to be questioned must:

(a) give at least _____ days notice of the date for the questioning; and,

(b) where the attached order says so, pay the witness appearance money.

5. You must arrange:

(a) to have the evidence recorded in a manner set out in the attached order; and

(b) where the order says so, to have it transcribed.

You must administer the following oath or affirmation to the person who records the evidence in shorthand and, where necessary, to the person who transcribes any written, audio or video recording of the evidence:

You ☐ swear
☐ affirm

that you will truly and accurately

☐ record

☐ transcribe
☐ record and transcribe

all questions put to all witnesses and their answers in keeping with the directions of the commissioner.

(In an oath, add the words: "So help you God.")

6. To each witness whose evidence you take, you must administer the following oath or affirmation:

You ☐ swear

☐ affirm

that the evidence that you are about to give about the matters in dispute between the parties in this case shall be the truth, the whole truth, and nothing but the truth. *(In an oath, add the words: "So help you God.")*

7. Where any witness does not understand the language in which he or she is being questioned or is deaf or mute, his or her evidence must be given through an interpreter. You must first administer the following oath or affirmation to the interpreter:

You ☐ swear

☐ affirm

that you understand the _____

language and the language in which the examination is to be conducted and that you will truly interpret the

☐ oath

☐ affirmation

to all witnesses, all questions put to the witness and the answers of the witness, to the best of your skill and understanding. *(In an oath, add the words: "So help you God.")*

8. You must:

(a) fill out the certificate on the next page;

(b) make a copy of

(i) the audio or video record of the evidence,

(ii) any transcript of the evidence, and

(iii) where possible, any exhibits;

(c) keep copies in your care until the court finishes this case;

(d) mail or deliver the originals, together with this commission and your certificate, to the clerk of the court; and

(e) immediately notify the party who asked for this questioning that the material has been sent to the clerk of the court.

COMMISSIONER'S CERTIFICATE

My name is *(full legal name)* _____

and I certify that:

☐ I administered the proper ☐ oath

☐ affirmation

to *(name)* _____

who was the person who ☐ recorded the evidence by shorthand.

☐ transcribed the evidence.

☐ I administered the proper ☐ oath
☐ affirmation

to *(name of witness(es))*

whose evidence was taken and recorded.

☐ I administered the proper ☐ oath
☐ affirmation

to *(name of interpreter)* _____

who was the interpreter through whom the evidence was given.

☐ The evidence of the witness(es) was properly taken and accurately ☐ recorded.
☐ recorded and transcribed.

_____   _____
Commissioner's signature   *Date of signature*

Form 20B

Letter of Request

ONTARIO

SEAL

_____
(Name of court)

at _____
Court office address

Court File Number

Form 20B: Letter of Request

Applicant(s)

Full legal name & address for service — street & number, municipality, postal code, telephone & fax numbers and e-mail address (if any).	Lawyer's name & address — street & number, municipality, postal code, telephone & fax numbers and e-mail address (if any).

Respondent(s)

Full legal name & address for service — street & number, municipality, postal code, telephone & fax numbers and e-mail address (if any).	Lawyer's name & address — street & number, municipality, postal code, telephone & fax numbers and e-mail address (if any).

TO THE JUDICIAL AUTHORITIES OF *(name of province, state or country):* _____

A CASE HAS BEEN STARTED IN THIS COURT INVOLVING THE PERSONS NAMED ABOVE. EVIDENCE BEFORE THIS COURT SHOWS THAT A WITNESS LIVING IN YOUR JURISDICTION SHOULD BE QUESTIONED THERE.

THIS COURT HAS ISSUED A COMMISSION TO *(name and address of commissioner)*

_____

TO QUESTION *(name and address of witness)* _____

_____

YOU ARE REQUESTED to have *(name of witness)* _____

    (a)   appear before the commissioner by the method normally used in your jurisdiction;

    (b)   answer questions under oath or affirmation; and

    (c)   bring to the examination the documents or things listed on Page 2 of this request.

YOU ARE ALSO REQUESTED TO allow the commissioner to have the witness questioned according to Ontario's law of evidence, to Ontario's rules of court and to the commission issued by this court.

AND WHEN YOU REQUEST IT, the courts in Ontario are ready and willing to do the same for you in a similar case.

THIS LETTER OF REQUEST is signed and sealed by a
court order made on *(date of order)* _____

_____   _____
Date of signature   *Clerk of the court*

(Give the date of every document that the witness should bring and give enough of a description of each document or thing that the witness must bring to identify it.)

Put a line through any blank space left on this page. If you need more space, add a sheet and number the page.

Form 20.2

Acknowledgement of Expert's Duty

ONTARIO

	Court File Number
_____	
(Name of court)	**Form 20.2: Acknowledgement**
at _____	**of Expert's Duty**
Court office address	_____

Applicant(s)

Full legal name & address for service — street & number, municipality, postal code, telephone & fax numbers and e-mail address (if any).	Lawyer's name & address — street & number, municipality, postal code, telephone & fax numbers and e-mail address (if any).

Respondent(s)

Full legal name & address for service — street & number, municipality, postal code, telephone & fax numbers and e-mail address (if any).	Lawyer's name & address — street & number, municipality, postal code, telephone & fax numbers and e-mail address (if any).

Children's Lawyer

Name & address of Children's Lawyer's agent for service (street & number, municipality, postal code, telephone & fax numbers and e-mail address (if any)) and name of person represented.

1. My name is *(full legal name)* _____ .

2. I live in *(municipality & province)* _____ .

3. I have been

    ☐ engaged by or on behalf of *(name of party/parties)* _____

    ☐ appointed by the court

    to provide evidence in relation to this court proceeding.

4. I acknowledge that in relation to this proceeding, it is my duty to provide:

    (a) opinion evidence that is fair, objective and non-partisan;

    (b) opinion evidence that is related only to matters that are within my area of expertise; and

    (c) such additional assistance as the court may reasonably require, to determine a matter in issue.

5. I acknowledge that the duty referred to above prevails over any obligation which I may owe to any party by whom or on whose behalf I am engaged.

_____   _____
Date   *Signature*

NOTE: This form must be attached to any report signed by a litigation expert or court-appointed expert and provided for the purpose of rules 20.1 to 20.3 of the *Family Law Rules*.

Form 22

Request to Admit

ONTARIO

Court File Number

_____
(Name of court)

**Form 22: Request
to Admit**

at _____
Court office address

Applicant(s)

Full legal name & address for service — street & number, municipality, postal code, telephone & fax numbers and e-mail address (if any).	Lawyer's name & address — street & number, municipality, postal code, telephone & fax numbers and e-mail address (if any).

Respondent(s)

Full legal name & address for service — street & number, municipality, postal code, telephone & fax numbers and e-mail address (if any).	Lawyer's name & address — street & number, municipality, postal code, telephone & fax numbers and e-mail address (if any).

TO: *(name of party)* _____

YOU MUST RESPOND TO THIS REQUEST WITHIN 20 DAYS AFTER BEING SERVED WITH IT.

You make your response by serving a response to request to admit in Form 22A, a blank copy of which should be attached to this request. If the blank form is missing, contact your own lawyer or the court office as soon as possible.

IF YOU DO NOT RESPOND WITHIN THE TIME GIVEN, THIS CASE WILL GO TO COURT ON THE BASIS THAT YOU ARE ADMITTING, FOR THE PURPOSE OF THIS CASE ONLY, THAT THE FACTS SET OUT BELOW ARE TRUE AND THAT THE DOCUMENTS DESCRIBED BELOW ARE GENUINE.

You are requested to admit, only for the purposes of this case, that the following facts are true. *(If you need more space to list additional facts, attach an extra sheet.)*

1. _____

2. _____

3. _____

4. _____

5. _____

You are requested to admit, only for the purposes of this case, that the following documents are genuine. *(Being "genuine" also means:*

- *that a document that claims to be an original was written, signed or sealed as it appears to have been;*
- *that a document claiming to be a copy is a true copy of the original; and*
- *where the document claims to be a copy of a letter, fax, electronic-mail message or other document ordinarily sent from one person to another, that it was sent as it appears to have been sent and received by the person to whom it was addressed.)*

Describe each document and identify it by date, type of document, author, name of person to whom it was sent, etc. Indicate whether the document is an original or a copy. If you need more space to list additional documents, attach a sheet.

1. _____

2. _____

3. _____

4. _____

5. _____

A copy of each document named above is attached to this request, except for: *(Give the number of any document that you are NOT attaching and state your reason for not doing so. Generally, you must attach copies of all the documents mentioned unless the other party already has a copy or it is impractical to attach a copy.)*

_____   _____
          Signature   *Date of signature*

989

Form 22A

Response to Request to Admit

ONTARIO

Court File Number

_____
(Name of court)

**Form 22A: Response
to Request to Admit**

at _____
Court office address

Applicant(s)

Full legal name & address for service — street & number, municipality, postal code, telephone & fax numbers and e-mail address (if any).	Lawyer's name & address — street & number, municipality, postal code, telephone & fax numbers and e-mail address (if any).

Respondent(s)

Full legal name & address for service — street & number, municipality, postal code, telephone & fax numbers and e-mail address (if any).	Lawyer's name & address — street & number, municipality, postal code, telephone & fax numbers and e-mail address (if any).

TO: *(name of party)* _____

This is my response to your *Request to Admit* of *(date)* _____

that was served on me on *(date)* _____

*(Refer to the facts and documents according to the numbering set out in the **Request to Admit**.)*

1. I admit that the following facts are true: *(fact numbers)* _____

2. I admit that the following documents are genuine: *(document numbers)* _____

3. I deny that the following facts are true: *(fact numbers)* _____

4. I deny that the following documents are genuine: *(document numbers)* _____

5. I refuse to admit the following facts for the following reasons: *(If you need more space, attach a sheet.)*

990

Fact number	My reasons

6. I refuse to admit that the following documents are genuine for the following reasons: *(If you need more space, attach a sheet.)*

Document number	My reasons

_____   _____
Signature   *Date of signature*

Form 23

Summons to Witness

ONTARIO

_____
(Name of court)

at _____
Court office address

Court File Number

Applicant(s)

Full legal name & address for service — street & number, municipality, postal code, telephone & fax numbers and e-mail address (if any).	Lawyer's name & address — street & number, municipality, postal code, telephone & fax numbers and e-mail address (if any).

Respondent(s)

Full legal name & address for service — street & number, municipality, postal code, telephone & fax numbers and e-mail address (if any).	Lawyer's name & address — street & number, municipality, postal code, telephone & fax numbers and e-mail address (if any).

TO: *(full legal name of witness)* _____

of *(address: street & number, municipality, postal code)* _____

YOU MUST:

(1) **come to** *(address: street & number, municipality)* _____

on *(date)* _____ , at _____ a.m./p.m.;

(2) **give evidence in the case or examination before** *(court or other person)*

_____

(3) **bring with you the documents and things listed on the back of this summons; and**

(4) **remain there until this case or examination is finished or until the person conducting it says otherwise.**

With this summons, you should get a fee that is calculated for ....day(s) of attendance as follows:

Appearance allowance of $ _____ daily $ _____

Travel allowance of $ _____ each way $ _____

Overnight hotel and meal allowance $ _____
                                              $ _____

TOTAL $ _____

If the case or examination takes up more of your time, you will be entitled to an additional fee.

_____
Date of issue

IF YOU DO NOT COME AND REMAIN AS REQUIRED BY THIS SUMMONS, A WARRANT MAY BE ISSUED FOR YOUR ARREST.

(Give the date of every document that the witness must bring and give enough of a description to identify each document or thing that the witness must bring.)

Draw a line through any blank space left on this page. If you need more space, you can add pages and number them.

Name, address, telephone & fax numbers and e-mail address (if any) of person or lawyer who prepared this summons.

Form 23A

Summons to Witness outside Ontario

ONTARIO

SEAL	_____
	(Name of court)

Court File Number

**Form 23A: Summons
to Witness outside
Ontario**

at _____
Court office address

Applicant(s)

Full legal name & address for service — street & number, municipality, postal code, telephone & fax numbers and e-mail address (if any).	Lawyer's name & address — street & number, municipality, postal code, telephone & fax numbers and e-mail address (if any).

Respondent(s)

Full legal name & address for service — street & number, municipality, postal code, telephone & fax numbers and e-mail address (if any).	Lawyer's name & address — street & number, municipality, postal code, telephone & fax numbers and e-mail address (if any).

TO: *(full legal name of witness)* _____

of *(address: street & number, municipality, postal code)* _____

_____

_____

YOU MUST:

(1) **come to** *(address: street & number, municipality)* _____

_____

on *(date)* _____ , at _____ **a.m/p.m.**

(2) **give evidence in the case or examination before** *(court or other person)*

_____

(3)   **bring with you the documents and things listed on page 2 of this *Summons*; and**

(4)   **remain there until this case or examination is finished or until the person conducting it says otherwise.**

With this *Summons*, you should get a fee that is calculated for .... day(s) of attendance as follows:

Appearance allowance of $20 for each day that
you are away from home ($60 minimum) $ _____

Travel allowance $ _____

Overnight hotel for minimum of 3 days ($60
minimum) $ _____

Meal allowance for minimum of 3 days ($60
minimum) $ _____

TOTAL $ _____

If the case of examination takes up more of your time, you will be entitled to an additional fee.

IF YOU DO NOT COME AND REMAIN AS REQUIRED BY THIS SUMMONS, A WARRANT MAY BE ISSUED FOR YOUR ARREST.

_____   _____
Date of issue   *Signature of the clerk of the court*

(Give the date of every document that the witness must bring and give enough of a description to identify each document or thing that the witness must bring.)

Draw a line through any blank space left on this page. If you need more space, you can add pages and number them.

This summons was issued at the request of and inquiries may be directed to:
(Name, address, telephone number & fax numbers and e-mail address [if any] of person or lawyer who requested this summons.)

JUDGE'S CERTIFICATE

I, *(name)* _____,

a judge of the *(name of court)* _____

CERTIFY THAT I have heard and examined *(name of party or parties who have asked for this summons or of his, her or their lawyer)*

_____

_____

_____

who seek(s) to compel the attendance of *(name of witness[es])*

_____

_____

_____

to produce documents or other articles or to testify, or both, in an Ontario case in the *(name of the court in which witness is to appear)* _____

involving *(names of parties in the case and court file number)*

_____

_____

I FURTHER CERTIFY THAT I am persuaded that the appearance of *(name of witness[es])*

_____

_____

_____

as a witness/witnesses in the case is necessary for the due adjudication of the case, and, in relation to the nature and importance of cause or proceeding, is reasonable and essential to the due administration of justice in Ontario.

The *Interprovincial Summonses Act* makes the following provision for the immunity of *(name of witness[es])*

_____

_____

A person who is required to attend before a court in Ontario by a summons adopted by a court outside Ontario shall be deemed, while within Ontario for the purposes of which the summons was issued, not to have submitted to the jurisdiction of the courts of Ontario other than as a witness in the proceedings in which the person is summoned and shall be absolutely immune from seizure of goods, service of process, execution of judgment, garnishment, imprisonment or molestation of any kind relating to a legal or judicial right, cause, action, proceeding or process within the jurisdiction of the Legislature of Ontario except only those proceedings grounded on events occurring during or after required attendance of the person in Ontario.

_____
(Signature of judge)

_____
(Date of signature)

SEAL

Form 23B
Order for Prisoner's Attendance
ONTARIO

	Court File Number

SEAL

(Name of court)

at _____

Court office address

Form 23B: Order for Prisoner's Attendance

Applicant(s)

Full legal name & address for service — street & number, municipality, postal code, telephone & fax numbers and e-mail address (if any).	Lawyer's name & address — street & number, municipality, postal code, telephone & fax numbers and e-mail address (if any).

Judge (print or type name)

Respondent(s)

Full legal name & address for service — street & number, municipality, postal code, telephone & fax numbers and e-mail address (if any).	Lawyer's name & address — street & number, municipality, postal code, telephone & fax numbers and e-mail address (if any).

Date of order

TO THE OFFICERS OF *(name of correctional institution)* _____

AND TO ALL PEACE OFFICERS IN ONTARIO:

THIS COURT has found that a prisoner at the institution or facility named above, *(prisoner's full legal name)*

_____

is ☐ a party in this case.

☐ a witness whose presence is necessary to decide an issue in this case.

THIS COURT ORDERS THAT:

1. You produce the prisoner before ☐ this court

1000

☐ *(Specify other officer before whom attendance is required.)* _____

_____

on *(date)* _____ , at _____ at *(address)*

_____

to enable the prisoner to come to court or to an examination in this case.

2. The prisoner be returned and re-admitted immediately afterwards to the correctional institution or other facility from which he/she was brought.

_____   _____
      Date of signature   *Signature of judge or clerk of the court*

Form 23C

Affidavit for Uncontested Trial

ONTARIO

	Court File Number

_____

(Name of court)

Form 23C: Affidavit for Uncontested Trial, dated

at _____

Court office address

_____

Applicant(s)

Full legal name & address for service — street & number, municipality, postal code, telephone & fax numbers and e-mail address (if any).	Lawyer's name & address — street & number, municipality, postal code, telephone & fax numbers and e-mail address (if any).

Respondent(s)

Full legal name & address for service — street & number, municipality, postal code, telephone & fax numbers and e-mail address (if any).	Lawyer's name & address — street & number, municipality, postal code, telephone & fax numbers and e-mail address (if any).

My name is *(full legal name)* _____

I live in *(municipality & province)* _____

and I swear/affirm that the following is true:

1. I am the applicant in this case.

2. There is/are *(number)* _____ child(ren) from our relationship, namely:

Full Legal Name	Age	Birthdate *(d, m, y)*	Resident in *(municipality & province)*	Now living with *(name of person and relationship to child)*

1002

3. I am asking for the following order:
   ☐ custody of the child(ren) named above
   ☐ access to the child(ren) named above
   ☐ support for *(name of recipient(s))* _____
   ☐ a restraining order against the respondent *(name)* _____
      (date of birth) _____
   ☐ other *(specify)* _____

4. The respondent and I were:
   ☐ married on *(date)* _____
   ☐ separated on *(date)* _____
   ☐ started living together on *(date)* _____
   ☐ never lived together. _____

CUSTODY AND ACCESS

Fill out this section if you are claiming custody of one or more of the children.

5. An order giving me custody of the child(ren) is in the best interests of the child(ren) because: *(Give reasons.)*

_____

_____

_____

_____

6. An order giving the respondent access to the children
   ☐ is   ☐ is not

   in the best interests of the child(ren) because: *(Give reasons.)*

_____

_____

_____

_____

_____

_____

_____

1003

7. If an order for access is made, it should be:

☐ reasonable access on reasonable notice;

☐ reasonable access on reasonable notice including but not limited to the terms below:

☐ on the following terms:

    ☐ every other weekend from _____ p.m. on Friday until _____ p.m. on Sunday or Monday, if Monday is a statutory holiday, starting on *(date)* _____

        ☐ alternate spring breaks, starting in *(year)* _____

        ☐ _____ weeks during the summer vacation, to be decided by the parties before April 1 of each year.

        ☐ one half of the winter break, starting on *(date)* _____ and ending on *(date)* _____ to be shared as follows:

        ☐ List any other special days such as religious festivals, Christmas Day, birthdays, Mother's Day, Father's Day, etc., and indicate with which person the children will be on each day. *(Specify dates and times.)*

        ☐ other *(Specify.)*

_____

_____

_____

_____

_____

CHILD SUPPORT

Fill out this section if you are claiming child support.

8. I am claiming support for *(number)* _____ child(ren).

9. To the best of my knowledge, the source(s) of the respondent's income is/are: *(Check one or more boxes as circumstances require.)*

    ☐ employment income at *(employer's name and address)*

    _____

    ☐ commissions, tips, overtime, bonuses, *etc.*

    ☐ self-employment as *(name or nature of respondent's business)*

    _____

    ☐ other *(specify.)*

10. I believe that the respondent's current annual income from all income sources is

    $ _____ for the following reasons: *(Give your reasons for believing the dollar amount set out.)*

    _____

    _____

    _____

    _____

    _____

    _____

SPOUSAL SUPPORT

Fill out this section if you are claiming support for yourself.

11. I need spousal support for the following reasons: *(Give details of your financial needs.)*

    _____

    _____

    _____

    _____

    _____

    _____

    _____

    _____

_____

_____

RESTRAINING ORDER

Fill out this section if you are claiming a restraining order against the respondent.

12. I need an order to restrain the respondent *(full legal name of person restrained)*

_____

(date of birth of person restrained) _____ from

a) ☐ contacting or communicating directly or indirectly with the following people *(full legal name and date(s) of birth of person[s] protected by this order)*

Name	Birthdate *(d,m,y)*

☐ except through *(name of person or agency)* _____

to arrange access to the child(ren).

☐ except to permit access to the child(ren) *(names and birth dates)*

_____

on *(dates/days and times)* _____

☐ except through or in the presence of counsel.

☐ except through or in the presence of counsel or a clinical investigator from the Office of the Children's Lawyer, if the Children's Lawyer is appointed to represent the child(ren).

b) ☐ coming within _____ ☐ metres ☐ yards ☐ feet of *(locations and addresses)*

_____

at any time or for any purpose

☐ except under the following conditions: *(provide details of conditions, including time(s), purpose(s) of exception(s) and address(es) as applicable)*

_____

_____

c) ☐ *(any additional terms)*

_____

I need a restraining order for the following reasons:

_____

_____

_____

_____

LACK OF SERVICE

Fill out this section if the respondent is not going to be served or has not been served.

> **NOTE:** *The* Family Law Rules *require all documents to be served on the opposing party. The court will make an order even without service, but only in very unusual circumstances such as:*
>
> 1. *An emergency situation where there is not enough time to serve documents or where serving them would put you or your child in danger or would have other serious consequences.*
> 2. *Where the court is satisfied that every effort has been made to find the other party and that it is impossible to serve him or her by any means.*

13. My application/motion is not being served on the respondent for the following reasons:

_____

_____

_____

_____

_____

OTHER ISSUES

_____
_____
_____
_____
_____
_____

Put a line through any blank space left on this page.

Sworn/Affirmed before me
at _____
                             municipality

in _____
         province, state, or country

                                                     _____
                                                   Signature
     (This form is to be signed in
     front of a lawyer, justice of
     the peace, notary public or
     commissioner for taking
     affidavits.)

on _____ _____
         Date   *Commissioner for taking*
                           affidavits
                (Type or print name below if
                signature is illegible.)

Form 25
Order (General)

ONTARIO

SEAL

Court File Number

_____
(Name of court)

at _____
Court office address

**Form 25: Order
(general)**

☐ **Temporary**
☐ **Final**

Applicant(s)

Full legal name & address for service — street & number, municipality, postal code, telephone & fax numbers and e-mail address (if any).	Lawyer's name & address — street & number, municipality, postal code, telephone & fax numbers and e-mail address (if any).

Judge (print or type name)

Respondent(s)

Full legal name & address for service — street & number, municipality, postal code, telephone & fax numbers and e-mail address (if any).	Lawyer's name & address — street & number, municipality, postal code, telephone & fax numbers and e-mail address (if any).

Date of order

The court heard an application/motion made by *(name of person or persons)* _____

_____

The following persons were in court *(names of parties and lawyers in court)* _____

_____

_____

_____

The court received evidence and heard submissions on behalf of *(name or names)* _____

_____

THIS COURT ORDERS THAT:

Put a line through any blank space left on this page. If additional space is needed, extra sheets may be attached.

_____

_____   _____
Date of signature   *Signature of judge or clerk of the court*

Form 25A

Divorce Order

ONTARIO

SEAL	Court file number

(Name of Court)

at _____

Court office address

Form 25A: Divorce Order

Applicant(s)

Full legal name & address for service — street & number, municipality, postal code, telephone & fax numbers and e-mail address (if any).	Lawyer's name & address — street & number, municipality, postal code, telephone & fax numbers and e-mail address (if any).

Judge (print or type name)

Respondent(s)

Full legal name & address for service — street & number, municipality, postal code, telephone & fax numbers and e-mail address (if any).	Lawyer's name & address — street & number, municipality, postal code, telephone & fax numbers and e-mail address (if any).

Date of order

The court considered an application of (name) _____

on (date) _____

The following persons were in court (Give names of parties and lawyers in court. This paragraph may be struck out if the divorce is uncontested.)

_____

The court received evidence and considered submissions on behalf of (name or names) _____

THIS COURT ORDERS THAT:

If the court decides that the divorce should take effect earlier, replace "31" with the smaller number.

1. (full legal names of spouses) _____

   who were married at (place) _____

   on (date) _____

   be divorced and that the divorce take effect 31 days after the date of this order.

   (Add further paragraphs where the court orders other relief.)

_____

Put a line through any blank space left on this page.

_____   _____

Date of signature   Signature of judge or clerk of the court

NOTE: Neither spouse is free to remarry until this order takes effect, at which time you can get a **Certificate of Divorce** from the court office.

FLR-A-25A-E (2009/08)

| Save Form | Print Form | | Clear Form |

ONTARIO

Form 25A
Divorce Order

		Court file number

SEAL

at _____

_____
(Name of Court)

_____
Court office address

Form 25A: Divorce Order

Judge (print or type name)

Applicant(s)

Full legal name & address for service — street & number, municipality, postal code, telephone & fax numbers and e-mail address (if any).	Lawyer's name & address — street & number, municipality, postal code, telephone & fax numbers and e-mail address (if any).

Respondent(s)

Date of order

Full legal name & address for service — street & number, municipality, postal code, telephone & fax numbers and e-mail address (if any).	Lawyer's name & address — street & number, municipality, postal code, telephone & fax numbers and e-mail address (if any).

The court considered an application of (name) _____

on (date) _____

The following persons were in court (Give names of parties and lawyers in court. This paragraph may be struck out if the divorce is uncontested.)

_____

The court received evidence and considered submissions on behalf of (name or names) _____

THIS COURT ORDERS THAT:

If the court decides that the divorce should take effect earlier, replace "31" with the smaller number.

1. (full legal names of spouses) _____

   who were married at (place) _____

   on (date) _____

   be divorced and that the divorce take effect 31 days after the date of this order.

   (Add further paragraphs where the court orders other relief.)

_____

Put a line through any blank space left on this page.

_____   _____
Date of signature   Signature of judge or clerk of the court

NOTE: Neither spouse is free to remarry until this order takes effect, at which time you can get a **Certificate of Divorce** from the court office.

FLR-A-25A-E (2009/08)

[Save Form]   [Print Form]   [Clear Form]

Form 25B

Secure Treatment Order

ONTARIO

	Court File Number

SEAL

....
(Name of court)

at ....
Court office address

Form 25B: Secure Treatment Order

Applicant(s)

Full legal name & address for service — street & number, municipality, postal code, telephone & fax numbers and e-mail address (if any).	Lawyer's name & address — street & number, municipality, postal code, telephone & fax numbers and e-mail address (if any).

Judge *(print or type name)*

Child

Full legal name of child:	Lawyer's name & address — street & number, municipality, postal code, telephone & fax numbers and e-mail address (if any).
Date of order — Birth date (d, m, y):	
Sex:	

The court heard an application of *(name of person or persons)*

....

The following persons were in court (names of parties and lawyers in court)

....

The court received evidence and heard submissions on behalf of *(name or names)*

....

THIS COURT ORDERS THAT:

☐ *(child's full legal name)* ....

be committed to the secure treatment program at *(name and address of program)*

....

for a period of .... days, beginning on *(date)* ....

☐ the commitment of *(child's full legal name)* ....

to the secure treatment program at *(name and address of program)*

....

be extended for a period of .... days, beginning on *(date)* ....

☐ this application for an order ☐ of commitment
                                                   ☐ extending the commitment

of *(child's full legal name)* ....

to the secure treatment program at *(name and address of program)*

....

be dismissed.

☐ *(Other; specify.)*

Form 25B: Secure Treatment Order (page 2)

Court File Number

Put a line through any blank space left on this page. If additional space is needed, extra sheets may be attached.

_____   _____
Date of signature   Signature of judge or clerk of the court

NOTE TO ADMINISTRATOR OF SECURE TREATMENT PROGRAM: Subsection 165(3) of the *Child, Youth and Family Services Act, 2017* states:

In the calculation of a child's period of commitment, time spent in the secure treatment program before an order has been made under section 164 (commitment) or pending an application under section 167 (extension) shall be counted.

NOTE FURTHER that section 172 of the *Child, Youth and Family Services Act, 2017* authorizes a peace officer to take a child to a place where there is a secure treatment program if an order for the child's commitment to the secure treatment program has been made under section 164.

FLR 25B (March 1, 2018)

Page 2 of 2

1014

Form 25C

Adoption Order

ONTARIO

	Court File Number

SEAL

at _____

(Name of court)

_____

Court office address

Form 25C: Adoption Order

Applicant(s)

	Full legal name & address for service — street & number, municipality, postal code, telephone & fax numbers and e-mail address (if any).	Lawyer's name & address — street & number, municipality, postal code, telephone & fax numbers and e-mail address (if any).
Judge (print or type name)		
Date of Order		

The court heard an application of *(name of person or persons)*

The following persons were in court *(names of parties and lawyers in court)*

The court received evidence and heard submissions on behalf of *(name or names)*

The person to be adopted is:

Name before adoption *(Give full legal name of person to be adopted, unless the court orders otherwise.)*	Date of birth	Place of birth *(municipality, province and country)*	Sex	Birth registration number

The application is for a(n) *(check all boxes that apply):*

☐ adoption of a child in extended society care   ☐ licensed adoption   ☐ CAS adoption of a child who is not in extended society care   ☐ section 199(1)(b) adoption

☐ international adoption   ☐ relative adoption   ☐ stepparent adoption *(complete additional section below)*

THIS COURT ORDERS THAT:

1. The person is adopted as the child of *(name of applicant or applicants)*

2. The name of the person shall now be *(person's full legal name)*

To be completed for a stepparent adoption:

As a result of this Order and pursuant to s. 217(2)(b) of the *Child, Youth and Family Services Act, 2017*, the parents of the person are *(full legal name of parents)*

_____

Date of signature

_____

Signature of judge or clerk of the court

FLR 25C (March 1, 2018)

Page 1 of 1

Form 25D

Order (Uncontested Trial)

ONTARIO

	Court File Number

SEAL _____
(Name of court)

at _____
Court office address

Form 25D: Order
(Uncontested Trial)
☐ Temporary
☐ Final

Applicant(s)

Full legal name & address for service — street & number, municipality, postal code, telephone & fax numbers and e-mail address (if any).	Lawyer's name & address — street & number, municipality, postal code, telephone & fax numbers and e-mail address (if any).

Judge
(print or type name)

Respondent(s)

Full legal name & address for service — street & number, municipality, postal code, telephone & fax numbers and e-mail address (if any).	Lawyer's name & address — street & number, municipality, postal code, telephone & fax numbers and e-mail address (if any).

Date of order

Name & address of Children's Lawyer's agent (street & number, municipality, postal code, telephone & fax numbers and e-mail address (if any)) and name of person represented.

The court considered an application/motion made by *(name of person or persons)*

The following persons were in court *(names of parties and lawyers in court)*

The court received evidence and submissions on behalf of *(name or names)*

This order affects the following children:

Child's full legal name	Date of birth (d, m, y)	Sex

PARENTAGE

☐ 1. **THIS COURT FINDS that:**

    ☐ each child mentioned above is a child of the marriage within the meaning of the *Divorce Act*.

    ☐ the applicant and respondent are parents of each child mentioned above within the meaning of the *Family Law Act* and the *Children's Law Reform Act*.

    ☐ other *(Specify.)*

Form 25D: Order (Uncontested Trial)   (page 2)   Court File Number [   ]

CUSTODY

☐ 2. **THIS COURT ORDERS that** *(name(s))* _____ shall have
  ☐ temporary   ☐ final
  ☐ sole   ☐ joint
  custody of each child mentioned above.

ACCESS

☐ 3. **THIS COURT ORDERS that** *(name(s))* _____ shall have
  ☐ temporary   ☐ final
  access to each child mentioned above. The terms of access are:

  ☐ reasonable access on reasonable notice;
  ☐ reasonable access on reasonable notice including but not limited to the terms below;
  ☐ as follows:
    ☐ every other weekend from _____ p.m. on Friday until _____ p.m. on Sunday or Monday,
      if Monday is a statutory holiday, starting on *(date)* _____
    ☐ alternate spring breaks, starting in *(year)* _____
    ☐ _____ weeks during the summer vacation, to be decided by the parties before April 1 of each year.
    ☐ one half of the winter break, starting on *(date)* _____
      and ending on *(date)* _____ to be shared as follows:

    ☐ List any other special days such as religious festivals, Christmas Day, birthdays, Mother's Day, Father's
      Day, etc., and indicate with which person the children will be on each day. *(Specify dates and times.)*
    ☐ other *(Specify.)*

CHILD SUPPORT

☐ 4. **THIS COURT FINDS that** *(name of payor)* _____ has an income of $ _____ **and IT**
  ORDERS that *(name of payor)* _____ pay to *(name of recipient)* _____
  _____ the sum of $ _____ per month for the support of the child(ren)
  named above, starting on *(date)* _____

Fill in this frame only if there is a claim for add-ons for the child(ren).

| **THIS COURT FINDS that** *(name of recipient)* _____ has an income of $ _____ **and** |
| **IT ORDERS that** *(name of payor)* _____ pay to *(name of recipient)* _____ |
| _____ the sum of $ _____ per month for the special |
| or extraordinary expenses (add-ons) of the child(ren) named above, starting on *(date)* _____ . |

The details of this amount are as follows:

Name of child	Nature of special or extraordinary expense	Amount
		$
		$
		$
		$

Form 25D: Order (Uncontested Trial)	(page 3)	Court File Number

---

SPOUSAL SUPPORT

☐ 5. **THIS COURT ORDERS that** *(name of payor)* _____

pay to *(name of recipient)* _____ ☐ ☐ temporary ☐ final

spousal support in the amount of $ _____ per _____ starting on

(date)

☐ 6. **THIS COURT ORDERS that** the support under paragraph 5 of this order be indexed and changed annually according to the indexing factor in subsection 34(6) of the *Family Law Act*.

SUPPORT MONEY OWED

☐ 7. **THIS COURT FINDS that** the amount of support owed is $ _____ as of *(date)*

AND THIS COURT ORDERS that *(name of payor)* _____

pay off this amount ☐ by *(date)* _____

☐ at the rate of $ _____ per _____ starting on *(date)*

SUPPORT – ENFORCEMENT

☐ 8. **THIS COURT ORDERS that** unless the support order is withdrawn from the office of the Director of the Family Responsibility Office, it shall be enforced by the Director and amounts owing under the order shall be paid to the Director, who shall pay them to the person to whom they are owed.

☐ 9. **THIS COURT ORDERS that** the clerk issue a support deduction order under section 11 of the *Family Responsibility and Support Arrears Enforcement Act* for the periodic support.

PROPERTY

☐ 10. **THIS COURT ORDERS that**

Form 25D: Order (Uncontested Trial)　　　　　**(page 4)**　　Court File Number

---

DISCLOSURE

☐ **11. THIS COURT ORDERS that** *(name)* _____

serve and file the following before the next court date:

　　☐ a current financial statement.

　　☐ other *(Specify.)*

OTHER MATTERS

☐ **12. THIS COURT ORDERS that**

COSTS

☐ **13. THIS COURT ORDERS that** costs be paid by *(name)* _____

to *(name)* _____ fixed at $ _____

ADJOURNMENT

☐ **14. THIS COURT ORDERS that** the matter(s) of

be adjourned to *(date)* _____ at *(time)* _____ for: *(purpose)* _____

INTEREST

☐ **15. THIS COURT ORDERS that** interest be payable on amounts owing under this order at the rate of

_____ % per year.

Put a line through any blank space left on this page. If additional space is needed, extra pages may be attached.

_____　　　　　　_____
Date of signature　　　　　　　　　　　　　　　*Signature of judge or clerk of the court*

Form 25E

Notice Disputing Approval of Order

ONTARIO

_____
(Name of court)

Court File Number

at _____
Court office address

Form 25E: Notice Disputing Approval of Order

Applicant(s)

Full legal name & address for service — street & number, municipality, postal code, telephone & fax numbers and e-mail address (if any).	Lawyer's name & address — street & number, municipality, postal code, telephone & fax numbers and e-mail address (if any).

Respondent(s)

Full legal name & address for service — street & number, municipality, postal code, telephone & fax numbers and e-mail address (if any).	Lawyer's name & address — street & number, municipality, postal code, telephone & fax numbers and e-mail address (if any).

TO: *(name of parties)* _____

I disagree with the proposed wording of the order in this case for the following reasons: *(Give your reasons.)*

_____

_____

_____

_____

_____

I am asking for a re-worded order. A copy of my version of the order is attached.
THE CLERK OF THE COURT WILL SETTLE THE WORDING OF THE ORDER
on *(date)* _____

at _____ **a.m/p.m., or as soon as possible after that time, at** *(place for settling order)*

IF YOU DO NOT COME, THE CLERK OF THE COURT MAY SIGN THE ORDER WITH WORDING THAT MAY BE DIFFERENT FROM THE VERSION FIRST PROPOSED.

_____   _____
          Signature   *Date of signature*

Form 25F

Restraining Order

ONTARIO

Court File Number

SEAL

at _____
(Name of court)

_____
Court office address

Form 25F: Restraining Order

☐ **Temporary** ☐ **Final**

Applicant(s)

Full legal name & address for service — street & number, municipality, postal code, telephone & fax numbers and e-mail address (if any).	Lawyer's name & address — street & number, municipality, postal code, telephone & fax numbers and e-mail address (if any).

Judge (print or type name)

Respondent(s)

Full legal name & address for service — street & number, municipality, postal code, telephone & fax numbers and e-mail address (if any).	Lawyer's name & address — street & number, municipality, postal code, telephone & fax numbers and e-mail address (if any).

Date of order

THIS COURT ORDERS THAT:

1. _____ , born _____ , shall not
(Court staff to insert here relevant clauses as ordered by judge in Endorsement.)

2. This restraining order is effective _____ .

3. This restraining order shall remain in effect until _____ .

1022

☐   A separate order with additional terms relating to this family case was also made on this date.

In support of this order,

this court heard a _____ made by the _____ for a restraining order under

_____ .

The _____ was made with notice to _____ .

The following persons were in court *(list names of parties and lawyers in court)*:

_____

_____

The court read the following materials filed in support of a request for this order:

_____

_____

The court heard submissions in support of a request for this order from:

_____

_____

_____   _____

Date of signature   *Signature of judge or clerk of the court*

Note: This order will be registered against the person being restrained on the Canadian Police Information Centre (CPIC) Database. Disobeying this order is a criminal offence punishable by fine or imprisonment. Any police or peace officer with jurisdiction over the place where the order was disobeyed may arrest the person being restrained without a warrant in accordance with section 495 of the *Criminal Code of Canada*.

Form 25G

Restraining Order on Motion without Notice

ONTARIO

SEAL	Court File Number

_____
(Name of court)

at _____
Court office address

Form 25G:
Restraining Order on
Motion without Notice

Applicant(s)

_____
Judge
(print or type
name)

Full legal name & address for service — street & number, municipality, postal code, telephone & fax numbers and e-mail address (if any).	Lawyer's name & address — street & number, municipality, postal code, telephone & fax numbers and e-mail address (if any).

Respondent(s)

_____
Date of
order

Full legal name & address for service — street & number, municipality, postal code, telephone & fax numbers and e-mail address (if any).	Lawyer's name & address — street & number, municipality, postal code, telephone & fax numbers and e-mail address (if any).

THIS COURT ORDERS THAT:

1. _____ , born _____ , shall not
(Court staff to insert here relevant clauses as ordered by judge in Endorsement.)

2. This restraining order is effective _____

3. This restraining order shall remain in effect until _____

4. This matter is adjourned to *(date and time)* to review this restraining order.

5. A copy of this order together with the notice of motion, dated _____ , and affidavit of

_____ , sworn/affirmed on

_____ , shall be served immediately on *(insert full legal name of person*

restrained by this order) _____ by *(specify type of service)*

_____ .

☐ A separate order with additional terms relating to this family case was also made on
   this date. _____

In support of this order,

this court heard a motion made by the _____ for a restraining order under

_____ .

The motion was made without notice to _____ .

The following persons were in court *(list names of parties and lawyers in court)*

_____

_____

The court read the following materials filed in support of a request for this order

_____

_____

The court heard submissions in support of a request for this order from

_____

_____

_____   _____
          Date of signature   *Signature of judge or clerk of the court*

NOTICE TO *(name)* _____

If you want to oppose this motion or to give your own views, you must serve an
Affidavit (general) (Form 14A). If you think the court should make a different order, you
must serve an Affidavit (general) (Form 14A) and a Notice of Motion (Form 14). In either
case, you must serve these materials on the other party and file the materials together with
proof of service at the court office on or before 2 p.m. on *(insert date)* _____ .
If you do not have a lawyer, you should ask the court office about serving the documents
for you.

Note: This order will be registered against the person being restrained on the Canadian Police Information Centre (CPIC) Database. Disobeying this order is a criminal offence punishable by fine or imprisonment. Any police or peace officer with jurisdiction over the place where the order was disobeyed may arrest the person being restrained without a warrant in accordance with section 495 of the *Criminal Code of Canada*.

Form 25H

Order Terminating Restraining Order

ONTARIO

SEAL

_____
(Name of court)

Court File Number

_____

**Form 25H: Order
Terminating
Restraining Order,
dated**

_____

at _____
Court office address

Applicant(s)

*Judge
(print or type
name)*

_____

Full legal name & address for service — street & number, municipality, postal code, telephone & fax numbers and e-mail address (if any).	Lawyer's name & address — street & number, municipality, postal code, telephone & fax numbers and e-mail address (if any).

Respondent(s)

*Date of
order*

_____

Full legal name & address for service — street & number, municipality, postal code, telephone & fax numbers and e-mail address (if any).	Lawyer's name & address — street & number, municipality, postal code, telephone & fax numbers and e-mail address (if any).

THIS COURT ORDERS THAT:

1. The restraining order made by Justice _____ ,

on _____ , shall be terminated, effective _____ .

In support of this order,

the following persons were in court *(names of parties and lawyers in court)*

_____

The court read the following materials filed in support of a request for this order

The court heard submissions in support of a request for this order from

_____   _____
Date of signature   Signature of judge or clerk of the court

Note: This order will be sent to police services to advise them to remove the terminated restraining order from the Canadian Police Information Centre (CPIC) Database.

Form 26

Statement of Money Owed

ONTARIO

	Court File Number

_____
(Name of court)

Form 26: Statement of Money Owed dated _____

at _____
                    Court office address

Recipient(s)

Full legal name & address for service — street & number, municipality, postal code, telephone & fax numbers and e-mail address (if any).	Lawyer's name & address — street & number, municipality, postal code, telephone & fax numbers and e-mail address (if any).

Payor

Full legal name & address for service — street & number, municipality, postal code, telephone & fax numbers and e-mail address (if any).	Lawyer's name & address — street & number, municipality, postal code, telephone & fax numbers and e-mail address (if any).

My name is *(full legal name)* _____

I live in *(municipality and province)* _____

and I swear/affirm that the following is true:

1. I am ☐ a person entitled to money under an order or a domestic contract that is enforceable in this court.
   ☐ a child's custodian or guardian entitled to money for the child's benefit under an order or a domestic contract that is enforceable in this court.
   ☐ an assignee of a person or of a child's custodian or guardian entitled to money under an order or a domestic contract that is enforceable in this court.
   ☐ an agent of the Director of the Family Responsibility Office.
   ☐ *(Other; specify.)* _____

2. I attach a copy of the ☐ court order   ☐ domestic contract   ☐ bond/recognizance
   and it has not been changed by a court order or agreement of the parties, except _____
   (Write "NIL" if there has been no change.)

3. The total of the periodic payments that remain unpaid today is $ _____ . The detailed calculation of the total is attached to this statement. *(See page 2 for instructions.)*

4. The amount of interest on the unpaid periodic payments between the date of each default and today
   is $ _____ . The detailed interest calculations are attached to this statement.
   (See page 2 for instructions.)

Put a line through any blank space left on this page.

Form 26: **Statement of Money Owed** **(page 2)** Court File Number

INSTRUCTIONS FOR COMPLETING FORM 26 (Statement of Money Owed)

Paragraph 3:

Write "NIL",

(a) if the periodic portion of your order or domestic contract is fully paid up today; or

(b) if your order or domestic contract does not require the payor to make periodic payments.

If you are claiming unpaid amounts of periodic payments under a support order, a fine or forfeiture to be paid by instalments or a domestic contract, you **MUST** attach one or more separate sheets as an appendix to this statement. There you must set out a history or a diary of the payor's payments and defaults. The diagram to the right shows one way to set out this history or diary. The final total in this diary of payments and defaults must be the same as the dollar amount in paragraph 3.

Date	Amount Due (Add to TOTAL)	Amount Paid (Subtract from TOTAL)	TOTAL Amount Owing
4 Sept. 1998	$250.00		$250.00
10 Sept. 1998		$250.00	$0.00
18 Sept. 1998	$250.00		$250.00
24 Sept. 1998		$150.00	$100.00
2 Oct. 1998	$250.00		$350.00
12 Oct. 1998		$125.00	$225.00
16 Oct. 1998	$250.00		$475.00
30 Oct. 1998	$250.00		$725.00
30 Oct. 1998	$250.00		$975.00

Paragraph 4:

Write "NIL",

(a) if you don't want to claim any interest on unpaid periodic payments; or

(b) if your order or domestic contract actually forbids you to claim interest. (If your order or domestic contract says nothing about interest, you can still claim it if you want.)

Even though the payor is fully paid up today on periodic payments and even though the dollar amount that you are claiming in paragraph 3 is "NIL", there may be interest owing from the times when the payor was behind in payments. You may therefore wish to make a claim for that unpaid interest here. If you are not barred from claiming interest and wish to do so, you **MUST** attach one or more work sheets as an appendix to this statement. On those work sheets,

(c) you must set out your method of computing interest. Unless the court order or domestic contract specifically allows you to compound interest, you must use simple interest.

(d) you must indicate the appropriate rate of interest. This rate can sometimes be set out in your order or domestic contract, but if it is not, then you must rely on the rate allowed by section 127 of the *Courts of Justice Act*. You can also get this information from the court office.

(e) for each overdue or partially overdue payment, calculate in dollars and cents the amount of interest allowed by subsection 129(2) of the *Courts of Justice Act*, from the date when it was due until today or until the date of full payment of that overdue amount, whichever is earlier.

Paragraph 5:

Write "NIL",

(a) if the lump sum (whether by way of order, forfeiture, fine or support in a domestic contract) is fully paid up today; or

(b) if there is no requirement on the payor to pay any lump sum.

If there have been partial payments on the lump sum, you **MUST** attach one or more separate sheets as an appendix to this statement. There, you must set out a history or a diary of the payor's partial payments, similar to the diagram on the right. The final total in this history must be the same as the dollar amount that you are claiming in paragraph 5.

Date	Amount Due (Add to TOTAL)	Amount Paid (Subtract from TOTAL)	TOTAL Amount Owing
1 Dec. 1998	$24,000.00		$24,000.00
29 Dec. 1998		$4,700.00	$19,300.00
12 Feb. 1999		$1,800.00	$17,500.00
6 May 1999		$1,226.00	$16,273.00

Paragraph 6:

Write "NIL",

(a) if you don't want to claim any interest on the lump-sum amount.

(b) if your order or domestic contract forbids you to claim interest.

Even though the lump sum has been paid up and even though the dollar amount that you are claiming in paragraph 5 is "NIL", the interest earned on it during a time when payment was overdue may still be owing and you may wish to claim it here. If you are not barred from claiming interest and wish to do so, you **MUST** attach one or more work sheets as an appendix to this statement. On those work sheets,

(c) you must set out your method of computing interest. You must use simple interest unless the court order or domestic contract specifically allows you to compound interest.

(d) you must indicate the appropriate rate of interest. This rate may sometimes be set out in your order or domestic contract, but if it is not, then you must rely on the rate allowed by section 127 of the *Courts of Justice Act*. You can also get this information from the court office.

(e) for each partial payment, calculate in dollars and cents the amount of interest from the date of the order or domestic contract until the date of the partial payment. Interest on any balance still outstanding today will be calculated from the date of the order, contract or agreement until today.

Form 26: **Statement of Money Owed** (page 3) Court File Number

5. The amount of the lump-sum ☐ support ☐ equalization payment
                                ☐ costs ☐ fine for contempt of court
                                ☐ (Other; specify.) _____

    that remains unpaid today is $ _____ . The detailed calculation is attached to this statement.
    (See page 4 for instructions.)

6. The total amount of unpaid interest on the lump sum up to today is $ _____ . The detailed
    calculation is attached to this statement.
    (See page 4 for instructions.)

7. The amount of court costs remaining unpaid today is $ _____ . The detailed calculation is attached
    to this statement.
    (See page 4 for instructions.)

8. The amount of unpaid interest on court costs up to today is $ _____ . The detailed calculation is
    attached to this statement.
    (See page 4 for instructions.)

CREDITOR'S RELIEF PROVISIONS

9. Of the money in paragraphs 5 and 6, I attribute $ _____ of the total lump-sum support.
    (See page 4 for instructions.)

10. Of the money in paragraphs 3 and 4, I attribute $ _____ of the total periodic support.
    (See page 4 for instructions.)

11. The total of the sums in paragraphs 9 and 10 is $ _____

12. I have carried out the computations in this statement and the attached sheets correctly to the best of my ability.

FINAL TOTAL

13. The total amount enforceable in this court that I am claiming against the payor is as follows:

    (a) unpaid amounts of periodic payments (paragraph 3) _____ $ _____

    (b) interest on unpaid amounts of periodic payments (paragraph 4) _____ $ _____

    (c) unpaid lump-sum debt (paragraph 5) _____ $ _____

    (d) interest on unpaid lump-sum debt (paragraph 6) _____ $ _____

    (e) unpaid court costs (paragraph 7) _____ $ _____

    (f) interest on unpaid court costs (paragraph 8) _____ $ _____

    TOTAL $ _____

Put a line through any blank space left on this page.

Sworn/Affirmed before me at _____
                              municipality

in _____
    province, state or country

on _____   _____
    date   *Commissioner for taking affidavits*   _____
                  (Type or print name below if signature is illegible.)   *Signature*

                                                                *(This form is to be signed in front of a
                                                                lawyer, justice of the peace, notary public
                                                                or commissioner for taking affidavits.)*

NOTE: To this statement, you must attach a photocopy of the order, domestic contract, bond or recognizance that you
will be enforcing through the court. In the case of a bond or recognizance, you must also attach a photocopy of the
order of forfeiture. If court costs were determined separately, you should include a photocopy of the order or certificate
of costs.
    Pages of computer print-out are acceptable provided that they generally conform to the examples or diagrams
    provided in the instructions above.

FLR 26 (April 12, 2016)   Page 3 of 6

Form 26:   Statement of Money Owed   (page 4)   Court File Number

INSTRUCTIONS FOR COMPLETING FORM 26 (Statement of Money Owed) *(continued)*

Paragraph 7:

Write "NIL",

(a) if the court costs are fully paid up today; or

(b) if the court did not award costs to you.

If there have been partial payments on the court costs, you **MUST** attach one or more separate sheets as an appendix to this statement. There, you must set out the history or diary of the payor's partial payments, as illustrated by the diagram alongside the note to paragraph 5. The final total in this diary must be the same as the dollar amount that you are claiming in paragraph 7.

Paragraph 8:

Write "NIL",

(a) if you don't want to claim any interest on court costs; or

(b) if your order forbids you to claim any interest on costs.

Even though the court costs may be paid up today and the dollar amount that you are claiming in paragraph 8 is "NIL", the interest earned on those costs during the time when payment on them was overdue may still be owing and you may wish to claim that interest here. If you are claiming interest on court costs, you **MUST** attach one or more work sheets as an appendix to this statement. On those work sheets,

(c) you must set out your method of computing interest. You must use simple accrual unless the court has specifically allowed you to compound your interest.

(d) you must indicate the appropriate rate of interest prevailing on the date when the order was made or the rate allowed by the court when it made the order. You can get this information from the court office.

(e) for each partial payment, you must calculate in dollars and cents the amount of interest from the date of the order until the date of the partial payment. Interest on any balance still outstanding today will run from the date of the order until today.

Paragraph 9:

Write "NIL" if your lump-sum claim has nothing to do with support or maintenance. Otherwise, figure out what portion of your lump-sum claim deals with support or maintenance. You are entitled to include the interest earned on that amount.

This figure will be needed by the clerk of the court and by others, such as the sheriff, because they are required by law to give your claim for lump-sum support priority over the claims of other people with orders against the payor under the *Creditors' Relief Act*. Section 4 of that Act states:

    4.   Priority for support orders – (1) A support or maintenance order has priority over other judgment debts regardless of when an enforcement process is issued or served.

        (a) if the order is for periodic payments, in the amount of the arrears owing under the order at the time of seizure or attachment; and

        (b) if the order for a lump sum payment, in the amount of the lump sum.

    (2) *Support orders rank equally.* – Support or maintenance orders rank equally with one another.

    (3) *Enforcement process.* – Process for the enforcement or a support or maintenance order shall be identified on its face as being for support or maintenance.

    (4) *Crown bound.* – Subsection (1) binds the Crown in right of Ontario.

Paragraph 10:

Write "NIL" if your claim has nothing to do with periodic support or maintenance. Otherwise, figure out what portion of your claim deals with periodic support or maintenance. You are entitled to include the interest earned on that amount. This figure together with the one in paragraph 9 will be needed by the clerk of the court and by others, such as the sheriff, to determine the priority that your support arrears should have over the claims of other people with orders against the payor. See subsection 4(1) of the *Creditors' Relief Act*.

Form 26:   Statement of Money Owed: APPENDIX _____ (page ____)

(A, B, C, etc.)

Court File Number _____

DATE	AMOUNT DUE _(Add to TOTAL)_	AMOUNT PAID _(Subtract from TOTAL)_	TOTAL _(Amount still owing)_
	$	$	$
	$	$	$
	$	$	$
	$	$	$
	$	$	$
	$	$	$
	$	$	$
	$	$	$
	$	$	$
	$	$	$
	$	$	$
	$	$	$
	$	$	$
	$	$	$
	$	$	$
	$	$	$
	$	$	$
	$	$	$
	$	$	$
	$	$	$
	$	$	$
	$	$	$
	$	$	$
	$	$	$
	$	$	$
	$	$	$
	$	$	$
	$	$	$
	$	$	$
	$	$	$
	$	$	$
	$	$	$
	$	$	$
	$	$	$
	$	$	$
	$	$	$
	$	$	$

FLR 26 (April 12, 2016)

Form 26: Statement of Money Owed: APPENDIX (page   ) Court File Number

(A, B, C, etc.)

CALCULATION OF INTEREST

1. The calculations below relate to interest earned on *(State nature of order, judgment or contract.)*

2. THE CALCULATIONS BELOW USE:

   ☐ SIMPLE INTEREST

   ☐ COMPOUND INTEREST, COMPOUNDED *(State frequency of compounding)*

   ☐ *(Other; specify.)*

3. The rate of interest permitted by law is   % per *(frequency)*

4. The calculation of the interest is detailed as follows:

Form 26A

Affidavit of Enforcement Expenses

ONTARIO

Court File Number

_____
(Name of court)

Form 26A: Affidavit of Enforcement Expenses

at _____
Court office address

dated _____

Recipient(s)

Full legal name & address for service — street & number, municipality, postal code, telephone & fax numbers and e-mail address (if any).	Lawyer's name & address — street & number, municipality, postal code, telephone & fax numbers and e-mail address (if any).

Payor

Full legal name & address for service — street & number, municipality, postal code, telephone & fax numbers and e-mail address (if any).	Lawyer's name & address — street & number, municipality, postal code, telephone & fax numbers and e-mail address (if any).

My name is *(full legal name)* _____

I live in *(municipality & province)* _____

and I swear/affirm that the following is true:

1. I am

   Attach copy of order, contract or agreement

   ☐ a person entitled to money under an order or a domestic contract that is enforceable in this court.

   ☐ child's custodian or guardian entitled to money for the child's benefit under an order or a domestic contract that is enforceable in this court.

   ☐ an assignee of a person or of a child's custodian or guardian entitled to money under an order or a domestic contract that is enforceable in this court.

   ☐ an agent of the Director of the Family Responsibility Office.

   ☐ *(Other; specify.)*

2. To enforce the order or domestic contract, I took the following steps for which I am claiming costs under the rules of the court:

   ☐ A financial examination of the payor was carried out.

   ☐ A writ of seizure and sale was issued, filed and enforced.

   ☐ A notice of garnishment was issued, served, filed and enforced.

   ☐ A writ of seizure and sale was changed by way of a statutory declaration.

   ☐ A notice of garnishment was changed by way of a statutory declaration.

   ☐ *(Other; specify.)*

Put a line through any blank space left on this page.

FLR 26A (April 12, 2016)

Page 1 of 2

Form 26A: **Affidavit of Enforcement Expenses**   **(page 2)**

Court File Number

3. The details of my claim are as follows: *(For each item of expense, give the date when it was paid and the amount. Where receipts are available, please attach them and identify them in numbered sequence.)*

ITEM OF EXPENSE	DATE	AMOUNT	Receipt No.
			1
			2
			3
			4
			5
			6
			7
			8
			9
			10
			11
			12
			13
			14
			15
			16
			17
			18
			19
			20
			21
			22
			23

If you need more space, you may attach extra sheets and number them.

Sworn/Affirmed before me at _____
_____ *municipality*

in _____
_____ *province, state or country*

on _____   _____
date   *Commissioner for taking affidavits*
         (Type or print name below if signature is illegible.)

_____
Signature
(This form is to be signed in front of a lawyer, justice of the peace, notary public or commissioner for taking affidavits.)

FLR 26A (April 12, 2016)

Page 2 of 2

Form 26B

Affidavit for Filing Domestic Contract with Court

ONTARIO

_____	**Court File Number**
(Name of court)	

at _____   **Form 26B: Affidavit**

Court office address   dated _____

for Filing Domestic Contract with Court

Recipient(s)

Full legal name & address for service — street & number, municipality, postal code, telephone & fax numbers and e-mail address (if any).	Lawyer's name & address — street & number, municipality, postal code, telephone & fax numbers and e-mail address (if any).

Payor

Full legal name & address for service — street & number, municipality, postal code, telephone & fax numbers and e-mail address (if any).	Lawyer's name & address — street & number, municipality, postal code, telephone & fax numbers and e-mail address (if any).

My name is *(full legal name)* _____

I live in *(municipality & province)* _____

and I swear/affirm that the following is true:

1. I attach a copy of a   ☐ marriage contract   ☐ cohabitation agreement

   ☐ separation agreement   ☐ paternity agreement

   for filing with the court so that its support provisions can be enforced or changed as if they were a court order.

2. The **contract/agreement** includes the following provisions relating to child support:

   a) *(Name of party)* _____ to pay *(name of party)* _____

   child support in the monthly amount of $ _____ for the following children: *(names and birthdates of children)*

   ☐ This amount includes the following special expenses:

Type	Amount
	$
	$
	$
	$

   b) Child support is based on the payor's gross annual income of $ _____ . The proportionate share of

   special expenses is based on the recipient's gross annual income of $ _____ .

Form 26B: Affidavit for Filing Domestic Contract (page 2) with Court	Court File Number

3. The **contract/agreement** has not been set aside or disregarded by a court nor has it been changed by agreement of the parties.

Sworn/Affirmed before me at _____

                                                  municipality

in _____

                    province, state, or country

on _____ _____

        date   *Commissioner for taking affidavits*

                    (Type or print name below if signature is illegible.)

_____

                        Signature

        (This form is to be signed in front of a

    lawyer, justice of the peace, notary public

    or commissioner for taking affidavits.)

Form 26C

Notice of Transfer of Enforcement

ONTARIO

Court File Number

_____

(Name of court)

Form 26C: Notice of
Transfer of Enforcement

at _____

Court office address

Recipient(s)

Full legal name & address for service — street & number, municipality, postal code, telephone & fax numbers and e-mail address (if any).	Lawyer's name & address — street & number, municipality, postal code, telephone & fax numbers and e-mail address (if any).

Payor

Full legal name & address for service — street & number, municipality, postal code, telephone & fax numbers and e-mail address (if any).	Lawyer's name & address — street & number, municipality, postal code, telephone & fax numbers and e-mail address (if any).

TO THE PARTIES IN THIS ENFORCEMENT,

TO THE CLERK OF THE COURT at *(list court locations out of which enforcement was carried out)*

AND TO THE SHERIFF FOR *(list areas where sheriff has been involved with enforcement)*

☐ I am the recipient named above. The attached
    ☐ order   ☐ domestic contract
has been withdrawn from the enforcement program run by the Director of the Family Responsibility Office. At my request, the Director assigned to me the enforcement measure(s) listed on page 2 of this form that were started by the Director.

☐ My name is *(full legal name)* _____
I am an authorized agent of the Director of the Family Responsibility Office. The recipient(s) *(name of recipient(s))*

filed the attached   ☐ order   ☐ domestic contract
in the Director's office to be enforced. At my request, the recipient(s) assigned to the Director the enforcement measure(s) listed on the back of this sheet that were started by the recipient(s).

_____   _____

Signature   *Date of signature*

Form 26C: Notice of Transfer of Enforcement   (page 2)   Court File Number

ENFORCEMENT MEASURES BEING TRANSFERRED		
Name of Enforcement Measure	Where Started	When Started

If you need more space, you may attach extra sheets and number them.

FLR 26C (April 12, 2016)   Page 2 of 2

Form 27

Request for Financial Statement

ONTARIO

Court File Number

_____
(Name of court)

at _____
Court office address

Form 27: Request for Financial Statement

Recipient(s)

Full legal name & address for service — street & number, municipality, postal code, telephone & fax numbers and e-mail address (if any).	Lawyer's name & address — street & number, municipality, postal code, telephone & fax numbers and e-mail address (if any).

Payor

Full legal name & address for service — street & number, municipality, postal code, telephone & fax numbers and e-mail address (if any).	Lawyer's name & address — street & number, municipality, postal code, telephone & fax numbers and e-mail address (if any).

TO: (name of party) _____

I claim that you have missed payments under an order or domestic contract, a copy of which is attached to this notice.

YOU MUST PREPARE A FINANCIAL STATEMENT (Form 13) within 15 days of being served with this notice. A blank form of financial statement should accompany or be attached to this notice. If it is missing, you should contact your own lawyer or the court office immediately.

YOU MUST MAIL your completed financial statement within the next 15 days to (person & address)

IF YOU DO NOT MAIL THE COMPLETED FINANCIAL STATEMENT AS REQUIRED BY THIS NOTICE, THE COURT MAY ORDER YOU TO DO SO AND YOU MAY THEN BE REQUIRED TO PAY THE COSTS. IF YOU DISOBEY THE ORDER, THE COURT MAY MAKE AN ORDER FOR YOUR IMPRISONMENT.

_____   _____
Signature   Date of signature

Form 27A

Request for Statement of Income

ONTARIO

	Court File Number

_____
(Name of court)

at _____
Court office address

Form 27A: Request for
Statement of Income

Recipient(s)

Full legal name & address for service — street & number, municipality, postal code, telephone & fax numbers and e-mail address (if any).	Lawyer's name & address — street & number, municipality, postal code, telephone & fax numbers and e-mail address (if any).

Payor

Full legal name & address for service — street & number, municipality, postal code, telephone & fax numbers and e-mail address (if any).	Lawyer's name & address — street & number, municipality, postal code, telephone & fax numbers and e-mail address (if any).

TO: *(name and address of income source)*

I claim that the payor has missed payments under an order or domestic contract.

YOU MUST PREPARE A STATEMENT OF INCOME in Form 27B concerning the payor named above. A blank form of statement of income should accompany or be attached to this notice. If it is missing, you should contact your own lawyer or the court office immediately.

YOU MUST MAIL the complete statement of income within 10 days of being served with this notice to *(person & address)*

IF YOU DO NOT MAIL THE COMPLETED STATEMENT OF INCOME AS REQUIRED BY THIS NOTICE, THE COURT MAY ORDER YOU TO DO SO AND YOU MAY THEN BE REQUIRED TO PAY THE COURT COSTS.

_____
Signature

_____
Date of Signature

FLR 27A (April 12, 2016)

Page 1 of 1

Form 27B

Statement of Income from Income Source

ONTARIO

_____

(Name of court)

at _____

Court office address

Court File Number

Form 27B: Statement of Income from Income Source

Recipients(s)

Full legal name & address for service — street & number, municipality, postal code, telephone & fax numbers and e-mail address (if any).	*Lawyer's name & address — street & number, municipality, postal code, telephone & fax numbers and e-mail address (if any).*

Payor

Full legal name & address for service — street & number, municipality, postal code, telephone & fax numbers and e-mail address (if any).	*Lawyer's name & address — street & number, municipality, postal code, telephone & fax numbers and e-mail address (if any).*

1. My name is *(full legal name)* _____

2. ☐ I am ☐ an income source of the payor.

   ☐ an employee of an income source of the payor.

   ☐ *(Other; specify.)* _____

   OR

   ☐ Neither I nor the organization for which I work is an income source of the payor for the following reasons:

   ☐ there is no money owed to the payor on any basis mentioned in paragraph 3 below.

   ☐ the payor has never worked for me or my organization.

   ☐ the payor has worked for me or my organization but stopped working

   on *(date)* _____

   ☐ *(Other; specify.)* _____

Strike out paragraph 3 if you are not an income source.

3. I owe money to the payor on the following basis: *(check one or more boxes below)*

☐ wages or salary of $ _____ per _____

☐ overtime that, over the past 6 months, has amounted to $ _____

☐ commission, bonus, piece-work allowance or other performance-related payment that, over the past 6 months, has amounted to $ _____

☐ benefits under an accident, disability or sickness plan that, over the past 6 months, has amounted to $ _____

☐ a disability, retirement or other pension of $ _____ per _____

☐ an annuity paying $ _____ per _____

☐ vacation pay/severance pay of $ _____

☐ *(Other; specify.)* _____

_____ _____
Signature *Date of signature*

Form 27C

Appointment for Financial Examination

ONTARIO

	Court File Number

_____
(Name of court)

at _____
Court office address

**Form 27C: Appointment
for Financial Examination**

Recipient(s)

Full legal name & address for service — street & number, municipality, postal code, telephone & fax numbers and e-mail address (if any).	Lawyer's name & address — street & number, municipality, postal code, telephone & fax numbers and e-mail address (if any).

Payor

Full legal name & address for service — street & number, municipality, postal code, telephone & fax numbers and e-mail address (if any).	Lawyer's name & address — street & number, municipality, postal code, telephone & fax numbers and e-mail address (if any).

TO: *(full legal name of person to be examined)* _____

I claim that you have missed payments under an order or domestic contract, a copy of which is attached. The purpose of this examination is to find out,

    (a) your ability to pay the amount of the money owing; and

    (b) your ability to continue obeying the order or domestic contract.

YOU MUST PREPARE a financial statement in Form 13 and serve it on the recipient or on the recipient's lawyer at least 7 days before the date of the examination. A blank form of financial statement should accompany or be attached to this notice. If it is missing, you should talk to your own lawyer or the court office immediately.

YOU MUST THEN COME TO A FINANCIAL EXAMINATION to be held on *(date)* _____

at _____ **a.m./p.m. at** *(place of examination):*

You can bring your own lawyer.

YOU MUST BRING WITH YOU TO THE FINANCIAL EXAMINATION the documents or things in your possession or control that are listed on the back of this sheet.

IF YOU DO NOT COME TO THE FINANCIAL EXAMINATION, THE COURT MAY MAKE AN ORDER WITHOUT YOU AND ENFORCE IT AGAINST YOU.

_____
Signature

_____
Date of signature

FLR 27C (April 12, 2016)

Page 1 of 2

Form 27C:	Appointment for Financial Examination	(page 2)	Court File Number

(Set out the nature and the date of every document and give enough details to identify every document and thing that the payor is to bring to the examination. Write "NIL" if no document or thing is to be brought to the examination.)

☐ A copy of the income tax return that you filed with the Canada Revenue Agency *(together with all material filed with the return)* for the years _____
and a copy of any notice of assessment or reassessment that you received from the Agency for those years.

☐ Proof of your income *(including pay stubs)* for the past _____ month(s).

☐ A print-out from every bank, trust company, loan corporation, credit union or caisse populaire in which you have maintained an account for the past _____ month(s) showing all the transactions carried out in account during that period of time.

Put a line through any blank space left on this page.

FLR 27C (April 12, 2016)

Form 28

Writ of Seizure and Sale

ONTARIO

	Court File Number

SEAL at

(Name of court)

Court office address

Form 28: Writ of Seizure and Sale

Recipient(s)

Full legal name & address for service — street & number, municipality, postal code, telephone & fax numbers and e-mail address (if any).	Lawyer's name & address — street & number, municipality, postal code, telephone & fax numbers and e-mail address (if any).

Payor

Full legal name & address for service — street & number, municipality, postal code, telephone & fax numbers and e-mail address (if any).	Lawyer's name & address — street & number, municipality, postal code, telephone & fax numbers and e-mail address (if any).

TO THE SHERIFF FOR THE _(name of area)_ _____

An order or domestic contract that is enforceable in this court and that requires the payor to make payments to the recipient is in default.

YOU ARE THEREFORE DIRECTED TO SEIZE AND TO SELL the personal and real property within your area of _(Give full legal name of person or corporation, etc., against whom the writ shall be issued.)_

Surname of payor or name of corporation, etc.		
First given name _(individual only)_	**Second given name, if any** _(individual only)_	**Third given name, if any** _(individual only)_

and to realize from that sale the following sums:

Insert amount to be realized from paragraph 4(b) of the request for a writ of seizure and sale. Insert date that statement of money owed was sworn/affirmed.

(a) $ _____ and interest on it at the rate of _____ % per year, beginning on

_____ _(date)_ _____ ; and

(b) your fees and expenses in enforcing this writ.

(Check appropriate box)

Priority for support payments: _insert amount from paragraph 3 of request for a writ of seizure and sale._

☐ The sum to be realized includes unpaid support of $ _____

YOU ARE THEREFORE REQUIRED, under subsection 4(1) of the _Creditors' Relief Act_, to give priority to this amount over other judgments and orders.

Assignment of costs to Legal Aid Ontario: _insert amount from paragraph 4(c) of request for writ of seizure and sale._

☐ An _Assignment of Judgment of Costs_ in the amount of $ _____ has been made in favour of Legal Aid Ontario.

YOU ARE THEREFORE REQUIRED, under subsections 46(4) and 47(1) of the _Legal Aid Services Act, 1998_, to deduct this sum from the proceeds of the sale and to pay it to Legal Aid Ontario.

Fine, bond or recognizance

☐ This Writ enforces the sum of $ _____ as

☐ a fine for contempt of this court

☐ a forfeited bond or a forfeited recognizance

and made payable to ☐ Her Majesty the Queen

☐ other _(Specify.)_

YOU ARE THEREFORE REQUIRED, under subsection 143(3) of the _Courts of Justice Act_, to proceed immediately to execute this Writ without a direction to enforce.

YOU ARE FURTHER DIRECTED TO PAY OUT THESE PROCEEDS ACCORDING TO LAW AND TO REPORT ON THE EXECUTION OF THIS WRIT IF REQUIRED BY THE PARTY OR BY THE PARTY'S LAWYER WHO FILED THIS WRIT.

_____ _____
Date of signature _Signature of the clerk of the court_

FLR 28 (April 12, 2016)

Page 1 of 2

Form 28: Writ of Seizure and Sale

Court File Number

Name of payor: _____

Name of recipient(s): _____

FEES					
Fee	Item	Officer			Full legal name of filing party:
$					
$				(Name of court)	Filing party's address for service:
$			**at**		
$				Court office address	Name, address, telephone & fax numbers and e-mail address (if any) of filing party's lawyer:
$					
$				**Writ of Seizure and Sale**	
$					
$					NOTE: *This writ has no automatic expiry date. It remains in effect:*
$					(a) *until it is withdrawn by or on behalf of the party who filed it; or*
$					(b) *until it is set aside or suspended by order of a court in Ontario.*
$					
$					
$					

FLR 28 (April 12, 2016)

Form 28A

Request for Writ of Seizure and Sale

ONTARIO

	Court File Number

_____
(Name of court)

at _____   **Form 28A: Request for**
                                                     Writ of Seizure and Sale
Court office address

Recipient(s)

Full legal name & address for service — street & number, municipality, postal code, telephone & fax numbers and e-mail address (if any).	Lawyer's name & address — street & number, municipality, postal code, telephone & fax numbers and e-mail address (if any).

Payor

Full legal name & address for service — street & number, municipality, postal code, telephone & fax numbers and e-mail address (if any).	Lawyer's name & address — street & number, municipality, postal code, telephone & fax numbers and e-mail address (if any).

TO THE CLERK OF THE COURT:

1. I am ☐ the person who signed the attached statement of money owed.

   ☐ the lawyer for the person who signed the attached statement of money owed.

   ☐ other *(Specify.)* _____

2. The attached statement of money owed contains a claim for $ _____
   (Insert the sum from paragraph 13 of the statement of money owed.)

3. This claim includes **unpaid support** of $ _____ , an amount that has priority over all

   other judgment debts of the payor's creditors.

4. I request that a writ of seizure and sale be issued, directed to the sheriff of each of the
   following areas:
   (list the areas)

_____

(a) to seize and sell the payor's real and personal property within that area;

(b) to realize from that seizure and sale ☐ the sum set out in paragraph 2 above;

☐ the sum of $ _____ *(Set out a sum less than that in paragraph 2 above if you do not want to have all of it enforced by seizure and sale.);* and

(c) to pay out the proceeds according to law, including payment of $ ____ *(write "NIL" if no assignment was made)* to Legal Aid Ontario in accordance with the attached *Assignment of Judgment of Costs* in favour of Legal Aid Ontario.

_____   _____
          Date of signature   *Signature*

NOTE: *You must file this request and a freshly prepared statement of money owed in Form 26 with the clerk of the court. If you completed paragraph 4(c) of this request with a dollar amount, a copy of the assignment of costs must be attached to this request and to each writ of seizure and sale that you file with a sheriff and a land registrar.*

Form 28B

Statuory Declaration to Sheriff

ONTARIO

_____	Court File Number
(Name of court)	

at _____

Court office address

Form 28B: Statutory Declaration to Sheriff

Recipient(s)

Full legal name & address for service — street & number, municipality, postal code, telephone & fax numbers and e-mail address (if any).	*Lawyer's name & address — street & number, municipality, postal code, telephone & fax numbers and e-mail address (if any).*

Payor

Full legal name & address for service — street & number, municipality, postal code, telephone & fax numbers and e-mail address (if any).	*Lawyer's name & address — street & number, municipality, postal code, telephone & fax numbers and e-mail address (if any).*

My name is *(full legal name)* _____

I live in *(municipality & province)* _____

and I declare that the following is true:

1. I am ☐ a recipient under a payment order.

   ☐ an assignee of a recipient under a payment order.

   ☐ an agent of the Director of the Family Responsibility Office.

   ☐ other *(Specify.)* _____

2. On *(date)* _____ a writ of seizure and sale was issued in this case, a copy of which is attached.

3. Since then, the amount owed by the payor has changed and, as of today, the amount owed stands at $ _____ with interest on it at the rate of _____ % per year beginning on *(date when interest begins)* _____

4. Since then, the payor has: ☐ legally changed his/her name from _____

to _____ .

☐ used the following alias(es): _____ .

☐ used the following spelling variations of his or her name or alias(es):

_____ .

5. The amount in paragraph 3 includes unpaid support of $ _____ which, under subsection 4(1) of the *Creditors' Relief Act*, gets priority over other judgments and orders.

6. An additional *Assignment of Judgment of Costs* in the amount of *(write NIL if none)* $ _____

has been made in favour of Legal Aid Ontario which, under subsections 46(4) and 47(1) of the *Legal Aid Services Act, 1998*, must be deducted from the proceeds of the sale and paid to Legal Aid Ontario.

7. The amount in paragraph 3 includes $ _____ as a fine for contempt of this court, a forfeited bond or a forfeited recognizance arising out of a civil proceeding and made payable to,

☐ Her Majesty the Queen   ☐ other *(Specify.)* _____

and, under subsection 143(3) of the *Courts of Justice Act*, the writ of seizure and sale can be executed immediately to collect that amount without a direction to enforce.

Declared before me at _____

municipality

in _____

province, state or country

on _____ _____

date   *Commissioner for taking affidavits (Type or print name below if signature is illegible.)*

_____

*Signature
(This form is to be signed in front of a lawyer, justice of the peace, notary public or commissioner for taking affidavits.)*

Form 28C

Writ of Temporary Seizure

ONTARIO

<table>
<tr><td>SEAL</td><td>at</td><td>_____
(Name of court)

_____
Court office address</td><td>Court File Number

**Form 28C: Writ of
Temporary Seizure**</td></tr>
</table>

Applicant(s)/Recipient(s) *(Strike out inapplicable term.)*

Full legal name & address for service — street & number, municipality, postal code, telephone & fax numbers & e-mail address (if any).	Lawyer's name & address — street & number, municipality, postal code, telephone & fax numbers & e-mail address (if any).

Respondent/Payor *(Strike out inapplicable term.)*

Full legal name & address for service — street & number, municipality, postal code, telephone & fax numbers & e-mail address (if any).	Lawyer's name & address — street & number, municipality, postal code, telephone & fax numbers & e-mail address (if any).

TO THE SHERIFF FOR THE *(name of area)* _____

On a motion made by *(name of moving party)* _____

the court gave its permission on *(date)* _____ to issue this writ.

YOU ARE THEREFORE DIRECTED TO SEIZE AND TO HOLD the following property within your area of *(Give full legal name of person or corporation, etc. against whom the writ shall be issued.)*

Surname of respondent/payor or name of corporation, etc.		
First given name *(individual only)*	**Second given name, if any** *(individual only)*	**Third given name, if any** *(individual only)*

Give description of property to be taken and held.

YOU ARE ALSO DIRECTED TO COLLECT AND TO HOLD any income from the property until the writ is withdrawn or until further order of the court.

_____
Date of signature

_____
Signature of the clerk of the court

Form 29

Request for Garnishment

ONTARIO

Court File Number

_____
(Name of court)

at _____
Court office address

Form 29: Request for Garnishment

Recipient(s)

Full legal name & address for service — street & number, municipality, postal code, telephone & fax numbers and e-mail address (if any).	Lawyer's name & address — street & number, municipality, postal code, telephone & fax numbers and e-mail address (if any).

Payor

Full legal name & address for service — street & number, municipality, postal code, telephone & fax numbers and e-mail address (if any).	Lawyer's name & address — street & number, municipality, postal code, telephone & fax numbers and e-mail address (if any).

TO THE CLERK OF THE COURT:

1. I am ☐ the person who signed the attached statement of money owed.
   ☐ the lawyer for the person who signed the attached statement of money owed.
   ☐ an agent for the Director of the Family Responsibility Office.
   ☐ *(Other; specify.)*

2. I want to enforce by way of garnishment the sum of $ _____ , which is the money claimed in the attached statement of money owed. *(If you want to collect ongoing periodic payments as well as arrears, check the box below.)*

   ☐ I also want the garnishment to collect ongoing payments of $ _____

   per *(period)* _____

3. I request that a separate notice of garnishment be issued and sent to each person named in the Appendix to this form, who, I have reason to believe, owes or will owe money to the payor in the amounts described in that Appendix.

_____   _____
Signature of person making request or of person's lawyer   _Date of signature_

NOTE: You must attach one or more sheets as an Appendix in which you name the person or persons who owe or will owe money to the payor. You must also prepare and attach a fresh statement of money owed in Form 26 (one prepared within the past 30 days) to this request and file it with the clerk of the court.

If (a) the payor's obligation to pay the order or domestic contract that you are enforcing by this garnishment should expire or be discharged, and

(b) there is no more money owed by the payor under that order or domestic contract,

or if you simply decide that you no longer want to enforce the order or domestic contract by means of this garnishment, you must immediately fill out and serve a notice to stop garnishment in Form 29I on the payor and on each garnishee and file it, together with proof of service, with the clerk of the court at the above court office.

Form 29: **Request for Garnishment – APPENDIX** (page _____)   Court File Number _____

Name of Garnishee: _____

Garnishee's address: _____

Amount that the garnishee owes or will owe to the payor:

☐ periodic amounts ☐ of $ _____
☐ whose dollar figure I do not know

that are or will be paid on (State frequency of payments. Write "UNKNOWN" if you do not know.) _____

☐ lump-sum amount ☐ of $ _____
☐ whose dollar figure I do not know.

Description of debt owed by the garnishee to the payor:
☐ wages, commissions or other employment income.   ☐ rental payments
☐ money held at a bank, credit union, etc.   ☐ pension payments
☐ (Other; specify.)

Name of Garnishee: _____

Garnishee's address: _____

Amount that the garnishee owes or will owe to the payor:

☐ periodic amounts ☐ of $ _____
☐ whose dollar figure I do not know

that are or will be paid on (State frequency of payments. Write "UNKNOWN" if you do not know.) _____

☐ lump-sum amount ☐ of $ _____
☐ whose dollar figure I do not know.

Description of debt owed by the garnishee to the payor:
☐ wages, commissions or other employment income.   ☐ rental payments
☐ money held at a bank, credit union, etc.   ☐ pension payments
☐ (Other; specify.)

Name of Garnishee: _____

Garnishee's address: _____

Amount that the garnishee owes or will owe to the payor:

☐ periodic amounts ☐ of $ _____
☐ whose dollar figure I do not know

that are or will be paid on (State frequency of payments. Write "UNKNOWN" if you do not know.) _____

☐ lump-sum amount ☐ of $ _____
☐ whose dollar figure I do not know.

Description of debt owed by the garnishee to the payor:
☐ wages, commissions or other employment income.   ☐ rental payments
☐ money held at a bank, credit union, etc.   ☐ pension payments
☐ (Other; specify.)

FLR 29 (April 12, 2016)   Page 2 of 2

Form 29A

Notice of Garnishment (Lump-Sum Debt)

ONTARIO

SEAL	Court File Number

_____
(Name of court)

at _____
Court office address

Form 29A:
Notice of
Garnishment
(lump-sum debt)

Recipient

Full legal name & address for service — street & number, municipality, postal code, telephone & fax numbers and e-mail address (if any).	*Lawyer's name & address — street & number, municipality, postal code, telephone & fax numbers and e-mail address (if any).*

Payor

Full legal name & address for service — street & number, municipality, postal code, telephone & fax numbers and e-mail address (if any).	*Lawyer's name & address — street & number, municipality, postal code, telephone & fax numbers and e-mail address (if any).*

TO: *(garnishee's full legal name and address)* _____

_____

ALL DEDUCTIONS MADE UNDER THIS NOTICE MUST BE PAID TO

☐ the clerk of the court   ☐ the Director of the Family Responsibility Office

at *(address)* _____

The payor *(name)* _____ has missed payments under a court order, a domestic contract or a paternity agreement that is enforceable in this court or that is enforceable by a garnishment process from outside Ontario and recognized by this court.

The recipient claims that you owe or will owe the payor a debt in the form of one or more lump-sum amounts. (A debt to the payor includes both a debt payable to the payor alone and a joint debt payable to the payor and one or more other persons.)

YOU MUST THEREFORE PAY TO the clerk of the court or the Director of the Family

Responsibility Office (as indicated above)

    (a)   within 10 days after service of this Notice upon you, ALL MONEY THAT IS NOW PAYABLE BY YOU TO THE PAYOR; and

    (b)   within 10 days after any future amount becomes payable, ALL MONEY THAT BECOMES PAYABLE BY YOU TO THE PAYOR.

The total amount of your payments is not to exceed $ _____ *(insert the dollar amount by adding the sums in paragraphs 5, 6, 7 and 8 of the statement of money owed or such lesser amount as the recipient chooses to have enforced by way of garnishment.)*

If your debt is jointly owed to the payor and to one or more other persons, you must pay half of the amount now payable or that becomes payable or such fraction as the court may order.

This notice is legally binding on you until it is changed or terminated.

(Check box below if appropriate.)

☐ This notice of garnishment enforces the support provisions of a court order, domestic contract or paternity agreement. Under subsection 4(1) of the *Creditors' Relief Act*, **YOU MUST GIVE THIS NOTICE OF GARNISHMENT PRIORITY OVER ALL OTHER NOTICES OF GARNISHMENT**, no matter when these other competing notices of garnishment were served on you. For details of the extent of this priority, you should talk to your own lawyer.

Your payment in accordance with this notice is, to the extent of the payment, a valid discharge of your debt to the payor and, in the case of a joint debt to the payor and one or more other persons, a valid discharge of your debt to the payor and the other person(s).

If your debt is jointly owed to the payor and to one or more other persons, **YOU MUST IMMEDIATELY MAIL a notice to co-owner of the debt (Form 29C) to the following persons:**

    (a)   each other person to whom the joint debt is owed, at the address shown in your own records;

    (b)   the recipient or the Director of the Family Responsibility Office, depending on who is enforcing the order; and

    (c)   the clerk of the court.

A blank Form 29C should be attached to this notice. If it is missing, you should talk to your own lawyer or the court office.

If you have reason to believe that you should not be making the payments required of you by this notice, you have the right to serve a dispute in Form 29F on the parties and file it at the court office within 10 days after service of this notice upon you. You may consult with your lawyer about this. A blank Form 29F (dispute from garnishee) should be attached to this notice. If it is missing, you should talk to your own lawyer or the court office. You can serve by any method set out in rule 6 of the *Family Law Rules*, including mail, courier and fax. If you serve Form 29F and file it at the court office, the court may hold a garnishment hearing to determine the rights of the parties. In the meantime, serving and filing a dispute does not stop the operation of this notice of garnishment.

If you are the payor's employer,

(a) Section 56.1 of Ontario's *Employment Standards Act* make it unlawful to dismiss or suspend an employee or to threaten to do so on the ground that a garnishment process has been issued in respect of the employee;

(b) section 7 of the Ontario's *Wages Act* says that you cannot deduct more than:

(i) 50% of any wages (after statutory deductions) payable to your employee for the enforcement of support; and

(ii) 20% of any wages (after statutory deductions) payable to your employee for the enforcement of money not connected to support.

These percentages can be increased or decreased only by an order of the court. If a copy of such an order is attached to this notice or if it is ever served on you, you must use the percentage given in that court order; and

(c) the *Family Law Rules* state that you MUST give to the clerk of the court and to the person who asked for this garnishment, within 10 days after the end of the payor's employment with you, a written notice,

(i) indicating that the payor has ceased to be employed by you, and

(ii) setting out the date on which the employment ended and the date of the payor's last remuneration from you.

IF YOU DO NOT OBEY THIS NOTICE, THE COURT MAY ORDER YOU TO PAY THE FULL AMOUNT OWED AND THE COSTS INCURRED BY THE RECIPIENT.

IF YOU PAY ANYONE OTHER THAN AS DIRECTED ON THE FRONT OF THIS SHEET, THE COURT MAY ORDER YOU TO MAKE ANOTHER PAYMENT, BUT THIS TIME, TO THE PERSON NAMED IN THIS NOTICE.

_____   _____
         Date of signature   *Signature of the clerk of the court*

NOTICE TO THE PAYOR: You have the right to serve and file a dispute in Form 29E at the court office within 10 days after service of this notice on you. You may want to talk to a lawyer about this. A blank Form 29E (dispute from payor) should have accompanied this notice when it was served on you. If it is missing, you should talk to your own lawyer or the court office immediately. You can serve by any method set out in rule 6 of the Family Law Rules, including mail, courier and fax. If you serve Form 29E and file it at the court office, the court may hold a garnishment hearing to decide the rights of the parties.

If the garnishee is your employer, the Family Law Rules says that you MUST, within 10 days after the end of your employment with the garnishee, give the clerk of the court and (depending on who is enforcing the garnishment) the recipient or the Director of the Family Responsibility Office, a written notice,

(a) indicating that your employment with the garnishee is ended; and

(b)   setting out the date on which your employment ended and the date of your last pay from the garnishee.

Within 10 days after you start any new job or go back to your old one, you MUST give a further written notice giving the name and address of your new employer or saying that you have gone back to work with your former employer.

Form 29B

Notice of Garnishment (Periodic Debt)

ONTARIO

	Court File Number

SEAL

_____
(Name of court)

Form 29B: Notice of Garnishment (periodic debt)

at _____
Court office address

Recipient

Full legal name & address for service — street & number, municipality, postal code, telephone & fax numbers and e-mail address (if any).	Lawyer's name & address — street & number, municipality, postal code, telephone & fax numbers and e-mail address (if any).

Payor

Full legal name & address for service — street & number, municipality, postal code, telephone & fax numbers and e-mail address (if any).	Lawyer's name & address — street & number, municipality, postal code, telephone & fax numbers and e-mail address (if any).

TO: *(garnishee's full legal name and address)*

_____

ALL DEDUCTIONS MADE UNDER THIS NOTICE MUST TO BE PAID TO

☐ the clerk of the court   ☐ the Director of the Family Responsibility Office

at *(address)* _____

The payor *(name)* _____ has missed payments under a court order or domestic contract that is enforceable in this court or that is enforceable by a garnishment process from outside Ontario and recognized by this court. The recipient claims that you owe or will owe the payor a debt in the form of wages, salary, pension payments, rent, annuity or other debt that you pay out periodically or by instalments. (A debt to the payor includes both a debt payable to the payor alone and a debt payable jointly to the payor and one or more other persons.)

Check the first circle if you want the garnishment to deduct fixed dollar amounts. If you want the garnishment to deduct by way of percentage, check the second circle below.

☐ **YOU MUST IMMEDIATELY THEREFORE DEDUCT FROM ALL SUCH PAYMENTS MADE BY YOU,**

☐ to satisfy the payor's ongoing duty to make periodic payments under the order or domestic contract THE SUM OF $ _____ on every *(state frequency)* _____ or the equivalent sum according to your regular or established cycle of payment to the payor;

Insert the dollar amount and frequency as stated in the periodic portion of the order or domestic contract.

and

"Accumulated debts" includes lump-sum orders, fines, forfeitures, accumulated arrears of periodic payments, court costs and interest.

☐ to reduce the payor's accumulated debts of $ _____ to the recipient under the order or domestic contract, THE SUM OF $ _____ on every *(state frequency)* _____ or the equivalent sum according to your regular or established cycle of payment to the payor, **OR**

Check this circle only if you want the garnishment to deduct by way of percentage.

Unless a court order says otherwise, you can deduct no more than 50% of the payor's wages to collect support and no more than 20% to collect money unrelated to support. There is no percentage ceiling on the deductions from non-wages.

☐ **YOU MUST IMMEDIATELY THEREFORE DEDUCT FROM ALL SUCH PAYMENTS MADE BY YOU,**

☐ _____ % of all wages that are now payable by you to the payor, and

☐ _____ % of any debt (other than wages) now payable by you to the payor periodically or by instalments.

AND YOU MUST PAY THIS DEDUCTION to the clerk of the Director (as indicated above) within 10 days after service of this notice upon you. If your debt is jointly owed to the payor and to one or more other persons, you must pay half of the amount now payable or that becomes payable or such fraction as the court may order.

THIS NOTICE LEGALLY BINDS YOU TO CONTINUE PAYING THESE DEDUCTIONS within 10 days after each payment becomes payable by you to the payor, until this notice is changed or terminated.

Form 29B	Notice of Garnishment (periodic debt)	(page 2)	Court File Number

(Check below if appropriate.)

☐   This notice of garnishment enforces the support provisions of a court order, domestic contract or paternity agreement.

Under subsection 4(1) of the *Creditors' Relief Act*, **YOU MUST GIVE THIS NOTICE OF GARNISHMENT PRIORITY OVER ALL OTHER NOTICES OF GARNISHMENT,** no matter when these other competing notices of garnishment were served to you. For details of the extent of this priority, you should talk to your own lawyer.

Your payment in accordance with this notice is, to the extent of the payment, a valid discharge of your debt to the payor and, in the case of a joint debt to the payor and one or more other persons, a valid discharge of your debt to the payor and the other person(s).

If your debt is jointly owed to the payor and to one or more other persons, **YOU MUST IMMEDIATELY MAIL a notice to co-owner of the debt (Form 29C) to the following persons:**

    (a)   each other person to whom the joint debt is owed, at the address shown in your own records;

    (b)   the recipient or the Director of the Family Responsibility Office, depending on who is enforcing the order; and

    (c)   the clerk of the court.

A blank Form 29C should be attached to this notice. If it is missing, you should talk to your own lawyer or the court office.

If you have reason to believe that you should not be making the payments required of you by this notice, you have the right to serve and file a dispute in Form 29F at the court office within 10 days after service of this notice upon you. You may consult with your lawyer about this. A blank Form 29F (dispute from garnishee) should be attached to this notice. If it is missing, you should talk to your own lawyer or the court office. You can serve by any method set out in rule 6 of the *Family Law Rules*, including mail, courier and fax. If you serve Form 29F and file it at the court office, the court may hold a garnishment hearing to determine the rights of the parties. In the meantime, serving and filing a dispute does not stop the operation of this notice of garnishment.

If you are the payor's employer

    (a)   Section 56.1 of Ontario's *Employment Standards Act* makes it unlawful to dismiss or suspend an employee or to threaten to do so on the ground that a garnishment process has been issued in respect of the employee;

    (b)   section 7 of Ontario's *Wages Act* says that you cannot deduct more than:

        (i)   50% of any wages (after statutory deductions) payable to your employee for the enforcement of support; and

        (ii)   20% of any wages (after statutory deductions) payable to your employee for the enforcement of money not connected to support.

        These percentages can be increased or decreased only by an order of the court. If a copy of such an order is attached to this notice or if it is ever served on you, you must use the percentage given in that court order; and

    (c)   the *Family Law Rules* state you MUST give to the clerk of the court and to the person who asked for this garnishment, within 10 days after the end of the payor's employment with you, a written notice,

        (i)   indicating that the payor has ceased to be employed by you, and

        (ii)   setting out the date on which the employment ended and the date of the payor's last remuneration from you.

IF YOU DO NOT OBEY THIS NOTICE, THE COURT MAY ORDER YOU TO PAY THE FULL AMOUNT OWED AND THE COSTS INCURRED BY THE RECIPIENT.

IF YOU PAY ANYONE OTHER THAN AS DIRECTED ON THE FRONT OF THIS SHEET, THE COURT MAY ORDER YOU TO MAKE ANOTHER PAYMENT, BUT THIS TIME, TO THE PERSON NAMED IN THIS NOTICE.

Date of signature	*Signature of the clerk of the court*

NOTICE TO THE PAYOR: You have the right to serve and file a dispute in Form 29E at the court office within 10 days after service of this notice on you. You may want to talk to a lawyer about this. A blank Form 29E (dispute from payor) should have accompanied this notice when it was served on you. If it is missing, you should talk to your own lawyer or the court office immediately. You can serve by any method set out in rule 6 of the *Family Law Rules*, including mail, courier and fax. If you serve From 29E and file it at the court office, the court may hold a garnishment hearing to decide the rights of the parties.

If the garnishee is your employer, the *Family Law Rules* say that you MUST, within 10 days after the end of your employment with the garnishee, give the clerk of the court and (depending on who is enforcing the garnishment) the recipient or the Director of the Family Responsibility Office, a written notice,

    (a)   indicating that your employment with the garnishee is ended; and

    (b)   setting out the date on which your employment ended and the date of your last pay from the garnishee.

Within 10 days after you start any new job or go back to your old one, you MUST give a further written notice giving the name and address of your new employer or saying that you have gone back to work with your former employer.

FLR 29B (April 12, 2016)   Page 2 of 2

Form 29C

Notice to Co-Owner of Debt

ONTARIO

	Court File Number

_____
(Name of court)

at _____

Court office address

Form 29C: Notice to Co-Owner of Debt

Recipient(s)

Full legal name & address for service — street & number, municipality, postal code, telephone & fax numbers and e-mail address (if any).	Lawyer's name & address — street & number, municipality, postal code, telephone & fax numbers and e-mail address (if any).

Payor

Full legal name & address for service — street & number, municipality, postal code, telephone & fax numbers and e-mail address (if any).	Lawyer's name & address — street & number, municipality, postal code, telephone & fax numbers and e-mail address (if any).

TO: *(co-owner's full legal name and address)* _____

_____

A court case between the recipient and the payor has resulted in a court order requiring the payor to pay money to the recipient. The recipient or a person enforcing this order on the recipient's behalf has served me or my business with a notice of garnishment, claiming to intercept a debt that I or my business is supposed to owe and to pay to the payor. Under the law, a debt to the payor includes both a debt payable to the payor alone and a debt payable jointly to the payor and one or more other persons. According to my records or the records of my business, you are such an "other person" who shares in the debt that I or my business owe to the payor.

☐ In accordance with this notice of garnishment, I have paid out one half

☐ In accordance with a court order, I have paid out $ _____

of the debt that I or my business jointly owes to you and the payor. This money is being held for 30 days by:

☐ the clerk of the court

☐ the Director of the Family Responsibility Office at *(address)* _____

1063

IF YOU BELIEVE THAT I OR MY BUSINESS HAVE PAID OUT MONEY THAT LEGALLY BELONGS TO YOU, you have 30 days from the service of this notice to serve Form 29G (dispute from co-owner of debt) and file it with the court. You can get a copy of this form from your own lawyer or from the court office. You must then serve a completed copy of this form on the following persons:

(a) me or my business at the address given below;

(b) the payor and the recipient; and

(c) the clerk of the court or the Director of the Family Responsibility Office, depending on who is holding the money.

You can serve by any method set out in rule 6 of the *Family Law Rules*, including mail, courier and fax. Once you have served this form, you must then file it with the court with proof of service (Form 6B). The court may then hold a garnishment hearing to determine your rights.

IF YOU FAIL TO DO THIS WITHIN 30 DAYS, you may not later challenge the recipient's garnishment of the debt that I or my business jointly owes to you and the payor.

_____
Signature of person making this notice or of person's lawyer

_____
Date of signature

Typed or printed name of person or of person's lawyer, address for service, telephone & fax number and e-mail address (if any).

Form 29D

Statutory Declaration of Indexed Support

ONTARIO

	Court File Number

_____
(Name of Court)

at _____
Court office address

Form 29D: Statutory Declaration of Indexed Support,

dated _____

Recipient(s)

Full legal name & address for service — street & number, municipality, postal code, telephone & fax numbers and e-mail address (if any).	Lawyer's name & address — street & number, municipality, postal code, telephone & fax numbers and e-mail address (if any).

Payor

Full legal name & address for service — street & number, municipality, postal code, telephone & fax numbers and e-mail address (if any).	Lawyer's name & address — street & number, municipality, postal code, telephone & fax numbers and e-mail address (if any).

Garnishee

Full legal name & address for service — street & number, municipality, postal code, telephone & fax numbers and e-mail address (if any).	Lawyer's name & address — street & number, municipality, postal code, telephone & fax numbers and e-mail address (if any).

My name is *(full legal name)* _____

I live in *(municipality & province)* _____

and I declare that the following is true:

1. I am
   - ☐ a recipient under a support order or the support provisions of a domestic contract.
   - ☐ an assignee of a recipient under a support order or the support provisions of a domestic contract.
   - ☐ an agent of the Director of the Family Responsibility Office.
   - ☐ *(Other; specify.)*

2. On *(date)* _____, a notice of garnishment was issued to the garnishee to enforce a support order or the support provisions of a domestic contract that indexed the periodic payments for inflation.

3. On *(date)* _____, the amount of support was automatically adjusted for inflation as set out in the order, contract or agreement.

4. As a result of this adjustment, the garnishee should now be making the following deductions: *(State new level of deductions.)*

Form 29D: **Statutory Declaration of Indexed Support**   (page 2)

Court File Number

Put a line through any blank space left on this page.

Sworn/Affirmed before me at _____

in _____
                    municipality

_____
province, state, or country

on _____   _____
        date   Commissioner for taking affidavits
                        (Type or print name below if signature is illegible.)

_____
Signature
(This form is to be signed in front of a lawyer, justice of the peace, notary public or commissioner for taking affidavits.)

NOTE: This declaration must be served on the garnishee and the payor together with blank forms of dispute and must then be filed with the clerk of the court. You can serve by any means allowed in rule 6 of the *Family Law Rules*, including mail, courier and fax. The filing with the clerk of the court must be accompanied by proof of service (Form 6B).

NOTICE TO GARNISHEE: From the moment that you are served with this declaration, you must treat the notice of garnishment as if it now required you to make the deductions set out in paragraph 4 of this declaration. Failure to do so is the same as disobeying the notice of garnishment.

NOTICE TO PAYOR AND GARNISHEE: You have the right to serve and file a dispute in Form 29E (dispute from payor) or Form 29F (dispute from garnishee) at the court office within 10 days after service of this declaration on you if you have legal reasons for objecting to the changes to the notice of garnishment. You may want to talk to a lawyer about this. A blank form of dispute should have accompanied this declaration when it was served on you. If it is missing, you should talk to your own lawyer or the court office immediately. If this is what you want to do, you must serve your dispute on the other parties. You can serve by any means allowed in rule 6 of the *Family Law Rules*, including mail, courier and fax. Once the dispute has been served, you must file it with the clerk of the court. The filing must be accompanied by proof of service (Form 6B). If you serve and file your dispute, the court may hold a garnishment hearing to decide the rights of the parties.

FLR 29D (April 12, 2016)   Page 2 of 2

Form 29E

Dispute (Payor)

ONTARIO

_____
(Name of court)

at _____
Court office address

Court File Number

Recipient(s)

Full legal name & address for service — street & number, municipality, postal code, telephone & fax numbers and e-mail address (if any).	Lawyer's name & address — street & number, municipality, postal code, telephone & fax numbers and e-mail address (if any).

Payor

Full legal name & address for service — street & number, municipality, postal code, telephone & fax numbers and e-mail address (if any).	Lawyer's name & address — street & number, municipality, postal code, telephone & fax numbers and e-mail address (if any).

Garnishee

Full legal name & address for service — street & number, municipality, postal code, telephone & fax numbers and e-mail address (if any).	Lawyer's name & address — street & number, municipality, postal code, telephone & fax numbers and e-mail address (if any).

My name is *(full legal name)* _____

I live in *(municipality & province)* _____

and I swear/affirm that the following is true:

1. I am the payor in this garnishment case.

2. I dispute ☐ the notice of garnishment issued on

☐ the statutory declaration of indexed support made on

(date) _____ , for the following reason(s):

(State the reason or reasons for your dispute in numbered paragraphs.)

1.

_____

Put a line through any blank space left on this page.

NOTE: *Merely serving and filling this dispute will not stop the garnishment process. It can be stopped at the recipient's request if the recipient agrees with the reasons for your dispute. It can also be stopped by a court order at a garnishment hearing. If you want the court to hold a hearing, you must check the box in the frame below.*

☐ **NOTICE TO THE CLERK OF THE COURT AND TO ALL PARTIES:** I am making a request for a garnishment hearing in which the court can rule on this dispute.

Sworn/Affirmed before me
at _____
municipality

in _____
province, state, or country

_____
Signature

on _____   _____
date   *Commissioner for taking*
affidavits
(Type or print name below if
signature is illegible.)

(This form is to be signed in front of a lawyer, justice of the peace, notary public or commissioner for taking affidavits.)

NOTICE TO RECIPIENT: Please examine this dispute. If you disagree with it and if the payer has not asked for a garnishment hearing, you yourself may ask to have a court hearing. You may want to talk to your own lawyer about this. You have 10 days from the date of being served with this document to decide whether to have a court hearing. If you want a hearing, you or your lawyer have 10 days within which to ask the clerk of the court, either in person or in writing, to mail out to you, to the payor, to the garnishee and to the co-owner of a joint debt (if any) a notice of garnishment hearing (Form 29H). At that hearing, the judge will give you and the other parties a chance to be heard and may make an order that can affect the rights of all parties.

Form 29F

Dispute (Garnishee)

ONTARIO

_____

(Name of court)

at _____

Court office address

Court File Number

Form 29F: Dispute (garnishee)

Recipient(s)

Full legal name & address for service — street & number, municipality, postal code, telephone & fax numbers and e-mail address (if any).	Lawyer's name & address — street & number, municipality, postal code, telephone & fax numbers and e-mail address (if any).

Payor

Full legal name & address for service — street & number, municipality, postal code, telephone & fax numbers and e-mail address (if any).	Lawyer's name & address — street & number, municipality, postal code, telephone & fax numbers and e-mail address (if any).

Garnishee

Full legal name & address for service — street & number, municipality, postal code, telephone & fax numbers and e-mail address (if any).	Lawyer's name & address — street & number, municipality, postal code, telephone & fax numbers and e-mail address (if any).

1. I am the garnishee in this garnishment case.

2. I am not legally required to pay ☐ the amounts set out in the notice of garnishment issued on *(date)*

    ☐ the changed amounts set out in the statutory declaration of indexed support

    made on *(date)* _____ ,

1070

for the following reason(s):

☐ I do not owe and do not expect to owe any money to the payor because:

    ☐ the payor has never worked for me.

    ☐ the payor stopped working for me on *(date)* _____

    ☐ I owed the payor money and paid it in full by *(date)* _____

    ☐ I do not hold any money in trust for or to the credit of the payor.

    ☐ *(Other; specify.)*

☐ I owe or will owe money to the payor, but it cannot be seized by garnishment because *(State reasons for legal exemption.)*

☐ *(Other grounds; specify.)*

Put a line through any blank space left on this page.

NOTE: *Merely serving and filing this dispute will not stop the garnishment process. It can be stopped at the recipient's request if the recipient agrees with the reasons for your dispute. It can also be stopped by a court order at a garnishment hearing. If you want the court to hold a hearing, you must check the box in the frame below.*

☐ **NOTICE TO THE CLERK OF THE COURT AND TO ALL PARTIES:** I am making a request for a garnishment hearing in which the court can rule on this dispute.

Signature of garnishee	*Date of signature*

NOTICE TO RECIPIENT: Please examine this dispute. If you disagree with it and if the garnishee has not asked for a garnishment hearing, you yourself may ask to have a court hearing. You may want to talk to your own lawyer about this. You have 10 days from the date of being served with this document to decide whether to have a court hearing. If you want a hearing, you or your lawyer have 10 days within which to ask the clerk of the court, either in person or in writing, to mail out to you, to the payor, to the garnishee and to the co-owner of a joint debt (if any) a notice of garnishment hearing (Form 29H). At that hearing, the judge will give you and the other parties a chance to be heard and may make an order that can affect the rights of all parties.

Form 29G

Dispute (Co-Owner of Debt)

ONTARIO

Court File Number

_____
(Name of court)

**Form 29G: Dispute
(co-owner of debt)**

at _____
Court office address

Recipient(s)

Full legal name & address for service — street & number, municipality, postal code, telephone & fax numbers and e-mail address (if any).	*Lawyer's name & address — street & number, municipality, postal code, telephone & fax numbers and e-mail address (if any).*

Payor

Full legal name & address for service — street & number, municipality, postal code, telephone & fax numbers and e-mail address (if any).	*Lawyer's name & address — street & number, municipality, postal code, telephone & fax numbers and e-mail address (if any).*

Garnishee

Full legal name & address for service — street & number, municipality, postal code, telephone & fax numbers and e-mail address (if any).	*Lawyer's name & address — street & number, municipality, postal code, telephone & fax numbers and e-mail address (if any).*

1. I am a person who shares in the debt that the garnishee in this garnishment case is supposed to owe to the payor.

2. I make a claim on the money that the garnishee paid out and that is being temporarily held for the recipient's benefit as follows:
    (In separately numbered paragraphs, indicate the amount that you are claiming to be yours and set out the legal basis for your claim.)

1073

1.

Put a line through any blank space left on this page.

NOTE: Merely serving and filing this dispute will not stop the garnishment process. It can be stopped at the recipient's request if the recipient agrees with the reasons for your dispute. It can also be stopped by a court order at a garnishment hearing. If you want the court to hold a hearing, you must check the box in the frame below.

☐ **NOTICE TO THE CLERK OF THE COURT AND TO ALL PARTIES**: I am making a request for a garnishment hearing in which the court can rule on this dispute.

_____   _____
Signature of co-owner of debt   *Date of signature*

NOTICE TO RECIPIENT: Please examine this dispute. If you disagree with it, and the co-owner of the debt has not asked for a garnishment hearing, you yourself may ask to have a court hearing. You may want to talk to your own lawyer about this. You have 10 days from the date of being served with this document to decide whether to have a court hearing. If you want a hearing, you or your lawyer have 10 days within which to ask the clerk of the court, either in person or in writing, to mail out to you, to the payor, to the garnishee and to the co-owner of a joint debt (if any) a notice of garnishment hearing (Form 29H). At that hearing, the judge will give you and the other parties a chance to be heard and may make an order that can affect the rights of all parties.

Form 29H

Notice of Garnishment Hearing

ONTARIO

<table>
<tr><td>

(SEAL)

at
</td><td>

_____
(Name of Court)

_____
Court office address
</td><td>

Court File Number
_____

Form 29H: Notice of Garnishment Hearing
</td></tr>
</table>

Recipient(s)

Full legal name & address for service — street & number, municipality, postal code, telephone & fax numbers and e-mail address (if any).	Lawyer's name & address — street & number, municipality, postal code, telephone & fax numbers and e-mail address (if any).

Payor

Full legal name & address for service — street & number, municipality, postal code, telephone & fax numbers and e-mail address (if any).	Lawyer's name & address — street & number, municipality, postal code, telephone & fax numbers and e-mail address (if any).

Garnishee

Full legal name & address for service — street & number, municipality, postal code, telephone & fax numbers and e-mail address (if any).	Lawyer's name & address — street & number, municipality, postal code, telephone & fax numbers and e-mail address (if any).

TO THE PARTIES:

THE COURT WILL HOLD A HEARING on *(date)* _____ **, at** _____ **a.m./p.m.**

or as soon as possible after that time, at *(place of hearing)* because *(Check the appropriate box or boxes.)*

☐ a dispute has been filed by ☐ payor   ☐ garnishee   ☐ co-owner of a
the   debt

☐ it is claimed that the garnishee has not paid any money

☐ it is claimed that the garnishee has paid less than the required amount money

and the clerk of the court has received a request that a garnishment hearing be held.

IF YOU DO NOT COME TO COURT, AN ORDER MAY BE MADE WITHOUT YOU AND ENFORCED AGAINST YOU.

Date of signature

Signature of the clerk of the court

NOTE: Where a dispute has been served and filed, a photocopy of it should be attached to this notice. If it is missing, you should talk to the court office immediately.

Form 29I

Notice to Stop Garnishment

ONTARIO

Court File Number

_____
(Name of court)

Form 29I: Notice to Stop Garnishment

at _____
Court office address

Recipient(s)

Full legal name & address for service — street & number, municipality, postal code, telephone & fax numbers and e-mail address (if any).	Lawyer's name & address — street & number, municipality, postal code, telephone & fax numbers and e-mail address (if any).

Payor

Full legal name & address for service — street & number, municipality, postal code, telephone & fax numbers and e-mail address (if any).	Lawyer's name & address — street & number, municipality, postal code, telephone & fax numbers and e-mail address (if any).

Garnishee

Full legal name & address for service — street & number, municipality, postal code, telephone & fax numbers and e-mail address (if any).	Lawyer's name & address — street & number, municipality, postal code, telephone & fax numbers and e-mail address (if any).

TO: *(name of garnishee)* _____

AND TO: ☐ **THE CLERK OF THE COURT** ☐ **THE SHERIFF OF** *(area)* _____

My name is: *(full legal name)* _____

I am ☐ the person who asked for the garnishment in this case.

☐ the lawyer for the person who asked for the garnishment in this case.

☐ the person who continued this garnishment under a transfer of enforcement.

☐ the lawyer for the person who continued this garnishment under a transfer of enforcement.

☐ an agent for the Director of the Family Responsibility Office.

☐ *(Other. Specify.)* _____

The notice of garnishment issued on *(date)* _____ , by the clerk of the court is withdrawn today.

YOU ARE THEREFORE DIRECTED TO STOP FURTHER PAYMENTS UNDER THE GARNISHMENT.

_____   _____
Signature of person withdrawing   *Date of signature*
garnishment

Form 29J

Statement to Garnishee Financial Institution re Support

ONTARIO

	Court File Number

_____

(Name of court)

at _____

Court office address

Form 29J: Statement to Garnishee Financial Institution re Support

Recipient(s)

Full legal name & address for service — street & number, municipality, postal code, telephone & fax numbers and e-mail address (if any).	Lawyer's name & address — street & number, municipality, postal code, telephone & fax numbers and e-mail address (if any).

Payor

Full legal name & address for service — street & number, municipality, postal code, telephone & fax numbers and e-mail address (if any).	Lawyer's name & address — street & number, municipality, postal code, telephone & fax numbers and e-mail address (if any).

Garnishee

Full legal name & address for service — street & number, municipality, postal code, telephone & fax numbers and e-mail address (if any).	Lawyer's name & address — street & number, municipality, postal code, telephone & fax numbers and e-mail address (if any).

My name is (*full legal name*) _____

I live in (*municipality & province*) _____

The following statements are true to the best of my knowledge:

1. I am ☐ a recipient under a support order or the support provisions of a domestic contract that is enforceable by this court

    ☐ an assignee of a recipient under a support order or the support provisions of a domestic contract

    ☐ an agent of the Director of the Family Responsibility Office

2. The payor's full name is ☐ _____

    ☐ unknown.

3. The payor commonly uses the name(s): _____

Form 29J :	**Statement to Garnishee** **Financial Institution re Support**	**(page 2)**	Court File Number

(Either paragraph 4 or 5 must be completed. If both known, complete both)

4.   The payor's date of birth is

5.   The payor's social insurance number is

_____   _____
Date of signature   *Signature*

NOTE: *Under rule 29(6.1) of the Family Law Rules, this form (29J) must be attached to Forms 29A, 29B, 29D, 29E, 29G, 29H or 29I when they are served on a bank or other financial institution at a central location. Under regulations made under the federal Bank Act, Cooperative Credit Associations Act and Trust and Loan Companies Act, a notice of garnishment for support payments against a bank or other federally regulated financial institution must be served on a central location established and published by each bank or financial institution.*

Form 30

Notice of Default Hearing

ONTARIO

SEAL	Court File Number

at _____
(Name of court)

_____
Court office address

Form 30: Notice of Default Hearing

Recipient(s)

Full legal name & address for service — street & number, municipality, postal code, telephone & fax numbers and e-mail address (if any).	Lawyer's name & address — street & number, municipality, postal code, telephone & fax numbers and e-mail address (if any).

Payor

Full legal name & address for service — street & number, municipality, postal code, telephone & fax numbers and e-mail address (if any).	Lawyer's name & address — street & number, municipality, postal code, telephone & fax numbers and e-mail address (if any).

TO *(name of payor)* _____

YOU MUST COME TO COURT on *(date)* _____ **, at** _____ **a.m./p.m.**

or as soon after that time as the court can hear the matter, at *(place of hearing)*

_____

It is claimed by the recipient or on the recipient's behalf that you have missed support payments under an order or a domestic contract. Details of the claim against you can be found in the attached copy of the statement of money owed. If it is missing, you should contact the court office immediately. The court has been asked to hold a default hearing under section 41 of the *Family Responsibility and Support Arrears Enforcement Act*, in which you will be required to explain not only the missed payments mentioned in the statement of money owed, but also any payments missed right up to the day when the court holds the hearing.

> **YOU MUST FILL OUT the attached blank forms of the financial statement (Form 13) and the default dispute (Form 30B), serve a copy of the completed forms on the recipient's lawyer, or on the recipient if the recipient has no lawyer, or on the Director of the Family Responsibility Office, and then file the completed forms, together with proof of service (Form 6B), at the court office, all within 10 days after service of this notice on you. You can use any method of service allowed under rule 6 of the *Family Law Rules*, including mail, courier or fax. If the blank forms are missing, you must talk to the court office immediately.**

IF YOU DO NOT FILL OUT AND SERVE THE FINANCIAL STATEMENT OR IF YOU DO NOT COME TO COURT AS REQUIRED BY THIS NOTICE, A WARRANT MAY BE ISSUED FOR YOUR ARREST TO BRING YOU TO COURT.

You should bring with you to the default hearing any documents (such as cancelled cheques) that you need to prove that you made payments that are claimed to be missing. You may bring your own lawyer with you.

AT THE DEFAULT HEARING, THE COURT MAY MAKE AN ORDER AGAINST YOU, INCLUDING AN ORDER FOR YOUR IMPRISONMENT FOR UP TO 180 DAYS. YOU MAY ALSO BE ORDERED TO PAY COSTS.

IF YOU PAY THE AMOUNT OF THE MISSING PAYMENTS ON OR BEFORE THE DAY OF THE HEARING, YOU MAY STILL BE REQUIRED TO COME TO COURT AND TO PAY COSTS.

_____	_____
Date of signature	*Signature of clerk of the court*

Form 30A

Request for Default Hearing

ONTARIO

Court File Number

_____

(Name of court)

**Form 30A: Request
for Default Hearing**

at _____

Court office address

Recipient(s)

Full legal name & address for service — street & number, municipality, postal code, telephone & fax numbers and e-mail address (if any).	*Lawyer's name & address — street & number, municipality, postal code, telephone & fax numbers and e-mail address (if any).*

Payor

Full legal name & address for service — street & number, municipality, postal code, telephone & fax numbers and e-mail address (if any).	*Lawyer's name & address — street & number, municipality, postal code, telephone & fax numbers and e-mail address (if any).*

TO THE CLERK OF THE COURT:

1. I am ☐ the person who signed the attached statement of money owed.

    ☐ the lawyer for the person who signed the attached statement of money owed.

    ☐ *(Other; specify.)*

    _____

2. The payor has missed support payments in the amount of $ ...., as detailed in the attached statement of money owed.

3. I request that a notice of default hearing be issued requiring the payor to come to court to explain the missed payments at a hearing under section 41 of the *Family Responsibility and Support Arrears Enforcement Act*.

_____	_____
Signature	*Date of signature*

NOTE: *You must prepare and attach a fresh statement of money owed (one that has been prepared within the past 30 days) to this request when you file it with the clerk of the court. Then, in the week leading up to the default hearing, you must file an updated statement of money owed.*

Form 30B

Default Dispute

ONTARIO

	Court File Number

_____

(Name of court)

Form 30B:
Default Dispute

at _____

Court office address

Recipient(s)

Full legal name & address for service — street & number, municipality, postal code, telephone & fax numbers and e-mail address (if any).	Lawyer's name & address — street & number, municipality, postal code, telephone & fax numbers and e-mail address (if any).

Payor

Full legal name & address for service — street & number, municipality, postal code, telephone & fax numbers and e-mail address (if any).	Lawyer's name & address — street & number, municipality, postal code, telephone & fax numbers and e-mail address (if any).

My name is *(full legal name)* _____

I live in *(municipality & province)* _____

and I that the following is true:

1. I am the person named as payor in this case.

Check off and fill in appropriate paragraphs below. Paragraphs that do not apply to you may be struck out and initialled.

☐ 2. I have not missed any support payments as claimed in the statement of money owed because:
   (Set out your reasons for saying that there are no missed payments.)

☐ **3.** I do not owe the amount claimed in the statement of money owed. I owe instead the sum of $ _____ .

The reason for the difference in the amounts is:

(Set out your explanation, if any and if known, for the difference. If you have paid all the money that you claim to owe here, ignore and strike out paragraphs 4 and 5 below; if not, go to paragraph 5 to give your reasons for non-payment.)

☐ **4.** I owe the amount claimed in the statement of money owed. *(Go to paragraph 5 below to give your reasons for not paying.)*

☐ **5.** My reasons for not paying the money that I owe are: *(State your reasons.)*

Put a line through any blank space left on this page.

Put a line through any blank space left on this page.

Sworn/Affirmed before me at _____

municipality

in _____

province, state, or country

on _____   _____

date   *Commissioner for taking affidavits*

(Type or print name below if signature is illegible.)

_____

Signature

(This form is to be signed in front of a lawyer, justice of the peace, notary public or commissioner for taking affidavits.)

Form 31

Notice of Contempt Motion

ONTARIO

	Court File Number

_____

(Name of court)

at _____

Court office address

Applicant(s)/Recipient(s) *(Strike out inapplicable term.)*

Full legal name & address for service — street & number, municipality, postal code, telephone & fax numbers and e-mail address (if any).	*Lawyer's name & address — street & number, municipality, postal code, telephone & fax numbers and e-mail address (if any).*

Respondent/Payor *(Strike out inapplicable term.)*

Full legal name & address for service — street & number, municipality, postal code, telephone & fax numbers and e-mail address (if any).	*Lawyer's name & address — street & number, municipality, postal code, telephone & fax numbers and e-mail address (if any).*

TO: *(name of person against whom contempt motion is made)* _____

The person making this motion or the person's lawyer must contact the clerk of the court by telephone or otherwise to choose a time and date when the court could hear this motion

YOU MUST COME TO COURT AT *(place of hearing)*

_____

ON *(date)* _____ ,

at _____ **a.m. /p.m. and to remain until the court has dealt with the case.**

A motion will be made by *(moving party's name)* _____

for a finding that you are in contempt of the court because you: *(Briefly state details of contempt.)*

_____

The evidence against you is set out in the affidavit(s) attached to this notice. If the document(s) is/are missing, you must talk to the court office immediately.

IF YOU ARE FOUND IN CONTEMPT OF THE COURT, THE COURT MAY MAKE AN ORDER TO IMPRISON YOU, TO PAY A FINE AND TO TEMPORARILY SEIZE YOUR PROPERTY. YOU MAY ALSO BE ORDERED TO PAY COSTS.

IF YOU DO NOT COME TO COURT, A WARRANT MAY BE ISSUED FOR YOUR ARREST TO BRING YOU TO COURT.

Signature of person making this motion or of person's lawyer

Date of signature

Typed or printed name, address for service, telephone and fax numbers and e-mail address of person or of person's lawyer

Form 32

Bond (Recognizance)

ONTARIO

Form 32: Bond
(recognizance)

Court File Number

SEAL

_____
(Name of court)

at _____
Court office address

Applicant(s)/Recipient(s) *(Strike out inapplicable term.)*

Full legal name & address for service — street & number, municipality, postal code, telephone & fax numbers and e-mail address (if any).	Lawyer's name & address — street & number, municipality, postal code, telephone & fax numbers and e-mail address (if any).

Respondent/Payor *(Strike out inapplicable term.)*

Full legal name & address for service — street & number, municipality, postal code, telephone & fax numbers and e-mail address (if any).	Lawyer's name & address — street & number, municipality, postal code, telephone & fax numbers and e-mail address (if any).

TO THE COURT:

My name is *(full legal name)* ....

I live in *(municipality and province)* ....

I ACKNOWLEDGE THAT I OWE

☐   Her Majesty the Queen

☐   *(name of person who can legally collect the money from me)* the amount of $ . . . . ,   ☐   that will be immediately deposited in full with the clerk of the court by me or by one or more of my sureties and that will be forfeited,

                           ☐   that, by the court's permission, will not need to be deposited with the clerk of the court but that can be collected from me and from one or more of my sureties in the same way that an order for the payment of money may be enforced by this court,

if I do not comply with any one or more of the following conditions:
(List the conditions in numbered paragraphs. Indicate the duration of each condition with the words, "... until [expiry date]" or a similar phrase wherever the judge has imposed an expiry date.)

Put a line through any blank space left on this page or on the reverse page.

NOTE: A recognizance must be signed in front of the clerk of the court or the judge. No seal is needed for a bond

_____
Signature of person under bond (recognizance)

(Complete the following unless the court did not require any surety. No seals are needed for a bond.)

By signing below, each surety agrees to become indebted in the same way as the person giving the bond or recognizance if that person does not comply with the terms on this form.

Full legal name and address of first surety	*Full legal name and address of second surety*
_____ *Signature of first surety*	_____ *Signature of second surety*
Full legal name and address of third surety	*Full legal name and address of fourth surety*
_____ *Signature of third surety*	_____ *Signature of fourth surety*

If this form is a recognizance, the following must be completed.
This recognizance was signed before me at *(municipality)*

....   _____
                                                                      Signature of judge or clerk of the court

on *(date)* ....

NOTE TO THE BOND GIVER AND TO ANY SURETY: If there is a material change in circumstances, you may make a motion to the court to change any condition of this bond (recognizance).

Form 32.1

Request to Enforce a Family Arbitration Award

ONTARIO

	Court File Number
_____ *(Name of court)*	
at _____ *Court office address*	**Form 32.1: Request to Enforce a Family Arbitration Award**

Applicant(s)

Full legal name & address for service – street & number, municipality, postal code, telephone & fax numbers and e-mail address (if any).	Lawyer's name & address – street & number, municipality, postal code, telephone & fax numbers and e-mail address (if any).

Respondent(s)

Full legal name & address for service – street & number, municipality, postal code, telephone & fax numbers and e-mail address (if any).	Lawyer's name & address – street & number, municipality, postal code, telephone & fax numbers and e-mail address (if any).

TO THE RESPONDENT(S):

A CASE HAS BEEN STARTED IN THIS COURT TO ENFORCE THE TERMS OF A FAMILY ARBITRATION AWARD THAT RELATES TO YOU. THE DETAILS ARE SET OUT ON THE ATTACHED PAGES.

IF YOU WANT TO OPPOSE THIS REQUEST, you or your lawyer must complete Form 32.1A: Dispute of Request for Enforcement (a blank copy should be attached), serve a copy on the applicant(s) and file a copy in the court office with an Affidavit of Service (Form 6A). **YOU HAVE ONLY 30 DAYS AFTER THIS REQUEST IS SERVED ON YOU (60 DAYS IF THE APPLICATION IS SERVED ON YOU OUTSIDE CANADA OR THE UNITED STATES) TO SERVE AND FILE THE DISPUTE. IF YOU DO NOT, THE CASE WILL GO AHEAD WITHOUT YOU AND THE COURT MAY MAKE AN ORDER AND ENFORCE IT AGAINST YOU.**

YOU SHOULD GET LEGAL ADVICE ABOUT THIS CASE RIGHT AWAY. If you cannot afford a lawyer, you may be able to get help from your local Legal Aid Ontario Office. (See your telephone directory under LEGAL AID.)

_____   _____
Date of Issue   *Clerk of the Court*

My name is *(full legal name)* _____

I live in *(municipality & province)* _____

And I swear/affirm that the following is true:

1. I attach a copy of a family arbitration agreement (attach certificates of independent legal advice for both parties)

    between myself and the Respondent that I signed on *(date)* _____ appointing

    (name) _____ to arbitrate the following issues:

    ☐ child custody/access   ☐ child support   ☐ spousal support   ☐ division of property

    ☐ other _____

2. The family arbitration agreement has not been set aside or changed in any way.

3. The arbitration was conducted in *(location)* _____

   on the following dates: _____

4. A family arbitration award was made
   on _____ *(date)* _____ . Attached is a copy of the award

   and the arbitrator's written reasons for it.

5. The family arbitration award has not been changed since it was issued.

6. ☐ Neither party to the arbitration agreement has sought to appeal or set aside the family arbitration award
      or brought any other proceeding relating to this arbitration.

   or

   ☐ Details of any steps taken by either party to appeal or set aside the family arbitration award or to have
      the arbitration declared invalid are as follows:

7. I am seeking a court order as set out in paragraphs _____ *(select particular clauses from the arbitration award)*
   _____ of the family arbitration award.

8. I am seeking an order for child support in accordance with the provisions of the family arbitration award.
   Additional information regarding that claim is set out in the FAMILY HISTORY section below.

   ☐ This amount is the table amount listed in the *Child Support Guidelines.*

   ☐ This amount is more than the table amount listed in the *Child Support Guidelines.*

   ☐ This amount is less than the table amount listed in the *Child Support Guidelines* for the following reasons:

9. Additional information that is important to this case is as follows:

Sworn/Affirmed before me
at _____
                       municipality

in _____
              province, state, or country

on _____   _____   _____
        date   *Commissioner for taking affidavits*   *Signature*
                        (Type or print name below if signature is illegible.)   *(This form is to be signed in front of a lawyer,*
                                                                justice of the peace, notary public or
                                                                commissioner for taking affidavits.)

Note: *If you are seeking an order that incorporates clauses relating to the custody of or access to a child, you must also serve and file a completed Form 35.1: Affidavit in Support of Claim for Custody or Access.*

FAMILY HISTORY

APPLICANT: Birthdate: *(d, m, y)* _____

RESPONDENT: Birthdate: *(d, m, y)* _____

RELATIONSHIP DATES:

☐ Married on *(date)* _____   ☐ Started living together on *(date)* _____

☐ Separated on *(date)* _____   ☐ Never lived together   ☐ Still living together

---

THE CHILD(REN)

List all children involved in this case, even if no claim is made for these children.

Full legal name	Age	Birthdate (d, m, y)	Resident in (municipality & province)	Now Living With (name of person and relationship to child)

IF CHILD SUPPORT IS TO BE PAID:

The ☐ Applicant ☐ Respondent   is to pay child support for the following children:

This child support is based on the ☐ Applicant's ☐ Respondent's   annual income(s) of $ _____

The special or extraordinary expenses for the children, if any, are as follows:

The ☐ Applicant ☐ Respondent   will pay _____ percent of the above expenses, or

$ _____ per _____ .

For information on accessibility of court services for
people with disability-related needs, contact:

Telephone: 416-326-2220 / 1-800-518-7901   TTY: 416-326-4012 / 1-877-425-0575

1094

Form 32.1A

Dispute of Request for Enforcement

ONTARIO

	Court File Number

_____

(Name of court)

at _____   **Form 32.1A: Dispute of Request for**

Court office address   **Enforcement**

Applicant(s)

Full legal name & address for service – street & number, municipality, postal code, telephone & fax numbers and e-mail address (if any).	Lawyer's name & address – street & number, municipality, postal code, telephone & fax numbers and e-mail address (if any).

Respondent(s)

Full legal name & address for service – street & number, municipality, postal code, telephone & fax numbers and e-mail address (if any).	Lawyer's name & address – street & number, municipality, postal code, telephone & fax numbers and e-mail address (if any).

My name is   *(full legal name)*   _____

I live in   *(municipality & province)*   _____

And I swear/affirm that the following is true:

1. I am the Respondent in this case.

2. I do not agree with the Applicant's request to enforce the terms of the family arbitration award dated

   _____

   (select the particular paragraphs of the request that you are

3. I dispute paragraphs   *disputing)* _____

   of the Applicant's Form 32.1: Request to Enforce a Family Arbitration Award for the following reasons:

4. ☐ The Applicant's FAMILY HISTORY is correct.

   ☐ The Applicant's FAMILY HISTORY is incorrect and should be corrected as follows:

Sworn/Affirmed before me at _____

                                                    municipality

in _____

                        province, state, or country

on _____   _____   _____
         date   *Commissioner for taking affidavits*   *Signature*
                           (Type or print name below if signature is illegible.)   *(This form is to be signed in front of a lawyer,*
                                                                                    justice of the peace, notary public or
                                                                                    commissioner for taking affidavits.)

     For information on accessibility of court services for
                              people with disability-related needs, contact:
                 elephone: 416-326-2220 / 1-800-518-7901   TTY: 416-326-4012 / 1-877-425-0575

Form 32A

Notice of Forfeiture Motion

ONTARIO

	Court File Number

_____

(Name of court)

at _____

Court office address

Form 32A: Notice of Forfeiture Motion

Applicant(s)/Recipient(s) *(Strike out inapplicable term.)*

Full legal name & address for service — street & number, municipality, postal code, telephone & fax numbers and e-mail address (if any).	Lawyer's name & address — street & number, municipality, postal code, telephone & fax numbers and e-mail address (if any).

Respondent/Payor *(Strike out inapplicable term.)*

Full legal name & address for service — street & number, municipality, postal code, telephone & fax numbers and e-mail address (if any).	Lawyer's name & address — street & number, municipality, postal code, telephone & fax numbers and e-mail address (if any).

TO: *(name of person who entered into recognizance or who posted bond)* _____

AND TO: *(name of surety or sureties)* _____

The person making this motion or the person's lawyer must contact the clerk of the court by telephone or otherwise to choose a time and date when the court could hear this motion

THE COURT WILL HEAR A MOTION ON *(date)* ...., **at** .... **a.m./p.m., or as soon as possible after that time at** *(place of hearing)*

_____

The motion is being made by *(moving party's name)* _____
who will be asking the court to make an order of forfeiture in respect of

☐ a recognizance entered into ☐ a bond posted

by *(name of person who entered into recognizance or who posted bond)* _____

on *(date)* _____ A copy of the bond/recognizance should be attached to this notice. Details of the grounds of the motion are set out in the affidavit(s) that accompany this notice. If the document(s) is/are missing, you should talk to the court office immediately.

IF YOU DO NOT COME TO COURT FOR THIS MOTION, AN ORDER OF FORFEITURE MAY BE MADE WITHOUT YOU AND MAY BE ENFORCED AGAINST YOU.

_____
Signature of person making this motion or of person's lawyer

_____
Date of signature

Typed or printed name, address for service, telephone and fax numbers and e-mail address (if any) of person or of person's lawyer

Form 32B

Warrant for Arrest

ONTARIO

	Court File Number

SEAL

_____
(Name of court)

Form 32B: Warrant for Arrest

at _____
Court office address

TO ALL PEACE OFFICERS IN THE PROVINCE OF ONTARIO:

I COMMAND YOU TO ARREST *(name of person to be arrested)* _____

on the grounds that this person is:

☐ a payor who has failed to file a financial statement at the request of the Director of the Family Responsibility Office.
*See subsection 40(4) of the **Family Responsibility and Support Arrears Enforcement Act**.*

☐ a payor who has failed to file a financial statement, as required by a notice of default hearing.
*See subsection 41(7) of the **Family Responsibility and Support Arrears Enforcement Act**.*

☐ a payor who has failed to appear before the court to explain a default in a support order or domestic contract that is enforceable in this court, as required by a notice of default hearing.
*See subsection 41(7) of the **Family Responsibility and Support Arrears Enforcement Act**.*

☐ a payor who is about to leave Ontario intending to evade his or her responsibilities under a support order or domestic contract that is enforceable in this court.
*See subsection 49(1) of the **Family Responsibility and Support Arrears Enforcement Act**.*

☐ a respondent in an application for support who is about to leave Ontario, intending to evade his or her responsibilities under the *Family Law Act*.
*See subsection 43(1) of the **Family Law Act**.*

☐ a respondent in an application to incorporate a paternity agreement in an order of the court, who is about to leave Ontario, intending to evade his or her responsibilities under the agreement.
*See subsection 59(2) of the **Family Law Act**.*

☐ a witness whose presence is necessary to determine an issue in a proceeding, who has been served with a summons to witness and who has failed to attend or to remain in attendance as required by the summons to witness.
*See subrules 20(9), 23(7) and 27(19) of the **Family Law Rules**.*

☐ a person who has failed to appear at a proceeding that may result in an order requiring him or her to enter into a recognizance or to post a bond.
*See rule 32(1) of the **Family Law Rules**.*

☐ a person who has failed to enter into a recognizance or to post a bond as required by an order of this court.
*See rule 32(1) of the **Family Law Rules**.*

☐ a person against whom a motion for contempt of the court is brought, whose attendance at the motion for contempt is necessary in the interests of the justice and who appears not likely to appear voluntarily at the motion.
*See subrule 31(4) of the **Family Law Rules**.*

☐ *(Other. Specify the grounds and the statutory of regulatory authority to issue this warrant.)*

AND I FURTHER COMMAND YOU to bring this person immediately to court in the municipality in which he or she may be found to be dealt with according to law, and if the court is not then sitting, to bring this person to a justice of the peace as soon as possible to be dealt with according to law.

_____
Signature of judge

_____
Date of issue

_____
Print or type name of judge

_____
Date on which this warrant expires

FLR 32B (April 12, 2016)

Page 1 of 2

(Insert all available information)

Full legal name of person to be arrested				Birth date (d,m,y)		Sex
Aliases or nicknames						
Residential address				Telephone number		
Employment address				Telephone number		
Height	Weight	Hair colour	Hair style	Eye colour		Complexion
Driver's licence			Year, make and model of automobile			
Licence plate & province			Social insurance number			
Clubs, associations or union affiliation						
Most recent date & occasion when residential address was verified by personal service						
Name & address of person to be contacted for further information				Telephone number		

(Name of court)

Court office address

WARRANT OF ARREST

I have informed this arrested person of his/her right to a lawyer.

Date of arrest

Signature of arresting officer

Printed name of arresting officer

(In space below, set out address and telephone number where arresting officer may be contacted.)

FLR 32B (April 12, 2016)

Form 32C

Affidavit for Warrant of Committal

ONTARIO

_____
(Name of court)

Court File Number

at _____
Court office address

**Form 32C: Affidavit for
Warrant of Committal**

dated _____

Applicant(s)/Recipient(s) *(Strike out inapplicable term.)*

Full legal name & address for service — street & number, municipality, postal code, telephone & fax numbers and e-mail address (if any).	Lawyer's name & address — street & number, municipality, postal code, telephone & fax numbers and e-mail address (if any).

Respondent/Payor *(Strike out inapplicable term.)*

Full legal name & address for service — street & number, municipality, postal code, telephone & fax numbers and e-mail address (if any).	Lawyer's name & address — street & number, municipality, postal code, telephone & fax numbers and e-mail address (if any).

My name is *(full legal name)* _____

I live in *(municipality & province)* _____

and I swear/affirm that the following is true:

1. I am
   ☐ a recipient under a payment order.
   ☐ an assignee of a recipient under a payment order.
   ☐ an agent of the Director of the Family Responsibility Office.
   ☐ *(Other; specify.)*

2. I am the person who
   ☐ asked the payor to file a financial statement.
   ☐ asked the payor to come to a financial examination.
   ☐ began a default hearing against the payor.
   ☐ made a contempt motion.
   ☐ *(Other; specify.)*

3. I make this motion to ask the court to issue a warrant of committal.

4. On *(date)* _____ , the court made an order of imprisonment,
a photocopy of which is attached to this affidavit, committing

☐ the payor to prison for disobeying the court's order to file a financial statement,

☐ the payor to prison for disobeying the court's order or direction about a financial examination,

☐ the payor to prison for missing support payments,

☐ *(name)* .... to prison for contempt of court,

☐ *(Other; specify.)*

for a period of .... days, but the committal was suspended on certain conditions set out in the order of imprisonment.

5. The respondent/payor was

☐ in court or his/her lawyer or agent was in court when this order of conditional imprisonment was made.

☐ not in court nor was his/her lawyer or agent in court when the order of conditional imprisonment was made, but the order was served on him/her on *(date)*
....

6. The conditions that were broken and the circumstances of the breach are as follows: *(Set out conditions of the suspended imprisonment that were broken and details of the breach.)*

☐ Payment of the sum of $ .... was due by *(date)* ....
but no payment was made by that day.

☐ Payment of the sum of $ .... was due by *(date)* ....
but only a partial payment of $ .... was made by that day.

☐ *(Other; specify.)*

Put a line through any blank space left on this page.

1101

Sworn/Affirmed before me at ....
                                    Municipality

in   _____

            province, state, or country

                                                            Signature
                                                    (This form is to be signed in
on   _____   *front of a lawyer, justice of the*
        date   *Commissioner for taking*   *peace, notary public or*
                              affidavits   *commissioner for taking*
                        (Type or print name below if   *affidavits.)*
                          signature is Ilegible.)

Note to Moving Party: You must attach a photocopy of the court's order of conditional imprisonment to this affidavit.

Form 32D

Warrant of Committal

ONTARIO

	Court File Number

(SEAL)

at _____
(Name of court)

_____
Court office address

Form 32D: Warrant
of Committal

TO ALL PEACE OFFICERS IN THE PROVINCE OF ONTARIO;

AND TO THE OFFICERS OF THE: *(name and address of correctional institution)*

_____

THIS WARRANT IS FOR THE COMMITTAL OF *(full legal name of person to be imprisoned)*

_____

THIS COURT FOUND THAT this person:

☐ disobeyed the court's order to file a financial statement;

☐ disobeyed the court's order or direction about a financial examination;

☐ without valid reason missed support payments as required by an order or domestic contract resulting in an order being made under the *Family Responsibility and Support Arrears Enforcement Act, 1996*;

☐ was in contempt of court;

☐ other *(Specify.)*

AS PUNISHMENT, THE COURT COMMITTED THIS PERSON to prison for a term of _____ days, to be served,

☐ continuously

☐ intermittently on *(pattern of intermittent sentence)* _____

and to be served   ☐   consecutively with any other term of imprisonment now being served or about to be served.

☐   *(Set out alternative arrangement with respect to other terms of imprisonment.)*

Check one
or both
boxes as
appropriate.
Otherwise
strike out
and initial.

☐ **AND THE COURT DIRECTED THAT** this order of imprisonment be suspended on one or more conditions. The court later found that this person broke one or more of the conditions and, as a result, the court has ordered the removal of the suspension from the order of imprisonment;

☐ **AND THE COURT ORDERED THAT** this person be subject to immediate release from custody upon receipt by the officers of the correctional institution or other secure facility of the sum of

(specify amount) $ _____ .

I THEREFORE COMMAND YOU TO BRING THIS PERSON SAFELY TO THE CORRECTIONAL INSTITUTION OR SECURE FACILITY NAMED ABOVE AND TO DELIVER HIM/HER TO THE OFFICERS OF THAT INSTITUTION OR FACILITY, TOGETHER WITH THIS WARRANT.

AND I COMMAND YOU, THE OFFICERS OF THE CORRECTIONAL INSTITUTION OR SECURE FACILITY, TO ADMIT THIS PERSON INTO CUSTODY IN YOUR INSTITUTION OR FACILITY AND TO DETAIN HIM/HER THERE UNTIL THIS WARRANT EXPIRES.

This warrant expires,

(a) in a case under the *Family Responsibility and Support Arrears Enforcement Act, 1996*, when this person has completed the prescribed term of imprisonment; or

(b) in other cases, when this person has completed the prescribed term of imprisonment, subject to section 28 (remission of sentence) of the *Ministry of Correctional Services Act*; or

(c) when you, the officers of the correctional institution or secure facility, receive the sum named above; or

(d) upon further order of this court,

whichever event happens first.

_____   _____
       Signature of judge   Date of issue

_____
       Print or type name of judge

NOTE: *Completion of the prescribed term of imprisonment does not discharge arrears of support or maintenance. A description of the person to be imprisoned is set out on page 2 of this warrant.*

FLR 32D (April 12, 2016)

Page 1 of 2

(Insert all available information)

Full legal name of person to be arrested				Birth date (d, m, y)		Sex
Aliases or nicknames						
Residential address				Telephone number		
Employment address				Telephone number		
Height	Weight	Hair colour	Hair style	Eye colour	Complexion	
Driver's licence			Year, make and model of automobile			
Licence plate & province			Social insurance number			
Clubs, associations or union affiliation						
Most recent date & occasion when residential address was verified by personal service				Family Responsibility Office Case No. (if applicable)		
Name & address of person to be contacted for further information				Telephone number		

(Name of court)

Court office address

WARRANT OF COMMITTAL

Form 33

Information for Warrant to Bring a Child to a Place of Safety

ONTARIO

Court File Number

at _____ *(Name of court)*

_____
Court office address

Form 33: Information for Warrant to Bring a Child to a Place of Safety

My name is *(full legal name)* _____

I live in *(municipality & province)* _____

and I swear/affirm that the following is true:

1. I am ☐ a child protection worker employed by *(full legal name of children's aid society)* _____

   ☐ *(Give occupation or title.)* _____
   a peace officer in the province of Ontario, employed in *(name of office out of which you work)* _____

2. I have reasonable and probable grounds to believe and do believe that *(child's full legal name)* _____

   is younger than 16 and is a child in need of protection for the following reasons: *(Set out grounds for belief.)*

3. I have reasonable and probable grounds to believe and do believe that a course of action less restrictive than the child's removal to a place of safety is not available or will not adequately protect the child, for the following reasons: *(Set out grounds for belief.)*

Strike out paragraph 4 if not applicable.

4. I have reasonable and probable grounds to believe that the child may be found at
   (Give full municipal address or a precise description of the premises where the child may be located.)

Put a line through any blank space left on this page.

Sworn/Affirmed before me at _____
municipality

in _____
province, state, or country

on _____
date

_____
Commissioner for taking affidavits
(Type or print name below if signature is illegible.)

_____
Signature
(This form is to be signed in front of a lawyer, justice of the peace, notary public or commissioner for taking affidavits.)

Form 33A

Warrant to Bring a Child to a Place of Safety

ONTARIO

	Court File Number
_____ *(Name of court)*	Form 33A: Warrant to Bring a Child to a Place of Safety
at _____ *Court office address*	

TO ALL CHILD PROTECTION WORKERS AND PEACE OFFICERS IN THE PROVINCE OF ONTARIO:

On the basis of an information sworn before me under Part V of the *Child, Youth and Family Services Act, 2017* respecting the child named or described at the bottom of this warrant, I am satisfied that there are reasonable and probable grounds to believe:

    (a)   that the child is younger than 16;

    (b)   that the child is in need of protection; and

    (c)   that a course of action less restrictive than the child's removal to a place of safety is not available or will not adequately protect the child.

Check box below only if the child's whereabouts are known. Otherwise, strike out the paragraph below and initial the deletion.

☐   I am further satisfied, on the basis of that information, that the child may now be found at *(Give full municipal address or a precise description of the premises where the child may be located.)*

_____

I THEREFORE AUTHORIZE YOU TO BRING THIS CHILD to a "place of safety" within the meaning of the *Child, Youth and Family Services Act, 2017.*

This warrant expires at _____ on *(date)* _____

_____ Signature of justice of the peace	_____ Date of signature
_____ Print or type name of justice of the peace	_____ Municipality where this warrant was signed

NOTE: *Any changes, alterations or corrections to this form must be initialled by the justice of the peace.* **It is a criminal offence for any other person to change the wording of this warrant after it has been signed by the justice of the peace.**

DESCRIPTION: *Insert all available information*

Full legal name of child to be brought to a place of safety				Birth date (d,m,y)	Sex
Aliases or nicknames					
Residential address				Telephone number	
Present whereabouts of child				Telephone number	
Height	Weight	Hair colour	Hair style	Eye colour	Complexion
Other features					
Name & address of person to be contacted for further information				Telephone number	

Error! Reference source not found.
(Name of court)

at

_____

Court office address

WARRANT TO BRING A CHILD TO A PLACE OF SAFETY

Form 33B

Plan of Care for Child(ren) (Children's Aid Society)

ONTARIO

	Court File Number

_____
(Name of court)

at _____
Court office address

Form 33B: Plan of
Care for Child(ren)
(Children's Aid Society)

Applicant(s) *(In most cases, the applicant will be a children's aid society.)*

Full legal name & address for service — street & number, municipality, postal code, telephone & fax numbers and e-mail address (if any).	Lawyer's name & address — street & number, municipality, postal code, telephone & fax numbers and e-mail address (if any).

Respondent(s) *(In most cases, a respondent will be a "parent" within the meaning of section 74 of the Child, Youth and Family Services Act, 2017)*

Full legal name & address for service — street & number, municipality, postal code, telephone & fax numbers and e-mail address (if any).	Lawyer's name & address — street & number, municipality, postal code, telephone & fax numbers and e-mail address (if any).

Children's Lawyer

Name & address of Children's Lawyer's agent for service (street & number, municipality, postal code, telephone & fax numbers and e-mail address (if any)) and name of person represented.

Fill out only those paragraphs that apply and strike out others.

1. I am/We are *(full legal name)* _____

    and I am/we are *(state your position with children's aid society)* _____

2. The child(ren) in this case is/are:

Child's Full Legal Name	Birthdate	Sex

3. ☐ After the court makes a finding that the child(ren) is/are in need of protection under Part V of the *Child, Youth and Family Services Act, 2017*, I/we ask the court to make an order.

    ☐ The court previously found on *(date)* _____ that the child(ren) was/were in

    need of protection under Part V of the *Child, Youth and Family Services Act, 2017*, and the court made an

    order on *(date)* _____ . I/We now ask the court to make a further order.

    The details of the order that I/we now ask the court to make are as follows: *(Give details of the order you now want the court to make. If you want the order to include any supervision by the children's aid society, give details of any terms and conditions of supervision.)*

Put a line through any blank space left on this page.

Form 33B:	Plan of Care for Child(ren) (Children's Aid Society)	(page 2)	Court File Number

4. The services that the family and child(ren) need and that will be provided are as follows: *(Give details of the service needed, who needs it and who will be providing it.)*

5. The children's aid society expects the respondent(s) to carry out certain conditions before it would feel that supervision or society care of the child(ren) is no longer needed. Very serious consequences could result if those conditions are broken. These conditions are: *(Set out conditions and estimate the time needed to achieve them.)*

Put a line through any blank space left on this page.

FLR 33B (March 1, 2018)

Form 33B:	Plan of Care for Child(ren) (Children's Aid Society)	(page 3)	Court File Number

6. The child(ren) cannot be adequately protected while in the care of the respondent(s) because: *(State reasons.)*

7. The following efforts have been made in the past to protect the child(ren) while in the care of the respondent(s): *(Describe the efforts made. If no efforts were made, give explanation.)*

8. The following efforts are planned to keep up the child(ren)'s contact with the respondent(s): *(Describe plans. Write "Nil" if there are no plans.)*

9. The following arrangements have been or are being made to recognize the importance of the child's culture and to preserve his/her heritage, traditions and cultural identity:

Put a line through any blank space left on this page.

FLR 33B (March 1, 2018)

Form 33B:	Plan of Care for Child(ren) (Children's Aid Society)	(page 4)	Court File Number

PART 3

10. The children's aid society has removed the child(ren) from the care of the respondent(s) and intends to make

this removal ☐ temporary.

☐ permanent. *(If the children's aid society is not seeking an order of extended society care, please provide details of the efforts by the children's aid society to provide a long-term, stable placement for the child.)*

11. *(To be completed if the children's aid society is seeking an order of extended society care.)*

Efforts will be made to assist the child to develop a positive, secure and enduring relationship within a family through one of the following methods:

☐ adoption   ☐ a custody order under s. 116(1)   ☐ a plan for customary care

☐ other *(Please provide available details.)*

12. This plan of care was served on and its details explained to the respondent(s) and others named below:

Print name of person to whom this plan was explained	Print name of person who explained plan	Date of explanation

Put a line through any blank space left on this page.

Date of signature	Signature

Date of signature	Signature

Form 33B.1

Answer and Plan of Care (Parties other than Children's Aid Society)

ONTARIO

_____	**Court File Number**
(Name of court)	
at _____	**Form 33B.1: Answer and Plan of Care (Parties other than Children's Aid Society)**
Court office address	

Applicant(s)

Full legal name & address for service — street & number, municipality, postal code, telephone & fax numbers and e-mail address (if any).	*Lawyer's name & address — street & number, municipality, postal code, telephone & fax numbers and e-mail address (if any).*

Respondent(s)

Full legal name & address for service — street & number, municipality, postal code, telephone & fax numbers and e-mail address (if any).	*Lawyer's name & address — street & number, municipality, postal code, telephone & fax numbers and e-mail address (if any).*

Children's Lawyer

Name & address for service for Children's Lawyer's agent — street & number, municipality, postal code, telephone & fax numbers and e-mail address (if any)) and name of person represented.

TO THE APPLICANT(S):

(Note to the respondent(s): If you are making a claim against someone who is not an applicant, insert the person's name and address here.)

AND TO: *(full legal name)* _____ **, an added respondent,**

of *(address for service of added party)*

(Note to the respondent(s): You must complete, serve, file and update this form if any significant changes regarding the child(ren)occur after you sign this form.)

I am/We are *(full legal name(s))* _____

and I am/we are *(state your relationship to the child(ren))*

Form 33B.1: **Answer and Plan of Care (Parties other** **(page 2)**
than Children's Aid Society)

Court File Number

PART 1

1.   The child(ren) in this case is/are:

Child's Full Legal Name	Birthdate	Age	Sex	Full Legal Name(s) of Parent(s)	Is the Child First Nations, Inuk, or Métis?	Child's Bands and First Nations, Inuit, or Métis Communities

2.   The following people have had the child(ren) in their care and custody during the past year:

Child's Name	Name of Other Caregiver(s)	Period of Time with Caregiver(s) (d,m,y to d,m,y)

Form 33B.1:	Answer and Plan of Care (Parties other (page 3) than Children's Aid Society)	Court File Number

PART 2

3. If this is a child protection application, complete this Part, then go to Part 4. *(If this is a status review, complete Part 3, then go to Part 4.)*

    (Check applicable box(es).)

    ☐ I/We agree with the following facts in

    ☐ paragraph 6 of the application (Form 8B).

    ☐ paragraph 3 of the application (Form 8B.1).

    (Refer to the numbered paragraph(s) under paragraph 6/paragraph 3 of the application.)

    ☐ I/We disagree with the following facts in

    ☐ paragraph 6 of the application (Form 8B).

    ☐ paragraph 3 of the application (Form 8B.1).

    (Refer to the numbered paragraph(s) under paragraph 6/paragraph 3 of the application.)

NOTE: *If you intend to dispute the children's aid society's position at the temporary care and custody hearing, an affidavit in Form 14A **MUST** also be served on the parties and filed at court.*

(Attach an additional page and number it if you need more space.)

Form 33B.1: Answer and Plan of Care (Parties other (page 4) than Children's Aid Society)

Court File Number

PART 3

4. If this is a status review, complete this Part, then go to Part 4. *(If this is a protection application, complete Part 2, then go to Part 4.)*

   (Check applicable box(es).)

   ☐ I/We agree with the following facts in

       ☐ paragraph 6 of the application (Form 8B).

       ☐ paragraph 3 of the application (Form 8B.1).

       (Refer to the numbered paragraph(s) under paragraph 6/paragraph 3 of the application.)

   ☐ I/We disagree with the following facts in

       ☐ paragraph 6 of the application (Form 8B).

       ☐ paragraph 3 of the application (Form 8B.1).

       (Refer to the numbered paragraph(s) under paragraph 6/paragraph 3 of the application.)

(Attach an additional page and number it if you need more space.)

FLR 33B.1 (March 1, 2018)

Form 33B.1:	Answer and Plan of Care (Parties other (page 5) than Children's Aid Society)	Court File Number

PART 4

5. What placement and terms of placement do you believe would be in the child(ren)'s best interests? *(You should include in your plan of care at least the following information. If your plan is not the same for a particular child, then complete a separate plan for that child.)*

    (a)   *Where will you live?*

    (b)   *Who, if anyone, will live with you?*

    (c)   *Where will the child(ren) live?*

    (d)   *What school or daycare will the child(ren) attend?*

    (e)   *What days and hours will the child(ren) attend school or daycare?*

    (f)   *Are you enrolled in school or counselling?*

    (g)   *If you are enrolled in counselling, where do you attend counselling?*

    (h)   *What support services will you be using for the child(ren)?*

    (i)   *Do you have support from your family or community?*

    (j)   *If you have support from your family or community, who will help you and how will they help you?*

    (k)   *What will the child(ren)'s activities be?*

    (l)   *What will your source of income be?*

    (m)   *Do you go to work or school?*

    (n)   *If you go to work or school, what are the details, including the days and hours you work or go to school, and who will look after your child(ren) while you are there?*

    (o)   *State why you feel that this plan would be in the child(ren)'s best interests. (Attach an additional page and number it if you need more space.)*

Form 33B.1: Answer and Plan of Care (Parties other (page 6) than Children's Aid Society)

6. These are the people who have information that would support my plan:

Name	Information

(Attach an additional page and number it if you need more space.)

Form 33B.1: Answer and Plan of Care (Parties other **(page 7)** than Children's Aid Society)

Court File Number

PART 5

Claims by Respondent(s)

(Fill out a separate claim page for each person against whom you are making a claim(s).)

7. **THIS CLAIM IS MADE AGAINST**

☐ **THE CHILDREN'S AID SOCIETY (OR OTHER APPLICANT)**

☐ **AN ADDED PARTY**, whose name is *(full legal name)* _____

(If you claim against an added party, make sure that the person's name appears on page 1 of this form.)

8. **I/WE ASK THE COURT FOR THE FOLLOWING ORDER:**

(Claims below include claims for temporary orders.)

Claims relating to child protection
☐ access
☐ lesser protection order
☐ return of child(ren) to my/our care
☐ place child(ren) into the custody of *(name)* _____
(s. 102, deemed custody order under the Children's Law Reform Act)
☐ place child(ren) into the custody of *(name)* _____
(s. 116(1)(b), custody order for child formerly in extended society care)
☐ interim society care for _____ months
☐ place child(ren) into the care and custody of *(name)* _____ subject to society supervision
☐ costs
☐ other *(Specify.)* _____

Give details of the order that you want the court to make. *(Include the name(s) of the child(ren) for whom custody or access is claimed.)*

IMPORTANT FACTS SUPPORTING MY/OUR CLAIM(S)

(In numbered paragraphs, set out the facts that form the legal basis for your claim(s). Attach an additional page and number it if you need more space.)

Put a line through any space left on this page.

_____
Date of signature

_____
Signature

_____
Date of signature

_____
Signature

Form 33B.2

Answer (*Child, Youth and Family Services Act, 2017* Cases other than Child Protection and Status Review)

ONTARIO

	Court File Number

_____
(Name of court)

Form 33B.2: Answer (*Child, Youth and Family Services Act, 2017* Cases other than Child Protection and Status Review)

at _____
Court office address

Applicant(s)

Full legal name & address for service — street & number, municipality, postal code, telephone & fax numbers and e-mail address (if any).	Lawyer's name & address — street & number, municipality, postal code, telephone & fax numbers and e-mail address (if any).

Respondent(s)

Full legal name & address for service — street & number, municipality, postal code, telephone & fax numbers and e-mail address (if any).	Lawyer's name & address — street & number, municipality, postal code, telephone & fax numbers and e-mail address (if any).

Children's Lawyer

Name & address for service for Children's Lawyer's agent - street & number, municipality, postal code, telephone & fax numbers and e-mail address (if any) and name of person represented.

TO THE APPLICANT(S):

(Note to the respondent(s): If you are making a claim against someone who is not an applicant, insert the person's name and address here.)

AND TO: *(full legal name)* _____ **, an added respondent,**

of *(address for service of added party)*

(Note to the respondent(s): You must complete, serve, file and update this form if any significant changes regarding the child(ren) occur after you sign this form.)

I am/We are *(full legal name(s))* _____

and I am/we are *(state your relationship to the child(ren))*

Form 33B.2: Answer (*Child, Youth and Family Services Act, 2017* Cases other than Child Protection and Status Review)   (page 2)

Court File Number

1. The child(ren) in this case is/are:

Child's Full Legal Name	Birthdate	Age	Sex	Full Legal Name(s) of Parent(s)	Is the Child First Nations, Inuk, or Métis?	Child's Bands and First Nations, Inuit, or Métis Communities

Form 33B.2:	Answer (*Child, Youth and Family Services Act, 2017* Cases other than Child Protection and Status Review)	(page 3)	Court File Number

2. ☐ I/We agree with the following facts in the application (Form 8B.2 or 34L). *(Refer to the numbered paragraph(s) in the application.)*

☐ I/We disagree with the following facts in the application (Form 8B.2 or 34L). *(Refer to the numbered paragraph(s) in the application.)*

(Attach an additional page and number it if you need more space.)

Form 33B.2:	Answer (*Child, Youth and Family Services Act, 2017* Cases other than Child Protection and Status Review)	(page 4)	Court File Number

3. Do you agree that the court should make the order requested?

☐ Yes   ☐ No

Give reasons:

(Attach an additional page and number it if you need more space.)

FLR 33B.2 (March 1, 2018)

FAMILY LAW RULES FORMS

Court File Number

IMPORTANT FACTS SUPPORTING MY/OUR POSITION

(In numbered paragraphs, set out the facts that form the legal basis for your position. Attach an additional page and number it if you need more space.)

Put a line through any blank space left on this page.

_____	_____
Date of signature	*Signature*
_____	_____
Date of signature	*Signature*

Form 33C

Statement of Agreed Facts (Child Protection)

ONTARIO

	Court File Number
_____ *(Name of court)*	

at _____
Court office address

Form 33C: Statement of Agreed Facts (Child Protection)

Applicant(s) *[In most cases, the applicant will be a children's aid society.]*

Full legal name & address for service — street & number, municipality, postal code, telephone & fax numbers and e-mail address (if any).	Lawyer's name & address — street & number, municipality, postal code, telephone & fax numbers and e-mail address (if any).

Respondent(s) *[In most cases, a respondent will be a "parent" within the meaning of section 74 of the Child, Youth and Family Services Act, 2017.]*

Full legal name & address for service — street & number, municipality, postal code, telephone & fax numbers and e-mail address (if any).	Lawyer's name & address — street & number, municipality, postal code, telephone & fax numbers and e-mail address (if any).

Children's Lawyer

Name & address of Children's Lawyer's agent for service (street & number, municipality, postal code, telephone & fax numbers and e-mail address (if any)) and name of person represented.

THE PEOPLE SIGNING THIS AGREEMENT ARE:

(Give full legal name. If you are a respondent, state your relationship to the child(ren). If you are an employee of the children's aid society, state your position within the society.)

Print or type full legal name	Relationship to child OR position within children's aid society
Signature	Date of signature

Print or type full legal name	Relationship to child OR position within children's aid society
Signature	Date of signature

Print or type full legal name	Relationship to child OR position within children's aid society
Signature	Date of signature

WE AGREE: (a) that the statements made on this form are true; and

(b) that this form may be filed with the court and may be read to the court as evidence, without affecting anyone's right to test that evidence by cross-examination or to bring in other evidence.

Form 33C: Statement of Agreed Facts (Child Protection) (page 2)

Court File Number

Note that "parent" means parent as defined in section 74 of the *Child, Youth and Family Services Act, 2017*.

1. The information about the child(ren) in this case is as follows:

Full legal name of first child:	Date of birth	Age	Sex
Is the child a First Nations, Inuk, or Métis person?			
Name of each of the child's bands and First Nations, Inuit, or Métis communities and their representative(s)			
If child was brought to a place of safety, address and identity of place from which the child was removed			
Full legal name(s) of child's parent(s) (List everyone who is a parent of the child as defined in section 74 of the Child, Youth and Family Services Act, 2017)			

Full legal name of second child:	Date of birth	Age	Sex
Is the child a First Nations, Inuk, or Métis person?			
Name of each of the child's bands and First Nations, Inuit, or Métis communities and their representative(s)			
If child was brought to a place of safety, address and identity of place from which the child was removed			
Full legal name(s) of child's parent(s) (List everyone who is a parent of the child as defined in section 74 of the Child, Youth and Family Services Act, 2017)			

Full legal name of third child:	Date of birth	Age	Sex
Is the child a First Nations, Inuk, or Métis person?			
Name of each of the child's bands and First Nations, Inuit, or Métis communities and their representative(s)			
If child was brought to a place of safety, address and identity of place from which the child was removed			
Full legal name(s) of child's parent(s) (List everyone who is a parent of the child as defined in section 74 of the Child, Youth and Family Services Act, 2017)			

If there are more children, attach a sheet and number it.

Form 33C:	Statement of Agreed Facts (Child Protection)	(page 3)	Court File Number

2. The details of the children's aid society's previous involvement with one or more of these children in this case are as follows:
(Write "Nil" if no involvement. Indicate any involvement with children's aid society in another part of Ontario or a child protection agency outside Ontario. Please remember that this is a statement of AGREED FACTS. That means that you must not set out something as a fact if another party disagrees with it. If you cannot agree at all about anything, write: "No agreement reached.")

3. The child(ren) was/were brought to a place of safety because:
(If the child(ren) was/were not brought to a place of safety, write "Nil". Again, there must be full agreement by all parties. Any point on which there is disagreement must be excluded. If there is no agreement at all on anything, write: "No agreement reached.")

4. We agree that the court should make a finding that the child(ren) is/are in need of protection on the following reasons:
(Use only the reasons listed on page 3 of the application [form 8B]. Any reason on which there is disagreement must be excluded. If there is no agreement at all, write: "No agreement reached." In any event, the court can always make some other finding.)

4.1 The following important events relating to the child(ren)'s best interests have occurred since the date this application began:

5. We agree that the order that would best serve the best interests of the child(ren) is:
(Again, list only the terms and conditions on which there is full agreement by all parties. If there is no agreement at all, write: "No agreement reached." In any event, the court is always free to make some other order. If the order on which you all agree would remove the child(ren) from the care of the person who had the child(ren) before the case started, explain why less disruptive options would not be enough to protect the child(ren).)

Put a line through any space left on this page

Form 33D

Statement of Agreed Facts (Status Review)

ONTARIO

	Court File Number

_____
(Name of court)

at _____
Court office address

Applicant(s) *[In most child protection cases, the applicant will be a children's aid society.]*

Full legal name & address for service — street & number, municipality, postal code, telephone & fax numbers and e-mail address (if any).	Lawyer's name & address — street & number, municipality, postal code, telephone & fax numbers and e-mail address (if any).

Respondent(s) *[In most cases, a respondent will be a "parent" within the meaning of section 74 of the Child, Youth and Family Services Act, 2017.]*

Full legal name & address for service — street & number, municipality, postal code, telephone & fax numbers and e-mail address (if any).	Lawyer's name & address — street & number, municipality, postal code, telephone & fax numbers and e-mail address (if any).

Children's Lawyer

Name & address of Children's Lawyer's agent for service (street & number, municipality, postal code, telephone & fax numbers and e-mail address (if any)) and name of person represented.

THE PEOPLE SIGNING THIS AGREEMENT ARE:

(Give full legal name. If you are a respondent, state your relationship to the child(ren). If you are an employee of the children's aid society, state your position within the society.)

Print or type full legal name	Relationship to child OR position within children's aid society
Signature	Date of signature

Print or type full legal name	Relationship to child OR position within children's aid society
Signature	Date of signature

Print or type full legal name	Relationship to child OR position within children's aid society
Signature	Date of signature

WE AGREE: (a) that the statements made on this form are true; and

(b) that this form may be filed with the court and may be read to the court as evidence, without affecting anyone's right to test that evidence by cross-examination or to bring in other evidence.

Form 33D:	Statement of Agreed Facts (Status Review)	(page 2)	Court File Number

Note that "parent" means parent as defined in section 74 of the *Child, Youth and Family Services Act, 2017*.

1. The information about the child(ren) in this case is as follows:

Full legal name of first child:		Date of birth	Age	Sex
Is the child a First Nations, Inuk, or Métis person?				
Name of each of the child's bands and First Nations, Inuit, or Métis communities and their representative(s)				
If child was brought to a place of safety, address and identity of place from which the child was removed				
Full legal name(s) of child's parent(s) (List everyone who is a parent of the child as defined in section 74 of the Child, Youth and Family Services Act, 2017)				

Full legal name of second child:		Date of birth	Age	Sex
Is the child a First Nations, Inuk, or Métis person?				
Name of each of the child's bands and First Nations, Inuit, or Métis communities and their representative(s)				
If child was brought to a place of safety, address and identity of place from which the child was removed				
Full legal name(s) of child's parent(s) (List everyone who is a parent of the child as defined in section 74 of the Child, Youth and Family Services Act, 2017)				

Full legal name of third child:		Date of birth	Age	Sex
Is the child a First Nations, Inuk, or Métis person?				
Name of each of the child's bands and First Nations, Inuit, or Métis communities and their representative(s)				
If child was brought to a place of safety, address and identity of place from which the child was removed				
Full legal name(s) of child's parent(s) (List everyone who is a parent of the child as defined in section 74 of the Child, Youth and Family Services Act, 2017)				

If there are more children, attach a sheet and number it.

| Form 33D: | **Statement of Agreed Facts** | (page 3) | Court File Number |
| | **(Status Review)** | | |

2. The most recent protection order dealing with the child(ren) in paragraph 1 was made on *(date)* _____
   _____ and it said that: *(State substance of order.)*

3. Since the order under review was made, the following person(s) has/have become a "parent" under Part V of the *Child, Youth and Family Services Act, 2017*:

Full legal name	Relationship to child

4. Since that order was made, the following important events have happened:
   (Describe only the events on which you can ALL agree. Please remember that this is a statement of AGREED FACTS. That means that you must not set out something as a fact if at least one of the persons signing this statement disagrees with it. If you cannot agree at all about anything, write: "No agreement reached.")

5. We agree that an order of the court is needed now and that it would best serve the best interests of the child(ren) because:
   (If there is no agreement that an order needs to be made, write: "No agreement reached on need for an order." If you agree that an order needs to be made, give reasons for it and set out its terms and conditions. If any person disagrees with a reason, term or condition, then you must not include that reason, term or condition. If you cannot agree on any reasons, write: "No agreement reached on reasons for order." If you cannot agree on any terms or conditions of the order, write: "No agreement reached on terms and conditions of order.")

Put a line through any space left on this page

Form 33E

Child's Consent to Secure Treatment

ONTARIO

	Court File Number

_____

(Name of court)

at _____

Court office address

Form 33E: Child's
Consent to Secure
Treatment

Applicant(s)

Full legal name & address for service — street & number, municipality, postal code, telephone & fax numbers and e-mail address (if any).	Lawyer's name & address — street & number, municipality, postal code, telephone & fax numbers and e-mail address (if any).

Child

Full legal name of child:	Lawyer's name & address — street & number, municipality, postal code, telephone & fax numbers and e-mail address (if any).
Birthdate:	
Sex:	

1. My name is *(child's full legal name)* _____

2. I know that the applicant(s) is/are asking the court to make an order

    ☐ to send me to and maybe have me locked up for my own protection at _____

    ☐ to keep me for a longer time and maybe keep me locked up for my own protection at _____

    ☐ to get me released from *(name and address of program)* _____

3. I know that ☐ I have a right to be in court when this case is heard by the judge, but I agree not to come to court and to let the court make whatever order needs to be made without me.

    ☐ the court usually needs to hear witnesses before it can make an order in this case, but I agree that the court can make the order without having to hear witnesses in person and can reach its decision on evidence found in the reports and other documents that the applicant(s) can show to the judge.

4. I have talked with a lawyer   (a)   who has explained these things to me, and

                                                       (b)   who has explained what it means for me to sign this consent, and

                                                       (c)   who is going to witness my signature of this form.

Signature of child

Signature of lawyer

Date of signatures

NOTE: _This consent must be witnessed by an independent lawyer who is to provide an affidavit of independent legal advice on page 2 of this form._

NOTE: A consent to dispense with oral evidence is not effective for more than 180 days after the court's order.

AFFIDAVIT OF EXECUTION AND INDEPENDENT LEGAL ADVICE

My name is _(full legal name)_ _____

and I swear/affirm that the following is true:

1. I am a member of the Bar of _(name of jurisdiction)_ _____

     and am not acting for any other person in this secure treatment case.

2. I explained to _(child's full legal name)_ _____

     ☐   the nature and effect of   ☐   secure treatment;

                                       ☐   an extension of secure treatment;

                                       ☐   release from secure treatment;

     ☐   the consequences of not attending the hearing; and

     ☐   the consequences of a hearing where a court proceeds without hearing oral evidence;

     in language appropriate to his/her age to the best of my knowledge and skills.

3. After my explanation, the child told me that he/she wanted to sign this consent.

4. I was present at and witnessed the signing of this consent by the child.

Sworn/Affirmed before me at _____

municipality

in _____

Province, state or country

on _____ _____

date   *Commissioner for taking*
               affidavits
               (Type or print name below if
               signature is illegible.)

_____

Signature
(This form is to be
signed in front of a
lawyer, justice of the
peace, notary public or
commissioner for taking
affidavits.)

Form 33F

Consent to Secure Treatment (Person other than Child)

ONTARIO

	Court File Number

(Name of court)

at _____

Court office address

Form 33F: Consent to
Secure Treatment
(person other than child)

Applicant(s)

Full legal name & address for service — street & number, municipality, postal code, telephone & fax numbers and e-mail address (if any).	Lawyer's name & address — street & number, municipality, postal code, telephone & fax numbers and e-mail address (if any).

Child

Full legal name of child:	Lawyer's name & address — street & number, municipality, postal code, telephone & fax numbers and e-mail address (if any).
Birthdate:	
Sex:	

Name and address of secure treatment program in this case

My name is *(full legal name)* _____ and I am

☐ the administrator of the secure treatment program. I consent to this application for
  ☐ the child's commitment to the program.
  ☐ an extension of the child's commitment to the program.
  ☐ an extension of the commitment to the program of the person admitted into it who has now attained the age of eighteen years.

☐ the child's parent. I consent to
  ☐ this application for the commitment of my child who is in the care of a person other than the administrator of the secure treatment program.
  ☐ my child's commitment to the secure treatment program for a period of 180 days in this application brought by *(full legal name of applicant children's aid society)* _____

  ☐ this application by the administrator of the secure treatment program for an extension of my child's admission to the program.

☐ an authorized representative of the Minister of Children and Youth Services for Ontario. I consent to the admission of the child who is less than twelve years old to the secure treatment program.
  ☐ temporarily while this case for an order of commitment or for an order extending it is adjourned.
  ☐ on the court's final order of commitment or extending commitment.

☐ an officer of *(full legal name of children's aid society)* _____
  I am authorized, on behalf of the society, to consent to this application of the administrator of the secure treatment program for an extension of the child's commitment to that program.

☐ the person who is the subject of this case. I am 18 years of age or more. I consent to this application to extend my commitment to the secure treatment program to which I am now admitted.

_____ _____
Signature *Date of signature*

Form 34

Child's Consent to Adoption

ONTARIO

	Court File Number
(Name of court)	

at _____

Court office address

Form 34: Child's Consent to Adoption

Applicant(s) *(The first letter of the applicant's surname may be used)*

Full legal name & address for service — street & number, municipality, postal code, telephone & fax numbers and e-mail address (if any).	Lawyer's name & address — street & number, municipality, postal code, telephone & fax numbers and e-mail address (if any).

Respondent(s) *(If there is a respondent, the first letter of the respondent's surname may be used)*

Full legal name & address for service — street & number, municipality, postal code, telephone & fax numbers and e-mail address (if any).	Lawyer's name & address — street & number, municipality, postal code, telephone & fax numbers and e-mail address (if any).

1. My name is *(child's full legal name)*

2. I was born on *(give date of birth)*

3. I know that the applicant(s) is/are asking the court to make an order to adopt me.

4. I agree to being adopted by the applicant(s).

5. I have been given a chance to get counselling.

6. I understand the nature and effect of this consent. I understand that I may withdraw this consent within 21 days by attending at the office of the lawyer who witnessed the consent located at *(give address)*

   or by attending at the office of another authorized representative of the Children's Lawyer and signing a written notice of withdrawal.

7. I understand that once I turn eighteen years old, I can apply for a copy of my original birth registration, if any, and a copy of my adoption order.

8. I understand that once I turn nineteen years old, my birth parent(s) can apply for information from my original birth registration, if any, any substituted birth registration and my adoption order. This information would include my full legal name after adoption.

9. I have spoken to a lawyer   ☐ who has explained adoption to me,

   ☐ who has explained what it means for me to sign this consent,

   ☐ who has told me what to do if I want to change my mind about this consent,

   ☐ who has told me about my rights and the rights of other persons with respect to the disclosure of adoption information, and

   ☐ who is going to witness my signing of this form.

To be completed only where the child is 12 years of age or older.

10. I agree that my name after adoption will be *(full legal name after adoption)*

_____   _____

Date of signatures   *Signature of child*

_____

Signature of Children's Lawyer

FLR 34 (November 1, 2018)

Page 1 of 2

1134

Form 34: **Child's Consent to Adoption** **(page 2)**

Court File Number

AFFIDAVIT OF EXECUTION AND INDEPENDENT LEGAL ADVICE

My name is *(full legal name)*

and I swear/affirm that the following is true:

1. I am a member of the Bar of *(name of jurisdiction)*
   and am an agent of the Office of the Children's Lawyer.

2. I am not acting for any other person in this adoption case.

3. I explained to *(child's full legal name)* _____ about

   ☐ the nature and effect of adoption under the law of Ontario

   ☐ the nature and effect of this consent

   ☐ the circumstances under which this consent may be withdrawn

   ☐ his/her rights and the rights of other persons with respect to the disclosure of adoption information

   in language appropriate to his/her age to the best of my knowledge and skills.

4. After my explanation, the child told me that he/she wanted to sign this consent.

5. I was present at and witnessed the signing of this consent by the child.

Sworn/Affirmed before me at _____ *municipality*	Signature
in _____ *province, state or country*	*(This form is to be signed in front of a lawyer, justice of the peace, notary public or commissioner for taking affidavits.)*
on _____ *date* _____ Commissioner for taking affidavits *(Type or print name below if signature is illegible.)*	

Form 34A

Affidavit of Parentage, Sworn/Affirmed

ONTARIO

	Court File Number
_____	
(Name of court)	**Form 34A: Affidavit of Parentage, sworn/affirmed**
at _____	
Court office address	

Applicant(s) *(If the applicant is unknown at the time this affidavit is sworn/affirmed or if the applicant's name is not to be disclosed to the person swearing/affirming this affidavit, leave this box blank)*

Full legal name & address for service — street & number, municipality, postal code, telephone & fax numbers and e-mail address (if any).	Lawyer's name & address — street & number, municipality, postal code, telephone & fax numbers and e-mail address (if any).

Respondent(s) *(If there is a respondent, the first letter of the respondent's surname may be used)*

Full legal name & address for service — street & number, municipality, postal code, telephone & fax numbers and e-mail address (if any).	Lawyer's name & address — street & number, municipality, postal code, telephone & fax numbers and e-mail address (if any).

My name is *(full legal name)* _____

I live in *(municipality & province)* _____

and I swear/affirm that the following is true:

1. The child's full legal name is: *(Give full legal name, date of birth, sex and birth registration number if known of person to be adopted. If this person was placed for adoption by a licensee or children's aid society, you may use an initial for the surname.)*

Full legal name	Date of birth	Sex	Birth registration number

2. I am *(State your relationship to the child.)* _____

3. The child was born on *(date)* _____, in *(municipality, province, etc.)* _____

4. The child's birth was registered or registration has been requested with the vital statistics register of *(province)* _____ under the following name(s):

Check applicable box(es).

5. *(Name of person familiar with legal meaning of "parent")* _____
has reviewed with me those categories of persons who qualify as "parents" for the purposes of the *Child, Youth and Family Services Act, 2017* and whose consents have to be obtained or dispensed with before the child can be adopted.

Check off all boxes below that apply to your situation. Note that "birth parent" means the person who gives birth to the child.

6. The review mentioned in paragraph 5 included an examination of the following checklist:

   (a) Within the 300-day period before the child's birth,

   ☐ the birth parent's spouse *(spouse's full legal name)* _____ died.

   ☐ the birth parent got a divorce or annulment from *(spouse's full legal name)* _____

   ☐ the birth parent was living in conjugal relationship outside marriage with *(person's full legal name)*

   _____

   that lasted for a period of *(State duration of relationship.)* _____
   and came to an end.

   ☐ the birth parent was not living in a conjugal relationship of some permanence outside of marriage with anyone.

Form 34A: Affidavit of Parentage   **(page 2)**

Court File Number

(b) At the time of the child's birth, the birth parent was

☐ not married.

☐ married to *(spouse's full legal name)* _____

☐ not living in a conjugal relationship outside marriage.

☐ living in a conjugal relationship outside marriage with *(spouse's full legal name)*
_____

for a period of *(state duration of relationship)* _____

(c) Where the child was conceived through assisted reproduction, at the time of the child's conception, the child's birth parent

☐ was not married.

☐ was married to *(spouse's full legal name)* _____

☐ was living in a conjugal relationship outside marriage with *(spouse's full legal name)*
_____

for a period of *(state duration of relationship)* _____

☐ *(not applicable)*

(d) Under Ontario's *Vital Statistics Act* or under similar legislation in another province or territory in Canada,

☐ no person, to the best of my knowledge and information,

☐ *(person's full legal name)* _____

has certified the child's birth as the child's parent.

(e) As of today's date,

☐ no other person has, to the best of my knowledge and information, been recognized by a court

☐ *(person's full legal name)* _____ has been recognized

by *(name of court)* _____

to be a parent to the child.

(f) In the 12 months before the child was placed for adoption,

☐ no person

☐ *(person's full legal name)* _____

has demonstrated a settled intention to treat the child as a child of his or her own family.

(g) In the 12 months before the child was placed for adoption,

☐ no person has acknowledged to me or, to the best of my knowledge and information, to any other person or agency

☐ *(person's full legal name)* _____ acknowledged

☐ to me

☐ to *(name of other person or agency)* _____

parentage of the child and provided for the child's support.

Form 34A: **Affidavit of Parentage**   (page 3)   Court File Number

(h) Prior to January 1, 2017, a statutory declaration

☐ has, to the best of my knowledge and information, never been filed by any person,

☐ was filed by *(person's full legal name)* _____

with the office of the Registrar General acknowledging parentage of the child.

(i) There is

☐ no written agreement or court order requiring any person,

☐ a written agreement made on *(date)* _____ , at

(municipality, etc.) _____ ,

requiring *(person's full legal name)* _____

☐ an order of *(name of court)* _____ , made

on *(date)* _____ , at

(municipality, etc.) _____ ,

requiring *(person's full legal name)* _____

to provide for the child's support.

(j) There is

☐ no written agreement or court order giving any person,

☐ a written agreement made on *(date)* _____ , at

(municipality, etc.) _____ ,

giving *(person's full legal name)* _____

☐ an order of *(name of court)* _____ , made

on *(date)* _____ , at

(municipality, etc.) _____ ,

giving *(person's full legal name)* _____

custody of or access to the child.

7. The review in paragraphs 5 and 6 indicates that, other than the person making this affidavit,

☐ no other person

☐ *(full legal name of person(s))*

meets/meet the definition of "parent" whose consent would therefore be required before the child could be adopted.

Sworn/Affirmed before me at _____
municipality

in _____
province, state or country

on _____   _____
date   *Commissioner for taking affidavits*
(Type or print name below if signature is illegible.)

_____
Signature
(This form is to be signed in front of a lawyer, justice of the peace, notary public or commissioner for taking affidavits.)

Form 34B

Non-Parent's Consent to Adoption by Spouse

ONTARIO

	Court File Number

....
(Name of court)

at ....
Court office address

**Form 34B: Non-Parent's
Consent to Adoption
by Spouse**

Applicant(s) *(The first letter of the applicant's surname may be used)*

Full legal name & address for service — street & number, municipality, postal code, telephone & fax numbers and e-mail address (if any).	Lawyer's name & address — street & number, municipality, postal code, telephone & fax numbers and e-mail address (if any).

Respondent(s) *(If there is a respondent, the first letter of the respondent's surname may be used)*

Full legal name & address for service — street & number, municipality, postal code, telephone & fax numbers and e-mail address (if any).	Lawyer's name & address — street & number, municipality, postal code, telephone & fax numbers and e-mail address (if any).

1. My name is *(full legal name)* ....
   and I live in *(municipality & province)* ....

2. The applicant is my "spouse" within the meaning of Part VIII of the *Child, Youth and Family Services Act, 2017.*

3. I am not a "parent" of the child in this case within the meaning of Part VIII of the *Child, Youth and Family Services Act, 2017.*

4. I consent to the adoption of: *(Give full legal name, date of birth, sex and birth registration number if known of person to be adopted. If this person is in extended society care or was placed for adoption by a licensee or children's aid society, you may use an initial for the surname.)*

....

Full legal name	*Date of birth*	*Sex*	*Birth registration number*

by my **spouse** *(spouse's full legal name)* ....

_____   _____
Date of signatures   *Signature of non-parent*

                                                _____
                                                Signature of independent lawyer

NOTE: This consent must be witnessed by an independent lawyer who is to provide an affidavit of execution and independent legal advice on the next sheet of this form.

Form 34B: Non-Parent's Consent to Adoption (page 2)
by Spouse

Court File Number

AFFIDAVIT OF EXECUTION AND INDEPENDENT LEGAL ADVICE

My name is *(full legal name)* _____

and I swear/affirm that the following is true:

1. I am a member of the Bar of *(name of jurisdiction)* _____
and I am not acting for any other person in this adoption case.

2. I explained to *(non-parent's full legal name)* _____ about

☐ the nature and effect of adoption under the law of Ontario;

☐ the nature and effect of this consent;

☐ the circumstances under which this consent may be withdrawn; and

☐ the right to counselling.

3. After my explanation, he/she told me that he/she wanted to sign this consent.

4. I was present at and witnessed the signing of this consent.

Sworn/Affirmed before me at _____

municipality

in _____

province, state or country

on _____

date   _____

Commissioner for taking affidavits
(Type or print name below if signature is illegible.)

_____

Signature

(This form is to be signed in front of a lawyer, justice of the peace, notary public or commissioner for taking affidavits.)

FLR 34B (March 1, 2018)

Page 2 of 2

Form 34C

Director's or Local Director's Statement on Adoption

ONTARIO

_____	Court File Number _____
(Name of court)	

Form 34C: Director's or Local Director's Statement on Adoption

at _____
Court office address

Applicant(s) *(The first letter of the applicant's surname may be used)*

Full legal name & address for service — street & number, municipality, postal code, telephone & fax numbers and e-mail address (if any).	Lawyer's name & address — street & number, municipality, postal code, telephone & fax numbers and e-mail address (if any).

Child _____

(Child's full legal name. If the child is in extended society care or was placed by a licensee or children's aid society, you may use an initial for the surname.)

Date of birth	Sex	Birth registration number

A local director of a children's aid society may complete this form only where the child was placed for adoption by the society and the child has resided in the home of the applicant(s) for at least 6 months.

1. My name is *(full legal name)* _____ and I am

   ☐ appointed as a Director under the *Child, Youth and Family Services Act, 2017*.

   ☐ the local director of *(full legal name of children's aid society)*

2. The child in this adoption case   ☐ is less than 16 years of age.

                    ☐ is 16 years of age or more but has not withdrawn from parental control.

3. The child has resided in the home of the applicant(s) since *(date)* _____

4. Having regard to the child's best interests, I recommend:

   ☐ that the period of residence be dispensed with and that an order be made for the child's adoption by the applicant(s).

   ☐ that the court make an order of temporary custody of the child in favour of the applicant(s) for a period not exceeding one year on the terms set out on the next sheet of this form.

   ☐ because the child has resided in the home of the applicant(s) for at least 6 months, that an order be made for the child's adoption by the applicant(s).

   ☐ that an order for the child's adoption not be made for reasons set out on the next sheet of this form.

5. The report on the child's adjustment in the home of the applicant(s) is attached to this form.

6. There are ☐ no additional circumstances to which I want to draw the court's attention.

            ☐ additional circumstances set out on the next sheet of this form to which I want to draw the court's attention.

_____	_____
Date of signature	Signature

NOTE TO DIRECTOR OR LOCAL DIRECTOR: If, in the Director's or local director's opinion, it would not be in the child's best interest to make the order, this form and any attachments must be filed with the court and served on the applicant(s) at least 30 days before the adoption hearing.

FLR 34C (March 1, 2018)   Page 1 of 2

Form 34C: Director's or Local Director's Statement on Adoption	(page 2)	Court File Number

(Set out any additional circumstances to which the court's attention should be drawn. If more space is needed, an additional page may be attached.)

(Set out the proposed terms of the temporary custody order or the reasons for recommending against the making of an adoption order. If more space is needed, an additional page may be attached.)

Form 34D

Affidavit of Adoption Applicant(s), Sworn/Affirmed

ONTARIO

_____ *(Name of court)*	Court File Number
at _____ *Court office address*	**Form 34D: Affidavit of Adoption Applicant(s), sworn/affirmed**

Applicant(s) *(The first letter of the applicant's surname may be used)*

Full legal name & address for service — street & number, municipality, postal code, telephone & fax numbers and e-mail address (if any).	Lawyer's name & address — street & number, municipality, postal code, telephone & fax numbers and e-mail address (if any).

Respondent(s) *(If there is a respondent, the first letter of the respondent's surname may be used)*

Full legal name & address for service — street & number, municipality, postal code, telephone & fax numbers and e-mail address (if any).	Lawyer's name & address — street & number, municipality, postal code, telephone & fax numbers and e-mail address (if any).

Child

_____

(Child's full legal name. If the child is in extended society care or was placed by a licensee or children's aid society, you may use an initial for the surname.)

_____ *Date of birth*	_____ *Sex*	_____ *Birth registration number*

My/Our name(s) is/are *(full legal name(s))* _____

I/We live in *(municipality & province)* _____

and I/we swear/affirm that the following is true:

1. I am/We are the applicant(s) for the adoption of the child in this case and reside in Ontario.

2. My/Our birthdate(s) is/are: *(For two persons, indicate which birthdate belongs to whom.)*

3. The details of my/our background are as follows: *(Give details of your health, education, employment, ability to support and care for the child and any other relevant background material. If you need more space, you may add a page.)*

Put a line through any blank space left on this page.

FLR 34D (March 1, 2018)

Page 1 of 3

Form 34D: Affidavit of Adoption Applicant(s)   (page 2)

Court File Number

4. The child is a resident of Ontario and is *(check all boxes that apply)*:
    - ☐ my/our grandchild.
    - ☐ my/our grandnephew/grandniece.
    - ☐ my/our nephew/niece.
    - ☐ a child of my spouse.
    - ☐ not related to me/us.
    - ☐ a First Nations, Inuk, or Métis child.
    - ☐ a member of the following band(s) or First Nations, Inuit, or Métis communities *(list the child's band(s) and/or First Nations, Inuit, or Métis community(ies))*:

5. The history of my/our relationship with the child is as follows: *(Give details of history of your relationship with the child. If you need more space, you may add a page.)*

Put a line through any blank space left on this page.

FLR 34D (March 1, 2018)

Page 2 of 3

1144

Form 34D: Affidavit of Adoption Applicant(s)   (page 3)

Court File Number

Check applicable box.

6. ☐ I am the sole applicant for this child's adoption and if an adoption order is made, I will be the child's only legal parent.

☐ I am the sole applicant for this child's adoption. If an adoption order is made, I will be joining with

(spouse's full legal name) .... ,
who is my spouse within the meaning of Part VIII of the *Child, Youth and Family Services Act, 2017*, and together, we will be the child's only legal parents.

☐ We are applying for this child's adoption jointly as spouses within the meaning of Part VIII of the *Child, Youth and Family Services Act, 2017*. If an adoption order is made, we will be the child's only legal parents.

7. I/We understand and appreciate the special role of an adopting parent.

8. No payment or reward of any kind was made, given, received or agreed to be made, given or received by me/us or, to the best of my/our knowledge, by any other person in connection with,

(a) the adoption of this child;

(b) this child's placement for adoption;

(c) the giving of any consent to this child's adoption; or

(d) any negotiations or arrangements leading up to this child's adoption,

except for what is permitted by the *Child, Youth and Family Services Act, 2017* and the regulations made under that Act.

9. I/We understand the importance of the child's culture and will make efforts to preserve his/her traditions, heritage and cultural identity.

10. I/We understand that once the child turns eighteen years old, he/she can apply for a copy of his/her original birth registration, if any, and a copy of his/her adoption order.

11. I/We understand that once the child turns nineteen years old, his/her birth parent(s) can apply for information from his/her original birth registration, if any, any substituted birth registration, and his/her adoption order. This information would include the child's full legal name after adoption.

12. I/We understand the provisions of the *Vital Statistics Act* and the *Child, Youth and Family Services Act, 2017* related to the disclosure of adoption information.

13. I/We want to bring to the court's attention the following additional facts about the child's best interests: *(Give any additional facts. If you need more space, you may add a page.)*

Put a line through any blank space left on this page.

Sworn/Affirmed before me at ....
municipality

in ....
province, state or country

on ....
date   *Commissioner for taking affidavits*
(Type or print name below if signature is illegible.)

....
Signature
(This form is to be signed in front of a lawyer, justice of the peace, notary public or commissioner for taking affidavits.)

Form 34E

Director's Consent to Adoption

ONTARIO

	Court File Number

_____

(Name of court)

at _____

Court office address

Form 34E: Director's Consent to
Adoption

Applicant(s) *(The first letter of the applicant's surname may be used)*

Full legal name & address for service — street & number, municipality, postal code, telephone & fax numbers and e-mail address (if any).	Lawyer's name & address — street & number, municipality, postal code, telephone & fax numbers and e-mail address (if any).

Child _____

(Child's full legal name. If the child is in extended society care or was placed by a licensee or children's aid society, you may use an initial for the surname.)

_____   _____   _____
Date of birth   Sex   Birth registration number

1.   My name is *(full legal name)* _____ and I am

appointed as a Director under the *Child, Youth and Family Services Act, 2017.*

2.   An order was made placing the child in extended society care on *(date)* _____

and was placed into the care of *(full legal name of children's aid society)* _____

_____

3.   I consent to this child's adoption by the applicant(s).

_____   _____
Date of signature   Signature

Form 34F

Parent's or Custodian's Consent to Adoption

ONTARIO

	Court File Number

_____
(Name of court)

at _____
Court office address

Form 34F: Parent's or Custodian's Consent to Adoption

1. **My name is** *(full legal name)* _____

   I was born on *(date of birth)* _____ **and I live**

   at *(address)* _____

2. The child in this case is: *(Give child's full legal name, date of birth, sex and birth registration number, if available.)*

   _____

Full legal name	Date of birth	Sex	Birth registration number

3. **I am a parent of the child within the meaning of Part VIII of the** *Child, Youth and Family Services Act, 2017* **because I am** *(Check appropriate paragraph below.)*

   ☐ a parent of the child under section 6, 8, 9, 10, 11 or 13 of the *Children's Law Reform Act (includes a birth parent, her spouse).* I am the child's *(state your relationship to the child)*

   ☐ an individual described in subsection 7(2) of the *Children's Law Reform Act.*

   ☐ an individual who has been found or recognized by a court of competent jurisdiction outside of Ontario to be a parent of the child.

   ☐ a parent under section 217 or 218 of the *Child, Youth and Family Services Act, 2017. (includes adoptive parents)*

   ☐ an individual having lawful custody of the child.

   ☐ an individual who, during the 12 months before the child was placed for adoption, has demonstrated a settled intention to treat the child as a member of his/her family.

   ☐ an individual who, during the 12 months before the child was placed for adoption, has acknowledged parentage of the child and has provided for the child's support.

   ☐ an individual who is required to provide for the child or who has custody of or access to the child under a written agreement or a court order.

   ☐ an individual who has acknowledged parentage of the child under section 12 of the *Children's Law Reform Act* as it read before January 1, 2017.

4. I consent to the adoption of this child.

5. I understand the nature and effect of this consent. I understand that I may withdraw this consent in one or more of the following ways:

   - If the child is placed for adoption by a children's aid society, by ensuring that the children's aid society located at

     (address) _____

     receives my written notice of withdrawal within 21 days after my consent was given.

   - If the child is placed for adoption by a licensee, by ensuring that the licensee located at *(address)*

     _____

     receives my written notice of withdrawal within 21 days after my consent was given.

   - If a relative of the child or the spouse of a parent proposes to apply to adopt the child, by ensuring that the proposed applicant receives my written notice of withdrawal within 21 days after my consent was given.

6. I understand that, after the 21 days have passed, I am not allowed to withdraw this consent unless I first get the court's permission, and then only if my child has not yet been placed for adoption and if I can show that it is in the child's best interests that this consent be withdrawn.

7. I understand the nature of an adoption order and that, if an adoption order is made, I will no longer be a legal parent to the child.

8. I understand that once the child turns eighteen years old, he/she can apply for a copy of his/her original birth registration, if any, and a copy of his/her adoption order. I understand that my full legal name may be included on such copies.

Form 34F: Parent's or Custodian's Consent to Adoption   (page 2)

Court File Number

9. I understand that once the child turns nineteen years old, his/her birth parent(s) may apply for information from his/her original birth registration, if any, any substituted birth registration, and his/her adoption order. This information would include the child's full legal name after adoption.

10. I understand my right to ask and to be told whether an adoption order has been made for the child.

11. I understand my rights and the rights of other persons with respect to the disclosure of adoption information.

12. No payment or reward of any kind was made, given, received or agreed to be made, given or received by me/us or, to the best of my/our knowledge, by any other person in connection with,

    (a) the adoption of this child;

    (b) this child's placement for adoption;

    (c) the giving of any consent to this child's adoption; or

    (d) any negotiations or arrangements leading up to this child's adoption,

except for what is permitted by the *Child, Youth and Family Services Act, 2017* and the regulations made under that Act.

13. I have had a chance to get counselling about this consent.

14. I have had independent legal advice about this consent.

_____   _____
Date of signatures   *Signature of parent*

NOTE: This consent must be witnessed by an independent lawyer who is to provide an affidavit of execution and independent legal advice below. If the person giving this consent is less than 18 years old, the consent must be accompanied by Form 34J (Affidavit of Execution and Independent Legal Advice (Children's Lawyer)), instead of the Affidavit of Execution and Independent Legal Advice that accompanies this form.

_____
Signature of independent lawyer

AFFIDAVIT OF EXECUTION AND INDEPENDENT LEGAL ADVICE

My name is *(full legal name)* _____

and I swear/affirm that the following is true:

    1. I am a member of the Bar of *(name of jurisdiction)* _____
    and I am not acting for any other person in this adoption case.

    2. I explained to *(parent's full legal name)* _____ about
    ☐ the nature and effect of adoption under the law of Ontario;
    ☐ the nature and effect of this consent;
    ☐ the circumstances under which this consent may be withdrawn;
    ☐ his/her rights and the rights of other persons with respect to the disclosure of adoption information;
    ☐ the right to counselling.

    3. After my explanation, he/she told me that he/she wanted to sign this consent.

    4. I was present at and witnessed the signing of this consent.

Sworn/Affirmed before me at _____

in _____

on _____

_____ *municipality*	
_____ *province, state or country*	_____ *Signature* *(This form is to be signed in front of a lawyer, justice of the peace, notary public or commissioner for taking affidavits.)*
_____ *date* *Commissioner for taking affidavits* *(Type or print name below if signature is illegible.)*	

Form 34G

Affidavit of Adoption Licensee or Society Employee, Sworn/Affirmed

ONTARIO

	Court File Number
_____ *(Name of court)*	
at _____ *Court office address*	**Form 34G: Affidavit of Adoption Licensee or Society Employee, sworn/affirmed**

Applicant(s) *(The first letter of the applicant's surname may be used)*

Full legal name & address for service — street & number, municipality, postal code, telephone & fax numbers and e-mail address (if any).	Lawyer's name & address — street & number, municipality, postal code, telephone & fax numbers and e-mail address (if any).

Respondent(s) *(If there is a respondent, the first letter of the respondent's surname may be used)*

Full legal name & address for service — street & number, municipality, postal code, telephone & fax numbers and e-mail address (if any).	Lawyer's name & address — street & number, municipality, postal code, telephone & fax numbers and e-mail address (if any).

My name is *(full legal name)* _____

I live in *(municipality & province)* _____

and I swear/affirm that the following is true:

1. The name of the child being placed for adoption is: *(Give full legal name, date of birth, sex and birth registration number if known of person to be adopted. If this person is in extended society care or was placed for adoption by a licensee or children's aid society, you may use an initial for the surname.)*

    _____

    Full legal name   Date of birth   Sex   Birth registration number

2. I am   ☐   a person licensed under Part VIII of the *Child, Youth and Family Services Act, 2017* to place the child for adoption.

    ☐   an employee of *(full legal name of children's aid society)* _____ authorized to place the child for adoption.

    ☐   an employee of *(full legal name of adoption agency)* _____ which is licensed under Part VIII of the *Child, Youth and Family Services Act, 2017* to place the child for adoption.

3. I have made reasonable inquiries about the existence of any outstanding orders of custody of or access to the child. To the best of my knowledge,

    ☐   there is no outstanding order.

    ☐   the outstanding order(s) is/are as follows: *(For each order, give the name of the court, date of order, name of judge, court file number and full legal name(s) of the person(s) given custody or access under the order.)*

Form 34G: **Affidavit of Adoption Licensee**   **(page 2)**
            or Society Employee

Court File Number

4.   I have made reasonable inquiries about the existence of any person — other than the person(s) who already filed a consent — who is a "parent" of the child within the meaning of Part VIII of the *Child, Youth and Family Services Act, 2017*. To the best of my knowledge,

☐   There is no other "parent".

☐   the other "parent(s)" is/are: *(For each person, state his or her full legal name, address and an explanation why a consent is not yet available.)*

5.   I have made reasonable inquiries about the existence of any other application for the adoption of this child. To the best of my knowledge,

☐   there has been no other adoption application with respect to this child.

☐   the details of the other adoption application(s) are as follows: *(For each application, state the name and location of the court before which the application was brought, the date of the application, the full legal name(s) of the applicant(s) and the result of the application.)*

6.   I have made reasonable inquiries whether the person(s) who filed the consent(s) in this application withdrew the consent(s) or whether a court had set aside the consent(s). To the best of my knowledge,

☐   no consent was withdrawn or set aside.

☐   the details of the withdrawal or of the setting aside are as follows: *(Specify details.)*

7.   The child in this adoption case

☐   is 7 or more years old and I have therefore offered the child a chance to get counselling about the consent. This offer of counselling

☐   was accepted and the child received counselling.

☐   was turned down by the child.

I also ensured that the child received independent legal advice from *(lawyer's name)*

☐   is less than 7 years old and no counselling or independent legal advice was offered.

8.   I offered the child's parent(s) a chance to get counselling about the consent and the offer

☐   was accepted by *(name of parent(s) who accepted offer)*

and counselling was provided.

☐   was turned down by *(name of parent(s) who refused offer)*

Put a line through any space left on this page
FLR 34G (March 1, 2018)

Page 2 of 3

Form 34G: **Affidavit of Adoption Licensee** **(page 3)** Court File Number
or Society Employee

9. The parent(s) received independent legal advice from *(name of lawyer(s))*

10. To the best of my knowledge, no person has given, received or agreed to give or receive any payment or reward of any kind in connection with

    (a) The adoption of the child;

    (b) The child's placement for adoption;

    (c) The giving of any consent to the child's adoption; or

    (d) Any negotiations or arrangements leading up to the child's adoption,

except for what is permitted by the *Child, Youth and Family Services Act, 2017* and the regulations made under it.

Sworn/Affirmed before me at _____

                            municipality

in _____

           province, state or country

on _____ _____

    date   *Commissioner for taking affidavits*
       (Type or print name below if signature is illegible.)

_____
Signature

(This form is to be signed in front of a lawyer, justice of the peace, notary public or commissioner for taking affidavits.)

Form 34G.1

Affidavit for Society Employee for Adoption of a Child in Extended Society Care, Sworn/Affirmed

ONTARIO

	Court File Number
_____ *(Name of court)*	
at _____ *Court office address*	**Form 34G.1: Affidavit of Society Employee for Adoption of a Child in Extended Society Care, sworn/affirmed**

Applicant(s) *(The first letter of the applicant's surname may be used)*

Full legal name & address for service — street & number, municipality, postal code, telephone & fax numbers and e-mail address (if any).	Lawyer's name & address — street & number, municipality, postal code, telephone & fax numbers and e-mail address (if any).

Respondent(s) *(If there is a respondent, the first letter of the respondent's surname may be used)*

Full legal name & address for service — street & number, municipality, postal code, telephone & fax numbers and e-mail address (if any).	Lawyer's name & address — street & number, municipality, postal code, telephone & fax numbers and e-mail address (if any).

My name is *(full legal name)* _____

I live in *(municipality & province)* _____

and I swear/affirm that the following is true:

1. The name of the child being placed for adoption is: *(Give full legal name, date of birth, sex and birth registration number if known of person to be adopted. You may use an initial for the surname.)*

Full legal name	*Date of birth*	*Sex*	*Birth registration number*

2. I am an employee of *(full legal name of children's aid society)* _____
   authorized to place the child for adoption.

3. The child was placed in extended society care by order of Justice *(name of judge)* _____
   on *(date)* _____ . A copy of the extended society care order and proof of service of the order are
   attached to this affidavit.

4. I have made reasonable inquiries about the existence of any outstanding orders of access to the child. To the best of
   my knowledge,

   ☐ there is no outstanding order.

   ☐ A copy of the order ending access to the child made under s. 104 of the *Child, Youth and Family Services Act, 2017* made by

   Justice *(name of judge)* _____ on *(date of order)* _____

   and proof of service of the order are attached to this affidavit.

Form 34G.1: Affidavit of Society Employee for **(page 2)**   Court File Number
Adoption of a Child in Extended
Society Care

☐ A copy of the order for access to the child made under s. 104 of the *Child, Youth and Family Services Act, 2017*

made by Justice *(name of judge)* _____ on *(date of order)* _____

is attached to this affidavit.

☐ On *(date)* _____ , *(name of children's aid society)* _____

gave notice to *(name(s) of person(s) entitled to notice)* _____

that the child would be placed for adoption as described in the affidavit(s) of service of *(name(s) of person(s) who*

served notice) _____ sworn/affirmed on *(date(s)*

affidavit(s) of service sworn or affirmed) _____ .

    ☐ This service was in accordance with the requirements in s. 195(4) of the *Child, Youth and Family Services*
Act, 2017.

    ☐ This service was in accordance with the order of Justice *(name of judge)* _____

pursuant to s. 195(5) of the *Child, Youth and Family Services Act, 2017.*

    ☐ Justice *(name of judge)* _____ made an order on *(date of order)*

_____ dispensing with service of notice on *(name(s) of person(s) entitled to access to*

or contact with the child who was(were) not served) _____

pursuant to s. 195(6) of the *Child, Youth and Family Services Act, 2017.*

☐ The child is a First Nations, Inuk, or Métis person and on *(date)* _____ ,

(name of children's aid society) _____ gave notice to

(name(s) of person(s) entitled to notice) _____

that the child would be placed for adoption as described in the affidavit(s) of service of *(name(s) of person(s)*

who served notice) _____ sworn/affirmed on *(date(s)*

affidavit(s) of service sworn or affirmed) _____ .

    ☐ This service was in accordance with the requirements in s. 197(4)(a) of the *Child, Youth and Family Services*
Act, 2017.

    ☐ This service was in accordance with the order of Justice *(name of judge)* _____

pursuant to s. 197(4)(b) of the *Child, Youth and Family Services Act, 2017.*

    ☐ Justice *(name of judge)* _____ made an order on *(date of order)*

_____ dispensing with service of notice on *(name(s) of person(s) entitled to notice and*

who was/were not served) _____

pursuant to s. 197(4)(b) of the *Child, Youth and Family Services Act, 2017.*

☐ No application for an openness order was filed with respect to this child and the access order of Justice *(name*

of judge) _____ , dated *(date of order)* _____ , was

terminated upon the placement of the child for adoption on *(date child placed for adoption)*

Form 34G.1:	Affidavit of Society Employee for Adoption of a Child in Extended Society Care	(page 3)	Court File Number

☐ An openness application was filed by *(name of person(s) seeking an openness order)*

_____ and the following order was made:

(Give the name of the court, date of order, name of judge, court file number, full legal name(s) of the person(s) permitted to communicate or have a relationship with the child under the order and details of the order.)

☐ An openness application was filed by *(name of person(s) seeking an openness order)*

_____ and has not yet been concluded.

The status of that application is as follows: *(Provide details of the order requested, position of other parties and any court dates that have been scheduled.)*

5. ☐ I have made reasonable inquiries about the existence of any outstanding appeals of orders relating to the child. To the best of my knowledge,

   ☐ There is no appeal in progress of the order(s) for extended society care or ending access to the child.

   ☐ The appeal period for the order(s) for extended society care and ending access to the child have expired without an appeal being filed.

   ☐ An appeal of the order for extended society care was filed on *(date)* _____, and was withdrawn on *(date)* _____.

   ☐ An appeal of the order for extended society care was filed and dismissed by *(name of judge or registrar of the Court of Appeal)* _____ on *(date of order)* _____

   ☐ An appeal of the order ending access was filed on *(date)* _____, and was withdrawn on *(date)* _____.

   ☐ An appeal of the order ending access was filed and dismissed by *(name of judge or registrar of the Court of Appeal)* _____ on *(date of order)* _____.

Sworn/Affirmed before me at _____	
municipality	Signature
in _____	
province, state or country	*(This form is to be signed in front of a lawyer, justice of the peace, notary public or commissioner for taking affidavits.)*
on _____	
date Commissioner for taking affidavits	
(Type or print name below if signature is illegible.)	

Form 34H

Affidavit of Adopting Relative or Stepparent, Sworn/Affirmed

ONTARIO

_____ *(Name of court)*	**Court File Number** _____
at _____ *Court office address*	**Form 34H: Affidavit of Adopting Relative or Stepparent, sworn/affirmed** _____

Applicant(s) *(The first letter of the applicant's surname may be used)*

Full legal name & address for service — street & number, municipality, postal code, telephone & fax numbers and e-mail address (if any).	Lawyer's name & address — street & number, municipality, postal code, telephone & fax numbers and e-mail address (if any).

Respondent(s) *(If there is a respondent, the first letter of the respondent's surname may be used)*

Full legal name & address for service — street & number, municipality, postal code, telephone & fax numbers and e-mail address (if any).	Lawyer's name & address — street & number, municipality, postal code, telephone & fax numbers and e-mail address (if any).

My name is *(full legal name)* _____

I live in *(municipality & province)* _____

and I swear/affirm that the following is true:

1. I was born on *(date of your own birth)* _____

2. The name of the child whom I want to adopt is *(Give full legal name, date of birth, sex and birth registration number if known)*

Full legal name	Date of birth	Sex	Birth registration number

3. I am the applicant in this adoption and am this child's

   ☐ stepparent.　　　　　　　　　☐ grandparent.

   ☐ aunt/uncle.　　　　　　　　　☐ great-aunt/great-uncle.

4. I have made reasonable inquiries about the existence of any outstanding orders of custody of or access to the child. To the best of my knowledge,

   ☐ there is no outstanding order.

   ☐ the outstanding order(s) is/are as follows: *(For each order, give the name of the court, date of order, name of judge, court file number and full legal name(s) of the person(s) given custody or access under the order.)*

Put a line through any space left on this page.

Form 34H: Affidavit of Adopting Relative or Stepparent (page 2)

Court File Number

5. I have made reasonable inquiries about the existence of any person — other than the person(s) who already filed a consent — who is a "parent" of the child within the meaning of Part VIII of the *Child, Youth and Family Services Act, 2017*. To the best of my knowledge,

☐ there is no other "parent".

☐ the other "parent(s)" is/are: *(For each parent, state his or her full legal name, address and an explanation why a consent is not yet available.)*

6. I have made reasonable inquiries about the existence of any other application for the adoption of this child. To the best of my knowledge,

☐ there has been no other adoption application with respect to this child.

☐ the details of the other adoption application(s) are as follows: *(For each application, state the name and location of the court before which the application was brought, the date of the application, the full legal name(s) of the applicant(s) and the result of the application.)*

7. I have made reasonable inquiries whether the person(s) who filed the consent(s) in this application withdrew the consent(s) or whether a court had set aside the consent(s). To the best of my knowledge,

☐ no consent was withdrawn or set aside.

☐ the details of the withdrawal or of the setting aside are as follows: *(Specify details.)*

8. The child in this adoption case

☐ is 7 or more years old and I have therefore offered the child a chance to get counselling about the consent. This offer of counselling

☐ was accepted and the child received counselling.

☐ was turned down by the child.

I also ensured that the child received independent legal advice from *(lawyer's name)*

☐ is less than 7 years old and no counselling or independent legal advice was offered.

9. I offered the child's parent(s) a chance to get counselling about the consent and the offer

☐ was accepted by *(name of parent(s) who accepted offer)*

_____ and counselling was provided.

☐ was turned down by *(name of parent(s) who refused offer)*

_____

Put a line through any space left on this page.

FAMILY LAW RULES FORMS

Form 34H: **Affidavit of Adopting Relative or Stepparent** **(page 3)**

Court File Number: _____

10. I also ensured that the parent(s) received independent legal advice from *(name of lawyer(s))*

_____

11. To the best of my knowledge, no person has given, received or agreed to give or receive any payment or reward of any kind in connection with,

    (a)   the adoption of the child;

    (b)   the child's placement for adoption;

    (c)   the giving of any consent to the child's adoption; or

    (d)   any negotiations or arrangements leading up to the child's adoption,

except for what is permitted by the *Child, Youth and Family Services Act, 2017* and the regulations made under it.

12. I understand that once the child turns eighteen years old, he/she can apply for a copy of his/her original birth registration, if any, and a copy of his/her adoption order.

13. I understand that once the child turns nineteen years old, his/her birth parent(s) can apply for information from his/her original birth registration, if any, any substituted birth registration and his/her adoption order. This information would include the child's full legal name after adoption.

14. I understand the provisions of the *Vital Statistics Act* and the *Child, Youth and Family Services Act, 2017* related to the disclosure of adoption information.

Sworn/Affirmed before me at _____
                                      municipality

in _____
                        province, state or country

on _____
    date   *Commissioner for taking affidavits*
                      (Type or print name below if signature is illegible.)

Signature

(This form is to be signed in front of a lawyer, justice of the peace, notary public or commissioner for taking affidavits.)

Form 34I

Parent's Consent to Adoption by Spouse

ONTARIO

_____
(Name of court)

at _____
Court office address

Court File Number

Form 34I: Parent's Consent to Adoption by Spouse

Applicant(s) *(The first letter of the applicant's surname may be used)*

Full legal name & address for service — street & number, municipality, postal code, telephone & fax numbers and e-mail address (if any).	Lawyer's name & address — street & number, municipality, postal code, telephone & fax numbers and e-mail address (if any).

Respondent(s) *(If there is a respondent, the first letter of the respondent's surname may be used)*

Full legal name & address for service — street & number, municipality, postal code, telephone & fax numbers and e-mail address (if any).	Lawyer's name & address — street & number, municipality, postal code, telephone & fax numbers and e-mail address (if any).

Child

(Child's full legal name. If this person is in extended society care or was placed by a licensee or children's aid society, you may use an initial for the surname.)

_____

Date of birth	Sex	Birth registration number

1. **My name is** *(full legal name)* _____

   I was born on *(date of birth)* _____ **and I live**

   at *(address)* _____

2. The applicant is my "spouse" within the meaning of Part VIII of the *Child, Youth and Family Services Act, 2017.*

3. I am a parent of the child within the meaning of Part VIII of the *Child, Youth and Family Services Act, 2017* because I am *(Check appropriate paragraph below.)*

   ☐ a parent of the child under section 6, 8, 9, 10, 11 or 13 of the *Children's Law Reform Act (includes a birth parent, her spouse).* I am the child's *(state your relationship to the child)*
   _____

   ☐ an individual described in subsection 7(2) of the *Children's Law Reform Act.*

   ☐ an individual who has been found or recognized by a court of competent jurisdiction outside of Ontario to be a parent of the child.

   ☐ a parent under section 217 or 218 of the *Child, Youth and Family Services Act, 2017. (includes adoptive parents)*

   ☐ an individual having lawful custody of the child.

   ☐ an individual who, during the 12 months before the child was placed for adoption, has demonstrated a settled intention to treat the child as a member of his/her family.

   ☐ an individual who, during the 12 months before the child was placed for adoption, has acknowledged parentage of the child and has provided for the child's support.

   ☐ an individual who is required to provide for the child or who has custody of or access to the child under a written agreement or a court order.

   ☐ an individual who has acknowledged parentage of the child under section 12 of the *Children's Law Reform Act* as it read before January 1, 2017.

4. I consent to the adoption of the child by my spouse.

5. I understand the nature and effect of this consent. I understand that I may withdraw my consent by ensuring that the proposed applicant and the licensee, if the child was placed for adoption by a licensee, receive(s) my written notice of withdrawal within 21 days after my consent was given.

Form 34I: Parent's Consent to Adoption by Spouse   (page 2)

6. I understand that, after the 21 days have passed, I am not allowed to withdraw this consent unless I first get the court's permission and if I can show that it is in the child's best interests that this consent be withdrawn.

7. I understand the nature of an adoption order. I understand that, if an adoption order were made, my spouse would be joining me in the role of a parent and, together, we would be the child's only legal parents. An adoption order would require me to share my parental rights and responsibilities with my spouse equally and permanently until a court ordered otherwise.

8. I understand my rights and the rights of other persons with respect to the disclosure of adoption information.

9. No payment or reward of any kind was made, given, received or agreed to be made, given or received by me/us or, to the best of my/our knowledge, by any other person in connection with,

      (a) the adoption of this child;

      (b) this child's placement for adoption;

      (c) the giving of any consent to this child's adoption; or

      (d) any negotiations or arrangements leading up to this child's adoption,

except for what is permitted by the *Child, Youth and Family Services Act, 2017* and the regulations made under that Act.

10. I had a chance to seek counselling with respect to this consent.

11. I have had independent legal advice with respect to this consent.

_____   _____
Date of signatures   *Signature of parent*

NOTE: This consent must be witnessed by an independent lawyer who is to provide an affidavit of execution and independent legal advice below. If the person giving this consent is less than 18 years old, the consent must be accompanied by Form 34J (Affidavit of Execution and Independent Legal Advice (Children's Lawyer)), instead of the Affidavit of Execution and Independent Legal Advice that accompanies this form.

_____
Signature of independent lawyer

AFFIDAVIT OF EXECUTION AND INDEPENDENT LEGAL ADVICE

My name is *(full legal name)* _____

and I swear/affirm that the following is true:

    1.   I am a member of the Bar of *(name of jurisdiction)* _____
          and I am not acting for any other person in this adoption case.

    2.   I explained to *(parent's full legal name)* _____ about

          ☐ the nature and effect of adoption under the law of Ontario;

          ☐ the nature and effect of this consent;

          ☐ the circumstances under which this consent may be withdrawn;

          ☐ his/her rights and the rights of other persons with respect to the disclosure of adoption information;

          ☐ the right to counselling.

    3.   After my explanation, he/she told me that he/she wanted to sign this consent.

    4.   I was present at and witnessed the signing of this consent.

Sworn/Affirmed before me at _____

                          municipality

in _____

                 province, state or country

on _____

       date   *Commissioner for taking affidavits*
                (Type or print name below if signature is illegible.)

_____
Signature
(This form is to be signed in front of a lawyer, justice of the peace, notary public or commissioner for taking affidavits.)

Form 34J

Affidavit of Execution and Independent Legal Advice (Children's Lawyer), Sworn/Affirmed

ONTARIO

_____
(Name of court)

at _____
Court office address

Court File Number

Form 34J: Affidavit of Execution
and Independent Legal Advice
(Children's Lawyer),
sworn/affirmed

My name is *(full legal name)* _____

and I swear/affirm that the following is true:

1. I am an authorized representative of the Office of the Children's Lawyer in the adoption of:

Full legal name of child	Date of birth (d, m, y) and sex

2. I explained to *(minor parent's full legal name)* _____ about
   - ☐ the nature and effect of adoption under the law of Ontario;
   - ☐ the nature and effect of a consent to adoption;
   - ☐ the right to counselling;
   - ☐ his/her rights and the rights of other persons with respect to the disclosure of adoption information;
   - ☐ the right upon request to be advised whether an adoption order has been made,

   in language appropriate to his/her age to the best of my knowledge and skills.

3. I also explained that he/she could withdraw the consent within 21 days by a written notice. I gave him/her the address where the written notice would have to be served. I also explained that, after the 21 days had passed, he/she could withdraw the consent only with the court's permission but only if the child had not yet been placed with a person for adoption and if he/she could convince the court that it would be in the child's best interests to have the consent withdrawn.

4. After my explanation, he/she told me that he/she wanted to sign the consent to adoption and I believe that this reflects his/her true wishes.

5. I was present at and witnessed the signing of the consent.

Sworn/Affirmed before me at _____
municipality

in _____
province, state or country

on _____
date

_____
Commissioner for taking affidavits
(Type or print name below if signature is illegible.)

_____
Signature
(This form is to be signed in front of a lawyer, justice of the peace, notary public or commissioner for taking affidavits.)

Form 34K

Certificate of Clerk (Adoption)

ONTARIO

	Court File Number

_____
(Name of court)

Form 34K: Certificate of Clerk (Adoption)

at _____
Court office address

Applicant(s) *(The first letter of the applicant's surname may be used)*

Full legal name & address for service — street & number, municipality, postal code, telephone & fax numbers and e-mail address (if any).	Lawyer's name & address — street & number, municipality, postal code, telephone & fax numbers and e-mail address (if any).

Respondent(s) *(If there is a respondent, the first letter of the surname may be used)*

Full legal name & address for service — street & number, municipality, postal code, telephone & fax numbers and e-mail address (if any).	Lawyer's name & address — street & number, municipality, postal code, telephone & fax numbers and e-mail address (if any).

If the appropriate box on the left cannot be checked, check the box on the right margin and describe the deficiency by the box.
The clerk of the court certifies as follows:

1.   MATERIAL COMMON TO ALL ADOPTION CASES

Deficiency

(a) ☐ An application for adoption (Form 8D in *Family Law Rules*) has been filed.   1(a) ☐

(b) ☐ A certified copy of the statement of live birth has been filed (Form 2 in regulation under *Vital Statistics Act*).   1(b) ☐

☐ A certified copy of a change of birth registration has been filed (Form 2 in regulation under *Vital Statistics Act*).

☐ Equivalent proof of details of birth has been filed.

(c) ☐ The person to be adopted is 7 years of age or over and has filed a consent to adoption (Form 34 in *Family Law Rules*).   1(c) ☐

☐ A court order dispensing with the consent of the person to be adopted has been filed.

(d) ☐ An affidavit of parentage has been filed (Form 34A in *Family Law Rules*).   1(d) ☐

☐ Other evidence of who is or is not a "parent" has been filed.

(e) ☐ A report on the child's adjustment in the applicant's home: 1(e) ☐

   ☐ is required by the Act (where a child had been "placed" for adoption through a licensee, a society or otherwise). That report has been filed.

   ☐ had been ordered by the court in the case of an adoption by a stepparent or relative. That report has been filed.

   ☐ has not been required in this case.

(f) ☐ The applicant has a 'spouse' who is not a 'parent' and who has not joined in the application. That spouse's consent (Form 34B in *Family Law Rules*) has been filed.   1(f) ☐

☐ A court order dispensing with the spouse's consent has been filed, together with,

   (i) ☐ proof of service of this order.

   (ii) ☐ a certified copy of an order dispensing with service.

Form 34K: **Certificate of Clerk (Adoption)** **(page 2)**

Court File Number

Deficiency

(g) ☐ The Director's or local director's statement (with recommendations) on the adoption (Form 34C in *Family Law Rules*): 1(g) ☐

    ☐ is required by the Act (where a child had been "placed" for adoption through a licensee, a society or otherwise). That statement has been filed.

    ☐ had been ordered by the court in the case of an adoption by a stepparent or relative. That statement has been filed.

    ☐ has not been required in this case.

(h) ☐ The affidavit of each adoption applicant (Form 34D in *Family Law Rules*) has been filed. 1(h) ☐

(i) ☐ A draft adoption order (Form 25C in *Family Law Rules*) has been filed. 1(i) ☐

(j) ☐ This is a joint application by spouses and 1(j) ☐

    (i) ☐ a certificate of the applicants' marriage had been filed.

    (ii) ☐ other proof of the applicants' spousal status has been filed.

(k) ☐ Other joint application *(Specify.)* 1(k) ☐

(l) ☐ *(Other. Specify.)* 1(l) ☐

2. ADDITIONAL MATERIAL FOR ADOPTIONS OF CHILDREN IN EXTENDED SOCIETY CARE

(a) ☐ The Director's consent to adoption (Form 34E in *Family Law Rules*) has been filed. 2(a) ☐

(b) ☐ There is no outstanding access order to this child in extended society care, and an affidavit (Form 34G.1) has been filed confirming that fact. 2(b) ☐

    ☐ A certified copy of an order terminating access to this child in extended society care has been filed, together with,

    (i) ☐ proof of service of this order.

    (ii) ☐ a certified copy of an order dispensing with service.

(c) ☐ The outstanding access order was terminated when the child was placed for adoption and the following document(s) were filed: 2(c) ☐

    ☐ A copy of each access order made under Part V of the *Child, Youth and Family Services Act, 2017*.

    ☐ A copy of every notice of intention to place for adoption.

    ☐ Proof of service of notice of intention to place for adoption.

    ☐ A copy of the order permitting an alternative method of service.

    ☐ Proof of service in accordance with order for alternative service.

    ☐ A copy of the order dispensing with notice.

(d) ☐ The child is a First Nations, Inuk, or Métis person and the following document(s) were filed: 2(d) ☐

    ☐ A copy of every notice of intention to place for adoption in accordance with section 197(2) of the *Child, Youth and Family Services Act, 2017*, unless the child's First Nations, Inuk or Métis community was not listed at the time the child was placed for adoption, or the child was placed under the old Act.

    ☐ Proof of service of notice in accordance with s. 197(4)(a) of the *Child, Youth and Family Services Act, 2017*.

    ☐ A copy of the order permitting an alternative method of service pursuant to s. 197(4)(b) of the *Child, Youth and Family Services Act, 2017*.

Form 34K: **Certificate of Clerk (Adoption)** **(page 3)**

Court File Number

Deficiency

☐ Proof of service in accordance with order for alternative service.

☐ A copy of the order dispensing with notice pursuant to s. 197(4)(b) of the *Child, Youth and Family Services Act, 2017.*

(e) ☐ A certified copy of the extended society care order has been filed together with,   2(e) ☐

   (i) ☐ proof of service of this order.

   (ii) ☐ a certified copy of an order dispensing with service.

(f) ☐ A copy of any openness order has been filed (if applicable).   2(f) ☐

(g) ☐ An affidavit from a society employee (Form 34G.1) has been filed, stating that no appeal of the orders mentioned in clause (b) above had been launched or that the appeal period had expired.   2(g) ☐

(h) ☐ The child is a First Nations, Inuk, or Métis person, and the following document(s) were filed: 2(h) ☐

   ☐ a copy of the notice provided by a society setting out the society's intention to begin planning for adoption of the child.

   ☐ proof of service of the notice(s).

(i) ☐ An affidavit (Form 34G.1 in *Family Law Rules*) of an authorized employee of the children's aid society has been filed.   2(i) ☐

(j) ☐ *(Other. Specify.)*   2(j) ☐

3. **ADDITIONAL MATERIAL FOR ADOPTIONS OF CHILDREN NOT IN EXTENDED SOCIETY CARE PLACED FOR ADOPTION BY LICENSEE OR SOCIETY**

(a) ☐ The child has been placed by a children's aid society.   3(a) ☐

   ☐ The child has been placed by a licensee, and a copy of the licensee's licence to make the placement at the time of placing the child for adoption has been filed.

(b) ☐ An affidavit (Form 34G in *Family Law Rules*) of the licensee or of an authorized employee of the children's aid society has been filed.   3(b) ☐

(c) ☐ The person filing the affidavit knows of no custody or access order involving the child.   3(c) ☐

   ☐ Certified copy/copies of the custody or access order(s) involving the child has/have been filed together with,

   (i) ☐ proof of service of this order.

   (ii) ☐ a certified copy of an order dispensing with service.

(d) ☐ A consent (Form 34F in *Family Law Rules*) to adoption from the birth parent has been filed.   3(d) ☐

   ☐ The consent, which was signed by the birth parent when she was under 18 years of age, is accompanied by a certificate of the Children's Lawyer (Form 34J in *Family Law Rules*).

   ☐ The child's birth parent has, outside Ontario, signed a form of consent that is not an Ontario consent form and that is accompanied by:

   (i) ☐ a certified translation of the document into English/French.

   (ii) ☐ evidence that the foreign consent complies with the laws of the place where the birth parent made it.

   ☐ A certified copy of an order dispensing with the birth parent's consent has been filed, together with proof of service of the order.

Form 34K: **Certificate of Clerk (Adoption)** **(page 4)**

Court File Number

Deficiency

(e) ☐ The child is presumed to have a "parent" as defined under paragraph 2 of section 180 of the *Child, Youth and Family Services Act, 2017* and the following document(s) have been filed:

    ☐ A consent (Form 34F in *Family Law Rules*) to adoption from the "parent."

    ☐ The consent, which was signed by the "parent" when he was under 18 years of age, is accompanied by a certificate of the Children's Lawyer (Form 34J in *Family Law Rules*).

    ☐ The "parent" has, outside Ontario, signed a form of consent that is not an Ontario consent form and that is accompanied by:

        (i) ☐ a certified translation of the document into English/French.

        (ii) ☐ evidence that the foreign consent complies with the laws of the place where the "parent" made it.

    ☐ A certified copy of an order dispensing with the "parent's" consent, together with proof of service of the order.

    ☐ The court has ruled that, on a balance of probabilities, the person does not have the status of "parent" under paragraph 2 of section 180 of the *Child, Youth and Family Services Act, 2017*.

3(e) ☐

(f) ☐ A consent (Form 34F in *Family Law Rules*) to adoption from any other person who is a "parent" under Part VIII of the *Child, Youth and Family Services Act, 2017* has been filed.

    ☐ The consent, which was signed by the other "parent" when he/she was under 18 years of age, is accompanied by a certificate of the Children's Lawyer (Form 34J in *Family Law Rules*).

    ☐ This other "parent" has, outside Ontario, signed a form of consent that is not an Ontario consent form and that is accompanied by:

        (i) ☐ a certified translation of the document into English/French.

        (ii) ☐ evidence that the foreign consent complies with the laws of the place where the other "parent" made it.

    ☐ A certified copy of an order dispensing with the other "parent's" consent has been filed, together with proof of service of the order.

3(f) ☐

(g) ☐ A consent (Form 34F in *Family Law Rules*) to adoption from any other person who is a "parent" under Part VIII of the *Child, Youth and Family Services Act, 2017* has been filed.

    ☐ The consent, which was signed by the other "parent" when he/she was under 18 years of age, is accompanied by a certificate of the Children's Lawyer (Form 34J in *Family Law Rules*).

    ☐ This other "parent" has, outside Ontario, signed a form of consent that is not an Ontario consent form and that is accompanied by:

        (i) ☐ a certified translation of the document into English/French.

        (ii) ☐ evidence that the foreign consent complies with the laws of the place where the other "parent" made it.

    ☐ A certified copy of an order dispensing with the other "parent's" consent has been filed, together with proof of service of the order.

3(g) ☐

(h) ☐ The child is a First Nations, Inuk, or Métis person, and the following document(s) were filed:

    ☐ a copy of the notice provided by a society setting out the society's intention to begin planning for adoption of the child.

    ☐ a copy of the notice provided by a licensee in accordance with regulations made under the Act setting out the licensee's intention to place the child for adoption.

3(h) ☐

FLR 34K (March 1, 2018)

Form 34K:	Certificate of Clerk (Adoption)	(page 5)	Court File Number

Deficiency

    ☐   proof of service of the notice(s).

(i)   ☐   *(Other. Specify.)*   3(j)   ☐

4. ADDITIONAL MATERIAL FOR ADOPTION OF CHILD RESIDENT IN CANADA BEFORE ADOPTION BY RELATIVE OR STEPPARENT OR WHERE CHILD HAS RESIDED WITH APPLICANT FOR AT LEAST TWO YEARS

(a)   ☐   There are no custody or access orders involving the child.   4(a)   ☐

     ☐   Certified copy/copies of the custody or access order(s) involving the child has/have been filed together with,

         (i)   ☐   proof of service of this order.

         (ii)   ☐   a certified copy of an order dispensing with service.

(b)   ☐   A consent (Form 34F in *Family Law Rules*) to adoption from the birth parent has been filed.   4(b)   ☐

     ☐   The consent, which was signed by the birth parent when she was under 18 years of age, is accompanied by a certificate of the Children's Lawyer (Form 34J in *Family Law Rules*).

     ☐   The child's birth parent has, outside Ontario, signed a form of consent that is not an Ontario consent form and that is accompanied by:

         (i)   ☐   a certified translation of the document into English/French.

         (ii)   ☐   evidence that the foreign consent complies with the laws of the place where the birth parent made it.

     ☐   A certified copy of an order dispensing with the birth parent's consent has been filed, together with proof of service of the order.

(c)   ☐   The child is presumed to have a "parent" as defined under paragraph 2 of section 180 of the *Child, Youth and Family Services Act, 2017* and the following document(s) have been filed: 4(c)   ☐

     ☐   A consent (Form 34F in *Family Law Rules*) to adoption from the "parent."

     ☐   The consent, which was signed by the "parent" when he was under 18 years of age, is accompanied by a certificate of the Children's Lawyer (Form 34J in *Family Law Rules*).

     ☐   The "parent" has, outside Ontario, signed a form of consent that is not an Ontario consent form and that is accompanied by:

         (i)   ☐   a certified translation of the document into English/French.

         (ii)   ☐   evidence that the foreign consent complies with the laws of the place where the "parent" made it.

     ☐   A certified copy of an order dispensing with the "parent's" consent has been filed, together with proof of service of the order.

     ☐   The court has ruled that, on a balance of probabilities, the person does not have the status of "parent" under paragraph 2 of section 180 of the *Child, Youth and Family Services Act, 2017*.

(d)   ☐   A consent (Form 34F in *Family Law Rules*) to adoption from any other person who is a "parent" under Part VIII of the *Child, Youth and Family Services Act, 2017* has been filed.   4(d)   ☐

     ☐   The consent, which was signed by the other "parent" when he/she was under 18 years of age, is accompanied by a certificate of the Children's Lawyer (Form 34J in *Family Law Rules*).

Form 34K: **Certificate of Clerk (Adoption)**   **(page 6)**

Court File Number

Deficiency

	☐	This other "parent" has, outside Ontario, signed a form of consent that is not an Ontario consent and that is accompanied by:		

   (i)   ☐   a certified translation of the document into English/French.

   (ii) ☐   evidence that the foreign consent complies with the laws of the place where the other "parent" made it.

   ☐   A certified copy of an order dispensing with the other "parent's" consent has been filed, together with proof of service of the order.

(e)   ☐   A consent (Form 34F in *Family Law Rules*) to adoption from any other person who is a "parent" under Part VIII of the *Child, Youth and Family Services Act, 2017* has been filed.   4(e)   ☐

   ☐   The consent, which was signed by the other "parent" when he/she was under 18 years of age, is accompanied by a certificate of the Children's Lawyer (Form 34J in *Family Law Rules*).

   ☐   This other "parent" has, outside Ontario, signed a form of consent that is not an Ontario consent and that is accompanied by:

   (i)   ☐   a certified translation of the document into English/French.

   (ii) ☐   evidence that the foreign consent complies with the laws of the place where the other "parent" made it.

   ☐   A certified copy of an order dispensing with the other "parent's" consent has been filed, together with proof of service of the order.

(f)   ☐   The affidavit (Form 34H in *Family Law Rules*) of the stepparent or of each adoption applicant has been filed.   4(f)   ☐

(g)   ☐   This is a stepparent adoption and the spouse of the adopting stepparent has filed a consent (Form 34I in *Family Law Rules*).   4(g)   ☐

(h)   ☐   *(Other. Specify.)*   4(h)   ☐

_____   _____
Date of Signature   Signature of clerk of the court

Form 34L

Application for Openness Order

ONTARIO

	Court File Number

(SEAL)

_____

(Name of court)

at _____

Court office address

Form 34L: Application for Openness Order

Applicant(s)

Full legal name & address for service — street & number, municipality, postal code, telephone & fax numbers and e-mail address (if any).	Lawyer's name & address — street & number, municipality, postal code, telephone & fax numbers and e-mail address (if any).

Respondent(s) *(Persons entitled to notice.)*

Full legal name & address for service — street & number, municipality, postal code, telephone & fax numbers and e-mail address (if any).	Lawyer's name & address — street & number, municipality, postal code, telephone & fax numbers and e-mail address (if any).

Children's Lawyer

Name & address of Children's Lawyer's agent for service (street & number, municipality, postal code, telephone & fax numbers and e-mail address (if any)) and name of person represented.

TO THE RESPONDENT(S):

A COURT APPLICATION HAS BEEN STARTED IN THIS COURT FOR AN OPENNESS ORDER. THE DETAILS ARE SET OUT ON THE ATTACHED PAGES.

THE FIRST COURT DATE IS *(date)* _____ **AT** _____ ☐ a.m. ☐ p.m.

or as soon as possible after that time, at: *(address)*

YOU SHOULD CONSIDER GETTING LEGAL ADVICE ABOUT THIS RIGHT AWAY. If you cannot afford a lawyer, you may be able to get help from Legal Aid Ontario. Call **1-800-668-8268 toll-free** to get legal aid help in over 120 languages. For more information about the services available through Legal Aid Ontario, visit www.legalaid.on.ca.

YOU HAVE ONLY 30 DAYS AFTER THIS APPLICATION IS SERVED ON YOU (60 DAYS IF THIS APPLICATION IS SERVED ON YOU OUTSIDE CANADA OR THE UNITED STATES) TO SERVE AND FILE AN ANSWER IN FORM 33B.2: Answer *(Child, Youth and Family Services Act, 2017* Cases other than Child Protection and Status Review). **IF YOU DO NOT, THE CASE WILL GO AHEAD WITHOUT YOU AND THE COURT MAY MAKE AN ORDER.**

_____   _____
Date of issue   *Clerk of the court*

FLR 34L (March 1, 2018)

Page 1 of 3

Form 34L: Application for Openness Order   **(page 2)**   Court File Number

THE CHILD

Child's Full Legal Name	Birthdate	Sex	Is the Child First Nations, Inuit, or Métis?	Child's Bands or First Nations, Inuit, or Métis Communities

Extended Society Care Order:

Court File Number	Court Office Address	Name of Judge	Date of Order

Details of Order

1. The applicant asks for an order that: *(Provide details of openness order.)*

2. ☐ (a) The openness order will permit the continuation of a relationship with a person that is beneficial and meaningful to the child in the following ways *(complete this section only if you are making this application under s. 194 or s. 196 of the Child, Youth and Family Services Act, 2017)*:

☐ (b) The openness order will help the child to develop or maintain a connection with the child's First Nations, Inuit or Métis cultures, heritages and traditions and to preserve the child's cultural identity and connection to community in the following ways *(complete this section only if you are making this application under s. 197 of the Child, Youth and Family Services Act, 2017)*:

For information on accessibility of court services for people with disability-related needs, contact:
Telephone: 416-326-2220 / 1-800-518-7901   TTY: 416-326-4012 / 1-877-425-0575

Form 34L: Application for Openness Order   **(page 3)**

3.   The openness order is in the best interests of the child for the following reasons:

Put a line through any blank space left on this page.

_____
Date of signature

_____
Signature

_____
If applicant is a children's aid society,
give office or position of person signing.

_____
Print or type name.

For information on accessibility of court services for people with disability-related needs, contact:
Telephone: 416-326-2220 / 1-800-518-7901   TTY: 416-326-4012 / 1-877-425-0575

Form 34M

Consent to Openness Order under s. 194 of the *Child, Youth and Family Services Act, 2017*

ONTARIO

	Court File Number

_____
(Name of court)

at _____
Court office address

Form 34M: Consent to Openness Order under s. 194 of the *Child, Youth and Family Services Act, 2017*

Applicant *(In all cases, the applicant will be a children's aid society.)*

Full legal name & address for service — street & number, municipality, postal code, telephone & fax numbers and e-mail address (if any).	Lawyer's name & address — street & number, municipality, postal code, telephone & fax numbers and e-mail address (if any).

Respondent(s) *(Persons entitled to notice.)*

Full legal name & address for service — street & number, municipality, postal code, telephone & fax numbers and e-mail address (if any).	Lawyer's name & address — street & number, municipality, postal code, telephone & fax numbers and e-mail address (if any).

Children's Lawyer

Name & address of Children's Lawyer's agent for service (street & number, municipality, postal code, telephone & fax numbers and e-mail address (if any)) and name of person represented.

THE CHILD

Child's Full Legal Name	Birthdate	Sex	Is the child First Nations, Inuit, or Métis?	Child's Bands or First Nations, Inuit, or Métis Communities

Extended Society Care Order:

Court File Number	Court Office Address	Name of Judge	Date of Order
Details of Order			

The parties and the child, if the child is 12 years of age or older, agree to the following:

1. The openness order will permit the continuation of a relationship with a person that is beneficial and meaningful to the child for the following reasons:

Form 34M: **Consent to Openness Order under s. 194 of the** **(page 2)**
Child, Youth and Family Services Act, 2017

Court File Number

2. The openness order is in the best interests of the child for the following reasons:

3. For the reasons set out above, we ask the court to make the following order: *(Provide details of openness order.)*

Applicant's name and position within the children's aid society:

_____   _____   _____
Date   *Applicant's signature*   *Witness' signature*

Signature of person who will be permitted to communicate with or have a relationship with the child if order is made:

_____   _____   _____
Date   *Respondent's signature*   *Witness' signature*

Signature of person with whom the children's aid society has placed or intends to place the child for adoption:

_____   _____   _____
Date   *Respondent's signature*   *Witness' signature*

If applicable, children's aid society that will supervise or participate in the arrangement under the openness order:

_____   _____   _____
Date   *Respondent's signature*   *Witness' signature*

FLR 34M (March 1, 2018)

Form 34M: Consent to Openness Order under s. 194 of the (page 3)
Child, Youth and Family Services Act, 2017

Court File Number

CHILD'S CONSENT

If child is 12 years of age or older:

_____ _____ _____
Date   Child's signature   Witness' signature

Form 34M.1

Consent to Openness Order under s. 196 or s. 197 of the *Child, Youth and Family Services Act, 2017*

ONTARIO

	Court File Number

_____
(Name of court)

at _____
Court office address

Form 34M.1: Consent to Openness Order under s. 196 or s. 197 of the *Child, Youth and Family Services Act, 2017*

Applicant

Full legal name & address for service — street & number, municipality, postal code, telephone & fax numbers and e-mail address (if any).	Lawyer's name & address — street & number, municipality, postal code, telephone & fax numbers and e-mail address (if any).

Respondent(s) *(Persons entitled to notice.)*

Full legal name & address for service — street & number, municipality, postal code, telephone & fax numbers and e-mail address (if any).	Lawyer's name & address — street & number, municipality, postal code, telephone & fax numbers and e-mail address (if any).

Children's Lawyer

Name & address of Children's Lawyer's agent for service (street & number, municipality, postal code, telephone & fax numbers and e-mail address (if any)) and name of person represented.

THE CHILD

Child's Full Legal Name	Birthdate	Sex	Is the Child First Nations, Inuit, or Métis?	Child's Bands or First Nations, Inuit, or Métis Communities

Extended Society Care Order:

Court File Number	Court Office Address	Name of Judge	Date of Order
Details of Order			

The parties and the child, if the child is 12 years of age or older, agree to the following:

1. The openness order is in the best interests of the child for the following reasons:

Form 34M.1: **Consent to Openness Order under s.** **(page 2)**
196 or s. 197 of the *Child, Youth and*
Family Services Act, 2017

Court File Number

2. The proposed openness order will permit the continuation of a relationship with a person that is beneficial and meaningful to the child for the following reasons (*complete this section only if you are seeking an openness order under s. 196 of the* Child, Youth and Family Services Act, 2017):

3. The person(s) with whom the children's aid society has placed or will place the child for adoption can comply with the terms of the proposed openness order. Details about the prospective adoptive parents' ability to comply are as follows (*complete this section only if you are seeking an openness order under s. 196 of the Child, Youth and Family Services Act, 2017*):

4. The proposed openness order would help the child to develop or maintain a connection with the child's First Nations, Inuit or Métis cultures, heritages and traditions and preserve the child's cultural identity and connection to community for the following reasons (*complete this section only if the society is intending to place a First Nations, Inuk or Métis child for adoption and you are seeking an openness order under s. 197 of the Child, Youth and Family Services Act, 2017*):

Form 34M.1: **Consent to Openness Order under s.** **(page 3)**
196 or s. 197 of the *Child, Youth and*
Family Services Act, 2017

Court File Number

5. For the reasons set out above, we ask the court to make the following order: *(Provide details of openness order.)*

Name of children's aid society representative and position within the children's aid society:

CONSENTS

Date	Applicant's signature	Witness' signature

Date	Respondent's signature	Witness' signature

If applicable, children's aid society that will supervise or participate in the arrangement under the openness order:

Date	Respondent's signature	Witness' signature

CHILD'S CONSENT

If child is 12 years of age or older:

Date	Child's signature	Witness' signature

Form 34N

Application to Change to Terminate Openness Order

ONTARIO

		Court File Number
SEAL at	_____ *(Name of court)* _____ *Court office address*	**Form 34N: Application to Change or Terminate Openness Order**

Applicant(s)

Full legal name & address for service — street & number, municipality, postal code, telephone & fax numbers and e-mail address (if any).	Lawyer's name & address — street & number, municipality, postal code, telephone & fax numbers and e-mail address (if any).

Respondent(s)

Full legal name & address for service — street & number, municipality, postal code, telephone & fax numbers and e-mail address (if any).	Lawyer's name & address — street & number, municipality, postal code, telephone & fax numbers and e-mail address (if any).

Children's Lawyer

Name & address of Children's Lawyer's agent for service (street & number, municipality, postal code, telephone & fax numbers and e-mail address (if any)) and name of person represented.

TO THE RESPONDENT(S):

A COURT CASE HAS BEEN STARTED AGAINST YOU IN THIS COURT. THE DETAILS ARE SET OUT ON THE ATTACHED PAGES.

THE FIRST COURT DATE IS *(date)* _____ **AT** _____ ☐ a.m. ☐ p.m.

or as soon as possible after that time, at: *(address)*

If you have also been served with a notice of motion, there may be an earlier court date, and you or your lawyer should come to court for the motion.

IF YOU WANT TO OPPOSE ANY CLAIM IN THIS CASE, you or your lawyer must prepare an Answer (*Child, Youth and Family Services Act, 2017* Cases other than Child Protection and Status Review) (Form 33B.2 – a blank copy should be attached), serve a copy on the children's aid society and all other parties and file a copy in the court office with an Affidavit of Service (Form 6B).

YOU HAVE ONLY 30 DAYS AFTER THIS APPLICATION IS SERVED ON YOU (60 DAYS IF THIS APPLICATION IS SERVED ON YOU OUTSIDE CANADA OR THE UNITED STATES) TO SERVE AND FILE AN ANSWER. IF YOU DO NOT, THE CASE WILL GO AHEAD WITHOUT YOU AND THE COURT MAY MAKE AN ORDER AND ENFORCE IT AGAINST YOU.

You should consider getting legal advice about this case right away. If you cannot afford a lawyer, you may be able to get help from your local legal aid office. *(See your telephone directory under LEGAL AID.)*

_____
Date of issue

_____
Clerk of the court

FLR 34N (March 1, 2018)

Page 1 of 5

Form 34N:	Application to Change or Terminate Openness Order	(page 2)	Court File Number

THE CHILD

Child's Full Legal name	Birthdate	Age	Sex	Date of Extended Society Care Order (if pre-adoption application under s. 198 of the Child, Youth and Family Services Act, 2017)	Date of Adoption Order (if post-adoption application under s. 207 of the Child, Youth and Family Services Act, 2017)

Details of Openness Order to be Changed or Terminated:

Name of Judge	Date of Order	Details of Openness Order

1. The applicant asks for an order: *(if applicable)*

   ☐ granting permission under s. 207(2) of the *Child, Youth and Family Services Act, 2017* to *(name of person seeking contact)*

   _____ to bring an application to change the order of

   Justice *(name of judge)* _____ ,

   dated *(date of order)* _____ for the following reasons:

2. The applicant asks for an order that:

   ☐ (a) the order, made by Justice *(name of judge)* _____

   on *(date of order)* _____ be changed as follows:

   OR

   ☐ (b) the order, made by Justice *(name of judge)* _____

   on *(date of order)* be terminated.

Form 34N: Application to Change or Terminate   **(page 3)**
Openness Order

Court File Number

3. The following circumstances have changed:

4. The proposed order is in the best interests of the child for the following reasons:

Form 34N: Application to Change or Terminate   **(page 4)**
          Openness Order

Court File Number

5.   If you are seeking to change (not terminate) an openness order:

☐ (a) In the case of an openness order made under s. 194 or s. 196 of the *Child, Youth and Family Services Act, 2017*, the proposed change to the openness order would continue a relationship that is beneficial and meaningful to the child for the following reasons:

☐ (b) in the case of an openness order made under s. 197 of the *Child, Youth and Family Services Act, 2017*, the proposed change to the openness order would help the child to develop or maintain a connection with the child's First Nations, Inuit or Métis cultures, heritages and traditions and preserve the child's cultural identity and connection to community for the following reasons:

Form 34N: Application to Change or Terminate   **(page 5)**
         Openness Order

Court File Number

6. If you are seeking to terminate (not change) an openness order made under s. 194 or 196 of the *Child, Youth and Family Services Act, 2017*, the proposed termination of the openness order would terminate a relationship that is no longer beneficial and meaningful to the child for the following reasons:

Put a line through any blank space left on this page.

_____
Date of signature

_____
Signature

_____
*If applicant is a children's aid society,
give office or position of person signing.*

_____
Print or type name

Form 35.1

Affidavit in Support of Claim for Custody or Access, Dated

ONTARIO

	Court File Number
_____	
(Name of court)	**Form 35.1: Affidavit in Support of**
at _____	**Claim for Custody or Access, dated**
Court office address	

Applicant(s)

Full legal name & address for service — street & number, municipality, postal code, telephone & fax numbers and e-mail address (if any).	Lawyer's name & address — street & number, municipality, postal code, telephone & fax numbers and e-mail address (if any).

Respondent(s)

Full legal name & address for service — street & number, municipality, postal code, telephone & fax numbers and e-mail address (if any).	Lawyer's name & address — street & number, municipality, postal code, telephone & fax numbers and e-mail address (if any).

Affidavit in Support of Claim for Custody or Access

(If you need more space, attach extra pages.)

My name is *(full legal name)* _____

My date of birth is *(d, m, y)* _____

I live in: *(name of city, town or municipality and province, state or country if outside of Ontario)* _____

I swear/affirm that the following is true:

PART A:
TO BE COMPLETED BY ALL PERSONS SEEKING CUSTODY OR ACCESS
(Write "N/A" if any of the paragraphs do not apply to you or the child(ren).)

1. During my life, I have also used or been known by the following names:

2. The child(ren) in this case is/are:

Child's full legal name	Birthdate (d, m, y)	Age	Full legal name(s) of parent(s)	Name(s) of all people the child lives with now *(include address if the child does not live with you)*	My relationship to the child *(specify if parent, grandparent, family friend, etc.)*

Form 35.1: Affidavit in Support of Claim for Custody or Access   (page 2)

Court File Number

Child's full legal name	Birthdate (d, m, y)	Age	Full legal name(s) of parent(s)	Name(s) of all people the child lives with now (include address if the child does not live with you)	My relationship to the child (specify if parent, grandparent, family friend, etc.)

3. **I am also the parent of or have acted as a parent (for example, as a step-parent, legal guardian etc.) to the following child(ren):** *(include the full legal names and birthdates of any child(ren) not already listed in paragraph 2)*

Child's Full Legal Name	Birthdate (d, m, y)	My relationship to the child (specify if parent, step-parent grandparent, etc.)	Name(s) of the person(s) with whom the child lives now (if the child is under 18 years old)

4. **I am or have been a party in the following court case(s) involving custody of or access to any child:** *(Including the child(ren) in this case or any other child(ren). Do not include cases involving a children's aid society in this section. Attach a copy of any custody or access court order(s) or endorsement(s) you have.)*

Court location	Names of parties in the case	Name(s) of child(ren)	Court orders made (include dates of orders)

Form 35.1: Affidavit in Support of Claim for Custody or Access   (page 3)

5. **I have been a party or person responsible for the care of a child in the following child protection court case(s):** (attach a copy of any relevant court order(s) or endorsement(s) you have)

Court location	Names of people involved in the case	Name of children's aid society	Court orders made (include dates of orders)

6. **I have been found guilty of the following criminal offence(s) for which I have not received a pardon:**

Charge	Approximate date of finding of guilt	Sentence received

7. **I am now charged with the following criminal offence(s):**

Charge	Date of next court appearance	Terms of release while waiting for trial (attach copy of bail or other release conditions, if any)

8. When the court is assessing a person's ability to act as a parent, s. 24 (4) of the *Children's Law Reform Act* requires the court to consider whether the person has at any time committed violence or abuse against:

- his or her spouse;
- a parent of the child to whom the claim for custody or access relates;
- a member of the person's household; or
- any child.

I am aware of the following violence or abuse the court should consider under s. 24 (4) of the *Children's Law Reform Act:* (describe incident(s) or episode(s) and provide information about the nature of the violence or abuse, who committed the violence and who the victim(s) was/were)

Form 35.1:	Affidavit in Support of Claim for Custody or Access	(page 4)	Court File Number

9. **To the best of my knowledge, since birth, the child(ren) in this case has/have lived with the following caregiver(s):** *(including a parent, legal guardian, children's aid society etc.)*

Child's Name	Name(s) of Caregiver(s) *(if the child was in the care of a children's aid society, give the name of that children's aid society)*	Period(s) of Time with Caregiver(s) *(d,m,y to d,m,y)*

10. **My plan for the care and upbringing of the child(ren) is as follows:**

    a) I plan to live at the following address: _____

    b) The following people (other than the child(ren) involved in this case) will be living with me:

Full legal name and other names this person has used	Birthdate *(d, m, y)*	Relationship to you	Has a child of this person ever been in the care of a children's aid society? *(if yes, give details)*	Has this person been found guilty of a criminal offence (for which he/she has not received a pardon) or is he/she currently facing criminal charges? *(if yes, give details)*

    c) **Decisions for the child(ren) (including education, medical care, religious upbringing, extra-curricular activities, etc.) will be made as follows:**

        ☐ jointly by me and *(name(s) of person(s))* _____

        ☐ by me

        ☐ by *(name(s) of person(s))* _____

           (If necessary, provide additional details below.)

Form 35.1: **Affidavit in Support of Claim for Custody or Access**   (page 5)   Court File Number

d)   ☐ **I am a stay-at-home parent.**

     ☐ **I work:**   ☐ **full time.**   ☐ **part time.**

     ☐ **I attend school:**   ☐ **full time.**   ☐ **part time.**

     at: *(name of your place of work or school)* _____

     ☐ **I anticipate that my plans for work and/or school may change as follows:** *(complete if you know or expect that you will be doing something different from what you are doing now))*

e)   **The child(ren) will attend school, daycare or be cared for by others on a regular basis as follows:**

f)   **My plan for the child(ren) to have regular contact with others, including the child(ren)'s parent(s) and family members, is as follows:**

g)   Check the appropriate box:

     ☐ **The child(ren) does not/do not have any special medical, educational, mental health or developmental needs.**

     ☐ **The child or one or more of the children has/have the following special needs and will receive support and services for those needs as follows:** *(if a child does not have special needs, you do not have to include information about that child below)*

Name of child	Special need(s)	Description of child's needs	Support or service child will be receiving *(include the names of any doctors, counsellors, treatment centres, etc. that are or will be providing support or services to the child)*
	☐ medical ☐ educational ☐ mental health ☐ developmental ☐ other		
	☐ medical ☐ educational ☐ mental health ☐ developmental ☐ other		
	☐ medical ☐ educational ☐ mental health ☐ developmental ☐ other		
	☐ medical ☐ educational ☐ mental health ☐ developmental ☐ other		
	☐ medical ☐ educational ☐ mental health ☐ developmental ☐ other		

FLR 35.1 (November 1, 2018)

Form 35.1:   Affidavit in Support of Claim for   **(page 6)** | Court File Number
Custody or Access

  h) I will have support from the following relatives, friends or community services in caring for the child(ren):

11. I acknowledge that the court needs up-to-date and accurate information about my plan in order to make a custody or access order in the best interests of the child(ren) (subrule 35.1 (7)). If, at any time before a final order is made in this case,

    a) there are any changes in my life or circumstances that affect the information provided in this affidavit; or

    b) I discover that the information in this affidavit is incorrect or incomplete,

  I will immediately serve and file either:

    a) an updated affidavit in support of claim for custody or access (Form 35.1); or,

    b) if the correction or change is minor, an affidavit in Form 14A describing the correction or change and indicating any effect it has on my plan for the care and upbringing of the child(ren).

          _____ *(Initial here to show you have read this paragraph and you understand it.)*

NOTE: If you are not a parent of the child, as determined under the *Children's Law Reform Act*, for whom you are seeking an order of custody, you must complete Part B of this affidavit.

For the purposes of this form and under the *Children's Law Reform Act*, a parent may include:

- The person who gives birth to a child (a "birth parent").

- Where a child is conceived through sexual intercourse, the person who is married to or living with the person who gives birth to the child at the time that the child is born (a "spouse").

- The person certified as a parent of the child under the *Vital Statistics Act*.

- A person found or recognized by a court as a parent to the child.

For more information about whether you are a parent for the purposes of this form, see the *Children's Law Reform Act* or talk to a lawyer.

If you are completing Part B, you do not have to swear/affirm the affidavit at this point. You will swear/affirm at the end of Part B.

Sworn/Affirmed before me at _____

                                municipality

in _____

                     province, state, or country

on _____ _____ | *Signature*

         Date   *Commissioner for taking affidavits*   *(This form is to be signed in front of a*
                        (Type or print name below if signature is illegible.)   *lawyer, justice of the peace, notary public*
                                                     or commissioner for taking affidavits.)

Form 35.1: Affidavit in Support of Claim for Custody or Access   **(page 7)**   Court File Number

PART B
TO BE COMPLETED ONLY BY A NON-PARENT SEEKING A CUSTODY ORDER

If you are a parent of the child, as determined under the *Children's Law Reform Act*, for whom you are seeking an order of custody, you are not required to complete this Part of the form.

Individuals who may <u>not</u> be a parent may include:

- A grandparent, aunt, or uncle.
- A sperm donor.
- A surrogate.
- A step-parent.

For more information about whether you are a parent for the purposes of this form, see the *Children's Law Reform Act* or talk to a lawyer.

NOTICE: If you are a non-parent claiming custody of a child, court staff will conduct a search of the databases maintained by the Ontario courts to identify previous or current family court cases in which you or the child(ren) may have been or may be involved and provide you with a list of those cases. This information will be shared with the court and you must provide a copy to any other party.

If the list contains information about someone other than you, you may swear or affirm an affidavit indicating that you are not the same person as the person named in the list.

In addition to the information in Part A, I swear/affirm that the following is true:

12. **To the best of my knowledge, the child(ren) in this case has/have been involved in the following custody/ access or child protection court cases:** *(do NOT include cases in which the child was charged under the* Youth Criminal Justice Act (Canada)*)*

Child(ren)'s name(s)	Type of Case	Details of Case

13. You must file a police records check with the court. Choose the option below that applies to you:

☐ **I have attached to this affidavit a copy of my police records check, dated** *(date of report from local police force)*

_____ **. Since the date that the attached police records check was completed, I have been found guilty of or charged with the following offence(s):**

☐ **On** *(date)* _____ **, I sent a request to** *(name of local police force)*

_____ **for a police records check.**

I agree to serve and file the police records check with the court within 10 days after the day I receive it. I understand that the court may not make an order for custody of the child(ren) until I have filed the police records check.

Form 35.1: Affidavit in Support of Claim for Custody or Access **(page 8)** | Court File Number

14. Since I turned 18 years old or became a parent, whichever was earlier, I have lived in the following places:

Approximate dates *(month/year to month/year)*	City, town or municipality where you lived *(if outside of Ontario, give name of province, state or country)*

15. I have provided a signed consent form to the court, which authorizes each of the children's aid societies listed below to send a report to me and to the court indicating:

. whether the society has any records within the meaning of the *Children's Law Reform Act* regulations relating to me; and

. the date(s) on which any files were opened and/or closed (if applicable).

i) Name of children's aid society: _____

ii) Name of children's aid society: _____

iii) Name of children's aid society: _____

iv) Name of children's aid society: _____

v) Name of children's aid society: _____

vi) Name of children's aid society: _____

16. I understand that if any report from a children's aid society indicates that the children's aid society has records related to me, then, unless the court orders otherwise, that report will be shared with:

a) the court;

b) any other parties in this case; and

c) the child(ren)'s lawyer, if there is one in this case.

If I wish to bring a motion asking the court not to release all or part of this report, I understand that I must file my motion with the court no later than **20 days** from the day that the last report is received by the court.

I also understand that any report indicating that a children's aid society has no records relating to me will not be shared with the court, any other party or the child(ren)'s lawyer.

_____ *(Initial here to show that you have read this paragraph and you understand it.)*

Sworn/Affirmed before me at _____
                                        Municipality

in _____
        province, state, or country

on _____ _____ | _____
        Date   *Commissioner for taking affidavits*   *Signature*
                      (Type or print name below if signature is illegible.) | *(This form is to be signed in front of a lawyer, justice of the peace, notary public or commissioner for taking affidavits.)*

Form 36

Affidavit for Divorce

ONTARIO

	Court File Number

_____
(Name of court)

at _____

Form 36:
Affidavit for Divorce

Court office address

Applicant(s)

Full legal name & address for service — street & number, municipality, postal code, telephone & fax numbers and e-mail address (if any).	Lawyer's name & address — street & number, municipality, postal code, telephone & fax numbers and e-mail address (if any).

Respondent(s)

Full legal name & address for service — street & number, municipality, postal code, telephone & fax numbers and e-mail address (if any).	Lawyer's name & address — street & number, municipality, postal code, telephone & fax numbers and e-mail address (if any).

My name is _(full legal name)_ _____

I live in _(municipality & province)_ _____

and I swear/affirm that the following is true:

1. I am the applicant in this divorce case.

2. There is no chance of a reconciliation between the respondent and me.

3. All the information in the application in this case is correct, except:
   (State any corrections or changes to the information in the application. Write "NONE" if there are no corrections or changes.)

_____

_____

4. ☐ The certificate or registration of my marriage to the respondent has been signed and sealed by the Registrar General of Ontario and:

   ☐ has been filed with the application.

1189

☐   is attached to this affidavit.

☐   The certificate of my marriage to the respondent was issued outside Ontario. It is called *(title of certificate)*

_____

It was issued at *(place of issue)*   _____

on *(date)*   _____

by *(name and title of person who issued certificate)*   _____

and the information in it about my marriage is correct.

☐   I have not been able to get a certificate or registration of my marriage. I was married to the respondent on *(date)* _____ at *(place of marriage)* _____

The marriage was performed by *(name and title)*   _____

who had the authority to perform marriages in that place.

5.   The legal basis for the divorce is:

☐   that the respondent and I have been separated for at least one year.

We separated on *(date)*   _____

☐   Other *(Specify.)*

_____

_____

6.   I do not know about and I am not involved in any arrangement to make up or to hide evidence or to deceive the court in this divorce case.

Strike out the following paragraphs if they do not apply.

7.   I do not want to make a claim for a division of property in this divorce case, even though I know that it may be legally impossible to make such a claim after the divorce.

8.   I want the divorce order to include the following paragraph numbers of the attached consent, settlement, separation agreement or previous court order: *(List the numbers of the paragraphs that you want included in the divorce order.)*

_____

9.   There are _____ *(number)* children of the marriage. They are:

Full legal name of child	Birth date (d, m, y)

10. The custody and access arrangements for the child(ren) are as follows: *(Give summary.)*

_____

_____

_____

_____

_____

_____

_____

11. These are the arrangements that have been made for the support of the child(ren) of the marriage:

   (a) The income of the party paying child support is $ _____ per year.

   (b) The number of children for whom support is supposed to be paid is *(number)* _____

   (c) The amount of support that should be paid according to the applicable table in the child support guidelines is $ _____ per month.

   (d) The amount of child support actually being paid is $ _____ per month.

     (NOTE: - Where the dollar amounts in clauses [c] and [d] are different, you must fill out the frame on the next page. If the amounts in clauses [c] and [d] are the same, skip the frame and go directly to paragraph 12.)

Fill out the information in this frame only if the amounts in paragraphs 11(c) and 11(d) are different. If they are the same, go to paragraph 12.

a) Child support is already covered by:

   (i) ☐ a court order dated *(date)* _____ that was made before the child support guidelines came into effect (before 1 May 1997). I attach a copy of the order.

   (ii) ☐ a domestic contract order dated *(date)* _____ that was made before the child support guidelines came into effect (before 1 May 1997). I attach a copy of the contract.

      (iii) ☐ a court order or written agreement dated *(date)* _____ made after the guidelines came into effect that has some direct or indirect benefits for the child(ren). I attach a copy.

      (iv) ☐ a written consent between the parties dated *(date)* _____ agreeing to the payment of an amount different from that set out in the guidelines.

b) The child support clauses of this order or agreement require payment of $ ___ per ____ in child support.

c) These child support clauses

    ☐ are not indexed for any automatic cost-of-living increases.

    ☐ are indexed according to *(Give indexing formula.)*

_____

_____

d) These child support clauses

    ☐ have not been changed since the day the order or agreement was made.

    ☐ have been changed on *(Give dates and details of changes.)*

_____

_____

e) *(If you ticked off box [i] above, you can go to paragraph 12. If you ticked off boxes [ii], [iii] or [iv] above, then fill out the information after box of the corresponding number below. For example, if you ticked off box [iii] above, you would fill out the information alongside box [iii] below.)*

      (ii) ☐ The amount being paid under this agreement is a fair and reasonable arrangement for the support of the child(ren) because: *(Give reasons.)*

_____

_____

      (iii) ☐ The order or agreement directly or indirectly benefits the child(ren) because: *(Give details or benefits.)*

_____

_____

(iv) ☐ The amount to which the parties have consented is reasonable for the support of the child(ren) because: *(Give reasons.)*

_____

_____

_____

12. I am claiming costs in this case. The details of this claim are as follows: *(Give details.)*

_____

_____

_____

_____

_____

_____

_____

_____

13. The respondent's address last known to me is: *(Give address.)*

_____

_____

_____

Put a line through any blank space left on this page.

1193

Sworn/Affirmed before me at _____
                                    municipality

in _____
              province, state or country

on _____ _____
        date   *Commissioner for taking*
                                    affidavits
                            (Type or print name below if
                            signature is illegible.)

_____
                                          Signature
                            (This form is to be signed in
                            front of a lawyer, justice of
                            the peace, notary public or
                            commissioner for taking
                            affidavits.)

Form 36A

Certificate of Clerk (Divorce)

ONTARIO

_____

(Name of court)

Court File Number

| Form 36A: Certificate of Clerk (Divorce) |

at _____

Court office address

Applicant's last name _____ **Respondent's last name** _____

If the appropriate box on the left cannot be checked, check the box on the right margin and describe the deficiency by that box. If the divorce application was filed electronically, write "N/A" in the blank spaces relating to the Continuing Record.

The clerk of the court certifies as follows:

Check if applicable and complete the rest of the certificate as if the divorce had been claimed by the applicant. 1 Divorce claimed only by the respondent.

Deficiency

1. PRELIMINARY

(a) ☐ Jurisdiction – Application filed in correct municipality 1(a) ☐

☐ No answer filed _____

☐ Answer was withdrawn – Continuing record tab/page number _____

☐ Order dated _____, under subrule 12(6), splitting divorce from rest of the case – continuing record tab/page number _____

☐ Answer struck out by order dated _____

- Continuing record tab/page number _____

☐ Joint application – no respondent

(b) ☐ Clearance certificate from Central Divorce Registry _____ 1(b) ☐

2. PROOF OF SERVICE 2 ☐

☐ Affidavit of service

☐ Person's lawyer accepted service

☐ Joint application – no service necessary

3. METHOD OF SERVICE 3 ☐

☐ Left copy with person to be served

☐ Left copy with person's lawyer

☐ Mailed copy to person and received acknowledgement signed by person

☐ Left copy at person's residence with adult resident and mailed another copy

☐ Signed acknowledgement of service filed

☐ Other _(specify.)_ _____

Service took place in _(province or country)_ _____

Service was carried out on _(date)_ _____

4. GROUNDS FOR DIVORCE 4 ☐

☐ Separation since _(date)_ _____, affidavit sworn more than one year after separation

☐ Adultery

☐ Cruelty

5. ONTARIO RESIDENCE 5 ☐

Application should indicate that at least one spouse must have been Ontario resident for at least a year.

☐ Applicant resident in Ontario since _(date)_ _____

☐ Respondent resident in Ontario since _(date)_ _____

6. CLAIMS 6 ☐

☐ Only claim for divorce

☐ Claim for child support _[details in part 9 below]_

☐ Claim for custody/access – details in application

☐ Claim for spousal support – details in application

☐ Claim for property – details in application

☐ Claim to include provisions of consent, agreement or previous court order – details in application

☐ Costs

Form 36A:	Certificate of Clerk (Divorce)	(page 2)	Court File Number

Deficiency

7. PROOF OF MARRIAGE   7 ☐

Marriage took place ☐ in Canada ☐ outside Canada

☐ Marriage certificate or registration of marriage filed – details agree with those in application

- Continuing record tab/page number ....

☐ No certificate – details of marriage set out in affidavit – Continuing record

tab/page number ....

☐ Previous divorce or death certificate filed – Continuing record tab/page number ....

8. AFFIDAVITS   8 ☐

☐ Applicant's affidavit – Continuing record tab/page number ....

☐ Respondent's affidavit – Continuing record tab/page number ....

☐ Affidavit of *(name)* ....

- Continuing record tab/page number ....

☐ Affidavit complies with Form 36 and is properly completed – Continuing record tab/page

number ....

9. CHILDREN   9 ☐

☐ No children of the marriage ☐ There are children of the marriage

☐ Child support guidelines information supplied – Continuing record

tab/page number ....

    ☐ Payor's income ☐ table amount

    ☐ recipient's income *[REQUIRED for special expenses (add-ons), split custody, shared custody, payor is stepparent, child over 18, payor's income more than $150,000, claim of undue hardship]*

    ☐ details of special expenses (add-ons)

    ☐ agreement/consent with explanation for claim less than table amount

10. DRAFT ORDER   10 ☐

The following material has been filed:

☐ Draft Order - no support claimed.

    ☐ 3 copies – filed in paper format ☐ Filed electronically

☐ Draft order and draft support deduction order – support claimed

    ☐ 4 copies of draft order + 2 copies of draft support deduction order – filed in paper format

    ☐ Filed electronically

☐ Service of order on parties

    ☐ Stamped envelope for each party – application filed in paper format

    ☐ Email address of at least one party – application filed electronically

☐ Address for service of order on respondent is same as

    ☐ on application ☐ on documents filed by respondent ☐ in applicant's affidavit

☐ Draft order in same terms as application

☐ Draft order in same terms as consent, minutes of settlement, or agreement filed

- Continuing record tab/page number ....

☐ Request for early effective date for divorce; agreements and undertakings filed not to appeal

- Continuing record tab/page number ....

11. NOTICE TO APPLICANT   11 ☐

☐ Applicant notified of deficiencies but requests to submit papers to judge despite them.

_____   _____

Date of signature   *Signature of clerk of the court*

FLR 36A (November 1, 2018)   Page 2 of 2

Form 36B

Certificate of Divorce

ONTARIO

_____

(Name of court)

at _____

Court office address

Court File Number

Form 36B:
Certificate of Divorce

Applicant(s)

Full legal name & address for service — street & number, municipality, postal code, telephone & fax numbers and e-mail address (if any).	Lawyer's name & address — street & number, municipality, postal code, telephone & fax numbers and e-mail address (if any).

Respondent(s)

Full legal name & address for service — street & number, municipality, postal code, telephone & fax numbers and e-mail address (if any).	Lawyer's name & address — street & number, municipality, postal code, telephone & fax numbers and e-mail address (if any).

I CERTIFY THAT the marriage of *(full legal names of the spouses)* ....

that was solemnized at *(place of marriage)* ....

on *(date of marriage)* ....

was dissolved by an order of this court made on *(date of divorce order)* ....

The divorce took effect on *(date when order took effect)* ....

SEAL

_____   _____
Date of signature   *Signature of clerk of the court*

NOTE: *This certificate can only be issued on or after the date on which the divorce takes effect.*

Form 37

Notice of Hearing

ONTARIO

Form 37: Notice of Hearing

SEAL	Court File Number

_____
(Name of Court)

at _____

Court office address

Applicant(s)

Full legal name & address for service — street & number, municipality, postal code, telephone & fax numbers and e-mail address (if any).	Lawyer's name & address — street & number, municipality, postal code, telephone & fax numbers and e-mail address (if any).

Respondent(s)

Full legal name & address for service — street & number, municipality, postal code, telephone & fax numbers and e-mail address (if any).	Lawyer's name & address — street & number, municipality, postal code, telephone & fax numbers and e-mail address (if any).

NOTICE:

THE COURT WILL HOLD A WRITTEN HEARING on *(date)* _____

at _____ **a.m./p.m.** _____ **, or as soon as possible after that date at** *(place of hearing)*

_____

This court has received

☐   An application under the *Interjurisdictional Support Orders Act, 2002* for
    ☐   an order   ☐   a change of an order

☐   A provisional   ☐   order   ☐   change of an order
                             ☐   in another part of   ☐   outside

1199

Ontario   Ontario

The details are set out in the attached materials.

IF YOU WANT TO OPPOSE ANY CLAIM IN THIS CASE, you or your lawyer must prepare an Answer (a blank copy of which is attached) and file a copy in the court office. **YOU HAVE ONLY 30 DAYS AFTER THIS NOTICE IS SERVED ON YOU TO FILE AN ANSWER TO THIS CASE.**

Whether or not you wish to oppose a claim in this case, **YOU MUST FILE A FINANCIAL STATEMENT** (a blank copy of which is attached) with the court office **WITHIN 30 DAYS AFTER THIS NOTICE IS SERVED ON YOU.**

If you want to ask for an oral hearing, you must prepare a motion (Form 14B – blank copy attached), and file a copy in the court office **WITHIN 30 DAYS AFTER THIS NOTICE IS SERVED ON YOU.**

The court will only consider the written materials in this case on the date noted above. UNLESS THE COURT ORDERS OTHERWISE, THERE IS NO NEED FOR YOU TO COME TO COURT OR TO HAVE A LAWYER THERE TO ARGUE YOUR CASE. If an order is made or the judge requires you to be present or provide further evidence, you will not be notified.

IF YOU DO NOT FILE WRITTEN MATERIALS, THE COURT MAY MAKE AN ORDER WITHOUT YOUR WRITTEN ANSWER AND ENFORCE IT AGAINST YOU.

You should get legal advice about this case right away. If you cannot afford a lawyer, you may be able to get help from your local Legal Aid Office. *(See your telephone directory under LEGAL AID)*

Date of signature	*Signature of registrar or clerk of the court*

NOTE: *A copy of the application should be attached to this notice, along with a copy of the applicant's financial statement, a copy of any provisional order and a copy of the applicant's evidence. Also attached to this notice should be blank Financial Statement that you must fill out and file. If a provisional order was made in another part of Ontario, you must serve and file your financial statement.*

If any of these documents is missing, you should talk to the court office at the address at the top of this form immediately.

Form 37A
Information Sheet

ONTARIO

Court File Number

_____

(Name of Court)

Form 37A:
Information Sheet

at _____

Court Office Address

Applicant(s)

Full legal name & address for service — street & number, municipality, postal code, telephone & fax numbers and e-mail address (if any).	Lawyer's name & address — street & number, municipality, postal code, telephone & fax numbers and e-mail address (if any).

Respondent(s)

Full legal name & address for service — street & number, municipality, postal code, telephone & fax numbers and e-mail address (if any).	Lawyer's name & address — street & number, municipality, postal code, telephone & fax numbers and e-mail address (if any).

TO THE APPLICANT(S):

The respondent(s) was/were served with a notice of

☐ *Interjurisdictional Support Orders Act, 2002* hearing.

☐ confirmation hearing.

A copy of this notice is attached to this sheet. It is being sent to you **FOR YOUR INFORMATION ONLY.**

THERE IS NO NEED FOR YOU TO COME TO THIS HEARING OR TO HAVE A LAWYER THERE TO ARGUE YOUR CASE FOR YOU.

You will be told about what happens at the hearing by the office where you submitted your application. If you have any questions, you should talk to your own lawyer or the office where you submitted your application.

_____

Date of signature

_____

Signature of registrar or clerk of the court

Form 37B

Direction to Request Further Information

ONTARIO

(SEAL)	**Court File Number**

_____
(Name of court)

at _____
Court Office Address

**Form 37B:
Direction to
Request Further
Information**

Applicant(s)

Full legal name & address for service — street & number, municipality, postal code, telephone & fax numbers and e-mail address (if any).	Lawyer's name & address — street & number, municipality, postal code, telephone & fax numbers and e-mail address (if any).

Respondent(s)

Full legal name & address for service — street & number, municipality, postal code, telephone & fax numbers and e-mail address (if any).	Lawyer's name & address — street & number, municipality, postal code, telephone & fax numbers and e-mail address (if any).

TO THE *(check appropriate box(es)* ☐ **APPLICANT(S):**

☐ **THE ONTARIO
INTERJURISDICTIONAL SUPPORT
ORDERS UNIT:**

This court considered the application for support or the application to change a support order

on *(date)* _____

THE COURT ADJOURNED THE HEARING OF THE CASE TO *(date)* _____

☐ You, the applicant, are directed to provide the information or documents required by the court.

☐ You, the Ontario Interjurisdictional Support Orders Unit, are directed to contact the applicant or appropriate authority in the reciprocating jurisdiction to request the information or documents required by the court.

This court requires the following information or documents: *(attach extra paper if necessary, or transcript noting information and documents required)*

The information or documents must be filed with this court at the address at the top of this form at least 30 days before the court date.

At the hearing, a temporary order:

☐   was not made;

☐   was made – details will be sent; or

☐   was made – a certified copy of the temporary order is attached.

           Date of signature   *Signature of registrar or clerk of the court*

NOTE: *A copy of the respondent's evidence and a copy of the court's reasons for seeking further evidence should be attached to this form. If either of these are missing, you should talk to the court office at the address at the top of this form immediately.*

Form 37C

Notice of Continuation of Hearing

ONTARIO

	Court File Number

SEAL

_____
(Name of court)

at _____

Court office address

Form 37C: Notice
of Continuation of
Hearing

Applicant(s)

Full legal name & address for service — street & number, municipality, postal code, telephone & fax numbers and e-mail address (if any).	*Lawyer's name & address — street & number, municipality, postal code, telephone & fax numbers and e-mail address (if any).*

Respondent(s)

Full legal name & address for service — street & number, municipality, postal code, telephone & fax numbers and e-mail address (if any).	*Lawyer's name & address — street & number, municipality, postal code, telephone & fax numbers and e-mail address (if any).*

TO THE RESPONDENT(S):

THE COURT WILL CONTINUE A WRITTEN HEARING on *(date)* _____

at _____ **a.m./p.m., or as soon as possible after that time at** *(place of hearing)* _____

_____

This case was adjourned on *(adjournment date)* _____
so that the case could be sent to the originating jurisdiction for further evidence.

The originating jurisdiction has now sent to this court further evidence, a copy of which is attached. This court will therefore consider this case at the time and place shown above.

IF YOU WISH TO RESPOND TO THE FURTHER EVIDENCE, YOU OR YOUR LAWYER MUST FILE AN AFFIDAVIT IN RESPONSE (Form 14A – blank copy attached) WITHIN 30 DAYS AFTER YOU RECEIVE THIS NOTICE.

If you want to ask for an oral hearing, you must prepare a motion (Form 14B – blank copy attached) and file a copy in the court office **WITHIN 30 DAYS AFTER THIS NOTICE IS SERVED ON YOU.**

The court will consider the written materials in this case on the date noted above. UNLESS THE COURT ORDERS OTHERWISE, THERE IS NO NEED FOR YOU TO COME TO COURT OR TO HAVE A LAWYER THERE TO ARGUE YOUR CASE. If an order is made or the judge requires you to be present or provide further evidence, you will be notified.

_____   _____
Date of signature   *Signature of registrar or clerk of the court*

NOTE: *A copy of the applicant's further evidence taken in the originating jurisdiction should be attached to this notice. If it is missing, you should talk to the court office at the address at the top of this form immediately.*

Form 37D

Notice of Registration of Order

ONTARIO

SEAL

_____
(Name of Court)

AT _____

Court office address

Court File Number _____

Applicant(s)

Full legal name & address for service — street & number, municipality, postal code, telephone & fax numbers and e-mail address (if any).	Lawyer's name & address — street & number, municipality, postal code, telephone & fax numbers and e-mail address (if any).

Respondent(s)

Full legal name & address for service — street & number, municipality, postal code, telephone & fax numbers and e-mail address (if any).	Lawyer's name & address — street & number, municipality, postal code, telephone & fax numbers and e-mail address (if any).

TO THE (check appropriate box(es)) ☐ **APPLICANT(S):**

☐ **RESPONDENT(S):**

The *(name of the court)* _____

at *(place where court presides)* _____

has asked the courts in Ontario to enforce ☐ an order for the payment of support for dependants.

☐ the support provisions of a written agreement between you and the other party.

This order or agreement has been registered with this Ontario court on *(date of registration)* .... under the *Interjurisdictional Support Orders Act 2002*.

If you have reason to believe that:

    a)   you did not have notice or a reasonable opportunity to be heard;

    b)   the order/agreement is contrary to public policy in Ontario; or

    c)   the court that made the order did not have jurisdiction to make it,

you may make a motion (Forms 14 and 14A) to have the registration set aside, but you must do so within 30 days after receiving this notice. You must mail notice of your own motion to the Ontario Interjurisdictional Support Orders Unit at: *(address)*

You may use any method of service set out in rule 6 of the *Family Law Rules* including mail, courier or fax.

If you choose not to challenge the registration, the order or agreement will be enforced against you as if it were an order of an Ontario court. You have the right at any time to apply for a change of this order or agreement if there has been a material change in circumstances since the making of the order or agreement.

_____	_____
Date of signature	*Signature of registrar or clerk of the court*

Form 37E

Notice for Taking Further Evidence

ONTARIO

SEAL

_____
(Name of Court)

at _____

Court office address

Court File Number

Form 37E: Notice for Taking Further Evidence

Applicant(s)

Full legal name & address for service — street & number, municipality, postal code, telephone & fax numbers and e-mail address (if any).	Lawyer's name & address — street & number, municipality, postal code, telephone & fax numbers and e-mail address (if any).

Respondent(s)

Full legal name & address for service — street & number, municipality, postal code, telephone & fax numbers and e-mail address (if any).	Lawyer's name & address — street & number, municipality, postal code, telephone & fax numbers and e-mail address (if any).

TO THE APPLICANT(S):

The provisional ☐ order in this case
☐ change of the order made by the
(name of court) _____

on *(date)* _____

has come before a judge of the *(name and address of court)* _____

That other court requires further evidence from you. The details are set out in the attached material.

If you want to continue your application for support or for a change in support, you or your lawyer must prepare an affidavit (Form 14A – blank copy attached) of your further evidence and file it in this court office.

The other court will continue the hearing on *(insert date, if known)* ....
Your affidavit evidence must be filed in this court 30 days before that date so it can be sent to the other court in time for the hearing.

IF YOU DO NOT FILE FURTHER AFFIDAVIT EVIDENCE, THE PROVISIONAL ORDER OR CHANGE OF AN ORDER MAY NOT BE CONFIRMED BY THE OTHER COURT.

Date of signature	*Signature of registrar or clerk of the court*

NOTE: A copy of the respondent's evidence and a copy of the other court's reasons for seeking further evidence should be attached to this notice. If either of these is missing, you should talk to the court office at the address at the top of this form immediately.

Form 38

Notice of Appeal

ONTARIO

Court File Number

_____
(Name of court)

Form 38:
Notice of Appeal

at _____
Court office address

Applicant(s) *Check the appropriate box:* ☐ **Appellant** ☐ **Respondent in this appeal**

Full legal name & address for service — street & number, municipality, postal code, telephone & fax numbers and e-mail address (if any).	*Lawyer's name & address — street & number, municipality, postal code, telephone & fax numbers and e-mail address (if any).*

Respondent(s) *Check the appropriate box:* ☐ **Appellant** ☐ **Respondent** **in this appeal**

Full legal name & address for service — street & number, municipality, postal code, telephone & fax numbers and e-mail address (if any).	*Lawyer's name & address — street & number, municipality, postal code, telephone & fax numbers and e-mail address (if any).*

Name & address of Children's Lawyer's agent (street & number, municipality, postal code, telephone & fax numbers and e-mail address (if any)) and name of person represented.

My name is *(name of party making this appeal)* _____

I APPEAL TO THE *(name of court)* _____

at *(municipality)* _____

from the following order or decision:

Date of order: _____

Name of court that made it: _____

Name of judge who made it: _____

Place where it was made: _____

It was: ☐ a final order. ☐ a temporary order.

I ask that this order be set aside and that an order be made as follows:
(Set out briefly the order that you want the appeal court to make.)

_____

_____

_____

The legal grounds for my appeal are: *(Set out in numbered paragraphs the legal basis of your appeal.)*

1. _____

_____

_____

_____

_____

_____

_____

_____

_____

_____

_____

_____

_____

_____

Draw a line through any space left on this page.

NOTE TO THE APPELLANT: You have 30 days to serve this notice on the other parties in the case and you must file it with the clerk of the appeal court with proof of service (Form 6B) within 10 days after that.

NOTE TO THE RESPONDENT: If you want to oppose this appeal, you or your lawyer must prepare a respondent's factum required by subrule 38(9) of the *Family Law Rules*, serve a copy on the appellant(s) and file a copy with the clerk of the appeal court with proof of service (Form 6B). You must serve and file a respondent's factum at least 3 days before the hearing of the appeal. If you do not, the appeal will go ahead without you and the court may make a new order and enforce it against you.

Date of signature	*Signature*

Form 39
Notice of Approaching Dismissal
ONTARIO

_____

(Name of court)

	Court File Number

at _____

Court office address

Form 39: Notice of Approaching Dismissal

Applicant(s)

Full legal name & address for service — street & number, municipality, postal code, telephone & fax numbers and e-mail address (if any).	Lawyer's name & address — street & number, municipality, postal code, telephone & fax numbers and e-mail address (if any).

Respondent(s)

Full legal name & address for service — street & number, municipality, postal code, telephone & fax numbers and e-mail address (if any).	Lawyer's name & address — street & number, municipality, postal code, telephone & fax numbers and e-mail address (if any).

TO ALL PARTIES:

1. THE CLERK OF THE COURT WILL DISMISS THIS CASE WITHOUT FURTHER NOTICE unless, within 60 days after service of this notice, one of the parties:

(a) obtains an order under subrule 39(3), 40(3) or 41(3) to lengthen the time to do anything described below;

(b) files an agreement signed by all parties and their lawyers, if any, for a final order disposing of all issues in the case, and a notice of motion for an order carrying out the agreement;

(c) serves on all parties and files a notice of withdrawal (Form 12) that discontinues all outstanding claims in the case;

(d) schedules or adjourns the case for trial; or

(e) arranges a case conference or settlement conference for the first available date.

2. If a case conference or settlement conference is arranged for a date as described in clause 1 (e) but the hearing does not take place on that date and is not adjourned by a judge, the case will be dismissed without further notice.

1214

3. Any temporary orders, including temporary orders for support and interim restraining orders under section 46 of the *Family Law Act* or under section 35 of the *Children's Law Reform Act*, will expire upon the dismissal of the case.

Put a line through any blank space left on this page.

_____   _____
       Date of signature   *Signature of clerk of the court*

CHECKLISTS

DOS AND DON'TS OF E-DISCOVERY PRACTICES IN ONTARIO

DO

- **Send a preservation letter at the very outset of the litigation**

  Purpose: To ensure upfront that the opposite party knows it must preserve electronic data and not destroy or alter it.

- **Ensure that e-discovery is canvassed in the discovery plan**

  Purpose: To make clear that there is to be a careful canvass of the electronic materials during the discovery process.

- **Speak to a computer expert before conducting an examination**

  Purpose: Lawyers sometimes don't have a very clear understanding of how computers store information, and hence it is important to speak to someone with extensive computer experience who can outline the ways that data is stored in specific cases and who can point to the lines of questioning that will be useful.

- **Show that electronic documents exist and are relevant**

  Purpose: If you need to bring motions for production, you will need to show more than a suspicion that electronic documents exist and that they are important to the case. For example, you may need to show that there were e-mail exchanges of draft documentation.

- **Examine how electronic documents are kept and preserved**

  Purpose: To prove the production sought is reasonable and not excessive. The Ontario Rules of Civil Procedure allow for production that is proportionate to the matters in dispute.

- **Examine how difficult a full review of the electronic data would be, and include cost estimates**

  Purpose: To prove the production sought is reasonable and not excessive. The Ontario Rules of Civil Procedure allow for production that is proportionate to the matters in dispute.

- **Examine in detail as to what searches were completed**

  Purpose: To establish that all proper searches have been completed or, more importantly, to see if they have been done at all. This will allow you to demand proper and full searches.

DON'T

- **Agree that only paper copies of e-mails are sufficient**

  Rationale: Agreeing to retain only paper copies of e-mails amounts to a waiver of a claim for electronic production. It also eliminates a lot of potentially useful information, such as when documents were created, etc.

CHECKLIST

- **Fail to examine the details of how electronic documents are kept and preserved**

   Rationale: Without this information, you will have great difficulty in showing that the production sought is reasonable.

- **Demand excessive disclosure — focus on what is actually necessary**

   Rationale: Excess production will be properly refused and judicial officers will be unwilling to assist an unreasonable litigant.

- **Fail to fulfil your discovery obligations**

   Rationale: If you fail to produce as required, it is hard to get production — do unto others as you would have done unto you!

- **Delay in bringing electronic production motions**

   Rationale: Motions brought just before trial will not be granted or, if they are, only at great cost.

CHECKLISTS

ONTARIO E-DISCOVERY IMPLEMENTATION COMMITTEE
MODEL DOCUMENT #8
ANNOTATED E-DISCOVERY CHECKLIST*
(with suggestions on how to minimize e-discovery costs)

PURPOSE OF THE DOCUMENT

This annotated e-discovery checklist is designed to provide guidance to counsel and their clients regarding the main steps to be taken with respect to the preservation, production and use of relevant documents,[1] including all types of electronically stored information, within an action or other legal proceeding. The annotations provide suggested methods of minimizing costs throughout the e-discovery process.

Every case is unique, and not all steps identified in the checklist may be required for all actions, while in some actions additional e-discovery steps may be called for.

PROPORTIONALITY

In any legal proceeding, the parties should ensure that all steps taken in the discovery process are proportionate, taking into account, among other things, the importance and complexity of the case, the amounts and interests at stake, and the costs, delay, burden and benefit associated with each step.

This annotated e-discovery checklist treats proportionality as a guiding principle, identifying circumstances in which certain e-discovery steps may not be required, or in which the steps may be accomplished more efficiently and with less cost and other burdens.

ANNOTATIONS

Annotations are included at various points throughout the model document, identifying issues that the parties may wish to consider. Many of the annotations refer to *The Sedona Canada Principles Addressing Electronic Discovery* (the "*Sedona Canada Principles*"). Civil litigants in Ontario are required, pursuant to Rule 29.1 of the *Rules of Civil Procedure*, to consult and have regard to the *Sedona Canada Principles* in preparing a discovery plan for an action. The *Sedona Canada Principles* are a set of national guidelines for e-discovery in Canada, which reflect both existing legal principles and a set of identified best practices. A copy of the *Sedona Canada Principles* may be downloaded from www.thesedonaconference.org, where they are found under the list of publications for Working Group 7.

NOTE REGARDING USE OF THIS DOCUMENT

This checklist and all of the EIC's model documents and other publications are available on the Ontario Bar Association's website at:

---

* Copyright 2010. Reproduced with permission of the Ontario E-Discovery Implementation Committee.

1 The word "document" is used in this Model Document in its broadest sense, as meaning "information recorded in any form, including electronically stored information". The word "document" is used interchangeably with the word "record".

http://www.oba.org/En/publicaffairs_en/E-Discovery/model_precedents.aspx

This model document has been prepared and made available to the public by the EIC for informational purposes. It is not provided as legal or technical advice and should not be relied upon as such.

FEEDBACK ON EIC MATERIALS

The EIC welcomes comments on all of its model documents and other publications. Any comments or suggestions can be provided to Michele A. Wright at mwright4@toronto.ca.

I. ADVISING THE CLIENT

1. **Address urgent preservation issues**: Determine immediately with the client whether there are urgent preservation issues because relevant records may be destroyed, altered or removed in the short term -- see subsection II-A below ("Address urgent issues").[2]

2. **Advise the client regarding the preservation obligation**: Advise the client orally to the extent required regarding:[3]

   - the obligation to preserve all relevant records, whether the records are helpful or not
   - the requirement to disclose and produce relevant non-privileged records
   - the requirement to disclose (but not produce) relevant privileged records
   - the need to preserve, disclose and produce electronic records as well as paper records
   - the different types of electronic records and different media in which they are stored
   - the importance of preserving electronic records in their original, unaltered form in order to ensure admissibility at trial
   - the potential consequences of spoliation
   - the cost savings and other benefits associated with a comprehensive and systematic approach to collecting relevant records
   - the proportionality principle and its application to documentary discovery
   - the application of the client's documentary discovery obligations to records that are not in the client's possession but that are under its power or control
   - the need to implement a litigation hold, and the steps involved — see subsection II-C below ("Initiate a litigation hold")
   - the utility of conferring with opposing parties regarding what is to be preserved, disclosed and produced and in what form -- see Section III below ("Conferring with opposing counsel")
   - the process for preserving, collecting, reviewing, processing and producing relevant records — see subsection II-B below ("Prepare the preservation plan").

3. **Explain the documentary discovery process**: Explain the documentary discovery process to the client, including:

   - all main steps involved in preserving, collecting, processing, reviewing and producing the client's records;

---

[2] Consider not only records in the client's possession, but also records held by opposing parties, and records held by non-parties.

[3] The nature of the communication with the client and the scope of the advice given will vary depending upon, among other things, the client's degree of knowledge and sophistication, and whether the client is a new or existing client. A more detailed discussion of possible advice to be given to the client is set out in the model memoranda regarding documentary discovery prepared by the Ontario E-Discovery Implementation Committee (Model Documents #3 and #4) for corporate clients and individuals.

- the personnel at the law firm and elsewhere (if applicable) who will be involved in the process;

- the demands that will be placed on the client in terms of time and personnel;

- the financial and other benefits of conducting the entire process electronically (including scanning of paper documents);

- the likely timeframe for completing the process; and

- the associated financial costs of all steps (being careful not to underestimate the potentially very significant financial cost).

4. **Deliver advice in writing**: Deliver an advice memorandum or letter to the client, if appropriate, describing:

- the client's obligations with respect to documentary discovery

- the essential steps in implementing a litigation hold in order to preserve potentially relevant records

- key issues to be addressed by the client in determining how best to fulfil its obligations to preserve, disclose and produce records in a strategic, proportionate and cost-effective manner.[4]

5. **Diarize to provide follow-up advice**: Diarize to remind the client of its preservation and production obligations at subsequent stages of the litigation (*e.g.*, after the initial affidavit of documents is served, after discoveries, etc.).

COST REDUCTION TIPS FOR THIS STEP:

Ways to reduce legal fees:

1. Counsel: Use a precedent memo regarding the documentary discovery process (such as the EIC's Model Documents #3 and #4), as an outline of the topics to review with the client orally, and as the starting point for an individualized advice memo or letter to the client.

2. Counsel: Maintain a model litigation hold policy and sample litigation hold notices to make available to the client.

3. Counsel: Become fully familiar in advance with the issues associated with preservation of electronic records, so that the client need not pay for counsel to inform themselves. The client can similarly reduce fees by achieving such familiarity itself, whether through in-house counsel or otherwise.

---

[4] In many cases, this step may be accomplished by way of a letter outlining the client's obligations with respect to the preservation of electronic evidence. For existing or sophisticated clients, particularly those with in-house legal counsel, it may not be necessary or desirable to provide a written advice memo in each case regarding obligations with respect to documentary discovery. Counsel must use their judgment in deciding what advice to provide in writing. The extent to which clients require assistance with preservation will vary from client to client and the assistance given should take account of the principle of proportionality. For model advice memos, see the E-Discovery Implementation Committee's Model Documents #3 and #4.

4. Client: Have an established litigation hold procedure in place as part of a litigation readiness plan.

In smaller cases:

1. Preservation advice may be provided at the same time as counsel is meeting with the client to collect records, gather facts and prepare file strategy.

2. Written advice regarding preservation may not be required if, for example, counsel is satisfied that all relevant records have been preserved and provided.

3. Counsel must give advice regarding the client's preservation obligations that is proportionate taking into account the dollar value, importance, and other features of the case. The obligation to preserve cannot reasonably be as onerous in smaller cases as it is in cases involving larger dollar values.

II. PRESERVING RELEVANT RECORDS

A. ADDRESS URGENT PRESERVATION ISSUES

1. **Identify imminent spoliation concerns**: Determine immediately whether:

    - the client has relevant records that may be destroyed, altered or removed in the short term

    - an opposing party has relevant records that there is reason to believe they may destroy, alter or remove in the short term

    - a non-party (such as a consultant, affiliate, *etc.*) has such records.

For the client, issues to consider in determining whether there is an imminent risk of destruction of relevant records include:

- whether the litigation is concerned with very recent or ongoing events, such that there is a risk of destruction of relevant records in "real time"

- the frequency with which the client recycles backup media

- whether the client has a regular email deletion policy under which emails are deleted routinely after a certain number of days if not otherwise filed

- the possibility of alteration to electronic records that are in continuing use, such as databases

- destruction of potentially relevant records in the ordinary course pursuant to the client's records retention policy

- the possibility of a relevant hard drive, portable device, *etc.* being scrubbed or otherwise rendered inaccessible (*e.g.*, the personal computer of a departing employee).

2. **Prepare and implement an urgent preservation plan**: If there are relevant records at imminent risk of destruction, immediately discuss with the client and implement a proportionate response to the need to preserve these records. Among other things:

    - Determine whether there is anything on the backup media that cannot be preserved otherwise[5]

- Identify the least expensive and least disruptive means of effectively preserving email that would otherwise be subject to an automatic email deletion process[6]

- Identify the least expensive and least disruptive means of effectively preserving records scheduled for destruction pursuant to the client's records retention policy[7]

- As appropriate, issue litigation hold notices immediately to persons who might otherwise destroy or discard relevant records — see subsection II-C below ("Initiate a litigation hold").

3. **Consider an urgent preservation motion**: Consider whether an immediate motion seeking the preservation of records held by opposing parties or non-parties is required (whether by way of *Anton Piller* order or otherwise).[8]

4. **Consider urgent preservation letters**: Consider whether to send a preservation letter to the opposing parties or to non-parties requesting preservation of records that may be imminently destroyed — see subsection II-D below ("Send preservation letters").

COST REDUCTION TIPS FOR THIS STEP:

Ways to reduce legal fees:

1. Client: Have an established litigation hold procedure in place as part of a litigation readiness plan and broader records management process, with provision for addressing urgent preservation issues.

2. Counsel and client: Maintain and use standard form preservation letters that may be quickly modified to the circumstances of the case. Preservation letters can be sent by the client rather than counsel if appropriate.

Ways to reduce consulting fees:

1. Limit the extent to which it is necessary to retain consultants to assist with urgent preservation steps relating to electronic records by:

- implementing a records management process through which company records are regularly or automatically filed;

- training internal IT staff on how to implement preservation procedures for electronic records (urgent and otherwise), if appropriate;

---

[5] The expense of taking backup media out of circulation, and preserving and restoring them, should be avoided if there is an alternative, less-expensive means of preserving the same data.

[6] Suspension of the email deletion process on a company-wide basis is not the preferred approach, if less expensive and less disruptive alternatives are available, such as email filing or copying.

[7] Suspension of destruction of all records under the records retention policy should be avoided if it is possible to identify specific subclasses of records, or specific records, that are potentially relevant to the litigation.

[8] An annotated model *Anton Piller* order has been prepared by the Ontario Commercial List Users Committee and is available online at the website of the Ontario Superior Court of Justice at http://www.ontariocourts.on.ca/scj/en/commerciallist/.

- acquiring some of the available affordable software tools that permit clients to make forensic copies of their own hard drives, if appropriate; and

- strictly limiting the retention period for backup media to the short time needed for disaster recovery purposes (where that is the sole purpose of the backup media).

In smaller cases:

1. Forensic copying of hard drives, whether by consultants or on a DIY basis, can be a relatively inexpensive means of preserving all relevant data in cases where few computers are involved.

2. Urgent preservation steps can be combined with all other preservation and collection steps in a single "blitz".

B. PREPARE THE PRESERVATION PLAN

1. **Identify an IT liaison**: Identify an information technology liaison person at the client, to coordinate the preservation of electronic records.

2. **Complete an IT questionnaire**: Ask the client and its IT liaison to complete an IT questionnaire,[9] or to provide information orally, regarding:

   - system architecture (network structure, geographic location of hardware, *etc.*);

   - types of hardware and software used by the client;

   - what forms of potentially relevant electronically stored information exist, such as emails, word processing documents, databases, Excel documents, voice mail records, web-based files or metadata;

   - methods of data storage, such as on servers, desktop computers, laptops, home computers, PDAs such as BlackBerrys or Palm Pilots, floppy disks, CDs, DVDs, zip drives, backup media, external hard drives and USB ("thumb") drives;

   - data storage by third parties such as banks, accountants, lawyers, insurers, third party service providers, affiliated companies or internet service providers;

   - the client's backup protocol, including types of backups performed and their schedule;

   - the physical location of backup media;

   - procedures for retrieving data from backup media;

   - the client's archiving protocol, if applicable, and procedures for retrieving data from archives;

   - costs and resources required to retrieve information from backup and other storage media.[10]

---

[9] For sample IT questionnaires, see *The Electronic Evidence and Discovery Handbook* (ABA Law Practice Management, 2006) at pp. 3 and following.

[10] Comment 3.c. of the *Sedona Canada Principles* recommends that counsel be prepared in a substantive way for a meet and confer session with opposing counsel by gaining "a thorough understanding of how

3. **Prepare an IT inventory**: Ask the IT liaison to prepare an inventory of storage media containing potentially relevant records.

4. **Prepare a preservation plan**: Meet or speak with the client, including the IT liaison, to prepare a preservation plan.[11] Topics for discussion and decision include:

- whether an e-discovery consultant or computer forensics specialist is needed in order to preserve and collect relevant records;

- the extent to which counsel or law firm personnel should be directly involved;

- the role to be played by the client in preserving and collecting records;

- what methods to use to search for the client's records, including the possible use of indexing software and other search tools;

- whether to preserve more broadly (such as by making forensic copies of hard drives and servers, with culling for relevance to occur later) or more narrowly based on specific relevance parameters;[12]

- the relevant search parameters to narrow the scope of preservation and collection, such as:

  - custodians;
  - date range;
  - geographic location;
  - file type;[13]
  - email suffix;

- search terms (such as employee names, key words in the litigation, names of persons on the other side, *etc.*);[14]

- whether and to what extent to preserve metadata;

- whether to preserve backup media and, if so, whether to seek to retrieve specific

---

electronically stored information is created, used and maintained by or for the client".

[11] Principle #3 of the *Sedona Canada Principles* states "[a]s soon as litigation is reasonably anticipated, parties must consider their obligation to take reasonable and good faith steps to preserve relevant electronically stored information." Note, though, that while most cases require thought to be given to e-discovery issues, not every case requires a strenuous chasing-down of electronic records and information. E-discovery can be an expensive diversion. Approaching it blindly can be counterproductive. Before starting any search for electronic evidence, counsel and client should analyze the issues in the case and prioritize them, and then determine the likely relevance of electronic records to those issues, in order of priority.

[12] Preserving broadly and then using culling software to identify relevant records will in some cases be quicker and more efficient than seeking to identify relevant records on an individualized basis.

[13] In most cases, the vast majority of electronic records will consist of e-mail, word processing documents and data within databases.

[14] Principle #7 of the *Sedona Canada Principles* states that parties may satisfy their obligations "by using electronic tools and processes such as data sampling, searching and/or the use of selection criteria to collect potentially relevant electronically stored information".

- records from the backup media;[15]
- whether and how to seek to preserve deleted or residual data;
- whether to make forensic copies of hard drives and servers;[16]
- the cost associated with all contemplated preservation steps;
- the risks associated with not undertaking the contemplated preservation steps; and
- a determination of what constitutes a proportionate preservation response, taking into account the amounts at issue, the importance of the case, the importance of various types of files, and other factors.

5. **Keep a written record of the preservation plan**: Make sure to maintain careful records of the preservation plan. Consider whether to send written confirmation to the client, documenting the preservation plan.

COST REDUCTION TIPS FOR THIS STEP:

Ways to reduce legal fees:

1. Limit the scope of the preservation plan by agreement among the parties.

2. Counsel: Maintain a precedent IT questionnaire.

3. Client: Provide complete and detailed information in response to the IT questionnaire, to reduce the need for legal time in gathering this background information.

4. Reduce or eliminate the role of lawyers in carrying out preservation steps once the preservation plan is prepared. As a general matter, this work can be carried out either by the client or by consultants, with only periodic consultation with counsel. If law firm personnel must be involved on a day-to-day basis, law clerks or contract lawyers should be considered where appropriate, given their lower billing rates.

Ways to reduce consulting fees:

1. Carry out preservation steps using client personnel, where appropriate. E-discovery consultants and computer forensics specialists play an important role in many cases, but their involvement is not required in all cases, especially where electronic records are not particularly important, or where the client is sufficiently sophisticated to be able to carry out preservation tasks without outside assistance.

2. Consider carefully whether the more complicated forms of preservation (involv-

---

[15] Comment 3.a. of the *Sedona Canada Principles* states that "[t]he general obligation to preserve evidence . . . must be balanced against the party's right to continue to manage its electronic information in an economically reasonable manner, including routinely overwriting electronic information in appropriate cases. It is unreasonable to expect organizations to take every conceivable step to preserve all electronically stored information that may be potentially relevant."

[16] In a smaller organization, the simplest and most effective way to preserve electronic evidence may be simply to make a forensic copy of the drives.

ing backup tapes, deleted and residual data, metadata, *etc.*) are required in the circumstances of the particular case.

Ways to reduce employee time:

1. Rely upon software tools rather than employee review to search for relevant records.

In smaller cases:

1. The client's preservation plan in smaller cases must take into account the proportionality principle. The cost of preservation efforts must be proportionate to the dollar value of the claim. Except in rare cases, this will mean that backup media need not be restored, deleted and residual data need not be preserved, and extraordinary preservation steps need not be taken.

2. Take advantage of inexpensive software tools that allow for relatively quick and easy indexing of records on a computer or computer network.

3. Focus on the records that truly matter.

C. INITIATE A LITIGATION HOLD

1. **Appoint an overseer**: Consider the appointment of one individual at the client to oversee the implementation of the litigation hold.

2. **Identify and implement the litigation hold policy**: Determine whether the client has an existing records retention policy that includes a litigation hold procedure.[17]

    • If so, consider obtaining a copy of the records retention policy, reviewing its adequacy, and advising the client of any deficiencies.

    • If not, provide the client with a model litigation hold procedure, including sample hold notices.[18]

3. **Issue litigation hold notices**: Issue litigation hold notices in writing to all employees, contract workers and third parties who may be custodians of potentially relevant documents to inform them of the need to preserve these documents in their original format without modification. Recipients of the litigation hold notice should include:

    • all persons at the client with direct knowledge of or involvement with the matters at issue;

    • all persons likely to have possession of records relevant to the matters at issue (including assistants to persons with direct knowledge, third parties with possession of records that remain in the control or power of the client,[19] *etc.*);

---

[17] A client may have several records retention policies for different divisions, departments or affiliates, and may have a separate retention policy for electronic records.

[18] A description of the litigation hold obligation, and a sample litigation hold notice, are found in the model memorandum to a corporate client regarding documentary discovery prepared by the Ontario E-Discovery Implementation Committee (Model Document #3).

[19] See Comments 3.d. and 5.c. of the *Sedona Canada Principles*. Consideration must be given to contacting outsourced vendors or non-party custodians of data of the client. As stated in Comment 5.c.,

- personnel responsible for archiving and storage of records at the client;
- personnel in charge of records retention procedures at the client; and
- appropriate IT personnel (including in particular the IT liaison person identified in preparing the preservation plan — see subsection C above).

4. **Ensure compliance with the litigation hold**: Client or counsel (if appropriate, with the assistance of an e-discovery consultant or computer forensics specialist) must work with the client's IT department to ensure that electronic records affected by the litigation hold are properly preserved. Counsel should follow up with the client to ensure the litigation hold has been implemented – see Section IV below ("Collecting Relevant Records").

5. **Issue follow up litigation hold notices**: Over the course of the litigation, issue litigation hold notices to new employees who will have access to relevant documents. Consider the necessity of additional litigation hold notices as issues in litigation evolve.

6. **Keep an audit trail**: Ensure that the chain of custody for the preserved records is properly documented,[20] to ensure the ability to prove the authenticity and integrity of the records at trial.[21]

- Consider whether any additional information is required to be preserved regarding the integrity of the system in which the records were stored.

COST REDUCTION TIPS FOR THIS STEP:

Ways to reduce legal fees:

1. Counsel: Maintain a model litigation hold policy with sample hold notices, as well as sample chain of custody documentation, to provide to clients as needed.

2. Client: Maintain an up-to-date litigation hold policy and records management system, including chain of custody procedures and documentation, to minimize the need for legal help in implementing the litigation hold.

3. Client: Implement the litigation hold using company employees, without the direct involvement of counsel in the implementation stage, where appropriate.

Ways to reduce consulting fees:

1. Where appropriate, implement the litigation hold without the involvement of outside consultants. The question of whether outside consultants are needed should be discussed with counsel.

"[m]any organizations outsource all or part of their information technology systems or share electronically stored information with third parties for processing, transmitting or for other business purposes." Note that where the client is an individual rather than a corporation, the obligation to ensure that certain third parties preserve relevant records still applies.

[20] For sample chain of custody documentation, see *The Electronic Evidence and Discovery Handbook* (ABA Law Practice Management, 2006) at pp. 14-15.

[21] See s. 34.1 of the *Evidence Act* (Ontario) and ss. 31.1 to 31.8 of the *Canada Evidence Act*, on establishing the authenticity and integrity of electronic records. See also *Electronic Records as Documentary Evidence*, published by the Canadian General Standards Board (CAN/CGSB 72.34-2005).

2. Limit the scope of the litigation hold, as part of preparing the preservation plan, to reduce the quantity of data and records to be preserved.

In smaller cases:

1. Prepare the preservation plan, implement the litigation hold and collect relevant records as part of a single meeting or exercise, where possible.

D. SEND PRESERVATION LETTERS

1. **Consider scope of preservation requests**: Consider carefully what preservation steps opposing parties should be asked to undertake.[22] Among other things:

   - Determine what relevant electronically stored information opposing parties may have

   - Determine as far as possible the relevant parameters that should be used to identify relevant documents. For example:

     - the persons, places and types of materials to be searched; and

     - the search terms and date ranges to be used.

   - Consider the steps that the other side will need to take to preserve relevant records, particularly in relation to metadata or deleted files.

2. **Send preservation letters**: Send preservation letters to opposing parties outlining some or all of the following, as appropriate:[23]

   - their e-discovery preservation obligations

   - the steps to be taken to preserve

   - the types of electronic records that should be preserved

   - the devices where that information may be located and identifying as far as possible the potentially relevant search terms

   - specific documents or classes of documents to be preserved, or specific custodians of relevant documents, or applicable date ranges, if known

   - a request that litigation hold notices be issued to third party custodians of electronically stored information

---

[22] Consider the proportionality principle in determining what preservation steps opposing parties should be asked to undertake. Extreme preservation efforts should not be requested except in unusual circumstances: see Comment 3.f. of the *Sedona Canada Principles*. Consider the client's ability and willingness to undertaking the same preservation steps, since any preservation demand made of the opposing parties may be reciprocated.

[23] See the sample preservation letters prepared by the Ontario E-Discovery Implementation Committee (Model Documents #5 and #6). A preservation letter should be sent to opposing counsel as soon as litigation is commenced, and sometimes before. At that time, counsel may have limited information about potentially relevant information in the possession of the other side. Therefore, it will usually be necessary to establish and enforce preservation obligations in a progressive manner. The first letter to opposing counsel may simply be a very general request to preserve relevant electronic information. It may be appropriate to then send one or more additional, more focused preservation letter with a defined scope in terms of date range, record types, custodians, search terms, etc.

- a request to meet and confer early in the proceedings to discuss appropriate preservation steps.

3. **Consider a preservation motion**: Consider whether a motion is necessary to compel preservation, where an opposing party refuses to confirm preservation steps have been taken or to participate in a meet and confer session. In this regard, consider the terms of the order you want, for example:

   - duration;
   - what is to be preserved;
   - how relevant documents are to be identified and where they may be found;
   - the search terms to be used;
   - how extensive preservation shall be;
   - the role of external consultants, if any; and
   - who bears the costs associated with preservation.[24]

4. **Consider preservation of records held by non-parties**: Consider whether to send preservation letters to non-parties.

COST REDUCTION TIPS FOR THIS STEP:

Ways to reduce legal fees:

1. Focus on the records that matter.

2. Avoid preservation demands that will generate unnecessary disputes over the scope of the preservation obligation.

3. Work cooperatively with opposing parties to identify and limit the scope of the preservation obligation.

4. Bring a preservation motion only where truly necessary to protect the client's interests.

5. Use model preservation letters as a basis for crafting a preservation demand appropriate to the circumstances of the case.

III. CONFERRING WITH OPPOSING COUNSEL

1. **Consider a meet and confer session**: Consider the appropriateness of conferring with opposing counsel early to attempt to agree on preservation and other discovery planning issues.[25]

---

[24] See the sample preservation order prepared by the Ontario E-Discovery Implementation Committee (Model Document #7).

[25] Rule 29.1 of the Ontario *Rules of Civil Procedure* requires parties to agree upon a written discovery plan for the action that addresses the intended scope of documentary discovery taking into account proportionality issues, dates for service of affidavits of documents, information regarding the timing, costs and

As an alternative, consider writing to opposing counsel with a proposal with respect to discovery planning, and inviting agreement.

2. **Consider topics of discussion**: Topics for discussion at the meet and confer include the following discovery planning issues:[26]

Preservation Steps Taken

- preservation steps taken to date to prevent destruction of records
- physical location of records
- whether to use a consultant to assist in preservation steps
- whether to send preservation notices to non-parties (*e.g.*, contractors, vendors)
- whether any additional preservation steps need to be taken

Searches to be Performed

- search parameters to be used to locate relevant records, such as:
- the physical locations to search;
- custodians whose records are to be searched;
- authors of records;
- file types; and
- the relevant date range
- whether, in light of the volume of records, it is appropriate to do sampling or to use a phased approach to production
- whether to produce metadata
- whether to produce information stored on back up media
- whether to use a consultant to search for relevant records

Exchanging Records

- format for exchange of electronic and paper records[27]

---

manner of production of documents, the names of discovery witnesses, information regarding the timing and length of examinations for discovery, and any other information intended to result in the expeditious and cost-effective completion of the discovery process in a manner that is proportionate to the importance and complexity of the action. The rule requires parties to consult and have regard to the *Sedona Canada Principles* in preparing the discovery plan. Principle #4 of the *Sedona Canada Principles* states that "Counsel and parties should meet and confer as soon as practicable, and on an ongoing basis, regarding the identification, preservation, collection, review and production of electronically stored information". Comment 4.a states that the purpose of the "meet and confer" is to identify and resolve e-discovery related issues in a timely fashion. Meeting early is "one of the keys to effective e-discovery for all sides".

[26] See the model discovery agreement prepared by the Ontario E-Discovery Implementation Committee (Model Document #1), for an annotated and expanded listing of topics for the meet and confer. See also Model Document #9: Checklist for Preparing a Discovery Plan.

[27] Recommended default standards for the format of exchange of electronic records are set out in the model discovery agreement prepared by the Ontario E-Discovery Implementation Committee (Model Document #1), at sections 6 and 10.

- whether specific software or hardware must be made available in order to allow electronically stored-information to be inspected
- whether to use common litigation support software, and in any event ensuring compatibility between software that is to be used and in the selection and coding of fields (*i.e.*, author, recipient, date, document number, *etc.*)
- whether to use a common third-party litigation support service provider to scan and/or code producible records
- whether to use a common protocol for coding records to be produced and for preparing affidavits of documents
- measures to be taken to protect privilege, privacy, trade secrets or other confidential information (including measures to address inadvertent production of privileged documents)
- whether a cost sharing/allocation agreement is desirable
- time frame for complying with obligations agreed upon
- electronic service of court documents, except if impractical
- agreement upon the authenticity and integrity of electronic records
- identification of an e-liaison person for each party to coordinate technical issues (*i.e.*, a litigation support clerk at each firm)

Subsequent events

- procedure if a party is unable to comply with an agreed step or if compliance becomes too onerous
- procedure where a party requests additional discovery steps beyond those agreed upon
- procedure with respect to inspection of records in their native or original form.[28]

3. **Confirm whether session is without prejudice**: Confirm whether the meet and confer session (or part of the session) is without prejudice.[29]

4. **Select method of confirmation of agreement**: Consider the most appropriate method of recording the parties' agreement (*e.g.*, by letter, by formal agreement, by consent court order).[30] Consider whether to record areas of disagreement and the basis for the disagreement.

---

[28] Counsel should consider the effect that entering into an agreement at the meet and confer session will have on their discovery rights. It may be appropriate to enter into an agreement with respect to some issues with a reservation of rights. For sample agreement language dealing with this point, see the model discovery agreement prepared by the Ontario E-Discovery Implementation Committee (Model Document #1), at section 4.

[29] It is recommended that counsel agree that negotiations be without prejudice, but that any agreement reached be with prejudice.

[30] See, for example, the following documents prepared by the Ontario E-Discovery Implementation Committee: (1) model long form discovery plan (Model Document #9A); (2) model short form discovery plan (Model Document #9B); (3) sample confirming letter regarding discovery plan (Sample Document #1); (4) model discovery agreement (Model Document #1); and (5) model preservation order (Model Document #7).

5. **Consider whether to bring a motion**: Consider whether to bring a motion in connection with matters of disagreement.

6. **Hold further meet and confer sessions**: Conduct additional meet and confer sessions as appropriate during the course of the litigation.[31]

COST REDUCTION TIPS FOR THIS STEP:

Ways to reduce legal fees:

1. The meet and confer process is itself a means of reducing legal fees, because it has the potential to narrow the scope of discovery, to streamline the discovery process, and to help the parties avoid costly discovery disputes.

2. Counsel: Maintain a checklist of topics to address at a meet and confer session, and a model discovery agreement and/or model confirming letter and/or model discovery planning proposal.

3. Client: Maintain precedent materials describing the organization's IT infrastructure (hardware, software, and networks) to assist counsel in preparing for a meet and confer session.

4. Seek to agree on the simplest, narrowest and most cost-efficient discovery plan that is appropriate to the circumstances of the case.

Ways to reduce consulting fees:

1. Consider carefully whether an outside consultant is required. In some cases, the retainer of an outside consultant is an essential expense, or results in a net cost saving because the consultant's involvement reduces legal fees. In other cases, using a consultant is unnecessary and the associated expense can be avoided or reduced.

In smaller cases:

1. The meet and confer session may consist of a phone call followed by a confirming letter.

2. Except in unusual cases, the parties should agree to a narrow scope of e-discovery using simple methods.

3. The importance of proceeding in a collaborative fashion is particularly acute in smaller matters, where any discovery dispute may result in disproportionately high transaction costs.

IV. COLLECTING RELEVANT RECORDS

1. **Decide who should collect records**: Decide with the client whether counsel or a con-

---

[31] In most cases, counsel may be able to deal with issues related to preservation, disclosure and production in the early stages. In more complex cases, it may be necessary to deal with various parts of these issues progressively in successive meetings. Principle #4 of the *Sedona Canada Principles* recommends that counsel and parties meet and confer "on an ongoing basis".

sultant should be involved in physically collecting the relevant records for delivery to counsel.[32]

2. **Instruct client on collection**: Instruct the client on proper methods of collection of records, if appropriate.

3. **Keep careful records of the collection process**: Make sure that the parties engaged in collecting the records maintain careful records of all collection steps, and maintain chain of custody documentation.[33]

4. **Ensure prompt collection**: Ensure that all records are collected promptly and comprehensively from all relevant sources, including third parties, in accordance with the preservation plan and any agreement reached with opposing parties.

5. **Review and assess results of data sampling**: When data sampling is being conducted to confirm whether relevant records are contained within a data set, counsel or the client should review the results of the data sampling and determine whether further sampling, or collection of records, is required.[34]

6. **Review and assess search results**: When software tools are being used to locate relevant records for collection through the use of search terms or other parameters, counsel or the client should review the results of the searches to determine whether the searches are effective in identifying relevant records. If necessary, modifications to the search terms should be made to ensure that relevant records are located and collected and, to the extent reasonably possible, irrelevant records are not captured (bearing in mind that further filtering can be conducted by counsel during the review stage).

COST REDUCTION TIPS FOR THIS STEP:

Ways to reduce legal fees:

1. Avoid involving counsel in the collection stage. Little if any of the work at this stage requires a direct role for lawyers.

Ways to reduce consulting fees:

1. Consider carefully whether the client or a consultant should carry out the collection of records. If the client has the ability and knowledge to conduct the collection exercise itself, consulting fees can be saved.

Ways to reduce employee time:

1. Employees collecting relevant records should be instructed not to engage in detailed relevance review. It is quicker and more efficient to collect a broader group of records, and then to filter them for relevance using software tools.

---

[32] Except in rare cases, counsel need not be involved in actually collecting the records.

[33] Counsel should be in a position to provide the client with sample chain of custody documentation, to make clear to the client what information relating to the chain of custody needs to be preserved.

[34] Principle #7 of the *Sedona Canada Principles* states that "[a] party may satisfy its obligation to preserve, collect, review and produce electronically stored information in good faith by using electronic tools and processes such as data sampling, searching or by using selection criteria to collect potentially relevant electronically stored information".

2. Electronic searches can be used to identify collections of records containing relevant material, thereby avoiding the need for detailed manual review by employees in identifying potentially relevant material for review by counsel.

In smaller cases:

1. There are inexpensive software programs capable of conducting electronic searches of a client's computer system to locate relevant records.

2. As a matter of proportionality (weighing the cost of retaining a consultant against the dollar value or importance of the case), the use of consultants to collect records in smaller cases should be rare.

V. PROCESSING AND REVIEWING THE RECORDS

1. **Decide on reviewing software**: Decide on the software tools to be used to filter and manage records collected by the client, such as:

   - e-discovery processing software (which reviews electronic data provided by a client, classifies it by file type, quantifies it, converts it into a form that may be loaded into litigation case management software, *etc.*)

   - culling software (through which irrelevant records can be culled by filtering based on parameters such as date, author, email suffix, search terms, *etc.*)

   - de-duplication software (through which duplicates or "near duplicates" are identified)

   - litigation case management software (the tool used to code records as relevant/ irrelevant, privileged/not privileged, *etc.*, and to manage records for use in the litigation)

   - web-hosted litigation case management software (through which parties may review records remotely through the Internet).

2. **Identify who will process the records**: Decide whether counsel or a consultant will conduct the processing, culling, de-duplicating, *etc.*

3. **Import the records from the client**: Import the collected records received from the client.

4. **Scan and code paper records**: Arrange for scanning and coding of paper records.[35]

5. **Assess the resources required in order to review**: Assess the volume of records requiring manual review for relevance, privilege, confidentiality, *etc.* and assess the human resource and time requirements to review these records. In this regard, consider:

   - whether to engage in manual review of records at all, or instead to rely upon software tools to search for relevant, non-privileged records (with audits of the search

---

[35] Scanning paper documents in a manner so that they are electronically text-searchable greatly increases the ease of searching paper records for relevance, privilege, *etc.* Note that, ideally, counsel should agree with opposing counsel in advance on the database fields to be coded and the format of coding, to ensure ease of exchange of records.

     results to confirm the effectiveness of the searches in filtering out irrelevant and privileged records)

- who should conduct the manual review of records (*e.g.*, counsel, contract lawyers, client representatives, *etc.*)
- what fields are to be coded during manual review (*e.g.*, relevance, privilege, confidentiality, key documents, issues, *etc.*).

6. **Review the records**: Conduct the manual review for relevance, privilege, *etc.*

7. **Redact**: Redact privileged or, where appropriate, confidential irrelevant text using a black box or other conspicuous marking.[36]

8. **Address confidentiality issues**: Address the requirements of any protective order regarding the identification of confidential records.

COST REDUCTION TIPS FOR THIS STEP:

Ways to reduce legal fees:

1. Use software tools to locate relevant or privileged records, to the extent reasonable and permitted in the circumstances. Seek to reach agreement with the opposing parties on the use of these tools if possible.

2. Minimize to the extent possible the number of records requiring manual review.

3. Use contract lawyers or other lower-priced labour to conduct manual review of records.

In smaller cases:

1. In smaller cases that nonetheless involve large volumes of records, the use of search tools to identify relevant and non-privileged material is recommended in lieu of broad ranging manual review, since the latter could be prohibitively expensive.

2. There are inexpensive and easily accessible software programs available for managing and reviewing records in smaller cases.

VI. DISCLOSING AND PRODUCING

1. **Agree on format of disclosure**: Seek to agree with the opposing parties on the format of disclosure (*i.e.*, the format of Schedules A, B and C to the affidavit of documents). In this regard:

- consider dispensing with unnecessary coding of fields such as the document description field, author, *etc.* — bearing in mind that the Schedules themselves are unlikely to be used to identify or search for records
- agreement on coded fields will make it easier to integrate each party's produc-

---

[36] Redactions in white are not recommended, as it may not be apparent to the parties receiving the redacted records whether a redaction exists, or its scope.

tions into the opposing parties' litigation case management software.

2. **Agree on format of production**: Seek to agree with the opposing parties on the format of production. In this regard, consider:

   - whether to produce native files

   - whether to produce OCR versions of scanned paper productions

   - what fields of data to produce (*e.g.*, all metadata, only selected metadata, *etc.*).[37]

3. **Address privilege and confidentiality issues**: Address privilege issues, as well as issues of privacy, trade secrets and other confidential information. Considerations here include:

   - entering into a "clawback" agreement with opposing parties, under which the parties agree to permit one another to retrieve inadvertently produced privileged records

   - whether to seek an order from the court endorsing or authorizing the claw back arrangement

   - redacting partially privileged or confidential records

   - determining how to produce native files that are partially privileged.[38]

4. **Advise client regarding continuing preservation**: Advise the client of the need to preserve, disclose and produce relevant documents on an ongoing basis. This relates to relevant documents created or obtained after initial documentary disclosure.

5. **Advise client regarding deemed undertaking**: Advise the client about its obligation of confidentiality pertaining to opposing parties' productions.

COST REDUCTION TIPS FOR THIS STEP:

Ways to reduce legal fees:

1. Clawback agreements can be effective in allowing a party to conduct their privilege review electronically (with or without manual audits of the results) rather than requiring the party to conduct a manual review of all relevant records for privilege.

2. Reaching agreement at an early stage on the format of disclosure and production can save considerable time spent by law clerks after the fact in seeking to reconcile incompatible production sets.

---

[37] Principle #8 of the *Sedona Canada Principles* states that "[p]arties should agree as early as possible in the litigation process on the format in which electronically stored information will be produced. Parties should also agree on the format, content and organization of information to be exchanged in any required list of documents as part of the discovery process".

[38] Principle #9 of the *Sedona Canada Principles* states that "[d]uring the discovery process parties should agree to or, if necessary, seek judicial direction on measures to protect privileges, privacy, trade secrets and other confidential information relating to the production of electronic documents and data".

In smaller cases:

1. Production of records in electronic form can be accomplished effectively and cheaply in smaller cases, even if counsel or the client does not have access to sophisticated litigation case management software.

VII. EXAMINATIONS FOR DISCOVERY

1. **Consider written e-discovery questions**: Consider whether it is appropriate to ask some questions relating to e-discovery in written form in advance of oral discovery so as to make the oral discovery more efficient. If so, contact opposing counsel to obtain agreement to use a combined written/oral process. Consider too whether it would be useful to provide opposing counsel in advance of the discovery with an outline of some technical areas to be covered in order to enable the examinee to become appropriately informed.

2. **Review available information**: Review what has previously been agreed upon between the parties with respect to preservation and production. Become familiar with any information provided on a with prejudice basis about the other parties' IT and records management systems through the process to date.[39]

3. **Use precedents**: Maintain and use precedent lists of e-discovery questions.[40]

4. **Prepare questions**: Whether the examination for discovery will proceed in writing, orally, or both, allow sufficient time to prepare detailed questions to be asked in respect of electronic records, if appropriate. In this regard:

   - prepare questions designed to confirm whether or not the agreed-upon steps at the meet and confer have been taken. Be prepared to question further if there appear to be gaps or inconsistencies with respect to the steps taken and/or there appear to be any issues of spoliation

   - consider questions with respect to any steps that were not agreed upon in the meet and confer stage and not submitted to the court for determination.

5. **Work with a consultant if appropriate**: If a third-party service provider has been retained, work with the provider to identify appropriate questions. If not, depending on the nature of the case, consider consulting a third-party service provider for the purpose of preparation for the examination.

6. **Address admissibility issues**: Review common law and statutory requirements with respect to admissibility of electronic evidence. See in particular s. 34.1 of the *Evidence*

---

[39] If the parties have engaged in a meet and confer process that resulted in an agreement on some or all issues, it is still important to ensure that what has been agreed upon forms part of the examination for discovery record. This could in some circumstances be done by making the agreement an exhibit. It is also important to ask questions to confirm what has been done and probe for any gaps or inconsistencies. The agreement can also be used as a template for questions.

[40] Useful lists of sample questions can be found in *The Electronic Evidence and Discovery Handbook* (Chicago: American Bar Association, Law Practice Management Section, 2006), especially in Chapter Five. Although designed for U.S. depositions, the lists can be readily adapted for examinations for discovery.

Act, R.S.O. 1990, c. E.23 and ss. 31.1-31.8 of the *Canada Evidence Act*, R.S.C. 1985, c. C-5 to determine what steps must be taken to ensure that the electronic evidence is admissible. Consider any challenges to the admissibility of the opposing party's electronic evidence.

7. **Maintain a reasonably narrow scope**: Consider the scope of the questions: while it may seem useful to obtain everything possible, the information received through very broad undertakings to produce could be overwhelming in relation to the issues.

COST REDUCTION TIPS FOR THIS STEP:

Ways to reduce legal fees:

1. Maintain and use precedent lists of e-discovery questions.

2. Be reasonable in assessing the need for oral discovery on e-discovery issues. Much can be addressed through agreement between counsel in most cases.

In smaller cases:

1. Do not spend time engaging in oral discovery on e-discovery issues unless it is of central importance to the case. It is a needless distraction in many instances.

2. The need for agreement on e-discovery matters is all the more acute in smaller cases, where any discovery dispute can be disproportionately costly.

VIII. ELECTRONIC TRIAL

1. **Confer with opposing counsel**: Prior to trial, confer with opposing counsel to determine if agreement can be reached with respect to admissibility, the manner of presentation of electronic evidence and, if appropriate, confidentiality.

2. **Follow e-trial checklist**: See Model Document #11: E-trial Checklist prepared by Ontario E-Discovery Implementation Committee, and the companion document "What is an Electronic Trial?".

ONTARIO E-DISCOVERY IMPLEMENTATION COMMITTEE
MODEL DOCUMENT #9
CHECKLIST FOR PREPARING A DISCOVERY PLAN[*]

PURPOSE OF THE DOCUMENT

Rule 29.1 of the Ontario *Rules of Civil Procedure* requires parties to an action to agree upon a discovery plan before proceeding with discovery.

This checklist provides a list of steps that may usefully be taken by parties and their counsel in the negotiation of an appropriate discovery plan for their case. The checklist is detailed, but not all steps will be required in all cases.

DISCOVERY PLAN TEMPLATES

The E-Discovery Implementation Committee (EIC) has also prepared two model precedents for a discovery plan – a long form template (Model Document #9A) and a short form template (Model Document #9B). Both templates are designed to incorporate all of the elements of a discovery plan mandated by Rule 29.1. Parties are invited to use and adapt these templates as appropriate for their case. Counsel may consider it appropriate to use the short form discovery plan in cases under Rule 76 or in other matters involving relatively straightforward or narrow legal and documentary production issues.

For a more comprehensive model agreement dealing with discovery issues, see Model Document #1: Discovery Agreement. For an example of a letter agreement confirming the elements of a discovery plan, see Sample Document #1: Letter Confirming Discovery Agreement. The EIC has also prepared an Annotated E-Discovery Checklist (Model Document #8), which is a comprehensive checklist designed to address all of the steps to be taken with respect to the preservation, production and use of relevant documents in a litigation matter, with annotations throughout on how to minimize e-discovery costs.

OVERVIEW OF REQUIREMENTS OF RULE 29.1

Rule 29.1.03(3) requires that the written discovery plan address:

a.   the intended scope of documentary discovery under rule 30.02, taking into account relevance, cost and the importance and complexity of the issues in the action;

b.   the dates for service of the parties' affidavits of documents;

c.   the timing, cost and manner of production of documents by the parties and any other persons;

d.   the names of discovery witnesses and information regarding the timing and length of the discoveries; and

e.   any other information intended to result in the expeditious and cost-effective completion of the discovery process in a manner that is proportionate to the importance and complexity of the action.

In considering whether proposed steps in the discovery process are proportionate, parties must

CHECKLIST

take into account the importance and complexity of the case, the amounts and interests at stake, and the costs, delay, burden and benefit associated with each step, among other things.

Rule 29.1.03(4) expressly directs parties to consult and have regard to *The Sedona Canada Principles Addressing Electronic Discovery* (the "*Sedona Canada Principles*"). The *Sedona Canada Principles* are a set of national guidelines for e-discovery in Canada, which reflect both existing legal principles and a set of identified best practices.[1]

Rule 29.1 requires that the discovery plan be prepared in the early stages of the litigation, before discovery begins. Rule 29.1.04 also requires parties to update their discovery plan during the conduct of the action. Under Rule 29.1.05, the court may refuse to grant discovery relief or to award costs if the parties have not agreed upon or updated a discovery plan.

NOTE REGARDING USE OF THIS DOCUMENT

The discovery plan templates and all of the EIC's model documents and other publications are available on the Ontario Bar Association's website at: http://www.oba.org/En/publicaffairs_en/E-Discovery/model_precedents.aspx

This model document has been prepared and made available to the public by the EIC for informational purposes. It is not provided as legal or technical advice and should not be relied upon as such.

Publications of the EIC are copyrighted by the Ontario E-Discovery Implementation Committee and all rights are reserved. Individuals may download these publications for their own use at no charge. Law firms and other organizations may download these publications and make them available internally for individual use within the firm or organization. EIC publications may be republished, copied or reprinted at no charge for non-profit purposes. Organizations and individuals may provide a link to the publications on the internet without charge provided that proper attribution to the Ontario E-Discovery Implementation Committee is included. For further information, or to request permission to republish, copy or reprint for commercial profit, contact the Chair of the Committee, David Outerbridge, at douterbridge@torys.com.

FEEDBACK ON EIC MATERIALS

The EIC welcomes comments on all of its model documents and other publications. Any comments or suggestions can be provided to Michele A. Wright at mwright4@toronto.ca.

PHASE I.   ISSUE IDENTIFICATION AND SCOPE OF DISCOVERY

1.   **Identify the issues in the litigation.**

- The parties should begin by identifying each cause of action and each defence raised in the action and the heads of damages. (The objective of the discovery plan is to assist parties in identifying and focusing on the important issues in the litigation in order to promote fair, expeditious, and efficient results.)
- It will be helpful for the parties to prepare, exchange and attempt to agree on out-

---

[1] A copy of the *Sedona Canada Principles* may be downloaded from www.thesedonaconference.org, where they are found under the list of publications for Working Group 7. http://www.thesedonaconference. org/content/miscFiles/publications_html?grp=wgs170 with the actual PDF at: http://www. thesedonaconference.org/dltForm?did=canada_pincpls_FINAL_108.pdf.

lines of the causes of action, defences and heads of damages in advance of the discovery plan negotiations.

2. **Identify the applicable legal tests.**

- For each cause of action, each defence and each head of damages, identify the specific legal test to be met or responded to (in order to articulate reasons why particular evidence may be relevant).

- Again, this is best accomplished by agreement in advance of the discovery plan negotiations.

3. **Consider, for each legal issue, the type of evidence required by each party.**

- For each cause of action, each defence and each head of damages, identify the type of evidence required to prove or defend that element of the case (*e.g.*, testimony, documents, other evidence), as part of the analysis as to the nature and scope of potentially relevant records.

PHASE II.   IDENTIFICATION OF RELEVANT RECORDS

4. **Identify, for each issue, the location of relevant records held by each party.**

- The purpose is to identify the location of all potentially relevant documents[2] in both paper and electronic formats.

- In respect of each cause of action, defence and head of damages, consider and identify:

  a. the individuals who had a role in the relevant events on behalf of the party, whether as a decision-maker, implementer, observer, or otherwise;

  b. other individuals who had a role in the events, as a decision-maker, implementer, observer, or otherwise, including agents of the party, consultants, or unrelated third parties and others; and

  c. other potential sources of records (including banks, accountants, lawyers, insurers, third party service providers, affiliated companies or internet service providers, for example).

- In identifying sources of documentary evidence, consideration must be given to how a party creates, stores, and maintains electronic records generally.[3]

---

[2] The word "document" is used in this Model Document in its broadest sense, as meaning "information recorded in any form, including electronically stored information". The word "document" is used interchangeably with the word "record".

[3] Comment 3.c. of the *Sedona Canada Principles* recommends that counsel be prepared in a substantive way to discuss their client's documentary discovery and production obligations with opposing counsel by gaining "a thorough understanding of how electronically stored information is created, used and maintained by or for the client." To this end, it is useful for counsel to ask the client and its IT representative to complete an IT questionnaire, or to provide information orally in advance of the discovery plan negotiations, regarding:

  a. system architecture (network structure, geographic location of hardware, *etc.*);

  b. types of hardware and software used by the client;

5. **Identify the types of potentially relevant records held by each party.**

- Consider with respect to each party and individual/organization identified above as an anticipated source of evidence:

    a. what types of documents it is anticipated that those individuals/organizations created or obtained that may be "relevant to an issue in the action";[4]

    b. during what time period is it anticipated that such records would have been created, obtained, archived, backed up and/or destroyed; and

    c. where these records may be located, if they still exist.[5]

- Prioritize who the most important records custodians are likely to be, the key time frames, and the most important and easily accessible locations where records are likely held.

- Where there are multiple copies of certain types of information, identify the sources that are the most readily available and easiest to preserve and retrieve.

---

c. what forms of potentially relevant electronically-stored information exist, such as emails, word processing documents, databases, Excel documents, voice mail records, web-based files or metadata;

d. methods of data storage, such as on servers, desktop computers, laptops, home computers, PDAs such as BlackBerrys or Palm Pilots, floppy disks, CDs, DVDs, zip drives, backup media, external hard drives and USB ("thumb") drives;

e. data storage by third parties such as banks, accountants, lawyers, insurers, third party service providers, affiliated companies or Internet service providers;

f. the client's backup protocol, including types of backups performed and their schedule;

g. the physical location of backup media;

h. procedures for retrieving data from backup media;

i. the client's archiving protocol, if applicable, and procedures for retrieving data from archives;

j. costs and resources required to retrieve information from backup and other storage media; and

k. any retention policies and/or schedules for the systematic destruction of paper and electronic records.

For sample IT questionnaires, see *The Electronic Evidence and Discovery Handbook* (ABA Law Practice Management, 2006) at pp. 3 and following.

[4] Rule 30.02 and 30.03 are amended effective January 1, 2010 to require that every document "relevant to any matter in issue" be produced. The broader language of "relating to any matter in issue" is repealed effective January 1, 2010.

[5] Review the party's record retention policy, if one exists. Consider providing written litigation hold notices to all employees, contract workers and third parties who may be custodians of potentially relevant documents to inform them of the need to preserve these documents in their original format without modification. Consider involving the client's IT department in the litigation hold process. A description of the litigation hold obligation, and a sample litigation hold notice, are found in the EIC's model memorandum to a corporate client regarding documentary discovery (Model Document #3).

PHASE III. PRESERVATION AND RETRIEVAL OF POTENTIALLY RELEVANT RE-CORDS

6. **Agree what is to be preserved by each party[6] and how urgently the preservation measures must be taken.[7]**

   - For each party, consider and determine:

      a. whether an e-discovery consultant or computer forensics specialist is needed in order to preserve and collect relevant records;

      b. whether to preserve more broadly (such as by making forensic/bitmap copies of hard drives and servers, with culling for relevance to occur later) or more narrowly based on specific relevance parameters;[8]

      c. whether forensic/bitmap copies of hard drives, servers or portable devices are needed for other reasons, such as in order to preserve the machine or device or for other evidentiary reasons;[9]

      d. what methods are to be used to search for the client's records, including

---

[6] Principle #3 of the *Sedona Canada Principles* states that "As soon as litigation is reasonably antici-pated, parties must consider their obligation to take reasonable and good faith steps to preserve potentially relevant electronically stored information". The *Sedona Canada Principles* also recognize, however, that "it is unreasonable to expect organizations to take every conceivable step to preserve all electronically stored information that may be potentially relevant" and a "reasonable inquiry based on good faith to iden-tify and preserve active and archival data should be sufficient".

[7] Determine immediately whether there are urgent preservation issues because relevant records may be destroyed, altered or removed in the short term, whether by your party/client, other parties, or non-parties. For example, consider: whether the litigation is concerned with very recent or ongoing events, such that there is a risk of destruction of relevant records in "real time"; the frequency with backup media may be recycled; whether there is any email deletion policy; the possibility of alteration to electronic records that are in continuing use, such as databases or portable devices including smart phones; destruction of po-tentially relevant records in the ordinary course pursuant to a records retention policy; and the possibility of a relevant hard drive, portable device, *etc.* being scrubbed or otherwise rendered inaccessible (*e.g.*, the personal computer of a departing employee). Refer to the EIC's Annotated E-Discovery Checklist (Model Document #8).

In addition, consideration should be given to sending a preservation letter to the opposing parties or their counsel as soon as litigation is commenced, and sometimes before. Consider that several preservation let-ters may be useful as the action proceeds and parties are able to better define the scope of preservation in terms of date range, record types, custodians, search terms, *etc.* See the EIC's model preservation letters (Model Documents #5 and #6) and the model preservation order (Model Document #7).

[8] Preserving broadly and then using culling software to identify relevant records will in some cases be quicker and more efficient than seeking to identify relevant records on an individualized basis. Consider what volume of information will have to be stored outside of the day-to-day business environment and the costs for any additional hardware or software or services that may be required.

[9] Comment 4.c of the *Sedona Canada Principles* suggests that "[w]hile the making of bit-level images of hard drives is useful in selective cases for the preservation phase, the further processing of the total con-tents of the drive should not be required unless the nature of the matter warrants the cost and burden. Mak-ing forensic image backups of computers is only the first step in a potentially expensive, complex, and dif-ficult process of data analysis. It can divert litigation into side issues involving the interpretation of ambiguous forensic evidence." Note that it is difficult in practice to make a forensic copy of a server, as servers are typically not able to be brought out of service for copying. However, in a smaller organization,

the possible use of indexing software and other search tools;

e. whether and to what extent to preserve metadata;[10]

f. whether to preserve archival and backup media and, if so, whether to seek to retrieve specific records from the archival and backup media;[11]

g. whether and how to seek to preserve deleted or residual data or records that use obsolete hardware or software;[12]

h. the cost associated with all contemplated preservation steps and resources required;

i. the cost associated with retrieval of all preserved records;

j. what constitutes a proportionate preservation response,[13] taking into account the amounts at issue, the importance of the case, the importance of various types of files, the total volume of material to be preserved, and retrieved and other factors;[14]

k. the risks associated with not undertaking the contemplated preservation steps; and

l. what steps will not be undertaken due to the cost, burden or delay associated with doing so.

---

the simplest and most effective way to preserve electronic evidence may be simply to make a forensic copy of the drives.

[10] Metadata is information about a particular data set or document which describes how, when and by whom it was collected, created, accessed, modified and how it is formatted. Metadata can be altered intentionally or inadvertently. It can be extracted when native files are converted to image. Some metadata, such as file dates and sizes, can easily be seen by users; other metadata can be hidden or embedded and unavailable to computer users who are not technically adept. Metadata is generally not reproduced in full form when a document is printed. Counsel are encouraged to refer to the EIC's Annotated E-Discovery Checklist (Model Document #8) for additional information regarding metadata.

[11] Relying upon backup media in order to locate relevant records is generally costly and inefficient. Backup media should be preserved only where they contain unique information that cannot otherwise be obtained, or where other special circumstances apply.

[12] Principle #6 of the *Sedona Canada Principles* states that "A party should not be required, absent agreement or a court order based on demonstrated need and relevance, to search for or collect deleted or residual electronically stored information." Comment 6.a suggests that deleted or residual data that can only be accessed through forensic means should not be presumed to be discoverable and ordinarily, searches for electronically sorted information" will be restricted to a search of active data and reasonably accessible online sources. The "evaluation of the need for and relevance of such discovery should be analyzed on a case by case basis" as "only exceptional cases will turn on "deleted" or "discarded" information".

[13] Rule 1.04(1.1) states that, in applying the rules, the court shall make orders and give directions that are proportionate to the importance and complexity of the issues, and to the amount involved, in the proceeding.

[14] In considering the proportionality principle, note that extreme preservation efforts should not be requested except in unusual circumstances: Comment 3f, *Sedona Canada Principles*. Consider also the party's own ability and willingness to undertake the same preservation steps, since any preservation demand made of opposing parties may be reciprocated. Also, make sure to maintain careful records of the preservation and retrieval plan as it is implemented. Counsel should consider whether to send written confirmation to the client, documenting the preservation plan.

- Consider what documentation shall be maintained to demonstrate compliance with the preservation measures agreed upon.
- Record the basis for decisions. Such a record may be important if parties are required to later defend a decision as having been reasonable, particularly where parties have (unilaterally or jointly) decided not to take a particular step or not to preserve or retrieve particular types or categories of records.
- Consider whether amendments to the pleadings are likely to be made and consider whether or how to preserve other records that may become relevant and the cost/benefit of taking such steps at the outset or in the future.
- Reference to the EIC's Model Document #8 (Annotated E-Discovery Checklist) is encouraged for further information regarding considerations relating to the preservation, review and production of electronic records in particular.

PHASE IV. SEARCHING AND FILTERING RECORDS

7. **Agree upon the parameters to be used in isolating records to be produced from within the records that have been preserved.**

- Within the subset of materials to be preserved, consider and discuss how to identify the relevant records for production and, if appropriate, use electronic tools and processes to assist in doing so.[15]
- Consider a phased approach to identifying relevant documents, based on the key custodians, record types or locations or other factors identified above.[16]
- Relevant electronic records may be identified using:

   a.   Keyword search terms (such as employee names, key words in the litigation, names of persons on the other side, *etc.*) using Boolean, whole language and fuzzy electronic searching tools;[17]

   b.   date range; and

---

[15] Principle #7 of the *Sedona Canada Principles* states that parties may satisfy their obligations "by using electronic tools and processes such as data sampling, searching and/or the use of selection criteria to collect potentially relevant electronically stored information". Comment 7.a indicates that, as it may be impractical or prohibitively expensive to review all information manually, parties and counsel should where possible agree in advance on targeted selection criteria. Comment 7.b suggests various processing techniques to use in searches including filtering, de-duplication, sampling and validation.

[16] Consider which custodians, time frame and/or locations are likely to produce the most significant information. Also evaluate whether there are alternate sources for information that may no longer be available or may be burdensome (whether due to cost or time) to retrieve, process, review, and/or produce. In a phased approach, the parties may agree, for example, that the records of specific custodians or found in specific locations are to be searched for relevance as part of a first phase, and then, after a review of those results, parties may consider whether or what additional steps are required in a second phase to search for and/or produce additional records.

[17] Obviously, narrow search terms will yield a more manageable volume of records, but parties face the risk of inadvertent omission of relevant records. The selection of appropriate search terms requires legal judgment, and the search results should be tested to evaluate whether relevant records are being caught. Consider collaborating with counsel for the other parties regarding appropriate search terms and developing search terms with advice from key individuals involved or from a review of the key documents iden-

c. file type.[18]

- Consider also using electronic analytic tools for clustering records, for concept mapping, for deduplicating records and for identifying e-mail strings.

- Relevant records may also be sought in some or all specific physical locations, whether in hard copy record storage or on servers, desktop computers, laptops, home computers, PDAs such as BlackBerrys or Palm Pilots, floppy disks, CDs, DVDs, zip drives, backup media, external hard drives and USB ("thumb") drives.

- Conduct a cost/benefit analysis. For all contemplated steps, evaluate what constitutes a proportionate response, taking into account: the amounts at issue; the importance of the case; the importance of various types of files;[19] the total volume of records that may be generated;[20] the cost and resources required in undertaking particular steps; and other factors.[21]

- Record the basis for the decisions made, particularly decisions made not to take a particular step. Consider whether there are any variables the full scope or impact of which cannot be assessed that may impact timing or cost.[22]

---

tified (to identify commonly used terms or names, for example). Keep careful records of the search terms and tools used and techniques employed.

The search tools used can also affect the reliability of the searches conducted. Determine whether your search tools permit only keyword searching, or also permits Boolean, whole language and fuzzy searching. Some tools permit concept mapping or clustering of related records using algorithms which analyze the records and look for patterns in the words used within the record.

[18] In most cases, the vast majority of electronic records will consist of e-mail, word processing documents and data within databases.

[19] Electronic searches for relevant records may omit nested emails, attachments, or compressed, encrypted or corrupted files, depending upon the process and software used. Address whether this is a concern.

[20] Pursuant to Rule 29.2.03, the court will consider the overall volume of documents that may be produced in response to a request before granting an order for production.

[21] Principle #5 of the *Sedona Canada Principles* states that "The parties should be prepared to produce relevant electronically stored information that is reasonably accessible in terms of cost and burden." Comment 5.a suggests that, given the volume and technical challenges associated with the discovery of electronically-stored information, the parties engage in a cost benefit analysis, weighing the "cost of identifying and retrieving the information from each potential source against the likelihood that the source will yield unique, necessary and relevant information". Counsel are encouraged to exercise judgment based on a reasonable good faith inquiry having regard to the location and cost of recovery or preservation. The more costly and burdensome the effort that will be required to access a particular source "the more certain the parties need to be that the source will yield responsive information". Comment 5.a suggests that, if potentially relevant documents exist in a format that is not "readily usable", cost-shifting may be appropriate. Refer to the EIC's Annotated E-Discovery Checklist (Model Document #8), which provides more detailed suggestions regarding steps to be considering in preserving, collecting, and processing and reviewing records.

[22] Parties should advise each other forthwith if, at any stage of the process, information becomes known that will impact on their ability to comply with their discovery plan obligations — for example, if records are discovered to be corrupt or inaccessible for a reason unknown at the time that the discovery plan was agreed upon.

PHASE V. REVIEW OF RECORDS

8. **Agree upon a protocol for reviewing and refining the records identified in any initial search as potentially relevant.**

   - Consider again whether a phased approach to reviewing records may be appropriate, based on the same cost/benefit considerations as outlined in Step #7 above.

   - Identify what measures can be taken to eliminate duplicate records.[23]

   - Identify what measures are to be taken with respect to private, personal or commercially sensitive information identified in the course of the search and review.[24]

   - Consider how processing and review of the records will be managed to ensure completeness, to track information as it is collected, and to avoid delays. Identify whether the use of specific software or specialist services are appropriate.

   - Record the basis for the decisions made, particularly decisions made not to pursue a particular step.

PHASE VI. EXCHANGING RECORDS

9. **Establish a protocol for the exchange of relevant records.**

   - Consider and, if possible, agree upon:

     a. the format for exchange of electronic and paper records (whether in paper, native file formats or .tif format, for example).[25] The production of electronic records in electronic form is to be preferred;[26]

---

[23] Consider, for example, whether there are types of emails, office documents or file types that can be automatically removed from collection (such as social notices, marketing, emails from lists, and news sources). Consider the use of technology to remove duplicate copies of records, facilitate identification and tracking of email chains, etc. Refer to the EIC's Annotated E-Discovery Checklist (Model Document #8) for additional suggestions and information.

[24] For example, counsel may consider employing a combination of electronic search techniques and manual review to identify private, personal or commercial sensitive information.

[25] Principle #8 of the *Sedona Canada Principles* states that "[p]arties should agree as early as possible in the litigation process on the format in which electronically stored information will be produced. Parties should also agree on the format, content and organization of information to be exchanged in any required list of documents as part of the discovery process." See the EIC's Annotated E-Discovery Checklist (Model Document #8) and the model Discovery Agreement (Model Document #1) for an annotated and expanded list of topics to consider. Also, it may be necessary to deal with certain issues in successive meetings during the proceedings; Principle 4 of the *Sedona Canada Principles* recommends that counsel and parties meet and confer on an ongoing basis.

[26] Comment 8.a of the *Sedona Canada Principles* states that "production of electronic documents and data should be made only in electronic format, unless the recipient is somehow disadvantaged and cannot effectively make use of a computer, or the volume of the documents to be produced is minimal and metadata is known (and agreed by all parties) to be irrelevant". Comment 8.a suggests that the practice of producing electronically stored information in paper form should be discouraged in most circumstances. Comment 8.b and 8.c suggest that parties attempt to agree on "methodology of production that (a) preserves metadata and allows it to be produced when relevant; (b) communicates accurately the content; (c) protects

    b.   whether specific software or hardware must be made available in order to allow electronically stored information to be inspected;

    c.   whether to use a common third-party litigation support service provider to scan and/or code or process producible records;

    d.   whether to use a common protocol for coding records to be produced (which is important to facilitate the exchange of records between parties) and for preparing affidavits of documents;

    e.   measures to be taken to redact documents;[27]

    f.   other measures to be taken to protect privilege, privacy, trade secrets or other confidential information (including measures to address inadvertent production of privileged documents);[28]

    g.   whether a cost sharing/allocation agreement is desirable; and

    h.   a time frame for complying with obligations agreed upon.

- Consider again whether a phased approach to producing records may be appropriate, based on the same cost/benefit considerations as outlined in Step #7 above.

10.   **Consider whether agreement can be reached or procedures are required to ensure the authenticity and integrity of records.**

- Identify specific procedures to be implemented to ensure the authenticity and integrity of producible electronically stored information.[29]

PHASE VII. EXAMINATIONS FOR DISCOVERY

11.   **Agree whether to exchange "contextual facts" in advance of oral discovery.**

- Contextual facts are the facts required in order to place other facts in their ap-

---

the integrity of the information; (d) allows for the creation of a version that can be redacted; (e) assigns a unique production identification number to each data item, and (f) can be readily imported into any industry-standard litigation review application". Recommended default standards for the format of exchange of electronic records are set out in the model Discovery Agreement prepared by the EIC (Model Document #1), at sections 6 and 10.

[27] Do not redact documents using white, as it may not be clear whether redaction has occurred or the extent of the redaction. Use black.

Also, if redacting electronically, ensure that the method of redacting images of electronic records also removes the associated text. Otherwise, the text will remain searchable even if the text is not visible within the image.

[28] Principle #9 of the *Sedona Canada Principles* states that "[d]uring the discovery process parties should agree to or, if necessary, seek judicial direction on measures to protect privileges, privacy, trade secrets and other confidential information relating to the production of electronic documents and data". Consider, for example, entering into a "clawback" agreement with opposing parties, under which the parties agree to permit one another to retrieve inadvertently produced privileged records. To mitigate the risk of inadvertent disclosure of privileged documents, conduct searches for the names of counsel, for example, during the search and review phase to identify potentially privileged documents. Consider how metadata and embedded data will be reviewed when native production is required.

[29] Section 12 of the EIC's model Discovery Agreement (Model Document #1) contains suggested provisions regarding authenticity and reliability.

propriate context. Examples of contextual facts that parties might wish to exchange in advance of oral discovery, in order to streamline the discovery process and reduce cost and delay, include: casts of characters, organizational charts, corporate structure charts, chronologies of events, IT infrastructure maps, information regarding the source of documentary productions, and the parties' records retention policies, among others.

12. **Identify who is to be produced for discovery as the representatives of each party.**

- Consider whether it would facilitate the discovery process to produce more than one representative per party, with each representative to be examined on a limited range of topics within their personal knowledge (with one representative to answer any other proper questions).

13. **Establish dates when oral examinations for discovery are to be conducted, and confirm the number of hours of discovery to be conducted by each examining party.**

- Rule 31.05.1 limits the duration of oral examinations conducted by any one party to seven hours, regardless of the number of parties or persons to be examined, unless the parties consent or leave of the court is obtained.

- If an increase in the number of hours for the conduct of examinations for discovery is to be negotiated, identify the considerations militating in favour of such an increase of time, and how much additional time is to be allocated.

- For simplified procedure actions, oral discovery is limited to two hours. A longer period of oral discovery is not permitted: Rule 76.04(2).

PHASE VIII.   OTHER FORMS OF DISCOVERY

14. **Agree whether part or all of the discovery is to be conducted through written questions and answers.**

- Consider and, if appropriate, agree whether some questions may be asked in written form in advance of oral discovery so as to make the oral discovery more efficient.

- Review Rule 35 regarding the procedure for written discoveries.

- Note that a party does not have the right to conduct both written and oral discovery except with leave of the court: Rule 31.02. However, the parties may consent to conduct both written and oral discovery.

- Written discovery is prohibited in simplified procedure actions: Rule 76.04(1).

15. **Consider whether the inspection of property is required.**

- Under Rule 32, the court may make an order for the inspection of real or personal property where it appears to be necessary for the proper determination of an issue in a proceeding. In cases where an inspection of property is appropriate, the parties should seek to agree in the discovery plan on the terms under which the inspection will occur.

16. **Consider whether a physical or mental examination of a party is required.**

- Under Rule 33, a party may bring a motion for an order for the physical or mental examination of a party whose physical or mental condition is in question. In cases where a physical or mental examination is appropriate, the parties should seek to agree in the discovery plan on the terms under which the examination will occur.

PHASE IX. OTHER ISSUES

17. **Address the possibility of changes to the discovery plan.**

- Parties should agree that, as additional information becomes available throughout the action, it may become apparent that: (a) it is impracticable or impossible for a party to complete all of the steps contemplated by the discovery plan or to do so in a cost and time-efficient manner, or (b) further steps, beyond those set out in the discovery plan, are required in order for a party to obtain access to relevant documents in the action.

- Parties should agree to notify each other promptly of such changes in circumstances and agree to negotiate in good faith with respect to any potential changes or, in appropriate cases, seek the assistance of the court.

- Note that Rule 29.1.04 requires that the parties ensure that the discovery plan is updated to reflect any changes in the information listed in subrule 29.1.03(3).

18. **Consider whether it is appropriate to share the reasonable costs required to comply with this discovery plan.**

- In general, parties may claim the reasonable costs incurred in complying with the discovery plan as "costs of and incidental to a proceeding or a step in a proceeding" for purposes of s. 131 of the *Courts of Justice Act*. Parties should consider whether it is appropriate to agree upon a different allocation or sharing of costs.

PRACTICE DIRECTIONS AND POLICIES*

PRACTICE DIRECTIONS AND POLICIES

PRACTICE DIRECTIONS AND POLICIES

In 2013-2014, the Superior Court of Justice undertook to review and consolidate all of its Regional and Provincial Practice Directions. The objective of the review was an administrative reset to identify and eliminate obsolete and redundant Practice Directions. The review also sought to consolidate, simplify and better organize the Practice Directions that were to remain in effect. The Court has now re-issued Consolidated Provincial and Regional Practice Directions for all proceedings in the Superior Court of Justice.

These Practice Directions took effect July 1, 2014 and all other previously issued Superior Court of Justice Practice Directions are revoked. The Practice Directions and Policies reproduced in this section are current to April 7, 2020. Counsel are advised to check the Superior Court's website for the most recent Practice Directions: http://www.ontariocourts.ca/scj/practice/practice-directions/

PRACTICE DIRECTIONS AND POLICIES

Practice Directions and Policies are reproduced with the permission of the Ontario Superior Court of Justice.

A. Consolidated Provincial Practice Direction (Latest Amendment: January 15, 2020)

Notice of Amendments:

Effective January 15, 2020, Part V: Rule 76 Simplified Procedure is added to the *Consolidated Provincial Practice Direction* to notify parties in Rule 76 cases that they must file the new Trial Management Plan form in accordance with subrules 76.10(2) and (4), as amended. Self-represented parties are encouraged to review the Instructions for Self-Represented Parties Preparing for Rule 76 Simplified Trials.

Effective May 17, 2019, Part II is amended to reflect the Court's adoption of the Canadian Bar Association's revised Canadian Judicial Protocol for the Management of Multi-Jurisdictional Class Actions and the Provision of Class Action Notice.

The Southwest Region civil long motions time in the chart in paragraph 46 is changed to 1 hour.

The confirmation deadlines in Part I C are updated.

Effective December 7, 2018, Part V G (Manner of Address for Masters) is added; Part III B is amended to provide that paragraphs 48 through 51 (motions to transfer a civil proceeding under rule 13.1.02 of the Rules of Civil Procedure) apply to motions to transfer a civil proceeding in any region.

Effective June 15, 2018, Part VI (Books of Authorities in Civil Proceedings) has been added; Part V C (Release of Digital Court Recordings) has been amended to clarify the process for obtaining a digital recording of a Small Claims Court proceeding and to provide that no digital recordings of civil and family motions are available to anyone unless a judge orders otherwise; and Paragraph 46 has been amended to update the information regarding long motion times in the Southwest Region.   See   http://www.ontariocourts.ca/scj/practice/practice-directions/provincial/.

Effective January 1, 2017, para 57 has been amended regarding the gowning policy of the court.

Effective July 1, 2016, Section F (Publication Bans) has been added to Part V.

Effective May 1, 2016, new provisions have been added in Part I C to clarify the court's expectations regarding the confirmation of events in a family case. Amendments were also made to permit a trial scheduling conference to be scheduled in order to ensure proper completion of the Trial Scheduling Endorsement Form, which has been consolidated into one document.

Effective April 1, 2016, Part 1B (Often Cited Family Law Cases) applies to all regions in Ontario.

Effective February 1, 2016, Para 49 of Part III B has also been amended to indicate that all motions to transfer a civil proceeding should be brought at the court location to which the moving party seeks to have the proceeding transferred.

Effective July 1, 2014

This Practice Direction governs proceedings in the Ontario Superior Court of Justice, province-wide *unless stated otherwise*, effective July 1, 2014.

This Practice Direction *supersedes* all previous province-wide Practice Directions issued prior to July 1, 2014, which are hereby revoked.

Counsel and parties are advised to refer to the relevant Parts of the Consolidated Practice Direction for Divisional Court Proceedings, as well as the applicable region-specific Practice Directions which are also available on the Superior Court of Justice website at: www.ontariocourts.ca/scj.

Table of Contents

Part I: Family Proceedings in the Superior Court of Justice

1. This Part applies to all Family Proceedings in the Superior Court of Justicein Ontario, *except where noted otherwise*. Counsel and parties are advised to refer to the relevant region-specific Practice Directions that supplement this Part.

A. Dispute Resolution Officer Program

Application

2.   Paragraphs 3 to 17 of this Practice Direction apply to *all* Dispute Resolution Officer (DRO) Programs in the Ontario Superior Court of Justice, including existing permanent programs, pilot projects, and any future programs.*

Role and Conduct of the DRO

3.   DRO lawyers hearing case conferences must be appointed by the Regional Senior Judge and the Senior Family Judge, pursuant to Rule 17(9) of the *Family Law Rules*.

4.   DROs shall:

   a)   hear *all* first case conferences for motions to change under Rule 15 of the *Family Law Rules*; and

   b)   complete a "Screening Report" after the conclusion of each DRO Case Conference, which will be included as part of the court file.

5.   DROs may:

   a)   hear first case conferences on matters other than motions to change *only* when referred to the DRO by a judge and when such matters are scheduled to DROs after all first case conferences on motions to change have received priority in scheduling;

   b)   attempt to identify, resolve or settle outstanding issues on a consent basis;

   c)   assist parties in organizing their issues and disclosure documents in order to make the case "judge-ready"; and/or

   d)   assist parties in obtaining a signed consent order from a judge, where the parties have consented in writing at the DRO Case Conference.

6.   DROs shall not:

   a)   write consents or draft orders on behalf of parties;

   b)   make orders, on consent or otherwise; or

   c)   award costs.

Role and Conduct of Parties Appearing before a DRO

7.   Rule 17 of the *Family Law Rules* applies to case conferences including those heard by a DRO pursuant to Rule 17(9).

8.   Parties attending a DRO Case Conference (DRC) must therefore comply with the document requirements under Rule 17 of the *Family Law Rules,* including advance filing of:

   a)   a case conference brief, which on a motion to change should at minimum include:

---

*   DROs are available in the Central East Region at the Newmarket, Durham and Barrie judicial centres, the Central West Region at the Milton and Brampton judicial centres, in the Central South Region at the Hamilton and St. Catharines judicial centres, in the South West Region at the London judicial centre and in Toronto at 393 University Avenue.

- a copy of the previous order that is the subject of the motion to change;
- documentation supporting the "change in circumstance";
- a description of the change being sought;

b) any relevant disclosure documents; and

c) a Form 14C Confirmation Form, filed not later than 2 pm, two business days prior to the date scheduled for the DRC.

Scheduling DRO Case Conferences (DRCs)

9. Wherever possible, motions to change will receive priority over other matters when DRCs are scheduled.

10. Wherever possible, litigants will receive the most immediate, next available date/time, accommodation may be made for reasonable conflicts.

11. Wherever possible, in advance of a DRC Hearing Date, the DRO will be advised of confirmed parties, in order to prevent any potential conflicts of interest.

DRO Screening Reports

12. At minimum, DRO Screening Reports shall include the following information, although additions may be made locally:

a) Name of DRO;

b) Whether parties were represented or unrepresented;

c) Whether the matter was scheduled before the DRO was a case conference on a motion to change or a case conference on an issue other than a motion to change;

d) Indication of whether the DRC was (1) "fully settled", (2) "partially settled", (3) resulted in no resolution, (4) resulted in disclosure only, upon conclusion;

e) Identification of any issues resolved and/or agreed upon for consideration by a judge,

f) Identification of any outstanding issues if only (1) "partially settled", (2) only disclosure arranged, or (3) no resolution;

g) Timelines for matters that must be completed (ie/disclosure by certain dates) by the parties, if issues were not resolved during the DRC; and

h) Indication of whether or not the conduct of any party has frustrated the objectives of the DRC.

13. A judge presiding at a subsequent court event for the parties may rely on the DRO's notations in the Screening Report, after hearing submissions on the issues, in determining if costs are appropriate.

Next Steps after the DRC

14. Wherever possible, on each DRC Hearing Date, at least one judge will be available to review any consent orders, minutes of settlement, or temporary orders arising out of the DRCs from the day's list. Where these settlements are reached at the end of a DRC, all efforts will be made to ensure parties and counsel will receive a judicial response on the same day as their DRC.

15. Upon completion of a DRC, parties shall be permitted to schedule as a next step:

    a) another case conference in front of a DRO if necessary;

    b) case conference in front of a judge;

    c) a settlement conference in front of a judge; or

    d) if necessary, a motion in front of a judge provided all of the necessary materials have already been filed.

Local Schedules & Procedures Regarding DRO Programs

16. Parties attending DRCs in their respective court locations should also consult their local courthouse for any specific local procedures.

17. Local DRO Schedules in each relevant court location will be provided in the *DRO Schedule Annex*, available on the Superior Court's website at: www.ontariocourts.ca/scj/practice/practice-directions/annex.

B. Often Cited Family Law Cases

18. Paragraphs 19 to 22 of this Practice Direction apply in all Regions.

19. A list of Often Cited Family Cases for Family Matters containing cases frequently relied on is available for each judge who presides over family cases. There will be additions to, and deletions from, the list from time to time. An up-to-date list is available on the Superior Court of Justice website at: www.ontariocourts.ca/scj/practice/practice-directions/list.

20. The cases in question appear on this list under various headings or topics which are not in any way intended to provide legal advice.

21. Parties in family law proceedings in the Superior Court of Justice need no longer include authorities on this list in any book of authorities relied on.

22. However, extracts from those authorities which counsel intend to refer to the court shall be included in the factum or book of authorities.

C. Confirmation Forms

22.1 Each party to a conference or motion must file a fully completed File 14C Confirmation no later than 2 p.m. three business days before the motion or conference, except as follows:

    a. Urgent motions that are being brought without notice to the other party do not need to be confirmed;

    b. Long motions must be confirmed earlier than three days in advance in several locations by regional practice direction.

22.2 Form 14C Confirmations must **only** list the specific issues that are to be addressed at that event and the specific materials that the judge should review.

22.3 Where Form 14C Confirmation forms have not been properly completed and filed by the appropriate deadline by at least one party, the event will not be heard on the scheduled day without the court's permission.

D. Form 14B Motions

23. Paragraphs 24 to 31 of this Practice Direction apply in all Regions *except* the Central East, East and Toronto Region. See the Practice Direction in your region for additional direction regarding 14B Motions.

24. The Superior Court's policy is to support timely case conferences in which parties are afforded sufficient judicial time to have a meaningful hearing. However, inadequate judicial resources present a scheduling challenge that makes consistent application of this policy across all judicial Regions difficult to achieve.

25. Consequently, in order to assist counsel and parties in making the best use of available conference time, the Superior Court will encourage greater use of Form 14B motions whenever it will make the case conference process more effective. Form 14B motions allow parties to address certain threshold issues prior to the case conference and are designed to streamline conferencing in Family Law proceedings. Such motions are limited to procedural, uncomplicated or unopposed matters that will promote the concept of fewer, but more meaningful, case conferences. In this respect, Form 14B motions procedures will be guided by paragraphs 26 to 31 (below).

26. Sub-rules 14(4.2) and (10) of the *Family Law Rules* provide that motions are permissible before a case conference, if there is a situation of urgency or hardship, or if the request for relief is limited to "procedural, uncomplicated or unopposed matters". Relief is requested using Form 14B.

27. Before a case conference is held, lawyers and self-represented litigants are strongly encouraged to use Form 14B to obtain any orders that are *needed to make the case conference a more meaningful and productive process.*

28. Examples of appropriate orders include:

    a) Orders of either a procedural or substantive nature that are on consent, or unopposed;

    b) A request for the appointment of the Office of the Children's Lawyer;

    c) Orders to add a party or obtain discovery from a third party;

    d) Orders for production of documents, permission for oral questioning or other issues pertaining to discovery;

    e) Enforcement of an order to provide information, produce a document or serve and file a financial statement or other document; and

    f) Any other procedural order or direction needed to promote a meaningful case conference including orders requiring that financial disclosure be provided by a party in accordance with rule 13.

29. Requests for an order shall be considered "uncomplicated" only if:

    a) Oral submissions can be made in five minutes or less for each side; and

    b) Affidavit material in support of the request for relief is three pages or less in length.

30. Requests that are without notice, on consent or unopposed will be determined by a judge in chambers. All other requests will be determined in motions court or by conference telephone call. The Form 14B should specify the court location, date and time

for the hearing unless a conference call had been arranged under Rule 14(8).

31. A copy of Form 14B is available at the courthouse and can also be downloaded from the government website at: www.ontariocourtforms.on.ca.

E. Settlement Conferences and Trial Scheduling Conferences

31.1 The settlement conference is an important step in family cases. The primary purpose of the settlement conference is to settle or at least narrow the issues in dispute.

31.2 Pursuant to rule 17(5) (g) of the Family Law Rules, if the case is not settled at the settlement conference, one of the additional purposes of the conference is to identify the witnesses and other evidence to be presented at trial, estimate the time needed for trial and, where appropriate, to schedule the case for trial.

31.3 If the case has not settled at the conclusion of the settlement conference, the court shall determine if the Trial Scheduling Endorsement Form can be completed at the conference or shortly thereafter and shall give directions to the parties regarding the completion of this form.

31.4 If necessary, the Court may require the parties to attend a trial scheduling conference to canvas issues regarding the scheduling of the trial and ensure proper completion of the trial scheduling endorsement form. Each party shall complete and file their portion of the Trial Scheduling Endorsement Form with the court in advance of a trial scheduling conference in accordance with the timelines in rule 17(13.1).

31.5 A trial scheduling conference's purposes include (i) ensuring that the case is ready to proceed to trial, (ii) considering each party's list of proposed witnesses and (iii) ensuring the accuracy of the estimated time for trial. Consideration should also be given to other conditions that would be appropriate under rule 1 in order to limit the duration and scope of the trial.

31.6 A trial date will not be made available until the court has reviewed and endorsed the complete Trial Scheduling Endorsement Form.

31.7 In exceptional circumstances, the court may provide litigants with a trial date before the court has endorsed the complete Trial Scheduling Endorsement form. Where this has occurred, the form must be finalized no later than 60 days in advance of the trial in order to retain the scheduled date.

F. Trial Management Conferences

31.8 A trial management conference should be held in all family cases that have not been resolved at or before the settlement conference in order to ensure trial readiness and canvas settlement. The trial management conference should be scheduled no more than two weeks in advance of the scheduled trial date, wherever possible.

31.9 The Trial Management Conference Brief: Form 17E is no longer required. Instead of the Trial Management Conference Brief, the following documents must be filed in advance of the trial management conference by the deadlines set out in rule 17(13.1):

    a. The completed Trial Scheduling Endorsement Form must be filed by either the Applicant or the party that requested the conference;

    b. Each party must file an offer to settle all outstanding issues; and,

    c.   Each party must file an outline of their opening statement for trial.

The Endorsement Volume of the continuing record should also be put before the judge at the trial management conference.

31.10   The completed Trial Scheduling Endorsement Form shall be filed with or added to the Trial Record. No offers to settle should be included in the Trial Record.

31.11   Attendance at an assignment court or other similar scheduling event shall not be necessary where a trial management conference has been held and the trial date has been confirmed.

31.12   Where the case has been settled and the trial is no longer required, one of the parties shall immediately advise the Trial Coordinator so that the trial date can be vacated. A copy of any Minutes of Settlement or consent should be filed at the same time.

Part II: Proceedings under the *Class Proceedings Act, 1992*

A. Adoption of the Canadian Bar Association's 2018 Protocol for Multi-jurisdictional Class Actions

32.   The Canadian Judicial Council endorsed the Canadian Bar Association's Resolution 18-03-A (Class Action Judicial Protocols (2018)), approving the Association's revised "Canadian Judicial Protocol for the Management of Multi-Jurisdictional Class Actions and the Provision of Class Action Notice", also known as the 2018 Protocol. The Ontario Superior Court of Justice adopted the 2018 Protocol and, as of June 1, 2019, parties to class proceedings shall comply with its terms.

33.   Plaintiff's counsel must post the pleadings in their class action on the Canadian Bar Association's National Class Action Database prior to the first attendance and confirm that they have done so at that attendance. To submit documents to the National Class Actions Database,

    1.

- Download and complete the Database Registration Form (Microsoft Word format)
- E-mail the completed Database Registration Form with accompanying scanned documents (e.g. original pleadings and certification motion) (PDF or Word format, character recognition preferred) to the CBA at classaction@cba.org.

    Questions about the National Class Actions Database can be emailed to: classaction@cba.org.

34.   At each attendance, the parties to a class action shall advise the court of any other action they are aware of and the status of each action.

35.   Plaintiff's counsel must compile a notification list setting out the names of all known counsel and judges in any action, together with their contact information. Prior to the date being set for the first case management conference, plaintiff's counsel must provide the court and all other counsel with the notification list.

36.   Additional required steps for class actions are set out in the 2018 Protocol.

B. Dedicated Class Proceedings Judges

37. To promote the goals of the *Class Proceeding Act, 1992*, including judicial economy and access to the courts, each Regional Senior Judge has assigned one or more judges to coordinate all class proceedings in that Region as the "Class Proceedings Judge". To increase efficiency and provide a degree of consistency, in keeping with the case management approach ascribed to the court by the Act, the Class Proceedings Judge will preside over the majority of pre-trial class proceedings motions and certifications in that Region.

38. Every class proceeding shall have appended to the court file number the letters CP, indicating that it is a class proceeding.

39. The names of assigned Class Proceedings Judges may be obtained from the Regional Managers in each Region:

Region	Telephone	Fax
Northwest	(807) 343-2727	(807) 343-2758
Northeast	(705) 564-7813	(705) 564-7902
East	(613) 239-1385	(613) 239-1007
Central East	(905) 853-4822	(905) 853-4826
Toronto	(416) 327-6104	(416) 325-2872
Central West	(905) 456-4838	(905) 456-4836
Central South	(905) 645-5323	(905) 645-5374
Southwest	(519) 660-2285	(519) 660-2294

Originating Process and Court Documents

40. The title of proceeding for every class proceeding shall state that it is a "Proceeding under the *Class Proceedings Act, 1992*."

41. Every class proceeding shall have appended to the court file number the letters CP, indicating that it is a class proceeding.

42. A copy of the originating process of any proceeding commenced under the *Class Proceedings Act, 1992* must be filed with the Class Proceedings Registry at the Civil Intake Office, 393 University Avenue, Toronto, Ontario, M5G 1E6, in addition to the court office in the jurisdiction where the matter was commenced. The originating process may be sent to the Registry by registered mail, ordinary mail, facsimile (416) 327-6187, or it may be filed.

43. The solicitor of record for the party who commences the proceeding must complete a Certificate of Compliance, verifying that a copy of the originating process has been filed with the Registry. The Certificate of Compliance must be filed forthwith in the court office where the action was commenced.

Procedure on Motions and other Hearings

44. In accordance with the statutory scheme, the judge hearing the pre-trial motions will case manage the proceeding.

Part III: Civil and Family Motions Procedure

A. Factums for Motions

45. The following requirements apply within all judicial Regions of the Ontario Superior Court of Justice for motions in civil and family proceedings:*

   a) Factums are **required** for long civil motions and encouraged for all other motions unless otherwise directed by a judge;

   b) Factums or Summaries of Argument under subrule 17(8) of the *Family Law Rules* are **required** for all long family motions unless otherwise directed by a case conference judge;

   c) No factum or Summary of Argument may exceed 20 pages, unless leave is granted;** and,

   d) The times for service and filing of factums or Summaries of Argument shall be in accordance with the times for service and filing of other motions materials respectively under the *Rules of Civil Procedure* or the *Family Law Rules,* **unless** a region-specific Practice Direction states otherwise.

46. The following chart sets out the times for short and long motions for civil and family proceedings in each judicial Region:

REGIONS	SHORT MOTIONS	LONG MOTIONS
Central East: Civil, Family	Under 1 hour	Over 1 hour
Central South: Civil, Family	Under 1 hour	Over 1 hour
Central West: Civil, Family	Under 1 hour	Over 1 hour
East: Civil, Family	Under 1 hour	Over 1 hour***
Northeast: Civil, Family	Under 1 hour	Over 1 hour
Northwest: Civil, Family	Under 2 hours	Over 2 hours
Southwest: Civil, Family	Civil: Under 1/2 hour Family: Under 1 hour	Civil: Over 1 hour Family: Over 1 hour
Toronto: Civil	Under 2 hours	Over 2 hours

§ The times stated in this chart for the Southwest Region are for general information only. It is recommended that you contact your court location to find out whether your motion will be treated as a short motion or a long motion.

B. Motions to Transfer a Civil Proceeding in the Central East, Central West, Central South and Toronto Regions under Rule 13.1.02 of the *Rules of Civil Procedure*

47. Paragraphs 48 to 51 of this Practice Direction govern all motions to transfer under rule 13.1.02.

---

* The *single exception* is family proceedings in the Toronto Region which are governed by the Consolidated Practice Direction Concerning Family Cases in the Toronto Region.

** In the Toronto Region no factum may exceed 30 pages, unless leave is granted.

*** The East Region has an additional "lengthy" category for long family motions more than 2 hours.

48.   A high volume of requests to transfer civil proceedings to another county, often in another Region, are being received. Counsel frequently seek to transfer a case, on consent. While the transfer may be appropriate in the circumstances of the case, the onus rests with the moving party to satisfy the court that a transfer is desirable in the interest of justice, having regard to the factors listed in rule 13.1.02(2)(b). It is not sufficient to bring a transfer motion orally, on consent, or to file a consent for an order to transfer a case to another county under rule 13.1.02.

49.   A motion to transfer a proceeding should be brought at the court location to which the moving party seeks to have the proceeding transferred. The moving party must file a Notice of Motion with a supporting affidavit, as required under rule 13.1.02(2). The moving party's affidavit must address the factors listed in rule 13.1.02(2)(b) and, as part of the relevant matters, must identify the current stage of the proceeding (i.e., whether further motions are anticipated in the proceeding, whether a pre-trial has occurred or is scheduled, and whether mediation has been held) and why the proceeding was originally commenced in the originating county. The affidavit should also address the estimated length of trial, whether it is a jury trial, and the number of parties and counsel.

50.   Counsel are *not* required to provide affidavit evidence about the availability of judges and court facilities in the other county to satisfy factor (viii) under rule 13.1.02(2). This factor shall be addressed by the Regional Senior Judge in the Region where the motion is brought, after consulting with the local administrative judge or Regional Senior Judge for the other county.

51.   The Regional Senior Judge, or his or her designate, will hear all motions to transfer. To allow the Regional Senior Judge to promptly determine all such motions, they shall be brought in writing. Responding parties are *strongly encouraged* to file and rely exclusively on written submissions to allow the motion to be heard and fully determined in writing. If an oral hearing becomes necessary, the motion shall be heard by teleconference arranged through the Office of the Regional Senior Judge in the Region where the motion is brought. In addition to filing motion material pursuant to the Rules, all parties on a motion to transfer are encouraged to submit an electronic, scanned version of their motion materials, saved as a PDF file and submitted on a USB stick appropriately tagged or marked indicating the court file number. This will facilitate the ability of the Regional Senior Judge to efficiently dispose of these motions, without the delay inherent in physical file transfers.

Part IV: Judicial Management of all Civil Proceedings not governed by Rule 77 of the *Rules of Civil Procedure*

52.   Counsel and parties are reminded that all civil proceedings in Ontario, not subject to case management under Rule 77, may be judicially managed under the present provisions of the *Rules of Civil Procedure*.

53.   Rule 37.15 provides that if a proceeding involves complicated issues or if two or more proceedings involve similar issues, parties and/or counsel who seek an order under the rule may make a request in writing to the Regional Senior Judge of their respective judicial Region to have a judge appointed.

54.   Pursuant to Rule 48.14, the court will supervise actions that are not set down for trial on a timely basis.

55. Status Notices (Form 48C) will be issued for actions that have not been placed on the trial list or terminated by any means within two years after the filing of a statement of defence, indicating that the proceeding will be dismissed for delay within 90 days, with costs, unless:

   a) the action is set down for trial; or

   b) the action has been terminated by any means; or

   c) a status hearing judge orders otherwise.

56. Any party who receives the Status Notice may request a Status Hearing, at which the plaintiff must show cause why the action should not be dismissed for delay and the court will review the action and may consider the range of orders set out in Rule 48.14(8).

Part V: Rule 76 Simplified Procedure

57. In accordance with subrules 76.10 (2) and (4), the Trial Management Plan must be filed with the court at least five days before the pre-trial conference.

58. Self-represented parties are encouraged to refer to the *Instructions for Self-Represented Parties Preparing for Rule 76 Simplified Procedure Trials*, available on the Superior Court's website, which offers guidance on how to prepare for trial.

Part VI: General Practice Directions Applicable to all Proceedings

A.   Gowning for Counsel

59. Counsel are required to gown for all trials, motions and appeals before the presiding judge in the Ontario Superior Court of Justice. Counsel who are pregnant are free to modify their traditional court attire in order to accommodate their pregnancy as they see fit, including dispensing with a waistcoat and tabs.

60. Counsel are not required to gown for appearances before masters or judges and deputy judges of the Small Claims Court (a branch of the Superior Court of Justice).

61. Counsel are not required to gown before a Superior Court Judge of Ontario when appearing in Assignment Court, case conferences, settlement conferences, trial management conferences, trial scheduling courts, or pre-trials, **unless** a region-specific Practice Direction states otherwise.

B.   Ensuring the Integrity of Scheduled Trials, Hearing and Appeals

62. This section is intended to ensure that trials, hearings and appeals are scheduled on the basis of the chronological order in which lawyers make their commitments to appear in court. It has three important objectives:

   a) to ensure that the trial lists of the Superior Court of Justice and the Ontario Court of Justice are respected;

   b) to reduce court delays, the waste of court resources and the unnecessary expense and inconvenience to the public brought about by adjournments; and

   c) to assist parties in civil or criminal cases in having adequate representation by a lawyer acceptable to them.

Trial Dates

63. Where a date for trial or for the hearing of a matter has been set by the Superior Court

of Justice or the Ontario Court of Justice, the trial or hearing is expected to take place on that date.

Presumption of Commitment

64. By agreeing to a trial or hearing date, a lawyer is presumed to have made a commitment to appear on that date and to be bound not to make any other commitments that would make the lawyer's appearance on that date impossible.

Duty to Inform of Previous Commitments

65. When setting a date for trials, hearings or appeals in the Superior Court of Justice or the Ontario Court of Justice, every lawyer has a duty to disclose previous commitments to another court that may conflict with a proposed date for a trial, hearing or appeal.

Respect for Previous Commitments

66. In setting dates for trials, hearings or appeals, the Superior Court of Justice and the Ontario Court of Justice, as much as possible, shall avoid setting dates that would make it impossible for lawyers to keep commitments already made in other courts.

C. Release of Digital Court Recordings

67. This section outlines the policy on the release of digital court recordings. Members of the public, counsel, litigants, accused or the media may obtain copies of digital court recordings (hereinafter referred to as "digital recordings") made from Digital Recording Devices (DRDs) of matters heard in open court, in accordance with the requirements of this section. The copies of digital court recordings will include annotations.

68. The release of digital recordings will be at the court's discretion and the use of all digital recordings will be subject to any court order and any common law or statutory restriction on publication applicable to the particular proceeding.

69. Unless this section provides otherwise, all persons must execute an undertaking with the court to access the digital recordings. The undertaking prescribes the way in which the digital recording is to be used and the terms and conditions under which the digital recording is being provided. All digital recordings are subject to the prohibition set out in s. 136 of the *Courts of Justice Act*, which prohibits the broadcast, reproduction and dissemination of audio recordings. Any person who contravenes s. 136 is guilty of an offence and subject to a penalty, in accordance with s. 136(4) of the *Courts of Justice Act*.

Exception, Small Claims Court Proceedings

70. A person requesting the release of a digital recording of a Small Claims Court proceeding must: (i) obtain a court order authorizing access, (ii) complete the "Undertaking to the Court for Access to Digital Court Recordings", and (iii) pay the prescribed fee. Paragraphs 87 to 90 of this practice direction apply to these requests. The release of a digital recording of a settlement conference is subject to rule 13.03 (4) of the *Rules of the Small Claims Court*.

71. For the purposes of obtaining an order for the release of a digital recording of a Small Claims Court proceeding, the provisions in paragraphs 87 to 90 apply and all refer-

ences to "judge" shall be read to include "deputy judge".

Definitions

72.　For the purposes of this section, "judge" means: all judges, traditional masters, and case management masters of the Superior Court of Justice.

Restrictions on Access to Digital Recordings from DRDs

73.　All copies or access to digital recordings are subject to any express order the presiding judge may make. The presiding judge may expand or restrict access to the digital recordings in any particular proceeding before him or her.

74.　Unless a judge of the Superior Court of Justice orders otherwise, no digital recordings are available to anyone in the following proceedings:

　　a)　*in camera* proceedings or any portion of a proceeding that is heard *in camera*;

　　b)　private or closed hearings (e.g. pursuant to s. 87 of the *Child, Youth and Family Services Act*);

　　c)　proceedings subject to a statutory, common law or court ordered restriction on the provision of transcripts or digital recordings of the proceeding (e.g., pre-trial conferences held in court with self-represented accused, pursuant to rule 28.05(4) of the *Criminal Proceedings Rules* of the Superior Court of Justice (Ontario), proceedings under the *Youth Criminal Justice Act*;

　　d)　case, settlement and trial management conferences pursuant to rule 17 of the *Family Law Rules*; and

　　e)　civil and family motions and applications (e.g. civil motions and applications under rule 37 and rule 38 of the *Rules of Civil Procedure*, family motions under rules 14 and 15 of the *Family Law Rules*).

Access to Digital Recordings from DRDs

Counsel of Record

75.　A counsel of record in a proceeding may obtain the digital recordings of that proceeding upon completion of the "Undertaking of Counsel/Licensed Paralegal of Record" and payment of the prescribed fee.

76.　Persons attending on behalf of counsel of record may obtain the digital recording if he or she: (i) provides a signed undertaking from counsel of record; (ii) signs the authorization included in the "Undertaking of Counsel/Licensed Paralegal of Record"; and (iii) pays the prescribed fee.

Litigant or Accused

77.　A litigant or accused in a proceeding may obtain the digital recordings of that proceeding upon completion of the "Undertaking to the Court for Access to Digital Court Recordings" and payment of the prescribed fee.

The Media

78.　Members of the media, identified on the "Joint Courts' List of Designated Media for Access to Digital Court Recordings" accessible on the Superior Court of Justice website: www.ontariocourts.ca/en/media-list.htm, may obtain the digital recordings upon completion of the "Undertaking to the Court for Access to Digital Court Recordings" and payment of the prescribed fee.

79. Members of the media who are not identified on the "Joint Courts' List of Designated Media for Access to Digital Court Recordings" may make an application for an order in accordance with this section authorizing him or her to obtain access to the digital recordings of the proceeding.

80. The applicant may obtain the digital recordings if he or she: (i) obtains a court order authorizing access, (ii) completes "Undertaking to the Court for Access to Digital Court Recordings", and (iii) pays the prescribed fee.

Members of the Public

81. Members of the public may make an application for an order in accordance with this section authorizing him or her to obtain access to the digital recordings of the proceeding.

82. The applicant may obtain the digital recording if he or she: (i) obtains a court order authorizing access, (ii) completes the "Undertaking to the Court for Access to Digital Court Recordings", and (iii) pays the prescribed fee.

Presiding Judge, Regional Senior Judge (RSJ) or Local Administrative Judge (LAJ)

83. Copies or access to digital recordings shall be provided, upon request, to the presiding judge for the proceeding in which the digital recording was prepared.

84. Copies or access to digital recordings shall be provided, upon request, to the RSJ or LAJ (or his or her designate), for administrative purposes, in the absence of the presiding judge. The presiding judge will be notified that access or copies of the digital recording were made available to the RSJ or LAJ (or his or her designate).

85. Where a judge wishes to access a digital recording from a proceeding in which another judge presided, the judge shall obtain the consent of the presiding judge to access the digital recording, subject to paragraph 83 (below).

86. Where a judge determines that he or she can deal more effectively and efficiently with a case by accessing a digital recording from a previous proceeding before another judge, in the same case or a related case, the judge can access the digital recording by obtaining permission from the presiding judge, the RSJ, the LAJ, or his or her designate, *unless it is in the interests of justice to dispense with such permission*. In that event, access to the digital recording shall be provided to the judge upon request. After access is provided, the judge who has obtained access shall notify the judge who presided at the earlier proceeding, if that judge was not notified when the issues arose.

Court Services Division Staff and Transcriptionists

87. Copies or access to digital recordings shall be provided upon request at no charge to the following:

   a) Court Services Division Staff who require access in the course of their employment responsibilities; and,

   b) Transcriptionists authorized by Regulation 158/03 under the *Evidence Act* who require access to transcribe court proceedings and who have signed an "Undertaking of Authorized Court Transcriptionist for Access to Audio Court Recordings".

Named Administrative Bodies or Organizations

88. Representatives of the bodies or organizations authorized pursuant to a Memorandum of Understanding with the Ministry of Attorney General to have access to digital audio recordings may obtain digital court recordings of court proceedings related directly to the matters under consideration by these bodies or organizations, upon completion of an Undertaking approved by the court and prescribed by the Memorandum of Understanding.

Hearing of the Application

89. Applications regarding access to the digital recording for any ongoing proceeding will be heard by the judge who is seized of the proceeding.

90. Applications shall be brought in accordance with the procedural rules that govern the court proceeding.

91. Applications regarding access to the digital recording for any other type of proceeding or for a proceeding that has concluded will be heard by the judge who presided at the hearing.

92. Where the judge who presided at the hearing is not available to hear the application or where no particular judge is associated with the proceeding, the RSJ, LAJ (or his or her delegate) may hear the application. Applicants should be aware that, especially for proceedings that have concluded or proceedings adjourned for a lengthy period of time, it may not always be possible to schedule an application before the appropriate judge on short notice because a judge may have many ongoing obligations in other proceedings.

93. Undertaking of Counsel/Licensed Paralegal of Record to the Court for Access to Digital Court Recordings can be obtained as Word or PDF documents on the Superior Court of Justice Website.

94. Undertaking to the Court for Access to Digital Court Recordings can be obtained as Word or PDF documents on the Superior Court of Justice Website.

D. Electronic Devices in the Courtroom

95. This section outlines the protocol on how electronic devices may be used in courtrooms of the Ontario Superior Court of Justice by counsel, licensed paralegals, law students and law clerks assisting counsel, self-represented litigants, and media or journalists.

Note: This section does not apply to persons who require electronic devices (or services requiring the use of electronic devices) to accommodate a disability.

Definitions

96. Electronic Devices

For the purposes of this section, "electronic devices" include all forms of computers, personal electronic and digital devices, and mobile, cellular, and smart phones.

97. Publicly Accessible Live Communications

For the purposes of this section, "publicly accessible live communications" are defined as the act of using an electronic device to transmit information from the courtroom to a publicly accessible medium (e.g. via Twitter or live blogs).

98.   Judge

For the purposes of this section, "judge" means:

a)   all judges, traditional masters, and case management masters of the Superior Court of Justice, and

b)   judges of the Small Claims Court and deputy judges.

Prohibited Use of Electronic Devices by the Public

99.   Members of the public are *not permitted* to use electronic devices in the courtroom unless the presiding judge orders otherwise.

Use of Electronic Devices in the Courtroom

100.   *Unless the presiding judge orders otherwise,* the use of electronic devices in silent mode and in a discreet and unobtrusive manner is *permitted* in the courtroom by:

a)   counsel;

b)   paralegals who are licensed by the Law Society of Ontario;

c)   law students and law clerks assisting counsel during the proceeding;

d)   self-represented parties; and,

e)   media or journalists

subject to the following restrictions:

i.   The electronic device cannot interfere with courtroom decorum or otherwise interfere with the proper administration of justice.

ii.   The electronic device cannot interfere with the court recording equipment or other technology in the courtroom.

iii.   The electronic device cannot be used to send publicly accessible live communications where to do so would breach a restriction on publication made in the proceeding.

Note: Anyone using an electronic device to transmit publicly accessible live communications from the courtroom has the responsibility to identify and comply with any publication bans, or other restrictions that have been imposed either by statute or by court order.

iv.   The electronic device cannot be used to take photographs or videos unless the judge has granted permission to do so, in accordance with s. 136 of the *Courts of Justice Act*.

v.   Only counsel, self-represented parties, the media and journalists are permitted to use electronic devices to make an audio recording of the proceeding and only for the purpose of note-taking. However, such audio recordings cannot be sent from the electronic device.

vi.   Talking on electronic devices is not permitted in the courtroom.

Enforcement

101.   Anyone who uses an electronic device in a manner that is inconsistent with this sec-

tion, any orders of the presiding judge or that the presiding judge determines to be unacceptable may be:

a) subject to prosecution for breaches of s. 136 of the *Courts of Justice Act*, a citation and prosecution for contempt of court, or prosecution for other offences;

b) ordered to turn off the device;

c) ordered to leave the device outside the courtroom;

d) ordered to leave the courtroom; and/or

e) ordered to abide by any other order the presiding judge may make.

E. Filing of Judicial Decisions from Electronic Databases and Citation of all Judicial Decisions

Filing of Judicial Decisions from Electronic Databases

102. Copies of judicial decisions obtained from approved electronic databases are acceptable for filing provided the report of the judicial decision contains paragraph numeration consistent with the numbering of the paragraphs in the decision as released by the court. "Approved electronic databases" are databases that are dedicated to the publication of judicial decisions (e.g. Quicklaw, CanLII, and Westlaw).

103. Counsel and parties should be aware that judicial decisions posted on electronic databases may be subject to correction or editing within a few days of the initial posting and, accordingly, parties should ensure that any decision obtained from an electronic database has not been subsequently amended.

Citation of all Judicial Decisions

104. Parties citing decisions from electronic databases should provide the citations for any paper versions of the decision in addition to the citation of the electronic database.

105. Parties should provide the date that the copy of any decision was obtained from an electronic database, as part of the citation information.

106. For decisions of the Ontario Superior Court of Justice released on or after January 1, 2010, parties should provide the neutral citation number (e.g. 2010 ONSC 1) in addition to the other required citations.

F. Publication Bans

Application of this Part

107. This part applies to all civil, criminal and family proceedings in the Superior Court of Justice and to proceedings in the Divisional Court.

108. This part applies to all applications or motions for discretionary publication bans. It does not apply to publication bans that are mandated by statute (i.e. those that either operate automatically by virtue of statute or that a statute provides are mandatory on request)

Formal Notice of Application/Motion Required

109. Unless otherwise directed by a judge, any person seeking a discretionary order restricting publication of any Superior Court proceeding must serve and file a notice

of motion or application and any supporting materials, in accordance with the applicable procedural rules.

Notification of the Media

110. Unless otherwise directed by a judge, the person seeking the publication ban (the requesting party) must provide notice to the media of the motion/application, using the procedure set out in this section.

111. The requesting party must complete and submit the "Notice of Request for Publication Ban" form available on the Superior Court of Justice website.

112. The length of notice required for the submission of the Notice of Request for Publication Ban is the same as the length of notice required under the applicable procedural rules for the serving and filing of the Notice of Application or Notice of Motion.

113. The information on the Notice of Request for Publication Ban will be distributed electronically to members of the media who have subscribed to receive notice of all publication ban applications/motions in the Superior Court.

114. Any member of the media who wishes to receive copies of the Notices prepared and submitted under this section should submit a request through the Superior Court of Justice website.

115. The requesting party may be required to produce a copy of the Notice of Request for Publication Ban to the Court at the hearing of the application/motion in order to establish that notice was provided in accordance with this section.

G. Manner of Address for Masters

116. Masters should be addressed in English as "Your Honour" and in French as "Votre Honneur".

Part VII: Books of Authorities in Civil Proceedings

A. Often-Cited Civil Cases

117. The List of Often-Cited Civil Cases in Civil Proceedings, which contains cases frequently relied upon, is available for each judge who presides over civil cases. There will be additions to, and deletions from, the list from time to time. The up-to-date list is available on the Superior Court of Justice website at: http://www.ontariocourts.ca/scj/practice/practice-directions/list-civil/.

118. The cases in question appear on the list under various headings or topics which are not in any way intended to provide legal advice.

119. Parties in civil proceedings need no longer include authorities on the list in any book of authorities relied on.

120. However, extracts from those authorities which counsel intend to refer to the court shall be included in the factum or book of authorities.

B. Requirements for Books of Authorities in Civil Proceedings

121. It is of great assistance to the Court to have books of authority filed by counsel containing copies of the authorities to which they intend to refer on the hearing of the matter. Such books of authorities:

a.   Should be printed double-sided.

b.   Should be bound in volumes no more than three inches thick.

c.   Should include only the cases to which counsel actually intend to refer in the oral argument. The particular passages in the cases to which counsel wish to refer should be clearly marked.

d.   Should be prepared jointly in accordance with this direction. Where counsel are unable to agree, then such case books should indicate whether they are filed by the appellant or the respondent. There should be consultation between counsel to avoid any duplication of the authorities included in their respective case books.

e.   Should have a tab for each case (either numerical or by letters), include an index of the authorities and indicate the tab where the authority is reproduced. It is not necessary to number the pages in the case book so long as the photocopies show the page numbers of each authority

Dated: April 11, 2014

Amended: January 15, 2020; May 17, 2019; December 7, 2018; June 15, 2018; January 1, 2017; July 1, 2016; May 1, 2016; April 1, 2016; February 1, 2016; April 28, 2015

Geoffrey B. Morawetz
Chief Justice
Superior Court of Justice (Ontario)

A.1 Practice Advisory Concerning the Provincial Civil Case Management Pilot – One Judge Model (Effective: February 1, 2019)

This practice advisory applies to Superior Court of Justice civil cases that are approved for inclusion in the pilot by the Regional Senior Judge. Simplified procedure cases under Rule 76 of the *Rules of Civil Procedure* are ineligible for the pilot.

This practice advisory *supplements existing practice directions*. Counsel and parties are advised to refer to the relevant parts of the Consolidated Provincial Practice Direction and any other applicable region-specific practice directions or guides, which are available on the Superior Court of Justice website at: www.ontariocourts.ca/scj.

In addition, this practice advisory *supplements* existing civil case management provisions under the *Rules of Civil Procedure*, including:

- Rule 77, applicable in Toronto, Ottawa and Windsor, in which certain proceedings can be directed into Rule 77 case management by the court's own initiative, at the request of a party, or on motion if required by the court (r. 77.05); and

- Rule 37.15, which provides that, where a proceeding involves complicated issues, or where there are two or more proceedings that involve similar issues, the Chief Justice, Associate Chief Justice, Regional Senior Judge, or his or her designate, may direct that all motions in the proceedings be heard by a particular judge (the case management judge). The case management judge can give directions and make procedural orders necessary to promote the most expeditious and least expensive determination of the proceeding.

What is one-judge case management?

The impetus for this pilot was a report of the Judiciary Committee of the American College of Trial Lawyers. The report, titled *Working Smarter But Not Harder in Canada: The Development of a Unified Approach to Case Management in Civil Litigation*, discussed the benefits of having the case management judge also preside at the trial of a matter.

The pilot includes the following features:

1. A judge that has been assigned to case-manage an action will preside over all pre-trial hearings, case management conferences, **and the trial**. This will allow the judge to become entirely familiar with the issues in the dispute. The only exception is for case conferences that are dedicated solely to settlement discussions; a different judge will preside over these case conferences in order to allow the parties to freely discuss the strengths and weaknesses of each party's case and discuss the parties' willingness to compromise their positions in an effort to find common ground.

2. No formal interlocutory motions will be scheduled in cases assigned to the pilot without the approval of the case management judge. Instead, informal procedures will be used wherever possible to resolve interlocutory disputes, such as meetings with counsel and self-represented parties in the judge's chambers or by teleconference. (*Exception*: motions for recusal would not require the approval of the case management judge.)

3. At a relatively early stage of the proceeding, the case management judge will fix a trial date, or order a trial to be heard in a particular sitting of the court, and impose a schedule for completing necessary steps prior to trial. The trial date would be adjourned only

in exceptional circumstances and would require the approval of the case management judge. For efficiency in the scheduling or conduct of the trial, the case management judge may make pre-trial orders concerning the admissibility of trial evidence.

The expected benefits of one-judge case management are the faster and less costly resolution of civil disputes. The pilot will be evaluated after two years.

How can I get my case included in the pilot?

Inclusion in the pilot is at the discretion of the Regional Senior Judge or his or her designate. The extent to which the pilot is available in the region, including the number of actions admitted into the pilot, will depend on available judicial resources and local scheduling practices.

When determining whether to include a case in the pilot, similar to Rule 77, the Regional Senior Judge or his or her designate will take into consideration a variety of factors, including:

- The complexity of the issues of fact or law
- The importance to the public of the issues of fact or law
- The number and type of parties or prospective parties, and whether they are represented
- The number of proceedings involving the same or similar parties or causes of action
- The amount of intervention by the court that the proceeding is likely to require
- The time required for discovery, if applicable, and for preparation for trial or hearing
- In the case of an action, the number of expert witnesses and other witnesses
- The time required for the trial or hearing
- Whether there has been substantial delay in the conduct of the proceeding.

Parties may apply to participate in the pilot by writing to the Regional Senior Judge or sending a completed application form (form available at: http://www.ontariocourts.ca/scj/files/forms/application-ccmp-EN.docx). The letter/application form must indicate the following:

1. The court file number
2. Title of proceeding
3. The court location where case was commenced (or to which it has been transferred)
4. The reasons why case management is needed to facilitate the resolution of the dispute
5. Confirmation that all parties consent to the following terms of the pilot:
   a. The case management judge will preside at the trial of the case, and
   b. Interlocutory disputes will be resolved though informal processes, such as case conferences, and no formal interlocutory motions will be scheduled unless the case management judge orders otherwise.

How will I know if my case has been accepted into the pilot?

You will receive written confirmation as to whether your case has been accepted into the pilot. If your case has been accepted, the confirmation will include the name of the case management judge. The case management judge may then direct the parties to attend a case conference pursuant to Rule 50.13 of the *Rules of Civil Procedure* to discuss the next steps.

How long will the pilot be and how will it be evaluated?

The expected duration of the pilot is two years. Participants are encouraged to complete an anonymous survey to assist in evaluating the one-judge civil case management model. The survey will be emailed to parties participating in the pilot.

Dated: January 3, 2019

Heather J. Smith
Chief Justice
Superior Court of Justice

B. Consolidated Practice Direction for Divisional Court Proceedings (Latest Amendment: May 17, 2019)

Notice of Amendments:

Effective May 17, 2019, Paragraphs 2 and 10 are amended to reflect January 2019 amendments to Rule 62.02 of the *Rules of Civil Procedure*.

Part I is amended to clarify where documents should be filed when a matter is to be heard by a single judge.

Part VII is amended to clarify where documents should be filed when a matter is to be heard by a panel.

On December 7, 2018, new requirements for motions for leave to appeal to the Divisional Court were added to Part II.

Effective July 1, 2017: A new Part II was created regarding motions for leave to appeal to Divisional Court (Part III to VII have been renumbered). As of July 1, 2017, rule 62.02 requires that leave to appeal to the Divisional Court under clause 19 (1) (b) of the Courts of Justice Act, regarding appeals of interlocutory orders of a judge, shall be obtained from a panel of that court, rather than by a single judge. Three printed copies of materials for motions for leave to appeal must now be filed in at the Divisional Court Office in Toronto.

Effective July 1, 2014

This Practice Direction applies to Divisional Court proceedings, effective July 1, 2014. It *supersedes* all Practice Directions for Divisional Court proceedings issued prior to July 1, 2014, which are hereby revoked.

Counsel and parties are advised to refer to the relevant Parts of the separate Consolidated Provincial Practice Direction and region-specific Practice Directions which may affect Divisional Court proceedings. All Superior Court of Justice Practice Directions are available on the Court's website at: www.ontariocourts.ca/scj.

Table of Contents

Part I: Proceedings to be Heard by a Single Judge

A.   Application

1. This Part applies only to motions, applications, and appeals before a single judge. It does not apply to matters to be heard by a Divisional Court panel.

2. The following proceedings in Divisional Court are directed for a hearing before one judge of the Divisional Court sitting in the Superior Court of Justice location where the hearing or other process that led to the decision appealed from took place:

> appeals of final orders of a masters or case management masters under s. 19(1)(c) of the *Courts of Justice Act*;

> appeals of Small Claims Court final orders under s. 31 of the Courts of Justice Act motions for leave to appeal from certain tribunals, as required by statute (e.g. *Assessment Act, Local Planning Appeal Tribunal Act*), but not motions for leave to appeal under Rule 62.02 which are heard by a Divisional Court panel in the Regional Centre (see Part VII below);

> urgent applications for judicial review, with leave, under section 6 (2) of the *Judicial Review Procedure Act*; and

> motions for interim relief.

B.   Proceedings in the Toronto Region

4. In the Toronto Region only, applications for judicial review under s. 6(2) of the *Judicial Review Procedure Act*, are directed to be brought in Divisional Court for a hearing before a single judge of that court sitting as a judge of the Superior Court of Justice.

The notice of application under s. 6(2), together with all other material, will be filed with the Divisional Court at Osgoode Hall.

Confirmation of Hearing

5. In the case of appeals to a single judge and other motions incidental to appeals or applications, counsel should contact the Divisional Court office by telephone, (416) 327-6202, to arrange a hearing date. In all three-judge proceedings, a hearing date must be obtained from the Registrar by telephone, (416) 326-5400.

6. Notwithstanding that a matter is set down for a hearing, and unless otherwise ordered by a judge, the papers will not be forwarded to the presiding judge and, unless otherwise ordered, the matter will not be heard on the date scheduled unless counsel for the moving party or applicant, by 2:00 p.m. three days prior to the scheduled hearing date, files all necessary material and confirms that the motion or application is to proceed as scheduled as required under the *Rules of Civil Procedure* (see rules 37.10.1 and 38.09.1).

Counsel for the moving party or applicant may confirm the hearing date by delivering the Confirmation Forms (Form 37B or Form 38B) to the Divisional Court office at Osgoode Hall or by fax transmission to (416) 327-5549. Motions under rule 62.02 for leave to appeal the interlocutory order of a Superior Court of Justice judge are exempt from this requirement, as these motions for leave are now heard by a panel in writing only (see Part II).

7. It is expected that a factum will be filed by each party on any matter. The presiding judge may decline to hear a matter if a factum has not been filed.

8. It is the responsibility of counsel to see that the material is filed as directed.

Time Estimates on Argument

9. When an application under s. 6(2) of the *Judicial Review Procedure Act* or an appeal under s. 19(1)(c) and 21(2) of the *Courts of Justice Act* will require more than one hour for hearing, counsel should advise the Registrar of their best estimate when the appointment is given.

Part II: Motions for leave to appeal to the Divisional Court

10. Rule 62.02 requires that motions for leave to appeal to the Divisional Court regarding an appeal of: an interlocutory order of a judge under clause 19 (1) (b) of the *Courts of Justice Act*, and a final order of a judge pertaining to costs under clauses 19 (1) (a) and 133 (b) of the *Courts of Justice Act*, must be obtained from a panel of that court, rather than by a single judge. These motions for leave to appeal are heard in writing and must be filed at the Divisional Court Office in Toronto at the following address in person or by mail/courier, together with payment of the filing fee:

Divisional Court Office
Osgoode Hall
130 Queen Street West
Toronto, ON M5H 2N5

The motion for leave will be heard in writing by a panel of three Divisional Court judges. Three printed copies of the motion record, factum and transcripts, if any, must be filed.

11. Counsel are reminded that all motions for leave to appeal must include, in the motion record, a copy of the signed and entered order from which leave to appeal is sought. In the materials filed with the court, parties should refer to themselves as "the moving party" or the "responding party". Both the moving party's and responding party's motion records must include costs submissions respecting the motion for leave to appeal, unless doing so would disclose an offer to settle. Costs submissions should include the proposed quantum of costs (win or lose) and a costs outline (Form 57B).

Part III: Factums in the Divisional Court

12. Counsel and parties should refer to rules 61.11, 61.12 and 68.04(3) and (6) of the *Rules of Civil Procedure* which deal with factums on appeals and applications for judicial review. These rules require a "concise summary" of fact and law and an estimate of the time required for oral argument. If in counsel's opinion a factum of more than 30 pages is necessary, counsel should arrange an appointment with a judge of the Divisional Court through the Registrar of the Court, before filing.

Part IV: Books of Authority

13. It is of great assistance to the Divisional Court to have books of authority filed by counsel containing copies of the authorities to which they intend to refer on the hearing of the matter. Such books of authorities:

    a) Should include only the cases to which counsel actually intend to refer in the oral argument. The particular passages in the cases to which counsel wish to refer should be clearly marked.

    b) Should be prepared jointly in accordance with this direction. Where counsel are unable to agree, then such case books should indicate whether they are filed by the appellant or the respondent. There should be consultation between counsel to avoid any duplication of the authorities included in their respective case books.

    c) Should have a tab for each case (either numerical or by letters), should include an index of the authorities and indicate the tab where the authority is reproduced. It is not necessary to number the pages in the case-book so long as the photocopies show the page numbers of each authority.

    d) Should be filed, if possible, not later than the Monday of the week preceding the hearing of the matter as they are of great assistance to the judges in preparing for the hearing.

Part V: Filing Electronic Versions of Documents in Civil Appeals and Judicial Review Applications

A. Application

14. This part is intended to establish a uniform approach to filing electronic documents for appeals and judicial review applications to the Divisional Court.

15. This part applies to civil appeals, including appeals from administrative tribunals, motions for leave to appeal under rule 62.02 and judicial review applications in the Divisional Court.

16. This part does not apply to motions other than motions for leave to appeal under rule 62.02. It does not apply to family appeals to the Divisional Court.

17. Parties filing electronic versions of material for Divisional Court proceedings must still file typed or printed copies of such material in accordance with Rules 61 – 62 and 68 of the *Rules of Civil Procedure*.

B. Appeals

18. Parties are required to file electronic versions of their factums and transcripts in appeals to the Divisional Court, in accordance with Rule 61 of the *Rules of Civil Procedure*.

18.1 Parties are also encouraged to file electronic versions of all materials (e.g. appeal books and compendiums, case books, record of proceedings) in the appeal.

C. Judicial Review Applications

19. The Court encourages parties to file electronic versions of their factums and transcripts in judicial review applications to the Divisional Court.

19.1 Parties are also encouraged to file electronic versions of all materials (e.g. application records, compendiums, case books, records of proceedings) in the judicial review application.

C.1 Motions for Leave to Appeal

20. The Court encourages parties to file electronic versions of their factums, transcripts, motion records and books of authorities in motions for leave to appeal from an interlocutory order of a judge under rule 62.02 of the *Rules of Civil Procedure*.

D. Providing Materials to Other Parties

21. Parties are also encouraged to give the electronic versions of documents that are filed electronically with the Court to all other parties to the proceeding.

E. Method of Filing Electronic Documents

22. Parties may file electronic documents on CD, DVD or USB key. Three copies of the CD, DVD or USB key should be filed with the Court where the matter is being heard by a panel of three judges.

23. The CD, DVD or USB key should be accompanied by a covering letter which identifies the materials contained on the CD, DVD or USB key.

USB Key: The cover letter should include a list of the files contained on the USB key, along with the title of proceedings, Court File #, Counsel Name(s), where applicable, and Party Name. If possible, the key should be labelled with the short style of cause and the Court File #.

CD or DVD: The CD or DVD should be labelled with the title of proceedings, Court File #, Counsel Name(s), where applicable, and Party Name. Include a list of the files contained on the CD or DVD in a cover letter.

24. The electronic documents should be filed together with the hard copy of the factum filed with the Court.

F. Format of Electronically Filed Documents

25. The electronic documents must be submitted in either Microsoft Word format (.doc or .docx) or text searchable PDF format.

26. The electronic version of factums or any other material filed in a Divisional Court appeal or judicial review application must be formatted and contained in one file and be virtually identical to the official printed version that is also filed with the Court. For example, a single file for a factum should contain the front and back pages, the index, the text and the schedules. Do not submit separate electronic files for the different sections of a factum or other document. Parties should refer to the Guide Concerning e-Delivery of Documents in the Superior Court of Justice with respect to the preparation and formatting of electronic materials to be filed with the Court.

G. Naming of Electronically Filed Documents

27. The file names for electronic versions of factums, transcripts and other documents filed must start with the Divisional Court appeal or judicial review application file number, followed by one of the character codes set out below. Any other parties not included in this list should include their full name together with the title of the document they are filing.

PRAC. DIR. AND POLICIES

Appeals

FAP	Factum of Appellant
FRE	Factum of Respondent
FXA	Factum of Cross-appellant
FXR	Factum of Cross-respondent
FOI	Factum of Intervener
FOAC	Factum of Amicus Curiae
AFAP	Amended Factum of Appellant
AFRE	Amended Factum of Respondent
FSE	Further Submissions – Appellant
FSR	Further Submissions – Respondent
ABC	Appellant's Appeal Book and Compendium
RBC	Respondent's Compendium
EXB	Exhibit Book
BOA	Book of Authorities of Appellant
BOR	Book of Authorities of Respondent

Transcripts

TRN	Transcript

Judicial Review Applications

FAPL	Factum of Applicant
FRP	Factum of Respondent
FIN	Factum of Intervener
ROP	Record of Proceeding
APAR	Application Record of Applicant
APRR	Application Record of Respondent
APINR	Application Record of Intervener
BAAP	Book of Authorities of Applicant
BARP	Book of Authorities of Respondent

Motions for Leave to Appeal

MPF	Factum of Moving Party
RPF	Factum of Responding Party
MMP	Motion Record of Moving Party
MRP	Motion Record of Responding Party

H.   Failure to Comply with this Practice Direction

28.   Please note that the Divisional Court may reject any electronic version of a factum or transcript that does not conform to the procedures set out in paragraphs 14-27 of this Practice Direction.

Part VI: Judges' Book of Authorities

29.   A Judges' Book of Authorities containing authorities frequently relied on is supplied

to each judge who sits in Divisional Court. There will be additions to, and deletions from, the book from time to time. An up-to-date list of the authorities in the Judges' Book will be available as of July 1, 2014, on the Court's website.

30.   In preparing books of authorities, counsel need no longer include authorities contained in the Judges' Book. However, extracts from those authorities which counsel intend to refer to the court should be included in the factum or book of authorities.

Part VII: Regional Centres for Divisional Court Filings

31.   The court locations listed below are the designated Divisional Court regional centres where panels of three Divisional Court judges hear appeals and applications for judicial review. Court documents relating to these hearings must be filed at the regional centre. (See Part I above regarding appeals heard by a single judge)

Region	Regional Centre
Central East Region	Durham Region Courthouse150 Bond St. E. Oshawa, ON L1G 0A2
Central South Region	Hamilton (John Sopinka) Courthouse 45 Main St. E. Hamilton, ON L8N 2B7
Central West Region	Brampton (A. Grenville & William Davis) Courthouse 7755 Hurontario St. Brampton, ON L6W 4T1
East Region	Ottawa Courthouse161 Elgin St., 2nd Fl. Ottawa On K2P 2K1
Northeast Region	Sudbury Courthouse155 Elm St. Sudbury, ON P3C 1T9
Northwest Region	Thunder Bay Courthouse125 Brodie St. N. Thunder Bay, ON P7C 0A3
Southwest Region	London Courthouse80 Dundas St. London, ON N6A 6A3
Toronto Region	Osgoode Hall130 Queen St. W. Toronto, ON M5H 2N5

Dated: April 11, 2014

Amended: May 17, 2019, December 7, 2018; July 1, 2017; May 10, 2016 (Part VI); January 25, 2016 (Part IV)

Heather J. Smith
Chief Justice
(Superior Court of Justice (Ontario))

C. Consolidated Practice Direction for the Central South Region (Latest Amendment: March 1, 2020)

Notice of Amendment:

Effective March 1, 2020, section G (Proceedings Heard in Hamilton by a Registrar in Bankruptcy) is added to Part IV (Civil Proceedings).

Part II C [paras. 42, 43, 48] was amended on May 17, 2019 to update confirmation deadlines. The deadline in subparagraph 48a is now Wednesday.

Part II B [para. 13], Part II C [paras. 40, 43, 55] were amended effective July 1, 2018 to coincide with changes to the Family Law Rules; Part III H [paras. 110 – 115] was revoked on May 1, 2017.

Effective June 1, 2016

This Practice Direction applies to proceedings in the Superior Court of Justice, Central South Region, effective June 1, 2016. It replaces the previous Consolidated Practice Direction for the Central South Region that was effective on July 1, 2014.

Counsel and parties are advised to refer to the relevant Parts of the Consolidated Provincial Practice Direction as well as the Consolidated Practice Direction for Divisional Court Proceedings which are available on the Superior Court of Justice website at: www.ontariocourts.ca/scj.

Table of Contents

Part I: General

A. Court Contact Information

1.   Contact information for each court location in the Central South Region is available in the Central South Region's Regional Court Calendar, available on the Superior Court of Justice website.

B. Schedule

2.   The schedule for proceedings in each of the eight court sites in the Central South Region is available in the Central South Region's Regional Court Calendar.

C. Gowning

3.   Counsel are not required to gown for the following court attendances:

     a.   Trial scheduling court (formerly known as assignment court, "speak to" court or "purge court") in family, criminal or civil proceedings.

     b.   Case conferences, settlement conferences, trial scheduling conferences or trial management conferences in family proceedings.

     c.   Pre-trial conferences in criminal proceedings.

     d.   Pre-trial conferences in civil proceedings.

     e.   Small Claims Court proceedings.

4.   Counsel must be gowned for all other proceedings.

D. Release of Digital Court Recordings

5.   Members of the public, counsel, litigants, accused or the media may obtain copies of digital court recordings of matters heard in open court, in accordance with the requirements of section C of part IV of the Court's Provincial Practice Direction.

E. Electronic Devices in the Courtroom

6.   The Superior Court of Justice's protocol relating to the use of electronic devices in the courtroom is set out in section D of part IV of the Court's Provincial Practice Direction.

Part II: Family Proceedings

7.   A reference in this part to a "rule" or the "rules" is a reference to the Family Law Rules.

A. Mandatory Information Program (MIP)

8. Attendance at the Mandatory Information Program (MIP) is required for all matters except the matters exempted under rule 8.1(2). MIP dates are provided by court staff at the time the documents starting the legal proceeding are issued.

9. Any request to change the date of a MIP should be made directly to the courthouse's Information Referral Coordinator whose contact information is on the Ministry of the Attorney General's website under Find an Ontario Court.

B. Conferences

Rules Applicable to all Conferences

10. All case conferences, settlement conferences, trial scheduling conferences and trial management conferences, are held before a Superior Court judge, subject to paragraph 77 (Motions to Change at locations with Dispute Resolution Officers).

11. All parties required to attend a MIP are expected to have done so and filed their certificate prior to their first case conference.

12. Briefs are required for all conferences, in accordance with rules 3 and 17.

13. Fully completed Form 17F Confirmation of Conference forms must be filed for all conferences, in accordance with rules 3 and 17 of the rules. The confirmation form must be filed with the court office or faxed to the trial coordinator no later than 2:00 p.m. three business days prior to the conference. If the conference has not been confirmed by at least one party, judicial permission will be required for the conference to proceed on the scheduled date. Failure to comply with the rules may also result in costs sanctions and/or postponement of the conference date.

14. Counsel and parties are expected to attend all conferences in person.

15. Counsel or a party who wishes to request to attend a conference by telephone conference call or by video under rule 17(16), must contact the trial coordinator at least 5 business days before the scheduled conference, who will seek permission from the presiding judge. Counsel or the party must make all other parties aware of the request so that they can communicate any objection to the trial coordinator. The party requesting the telephone conference call or video shall be responsible for any costs associated with it.

16. Any request for an adjournment of a conference shall initially be made through the trial coordinator. Absent an order or direction from a judge, or a consent signed by counsel or the parties and filed with the trial coordinator at least three business days before the date of the conference, counsel and the parties will be required to attend at the scheduled time to request the adjournment. This procedure is permitted for one adjournment and thereafter the parties or their counsel must attend before the court, unless a judge directs otherwise.

Costs for Conferences

17. Rule 24 requires the presiding judge at every court event to fix costs. If a party is seeking costs for preparation for and attendance at a conference, those submissions and a costs outline should be provided to the presiding judge during the conference so that the amount of the costs can be fixed by the presiding judge who will have

knowledge of the issues, the time spent, the degree of preparation required and the conduct of the parties which may entitle them or disentitle them to an order for costs. If a costs outline is not provided to the presiding judge, the judge may decline to make any costs award.

Case Conferences

18. Case conference dates may be obtained directly from the trial coordinator, subject to the practice in Family Court locations. A date will not be provided until at least one party serves and files a case conference brief. Each party must file its Form 17A: Case Conference Brief and Form 13A: Certificate of Financial Disclosure in advance of the case conference as set out in rules 13 and 17(13 and 13.1). Each party must also complete the financial disclosure required under rule 13.

19. If no answer or response to a Motion to Change is filed as required by the rules, no case conference is required and a date for an uncontested hearing may be obtained from the trial coordinator.

Settlement Conferences

20. Settlement conference dates will be set at the case conference or may be obtained directly from the trial coordinator.

21. A party attending a settlement conference must prepare a Form 17C Settlement Conference Brief with all necessary attachments and file it as required by rule 17(13.1).

22. Each party must complete their respective portion of the Trial Scheduling Endorsement Form and give it to the presiding judge at the outset of the settlement conference. Part 3 of the form will be completed by the judge after the issues have been reviewed with the parties.

23. The judge at the settlement conference may, in his or her discretion, convert the settlement conference into a trial management conference (as permitted by rule 17(7)) and have Part 3 of the Trial Scheduling Endorsement Form fully completed at that time.

24. The Trial Scheduling Endorsement Form must be fully completed before a trial date will be assigned.

25. Whenever possible, the trial date will be fixed at the conclusion of the settlement conference. A trial management conference date will be assigned at the same time, unless the presiding judge in his/her discretion feels that it will not be needed. Those will be rare and exceptional cases.

26. If there are matters that need to be completed by the parties before the case is ready for trial, the judge will fix a schedule to be followed by the parties to ensure that the case is trial ready. If the schedule is not adhered to by a party, this may be addressed by serving and filing a notice of motion to enforce the schedule, returnable at a regular motions court of the particular court location.

Trial Management Conferences

27. A trial management conference should be held in all family proceedings that have not been resolved at or before the settlement conference, no more than two weeks before the trial wherever possible, subject to paragraph 23.

28. The purposes of a trial management conference include exploring the chances of set-

PRAC. DIR. AND POLICIES

tling the case, ensuring that the parties know what witnesses will testify and what other evidence will be presented at trial and ensuring the accuracy of the estimated time needed for trial.

29. In advance of the trial management conference, the following documents must be filed by the deadlines set out in rule 17(13.1):

   a. The completed Trial Scheduling Endorsement Form as endorsed by the court must be filed by either the Applicant or the party that requested the conference;

   b. Each party must file an offer to settle all outstanding issues; and,

   c. Each party must file an outline of their opening statement for trial.

These documents are to be filed in lieu of the requirement to file a Trial Management Conference Brief: Form 17E under rule 17(13).

30. The final Trial Scheduling Endorsement Form shall be filed with or added to the Trial Record. The parties' offers to settle must not be filed with the Trial Record.

C. Motions

Form 14B Motions

31. Rules 14(4.2) and (10) of the rules provide that motions are permissible before a case conference if there is a situation of urgency or hardship, or if the request for relief is limited to "procedural, uncomplicated or unopposed matters". In most cases, relief should be requested using Form 14B: Motion.

32. In exceptional circumstances of urgency or hardship, permission to bring a motion before a case conference pursuant to rule (14(4.2)) can be sought when the motion is brought. A comprehensive affidavit explaining the reasons for the order sought must be filed with the motion.

33. In order to assist counsel and parties in making the best use of available conference time, the Superior Court will encourage greater use of Form 14B motions whenever it will make the case conference process more effective. Form 14B motions allow parties to address certain threshold issues prior to the case conference and are designed to streamline conferencing in family law proceedings. Such motions are limited to procedural, uncomplicated or unopposed matters that will promote the concept of fewer, but more meaningful case conferences. In this respect, Form 14B motions will be guided by the paragraphs 34 – 35.

34. Before a case conference is held, lawyers and self-represented litigants are strongly encouraged to use Form 14B to obtain any orders that are needed to make the case conference productive. Examples of appropriate orders include:

   a. orders of either a procedural or substantive nature that are on consent, or unopposed;

   b. a request for the appointment of the Office of the Children's Lawyer;

   c. orders to add a party or obtain discovery from a third party;

   d. orders for production of documents, permission for questioning or other issues pertaining to discovery;

   e. enforcement of an order to provide information, produce a document or serve and file a financial statement or other document;

    f.   any other procedural order or direction needed to promote a meaningful case conference.

35.   Motions that are without notice, on consent or unopposed will be determined by a judge in chambers, unless the court directs otherwise.

Short Motions

36.   A short motion is a motion that will be argued by the parties in less than one hour including reply argument (but excluding the time required for the judge to consider the matter and render a decision).

37.   Short motions shall be made returnable to a regularly scheduled motions day. These dates are listed in the Central South Region's Regional Court Calendar, available on the Superior Court of Justice website.

Factums and Other Materials

38.   A factum or summary of argument is not required on a short motion, although such documents are encouraged because they provide significant assistance to the presiding judge. A factum or summary of argument shall not exceed 20 double spaced typed pages, unless leave is granted.

39.   Parties are encouraged to submit draft orders with their motion materials.

40.   Where a factum is being filed, the court also strongly encourages parties to deliver an electronic copy of the factum, in Word Format, at least three business days before the hearing of the motion, which can be sent to the email address for the court location where the motion will be argued:

Hamilton Family Court: Hamilton.family.superior.court@ontario.ca
Kitchener: Kitchener.superior.court@ontario.ca
Brantford: Brantford.superior.court@ontario.ca
St. Catharines: St.Catharines.superior.court@ontario.ca
Simcoe: Simcoe.superior.court@ontario.ca
Welland: Welland.superior.court@ontario.ca
Cayuga: Cayuga.superior.court@ontario.ca

The covering email should identify the style of cause, the court file number and the date scheduled for the argument of the motion.

Costs

41.   If counsel or a party is seeking costs for appearing on a motion, they must attend with a costs outline to be given to the presiding judge. The costs outline should specify the number of hours of work which was necessary to prepare for the motion, the nature of the work, the lawyer/clerk or other person who did the work, the number of years a lawyer has been at the bar and an itemized list of disbursements incurred with supporting invoices, if available. If the outline is not available to be given to the presiding judge, the judge may decline to make any costs award.

Adjournments of Short Motions

42.   If the trial coordinator receives written confirmation that the parties have agreed to a consent adjournment not later than 2:00 p.m. three business days before the motion

is returnable, the adjournment will be granted, subject to the discretion of the presiding judge and provided that the adjournment has only been requested once. The written consent must specify the date to which the matter is to be adjourned, unless the motion has been settled. If these requirements have been met, counsel and parties are not required to attend before the presiding judge at the motion date.

43. No confirmations will be accepted after 2:00 p.m. three business days before the motion is returnable.

44. If counsel and/or a self-represented party wish(es) to adjourn a matter and it is past the filing deadline for the confirmation form, they should email or fax the trial coordinator as soon as possible to advise the court of the request. If the request is opposed this should also be noted. This should be done so that the presiding judge need not read the file in preparation for the motion. However, the parties or their counsel must still attend court in these circumstances.

Long Motions

45. A long motion is a motion that is expected to require more than one hour of oral argument, including reply argument (but excluding the time required for the presiding judge to consider the matter and render his/her decision).

46. A date for a long motion must be obtained through the trial coordinator. These motions are generally set to be argued during a specified week rather than a specific date but they are scheduled on a fixed date at certain locations in the Central South Region. The trial coordinator at the specific court site should be contacted to determine the local practice.

47. The notice of motion for a long motion must be served and filed and made returnable to a regularly scheduled weekly motions list in accordance with the rules. The notice of motion must indicate whether:

   a. the long motion is being scheduled to a day or week provided by the trial coordinator on consent of all parties, in which case the parties do not need to attend the regular motion date; or

   b. the parties have been unable to agree on a date for the motion, in which case the parties must attend the regular motion date so that a hearing date for the long motion can be set; in these circumstances, the appearance in regular motions court must be confirmed in writing in accordance with the rules.

48. Once the date has been set for the hearing of the motion:

   a. if the long motion is to be called for argument during a given week, a confirmation for the Long Motion (Form 14C) must be filed with the trial coordinator no later than 2:00 p.m. on the Wednesday prior to the chosen week confirming that the motion will proceed, indicating how long the matter will be argued in total and what material is to be read by the judge hearing the long motion.

   b. if the motion has been scheduled on a fixed date, a confirmation for argument of the Long Motion (Form 14C) must be filed with the trial coordinator no later than 2:00 p.m. three business days prior to the scheduled date confirming that the motion will proceed, indicating how long the matter will be argued in total and what material is to be read by the judge hearing the long motion.

Adjournments of Long Motions

49.   Adjournments of long motions will not be readily granted. Any request for an adjournment of a long motion must be immediately communicated to the office of the trial coordinator. Unless otherwise directed by a judge, a request for an adjournment of a long motion must be made in court.

Long Motions Not Reached

50.   If a long motion is not reached on the scheduled date or during the scheduled week, counsel and the parties are to arrange a new date with the trial coordinator. If a date cannot be agreed upon, the matter will be placed before a judge by the trial coordinator and the parties (or their counsel) will be required to attend.

51.   The trial coordinator must be immediately advised in writing of settlement of any or all of the issues prior to the hearing date.

Factums and Other Materials

52.   Factums are required for all long motions. The times for service and filing of factums shall be in accordance with the times for service and filing of other motion materials under the rules.

53.   If case law will be relied on by a party (other than cases referred to in the Court's list of Often Cited Family Cases), a Book of Authorities should be served and filed with the factum or summary of argument with appropriate excerpts from each case highlighted or side barred.

54.   A factum shall not exceed 20 double spaced typed pages, unless leave is granted. The parties are encouraged to submit draft orders with their motion materials.

55.   In addition, the court strongly encourages parties to deliver an electronic copy of a factum, in Word format, at least three business days before the hearing of the motion, which can be sent to the email address for the location where the motion will be argued:

Hamilton Family Court: Hamilton.family.superior.court@ontario.ca
Kitchener: Kitchener.superior.court@ontario.ca
Brantford: Brantford.superior.court@ontario.ca
St. Catharines: St.Catharines.superior.court@ontario.ca
Simcoe: Simcoe.superior.court@ontario.ca
Welland: Welland.superior.court@ontario.ca
Cayuga: Cayuga.superior.court@ontario.ca

The covering email should identify the style of cause, the court file number and the date scheduled for the argument of the motion.

56.   A factum shall include the following:

    a.   a statement of the facts which are relevant to the motion or application;

    b.   the legal questions to be considered by the court;

    c.   the law and prior case law relating to the issues;

    d.   the argument of the party relating to each legal question;

    e.   the order which is sought from the court.

D. Trials

Short Trials

57. A short trial is a trial that will take 15 court days or less.

Court Schedule

58. Each court location in the region holds trial sittings at different times throughout the calendar year. The trial sittings are listed in the Central South Region's Regional Court Calendar.

Trial Scheduling Court

59. Attendance at trial scheduling court will only be required by the parties where a trial date has not already been set either at the settlement conference or arranged through the trial coordinator as set out below.

60. If a trial date has not been set at the settlement conference, it should be arranged with the trial coordinator.

61. If the parties consent to a trial date or trial sittings, the consent must be filed with the trial coordinator at least three business days before that trial scheduling court date and if done, the parties do not need to attend.

62. If the parties are unable to agree on a trial date, they may speak to the matter at trial scheduling court. As a general rule, trial dates will not be arranged at the trial scheduling court unless counsel and self-represented parties have contacted the trial coordinator and tried to arrange dates in advance.

63. Subject to the practice in Family Court sites, trial scheduling courts in family proceedings are held each month at each court site in the Central South Region; these dates are listed in the Central South Region's Regional Court Calendar.

64. If there is an issue that must be addressed by the presiding judge at trial scheduling court, counsel and self-represented parties are to attend in person. In certain cases, with prior direction from a judge, counsel and/or self-represented parties may attend by telephone conference call. That conference call will take place in the courtroom on the record. A telephone conference call must be arranged through the trial coordinator at least three business days before the date of the trial scheduling court. The party requesting the telephone conference call shall be responsible for the costs associated with it.

Trial Lists

65. Cases that have been placed on the trial list will be deemed ready to proceed.

66. Counsel and parties have a duty to inform the trial coordinator of any pertinent information that may affect the trial (e.g. a case has settled or a change has occurred that will affect the status of the trial).

Trial Adjournment Requests

67. Any request for an adjournment of the trial must be communicated to the trial coordinator immediately. A motion to adjourn shall be brought on a regular weekly motion list. An adjournment can only be granted by order of a judge, even if all parties consent to the adjournment.

Long Trial Sittings

68. All trials which are expected to last longer than 15 days are deemed to be long trials.

69. There are two long trial sittings each year in the Central South Region, usually in March (commencing just after the March School Breaks) and in October. These dates are listed in the Central South Region's Regional Court Calendar.

70. Any matter placed on the long trial list is given a fixed date to commence and a judge will be made available to hear the matter in its entirety. Once a matter is placed on the long trial sittings list and a trial date is fixed, adjournments are rarely granted without significant costs ramifications.

71. Counsel and parties have a duty to inform the trial coordinator of any pertinent information that may affect the trial (e.g. a case has settled or a change has occurred that will affect the status of the trial).

72. All family cases requiring more than 15 days for trial must be referred to the Office of the Regional Senior Justice for possible assignment to a Long Trial. Where a judge determines that a matter should be referred to the long trial list, the judge will endorse the Trial Record and the Trial Scheduling Endorsement Form accordingly and forward the Form to the Office of the Regional Senior Justice.

73. The Office of the Regional Senior Justice will arrange a conference call with all parties or their counsel to assign the case to a particular long trial sittings, may order a schedule to be followed to ensure that the case is ready to proceed on the sittings to which it has been assigned and schedule a trial management conference to be held before the trial date.

74. All motions for an adjournment of a trial on the long trial list, including a consent adjournment, must be made returnable before the Regional Senior Judge or his/her designate.

E. Family Court Sites

75. St. Catharines and Hamilton are Family Court sites; they are the only two Superior Court of Justice locations in the Central South Region where hearings under the *Children and Family Services Act* (child protection cases), Family Responsibility Office cases and fast track cases (under rule 39) are heard.

76. Dates for child protection, Family Responsibility Office and first appearance courts (for fast track cases) are available in the Central South Region's Regional Court Calendar or from the trial coordinator.

77. Dispute Resolution Officer programs are available in St. Catharines and Hamilton. In those locations, the first case conference on a Motion to Change a final order or agreement shall be scheduled before a Dispute Resolution Officer (DRO) in accordance with Part I of the Consolidated Provincial Practice Direction, unless the court orders otherwise.

Part III: Criminal Proceedings

78. Any change regarding the status of a criminal matter must be brought to the immediate attention of the trial coordinator.

79. A reference in this part to a "rule" or "rules" is a reference to the Criminal Proceeding

Rules for the Superior Court of Justice.

A. Committal to Superior Court of Justice

80. Upon committal in the Ontario Court of Justice, the accused will be remanded to the next trial scheduling court (formerly assignment court) in the Superior Court of Justice that is at least three days from the date of the committal.

81. The indictment committing the accused to stand trial shall be filed in the Superior Court of Justice returnable on a fixed date at least three days before the accused's first appearance in the trial scheduling court.

B. Trial Scheduling Court (formerly Assignment Court)

82. Criminal trial scheduling courts are held at each court site in the Central South Region one day per calendar month. These schedules can be found in the Central South Region's Regional Court Calendar, available on the Superior Court of Justice website.

Designations of Counsel

83. Counsel are encouraged to file "designations of counsel" in the Superior Court of Justice at the earliest opportunity to save clients the time and expense of attending court to address scheduling matters at trial scheduling court.

84. A designation filed in the Ontario Court of Justice does not apply in the Superior Court of Justice.

85. An original designation of counsel for the Superior Court of Justice should be filed in advance of trial scheduling court if counsel intends to appear pursuant to the Designation.

Appearance by Telephone Conference Call

86. If there is an issue that must be addressed by the presiding judge at trial scheduling court, counsel may attend in person or, subject to the discretion of the presiding judge, may attend by telephone conference call or any technological means satisfactory to the court that permits the court and all counsel to communicate simultaneously in the courtroom and will be "on the record".

87. A telephone conference call must be arranged through the office of the trial coordinator at least three business days before the date of the appearance in the trial scheduling court. Counsel attending by telephone conference call must give his/her office and cellphone numbers to the trial coordinator and must indicate the number at which he/she will be available for the conference call.

88. Telephone conference calls can be arranged between the court and counsel even when the accused is in custody and is attending by video remand, provided that the judge is satisfied that the conditions of s. 848 of the *Criminal Code* are satisfied.

Video Remands

89. In Kitchener and Hamilton, accused persons who are in custody may elect to appear at trial scheduling court by video remand, unless otherwise directed by a judge.

90. In St. Catharines, an accused who is held at the Niagara Detention Centre may attend by video remand, unless otherwise directed by a judge.

91. Where the accused has not previously appeared before the Superior Court of Justice by video on the indictment before the court, defence counsel or the accused must notify the custodian of the institution where the accused is held that he/she wishes to attend trial scheduling court by video instead of "in person". Thereafter, the accused can simply be adjourned to his or her next appearance to appear by video remand if requested by the accused, unless otherwise directed by a judge.

C. Pre-Trial Conferences in Criminal Cases

92. A pre-trial conference date and time can be arranged by counsel with the trial coordinator and held without a judge's order and prior to the accused's first appearance in trial scheduling court.

93. Where a pre-trial conference has not been scheduled or held prior to the accused's appearance in trial scheduling court, the parties shall schedule a pre-trial conference with the trial coordinator on a date that is at least three business days before the accused's appearance in trial scheduling court; otherwise, the matter will be adjourned to the next trial scheduling court, subject to the discretion of the presiding judge.

94. A pre-trial conference in a criminal matter must be held within 60 days of the order to stand trial in the Superior Court of Justice.

95. The purpose of the pre-trial conference is to discuss the issues in the case, possible resolution of some or all of the issues, the scheduling of pre-trial motions, the scheduling of the trial and any other matter that the pre-trial conference judge feels may promote a fair and expeditious hearing of the charges contained on the indictment.

96. Where the accused is represented by counsel, the pre-trial conference will be held before a judge of the court, in the presence of counsel and not the accused, unless the judge orders the accused to be present, in accordance with rule 28.05(8).

97. Where an accused person is self-represented, the pre-trial conference will be held in a court room closed to the public pursuant to rule 28.05(2). The conference shall be recorded, however, the recording and any transcript of the pre-trial conference will not be made available to anyone without notice to all parties and the prior written approval of the presiding judge or another judge of the court, in accordance with rules 28.05(3) and (4). Anything said in the pre-trial cannot be used for or against an accused during his/her trial.

98. Pre-trial conference reports are to be served and filed with the trial coordinator pursuant to rules 28.04(7) and (8).

99. Crown counsel and counsel of record for each accused must attend the pre-trial conference fully briefed and with specific authority to act on the matter.

100. The judge who presides at the pre-trial conference will not be the trial judge unless the parties consent.

D. Scheduling Trial Dates for Criminal Cases

101. A trial date will not be scheduled until a pre-trial conference has taken place.

102. Trial dates must be canvassed with the trial coordinator before they can be scheduled in trial scheduling court. Counsel wishing to set a trial date must canvass trial dates with the trial coordinator at least three business days prior to trial scheduling court;

otherwise the matter will be adjourned to the next trial scheduling court date to achieve compliance with this rule.

103. If the accused intends to bring a pre-trial application under s. 11(b) of the Charter (unreasonable delay in time to trial), that should be indicated to the trial coordinator and to the trial scheduling court so that the earliest possible trial dates can be identified and offered by the court.

E. Adjournment of Trial or Pre-Trial Applications

104. In the event that the Crown or a defendant should need to seek an adjournment of a trial date or pre-trial application date after the date has been fixed, the trial coordinator and the opposing counsel/party shall immediately be given written notice of the request so that a date can be set for the adjournment application to be heard.

105. A formal notice of application and supporting affidavit for an adjournment must be served and filed in accordance with rules 26.03 and 26.04, unless otherwise directed by a judge.

106. The parties shall attend before the presiding judge on the date and at the time obtained from the trial coordinator. If an accused is in custody, the applicant shall take the appropriate steps to have the accused transported from the custodial institution where he/she is being held to the court house for the attendance before the presiding judge or, alternatively, to attend by video if the technology is available and appropriate and if the accused consents to an appearance by video.

F. Abandonment of Pre-Trial Applications

107. If time has been scheduled for a pre-trial application and the applicant determines that the application will not be necessary, the applicant must immediately serve and file a Notice of Abandonment (Form 9 prescribed under the rules) and also give a copy to the trial coordinator.

G. Non Compliance with Court Ordered Deadlines

108. In the event that a party does not comply with an order or rule of the court stipulating the date by which a party bringing a pre-trial application shall serve and file its materials and/or an order or rule stipulating the date by which a party responding to a pre-trial application must serve and file its materials, the trial coordinator is to be immediately notified.

109. If any party feels that the matter needs to be addressed in open court, the party must inform the trial coordinator, who will advise the parties when the matter is to be spoken to in open court, and the parties shall attend before the presiding judge on the date and at the time assigned. The accused shall also attend before the court at the assigned date and time. If an accused is in custody, the Crown shall take the appropriate steps to have the accused transported from the custodial institution where he/she is being held to the court house for the attendance before the presiding judge.

H. Bail Variations pursuant to section 515.1 of the *Criminal Code*

This section (paragraphs 110 to 115) has been revoked and replaced by part V of the Provincial Practice Direction Regarding Criminal Proceedings.

I. Other Bail Applications

110. Unless the application is under s. 522 or 518(2) of the *Criminal Code*, if an application for bail has never been brought by the accused at any time, it must be brought in the Ontario Court of Justice, even if the accused has been committed for trial in the Superior Court of Justice.

J. Summary Conviction Appeals

111. Summary Conviction Appeals shall be placed on a trial scheduling court list to be spoken to, in accordance with the following timelines.

   a. Defence appeals involving appellants who are out of custody shall be placed on a trial scheduling court list no more than three months from the date of the filing of Notice of Appeal. When the appeal is perfected, the court will assign a hearing date and time.

   b. Crown appeals and defence appeals involving appellants who are in custody on the matter from which the appeal is taken shall be placed on a trial scheduling court list which is no longer than 30 days from the date of filing the appeal.

112. In certain cases, where circumstances require it, counsel or a party may seek leave to argue an appeal without transcripts but by using alternative means, including the digital recording of the event from which the appeal is being brought.

K. 90 Day Detention Reviews

113. Upon receipt of a Notice of Application for a 90 Day Detention Review pursuant to section 525(1) of the *Criminal Code*, the matter will be placed on the trial scheduling court list, in accordance with the procedures set out in the section.

114. If the accused is not represented by counsel,

   a. The 90-Day Detention Review will be heard at the next trial scheduling court or any earlier date that is agreeable to the Crown and the accused.

   b. Notice of this hearing date will be sent to the institution in which the accused is detained and the Crown Attorney's office by the trial coordinator.

   c. Where necessary, the Crown Attorney's office will obtain an Order to Procure Attendance of a Prisoner to have the accused brought to the courthouse for the hearing.

115. If the accused is represented by counsel,

   a. Defence counsel will be contacted by the trial coordinator and asked whether he/she requests a hearing date be set or whether there will be a waiver of the hearing.

   b. If counsel waives the hearing, he/she shall immediately provide the trial coordinator with a written waiver of the hearing signed by the accused or counsel, which the trial coordinator will forward to the institution in which the accused is detained in custody and the Crown Attorney's office.

   c. If counsel indicates that a hearing date is to be set,

      i. The matter will be placed on the next trial scheduling court date list, so that a hearing date will be set by a judge.

    ii.   The accused will attend the trial scheduling court either in person or by video remand where the appropriate technology is available and the accused consents.

    iii.   After the hearing date is set, the trial coordinator will send a copy of the Notice of the Hearing Date to the institution in which the accused is detained.

    iv.   If the date is set in the absence of the accused, where necessary, the Crown Attorney's office will obtain a judge's order to have the accused brought to the courthouse for the trial scheduling court and/or for the hearing.

116.   Counsel and the accused shall attend at the trial scheduling court unless a waiver signed by the accused has been received by the trial coordinator at least three days before trial scheduling court. Counsel may attend by telephone conference call in accordance with paragraphs 86-88.

Part IV: Civil Proceedings

117.   A reference in this part to a "rule" or the "rules" is a reference to the Rules of Civil Procedure.

A. Motions and Applications

118.   In the Central South Region, motions and applications in civil proceedings are classified as "long" or "short" for scheduling purposes.

Short Motions and Applications

119.   A "short" motion or application is one that will be argued by the parties in less than one hour including reply argument (but excluding the time required for the judge to consider the matter and render a decision).

120.   Short motions and applications are heard at the regular motions court during the weeks that the Court is scheduled to sit. The motion or application shall be made returnable to a regularly scheduled motions day. These dates are listed in the Central South Region's Regional Court Calendar on the Superior Court of Justice's website.

Long Motions and Applications

121.   A "long" motion or application is one which is expected to require more than one hour for argument, including reply argument (but excluding the time required by the judge to consider the matter and render a decision).

122.   A date for a long motion or application must be obtained through the trial coordinator. These motions and applications are generally set to be argued during a specified week rather than a specific date, but they are scheduled on a fixed date at certain locations in the Region. The trial coordinator at the specific court site should be contacted to determine the local practice.

123.   The notice of motion or notice of application must be served and filed and made initially returnable to a regularly scheduled motions day in accordance with the rules. This date is an interim date for the matter to be spoken to, until an actual date for the hearing can be obtained from the trial coordinator and confirmed with the opposing party(ies).

a. If the parties can agree to a date/week for the long motion or application to be argued, a confirmation in writing shall be filed with the trial coordinator at least three business days before the return of the originally scheduled motion (i.e., the regularly scheduled motions day). The written confirmation must indicate:

   1. that the parties have agreed to the hearing date;

   2. that the parties are ready to proceed on that date;

   3. the time required for the hearing of the motion or application; and

   4. whether oral evidence may be required.

   Once the written confirmation is received, the motion record will be endorsed to adjourn the matter to the date or week scheduled for the hearing. In that case, counsel or the parties do not have to attend at the originally scheduled motions court.

b. If the parties cannot agree to a date/week for the long motion or application to be argued, all parties must attend the originally scheduled motions court so that a date for the hearing and timetable of events (e.g., dates for responding materials to be filed, productions to be complete, cross-examinations, delivery of factums) can be ordered by the presiding judge at motions court.

124. Where a motion or application is scheduled for a specified week, the trial coordinator will contact parties or their counsel to advise when the matter will be argued during that week. When the matter is called for argument, the matter is expected to proceed.

Timetable for Long Motions and Applications

125. Parties are expected to agree and adhere to a timetable of events prior to a hearing of a long motion or application (e.g., dates for responding materials to be filed, productions to be complete, cross-examinations, delivery of factums, etc.). If an agreed upon or court ordered timetable is not complied with after a date for a long motion or application has been assigned, a party shall bring a motion returnable at an earlier regularly scheduled motions date to have the matter spoken to by all parties.

Factums & Other Material for Motions and Applications

126. A factum is required on a long motion or application. A factum is not required on a short motion or application, although factums are strongly encouraged because they provide significant assistance to the presiding judge. In either case, a factum shall not exceed 20 double spaced typed pages, unless leave is granted.

127. A factum shall include the following:

   a. a statement of the facts which are relevant to the motion or application.

   b. the legal questions to be considered by the court.

   c. the law and prior case law relating to the issues.

   d. the argument of the party relating to each legal question.

   e. the order which is sought from the court.

128. When a factum is prepared, it shall be served and filed pursuant to rules 37.10(6), (7) and (8).

129. In addition, the court strongly encourages parties to deliver an electronic copy of a factum in Word format, at least two business days before the argument of the motion. The factum should be sent to by email to the court location where the motion will be argued:

Hamilton Sopinka: Hamilton.superior.court@ontario.ca
Kitchener: Kitchener.superior.court@ontario.ca
Brantford: Brantford.superior.court@ontario.ca
St. Catharines: St. Catharines.superior.court@ontario.ca
Simcoe: Simcoe.superior.court@ontario.ca
Welland: Welland.superior.court@ontario.ca
Cayuga: Cayuga.superior.court@ontario.ca

The covering email should identify the style of cause, the court file number and the date scheduled for the argument of the motion.

130. Parties are also encouraged to submit draft orders with their motion materials.

131. If case law will be relied on by a party, a book of authorities should be served and filed with the factum with appropriate excerpts from each case highlighted or side barred.

132. For long motions and applications,

    a. Counsel are to consult with each other and where possible file a joint compendium, which shall contain the key material documents to be relied on during oral argument. Where counsel cannot agree on a joint compendium, each will file their own separate compendium, which shall contain the key material documents to be relied on during oral argument. This may include extracts of relevant transcripts, relevant documents, photographs, etc. The compendium should not exceed 30 pages in length.

    b. Counsel are strongly encouraged to deliver an electronic version of their factum, the joint compendium (or separate compendium), and book of authorities on CD, DVD or USB key to the court. These materials may not be sent by email because of the size of the materials. The electronic documents must be submitted in either Word format (.doc or .docx) or text searchable PDF The CD, DVD or USB key should be accompanied by a covering letter which identifies the materials contained on the CD, DVD or USB key, as follows:

USB Key: The cover letter should include a list of the files contained on the USB key, along with the title of proceedings, Court File #, Counsel Name(s), where applicable, and Party Name. If possible, the key should be labelled with the short style of cause and the Court File #.

CD or DVD: The CD or DVD should be labelled with the title of proceedings, Court File #, Counsel Name(s), where applicable, and Party Name. Include a list of the files contained on the CD or DVD in the cover letter.

Confirmation of Motions and Applications

133. Motion and application confirmation forms advise the trial coordinator that the matter will be proceeding as scheduled. As required under rule 37.10.1 and 38.09.1, a Confirmation Form (Form 37B or 38B) must be delivered or faxed to the trial coordinator for all motions and applications no later than 2:00 p.m. three days before the hearing date. A copy must also be faxed or emailed to the other party(ies). Parties

or their counsel must ensure all confirmation forms are fully completed. Failure to do so may result in an adjournment and/or cost sanctions.

134.   Subject to the discretion of the presiding judge, only the documents and material filed by parties or their counsel on the motion and specifically referred to in the confirmation form will be before the court.

Adjournments of Short Motions or Applications

135.   If the trial coordinator receives an updated confirmation form advising that the parties have agreed to a consent adjournment by 2:00 p.m. the day before the short motion or application is returnable, the adjournment will be granted, subject to the discretion of the presiding judge. The updated confirmation form must specify the date to which the matter is to be adjourned, unless the motion has been settled.

136.   Parties or their counsel are not required to attend before the presiding judge if the appropriate information relating to the consent adjournment is provided by 2:00 p.m. the day before the short motion or application is returnable. No confirmations will be accepted after 2:00 p.m. on the day before the motion or application is returnable.

137.   If a consent or contested adjournment is sought after 2:00 pm on the day before the return of the short motion or application, counsel and/or the self-represented party should email or fax the trial coordinator that the motion will be adjourned or a contested request for adjournment will take place. It is the responsibility of parties or their counsel to address the motion in court in these circumstances.

138.   Parties will be permitted three consent adjournments on a short motion or application. If a further adjournment is sought, parties or their counsel are required to attend in person, unless otherwise ordered by a judge.

Adjournment of Long Motions or Applications

139.   The trial coordinator must be immediately advised of any adjournment requests for a long motion or application, and of any settlements prior to the hearing date. In particular,

    a.   If a fixed date has been set for the long motion to be argued and a party wishes an adjournment, that request must be spoken to before a judge. The party must bring a motion on a regularly scheduled motions day to obtain the adjournment. If the adjournment is granted, the motion will be assigned to the Long Motions List.

    b.   If a long motion to be argued during a given week has been adjourned, and parties consent to a further adjournment, the long motion may be adjourned by filing a consent with the trial coordinator at least three business days before the scheduled week.

    c.   If a long motion to be argued during a given week has been adjourned, and parties do not consent to a further adjournment, the party seeking an adjournment shall bring a motion before a judge who is presiding at a regularly scheduled motions day. If the adjournment is granted, the motion will be assigned to the Long Motions List.

Ex Parte Motions

140.   All *ex parte* motions in writing must be filed with the court office with payment of

the applicable filing fee. They will be placed before a judge in chambers for review in the normal course. *Ex parte* motions may not be "filed" by delivering them to the trial coordinator for a judge to review, or by sending them by email or otherwise directly to a judge of the court.

Consent Orders in Civil Motions

141. Where parties or their counsel have agreed to a consent order in a civil motion scheduled for hearing, a fully executed consent, together with a draft order, must be sent to the trial coordinator with a motion Confirmation Form (Form 37B) by 2 p.m. three days before the scheduled hearing, as required by rule 37.10.1. The materials will be put before the presiding judge in chambers for review. If satisfied that the order should issue, the presiding judge will sign the draft order. The moving party or their counsel will be notified by the court that the order is ready to be picked up and entered. Unless otherwise advised by the court, parties or their counsel do not have to attend at court on the scheduled hearing date, which shall be vacated.

142. Where parties or their counsel have resolved a motion scheduled for hearing by way of a fully executed consent and draft order *after the motion confirmation form is filed*, the trial coordinator should be advised as soon as possible. The moving party or their counsel may attend at 9:30 a.m. on the morning scheduled for the hearing of the motion, and leave the consent and draft order with the courtroom registrar. The consent and draft order will be put before the presiding judge in chambers for review. If the presiding judge is satisfied that the order should issue, he/she will sign the draft order. The registrar will return the signed order to counsel to be entered.

B. Construction Liens

143. All construction lien actions will proceed in a summary fashion as envisioned by the *Construction Lien Act*, R.S.O. 1990, c. 30.

C. Trials

144. A civil action is set down for trial by filing a trial record. The filing of a trial record with proof of service shall be accompanied by a Trial Data Form.

Court Schedule

145. Each court location in the region holds trial sittings at different times throughout the calendar year. Trial scheduling courts for short civil trials (15 days or less) are held monthly in each of the court locations in the Central South Region. Dates for trial scheduling court and trial sittings can be found in the Central South Region's Regional Court Calendar.

Short Trials

146. A short civil trial is a trial that is expected to be completed in 15 days or less.

Short Trials – Trial Scheduling Court

147. Upon filing of the trial record, the registrar shall provide the listing party or their counsel with the notice of trial scheduling court. Within five days of receipt, the listing party or their counsel must serve the notice of trial scheduling court on all other parties or their counsel.

148. In advance of trial scheduling court, the listing party is expected to obtain available

trial dates from the trial coordinator and canvass those dates with the other parties. Parties are then expected to agree upon a date among the available trial dates.

149. Dates for short trials will then be assigned in one of the following methods:

a. Where the parties agree to a trial date, they may file a written consent with the trial coordinator requesting that the agreed upon trial date/week be assigned to the case. If the trial coordinator receives the consent by 2:00 p.m. three business days before the scheduled trial scheduling court the parties do not need to attend trial scheduling court. The trial record will be endorsed in chambers.

b. Where the parties do not agree to a trial date, they must attend to speak to the matter at trial scheduling court so that a trial date/week will be assigned.

150. Consent procedural orders, including consent adjournments of the trial scheduling court date, will not be granted at trial scheduling court.

151. All actions may be adjourned on consent to another trial scheduling court through the trial coordinator in advance of the trial scheduling court date. Parties or their counsel must file or fax a written consent for the adjournment, signed on behalf of all parties, with the trial coordinator by 2:00 p.m. three business days before the trial scheduling court date. An action listed on the trial scheduling court list may only be adjourned two times on consent without the parties having to appear personally at trial scheduling court. After two adjournments have been granted, all parties must attend trial scheduling court in person by or telephone conference call for a further adjournment.

152. Absent a consent adjournment, or a consent to place a matter on a trial sittings of the court, parties or their counsel are expected to appear in person at trial scheduling court, although they may, in the discretion of the presiding judge, attend by telephone conference call which will be received in the courtroom and will be "on the record". A telephone conference call must be arranged through the trial coordinator by 2:00 p.m. Three business days before the date of the trial scheduling court. Counsel attending by telephone conference call must give their office and cell phone numbers to the trial coordinator and must indicate the number at which they will be available for the conference call.

Long Trials

153. A long civil trial is a trial that is expected to take more than 15 days.

Procedure for Obtaining Long Trial Dates

154. Any matter placed on the long trial list is given a fixed date to commence and a judge will be available to hear the matter in its entirety. Once a matter is placed on the long trial list and a trial date is fixed, adjournments are rarely granted without significant costs ramifications.

155. All civil cases requiring more than 15 days in length for trial must be referred to the Office of the Regional Senior Justice. After a trial record is filed, cases are referred to the Office of the Regional Senior Justice for possible assignment to a long trial list in one of three ways:

a. A judge may determine that a short trial should be referred to the long trial list. The judge will endorse the trial record accordingly and refer the case to the Office of the Regional Senior Justice.

b. If all parties agree that a trial will last more than 15 days, a consent request for a long trial date can be delivered to the Office of the Regional Senior Justice.

c. If all parties do not agree that a trial will last more than 15 days, any party may write to the Office of the Regional Senior Justice seeking a teleconference to determine whether the matter should be placed on the long trial list.

156. Where a matter is referred to the Office of the Regional Senior Justice for possible assignment to a long trial list, parties or their counsel must complete the Long Trial Sittings Intake Form, available on the Superior Court of Justice website and from the registrar in each courtroom or from the trial coordinator's office. The form must be submitted to the Office of the Regional Senior Judge of the Superior Court of Justice, 45 Main Street East, Suite 721, Hamilton, ON, L8N 2B7 within 10 days of a party's request for a long trial date, or an order of judge referring the case to the Office of the Regional Senior Justice for assignment of a long trial date.

157. The Office of the Regional Senior Justice will then arrange a conference call with parties or their counsel to assign the case to a particular long trial sitting and order a schedule to be followed to ensure that the case is ready for trial at the sittings to which it has been assigned. The matter will be determined by the Regional Senior Justice in a telephone conference call arranged with counsel or, if one of the parties is self-represented, at an "in court" attendance or by a telephone conference call which will be recorded by a court reporter.

Adjournment of Cases Set Down for Trial – Short and Long Trials

158. Once an action is placed on a short or long trial list, parties are deemed ready to proceed to trial as per rule 48.07. Cases scheduled for trial will proceed during a scheduled sitting week or designated trial week, or in the case of long trials, on the date scheduled for commencement of the long trial. Where a case is scheduled to proceed during a sitting week, parties or their counsel are expected to proceed when called.

159. All requests to adjourn a short trial or a long trial must be communicated immediately to the trial coordinator's office.

160. To obtain an adjournment of a short trial, including a consent adjournment, a motion must be served and filed to be argued before a judge at a regular weekly motions day or at the monthly trial scheduling court, supported by affidavit evidence indicating the reason for the requested adjournment. An adjournment can only be granted by the order of a judge, even if all parties agree to the adjournment.

161. To obtain an adjournment of a long trial, including a consent adjournment, a motion must be served and filed, supported by affidavit evidence indicating the reason for the requested adjournment. The motion shall be returnable before the Regional Senior Judge or his/her designate.

162. Counsel and parties are responsible to advise the trial coordinator of the status of an upcoming trial. Some examples of the information which must be communicated to the trial coordinator, as soon as it is apparent to a party, include:

a. settlement of the action or pending settlement of the action;

b. whether it is likely that a request for adjournment will be sought;

c. whether there will be any motions at the outset of the trial;

d. whether the parties may consent to dispensing with a jury;

e. the need for an interpreter to assist with the testimony of one or more witnesses; and

f. the name of a particular judge who may not be able to preside due to a potential conflict.

Restoring an Action to a Trial List

163. An action that is struck off a trial list must be restored by order of a judge, obtained at a motion, pursuant to rule 48.11. An affidavit of counsel detailing the reason for the action being removed from the trial list, along with the current status of the action, shall be filed in support of the motion. If an action is restored to the trial list, the order shall include a specific trial scheduling court date or trial sittings, or in the case of a long trial, it shall be referred to the Office of the Regional Senior Justice.

Pre Trial Conferences – for Short and Long Trials

164. Pre-trials are mandatory in all civil cases for both short and long trials. Pre-trials are scheduled for 45 minute intervals. Parties or their counsel must obtain pre-trial dates from the trial coordinator and when scheduling the pre-trial, advise if additional time is required for complex actions. Failure to provide this information in a timely manner may result in an adjournment of the pre-trial and possible cost sanctions.

165. Pre-trial conference briefs must be filed, with proof of service five business days prior to the pre-trial date, pursuant to rule 50.04. Failure to comply may result in cancellation of the pre-trial and possible cost sanctions. Self-represented parties are not excused from filing a pre-trial conference brief.

166. Pre-trial conference briefs shall contain no more than 20 double spaced typed pages. Medical reports, contracts, experts' reports and other documents are not to be attached. Relevant excerpts from such documents should be included in the typed pre-trial brief. The documents should be brought to the pre-trial conference in case the presiding judge needs to review one or more of them. The first page or two of the pre-trial brief should contain an "executive summary" of the case so that the presiding judge can quickly get a "snapshot' of the facts and issues.

167. Parties are also strongly encouraged to deliver an electronic copy of the pre-trial conference brief to the email account at the Superior Court office where the pre-trial will be held at least five days before the pre-trial. Those email addresses are found at paragraph 135 above. The covering email should indicate the title of proceedings, the court file number, for which party the pre-trial conference brief is being submitted, counsel's name or the party's name where the party is self-represented, and the date of the pre-trial conference.

168. Counsel of record, or counsel fully briefed with full authority, must attend the pre-trial with their clients, unless there is a prior order excusing counsel and/or the instructing client from attending.

169. All parties are required to participate at the pre-trial conference unless otherwise ordered by the court in advance as per rule 50.05.

170. Arrangements for a pre-trial conference by telephone for any party must be made in writing and received at least 10 days in advance so that the presiding judge can de-

termine if such a telephone attendance is appropriate.

D. Transfer of Cases

From Central South Region to another Region

171. If a party seeks to transfer an action commenced in the Central South Region to another region, a motion to transfer shall be filed in the court office of the county to which the transfer is sought (the receiving region), as per rules 4.05(2)4 and 13.1.02(3.1).

172. In the Central East, Central West and Toronto regions, the motion to transfer will be heard by the Regional Senior Justice, in writing. Please refer to section B of part IV of the Consolidated Provincial Practice Direction which sets out the process for motions to transfer a civil proceeding to the Central East, Central West, Central South and Toronto regions.

173. If the transfer is approved, the signed order must be issued and entered in the court location where the action was started and a requisition must then be made to transfer the file to the court location in the receiving region which has been approved in the signed transfer order.

From another Region to Central South

174. If a party seeks to transfer an action commenced in another region to the Central South Region, a motion to transfer shall be filed in the court office of the county within Central South to which the transfer is sought, as per rules 4.05(2)4 and 13.1.02(3.1).

175. The motion shall be heard by the Regional Senior Judge of the Central South Region, in writing. A copy of the materials and evidence of payment of the filing fee shall be sent to the Office of the Regional Senior Justice of the Central South Region. Please refer to section B of part IV of the Consolidated Provincial Practice Direction which sets out the process for motions to transfer a civil proceeding to the Central East, Central West, Central South and Toronto regions.

176. If the transfer is approved, the signed order must be issued and entered in the court location where the action was started and a requisition must then be made to transfer the file to the court location in the Central South Region which has been approved in the signed transfer order.

From one Superior Court location to another Superior Court location in the same Region

177. A motion to transfer a civil case from one location in the Central South Region to another location in the Central South Region should be brought in the court location in which the action was commenced.

178. If it is a consent motion, the motion shall be considered by the Local Administrative Judge at that court site. If it appears appropriate to transfer the case, before signing the order, the Local Administrative Judge will verify with the Local Administrative Judge of the court location to which the action is to be transferred that the case can be accommodated at that court site.

179. If it is not a consent motion, the motion shall be made returnable at a weekly motions

court. If the presiding judge determines that the transfer order should be made, before signing the order he/she will verify with the Local Administrative Judge of the court location to which the action is to be transferred that the case can be accommodated at that court site.

E. Mortgage Proceedings

180. Pursuant to rule 13.1.01(3), Brantford, Cayuga, Hamilton, Kitchener, St. Catharines, Simcoe, and Welland are designated as places where mortgage proceedings may be commenced for property located anywhere in the Central South Region.

F. Class Actions: Proceedings under the *Class Proceedings Act, 1992*

181. Counsel or parties commencing a class action to be issued in the Central South Region are urged to read part II of the Consolidated Provincial Practice Direction, which applies to class proceedings throughout the province.

182. In the Central South Region, two judges have been designated as Class Action judges. The names of assigned Class Proceedings judges may be obtained from the office of the Regional Manager, Judicial Services for the Central South Region (telephone number (905) 645-5323; fax number (905) 645-5374). The Regional Manager should be notified in writing when a class action has been or is about to be commenced in the Central South Region.

G. Proceedings Heard in Hamilton by a Registrar in Bankruptcy

183. As of March 1, 2020 new Bankruptcy and Insolvency Act (Canada) matters to be determined by a Registrar in Bankruptcy under section 192 of the Act shall be filed and heard in Hamilton, provided that the matter originated in one of the following areas:

- Hamilton
- Norfolk
- Haldimand
- Brant
- Niagara

184. Matters originating in one of the above areas, but commenced in Toronto prior to March 1, 2020, will continue to be heard in Toronto, unless the court orders otherwise.

Dated: June 1, 2016

Amended: March 1, 2020; May 17, 2019; July 1, 2018 (Part II B [para. 13], Part II C [paras. 40, 43, 55]); May 1, 2017 (revocation of part III H (paragraphs 110 – 115))

Geoffrey B. Morawetz
Chief Justice
Superior Court of Justice (Ontario)

Harrison J. Arrell
Regional Senior Judge
Central South Region

D. Practice Direction Concerning Civil Proceedings in Central East Region (Effective: January 1, 2017)

Effective January 1, 2017

This Practice Direction applies to all civil proceedings in the Superior Court of Justice, Central East Region, effective January 1, 2017. It *supersedes* all previous region-specific Practice Directions concerning civil proceedings for the Central East Region issued prior to January 1, 2017, which are hereby revoked.

Counsel and parties are advised to refer to the relevant Parts of the Consolidated Provincial Practice Direction as well as the Consolidated Practice Direction for Divisional Court Proceedings which are available on the Superior Court of Justice website at: www.ontariocourts.ca/scj.

Table of Contents

Part I: General

1. In addition to this Practice Direction, counsel and parties to civil proceedings are advised to refer to the Consolidated Provincial Practice Direction.

2. In this Practice Direction, any reference to "counsel" includes a self-represented party.

Part II: Motions to Transfer

3. All requests for a transfer of a civil proceeding from one county to another shall be pursuant to rule 13.1.02 of the *Rules of Civil Procedure*. The motion will be granted or denied based on its merits. Counsel and parties are advised to refer to Part III of the Con-

solidated Provincial Practice Direction which prescribes specific requirements for motions to transfer a civil proceeding.

Part III: Mortgage Proceedings

4.   Pursuant to rule 13.1.01(3) of the *Rules of Civil Procedure*, Barrie or Oshawa are designated as the places where mortgage proceedings may be commenced for property located anywhere in the Central East Region.

Part IV: Construction Liens

5.   Construction lien pre-trials will be scheduled at intervals at the Newmarket, Barrie, and Oshawa judicial centres. To ensure continuity and efficient management, the pre-trials will be assigned to designated judges at each of the centres.

6.   Construction lien pre-trials in Peterborough, Cobourg and Lindsay will be scheduled on an "as needed basis" with the Trial Co-ordinator.

7.   Construction lien pre-trials from Bracebridge will be scheduled to be heard in Barrie.

8.   In order to accommodate counsel, the pre-trials in construction lien matters will be scheduled on different weeks at each of the judicial centres. For a list of the scheduled dates for the pre-trials, and telephone numbers of the Trial Co-ordinator for each judicial centre, please see the "Court Locations & Schedules" section of the Court's website at: ontariocourts.ca/scj/locations/.

A.   First Pre-Trial Conference

9.   It is preferred that counsel who will appear at trial and their clients attend the first pre-trial conference. Every effort will be made to discuss a resolution of the proceeding at this first appearance. In the event that a settlement cannot be achieved at this stage, then the pre-trial judge shall order:

    i.   the exchange of Affidavits of Documents together with a copy of each document referred to in Schedule A;

    ii.   the date for examinations, as well as the answering of undertakings;

    iii.   the date for a motion relating to refusals on examinations and any other contemplated motions;

    iv.   that a "Scott" Schedule and any responding Schedule be prepared and delivered prior to the next appearance date;

    v.   the next pre-trial date; and,

    vi.   that Plaintiff's counsel take out an order incorporating the above-noted terms.

B.   Second Pre-Trial Conference

10.   It is mandatory that all counsel who will appear at trial and their respective clients attend the second (and, if necessary, any subsequent) pre-trial conference.

11.   The pre-trial judge will discuss and assess the progress of the proceeding and will consider an appropriate award of costs for non-compliance with the First Appearance Order.

12.   At the second pre-trial conference, the parties will be required to detail their respec-

tive positions with supporting documentation.

13. In the event that the proceeding is not settled at the conclusion of this second or subsequent pre-trial conference, the pre-trial conference judge shall fix a date for trial within the Civil Trial Sittings.

Part V: Ex Parte Motions in Writing

14. All ex parte motions in writing must be filed with the court office and payment of the applicable filing fee made. They will be put before a judge in chambers for review in the normal course. Ex parte motions may not be "filed" by delivering them to the Trial Co-ordinator for a judge to review, or by sending them by email or otherwise directly to a judge of the court.

Part VI: Civil Proceedings in Newmarket

A. Elimination of "Placeholder" Motions

15. Where counsel or a party has booked with the Trial Co-ordinator a date for the hearing of a motion, a Notice of Motion must be filed (and the necessary filing fee paid) no later than 10 days after the motion date is booked. Unless a Notice of Motion is filed (and the necessary payment made) within this time period, any booked motion date will be vacated without notice to counsel or the moving party. The booking of "placeholder" motions will cease.

B. Civil Motions Consent Orders

16. Where counsel and/or the parties have agreed to a consent order in a civil motion scheduled for hearing, a fully executed consent, together with a draft order, shall be emailed to the court at Newmarket.SCJ.TC@ontario.ca, along with the motion confirmation form (Form 37B) by 2 pm three days before the scheduled hearing, as required by rule 37.10.1. The materials will be put before the presiding judge in chambers for review. If satisfied that the order should issue, the presiding judge will sign the draft order. Counsel for the moving party will be notified by the court that the order is ready to be picked up and entered. Unless otherwise advised by the court, counsel and/or the parties do not have to attend at court on the scheduled hearing date, which shall be vacated.

17. Where counsel and/or the parties have resolved a motion scheduled for hearing by way of a fully executed consent and draft order, after the motion confirmation form is filed, counsel for the moving party may attend at 9:00 a.m. on the morning scheduled for hearing of the motion, and file the consent and draft order with the courtroom registrar. The consent and draft order will be put before the presiding judge in chambers for review. If the presiding judge is satisfied that the order should issue, he/she will sign the draft order. The registrar will return the signed order to counsel to be entered. Counsel is not required to remain in the courtroom after receiving the signed order.

Part VII: Long Motions and Motions for Summary Judgment in Barrie, Bracebridge, Cobourg, Lindsay, Newmarket, Oshawa and Peterborough

18. Dates for all long motions (exceeding one hour) and all motions for summary judgment must be obtained from the Trial Co-ordinator.

19. For all motions exceeding one hour and for all summary judgment motions, counsel

(and parties who are self-represented) shall file a factum no longer than 25 pages. In addition to a factum, counsel are to consult with each other and where possible file a Joint Compendium, which shall contain the key material documents to be relied on during oral argument. Where counsel cannot agree on a Joint Compendium, each will file their own separate Compendium, which shall contain the key material documents to be relied on during oral argument. The Compendium should not exceed 30 pages in length.

20. Where counsel intends to rely on case law, he or she shall file a case brief containing only those cases that will be referred to in oral argument, with the relevant passages side-barred.

21. Counsel are encouraged to file an electronic version of the factum, the Joint Compendium (or separate Compendium), and case brief on CD, DVD or USB key. The electronic documents must be submitted in either Microsoft Word format (.doc or .docx) or text searchable PDF format. The CD, DVD or USB key should be accompanied by a covering letter which identifies the materials contained on the CD, DVD or USB key, as follows:

> **USB Key**: The cover letter should include a list of the files contained on the USB key, along with the title of proceedings, Court File #, Counsel Name(s), where applicable, and Party Name. If possible, the key should be labelled with the short style of cause and the Court File #.

> **CD or DVD**: The CD or DVD should be labelled with the title of proceedings, Court File #, Counsel Name(s), where applicable, and Party Name. Include a list of the files contained on the CD or DVD in the cover letter.

Part VIII: Pre-Trial Conferences

A. Purpose

22. The purpose of this Part is to ensure that civil cases proceed to trial only after they have been properly pre-tried and endorsed as ready for trial by the presiding pre-trial conference judge. This will be achieved by the assignment of civil pre-trial conferences to judges who are experienced in civil litigation matters. Those judges will conduct all pre-trial conferences in the Region. It will also be achieved by the establishment of a Central East Trial Scheduling Court ("CETSC"), which will be held in Oshawa and presided over by the Regional Senior Judge or a judge designated by him or her. The CETSC replaces all other Trial Scheduling Courts in the Region and they will be discontinued.

B. Obtaining a Pre-Trial Conference Date

23. All civil cases will proceed to a pre-trial conference once they are certified ready for trial by the filing of a Trial Record.

24. The existing Trial Scheduling Notice and Consent Form is replaced with a Pre-Trial Conference Confirmation Form. Counsel are required to contact the Trial Co-ordinator in the centre where the action is outstanding, to book a pre-trial conference date that is agreed to by all counsel. Counsel are to record this date on the Pre-Trial Conference Confirmation Form, and transmit it to the Trial Co-ordinator within seven days of booking the pre-trial conference date to the appropriate court location.

Barrie/Bracebridge: Barrie.SCJ.TC@ontario.ca (705-739-6099)

Newmarket: Newmarket.SCJ.TC@ontario.ca (905-853-4863)
Oshawa: Oshawa.SCJ.TC@ontario.ca (905-743-2652)
Peterborough/Cobourg/Lindsay: Peterborough.SCJ.TC@ontario.ca (705-745-3526)

25. In the event that counsel who seeks a pre-trial conference date cannot obtain the agreement of opposing counsel to one of the dates provided by the Trial Co-ordinator, counsel seeking to book the pre-trial conference shall notify the Trial Co-ordinator who will add the case to the next available CETSC.

26. All counsel are required to appear at the CETSC. Counsel opposing the fixing of the pre-trial date must establish good reason why the pre-trial conference cannot proceed on one of the dates provided by the Trial Co-ordinator. The presiding judge shall fix a date for the pre-trial conference. If the presiding judge is satisfied that no good reason was established for counsel's failure to agree to one of the dates provided by the Trial Co-ordinator, the presiding judge may make a costs award against the offending party.

C. Pre-Trial Conference Memorandums

27. Counsel shall file their pre-trial conference memorandums with the court administration office in the centre where the action is outstanding, no later than five (5) business days before the pre-trial conference. Pre-trial memorandums will *not* be accepted for late filing. This filing requirement is intended to ensure that the pre-trial conference judge has adequate time to review the pre-trial conference memorandums in advance of the pre-trial conference.

28. If counsel fails to file the pre-trial conference memorandum in time, the pre-trial conference will be cancelled by the Trial Co-ordinator. Cancellation of the pre-trial conference, absent exceptional circumstances, may result in a costs award against the offending party.

29. If a pre-trial conference is cancelled because counsel for a party failed to file the pre-trial conference memorandum in time, counsel for any other party to the action may unilaterally fix a fresh pre-trial conference date with the Trial Co-ordinator.

30. Where a second pre-trial conference date is cancelled due again to late filing of the pre-trial conference memorandum, the Trial Co-ordinator will put the case to be spoken to at the next available CETSC. All counsel are required to attend the CETSC.

D. The Pre-Trial Conference

31. To ensure that adequate time is allocated for a meaningful pre-trial conference, generally no more than four (4) pre-trial conferences per day will be scheduled before a single judge.

32. The pre-trial conference judge will, in accordance with rule 52.07, assist the parties in working toward a full or partial resolution of the issues in the action. In addition, the pre-trial conference judge will make such case management orders as are appropriate to ensure that the case is ready for trial. This may necessitate the holding of more than one pre-trial conference in a case.

33. The pre-trial conference judge will endorse that the case is ready for trial only when he or she is satisfied of this. The pre-trial conference judge will complete a Pre-Trial Conference Report, which will be provided to the judge presiding at the CETSC, and

1320

also to the trial judge. It will include the estimated length of the trial.

E. Central East Trial Scheduling Court

34. Once the pre-trial conference judge has endorsed that the case is ready for trial, the case will be listed for appearance in the CETSC. The CETSC will take place in Oshawa at least once per month, usually on the last Thursday of the month. It will be presided over by the Regional Senior Judge or his or her designate.

35. Counsel of record for each party is expected to attend the CETSC. While it is preferable that counsel attend in person, attendance by telephone conference call at pre-booked times during the course of the day is permissible. Arrangements for attendance by telephone conference call can be made through the Trial Co-ordinator in the centre where the action is outstanding, or the Oshawa Trial Co-ordinator, no later than the Friday before the scheduled CETSC. In the event that counsel of record is not available to attend in person or by telephone conference call, a fully instructed lawyer acting as counsel's agent must attend the CETSC in person.

36. The purpose of the CETSC is to confirm the length of the trial and to ensure that the case is ready for trial. Civil cases will be listed to be tried at the twice-yearly regional Civil Trial Sittings. The judge presiding at the CETSC will canvass with counsel on which Civil Trial Sittings list the action will be placed. If counsel has more than one case on a particular Civil Trial Sittings list, the presiding judge must be informed of all other cases counsel has on that list and their present status. The purpose of such enquiry is to avoid the adjournments that result when counsel set multiple cases for trial at the same Civil Trial Sittings.

37. If a trial is estimated to take longer than three weeks, the judge presiding at the CETSC will decide whether the case can be tried within the twice-yearly Civil Trial Sittings, or whether the Regional Senior Judge should be asked to assign a fixed trial date.

38. A further purpose of the CETSC is to canvass whether there is any reason why a case cannot be tried at any of the courthouses in the region, so that courtroom and judicial resources can be maximized. Counsel and the parties will be required to show good reason why a case must be tried at a particular courthouse.

F. Adjournments

39. Counsel should be prepared to proceed to trial during the Civil Trial Sittings to which the case has been assigned or on the fixed date set. Any requests to adjourn a trial must be brought at a CETSC. Counsel should expect that adjournments sought when the case is called for trial will not be granted, absent compelling reasons.

Dated: January 1, 2017

Heather J. Smith - Chief Justice (Superior Court of Justice (Ontario))

Michelle Fuerst - Regional Senior Judge (Superior Court of Justice, Central East Region)

D.1 Practice Advisory Concerning Long Motions in the Central East Region (Effective: June 19, 2017)

Effective June 19, 2017

This Practice Advisory applies to all civil, family and stand-alone pre-trial criminal long motions (e.g. 11b applications) that are scheduled for one or more hours. It *supplements* existing practice directions, including:

- Consolidated Practice Direction Concerning Family Cases in Central East Region (Regional) *Effective May 1, 2016*

- Practice Direction Concerning Civil Proceedings in the Central East Region (Regional) *Effective January 1, 2017*

Counsel and parties are advised to refer to the relevant parts of the Consolidated Provincial Practice Direction and any other applicable Central East region-specific Practice Directions or Guides, which are available on the Superior Court of Justice website at: www.ontariocourts.ca/scj.

Requirement to File Electronic Copies of Documents on USB

For civil, family and criminal long motions, parties must file electronic copies of their materials on a USB stick, in addition to paper copies. The pilot excludes child protection cases, criminal third party records applications, and criminal long motions heard during trial. Only stand-alone pre-trial criminal long motions (e.g. 11b applications) are included.

The USB must include a copy of the motion materials, including the factum, where required. *Paper copies of the motion materials must also be filed as required by the rules of court.*

Acceptable Formats for Electronic Documents

Two electronic versions of *each* document are required:

1. Electronic One copy must be created using Microsoft Word (.DOC), and

2. One copy must be saved in PDF format. Documents converted from Word to PDF are preferable to scanned PDF documents.

Electronic Documents Naming Convention

In order to assist court staff in storing the electronic materials and the judge in accessing them, when saving electronic documents on the USB, each document must be named using one of the prefixes below, followed by the short style of cause and court file number (e.g. MPL Brown v. Brown CV-17-12345-0000):

Motion Record (containing the Notice of Motion)

MPL = Motion Record of the Plaintiff
MDE = Motion Record of the Defendant
MDM = Motion Record of the Defendant to Counterclaim
MTP = Motion Record of the Third Party
M4P = Motion Record of the Fourth Party
M5P = Motion Record of the Fifth Party
M6P = Motion Record of the Sixth Party
M7P = Motion Record of the Seventh Party

MAP = Motion Record of the Applicant
MRP = Motion Record of the Respondent
MIN = Motion Record of the Intervener
MAN = Motion Record of the Agency (Agency/Person/Special Interest)
MSL = Motion Record of the Solicitor (under the *Solicitors Act*)
MCL = Motion Record of the Client (under the *Solicitors Act*)
MNP = Motion Record of a Non-party

All relevant prior court orders and endorsements *(if not already included in the Motion Record)*
    COE = Court Orders and Endorsements
Note: Include only court orders and judge's endorsements that relate to the long motion.

Affidavits

AFPL = Affidavit of or on behalf of the Plaintiff
AFDE = Affidavit of or on behalf of the Defendant
AFDM = Affidavit of or on behalf of the Defendant to Counterclaim
AFTP = Affidavit of or on behalf of the Third Party
AF4P = Affidavit of or on behalf of the Fourth Party
AF5P = Affidavit of or on behalf of the Fifth Party
AF6P = Affidavit of or on behalf of the Sixth Party
AF7P = Affidavit of or on behalf of the Seventh Party
AFAP = Affidavit of or on behalf of the Applicant
AFRP = Affidavit of or on behalf of the Respondent
AFIN = Affidavit of or on behalf of the Intervener
AFAN = Affidavit of or on behalf of the Agency (Agency/Person/Special Interest)
AFSL = Affidavit of or on behalf of the Solicitor (under the *Solicitors Act*)
AFCL = Affidavit of or on behalf of the Client (under the *Solicitors Act*)
AFNP = Affidavit of or on behalf of a Non-party

Affidavits of Service/Proof of Service

AFSPL = Affidavit of Service or Proof of Service of or on behalf of the Plaintiff
AFSDE = Affidavit of Service or Proof of Service of or on behalf of the Defendant
AFSDM = Affidavit of Service or Proof of Service of or on behalf of the Defendant to Counterclaim
AFSTP = Affidavit of Service or Proof of Service of or on behalf of the Third Party
AFS4P = Affidavit of Service or Proof of Service of or on behalf of the Fourth Party
AFS5P = Affidavit of Service or Proof of Service of or on behalf of the Fifth Party
AFS6P = Affidavit of Service or Proof of Service of or on behalf of the Sixth Party
AFS7P = Affidavit of Service or Proof of Service of or on behalf of the Seventh Party
AFSAP = Affidavit of Service or Proof of Service of or on behalf of the Applicant
AFSRP = Affidavit of Service or Proof of Service of or on behalf of the Respondent
AFSIN = Affidavit of Service or Proof of Service of or on behalf of the Intervener
AFSAN = Affidavit of Service or Proof of Service of or on behalf of the Agency (Agency/Person/Special Interest)

AFSSL = Affidavit of Service or Proof of Service of or on behalf of the Solicitor (under the *Solicitors Act*)

AFSCL = Affidavit of Service or Proof of Service of or on behalf of the Client (under the *Solicitors Act*)

AFSNP = Affidavit of Service or Proof of Service of or on behalf of a Non-party

Book of Authorities

BAPL = Book of Authorities of the Plaintiff

BADE = Book of Authorities of the Defendant

BADM = Book of Authorities of the Defendant to Counterclaim

BATP = Book of Authorities of the Third Party

BA4P = Book of Authorities of the Fourth Party

BA5P = Book of Authorities of the Fifth Party

BA6P = Book of Authorities of the Sixth Party

BA7P = Book of Authorities of the Seventh Party

BAAP = Book of Authorities of the Applicant

BARP = Book of Authorities of the Respondent

BAIN = Book of Authorities of the Intervener

BAAN = Book of Authorities of the Agency (Agency/Person/Special Interest)

BASL = Book of Authorities of the Solicitor (under the *Solicitors Act*)

BACL = Book of Authorities of the Client (under the *Solicitors Act*)

BANP = Book of Authorities of Non-party

Factums, including Amended and Supplementary

FPL = Factum of the Plaintiff

FDE = Factum of the Defendant

FDM = Factum of the Defendant to Counterclaim

FTP = Factum of the Third Party

F4P = Factum of the Fourth Party

F5P = Factum of the Fifth Party

F6P = Factum of the Sixth Party

F7P = Factum of the Seventh Party

FAP = Factum of the Applicant

FRP = Factum of the Respondent

FIN = Factum of the Intervener

FAN = Factum of the Agency (Agency/Person/Special Interest)

FSL = Factum of the Solicitor (under the *Solicitors Act*)

FCL = Factum of the Client (under the *Solicitors Act*)

FNP = Factum of a Non-party

Note: Add the suffix AM or SUP to indicate Amended or Supplemental Factum

Costs Outline

COPL = Cost Outline of the Plaintiff
CODE = Cost Outline of the Defendant
CODM = Cost Outline of the Defendant to Counterclaim
COTP = Cost Outline of the Third Party
CO4P = Cost Outline of the Fourth Party
CO5P = Cost Outline of the Fifth Party
CO6P = Cost Outline of the Sixth Party
CO7P = Cost Outline of the Seventh Party
COAP = Cost Outline of the Applicant
CORP = Cost Outline of the Respondent
COIN = Cost Outline of the Intervener
COAN = Cost Outline of the Agency (Agency/Person/Special Interest)
COSL = Cost Outline of the Solicitor (under the *Solicitors Act*)
COCL = Cost Outline of the Client (under the *Solicitors Act*)
CONP = Cost Outline of a non-party

Transcripts

TRN = Transcript

Compendiums

CPL = Compendium of the Plaintiff
CDE = Compendium of the Defendant
CDM = Compendium of the Defendant to Counterclaim
CTP = Compendium of the Third Party
C4P = Compendium of the Fourth Party
C5P = Compendium of the Fifth Party
C6P = Compendium of the Sixth Party
C7P = Compendium of the Seventh Party
CAP = Compendium of the Applicant
CRP = Compendium of the Respondent
CIN = Compendium of the Intervener
CAN = Compendium of the Agency (Agency/Person/Special Interest)
CSL = Compendium of the Solicitor (under the *Solicitors Act*)
CCL = Compendium of the Client (under the *Solicitors Act*)
CNP = Compendium of a Non-party

Note: When there is a joint compendium filed, suffix the file name with the parties (i.e. PL for plaintiff; DE for defendant, DM defendant to counterclaim, etc.)

Note: When there are multiple documents of the same type filed, suffix the file name with 001, 002, 003, 004, 005, etc.

Counsel and parties may also refer to the Guide Concerning e-Delivery of Documents in the Ontario Superior Court of Justice available on the Superior Court's website.

Date: May 29, 2017

Michelle Fuerst - Regional Senior Judge (Superior Court of Justice, Central East Region)

E. Consolidated Practice Direction for the Central West Region (Latest Amendment: February 3, 2020)

Notice of Amendment:

Paragraphs 26.5 through 26.9 are added to Part I J (Case Conferences and Settlement Conferences) effective February 3, 2020;

Part I A [paras. 2 – 6] was amended on July 1, 2018;

Part III A [paras. 75 – 80] was revoked on May 1, 2017;

Part I J [paragraphs 26 and 27] (family proceedings – case conferences and settlement conferences) was replaced on January 1, 2017.

Effective July 1, 2014

This Practice Direction applies to proceedings in the Superior Court of Justice, Central West Region, effective July 1, 2014. It *supersedes* all previous region-specific Practice Directions for the Central West Region issued prior to July 1, 2014, which are hereby revoked.

Counsel and parties are advised to refer to the relevant Parts of the Consolidated Provincial Practice Direction as well as the Consolidated Practice Direction for Divisional Court Proceedings which are available on the Superior Court of Justice website at: www.ontariocourts.ca/scj.

Table of Contents

      E.   **Emergency/Walk-in Motions**
      F.   **Certification of an Action to Set Pre-Trial and Trial Dates**
      G.   **Material for use of the Court**
      H.   **Confirmations for Motions and Applications**
      I.   **Cost Orders in Civil Motions and Applications**

Part III: Criminal Proceedings

      A.   **Bail Variations pursuant to section 515.1 of the Criminal Code**

Part I: Family Proceedings

1. In addition to this Part, counsel and parties in family proceedings are advised to refer to Part I of the Consolidated Provincial Practice Direction.

A. Confirmations

2. Each party to a motion or conference must file a <u>Form 14C Confirmation of Motion or Form 17F Confirmation of Conference</u> no later than 2 p.m. three business days before the date of the motion or conference. The parties may file a Form 14C or Form 17F Confirmation jointly.

3. The parties or their counsel should consult with each other prior to filing their Form 14C or Form 17F Confirmations, unless the parties are self-represented and prohibited from communicating by court order.

4. Where Form 14C Confirmation of Motion or Form 17F Confirmation of Conference forms have not been filed, the conference or motion will not be scheduled on the event list and, as a result, will not be heard by the court. *Costs may be ordered against a party who has not filed the Confirmation.*

5. Form 14C Confirmation of Motion or Form 17F Confirmation of Conference forms must only list the specific issues that are to be addressed at the event. They should also indicate which materials the judge should review with clear reference to the specific volume, tab and page numbers of the Continuing Record. *Failure to provide this information may result in the materials not being reviewed by the judge or the motion not being heard on that day.*

6. Form 14C Confirmation of Motion or Form 17F Confirmation of Conference must also include an appropriate time estimate for the entire motion or conference, including time required by the other party. Parties will be held to the time stated on their Confirmations.

B. Short Motions

7. Motions that are expected to take one hour or less may be scheduled on a regular motions day serving and filing the motion material at the court office at the location where the motion is to be heard within the timelines set out in the *Family Law Rules*.

C. Long Motions

8. Motions that are expected to take more than one hour (including the other party's reply and cross motion, if any) must be scheduled as long motions and scheduled through the Trial Coordinator in the location where the motion is to be heard.

(i) Long Motions in Milton

9. In Milton, a long motion must be confirmed no later than three weeks prior to the date the motion is to be heard, and all material must be filed by the moving party by that date. Counsel and parties will be advised of this requirement at the time the motion is booked.

10. If the material and the confirmation are not filed at least three weeks in advance of the date the motion is to be heard, the motion will be removed from the list and will not be heard. If possible, the time can be used to hear another motion by arrangement with the trial office.

(ii) Long Motions in Owen Sound and Walkerton

11. In Owen Sound and Walkerton, a long motion must be confirmed no later than three weeks prior to the date the motion is to be heard. The moving party's factum must be served and filed four weeks prior to the hearing date. The respondent's factum must be served and filed three weeks prior to the hearing date. The litigant, or counsel, as the case may be, will be advised of this requirement at the time the motion is booked.

12. If the moving party's factum and the confirmation are not filed in accordance with these timelines, the motion will be removed from the list and will not be heard. If possible, the time can be used to hear another motion by arrangement with the trial office.

13. The respondent's failure to file its factum in accordance with these timelines will be addressed by the judge hearing the long motion.

14. Any request to adjourn a long motion, even if on consent, must be made by Notice of Motion, with a supporting Affidavit, returnable on the earliest available regular motions date.

D. Form 14B Motions

15. A Form 14B Motion must be filed at the court office and cannot be filed by fax. A Form 14B Motion Form should be accompanied by four copies of a proposed Order (Form 25), a completed endorsement sheet and a self-addressed and stamped envelope for each party.

16. The 14B Motion Form shall be filed in the Continuing Record and a copy of the proposed Order shall be attached to the appropriate place in the Endorsement Volume.

17. In addition to this section, counsel and parties are advised to refer to Part I of the Consolidated Provincial Practice Direction regarding Form 14B Motions.

E. Urgent Motions on Notice

18. A party may seek an urgent motion on notice without a case conference in situations of urgency or hardship including issues such as abduction and threats of harm where an Early Case Conference is not available. A party seeking such a motion must file all of the required materials except for a Form 14C Confirmation.

F. Urgent Motions without Notice

19. A party that is seeking a motion without notice to the other party must also set out why notice is unnecessary or not reasonably possible. A factum or Summary of Argument is not required for an urgent motion that has been brought without notice.

G. Factums Summaries of Arguments and Briefs of Authorities

20. A properly drafted factum or Summary of Argument is required on all long motions except where noted otherwise. If the moving party does not file a factum or Summary of Argument where required, the motion will not be scheduled.

21. For long motions, each party's factum or Summary of Argument must be filed at least seven days before the hearing of the motion.

22. No factum or Summary of Argument may exceed 20 pages without leave of the court.

23. The authorities that are included on the court's list of Often Cited Family Cases do not need to be provided to the court. Counsel and parties are advised to refer to Part I of the Consolidated Provincial Practice Direction for further direction.

H. Compendiums

24. A Compendium containing the documents and evidence that are essential to the hearing of the motion may be provided for long or complex motions. A party wishing to file a Compendium should file it with their factum. A joint Compendium may be filed with the respondent's factum. A Compendium would normally include the Notice of Motion, Affidavits and Financial Statements, as well as excerpts from the evidence and exhibits that will be referred to in the argument of the motion.

I. Electronic Copies of Material

25. Whenever the volume of materials is large or the motion is complex, the parties should file an electronic copy of their motion materials as well as paper copies. Counsel and parties are advised to refer to the Guide Concerning e-Delivery of documents available on the Superior Court of Justice Website.

J. Case Conferences and Settlement Conferences

26.1 Counsel and parties are expected to attend all conferences in person.

26.2 Parties may arrange for a conference to occur by teleconference with the consent of both parties and their counsel. If the other party will not consent, a request for a teleconference may be made by filing a Form 14B Motion Form.

26.3 Counsel or the parties should communicate before any conference in order to attempt to resolve the issues that are in dispute unless the parties are self-represented and prohibited from communication by court order.

26.4 A date for a case conference may only be obtained upon one side filing a case conference brief.

26.5 Parties shall serve and file a case conference brief (Form 17A) for case conferences and a settlement conference brief (Form 17C) for settlement conferences with any necessary attachments. The purposes of a case conference are set out in Rule 17(4) and the purposes of a settlement conference are set out in Rule 17(5). Parties should prepare their briefs with a view to a realistic agenda that can be completed in the time that has been scheduled for the conference.

26.6 Conference briefs were designed to replace adversarial pleadings and affidavits. These briefs shall be prepared in a manner that will promote settlement and shall include the party's proposal for any unresolved issues. They should also be prepared so that they can realistically be read by the conference judge in the time scheduled for the event that day.

26.7 Conference briefs shall be limited to the 4 page form set out in the Family Law Rules. In addition to the standard form, briefs must contain documents mandated by the rules (including for example Net Family Property Statements) and may contain attachments that are necessary to facilitate settlement, such as expert reports, proposed parenting plans and lists of outstanding disclosure.

26.8 In exceptional circumstances, a conference brief may include necessary and additional facts that will assist in resolving the outstanding issues. However, in no case shall a conference brief exceed 6 double spaced pages (excluding the attachments referred to in paragraph 26.7 above).

26.9 Conference briefs that exceed the length set out above may be returned to the parties. Lengthy or unduly adversarial conference briefs may not be read. The matter may also be placed at the bottom of the list and costs may be awarded.

26.10 Once a case or settlement conference has been scheduled no adjournments will be permitted except in **exceptional** circumstances. If exceptional circumstances arise, the party requesting the adjournment must obtain the permission, in writing, of a Superior Court Justice.

26.11 Trial management conferences may not be adjourned without a judge's order, which must be obtained either by 14B motion or by appearing before the court. The adjournment request must set out compelling reasons why the parties are not ready to go ahead, along with a proposed timetable to move the case forward.

27. Parties must serve and file a Trial Scheduling Endorsement Form with their Settlement Conference briefs, so that if the matter does not settle at the Settlement Conference a trial date can be scheduled.

K. Dispute Resolution Officer Program – Brampton and Milton

28. If the matter is not resolved at a Settlement Conference, a Trial Scheduling Endorsement Form must be completed prior to the matter being scheduled for trial.

29. The first Case Conference on a motion to change a final order or agreement in Brampton or Milton shall be scheduled before a Dispute Resolution Officer (DRO) in accordance with Part I of the Consolidated Provincial Practice Direction. Counsel and parties are advised to refer to Part I of the Provincial Practice Direction for further direction.

30. A DRO conference may be held on matters other than motions to change only as directed by the court upon request by a 14B Motion or at another court event.

L. Early Case Conferences – Brampton and Milton

31. Litigants who are represented by counsel, and those who are self-represented, can participate in an early case conference.

32. The case conferences will be held on Mondays. They will be listed as "Early Case Conference" (ECC) and are available only if a case conference has not already been held.

33. Fifteen ECCs will be scheduled for 10 a.m.

34. Both parties must certify they have fully discussed the issues to be litigated with the other side before their attendance at court for the ECC, or have attended court not later than 9 a.m. on the scheduled date to fully discuss the issues. If the parties have not discussed the issues fully in advance of 10 a.m., the conference will be rescheduled.

35. Litigants are required to attend the ECC.

36. Each ECC will be *limited to a total of 15 minutes* for all submissions, discussion and endorsements.

37. The litigants must file updated financial statements. Case Conference Briefs must *not exceed five double spaced pages* setting out their positions and *must not include lengthy schedules.*

38. The parties are limited to factual assertions contained in the written material, and will not be permitted to add additional facts in submissions.

M. Trial Records

39. If the matter is not resolved at a case conference, a completed Trial Scheduling Endorsement Form must be completed by the parties and endorsed by the court prior to the matter being scheduled for trial.

40. The Applicant must file a Trial Record at least 30 days prior to the scheduled Trial date. Failure to do so will result in the matter being removed from the Trial list, unless the court orders otherwise.

N. Cost Orders in Family Law Motions and Applications

41. Rule 57.01(6) of the *Rules of Civil Procedure* requires that, unless the parties have agreed on costs:

    every party who intends to seek costs for that step shall give to every other party involved in the same step, and bring to the hearing, a costs outline (Form 57B) not exceeding three pages in length.

42. This is to permit the presiding judge, where feasible, to summarily determine the issue of costs. The overriding principle is that "the court shall devise and adopt the simplest, least expensive, and most expeditious process for fixing costs. . ." Rule 57.01(7).

43. While Rule 24 of the *Family Law Rules*, in addressing costs, does not refer to costs outlines or bills of costs, Rule 1(7) states that if a matter is not covered by the rules, the court may give direction, and the practice shall be decided by analogy to these rules, by reference to the *Courts of Justice Act* and, if the court considers it appropriate, by reference to the *Rules of Civil Procedure.*

44. Too frequently counsel are attending motions and applications without costs outlines, and seeking to make submissions regarding the costs to be awarded. When judges ask for the outlines or bills of costs, counsel often seek to file written submissions as to costs. This is contrary to the intention of the Rules, delays the determination of the issue, and requires judges to determine costs issues for motions and applications that were often decided months before.

45. All counsel appearing on motions and applications should attend the hearing with

their costs outline in accordance with Rule 57.01 available, to provide to the presiding judge. If the outline is not available to be given to the presiding judge, the judge may decline to make any costs award.

Part II: Civil Proceedings

46. In addition to this Part, counsel and parties to civil proceedings are advised to refer to Part III of the Consolidated Provincial Practice Direction.

A. Motions to Transfer a Civil Proceeding under Rule 13.1.02 of the *Rules of Civil Procedure*

47. All requests for a transfer of a civil proceeding from one county to another shall be pursuant to rule 13.1.02 of the *Rules of Civil Procedure*. The motion will be granted or denied based on its merits. Counsel and parties are advised to refer to Part III of the Consolidated Provincial Practice Direction which prescribes specific requirements for motions to transfer a civil proceeding.

A.1 Designated Counties for the Commencement of Mortgage Proceedings under rule 13.1.01(3)

47.1 Pursuant to rule 13.1.01(3) of the *Rules of Civil Procedure*, which comes into effect on March 31, 2015, Brampton, Milton, Orangeville or Owen Sound have been designated as the place for commencement of mortgage proceedings for property located anywhere in the Central West Region.

B. Applications and Motions

48. Applications and motions that require one hour or less for all parties to argue are considered short. Applications and motions that require more than one hour for all parties to argue are considered long.

C. Short Applications or Short Motions before a Judge

49. All the materials for short motions and applications are filed in the Registrar's office. Parties must consult with each other to select a return date convenient to all parties and which will permit all parties to file all necessary materials and conduct any examinations before the return date. At the time of filing the Notice of Motion, a realistic estimate of the time required by all parties for argument must be provided.

D. Long Motions

50. Motions that are expected to take more than one hour (including the other party's reply and cross motion, if any) must be scheduled as Long Motions and scheduled through the Trial Coordinator in the location where the motion is to be heard.

(i) Long Motions in Milton

51. In Milton a long motion must be confirmed no later than three weeks prior to the date the motion is to be heard, and all material must be filed by the moving party by that date. The litigant, or counsel, as the case may be, will be advised of this requirement at the time the motion is booked.

52. If the material and the confirmation are not filed at least three weeks in advance of the

date the motion is to be heard, the motion will be removed from the list and will not be heard. If possible, the time can be used to hear another motion by arrangement with the trial office.

(ii) Long Motions in Owen Sound and Walkerton

53. In Owen Sound and Walkerton, a long motion must be confirmed no later than three weeks prior to the date the motion is to be heard. The moving party's factum must be served and filed four weeks prior to the hearing date. The respondent's factum must be served and filed three weeks prior to the hearing date. The litigant, or counsel, as the case may be, will be advised of this requirement at the time the motion is booked.

54. If the moving party's factum and the confirmation are not filed in accordance with these timelines, the motion will be removed from the list and will not be heard. If possible, the time can be used to hear another motion by arrangement with the trial office.

55. The respondent's failure to file its factum in accordance with these timelines will be addressed by the judge hearing the long motion.

56. Any request to adjourn a long motion, even if on consent, must be made by Notice of Motion, with a supporting Affidavit, returnable on the earliest available regular motions date.

E. Emergency/Walk-in Motions

57. Counsel and parties who wish to have a motion added to a motions list must attend the trial office before bringing the motion into court. Counsel will be provided with a form to be completed. The trial office staff will then assign the application for leave to be added to the list to a judge who is presiding in motions court that day. The application for leave must be brought in the assigned court, unless the assigned judge directs otherwise.

58. If counsel and parties have not gone to the trial office before attending the courtroom, they will be required to go to the trial office and complete the form before the leave application is heard.

F. Certification of an Action to Set Pre-Trial and Trial Dates

59. The practice of certifying an action ready for trial continues in Brampton. Once the trial record is filed, the Registrar will hand to the party who set the action down for trial a Certification Form to Set Pre-Trial and Trial Dates. After consultation with the opposing counsel or party, the party who received the form must complete and return the Certification Form to the trial office.

60. If a completed Certification Form is not returned within 90 days of the matter being set down for trial, the parties will be required to attend at the Assignment Court. If the parties are not ready for trial, the action will be struck from the list.

61. In order to restore an action that has been struck from the trial list, the parties must obtain an order granting leave from a judge under rule 48.11 to restore it to the trial list.

62. Once trial dates are set, the parties may adjourn the date if on consent of all parties.

63. Rule 48.04 provides that a party who sets an action down for trial or consents to placing the action on the trial list cannot initiate or continue any form of discovery or in-

terlocutory motion without leave of the court. Leave will be granted only in rare circumstances.

G. Material for use of the Court

Factums

64. Factums are required for all applications. Factums are required for all motions over one hour and are strongly encouraged for all other motions. No factum may exceed 20 pages, unless leave is granted. For longer or more complex motions, the court always finds it helpful for the parties to file electronic copies of their factums in Word format. Electronic copies should be attached to the hard copy of the factum with the court and should be labelled with the court file name and number, event and content of the electronic document (e.g. flash drive), as well as the return date of the matter.

Books of Authority

65. Cases contained in books of authorities should be copied on both sides of a page. Electronic copies of books of authorities are helpful in longer or more complex motions.

H. Confirmations for Motions and Applications

66. Confirmation notices for short motions/applications must be received by fax or delivered to the court office not later than 2:00 p.m. three business days before the matter is to be heard. For example, for matters to be heard on Monday, they must be confirmed by 2:00 p.m. on the preceding Wednesday.

67. Confirmations must list only the specific issues to be addressed at the motion/application. They should also indicate the materials that the judge should review.

68. Except as otherwise provided in the Practice Direction, confirmation notices for long motions/applications must be received five business days before the matter is to proceed.

69. Only Central West confirmation notices will be accepted.

70. In Brampton and Milton, counsel should indicate on the form if they have other matters to be heard on that date, so that the court office may attempt to put their matters on one list if two or more judges are scheduled to hear the motion/application.

I. Cost Orders in Civil Motions and Applications

71. Rule 57.01(6) of the *Rules of Civil Procedure* requires that, unless the parties have agreed on costs:

    every party who intends to seek costs for that step shall give to every other party involved in the same step, and bring to the hearing, a costs outline (Form 57B) not exceeding three pages in length.

72. This is to permit the presiding judge, where feasible, to summarily determine the issue of costs. The overriding principle is that "the court shall devise and adopt the simplest, least expensive, and most expeditious process for fixing costs. . ." Rule 57.01(7).

73. Too frequently counsel are attending motions and applications without costs outlines, and seeking to make submissions regarding the costs to be awarded. When judges ask

for the outlines or bills of costs, counsel often seek to file written submissions as to costs. This is contrary to the intention of the Rules, delays the determination of the issue, and requires judges to determine costs issues for motions and applications that were often decided months before.

74. All counsel appearing on motions and applications should attend the hearing with their costs outline in accordance with Rule 57.01 available, to provide to the presiding judge. If the outline is not available to be given to the presiding judge, the judge may decline to make any costs award.

Part III: Criminal Proceedings

A. Bail Variations pursuant to section 515.1 of the *Criminal Code*

This section (paragraphs 75 to 80) has been revoked and replaced by part V of the Provincial Practice Direction Regarding Criminal Proceedings.

Dated: April 11, 2014

Amended: February 3, 2020; July 1, 2018 (modification to Part I A [paras. 2 – 6]); May 1, 2017 (revocation of part III A (paras. 75 – 80)); January 1, 2017 [paragraphs 26 and 27], July 1, 2015 [modification to paragraph 39]; February 27, 2015 [addition of para 47.1], November 7, 2014 [addition of paras 11 – 14 and 53 – 56]

G. Morawetz
Chief Justice
Superior Court of Justice (Ontario)

Peter A. Daley
Regional Senior Judge
Superior Court of Justice, Central West Region

F. Consolidated Practice Direction for the East Region (Latest Amendment: August 1, 2016)

Notice of Amendments:

Effective August 1, 2016, Part 1 (Family Proceedings) is revoked and replaced by the Practice Direction Regarding Family Cases in the Superior Court of Justice East Region.

Part II A.1 (Designated Counties for the Commencement of Mortgage Proceedings under rule 13.1.01) has been amended to change the place of commencement of Mortgage Proceedings. These amendments were made March 11, 2016 and are in effect April 1, 2016.

Part II A.1 (Designated Counties for the Commencement of Mortgage Proceedings under rule 13.1.01) was added on February 27, 2015 and comes into effect on March 31, 2015.

Effective July 1, 2014

This Practice Direction applies to proceedings in the Superior Court of Justice, East Region, effective July 1, 2014. It *supersedes* all previous region-specific Practice Directions for the East Region issued prior to July 1, 2014, which are hereby revoked.

Counsel and parties are advised to refer to the relevant Parts of the Consolidated Provincial Practice Direction as well as the Consolidated Practice Direction for Divisional Court Proceedings which are available on the Superior Court of Justice website at: www.ontariocourts.ca/scj.

Table of Contents

Part I: Family Proceedings

1. This part (paragraphs 1 to 19) has been revoked and replaced by the Practice Direction Regarding Family Cases in the Superior Court of Justice East Region.

Part II: Civil Proceedings

20. In addition to this Part, counsel and parties in civil proceedings are advised to refer to Part III of the Consolidated Provincial Practice Direction.

A. Civil Motions Court in Perth

21. In Perth, to respond to the issue of over scheduling in Friday motion courts, it is nec-

essary to limit the number of civil motions that are set down weekly based on the time estimates provided by counsel and parties.

22. Counsel and parties must contact Court Administration to book motion time into the schedule. Counsel and parties will be held to the time estimate provided.

23. Long motions, in excess of one hour, will continue to be scheduled through the Trial Coordinator's office.

A.1 Designated Counties for the Commencement of Mortgage Proceedings under rule 13.1.01(3)

23.1 Pursuant to rule 13.1.01(3) of the *Rules of Civil Procedure*, Belleville, Brockville, Cornwall, Kingston, L'Orignal, Napanee, Picton, Pembroke, Perth and Ottawa have been designated as places where mortgage proceedings may be commenced for property located anywhere in the East Region.

Part III: Criminal Proceedings

A. Criminal Case Management Procedures for Ottawa under Rule 28 of the *Criminal Proceedings Rules*

24. The following criminal case management procedures, in paragraphs 25 to 29, apply in Ottawa regarding Rule 28 and the requirement for Pre-Trial Conference Reports (Rule 28.04 and Form 17), Trial Readiness Courts (Rule 28.04(18)(a)) and Trial Readiness Reports (Rule 28.04(18)(b) and Form 18-C-1).

25. Pre-Trial Conference Reports (Form 17) are not required to be filed at or before the first pre-trial in Superior Court. They may be required at a later time as directed by the pre-trial judge.

26. When the trial date is set, two other dates will be set at the same time and recorded on the indictment. The first is the filing date (usually 30 days before the trial date) for the Trial Readiness Report in Form 18-C-1. The second is a mandatory appearance in Trial Readiness Court at 12:30 p.m. on the Thursday immediately prior to the trial date.

27. Trial Readiness Court will be held each Thursday at 12:30 p.m. with a justice presiding, usually in a courtroom on the 3rd floor. Counsel are not required to gown.

28. The purpose of the Trial Readiness Report (Form 18-C-1) is to inform the court and other counsel that the case is proceeding as discussed at the most recent pre-trial.

29. If counsel or parties do not file a Trial Readiness Report by the filing date as recorded on the indictment or, if since the most recent pre-trial, there has been a change affecting the trial, all counsel and parties are required to attend the next Trial Readiness Court immediately following that filing date.

B. Notice of Application for a 90 Day Detention Review

30. Upon receipt of a Notice of Application for a 90 Day Detention Review pursuant to section 525(1) and (2) of the *Criminal Code of Canada*, the following practice in paragraphs 31 to 34 will be followed.

31. If the accused is not represented by counsel, a hearing date will be scheduled for the next bail review court date. Notice of this hearing date will be sent to the Regional

Detention Centre and the Crown Attorney's office by the Trial Coordinator. The Crown Attorney's office will prepare an Order to Produce to have the prisoner brought to the hearing.

32. If the accused is represented by counsel, defence counsel will be contacted by the Trial Coordinator and asked whether he/she requests a hearing date be set or whether there will be a waiver of the hearing.

33. If counsel waives the hearing, he/she will immediately send a letter to the Trial Co-ordinator confirming this waiver and a copy of this waiver will then be forwarded to the Regional Detention Centre and the Crown Attorney's office by the Trial Coordinator.

34. If counsel indicates that a hearing date is to be set, that hearing date will be set by a judge at the next bail review court date in the absence of the accused, but in the presence of defence counsel, after which a copy of the Notice of the Hearing Date will be sent to the Regional Detention Centre, defence counsel and the Crown Attorney's office by the Trial Coordinator. The Crown Attorney's office will prepare an Order to Produce to have the prisoner brought to the hearing.

Dated: April 11, 2014

Amended: August 1, 2016; March 11, 2016; Amended: February 27, 2015 (addition of para 23.1)

Heather J. Smith – Chief Justice (Superior Court of Justice (Ontario))

James McNamara – Regional Senior Judge (Superior Court of Justice, East Region)

G. Consolidated Practice Direction for the Northeast Region (Latest Amendment: October 26, 2018)

Notice of Amendments:

On October 26, 2018, Section B (Solicitor-Client Costs Assessments) was added to Part III.

Part III A (Designated Counties for the Commencement of Mortgage Proceedings under r. 13.1.01) was added on February 27, 2015 and comes into effect on March 31, 2015.

Effective July 1, 2014

This Practice Direction applies to proceedings in the Superior Court of Justice, Northeast Region, effective July 1, 2014. It *supersedes* all previous region-specific Practice Directions for the Northeast Region issued prior to July 1, 2014, which are hereby revoked.

Counsel and parties are advised to refer to the relevant Parts of the Consolidated Provincial Practice Direction as well as the Consolidated Practice Direction for Divisional Court Proceedings which are available on the Superior Court of Justice website at: www.ontariocourts.ca/scj.

Table of Contents

Part I: Family Proceedings

1. In addition to this part, counsel and parties in family proceedings are advised to refer to Part I of the Consolidated Provincial Practice Direction.

A. Form 14B Motions

2. Form 14B motions procedures are governed by Part I of the Consolidated Provincial Practice Direction. Counsel and parties are advised to refer to that Practice Direction for further direction.

Part II: Criminal Proceedings

A. Criminal Matters arising in Chapleau and Gogama

3. The following Superior Court of Justice matters of a criminal nature arising in Chapleau or Gogama, in the District of Sudbury, may proceed at the Superior Court of Justice in Timmins, in the District of Cochrane:

a) Trials emanating from committals to stand trial in the Ontario Court of Justice in Chapleau or Gogama rendered after June 30, 2010, or preferred indictments in matters arising out of Chapleau or Gogama filed after June 30, 2010;

b) Appeals from summary convictions in the Ontario Court of Justice in Chapleau or Gogama rendered after June 30, 2010;

c) Applications for prerogative remedies relating to decisions of the Ontario Court of Justice in Chapleau or Gogama rendered after June 30, 2010;

d) Reviews of bail decisions of the Ontario Court of Justice for Chapleau or Gogama matters rendered after June 30, 2010; and,

e) Any other matters relating to charges with an alleged offence date after June 30, 2010.

Part III: Civil Proceedings

A.   Designated Counties for the Commencement of Mortgage Proceedings under rule 13.1.01(3)

4.   Pursuant to rule 13.1.01(3) of the *Rules of Civil Procedure*, which comes into effect on March 31, 2015, North Bay, Parry Sound, Sudbury, Haileybury, Sault St. Marie, Cochrane or Gore Bay have been designated as the place for commencement of mortgage proceedings for property located anywhere in the Northeast Region.

B.   Solicitor-Client Costs Assessments

5.   A pre-assessment hearing will be scheduled for all solicitor/client costs assessments.

6.   The hearing is meant to assist the parties in the mediation of their dispute and, failing settlement, to ensure that the matter is ready for hearing.

7.   When the documents needed to obtain a Notice of Appointment for Assessment of Costs (Form 58A) are filed, the court shall:

    a.   Set a date for a pre-assessment hearing, to be held by teleconference; and

    b.   Issue a Notice of Assessment – Pre-Assessment Hearing Form to the filing party.

8.   The filing party shall serve the Notice and the bill of costs on every party interested in the assessment at least seven days before the date fixed for the pre-assessment hearing. The filing party shall file proof of service with the court immediately afterwards.

9.   At the pre-assessment hearing, the presiding officer will assist the parties in resolving their dispute through mediation.

10.   If the dispute is settled at the pre-assessment hearing, the presiding officer will complete a written endorsement to reflect the terms of the settlement. The court office will then prepare a certificate of assessment, attaching the written endorsement, and provide a copy to each party as soon as possible afterwards.

11.   If the dispute does not settle at the pre-assessment hearing and the parties wish to participate in an extended mediation, the presiding officer shall:

    a.   Schedule an extended mediation;

    b.   Prepare a written endorsement stating that the parties wish to enter into extended mediation; and

    c.   File the endorsement with the court office.

12.   If the dispute does not settle in the pre-assessment hearing or subsequent extended mediation, then the presiding officer shall:

    a.   Ensure that all required filings have been made;

    b.   Verify proof of service;

    c.   Confirm the bill(s) of costs being assessed and the amount(s) of costs in dispute;

    d.   Attempt to narrow the issues;

    e.   Determine the amount of time required for the assessment hearing;

    f.   Set a date for the assessment hearing; and

    g.   Prepare a written endorsement dealing with subparagraphs a. through f., and file it with the court office immediately afterwards.

13.   Within seven days of receiving the endorsement, the court shall prepare a Notice of Appointment for Assessment of Costs and mail it to each party.

14.   If a party fails to attend the pre-assessment hearing, the party will not be entitled to notice of any further step in the proceeding or served with any document in respect of the matter. The presiding officer may schedule the assessment hearing without notice to the party and provide the court office with a written endorsement to that effect.

Dated: April 11, 2014

Amended: October 26, 2018 (Part III); February 27, 2015 (addition of para 4)

Heather J. Smith – Chief Justice (Superior Court of Justice (Ontario))

Robbie D. Gordon – Regional Senior Judge (Superior Court of Justice, Northeast Region)

H. Consolidated Practice Direction for the Northwest Region (Latest Amendment: October 26, 2018)

Notice of Amendments:

On October 26, 2018, Part IV (Civil Proceedings) was added. The former Part I A.1 (Designated Counties for the Commencement of Mortgage Proceedings under rule 13.1.01(3)) is now Part IV A. Part IV B addresses solicitor-client costs assessments.

On September 4, 2018, Part I B was amended to provide direction regarding the use of CourtCall, a remote-appearance service, for telephone and video conferences.

Part I A.1 (as of October 26, 2018, Part IV A) (Designated Counties for the Commencement of Mortgage Proceedings under r. 13.1.01) was added on February 27, 2015 and comes into effect on March 31, 2015.

Effective July 1, 2014

This Practice Direction applies to proceedings in the Superior Court of Justice, Northwest Region, effective July 1, 2014. It *supersedes* all previous region-specific Practice Directions for the Northwest Region issued prior to July 1, 2014, which are hereby revoked.

Counsel and parties are advised to refer to the relevant Parts of the Consolidated Provincial Practice Direction as well as the Consolidated Practice Direction for Divisional Court Proceedings which are available on the Superior Court of Justice website at: www.ontariocourts.ca/scj.

Table of Contents

Part I: All Proceedings

A. Faxing or Emailing Documents and Late Filings of Documents and Confirmation Forms in all Civil, Family and Criminal Proceedings

1.   There has been a marked increase in civil, family and criminal materials being faxed or e-mailed to the Superior Court of Justice, Northwest Region. This includes case con-

ference, settlement conference, and pre-trial briefs, motion records and briefs of authorities. Often these materials are sent at the last minute. Some of the materials are voluminous.

2. In addition, there has been an increase in the number of late filings of confirmation forms and documents for specific hearings.

3. This flood of materials has, at times, overwhelmed the court's capacity to receive and process them. Faxed materials are generally less legible than original materials. They may be out of alignment. In addition, it is far from certain that all pages transmitted will be received by the court. Finally, there is a concern that pages of one document being pulled from the fax machine may be intermingled with another unrelated document.

4. Similar problems apply to the printing of e-mailed documents at the court office. Current staffing does not allow for printing and collating of e-mailed materials.

5. With respect to late filings of materials and confirmation forms as required under the applicable rules, staff are in a difficult position, not knowing whether they should accept or refuse documents.

6. In order that documents to be filed are received in a complete and legible form, all parties are asked to file original documents at the Registrar's office, complete with original affidavits of service, in compliance with the rule setting out the time for filing. Unless the filing is of an urgent nature, or the presiding judge has requested material to be delivered in this fashion, documents *should not* be sent to the court for filing by fax or e-mail. The single exception is a Pre-Trial Conference Report (From 17) which may be faxed or delivered to the trial office in accordance with timelines noted on the Form.

7. With respect to late filing of documents and confirmation forms, specific direction has been provided to staff that, if confirmations and material are not received within the prescribed time, the court file must not be forwarded to the judge. If counsel or self-represented parties appear on a specific day (and their filings are not complete) they will need to complete a fiat to be presented to the judge and she/he will decide whether or not they will hear the matter or order the parties to select a new date.

B. Requests to Attend Proceedings via Teleconference or Videoconference in all Proceedings

8. Counsel and parties requesting to attend their matter via teleconference or videoconference may, in proceedings for which CourtCall is available, arrange their attendance via CourtCall in accordance with paragraphs 11 through 13. Otherwise, they must submit the appropriate Request Form. (See paragraphs 14 through 19 for more information).

CourtCall

9. CourtCall, a third-party videoconferencing service, is available for the following matters:

    a. Assignment Court matters;

    b. Regular Motions Court matters;

    c. civil and criminal pre-trials;

    d.   family conferences; and

    e.   any other matter for which telephone appearances are currently authorized.

10.   All persons who have made the necessary arrangements with CourtCall and advised the Court and any other party in accordance with paragraphs 11 and 12 may assume that they have the Court's permission to appear for the event using CourtCall, unless otherwise directed by a judge.

11.   Any party or counsel wishing to appear by CourtCall must make the necessary arrangements with CourtCall. The process for doing so is as follows:

    a.   If not already registered with CourtCall as a client, register at courtcall.com.

    b.   **At least two (2) business days before the hearing**, book the appearance by logging into the CourtCall website (courtcall.com) and completing a "New Appearance" request, or by contacting CourtCall at 1-888-882-6878.

    c.   Pay the fee set by CourtCall for the video appearance.

    d.   CourtCall will email or fax a confirmation upon completion of the booking and payment.

    e.   The party or counsel appearing by video must supply his or her own telephone and computer with a camera and internet connection with sufficient bandwidth to allow them to connect and participate.

    f.   On the day of the hearing, the party or counsel must initiate the video appearance by clicking on the link and dialing the toll-free teleconference number provided in the confirmation sent by CourtCall.

    g.   A pre-hearing check-in is required fifteen minutes before the scheduled hearing time.

12.   The party or counsel must also advise the Court and any other party, in writing, that they will be attending the court event by using the CourtCall service. This can be done by completing the appropriate section on the scheduling or confirmation form filed with the Court.

13.   If the requesting party or counsel fails to provide this notice, then they must obtain the permission of the presiding judge to attend the matter by any means other than in person.

Teleconference or videoconference attendances not through CourtCall

14.   If a party or counsel is requesting teleconference or videoconference attendance, but not through CourtCall, the request must be made by submitting a Request Form no less than five (5) days prior to the event.

15.   No request shall be considered approved until approval has been duly granted by a judge of the Superior Court of Justice acting for, or in, the Northwest Region.

16.   To receive a Request Form for matters in Thunder Bay contact the Trial Coordinator.

17.   To receive a Request Form for matters in Kenora and Fort Frances, please contact the Assistant Trial Coordinator.

18.   The contact information for the Trial Coordinator and Assistant Trial Coordinator are

available on the Superior Court's website at: www.ontariocourts.ca/scj/practice/schedules/nw/directory.

19. This process is authorized for civil proceedings under Rule 1.08 of the *Rules of Civil Procedure*, for family proceedings under subrule 5 (2) (g) of the *Family Law Rules* and for criminal proceedings under the Superior Court's *Provincial Practice Direction Regarding Criminal Proceedings* and various provisions of the *Criminal Code*.

Part II: Family Proceedings

20. In addition to this Part, counsel and parties in family proceedings are advised to refer to Part I of the Consolidated Provincial Practice Direction.

A. 14B Motions

21. Form 14B motions procedures are governed by Part I of the Consolidated Provincial Practice Direction. Counsel and parties are advised to refer to that Practice Direction for further direction.

Part III: Criminal Proceedings

A. Gowning for Criminal Pre-trials

22. In addition to the gowning requirements outlined in the Consolidated Provincial Practice Direction, counsel are required to gown for criminal pre-trials in the Northwest Region.

Part IV: Civil Proceedings

A. Designated Counties for the Commencement of Mortgage Proceedings under rule 13.1.01(3)

23. Pursuant to rule 13.1.01(3) of the *Rules of Civil Procedure*, which comes into effect on March 31, 2015, Fort Frances, Thunder Bay or Kenora have been designated as the place for commencement of mortgage proceedings for property located anywhere in the Northwest Region.

B. Solicitor-Client Costs Assessments

24. A pre-assessment hearing will be scheduled for all solicitor/client costs assessments.

25. The hearing is meant to assist the parties in the mediation of their dispute and, failing settlement, to ensure that the matter is ready for hearing.

26. When the documents needed to obtain a Notice of Appointment for Assessment of Costs (Form 58A) are filed, the court shall:

   a. Set a date for a pre-assessment hearing, to be held by teleconference; and

   b. Issue a Notice of Assessment – Pre-Assessment Hearing Form to the filing party.

27. The filing party shall serve the Notice and the bill of costs on every party interested in the assessment at least seven days before the date fixed for the pre-assessment hearing. The filing party shall file proof of service with the court immediately afterwards.

28. At the pre-assessment hearing, the presiding officer will assist the parties in resolving their dispute through mediation.

29. If the dispute is settled at the pre-assessment hearing, the presiding officer will make a written endorsement reflecting the terms of the settlement. The court office will then prepare a certificate of assessment, with the endorsement attached, and provide a copy to each party as soon as possible afterwards.

30. If the dispute is not settled at the pre-assessment hearing and the parties wish to participate in an extended mediation, the presiding officer shall:

    a. Schedule an extended mediation;

    b. Prepare a written endorsement stating that the parties wish to enter into extended mediation; and

    c. File the endorsement with the court office.

31. If the dispute is not settled at the pre-assessment hearing or subsequent extended mediation, then the presiding officer shall:

    a. Ensure that all required filings have been made;

    b. Verify proof of service;

    c. Confirm the bill(s) of costs being assessed and the amount(s) of costs in dispute;

    d. Attempt to narrow the issues;

    e. Determine the amount of time required for the assessment hearing;

    f. Set a date for the assessment hearing; and

    g. Prepare a written endorsement dealing with subparagraphs a. through f., and file it with the court office immediately afterwards.

32. If either party fails to attend the pre-assessment hearing, the presiding officer may schedule the matter for default hearing and provide the court office with an endorsement to that effect.

Dated: April 11, 2014

Amended: October 26, 2018; September 4, 2018; February 27, 2015 (addition of para 7.1)

Heather J. Smith – Chief Justice (Superior Court of Justice (Ontario))

Douglas Shaw – Regional Senior Judge (Superior Court of Justice, Northwest Region)

I. Consolidated Practice Direction for the Southwest Region (Latest Amendment: May 17, 2019)

Notice of Amendment:

Effective May 17, 2019, paragraphs 5, 6, 10 and 60 are amended to reflect the change in the civil long motions time from 30 minutes to 60 minutes.

Part II C [paras. 25 – 27], Part II D [para. 30] were amended on July 1, 2018.

Effective August 1, 2016

This Practice Direction applies to proceedings in the Superior Court of Justice, Southwest Region, effective August 1, 2016. It replaces the previous Consolidated Practice Direction for the Southwest Region that was effective on July 1, 2014.

Counsel and parties are advised to refer to the relevant Parts of the Consolidated Provincial Practice Direction as well as the Consolidated Practice Direction for Divisional Court Proceedings which are available on the Superior Court of Justice website at: www.ontariocourts.ca/scj.

Table of Contents

Part I: Civil Proceedings

A. Introduction

1. This Part identifies scheduling and administrative changes to facilitate more expeditious and efficient litigation under the *Rules of Civil Procedure*.

2. Subject to paragraph 60, this Part *does not* apply to commercial motions or applications heard in London as described in Part IV of this Practice Direction. This Part does apply to contested estates matters as described in Part V below.

3. A reference in this part to a "rule" or the "rules" is a reference to the *Rules of Civil Procedure*.

B. Applications and Motions

4. All applications and motions will be heard on the assigned motions court day for each respective county in the Southwest Region commencing at 10:00 a.m. unless specified otherwise in this practice direction or by court order.

5. Any motion or application that requires more than 60 minutes for all parties to argue, or requires a court reporter, will be adjourned to a special appointment date.

6. Two consent adjournments of short motions (motions scheduled for 60 minutes or less) are permitted. Any further adjournment will, if permitted, be sine die returnable on four days' notice unless otherwise ordered by the presiding judge.

7. All motions and applications (including those requiring a special appointment date) must be confirmed. Confirmation forms must be filed no later than 2:00 p.m. three days before the hearing date, as required under rules 37.10.1(1) and 38.09.1(1). Communication and cooperation in completing all parts of the prescribed form is expected by the Court. The form should accurately and fully describe all materials to which the presiding judge will be referred by any party.

8. Rules 37.10.1(2) and 38.09.1(2) provide that motions and applications that are not confirmed will not be heard by the Court. Parties will not be permitted to take unconfirmed matters into motions court to request that they be added to the list.

9. For greater certainty, the *Rules of Civil Procedure*, including all timelines, are to be strictly adhered to.

C. Special Appointments for Motions and Applications

10. Special appointments are required for motions and applications that require more than 60 minutes for all parties to argue or require a court reporter.

11. Special appointments are scheduled for a date made available by the Trial Coordinator. To obtain a date, all parties or their counsel must complete a Certificate of Readiness of Special Appointment confirming they are, or will be on the assigned date, ready to proceed, the time required for the motion and whether a court reporter is required. The Certificate of Readiness of Special Appointment also includes a timetable for the completion of any step that remains to be completed at the time a special appointment is scheduled. The judge presiding in motions court will resolve any disputes relating to a date for such appointment and/or the timetable in motions court. Counsel and self-represented parties will be expected to strictly abide by the timetable and be ready to argue the matter on the assigned date.

12. Factums are required for all special appointments. Pursuant to the *Rules of Civil Procedure*, the moving party's factum shall be served and filed at least seven days before the scheduled hearing date of the special appointment. The responding party's factum shall be served and filed at least four days before the hearing.

13. Once the special appointment has been scheduled by the court, any adjournment requests must be spoken to before a judge. The Trial Coordinator must be advised of any adjournment requests and any settlements as far in advance of the hearing date as possible. In person attendance is required to speak to requests for an adjournment or to vacate a special appointment date. Adjournments will only be granted in exceptional cases.

14. Paragraphs 7 and 8 (confirmation forms) also apply to motions and applications that are scheduled as special appointments.

D. Pre-Trials

15. In order to make civil pre-trials more productive and efficient, the following guidelines should be adhered to:

   a. Copies of medical records and reports need not be filed with your pre-trial conference brief. Instead, relevant passages from these documents shall be copied and pasted within the pre-trial conference brief itself;

   b. Each party shall bring to the conference a separate brief containing all medical and other expert reports to the conference as required by rule 50.11;

   c. Pre-trial conference briefs should not exceed 20 pages in length, except in the rarest of cases. Briefs that are concise tend to be the most focused and useful for the Court;

   d. Pre-trial conference briefs must contain all of the information mandated by rule 50 including the names and anticipated length of the evidence of each witness a party is likely to call (the "witness list") and details of all steps that need to be completed before the matter is ready to be heard (including the delivery of any other expert report) and the estimated time for completion of each outstanding step. Each witness list shall be set forth in a separate, stand-alone schedule capable of being removed from the pre-trial conference brief and attached to the pre-trial conference report completed by the presiding judge pursuant to rule 50.08(1).

E. Designated Counties for the Commencement of Mortgage Proceedings under rule 13.1.01(3)

16. Pursuant to rule 13.1.01(3), London, Windsor, St. Thomas, Chatham, Sarnia, Woodstock, Stratford and Goderich have been designated as the place for commencement of mortgage proceedings for property located anywhere in the Southwest Region.

Part II: Family Proceedings

A. Introduction

17. This Part identifies scheduling and administrative changes to facilitate more expeditious and efficient litigation under the *Family Law Rules*.

18. Unless otherwise stated, this Part applies to **all** family proceedings, including those in the Unified Family Court – London.

19. A reference in this part to a "rule" or the "rules" is a reference to the *Family Law Rules*.

B. Family Motions

20. Any motion that requires less than one hour for all parties to argue is treated as a regular motion.

21. All regular motions will be heard on the assigned motions court day for each respective county in the Southwest Region commencing at 10:00 a.m. unless otherwise ordered by the court.

22. All motions requiring more than one hour to argue will require a special appointment.

23. Paragraphs 11 and 12 relating to special appointments in civil cases also apply to special appointments in family cases, including the requirements for the filing of factums. However, if the Certificate of Readiness of Special Appointment – Family Cases has been completed at the case conference, no further attendance will be required in order to obtain the date for a special appointment.

14B Motions

24. Form 14B motions are governed by Part I of the Consolidated Provincial Practice Direction. Counsel and parties are advised to refer to that Practice Direction for further direction.

C. Confirmation Forms

25. Each party to a conference or motion must file a fully completed <u>Form 14C Confirmation of Motion</u> or <u>Form 17F Confirmation of Conference</u> no later than 2 p.m. three business days before the motion or conference, except urgent motions that are being brought without notice to the other party do not need to be confirmed.

26. Form 14C Confirmation of Motion or Form 17F Confirmation of Conference forms must only list the specific issues that are to be addressed at that event and the specific materials that the judge should review. Communication and cooperation in completing all parts of the prescribed form is expected. The materials which the presiding judge will be referred to, by any party, should be fully and accurately described.

27. Where Form 14C Confirmation of Motion or Form 17F Confirmation of Conference forms have not been properly completed and filed by the appropriate deadline, the event will not be heard on the scheduled day without the permission of the presiding judge.

D. Conference Briefs

28. No brief or other document for use at the conference that is required to be served or filed may be served or filed after 2:00 p.m. four business days before the date scheduled for the conference (rule 17(14.1)).

29. Any attempt to file conference briefs outside of the filing dates set out in the *Family Law Rules* will be refused at the counter. However, the parties may attend in person no later than 9:00 a.m. on the day of the conference with their conference brief and file with the Trial Coordinator provided it has been served on the other party as required in the above paragraph 24 and proof of service is attached. The Trial Coordinator will stamp the brief "FILED LATE" and place it with the materials for the pre-

siding judge to review or not, at the judge's discretion. This process allows the court staff to comply with the Rules and for conferences to proceed in a timely manner, giving the presiding judge an opportunity to read the conference brief or refuse the brief.

E. Scheduling Family Conferences

30. Case Conferences will be limited to 7 per day to allow approximately 45 minutes for each matter scheduled.

31. Settlement Conferences will be limited to 5 per day to allow 60 minutes scheduled for each matter.

F. Settlement Conferences and Trial Scheduling Conferences

32. The settlement conference is an important step in family cases. The primary purpose of the settlement conference is to settle or at least narrow the issues in dispute. Parties (or their counsel) are required to communicate before any conference in order to attempt to narrow or resolve the issues that are in dispute, unless the parties are self-represented and are also prohibited from communicating by court order.

33. Pursuant to rule 17(5) (g), if the case is not settled at the settlement conference, one of the additional purposes of the conference is to identify the witnesses and other evidence to be presented at trial, estimate the time needed for trial and, where appropriate, to schedule the case for trial.

34. Parties are to come to the settlement conference having completed Parts 1 and 2 of the Trial Scheduling Endorsement Form. If the case has not settled at the conclusion of the settlement conference, the presiding judge will complete Part 3 of the form, or shall give directions to the parties regarding the completion of this form.

35. If necessary, the court may require the parties to attend a trial scheduling conference to canvass issues regarding the scheduling of the trial and ensure proper completion of the Trial Scheduling Endorsement Form. Each party shall complete and file their portion of the Trial Scheduling Endorsement Form with the court in advance of a trial scheduling conference in accordance with the timelines in rule 17(13.1).

36. The purpose of a trial scheduling conference includes (i) ensuring that the case is ready to proceed to trial, (ii) considering each party's list of proposed witnesses and (iii) ensuring the accuracy of the estimated time for trial. Consideration should also be given to other conditions that would be appropriate under rule 1 in order to limit the duration and scope of the trial.

37. A trial date will not normally be made available until the court has reviewed and endorsed the complete Trial Scheduling Endorsement Form. The court may however, in its discretion, provide litigants with a provisional trial date before the court has endorsed the complete Trial Scheduling Endorsement Form, where necessary. Where this has occurred, the form must be finalized no later than 60 days in advance of the trial or as directed by the presiding judge in order to retain the scheduled trial date.

G. Trial Management Conferences

38. A trial management conference should be held in family cases that have not been resolved at or before the settlement conference in order to ensure trial readiness and canvas settlement. The trial management conference should be scheduled no more than two weeks in advance of the scheduled trial date, wherever possible.

39. The purpose of a trial management conference is to confirm that parties are ready for trial, have filed their Trial Record exchanged all other material required by the Trial Scheduling Endorsement Form, provide any further directions or revisions to the Trial Scheduling Endorsement Form, and to explore any final possibilities for settlement to resolve the trial.

40. The Trial Management Conference Brief: Form 17E is no longer required. Instead the following documents must be filed at least 7 days before the Trial Management Conference:

   a. The completed Trial Scheduling Endorsement Form must be filed by either the Applicant or the party that requested the conference;

   b. Each party must file an offer to settle all outstanding issues; and,

   c. Each party must file an outline of their opening statement for trial.

41. The Endorsement Volume of the continuing record should also be put before the judge at the trial management conference.

42. The judge will make any changes to Part 3 of the Trial Scheduling Endorsement Form to reflect any changes in the outstanding issues, witnesses and positions of the parties since the form was initially completed, ensure that the case is trial ready and confirm the trial sittings.

43. The completed Trial Scheduling Endorsement Form shall be filed with or added to the Trial Record. No offers to settle should be included in the Trial Record.

44. Where the case has been settled and the trial is no longer required, one of the parties shall immediately advise the Trial Coordinator so that the trial date can be vacated. A copy of any Minutes of Settlement or consent should be filed at the same time.

45. The Trial Record is to be served and filed within the timelines set out in the *Family Law Rules.*

Part III: Additional Provisions Regarding the Unified Family Court – London

A.   Family Law matters

46. Paragraphs 17 – 23 also apply to all family law matters being heard in the Unified Family Court – London except for *Child, Youth and Family Services Act.*

47. Previously scheduled settlement conferences, motions, special appointments or summary hearings may be adjourned on consent by obtaining a new date from the Trial Coordinator. A confirmation must then be sent in changing the dates. If the confirmation is sent there is no need for attendance by counsel/party. A separate confirmation must be filed to confirm attendance on the new date in accordance with the *Family Law Rules.* No more than two consent adjournments will be permitted before an in-person attendance is required.

48. Trial management conferences with a set trial sittings date may only be adjourned by attendance before the Local Administrative Judge or his/her designate at a time that may be arranged through the Trial Coordinator.

49. Trial adjournment requests may be made at the Trial Readiness Court if they have not already been addressed at the Trial Management Conference. Attendance is required. It is expected that if a matter is on the trial list it is ready for trial and, if not, it will

be removed, and placed on another trial list, or adjourned to a date to be spoken to, at the presiding judge's discretion. At the Trial Readiness Court no order will be given to the trials and the parties will be expected to be ready when called.

B. *Child and Family Services Act* matters

50. Paragraphs 51 – 54 apply to all *Child, Youth and Family Services Act* matters being heard in the Unified Family Court – London.

51. Trials can only be adjourned to a subsequent trial date on motion with supporting affidavit material. These motions may be brought at the Trial Readiness Court or earlier before the Local Administrative Judge or his/her designate at a time that may be arranged through the Trial Coordinator. This direction applies to requests for adjournments by Children Aid Societies and any other party.

52. Temporary Care and Custody hearings and other motions may be adjourned to a subsequent date as set out above in paragraph 47 for family matters without the necessity of attendance by counsel or parties, provided that no more than two consent adjournments will be permitted before an in-person attendance is required.

53. Even with the consent of both parties, settlement conferences and trial management conferences may only be adjourned by filing a confirmation indicating an intention to adjourn accompanied by a personal attendance to explain the reasons for the adjournment. If the parties know ahead that a request to adjourn the settlement conference will be made, the matter may be brought forward to be spoken to. Where an adjournment has been granted, a confirmation form will have to be filed in advance of the new date as required by the *Family Law Rules*.

54. For child protection matters, the child protection Trial Scheduling Endorsement Form must be filed by all parties at the final Settlement Conference. This form is available on the Superior Court of Justice website.

C. General

55. Trial lists are blended with *Family Law Act/Children's Law Reform Act* matters and *Child, Youth and Family Services Act* matters, bearing in mind that *Child, Youth and Family Services Act* matters have statutory timelines under both the *Child, Youth and Family Services Act* and the *Family Law Rules* that must be respected, and will be given priority.

56. Any requests for adjournments of settlement conferences, special appointments or Temporary Care and Custody hearings should be made as early as possible so that other matters may be scheduled in their stead. This will assist in reducing time-outs for these events.

Part IV: Commercial Proceedings in London

57. The purpose of this Part is to ensure administrative steps are in place for the appropriate and timely scheduling of commercial matters.

A. Application

58. This Part applies to commercial matters in London involving the following statutes:

   a. those arising under the *Bankruptcy and Insolvency Act* (BIA) to the extent they

1354

are beyond the jurisdiction of the Deputy Registrar under section 192 of the BIA. Such matters would include, by way of example only, opposed applications for a bankruptcy order, interim receiverships;

b. matters involving the *Companies' Creditors Arrangement Act* from the initial application until completion;

c. matters involving the *Personal Property Security Act*;

d. matters involving receivers appointed under the *Courts of Justice Act* whether in conjunction with or separate from an appointment under the BIA;

e. matters involving issues arising under the *Farm Debt Mediation Act*;

f. matters involving realization or the determination of priorities of claims arising under the *Bank Act*;

g. matters under either the *Ontario Business Corporations Act* or the *Canada Business Corporations Act*;

h. matters under the *Partnerships Act* or *Limited Partnerships Act*;

i. matters under the *Bulk Sales Act*; and

j. matters incidental to a proceeding involving a statute or subject mentioned above.

B. Procedure

59. Counsel shall identify to the Trial Coordinator that a commercial matter is time sensitive by completing the Time Sensitive – Commercial Scheduling Request A date for hearing shall be scheduled directly with the Trial Coordinator.

60. If a commercial matter is not time sensitive, motions or applications shall initially be made returnable on a regular motions date. If such a motion or application requires more than 60 minutes for all parties to argue or requires a court reporter, counsel shall complete the Certificate of Readiness of Special Appointment of Commercial Matter Form and the Region's usual procedures with respect to special appointments as set out in Part I shall apply.

61. Factums are required for all special appointments involving commercial matters. Pursuant to the *Rules of Civil Procedure*, the moving party's factum shall be served and filed at least seven days before the scheduled hearing date of the special appointment. The responding party's factum shall be served and filed at least four days before the hearing.

62. Paragraphs 7 and 8 (confirmation forms) also apply to all motions and applications for commercial proceedings in London.

63. Counsel and parties are directed to the provisions of rule 37.15 and encouraged to consider the appropriateness of a request for a direction that all motions in the commercial proceeding be heard by a single judge.

Part V: Additional Provisions Regarding Contested Estate Matters including a Contested Passing of Accounts

64. This part (in addition to Part I) applies to all contested estates matters, including a contested passing of accounts, in the Southwest Region.

65. Unless a judge has dispensed with the requirement, a contested estate matter, including a contested passing of accounts, estimated by any party to require a hearing of more than one day will not be scheduled except in accordance with an order giving directions. An order dispensing with the requirement will only be made in exceptional circumstances. Motions for directions may also be sought for a shorter contested estate matter.

66. Orders giving directions in contested matters are designed to provide the parties with a procedural framework in which to prepare the proceeding for final adjudication. Rule 75.06 provides the court with considerable discretion and flexibility to put in place a process that will ensure the just, expeditious and least expensive determination of a proceeding on its merits. Parties are expected to take time and care in preparing proposed orders giving directions for consideration by the court.

67. Draft orders giving directions should address the following matters to the extent applicable:

   a. the issue(s) to be decided;

   b. the identity of the parties;

   c. whether there is any party under disability who requires representation and, if so, whether notice to the Public Guardian and Trustee or the Office of the Children's Lawyer should be directed;

   d. whether an estate trustee should be appointed during litigation and the amount of security, if any, such an estate trustee should file;

   e. who shall be served with the order for directions, and the method of and times for service;

   f. whether the parties will exchange pleadings or put before the court their respective positions and the material facts upon which they rely by some other means;

   g. procedures for bringing the matter before the court in a summary way;

   h. any other pre-hearing steps to be undertaken, including the scope of documentary disclosure and examinations for discovery;

   i. the necessity of and means of obtaining third party records including accounting or legal records;

   j. the nature of any pre-hearing motion;

   k. the delivery of any expert report and the utility of a pre-hearing meeting between experts to narrow the issues in dispute;

   l. the date by which the matter must be set down for hearing;

   m. a pre-trial conference;

   n. the witnesses each party intends to call, the issues each witness intends to address, and the anticipated length of each witness' testimony including cross-examination;

   o. a timetable for each applicable step outlined above; and

   p. any matter relating to the conduct of the trial or hearing, including whether affidavit(s) may or will be used as the evidence-in-chief of a witness.

68. A motion for an order giving directions should be scheduled through the Trial Co-ordinator at 9:30 a.m. for 15-minutes if on consent and 30-minutes if contested. If the parties cannot agree on the terms of an order giving directions, each party must file with its motion material a copy of the draft order giving directions it is seeking. Under no circumstances should any order giving directions provide that an affidavit is or affidavits are to constitute or form part of the pleadings.

69. The parties' time estimate for the hearing will be re-evaluated at the pre-trial conference. The hearing date may be vacated if the presiding judge concludes the parties have underestimated the time required.

Part VI: Forms

70. Each of the forms prescribed under the *Rules of Civil Procedure* and the Family Law Rules are available on the Ontario Court Forms website

71. Additional forms referred to in this Practice Direction are as follows:

    A. Certificate of Readiness of Special Appointment

    B. Certificate of Readiness of Special Appointment – Family Cases

    C. Time Sensitive – Commercial Scheduling Request

    D. Certificate of Readiness of Special Appointment for Commercial Matter

    E. Trial Scheduling Endorsement Form (TSEF – Family)

    F. Trial Scheduling Endorsement Form (TSEF – Child Protection)

Dated: July 21, 2016

Amendments: May 17, 2019; July 1, 2018 (Part II C [paras. 25 – 27], Part II D [para. 30])

Heather J. Smith
Chief Justice
Superior Court of Justice (Ontario)

Thomas A. Heeney
Regional Senior Judge
Superior Court of Justice, Southwest Region

J. Consolidated Practice Direction Concerning Family Cases in Central East Region (Latest Amendment: July 1, 2018)

Notice of Amendment:

Amended July 1, 2018 (to coincide with changes to the Family Law Rules regarding the filing of materials and confirmations for conferences and motions), May 1, 2016 and December 1, 2017.

Effective July 1, 2014

This Practice Direction applies to family law proceedings in Central East Region, other than Child Protection cases under the *Child, Youth and Family Services Act*. It supersedes all previous Practice Directions concerning family proceedings in Central East Region, which are hereby revoked. All family proceedings throughout Central East Region are conducted in the Family Court Branch of the Superior Court of Justice and are governed by the *Family Law Rules*. Counsel and parties can generally expect to attend the following court events with a judge prior to trial: one case conference; one settlement conference; one trial scheduling conference; and one trial management conference. In exceptional cases, a judge may schedule additional conferences or combine some of these conferences into one event, as permitted by the *Family Law Rules*. If a judicial decision is required prior to trial, parties may also schedule a motion as permitted by rules 14(4) to (16).

This Practice Direction explains the filing requirements and scheduling procedures for each of these events to ensure that each attendance is a meaningful appearance. Where there is a conflict between the filing requirements of the Family Law Rules and this Practice Direction, the Practice Direction shall apply. All filing should be done at the Family Court Filing Office for the centre in which the proceedings have been started. All references to the Trial Coordinator refer to the Family Court Trial Coordinator in the same centre. Each Family Court site also has a Family Law Information Centre (FLIC) and Mediation Service. Contact information for these services is available on the Ministry's website.

Contact information for the various court offices at each site in Central East is included at the end of this Practice Direction. Counsel and parties should also refer to the relevant parts of the Consolidated Provincial Practice Direction (Part 1 in particular). There are also additional resources that may be helpful to family law litigants at the end of this Practice Direction.

Each of the forms that are required by the *Family Law Rules* are available at the Ontario Court Forms website at: http://www.ontariocourtforms.on.ca/en/family-law-rules-forms/. In addition, the Trial Scheduling Endorsement Form for family cases is available on the Superior Court of Justice's website at: http://www.ontariocourts.ca/scj/practice/rules-forms/.

Table of Contents

Part I: Confirmations

1.   Each party to a conference or motion must file a fully completed <u>Form 17F Confirmation of Conference</u> or <u>Form 14C Confirmation of Motion</u>. If the parties consult and agree on the content, they may file one joint Form 17F or Form 14C. The Confirmation Forms must be filed no later than 2 p.m. three business days before the date of the motion or conference, **except for long motions which must be filed by 2 p.m. seven days before the motion.** The Form 14C or Form 17F may be faxed to the Filing Office for the court in which the event is scheduled.

2.   Unless the parties do not have counsel **and** are prohibited by court order or safety issues from communicating with each other, the parties or their counsel should consult with each other in advance of the scheduled court date in order to (i) set a joint agenda of the issues they wish addressed at the conference or motion; (ii) attempt to resolve the issues in dispute; and (iii) determine how much of the scheduled time each of them will require at the court attendance to address those issues. The parties are expected to exchange proposals in advance of filing their Form 14C Confirmation of Motion or Form 17F Confirmation of Conference forms. The Form 14C or Form 17F should confirm that these discussions have taken place, or set out reasons why not, otherwise the matter may not be heard. Priority will be given to matters for which the Form 14C or Form 17F Confirmation has been fully and properly completed and reasonable efforts have been made by the parties to consult in advance, as set out above.

3.   If direct communication is problematic, as only one of the two parties is represented, counsel may communicate with the other party in writing before filing their Form 14C or Form 17F. Counsel should indicate (i) the issues that must be addressed; (ii) their client's proposal to resolve the issues; and (iii) how much of the scheduled time he or she requires. The Form 14C or Form 17F should confirm that this communication has been sent and counsel should bring a copy of the communications to the conference or motion.

4.   Where Form 14C Confirmation of Motion or Form 17F Confirmation of Conference forms have not been filed, the conference or motion will be crossed off the court's daily schedule or event list and will not be heard by the court, unless the parties obtain a judge's order to restore it to the list. Costs may also be ordered against a party who has

not filed a properly completed Form 14C Confirmation of Motion or Form 17F Confirmation of Conference.

5.   Form 14C Confirmation of Motion or Form 17 Confirmation of Conference forms must **only** list the specific issues that are to be addressed at that event. They should also indicate which materials the judge should review. The Form 14C or 17F Confirmation should not direct the judge to read the entire file or any material that is not necessary for that day. A judge will generally only read the briefs and financial documents for case or settlement conferences. For motions, the Form 14C or 17F Confirmation should provide a clear reference to the specific volume, tab and page numbers of the Continuing Record that need to be read for the event. Normally, this will be the Notice of Motion and affidavits filed by both parties. *Failure to provide this information may result in the materials not being reviewed by the judge, the matter being placed at the bottom of the list, or the matter not being heard on that day.*

6.   Form 14C Confirmation of Motion or Form 17F Confirmation of Conference forms must also include a realistic time estimate for the **entire motion or conference to be completed in the time that has been booked**, including time required by the other party. See paragraphs 39 and 42 below regarding the allocation of time for motions. *Parties will be held to the time stated on their Confirmations.*

Part II: Adjournments

7.   Once a date has been booked, the court expects counsel or parties to be ready to proceed on the scheduled day and time. In most centres, a number of cases will be scheduled at the same time, as the court cannot anticipate who will be delayed waiting to see duty counsel. Every effort will be made to give priority to cases in which the parties have exchanged properly completed material and negotiated in advance, so that they are ready to proceed at their scheduled time. However, counsel or parties should be prepared for the possibility of lengthy wait times, as the court works through the scheduled list. The court's schedule is posted <u>online</u> at 4:30 p.m. on the day before the scheduled attendance.

8.   Due to the number of litigants requiring court dates, it is important that scheduled events are not adjourned, unless there is a reason that the parties cannot proceed. If circumstances arise that necessitate an adjournment, it should be requested as soon as possible so that the time can be made available for other matters. Unless otherwise provided in this Practice Direction, up to two administrative adjournments per case may be obtained by contacting the Trial Coordinator no later than 2:00 p.m. two business days before the scheduled event. After two administrative adjournments of any case, the parties must attend personally before the court to request an adjournment, otherwise the proceeding may be dismissed.

9.   Trial scheduling conferences may not be adjourned without a judge's order, which must be obtained either by 14B motion, if there have not been two previous administrative adjournments for the case, or by appearing before the court. The adjournment request must set out strong reasons why the parties are not ready to go ahead, along with a proposed timetable to move the case forward.

10.   Trial management conferences are peremptory on all parties and may not be adjourned without appearing before the court. Trial management conferences will only be adjourned in compelling and unforeseen circumstances, such as illness.

11. Unless a judge has ordered otherwise, once a matter has been placed on a trial list, parties and counsel must be ready to proceed on one-half days' notice at any time during that trial sittings. A trial may not be adjourned without a judge's order, which can only be obtained by attending personally, and which will only be granted in compelling and unforeseen circumstances, such as illness.

Part III: First Appearance

12. For cases to which Rule 39 applies (fast track matters, which do not involve claims relating to property or divorce), the first court date will be scheduled before a Rule 39 clerk. Parties must attend to ensure their case will be ready for a case conference. However, if both parties have filed all material required by the *Rules* (Application and Answer; Financial Statements; Certificate of Financial Disclosure; and Form 35.1 Affidavit in support of Custody or Access), they may jointly consent to waive the first appearance date. This may be done by filing a Joint Waiver of the first appearance with the Trial Coordinator who will then schedule a case conference date for the parties.

13. The first appearance Clerk can assist the parties by providing information and forms that need to be filed to proceed to a case conference. Duty counsel is available to provide advice to parties who qualify financially. Duty counsel and mediation services are also available to try to assist the parties to negotiate a temporary or final resolution of their issues at the first appearance date.

Part IV: Conferences

A. Case Conferences and Settlement Conferences

14. The parties may obtain a case conference date at their first appearance date or, if permitted by the Family Law Rules, by serving and filing a Notice of Case Conference with a date that has been obtained from the Trial Coordinator. To avoid unnecessary adjournment requests, the other side should be consulted before scheduling a date for any conference wherever possible.

15. Counsel or the parties are required to communicate before any conference in order to attempt to narrow or resolve the issues that are in dispute, unless the parties are self-represented **and** prohibited from communicating by court order.

16. Parties should serve and file a case conference brief (Form 17A) for case conferences and a settlement conference brief (Form 17C) for settlement conferences with any necessary attachments. The purposes of a case conference are set out in Rule 17(4) and the purposes of a settlement conference are set out in Rule 17(5). Parties should prepare their briefs with a view to a realistic agenda that can be completed in the time that has been scheduled for the conference.

17. Conference briefs were designed to replace adversarial pleadings and affidavits. Absent exceptional circumstances, the briefs should be prepared in a manner that will promote a climate for settlement and can realistically be read by the conference judge in the time scheduled that day. The briefs should also set out the party's proposal for any unresolved issues. **Case conference briefs should be limited to the four page form set out in the *Family Law Rules* with a maximum of two additional pages of narrative and proposals**, other than supporting material such as lists of outstanding disclosure or professional reports. Case conference briefs that exceed the six page

maximum may be returned to the parties, and the matter may be placed at the bottom of the list. Lengthy or unduly adversarial case or settlement conference briefs may not be read. The matter may also be placed at the bottom of the list and costs may be awarded.

18. At the conclusion of the case conference, the presiding judge will either schedule a settlement conference or give directions to the parties about scheduling their next step. If a motion is required, the parties should agree to deadlines to file their material, so that all material will be filed no later than 2 p.m. three business days before the motion is scheduled to be heard.

Teleconferences

19. Parties may arrange for a conference to occur by teleconference with permission obtained in advance from the judge who is scheduled to conduct the conference. The request should indicate whether the other side is consenting and, if not, the reasons. If the other party will not consent, a request for a teleconference may be made by filing a Form 14B Motion or by faxing a letter to the Trial Coordinator to be considered by the conference judge.

Motions to Change

20. A request to change a final order is made by filing a motion to change under Rule 15. The first case conference on a motion to change a final order or agreement shall be scheduled before a Dispute Resolution Officer (DRO) for those centres that have a DRO program (Barrie, Newmarket and Oshawa) in accordance with Part I of the Consolidated Provincial Practice Direction.

21. A DRO conference can be held on matters other than motions to change only as directed by the court. This may be requested by a Form 14B Motion or at another court event.

B. Trial Scheduling Conferences

22. If the matter is not resolved at a settlement conference, the next event will be a trial scheduling conference. Where possible, the trial scheduling conference will be heard within 30 days of the settlement conference by the same judge. A trial scheduling conference will normally be scheduled by the settlement conference judge at the conclusion of the settlement conference, unless a judge has directed that the settlement conference and trial scheduling conference be combined. If the settlement conference and trial scheduling conference have been combined, the court will ensure that the Trial Scheduling Endorsement Form is completed prior to the conclusion of the combined conference.

23. The purposes of a trial scheduling conference are to ensure trial readiness and make directions regarding how the trial will proceed. The parties should serve and file a Trial Scheduling Endorsement Form in advance of the trial scheduling conference in accordance with the timelines in Rule 17(13.1), with the appropriate portions completed by each party, in lieu of the Trial Management Conference Brief (Form 17E).

24. Prior to a matter being scheduled for trial, the Trial Scheduling Endorsement Form must be fully completed and endorsed by the trial scheduling conference judge. In exceptional cases of urgency, a judge may place a matter on the trial list to secure a trial

date before the Trial Scheduling Endorsement Form is completed. In those cases, specific directions will be given about when the Trial Scheduling Endorsement Form is to be completed and when the trial management conference is to be held.

25. At the conclusion of the trial scheduling conference, a trial management conference will generally be scheduled by the presiding judge. Parties are required to advise the Trial Coordinator immediately if a matter settles so that this date can be made available to other matters.

C. Trial Management Conferences

26. Unless otherwise ordered, a trial management conference will be held for any case that has not resolved 30 days prior to the scheduled trial date. Where possible, this event will be held within 2 weeks of the scheduled trial date. The purpose of the trial management conference is to confirm that parties are ready for trial, have filed their Trial Record and exchanged all other material required by the Trial Scheduling Endorsement Form, provide any further directions or revisions to the Trial Scheduling Endorsement Form and to explore any final possibilities for settlement to resolve the trial.

27. Additional requirements relating to the trial management conference are contained in paragraphs 47 to 50 below.

Part V: Motions

28. If the parties require a judge's order related to some aspect of the case, they may schedule a motion. Rule 14(4) provides that, except in urgent situations, no motion should be brought before a conference on the substantive issues in a case has been completed. Short motions are defined as motions that can be completed in less than one hour. Long motions are motions that are expected to take longer than one hour. 14B motions, which do not require a court attendance, and urgent motions, with or without notice, are also discussed below.

A. 14B Motions

29. A Form 14B Motion may be filed for matters that are procedural, uncomplicated or unopposed, as set out in Rule 14(10). A 14B must be filed at the family court office and cannot be filed by fax.

30. The 14B Motion and supporting materials must be filed in the Continuing Record.

B. Urgent Motions on Notice

31. A party may seek an urgent motion **on notice** without a case conference in situations of urgency or hardship regarding serious issues such as abduction, safety issues or dire financial harm. A party seeking such a motion must serve and file all of the required materials except for a Form 14C Confirmation. Prior to bringing an urgent motion, the Trial Coordinator should be contacted to see if an urgent case conference can be scheduled before the motion is heard.

32. In order to assist with having the order issued quickly, parties are encouraged to provide the court with a draft order for urgent motions.

C. Urgent Motions without Notice

33. Motions without notice may be brought only in exceptional circumstances as set out in Rule 14(12).

34. A court will not generally make an order without allowing both parties an opportunity to participate. In addition to addressing the requirements of paragraph 31 above, a party who is seeking a motion without notice to the other party **must** address why the other party has not been served. **The motion materials should set out specifically and clearly why notice is unnecessary, not reasonably possible, or any other grounds that would justify the motion being heard without notice to the other side.**

35. An order obtained without notice will need to be served on the other party and the matter must be scheduled to return for another court date within 14 days, as set out in Rule 14(14).

36. If a person is requesting a restraining order as part of his or her urgent motion, he or she should also complete the pink restraining order endorsement form with the required information (such as names and birthdates of those affected, as well as addresses at which the other side is to be prohibited from attending). This form is available at the Filing Office where the urgent motion is filed.

37. If a restraining order has been granted, the court can arrange for service of the material on the other side, if requested by a party who is not represented by counsel.

D. Short Motions

38. Motions that are expected to take one hour or less may be scheduled on the regular motion day for that centre. This date must be obtained from the Trial Coordinator. No factum should be filed for a short motion, unless ordered by the case conference or case management judge. The Notice of Motion and supporting material should be served and filed at the Family Court Office within the timelines set out in the Family Law Rules.

39. If a motion is booked for one hour, each party will be permitted a maximum of 20 minutes for argument and five minutes will be available for reply. The remaining 15 minutes is for the judge's decision and submissions regarding costs. If parties are not able to adequately deal with their matter within that time, they should schedule a long motion.

40. If a party wishes to bring a cross-motion or responding motion on the same day, it must also be scheduled through the Trial Coordinator. If no additional time is required for argument, as the issues are the same as those already raised in the motion, the responding motion may be booked for the same day. If additional time will be required for argument, and time is not available on the same short motion day, the responding motion must be scheduled on another regular motion day that has time available. Alternatively, the parties may avoid two attendances by agreeing to have both motions heard together by the same judge on a long motions day.

E. Long Motions

41. Motions that are expected to take more than one hour, as allocated in paragraph 39, must be scheduled as long motions through the Trial Coordinator or by the presiding

judge at a conference. Long motions can be scheduled either (a) with the other party's written consent or (b) with the court's permission. **The moving party must serve and file all their motion material and an Offer to Settle at least 30 days prior to the scheduled motion date, otherwise the date will be vacated**. The responding party must serve and file their responding material **and an Offer to Settle** at least **15** days before the scheduled motion date. Reply material, if any, and a properly completed 14C, confirming the motion date and material to be read, must be served and filed by 2 p.m. **seven** days prior to the scheduled motion date. **If a long motion is not confirmed by 2 p.m. seven days in advance, it will be removed from the list and the date will be vacated.**

42. The time for argument of a long motion will be allocated as follows: one third of the time scheduled for the motion will be allotted to the applicant for argument; one third of the time will be allotted to the respondent; and five minutes for each hour that has been booked will be allotted for reply. The remaining time will be for allocated for the judge's decision and submissions regarding costs. The parties will be held to the time that they have scheduled.

F. Factums and Briefs of Authorities

43. Unless otherwise directed by the conference judge, no factum should be filed for a short motion but a properly drafted factum is required on all long motions, other than Motions to Change. Each party's factum must be served and filed by no later than 2 p.m. two business days before the hearing of the motion.

44. No factum may exceed 20 pages without leave of the court.

45. The authorities that are included on the court's list of Often Cited Family Cases do not need to be provided to the court with a party's factum. Counsel and parties are advised to refer to Part I-B of the Consolidated Provincial Practice Direction. An updated list of family cases is available on the Superior Court's website at: www.ontariocourts.ca/scj.

G. Electronic Copies of Materials

46. When a motion is complex or the volume of materials is large, the parties may file an electronic copy of their materials by providing them by USB. The USB should include a copy of their motion materials, including their factum, where required. Paper copies of the motion materials must also be filed in the Continuing Record. The factum should be filed as a separate document, which does not form part of the Continuing Record. Counsel and parties should refer to the Guide Concerning e-Delivery of Documents available on the Superior Court's website.

Part VI – Trials and Trial Records

47. The Applicant must file a completed Trial Record, no later than **7 days before the trial management conference**, containing the documents set out in Rule 23(1) and the completed Trial Scheduling Endorsement Form. The Respondent may add any documents that should have been included in the Trial Record, as set out in Rule 23(2), up to 2 p.m. **two** business days before the trial management conference. A current financial statement for each party and comparative net family property statement shall be included in the Trial Record. **The parties do not need to update their financial statements and net family property statements again prior to trial unless**

there is a change or an updated statement has been requested by the court.

48. No later than 2 p.m. two business days before the trial management conference, each party must also serve and file an Offer to Settle, an outline of their Opening Trial Statement and a Draft Order.

49. If the trial record has not been filed by the trial management conference, an order may be made requiring that the trial record be prepared on an urgent basis and that costs are to be paid or alternatively the matter may be removed from the trial list.

50. Any requests to adjourn the trial should be dealt with at the trial management conference in accordance with paragraph 10 above.

Part VII – Uncontested Trials

51. If no Answer has been filed within 30 days of the Application being served, Rule 23 allows a party to request a final order on affidavit evidence (Form 23C). Where a first appearance or case conference has been scheduled, or there is another upcoming court date, the Form 23C will not be considered by a judge in advance of the scheduled date.

52. The party filing the Form 23C should ensure that all orders requested have been claimed in the Application. As the uncontested trial is a substitute for a full trial with oral evidence, he or she should also ensure that all evidence relied upon in support of the requested order is filed as part of the 23C.

Dated: December 1, 2017

Amended: July 1, 2018; December 1, 2017; May 1, 2016

Heather J. Smith, Chief Justice (Superior Court of Justice (Ontario))

Michelle Fuerst, Regional Senior Judge (Superior Court of Justice, Central East Region)

Contact information for the Family Courts in this region, including each Trial Coordinator for family cases, is attached as **Schedule A**.

Additional information about family cases in the Superior Court of Justice is available in the **Guide to Process for Family Cases** at www.ontariocourts.ca/scj/family/.

General information about family law and family cases is available from Community Legal Education Ontario at: http://yourlegalrights.on.ca/legal-topic/family-law.

Information about the mediation and information services that are available at the Family Courts in this region is available on the Ministry's website at www.attorneygeneral.jus.gov.on.ca/english/family/mediation.php.

Schedule A Barrie / Bracebridge / Cobourg / Lindsay / Newmarket / Oshawa / Peterborough

Barrie

Family Office
Telephone: 705-739-6116
Fax: 705-739-6109

Family Trial Coordinator
Telephone: 705-739-6442
Toll Free: 1-800-410-1061
Fax: 705-739-6099

Bracebridge

Family Office
Telephone: 705-645-8793
Fax: 705-645-7901

Family Trial Coordinator
Telephone: 705-739-7121
Toll Free: 1-800-410-1061
Fax: 705-739-6099

Cobourg

Family Office
Telephone: 905-372-3751
Fax: 905-372-9952

Family Trial Coordinator
Telephone: 705-876-3823
Toll Free: 1-800-788-0977
Fax: 705-745-3526

Lindsay

Family Office
Telephone: 705-324-1400
Fax: 705-324-1401

Family Trial Coordinator
Telephone: 705-876-3823
Toll Free: 1-800-788-0977
Fax: 705-745-3526

Newmarket

Family Office
Telephone: 905-853-4809
Fax: 905-853-4864

Family Trial Coordinator
Telephone: 905-853-4823
Fax: 905-853-4880

Oshawa

Family Office
Telephone: 905-743-2800, ext 7010
Fax: 905-743-2622

Family Trial Coordinator
Telephone: 905-743-2800, ext. 7012
Fax: 905-743-2693

Peterborough

Family Office
Telephone: 705-876-3815
Fax: 705-876-3813

Family Trial Coordinator
Telephone: 705-876-3823
Toll Free: 1-800-788-0977
Fax: 705-745-3526

K. Practice Direction Regarding Family Cases in the Superior Court of Justice East Region (Latest Amendment: July 1, 2018)

Notice of Amendment:

Part III [paras. 7 – 12] were amended on July 1, 2018.

Effective August 1, 2016

This Practice Direction applies to family law proceedings in the Superior Court of Justice in the East Region. It supersedes Part I: Family Proceedings of the Consolidated Practice Direction for the East Region.

Counsel and parties are advised to refer also to the relevant parts of the Consolidated Provincial Practice Direction which is available on the Superior Court of Justice website at www.ontariocourts.ca/scj.

This Practice Direction provides clarification of the process for motions (including urgent motions), case conferences, settlement conferences, trial management conferences and trials that are required under the *Family Law Rules*. This Practice Direction does not apply to cases under the *Child, Youth and Family Services Act*.

Part I: General Information

    A.   **Court Contact Information:**

    B.   **Schedule:**

    C.   **Forms:**

Part II: Obtaining Dates

Part III: Confirmations

Part IV: Motions

    A.   **Regular Motions**

    B.   **Long Motions**

Part V: Compendiums – Family Law Motions

    A.   **14B Motions**

    B.   **Procedural Motions: Ottawa Only**

    C.   **Urgent Motions on Notice**

    D.   **Urgent Motions without Notice**

Part VI: Consent Adjournments

Part VII: Conference Attendance by Video or Teleconference

Part VIII: Trial Scheduling

Part IX: Trial Records

Part I: General Information

A. Court Contact Information

1.   The contact information for the ten court sites in the East Region can be found on the regional court schedule section of the website of the Superior Court of Justice.

B. Schedule

2.   The schedule for proceedings in Family Court for the ten court sites in the East Region can also be found on the regional court schedule section of the website of the Superior Court of Justice.

C. Forms

3. Each of the forms prescribed under the Family Law Rules is available on the Ontario Court Forms. The Trial Scheduling Endorsement Form, referred to below, is available on the Superior Court of Justice website.

Part II: Obtaining Dates

4. Dates for conferences and motions shall be obtained at the Family Law Counter in conjunction with the Trial Coordinator's Office. The party scheduling the date should consult in advance with the other party so that the date set is available for both parties.

5. Strict attention should be paid to the estimate of time required for the event. The parties should consult in advance so that the time estimate will include sufficient time for both parties, including for any cross motion that is expected to be heard on the same date.

6. Time allotments on the daily event lists are based on the time estimate provided when the date is obtained. Parties may be held to that time estimate, or, the motion may not be heard if the actual time required for it exceeds the initial time estimate.

Part III: Confirmations

7. Each party to a motion or conference must file a Form 14C Confirmation of Motion or Form 17F Confirmation of Conference, or the parties may file one jointly, no later than 2 p.m. three business days before the date of the motion or conference.

8. These may be filed at the Family Law Counter in the courthouse or they may be faxed to the Family Court Office. Please see the Court Contact Information link above.

9. The parties or their counsel should consult with each other prior to filing their Form 14C Confirmation of Motion/Form 17F Confirmation of Conference forms, unless the parties are self-represented and prohibited from communicating by court order or by a term of judicial release.

10. Where no Form 14C Confirmation of Motion or Form 17 Confirmation of Conference has been filed by any party, the conference or motion will be not be heard on that day. Costs may also be ordered against a party who has not filed a Confirmation.

11. Form 14C Confirmation of Motion or Form 17F Confirmation of Conference forms must only list the specific issues that are to be addressed at the event. They should also indicate which materials the judge should review with clear reference to the specific volume, tab, and page numbers of the Continuing Record. *Failure to provide this information may result in the materials not being reviewed by the judge or the motion not being heard on that day.*

12. Form 14C Confirmation of Motion or Form 17F Confirmation of Conference forms must also include an up-to-date time estimate for the entire motion or conference, including time required by the other party. Parties should not expect more time than originally requested nor will they be permitted more time than specified in the confirmation forms.

13. If the matter settles or the issues narrow or change parties are asked to notify the court by fax as soon as possible.

Part IV: Motions

A. Regular Motions

14. Regular motions are determined by the amount of time they will require to be argued. The duration for regular motions in each judicial centre is set out in Schedule 1 to this Practice Direction.

15. In all judicial centres, any regular motion requiring one hour or more for argument requires a Factum. Motion materials shall be served and filed in accordance with the timelines set out in the Family Law Rules. Motion materials must be filed at the Family Law Counter.

B. Long Motions

16. Long Motions are all motions expected to exceed the regular motion duration in the applicable judicial centre (including the other party's reply and cross motion, if any). Long motions must be scheduled through the Trial Coordinator's Office. Long motions should be scheduled with the other party's consent as to the date.

17. A factum is required for all motions that are one hour or more. The moving party shall serve and file its Factum at least four business days before the hearing of the motion. The responding party shall serve and file its Factum at least 2 business days before the hearing of the motion.

18. No Factum may exceed 20 pages without leave of the court.

19. The authorities that are included in the Superior Court of Justice List of Often Cited Family Cases do not need to be provided to the court. However the specific paragraphs on which a party relies shall be reproduced in its Factum.

Ottawa Only

20. The moving party must provide its material for the long motion not later than ten days after the long motion date is scheduled. *Failure to do so will result in the long motion date being vacated without further notice to either party.*

Part V: Compendiums – Family Law Motions

21. A Compendium containing the documents and evidence essential to the hearing of a long or complex motion (e.g. summary judgment) may be served and filed with a Factum. A joint Compendium may be filed with the Respondent's Factum.

22. Normally a Compendium would include: the Notice of Motion, Affidavits or essential portions of Affidavits, Financial Statements, Net Family Property Statements, essential Exhibits and excerpts from any other evidence (e.g. transcripts) that will be referred to when arguing the motion.

A. 14B Motions

23. A 14B Motion must be filed at the Family Law Counter and cannot be filed by fax. A Form 14B Motion Form should be accompanied by 4 copies of a proposed Order (Form 25), a self-addressed and stamped envelope for each party. For local counsel, the address may be the lawyer's court office box and no stamp is required.

24. Service requirements of a Form 14B motion are governed by the *Family Law Rules*.

25.   Where a party would be unable to file documents due to their inability to obtain Canada Revenue Agency documents in a timely way, a Form 14B motion may be filed with their documents together with an affidavit stating: (a) they have filed tax returns for the particular year and have provided a copy of the return to the other party but do not yet have a notice of assessment; or (b) they have filed their tax returns for the particular year but do not have a copy or a copy of the notice of assessment – and explain why; or (c) they do not have Canadian tax returns for the particular year because they lived somewhere else and they have either provided the other return to the other party or are unable to do so for some explicable reason, and they have written to Canada Revenue Agency for the Income and Deductions printout required by *rule 13(7)(2)(B)* but have not yet received it and they attach a copy of the letter to CRA as an exhibit.

B.   Procedural Motions: Ottawa Only

26.   Dates are posted at the Family Law Counter and in Family Law Information Centre when procedural motions may be brought in court. Attendance at the Family Counter by no later than 9:30 a.m. on the motion date with the served motion materials and proof of service is required.

27.   A procedural motion includes a motion for a determination of urgency or hardship, seeking permission to bring a substantive motion before case conference.

28.   A procedural motion should only be brought without notice to the other party in compliance with *rule 14(12)*.

29.   All procedural motions, whether opposed or unopposed, are confined to 15 minutes or less in duration.

C.   Urgent Motions on Notice

30.   A party may seek an urgent motion on notice without a case conference in situations of urgency or hardship including issues such as abduction, threats of harm or dire financial harm. A party seeking such a Motion must file all of the required materials.

D.   Urgent Motions without Notice

31.   A party that is seeking a motion without notice to the other party must also set out why notice is unnecessary or not reasonably possible. A Factum or Summary of Argument is not required for an urgent motion that has been brought without notice.

Part VI: Consent Adjournments

32.   Although the court requests notice of consent adjournments as early as possible, consent adjournments of regular motions may be obtained by faxing notice to the court office not later than 4 p.m. on the last business day before the scheduled event. A notice of return of motion must be delivered to obtain a subsequent date.

33.   If the motion is to be adjourned on consent on terms or on the basis of a consent order, the original signed consent and approved draft order must be filed before the matter will be taken off the list.

34.   Adjournments of conferences scheduled in response to a Notice of Approaching Dismissal are only available by permission of a judge.

Part VII: Conference Attendance by Video or Teleconference

35. Parties may arrange through the Family Law Counter in conjunction with the Trial Office for a case conference to occur by teleconference with the consent of both parties and their counsel.

36. For other conferences, or if the other party to the case conference does not consent, a request for a teleconference may be made by a *Form 14B*.

37. Videoconferencing may be available in certain centres and can be used with prior judicial approval. For information contact the local Trial Coordinator.

Part VIII: Trial Scheduling

38. If a case is not resolved at a settlement conference, the Trial Scheduling Endorsement Forms must be completed and endorsed by the Court prior to the case being listed for trial.

39. The completed Forms shall be entered into the yellow Endorsement book of the Continuing Record for use at a Trial Management Conference.

40. Where the Court has directed that a Trial Scheduling Conference should be held, the parties must confirm their attendance at this conference in accordance with Rule 17(14) and file their respective portions of the Trial Scheduling Endorsement Form in advance of the conference in accordance with the timelines in rule 17(13.1).

41. Parties should refer to section 31.9 of Part 1 of the Provincial Practice Direction regarding the materials that must to be filed in advance of a Trial Management Conference.

Part IX: Trial Records

42. The Applicant must serve and file a Trial Record at least 30 days prior to the scheduled Trial date, in compliance with *rule 23(1) and (2)*.

43. If the Applicant fails to do so, the Respondent may serve and file a Trial Record at least 20 days before the scheduled Trial date.

44. Failure of either party to file the Trial Record shall result in the case being removed from the Trial list, unless the court orders otherwise.

Dated: July 21, 2016

Amended: July 1, 2018 (Part III [paras. 7 – 12])

Heather J. Smith, Chief Justice (Superior Court of Justice (Ontario))

James E. McNamara, Regional Senior Judge (Superior Court of Justice, East Region)

L. Consolidated Practice Direction Concerning Family Cases in the Northeast Region (Latest Amendment: July 1, 2018)

Notice of Amendment:

Part I [paras. 1 – 5], Part III C [para. 11] were amended on July 1, 2018.

Effective May 1, 2016

This Practice Direction applies to family law proceedings in the Superior Court of Justice in the Northeast Region. It supersedes Part I: Family Proceedings of the Consolidated Practice Direction for the Northeast Region.

Counsel and parties are advised to refer also to the relevant parts of the Consolidated Provincial Practice Direction which is available on the Superior Court of Justice website at www.ontariocourts.ca/scj.

Part I: Confirmations

Part II: Motions

- A. **Short Motions**
- B. **Long Motions**
- C. **Factums and Briefs of Authorities**
- D. **14B Motions**
- E. **Compendiums**
- F. **Electronic Copies of Materials**
- G. **Urgent Motions on Notice**
- H. **Urgent Motions without Notice**
- I. **Case Conferences and Settlement Conferences**
- J. **Trial Management Conferences**
- K. **Trial Records**

Part I: Confirmations

1.   Each party to a motion or conference must file a Form 14C Confirmation of Motion or Form 17F Confirmation of Conference, or the parties may file one jointly, no later than 2 p.m. three business days before the date of the motion or conference.

2.   The parties or their counsel should consult with each other prior to filing their Form 14C Confirmation of Motion or Form 17F Confirmation of Conference, unless the parties are self-represented and prohibited from communicating by court order.

3.   Where Form 14C Confirmation of Motion or Form 17F Confirmation of Conference forms have not been filed by at least one party, the conference or motion will not be scheduled on the event list and, as a result, will not be heard by the court. Costs may also be ordered against a party who has not filed the confirmation.

4.   Form 14C Confirmation of Motion or Form 17F Confirmation of Conference forms must only list the specific issues that are to be addressed at the event. They should also indicate which materials the judge should review with clear reference to the specific volume, tab and page numbers of the Continuing Record. Failure to provide this information may result in the materials not being reviewed by the judge or the motion or conference not being heard on that day, and costs consequences.

5.   Form 14C Confirmation of Motion or Form 17F Confirmation of Conference forms

1374

must also include an appropriate time estimate for the entire motion or conference, including time required by the other party. Parties will be held to the time stated on their confirmations.

6. If a Confirmation is filed for a consent adjournment, no one needs to appear to speak to the court about the adjournment unless directed to do so by the court.

Part II: Motions

A. Short Motions

7. Motions that are expected to take one hour or less may be scheduled on a regular motions day by serving and filing the motion material at the court office within the timelines set out in the *Family Law Rules*.

B. Long Motions

8. In those court centres that have adopted a long motions protocol for family law matters, the protocol must be followed unless an order is obtained to the contrary. Contact the Trial Coordinator in the centre that the case is in for the latest information about long motion protocols.

9. In those court centres that have not adopted a long motions protocol,

   a. Motions that are expected to take more than 1 hour (including the other party's reply and cross motion, if any) must be scheduled as long motions through the Trial Coordinator in the court office. Long motions can be scheduled either (i) with the other party's written consent or (ii) with the court's permission, by filing a Form 14B Motion Form under section 14(10) of the *Family Law Rules*; and

   b. The moving party must serve and file all their motion material and an Offer to Settle at least 30 days prior to the scheduled motion date, or the date will be vacated. The responding party must serve and file their responding material and an Offer to Settle at least 15 days before the scheduled motion date. Reply material, if any, and a properly completed Form 14C Confirmation, confirming the motion date and material to be read, must be served and filed by 2 p.m. seven days prior to the scheduled motion date. If a long motion is not confirmed by 2 p.m. seven days in advance, it will be removed from the list and the date will be vacated.

C. Factums and Briefs of Authorities

10. A properly drafted factum is required on all long motions and is optional for short motions. If the moving party does not file a factum where required, the motion will not be scheduled.

11. Each party's factum must be filed by no later than 2 p.m. three business days before the hearing of the motion.

12. No factum may exceed 20 pages without leave of the court.

13. The authorities that are included on the court's list of Often Cited Family Cases do not need to be provided to the court with a party's factum. An updated list of often cited family cases is available on the Superior Court's website at: www.ontariocourts.ca/scj. However, extracts from those authorities which the court will be referred to shall be included in the factum or book of authorities, in addition to copies of any other cases that a party relies on.

D. 14B Motions

14. A Form 14B Motion must be filed at the family court office and cannot be filed by fax. A Form 14B Motion Form should be accompanied by one copy of a proposed Order (Form 25) and a self-addressed and stamped envelope for each party.

15. The 14B Motion Form shall be filed in the Continuing Record and a copy of the proposed Order shall be attached to the appropriate place in the Endorsement Volume.

E. Compendiums

16. A Compendium* containing the documents and evidence that are essential to the hearing of the motion may be provided for long or complex motions. A party wishing to file a Compendium should file it with their factum. A joint Compendium may be filed with the respondent's factum.

F. Electronic Copies of Materials

17. Whenever the volume of materials is large or the motion is complex, the parties should file an electronic copy of their motion materials as well as paper copies.

G. Urgent Motions on Notice

18. A party may seek an urgent motion on notice without a case conference in situations of urgency or hardship including issues such as abduction, threats of harm or dire financial harm. A party seeking such a motion must file all of the required materials for a motion except for a Form 14C Confirmation.

H. Urgent Motions without Notice

19. A party that is seeking a motion without notice to the other party must also set out why giving notice is unnecessary, is not reasonably possible, or would have serious consequences.

I. Case Conferences and Settlement Conferences

20. A party may by written request through the Trial Coordinator ask that a conference be conducted by teleconference or, where available, by videoconference. In any such request, the party shall indicate whether or not it is being made with consent of the opposing party and, if it is not, the reasons for the request.

21. Counsel or the parties should communicate before any conference in order to attempt to resolve the issues that are in dispute, unless the parties are self-represented and prohibited from communicating by court order.

22. The parties should each bring their Trial Scheduling Endorsement Forms to the settlement conference with their respective portions completed. If the matter is not resolved at a settlement conference, the complete Trial Scheduling Endorsement form must be endorsed by the court prior to the matter being scheduled for trial.

J. Trial Management Conferences

23. A trial management conference will be scheduled by the court office for a date before the assigned trial date.

---

* *A compendium would normally include the Notice of Motion, Affidavits and Financial Statements, as well as excerpts from the evidence and exhibits that will be referred to in the argument of the motion.*

24. In advance of the Trial Management Conference, each party must file an Offer to Settle and Outline of Opening Statement in lieu of the Form 17E Trial Management Conference Brief. A copy of the completed Trial Scheduling Endorsement form shall be attached to these materials by the court.

K. Trial Records

25. The Applicant must serve and file a Trial Record at least 30 days prior to the scheduled trial date. Failure to do so will result in the matter being removed from the trial list, unless the court orders otherwise. Financial Statements do not need to be updated again after the Trial Record is filed as required by Rule 13(12) unless this is required by the Trial Scheduling Endorsement Form.

Dated: May 1, 2016

Amended: July 1, 2018 (Part I [paras. 1 – 5], Part III C [para. 11])

Heather J. Smith, Chief Justice (Superior Court of Justice (Ontario))

Robbie D. Gordon, Regional Senior Judge (Superior Court of Justice, Northeast Region)

M. Consolidated Practice Direction Concerning Family Cases in the Northwest Region (Latest Amendment: September 4, 2018)

Notice of Amendment:

On September 4, 2018,

- **Part II was amended to clarify how to schedule long motions and to provide for filing of electronic copies of motion materials by USB; and**

- **Part III was amended in respect of the length of conferences and requests for court approval for teleconferences and videoconferences.**

Part I A [paras. 2 – 6], Part II G [para. 17] was amended on July 1, 2018

Effective June 1, 2016

This Practice Direction applies to family law proceedings in the Superior Court of Justice in the Northwest Region (Thunder Bay, Fort Frances and Kenora). It supersedes all previous Practice Directions concerning family proceedings in the Northwest Region which are hereby revoked.

Counsel and parties should also refer to the relevant parts of the Consolidated Provincial Practice Direction (Part I in particular).

All documents must be filed at the Registrar's Office in which the proceedings are commenced.

Each of the forms required by the Family Law Rules is available at the Ontario Court Forms website at: http://www.ontariocourtforms.on.ca/en/family-law-rules-forms/. In addition, the Trial Scheduling Endorsement Form for family cases is available on the website of the Superior Court of Justice at: http://www.ontariocourts.ca/scj/practice/rules-forms/

Forms to request to attend any proceeding by teleconference or videoconference are available by contacting the Trial Coordinator's office at the location in which proceedings are commenced. Contact information for the Trial Coordinator's office each centre is available in the regional schedule.

Information about additional family law services that are available in the Northwest Region is attached at Appendix A.

Table of Contents

Part III: Case Conferences, Settlement Conferences, Trial Scheduling Conferences

Part I: Confirmations

1. Each party to a motion or conference must file, at the Registrar's Office, a <u>Form 14C Confirmation of Motion</u> or <u>Form 17F Confirmation of Conference</u>, or the parties may file one jointly, no later than 2 p.m. three business days before the date of the motion or conference except for long motions, which must be filed by 2:00 p.m. seven days before the motion.

2. The parties or their counsel should consult with each other prior to filing their Form 14C Confirmation of Motion or Form 17F Confirmation of Conference, unless the parties are self-represented and prohibited from communicating by court order.

3. Where Form 14C Confirmation of Motion or Form 17F Confirmation of Conference forms have not been filed by at least one party, the conference or motion will not be placed on the daily event list and, as a result, will not be heard by the court.

4. Form 14C Confirmation of Motion or Form 17F Confirmation of Conference forms must only list the specific issues that are to be addressed at the event. They should also include a list of which materials the judge should review with clear reference to the specific volume, tab and page numbers of the Continuing Record. Failure to provide this information may result in the materials not being reviewed by the judge or the motion or conference not being heard on that day, and costs consequences.

5. Form 114C Confirmation of Motion or Form 17F Confirmation of Conference forms must also include an appropriate time estimate for the entire motion or conference, including time required by the other party. Parties will be held to the time stated on their confirmations.

6. If a Form 14C Confirmation of Motion or Form 17F Confirmation of Conference is filed for a consent adjournment, no one needs to appear to speak to the court about the adjournment unless directed to do so by the court.

Part I.1:   Telephone and Video Attendances

7. Counsel and parties requesting to attend their matter by teleconference or videoconference may, in matters for which CourtCall is available, arrange their attendance via CourtCall in accordance with the *Consolidated Practice Direction for the Northwest Region*. If attending a matter remotely but not through CourtCall, they must submit the appropriate Request Form. Counsel and parties are advised to consult the *Consolidated Practice Direction for the Northwest Region* for further direction on CourtCall and Request Forms.

Part II: Motions

A.   Short Motions

8. Motions that will take less than two hours (including the other party's reply and cross

motion, if any) may be scheduled on a regular motions day by serving and filing the motion material at the court office within the timelines set out in the Family Law Rules.

B. Long Motions

9. Motions that will take two hours or more (including the other party's reply and cross motion, if any) must be scheduled by obtaining a special date from the Regional Manager or Trial Coordinator. The moving party must serve and file all their motion material at least 30 days prior to the scheduled long motion date, or the date will be vacated. The responding party must serve and file their responding material at least 15 days before the scheduled long motion date. Reply material, if any, and a properly completed Form 14C (Confirmation), confirming the long motion date and material to be read, must be served and filed by 2 p.m. seven days prior to the scheduled long motion date. If a long motion is not confirmed by 2 p.m. seven days in advance, it will be removed from the list and the date will be vacated.

C. Factums and Briefs of Authorities

10. A properly drafted factum is required on all long motions but is optional for short motions. If the moving party does not file a factum where required, the motion will not proceed. The text of the factum shall be printed on good quality white paper 216 millimeters by 279 millimeters in size, on one side only, with double spaces between the lines except for quotations which may be single spaced, and margins of approximately 40 millimeters on the left hand side. The characters used shall be at least 12 point or 10 pitch size.

11. Any factum must be filed with the parties' motion materials.

12. No factum may exceed 20 pages without leave of the court.

13. The authorities that are included on the court's list of often cited family cases do not need to be provided to the court with a party's factum. An updated list of often cited family cases referred to is available on the Superior Court's website at: www.ontariocourts.ca/scj. However, extracts from those authorities which the court will be referred to shall be included in the factum or book of authorities, in addition to copies of any other cases that a party relies on.

D. 14B Motions

14. A Form 14B Motion must be filed at the Registrar's Office and cannot be filed by fax. A Form 14B Motion should be accompanied by one copy of a proposed Order (Form 25) and a self-addressed and stamped envelope for each party.

15. The Form 14B Motion shall be filed in the Continuing Record and a copy of the proposed Order shall be attached to the appropriate place in the Endorsement Volume.

E. Compendium

16. A Compendium* containing the documents and evidence that are essential to the hearing of the motion may be provided for long or complex motions. A party wishing to

---

* A Compendium would normally include the Notice of Motion, Affidavits and Financial Statements, as well as excerpts from the evidence and exhibits that will be referred to in the argument of the motion.

file a Compendium should file it with their factum. A joint Compendium may be filed with the respondent's factum.

F. Electronic Copies of Materials

17. Whenever the volume of materials is large or the motion is complex, the parties should file an electronic copy of their motion materials on a USB key at the Registrar's Office, with the file name clearly identified for each document, as well as paper copies.

18. The USB key should be accompanied by a list of the files on the USB key, the title of proceedings, court file number, counsel names (where applicable) and party name. Where possible, the USB key should be labelled with the short style of cause and court file number.

19. Neither the USB key nor any file on it should be password-protected.

G. Urgent Motions With Notice

20. A party may seek an urgent motion with notice without a case conference in situations of urgency or hardship, as set out in Rule 14(4.2). A party seeking such a motion must serve and file all of the required materials except for a Form 14C Confirmation of Motion. Prior to bringing an urgent motion, the Trial Coordinator should be contacted to see if an urgent case conference can be scheduled before the motion is heard.

21. To enable the order to be issued quickly, parties are encouraged to provide the court with a draft order.

H. Urgent Motions Without Notice

22. Motions without notice may be brought only in exceptional circumstances as set out in Rule 14(12).

23. A Court will not generally make an order without allowing both parties an opportunity to participate. In addition to addressing the requirements of paragraph 17 above, a party who is seeking a motion without notice to the other party must address why the other party has not been served. The motions materials should set out specifically and clearly why notice is unnecessary, not reasonably possible, or any other grounds that would justify the motion being heard without notice to the other side.

24. An order obtained without notice, together with all documents used on the motion, shall be served on the other party, unless the court orders otherwise. The matter must be scheduled to come back to the court within 14 days, as set out in Rule 14(14).

25. If a person is requesting a restraining order as part of his/her urgent motion, he or she should also complete the pink restraining order endorsement form with the required information (such as names and birth dates of those affected, as well as addresses at which the other side is to be prohibited from attending.) This form is available at the Registrars' Office, where the urgent motion is filed.

26. If a restraining order has been granted, the court can arrange for service of the material on the other side, if requested by a party who is not represented by counsel.

Part III: Case Conferences, Settlement Conferences, Trial Scheduling Conferences

I.   Conferences

27.   Counsel or the parties should communicate before any conference in order to attempt to resolve the issues that are in dispute, unless the parties are self-represented and prohibited from communicating by court order.

28.   Case conference briefs and settlement conference briefs must be filed in accordance with the Family Law Rules.

29.   All conferences will be scheduled for a duration of one hour.

30.   The parties should bring their Trial Scheduling Endorsement Forms to the settlement conference with their respective portions completed.

31.   If the case has not settled at the conclusion of the settlement conference, the court shall determine if the Trial Scheduling Endorsement Form can be completed at the conference or shortly thereafter and shall give directions to the parties regarding the completion of this form.

32.   If necessary, the Court may require the parties to attend a trial scheduling conference to canvas issues regarding the scheduling of the trial and ensure proper completion of the Trial Scheduling Endorsement Form. Each party shall complete and file his or her portion of the Trial Scheduling Endorsement Form with the court in advance of a trial scheduling conference in accordance with the timelines in rule 17(13.1).

33.   The purpose of a Trial Scheduling Conference includes (i) ensuring that the case is ready to proceed to trial, (ii) considering each party's list of proposed witnesses and (iii) ensuring the accuracy of the estimated time for trial. Consideration should also be given to other factors that would be appropriate under rule 1 in order to limit the duration and scope of the trial.

34.   A trial date will not be made available until the court has reviewed and endorsed the completed trial scheduling endorsement form.

J.   Trial Management Conferences

35.   A trial management conference shall be scheduled by the parties at the time that the trial date is assigned. The trial management conference should be scheduled to be held within two weeks of the scheduled trial date, dependent on the availability of judicial resources.

36.   The Trial Management Conference Brief, Form 17E, is no longer required. Instead of the Trial Management Conference Brief, the following documents must be filed in advance of the trial management conference by the deadlines set out in rule 17(13.1)

   a.   The completed Trial Scheduling Endorsement Form must be filed by the applicant;

   b.   Each party must file an outline of his or her opening statement for trial, and

   c.   Each party must serve and bring to the conference, an offer to settle all outstanding issues.

37.   The Trial Scheduling Endorsement Form shall be filed with or added to the Trial Record.

38.   The purpose of the trial management conference is to confirm that the parties are ready for trial, have filed the Trial Record and exchanged all material required by the Trial Scheduling Endorsement Form, and to explore the final possibility of settlement of any or all trial issues.

39.   Where the case has been settled and the trial is no longer required, one of the parties shall immediately advise the Trial Coordinator so that the trial date can be vacated. A copy of any Minutes of Settlement or consent should be filed with the Registrar's Office at the same time.

K.   Trial Records

40.   The applicant must serve and file a Trial Record at least 30 days prior to the scheduled trial date. Failure to do so will result in the matter being removed from the trial list, unless the court orders otherwise. Financial Statements do not need to be updated again after the Trial Record is filed as required by Rule 13(12) unless this is required by the Trial Scheduling Endorsement Form.

L.   Trial Dates

41.   Trials are placed on specific Running List sessions scheduled throughout the year, at each location with the Northwest Region. Please contact the appropriate Trial Coordinator for trial dates in the selected location.

42.   Uncontested trial dates are also provided by contacting the Trial Coordinator at the selected location.

Dated May 24, 2016
Amended: September 4, 2018; July 1, 2018

Heather J. Smith, Chief Justice (Superior Court of Justice (Ontario))

Douglas C. Shaw, Regional Senior Judge (Superior Court of Justice, Northwest Region)

Bonnie Warkentin, Regional Senior Judge (Superior Court of Justice, Northwest Region)

Appendix A

The Family Law Information Centre

1.   Mediation North is responsible for information on Family Law MIP Sessions, etc. held throughout the Northwest Region. To contact the Information Referral Coordinator please dial: 1-888-935-5455.

2.   Thunder Bay has a drop-in **Family Law Information (FLIC) Office**: open daily from 8:30 a.m. until 5:00 p.m. Monday- Friday and is located on the 1st floor of the Thunder Bay Court House.– Kenora and Fort Frances do not have a local FLIC office.

3.   **Duty counsel** at Thunder Bay is available Tuesdays 9:00 a.m. – 11:30 a.m. and 1:30 p.m. – 4:00 p.m., and Thursdays 1:30 p.m.- 4:00 p.m., at no cost for consultation with qualified individuals seeking legal advice.– Kenora and Fort Frances do not have Duty Counsel available for SCJ files.

N. Consolidated Practice Direction for Civil Actions, Applications, Motions and Procedural Matters in the Toronto Region (Latest Amendment: March 1, 2020)

Notice of Amendments:

Effective March 1, 2020, section H (Proceedings Heard in Hamilton by a Registrar in Bankruptcy) is added to Part I (Applications and Motions).

Effective December 7, 2018, Paragraph 14 has been amended. Short motions and short applications may not be booked by telephone.

Effective June 15, 2018: Paragraph 9 has been amended to provide that the Court requires a chronology of events and compendium on all long motions and motions for summary judgment; and Part IV (Certification of an Action to Set Pre-Trial and Trial Dates) has been amended to require the filing of a Timetable for Service of Expert Reports form. See http://www.ontariocourts.ca/scj/practice/practice-directions/toronto/t/.

Effective May 1, 2017, para 57 and the related certificate have been amended regarding mediation prior to setting an action down for trial.

Effective July 1, 2015

This Practice Direction applies to actions, applications, motions and procedural matters in the Toronto Region, effective July 1, 2015. It replaces the previous Consolidated Practice Direction for Civil Actions, Applications, Motions and Procedural Matters in the Toronto Region that was effective on July 1, 2014. Changes have been made to incorporate the numerous scheduling improvements that were introduced by the Toronto Region Pilot Practice Advisory issued by Regional Senior Justice Morawetz on October 14, 2014. These changes have proven successful in bringing about greater scheduling efficiencies. They are now been implemented on a permanent basis in Toronto through this Practice Direction.

This Practice Direction *does not apply* to motions or applications heard on the Commercial and Bankruptcy Lists, Estates List, or under the *Class Proceedings Act, 1992*, unless specifically mentioned.

Counsel and parties are advised to refer to the relevant Parts of the Consolidated Provincial Practice Direction, the Consolidated Practice Direction for Divisional Court Proceedings as well as any other relevant Toronto region-specific Practice Directions and Guides (e.g. the Guide Concerning Best Practices for Civil Actions, Applications and Motions in the Toronto Region).

All Superior Court of Justice Practice Directions are available on the Superior Court's website at: www.ontariocourts.ca/scj.

Table of Contents

Part I.   Applications and Motions

A.   Civil Practice Court

1.   Civil Practice Court ("CPC") has been instituted in the Toronto region. It replaces the former Motions Scheduling Court. It serves the following purposes:

    a.   To curtail the motions culture in Toronto and to ensure that motions and applications that are ready to proceed can be heard on a timely basis.

    b.   To permit the CPC judge to identify cases, at any stage, which require a degree of case management. Case management, most typically, will only be invoked in complex cases or where long motions are involved.

    c.   To assist in the orderly hearing of long motions, long applications, and any summary judgment motion. Parties will be encouraged to submit agreed upon timetables, and where necessary, case conferences will be scheduled in advance. The CPC judge will consider the option of directing long motions to the trial list.

    d.   To create a judicial mechanism whereby the CPC judge can assign those cases in need of the courts intervention before other available judges.

2.   The CPC is supported administratively by the Civil Practice Unit. Staff in the Civil Practice Court serve as the first contact for any long motion, long application and any summary judgment motion. They are supported by an enhanced computerized scheduling program.

B.   Rules Applicable to All Motions & Applications

3.   There are four different streams for scheduling motions and applications, depending on how they are heard, their duration and the judicial officer who is to hear the motion or application:

    a.   **Short Applications & Short Motions before Judge or Master:** Applications and motions before a Judge or Master that require two hours or less for all parties to argue are considered short applications and short motions. These motions are to be booked through the Civil Scheduling Unit, per the direction below.

    b.   **Long Applications, Long Motions, Summary Judgment Motions and Urgent Matters before a Judge:** Applications and motions before a Judge that require more than two hours for all parties to argue are considered long applications and long motions. These applications and motions are booked first by contacting the Civil Practice Unit for a date in Civil Practice Court. The Civil Practice Court will confirm the date for hearing the motion, and make any necessary procedural orders that are required.

c. **Motions before Masters.** Different procedures exist for scheduling long motions, short motions and *ex parte* motions before a Master. Different procedures are also outlined below for booking long motions before a master in case-managed actions and in construction lien actions or within a reference.

d. **Motions before Judges or Masters in Writing.** Counsel are strongly encouraged to bring in-writing motions when appropriate, to reduce unnecessary court appearances that drain limited judicial resources and which unnecessarily add to cost.

4. **Elimination of "Placeholder" Motions.** Any date requisitioned for a motion before a judge or master will be vacated if the Notice of Motion is not filed with payment of the motion fee within 10 business days after the motion date is requisitioned.

5. **Matters to be Heard within 100 Days of Booking.** All motions will only be booked when the parties are able to confirm their availability to have the motion heard within the 100 days (14 weeks) from the date of booking. Parties who cannot proceed within that timeframe will not be provided with a motion date, except in extenuating and exceptional circumstances.

6. **Costs Outline Required.** On all motions before a judge or master, parties are reminded to prepare in advance, and bring to the hearing, a costs outline to the motion, as required by r. 57.01(6).

7. **No Adjournments 2 Days Prior to Hearing.** No adjournment for any motion before a judge or master will be granted within 2 days of the scheduled hearing date, except in extenuating and exceptional circumstances.

8. **Parties' Responsibilities for All Adjourned Hearings.** Where a matter has been adjourned and materials have been previously filed with the court, parties are responsible to ensure that all previously filed materials to be relied upon are pulled from the file or ordered from storage, if applicable, and brought to staff in the court office, at least one week prior to the new hearing date.

9. **Materials for use of the Court.** The following materials, including material in electronic format, are required by the Court:

a. Factums are required for all applications.

b. Factums are required for all motions over two hours (except undertakings and refusals motions) and are strongly encouraged for all other motions.

c. No factum may exceed 30 pages, unless leave is granted.

d. For longer or more complex motions, the court strongly encourages parties to file electronic copies of their factums in Word format. Electronic copies should be attached to the hard copy of the factum filed with the court and should be labelled with the court file name and number, event and content of the disk, as well as the return date of the matter. Counsel and parties should refer to the Guide Concerning e-Delivery of Documents available on the Superior Court's website.

e. Chronology of events and compendium on all long motions and motions for summary judgment.

f. Cases contained in books of authorities should be copied on both sides of a page. If possible, electronic copies of books of authorities are helpful in longer or more complex motions.

g. Parties are encouraged to refer to the Guide Concerning Best Practices for Civil Actions, Applications and Motions, available on the Superior Court's website, which offers further guidance to counsel and parties when bringing motions or applications, particularly on matters involving voluminous materials.

10. **Motions to Transfer a Civil Proceeding.** All requests for a transfer of a civil proceeding (action or application) from one county to another shall be pursuant to rule 13.1.02 of the *Rules of Civil Procedure.* The motion will be granted or denied based on its merits. Counsel and parties are advised to refer to Part III of the Consolidated Provincial Practice Direction which prescribes specific requirements for motions to transfer a civil proceeding.

11. **Motions to be Heard by Masters.** A master has jurisdiction to hear any motion in a civil proceeding except those specified rule 37.02(2). Masters' motions must be made to a master. Unless the relief requested in the motion is within the exclusive jurisdiction of a judge, a motion returnable by attendance or in writing must be made to "the Court" and heard by a master. Judges may refuse to hear any motion that is within the jurisdiction of a master.

12. **Simplified Procedure Discovery Motions.** Motions concerning issues arising from examinations for discovery in Simplified Procedure actions will be scheduled for a maximum of 30 minutes in total. All parties are expected to complete oral argument of the motion within the time scheduled, subject to leave from the presiding master in exceptional cases. Parties are encouraged to use rule 34.12 and answer questions that are objected to.

13. **Confirmation of Applications and Motions.** In accordance with rules 37.10.1 and 38.09.1, the Confirmation Form for motions and applications must be filed by the applicant or moving party with the Registrar not later than 2 p.m. three days before the hearing date. Parties must confer as to the time required before sending in the Confirmation Form. Estimated time must not exceed time booked. Parties are expected to adhere to the time requested.

C. Scheduling a Short Application or Short Motion Before a Judge or Master

14. Short applications and short motions must be booked through the Civil Practice Unit [Or Civil Scheduling Unit] (except summary judgment motions, masters' motions in construction lien actions or within a reference). These matters are to be booked by emailing the Civil Scheduling/Practice Unit at JUS.G.MAG.CSD.CivilMotionsScheduling@ontario.ca. Alternatively, parties may attend in person at 10th Floor, 393 University Ave., M5G 1E6.

15. Parties shall consult with each other to select a return date that is convenient to all parties and which will permit all parties to file all necessary materials and conduct any examinations before the return date. At the time of booking, a realistic estimate of the time required by all parties for argument must be provided.

16. When a party books a return date for a short application or short motion by email to the Civil *Scheduling/Practice* Unit, it shall send by email a completed Requisition to Schedule Short Motion or Application If booking by phone, the information contained in the Requisition to Schedule Short Motion or Application form must be communicated to the booking staff. The form must be included with the motion material when filed.

17. Short motions in construction lien actions and hearings for directions within a reference are not booked through the Civil Scheduling/Practice Unit. See instructions below on booking motions before Masters.

D. Scheduling a Long Application, Long Motion, Summary Judgment Motion or Urgent Matter before a Judge

18. An attendance at Civil Practice Court before a judge is required to schedule:

   a. Long applications or long motions before a judge;

   b. All summary judgment motions before a judge;

   c. The urgent hearing of motions or applications before a judge; and

   d. Contested requests for case management by a judge under rule 77.

   e. Appeals from the Consent and Capacity Board under the Health Care Consent Act.

19. CPC commences at 9:30 a.m. Gowns are not required in CPC. Several CPC's may sit on a given day.

20. Appointments to appear in CPC may be booked by emailing the Civil Practice Unit at CivilPracticeCourt@ontario.ca, along with a completed Requisition to Attend Civil Practice Court.

21. Information about the current start time, location, and contact information for the CPC can be found on the Superior Court of Justice website at www.ontariocourts.ca/scj/practice/schedules/t/.

22. Before appearing at CPC, parties must seek to establish an agreed timetable for the completion of all steps required prior to the hearing of the application or motion and to bring a copy of the timetable to Civil Practice Court for approval by the judge.

23. Rule 20 of the *Rules of Civil Procedure* contemplates that some summary judgment motions will proceed by way of a hybrid hearing (written record, plus some oral evidence) or by way of a hearing on the written record followed closely by a tailored trial of issues. Scheduling the expeditious hearing of these Rule 20 motions will require greater management by the judiciary. Accordingly, all motions for summary judgment will undergo a scheduling and monitoring process commencing with an attendance at Civil Practice Court (see Summary Judgment Case Information Sheet available through court staff).

24. Parties are to advise the Civil Motions Coordinator 30 days prior to the motion hearing date about the status of the motion. In addition, in the normal course, the court will contact the parties one week before the hearing of the long motion, long application or summary judgment motion before a judge to inquire into its status, its readiness for hearing, and whether oral evidence may be required at the hearing of the mo-

tion. If the parties advise or the court determines that the motion is not ready for hearing, the parties may receive further directions from the court regarding the scheduling of the hearing of the motion.

E. Scheduling Motions before Masters

Long Motions before a Master

25. To schedule a long motion before a master, a Requisition to Schedule Long Motion must be completed and e-mailed to Masters.Long.Motions@ontario.ca or delivered to Masters Administration on the 6th floor 393 University Ave., or by fax to 416-327-6405. Once the requisition is received, a master will be assigned to hear the motion.

26. If the action is case managed, a Requisition is not necessary and a request for a long motion may be sent directly to the Assistant Trial Coordinator for the master who is managing the action.

27. If the motion is for refusals and undertakings, both moving and responding parties are expected to have completed refusals and undertaking charts grouped by issue and completed in accordance with rules 37.10(10)(a) and (b) prior to the case conference to allow a realistic time for the hearing to be set.

Ex-Parte motions before a Master

28. After attending at the motions office, motions made without notice or consent motions may be walked into Masters' Ex-Parte Motions Court any day that a master is sitting.

29. If the motion must be heard before the next date that an ex-parte master is sitting, or if the motion must be on notice, the Civil Practice Unit will direct the moving party to appear before the Duty Master. The Duty Master will determine if the matter is urgent and if urgent, will hear the motion or attempt to have it heard by another master.

Construction Lien Motions & References before a Master

30. Long and short motions in construction lien actions require an appointment with the Construction Lien Master to be arranged through the Assistant Trial Coordinator for the Construction Lien Masters on the 6th Floor 393 University Ave., or by telephone to 416-212-9783 or 416-327-9404. All long motions require a telephone case conference with the master who will be hearing the motion in order to determine the length of time required, set a timetable for any remaining steps before the hearing of the motion and fix a return date for the motion.

31. Motions made without notice and consent motions in construction lien actions are heard daily from 9:30 to 10:00 a.m.

32. Short motions and hearings for directions within a reference are booked through the Assistant Trial Coordinator for the master assigned to conduct the reference.

Motions before a Master from the Class Proceedings, Commercial and Estates Lists

33. If the motion is under the *Class Proceedings Act, 1992*, or a proceeding on the Commercial List or Estates List, a written direction will be required from a judge on the respective list permitting the motion to be heard by a master.

34. Similarly, if the action has been assigned to a judge under rule 37.15 or rule 77.06, a direction from that judge that a master be appointed to hear motions within the master's jurisdiction will be necessary.

35.   The requirement for a judge's written direction does not apply to motions under the *Bankruptcy and Insolvency Act* heard by a master exercising the authority of a registrar of the court in bankruptcy under that Act.

F.   Motions in Writing

36.   Counsel are encouraged to bring in-writing motions when appropriate under Rule 37.12.1 for *ex parte*, consent, and unopposed matters. Counsel must provide the consent (under Rule 37.12.1(2)) or notice that the motion is unopposed (Rule 37.12.1(3)), along with a draft order for the court. In particular, motions such as default judgments, Norwich orders, non-party production or substituted service orders may be well-suited to in-writing motions.

37.   With the exception of construction lien actions and references, unless otherwise directed by a judge or master, motions in writing should be filed in the Civil Intake Office, 10th Floor, 393 University Avenue.

38.   Motions in writing in a construction lien file or reference should be filed with the Assistant Trial Coordinator for the Construction Lien Masters located on the 6th Floor, 393 University Avenue.

39.   A motion under Rule 7.08 must be brought in accordance with the Best Practice's Guidelines and Checklist for Rule 7.08 matters.

G.   Adjournments

40.   Short applications and short motions can be adjourned once through the Civil Practice Unit (or the assistant trial coordinator for the Construction Lien Masters, if applicable); any further adjournments of these matters must be spoken to in court.

41.   To adjourn a long application or long motion scheduled before a judge, counsel must appear in CPC and speak to the adjournment.

42.   Long motion dates before a master may be adjourned only with leave of the assigned master at a case conference requested for that purpose before the motion date.

43.   No adjournment for any motion before a judge or master will be granted within 2 days of the scheduled hearing date, except in extenuating and exceptional circumstances.

44.   Where a matter has been adjourned and materials have been previously filed with the court, parties are responsible to ensure that all previously filed materials to be relied upon are pulled from the file or ordered from storage within 30 days prior to the motion, if applicable, and brought to staff in the court office, at least one week prior to the new hearing date.

H.   Proceedings Heard in Hamilton by a Registrar in Bankruptcy

45.   As of March 1, 2020, new *Bankruptcy and Insolvency Act* (Canada) matters to be determined by a Registrar in Bankruptcy under section 192 of the Act shall be filed and heard in Hamilton, provided that the matter originated in one of the following areas:

- Hamilton
- Norfolk
- Haldimand
- Brant

- Niagara

46. Matters originating in one of the above areas, but commenced in Toronto prior to March 1, 2020, will continue to be heard in Toronto, unless the court orders otherwise.

Part II: Requests for Assignment to Case Management – Rule 77.05

47. Under rule 77.01(2)1, parties are required to assume the greater share of responsibility for managing their own actions. However, "light touch" case management under Rule 77 is available on an "as needed/as requested" basis in accordance with the provisions of the rule.

A. Consent Requests

48. Consent or unopposed requests for assignment to case management may be made to the Team Leader Toronto Master, or the Regional Senior Judge, or designate, in the case of a request for case management by a judge, by completing a Request for Case Management.

49. Consent by itself is insufficient and parties must explain why case management is necessary having regard to the circumstances and the criteria set out in rule 77.05(4). Case management will not be assigned to actions that fail to meet the prescribed criteria.

50. If the request is granted, the Team Leader Toronto Masters or Regional Senior Judge, or designate, will assign a master or judge to case manage the action.

B. Opposed Requests

51. Opposed requests for assignment to case management must be brought by way of motion:

  a. in the case of a request for case management by a master, on notice returnable in Masters' Motions Court before any case management master; or,

  b. in the case of a request for case management by a judge, on notice returnable in Civil Practice Court.

52. If the master grants the motion he or she will become the managing master.

53. Once a master is assigned to case manage a proceeding he or she will hear all motions in that proceeding within the jurisdiction of a master and will be available for case conferences.

54. If a motion for case management by a judge is granted, the Regional Senior Judge or designate will assign a judge to case manage the proceeding.

55. Requests under rules 37.15 or 77.06 for the appointment of a judge to hear all motions or steps in a proceeding shall be made in writing to the Regional Senior Judge, or designate.

56. A judge normally will not be assigned under rules 37.15 or 77.06 unless there is a likelihood of a significant number of motions or other steps in the proceeding that are within the exclusive jurisdiction of a judge.

Part III: Mandatory Mediation

57.   All actions commenced in or transferred to the Toronto Region are subject to mandatory mediation under rule 24.1 except those actions excluded in rules 24.1.04(2) and (2.1).

58.   A mediation session must take place within 180 days after the first defence has been filed, unless a consent under rule 24.1.09(3) has been filed or the court orders otherwise.

59.   Court staff will not accept for filing a trial record (ordinary action) or a notice of readiness for pre-trial conference (Simplified Procedure action) unless the party setting the action down for trial files a Certificate that:

   a.   Form 24.1A (Notice of Name of Mediator and Date of Session) has been filed with the mediation coordinator and the mediation session has taken place;

   b.   the report by mediator (indicating that the mediation has been concluded) has been filed with the mediation coordinator;

   c.   an order has been obtained from a judge or case management master exempting the action from mediation; or,

   d.   an order has been obtained from a judge or case management master extending the deadline for mediation until after the action is set down for trial.

These requirements will apply even where the parties have agreed to postpone a mediation session to a date more than 180 days after the first defence has been filed as permitted by rule 24.1.

60.   A motion for an order exempting the action from mediation should be made to any master (unless the action is being case managed by a judge or a specific master). The motion should be returnable in motions court or by case conference if the action is case managed. Motions in writing on consent will be considered if sufficient reasons are given.

61.   In keeping with the requirement for mandatory mediation and *Rule 1.05*, a judge may, at any stage in the proceeding, order that the parties not take any further steps in the proceeding, without leave of a judge, until a mandatory mediation has taken place.

Part IV: Certification of an Action to Set Pre-Trial and Trial Dates

62.   The practice of certifying an action ready for trial continues in the Toronto Region.

63.   Approximately 60 days after a trial record is filed, the Civil Trial Office will send to the party who set the action down for trial a Certification Form to Set Pre-Trial and Trial Dates, together with a list of available trial dates.

64.   After consultation with the opposing counsel or party, the party who received the form must complete and return the Certification Form to the Civil Trial Office.

65.   If a completed Certification Form is not returned by the date specified on the covering memo, the action will be struck from the trial list.

66.   In order to restore an action that has been struck from the trial list the parties must:

   a.   Obtain an order granting leave from a case management master or judge under rule 48.11 to restore it to the trial list; and thereafter,

b.   Attend the main file room on the 10th floor of 393 University Ave. and arrange to have the original trial record pulled and taken with the court order to the Civil Intake Counter.

The action will then be re-instated to the trial list and the trial record returned to the trial office. The trial office will treat the action as a new matter and forward new certification forms.

67.   If an opposing party will not cooperate in completing the Certification Form within a reasonable time, for cases 10 days or less, a party can arrange an appearance before a judge in a "To Be Spoken To Court" which usually is held each Monday at 9:30 a.m. Contact the trial coordinator for additional information at 416-327-5320.

68.   If an opposing party will not cooperate in completing the Certification Form within a reasonable time, and if a trial is anticipated to be over 10 days and, a party can arrange an appearance before the Long Trial Scheduling Court, which is normally held on Wednesdays at 9:30 a.m.

69.   Parties appearing in To Be Spoken To Court or Long Trial Scheduling Court are required to complete and provide the presiding judge with a Timetable For Service of Expert Reports Form before trial and pre-trial dates will be scheduled.

70.   In cases where the trial date is fixed by the trial office, the parties are required to file a Timetable For Service of Expert Reports Form within 10 business days after receipt of the trial date, failing which the action will be struck from the trial list.

71.   Once trial dates are set, there will be no adjournments of the trial except in extenuating and exceptional circumstances.

72.   Rule 48.04 provides that a party who sets an action down for trial or consents to placing the action on the trial list cannot initiate or continue any form of discovery or interlocutory motion without leave of the court. Leave will be granted only in rare circumstances.

Part V: Administrative Forms

73.   Administrative forms not prescribed under the *Rules of Civil Procedure* and used by the Civil Practice Unit may be obtained from the Civil Practice Unit or can be found on the Superior Court of Justice website.

Part VI: Designated Counties for the Commencement of Mortgage Proceedings under rule 13.1.01(3)

74.   Pursuant to rule 13.1.01(3) of the *Rules of Civil Procedure*, which comes into effect on March 31, 2015, Toronto shall be the place for commencement of mortgage proceedings for property located anywhere in the Toronto Region.

Dated: June 26, 2015

Amended: March 1, 2020; December 7, 2018; June 15, 2018; May 1, 2017

Geoffrey B. Morawetz
Chief Justice
Superior Court of Justice (Ontario)

Stephen Firestone
Regional Senior Judge
Superior Court of Justice, Toronto Region

O. Consolidated Practice Direction Concerning Family Cases in the Toronto Region (Latest Amendment: July 1, 2018)

Notice of Amendment:

Changes have been made to paragraphs 1-5 below which came into effect on July 1, 2018.

Changes have been made to paragraphs 3, 19, 23 and 25 below which came into effect on July 1, 2015.

Effective July 1, 2014

This Practice Direction applies to family law proceedings in the Toronto Region. It *supersedes* Part III of the Consolidated Provincial Practice Direction *for family cases in Toronto*. It also *supersedes* all previous Practice Directions concerning family proceedings in the Toronto Region issued prior to July 1, 2014, which are hereby revoked.

Counsel and parties are advised to refer to the relevant parts of the Consolidated Provincial Practice Direction, the Consolidated Practice Direction for Divisional Court Proceedings as well as any other applicable Toronto region-specific Practice Directions or Guides, which are available on the Superior Court of Justice website at: uat.ontariocourts.ca/scj.

Part I: Confirmations

1. Each party to a motion or conference must file either a Form 14C Confirmation of Motion or Form 17F Confirmation of Conference, or the parties may file one jointly, no later than 2 p.m. three business days before the date of the motion or conference.

2. The parties or their counsel should consult with each other prior to filing their Form 14C Confirmation of Motion or Form 17F Confirmation of Conference, unless the parties are self-represented and prohibited from communicating by court order.

3. Where Form 14C Confirmation of Motion or Form 17F Confirmation of Conference forms have not been filed by at least one party, the conference or motion will not be

scheduled on the event list and, as a result, will not be heard by the court. *Costs may also be ordered against a party who has not filed the confirmation.*

4. Form 14C Confirmations of Motion or Form 17F Confirmation of Conference forms must **only** list the specific issues that are to be addressed at the event. They should also indicate which materials the judge should review with clear reference to the specific volume, tab and page numbers of the Continuing Record. *Failure to provide this information may result in the materials not being reviewed by the judge or the motion not being heard on that day.*

5. Form 14C Confirmation of Motion or Form 17F Conformation of Conference forms must also include an appropriate time estimate for the **entire motion or conference**, including time required by the other party. Parties will be held to the time stated on their confirmations.

Part II: Motions

A. Short Motions

6. Motions that are expected to take one hour or less may be scheduled on a Tuesday or Thursday by serving and filing the motion material (including a factum or Summary of Argument) at the family court office within the timelines set out in the *Family Law Rules*.

B. Long Motions

7. Motions that are expected to take more than 1 hour (including the other party's reply and cross motion, if any) must be scheduled as long motions and scheduled through the Trial Coordinator in the family court office. Long motions can be scheduled either (a) with the other party's written consent or (b) with the court's permission, by filing a Form 14B Motion Form under section 14(10) of the *Family Law Rules*.

C. Factums, Summaries of Arguments and Briefs of Authorities

8. A properly drafted factum or Summary of Argument is required on all motions except as noted below. If the moving party does not file a factum or Summary of Argument where required, the motion will not be scheduled.

9. For short motions, the times for service and filing of moving party's factum or Summary of Argument should be filed in accordance with the requirements relating to other motion materials in section 14(11) and 14(11.1) of the *Family Law Rules*.

10. For long motions, each party's factum or Summary of Argument must be filed at least seven days before the hearing of the motion.

11. No factum or Summary of Argument may exceed 20 pages without leave of the court.

12. The authorities that are included on the court's list of Often Cited Family Cases do not need to be provided to the court with a party's factum or Summary of Argument. Counsel and parties are advised to refer to Part I-B of the Consolidated Provincial Practice Direction. An updated list of family cases is available on the Superior Court's website at: uat.ontariocourts.ca/scj.

D. 14 B Motions

13. A Form 14B Motion must be filed at the family court office and cannot be filed by fax.

A Form 14B Motion Form should be accompanied by four copies of a proposed Order (Form 25), a completed endorsement sheet and a self-addressed and stamped envelope for each party.

14. The 14B Motion Form shall be filed in the Continuing Record and a copy of the proposed Order shall be attached to the appropriate place in the Endorsement Volume.

E. Compendiums

15. A Compendium* containing the documents and evidence that are essential to the hearing of the motion may be provided for long or complex motions. A party wishing to file a Compendium should file it with their factum. A joint Compendium may be filed with the respondent's factum.

F. Electronic Copies of Materials

16. Whenever the volume of materials is large or the motion is complex, the parties should file an electronic copy of their motion materials as well as paper copies. Counsel and parties should refer to the Guide Concerning e-Delivery of Documents available on the Superior Court's website.

G. Urgent Motions on Notice

17. A party may seek an urgent motion **on notice** without a case conference in situations of urgency or hardship including issues such as abduction, threats of harm or dire financial harm. A party seeking such a motion must file all of the required materials except for a Form 14C Confirmation.

H. Urgent Motions without Notice

18. A party that is seeking a motion **without notice** to the other party must also set out why notice is unnecessary or not reasonably possible. A factum or Summary of Argument is not required for an urgent motion that has been brought without notice.

I. Case Conferences and Settlement Conferences

19. Parties may request that a conference occur by teleconference with or without the consent of both parties or their counsel by filing a Form 14B Motion Form.

20. Counsel or the parties should communicate before any conference in order to attempt to resolve the issues that are in dispute, unless the parties are self-represented and prohibited from communicating by court order.

21. The first case conference on a motion to change a final order or agreement shall be scheduled before a Dispute Resolution Officer (DRO) in accordance with Part I of the Consolidated Provincial Practice Direction.

22. A DRO conference can be held on matters other than motions to change only as directed by the court upon request by a 14B Motion or at another court event.

23. If the matter is not resolved at a settlement conference, a Trial Scheduling Endorsement Form, endorsed by the Court) must be completed prior to the matter being scheduled for trial.

---

* A compendium would normally include the Notice of Motion, Affidavits and Financial Statements, as well as excerpts from the evidence and exhibits that will be referred to in the argument of the motion.

J. Trial Management Conferences

24. A trial management conference will normally be scheduled by the family court office for the week before the assigned trial date.

25. The completed Trial Scheduling Endorsement Form must be filed by one of the parties in advance of the Trial Management Conference and each party must file an Offer to Settle and Outline of Opening Statement, in lieu of the Trial Management Conference Brief.

K. Trial Records

26. The Applicant must file a Trial Record at least 30 days prior to the scheduled trial date. Failure to do so will result in the matter being removed from the trial list, unless the court orders otherwise.

Additional information about family cases and the mediation and information services that are available at the Toronto Superior Court of Justice, 393 University Avenue, 9th Floor, is available from Mediate 393 which is available on their <u>*website*</u>.

Dated: April 11, 2014
Amended: July 1, 2018 (Para. 1-5); July 1, 2015 (Para. 3, 19, 23 and 25)

Heather J. Smith
Chief Justice
Superior Court of Justice (Ontario)

Geoffrey B. Morawetz
Regional Senior Judge
Superior Court of Justice, Toronto Region

P. Consolidated Practice Direction Concerning the Commercial List in the Toronto Region (Effective: July 1, 2014)

Effective July 1, 2014

This Practice Direction applies to matters on the commercial list in the Toronto Region. It *supersedes* all Toronto Region Practice Directions concerning the commercial list issued before July 1, 2014, which are hereby revoked.

Counsel and parties are advised to refer to the relevant Parts of the Consolidated Provincial Practice Direction, the Consolidated Practice Direction for Divisional Court Proceedings as well as any other relevant Toronto region-specific Practice Directions and Guides which are available on the Superior Court of Justice website at: www.ontariocourts.ca/scj.

See also Changes to Commercial List operations in light of COVID-19 (Issued March 16, 2020) https://www.ontariocourts.ca/scj/changes-to-commercial-list-operations-in-light-of-covid-19/

Table of Contents

Part I: Introduction

The Commercial List was established in 1991 for the hearing of certain actions, applications and motions in the Toronto Region involving issues of commercial law. The special procedures adopted for the hearing of matters on the Commercial List expedite the hearing and determination of these matters and have been met with considerable approval.

All counsel appearing in matters on the Commercial List are expected to know and follow the current Practice Direction.

The Commercial List remains, in the first instance, voluntary, except for bankruptcy matters. Applicants and plaintiffs may continue to set other matters that qualify for the Commercial List down for hearing either on the Commercial List or elsewhere. There is, however, a provision for any party to have a matter transferred to, or removed from, the Commercial List.

A continuous re-evaluation process by the court and the Commercial List Users' Committee determines whether (i) other matters should be added to those matters which may be listed on the Commercial List or (ii) its procedures should be further modified or continued.

This Practice Direction is to govern the conduct of matters on the Commercial List subject to further amendments as required.

Part II: Matters Eligible for the Commercial List

1. Matters which may be listed on the Commercial List are applications, motions and actions which in essence involve the following:

   a) *Bankruptcy and Insolvency Act;*

   b) *Bank Act*, relating to realizations and priority disputes;

   c) *Bulk Sales Act;*

   d) *Business Corporations Act (Ontario) and Canada Business Corporations Act;*

   e) *Companies' Creditors Arrangement Act;*

   f) *Limited Partnerships Act;*

   g) *Pension Benefits Act;*

   h) *Personal Property Security Act;*

   i) receivership applications and all interlocutory motions to appoint, or give directions to, receivers and receiver/managers;

   j) *Securities Act;*

   k) *Winding-Up and Restructuring Act;*

   l) *Credit Unions and Caisses Populaires Act*, relating to credit unions and caisses populaires under administration or that are being wound up or liquidated; and

   m) such other commercial matters as a judge presiding over the Commercial List may direct to be listed on the Commercial List, including: suitably complex cases under the *Arthur Wishart Act* (Franchise Disclosure), suitable commercial matters under the *International Commercial Arbitration Act* (Ontario), *Arbitration Act, 1991* (Ontario) and *Commercial Arbitration Act* (Canada). [See *771225 Ontario Inc. v. Bramco Holdings Co. Ltd.*, [1993] O.J. No. 1772 and

1399

Maple Valley Acres Limited v. CIBC, [1992] O.J. No. 2610), *Piedra v. TSX Inc.*, [2009] O.J. No. 5351 (Div. Ct.)].

In considering whether to make a direction under sub-paragraph 1m), the judge may take into account the current and expected caseload of matters listed on the Commercial List.

Part III: Judges, Court Officials, Courtrooms and General Procedures

2. The Commercial List shall be administered through the facilities of the Commercial List Office, 7th Floor, 330 University Avenue, Toronto M5G 1R7 fax: (416) 327-6228.

3. Matters listed on the Commercial List, including bankruptcy matters, shall usually be heard in courtrooms at 330 University Avenue, Toronto.

4. If counsel are aware that a judge sitting on the Commercial List should not hear a particular matter, the Commercial List Office should be advised.

5. Cooperation, communication and common sense shall continue to be the principles of operation of the Commercial List.

Part IV: Originating Process

6. Actions and applications under sub-paragraphs 1a) to l) (above) intended to be listed on the Commercial List may be issued in the Commercial List Office. Otherwise, all originating processes shall be issued from the appropriate office of the Superior Court of Justice as provided in the *Rules of Civil Procedure*.

7. For all applications, an initial return date must be obtained from the Commercial List Office or selected by counsel in conformity with the provisions of paragraphs 16 to 22 (below).

Part V: Place of Hearing

8. Only Toronto Region matters can be listed on the Commercial List (unless, for special reasons, authorization is given by the supervising judge). Aside from urgent insolvency matters, there should be a material connection to the Toronto Region over and above the location of counsel. Matters listed on the Commercial List shall only be heard in Toronto.

Part VI: Applications for Transfer to/from the Commercial List

9. Matters may be transferred to or removed from the Commercial List on a motion to a judge sitting to hear matters on the Commercial List.

10. A matter may be provisionally transferred to the Commercial List by a judge who is hearing the matter or a proceeding in the matter but who is not sitting to hear matters on the Commercial List, with the consent of all parties appearing. Such provisional transfer shall be for the purpose of bringing an application for transfer in accordance with paragraph 9 by one of the parties or as the judge may direct.

11. A matter may be transferred to the Commercial List by the Commercial List Office staff if the transfer is on consent of all parties, a Request Form and Case Timetable are fully completed and the matter is a Toronto Region matter which clearly falls within the categories of sub-paragraphs 1a) to l) (above).

Part VII: Court Documents

12. The name of the court in the title of proceedings of matters listed on the Commercial

List shall be: "Superior Court of Justice – Commercial List". All Notices of Application and Notices of Motion involving the Commercial List shall state that the application or motion will be made to "a judge presiding over the Commercial List at 330 University Avenue, Toronto".

13. All parts of the front and the back of a Request Form must be completed for all cases and for each proceeding (including 9:30 a.m. matters, matters added to the Commercial List and all other attendances) and the form must be signed by all counsel or an explanation for not doing so must be given. If all counsel cannot sign the same form, they may sign individual copies. Completed Request Forms may be faxed to the Commercial List Office at (416) 327-6228. Copies of the current Request Forms are available from the Commercial List Office.

14. For matters that are scheduled for a hearing time of one day or more, the Request Form shall set out an estimate of the amount of time it will take a judge to read the materials in advance.

15. A Case Timetable should be completed. If this cannot be done before the matter is first spoken to (it being recognized that the schedule may depend on the setting of a hearing date), a Case Timetable should be agreed among counsel as soon as possible thereafter and a copy sent to the Commercial List Office. In the event that counsel cannot agree on a schedule, counsel should attend before the supervising judge in chambers (see paragraph 26). It is expected that preliminary procedures shall be completed sufficiently in advance of the deadline dates to allow for consideration of the matter by counsel and for some subsequent slippage in the timetable. If a step is not completed in accordance with the Case Timetable, counsel are expected to get the matter back on schedule as soon as possible: (see *Re: Mernick* (1992), 14 C.B.R. (3d) 263). Copies of the current Case Timetable form are available from the Commercial List Office.

Part VIII: Dates for Applications, Motions and Trials

16. The Commercial List Office shall maintain the Commercial List. Subject to paragraphs 41 and 42 (below), the office staff, acting under the direction of the supervising judge, may assign initial hearing dates for matters other than trials.

17. The supervising judge or designate may assign initial hearing dates for matters not assigned by the office staff and for trials which, may be made in chambers at 9:30 a.m.

18. For trials and trials of issues, a motion to set a hearing date shall be made, unless the matter is otherwise scheduled by the supervising judge or designate in chambers on consent or on the appearance of all parties. The motion should be made to the supervising judge or designate, either as a chambers motion under paragraph 25 (below), or by special appointment. A trial date shall not be set unless the parties have completed a Trial Requirements Memorandum, including a brief outline of the case and its issues and witness time estimates. The Trial Requirements Memorandum form may be obtained from the Commercial List Office.

19. For a scheduling motion to a judge to be heard in chambers, counsel should try to provide a list of three mutually convenient and disparate dates from which the judge may select. Counsel are expected to check with the Commercial List Office for available dates immediately prior to the motion.

20. Except where special circumstances otherwise require, in selecting a return date for a matter, counsel are expected to allow reasonable time for all preliminary steps to take place before the return date (see paragraph 14). Counsel are encouraged and expected to consult among themselves in this regard, so that matters can be dealt with on the scheduled return date without further adjournment.

21. Counsel may specify the return date for a matter as "on a date to be established by the Commercial List Office" if there is no agreement on the return date.

22. A list of matters scheduled to be heard the following day will be posted on the bulletin board at 330 University Avenue by 4:00 p.m. Information about matters listed for the following day may also be obtained by calling (416) 327-5045 after 4:00 p.m.

Part IX: Estimates of Required Time

23. A realistic estimate of the time required for hearing the matter must be stated in the Request Form. If such an estimate cannot be given on the initial return of a matter, the Request Form must be appropriately amended when the matter is subsequently rescheduled. If all parties do not sign the Request Form, the initial return of the matter shall be for only a 10 minute scheduling hearing. Counsel should allocate the estimated hearing time appropriately among themselves, failing which the court shall assume that counsel have agreed to an equal division of time. If the time estimates in the Request Form becomes obsolete, then it is to be revised by notice to the Commercial List Office, giving the reason for the change. The court expects counsel to adhere to their time estimates.

24. The court may attempt to fix not only the date, but also the time, of the hearing, in appropriate situations. This shall require the cooperation of all counsel to correctly estimate the time required for their matters, to complete them within the time previously scheduled and to minimize wasted time for all concerned.

Part X: Chambers Matters

25. Commercial List judges will be available in chambers at 9:30 a.m. on each day to deal with ex parte, urgent, scheduling and consent matters, each of which must take not more than 10 minutes. Counsel must book these chambers matters through the Commercial List Office and these bookings will be made to allow the Chambers Judge to hear all chambers matters by 10:00 a.m. Counsel are expected to have discussed the matter in advance and to have prepared a draft resolution for consideration by the Chambers Judge. Counsel should file the materials for the appointment on the previous day, so that the judge is aware of the nature of the matter to be considered.

26. *Ex parte* matters on the Commercial List will be rare. Counsel shall be required to justify the reason for not notifying the respondents. In most cases, notice shall be required, particularly if the matter is part of an ongoing dispute and there are solicitors known to be representing the respondents, even if in respect of other matters.

27. Motions to have matters listed on the Commercial List under sub-paragraph 1m), should be accompanied by the consent of the other counsel involved or a completed Request Form so that the judge may make an order either granting or refusing the motion.

Part XI: Adjournments and Settlements

28. Counsel shall be expected to be ready to proceed with matters for which hearing times have been agreed to or set; adjournments of previously scheduled matters shall be granted only in special circumstances and for a material reason. Counsel are expected conscientiously to have sought to resolve most adjournments and waiting periods among themselves before a hearing, in a way which minimizes inconvenience and difficulty for the parties. Parties are expected to have retained counsel promptly and requests for adjournments because counsel have not been retained promptly or because new counsel have been retained just prior to the hearing shall be dealt with accordingly. Applications for adjournments on consent should be forwarded to the Commercial List Office or, if directed by the supervising judge, shall be spoken to at the next available 9:30 a.m. sittings; counsel are expected to ensure that adjournments are sought at the earliest opportunity, so that time is not blocked which could be used for other matters. It is expected that the first counsel to speak to a proposed adjournment shall be in a position to outline the position of other counsel appearing.

29. If an adjournment of a previously scheduled matter is to be sought or appears likely to be required, the Commercial List Office must be alerted as soon as possible to accommodate rescheduling of another matter or alerting counsel on standby matters.

30. If a matter is adjourned to permit the continuation of realistic settlement discussions and the matter is not settled within a reasonable time, a report should be made to the supervising judge through the Commercial List Office on the status of those discussions. This report should be made within 30 days and may be made in court, in chambers or by letter, as appropriate.

31. Where appropriate, matters may be scheduled to be heard on a "standby" basis for a particular date. In these cases, counsel should be prepared to proceed on short notice or they must keep the Commercial List Office advised of times when they become unavailable.

32. Counsel on Commercial List matters are expected to conscientiously and continuously canvass the matter of settlement and to advise promptly of all concluded settlements, or matters which are reasonably likely to settle, so that other matters may be rescheduled.

Part XII: Judge to Hear Whole Matter

33. It is anticipated that a judge who determines a substantive component of a proceeding will continue to hear all subsequent substantive components in that proceeding. Arrangements for these subsequent proceedings may be made directly with the Commercial List Office. The continuing judge should be contacted in writing about the nature of the matter to be heard and a list of times which are convenient to all counsel, so that the judge can conveniently schedule the matter or can refer it back to the Commercial List Office for re-assignment. For matters of sufficient complexity or duration, in the event that the original judge is not sitting on the Commercial List at the time or has not then been assigned to a future Commercial List team, a request may be made for the appointment of a new continuing judge.

Part XIII: Case Management

34. It is expected that most matters of substance and of an ongoing nature on the Commercial List shall be subject to a form of case management by a Commercial List judge. Paragraph 33 already provides for significant informal case management for each case on the Commercial List. When a matter is transferred to the Commercial List, when the trial of an issue is directed or in any other matter where a party moves for case management and a Commercial List judge so directs, a specific case management judge may be appointed.

35. Where a Commercial List matter is subject to specific case management, a Scheduling Conference (if not already held at the time of transfer or otherwise) shall be held with the case management judge not later than one month after the close of pleadings or the date of the order (referred in paragraph 34) to determine a plan to process the case in a timely and reasonable fashion and to deal with any matters of a procedural nature which should be addressed at an early stage of the proceedings. The prospects for settlement should also be addressed. The results of a Scheduling Conference will be recorded in a Case Timetable.

36. Counsel will be expected to have conferred among themselves, prior to the Scheduling Conference, for the purpose of preparing a plan to process the case, including a discovery plan pursuant to rule 29.1 and a Case Timetable, for review with the case management judge.

37. Unless otherwise ordered, a Case Conference shall also be held with the case management judge not later than one month after the completion of discoveries. The plaintiff or applicant shall have the onus of arranging the Case Conference. The purpose of the Case Conference is to monitor the progress of the matter, to canvass settlement or other disposition of all or as many of the issues as possible, and to provide whatever directions as may be necessary or appropriate with respect to the disposition of the matter.

38. A Case Conference may be held at any other time during the proceeding where the parties consent or where a party moves for the scheduling of a Case Conference and the case management judge so directs.

Part XIV: Commercial List Motions before a Master

39. No Commercial List motions should be heard by a master unless referred by a Commercial List judge. The judge should indicate his/her referral by a written endorsement or direction to that effect.

40. Once there has been a referral from a Commercial List judge, counsel may book a short (two hours or less) master's motion through the scheduling unit on the 10th Floor at 393 University Avenue, but if the motion is a half day or longer or if a series of motions are anticipated where it would be beneficial for one master to be seized, no such motions shall be booked until a master is assigned by the Team Leader – Toronto Masters. The assigned Master's Registrar will then contact counsel to arrange for scheduling of the motion.

Part XV: Motions for Summary Judgment

41. If a motion for summary judgment is brought in a proceeding on the Commercial List, a motion date will not in the ordinary course be booked until:

a) The parties have exchanged all motion materials, on an agreed schedule or one fixed at a 9:30 a.m. chambers appointment, and are sufficiently advanced in the preparation of the motion to crystallize the issues and the evidence relating to them;

b) A case conference has been booked at which counsel must be prepared to address whether oral evidence should be heard on the motion in accordance with subrule 20.04(2.2), the length of time necessary for the hearing of the motion, judicial preparation time necessary and any other directions that may be required;

c) The judge hearing the case conference has directed that a motion date be booked, bearing in mind that it is expected that the case conference judge will hear the motion.

Part XVI: Applications

42. It is expected that applications, which can require some oral evidence, will be managed in the same manner as motions for summary judgment in paragraph 41.

Part XVII: Alternative Dispute Resolution and Pre-Trials

43. Resort to the techniques of "alternative dispute resolution" (ADR), where appropriate, is recognized and encouraged as an effective aid in the disposition of issues and matters on the Commercial List. Pursuant to Rule 24.01.04(2) (c), mandatory mediation does not apply to cases on the Commercial List.

44. It shall be the duty of the case management judge and the obligation of counsel to explore methods to resolve the contested issues between the parties, including the resort to ADR, at the case conferences and on whatever other occasions it may be fitting to do so.

45. At any time, particularly on consent of the parties, the case management judge may refer any issue for ADR, as appears appropriate.

46. When a matter, or any issue within a matter, has been referred to ADR, counsel shall report to the case management judge at regular intervals as to the progress of the ADR proceedings. The timing of such reports shall be agreed upon between counsel and the case management judge.

47. The court may schedule intensive pre-trials for either entire cases or for significant matters within cases. These pre-trials should be booked through the Commercial List Office, with enough time for the matters in issue and the possibility of settlement to be canvassed thoroughly. At least five days before the pre-trial, each party shall deliver to the other parties a pre-trial brief containing:

a) a concise statement of facts including the agreed facts and admissions;

b) where necessary, a concise summary of the issues;

c) any outstanding procedural issues;

d) the current settlement position of each party; and

e) an estimate of the trial time, including a list of witnesses and an estimate of the time required for hearing the evidence of each.

48. A trial management conference, which is to be arranged by counsel at least two months before trial, is to be held to deal with arrangements for managing the trial or hearing.

Part XVIII: Materials for use of Court

49. It is expected that materials filed for the use of the court will be filed with the Commercial List Office at least within the time prescribed by the Rules. Early filing is recommended. All moving party or applicant material must be filed seven days (excluding holidays) before the hearing. All responding material must be filed four days (excluding holidays) before the hearing.

50. The Commercial List Office should be advised of what specific materials from its files are required for the hearing of any particular proceeding. This is particularly important where the matter is on-going or the materials in the court files are voluminous. It is suggested that counsel co-ordinate on a common numbering scheme for the records, transcripts, factums, authorities and other materials intended for use by the court and that a representative attend at the Commercial List Office before a hearing to ensure that the correct materials are available to the judge.

51. In appropriate cases, to supplement any required formal Record, counsel are requested to consider preparing an informal Compendium of the key materials to be referred to in argument (fair extracts of documents, transcripts, previous orders, authorities, etc.) to assist in focusing the case for the court: (see *Saskatchewan Egg Producers' Marketing Board v. Ontario*, [1993] O.J. No. 434.) Relevant portions of the Compendium should be highlighted or marked. Counsel are urged to consult among themselves in the preparation of a joint Compendium, if possible. The Compendium should contain only essential materials. The use of a loose-leaf format is particularly helpful to the court both for conducting hearings and for writing decisions.

52. All records and submissions should note on the cover page and the back page the nature of the proceeding for which the material is filed and the scheduled hearing date. When there is more than one affidavit of an individual filed in any proceeding, the affidavits should be numbered sequentially.

53. Factums should not, in the ordinary course, exceed 25 pages in length.

54. Unless it is not possible, briefs of authorities and substantial documents should be reproduced using both sides of the page.

55. Books of Authorities must be highlighted or side-barred to indicate the passages that will be referred to in argument.

56. The court invites the use of diagrams, corporate organization charts, list of persons involved, point-form chronologies and other synopses of complex or technical evidence.

57. The prior preparation of draft orders for consideration by the court at the end of a hearing will greatly expedite the issuance of orders. Where relevant model orders have been approved by the Commercial List Users' Committee, a copy of the draft order blacklined to the model order and indicating all variations sought from the model order must be filed.

58. For trials, the court encourages the use of sworn witness statements to replace ex-

amination in chief, in whole or in part, in appropriate circumstances. All such witness statements must be exchanged with all other parties and counsel well in advance of the hearing and, unless a prior order is made, the witness should be available for cross-examination at the trial. (Also see rule 53.02)

Part XIX: Expert Witnesses

59.   It is expected that counsel will comply with requirements set out in subrule 53.03(1) and (2) so as to provide notice of the intention to call an expert witness, including delivery of a signed report which contains the information mandated by subrule 53.03(2.1) within the expert report. Counsel must bring to the attention of their expert witness the duties of an expert set out in rule 4.1. Best practice should include providing the expert with the language of rule 4.1 and rule 53.03, subrules (1), (2) and (2.1).

Part XX: Reasons for Decision

60.   If an endorsement, order or decision is hand-written or dictated and not transcribed by the court, counsel for the plaintiff or moving party shall assist the court in preparing a typed draft and providing to the court the typed draft for editing by the judge, along with an electronic version of the draft and a copy of the hand-written version or dictation media, highlighting any passages which were difficult to read.

Part XXI: Costs

61.   The court will seek to award and fix costs at the end of the hearing of a matter. Counsel must submit a costs outline [subrule 57.01(6)] and be prepared to deal with costs (including liability, scale and amount) at the conclusion of the hearing of the matter or, if absolutely necessary, by written submissions immediately thereafter.

Part XXII: Users' Committee

62.   A Commercial List Users' Committee has been established. It is comprised of members of the judiciary who sit on the Commercial List from time to time, of practitioners who are familiar with the operation of the Commercial List and who are nominated by relevant user organizations in conjunction with the Users' Committee and of a representative of Courts Administration from the Commercial List Office. The names of the members of the Users' Committee may be obtained from the Commercial List Office. The Users' Committee meets regularly to consider improvements to the organization and operation of the Commercial List and to make recommendations to the Regional Senior Justice and the Chief Justice in that regard. The Users' Committee welcomes suggestions, compliments and complaints from other practitioners who have had cases on the Commercial List. Communications may be sent to the Commercial List Office, which will direct them to the office of the Regional Senior Justice.

Part XXIII: Enquiries

63.   The supervising judge of the Commercial List may be contacted about the scheduling of trials, long matters and urgent matters. In such cases, it is expected that counsel shall give details of the matter, the urgency, if any, expected length and mutually convenient dates. A Request Form and Case Timetable may be used for this purpose.

Part XXIV: Commercial List Forms

64. Current versions of the Request Forms, Case Timetable and Trial Requirements Memorandum may be obtained from the Commercial List Office.

Part XXV: Frequently Cited Cases in Commercial Proceedings

65. An Authorities Book for Commercial List matters containing cases frequently relied on, has been developed and approved for use in matters assigned to the Toronto Commercial List. There will be additions to, and deletions from, the list from time to time. The Authorities Book is available on the Superior Court's website at: www. ontariocourts.ca/scj/practice/practice-directions/toronto/commercial-list-authorities-book.

66. The cases in question appear on this list under various headings or topics which are not in any way intended to provide legal advice.

67. If you are relying on an authority that is contained in the Authorities Book, it need not be reproduced as part of the materials filed for the matters before the Commercial List in Toronto.

Part XXVI: Protocol Concerning Court-to-Court Communications in Cross Border Cases

68. The Commercial List has approved the adoption of the Guidelines Applicable to Court-to-Court Communications in Cross Border Cases ("Guidelines") prepared by the American Law Institute, for matters on the Commercial List. The Guidelines are available at: www.iiiglobal.org/component/jdownloads. The Guidelines have already been applied to international insolvency cases on the Commercial List. It is expected that these Guidelines will facilitate cooperative procedures for insolvency proceedings and other types of commercial disputes involving cross-border proceedings, where court-to-court communications might facilitate in harmonizing proceedings to help ensure consistent results and increase efficiency.

69. The Guidelines will only be applied in specific cases, following adequate notice to the parties.

70. Although the Guidelines were prepared for court-to-court communications as between Canada and the United States, the Commercial List endorses their application in court-to-court communications between Canada and other countries, and as between Ontario and the other provinces and territories.

71. Counsel and/or the parties should ensure that any issues concerning the confidentiality of materials to be transmitted by the Commercial List to another jurisdiction, including the deemed undertaking rule, Rule 30.1 of the *Rules of Civil Procedure*, be addressed when consideration is given by the court to the transmittal of evidentiary or written materials from the Commercial List to another court. The Guidelines are to apply only in a manner that is consistent with the *Rules of Civil Procedure* and the practice in this jurisdiction.

72. The Commercial List confirms, as noted in the Guidelines, that the Guidelines are not meant to be static, but are meant to be adapted an modified to fit the circumstances of individual cases, and to change and evolve as experience is gained from working with them.

73. A copy of the Guidelines may also be obtained from the Commercial List Office at 393 University Avenue, 10th Floor, Toronto, Ontario M5G 1E6, Telephone 416-327-5043, Fax 416-327-6228.

Dated: April 11, 2014

Heather J. Smith - Chief Justice (Superior Court of Justice (Ontario))

Geoffrey B. Morawetz - Regional Senior Judge (Superior Court of Justice (Toronto Region))

Q. Consolidated Practice Direction Concerning the Estates List in the Toronto Region (Latest Amendment: June 15, 2018)

Notice of Amendment:

Effective June 15, 2018, Part V D (Guardianship Applications) has been amended regarding the process for commencing a guardianship application.

Effective July 1, 2014

The Estates List has been established for the hearing of certain proceedings in the Toronto Region involving issues of estate, trust and capacity law.

This Practice Direction applies to matters on the Estates List in the Toronto Region, effective July 1, 2014. It *supersedes* all previous Practice Directions concerning Estates List matters in the Toronto Region issued before July 1, 2014, which are hereby revoked.

Counsel and parties are advised to refer to the relevant Parts of the Consolidated Provincial Practice Direction, the Consolidated Practice Direction for Divisional Court Proceedings as well as any other relevant Toronto region-specific Practice Directions and Guides which are available on the Superior Court of Justice website at: www.ontariocourts.ca/scj.

Table of Contents

Part IX: Materials for Use of the Court
    A.   **General Requirements**
    B.   **Multiple-appearance Proceedings: Records for use at the Hearing**
    C.   **Multiple-appearance Proceedings: On-going Endorsements/Orders Record**
    D.   **Compendium of Documents**
    E.   **Factums and Short Statements of Issues**
    F.   **Evidence at Trial**

Part X: Matters Without a hearing

Part XI: Costs

Part XII: Applications for the Appointment of Guardians Under the *Substitute Decisions Act* or *Children's Law Reform Act*

Part XIII: Settlements Affecting Parties Under a Disability
    A.   **Settlements of Estates List Proceedings**
    B.   **Settlements of other Civil Proceedings**

Part XIV: Applications Under Part V of the *Succession Law Reform Act*

Part XV: *Family Law Act* Elections

Part I: The Estates Office

1.   The Toronto Region Estates List is administered through the Estates Office, 7th floor, 330 University Avenue, Toronto, telephone number 416.326.2940 and fax number 416.326.2939. All filings relating to Estates List matters are done through the Estates Office.

Part II: Principles Guiding the Estates List

2.   The following principles shall guide all proceedings conducted on the Estates List:

    a)   The time and expense devoted to a proceeding should be proportionate to what is at stake in the proceeding; and,

    b)   Co-operation, communication, civility and common sense should prevail amongst all parties and counsel.

Part III: Matters Heard on the Estates List

3.   The Estates List hears the following matters:

    a)   all matters arising under Rules 74 and 75 of the *Rules of Civil Procedure*;

    b)   applications under Rule 14.05 regarding estates, wills and trusts, including applications for advice under section 60 of the *Trustee Act*;

    c)   applications relating to inter vivos trusts, whether under Rule 14.05, the *Variation of Trusts Act*, or otherwise;

    d)   proceedings involving the proof or validity of wills, including lost wills;

    e)   proceedings concerning the administration of estates;

    f)   summary procedures for claims against estates pursuant to the *Estates Act*, ss. 44 and 45;

    g)   passing of accounts of estate trustees or any other person acting in a fiduciary capacity, including guardianships and those acting under powers of attorney;

h) applications under the *Succession Law Reform Act*;

i) proceedings under the *Substitute Decisions Act, 1992*, including proceedings under that Act involving powers of attorney;

j) applications for the appointment of a guardian of property of a child under s. 47 of the *Children's Law Reform Act*, if brought in the Superior Court of Justice;

k) appeals from the Consent Capacity Board under the *Health Care Consent Act, 1996* or the *Mental Health Act*;

l) proceedings under the *Declarations of Death Act, 2002* or *Absentees Act*;

m) proceedings under the *Charities Accounting Act, Charitable Gifts Act* or *Religious Organizations' Lands Act*;

n) applications for the extension of time to make an election under s. 6(1) of the *Family Law Act* regarding the interest of a spouse under section 5(2) of that Act; and,

o) such other matters concerning estate, trust or capacity law as a judge may direct be heard on the Estates List. In considering whether to make such a direction, the judge may take into account the current and expected case load of matters on the Estates List.

4. Where an estate trustee(s) is either plaintiff or defendant in a civil action which does not specifically concern estate or trust law, or where an estate trustee becomes a party in such an action by virtue only of an order to continue under Rule 11.02, the action shall proceed as any other action and shall not be placed on the Estates List unless the court orders otherwise.

A. Transfers of matters to the Estates List

5. A matter that should have been commenced on the Estates List may be transferred to it by a judge who is hearing the matter, but who is not sitting on the Estates List.

6. Matters may be transferred to the Estates List on consent, provided the matters fall within the categories outlined in sub-paragraphs 3(a) – (o), or on a motion to a judge sitting to hear matters on the Estates List.

7. The place of commencement of a proceeding is governed by Rule 13.1.01. Requests to transfer matters commenced outside the Toronto Region to the Estates List are governed by Part III of the Consolidated Provincial Practice Direction.

Part IV: Administrative Matters

A. Courtrooms and Gowning

8. Matters listed on the Estates List usually are heard at 330 University Avenue, Toronto, unless notice to the contrary is given.

9. Counsel shall gown for all hearings or attendances, except pre-trial conferences and 9:30 Appointments.

B. Estates List Documents and Forms

10. Copies of forms specified by the *Rules of Civil Procedure* can be found on the Court

Services Division Forms website: ontariocourtforms.on.ca/en/. Confirmation and other administrative forms used by the Estates List may be obtained from the Estates List Office or can be found on the Estates List webpage on the Superior Court of Justice website: www.ontariocourts.ca/scj. Counsel and parties using documents obtained from a website must remember that the *Rules of Civil Procedure* require that all documents filed in a proceeding must use characters of at least 12 point, or 10 pitch, size; as a result, some conversion of the font size of web-sourced documents may be required.

Part V: Scheduling Matters on the Estates List

A. The Daily List 9:30 Appointments and the Hearing List

11. The daily list of matters heard by a judge sitting on the Estates List consists of two parts: (i) the hearing of 9:30 Appointments of 10-minutes each, immediately followed by (ii) the hearing of contested matters or unopposed matters that require some time for a judge to review ("Hearing Matters"). 9:30 Appointments take place in chambers and deal with minor and/or unopposed matters. Counsel are not required to gown. Contested matters and application or motions are conducted in open court commencing 10:00 a.m.

12. Booking dates for a 9:30 Appointment or a Hearing Matter can be done through the Estates Office.

13. 9:30 Appointments will be for no more than 10 minutes for each matter booked and must be booked at least two days in advance. Any materials required for a 9:30 Appointment should be filed no later than 12 noon the day before the appointment.

14. If a party fails to appear at a 9:30 Appointment, the court may set a timetable and hearing date for the matter in the party's absence.

15. In order to ensure the most efficient use of court time and to enable contested matters to be heard at the earliest reasonable date, procedures for booking time on the Estates List for the hearing of a proceeding vary according to the type and length of proceeding as described below.

B. Passing of Accounts Applications

16. When initiating an application for the passing of accounts in all circumstances – whether the passing of accounts of estate trustees or of any other person acting in a fiduciary capacity, including guardianships and those acting under powers of attorney – the applicant should book only 10 minutes on the list for Hearing Matters for the initial return date of the application.

17. If no notices of objection are received or if notices of objection are received but are withdrawn within the prescribed time in respect of the application to pass accounts, and no request for increased costs has been filed and served, the applicant may request, upon filing the material required by subrule 74.18(9), that the application proceed as an unopposed matter to be dealt with by a judge in chambers without the need for the parties to attend.

18. If no notices of objection are received or if notices of objection are received but are withdrawn within the prescribed time in respect of the application to pass accounts, and a request for increased costs has been filed and served, the judge hearing the mat-

ter on the initial return date may determine the amount of the costs at that time or, if the judge is of the view that there is not sufficient time on the initial return date to hear the matter on the initial return date, the judge can schedule a date for a further hearing on the costs issue.

19. If notices of objection are received and not withdrawn in response to the application to pass accounts, and if the parties can agree in advance of the initial return date on the terms of an order giving directions (including a timetable for each pre-hearing step and, where practicable, the hearing date), then parties can obtain a consent order giving directions on the scheduled initial 10 minute return date for the application.

20. If notices of objection are received and not withdrawn and if the parties cannot agree on an order for directions prior to the initial return date, the parties should file, at least two days in advance of the initial return date, copies of their respective draft orders giving directions, including timetables for each pre-hearing step and proposed hearing dates. If the dispute about directions can be resolved during the 10 minute appointment on the initial return date, the judge can issue an order giving directions, including a timetable for pre-hearing steps and a hearing date. If the argument about the terms of an order giving directions will require longer than the 10 minute appointment on the initial return date, the judge can schedule a date for the hearing of a contested motion for directions.

21. Draft orders giving directions should address the items described in paragraph 43 (below).

C. Applications Involving Wills Where an Order Giving Directions is Required

22. Where a notice of objection has been filed to the issuance of a certificate of appointment of estate trustee and an application for directions is required, the applicant, or other person applying for directions, should book an initial 10 minute 9:30 Appointment for the initial return date of the application for directions.

23. If prior to their attendance at the 9:30 Appointment the parties can agree on the terms of a consent order giving directions, including a timetable for each pre-hearing step agreed upon, the judge at the 9:30 Appointment may issue a consent order giving directions.

24. If the parties cannot agree on an order giving directions prior to the 9:30 Appointment, the parties should file, at least two days in advance of the 9:30 Appointment, copies of their respective draft orders giving directions, including timetables for each pre-hearing step. If the dispute about directions can be resolved during the 10 minute 9:30 Appointment, the judge may issue the order giving directions, including a timetable for pre-hearing steps. If the argument about the terms of an order giving directions will require longer than the 10 minute 9:30 Appointment, the judge can schedule a date for the hearing of a contested application for directions.

D. Guardianship Applications

25. Applications for the appointment of a guardian under the *Substitute Decisions Act, 1992* or *Children's Law Reform Act* should be commenced by filing an application record. Applicants should advise the court of the expected length of time for the application and whether the application is opposed, unopposed or on consent.

E. Any Other Type of Application or Motion Brought on the Estates List

Matters that will require less than one hour to argue on the merits

26. For other matters heard on the Estates List where the applicant or moving party realistically estimates that the argument of the matter by all parties involved will take less than one hour, an appointment may be booked on the list for Hearing Matters, through the Estates Office, for a hearing of up to one hour.

Matters that will require more than one hour to argue on the merits

27. Where an application or a motion will require more than one hour to argue on the merits and all parties to the application or motion can agree on a timetable for all pre-hearing steps and on the hearing date for argument, the applicant or moving party may obtain from the Estates Office a consent hearing date upon filing a Hearing Date Request Form that:

    a) confirms that the parties have agreed on a timetable for all pre-hearing steps;

    b) sets out the agreed upon timetable; and

    c) sets out the agreed hearing date.

    The hearing date for such a motion may be reserved by contacting the Estates Office. Confirmation of the hearing date will require the applicant or moving party to file a completed Hearing Date Request Form with the Estates Office.

28. If the parties to an application or motion that will require more than one hour to argue on the merits cannot agree on a timetable for all pre-hearing steps or on a hearing date, the applicant or moving party, on notice to all other parties, shall book a 9:30 Appointment for the Court to set a timetable for pre-hearing steps and a hearing date for the application or motion to be argued on the merits. The parties should file, at least two days in advance of the 9:30 Appointment, copies of their proposed pre-hearing timetables and their proposed hearing dates.

F. Other Matters that Can be Dealt with at a 9:30 Appointment

29. Apart from the circumstances described above, there may be other occasions during a proceeding when the parties may wish to book a 9:30 Appointment to obtain the assistance of the court in setting timetables for further steps in the proceeding, including steps required to ready the matter for trial, or to obtain consent orders. On notice to other interested parties, such 9:30 Appointments may be booked on two days' notice.

G. Adjournments

General Principles

30. Parties are expected to be ready to proceed with matters for which hearing dates have been agreed to or set by the court; adjournments of previously scheduled matters shall be granted only in special circumstances and for a material reason. Parties are expected conscientiously to have sought to resolve most adjournments and waiting periods among themselves before a hearing in a way which minimizes inconvenience and difficulty for the parties.

31. Parties are expected to retain counsel promptly. A request for an adjournment because counsel has not been retained promptly or because new counsel has been retained just prior to the hearing shall be dealt with accordingly.

Where the Hearing Date Was Set at a 9:30 Appointment

32.   Requests for adjournments of hearing dates which were set as a result of attendances at a 9:30 Appointment should occur infrequently since the reasonableness of the hearing date would have been canvassed at that appointment. Any such request for an adjournment, even on consent, should be made through a further 9:30 Appointment so that the Court can be satisfied that the matter has reached a stage of readiness which justifies assigning a new hearing date. If the matter is not ready for hearing, it may be removed from the hearing list, leaving it to the parties to re-apply subsequently through a 9:30 Appointment for a new hearing date once the matter is ready to be heard.

Where the Hearing Date Was Not Set at a 9:30 Appointment

33.   Where the hearing date for a matter was not set through a 9:30 appointment attendance, a first consent adjournment of the hearing of the matter may be arranged through the Estates Office.

34.   If the parties wish to seek a second consent adjournment of the matter, they should adjourn the matter, in advance of the scheduled hearing date, to a 9:30 Appointment. If the request for a second adjournment is not made until the appearance before the judge scheduled to hear the matter, that judge may direct the matter to be adjourned to a 9:30 Appointment before it proceeds further. On the return of the matter at a 9:30 Appointment the Court can determine whether the matter is ready for hearing, or whether it would be more appropriate to remove the matter from the hearing list, leaving it to the parties to reapply subsequently through a 9:30 Appointment for a new hearing date once the matter is ready to be heard.

Part VI: Contested Matters – General

A.   Confirmation of Applications and Motions

35.   Parties must confirm the hearing of an application or motion at least three days in advance of the hearing date using the Confirmation Form (9:30 Appointment and Hearing Matter) available from the Estates Office.

B.   Urgent Applications or Motions

36.   A party who considers a matter to be urgent may complete and submit to the Estates Office an Urgent Hearing Request form describing the nature of the matter, the reason for the urgency, the time required for the matter, and any scheduling discussions the party has been able to engage in with the other party or parties in the circumstances, as well as attaching a copy of the proposed Notice of Application or Notice of Motion.

37.   Requests for the hearing of urgent applications or motions will be heard on an "as required" basis, by the supervising judge or designate. The Estates Office will notify the parties of the time and location for the hearing of the urgent request.

C.   Pre-Trial Conference and Trial Dates

38.   Pre-trial conferences must be held in all matters proceeding to trial. Dates for pre-trial conferences and trials should be obtained from the Estates Office at the time the proceeding is set down for trial.

39.   Two hours normally will be assigned for a pre-trial conference. If the parties think

that a longer pre-trial conference would be appropriate in the circumstances of their case, they may book a 9:30 Appointment to secure a date for a longer pre-trial conference. If the parties are unable to agree upon a pre-trial conference date, trial date, the length of time for the trial, or any other matter concerning the conduct of the trial, a party may book a 9:30 Appointment to determine such matters.

40. At least five days prior to the date of a pre-trial conference each party must serve and file with the Estates Office an Estates List Pre-Trial Conference Form.

Part VII: Contested Matters – Estates

A. Orders Giving Directions: General

41. Orders giving directions in contested matters are designed to provide the parties with a procedural framework in which to prepare the proceeding for final adjudication. Rule 75.06 provides the court with considerable discretion and flexibility to put in place a process that will ensure the just, expeditious and least expensive determination of a proceeding on its merits. Parties are expected to take time and care in preparing proposed orders giving directions for consideration by the court.

42. If the parties cannot agree upon an order giving directions before or at a 9:30 Appointment and a contested motion for directions is required, each party must file with its motion materials a copy of the draft order giving directions it is seeking.

43. Draft orders giving directions should address, where applicable, the following matters:

   a) the issues to be decided;

   b) who are the parties – who is propounding the will(s) and who is challenging the will(s), and who is submitting rights to the court;

   c) whether there is any party under disability who requires representation and, if so, whether notice to the Public Guardian and Trustee or the Office of the Children's Lawyer should be directed;

   d) whether an estate trustee should be appointed during litigation and the amount of security, if any, such an estate trustee should file;

   e) who shall be served with the order for directions, and the method of and times for service;

   f) whether the parties should exchange pleadings or put before the court their respective positions and the material facts upon which they rely by some other means;

   g) procedures for bringing the matter before the court in a summary way;

   h) the timing of a mediation session under Rule 75.1 and its conduct, including (i) whether the parties wish the mediator to provide any report to the court on procedural issues, (ii) the desirability of multiple mediation sessions, and (iii) when a pre-trial conference should be held in the event the mediation does not result in a settlement of the proceeding;

   i) any other pre-hearing steps to be undertaken, including documentary disclosure, obtaining medical, accounting or legal records, examinations for discovery, and the availability of a motion for summary judgment;

j) the timing for the delivery of any expert report and the utility of a pre-hearing meeting between experts to narrow the issues in dispute;

k) the timing of a pre-trial conference, including how long after an unsuccessful mediation session the pre-trial conference should be held; and,

l) any matter relating to the conduct of the trial or hearing, including whether affidavits be used as witnesses' evidence-in-chief.

B. Orders Giving Directions: Contested Passing of Accounts

44. Where a hearing will be held on a passing of accounts, orders giving directions proposed by the parties should address the following issues, where applicable:

a) the timing and conduct of a mediation;

b) the issues to be tried and each party's position on each issue;

c) the timing and scope of relevant disclosure;

d) the witnesses each party intends to call, the issues each witness intends to address, and the anticipated length of each witness' testimony (examination-in-chief and cross-examination); and,

e) the procedure to be followed at the hearing, including the method of adducing evidence-in-chief.

Part VIII: Mandatory Mediation – Rule 75.1

45. Rule 75.1.02(1) stipulates that mandatory mediation applies to the following proceedings:

a) contested applications to pass accounts;

b) formal proof of testamentary instruments;

c) objections to issuing a certificate of appointment;

d) return of a certificate of appointment;

e) claims against an estate;

f) proceedings under Part V of the *Succession Law Reform Act*;

g) proceedings under the *Substitute Decisions Act, 1992*;

h) proceedings under the *Absentees Act*, the *Charities Accounting Act*, the *Estates Act*, the *Trustee Act* or the *Variation of Trusts Act*;

i) applications under Rule 14.05(3) whether the matters at issue relate to an estate or trust; and,

j) proceedings under s. 5(2) of the *Family Law Act*.

46. On contested passing of accounts applications parties should be prepared to deal with the issue of directions for mandatory mediation on the initial return date specified in the notice of application.

47. In all other matters, motions for directions for the conduct of a mandatory mediation normally should form part of, or be combined with, a motion for directions under Rule 75.06. Consent mediation orders can be obtained through a 9:30 Appointment.

48. In addition to addressing the matters set out in Rule 75.1.05(4), an order giving di-

rections for mediation should, where appropriate, deal with any further information the parties require in advance of the mediation in order to ensure a productive mediation session.

Part IX: Materials for Use of the Court

A.   General Requirements

49.   Parties are strongly encouraged to file any materials for use of the court earlier than the dates specified in the Rules, especially for more complex hearings. All materials must be filed by the moving party at least seven days before the hearing. All material must be filed by the responding party at least four days before the hearing.

50.   Application/Motion Confirmation Forms must clearly specify the materials that each party wishes the court to read for use on the application/motion.

B.   Multiple-appearance Proceedings: Records for use at the Hearing

51.   Many proceedings on the Estates List involve multiple attendances before the Court. Over time materials can become voluminous. Parties are reminded that the Rules require that the application and motion records used at a hearing must contain *all* materials that the parties intend to use on that particular hearing.

52.   The Estates List strongly discourages the practice of relying at a hearing on materials used at previously disposed of hearings in a proceeding. If a party intends to do so, the party must ensure that a representative attends at the Estates Office sufficiently in advance of the hearing to ensure that the correct materials are available for the judge. It is the responsibility of the parties, not the Estates Office or the judge, to ensure that materials from previously disposed of hearings are available for a current hearing.

53.   In complex cases where a large volume of materials will be placed before the hearing judge, it is of great assistance to the court for the parties to coordinate on a common numbering scheme for the records, transcripts, factums, authorities and other materials intended for use by the court and to ensure that the materials are properly organized for use on the hearing.

C.   Multiple-Appearance Proceedings: On-Going Endorsements/Orders Record

54.   Where a proceeding likely will involve multiple attendances before the court, it is of assistance to judges hearing matters in the proceeding to be able to review previous orders, endorsements and reasons for judgment. In such cases the person starting a case is responsible for preparing and filing with the Estates Office a red three-ring binder, bearing the proceeding's style of cause, entitled "Endorsements/Orders Record", and containing numbered tabs.

55.   The person who started the case shall keep the Endorsements/Orders Record up-to-date, under the supervision of the Estates Office personnel, by using the following procedure. Within five days of the date of the issuance of a new endorsement or reasons for judgment, or the entry of a new order in the proceeding, the person who started the case shall provide the Estates Office with (i) a copy of the new endorsement, order or reasons for judgment, (ii) a consecutively numbered tab for the new document, and (iii) an updated table of contents for filing in the *Endorsements/Orders Record* so that a continuous record of all judicial decisions in the proceeding can be kept in an ordered fashion in the court file. Where an endorsement is hand-written, the

applicant should assist the Court by preparing a typed draft, in consultation with other parties, for inclusion in the *Endorsements/Order Record*.

56. An order giving directions in a proceeding may include a provision requiring the applicant to prepare and maintain such an *Endorsements/Orders Record*.

D. Compendium of Documents

57. In appropriate cases, to supplement any required formal record, parties are requested to consider preparing a Compendium of the key materials to be referred to during oral argument (fair extracts of documents, transcripts, previous orders, authorities, etc.) to assist in focusing the case for the Court. Relevant portions of the Compendium should be highlighted or marked. Parties are encouraged to consult among themselves to prepare a joint Compendium, if possible.

58. The Court encourages the use of diagrams, family trees, lists of persons involved, corporate organization charts, point-form chronologies, and other synopses of complex or technical evidence.

59. The prior preparation of draft orders for consideration by the Court at the end of a hearing will greatly expedite the issuance of orders.

E. Factums and Short Statements of Issues

60. The Rules require that on applications each party must file a factum for use at the hearing.

61. Although under the Rules factums are not mandatory on the hearing of a motion, parties are reminded that factums are of great assistance to the Court where the motion will be contested or where an understanding of a large amount of materials will be required in order for a court to deal with an unopposed matter. In appropriate cases filing a short, point-form or simple statement of issues, fact and/or law may provide an alternative way by which parties can assist the Court in understanding the issues on the motion.

F. Evidence at Trial

62. The court encourages the use, in appropriate circumstances, of sworn witness statements at trial in substitution for the examination-in-chief of witnesses, in whole or in part. Where sworn witness statements will be used, they must be exchanged with all other parties and counsel well in advance of the hearing and, unless a prior order is made, the witnesses should be available for cross-examination at the trial.

Part X: Matters Without a Hearing

63. Judges on the Estates List deal with a variety of applications without a hearing. The most common applications involve requests to dispense with administration bonds and uncontested passing of accounts. It is important that parties filing applications without a hearing ensure that their materials contain all the information and evidence required by statute, the Rules or any published filing endorsements emanating from the Estates List, and also provide clear, detailed explanations of the reasons for the relief they are requesting.

64. Filing requirements for requests to dispense with administration bonds are set out in *Re Henderson Estate*, 2008 CanLII 69136 (ON S.C.).

65. Two copies of the draft order sought must be filed with the application materials.

Part XI: Costs

66. Parties are reminded that the traditional practice of awarding costs in estate litigation to all parties out of the estate has been tempered by recent jurisprudence relating to the conduct of parties and their relative success in the litigation. Parties are expected to be aware of this jurisprudence and to be prepared to make submissions with respect to its application in particular cases.

Part XII: Applications for the Appointment of Guardians Under the *Substitute Decisions Act* or *Children's Law Reform Act*

67. Part III of the *Substitute Decisions Act, 1992* specifies the procedure and filing requirements for applications to appoint guardians of adults. Part III of the *Children's Law Reform Act* sets out the procedure and filing requirements for applications to appoint guardians of minors. In addition, the general requirements of Rule 38 governing applications apply to applications to appoint guardians.

68. Parties should refer to paragraphs 25 to 28 (above) regarding the requirements for scheduling applications for the appointments of guardians.

Part XIII: Settlements Affecting Parties Under a Disability

69. The partial or full settlement of a claim made by or against a person under disability requires the approval of a judge under Rule 7.08. Often the implementation of such a settlement will require the appointment of a guardian of property under Parts I and III of the *Substitute Decisions Act* or section 47 of the *Children's Law Reform Act.*

A. Settlements of Estates List Proceedings

70. Where the settlement of a proceeding on the Estates List requires court approval, the motion for approval of the settlement and the application for the appointment of a guardian of property should be brought before a judge on the Estates List.

B. Settlements of Other Civil Proceedings

71. Where the settlement of any other civil proceeding will require the appointment of a guardian of property for a person under disability, the application for the appointment of a guardian should be brought on the Estates List. However, where the settlement occurs during the trial or pre-trial conference of a civil matter, the trial or pre-trial judge may deal with the application to appoint a guardian of property where the circumstances make it more practical to do so.

72. Where the settlement involves an adult under disability, in most circumstances the application to appoint a guardian of property should be brought on the Estates List prior to the filing of a motion for approval of the settlement so that an authorized person exists to receive any settlement funds on behalf of the party under disability prior to the approval of the settlement.

73. Since the *Children's Law Reform Act* does not authorize an amendment to a management plan for a guardian of property of a minor except by court order, where the settlement involves a minor under disability the application to appoint a guardian of property initially should be made returnable at a 9:30 Appointment on the Estates List

so that the court can coordinate the hearing of the application to appoint a guardian with the motion to approve the settlement.

Part XIV: Applications Under Part V of the *Succession Law Reform Act*

74. In considering an application for dependant's support under Part V of the *Succession Law Reform Act*, a court must consider numerous circumstances, including the dependant's current assets and means, the assets and means that the dependant is likely to have in the future, and the dependant's needs in light of the dependant's accustomed standard of living. Although the *Rules of Civil Procedure* do not prescribe the manner by which an applicant should place before the court evidence about these matters, applicants are encouraged to include in their application materials comprehensive lists of the dependant's assets and liabilities, as well as information about the dependant's income and expenses.

Part XV: *Family Law Act* Elections

75. An application for the extension of time to make an election under s. 6(1) of the *Family Law Act* regarding the interest of a spouse under section 5(2) of that Act should be brought on the Estates List.

Dated: April 11, 2014

Amended: June 15, 2018

Heather J. Smith
Chief Justice
Superior Court of Justice (Ontario)

Geoffrey B. Morawetz
Regional Senior Judge
Superior Court of Justice, Toronto Region

R. The Guide Concerning Best Practices for Civil Actions, Applications and Motions in the Toronto Region (Effective: July 1, 2014)

Effective July 1, 2014

This Guide applies to civil actions, applications and motions in the Toronto Region, effective July 1, 2014. It *supersedes* the previous best practice document concerning civil applications and motions, which is hereby revoked.

Counsel and parties are advised to refer to the relevant Parts of the Consolidated Provincial Practice Direction, the Consolidated Practice Direction for Divisional Court Proceedings as well as other relevant Toronto region-specific Practice Directions and Guides (e.g. the Consolidated Practice Direction for Civil Actions, Applications, Motions and Procedural Matters in the Toronto Region).

All Superior Court of Justice Practice Directions and Guides are available on the Superior Court's website at: www.ontariocourts.ca/scj.

Table of Contents

Part I: Purpose

1.   The Consolidated Practice Direction for Civil Actions, Applications, Motions and Procedural Matters in the Toronto Region encourages parties to refer to this Guide. *This Guide* describes the practices the court encourages both counsel and self-represented parties to use in preparing and conducting civil actions, applications and motions.

Part II: Co-operation and Civility between Counsel and between Counsel and Self-Represented Parties

2.   To be fair and just an adversarial system of litigation requires the opponents to resolve their differences in a civilized manner. Although parties conduct civil actions, appli-

cations and motions within the context of an adversarial system, the court expects counsel and self-represented parties to conduct themselves, at all times, in ways that promote cooperation, effective and timely communication, and civility, as well as applying common sense to the resolution of issues that arise during the course of a proceeding.

3. The court expects counsel to conduct applications and motions having regard to the *Principles of Professionalism for Advocates* and the *Principles of Civility for Advocates* published by The Advocates' Society, found at: https://www.advocates.ca/ Upload/Files/PDF/Advocacy/BestPracticesPublications/Principles_of_Civility_ English.pdf.

Part III: Assistance for Self-Represented Parties in Preparing Materials for Civil Proceedings

4. Counsel who are involved in civil proceedings involving a self-represented party are encouraged to consult and be guided by the *Canadian Code of Conduct for Trial Lawyers Involved in Civil Actions Involving Unrepresented Litigants* published by the American College of Trial Lawyers and found at: www.actl.com/.

Part IV: Electronic Document Disclosure

5. Parties are reminded of their obligation under Rule 29.1.03(4) to consult and have regard to the document titled *The Sedona Canada Principles Addressing Electronic Discovery* developed and available from the Sedona Conference. Applying the *Sedona Canada Principles Addressing Electronic Discovery* is particularly important in complex applications or motions which may involve significant documentary disclosure.

6. The *Sedona Canada Principles Addressing Electronic Discovery* may be found at: www.thesedonaconference.org/publications.

Part V: Materials for Use of the Court in Civil Proceedings

A. Confirmation of Applications and Motions Required

7. Parties are reminded that their confirmation form must be sent to the motions office no later than 2:00 p.m. three days before the scheduled hearing date under Rule 37.10.1.

B. Factums or Written Arguments

8. Factums are required for all applications.

9. Factums are required for all motions over two hours (except undertakings and refusals motions) and are strongly encouraged for all other motions.

10. All factums should be clear and concise.

11. For longer or more complex motions, the court finds it helpful for the parties to file electronic copies of their factums in Word format. Electronic copies of factums should be attached to the hard copy of the factum filed with the court on a disk and should be labelled with the court file name and number, event and content of the disk, as well as the return date of the matter. Counsel and parties should refer to the Guide Concerning e-Delivery of Documents available on the Superior Court's website.

C. Books of Authorities

12. Cases contained in books of authorities should be copied on both sides of a page.

Electronic copies of books of authorities are helpful in longer or more complex motions. Disks should be labelled with the court file name and number, event and content of the disk, as well as the return date of the matter.

D. Complex Applications and Motions

13. Where a matter is on-going or the materials in the court files are voluminous, counsel are requested to facilitate the hearing of the matter by:

    a) preparing a consolidated record;

    b) preparing a consolidated compendium;

    c) preparing a numbered list of all motion records, transcripts, casebooks and other materials; or

    d) by having a representative attend at the Civil Motions List Office before a hearing to ensure that all the materials needed for the motion, application or trial are available to the court.

14. In appropriate cases, to supplement any required formal record, counsel are requested to consider preparing a compendium of the key materials to be referred to in argument (fair extracts of documents, transcripts, previous orders, authorities, etc.) to assist in focusing the case for the court. Relevant portions of the compendium should be highlighted or marked. Counsel are urged to consult among themselves in the preparation of a joint compendium, if possible.

E. Charts and Diagrams

15. The court invites the use of diagrams, corporate organization charts, list of persons involved, point-form chronologies and other synopses of complex or technical evidence.

F. Organization of Materials on Continuing Matters

16. Where a matter has been adjourned, parties are responsible to ensure that all the materials for the adjourned are available at least one week before the new hearing date. (This responsibility requires reviewing the court file and may require requisition documents that may have been transferred to storage.)

17. Where there are prior endorsements, orders or judgments that are relevant to a continuing matter, parties are encouraged to file an Orders Brief containing the relevant material.

18. Between 12 noon and 2:30 p.m. two days before the hearing date of a long or complex motion or application, it is recommended that a representative of the moving party attend the Civil Motions Office and organize the court file to put all relevant documents, particularly where materials are voluminous or where a matter is scheduled to reconvene.

G. Costs

19. Parties are reminded that unless they have agreed on the costs of a motion or application, Rule 57.01(6) requires every party who intends to seek costs for a motion or application to give to the other party before the hearing of the motion or application a costs outline not exceeding three pages in length (Form 57B) and bring a copy to

the hearing. It is within the discretion of the court not to entertain cost submissions unless the parties have complied with this rule.

Part VI: Court Contact Information for Applications and Motions

A. Civil Scheduling Unit

20. 10th Fl. 393 University Ave.
    Tel: 416-327-5535
    Fax: 416-327-9470

    Short Motions or Applications (Under 2 hours before a Judge or Master)
    Email: JUS.G.MAG.CSD.CivilMotionsScheduling@Ontario.ca

    Motion Scheduling Court (Over 2 hours, before a Judge)
    Email: MotionsSchedulingCourt@Ontario.ca

    Motion Scheduling Court: Summary Judgment
    Email: MotionsSchedulingCourt@Ontario.ca

    Confirmations for Motions and Applications
    Email: JUS.G.MAG.CSD.CivilMotionsConfirmation@Ontario.ca
    Fax: 416-327-5484

B. Masters Administration

23. 6th Fl. 393 University Ave.
    Tel: 416-327-0506
    Fax: 416-326-5416

    Long Motions before a Master
    Email: Civil.Masters.Long.Motions@Ontario.ca

    Motions in Construction Lien or References
    416-327-9404 or 416-212-9783

    References
    Telephone 416-327-0506 or attend in person to the Masters Administration on the 6th Floor, 393 University Avenue

    Case Management Masters
    Fax: 416-326-5416

C. Trial Coordinators Office

24. 7th Fl. 330 University Ave.
    Tel: 416-327-5320
    Fax: 416-327-5697

    Pre-Trial Conference (Ordinary and Simplified Procedure)
    Email: Toronto.SCJ.Civil.Pre-Trials@Ontario.ca

    Trial Dates
    Email: MAG.CSD.Trials@Ontario.ca

S. Practice Advisory re Video Conferencing for Civil Practice Court, Commercial List Chambers Matters and Estates List 9:30 appointments in the Toronto Region (Effective: March 8, 2017)

The following Practice Advisory is in effect as of March 8, 2017.

1. In accordance with rule 1.08 of the *Rules of Civil Procedure*, counsel and/or parties may appear by video conference, unless otherwise directed by the court, for (i) consent matters, (ii) unopposed matters and (iii) scheduling matters in the following types of events:

    a. Civil Practice Court appearances (as described in paragraphs 1 – 2 of the Consolidated Practice Direction for Civil Actions, Applications, Motions and Procedural Matters in the Toronto Region)

    b. Commercial List Chambers Matters (as described in paragraphs 25 – 27 of the Consolidated Practice Direction Concerning the Commercial List)

    c. Estates List 9:30 appointments (as described in paragraphs 11 – 15 of the Consolidated Practice Direction Concerning the Estates List in the Toronto Region).

2. Parties or counsel who choose to appear by video conference for one of these events must make their own arrangements to do so, in accordance with rule 1.08(6); they may do so through one of the two methods set out below.

Appearing by video conference using CourtCall (no prior Court approval required)

3. CourtCall is a third-party video conferencing service that is available for the court matters and events described in section 1.

4. A CourtCall video appearance is voluntary. Any party or counsel wishing to appear by video using CourtCall must contact CourtCall directly to make the necessary arrangements, which include the following:

    i. If not already registered with CourtCall as a client, register at courtcall.com.

    ii. **At least two (2) business days before the hearing,** book the appearance by logging into the CourtCall website (courtcall.com) and completing a "New Appearance" request, or by contacting CourtCall at 1-888-882-6878.

    iii. Pay the fee set by CourtCall for the video appearance.

    iv. CourtCall will email or fax a confirmation upon completion of the booking and payment.

    v. The participant appearing by video must supply his or her own telephone and computer with a camera and internet connection with sufficient bandwidth to allow them to connect and participate.

    vi. On the day of the hearing, the participant must initiate the video appearance by clicking on the link and dialing the toll-free teleconference number provided in the confirmation sent by CourtCall.

    vii. A pre-hearing check-in is required fifteen minutes before the scheduled hearing time.

    viii. For further information, please refer to the CourtCall website (courtcall.com) or contact CourtCall at 1-888-882-6878.

5. The party/counsel must also advise the Court, in writing, that he/she will be attending the court event by video using the CourtCall service. This can be done by completing the appropriate section on the scheduling/confirmation form filed with the Court.

6. All persons who have completed the necessary arrangements with CourtCall and advised the Court, in accordance with the steps outlined above, may assume that they have the Court's permission to appear for the event by video, unless otherwise directed by a judge.

Appearing by other means (prior Court approval required):

7. A party or counsel who wishes to appear for one of the court matters/events described in section 1 by video conference through means other than the CourtCall service or by telephone conference must (i) obtain the Court's prior approval to appear by the means proposed (in accordance with rule 1.08(2) or (3)) and (ii) then make the necessary arrangement in accordance with rule 1.08(6).

Dated: March 8, 2017

Heather J. Smith
Chief Justice
Superior Court of Justice (Ontario)

Geoffrey B. Morawetz
Regional Senior Judge
Superior Court of Justice, Toronto Region

Note: CourtCall can be used for video appearances at **court dates on or after March 27 2017**. Counsel/parties can begin scheduling appearances on CourtCall's website as of March 20, 2017.

T. The Guide Concerning e-Delivery of Documents in the Ontario Superior Court of Justice (Effective: July 1, 2014)

This Guide applies to the e-Delivery of documents in the Ontario Superior Court of Justice, effective July 1, 2014. It *supersedes the* previous Guidelines concerning the Commercial List e-Delivery Pilot Project issued in June 2012, which is hereby revoked.

Counsel and parties are advised to refer to the relevant Parts of the Consolidated Provincial Practice Direction, the Consolidated Practice Direction for Divisional Court Proceedings as well as any other relevant Toronto region-specific Practice Directions and Guides which are available on the Superior Court of Justice web-site at: www.ontariocourts.ca/scj.

Table of Contents

Introduction

Often judges sitting on the Commercial List ask counsel to provide them with an electronic copy of the materials filed for a hearing. Experience has shown that significant differences exist amongst the formats used by counsel when preparing electronic copies. As a result, the usefulness to the judge of electronic copies varies from case to case – some formats do not permit a judge to cut and paste text; some formats do not organize the scanned file by document, making quick reference to an item difficult; and, some formats are not searchable.

For electronic copies of documents to be useful to judges they must: (i) be well organized and searchable so that judges can locate quickly specific pieces of evidence or argument; (ii) enable a judge to cut and paste argument or evidence; and, (iii) enable the portability of all hearing materials.

In order to meet these needs a working group of the Commercial List Users Committee has prepared this Guide. The purpose is simple: when a judge asks counsel to submit electronic documents of filed materials, counsel now will be able to follow a uniform approach to preparing electronic copies thereby enhancing their usefulness to judges.

This Guide contemplate that in most cases counsel will deliver electronic copies of documents to the judge via a USB key, with factums in Word format and the remaining hearing materials placed in an organized PDF file. Guidelines for emailing documents to judges are also included.

Three key points should be made about the scope of this Guide:

a)   Electronic copies of documents subject to a sealing order, or for which a request for a sealing order will be made, should NOT be sent to a judge. Such documents should be submitted to the court in the normal fashion for confidential documents;

b)   Electronic documents sent to a judge should NOT be password protected or subject to security settings; and,

c)   USB keys or, where directed, CD-ROMs, are to be delivered to a judge through the Commercial List Office.

This Guide is organized into four parts:

Part I: A **Sample Checklist** which judges may use when discussing with counsel the requirements for electronic copies of documents in any specific case;

Part II: A **Description of the Basic Steps** involved in preparing electronic copies of documents for filing with a judge;

Part III: An **Outline of the Technical Specifications** for electronic copies of documents, including Hardware and Software Requirements. The procedures set out in this Guide seek to use hardware and software which is readily accessible to all counsel at a reasonable cost. This section describes readily available software and hardware options; and,

Part IV: Detailed **Instructions on How to Create** simple and complex PDF documents.

Although the product of consultation with both the Bench and the Bar, no doubt areas of improvement will emerge as greater use is made of this Guide. The Commercial List Users Committee intends to monitor the use of the "e-Delivery" of documents and make improvements to this Guide based on the experience of the Commercial List.

Part I: Sample Checklist for the Use of Commercial List Judges

Please note: a word version of the Sample Checklist is also available on the Superior Court's website at: www.ontariocourts.ca/scj.

Judge: Court File No.:
Title of Proceedings: Hearing Date:

No.	Description	Yes / No
1.	Submit electronic copy of facta in Word format?	Yes No
2.	Submit PDF copy of facta and application/motion record? (select # 3 Simple Format or # 5 Complex Format)	Yes No
3.	**Simple format:** Create bookmarks within PDF (refer to "Guidelines" document)	Yes No
4.	Make PDF OCR text searchable?	Yes No
5.	**Complex format:** Create hyperlinks & bookmarks within PDF (refer to "Guidelines" document)	Yes No
6.	File paper copies of facta and application/motion record with the Commercial List Office?	Yes No
7.	Receipt of hyperlinked PDF within 1-5 business days (based on number of pages, number of potential links and available resources)	Yes No

NOTE: CONFIDENTIAL DOCUMENTS SHOULD NOT BE FILED ELECTRONI-CALLY

Parties	Names, Contact Information & File Naming Instructions
Plaintiff/Applicant	
Defendant/Respondent	
Third Party	
Intervener	

Additional Instructions: _____

Part II: The Basic Steps in Preparing and Filing Electronic Copies of Court Documents with a Judge

A. Preparation of Electronic Word File Copy

1. Document(s) is created and finalized in word processing software. Microsoft Word (.DOC) is the standard format.

2. Create front and back covers, indices and schedules in Microsoft Word format.

3. One copy of the official court document(s), along with all attachments, is to be printed and filed as the official court copy.

4. One copy of factum is to be uploaded to the Digital Hearing Workspace in Word format, as well as one copy in PDF format (if requested by the judge).

B. Preparation of Electronic PDF Copy

5. Convert or scan Word document to PDF format. Conversion is preferable.

6. Convert or scan front and back covers, indices, schedules, etc., and combine with PDF.

7. Combined PDF should contain identical content and should appear the same as the official paper copy filed with the court. The PDF copy should conform to the same requirements in the *Rules of Civil Procedure* as the paper copy.

8. Scanned or converted documents are to be provided as black and white documents unless there is a relevant reason to include content in colour.

9. Image quality of scanned or converted documents is to be 200 – 300 dpi.

10. Update page numbering in the PDF file to reflect actual page numbers based on paper copy (see Part III: Outline of Technical Specifications).

11. Name PDF file based on pre-defined nomenclature (see Part III: Outline of Technical Specifications).

12. Perform Optical Character Recognition (OCR) within PDF to enable text searching.

13. Create bookmarks and hyperlinks within PDF to link to page references within attachments (if requested).

14. Do not apply any security settings or modification to the file properties of the PDF that may prevent the court from opening, viewing, saving, printing or searching the document.

15. Confirm the size of the Word document and / or PDF document in the properties of the file.

16. Deliver a copy of PDF document to all other parties. This will be accomplished by uploading the document to the Digital Hearing Workspace.

C. Transcripts

17. Electronic copies of transcripts may be filed in PDF and DOC formats as long as the copies are searchable.

D. Sending the electronic copies to the judge

18. It is anticipated that in most circumstances judges will ask counsel to provide them with electronic copies of documents on a USB key or CD ROM. Where such a request is made by the judge, counsel should deliver the materials to the judge through the Commercial List Office. The USB key or CD ROM should be accompanied by a covering letter which identifies the materials contained on the USB key or CD ROM.

   a) **USB Key:** In the cover letter include a list of the files contained on the USB key, along with the title of proceedings, Court File #, Counsel Name(s) and Party Name. If possible, label the key with the short style of cause and the Court File #.

   b) **CD ROM:** Label the CD ROM with the title of proceedings, Court File #, Counsel Name(s) and Party Name. Include a list of the files contained on the CD in a cover letter.

19. In cases where the judge has requested counsel to deliver the electronic copies by email, the cover email should include the title of proceedings, Court File #, Counsel Name(s), Party Name and type of filing. A list of the email attachments is to be included in the body of the email. See the example below.

20. **PLEASE NOTE: A judge's email system cannot accept emails containing attachments of more than 6 Mb in size.**

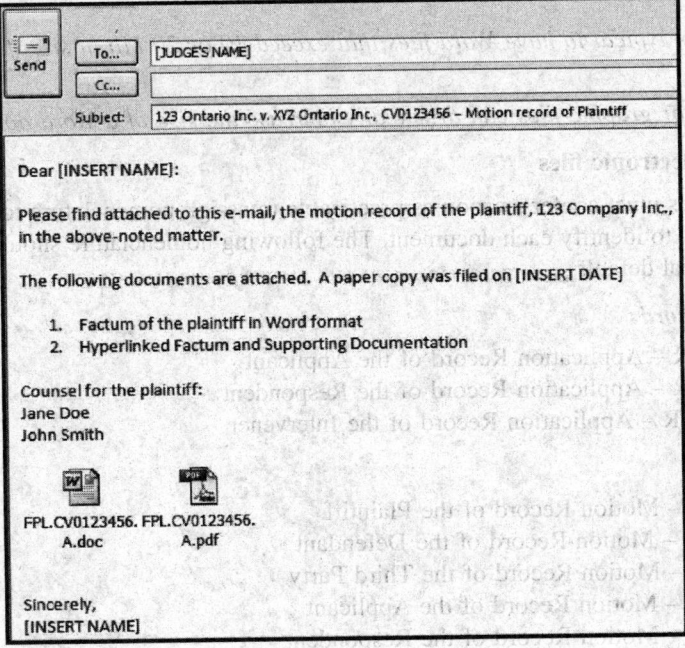

Part III: Outline of Technical Specifications

A. General Information on .PDF and .DOC file sizes

21. An approximation of the number of paper pages contained in a unit of PDF

Data size	Approximate Pages
1 Mb PDF	20 pages
2 Mb PDF	40 pages
5 Mb PDF	100 pages
10 Mb PDF	200 pages
100 Mb PDF	2,000 pages (3/4 – full bankers box, single sided)
1024 Mb or 1 Gig	20,480 pages (8-12 bankers boxes, single sided)
2048 Mb or 2 Gigs	40,960 pages (16-24 bankers boxes, single sided)

Note 1: Bookmarks and a table of contents somewhat affect the size of a PDF file. Hyperlinks can drastically increase the size of a PDF file. Approximate pages in Word documents versus file sizes

Data size	Approximate Pages
1 Mb .DOC	60 pages
2 Mb DOC	120 pages
5 Mb DOC	300 pages
10 Mb DOC	600 pages

| 100 Mb DOC | 6,000 pages (2-3 full bankers boxes, single sided) |
| 1024 Mb or 1 Gig | 61,440 pages (24-30 bankers boxes, single sided) |

Note 2: It is not typical to have Word files that exceed 10 or 20 Mb in size if the file contains text only.

Note 3: Image or graphic files can drastically increase the size of a Word document.

B. Naming electronic files

22. Parties must confer as soon as practicable to assign nomenclature to be used consistently to identify each document. The following nomenclature should be used as the general default:

Application Record

23. APAR – Application Record of the Applicant
APRR – Application Record of the Respondent
APINR – Application Record of the Intervener

Motion Record

24. MPL – Motion Record of the Plaintiff
MDE – Motion Record of the Defendant
MTP – Motion Record of the Third Party
MAP – Motion Record of the Applicant
MRP – Motion Record of the Respondent
MIN – Motion Record of the Intervener

Affidavits

25. AFPL – Affidavit of or on behalf of the Plaintiff
AFDE – Affidavit of or on behalf of the Defendant
AFTP – Affidavit of or on behalf of the Third Party
AFAP – Affidavit of or on behalf of the Applicant
AFRP – Affidavit of or on behalf of the Respondent
AFIN – Affidavit of or on behalf of the Intervener

Book of Authorities

26. BAPL – Book of Authorities of the Plaintiff
BADE – Book of Authorities of the Defendant
BATP – Book of Authorities of the Third Party
BAAP – Book of Authorities of the Applicant
BARP – Book of Authorities of the Respondent
BAIN – Book of Authorities of the Intervener

Factums, including Amended and Supplementary

27. FPL – Factum of the Plaintiff
FDE – Factum of the Defendant
FTP – Factum of the Third Party
FAP – Factum of the Applicant
FRP – Factum of the Respondent
FIN – Factum of the Intervener

Note 4: suffix AM or SUP to indicate Amended or Supplemental Factum

Costs Outline

28.   COPL – Cost Outline of the Plaintiff CODE – Cost Outline of the Defendant COTP
      – Cost Outline of the Third Party COAP – Cost Outline of the Applicant CORP – Cost
      Outline of the Respondent

Note 5: when there are multiple documents of the same type filed, suffix the file name with 001, 002, 003, 004, 005, etc.

C.   Page numbering in PDF files for Facta

Title page has no page number

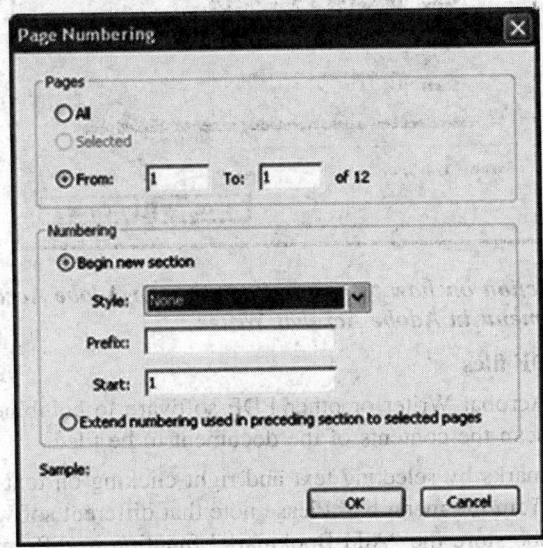

Index page numbers set using Roman numerals; e.g. i, ii, iii, iv, etc.

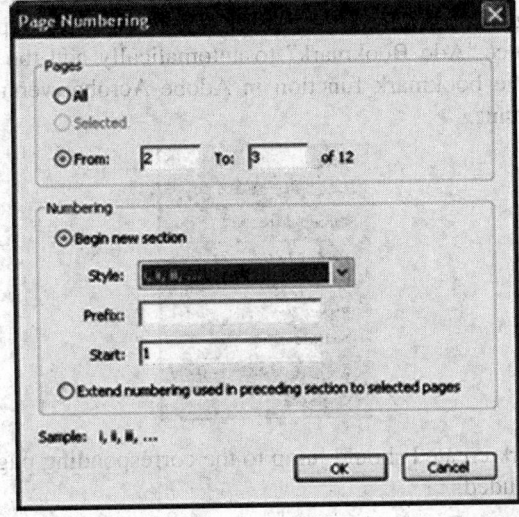

Factum pages set to use actual "hard copy" page numbers. Set pages in body of Factum to be numbered consecutively; e.g. 1, 2, 3, 4, 5, 6, etc.

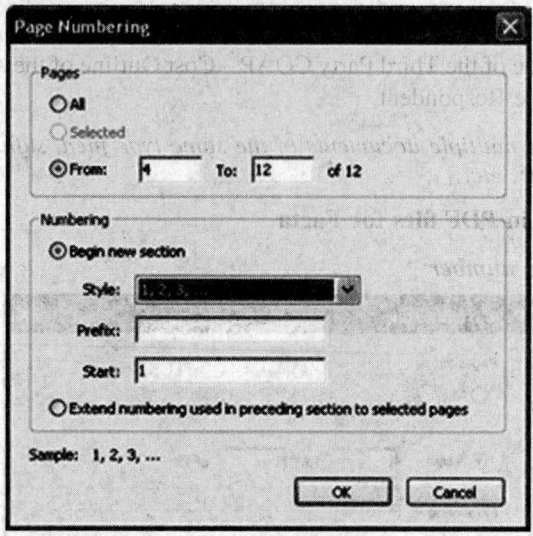

Note 6: Further instruction on how to re-number pages in Adobe Acrobat can be found by searching the "Help" menu in Adobe Acrobat Writer.

D. Bookmarks in PDF files

29. Use Adobe Acrobat Writer or other PDF software to combine documents into one PDF file or scan the contents of the document to be filed,

30. Create bookmarks by selecting text and right clicking on text or by selecting "Add Bookmark" from the menu bar. Please note that different software and different versions of Adobe store the "Add Bookmark" function in different areas of the menu. Consult the "Help" menu for your software for more specific information.

31. The PDF document must be OCR searchable in order to highlight text. In Adobe Acrobat, highlight the heading of text in the document as it appears in the Index, right click and select "Add Bookmark" to automatically add the highlighted text to the bookmark. The bookmark function in Adobe Acrobat version X is located in the "Content" menu:

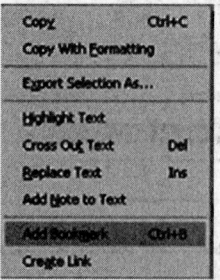

32. Each bookmark created should jump to the corresponding page of the PDF based on the Index included.

33. In the "Document Properties" of the PDF, set the "Initial View" to show the Book-

marks panel and pages. Set the "Magnification" to "Fit to Page".

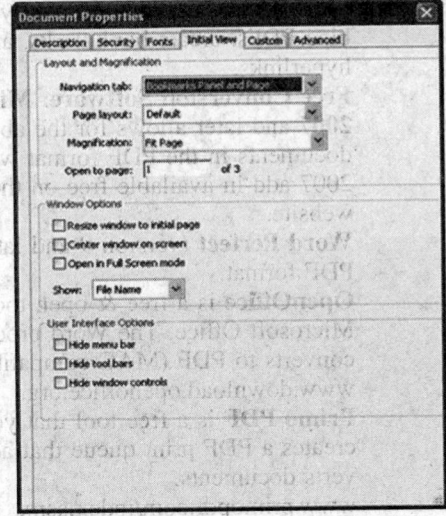

34. Where possible (and if requested) create a hyperlink to other documents contained in the PDF such as Authorities, Transcripts, Affidavits, etc.

35. Hyperlinks should only be created to documents that exist within the PDF document. Consult the "Help" menu for your software for more specific information.

E. Hardware and Software Required

Software / Hardware	Options
Computer or Laptop	Minimum requirements will be included with software purchases however at this time, common minimum requirements include: • 1.3 GHz or faster processor, 512 MB RAM; • 1 GB of available hard drive space; Windows XP or above;
Scanner	Scanner with automatic document feeder is preferable (ADF)
Word Processing software	Microsoft Word or Corel Word Perfect

Software / Hardware	Options
PDF Software	Software should have capability to OCR, combine PDFs, create bookmarks, and create hyperlinks. **Free Conversion Software: Microsoft Office 2007** and later allows for the ability to save documents in the PDF format with an Office 2007 add-in available free on the Microsoft website. **Word Perfect** (version 9 and later) saves to PDF format. **OpenOffice** is a free & open tool similar to Microsoft Office. The Word processing tool converts to PDF (MAC compatible). www.download.openoffice.org. **Primo PDF** is a free tool that you install that creates a PDF print queue that actually converts documents. www.primopdf.com/index.aspx **Other cost efficient software options: Adobe Acrobat Standard X** is one of the most commonly used PDF conversions, viewing and writing software. (Recommended). www.adobe.com/products/acrobatstandard.html. **Nuance PDF Converter Pro 7** is another commonly used PDF conversion, view and writing software www.nuance.com/products/pdf-converter-professional7/index.htm.
Scanning Software	Scanning software should be bundled with the scanner at time of installation. Consult the manual or other documentation provided with your scanner
Email application	Microsoft Outlook, Lotus Notes or other email program
Internet connection	High speed internet access preferable
Phone or other device capable of receiving SMS messages	Setting up an account to access the Digital Hearing Workspace may require the user to enter a verification code sent by SMS message
Useful Resource Links	PDF help: www.pdfforlawyers.com. Consult the Help menu of your PDF software

Note: The availability of the software or hardware referred to in the above table may vary from time to time.

F. Additional/ Optional Software

36. Meta-data cleaner to scrub Word documents and PDF documents of meta-data. A no cost option for scrubbing Word documents could be to copy the contents of a document into a new "clean" document (ensure pagination is the same). Alternately, print and scan your document to PDF.

37. Most Meta-data in PDF documents can be removed from the properties menu of the PDF or by using a compatible PDF meta-data cleaner.

38. Do not compress files using ZIP or any other file compression format. Files should not be compressed for delivery by any method.

G. Software Options Matrix[*]

Function / Feature	Nuance PDF Converter Pro 7	Adobe Acrobat X Standard	Adobe Acrobat Reader	Foxit Reader
View, Search & Print PDF File	Yes	Yes	Yes	Yes
Preserves Hyperlink, Bookmarks & Comments	Yes	Yes	Yes	Yes
Document Review: Comments, Annotations, highlights (use arrows, sticky notes)	Yes	Yes	Yes	Yes
Modify text using "typewriter"	Yes	Yes	No	No
Export Comments or Notes in Summary	Yes	Yes	No	No
Text Search (if OCR text exists)	Yes	Yes	Yes	Yes
Digital Signature	Yes	Yes	No	No
Encryption / Security Settings	Yes	Yes	No	No
Convert from Word	Yes	Yes	No	No
Combine PDFs	Yes	Yes	No	No
OCR Capabilities	Yes	Yes	No	No
Bookmarking	Yes	Yes	No	No
Hyperlinking	Yes	Yes	No	No
Ability to support scanning	Yes	Yes	No	No
Mac Compatible Version	Yes	Yes	Yes	Yes
PRICING	$99.99	$199.00	FREE	FREE

Part IV: How to Create Simple and Complex PDF Documents

39. There are two ways to create PDF documents. PDF documents can be created by converting a text document into PDF format using software such as Adobe Acrobat, Adobe Distiller, Nuance, PDF Maker, or scanning documents from paper in PDF.

A. Converting a text file to a PDF file

40. Converting text files into PDF format is the preferred method for two reasons: text conversion creates a more searchable document than scanning from paper and text conversion creates a smaller file size then scanned or imaged documents. Always convert the final version of documents to PDF format to ensure the PDF copy is the same in content and pagination as the court filed paper copy.

   a) Open the document in word processing application (Microsoft Word or Corel WordPerfect, for example)

---

[*] This Matrix is not exhaustive. Further, the software programs and pricing in are not current. They reflect pricing in effect in 2012. Users are advised to check for updated programs and pricing.

b) From the File menu select the Print and choose the PDF printer installed.

c) Click on the settings of the printer and confirm the PDF printer is set to print to a resolution of 200 or 300 dpi.

d) Set the magnification to "Fit to Page" via File – Properties.

e) Click Print and Save the PDF file with the proper naming convention. Be sure the file has a file extension of .PDF.

B. Creating a PDF file from a scanned document

41. For documents that must be scanned because a text version does not exist, documents should be scanned directly into PDF format using available software in conjunction with the scanner. Scanning documents into image format will require OCR to be run against the documents making the PDF searchable.

a) Refer to the manual that accompanied the scanner being used for specific details on how to scan a document.

b) Use the automatic document feeder (ADF) to scan multiple pages if one is available.

c) Ensure the resolution for scanning is set to a resolution of 200 or 300 dpi.

d) Set the magnification to "Fit to Page" via File – Properties.

e) Save scanned documents to PDF format with the proper naming convention. Ensure the file has a file extension of .PDF.

C. How to Combine PDFs

42. If there are multiple PDF documents to be combined into one file, this must be done before Bookmarks can be created. Depending on the software used, bookmarks may be automatically created at the time of combining or merging PDF files. PDF "Creator" or "Writer" is required to merge PDF files.

a) From within Adobe Acrobat Standard or Professional, click on "Create PDF" from the toolbar on the main screen.

b) The Create PDF from Multiple Documents window will appear. From the "Browse" button, browse to the location of the PDF files and add them in the order in which they should be combined.

c) Once the PDF files are in a list, they can be moved up or down depending on the location where they should be in the combined PDF document.

d) Click "OK" to begin the merge of files.

e) Select "File" – "Save As" to save the PDF with the proper naming convention. Ensure the file has a file extension of PDF.

f) Set the magnification to "Fit to Page" via File – Properties.

D. How to Create Bookmarks

43. Bookmarks appear on the left side of a PDF document. To view bookmarks, choose Bookmarks or show Bookmarks from the View menu of your Adobe Acrobat software (the location of this menu will depend on the version of Adobe Acrobat or other

software being used). Use the Table of Contents as a guideline for creating book-marks.

   a) Using Adobe Acrobat to create a bookmark, navigate to the page to be book-marked.

   b) Choose "New Bookmark" from the Document menu, click on the New Book-mark button or click "Ctrl, B" on the keyboard to create a new bookmark.

   c) Click on the new untitled bookmark and enter a name for it (for example, if the bookmark is for the table of contents, enter "Table of Contents" as the name of the bookmark.

   d) Repeat for each bookmark to be created.

   e) Set the Initial View of the Bookmarked PDF to be "Bookmarks Panel and Page" via File – Properties – Initial View.

   f) Use plain black text as the display properties for text in bookmarks. No colours, no italics.

E. How to Rename or Delete Bookmarks

44. If bookmarks need to be renamed to match the table of contents, follow the below steps.

   a) Using Adobe Acrobat, right click on the bookmark and select "Rename";

   b) Type in the name as it appears in the Table of Contents;

   c) To delete a bookmark, right click on it and select "Delete".

F. How to Create Hyperlinks

45. Hyperlinks appear throughout a PDF. In a factum hyperlinks can be made to docu-mentary evidence, oral evidence, authorities, exhibits and affidavits, etc.

   a) Using Adobe Acrobat to create a hyperlink, navigate to the page where a hy-perlink will be created.

   b) Choose "Link Tool" from the Document menu, click on the New Bookmark but-ton or click "Ctrl, B" on the keyboard to create a new bookmark.

   c) Click on the new untitled bookmark and enter a name for it (for example, if the bookmark is for the table of contents, enter "Table of Contents" as the name of the bookmark.

   d) Repeat for each bookmark to be created.

   e) Set the Initial View of the Bookmarked PDF to be "Bookmarks Panel and Page" via File – Properties – Initial View.

   f) Use a consistent method for creating hyperlinks. Hyperlinks should be visible on the document by either underlining, highlighting or text box using a consistent colour that does not obstruct the display of text.

G. How to Update Page Numbering

46. Title page and back page have no page number.

47. Index page numbers set using Roman numerals; e.g., i, ii, iii, iv, etc.

48. Factum pages set to use actual "hard copy" page numbers. Set pages in body of Factum to be numbered consecutively; e.g., 1, 2, 3, 4, 5, 6, etc.

49. Update page numbering via page numbering section of the PDF software. Page numbers can be manually assigned to match the paper copy.

50. Further instruction on how to re-number pages in Adobe Acrobat or other PDF software can be found by searching the "Help" menu of the software.

H. Questions/ Answers and FAQ

51. What is 200 or 300 dpi and why is this important?

The quality of a scanned document largely depends on the condition of the paper document itself. If the document is older (created before 1995) or the quality of the paper is poor, the quality of the image may also be poor. If the scanning software is set to a resolution of 200 or 300 dpi, the best possible quality of image will be created, while keeping the file size to a minimum. Resolution is measured in dots per inch (dpi). A higher resolution is slower to scan (this is also dependent on the scanner and the number of pages that are scanned). The recommended resolution is 200 or 300 dpi.

52. What is OCR?

OCR stands for Optical Character Recognition. OCR is a technology that once run against PDF files makes the files searchable and editable. OCR quality is not always 100% accurate. Accuracy of OCR text depends largely on the quality of the paper being scanned and the scanning resolution used.

53. What is PDF?

PDF stands for Portable Document Format. It is a universal file format that preserves the fonts, images, graphics, and layout of any source document, regardless of the application and platform used to create it.

54. What is USB?

USB stands for Universal Serial Bus. USB is a hardware format used to store and transfer files.

55. How do I know what the size is of my PDF file?

Right click on the PDF file and check the properties tab to determine the size of the PDF file.

56. How should the PDF be named?

Follow the guidelines provided in the naming convention list and those provided on the initial meeting checklist.

U. The Guide Concerning Commercial List E-Service (Effective: July 1, 2014)

Effective July 1, 2014

This Guide applies to proceedings on the commercial list in the Toronto Region, effective July 1, 2014. It *supersedes all* E-Service Protocols for the Commercial List in the Toronto Region, issued before July 1, 2014, which are hereby revoked.

Counsel and parties are advised to refer to the relevant Parts of the Consolidated Provincial Practice Direction, the Consolidated Practice Direction for Divisional Court Proceedings as well as any other relevant Toronto region-specific Practice Directions and Guides which are available on the Superior Court of Justice website at: www.ontariocourts.ca/scj.

Table of Contents

Part I: Introduction

Proceedings on the Ontario Superior Court (Commercial List) (the "**Court**" or the "**Commercial List**") frequently involve multiple and evolving stakeholders located nationally and internationally. These proceedings involve "real time litigation" which, by its nature, requires efficient, effective and cost efficient methods of providing service and notice to stakeholders.

The usual methods of service provided for under the *Rules of Civil Procedure (Ontario)* (the "**Rules**") do not always operate efficiently in multi-party, multi-jurisdictional proceedings, nor do they take advantage of the most current technologies. Service provisions in Commercial List orders before the development of this guide evolved in an *ad hoc* manner without precision or specificity with respect to such fundamental terms as the "service list".

The purpose of this Commercial List E-Service Guide ("**E-Service Guide**") is to provide a uniform method of "substituted service", under the Rules, that engages modern and efficient processes to effect service and give notice in certain Commercial List proceedings. In order to achieve this purpose the E-Service Guide utilizes three tools:

a)   Service of documents by electronic mail;

b)   A "service list" with defined parameters; and

c)   Mandatory websites containing defined minimum levels of information.

The E-Service Guide will be incorporated by reference in orders at the initial stages of certain Commercial List proceedings as a form of substituted service pursuant to Rule 16.04 of the Rules subject to Rule 17.05.[1] A copy of the E-Service Guide will be available on the Commercial List website at: www.ontariocourts.ca/scj/practice/practice-directions/toronto/#Commercial_List and need not be appended to the incorporating order.

The E-Service Guide permits service upon persons on the E-Service List [2] by those who have the right to serve and file material in the proceeding under the Rules, an order of the Court or otherwise. The E-Service Guide does not itself give any person the right to serve and file material. To that end, the E-Service Guide is not meant to alter or replace requirements under the Rules with respect to such matters as the delivery of Notices of Appearance. The E-Service Guide is subject to modification by the Court in appropriate cases.

Nothing in this E-Service Guide varies any requirements under the Rules or applicable practice directions with respect to the filing of Court Documents with the Court.

The E-Service Guide will be used in the following insolvency proceedings (collectively, the "**Insolvency Proceedings**") pending before the Commercial List:

a) Proceedings under the *Companies' Creditors Arrangement Act (Canada)* ("**CCAA**");

b) Receivership proceedings, including proceedings under the *Bankruptcy and Insolvency Act (Canada) ("BIA"), the Courts of Justice Act (Ontario),* the *Securities Act (Ontario)* and other legislation which provides for the appointment of court officers;

c) Proceedings under the *Winding-Up and Restructuring Act*;

d) Division I proposal proceedings under the BIA; and

e) Any other insolvency-related proceedings, including bankruptcy proceedings under the BIA or other Commercial List proceedings, where the Court determines that it would be beneficial to use the E-Service Guide.[3]

In addition to the Insolvency Proceedings, the E-Service Guide may be used in large or complex arrangement, re-organization or similar court proceedings under the *Business Corporations Act (Canada)* and the *Business Corporations Act (Ontario)* where the Court determines that its use would be beneficial ("**Reorganization Proceedings**").[4] Insolvency Proceedings and Reorganization Proceedings are referred to collectively as "**Commercial List Proceedings**".

Part II: Service by Email

1. Electronic mail ("**Email**") will be the required mechanism to serve documents to be filed in court ("**Court Documents**") in Commercial List Proceedings. If service by Email is not practicable Court Documents may be served as provided in the Rules.

2. Court Documents are documents that must be served under the Rules with respect to motions or applications in Commercial List Proceedings such as notices of motion, notices of application, affidavits, facta, Court Officer [5] reports and orders.

3. Service by Email on the E-Service List shall be used only for the following purposes:

a) Service of Court Documents;

b) Delivery of correspondence containing information with respect to motions or applications such as the location or timing of a Commercial List Proceeding or other directions with respect to a proceeding; and

c) Circulation of material related to motions or applications such as draft orders.

4. Email sent to the E-Service List shall not be used in order to provide a party's general comments on the proceedings or to advocate positions or for any other use not specifically provided for herein.

5. The moving party in a Commercial List Proceeding shall seek Court adoption of the E-Service Guide in the order initiating the proceeding (or as soon as practicable thereafter). The following provision shall be included in such order unless varied by the Court:

"Substituted Service and Case Website[6]

THIS COURT ORDERS THAT the E-Service Guide of the Commercial List (the "Guide") is approved and adopted by reference herein and, in this proceeding, the service of documents made in accordance with the Guide (which can be found on the Commercial List website at: www.ontariocourts.ca/scj/practice/practice-directions/toronto/#Commercial_List) shall be valid and effective service. Subject to Rule 17.05 [7] this Order shall constitute an order for substituted service pursuant to Rule 16.04 of the Rules of Civil Procedure. Subject to Rule 3.01(d) of the Rules of Civil Procedure and paragraph 13 of the Guide, service of documents in accordance with the Guide will be effective on transmission. This Court further orders that a Case Website shall be established in accordance with the Guide with the following URL '<@>'."

6. Except as otherwise provided herein, Email service is a sufficient mode of service of Court Documents without duplicating service by facsimile, hard copy delivery or other method of service.

7. Court Documents should be served by Email by way of HTML link or PDF files. If the party serving the Court Document can create an HTML link to the Court Document prior to serving the Court Document, service of such document by PDF file shall not be necessary. The HTML link must be a link directly to the document being served.[8]

8. To the extent practicable, Court Documents shall be in a format which is compliant with the Guide Concerning e-Delivery.

9. Where a party is serving more than one document by Email of HTML links, the Email shall specify each document being served and shall include a separate HTML link for each document being served.

10. If a Court Document is being served by way of an Email of a PDF file, the party serving the Court Document shall be cognizant of the size of the file and send the Court Document in multiple Emails if the PDF file would appear to be too large to serve in a single Email.

11. If the party serving the Court Document by Email receives notification of a transmission failure, the party serving the Court Document shall make reasonable efforts to ensure that successful Email transmission of the Court Document occurs or that the Email comes to the attention of the intended recipient or his or her firm.[9]

12. Any Court Document served by Email should clearly state in the subject line of the Email: (i) notification that a Court Document is being served; (ii) a recognizable short form name of the Commercial List Proceeding; (iii) the nature of the proceeding; and (iv) the nature of the Court Document.[10] The body of the Email should contain a description of the party serving the Court Document, a brief description of the nature of the Court Document being served, the date of the proceeding and any other specific information with respect to the proceeding such as, for example, a specific commencement time or court location if known.

13. In accordance with Rule 3.01(1)(d), a Court Document served by Email before 4:00 p.m. shall be deemed to be received that day and Court Documents served after 4:00 p.m. or at any time on a holiday shall be deemed to be received on the next day that is not a holiday.

14. Each party serving a Court Document in a Commercial List Proceeding is responsible

for complying with the E-Service Guide. Nothing herein, however, is intended to change the substantive law about who is required to be served with materials in respect of any particular motion or proceeding brought within a Commercial List Proceeding.

15. Even though a Court Document has been served in accordance with this E-Service Guide, a person may show that the Court Document:

   a) did not come to the person's notice;

   b) came to the person's notice later than when it was served or effectively served, or

   c) was incomplete or illegible.

16. Each party serving a Court Document by Email shall prepare an affidavit of service containing the particulars of the service including the E-Service List served, the Email addresses to which Court Documents were sent and the time of the Emailing. A copy of the affidavit of service shall be filed with the Court.

Part III: The E-Service List

17. The E-Service List in a Commercial List Proceeding ("**E-Service List**") is a mechanism to facilitate service of Court Documents on stakeholders who should be served with Court Documents ("**Stakeholders**"). Stakeholders include a corporation, body corporate, partnership or individual that has a legal interest in the Commercial List Proceeding. The E-Service List is not intended as a mechanism to generally disseminate information with respect to the status of a Commercial List Proceeding.

18. The E-Service List shall list the names, contact coordinates, including Email addresses, of Stakeholders or their counsel, who may be served by Email in accordance with Part III hereof. Inclusion of a party on the E-Service List allows effective service of Court Documents on such party by Email.

19. After the order is issued authorizing the use of the E-Service Guide in a Commercial List Proceeding, counsel for the party initiating the proceeding, or the appointed Court Officer, if appropriate, (the "**E-Service List Keeper**") shall prepare the initial E-Service List containing the names and e-mail addresses of Stakeholders upon whom service is to be effected by Email.

20. The E-Service List Keeper shall use its best efforts to ensure that the Email address of a Stakeholder is correct and will result in an effective transmission of Court Documents to the intended recipient when initially placed on the E-Service List. Stakeholders on the E-Service List shall notify the E-Service List Keeper of any subsequent change of their Email address.

21. The E-Service List Keeper shall send an Email to each proposed Stakeholder identifying themselves as the E-Service List Keeper and advising that: (i) the proposed Stakeholder has been placed upon the E-Service List, (ii) Court Documents will be validly served upon the proposed Stakeholder by Email; and (iii) that any Stakeholder on the E-Service List may serve Court Documents on any other Stakeholder on the E-Service List in accordance with this E-Service Guide.

22. During the course of the Commercial List Proceeding, the E-Service List Keeper shall add Stakeholders to the E-Service List from time to time as required subject to the procedure set out in paragraph 21.

23. The E-Service List must include the following parties:

   a) Counsel for the applicant/moving party in the Commercial List Proceeding;

   b) The Court Officer appointed in the Commercial List Proceeding and counsel for the Court Officer;

   c) Counsel for any party that has delivered a Notice of Appearance under the Rules from time to time;

   d) Any party or counsel to any party who should be served with Court Documents in accordance with the Rules and the practice in the Commercial List; and

   e) Any Stakeholder or counsel to a Stakeholder who has filed a Request for Electronic Service (**"RES"**).[11]

24. Stakeholders who wish to be placed on the E-Service List in order to receive service of Court Documents in a timely and efficient manner shall Email to the E-Service List Keeper a duly completed RES in the form attached as Schedule "A" hereto[12].

25. If a Stakeholder on the E-Service List no longer has an ongoing legal interest in a Commercial List Proceeding, that Stakeholder may request that the E-Service List Keeper delete that Stakeholder from the E-Service List.

26. Those persons who are interested in monitoring a Commercial List Proceeding but are not required to be served with Court Documents in accordance with the Rules or the practice in the Commercial List are not to be placed on the E-Service List. Such parties should monitor the Commercial List Proceeding by accessing the Case Website.[13]

27. A lawyer who files an RES on behalf of a client must identify such client. Lawyers receiving E-Service of Court Documents on behalf of clients must be properly accredited lawyers within the jurisdiction in which they practice. By delivery of such RES, the lawyer warrants his or her authority to receive service on behalf of his/her client.

28. In addition to the E-Service List referred to in paragraph 18 hereof, the E-Service List Keeper shall create and maintain a copyable Word document containing up to date Email addresses of the Stakeholders on the E-Service List (the "**Address List**"). The purpose of the Address List is to allow Stakeholders on the Service List to copy and paste the Email addresses of the current Stakeholders on the E-Service List into Emails serving Court Documents. This process is designed to avoid E-Service of Court Documents using out of date or inaccurate E-Service Lists. The practice of serving Court Documents by "replying to all" on a previous Email is discouraged. The E-Service List Keeper shall provide a current copy of the Address List to the WebHost[14] each time the list is updated, as Stakeholders are added or removed.

29. Any party wishing to serve a Court Document in a Commercial List Proceeding shall use the then current copy of the Address List posted on the Case Website to serve the Court Documents. If possible, the serving party shall make enquiries of the E-Service List Keeper to determine if the E-Service List Keeper is aware of parties to be added to the Address List who have not yet been added.

30. During the course of a Commercial List Proceeding, certain motions or applications require service of Court Documents on respondents with an interest in that particular

motion or application only; for example, service on lien claimants with an interest only on specific property with respect to a sale approval and vesting order. In such circumstances, the party bringing the motion or application shall prepare a Supplementary E-Service List listing the names and Email addresses of the "one time" respondents that the moving party wishes to serve by Email. The cover Email shall contain the information designated in paragraph 12 and 21 hereof. The affidavit of service with respect to that motion shall include the Supplementary E-Service List.

31. The E-Service List Keeper shall use its best efforts to maintain the E-Service List current and accurate. In addition to any other protection that may be available to it by statute or Court order, the E-Service List Keeper shall incur no liability in carrying out the provisions of this E-Service Guide and, in particular, with respect to the creation or maintenance of the E-Service List, except for any gross negligence or wilful misconduct on its part.

Part IV: The Case Website

32. The case website hereinafter described (the "**Case Website**") will be established for the purpose of:

a) Creating a comprehensive and current record of Commercial List Proceedings;

b) Allowing easy and inexpensive access to the record of proceedings to Stakeholders involved in Commercial List Proceedings and to parties with a potential interest in the proceedings;

c) Providing a mechanism to facilitate service of Court Documents by Email with HTML links to particular Court Documents; and

d) Provide a mechanism to facilitate the dissemination of notices and information to larger groups of interested parties such as employees, retirees or general unsecured creditors.

33. The Case Website shall be hosted by the Court Officer appointed in the Insolvency Proceeding or by counsel to the applicant in Reorganization Proceedings (the "**WebHost**") or as the Court may order.

34. The Case Website, or a link to the Case Website, shall be located on the WebHost's website and shall be prominently identified to ensure easy public access to the Case Website and the Court Documents posted thereon. The Case Website shall be specifically devoted to the posting, organization, storage and display of electronic versions of all Court Documents delivered in a Commercial List Proceeding.

35. The Case Website shall be organized in a manner that facilitates the ability of any interested party to easily locate Court Documents delivered in the Commercial List Proceedings and other documentation relevant to the Commercial List Proceedings such as proof of claim forms and creditor meeting documentation.

36. The WebHost shall post the following categories of documents, as served or to be served:

a) Notices of application/notices of motion;

b) All affidavits, including exhibits, and other material filed by an applicant/ moving party with respect to an application/motion;

c)   All responding affidavits, including exhibits, and other material delivered in response to the application or motion by all respondents;

d)   All facta and written arguments delivered by any party to an application or to a motion;

e)   Books of authorities;

f)   All court reports filed by Court Officers;

g)   All Court Orders, Reasons for Decision and Endorsements;

h)   The current version of the E-Service List and Address List;

i)   The name and Email address of the E-Service List Keeper; and

j)   Any document that requires dissemination to interested parties, such as proof of claim forms, notices of creditor meetings, plan disclosure statements, plans of reorganization and voting letters as requested by the restructuring debtor or the Court Officer.

If the WebHost is uncertain whether a document should be posted on the Case Website as a result of its content, the WebHost may seek directions from the Court at a 9:30 appointment.

37.   This list of information to be posted to the Case Website is not meant to be an exhaustive list. The WebHost may post other case-related information to the Case Website in its discretion. In the case of a Monitor under the CCAA, nothing in this E-Service Guide shall affect any requirements set out in the CCAA or the regulations thereunder with respect to the posting of documents to a website by the Monitor.

38.   Documents that have been sealed by Court order or documents in respect of which sealing orders are being requested shall not be posted on the Case Website.

39.   Any party intending to bring a motion or application in a Commercial List Proceeding shall, if reasonably possible, provide an electronic copy of the motion or application record to the WebHost for posting on the Case Website prior to service. If the motion or application record has been posted on the Case Website, the moving party or applicant may serve the proceeding by Email using a HTML link to the Case Website. Where time does not permit the prior posting of motion or application records on the Case Website, the applicant or moving party shall serve the Court Documents on the E-Service List by Email of a PDF or by HTML link in accordance with paragraph 7.

40.   Counsel shall send an electronic copy of Court Documents to the WebHost at the time of service of the Court Documents on the E-Service List.

41.   The WebHost shall use its best efforts to post documents provided to it by counsel in PDF format on the Case Website as soon as practicable.

42.   The WebHost shall maintain the Case Website for a period of at least six months after the earlier of completion of the Commercial List Proceeding or the discharge of the WebHost if a Court Officer.

43.   To the extent practicable the WebHost shall post links to foreign proceedings related to the Commercial List Proceedings on the Case Website.

44.   The WebHost is entitled to charge for the time spent maintaining the Case Website at

the usual hourly rates charged by its staff. No additional charges or fees may be claimed with respect to the establishment and maintenance of the Case Website.

45. The WebHost shall use its best efforts to maintain the Case Website current and complete. In addition to any other protection that may be available to the WebHost by statute or Court order, the WebHost shall incur no liability or obligation in carrying out the provisions of this E-Service Guide and, in particular, with respect to the creation and maintenance of the Case Website, except for any gross negligence or wilful misconduct on its part.

SCHEDULE "A"

REQUEST FOR ELECTRONIC SERVICE ("RES")

Please refer to important notes below

In the Matter of the ❑ CCAA ❑ Receivership ❑ BIA Proposal ❑ Other_____	XYZ Company Ltd (the "Debtor") of: < http://www.caseurl.com>
Legal Counsel to Stakeholder listed below: (please provide firm name, lawyer's name, address and email address) Please indicate your preference (by checking applicable box below): ❑ Serve counsel only ❑ Serve counsel & Stakeholder listed below	\<LawfirmLLP . . . . > \<Lawyer name . . . . > \<Address line 1 . . . . > \<Address line 2 . . . . > \<email address . . . . >
Name of Stakeholder requesting E-Service: (please provide full legal name, address, email address and describe Stakeholder's legal relationship to the Debtor)	ABC Company Inc. \<Address line 1 . . . . > \<Address line 2 . . . . > \<email address . . . . >
Date:	< Insert current date . . . . . >

I acknowledge having read the Ontario Superior Court of Justice Commercial List E-Service Guide. I hereby request to be placed on the E-Service List. By so doing, I agree as a Stakeholder or as counsel to a Stakeholder that the Stakeholder accepts service by electronic means in this case and will be bound by that service:

Stakeholder/ Counsel to Stakeholder

PLEASE RETURN SIGNED COPY OF FORM TO *<insert name of E-Service List Keeper here>: <email address> | 416-xxx-xxxx*

IMPORTANT NOTES

1. The E-Service List is intended to provide a timely and efficient method for effecting service in Commercial List Proceedings in accordance with the **E-Service Guide**, a copy of which has been posted on the Commercial List website at: www.ontariocourts. ca/scj/practice/practice-directions/toronto/#Commercial_List.

2. Persons interested solely in monitoring the proceedings should do so by reference to the Case Website noted above and should not request to be placed on the E-Service List.

3. By filing this RES form, you hereby agree that the Stakeholder accepts service by elec-

tronic means as the sole means of service and will be bound by that service.

4.   Parties residing outside of Ontario should consider whether, based on substantive law, the delivery of an RES constitutes an attornment to the Ontario proceedings.

---

[1]   Rule 17.05 deals with service of parties in a "contracting state" within the Convention on the Service Abroad of Judicial and Extrajudicial Documents in Civil or Commercial Matters signed at The Hague on November 15, 1965 – Special requirements may apply to such service which are outside the scope of this E-Service Guide.

[2]   As defined in Part III below.

[3]   CCAA proceedings involve, by definition, cases with more than $5 million of debt. No debt level criteria have been provided for other Insolvency Proceedings that may take advantage of the E-Service Guide – though the E-Service Guide, and in particular, the Case Website, may be inappropriate for smaller cases.

[4]   Before seeking an order incorporating the E-Service Guide in Reorganization Proceedings, counsel should ensure that their firm has the capability to host the Case Website or that other suitable arrangements are made for the hosting of the site.

[5]   Court Officers include Monitors, Receivers, Information Officers, Interim Receivers, Trustees in Bankruptcy, Proposal Trustees and other similar persons.

[6]   As defined in Part IV below.

[7]   See Note 1.

[8]   Where the HTML link is not to the Case Website, the party serving the Court Document shall ensure that the link remains active until the completion of the motion or proceeding relating to that Court Document.

[9]   Parties who are on the E-Service List shall ensure that "out of town notifications" or other similar notifications contain the name and Email address of another member of that person's firm or business to whom the Court Document should be sent.

[10]   By way of example – E-SERVICE: Nortel – Approval of Sale of Assets – Motion Record.

[11]   As defined in paragraph 24 below.

[12]   Parties who do not reside in Ontario should consider whether, based upon the substantive law, the delivery of an RES constitutes attornment to the Ontario proceeding.

[13]   As defined in Part IV below.

[14]   As defined in Part IV herein.

V. Practice Direction Concerning Civil Appeals at the Court of Appeal for Ontario (Latest Amendment: July 10, 2018)[1]

Effective: March 1, 2017

Amended: July 10, 2018

TABLE OF CONTENTS

---

[1] See online: https://www.ontariocourts.ca/coa/en/notices/pd/civil.htm.

1. EFFECTIVE DATE

This Practice Direction Concerning Civil Appeals at the Court of Appeal for Ontario revokes and replaces the Court of Appeal's previously issued Practice Direction Concerning Civil Appeals (effective 1 January 2004, updated November 2008).

This Practice Direction was filed with the Secretary of the Civil Rules Committee on 24 January 2017 and is published pursuant to rule 1.07 of the *Rules of Civil Procedure*. It is effective as of 1 March 2017.

2. APPLICATION OF THE RULES OF CIVIL PROCEDURE

When bringing an appeal or motion in the Court of Appeal, parties must consult the *Rules of Civil Procedure*, R.R.O. 1990, Reg. 194.

Rule 61 is the primary rule governing procedures for bringing appeals and motions in writing for leave to appeal in the Court of Appeal. Rule 61.03.1 governs motions for leave to appeal. Rule 61.16 and Rule 37 are the primary rules governing procedures for bringing motions to a single judge and motions to a three-judge panel of the Court of Appeal, except for motions for leave to appeal.

Other rules that more commonly apply to appeals and motions in the Court of Appeal include:

- Rule 2 (Non-compliance with the Rules)
- Rule 2.1 (General Powers to Stay or Dismiss a Proceeding/Motion if Vexatious, etc.)
- Rule 3 (Time)
- Rule 4 (Court Documents)
- Rule 16.01(3)-(4); 16.03-16.09 (Service)
- Rule 57 (Costs of Proceedings)
- Rule 58 (Assessment of Costs)
- Rule 63 (Stay Pending Appeal)

Practice directions supplement the *Rules of Civil Procedure* and provide guidance and direction about matters not covered by the *Rules*. If there is a conflict between the *Rules of Civil Procedure* and this Practice Direction, the *Rules of Civil Procedure* take precedence.

3. ACCESS TO COURT SERVICES IN FRENCH

Motions and appeals are equally available in English and French without delay. Where you are proceeding in French or in both English and French, please note this in your correspondence.

The staff of the Court of Appeal for Ontario is pleased to serve the public in English and French. Staff will direct French inquiries to bilingual staff members.

---

4. CORRESPONDENCE

4.1 Providing a Copy of all Correspondence to Opposing Parties

1. Any correspondence addressed to the Court of Appeal in relation to a court file must be copied to all parties to the proceeding or, if the parties are represented by a lawyer(s), to their lawyer(s) of record. This requirement applies, without limitation, to any correspondence addressed to the Registrar, Deputy Registrar, Senior Legal Officer, the Appeal Scheduling Unit and/or the Motions Clerk. All such correspondence must contain the Court of Appeal file number (where applicable) and title of proceeding.

2. In the event that correspondence addressed to the Court of Appeal or any of its staff is not copied to all parties or their lawyers, it will not be received, reviewed or answered.

4.2 Correspondence to a Judge Must be Addressed to the Registrar of the Court of Appeal

1. Rule 1.09 of the *Rules of Civil Procedure* requires that all parties must consent to out-of-court communications with a judge about a court proceeding unless the court directs otherwise.

   All correspondence intended to be reviewed by a judge or judges must be addressed to the Registrar and copied to all parties to the proceeding or, if the parties are represented by a lawyer(s), to their lawyer(s) of record. The Registrar will consult with the judge(s) to whom the correspondence is directed for directions as to whether the judge(s) will receive the correspondence.

2. In the event that correspondence intended to be reviewed by a judge or judges is not addressed to the Registrar or is not copied to all parties or their lawyers, it will not be received, reviewed or answered.

4.3. Restrictions on Sending Correspondence by Email

1. The Court of Appeal E-filing address, COA.E-file@ontario.ca, must only be used to deliver electronic versions of factums, transcripts and other documents specified in this Practice Direction and in the Guidelines for Filing Electronic Documents at the Court of Appeal for Ontario. This email address is not designed or intended to receive any inquiries or other communications about court proceedings.

2. Please consult the Guidelines for Filing Electronic Documents at the Court of Appeal for Ontario for the complete list of the type of documents that may be sent to COA. E-file@ontario.ca.

3. In order to receive a timely response to an inquiry involving proceedings in the Court of Appeal, including case searches, status inquiries, or inquiries about filing requirements, please call 416-327-5020 or toll free at 1-855-718-1756. Inquiries may also be sent via fax to (416) 327-5032. Alternatively, you may consult the Court of Appeal's website for detailed information about how best to direct your inquiry: http://www.ontariocourts.ca/coa/en/about/information.htm.

5. SERVICE

5.1 Service

1. The Registrar will accept copies of affidavits of service. The court will address any issues associated with proof of service as necessary.

2. The requirement in the *Rules of Civil Procedure* to serve and file electronic versions of appeal material (factums and transcripts) may be met by satisfying the Registrar that the electronic version was emailed to the opposing party(ies), together with proof of service of the paper version of the factum and transcript.

5.2 Service on a Party Acting in Person

Rule 16 of the *Rules of Civil Procedure* describes the ways that service shall be made on a party acting in person ("self-represented party") and a party with a lawyer of record. To clarify, in the case of service on a party acting in person, service may be made by regular mail, registered mail, or by courier. If service is by courier, the deponent of the affidavit of service must indicate the date when the document was provided to the courier <u>and</u> the date that the courier provided the document to the self-represented party.

5.3 Alternative Arrangements for Service of Court Documents

When a judge of the Ontario Superior Court of Justice has made an order approving a form of substituted service pursuant to rule 16.04 of the *Rules of Civil Procedure*, including an order approving and adopting the "Commercial List E-Service Guide", the parties should file a copy of such order with the Registrar of the Court of Appeal, together with the notice of appeal. When such an order has been filed, the service of documents in accordance with the order shall be considered as valid and effective service for all documents filed in the Court of Appeal, unless a judge of the Court of Appeal directs otherwise.

6. NOTICE OF APPEAL IN CIVIL APPEALS

6.1 Time for Commencing an Appeal

1. A party must serve a notice of appeal together with the certificate required by rule 61.05(1) of the *Rules of Civil Procedure* within 30 days after the order appealed from was made, unless a statute or the *Rules* provide otherwise. The notice of appeal, with proof of service, must be filed in the Registrar's Office in person or by mail within 10 days after service.

    The time limit for serving the notice of appeal is 30 days from the making of the order or judgment that the party is appealing from and <u>not</u> 30 days from the making of a subsequent, related order, such as an order dealing with costs.

2. Rules 16.05 and 16.06 specify when service of a document becomes effective. For example, if a notice of appeal is served by mail, then service of the notice of appeal only becomes effective on the fifth day after the document is mailed. In other words, the notice of appeal must be mailed at least five days before the expiry of the 30-day time period for filing the notice of appeal. Rule 3 regulates the computation of time under the *Rules of Civil Procedure*.

6.2 Title of Proceeding

The title of a proceeding in the Court of Appeal must conform to rule 61.04(2) of the *Rules of Civil Procedure* and Form 61B. The title of proceeding should set out the parties in the same order as they appear in the title of proceeding in the court appealed from. Clearly identify the appellant and respondent as indicated in Form 61B.

The title of proceeding should include any person who has been added as a party to the proceeding by an order of the court under rule 13.01 or 13.03(2) of the *Rules of Civil Procedure*. The title of proceeding should <u>not</u> include any person who has been granted leave to intervene as a friend of the court under rule 13.02 or 13.03(2).

6.3 Jurisdictional Statement – Ensuring the Court of Appeal has Jurisdiction

1. The *Rules of Civil Procedure* require that the notice of appeal includes a jurisdictional statement identifying the statutory or other basis for filing an appeal in a particular appellate court. This requirement is intended to avoid the problem of appeals being filed in the wrong court, or appeals being commenced even though there is no right to appeal from the order in question, or leave to appeal from the order is required before an appeal may be brought.

2. Parties need to be aware that there is no common law or inherent right of appeal. For there to be a right of appeal from any order or judgment, the right of appeal must be conferred by a statute. Accordingly, the jurisdictional statement in the notice of appeal must set out the basis upon which the appellant claims that the Court of Appeal has jurisdiction to entertain the appeal, including any relevant statute that provides for an appeal to the Court of Appeal.

3. The *Courts of Justice Act*, R.S.O. 1990, c. C.43, provides for the general appellate jurisdiction of the Court of Appeal and the Divisional Court in civil matters (see ss. 6, 19 and 21.9.1 of the *Courts of Justice Act*). Parties to an appeal need to consider and indicate whether the order under appeal is final or interlocutory (see s. 6(1)(b) of the *Courts of Justice Act*). In addition, if the order is only for the payment of money, then the parties need to review s. 19(1.2) of the *Courts of Justice Act* to determine if the appeal lies to the Court of Appeal or to the Divisional Court. In family law matters, the parties need to consider the application of s. 21.9.1 of the *Courts of Justice Act* to determine if the appeal lies to the Divisional Court rather than to the Court of Appeal.

4. In preparing the jurisdictional statement, parties must be aware that provisions of other statutes that govern certain types of litigation may displace the general provisions of the *Courts of Justice Act* by providing that an appeal from an order lies to the Divisional Court (for example, see s. 255 of the Ontario *Business Corporations Act*, R.S.O. 1990, c. B.16, and s. 30 of the *Class Proceedings Act, 1992*, S.O. 1992, c. 6). Parties must also consider that orders may not be appealed if they were made under a statute that explicitly precludes a right of appeal (e.g., see the *Arbitration Act, 1991*, S.O. 1991, c. 17, ss. 7(6), 10(2), 15 and 17). In addition, some legislation requires leave to appeal before an appeal may be filed (e.g., see the *Arbitration Act, 1991*, S.O. 1991, c. 17, s. 49).

6.4 Additional Information to Provide to the Court

On all documents filed with the court, parties shall include their telephone number, fax number, mailing address, email address (if available) and, in the case of lawyers, Law Society number.

Lawyers and self-represented parties should promptly advise the court and the other parties of any changes to their mailing or email address by emailing the Registrar's Office at COA.E-file@ontario.ca or by fax to 416-327-5032. Please include in the subject line of the email the title of proceeding and the court file number and the nature of the information being provided.

7. MOTIONS TO THE COURT OF APPEAL IN CIVIL MATTERS

7.1 Motions to a Single Judge

7.1.1 General

1. A single judge of the Court of Appeal hears motions Monday through Friday in chambers court located in Courtroom 7 at Osgoode Hall. From September to June, motions court starts at 10 a.m., unless the court orders otherwise. In July and August, motions court starts at 9:30 a.m., unless the court orders otherwise.

2. Lawyers do not need to wear gowns when they appear on motions before a single judge in chambers.

7.1.2 Notice of Motion

1. The notice of motion must be formatted in accordance with Form 37A of the *Rules of Civil Procedure*.

2. The moving party may select the date for the hearing of a motion if the time limits in Rule 37 of the *Rules of Civil Procedure* for serving and filing the notice of motion and the motion record are met. Section 7.1.5 of this Practice Direction discusses the deadlines for filing a notice of motion and motion record.

3. The notice of motion must contain a statement outlining the jurisdiction of a single judge to hear the motion and to grant the relief requested.

4. The notice of motion must contain an estimated length of time for the oral argument of the motion.

5. If the hearing of a motion is expected to take more than 30 minutes, the moving party is strongly encouraged to contact the motions desk at 416-327-5020 (select your language of choice, followed by option 3) to determine the current status of the list before selecting a hearing date and serving and filing the motion material.

7.1.3 Scheduling Motions

1. Self-represented parties, and lawyers who are bringing motions involving self-represented parties, are encouraged to schedule motions on Wednesdays or Thursdays when pro bono (free) duty counsel will be present at the court to provide advice and assistance to self-represented parties.

2. Parties who are self-represented in family law matters, and lawyers who are bringing motions against self-represented parties in family law matters, are encouraged to schedule motions on Wednesdays when pro bono (free) family law duty counsel will be available to provide advice and assistance to self-represented parties.

3. Duty counsel in motions court assists self-represented parties as *amicus curiae*, or "friend of the court".

4. More information about the duty counsel and family law duty counsel program can be

obtained at the following link: http://www.ontariocourts.ca/coa/en/info/civfam/legalaid.htm

5. On Wednesdays and Thursdays, motions brought by or against self-represented parties receive priority. When all parties are represented by lawyers, they are advised to schedule motions on other days of the week if possible in order to avoid delays in having their motion heard.

6. If the moving party's estimated time for arguing a motion is 15 minutes or more, the moving party must serve and file a factum. If the moving party does not file a factum, then the moving party's time for oral argument shall be limited to 15 minutes.

7. In order to ensure the efficient use of court resources, the Registrar may direct that a motion scheduled for hearing be removed from the list and rescheduled to a different date. The parties will be consulted before the motion is removed from the list and the hearing rescheduled.

7.1.4 Motions on Consent

1. Where all parties consent to an order, the moving party should file a notice of motion, two copies of the draft order, and a document indicating the parties' consent to the order. This document must be signed by the parties or their lawyers and contain the relevant court file number(s) and the title of proceeding. Parties are advised to include an affidavit or covering letter addressed to the Office of the Registrar setting out why the consent order is appropriate.

2. If a judge considering the proposed consent order is satisfied that it should issue, the order will be issued, usually within 2-3 business days.

3. If a judge considering the proposed order is not satisfied that it is appropriate or that it should issue, the parties will be advised and will be given an opportunity to provide oral or written argument.

7.1.5 Requirement to Deliver a Motion Record and the Time Limits for Service and Filing

1. Rule 37.10 of the *Rules of Civil Procedure* requires the moving party to serve and file a notice of motion and a motion record together with proof of service at least seven days before the hearing date. To ensure the efficient hearing of motions by a single judge, the Registrar's office will only schedule a motion for hearing if the notice of motion and the motion record are served and filed at least seven days before the hearing date, subject to the exceptions noted in paragraphs 3 and 4 below.

2. The motion record should include the materials referred to in rule 37.10(2). In accordance with rule 37.10(2)(e), the moving party should include in the motion record a copy of the Notice of Appeal or, if the party is seeking an extension of time, the proposed Notice of Appeal. The motion record should also include any previous court order(s) made in the proceeding that is (are) relevant to the issues on the motion together with the court's reasons for the prior order(s).

3. As provided in rule 37.10(1), the moving party may seek to obtain court approval dispensing with the requirement to file a motion record. To obtain such approval, the moving party should send a letter to the attention of the Registrar setting out the reasons for the request. The letter should be copied to the responding party(ies) and be sent by

email to COA.E-file@ontario.ca or by fax to 416-327-5032. The request and any response by the responding party(ies) will be placed before a judge of the Court of Appeal in advance of the hearing.

4. In situations of urgency or in unanticipated circumstances where the time limits for filing a notice of motion and/or motion record cannot be complied with, the material may be served and/or filed on shorter notice only by filing a consent or with leave of a judge.

5. When a party seeks an abridgement of the time to serve and/or file motion materials, the notice of motion should include in the relief sought a request for an abridgement of the time limits for serving and/or filing the relevant motion material. The request for an abridgement of time should be supported by a letter or affidavit explaining the reason for the request. The moving party shall deliver the letter or affidavit and accompanying motion materials to the Registrar's Office in person or by email to COA.E-file@ ontario.ca or by fax to 416-327-5032. The Registrar will present the materials to a judge to determine if the material may be filed and if the motion may be heard on the date requested, and the parties will be promptly advised of the outcome.

7.1.6 Including Materials from the Court File in the Motion Record

If the parties wish to refer at the hearing of the motion to any material from the court file that is associated with the appeal, or if they wish to refer to any material from a prior motion, the moving party must submit a letter addressed to the motions clerk asking for the specified material to be placed before the motions judge. The letter should be submitted at the same time that the motion materials must be filed pursuant to rule 37.10 of the *Rules of Civil Procedure*.

7.1.7 Factums for Use on Motions

1. Factums greatly assist the judges in hearing and deciding motions. At the same time, it is understood that the filing of factums in some relatively simple motions may not be necessary and may cause undue expense to the parties.

2. As a result, a factum must be served and filed in motions before a single judge if the moving party's estimated time for argument is 15 minutes or more.

3. The last paragraph of a factum for a motion must indicate the amount of time estimated to argue the motion, not including reply.

4. The court requests that the parties file an electronic copy of any factum filed on a motion. For details on the procedures for filing electronic material, please consult the Guidelines for Filing Electronic Documents at the Court of Appeal for Ontario.

5. In the majority of motions, the length of the factums should be 10 pages or less. Factums shall not be more than 30 pages without a court order authorizing the filing of a longer factum.

6. If a party does not file a factum on a motion, the party will be limited to 15 minutes of oral argument at the hearing of the motion.

7.1.8 Motions to Expedite

1. Motions to expedite the production of transcripts must be served on the opposing party and the authorized court transcriptionist.

2. Motions to expedite appeals may be brought to a judge in chambers. For more infor-

mation on expedited appeals, see section 12.1 of this Practice Direction.

7.1.9   Ex Parte Motions (Motions Without Notice to the Other Party)

When a party seeks to bring a motion without serving the notice of motion on the opposing party(ies), the moving party must indicate in the notice of motion the reasons for seeking to bring the motion without notice. A judge of the court will review the notice of motion and may grant the request to move without notice if the judge is satisfied that the nature of the motion or the circumstances render service of the notice of motion impracticable or unnecessary.

7.1.10   Motions to Intervene in an Appeal

1. Motions to intervene in a civil proceeding in the Court of Appeal are heard by the Chief Justice or Associate Chief Justice or a judge designated for the purpose: see rule 13.03(2) of the *Rules of Civil Procedure*.

2. The parties should consult with each other to obtain mutually agreeable dates for hearing the motion and present these dates to the court through correspondence addressed to the court's Senior Legal Officer. If the parties cannot agree on suitable dates, the court will fix the date of the hearing. The moving party will be advised of the hearing date selected by the court and will be responsible for notifying the other parties.

3. After the date for the hearing of the motion to intervene is confirmed, the moving party must file a notice of motion, motion record, factum, and other material for use by the court in accordance with rule 37.10 of the *Rules of Civil Procedure* and this Practice Direction.

4. The parties may request that the motion for intervention be heard by teleconference call or videoconference. This request should be included in correspondence addressed to the Senior Legal Officer, who will put the request to the judge assigned to hear the motion.

7.2   Motions before Three Judges

7.2.1.   Panel Motions (Except for Motions for Leave to Appeal to the Court of Appeal)

A three-judge panel of the Court of Appeal holds oral hearings on the following types of motions ("panel motions"):

*   motions to quash an appeal pursuant to s. 134(3) of the *Courts of Justice Act*;

*   motions under s. 7(5) of the *Courts of Justice Act* to set aside or vary the decision of a single judge of the Court of Appeal on a motion; and

*   motions to introduce further evidence under s. 134(4)(b) of the *Courts of Justice Act*.

7.2.2   Notice of Motion

1. The notice of motion must be in accordance with Form 37A of the *Rules of Civil Procedure*. The notice of motion must contain a statement outlining the jurisdiction of a panel to hear the motion and to grant the relief requested.

2. As provided in rule 61.16(3), the notice of motion should state that the moving party will make a motion to the court on a date to be fixed by the Registrar.

7.2.3   Scheduling Panel Motions

1. Except in cases of urgency, panel motions will not be scheduled for hearing until the

moving party has filed the motion record, factum and transcript, if any.

2. The oral argument for panel motions shall be limited to 15 minutes for the moving party, 10 minutes for the responding party, and 5 minutes for reply.

3. A party who seeks more time for oral argument must make a request to the civil List Judge. For details on requesting more time for oral argument, please see section 12.2 of this Practice Direction.

7.2.4 Factums for use on Panel Motions

1. In the majority of panel motions, the length of the factums should be 10 pages or less. Factums shall not be more than 30 pages without a court order authorizing the filing of a longer factum.

2. The court requests that the parties file an electronic copy of any factum or transcript filed on a motion before a panel. For details on the procedures for filing electronic material, please consult the Guidelines for Filing Electronic Documents at the Court of Appeal for Ontario.

7.2.5 Motion to Quash an Appeal

1. Where the basis for a motion to quash an appeal is that the court lacks jurisdiction to hear the appeal, the motion will be scheduled at an early date.

2. A motion to quash an appeal based on an argument that the appeal is devoid of merit is heard together with the appeal because the court must consider the merits of the appeal in deciding the motion.

7.2.6 Motion to Introduce Further Evidence

1. When a party seeks leave to file further evidence on an appeal pursuant to s. 134(4)(b) of the *Courts of Justice Act*, rule 61.16(2) of the *Rules of Civil Procedure* requires the party to bring such a motion to the panel of judges hearing the appeal.

2. The party must file three copies of the proposed further evidence in a document that is bound front and back in orange covers and identified on the cover as "Fresh Evidence Tendered by the Appellant" or "Fresh Evidence Tendered by the Respondent", as appropriate.

3. The parties should file a factum on the motion containing their arguments for or against admitting the further evidence on the appeal, including any impact the evidence may have on the resolution of the appeal.

4. Parties should consult rule 61.16(4) of the *Rules of Civil Procedure* for the timelines for serving and filing motion records and factums on a motion to introduce further evidence under s. 134(4)(b) of the *Courts of Justice Act*.

5. In situations of urgency or in unanticipated circumstances where the time limits for filing a motion record and/or factum cannot be complied with, the material may be served and/or filed on shorter notice only with the permission of a judge. For information on bringing a request to abridge the time for serving and/or filing motion materials, please refer to section 7.1.5 of this Practice Direction.

7.2.7 Motions in Writing for Leave to Appeal

1. Pursuant to rule 61.03.1 of the *Rules of Civil Procedure*, a three-judge panel hears mo-

tions for leave to appeal to the Court of Appeal in writing without an oral hearing.

2. The court requests that the parties file an electronic copy of any factum filed on a motion in writing for leave to appeal brought under rule 61.03.1. For details on the procedures for filing electronic material, please consult the Guidelines for Filing Electronic Documents at the Court of Appeal for Ontario.

3. On a motion for leave to appeal, the court may consider whether the issue raised by the moving party involves a question of public importance. Any party that seeks to introduce additional evidence on the question of public importance must file a motion to admit this evidence and a supporting affidavit together with the motion for leave to appeal.

4. The moving party should file three copies of the proposed additional evidence bound front and back in orange covers and identified as "Additional Evidence Tendered by the Moving Party". If the respondent seeks to file its own additional evidence on the question of public importance, the respondent should file three copies of the proposed further evidence bound front and back in orange covers and identified as "Additional Evidence Tendered by the Respondent".

5. The parties may include submissions regarding the admissibility and significance of the proposed additional evidence in their factums filed on the motion for leave to appeal, provided that the factum clearly indicates that the evidence in question is being tendered as additional evidence on the leave motion.

6. Motions to strike or reject affidavits concerning the question of public importance and motions to cross-examine any witness who has sworn such an affidavit should be brought to a single judge in chambers.

7.3 Formatting and Binding of Motion Material

1. With the exception of motions to file further or additional evidence as discussed in section 7.2.6, motion records shall have a white front cover and a light blue back sheet. Responding motion records shall have a green front cover and a light blue back sheet. The moving party's factum shall be bound in front and back white covers while the responding party's factum shall be bound in green front and back covers.

2. Parties should consult Rule 4 of the *Rules of Civil Procedure* for further information on the formatting and binding of motion material filed at the court. All text in factums must be double-spaced, except for quotations longer than four lines and footnotes. The Court of Appeal requires the use of 12-point or larger font and encourages the use of Arial or Times New Roman for all text in factums, including citations and footnotes.

3. The Registrar may refuse to accept documents or materials for filing if they do not comply with the *Rules* and/or this Practice Direction, or if they are not legible.

7.4 Power to Stay or Dismiss a Motion

Parties should be aware that, pursuant to rule 2.1.02 of the *Rules of Civil Procedure*, the court may, on its own initiative, stay or dismiss a motion if the motion appears on its face to be frivolous or vexatious or otherwise an abuse of the process of the court.

At the Court of Appeal, the review process contemplated by rule 2.1.02 will primarily be used in relation to motions brought to a panel seeking to have a judgment of the court set aside or varied under rule 59.06 of the *Rules of Civil Procedure*. Parties who bring this type of motion should expect that the court will screen their motion in accordance with rule 2.1.02.

7.5 Adjournment Requests

7.5.1 Single Judge Motions

1. If all parties are prepared to consent to an adjournment of a single judge motion, then the moving party should provide a letter addressed to the motions clerk and copied to all parties advising of the adjournment request. The requesting letter may be submitted by email to COA.E-file@ontario.ca (please include "Adjournment Request" and the court file number and title of proceeding in the subject line of the email) or by fax (416-327-5032). The motions clerk will adjourn the motion to a date as agreed by the parties.

2. If the request to adjourn a single judge motion is opposed, then the party requesting the adjournment should provide a letter addressed to the motions clerk and copied to all parties advising of the reason for the adjournment request. The party opposing the request should provide a letter addressed to the motions clerk and copied to all parties advising of the reasons for opposing the adjournment request. This correspondence should be submitted by email to COA.E-file@ontario.ca (please include "Adjournment Request" and the court file number and title of proceeding in the subject line of the email) or by fax (416-327-5032). The motions clerk will present the correspondence to the motions judge for review and his or her determination will be communicated to the parties by the motions clerk before the hearing date of the motion.

7.5.2 Panel Motions

1. If a hearing date for a panel motion is more than three weeks away, and if all parties are prepared to consent to an adjournment, then the moving party should provide a letter addressed to the Appeal Scheduling Unit and copied to all parties advising of the adjournment request. The requesting letter may be submitted by email to COA.E-file@ontario.ca (please include "Adjournment Request" and the court file number and title of proceeding in the subject line of the email) or by fax (416-327-6256). The Appeal Scheduling Unit will confirm if the matter will be adjourned and if so, will advise the parties of the new hearing date.

2. If a hearing date for a panel motion is more than three weeks away, and if the adjournment request is opposed by one or more of the parties, then the party seeking the adjournment must make the adjournment request to a judge of the court who has been designated by the Chief Justice to serve as the civil List Judge.

3. A conference call before the civil List Judge to change a hearing date must be arranged through the Appeal Scheduling Unit by contacting 416-327-5020 (select your language of choice, followed by option 4, and then press 2) or by fax (416-327-6256). The Appeal Scheduling Unit will contact the parties with the date, time and the dial-in details for the conference call.

4. If the hearing date for a panel motion is three weeks or less away, any adjournment request - whether on consent or opposed - must be made in writing to the attention of the Appeal Scheduling Unit. The requesting letter may be submitted by email to COA.E-file@ontario.ca (please include "Adjournment Request" and the court file number and title of proceeding in the subject line of the email) or by fax (416-327-6256). The request will be forwarded to the president of the panel for review and his or her deter-

mination will be communicated to the parties by the Appeal Scheduling Unit.

7.6 Withdrawing or Abandoning a Motion

1. If the moving party withdraws or abandons a motion to be heard by a single judge or by a panel of judges, the party must serve and file a notice of abandonment in accordance with rule 37.09 (use Form 61K with necessary modifications). The moving party should also send a letter addressed to the Registrar advising that the motion has been withdrawn or abandoned. The letter should be copied to all parties and be sent by email to COA.E-file@ontario.ca (please include "Notice of Abandonment of a Motion" and the court file number and title of proceeding in the subject line of the email) or by fax to (416) 327-5032. The letter should indicate how the issue of costs has been resolved.

2. If a motion before a single judge is withdrawn or abandoned within two days of the scheduled hearing date, the moving party must advise the motions clerk that the motion will not be proceeding by calling 416-327-5020 (select your language of choice, followed by option 3).

3. If a motion before a panel of three judges is abandoned after it has been listed for hearing, the moving party must promptly advise the Appeal Scheduling Unit by contacting 416-327-5020 (select your language of choice, followed by option 4, and then press 2) or by fax (416-327-6256).

8. APPEAL MANAGEMENT

1. In especially complicated appeals, such as appeals involving multiple parties or grouped appeals, it may be appropriate for a judge to be assigned to manage the conduct of the appeal(s). A request for the assignment of an appeal management judge should be made to the court by letter addressed to the Senior Legal Officer. The request should contain enough information to satisfy the court that such an appointment is appropriate. The decision to appoint an appeal management judge is made by the Chief Justice or Associate Chief Justice and is communicated to the parties.

2. The appeal management judge will conduct appeal management conferences to ensure the efficient conduct of the appeal. Appeal management conferences are held to deal with matters not otherwise governed by the *Rules of Civil Procedure*, including: the order of argument; time allocations for oral argument; the hearing date; the issues to be argued; the possibility of settling the appeal or any issues under appeal; coordination, if necessary, of the scheduling of prehearing motions; creating customized electronic appeal records; and similar matters. Such conferences are conducted in person or by teleconference or videoconference and are arranged through the Appeal Scheduling Office of the Court of Appeal.

3. In order to ensure the efficient conduct of the appeal, the appeal management judge's decisions at appeal management conferences will be communicated as required to the panel hearing the appeal, the parties, and the court's staff.

4. When the parties to a case-managed appeal seek to obtain relief from compliance with any requirements of the *Rules of Civil Procedure* or of this Practice Direction, an order of the appeal management judge dispensing with such compliance will be required. Such an order may be obtained on consent of all parties by providing two copies of the draft order, a document indicating the signed consent of the parties, and an affidavit or

letter addressed to the appeal management judge with sufficient information to satisfy the appeal management judge that the order is appropriate.

9. PRE-HEARING SETTLEMENT CONFERENCES IN FAMILY LAW APPEALS

9.1 General

The Court of Appeal for Ontario offers a voluntary pre-hearing settlement conference program. Its purpose is to attempt to resolve family law appeals at an earlier stage in order to reduce costs for litigants. The court makes available a roster of appellate judges who have particular interest in family law matters. The pre-hearing settlement conference is for those parties who would like to explore a final resolution of their legal differences before a full hearing or a narrowing of the issues requiring resolution. The court will hold a pre-hearing settlement conference only if all parties believe that a judge's assistance may assist them in resolving or narrowing the issues on appeal.

9.2 Two-Stage Process

Pre-hearing settlement conferences are offered at two stages, as the parties require. A Stage 1 conference will take place as soon as possible after the Notice of Appeal has been filed but before the transcript has been prepared. The purpose of the conference at this stage of the proceedings is to minimize cost, if at all possible, especially the cost of the production of the transcripts. However, the parties must comply with rule 61.05(5) of the *Rules of Civil Procedure*.

A Stage 2 conference will take place after perfection of the appeal. It is designed to attempt a global resolution of the issues under appeal but, if unsuccessful, at least to offer a "good, hard look" at the issues and explore alternatives to see if the appeal, or at least some issues, can be resolved.

9.3 Application for a Pre-hearing Settlement Conference

In order to request a conference, the parties must complete a Form entitled "Joint Request for Pre-hearing Settlement Conference" Word, PDF. They are to specify whether they are seeking a Stage 1 or Stage 2 conference although, in most cases, the timing of the application will be sufficient to advise the court. The Form must be submitted to the Appeal Scheduling Unit by email to COA.E-file@ontario.ca or by facsimile (416-327-6256). The parties should propose a range of dates and times for the conference that are suitable to all participants. The request should also contain a reasonable estimate for the length of the conference, although the court will be as flexible as required by the circumstances.

Once the "Joint Request" is received by the court, the Appeal Scheduling Unit will schedule a conference, usually within 7 to 30 days. The court will make every effort, especially in respect of Stage 1 conferences, to convene counsel and the parties as quickly as possible. Because the pre-hearing settlement conference is not intended to delay the normal progress of the appeal, a request for such a conference does not operate to suspend the obligation of the parties to comply with the requirements of Rule 61 of the *Rules of Civil Procedure*.

9.4 Memoranda

If the parties request a Stage 1 conference, they will be required to file a copy of the reasons for judgment and a memorandum outlining the issues. It is the appellant's responsibility to deliver the reasons for judgment to the court for use at the conference. The memorandum of each party shall be no longer than 6 pages. If either party requires an exhibit from the trial or the proceeding being appealed, it may be attached to the memorandum. The court expects that the parties will attempt to isolate the real points in issue and consider ways in which they may be resolved. Since the court file will be available to the judge at the conference, the parties need not include material in the memorandums that is referred to in the notice of appeal. The parties shall serve their memorandum on the other parties.

The judgment and memorandums should be filed with the court at least 2 days before the conference.

If the parties wish a Stage 2 conference, they must file memorandums as in Stage 1. The court will also rely on the appeal book and the factums filed in preparing for the conference.

9.5   The Conference

A Court of Appeal judge will preside over the conference. The parties and those who may have a significant influence on the outcome of the conference must be present, since they are the ultimate decision-makers. The parties are free to ask the court for whatever arrangement counsel believes to be appropriate and necessary. The process is meant to be as flexible as the parties wish. The pre-hearing settlement conference will not result in an adjournment of the appeal. The judge conducting the conference will not be assigned to the panel ultimately hearing the appeal and will not discuss any aspect of the conference with the panel.

9.6   The Results

If the pre-hearing settlement conference results in a successful resolution of some or all of the issues, the court will expect an agreement to be drafted and signed by the parties. Counsel may also be required to provide a draft order and to speak to the settlement in court. This will depend on the circumstances of the settlement.

Except for such an agreement and draft order, the fact of the pre-hearing settlement conference, the memorandums filed and all deliberations in the process will remain strictly confidential and without prejudice to the parties' legal positions.

If the pre-hearing settlement conference is unsuccessful, the appeal will proceed as scheduled.

9.7   Notice to Parties

To encourage parties to use the pre-hearing settlement conference facility, counsel filing or responding to a family law appeal will be required to advise their client of the availability of this service.

9.8   Inquiries

Further information, if required, may be obtained from the Court's Appeal Scheduling Unit by telephone (416-327-5028/4615). A pre-hearing conference may be arranged by contacting the court's Appeal Scheduling Unit by telephone (416-327-5028/4615) or fax (416-327-6256).

_____

10.   PRE-HEARING SETTLEMENT CONFERENCES IN OTHER APPEALS

A judge of the court may conduct a pre-hearing settlement conference in any appeal in which all counsel request such a conference. Arrangements for a pre-hearing conference shall be made through the court's Appeal Scheduling Unit by telephone (416-327-5028/4615) or by fax (416-327-5256). The parties should proceed by way of analogy to the procedures set out in the program for pre-hearing settlement conferences in family law appeals.

11. PERFECTING AN APPEAL

11.1 Perfection: Steps Required

1. The appellant is responsible for taking the steps prescribed by rules 61.09(2) and (3) of the *Rules of Civil Procedure* for perfecting an appeal. The appellant must file with the Registrar a certificate of perfection as described in rule 61.09(3)(c) before the appeal is perfected. After an appeal is perfected, the Registrar will assign a date for hearing the appeal.

2. Rule 61.09(4) permits an appellant to bring a motion to a single judge of the Court of Appeal for directions to vary the rules governing the material that must be served and filed to perfect an appeal. The moving party must satisfy the judge that it is in the interest of justice to grant relief from compliance with any of the *Rules*. Details about bringing motions to a single judge are found in section 7.1 of this Practice Direction and in rules 61.16 and 37 of the *Rules of Civil Procedure*.

11.2 *Child, Youth and Family Services Act Appeals*

Rule 38(2) of the *Family Law Rules* modifies certain time periods that apply in appeals under the *Child, Youth and Family Services Act, 2017*, S.O. 2017, c. 14, Sched. 1, including the time for perfecting the appeal. The parties should consult this rule for the deadlines that apply in these types of appeals. These deadlines are generally shorter than the time periods prescribed in the *Rules of Civil Procedure*.

11.3 Transcripts and Exhibits

1. The phrase "transcript of evidence" as used in rule 61.09(1) of the *Rules of Civil Procedure* refers only to the oral testimony of witnesses given in the presence of a judge. Oral arguments by a lawyer or a self-represented party do not qualify as "evidence" under the *Rules*.

2. Attention is directed to rule 61.05 regarding the service of certificates (Form 61C and Form 61D) and/or an agreement respecting evidence. The appellant's certificate respecting evidence should be served and filed together with the notice of appeal. The respondent's certificate respecting evidence must be served on the appellant within 15 days of service of the appellant's certificate.

3. When a lawyer who acted at trial is not acting on the appeal, the court expects that the trial lawyer will provide timely assistance to the appellate lawyer or to the self-represented party in completing the certificates or in making an agreement respecting evidence.

4. According to rule 61.05(5), the appellant must order a transcript of all the oral evidence that the parties have not agreed to exclude.

5. In the vast majority of appeals, it is not necessary to transcribe all the testimony of the witnesses who testified in the lower court. Oral evidence should be transcribed only if the Court of Appeal needs to review the evidence in order to properly analyze the grounds of appeal and any cross-appeal.

Unnecessary transcription of the evidence of witnesses in the lower court delays the hearing of appeals and substantially increases the cost of litigation. The parties should give serious consideration to the issue of what evidence is really necessary for a proper adjudication of the appeal.

6. In appeals where the facts are not in dispute, the parties are encouraged to file an agreed statement of facts, which will take the place of a transcript. The agreed statement of facts shall be filed in the appeal book and compendium.

7. The court may impose costs sanctions where evidence is transcribed unnecessarily.

8. Unless otherwise ordered by a judge of the Court of Appeal, the transcripts of trial proceedings shall omit the following aspects of the proceedings:

   (a) all proceedings on the challenge of the array or of jurors for cause;

   (b) any opening address of the trial judge;

   (c) the opening address of a lawyer and/or a self-represented party;

   (d) all proceedings in the absence of the jury and all argument in the absence of the jury (except objections to a charge and the trial judge's related rulings together with any reasons for the rulings);

   (e) all objections to the admissibility of evidence, except for a notation that an objection was made (note: the ruling of the trial judge on the objection, including any reasons for the ruling, will be transcribed.)

9. When any aspect of the proceedings mentioned in paragraph 8 is the subject of a ground of appeal, the relevant material may be transcribed without the need for a judge's order.

11.4 Timely Preparation of Transcripts

1. Authorized court transcriptionists have been instructed that after a transcript has been ordered for a civil appeal, the completion of the transcript is not to be suspended without an order of a judge of the Court of Appeal or the receipt of a notice of abandonment of the appeal.

2. This instruction does not apply to appeals where the Area Committee has not yet decided whether to grant a Legal Aid certificate to cover the client's appeal. To ensure the timely determination of Legal Aid applications, trial lawyers are reminded of their primary responsibility to prepare an opinion letter for use on the application for Legal Aid. Every effort should be made to prepare and submit this opinion letter to Legal Aid within 30 days of the filing of the notice of appeal.

3. Lawyers are reminded that interim payments for transcripts may be obtained from Legal Aid Ontario in cases where a Legal Aid certificate has been issued.

4. The authorized court transcriptionist is requested to file with the Court of Appeal a Certificate/Proof of Ordering when the transcript has been ordered and a Certificate/Notification of Completion when the transcript has been completed. This request is in addition to any obligation imposed on the parties by the *Rules of Civil Procedure*.

5. Transcripts are generally completed within 90 days of the date of being ordered, subject to extensions for exceptional circumstances.

6. If a transcriptionist's Certificate of Completion has not been filed by the expected

completion date of the transcript, the court will inquire about the status of the transcript and ascertain if the court's assistance is required to ensure its timely completion. The court may refer the issue of the outstanding transcript to a status court hearing before a judge of the Court of Appeal. The ordering party must attend the hearing, and the other parties may choose to attend in order to make submissions. The parties may attend either by way of teleconference or in person. At the hearing, the judge may order the transcriptionist to appear in order to explain the delay and to provide a plan for the timely completion of the transcript.

11.5 Filing Transcripts

The authorized court transcriptionist must prepare an electronic version of the transcript for the court's use, and for the parties' use if they request it. The appellant is required to file an electronic version of the transcript with the court, together with a paper copy. The line and page numbering of the transcript in electronic form must correspond with that in the hard copy.

For details on the proper formatting and procedures for filing electronic documents in the Court of Appeal, please consult the Guidelines for Filing Electronic Documents at the Court of Appeal for Ontario.

11.6 Compendiums and Exhibit Books

1. Rules 61.09 and 61.10 of the *Rules of Civil Procedure* require the appellant to file three copies of an appeal book and compendium together with the factum in order to perfect an appeal. Rule 61.12 requires a respondent to file three copies of a respondent's compendium. The appellant's appeal book and compendium shall be bound front and back in buff covers. The respondent's compendium shall be bound front and back in green covers.

2. Rules 61.09 and 61.10.1 require the appellant to file one copy of an exhibit book. The exhibit book shall be bound front and back in buff covers.

3. If an appeal is from an order made on an application or on a motion in which no exhibits were filed, then the court will not require the appellant to serve and file an exhibit book in order to perfect the appeal. The appellant shall serve the certificate of perfection on the other parties to the appeal and shall state in the certificate that an exhibit book is not required because no exhibits were filed on the application or motion.

4. The appellant's appeal book and compendium and the respondent's compendium contain documents essential to the hearing of the appeal, including the excerpts from the transcript and any exhibits that the parties will refer to in oral argument. Since the parties are only required to file one paper copy of the transcript and one paper copy of the exhibit book, it is essential to include in the compendiums all portions of the transcript that are relevant to the grounds of appeal and all relevant exhibits.

5. When the proceedings in the lower court were conducted in full or in part based on affidavit evidence, all relevant affidavits and any attached exhibits must be included in the appeal book and compendium or in the respondent's compendium.

6. In appeals from civil jury trials, if any ground of appeal relates to the charge to the jury, the trial judge's charge must be included in the appeal book and compendium.

7. In the event that the appeal book and compendium includes all the affidavits and exhibits that were filed in the lower court, then the appellant does not need to also serve

and file an exhibit book in order to perfect the appeal. In such cases, the appellant's certificate of perfection should state: "All the exhibits required for this appeal are included in the appeal book and compendium." Parties should be aware, however, that the appeal book and compendium is far less useful if unnecessary exhibits or materials are included in it.

8. Filing compendiums is critical to the efficient preparation and effective argument of appeals. Thus, the requirement to file an appeal book and compendium and a respondent's compendium in all civil matters is mandatory and must be complied with, unless a judge orders relief from compliance on a motion brought under rule 61.09(4).

9. The appeal book and compendium and the respondent's compendium should be organized as described in rules 61.10(1) and 61.12(7) of the *Rules of Civil Procedure*, and should be organized in a way that enables the court to easily locate all of the documents that are referred to in the parties' factums.

10. Extracts of transcripts, affidavits or exhibits in the compendiums should include as much material as is needed to understand the context for the part of the extract that the party is relying on.

11. The Court of Appeal encourages parties to submit electronic copies of compendiums and exhibit books by CD/DVD-ROM or USB Flash Drive/USB Key, in addition to serving and filing paper copies of these materials. For details on the procedures for filing electronic material, please consult the Guidelines for Filing Electronic Documents at the Court of Appeal for Ontario.

11.7 Factums

1. Rules 61.11 and 61.12 of the *Rules of Civil Procedure* deal with the appellant's and the respondent's factums. These rules emphasize the need for a concise summary of the relevant facts, a concise argument of the law relating to each issue, and the requirement to cross-reference the factum to the compendium. The court may impose cost sanctions on respondents who do not file their factums within the time provided in rule 61.12(2).

2. The Court of Appeal encourages the use of hyperlinks to case law referred to in electronically-filed factums. Parties may hyperlink authorities to the judgments database found on the websites of Canadian courts, www.canlii.org/en/index.html, in addition to LexisNexis Quicklaw and WestlawNext Canada.

3. The Court of Appeal requires the use of 12-point or larger font and encourages the use of Arial or Times New Roman for all text in factums, including citations and footnotes. All text in factums must be double-spaced, except for quotations longer than four lines and footnotes. The appellant's factum shall be bound in front and back white covers while the respondent's factum shall be bound in green front and back covers. The Registrar may refuse to accept materials for filing if they do not comply with the *Rules* and/or this Practice Direction, or if they are not legible.

4. In the majority of appeals, the length of the factum should be 30 pages or less. The Registrar will refuse to accept factums that use excessive footnotes or that use formatting that is inconsistent with rule 4.01(1) of the *Rules of Civil Procedure* in order to meet the 30-page limit.

5. To file a factum of longer than 30 pages, permission must be obtained by bringing a motion to a single judge of the Court of Appeal. On any such motion, the moving party

must, other than in exceptional cases, include a copy of the proposed factum in the motion record.

6. If the factum refers to information that is subject to a publication ban or sealing order imposed by a court in the proceedings, or contains information the release of which would violate a legislative provision, then the party must include a prominent reference to the terms of the applicable order or legislative provision on the front cover of the factum.

7. The *Rules of Civil Procedure* require the filing of an electronic copy of all factums for use on appeals. For details on the proper formatting and procedures for preparing electronic documents for filing at the Court of Appeal, please consult the Guidelines for Filing Electronic Documents at the Court of Appeal for Ontario.

8. Parties are encouraged to consult the Reference Guide for Citation Practices at the Court of Appeal for Ontario for assistance in preparing their factums and other appeal material. This reference guide is for information purposes only.

11.8 Books of Authorities

1. Although not required to perfect an appeal, the Court of Appeal is greatly assisted by books of authorities containing copies of the cases and relevant extracts from secondary authorities to which the parties intend to refer in arguing their appeal.

2. Parties are welcome to file joint books of authorities whenever possible.

3. If it is not feasible to provide a joint book of authorities, then do not include copies of cases that are in the other party's book of authorities. The factum should cite to the version of the case that is found in the other party's book of authorities.

4. The following practices should be followed when preparing and filing books of authorities:

   (i) Include the cases being relied on in the factum and in oral argument, subject to the exception noted next.

   (ii) The Court of Appeal has adopted a List of Frequently Cited Civil Authorities. Authorities on this list do not need to be included in the books of authorities. Instead, when a party's factum refers to an authority on this list, the book of authorities should only include the headnote and particular passage(s) from the authority being relied on. A complete version of the authorities on this list is available for the judges' use.

   (iii) Separate the authorities in the book of authorities with a tab (either numerical or alphabetical) and include a table of contents listing where to find each authority. The authorities may be printed on both sides of the page.

   (iv) Clearly mark in each authority the passage(s) that is(are) being relying on.

   (v) Joint books of authorities should be bound front and back in yellow covers and marked "Joint Book of Authorities". A book of authorities filed only by the appellant should be bound front and back in white covers and marked "Appellant's Book of Authorities". A book of authorities filed only by the respondent should be bound front and back in green covers and marked "Respondent's Book of Authorities".

(vi)   Because books of authorities are of great assistance to the judges in preparing for the hearing, they should be filed whenever possible at the same time as the factum. If this is not possible, then they should be filed no later than one month before the hearing date.

5.   The order for selecting which print version of a case to include in the book of authorities is as follows:

(i)   the decision as posted on the relevant court's website, preferably using the PDF format;

(ii)   the decision as posted on CanLII (www.canlii.org), preferably using the PDF format;

(iii)   the decision as it appears in an official or semi-official reporter (e.g., Supreme Court of Canada Reports, Ontario Reports, Federal Reports, and other provincial reporter series such as the B.C.L.R.'s, etc.);

(iv)   the decision as it appears in an unofficial reporter (e.g., Dominion Law Reports, Business Law Reports, etc.);

(v)   the decision as posted on subscription-based databases (e.g., WestlawNext Canada, LexisNexis Quicklaw, etc.).

11.9   Materials for Consolidated and Grouped Appeals

1.   When two or more appeals are to be heard together because the appeals are from the same or related court orders, if all parties consent to filing consolidated material for the appeals, then the parties may file a letter of consent together with the consolidated material, including consolidated appeal books and compendiums, exhibit books, factums and the books of authorities for use on all the appeals.

2.   If the parties to consolidated appeals are unable to agree on the use of consolidated material, a motion for directions may be brought before a single judge of the court to authorize the preparation and filing of consolidated material as the court may approve.

3.   The material filed in consolidated appeals should include the court file number of each appeal that is being heard together.

4.   When two or more appeals are grouped for hearing together because they raise similar issues but the appeals are from orders made in separate proceedings, the parties must file separate material for each appeal unless a judge directs otherwise on a motion for directions.

5.   Parties to consolidated or grouped appeals may seek the assistance of an appeal management judge early in the appellate process. Section 8 of this Practice Direction discusses the process for requesting the assignment of an appeal management judge.

11.10   Electronic Appeals

1.   When the volume of material is large or the appeal is complex, the appeal will be much more efficiently presented to the court if the paper appeal materials are also filed in an electronic format. Thus, parties should consider the desirability of filing an electronic copy of not only the factums and transcripts but also the materials in the compendiums.

2.   The electronic copies of the factums should be hyperlinked to the authorities that are cited in the factums and to the materials found in the electronic compendiums.

3. If electronic copies of any of the materials referred to in the factum are not available, then paper copies of the materials should be scanned using an optical character recognition feature to convert the scanned document into a searchable format. Generally speaking, it is not helpful to provide the court with non-searchable PDF files. To confirm that your document is searchable, use the word search feature of your software program.

12. APPEAL SCHEDULING PROCEDURES

12.1 Expedited Appeals

1. Most civil appeals will be heard within four to six months of perfection. However, it is recognized that some appeals must be heard more quickly.

2. The court automatically expedites the following types of appeals:

    (a) family law appeals;

    (b) appeals under the *Child, Youth and Family Services Act, 2017*, S.O. 2017, c. 14, Sched. 1; and

    (c) appeals that may delay the progress of an ongoing proceeding.

3. Such appeals will be heard at the earliest practicable date, usually within three months of perfection.

4. Appeals other than those listed in paragraph 2 may be expedited by bringing a motion to a judge of the Court of Appeal for an order expediting the appeal. The judge must be satisfied that the urgency of the matter requires an earlier hearing date.

12.2 Estimate of Time Required for Oral Argument

1. Parties shall certify in the factum a realistic estimate of the time for oral argument of the appeal, not including reply, in fractions of an hour or hours (e.g., ¾ of an hour, 1½ hours).

2. Prior to scheduling the appeal for a hearing date, a judge of the court will review the time estimate of the appellant and will assign time for the oral argument of each party, including any time for reply.

3. The parties will be notified of the time assignment for oral argument when they are notified of the hearing date of the appeal.

4. The time assignments are provided to the panel hearing the appeal. The court expects the parties to adhere to their time assignments.

5. Parties who seek more time for oral argument must make a request to a judge of the court who has been designated by the Chief Justice to serve as the civil List Judge.

6. A conference before the civil List Judge for more time for oral argument must be arranged through the Appeal Scheduling Unit by contacting 416-327-5020 (select your language of choice, followed by option 4, and then press 2) or by fax (416-327-6256).

7. Requests made for the assistance of the List Judge will be dealt with by conference call. The Appeal Scheduling Unit will contact the parties with the date, time and the dial-in details for the List Judge conference call.

12.3 Adjournment Requests

1. If a hearing date for an appeal is more than three weeks away, and if all parties are prepared to consent to an adjournment, then the appellant should provide a letter addressed to the Appeal Scheduling Unit and copied to all parties advising of the adjournment request. The requesting letter may be submitted by email to COA.E-file@ontario.ca (please include "Adjournment Request" and the court file number and title of proceeding in the subject line of the email) or by fax (416-327-6256). The Appeal Scheduling Unit will confirm if the matter will be adjourned and if so, will advise the parties of the new hearing date.

2. If a hearing date for an appeal is more than three weeks away, and if the adjournment request is opposed by one or more of the parties, then the party seeking the adjournment must make the adjournment request to a judge of the court who has been designated by the Chief Justice to serve as the civil List Judge.

3. A conference call before the civil List Judge to change a hearing date must be arranged through the Appeal Scheduling Unit by contacting 416-327-5020 (select your language of choice, followed by option 4, and then press 2) or by fax (416-327-6256). The Appeal Scheduling Unit will contact the parties with the date, time and the dial-in details for the conference call.

4. If the hearing date for an appeal is three weeks or less away, any adjournment request – whether on consent or opposed – must be made in writing to the attention of the Appeal Scheduling Unit. The requesting letter may be submitted by email to COA.E-file@ontario.ca (please include "Adjournment Request" and the court file number and title of proceeding in the subject line of the email) or by fax (416-327-6256). The request will be forwarded to the president of the panel for review and his or her determination will be communicated to the parties by the Appeal Scheduling Unit.

12.4 Appeals without Oral Argument

1. The court may decide appeals without oral argument on the consent of the parties. Parties who seek to have an appeal decided without oral argument shall, after delivering their factums, file a written consent with the Registrar to hear the appeal in writing.

2. In appeals without oral argument, the appellant shall be permitted to file a reply factum, which must be served and filed within ten days of the filing of the respondent's factum.

3. Where practical, the court shall render judgment within 60 days of the filing of the consent.

12.5 The Composition of the Panel

The parties may consult the Court of Appeal's website at http://www.ontariocourts.ca/coa/en/caselist/ to see the weekly hearings lists and the composition of the panel for their appeal. The weekly hearing lists are posted on Friday at noon on the week prior to the next week's hearings.

13. REQUEST TO RECONSIDER A PRIOR PRECEDENTIAL DECISION OF THE COURT OF APPEAL

1. When a party wishes to ask the court to decline to follow a prior precedential decision

of the Court of Appeal for Ontario, the party should send a letter to the attention of the Senior Legal Officer requesting that the court convene a five-judge panel to hear the appeal. The letter should explain why there is reason to think that the court's prior precedential decision should not be followed. The letter should be copied to all parties and be submitted not later than the time for filing the requesting party's factum.

2. Any party to the proceeding in the Court of Appeal may send a letter responding to the request to convene a five-judge panel to hear the appeal.

3. The Chief or the Associate Chief Justice will review a party's request for a five-judge panel and his or her decision on the matter is final.

14. SETTLING OR ABANDONING AN APPEAL OR CROSS-APPEAL

1. If the parties agree to settle an appeal or cross-appeal, they are required to promptly submit a letter addressed to the Registrar advising that the matter has been settled. The letter should be copied to all parties and be sent by email to COA.E-file@ontario.ca (please include "Notice of Abandonment" or "Notice of Settlement" and the court file number and title of proceeding in the subject line of the email) or by fax to (416) 327-5032. The letter should indicate how the issue of costs has been resolved. The parties may attach a copy of any minutes of settlement with the letter advising of the settlement.

2. In accordance with rule 61.16(2.2) of the *Rules of Civil Procedure*, an order dismissing an appeal on consent of the parties may be obtained from a judge in chambers. When the parties settle an appeal and seek relief other than an order dismissing the appeal on consent, at least one of the parties may be directed by the court to appear in order to satisfy the court that the requested order is not inappropriate.

3. If an appeal or cross-appeal is abandoned, the relevant party is required to promptly file a notice of abandonment (Form 61K) in accordance with rule 61.14(1).

4. If an appeal and/or cross-appeal is settled or abandoned after it has been listed for hearing, the relevant party must promptly advise the Appeal Scheduling Unit of the settlement or abandonment by contacting 416-327-5020 (select your language of choice, followed by option 4, and then press 2) or by fax (416-327-6256) to ensure the efficient use of courtrooms and court resources.

15. COURTROOM DECORUM

15.1 Addressing the Court

Members of the Court of Appeal should be addressed as "Chief Justice", "Associate Chief Justice", "Justice" or "Justice (Surname)", as appropriate, and not as Madam Justice, My Lady, My Lord, Your Ladyship, Your Lordship or Your Honour.

15.2 Courtroom Attire

Lawyers do not need to wear gowns when they appear on motions before a single judge in chambers.

Counsel who are pregnant when appearing before a panel in the Court of Appeal for Ontario are free to modify their traditional court attire in order to accommodate their pregnancy as they see fit, including dispensing with a waistcoat and tabs.

15.3 Use of Electronic Communication Devices in the Courtroom

Unless a judge orders otherwise, electronic communication devices including cell phones and laptop computers may be used in the courtroom in a manner that is not disruptive of the proceedings. Anyone using an electronic communication device to transmit information about a court hearing has the responsibility to identify and comply with the terms of any applicable publication ban, sealing order, or other restriction on publication that has been imposed by court order or by statute. [1]

Photography and video recording of a court hearing without the authorization of a judge is prohibited by s. 136(1) of the *Courts of Justice Act*. Audio recording of a court hearing is permissible for note-taking purposes, but these audio recordings may not be transmitted. Anyone who uses an electronic communication device in a way that violates this Practice Direction may be ordered to turn off the device, leave the device outside the courtroom, leave the courtroom, abide by any other court order, and may also be subject to prosecution.

---

16. ELECTRONIC DELIVERY OF REASONS FOR JUDGMENT

The court will send an HTML and PDF copy of the signed judgment by email to those lawyers and self-represented parties who have provided an email address on their materials filed with the court. Paper copies of judgments are also available at the Registrar's Office to those parties who do not have an email address, and to members of the public (who must pay the prescribed fee).

Judgments are posted on the court's website shortly after release at http://www.ontariocourts.ca/decisions_index/en/.

The court provides advance notice of release of its reserved decisions at http://www.Ontariocourts.ca/decisions_index/notice.htm.

---

17. DIGITAL AUDIO RECORDINGS

1. The Court of Appeal is not a "court of record". Its oral hearings are not monitored or transcribed as a matter of routine. However, the Court of Appeal records all hearings that are held in open court through the use of digital audio recording. Unless a judge orders otherwise, a copy of a digital audio recording is available upon request, provided that the proceedings are not subject to a statutory publication ban or other court order that prevents the release of the digital audio recording.

2. Requests for access to digital audio recordings should be made in the Registrar's Office and are subject to payment of the prescribed fee, unless a fee waiver certificate is produced. Such recordings are for personal use, and will not be released unless the person requesting the recording signs an undertaking agreeing to respect the limits on the permitted uses of the recording.

3. If a person wishes to have a transcript of a hearing made, he or she must first bring a motion for permission to do so before a single judge. Once the order is obtained, the person may have the recording transcribed at her or her own expense.

4. The publication, broadcasting, reproduction or other dissemination of an audio record-

ing of a court hearing is prohibited unless expressly authorized by a court order.

18. COSTS IN THE COURT OF APPEAL

1. Parties should be prepared to address all issues of costs, including the quantum of costs, at the hearing of an appeal or a motion.

2. Parties who may be entitled to costs must prepare and exchange their proposed bills of costs, to be filed at the time of argument if requested by the court. This bill should be complete to the day before the hearing and include an estimate of the costs associated with the hearing of the appeal or motion.

3. If the decision on the appeal or motion is released orally immediately after the hearing, the parties will have an opportunity to make brief submissions as to the quantum and scale of costs to be paid.

4. If the decision on the appeal or motion is reserved, the filing of the bill of costs and submissions will usually occur at the hearing.

5. The court may determine that it would be preferable to receive costs submissions after releasing its decision. In such cases, a party entitled to receive costs will deliver a bill of costs together with any submissions, in writing, in support of the requested order for costs within seven days of the release of the decision. Any party liable to pay costs may deliver a response, in writing, within 14 days of the release of the decision. The party entitled to receive costs may deliver a brief reply within 17 days of the release of the decision. These deadlines apply unless the court directs different deadlines at the hearing.

6. Unless the court orders otherwise, such material should be filed at the Registrar's Office in triplicate, together with proof of service, to the attention of the Appeal Scheduling Unit.

7. Unless the court orders otherwise, any material received in relation to costs will be forwarded to the panel for consideration 18 days after the release of the decision. The parties will be notified of the decision as to costs by way of an addendum to the decision.

19. POST-HEARING SUBMISSIONS

1. The parties are expected to fully argue all issues on an appeal in the factum and in oral submissions at the hearing of the appeal. Attempts by the parties to provide the court with additional written submissions, authorities, or other material after the hearing are improper, subject to the exceptions discussed here.

2. On occasion, after the hearing of an appeal, the court may wish to receive further submissions from the parties in respect of one or more issues. The Senior Legal Officer will advise the parties of any request by the court for further submissions and will give a timetable within which to serve and file this material.

3. The parties may become aware of a newly-decided authority that might have an impact on a reserved appeal. The authority may be sent, without submissions, to the attention of the Senior Legal Officer, who will ensure that the material is transmitted to the panel that heard the appeal.

PRAC. DIR. AND POLICIES

4.   If a party wishes to make submissions concerning the impact of a new authority, a request to do so should be included in a covering letter addressed to the Senior Legal Officer and copied to the other parties. The Senior Legal Officer will advise the parties whether the court is prepared to entertain such submissions and, if necessary, will give a timetable for serving and filing submissions.

5.   In exceptional circumstances, a party may seek to make additional submissions to the court while an appeal is under reserve. The request, outlining the essentials of the argument and the reasons the argument was not made at the hearing of the appeal, should be made in writing to the attention of the Senior Legal Officer. Opposing parties may respond in writing to the request. The Senior Legal Officer will advise the parties whether the panel will receive further submissions. This process is not to be viewed as a substitute for properly preparing the factum and fully arguing the issues at the hearing of the appeal.

6.   After a panel has released its reasons for judgment, the decision of the court is final. The normal recourse for a party who objects to the court's decision is by way of an application for leave to appeal to the Supreme Court of Canada.

7.   In accordance with rule 61.16(6.1) of the *Rules of Civil Procedure*, an order or decision of a panel of the Court of Appeal may not be set aside or varied except in accordance with rules 37.14 and 59.06. Parties should be aware that rule 59.06 provides for a very narrow jurisdiction to set aside or vary an order made by a panel. This rule and the authorities that have interpreted it should be consulted before commencing a motion under rule 59.06.

8.   In accordance with rule 2.1.02 of the *Rules of Civil Procedure*, the Court of Appeal will automatically screen motions under rule 59.06(2) in order to ensure that the motion is not frivolous, vexatious, or otherwise an abuse of the process of the court.

20. CONTACT INFORMATION FOR THE COURT'S REGISTRAR

The office of the Registrar may be contacted at COA.Registrar@ontario.ca or by fax at 416-327-5032.

21. CONTACT INFORMATION FOR THE COURT'S SENIOR LEGAL OFFICER

The office of the Senior Legal Officer may be contacted at COA.SeniorLegalOfficer@ontario.ca or by fax at 416-327-6256.

Chief Justice George R. Strathy

January 30, 2017
Date

---

[1] For example, see *Child, Youth and Family Services Act, 2017*, S.O. 2017, c. 14, Sched. 1 s. 134(11); *Criminal Code of Canada*, R.S.C. 1985, c. C-46, ss. 486, 486.4-486.6, 517, 539; *Youth Criminal Justice Act*, S.C. 2002, c. 1, ss. 110, 111.

W. Bringing and Responding to Motions in Civil and Family Appeals (Latest Amendment: February 17, 2017)[2]

Table of Contents

1. General

From time to time you may find it necessary to bring a motion in relation to an appeal or proposed appeal in the Court of Appeal. As it would be impossible to anticipate every situation that might arise in a guide such as this, these notes will only serve to highlight procedures that apply to bringing motions in the court.

Procedures for motions in the Court of Appeal are governed by rule 61.16 of the *Rules of Civil Procedure*. This rule incorporates many of the provisions found in the general rule for motions, rule 37. Additionally, other rules dealing with the format of documents, computation of time, serving of documents on the other side and so on are also dealt with in the *Rules of Civil Procedure*. As a result you really must review the *Rules of Civil Procedure* before taking any step on an appeal or motion. You may review the *Rules of Civil Procedure* at the following link: https://www.ontario.ca/laws/regulation/900194

Forms, where referred to in the rules, can be found at the following link: http://ontariocourtforms.on.ca/en/

Please note that the court does not provide blank forms. You will have to type or copy the forms yourself or download them from one of the sites above.

Additionally, the court has issued practice directions that outline practical matters not covered in the rules. Section 7 of the Practice Direction concerning Civil Appeals deals with motions. You may (and should) review this practice direction, which can be found at the following link: http://www.ontariocourts.ca/coa/en/notices/pd/civil.htm.

Carefully review the applicable rules and practice directions before attempting to file or respond to a motion. They set out the "when, where, what, and how" of bringing and responding to mo-

---

[2] See online: https://www.ontariocourts.ca/coa/en/info/civfam/motion.htm.

tions. Generally speaking, the rules and practice directions set out what must be filed, what must be included in your filings, and when you must file your materials.

If you do not comply with the rules and practice directions, the staff of the court will not be able to accept your material for filing. To avoid frustration, a review of the applicable rules and careful planning are essential. For example, you should expect that it would be necessary to serve your opponent with all of the documents you wish to file on the motion. Only in exceedingly rare circumstances is a motion heard without the other side having been served with all of the materials. Similarly you should expect that it would be necessary to serve and file your materials within the timeline set out in the rules and the practice directions. While there is a provision for seeking permission of the registrar or a judge for late filing, such permission is usually granted only in emergencies or urgent situations. Keep in mind that bad planning does not necessarily create an emergency.

You should also be aware that bringing frivolous, unmeritorious, vexatious or even merely unsuccessful motions may result in an award of costs being made against you. Similarly, unsuccessfully opposing a motion may lead to a costs order against you. In fact, costs are usually awarded in favour of the party that succeeds on the motion. In some circumstances, a failure to pay such costs may prejudice your ability to argue the appeal.

2. Types of Motions

Most motions are heard by a single judge. A panel of three judges hears some motions, but only when required by statute or a rule. The procedure for motions to a single judge and motions to a panel of three judges are different, as generally described below.

2.1 Motions heard by three judges

The most common types of panel motions are:

- A motion to quash an appeal (on the basis that the Court of Appeal does not even have jurisdiction to hear the appeal).
- A motion to introduce new or "fresh" evidence on the appeal.
- A motion to review a decision of a single judge who heard an earlier motion.
- A motion seeking leave to appeal a decision of Divisional Court

The law as to if, when and how these motions can be brought is rather extensive. You should carefully research the law or seek legal advice before attempting to bring such a motion. For example, motions for leave to appeal have a specific rule (61.03.1) that provides for procedures that are somewhat different than the procedure to be followed for other motions to a panel of judges (see rule 61.16).

2.1.1 Motions for Leave to Appeal from a decision of Divisional Court

As mentioned above, these motions to a panel of three judges have a special rule setting up the procedure to follow. These motions are dealt with in writing without oral argument. As a result, specialized procedures are contained within a rule 61.03.1 ensure that the parties can make full argument in writing and to permit the court to deal with the matter properly without an oral hearing.

2.1.2 Other Motions Heard by Three Judges

The details outlining the procedure for bringing other motions to a panel of judges are set out in the rules (especially rule 61.16) and the practice direction noted above. Generally a motion brought to a panel must state that it will be heard "on a date to be fixed by the registrar". The person bringing the motion cannot unilaterally pick the date for the hearing of the motion. The court will advise you of the hearing date after you have served and filed the necessary documents in support of your motion, (a motion record and a factum in triplicate-one for each judge). The rules provide timelines within which material must be filed. If you do not comply with these timelines, your motion may be dismissed by the registrar without a hearing.

A party responding to such a motion may also file a motion record and factum for each judge. As you might expect, the rules provide timelines for serving and filing responding materials as well.

As the hearing date approaches, the parties should consult with each other to attempt to narrow the issues. The party bringing the motion must file a "confirmation of motion" form (Form 37 B) no later than 2 p.m. two days before the hearing. If such a confirmation is not provided to the court, the motion will not be heard without permission from a judge.

2.2 Motions heard by a single judge

Most motions in the Court of Appeal are brought before one judge. The most common examples of motions brought to a single judge are:

- A motion to extend the time in which to file an appeal, if you missed the deadline for doing so.
- A motion to extend the time to perfect an appeal, if you missed that deadline.
- A motion to expedite the hearing of an appeal if there is some urgency.
- A motion to adjust the timelines for filing materials, either shortening lengthening them, depending on circumstances of the case.
- A motion to dispense with the filing of certain materials, the filing of which may be required by the rules but which are unnecessary for the hearing of the appeal.
- A motion to "stay" the order under appeal, if it was not one that was automatically stayed on the filing of the appeal (see for example rule 63 of the *Rules of Civil Procedure*)
- A motion to remove the "stay" if one was automatically imposed by the filing of the appeal.

As mentioned above, you should review the Practice Direction and the *Rules of Civil Procedure* generally and rules 61.16 and 37 in particular for the procedure for bringing motions to a judge.

If you are the party bringing the motion to a single judge, generally you must:

- Choose a date (at 10 a.m.) for the hearing of the motion.
- Serve your notice of motion on all parties at least seven business days before the hearing date. Note: The rules provide for minimum notice periods. You may give more notice and file your motion well in advance of the selected hearing date.
- If you choose to file a factum containing your legal argument, you must also serve it at least four business days before the hearing.
- File your notice of motion and motion record at least seven business days before the hearing.

- File your factum, if any, at least seven business days before the hearing. (Since you will have served it at least seven business days before the hearing, it might be more convenient to file it when you file your notice of motion and motion record so as to avoid making additional trips to the Court of Appeal).

If you are a party responding to a motion you may file a responding motion record and respondent's factum. If you wish to do so you must serve and file it at least four business days before the hearing.

The parties should consult with each other to attempt to narrow the issues or determine whether the responding party will consent to the order. The party bringing the motion must file a "confirmation of motion" (Form 37 B) no later than 2 p.m. three business days before the hearing. If such a confirmation is not provided to the court, the motion will not be heard without permission from a judge.

As mentioned earlier, in cases of emergency or urgency a party that is unable to comply with these timelines may seek the approval of the registrar or a judge to file the material on short notice. However, as noted above, bad planning may not be a good enough reason for obtaining permission to file late.

The notice of motion and the confirmation of motion both require an estimate for the anticipated length of the oral argument of the motion. Note, however, that if any party does not file a factum of their argument (which is not mandatory on a motion before a single judge) that party's argument will be limited to 15 minutes. Similarly, a judge may cut short the time requested for oral argument if it appears that the party's estimate was unreasonable.

3. Legal assistance

You may wish to read the self-help information, which may be found elsewhere on this web site under the title "Getting Legal Assistance".

3.1.1 Pro Bono Law Ontario

If you are representing yourself, either because you do not qualify for Legal Aid or because you choose to do so, you may nevertheless wish some assistance with your appeal or motion before your appeal is heard. Pro Bono Ontario (PBO) helps self-represented persons in the Court of Appeal in three ways.

Please note that due to the timelines involved in bringing appeals and motions pending appeal, especially motions to a single judge, you may well wish to consult PBO about these services before commencing an appeal or motion so that you can determine whether you can get "pro bono" assistance before you take your first step. While an appeal or motion may be adjourned to permit either side to obtain or try to obtain legal assistance, you should not assume that an adjournment will be permitted in your case. You should also be aware that the other party may ask for costs arising out of a request for an adjournment. Therefore if you are going to attempt to seek the assistance of a lawyer privately, through Legal Aid, or with the assistance of PBO, it is important to do so without delay.

3.1.2 Summary advice on the basic elements of an appeal – CIVIL APPEALS ONLY (not family law appeals)

For civil appeals, PBO operates a summary advice service that helps self-represented litigants understand the nature of an appeal, the proper court for an appeal, the timelines, and the documents for commencing an appeal. This service is not available for all stages of an appeal. It is designed to give individuals some basic guidance at the beginning of the process and to help them preserve their rights.

This service is available in-person at court-based help centres in Toronto (393 University Avenue, Suite 110) and Ottawa (161 Elgin Street, Suite 5027). The centres are open Monday to Friday from 9:30 a.m. to 4:00 p.m. but are closed from 12:00 p.m. to 1:00 p.m. If you cannot attend in person, you may apply online at www.probonoontario.org/application or by toll-free call to 1-855-255-7256.

3.1.3 Merit assessment and possible pro bono representation – CIVIL AND FAMILY APPEALS

Administered in partnership with The Advocates' Society, this PBO service is an effort to assess the merit of civil and family appeals and match self-represented litigants with volunteer lawyers in appropriate cases. If a case is "matched" following a merit assessment, the services provided range from summary advice to discrete tasks (such as helping draft a factum or making submissions in court) to full representation in some cases. However, the service does not guarantee any particular type of assistance.

To apply for this service, self-represented litigants can visit a PBO court-based help centre in Toronto (393 University Avenue, Suite 110) or Ottawa (161 Elgin Street, Suite 5027); or apply online at www.probonoontario.org/application or by toll-free call to 1-855-255-7256.

3.1.4 Amicus duty counsel project for motions - CIVIL AND FAMILY APPEALS

Also administered in partnership with The Advocates' Society, this PBO service provides "amicus duty counsel" to assist the court by helping self-represented individuals who are bringing or responding to motions in the Court of Appeal. "Amicus" means that duty counsel is a friend of the court. Duty counsel is there to help you but is not your lawyer. This means that duty counsel will try to come up with any arguments that can help your case, but is not obliged to make arguments or take positions for you that are not supported by the facts or law.

Duty counsel will be available at the court to help with civil motions on Wednesdays and Thursdays, and to help with family motions on Wednesdays. You are encouraged to schedule your motion for hearing on a day when duty counsel is present to provide you with guidance. If appropriate, duty counsel may also be able to make submissions to the Court and/or help you resolve the dispute.

If you schedule the hearing for a day when duty counsel is available, you should also give court staff your full contact information so that duty counsel has the opportunity to contact you in advance (but please note that duty counsel is not obliged to do so). You should also file material as soon as possible (so that duty counsel has a chance to review it) and arrive early on the day of the hearing (so that you can consult with duty counsel).

4. Disclaimer

The foregoing is provided for your information only. Pro Bono Law Ontario is not affiliated with the courts in any way. Court staff may not recommend that a litigant retain a particular counsel or seek the assistance of a program such as the one provided by PBLO.

Last Updated: February 17, 2017

X. Class Proceedings: Class Proceedings Committee Practice Directions

Practice Direction #1 — Application Process (Amended: May 2019)

CLASS PROCEEDINGS COMMITTEE

PRACTICE DIRECTION #1

(MAY 2019)[3]

Application process

Purpose of the Class Proceedings Committee

The *Law Society Act*, R.S.O. 1990, c. L.8, as amended (the *"Act"*) created the Class Proceedings Committee (the "Committee") to determine whether and which plaintiffs in class proceedings should receive financial support from the Class Proceedings Fund (the "Fund") and the amount of such support.

How to prepare an application

Staged funding

1. Pursuant to section 2 of O. Reg 771/92, applicants must make separate applications for funding in respect of the following different stages of a proceeding:

   1. Steps taken up to the end of the hearing of a motion for an order certifying the proceeding as a class proceeding.

   2. Appeals of orders relating to certification.

   3. Steps other than those described in paragraphs 1 and 2 taken up to the end of discovery or cross-examination on affidavits.

   4. Steps other than those described in paragraphs 1 to 3 concerning the determination of common issues.

   5. Appeals from a judgment on common issues.

   6. Steps other than those described in paragraphs 1 to 5. O. Reg. 771/92, s. 2.

The initial application

2. Pursuant to section 3 of O. Reg. 771/92 applicants must provide the following materials as part of an initial application for funding:

   Tab 1   If the applicant is an individual, his or her name, address, telephone number and fax number, if any.

   Tab 2   If the applicant is a corporation, its name, head office address, telephone number and fax number and a copy of its articles of incorporation.

   Tab 3   Each defendant's name.

   Tab 4   A statement indicating which of the stages in the proceeding, as set out in paragraphs 1 to 6 of section 2, the application addresses.

   Tab 5   A copy of the pleadings and any court orders relating to the proceeding, in

---

[3] See online https://lawfoundation.on.ca/download/practice-direction-1.

particular any statements of defence, certification materials and facta related to any motion in the case to date.

Tab 6   A description of the class and an estimate of the number of members in the class.

Tab 7   A legal opinion describing and assessing the merits of the applicant's case, and any other information and documents the applicant considers appropriate for this purpose.

Tab 8   If the applicant has not yet applied for certification of the proceeding as a class proceeding, a statement indicating when the applicant will do so.

Tab 9   If the proceeding has not yet been certified as a class proceeding, a legal opinion assessing the likelihood that it will be certified.

Tab 10   A statement of the financial support being requested, itemized according to the purposes for which it is being requested.

Tab 11   Such information and documents as the applicant considers appropriate to address the following matters:

   a.   whether the applicant has made reasonable efforts to raise funds from other sources. The applicant's counsel should disclose the amount, if any, of funds the applicant has or expects to raise to supplement any funding granted by the Committee, taking into account the nature of the case and the circumstances of the applicant;

   b.   whether the applicant has a clear and reasonable proposal for the use of any funds awarded; and

   c.   whether the applicant has appropriate financial controls to ensure that any funds awarded are spent for the purposes of the award. (See s. 59.3(4) of the Law Society Act.)

Tab 12   An affidavit by the applicant stating that the information provided by him, her or it in connection with the application is true.

Tab 13   Authorization to the Committee and to the Board of Trustees of The Law Foundation of Ontario (the "Board") to verify the information provided by the applicant in connection with the application.

Tab 14   The name and address of the applicant's lawyer.

Tab 15   A statement by the lawyer indicating that he or she will accept payments from the Class Proceedings Fund in connection with the applicant and will use them for the purposes for which the payments are made. O. Reg. 771/ 92, s. 3 (1).

The Committee requests that the initial application record also contain the following Tabs:

Tab 16   A list of the individual lawyers expected to participate in the prosecution of the case, a description of their experience and qualifications, a statement as to whether a contingency fee agreement has been entered into under s. 33 of the Class Proceedings Act, 1992, and an estimate of the aggregate number of hours the applicant's counsel expects to and is prepared to devote to the case;

Tab 17   Material addressing the issue of the defendant's ability to pay any judgment and comply with any non-monetary relief which may ultimately be granted against it, and, if it appears the defendant will not be able to pay or comply, explaining why financial support should nevertheless be granted;

Tab 18   The plan or draft plan which has been or is intended to be filed pursuant to s. 5(I)(e)(ii) of the *Class Proceedings Act, 1992*;

Tab 19   The applicant counsel's best estimate as to all disbursements expected to be incurred up to and including trial; and

Tab 20   The applicant counsel's summary of all anticipated expert evidence which will be required. For greater clarity, the name of the expert will not be required at this stage if the identity is unknown, but the applicant's counsel must provide a summary of all types of experts anticipated as well as the type of expert testimony they will provide and the expected cost. The applicant must also provide a summary of all anticipated disbursements which will be requested up to and including any appeals.

3.   With respect to Tabs 7 and 9 (the legal opinion describing and assessing the merits of the applicant's case and the legal opinion assessing the likelihood of certification), the applicant should comply with the attached guidelines entitled "Opinion on the Merits" and "Opinion on Certification". The applicant is reminded that this is not a typical advocacy process. In most cases, the Committee will not have the benefit of written submissions from the defendants, nor will the Committee have the opportunity to meet with defence counsel to ask questions. The Committee therefore asks the applicant to fairly present and comment on defences or positions which either have been raised by the defendant(s), or which the applicant anticipates could be raised by the defendant(s).

4.   With respect to Tabs 10 and 19, the applicant must comply with the Class Proceedings Funding Disbursement Policy.

5.   Applicants must also provide copies of any relevant documents or cases which they refer to in their application record.

6.   Counsel are reminded that the failure to produce all required information/ documents may result in follow-up questions and a possible adjournment of the scheduled date.

How to submit an application

7.   Applicants should submit (1) copy of the application materials in a Class Proceedings Funding Application in electronic format only in a PDF document with bookmarks. The materials should contain an index with the Tabs above corresponding to the PDF bookmarks.

Supplementary applications

8.   The materials for subsequent applications, if any, should also be submitted electronically in a PDF document with bookmarks and should be called a First or Second or Third etc. Supplementary Class Proceeding Funding Application (as the case may be). Supplementary Funding Applications should not duplicate the contents of any previous application, and should contain:

a.   Copies of any materials the applicant thinks necessary;

b.   Copies of any pleadings filed and orders made by the court in the proceedings which have not already been submitted in a previous funding application;

c.   A concise report on the status of the class proceeding including an estimated timetable; and

d.   Written submissions addressing why the additional funding is necessary.

Confidentiality

9.   Some of the information/documents submitted pursuant to paragraphs 2 to 8 above may be confidential. The Committee expects and encourages full and frank disclosure and will protect the confidentiality of such materials except as may be compelled by law.

How applications will be considered

10.   With respect to the applicant's initial application, <u>after a complete application is received</u> the Committee will advise the applicant of the time and place of the Committee's meeting to consider the application. The Committee typically holds its meetings at the Committee's office located at 20 Queen Street West, Suite 3002, Toronto, Ontario M5H 3R3. The Committee will meet *in camera* with the applicant's counsel who will be given an opportunity to make oral submissions and the Committee may ask the applicant's counsel questions.

11.   While the applicant (proposed representative plaintiff) is welcome to attend the meeting in person, he or she is not required to.

12.   The Committee's meetings with the applicant's counsel typically take between 20 minutes and one hour. The Committee will reserve its decision and advise the applicant's counsel of its decision in writing in due course.

13.   Applications by conference call may be arranged if appropriate in the circumstances. The Committee's meetings will not be open to the public.

14.   Supplementary applications will ordinarily be considered in writing unless circumstances warrant an oral presentation to the Committee as described in Practice Direction 4 or unless the Committee grant's the applicant leave to make oral submissions because of special circumstances or on the Committee's own motion. The Committee will advise the applicant of its decision in writing in due course.

How funding is received

15.   In the event an application is granted in whole or in part, payments will be made to the applicant in accordance with the Class Proceedings Committee Funding Disbursement Policy.

If funding is refused

16.   Where an application is refused, the applicant may re-apply if so desired.

Levy against awards and settlement funds

17.   If an applicant is financially supported by the Fund and the class proceeding is successful, the applicant will be required to return to the Fund any amount advanced to the applicant from the Fund, which has not yet been repaid, plus 10% of the settle-

ment funds or monetary award. Pursuant to rule 12.05 of the Rules of Civil Procedure, payment of this levy must be addressed in the order approving the settlement or in the judgment.

How to contact the Committee

18.   The Committee's address is Suite 3002, 20 Queen Street West, Toronto, M5H 3R3, and its telephone number is 416-595-1425. More information about the Committee and the Fund can be found on the website: http://www.lawfoundation.on.ca

Dated: this 15th day of May, 2019

_____

Wendy Earle
Chair
Class Proceedings Committee

Practice Direction #2 — Defendant Submissions (Amended: May 2019)[4]

CLASS PROCEEDINGS COMMITTEE

PRACTICE DIRECTION #2

(MAY 2019)

Defendant's request for payment of costs and defendant's submissions to the Committee

Applications for defendant's costs

1.   Pursuant to section 59.4(1) of the *Law Society Act*, R.S.O. 1990, c. L.8, as amended (the "*Act*"), where a matter is funded by the Class Proceedings Committee (the "Committee") and the case is unsuccessful, the defendant has a right to apply for payment from the Class Proceedings Fund (the "Fund") of any costs award.

2.   Pursuant to section 59.4(3) of the Act, a defendant who has the right to apply for payment from the Fund may not recover any part of any costs award from the plaintiff.

Defendants' submissions regarding funding applications

3.   An application for funding brought by a representative plaintiff (the "applicant") under s. 59.3 of the Act is not an adversarial proceeding and the Act does not provide the defendant in the class proceeding with a right to oppose the application, make any submissions, or see any part of the applicant's funding application.

Plaintiff's consent required

4.   The Committee has a broad discretion under s. 59.3(4)(e) of the Act to consider any matter relevant to the funding application and is at liberty to seek information from any available source without compromising the confidentiality of the funding application. The Committee may ask the applicant for permission to seek from the defendant written submissions subject to certain safeguards to protect the applicant and the funding process.

5.   Without the express consent of the applicant the Committee will never:

a.   request submissions from a defendant;

---

[4]   See online: https://lawfoundation.on.ca/download/practice-direction-2/.

Y. Costs (July 1, 2005)

In preparing its report to the Rules Committee that led to the changes in fixing costs to be implemented on July 1, 2005, the Costs Subcommittee gathered substantial information and consulted widely. Based on this, the following may provide some guidance to the profession as these changes are implemented.

It is anticipated that in considering rates, as one of the various relevant factors, courts will normally treat the rates set out below as maximum rates when fixing partial indemnity costs. These rates are the maximums that were available under the costs grid. It is further anticipated that the maximum rates would apply only to the more complicated matters and to the more experienced counsel within each category. The rates used in costs submissions will normally come within the range established by these maximums as appropriate to the particular matter after giving consideration to the factors set out in r. 57.01(1) which now include the amount an unsuccessful party could reasonably expect to pay and the principle of indemnity. Finally, it is the intention that these guidelines will be reviewed periodically so that their currency can be maintained, in light of accumulated experience.

In addition to the hearing itself, these guidelines encompass mediation under r. 24.1, discovery of documents, drawing and settling issues on a special case, setting down for trial, pre-motion conferences, examinations, pre-trial conferences, settlement conferences, notices or offers, preparation for hearing, attendance at assignment court, orders issuing or renewing a writ of execution or notice of garnishment, seizure under writ of execution, seizure and sale under writ of execution, notices of garnishment or any other procedure authorized by the *Rules of Civil Procedure*.

Law Clerks	Maximum of $80.00 per hour
Student-at-law	Maximum of $60.00 per hour
Lawyer (less than 10 years)	Maximum of $225.00 per hour
Lawyer (10 or more but less than 20 years)	Maximum of $300.00 per hour
Lawyer (20 years and over)	Maximum of $350.00 per hour

Z. Others: Procedure in Construction Lien Actions

Actions under the *Construction Lien Act* are subject to additional or alternative provisions designed to streamline the proceeding. Master Sandler in *Pineau v. Kretschmar Inc.*, [2004] O.J. No. 396 (Master), explained how the statutory steps differed from those under the rules in the passage below (at paras. 3-16):

[The proper procedure for processing a Toronto construction lien claim to trial] still seems to be a mystery to many lawyers although the current system has been in place since at least 1983 when the Construction Lien Act came into force, and I believe is the same system that was used under the Mechanics' Lien Act for Toronto lien cases, going back at least to the late 1960's.

If the premises are situate within the legal limits of the City of Toronto, the action must be commenced by the issuing of a statement of claim in the Toronto office of the Superior Court of Justice - s. 53(1). The statement of claim must then be served, within 90 days, subject to extension - see s. 53(2).

The exchange of pleadings is governed by sections 54(1) and 53(3), and sections 55 and 56. Noting in default is provided by s. 54(2).

At this point, a decision must be made as to whether the case is to be tried by a judge or by a master. The election is usually made by the plaintiff but can, in fact, be made as well by any defending party.

If any party wants a judge to hear the case, it sets the action down for trial under rules 48.01 and 48.02, (serving and filing a trial record), but it must also have regard to rule 48.04 about not thereafter initiating or continuing any form of discovery or any motions (except with leave of the court). And leave (consent) for any discovery or any motions is, in any event, required by s. 67(2), so any discovery or other interlocutory proceeding must be proceeded with first. Such leave (consent) is dealt with by the Toronto construction lien motions master (currently, Master Saunders) on Mondays. This party must then also serve a notice of trial (statutory form) as required by s. 60(4), on all persons described in s. 60(2). This is a requirement of the Act and not the rules. Presumably, the form of notice of trial for Toronto lien actions to be tried by judges must be modified so that it is returnable in Trial Scheduling Court at the same date/time as the Trial Scheduling Unit's notice and this is because of the use of the Trial Scheduling Court procedure in Toronto. (It is to be noted that s. 67(3) of the Act provides that the *Courts of Justice Act* and the rules of court (*i.e.*, the Rules of Civil Procedure) apply to cases under the Act, except where inconsistent with the Act, and subject to s. 67(2).) Once the trial record has been served, and proof of service filed, the Toronto Trial Scheduling Office will issue a Trial Scheduling Court Notice which eventually results in the case ending up in Trial Scheduling Court (every Wednesday), about 5 to 6 months after the trial record was filed. While there is no case or practice direction on point, I think the s. 60(4) notice of trial, duly modified, should be returnable for the scheduled Trial Scheduling Court date. The case will be assigned to one of the four Toronto Teams and the presiding Trial Scheduling Court judge will fix a trial date in the presence of counsel for all parties and other affected persons such as other lien claimants, or possibly, give other directions. For who are the other affected persons, see s. 60(4) and especially, s. 60(2).

This path is very rarely followed in Toronto. Even if it is, s. 58(3) of the Act provides that, at trial, (or presumably at Trial Scheduling Court), the trial judge may, on his or her own motion, direct a reference to a Toronto master, or to a case management master. This has often been done by Toronto trial judges, especially where there are multiple parties, or, in a two-party dispute, or where the trial will be lengthy, or where there are a large number of disputed extras and deficiencies in issue, often in a house construction or house renovation case or where the amount in issue is small.

If any party (usually, the plaintiff) wants a master to hear the case, (the usual procedure), then

this party must obtain a judgment of reference under s. 58(1) of the Act to a Toronto mas
case management master. Section 58(1) and s. 67(6), detail how the motion for this judgmei.
reference is to be made. Either all parties must consent or notice of the motion must be given
any defending party who won't consent. (For non-defending parties who have been noted in default - see s. 54(4).)

The form of this judgment of reference is mandated by Ont. Reg. 175, R.R.O. 1990, s. 2(16) and
Form 16. Note that this Regulation provides that the judgment under s. 58 "shall be in Form 16".
Form 16 contains four specific paragraphs, the most important of which provides that ". . . this
action be referred to the master at Toronto . . . for trial" who is to issue a report that must then
be confirmed - see s. 62(1)(b) and rules 54.07(1) and 54.09(1).

Once the judgment of reference has been obtained, then the party obtaining that judgment (or, in
fact, any other party) must make a motion to the court (a master), without notice, to have a date,
time and place fixed for the trial of the action. This is a routine motion. The date so fixed is called,
colloquially the "first construction lien pre-trial" but is really the first day of the trial. I have previously described this procedure in the case of *Ontario Electrical Construction v. Stern* (1997),
31 C.L.R. (2d) 150, at pp. 166-167, and this procedure has also been described and approved of
by Beaulieu J. in *York Marble v. Exim* (1999), 41 C.L.R. (2d) 110 at pp. 112.

Once this order has been obtained, the party who obtained it (usually the plaintiff) must serve a
properly worded notice of trial (and because masters require it, a copy of the order) on all persons
described in s. 60(2) - see s. 60(4). This is, in the main, all other lien claimants, if any. A notice
of trial may be in Form 17 but it must be served - (see the word "shall" in s. 60(4)). This notice
of trial is a critical document. The person serving this notice of trial, and all persons served with
it are "parties to the action" - see s. 57(2).

Once a master conducts the first "pre-trial", he or she is seized of the reference (trial), but is not
so seized by reason only of having appointed the day, time and place for the trial (first "pre-trial")
under s. 60(1) - see s. 52. So I became seized with this case on November 28.

As a matter of practice, Toronto construction lien masters do not order settlement meetings to
take place, under s. 60(1), in Toronto lien actions, because the first "pre-trial", which is supervised by the master, is a more effective procedure than an unsupervised settlement meeting under
s. 61. (Sometimes, the trial master may establish a Vetting Committee to scrutinize the various
lien claim[s] and report back but this is a totally different procedure than a settlement meeting
under s. 61). Outside of Toronto, in some jurisdictions, settlement meetings are often ordered.
The practice varies across the Province.

It is critical to note that under s. 37(1) of the Act, there is a provision that if, within two years
after the date of the statement of claim, the action, or an action in which the lien may be enforced
(a subtle distinction) has not been set down for trial, or an order has not been made fixing a trial
date under s. 60(2), the lien expires, and a motion may then be brought to declare the lien expired
under s. 46. This motion may be brought without notice, unless costs are claimed (or unless notice is directed to be given on the original without-notice motion, by the court, because of the pe-
culiar circumstances-something I sometimes do and now seem to be doing more frequently.).

I have previously ruled that a judgment of reference under s. 58(1) is not an "order fixing a trial
date" under s. 37(1)1. An order under s. 60(1) is required in order to stop the time running. But
I have seen an order of a judge that combined both a s. 58(1) order and a s. 60(1) order, this being
done when the time limit was about to expire. But it was on consent.